T0292640

The
Minimum
Description
Length
Principle

The Minimum Description Length Principle

Peter D. Grünwald

The MIT Press
Cambridge, Massachusetts
London, England

Typeset in Palatino by the author using LATEX 2_ε with C. Manning's `fbook.cls` and `statnlpbook.sty` macros.

Library of Congress Cataloging-in-Publication Information

Grünwald, Peter D.
    The minimum description length principle / Peter D. Grünwald.
        p.   cm.—(Adaptive computation and machine learning)
    Includes bibliographical references and index.
    ISBN-13: 978-0-262-07281-6 (hc. alk. paper)—978-0-262-52963-1 (pb. alk. paper)
    1. Minimum description length (Information theory) I. Title

 QA276.9G78 2007
 003′.54—dc22

                                                                    2006046646

The MIT Press is pleased to keep this title available in print by manufacturing single copies, on demand, via digital printing technology.

To my father

Brief Contents

IV Additional Background   597

Contents

List of Figures

Series Foreword

The goal of building systems that can adapt to their environments and learn from their experience has attracted researchers from many fields, including computer science, engineering, mathematics, physics, neuroscience, and cognitive science. Out of this research has come a wide variety of learning techniques that have the potential to transform many scientific and industrial fields. Recently, several research communities have converged on a common set of issues surrounding supervised, unsupervised and reinforcement learning problems. The MIT Press series on Adaptive Computation and Machine Learning seeks to unify the many diverse strands of machine learning research and to foster high-quality research and innovative applications.

Thomas Dietterich

Foreword

This is a splendid account of the latest developments on the minimum description length (MDL) principle and the related theory of stochastic complexity. The MDL principle seeks to place the age-old statistical or inductive inference on a sound foundation. In order to achieve this it requires the drastically different and, for many, unpalatable view that the objective is not to estimate any "true" data-generating mechanism but simply to find a good explanation of data, technically called a model. The author gives an impassionate balanced discussion of the deep philosophical implications of the principle, and he traces the tortuous path from the roots to the current refined stage of the principle, in which the idea of a *universal* model plays a central role. This is a model that allows for an objective comparison of alternative models regardless of their form or number of parameters in case the interest is in model selection. Further, it provides a basis for prediction and classification.

The author describes painstakingly the information- and probability-theoretic notions needed for the reader with a minimum of prerequisites to apply the principle to a variety of statistical problems. This involves an in-depth treatment of the theory of "universal models," which in its general form is deep and complex. The author's treatment of it, however, is highly accessible. He achieves this by devoting an extensive section on discussing finite universal models, which are much simpler than the general case but do serve to illustrate the general ideas.

Based on this treatment, he then introduces the MDL principle in its modern, refined form, always emphasizing the ideas that give rise to the actual formulas. He starts out with the simple case of comparing a finite number of parametric models, and gradually builds up the theory to general problems of model selection. He also briefly discusses parameter estimation and nonparametric inference. For the reader with deeper statistical knowledge, in Chapter 17 he compares MDL to some other more customary statistical techniques.

Jorma Rissanen
Helsinki Institute for Information Technology
Helsinki, Finland
December 2005

Preface

How does one decide among competing explanations of data given limited observations? This is the problem of *model selection*. A central concern in model selection is the danger of *overfitting*: the selection of an overly complex model that, while fitting observed data very well, predicts future data very badly. Overfitting is one of the most important issues in inductive and statistical inference: besides model selection, it also pervades applications such as prediction, pattern classification and parameter estimation.

The minimum description length (MDL) principle is a relatively recent method for inductive inference that provides a generic solution to the model selection problem, and, more generally, to the overfitting problem. MDL is based on the following insight: any regularity in the data can be used to *compress* the data, i.e. to describe it using fewer symbols than the number of symbols needed to describe the data literally. The more regularities there are, the more the data can be compressed. Equating "learning" with "finding regularity," we can therefore say that the more we are able to compress the data, the more we have *learned* about the data. Formalizing this idea leads to a general theory of inductive inference with several attractive properties:

1. **Occam's razor.** MDL chooses a model that trades off goodness-of-fit on the observed data with "complexity" or "richness" of the model. As such, MDL embodies a form of Occam's razor, a principle that is both intuitively appealing and informally applied throughout all the sciences.

2. **No overfitting, *automatically*.** MDL methods *automatically* and *inherently* protect against overfitting and can be used to estimate both the parameters and the structure (e.g., number of parameters) of a model. In contrast, to avoid overfitting when estimating the structure of a model, traditional

methods such as maximum likelihood must be *modified* and extended with additional, typically ad hoc principles.

3. **Bayesian interpretation.** Some (not all) MDL procedures are closely related to Bayesian inference. Yet they avoid some of the interpretation difficulties of the Bayesian approach, especially in the realistic case when it is known a priori to the modeler that none of the models under consideration is true. In fact:

4. **No need for "underlying truth."** In contrast to other statistical methods, MDL procedures have a clear interpretation independent of whether or not there exists some underlying "true" model.

5. **Predictive interpretation.** Because data compression is formally equivalent to a form of probabilistic prediction, MDL methods can be interpreted as searching for a model with good predictive performance on *unseen* data. This makes MDL related to, yet different from, data-oriented model selection techniques such as cross-validation.

This Book

This book provides an extensive, step-by-step introduction to the MDL principle, with an emphasis on conceptual issues. From the many talks that I have given on the subject, I have noticed that the same questions about MDL pop up over and over again. Often, the corresponding answers can be found only — if at all — in highly technical journal articles. The main aim of this book is to serve as a reference guide, in which such answers can be found in a much more accessible form. There seems to be a real need for such an exposition because, quoting Lanterman (2001), of "the challenging nature of the original works and the preponderance of misinterpretations and misunderstandings in the applied literature." Correcting such misunderstandings is the second main aim of this book.

First Aim: Accessibility I first learned about MDL in 1993, just before finishing my master's in computer science. As such, I knew some basic probability theory and linear algebra, but I knew next to nothing about advanced measure-theoretic probability, statistics, and information theory. To my surprise, I found that to access the MDL literature, I needed substantial knowledge about all three subjects! This experience has had a profound influence on this book: in a way, I wanted to write a book which I would have been able to understand when I was a beginning graduate student. Therefore, since with some difficulty its use can be avoided, there is no measure theory whatsoever in this book. On the other hand, this book is full of statistics and information theory, since these are essential to any understanding of MDL. Still, both subjects are introduced at a very basic level in Part I of the book, which provides an initial introduction to MDL. At least this part of the book should be readable without any prior exposure to statistics or information theory.

If my main aim has succeeded, then this book should be accessible to (a) researchers from the diverse areas dealing with inductive inference, such as statistics, pattern classification, and branches of computer science such as machine learning and data mining; (b) researchers from biology, econometrics, experimental psychology, and other applied sciences that frequently have to deal with inductive inference, especially model selection; and (c) philosophers interested in the foundations of inductive inference. This book should enable such readers to understand what MDL is, how it can be used, and what it does.

Second Aim: A Coherent, Detailed Overview In the year 2000, when I first thought about writing this book, the field had just witnessed a number of advances and breakthroughs, involving the so-called *normalized maximum likelihood code*. These advances had not received much attention outside of a very small research community; most practical applications and assessments of MDL were based on "old" (early 1980s) methods and ideas. At the time, some pervasive myths were that "MDL is just two-part coding", "MDL is BIC" (an asymptotic Bayesian method for model selection), or "MDL is just Bayes." This prompted me and several other researchers to write papers and give talks about the new ideas, related to the normalized maximum likelihood. Unfortunately, this may have had somewhat of an adverse effect: I now frequently talk to people who think that MDL is just "normalized maximum likelihood coding." This is just as much of a myth as the earlier ones! In reality, MDL in its modern form is based on a general notion known in the information-theoretic literature as *universal coding*. There exist many types of universal codes, the main four types being the Bayesian, two-part, normalized maximum likelihood, and prequential plug-in codes. All of these can be used in MDL inference, and which one to use depends on the application at hand. While this emphasis on universal codes is already present in the overview (Barron, Rissanen, and Yu 1998), their paper requires substan-

tial knowledge of information theory and statistics. With this book, I hope
to make the universal coding-based MDL theory accessible to a much wider
audience.

A Guide for the Reader

This book consists of four parts. Part I is really almost a separate book. It provides a very basic introduction to MDL, as well as an introductory overview
of the statistical and information-theoretic concepts needed to understand
MDL. Part II is entirely devoted to universal coding, the information-theoretic
notion on which MDL is built. Universal coding is really a theory about data
compression. It is easiest to introduce without directly connecting it to inductive inference, and this is the way we treat it in Part II. In fact though, there
is a very strong relation between universal coding and inductive inference.
This connection is formalized in Part III, where we give a detailed treatment
of MDL theory as a theory of inductive inference based on universal coding. Part IV can once again be read separately, providing an overview of the
statistical theory of *exponential families*. It provides background knowledge
needed in the proofs of theorems in Part II.

The Fast Track — How to Avoid Reading Most of This Book I do not
suppose that any reader will find the time to read all four parts in detail.
Indeed, for readers with prior exposure to MDL, this book may serve more
like a reference guide than an introduction in itself. For the benefit of readers
with no such prior knowledge, each chapter in Part I and Part II starts with
a brief list of its contents as well as a *fast track*–paragraph, which indicates
the parts that should definitely be read, and the parts that can be skipped at
first reading. This allows a "fast track" through Part I and Part II, so that the
reader can quickly reach Part III, which treats state-of-the-art MDL inference.
Additionally, some sections are marked with an asterisk (*). Such sections
contain advanced material and may certainly be skipped at first reading.

> Also, the reader will frequently find paragraphs such as the present one, which
> are set in smaller font. These provide additional, more detailed discussion of
> the issues arising in the main text, and may also be skipped at first reading.

Also, at several places, the reader will find boxes like the one below:

Boxes Contain the Most Important Ideas
Each chapter contains several boxes like this one. These contain the most important insights. Together, they form a summary of the chapter.

To further benefit the hurried reader, we now give a brief overview of each part:

Part I Chapter 1 discusses some of the basic ideas underlying MDL in a mostly nonmathematical manner. Chapter 2 briefly reviews general mathematical and probabilistic preliminaries. Chapter 3 gives a detailed discussion of some essential information-theoretic ideas. Chapter 4 applies these notions to statistical models. This chapter gives an extensive analysis of the log-likelihood function and its expectation. It may be of interest for teachers of introductory statistics, since the treatment emphasizes some, in my view, quite important aspects usually not considered in statistics textbooks. For example, we consider in detail what happens if we vary the data, rather than the parameters. Chapter 5 then gives a first mathematically precise implementation of MDL. This is the so-called crude two-part code MDL. I call it "crude" because it is suboptimal, and not explicitly based on universal coding. I included it because it is easy to explain — especially the fact that it has obvious defects raises some serious questions, and thinking about these questions seems the perfect introduction to the "refined" MDL that we introduce in Part III of the book.

> Although some basic familiarity with elementary probability theory is assumed throughout the text, all probabilistic concepts needed are briefly reviewed in Chapter 2. They are typically taught in undergraduate courses and can be found in books such as (Ross 1998). Strictly speaking, the text can be read without any prior knowledge of statistics or information theory — all concepts and ideas are introduced in Chapters 3 and 4. Nevertheless, some prior exposure to these subjects is probably needed to fully appreciate the developments in Part II and Part III. More extensive introductions to the statistical concepts needed can be found in, for example (Bain and Engelhardt 1989; Casella and Berger ; Rice 1995).

Part II Part II then treats the general theory of universal coding, with an emphasis on issues that are relevant to MDL. It starts with a brief introduction which gives a high-level overview of the chapters contained in Part II. Its first chapter, Chapter 6, then contains a detailed introduction to the main ideas, in the restricted context of countable model classes. Each of the four subsequent chapters gives a detailed discussion of one of the four main types of universal codes, in the still restricted context of "parametric models" with (essentially) compact parameter spaces. Chapters 11, 12, and 13 deal with general parametric models — including linear regression models — as well as nonparametric models.

Part III Part III gives a detailed treatment of refined MDL. We call it "refined" so as to mark the contrast with the "crude" form of MDL of Chapter 5. It starts with a brief introduction which gives a high-level overview of refined MDL. Chapter 14 deals with refined MDL for model selection. Chapter 15 is about its other two main applications: hypothesis selection (a basis for parametric and nonparametric density estimation) and prediction. Consistency and rate-of-convergence results for refined MDL are detailed in Chapter 16. Refined MDL is placed in its proper context in Chapter 17, in which we discuss its underlying philosophy and compare it to various other approaches.

Compared to Part I, Part II and Part III contain more advanced material, and some prior exposure to statistics may be needed to fully appreciate the developments. Still, all required information-theoretic concepts — invariably related to *universal coding* — are once again discussed at a very basic level. These parts of the book mainly serve as a reference guide, providing a detailed exposition of the main topics in MDL inference. The discussion of each topic includes details which are often left open in the existing literature, but which are important when devising practical applications of MDL. When pondering these details, I noticed that there are several open questions in MDL theory which previously have not been explicitly posed. We explicitly list and number such open questions in Part II and Part III. These parts also contain several new developments: in order to tell a coherent story about MDL, I provide some new results — not published elsewhere — that connect various notions devised by different authors.

> The main innovations are the "distinguishability" interpretation of MDL for finite models in Chapter 6, the "phase transition" view on two-part coding in Chapter 10, the luckiness framework as well as the CNML-1 and CNML-2 extensions of the normalized maximum likelihood code in Chapter 11, and the connections between Césaro and standard KL risk and the use of redundancy rather than resolvability in the convergence theorem for two-part MDL in Chapter 15.

I also found it useful to rephrase and re-prove existing mathematical theorems in a unified way. The many theorems in Part II and Part III usually express results that are similar to existing theorems by various authors, mainly Andrew Barron, Jorma Rissanen, and Bin Yu. Since these theorems were often stated in slightly different contexts, they are hard to compare. In our version, they become easily comparable. Specifically, in Part II, we restrict the treatment to so-called *exponential families* of distributions, which is a weakening of existing results. Yet, the theorems invariably deal with uniform convergence, which is often a strengthening of existing results.

Part IV: Exponential Family Theory   The theorems in Part II make heavy use of the general and beautiful theory of *exponential* or, relatedly, *maximum entropy* families of probability distributions. Part IV is an appendix that contains an overview of these families and their mathematical properties. When writing the book, I found that most existing treatments are much too restricted to contain the results that we need in this book. The only general treatments I am aware of (Barndorff-Nielsen 1978; Brown 1986) use measure theory, and give a detailed treatment of behavior at parameters tending to the boundaries of the parameter space. For this reason, they are quite hard to follow. Thus, I decided to write my own overview, which avoids measure theory and boundary issues, but otherwise contains most essential ideas such as sufficiency, mean-value and canonical parameterizations, duality, and maximum entropy interpretations.

Acknowledgments

Tim van Erven, Peter Harremoës, Wouter Koolen, In Jae Myung, Mark Pitt, Teemu Roos, Steven de Rooij, and Tomi Silander read and commented on parts of this text. I would especially like to thank Tim, who provided comments on the entire manuscript.

Mistakes
Of course, the many mistakes which undoubtedly remain in this text are all my (the author's) sole responsibility. I welcome all emails that point out mistakes in the text!

Among those who have helped shape my views on statistical inference, two people stand out: Phil Dawid and Jorma Rissanen. Other people who have strongly influenced my thinking on these matters are Vijay Balasubramanian, Andrew Barron, Richard Gill, Teemu Roos, Paul Vitányi, Volodya Vovk, and Eric-Jan Wagenmakers. My wife Louise de Rooij made a very visible and colourful contribution. Among the many other people who in some way or other had an impact on this book I should mention Petri Myllymäki, Henry Tirri, Richard Shiffrin, Johan van Benthem, and, last but not least, Herbert, Christa and Wiske Grünwald. As leaders of our research group at CWI (the National Research Institute for Mathematics and Computer Science in the Netherlands), Harry Buhrman and Paul Vitányi provided the pleasant working environment in which this book could be written. The initial parts of this book were written in 2001, while I was visiting the University of California at Santa Cruz. I would like to thank Manfred Warmuth and David Draper for hosting me. Finally and most importantly, I would like to thank my lovely wife Louise for putting up with my foolishness for so long.

PART I

Introductory Material

1 *Learning, Regularity, and Compression*

Overview The task of inductive inference is to find laws or regularities underlying some given set of data. These laws are then used to gain insight into the data or to classify or predict future data. The minimum description length (MDL) principle is a general method for inductive inference, based on the idea that the more we are able to *compress* (describe in a compact manner) a set of data, the more regularities we have found in it and therefore, the more we have *learned* from the data. In this chapter we give a first, preliminary and informal introduction to this principle.

Contents In Sections 1.1 and 1.2 we discuss some of the fundamental ideas relating description length and regularity. In Section 1.3 we describe what was historically the first attempt to formalize these ideas. In Section 1.4 we explain the problems with using the original formalization in practice, and indicate what must be done to make the ideas practicable. Section 1.5 introduces the practical forms of MDL we deal with in this book, as well as the crucial concept of "universal coding." Section 1.6 deals with some issues concerning *model selection*, which is one of the main MDL applications. The philosophy underlying MDL is discussed in Section 1.7. Section 1.8 shows how the ideas behind MDL are related to "Occam's razor." We end in Section 1.9 with a brief historical overview of the field and its literature.

Fast Track This chapter discusses, in an informal manner, several of the complicated issues we will deal with in this book. It is therefore essential for readers without prior exposure to MDL. Readers who are familiar with the basic ideas behind MDL may just want to look at the boxes.

1.1   Regularity and Learning

We are interested in developing a method for *learning* the laws and regularities in data. The following example will illustrate what we mean by this and give a first idea of how it can be related to descriptions of data.

Example 1.1 We start by considering binary data. Consider the following three sequences. We assume that each sequence is 10000 bits long, and we just list the beginning and the end of each sequence.

$$00010001000100010001\ldots00010001000100010001000100010001 \quad (1.1)$$

$$01110100110100100110\ldots10101110101110110001011000010 \quad (1.2)$$

$$00011000001010100000\ldots00100010000100000001000110000 \quad (1.3)$$

The first of these three sequences is a 2500-fold repetition of 0001. Intuitively, the sequence looks regular; there seems to be a simple "law" underlying it; it might make sense to conjecture that future data will also be subject to this law, and to predict that future data will behave according to this law. The second sequence has been generated by tosses of a fair coin. It is, intuitively speaking, as "random as possible," and in this sense there is no regularity underlying it.[1] Indeed, we cannot seem to find such a regularity either when we look at the data. The third sequence contains exactly four times as many 0s as 1s. It looks less regular, more random than the first; but it looks less random than the second. There is still some discernible regularity in these data, but of a statistical rather than of a deterministic kind. Again, noticing that such a regularity is there and predicting that future data will behave according to the same regularity seems sensible.

1.2   Regularity and Compression

What do we mean by a "regularity"? The fundamental idea behind the MDL principle is the following insight: every regularity in the data can be used to *compress* the data, i.e. to describe it using fewer symbols than the number of symbols needed to describe the data literally. Such a description should always uniquely specify the data it describes - hence given a description or

---

1. Unless we call "generated by a fair coin toss" a "regularity" too. There is nothing wrong with that view - the point is that, the *more* we can compress a sequence, the *more* regularity we have found. One can avoid all terminological confusion about the concept of "regularity" by making it *relative* to something called a "base measure," but that is beyond the scope of this book (Li and Vitányi 1997).

encoding D' of a particular sequence of data D, we should always be able to fully reconstruct D using D'.

For example, sequence (1.1) above can be described using only a few words; we have actually done so already: we have not given the complete sequence — which would have taken about the whole page — but rather just a one-sentence description of it that nevertheless allows you to reproduce the complete sequence if necessary. Of course, the description was done using natural language and we may want to do it in some more formal manner.

If we want to identify regularity with compressibility, then it should also be the case that nonregular sequences can *not* be compressed. Since sequence (1.2) has been generated by fair coin tosses, it should not be compressible. As we will show below, we can indeed prove that *whatever* description method C one uses, the length of the description of a sequence like (1.2) will, with overwhelming probability, be not much shorter than sequence (1.2) itself.

Note that the description of sequence (1.3) that we gave above does not uniquely define sequence (1.3). Therefore, it does not count as a "real" description: one cannot regenerate the whole sequence if one has the description. A unique description that still takes only a few words may look like this: "Sequence (1.3) is one of those sequences of 10000 bits in which there are four times as many 0s as there are 1s. In the lexicographical ordering of those sequences, it is number i." Here i is some large number that is explicitly spelled out in the description. In general, there are 2^n binary sequences of length n, while there are only $\binom{n}{\nu n}$ sequences of length n with a fraction of ν 1s. For every rational number ν except $\nu = 1/2$, the ratio of $\binom{n}{\nu n}$ to 2^n goes to 0 exponentially fast as n increases (this is shown formally in Chapter 4; see Equation (4.36) on page 129 and the text thereunder; by the method used there one can also show that for $\nu = 1/2$, it goes to 0 as $O(1/\sqrt{n})$). It follows that compared to the total number of binary sequences of length 10000, the number of sequences of length 10000 with four times as many 0s as 1s is vanishingly small. Direct computation shows it is smaller than 2^{7213}, so that the ratio between the number of sequences with four times as many 0s than 1s and the total number of sequences is smaller than 2^{-2787}. Thus, $i < 2^{7213} \ll 2^{10000}$ and to write down i in binary we need approximately $(\log_2 i) < 7213 \ll 10000$ bits.

Example 1.2 [Compressing Various Regular Sequences] The regularities underlying sequences (1) and (3) were of a very particular kind. To illustrate that *any* type of regularity in a sequence may be exploited to compress that sequence, we give a few more examples:

The Number π Evidently, there exists a computer program for generating the first n digits of π – such a program could be based, for example, on an infinite series expansion of π. This computer program has constant size, except for the specification of n which takes no more than $O(\log n)$ bits. Thus, when n is very large, the size of the program generating the first n digits of π will be very small compared to n: the π-digit sequence is deterministic, and therefore extremely regular.

Physics Data   Consider a two-column table where the first column contains numbers representing various heights from which an object was dropped. The second column contains the corresponding times it took for the object to reach the ground. Assume both heights and times are recorded to some finite precision. In Section 1.5 we illustrate that such a table can be substantially compressed by first describing the coefficients of the second-degree polynomial H that expresses Newton's law; then describing the heights; and then describing the deviation of the time points from the numbers predicted by H.

Natural Language   Most sequences of words are not valid sentences according to the English language. This fact can be exploited to substantially compress English text, as long as it is syntactically mostly correct: by first describing a grammar for English, and then describing an English text D with the help of that grammar (Grünwald 1996), D can be described using much less bits than are needed without the assumption that word order is constrained.

Description Methods   In order to formalize our idea, we have to replace the part of the descriptions above that made use of natural language by some formal language. For this, we need to fix a *description method* that maps sequences of data to their descriptions. Each such sequence will be encoded as another sequence of symbols coming from some finite or countably infinite *coding alphabet*. An *alphabet* is simply a countable set of distinct symbols. An example of an alphabet is the binary alphabet $\mathbb{B} = \{0, 1\}$; the three data sequences above are sequences over the binary alphabet. A sequence over a binary alphabet will also be called a binary *string*. Sometimes our data will consist of real numbers rather than binary strings. In practice, however, such numbers are always truncated to some finite precision. We can then again model them as symbols coming from a finite data alphabet.

More precisely, we are given a *sample* or equivalently *data sequence* $D = (x_1, \ldots, x_n)$ where each x_i is a member of some set $\mathcal{X}$, called the *space of observations* or the *sample space for one observation*. The set of all potential samples of length n is denoted $\mathcal{X}^n$ and is called the *sample space*. We call

x_i a single *observation* or, equivalently, a *data item*. For a general note about how our terminology relates to the usual terminology in statistics, machine learning and pattern recognition, we refer to the box on page 72.

Without any loss of generality we may describe our data sequences as binary strings (this is explained in Chapter 3, Section 3.2.2). Hence all the description methods we consider map data sequences to sequences of bits. All description methods considered in MDL satisfy the *unique decodability property*: given a description D', there is at most one ("unique") D that is encoded as D'. Therefore, given any description D', one should be able to fully reconstruct the original sequence D. Semiformally:

Description Methods

Definition 1.1 A *description method* is a *one-many* relation from the sample space to the set of binary strings of arbitrary length.

A truly formal definition will be given in Chapter 3, Section 3.1. There we also explain how our notion of "description method" relates to the more common and closely related notion of a "code." Until then, the distinction between codes an description methods is not that important, and we use the symbol C to denote both concepts.

Compression and Small Subsets   We are now in a position to show that strings which are "intuitively" random cannot be substantially compressed. We equate intuitively random with "having been generated by independent tosses of a fair coin." We therefore have to prove that it is virtually impossible to substantially compress sequences that have been generated by fair coin tosses. By "it is virtually impossible" we mean "it happens with vanishing probability." Let us take some arbitrary but fixed description method C over the data alphabet consisting of the set of all binary sequences of length ≥ 1. Such a code maps binary strings to binary strings. Suppose we are given a data sequence of length n (in Example 1.1, $n = 10000$). Clearly, there are 2^n possible data sequences of length n. We see that only two of these can be mapped to a description of length 1 (since there are only two binary strings of length 1: 0 and 1). Similarly, only a subset of at most 2^m sequences can have a description of length m. This means that at most $\sum_{i=1}^{m} 2^i < 2^{m+1}$ data sequences can have a description length $\leq m$. The fraction of data sequences of length n that can be compressed by more than k bits is therefore at most 2^{-k} and as such decreases exponentially in k. If data are generated by n tosses of a fair coin, then all 2^n possibilities for the data are equally probable, so the probability that we can compress the data by more than k bits is smaller than 2^{-k}. For example, the probability that we can compress the data by more than 20 bits is smaller than one in a million.

Most Data Sets Are Incompressible

Suppose our goal is to encode a binary sequence of length n. Then

- No matter what description method we use, only a fraction of at most 2^{-k} sequences can be compressed by more than k bits.

- Thus, if data are generated by fair coin tosses, then no matter what code we use, the probability that we can compress a sequence by more than k bits is at most 2^{-k}.

- This observation will be generalized to data generated by an arbitrary distribution in Chapter 3. We then call it the *no-hypercompression inequality*. It can be found in the box on page 103.

Seen in this light, having a short description length for the data is equivalent to identifying the data as belonging to a tiny, very *special* subset out of all a priori possible data sequences; see also the box on page 31.

1.3   Solomonoff's Breakthrough – Kolmogorov Complexity

It seems that what data are compressible and what are not is extremely dependent on the specific description method used. In 1964 – in a pioneering paper that may be regarded as the starting point of all MDL-related research (Solomonoff 1964) – Ray Solomonoff suggested the use of a *universal computer language* as a description method. By a universal language we mean a computer language in which a universal Turing machine can be implemented. All commonly used computer languages, like Pascal, LISP, C, are "universal." Every data sequence D can be encoded by a computer program P that prints D and then halts. We can define a description method that maps each data sequence D to the *shortest program* that prints D and then halts.[2] Clearly, this is a description method in our sense of the word in that it defines a 1-many (even 1-1) mapping from sequences over the data alphabet to a subset of the binary sequences.

The shortest program for a sequence D is then interpreted as the *optimal hypothesis* for D. Let us see how this works for sequence (1.1) above. Using a language similar to C, we can write a program

> for i = 1 to 2500 ; do {print '0001'} ; halt

which prints sequence (1.1) but is clearly a lot shorter than it. If we want to make a fair comparison, we should rewrite this program in a binary alphabet; the resulting number of bits is still much smaller than 10000. The shortest program printing sequence (1.1) is at least as short as the program above, which means that sequence (1.1) is indeed highly compressible using Solomonoff's code. By the arguments of the previous section we see that, given an arbitrary description method C, sequences like (1.2) that have been generated by tosses of a fair coin are very likely not substantially compressible using C. In other words, the shortest program for sequence (1.1) is, with extremely high probability, not much shorter than the following:

> print '01110100110100001010........10111011000101100010'; halt

This program has size about equal to the length of the sequence. Clearly, it is nothing more than a repetition of the sequence.

Kolmogorov Complexity   We define the *Kolmogorov complexity* of a sequence as the length of the shortest program that prints the sequence and then halts. Kolmogorov complexity has become a large subject in its own right; see (Li and Vitányi 1997) for a comprehensive introduction.

The lower the Kolmogorov complexity of a sequence, the *more regular* or equivalently, the *less random*, or, yet equivalently, the *simpler* it is. Measuring regularity in this way confronts us with a problem, since it depends on the particular programming language used. However, in his 1964 paper, Ray Solomonoff (Solomonoff 1964) showed that *asymptotically* it does not matter what programming language one uses, as long as it is universal: for every sequence of data $D = (x_1, \ldots, x_n)$, let us denote by $L_{\mathrm{UL}}(D)$ the length of the shortest program for D using universal language UL. We can show that for

---

2. If there exists more than one shortest program, we pick the one that comes first in enumeration order.

every two universal languages UL_1 and UL_2, the difference between the two lengths $L_{UL_1}(D) - L_{UL_2}(D)$ is bounded by a constant that depends on UL_1 and UL_2 but not on the length n of the data sequence D. This implies that if we have a lot of data (n is large), then the difference in the two description lengths is negligible compared to the size of the data sequence. This result is known as the *invariance theorem* and was proved independently in (Solomonoff 1964), (Kolmogorov 1965) (hence the name Kolmogorov complexity), and (Chaitin 1969). The proof is based on the fact that one can write a compiler for every universal language UL_1 in every other universal language UL_2. Such a compiler is a computer program with length $L_{1\to2}$. For example, we can write a program in Pascal that translates every C program into an equivalent Pascal program. The length (in bits) of this program would then be $L_{C\to Pascal}$. We can simulate each program P_1 written in language UL_1 by program P_2 written in UL_2 as follows: P_2 consists of the compiler from UL_1 to UL_2, followed by P_1. The length of program P_2 is bounded by the length of P_1 plus $L_{1\to2}$. Hence for all data D, the maximal difference between $L_{UL_1}(D)$ and $L_{UL_2}(D)$ is bounded by $\max\{L_{1\to2}, L_{2\to1}\}$, a constant which only depends on UL_1 and UL_2 but not on D.

1.4 Making the Idea Applicable

Problems   There are two major problems with applying Kolmogorov complexity to practical learning problems:

1. **Uncomputability.** The Kolmogorov complexity cannot be computed in general;

2. **Large constants.** The description length of any sequence of data involves a constant depending on the description method used.

By "Kolmogorov complexity cannot be computed" we mean the following: there is no computer program that, for every sequence of data D, when given D as input, returns the shortest program that prints D and halts. Neither can there be a program, that for every data D returns only the *length* of the shortest program that prints D and then halts. Assuming such a program exists leads to a contradiction (Li and Vitányi 1997).

The second problem relates to the fact that in many realistic settings, we are confronted with very small data sequences for which the invariance theorem is not very relevant since the length of D is small compared to the constant $L_{1\to2}$.

"Idealized" or "Algorithmic" MDL   If we ignore these problems, we may use Kolmogorov complexity as our fundamental concept and   build a theory of idealized inductive inference on top of it. This road has been taken by Solomonoff (1964, 1978), starting with the 1964 paper in which he introduced Kolmogorov complexity, and by Kolmogorov, when he introduced the *Kolmogorov minimum sufficient statistic* (Li and Vitányi 1997; Cover and Thomas 1991). Both Solomonoff's and Kolmogorov's ideas have been substantially refined by several authors. We mention here P. Vitányi (Li and Vitányi 1997; Gács, Tromp, and Vitányi 2001; Vereshchagin and Vitányi 2002; Vereshchagin and Vitányi 2004; Vitányi 2005), who concentrated on Kolmogorov's ideas, and M. Hutter (2004), who concentrated on Solomonoff's ideas. Different authors have used different names for this area of research: "ideal MDL," "idealized MDL," or "algorithmic statistics." It is closely related to the celebrated theory of *random sequences* due to P. Martin-Löf and Kolmogorov (Li and Vitányi 1997). We briefly return to idealized MDL in Chapter 17, Section 17.8.

Practical MDL   Like most authors in the field, we concentrate here on non-idealized, practical versions of MDL that explicitly deal with the two problems mentioned above. The basic idea is to scale down Solomonoff's approach so that it does become applicable. This is achieved by using description methods that are less expressive than general-purpose computer languages. Such description methods C should be restrictive enough so that for any data sequence D, we can always compute the length of the shortest description of D that is attainable using method C; but they should be general enough to allow us to compress many of the intuitively "regular" sequences. The price we pay is that, using the "practical" MDL principle, there will always be some regular sequences which we will not be able to compress. But we already know that there can be *no* method for inductive inference at all which will always give us all the regularity there is — simply because there can be no automated method which for any sequence D finds the shortest computer program that prints D and then halts. Moreover, it will often be possible to guide a suitable choice of C by a priori knowledge we have about our problem domain. For example, below we consider a description method C that is based on the class of all polynomials, such that with the help of C we can compress all data sets which can meaningfully be seen as points on some polynomial.

1.5   Crude MDL, Refined MDL and Universal Coding

Let us recapitulate our main insights so far:

MDL: The Basic Idea

The goal of statistical inference may be cast as trying to find regularity in the data. "Regularity" may be identified with "ability to compress." MDL combines these two insights by *viewing learning as data compression*: it tells us that, for a given set of hypotheses $\mathcal{H}$ and data set D, we should try to find the hypothesis or combination of hypotheses in $\mathcal{H}$ that compresses D most.

This idea can be applied to all sorts of inductive inference problems, but it turns out to be most fruitful in (and its development has mostly concentrated on) problems of *model selection* and, more generally, dealing with *overfitting*. Here is a standard example (we explain the difference between "model" and "hypothesis" after the example).

Example 1.3 [Model Selection and Overfitting] Consider the points in Figure 1.1. We would like to learn how the y-values depend on the x-values. To this end, we may want to fit a polynomial to the points. Straightforward linear regression will give us the leftmost polynomial - a straight line that seems overly simple: it does not capture the regularities in the data well. Since for any set of n points there exists a polynomial of the $(n-1)$st degree that goes exactly through all these points, simply looking for the polynomial with the least error will give us a polynomial like the one in the second picture. This polynomial seems overly complex: it reflects the random fluctuations in the data rather than the general pattern underlying it. Instead of picking the overly simple or the overly complex polynomial, it seems more reasonable to prefer a relatively simple polynomial with small but nonzero error, as in the rightmost picture. This intuition is confirmed by numerous experiments on real-world data from a broad variety of sources (Rissanen 1989; Vapnik 1998; Ripley 1996): if one naively fits a high-degree polynomial to a small sample (set of data points), then one obtains a very good fit to the data. Yet if one *tests* the inferred polynomial on a second set of data coming from the same source, it typically fits this test data very badly in the sense that there is a large distance between the polynomial and the new data points. We say that the polynomial *overfits* the data. Indeed, all model selection methods that are used in practice either implicitly or explicitly choose

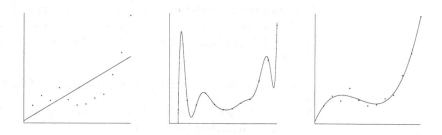

Figure 1.1 A simple, a complex and a tradeoff (third-degree) polynomial.

a tradeoff between goodness-of-fit and complexity of the models involved. In practice, such tradeoffs lead to much better predictions of test data than one would get by adopting the "simplest" (one degree) or most "complex"[3] ($n - 1$-degree) polynomial. MDL provides one particular means of achieving such a tradeoff.

It will be useful to distinguish between "model", "model class" and "(point) hypothesis." This terminology is explained in the box on page 15, and will be discussed in more detail in Section 2.4, page 69.   In our terminology, the problem described in Example 1.3 is a "point hypothesis selection problem" if we are interested in selecting both the degree of a polynomial and the corresponding parameters; it is a "model selection problem" if we are mainly interested in selecting the degree.

To apply MDL to polynomial or other types of hypothesis and model selection, we have to make precise the somewhat vague insight "learning may be viewed as data compression." This can be done in various ways. We first explain the earliest and simplest implementation of the idea. This is the so-called *two-part code* version of MDL:

---

3. Strictly speaking, in our context it is not very accurate to speak of "simple" or "complex" polynomials; instead we should call the *set* of first degree polynomials "simple," and the *set* of 100th-degree polynomials "complex."

> **Crude Two-Part Version of MDL Principle (Informally Stated)**
>
> Let $\mathcal{H}_1, \mathcal{H}_2, \ldots$ be a list of candidate models (e.g., $\mathcal{H}_\gamma$ is the set of γth degree polynomials), each containing a set of point hypotheses (e.g., individual polynomials). The best point hypothesis $H \in \mathcal{H} = \mathcal{H}_1 \cup \mathcal{H}_2 \cup \ldots$ to explain the data D is the one which minimizes the sum $L(H)+L(D|H)$, where
>
> - $L(H)$ is the length, in bits, of the description of the hypothesis; and
>
> - $L(D|H)$ is the length, in bits, of the description of the data when encoded with the help of the hypothesis.
>
> The best *model* to explain D is the smallest model containing the selected H.

The terminology "crude MDL" is explained in the next subsection. It is not standard, and it is introduced here for pedagogical reasons.

Example 1.4 [Polynomials, cont.] In our previous example, the candidate hypotheses were polynomials. We can describe a polynomial by describing its coefficients at a certain precision (number of bits per parameter). Thus, the higher the degree of a polynomial or the precision, the more bits we need to describe it and the more "complex" it becomes. A description of the data "with the help of" a hypothesis means that the better the hypothesis fits the data, the shorter the description will be. A hypothesis that fits the data well gives us a lot of *information* about the data. Such information can always be used to compress the data. Intuitively, this is because we only have to code the *errors* the hypothesis makes on the data rather than the full data. In our polynomial example, the better a polynomial H fits D, the fewer bits we need to encode the discrepancies between the actual y-values y_i and the predicted y-values $H(x_i)$. We can typically find a very complex point hypothesis (large $L(H)$) with a very good fit (small $L(D|H)$). We can also typically find a very simple point hypothesis (small $L(H)$) with a rather bad fit (large $L(D|H)$). The sum of the two description lengths will be minimized at a hypothesis that is quite (but not too) "simple," with a good (but not perfect) fit.

1.5.1 From Crude to Refined MDL

Crude MDL picks the H minimizing the sum $L(H) + L(D|H)$. To make this procedure well defined, we need to agree on precise definitions for the

---

Models and Model Classes; (Point) Hypotheses

We use the word *model* to refer to a *set* of probability distributions or functions of the same functional form. E.g., the "first-order Markov model" is
the set of all probability distributions that are first-order Markov chains.
The "model of kth degree polynomials" is the set of all kth degree polynomials for some fixed k.

We use the word *model class* to refer to a family (set) of models, e.g. "the
model class of all polynomials" or "the model class of all Markov chains
of each order." The definitions of "model" and "model class" are chosen
so that they agree with how these words are used in statistical practice.
Therefore they are intentionally left somewhat imprecise.

We use the word *hypothesis* to refer to an *arbitrary* set of probability distributions or functions. We use the word *point hypothesis* to refer to a
single probability distribution (e.g. a Markov chain with all parameter
values specified) or function (e.g. a particular polynomial). In parametric
inference (Chapter 2), a point hypothesis corresponds to a particular parameter value. A point hypothesis may also be viewed as an *instantiation*
of a model.

What we call "point hypothesis" is called "*simple* hypothesis" in the
statistics literature; our use of the word "model (selection)" coincides
with its use in much of the statistics literature; see Section 2.3, page 62
where we give several examples to clarify our terminology.

Figure 1.2   Models and Model Classes; (Point) Hypotheses.

codes (description methods) giving rise to lengths $L(D|H)$ and $L(H)$. We
now discuss these codes in more detail. We will see that the definition of
$L(H)$ is problematic, indicating that we somehow need to "refine" our crude
MDL principle.

Definition of $L(D|H)$ Consider a two-part code as described above, and
assume for the time being that all H under consideration define probability
distributions. If H is a polynomial, we can turn it into a distribution by mak-

ing the additional assumption that the Y-values are given by $Y = H(X) + Z$, where Z is a normally distributed noise term with mean 0.

For each H we need to define a code with length $L(\cdot \mid H)$ such that $L(D|H)$ can be interpreted as "the codelength of D when encoded with the help of H." It turns out that for probabilistic hypotheses, there is only one reasonable choice for this code; this is explained at length in Chapter 5. It it is the so-called *Shannon-Fano code*, satisfying, for all data sequences D, $L(D|H) = -\log P(D|H)$, where $P(D|H)$ is the probability mass or density of D according to H. Such a code always exists, as we explain in Chapter 3, in the box on page 96.

Definition of $L(H)$: A Problem for Crude MDL   It is more problematic to find a good code for hypotheses H. Some authors have simply used "intuitively reasonable" codes in the past, but this is not satisfactory: since the description length $L(H)$ of any fixed point hypothesis H can be very large under one code, but quite short under another, our procedure is in danger of becoming arbitrary. Instead, *we need some additional principle for designing a code for $\mathcal{H}$.*

In the first publications on MDL (Rissanen 1978; Rissanen 1983), it was implicitly advocated to choose some sort of *minimax code* for each $\mathcal{H}_\gamma$, minimizing the shortest worst-case total description length $L(H) + L(D|H)$, where the worst-case is over all possible data sequences. Thus, the MDL principle is employed at a "meta-level" to choose a code for $\mathcal{H}_\gamma$. This idea, already implicit in Rissanen's early work abut perhaps for the first time stated and formalized in a completely precise way Barron and Cover (1991), is the first step towards "refined" MDL.

More Problems for Crude MDL   We can use crude MDL to code any sequence of data D with a total description length $L(D) := \min_H \{L(D|H) + L(H)\}$. But it turns out that this code is *incomplete*: one can show that there exist other codes L' which for some D achieve strictly smaller codelength $(L'(D) < L(D))$, and for no D achieve larger codelength (Chapter 6, Example 6.4). It seems strange that our "minimum description length" principle should be based on codes which are incomplete (inefficient) in this sense. Another, less fundamental problem with two-part codes is that, if designed in a minimax way as indicated above, they require a cumbersome discretization of the model space $\mathcal{H}$, which is not always feasible in practice. The final problem we mention is that, while it is clear how to use crude two-part codes for point hypothesis and model selection, it is not immediately clear how they can be used for *prediction*.

Later, Rissanen (1984) realized that these problems could be side-stepped by using *one-part* rather than *two-part codes*. As we explain below, it depends on the situation at hand whether a one-part or a two-part code should be used. Combining the idea of designing codes so as to achieve essentially minimax optimal codelengths with the combined use of one-part and two-part codes (whichever is appropriate for the situation at hand) has culminated in a theory of inductive inference that we call *refined MDL*. We discuss it in more detail in the next subsection.

Crude Two-Part MDL (Part I, Chapter 5 of this book)

In this book, we use the term "crude MDL" to refer to applications of MDL for model and hypothesis selection of the type described in the box on page 14, as long as the hypotheses $H \in \mathcal{H}$ are encoded in "intuitively reasonable" but ad-hoc ways.

Refined MDL is sometimes based on one-part codes, sometimes on two-part codes, and sometimes on a combination of these, but, in contrast to crude MDL, the codes are invariably designed according to some minimax principles. If there is a choice, one should always prefer refined MDL, but in some exotic modeling situations, the use of crude MDL is inevitable.

Part I of this book first discusses all probabilistic, statistical and information-theoretic preliminaries (Chapters 2–4) and culminates in a description of crude two-part MDL (Chapter 5). Refined MDL is described only in Part III.

1.5.2 Universal Coding and Refined MDL

In refined MDL, we associate a code for encoding D *not with a single $H \in \mathcal{H}$,* but with the full model $\mathcal{H}$. Thus, given model $\mathcal{H}$, we encode data not in two parts but we design a single *one-part code* with lengths $\bar{L}(D|\mathcal{H})$. This code is designed such that *whenever there is a member of (parameter in) $\mathcal{H}$ that fits the data well, in the sense that $L(D \mid H)$ is small, then the codelength $\bar{L}(D|\mathcal{H})$ will also be small.* Codes with this property are called *universal codes* in the information-theoretic literature (Barron, Rissanen, and Yu 1998):

Universal Coding (Part II of This Book)
There exist at least four types of universal codes:

1. The normalized maximum likelihood (NML) code and its variations.

2. The Bayesian mixture code and its variations.

3. The prequential plug-in code

4. The two-part code

These codes are all based on entirely different coding schemes, but in practice, lead to very similar codelengths $\bar{L}(D|\mathcal{H})$. Part II of this book is entirely devoted to universal coding. The four types of codes are introduced in Chapter 6. This is follows by a separate chapter for each code.

For each model $\mathcal{H}$, there are many different universal codes we can associate with $\mathcal{H}$. When applying MDL, we have a preference for the one that is *minimax optimal* in a sense made precise in Chapter 6. For example, the set $\mathcal{H}_3$ of third-degree polynomials is associated with a code with lengths $\bar{L}(\cdot \mid \mathcal{H}_3)$ such that, the better the data D are fit by the best-fitting third-degree polynomial, the shorter the codelength $\bar{L}(D \mid \mathcal{H})$. $\bar{L}(D \mid \mathcal{H})$ is called the *stochastic complexity* of the data given the model.

Refined MDL is a general theory of inductive inference based on universal codes that are designed to be minimax, or close to minimax optimal. It has mostly been developed for model selection, estimation and prediction. To give a first flavor, we initially discuss model selection, where, arguably, it has the most new insights to offer:

1.5.3   Refined MDL for Model Selection

Parametric Complexity   A fundamental concept of refined MDL for model selection is the *parametric complexity* of a parametric model $\mathcal{H}$ which we denote by COMP($\mathcal{H}$). This is a measure of the "richness" of model $\mathcal{H}$, indicating its ability to fit random data. This complexity is related to the number of degrees-of-freedom (parameters) in $\mathcal{H}$, but also to the geometrical structure of $\mathcal{H}$; see Example 1.5. To see how it relates to stochastic complexity, let, for given data D, $\hat{H}$ denote the distribution in $\mathcal{H}$ which maximizes the probability, and hence minimizes the codelength $L(D \mid \hat{H})$ of D. It turns out that

$$\bar{L}(D \mid \mathcal{H}) = \text{stochastic complexity of } D \text{ given } \mathcal{H} = L(D \mid \hat{H}) + \text{COMP}(\mathcal{H}).$$

Refined MDL model selection between two parametric models $\mathcal{H}_1$ and $\mathcal{H}_2$ (such as the models of first and second degree polynomials) now proceeds as follows. We encode data D in two stages. In the first stage, we encode a number $j \in \{1, 2\}$. In the second stage, we encode the data using the universal code with lengths $\bar{L}(D \mid \mathcal{H}_j)$. As in the two-part code principle, we then select the $\mathcal{M}_j$ achieving the minimum total two-part codelength,

$$\min_{j \in \{1,2\}} \{L(j) + \bar{L}(D \mid \mathcal{H}_j)\} = \min_{j \in \{1,2\}} \{L(j) + L(D \mid \hat{H}) + \text{COMP}(\mathcal{H})\}. \quad (1.4)$$

Since the worst-case optimal code to encode j needs only 1 bit to encode either $j = 1$ or $j = 2$, we use a code for the first-part such that $L(1) = L(2) = 1$. But this means that $L(j)$ plays no role in the minimization, and we are effectively selecting the model such that the stochastic complexity of the given data D is smallest.[4] Thus, in the end we select the model *minimizing the one-part codelength of the data*. Nevertheless, refined MDL model selection involves a tradeoff between two terms: a goodness-of-fit term $L(D \mid \hat{H})$ and a complexity term $\text{COMP}(\mathcal{H})$. However, because we do not explicitly encode hypotheses H anymore, there is no potential for arbitrary codelengths anymore. The resulting procedure can be interpreted in several different ways, some of which provide us with rationales for MDL model selection beyond the pure coding interpretation (Chapter 14):

1. **Counting/differential geometric interpretation** The parametric complexity of a model is the logarithm of the number of *essentially different, distinguishable* point hypotheses within the model.

2. **Two-part code interpretation** For large samples, the stochastic complexity can be interpreted as a two-part codelength of the data after all, where hypotheses H are encoded with a special code that works by first discretizing the model space $\mathcal{H}$ into a set of "maximally distinguishable hypotheses," and then assigning equal codelength to each of these.

3. **Bayesian interpretation** In many cases, refined MDL model selection coincides with Bayes factor model selection based on a *noninformative prior* such as *Jeffreys' prior* (Bernardo and Smith 1994).

---

4. The reason we include $L(j)$ at all in (1.4) is to maintain consistency with the case where we need to select between an infinite number of models. In that case, it is necessary to include $L(j)$.

4. Prequential interpretation MDL model selection can be interpreted as selecting the model with the best predictive performance when sequentially
predicting *unseen* test data, in the sense described in Chapter 6, Section 6.4
and Chapter 9. This makes it an instance of Dawid's (1984) *prequential*
model validation and also relates it to *cross-validation* methods; see Chapter 17, Sections 17.5 and 17.6.

In Section 1.6.1 we show that refined MDL allows us to compare models of
different functional form. It even accounts for the phenomenon that different
models with the same number of parameters may not be equally "complex."

1.5.4   General Refined MDL: Prediction and Hypothesis Selection

Model selection is just one application of refined MDL. The two other main
applications are *point hypothesis selection* and *prediction*. These applications
can also be interpreted as methods for parametric and nonparametric *estimation*. In fact, it turns out that large parts of MDL theory can be reinterpreted as
a theory about *sequential prediction of future data given previously seen data*. This
"prequential" interpretation of MDL (Chapter 15) is at least as important as
the coding interpretation. It is based on the fundamental correspondence between probability distributions and codes via the Shannon-Fano code that
we alluded to before, when explaining the code with lengths $L(D \mid H)$; see
the box on page 96. This correspondence allows us to view any universal
code $\bar{L}(\cdot \mid \mathcal{H})$ as a strategy for sequentially predicting data, such that the
better $\mathcal{H}$ is suited as a model for the data, the better the predictions will be.

   MDL prediction and hypothesis selection are mathematically cleaner than
MDL model selection: in Chapter 15, we provide theorems (Theorem 15.1
and Theorem 15.3) which, in the respective contexts of prediction and hypothesis selection, express that, in full generality, *good data compression implies
fast learning*, where "learning" is defined as "finding a hypothesis that is in
some sense close to an imagined "true state of the world." There are similar theorems for model selection, but these lack some of the simplicity and
elegance of Theorem 15.1 and Theorem 15.3.

Probabilistic vs. Nonprobabilistic MDL   Like most other authors on MDL,
in this book we confine ourselves to *probabilistic hypotheses*, also known as
probabilistic sources. These are hypotheses that take the form of *probability distributions* over the space of possible data sequences. The examples we give in
this chapter (Examples 1.3 and 1.5) involve hypotheses H that are functions

from some space $\mathcal{X}$ to another space $\mathcal{Y}$; at first sight, these are not "probabilistic." We will usually assume that for any given x, we have $y = H(x) + Z$ where Z is a *noise term* with a known distribution. Typically, the noise Z will be assumed to be Gaussian (normally) distributed. With such an additional assumption, we may view "functional" hypotheses $H : \mathcal{X} \to \mathcal{Y}$ as "probabilistic" after all. Such a technique of turning functions into probability distributions is customary in statistics, and we will use it throughout large parts of this book. Whenever we refer to MDL, we implicitly assume that we deal with probabilistic models. We should note though that there exists variations of MDL that *directly* work with universal codes relative to functional hypotheses such as polynomials (see Section 1.9.1, and Chapter 17, Section 17.10).

Fixing Notation

We use the symbol H for general point hypotheses, that may either represent a probabilistic source or a deterministic function. We use $\mathcal{H}$ for sets of such general point hypotheses. We reserve the symbol $\mathcal{M}$ for probabilistic models and model classes. We denote probabilistic point hypotheses by P, and point hypotheses that are deterministic functions by h.

Individual-Sequence vs. Expectation-based MDL   Refined MDL is based on minimax optimal universal codes. Broadly speaking, there are two different ways to define what we mean by minimax optimality. One is to look at the worst-case codelength over *all possible sequences*. We call this *individual-sequence MDL*. An alternative is to look at *expected codelength*, where the expectation is taken over some probability distribution, usually but not always assumed to be a member of the model class $\mathcal{M}$ under consideration. We call this *expectation-based MDL*. We discuss the distinction in detail in Part III of the book; see also the box on page 407. The individual-sequence approach is the one taken by Rissanen, the main originator of MDL, and we will mostly follow it throughout this book.

The Luckiness Principle   In the individual-sequence approach, the minimax optimal universal code is given by the normalized maximum likelihood (NML) code that we mentioned above. A problem is that for many (in fact, most) practically interesting models, the NML code is not well defined. In such cases, a minimax optimal code does not exist. As we explain in Chapter 11, in some cases one can get around this problem using so-called "conditional NML" codes, but in general, one needs to use codes based on a modified minimax principle, which we call the *luckiness principle*. Although it has been implicitly used in MDL since its inception, I am the first to use the term "luckiness principle" in an MDL context; see the box on page 92, Chapter 3; the developments in Chapter 11, Section 11.3, where we introduce the concept of a *luckiness function*; and the discussion in Chapter 17, Section 17.2.1.

The luckiness principle reintroduces some subjectivity in MDL code design. This seems to bring us back to the ad-hoc codes used in crude two-part MDL. The difference however is that with luckiness functions, we can precisely quantify the effects of this subjectivity: for each possible data sample D that we may observe, we can indicate how "lucky" we are on the sample, i.e. how many extra bits we need compared to encode D compared to the best hypothesis that we have available for D. This idea significantly extends the applicability of refined MDL methods.

MDL is a Principle   Contrary to what is often thought, MDL, and even, "modern, refined MDL" is *not* a unique, single method of inductive inference. Rather, it represents a general *principle* for doing inductive inference. The principle may (and will) be formulated precisely enough to allow us to establish, for many given methods (procedures, learning algorithms) "this method is an instance of MDL" or "this is *not* an instance of MDL. But nevertheless:

MDL Is a Principle, Not a Unique Method
Being a *principle*, MDL gives rise to several *methods* of inductive inference.   There is no single "uniquely optimal MDL method/procedure/algorithm." Nevertheless, in *some special situations* (e.g. simple parametric statistical models), one can clearly distinguish between good and not so good versions of MDL, and something close to "an optimal MDL method" exists.

Summary: Refined MDL (Part III of This Book)

Refined MDL is a method of inductive inference based on *universal codes* which are designed to have some *minimax optimality properties*. Each model $\mathcal{H}$ under consideration is associated with a corresponding universal code. In this book we restrict ourselves to probabilistic $\mathcal{H}$. Refined MDL has mainly been developed for model selection, point hypothesis selection and prediction.

Refined MDL comes in two versions: individual-sequence and expectation-based refined MDL, depending on whether the universal codes are designed to be optimal in an individual-sequence or in an expected sense. If the minimax optimal code relative to a model $\mathcal{M}$ is not defined, some element of subjectivity is introduced into the coding using a *luckiness function*. A more precise overview is given in the box on page 406.

In the remainder of this chapter we will mostly concentrate on MDL for model selection.

1.6 Some Remarks on Model Selection

Model selection is a controversial topic in statistics. Although most people agree that it is important, many say it can only be done on external grounds, and never by merely looking at the data. Still, a plethora of automatic model selection methods has been suggested in the literature. These can give wildly different results on the same data, one of the main reasons being that they have often been designed with different goals in mind. This section starts with a further example that motivates the need for model selection, and it then discusses several goals that one may have in mind when doing model selection. These issues are discussed in a lot more detail in Chapter 14. See also Chapter 17, especially Section 17.3, where we compare MDL model selection to the standard model selection methods AIC and BIC.

1.6.1 Model Selection among Non-Nested Models

Model selection is often used in the following context: two researchers or research groups A and B propose entirely different models $\mathcal{M}_A$ and $\mathcal{M}_B$ as an explanation for the same data D. This situation occurs all the time in applied sciences like econometrics, biology, experimental psychology, etc. For example, group A may have some general theory about the phenomenon at hand which prescribes that the trend in data D is given by some polynomial. Group B may think that the trend is better described by some neural network; a concrete case will be given in Example 1.3 below. A and B would like to have some way of deciding which of their two models is better suited for the data at hand. If they simply decide on the model containing the hypothesis (parameter instantiation) that best fits the data, they once again run the risk of overfitting: if model $\mathcal{M}_A$ has more degrees of freedom (parameters) than model $\mathcal{M}_B$, it will typically be able to better fit random noise in the data. It may then be selected even if $\mathcal{M}_B$ actually better captures the underlying trend (regularity) in the data. Therefore, just as in the hypothesis selection example, deciding whether $\mathcal{M}_A$ or $\mathcal{M}_B$ is a better explanation for the data should somehow depend on how well $\mathcal{M}_A$ and $\mathcal{M}_B$ fit the data and on the respective "complexities" of $\mathcal{M}_A$ and $\mathcal{M}_B$.

In the polynomial case discussed before, there was a countably infinite number of "nested" $\mathcal{M}_\gamma$ (i.e. $\mathcal{M}_\gamma \subset \mathcal{M}_{\gamma+1}$). In contrast, we now deal with a finite number of entirely unrelated models $\mathcal{M}_\gamma$. But there is nothing that stops us from using MDL model selection as "defined" above.

Example 1.5 [Selecting Between Models of Different Functional Form]
Consider two models from psychophysics describing the relationship between physical dimensions (e.g., light intensity) and their psychological counterparts (e.g. brightness) (Myung, Balasubramanian, and Pitt 2000): $y = ax^b + Z$ (Stevens's model) and $y = a \ln(x + b) + Z$ (Fechner's model) where Z is a normally distributed noise term. Both models have two free parameters; nevertheless, according to the refined version of MDL model selection to be introduced in Part III, Chapter 14 of this book, Stevens's model is in a sense "more complex" than Fechner's (see page 417). Roughly speaking, this means there are a lot more data patterns that can be *explained* by Stevens's model than can be explained by Fechner's model. Somewhat more precisely, the number of data patterns (sequences of data) of a given length that can be fit well by Stevens's model is much larger than the number of data patterns of the same length that can be fit well by Fechner's model. Therefore, using Stevens's model we run a larger risk of "overfitting."

In the example above, the goal was to select between a power law and a logarithmic relationship. In general, we may of course come across model selection problems involving neural networks, polynomials, Fourier or wavelet expansions, exponential functions - anything may be proposed and tested.

1.6.2   Goals of Model vs. Point Hypothesis Selection

The goal of point hypothesis selection is usually just to infer a hypothesis from the data and use that to make predictions of, or decisions about, future data coming from the same source. Model selection may be done for several reasons:

1. **Deciding between "general" theories.** This is the application that was illustrated in the example above. Often, the research groups A and B are only interested in the models $\mathcal{M}_A$ and $\mathcal{M}_B$, and not in particular hypotheses (corresponding to parameter settings) within those models. The reason is that the models $\mathcal{M}_A$ and $\mathcal{M}_B$ are proposed as *general* theories for the phenomenon at hand. The claim is that they work not only under the exact circumstances under which the experiment giving rise to data D took place but in many other situations as well. In our case, the research group proposing model $\mathcal{M}_A$ may claim that the functional relationship underlying model $\mathcal{M}_A$ provides a good description of the relationship between light intensity and brightness under a variety of circumstances; however, the specific parameter settings may vary from situation to situation. For example, it should be an appropriate model both in daylight (for parameter setting (a_0, b_0)) and in artificial light (for parameter setting (a_1, b_1)).

2. **Gaining insight.** Sometimes, the goal is not to make specific predictions but just to get a first idea of the process underlying the data. Such a rough, first impression may then be used to guide further experimentation about the phenomenon under investigation.

3. **Determining relevant variables.** In Example 1.3 the instances x_i were all real numbers. In practice, the y_i may often depend on several quantities, which may be modeled by taking the x_i to be *real vectors* $x_i = x_{i1}, \ldots, x_{ik}$. We say that there are k *regressor variables*. In such a setting, an important model selection problem is to determine which variables are relevant and which are not. This is sometimes called the *selection-of-variables problem*. Often, for each j, there is a cost associated with measuring x_{ij}. We would therefore like to learn, from some given set of empirical data, which of the regressor variables are truly relevant for predicting the values of y. If there are k regressor variables, this involves model selection between 2^k different models. Each model corresponds to the set of all linear relationships between a particular subset of the regressor variables and y.

4. Prediction by weighted averaging. Even if our sole goal is prediction of future data, model selection may be useful. In this context, we first infer a model (set of hypotheses) for the data at hand. We then predict future data by *combining all the point hypotheses within the model to arrive at a prediction*. Usually this is done by taking a weighted average of the predictions that would be optimal according to the different hypotheses within the model. Here the weights of these predictions are determined by the performance of the corresponding hypotheses on past data. There are abundant examples in the literature on Bayesian statistics (Lee 1997; Berger 1985; Bernardo and Smith 1994) which show that, both in theory and in "the real world," prediction by weighting averaging usually works substantially better than prediction by a single hypothesis. In Chapter 15, we discuss model-based MDL prediction, which is quite similar to Bayesian prediction.

1.7   The MDL Philosophy

The first central MDL idea is that every regularity in data may be used to compress that data; the second central idea is that learning can be equated with finding regularities in data. Whereas the first part is relatively straightforward, the second part of the idea implies that *methods for learning from data must have a clear interpretation independent of whether any of the models under consideration is "true" or not.* Quoting J. Rissanen (1989), the main originator of MDL:

> "We never want to make the false assumption that the observed data actually were generated by a distribution of some kind, say Gaussian, and then go on to analyze the consequences and make further deductions. Our deductions may be entertaining but quite irrelevant to the task at hand, namely, to learn useful properties from the data."

Jorma Rissanen [1989]

Based on such ideas, Rissanen has developed a radical philosophy of learning and statistical inference that is considerably different from the ideas underlying mainstream statistics, both frequentist and Bayesian. We now describe this philosophy in more detail; see also Chapter 17, where we compare the MDL philosophy to the ideas underlying other statistical paradigms.

1. Regularity as Compression   According to Rissanen, the goal of inductive inference should be to "squeeze out as much regularity as possible"
from the given data. The main task is to distill the meaningful information
present in the data, i.e. to separate structure (interpreted as the regularity,
the "meaningful information") from noise (interpreted as the "accidental information"). For the three sequences of Example 1.1, this would amount to
the following: the first sequence would be considered as entirely regular and
"noiseless." The second sequence would be considered as entirely random -
all information in the sequence is accidental, there is no structure present. In
the third sequence, the structural part would (roughly) be the pattern that 4
times as many 0s as 1s occur; given this regularity, the description of exactly
which one among all sequences with four times as many 0s as 1s actually
occurs, is the accidental information.

2. Models as Languages   Rissanen interprets models (sets of hypotheses) as
nothing more than languages for describing useful properties of the data – a
model $\mathcal{H}$ is *identified* with its corresponding universal code $\bar{L}(\cdot \mid \mathcal{H})$. Different
individual hypotheses within the models express different regularities in the
data, and may simply be regarded as *statistics*, that is, summaries of certain
regularities in the data. *These regularities are present and meaningful independently of whether some $H^* \in \mathcal{H}$ is the "true state of nature" or not.* Suppose that
the model $\mathcal{H} = \mathcal{M}$ under consideration is probabilistic. In traditional theories, one typically assumes that some $P^* \in \mathcal{M}$ generates the data, and then
"noise" is defined as a random quantity relative to this P^*. In the MDL view
"noise" is defined relative to the model $\mathcal{M}$ as the residual number of bits
needed to encode the data once the model $\mathcal{M}$ is given. Thus, noise is *not* a
random variable: it is a function only of the chosen model and the *actually observed data*. Indeed, there is no place for a "true distribution" or a "true state
of nature" in this view – there are only models and data. To bring out the
difference to the ordinary statistical viewpoint, consider the phrase "these
experimental data are quite noisy." According to a traditional interpretation,
such a statement means that the data were generated by a distribution with
high variance. According to the MDL philosophy, such a phrase means only
that the data are not compressible with the currently hypothesized model –
as a matter of principle, it can *never* be ruled out that there exists a different
model under which the data are very compressible (not noisy) after all!

3. We Have Only the Data   Many (but not all[5]) other methods of inductive inference are based on the idea that there exists some "true state of nature," typically a distribution assumed to lie in some model $\mathcal{M}$. The methods are then designed as a means to identify or approximate this state of nature based on as little data as possible. According to Rissanen,[6] such methods are fundamentally flawed. The main reason is that the methods are designed under the assumption that the true state of nature is in the assumed model $\mathcal{M}$, which is often not the case. Therefore, *such methods only admit a clear interpretation under assumptions that are typically violated in practice.* Many cherished statistical methods have been designed in this way - we mention hypothesis testing, minimum-variance unbiased estimation, several nonparametric methods, and even some forms of Bayesian inference – see Chapter 17, Section 17.2.1. In contrast, MDL has a clear interpretation which *depends only on the data*, and not on the assumption of any underlying "state of nature."

> **Example 1.6 [Models That are Wrong, Yet Useful]** Even though the models under consideration are often wrong, they can nevertheless be very *useful*. Examples are the successful "Naive Bayes" model for spam filtering, hidden Markov models for speech recognition (is speech a stationary ergodic process? probably not), and the use of linear models in econometrics and psychology. Since these models are evidently wrong, it seems strange to base inferences on them using methods that are designed under the assumption that they contain the true distribution. To be fair, we should add that domains such as spam filtering and speech recognition are not what the fathers of modern statistics had in mind when they designed their procedures – they were usually thinking about much simpler domains, where the assumption that some distribution $P^* \in \mathcal{M}$ is "true" may not be so unreasonable; see also Chapter 17, Section 17.1.1.

4. MDL and Consistency   Let $\mathcal{M}$ be a probabilistic model, such that each $P \in \mathcal{M}$ is a probability distribution. Roughly, a statistical procedure is called *consistent* relative to $\mathcal{M}$ if, for all $P^* \in \mathcal{M}$, the following holds: suppose data are distributed according to P^*. Then given enough data, the learning method will learn a good approximation of P^* with high probability. Many traditional statistical methods have been designed with consistency in mind (Chapter 2, Section 2.5).

---

5. For example, cross-validation cannot easily be interpreted in such terms of "a method hunting for the true distribution." The same holds for some – not all – Bayesian methods; see Chapter 17.

6. The present author's own views are somewhat milder in this respect, but this is not the place to discuss them.

The fact that in MDL, we do not assume a true distribution may suggest that we do not care about statistical consistency. But this is not the case: we would still like our statistical method to be such that in the *idealized* case where one of the distributions in one of the models under consideration actually generates the data, our method is able to identify this distribution, given enough data. If even in the idealized special case where a "truth" exists within our models, the method fails to learn it, then we certainly cannot trust it to do something reasonable in the more general case, where there may not be a "true distribution" underlying the data at all. So: consistency *is* important in the MDL philosophy, but it is used *as a sanity check (for a method that has been developed without making distributional assumptions) rather than as a design principle*; see also Chapter 17, Section 17.1.1.

In fact, mere consistency is not sufficient. We would like our method to converge to the imagined true P^* *fast*, based on as small a sample as possible. Theorems 15.1 and 15.3 of Chapter 15 show that this indeed happens for MDL prediction and hypothesis selection – as explained in Chapter 16, MDL convergence rates for estimation and prediction are typically either minimax optimal or within a factor $\log n$ of minimax optimal.

Summarizing this section, the MDL philosophy is agnostic about whether any of the models under consideration is "true," or whether something like a "true distribution" even exists. Nevertheless, it has been suggested (Webb 1996; Domingos 1999) that MDL embodies a naive belief that "simple models" are "a priori more likely to be true" than complex models. Below we explain why such claims are mistaken.

1.8   Does It Make Any Sense?
MDL, Occam's Razor, and the "True Model"

When two models fit the data equally well, MDL will choose the one that is the "simplest" in the sense that it allows for a shorter description of the data. As such, it implements a precise form of Occam's razor – *even though as more and more data become available, the model selected by MDL may become more and more complex!* Throughout the ages, Occam's razor has received a lot of praise as well as criticism. Some of these criticisms (Webb 1996; Domingos 1999) seem applicable to MDL as well. The following two are probably heard most often:

"1. Occam's razor (and MDL) is arbitrary." Because "description length" is
a syntactic notion it may seem that MDL selects an arbitrary model: different
codes would have led to different description lengths, and therefore, to different models. By changing the encoding method, we can make "complex'
things "simple" and vice versa.

"2. Occam's razor is false." It is sometimes claimed that Occam's razor is
false: we often try to model real-world situations that are arbitrarily complex,
so why should we favor simple models? In the words of G. Webb:[7] "What
good are simple models of a complex world?"

  The short answer to 1 is that this argument overlooks the fact that we are
not allowed to use just any code we like! "Refined MDL" severely restricts
the set of codes one is allowed to use. As we explain below, and in more
detail in Chapter 7, this leads to a notion of complexity that can also be interpreted as a kind of "model volume," without any reference to "description
lengths." The short answer to 2 is that even if the true data-generating machinery is very complex, it may often be a good *strategy* to prefer simple
models for small sample sizes.. Below we give more elaborate answers to
both criticisms.

1.8.1 Answer to Criticism No. 1: Refined MDL's Notion of "Complexity" Is Not Arbitrary

In "algorithmic" or "idealized" MDL (Section 1.4), it is possible to define the
Kolmogorov complexity of a *point* hypothesis H as the length of the shortest program that computes the function value or probability $H(x)$ up to r
bits precision when input (x, r). In our practical version of MDL, there is
no single "universal" description method used to encode point hypotheses.
A hypothesis with a very short description under one description method
may have a very long description under another method. Therefore it is
usually meaningless to say that a particular point hypothesis is "simple" or
"complex." However, for many types of models, it *is* possible to define the
complexity of a *model* (interrelated set of point hypotheses) in an unambiguous manner, that does not depend on the way we parameterize the model.
This is the "parametric complexity" that we mentioned in Section 1.5.3.[8] It

---

7. Quoted with permission from KDD Nuggets 96:28, 1996.
8. The parametric complexity of a probabilistic model $\mathcal{M} = \{P\}$ that consists only of one hypothesis, is always 0, no matter how large the Kolmogorov complexity of P; see Chapter 17,
Example 17.5.

will be defined for finite models in Chapter 6. In Chapter 7 we extend the definition to general models that contain uncountably many hypotheses.

> There exists a close connection between the algorithmic complexity of a hypothesis and the parametric complexity of any large model that contains the hypothesis. Broadly speaking, for *most* hypotheses that are contained in any given model, the Kolmogorov complexity of the hypothesis will be approximately equal to the parametric complexity of the model.

In Example 1.3 we did speak of a "complex" point hypothesis. This is really sloppy terminology: since only the complexity of *models* rather than hypotheses can be given an unambiguous meaning, we should instead have spoken of "a point hypothesis that, relative to the set of models under consideration, is a member only of a complex model and not of a simple model." Such sloppy terminology is commonly used in papers on MDL. Unfortunately, it has caused a lot of confusion in the past. Specifically, it has led people to think that MDL model selection is a mostly arbitrary procedure leading to completely different results according to how the details in the procedure are filled in (Shaffer 1993). At least for the refined versions of MDL we discuss in Part III of this book, this is just plain false.

Complexity of Models vs. Complexity of Hypotheses

In *algorithmic* MDL, we may define the complexity of an *individual* (i.e., *point*) hypothesis (function or probability distribution). In *practical* MDL, as studied here, this is not possible: complexity becomes a property of *models* (sets of point hypotheses) rather than individual point hypotheses (instantiations of models).

MDL-based, or *parametric* complexity, is a property of a model that does not depend on any particular description method used, or any parameterization of the hypotheses within the model. It is related to (but not quite the same as) the number of substantially different hypotheses in a model (Part II of this book, Chapter 6, Chapter 7). A "simple model" then roughly corresponds to "a small set of hypotheses."

In practice, we often use models for which the parametric complexity is undefined. We then use an extended notion of complexity, based on a "luckiness function." While such a complexity measure does have a subjective component, it is still far from arbitrary, and it cannot be used to make a complex model "simple"; see Chapter 17, Section 17.2.1.

1.8.2   Answer to Criticism No. 2

In light of the previous discussions in this chapter, preferring "simpler" over more "complex" models seems to make a lot of sense: one should try to avoid overfitting (i.e. one should try to avoid modeling the noise rather than the "pattern" or "regularity" in the data). It seems plausible that this may be achieved by somehow taking into account the "complexity", "richness", or "(non-) smoothness" of the models under consideration. But from another viewpoint, the whole enterprise may seem misguided: as the example below shows, it seems to imply that, when we apply MDL, we are implicitly assuming that "simpler" models are somehow a priori more likely to be "true." Yet in many cases of interest, the phenomena we try to model are very complex, so then preferring simpler models for the data at hand would not seem to make a lot of sense. How can these two conflicting intuitions be reconciled?

> Authors criticizing Occam's razor (Domingos 1999; Webb 1996) usually do think that in some cases "simpler" models should be preferred over more "complex" ones since the former are more understandable, and in that sense more useful. But they argue that the "simpler" model will usually not lead to better predictions of future data coming from the same source. We claim that on the contrary, for the MDL-based definitions of "simple" and "complex" we will introduce in this book, selecting the simpler model in many cases *does* lead to better predictions, even in a complex environment.

Example 1.7   [MDL Hypothesis/Model Selection for Polynomials, cont.]
Let us focus on point hypothesis selection of polynomials. Let $\mathcal{H}_\gamma$ be the set of γth degree polynomials. Suppose a "truth" exists in the following sense: there exists some distribution P_X^* such that the x_i are all independently distributed according to P_X^*. We assume that all x_i must fall within some interval $[a, b]$, i.e. $P_X^*([a, b]) = 1$. There also exists a function h^* such that for all x_i generated by P_X^*, we have $y_i = h^*(x_i) + Z_i$. Here the Z_i are noise or "error" terms. We assume the Z_i to be identical, independent, normally (Gaussian) distributed random variables, with mean 0 and some variance σ^2. For concreteness we will assume $h^*(x) = x^3 - 8x^2 + 19x + 9$ and $\sigma^2 = 1$.

> This is actually the polynomial/error-combination that was used to generate the points in Figure 1.1 on page 13. However, the x_i in that graph were not drawn according to some distribution such as in the present scenario. Instead, they were preset to be $0.5, 1, 1.5, \ldots, 12$. This is similar to the practical case where the *experimental design* is controlled by the experimenter: the experimenter determines the x_i values for which corresponding y_i-values will be

measured. In this setup similar analyses as those below may still be made (see, e.g. (Wei 1992)).

In such a scenario with a "true" h^* and P_X^*, as more and more data pairs (x_i, y_i) are made available, with high probability something like the following will happen (Chapter 16): for very small n, MDL model selection will select a 0th-degree polynomial, i.e. $y = c$ for some constant c. Then as n grows larger, MDL will start selecting models of higher degree. At some sample size n it will select a third-order polynomial for the first time. It will then for a while (as n increases further) fluctuate between second-, third- and fourth-order polynomials. But for *all* n larger than some critical n_0, MDL will select the correct third order $\mathcal{H}_3$. It turns out that for all n, the point hypothesis $\ddot{h}_n$ selected by two-part MDL hypothesis selection is (approximately) the polynomial within the selected $\mathcal{H}_\gamma$ that best fits data $D = ((x_1, y_1), \dots, (x_n, y_n))$. As n goes to infinity, $\ddot{h}_n$ will with high probability converge to h^* in the sense that all coefficients converge to the corresponding coefficients of h^*.

Two-part code MDL behaves like this not just when applied to the model class of polynomials, but for most other potentially interesting model classes at well. The upshot is that, *for small sample sizes*, MDL has a built-in preference for "simple" models. This preference may seem unjustified, since "reality" may be more complex. We claim that on the contrary, such a preference (if implemented carefully) has ample justification.

To back our claim, we first note that MDL (and the corresponding form of Occam's razor) is just a *strategy* for inferring models from data ("choose simple models at small sample sizes"), not a statement about how the world works ("simple models are more likely to be true") – indeed, a strategy cannot be true or false, it is "clever" or "stupid." And the strategy of preferring simpler models is clever even if the data-generating process is highly complex, as illustrated by the following example:

Example 1.8 ["Infinitely" Complex Sources] Suppose that data are subject to the law $Y = g(X) + Z$ where g is some continuous function and Z is some noise term with mean 0. If g is not a polynomial, but X only takes values in a finite interval, say $[-1, 1]$, we may still approximate g arbitrarily well by taking higher and higher degree polynomials. For example, let $g(x) = \exp(x)$. Then, if we use MDL to learn a polynomial for data $D = ((x_1, y_1), \dots, (x_n, y_n))$, the degree of the polynomial $\ddot{h}_n$ selected by MDL at sample size n will increase with n, and with high probability, $\ddot{h}_n$ converges to $g(x) = \exp(x)$ in the sense that $\max_{x \in [-1,1]} |\ddot{h}_n(x) - g(x)| \to 0$ (Chapter 16). Of course, if we had better prior knowledge about the problem we could have tried to learn g using a model class $\mathcal{H}$ containing the function $y = \exp(x)$. But in general, both our imagination and our computational resources are limited, and we may be forced to use imperfect models.

If, based on a small sample, we choose the best-fitting polynomial $\hat{h}$ within the set of *all* polynomials, then, even though $\hat{h}$ will fit the data very well, it is likely to be quite unrelated to the "true" g, and $\hat{h}$ may lead to disastrous predictions of future data. The reason is that, for small samples, the set of all polynomials is very large compared to the set of possible data patterns that we might have observed. Therefore, any particular data pattern can only give us very limited information about which high-degree polynomial best approximates g. On the other hand, if we choose the best-fitting $\hat{h}^\circ$ in some much smaller set such as the set of second-degree polynomials, then it is highly probable that the prediction quality (mean squared error) of $\hat{h}^\circ$ on future data is about the same as its mean squared error on the data we observed: the size (complexity) of the contemplated model is relatively small compared to the set of possible data patterns that we might have observed. Therefore, the particular pattern that we do observe gives us a lot of information on what second-degree polynomial best approximates g.

Thus, (a) $\hat{h}^\circ$ typically leads to better predictions of future data than $\hat{h}$; and (b) unlike $\hat{h}$, $\hat{h}^\circ$ is *reliable* in that it gives a correct impression of how good it will predict future data *even if the "true" g is "infinitely" complex*. This idea does not just appear in MDL, but is also the basis of the structural risk minimization approach (Vapnik 1998) and many standard statistical methods for nonparametric inference; see Chapter 17, Section 17.10. In such approaches one acknowledges that the data-generating machinery can be infinitely complex (e.g., not describable by a finite degree polynomial). Nevertheless, it is still a good strategy to approximate it by simple hypotheses (low-degree polynomials) as long as the sample size is small. Summarizing:

The Inherent Difference between Under- and Overfitting

If we choose an overly simple model for our data, then the best-fitting point hypothesis within the model is likely to be almost the best predictor, within the simple model, of future data coming from the same source. If we overfit (choose a very complex model) and there is noise in our data, then, *even if the complex model contains the "true" point hypothesis*, the best-fitting point hypothesis within the model may lead to very bad predictions of future data coming from the same source.

This statement is very imprecise and is meant more to convey the general idea than to be completely true. The fundamental consistency theorems for MDL prediction and hypothesis selection (Chapter 15, Theorem 15.1 and Theorem 15.3), as well as their extension to model selection (Chapter 16), are essentially just variations of this statement that are provably true.

The Future and The Past Our analysis depends on the data items (x_i, y_i) to be probabilistically independent. While this assumption may be substantially weakened, we can justify the use of MDL and other forms of Occam's razor *only* if we are willing to adopt some (possibly very weak) assumption of the sort "training data and future data are from the same source": future data should (at least with high probability) be subject to some of the same regularities as training data. Otherwise, D and D' may be completely unrelated and *no* method of inductive inference can be expected to work well. This is indirectly related to the *grue*-paradox (Goodman 1955).

MDL and Occam's Razor

While MDL does have a built-in preference for selecting "simple" models (with small "parametric complexity"), this does *not at all* mean that applying MDL only makes sense in situations where simpler models are more likely to be true. MDL is a *methodology for inferring models from data, not a statement about how the world works!* For small sample sizes, it prefers simple models. It does so not because these are "more likely to be true" (they often are not). Instead, it does so because this tends to select the model that leads to the best predictions of future data from the same source. For small sample sizes this may be a model much simpler than the model containing the "truth" (assuming for the time being that such a model containing the "truth" exists in the first place).

In fact, some of MDL's most useful and successful applications are in nonparametric statistics where the "truth" underlying data is typically assumed to be "infinitely" complex (see Chapter 13 and Chapter 15).

1.9   History and Forms of MDL

The practical MDL principle that we discuss in this book has mainly been developed by J. Rissanen in a series of papers starting with (Rissanen 1978). It has its roots in the theory of Kolmogorov complexity (Li and Vitányi 1997), developed in the 1960s by Solomonoff (1964), Kolmogorov (1965) and Chaitin (1966, 1969). Among these authors, Solomonoff (a former student of the famous philosopher of science, Rudolf Carnap) was explicitly interested in inductive inference. The 1964 paper contains explicit suggestions on how the underlying ideas could be made practical, thereby foreshadowing some of the later work on two-part MDL. While Rissanen was not aware of Solomonoff's work at the time, Kolmogorov's [1965] paper did serve as an inspiration for Rissanen's (1978) development of MDL. Still, Rissanen's practical MDL is quite different from the idealized forms of MDL that have been directly based on Kolmogorov complexity, which we discussed in Section 1.4.

Another important inspiration for Rissanen was Akaike's AIC method for model selection (Chapter 17, Section 17.3), essentially the first model selection method based on information-theoretic ideas (Akaike 1973). Even though Rissanen was inspired by AIC, both the actual method and the underlying philosophy are substantially different from MDL.

Minimum *Message* Length   MDL is much closer related to the *Minimum Message Length (MML) Principle* (Wallace 2005), developed by Wallace and his coworkers in a series of papers starting with the groundbreaking (Wallace and Boulton 1968); other milestones are (Wallace and Boulton 1975) and (Wallace and Freeman 1987). Remarkably, Wallace developed his ideas without being aware of the notion of Kolmogorov complexity. Although Rissanen became aware of Wallace's work before the publication of (Rissanen 1978), he developed his ideas mostly independently, being influenced rather by Akaike and Kolmogorov. Indeed, despite the close resemblance of both methods in practice, the underlying philosophy is very different - see Chapter 17, Section 17.4.

Refined MDL   The first publications on MDL only mention two-part codes. Important progress was made by Rissanen (1984), in which prequential codes are employed for the first time and Rissanen (1987), who introduced the Bayesian mixture codes into MDL. This led to the development of the notion of stochastic complexity as the shortest codelength of the data given a model

(Rissanen 1986c; Rissanen 1987). However, the connection to Shtarkov's *normalized maximum likelihood code* was not made until 1996, and this prevented the full development of the notion of "parametric complexity." In the mean time, in his impressive Ph.D. thesis, Barron (1985) showed how a specific version of the two-part code criterion has excellent frequentist statistical consistency properties. This was extended by Barron and Cover (1991) who achieved a breakthrough for two-part codes: they gave clear prescriptions on how to design codes for hypotheses, relating codes with good minimax codelength properties to rates of convergence in statistical consistency theorems. Some of the ideas of Rissanen (1987) and Barron and Cover (1991) were, as it were, unified when Rissanen (1996) introduced the normalized maximum likelihood code. The resulting theory was summarized for the first time by Barron, Rissanen, and Yu (1998), and is the subject of this book. Whenever we need to distinguish it from other forms of MDL, we call it "refined MDL."

1.9.1 What Is MDL?

"MDL" is used by different authors in somewhat different meanings, and it may be useful to review these. Some authors use MDL as a broad umbrella term for all types of inductive inference based on finding a short codelength for the data. This would, for example, include the "idealized" versions of MDL based on Kolmogorov complexity (page 11) and Wallaces's MML principle (see above). Some authors take an even broader view and include all inductive inference that is based on data compression, even if it cannot be directly interpreted in terms of codelength minimization. This includes, for example the work on similarity analysis and clustering based on the *normalized compression distance* (Cilibrasi and Vitányi 2005).

On the other extreme, for historical reasons, some authors use the *MDL Criterion* to describe a very specific (and often not very successful) model selection criterion equivalent to BIC (see Chapter 17, Section 17.3).

As already indicated, we adopt the meaning of the term that is embraced in the survey (Barron, Rissanen, and Yu 1998), written by arguably the three most important contributors to the field: we use MDL for general *inference based on universal models*. Although we concentrate on hypothesis selection, model selection and prediction, this idea can be further extended to many other types of inductive inference. These include *denoising* (Rissanen 2000; Hansen and Yu 2000; Roos, Myllymäki, and Tirri 2005), *similarity analysis* and *clustering* (Kontkanen, Myllymäki, Buntine, Rissanen, and Tirri 2005), *outlier detection* and *transduction* (as defined in (Vapnik 1998)), and many others. In such areas there has been less research and a "definitive" universal-model based MDL approach has not yet been formulated. We do expect, however, that such research will take place in the future: one of the main strengths of "MDL" in this broad sense is that it can be applied to ever more exotic modeling situations, in which the models do not resemble anything that is usually encountered in statistical practice. An example is the model of context-free grammars, already considered by Solomonoff (1964).

Another application of universal-model based MDL is the type of problem usually studied in *statistical learning theory* (Vapnik 1998); see also Chapter 17, Section 17.10. Here the goal is to directly learn functions (such as polynomials) to predict Y given X, without making any specific probabilistic assumptions about the noise. MDL has been developed in some detail for such problems, most notably *classification* problems, where Y takes its values in a finite set – spam filtering is a prototypical example; here X stands for an email message, and Y encodes whether or not it is spam. An example is the application of MDL to decision tree learning (Quinlan and Rivest 1989; Wallace and Patrick 1993; Mehta, Rissanen, and Agrawal 1995). Some MDL theory for such cases has been developed (Meir and Merhav 1995; Yamanishi 1998; Grünwald 1998), but the existing MDL methods in this area can behave suboptimally. This is explained in Chapter 17, Section 17.10.2. Although we certainly consider it a part of "refined" MDL, we do not consider this "nonprobabilistic" MDL further in this book, except in Section 17.10.2.

1.9.2   MDL Literature

Theoretical Contributions   There have been numerous contributors to refined MDL theory, but there are three researchers that I should mention explicitly: J. Rissanen, B. Yu and A. Barron, who jointly wrote (Barron, Rissanen, and Yu 1998). For example, most of the results that connect MDL to traditional statistics (including Theorem 15.1 and Theorem 15.3 in Chapter 15) are due to A. Barron. This book contains numerous references to their work.

There is a close connection between MDL theory and work in *universal coding* ((Merhav and Feder 1998); see also Chapter 6) and *universal prediction* ((Cesa-Bianchi and Lugosi 2006); see also Chapter 17, Section 17.9).

Practical Contributions   There have been numerous practical applications of MDL. The only three applications we describe in detail are a crude MDL method for learning Markov chains (Chapter 5); a refined MDL method for learning densities based on histograms (Chapter 13 and Chapter 15); and MDL regression (Chapter 12 and Chapter 14). Below we give a few representative examples of other applications and experimental results that have appeared in the literature. We warn the reader that this list is by no means complete! Hansen and Yu (2001) apply MDL to a variety of practical problems involving regression, clustering analysis, and time series analysis. In (Tabus, Rissanen, and Astola 2002; Tabus, Rissanen, and Astola 2003), MDL is used for classification problems arising in genomics. Lee (2002a,b) describes additive clustering with MDL. use MDL for image denoising and apply MDL to decision tree learning. use MDL for sequential prediction. In (Myung, Pitt, Zhang, and Balasubramanian 2000; Myung, Balasubramanian, and Pitt 2000), MDL is applied to a variety of model selection problems arising in cognitive psychology. All these authors apply modern, "refined" versions of MDL. Some references to older work, in which "crude" (but often quite sensible) ad-hoc codes are used, are (Friedman, Geiger, and Goldszmidt 1997; Allen and Greiner 2000; Allen, Madani, and Greiner 2003; Rissanen and Ristad 1994; Quinlan and Rivest 1989; Nowak and Figueiredo 2000; Liu and Moulin 1998; Ndili, Nowak, and Figueiredo 2001; Figueiredo, J. Leitão, and A.K.Jain 2000; Gao and Li 1989). In these papers, MDL is applied to learning Bayesian networks, grammar inference and language acquisition, learning decision trees, analysis of Poisson point processes (for biomedical imaging applications), image denoising, image segmentation, contour estimation, and Chinese handwritten character recognition respectively. MDL has also been extensively studied in time-series analysis, both in theory (Hannan and Rissanen 1982; Gerenscér 1987; Wax 1988; Hannan, McDougall, and Poskitt 1989; Hemerly and Davis 1989b; Hemerly and Davis 1989a; Gerencsér 1994) and practice (Wei 1992; Wagenmakers, Grünwald, and Steyvers 2006).

Finally, we should note that there have been a number of applications, especially in *natural language learning*, which, although practically viable, have been primarily inspired by "idealized MDL" and Kolmogorov complexity, rather than by the Rissanen-Barron-Yu style of MDL that we consider here. These include (Adriaans and Jacobs 2006; Osborne 1999; Starkie 2001) and my own (Grünwald 1996).

Other Tutorials, Introductions and Overviews   The reader who prefers a shorter introduction to MDL than the present one may want to have a look at (Barron, Rissanen, and Yu 1998) (very theoretical and very comprehensive; presumes knowledge of information theory), (Hansen and Yu 2001) (presumes knowledge of statistics; describes several practical applications), (Lanterman 2001) (about comparing MDL, MML and asymptotic Bayesian approaches to model selection), or perhaps my own (Grünwald 2005), which is part of (Grünwald, Myung, and Pitt 2005), a "source book" for MDL theory and applications that contains chapters by most of the main contributors to the field.

Rissanen (1989,2007) has written two books on MDL. While outdated as an introduction to MDL, the "little green book" (Rissanen 1989) is still very much worth reading for its clear exposition of the philosophy underlying MDL. (Rissanen 2007) contains a brief general introduction and then focuses on some recent research of Rissanen's, applying the renormalized maximum likelihood (RNML) distribution (Chapter 11) in regression and denoising, and formalizing the connection between MDL and Kolmogorov's structure function. In contrast to myself, Rissanen writes in accord with his own principle: while containing a lot of information, both texts are quite short.

1.10   Summary and Outlook

We have discussed the relationship between compression, regularity, and learning. We have given a first idea of what the MDL principle is all about, and of the kind of problems we can apply it to. In the next chapters, we present the mathematical background needed to describe such applications in detail.

2 *Probabilistic and Statistical Preliminaries*

Overview   In the previous chapter, we informally presented the basic ideas behind the MDL principle. In Part II and Part III of this book we make these ideas more precise. To prepare for this, we need to review some basic facts of probability theory, statistics, and information theory. In this chapter we concentrate on probability theory and statistics. Once we have introduced the basic quantities, we are in a position to explain the terminology used in this book, and to contrast the goals of MDL–based inference with the goals implicit in other theories of inductive inference.

Contents   Section 2.1 starts with some general mathematical preliminaries. Section 2.2 discusses most of the probability theory needed in this book; it also introduces *probabilistic sources*, which may be thought of as probability distributions over infinite sequences. Section 2.3 introduces the type of statistical models that we will typically be dealing with. Section 2.4 explains the terminology used in this book, and Section 2.5 discusses the goals implicit in MDL.

Fast Track   Readers without basic knowledge of probability theory should read Sections 2.2 and 2.4. Section 2.3 on statistical modeling is quite detailed and may be skipped at first reading. Readers more familiar with probability and statistics may just want to look at the boxes on pages 72 and 73 about the terminology and the goals of different forms of inductive inference.

2.1   General Mathematical Preliminaries

Sets   Throughout this book, $\mathbb{R}$ denotes the set of the real numbers, $\mathbb{R}^+ = \{z \in \mathbb{R} \mid z > 0\}$ denotes the set of positive reals, $\mathbb{N}$ denotes the set of natural numbers $\{1, 2, \ldots\}$, $\mathbb{Z}$ denotes the set of integers $\{\ldots, -2, -1, 0, 1, 2, \ldots\}$, and $\mathbb{B} = \{0, 1\}$ denotes the set of *Booleans*. For any set $\mathcal{U}$, $\mathcal{U}^m$ denotes the m-fold Cartesian product of $\mathcal{U}$. In particular $\mathbb{R}^m$ is an m-dimensional vector space. $\Delta^{(m)}$ denotes the m-dimensional *unit simplex*. This is the set of m-component vectors with nonnegative entries and components summing to 1, i.e.

$$\Delta^{(m)} := \{(\alpha_1, \ldots, \alpha_m) \mid \alpha_1, \ldots \alpha_m \geq 0, \sum_{j=1}^{m} \alpha_j = 1\}. \tag{2.1}$$

(:= means "is defined as").

For $a, b \in \mathbb{R}$, $a < b$, the *closed interval* $[a, b]$ is defined as the set $\{x : a \leq x \leq b\}$. For $a, b \in \mathbb{R} \cup \{-\infty, \infty\}$, $a < b$, the *open interval* (a, b) is defined as the set $\{x : a < x < b\}$. Similarly, $[a, b]^2$, $[a, b]^3$, and, for arbitrary $m \in \mathbb{N}$, $[a, b]^m$, are called a *closed square, closed cube,* and *closed hypercube* respectively; similarly for open squares, cubes, and hypercubes.

A set $\mathcal{U} \subseteq \mathbb{R}^l$ is called *convex* if it is closed under taking mixtures, i.e. for all $x_0, x_1 \in \mathcal{U}$, $\lambda \in [0, 1]$, $\lambda x_1 + (1 - \lambda)x_0 \in \mathcal{U}$. For example, $\mathbb{R}$, $\Delta^{(m)}$, the open $(0, 1)$ and the closed $[0, 1]$ *unit interval* are all convex, but $[0, 1] \cup [2, 3]$ is not.

Functions   A function $f : \mathcal{U} \to \mathcal{U}'$ is called *one-to-one* if there are no $x_1, x_2 \in \mathcal{U}$, $x_1 \neq x_2$ such that $f(x_1) = f(x_2)$. Otherwise, the function is called *many-to-one*.

Let $\mathcal{U} \subseteq \mathbb{R}^m$. A function $f : \mathbb{R}^m \to \mathbb{R}$ is called *convex* on $\mathcal{U}$ if for $x_0, x_1 \in \mathcal{U}$, all $\lambda \in [0, 1]$,

$$f(\lambda x_1 + (1 - \lambda)x_0) \leq \lambda f(x_1) + (1 - \lambda)f(x_0). \tag{2.2}$$

It is called *strictly* convex if (2.2) holds with strict inequality. f is called (strictly) concave if $-f$ is (strictly) convex.   The relation between convex sets and functions is as follows: the *epigraph* (points (x, y) lying on or above the graph $(x, f(x))$) of a convex function f is a convex set.

Let $\mathcal{U} \subset \mathbb{R}^1$ and suppose $f : \mathbb{R}^1 \to \mathbb{R}$ is twice differentiable on $\mathcal{U}$. It is easy to show that if $f''(x) \equiv d^2/dx^2 f(x) \geq 0$ for all $x \in \mathcal{U}$, then the function is convex on $\mathcal{U}$. If the inequality is strict, then the function is strictly convex (note that the converse of this statement is not true!). The generalization of this statement to multidimensional $\mathcal{U} \subset \mathbb{R}^m$, $f : \mathbb{R}^m \to \mathbb{R}$, $m > 1$ is as follows. If the *Hessian matrix* of $f(x)$ is positive semidefinite at all $x \in \mathcal{U}$, the function is convex on $\mathcal{U}$. If the Hessian matrix is positive definite, then the function is strictly convex. Positive (semi-) definiteness is defined below. The Hessian matrix is defined as the $m \times m$ matrix of second partial derivatives of $f(x)$: let $x = (x_1, \ldots, x_m)$. Then the ith row, jth column entry of the Hessian matrix at x is given by $(\partial^2 / \partial x_i \partial x_j) f(x)$.

Vectors and Matrices We assume the reader is familiar with basic linear algebra, and we just list the notational conventions used in this book. Most vectors in this book are a *column vector*. The jth component of vector $x \in \mathbb{R}^m$ is denoted x_j, so that

$$x = \begin{pmatrix} x_1 \\ \vdots \\ x_m \end{pmatrix}.$$

The symbol $\top$ is used to denote the transpose of a vector or matrix, so that $x^\top = (x_1, \ldots, x_m)$ is the row vector with entries $x_1, \ldots, x_m$. In the remainder of this book, vectors that represent data sequences (page 52) are row vectors, and, unless stated otherwise, all other vectors are column vectors. When we display such a vector's components inline rather than in an equation, we sloppily omit the transpose signs. That is, $(v_1, \ldots, v_m)$, written, as here, inside a line, denotes a column rather than a row vector.

An $m \times m$ matrix M is *symmetric* if $M = M^\top$, i.e. we have $M_{ij} = M_{ji}$, where M_{ab} is the ath row, bth column element of M. The *inverse* of a matrix M, if it exists, is denoted M^{-1}.

The *inner product* between vectors $x = (x_1, \ldots, x_m)$ and $y = (y_1, \ldots, y_m)$ is defined as

$$\sum_{i=1}^{m} x_i y_i \equiv x^\top y.$$

Throughout this book we use the notation $x^\top y$ for inner product. The *Euclidean norm* (distance from the origin $\mathbf{0} := (0, \ldots, 0)^\top$) of x, denoted $\|x\|$, is defined as

$$\|x\| := \sqrt{x^\top x} = \sqrt{\sum_{i=1}^{m} x_i^2}.$$

The only slightly advanced notion of linear algebra that we use is *positive (semi-) definiteness*. An $m \times m$ matrix M is called positive semidefinite if for all vectors $v = (v_1, \ldots, v_m) \in \mathbb{R}^m$ with $v \neq 0$, we have $v^\top M v \geq 0$. It is called positive definite if the inequality is strict. It can be shown that a matrix is positive definite if and only if all its eigenvalues are larger than 0. Since the determinant $\det M$ of a matrix M is equal to the product of its eigenvalues, this implies that a positive definite matrix has positive determinant and is therefore invertible.

Topological Concepts   The *closed ϵ-ball* $B(\epsilon)$ in $\mathbb{R}^m$ is the set of all points with distance $\leq \epsilon$ from the origin $\mathbf{0} = (0, \dots, 0)^\top$. That is,

$$B(\epsilon) = \{x : \|x\| \leq \epsilon\}.$$

Let $\mathcal{U} \subseteq \mathbb{R}^m$. The *closure* of $\mathcal{U}$, denoted $\mathrm{cl}\,\mathcal{U}$, is given by

$$\mathrm{cl}\,\mathcal{U} := \bigcap_{\epsilon > 0} (\mathcal{U} + B(\epsilon)),$$

where for two sets $\mathcal{U}_1, \mathcal{U}_2$, the set $\mathcal{U}_1 + \mathcal{U}_2$ is defined as $\{x : x = y + z, y \in \mathcal{U}_1, z \in \mathcal{U}_2\}$. The *interior* of $\mathcal{U}$, denoted $\mathrm{int}\,\mathcal{U}$, is given by

$$\mathrm{int}\,\mathcal{U} := \{x : \text{There exists } \epsilon > 0, \{x\} + B(\epsilon) \subset \mathcal{U}\}.$$

$\mathcal{U}$ is called *closed* if it is equal to its closure. It is called *open* if it is equal to its interior. The *boundary* of $\mathcal{U}$ is defined as $\mathrm{cl}\,\mathcal{U} \setminus \mathrm{int}\,\mathcal{U}$.

The set $\mathcal{U}$ is called *bounded* if there exists some hypercube $[a, b]^m$, $a, b \in \mathbb{R}$, such that $\mathcal{U} \subset [a, b]^m$. A set is *compact* if it is closed and bounded. A set $\mathcal{U} \subset \mathbb{R}^m$ is called *connected* if for every pair of points x, y in $\mathcal{U}$, there exists a continuous function $f : [0, 1] \to \mathbb{R}^m$ so that $f(0) = x$ and $f(1) = y$, and for all $\lambda \in [0, 1]$, $f(\lambda) \in \mathcal{U}$. Note that this is the case precisely if the points are "connected" within the set in the informal sense.

Minimum, Maximum, Infimum, Supremum   We often try to minimize or maximize some functions. For such optimizations we use the symbols $\min$, $\max$, and $\arg\min, \arg\max$. For a given function $f : \mathcal{U} \to \mathbb{R}$, $\min_{x \in \mathcal{U}} f(x)$ denotes the minimum of $f(x)$ where x ranges over the set $\mathcal{U}$. $\arg\min_{x \in \mathcal{U}} f(x)$ denotes the $x \in \mathcal{U}$ for which the minimum of f is achieved. If there are several minima, then $\arg\min_{x \in \mathcal{U}} f(x)$ is undefined. For example, $\min_{x \in \mathbb{R}}\{x^2 + 1\} = 1$, $\arg\min_{x \in \mathbb{R}}\{x^2 + 1\} = 0$. Sometimes a function may be lower-bounded by some y such that the function f comes arbitrarily close to y but never achieves it. In that case, $\min f(x)$ is undefined. We can then use a generalization of the concept of minimum called "infimum," abbreviated to $\inf$. If $\min f(x)$ is defined, then $\inf f(x)$ coincides with $\min f(x)$; but in contrast to $\min$, $\inf f(x)$ is defined for *every* f. For example, $\min_{x \in \mathbb{R}}\{x^2\} = \inf_{x \in \mathbb{R}}\{x^2\} = 0$, but $\min_{x \geq 0}\{1/x\}$ is undefined whereas $\inf_{x \geq 0}\{1/x\} = 0$. The *supremum* of f, abbreviated $\sup_x f(x)$, is the corresponding analogue to the maximum.

Order and Asymptotics Notation We frequently deal with functions f : $\mathbb{N} \rightarrow \mathbb{R}$ that increase or decrease in a certain manner with n. To concisely express how $f(n)$ grows with n, we use *order notation*. For two functions $f, g : \mathbb{N} \rightarrow \mathbb{R}$, we say "$f$ is large O of g," written as $f(n) = O(g(n))$, if there exists a constant $c > 0$ such that for all n, $|f(n)| \leq c|g(n)|$. For example, if f is $O(n^2)$, then $|f(n)|$ increases at most as fast as some constant times n^2; if f is $O(1/n)$, then $|f(n)|$ goes to 0 at "rate" at least $1/n$. We say "f is small o of g," written as $f(n) = o(g(n))$, if $\lim_{n \to \infty} f(n)/g(n) = 0$. For example, if $f(n) = o(1)$, then $f(n)$ goes to 0 for large n. We write $f(n) = \text{ORDER}(g(n))$ if there exist constants $c, c' > 0$ such that for all n, $cg(n) \leq f(n) \leq c'g(n)$. A more common notation for ORDER is the symbol Θ, but we already use that (as is even more common) to denote the parameter set of a statistical model. Note that the sign of $f(n)$ is irrelevant in the definition of $O(\cdot)$, but it is relevant in our definition of ORDER.

For functions $f_1, f_2, h : \mathbb{N} \rightarrow \mathbb{R}$ such that $\lim_{n \to \infty} h(n) = 0$, we sometimes want to express relations such as

$$f_1(n) \leq f_2(n) + O(h(n)). \tag{2.3}$$

This notation, a combination of O notation with inequalities, is nonstandard. (2.3) means that there exists a function g such that $g(n) = O(h(n))$, and for all n, $f_1(n) \leq f_2(n) + g(n)$. Finally, we write $f(n) \sim g(n)$ to indicate asymptotic approximate equality, in the sense that the ratio of f and g tends to one. Formally, $f(n) \sim g(n)$ is an abbreviation of $\lim_{n \to \infty} f(n)/g(n) = 1$; $f(\epsilon) \sim g(\epsilon)$ indicates that $\lim_{\epsilon \downarrow 0} f(\epsilon)/g(\epsilon) = 1$.

Other Notation The symbol $\propto$ means "proportional to". More precisely, let $f : \Theta \rightarrow \mathbb{R}$ and $g : \Theta \rightarrow \mathbb{R}$ be two functions, where Θ is some subset of $\mathbb{R}$. Then $f(x) \propto g(x)$ means that there is a $c > 0$ such that for all $x \in \Theta$, $f(x) = cg(x)$. For $x \in \mathbb{R}$, the *ceiling* of x, denoted by $\lceil x \rceil$, stands for the smallest integer that is greater than or equal to x. For a finite set $\mathcal{U}$, we use $|\mathcal{U}|$ to denote the number of elements in $\mathcal{U}$. For numbers x, $|x|$ also stands for the absolute value of x. We use "log" for logarithm to base two, and "ln" for natural logarithm. For $z \in \mathbb{R}^+$, the well-known *gamma function* is defined as $\Gamma(z) = \int_0^\infty t^{z-1}e^{-t}dt$. This function generalizes the factorial $n! = 1 \cdot 2 \cdot 3 \cdot \ldots \cdot n$, in the sense that for integer $n > 1$, $\Gamma(n) = (n-1)!$ (Weisstein 2006).

2.2   Probabilistic Preliminaries

2.2.1   Definitions; Notational Conventions

Sample Spaces   Probability distributions P are always defined on a *sample space* (set of outcomes) $\mathcal{X}$. Intuitively, this is the set of outcomes (samples) that may potentially be observed.   Throughout this book, $\mathcal{X}$ will always be either finite, countably infinite, or a connected subset of $\mathbb{R}^l$. Here $\mathbb{R}$ stands for the real numbers and $l \geq 1$. In the latter case we call $\mathcal{X}$ *continuous*.

Probability Distributions   We first consider finite or countable $\mathcal{X}$. In this case, a *probability mass function* on $\mathcal{X}$ is any function $P : \mathcal{X} \to [0,1]$ such that $\sum_{x \in \mathcal{X}} P(x) = 1$. If $\mathcal{X}$ is finite and has m elements, then the set of probability mass functions on $\mathcal{X}$ may be identified with the m-dimensional unit simplex $\Delta^{(m)}$. An *event* is any subset of $\mathcal{X}$. Every probability mass function P uniquely determines a *probability distribution P'* which is a function from *events* to $[0,1]$, such that for all $x \in \mathcal{X}$, $P'(\{x\}) = P(x)$, and for all $\mathcal{E} \subseteq \mathcal{X}$, $P'(\mathcal{E}) = \sum_{x \in \mathcal{E}} P(x)$. We typically use the same symbol P both for a probability mass function and its corresponding distribution, freely writing both $P(x)$ and $P(\{x\})$.

In case $\mathcal{X}$ is continuous, we start with a *density function*. This is the analogue of the probability mass function for the continuous case. A density function is any function $f : \mathcal{X} \to [0, \infty)$ such that $\int_{x \in \mathcal{X}} f(x) dx = 1$. With each density function we can associate a corresponding probability distribution P such that, for all events $\mathcal{E} \subseteq \mathcal{X}$,

$$P(\mathcal{E}) = \int_{x \in \mathcal{E}} f(x) d(x),$$

as long as $\int_{x \in \mathcal{E}} f(x) d(x)$ is well-defined. If $\int_{x \in \mathcal{E}} f(x) d(x)$ is undefined, then $P(\mathcal{E})$ is undefined. Note that P is once again a function from events (subsets of $\mathcal{X}$) to $[0,1]$. In general, one can define probability distributions on continuous sample spaces that cannot be expressed in terms of density functions, but in this book we will not consider those. For an example of a distribution on a continuous sample space, see Example 2.2.

We often deal with sample spaces that are allowed to be either countable or continuous. In that case, we give the formulas only for the countable case. The appropriate formulas for the continuous case can be arrived at by substituting $f(x)$ for $P(x)$ and replacing all sums by corresponding integrals. For example, $\sum_{x \in \mathcal{X}} P(x)\phi(x)$ becomes $\int_{x \in \mathcal{X}} f(x)\phi(x) dx$.

Random Variables   A *random variable* is a function from the sample space to the real numbers. While many find this definition counterintuitive[1], it is definitely the right one as we hope to illustrate with Example 2.1.

Formally, let P be a distribution on a sample space $\mathcal{Z}$ and $X : \mathcal{Z} \to \mathbb{R}$ be a random variable on $\mathcal{Z}$ (it is convenient to use the symbol $\mathcal{Z}$ for the sample space here, in contrast to the $\mathcal{X}$ we used before). We define for all $x \in \mathbb{R}$,

$$P(X = x) := P(\{z : X(z) = x\}).$$

We call $P(X = \cdot)$ the *distribution of random variable X*, and, overloading the symbol "$\sim$", we write "$X \sim P$".

Example 2.1   Suppose we toss a die twice in a row. Then the sample space $\mathcal{Z} = \mathcal{X} \times \mathcal{X}$, where $\mathcal{X} = \{1, \dots, 6\}$. An outcome is of the form $(a, b) \in \mathcal{Z}$, where a denotes the result of the first throw and b denotes the result of the second throw. We may denote the outcome of the first throw by X_1 and the outcome of the second throw by X_2. Then X_1 may be thought of as a *function* from $\mathcal{Z}$ to $\mathcal{X}$, such that, for all $(a, b) \in \mathcal{Z}$, $X_1(a, b) = a$. Similarly, X_2 is a function such that for all $(a, b) \in \mathcal{Z}$, $X_2(a, b) = b$. We can write the probability that the outcome of the first throw was s as $P(X_1 = s)$. By definition, $P(X_1 = s) = \sum_{(a,b) \in \mathcal{Z}: a = s} P(a, b) = \sum_{b \in \mathcal{X}} P(s, b)$.

The notion of random variable that we use in this book is slightly more general than usual: we allow a random variable to take on the value $+\infty$ or $-\infty$, but not both. Moreover, we allow random variables to be *partial* functions, which can be undefined for certain values. Formally, a *partial random variable* is a function $X : \mathcal{Z} \to \mathbb{R} \cup \{\uparrow\}$, where $\uparrow$ stands for "undefined." In the context of Example 2.1, the random variable Y defined as $Y := (X_1 - 1)/(X_2 - 1)$ is undefined if X_2 takes on the value 1. Finally, the *support* of the marginal distribution of P for random variable X is the smallest closed subset of $\mathbb{R}$ such that X lies in this set with probability 1.

Random Vectors   An m-dimensional *random vector* on sample space $\mathcal{Z}$ is a tuple $(X_1, \dots, X_m)^\top$ where each X_j is a random variable on $\mathcal{Z}$. We use the same symbols (capitals) for random vectors as for random variables. A random vector $X = (X_1, \dots, X_m)^\top$ may be thought of as a function from the sample space to $\mathbb{R}^m$. The random vector denoted by the same letter as

---

1. In the words of Joe Halpern, "a random variable is neither random nor a variable," rather it is a deterministic function. It only becomes "random" because it is applied to outcomes of a random process.

the sample space always denotes the identity function. So, when the sample space is $\mathcal{X}$, then for all $x \in \mathcal{X}$, $X(x):=x$; when the space is $\mathcal{Z}$, then for all $z \in \mathcal{Z}$, $Z(z):=z$. In Example 2.1, we have $Z = (X_1, X_2)^\top$.

Expectation, Mean, (Co-) Variance   Let P be a distribution on sample space $\mathcal{Z}$ and let $X : \mathcal{Z} \to \mathbb{R}$ be a random variable. The *expectation $E_P[X]$ of X* "under" distribution P is defined as $E_P[X]:=\sum_{z \in \mathcal{Z}} P(z)X(z)$. In case X is a partial random variable so that $X(z) = \uparrow$ (undefined) for some $z \in \mathcal{Z}$, we define

$$E_P[X]:= \begin{cases} \sum_{z \in \mathcal{Z}; P(z) > 0} P(z)X(z) & \text{if } X(z) \neq \uparrow \text{ for all } z \text{ with } P(z) > 0. \\ \uparrow & \text{otherwise.} \end{cases}$$

Whenever P is clear from the context, we omit it as a subscript. Since Z denotes the basic outcomes in space $\mathcal{Z}$, we get that $E_P[Z] = \sum_{z \in \mathcal{Z}} P(z)z$, and that $E_P[X]$ may equivalently be written as $E_P[X(Z)]$.

In some cases, we want to determine the expectation of a function of several random variables, and it is not clear which one we average over. In that case, we denote the random variables over which we average in the subscript. For example, let X_1, X_2 be independent random variables on $\mathcal{Z}$ with domains $\mathcal{X}_1$ and $\mathcal{X}_2$ respectively, and let $f : \mathcal{X}_1 \times \mathcal{X}_2 \to \mathbb{R}$ be some function. Then $E_{X_1 \sim P}[f(X_1, X_2)]$ stands for $\sum_{x \in \mathcal{X}_1} P(x_1)f(x_1, X_2)$. Note that this expression is itself a random variable: we can write $Y:=E_{X_1 \sim P}[f(X_1, X_2)]$ and then Y is a random variable on $\mathcal{Z}$ with $Y(z) = \sum_{x \in \mathcal{X}_1} P(x_1)f(x_1, X_2(z))$.

For a random variable X, $E[X]$ is called the *mean* of X; $E[X^m]$ is called the *mth moment of X*, so that the mean is equal to the "first moment." The *variance* of random variable X is defined as the expected squared difference between the value of X and its mean: $\text{var}[X]:=E[X - E[X]]^2$. An easy calculation shows that

$$\text{var}[X] = E[X - E[X]]^2 = E[X^2] - (E[X])^2. \tag{2.4}$$

The *covariance* between random variables X and Y is defined as

$$\text{cov}[X, Y]:=E[(X - E[X])(Y - E[Y])].$$

An easy calculation shows that

$$\text{cov}[X, Y] = E[(X - E[X])(Y - E[Y])] = E[XY] - E[X]E[Y]. \tag{2.5}$$

Example 2.2 [Normal Distribution] As an example of a distribution on the real line $\mathbb{R}$, consider the *normal* or *Gaussian* distribution with mean μ and variance σ^2. This most important distribution is identified by its density

$$f_{\mu,\sigma^2}(x):=\frac{1}{\sqrt{2\pi}\sigma}e^{-\frac{(x-\mu)^2}{2\sigma^2}},$$

the familiar bell-shaped curve (for a picture, see Figure 4.1, page 114). The *standard normal distribution* is the distribution with mean $\mu = 0$ and variance $\sigma^2 = 1$.

Joint, Marginal, and Conditional Probability   Let P be a distribution on sample space $\mathcal{Z}$. Let X and Y be two random variables on $\mathcal{Z}$ with ranges $\mathcal{X}$ and $\mathcal{Y}$ respectively. The *joint distribution* of X and Y is the distribution on $\mathcal{X} \times \mathcal{Y}$ with probability mass/density function

$$P(x,y):=P\{z : X(z) = x, Y(z) = y\}.$$

In general, whenever X is not the only random variable defined on a sample space $\mathcal{Z}$, we call the distribution $P(X = \cdot)$ the *marginal* distribution of X. This distribution is defined by

$$P(X = x):=P\{z : X(z) = x\} = \sum_{y\in\mathcal{Y}} P(x,y).$$

For example, in Example 2.1, $P(X_1 = \cdot)$ is the marginal distribution of X_1.

The terminology stems from the following fact: suppose we write the distribution P on $\mathcal{Z}$ as a two-dimensional table, where the entry in the ith row and jth column represents the probability $P(X = i, Y = j)$. In the *margin* of the ith row, we write the sum of all entries of the ith row. Then the margin represents the distribution $P(X = \cdot)$.

The *conditional distribution* $P(Y = \cdot \mid X = x)$ is the distribution on $\mathcal{Y}$ with probability mass/density function $P(y|x)$ defined as

$$P(y|x):=\frac{P(x,y)}{P(x)} = \frac{P\{z : X(z) = x, Y(z) = y\}}{P\{z : X(z) = x\}}.$$

We say "$P(y|x)$ is the probability of y conditioned on x," or "$P(y|x)$ is the probability of y *given x*." Intuitively, $P(y|x)$ represents the probability that y obtains after x has been observed.

Relations between Joint, Marginal and Conditional; Bayes Formula   We now slightly rewrite the definitions of joint, marginal and conditional distributions, which allows us to write them in a different manner. These rewritings are just as important as the original definitions; they will be used over and over again in this book. First, by the definition of conditional probability, we note that the joint distribution of X and Y satisfies, for all x, y,

$$P(x, y) = P(x \mid y)P(y), \tag{2.6}$$

where $P(y) = \sum_z P(Y(z) = z)$ is the marginal distribution of Y. (2.6) can be interpreted as saying that 'the probability that x and y both obtain is the probability that y obtains times the probability that x obtains given that y is the case. (2.6) is a special case of the enormously important chain rule, described in the box on page 54.

Second, by (2.6), for each $x \in \mathcal{X}$, the probability $P(x)$ under the marginal distribution of X can be written as a *weighted average of the conditional probability of x*:

$$P(x) = \sum_{y \in \mathcal{Y}} P(x \mid y)P(y). \tag{2.7}$$

Third, and perhaps most important, we have *Bayes formula*. In many applications of probability theory, we observe some $x \in \mathcal{X}$ and, for each $y \in \mathcal{Y}$, we have direct access to (a) the marginal distribution $P(y)$, and (b), the conditional probability $P(x \mid y)$. We would like to calculate the probabilities $P(y \mid x)$. This can be done using *Bayes formula:*

$$P(y \mid x) = \frac{P(x \mid y)P(y)}{P(x)}. \tag{2.8}$$

For a concrete example, see Section 2.5.2. Bayes formula follows by rewriting $P(y \mid x)$ as $P(x, y)/P(x)$, using the definition of conditional probability. Next, $P(x, y)$ is rewritten in terms of (2.6), which itself was also a consequence of the definition of conditional probability.

Example 2.3 [Multivariate Normal Distribution] As an example of a joint distribution, consider the k-dimensional *multivariate normal* distribution for $k \geq 1$ on sample space $\mathbb{R}^k$. Such a distribution is identified by an arbitrary vector $\mu = (\mu_1, \ldots, \mu_k)^\top$ and by any symmetric positive definite $k \times k$ matrix Σ. The joint density of $x = (x_1, \ldots, x_k)^\top$ is given by

$$f_{\mu, \Sigma}(x) := \sqrt{\frac{\det \Sigma^{-1}}{(2\pi)^k}} e^{-\frac{1}{2}(x-\mu)^\top \Sigma^{-1}(x-\mu)}. \tag{2.9}$$

A straightforward calculation shows that, with the density (2.9), we have, for $j = 1, \ldots, k$, $E[X_j] = \mu_j$ and $\text{cov}[X_i, X_j] = \Sigma_{ij}$. Therefore, μ is the *mean* (vector) and Σ is the *covariance matrix* of the multivariate normal. Note that the one-dimensional normal distribution, Example 2.2, arises as a special case of (2.9).

If $X \equiv (X_1, \ldots, X_k)$ is normally distributed with mean μ and covariance matrix Σ, we write

$$X \sim \text{N}(\mu, \Sigma).$$

We can think of the multivariate normal density as a bell-shaped curve in many dimensions, such that along each (one-dimensional) line going through the mean μ, the corresponding marginal distribution is itself normal: it can be shown that $X \equiv (X_1, \ldots, X_k)$ have a multivariate normal distribution if and only if for each $\lambda \in \mathbb{R}^k$, $\lambda \neq 0$, $\lambda^\top X$ is univariate normal.

Independence   We say "X is independent of Y" if for all x with $P(x) > 0$, for all $y \in \mathcal{Y}$,

$$P(y \mid x) = P(y). \tag{2.10}$$

In words, the value of X does not influence the probability distribution on Y. In terms of "conditional" and "marginal distributions" this becomes: for all x, *the conditional distribution of Y given $X = x$ is equal to the marginal distribution of Y*. Using (2.6), (2.10) can be rewritten as: for all $x \in \mathcal{X}, y \in \mathcal{Y}$,

$$P(x, y) = P(x) \cdot P(y), \tag{2.11}$$

which shows that X is independent of Y iff Y is independent of X. If X and Y are independent, then $E[XY] = E[X]E[Y]$ so that $\text{cov}[X, Y] = 0$.

Product Distributions   Let P_X be a distribution on $\mathcal{X}$ and let P_Y be a distribution on $\mathcal{Y}$, and let $\mathcal{Z} = \mathcal{X} \times \mathcal{Y}$. There are many different distributions on $\mathcal{Z}$ with marginal distributions P_X and P_Y. Only one of these will satisfy (2.11). This distribution is called the *product distribution* of P_X and P_Y.

The Joy of the Product Distribution If X and Y are independent, then their joint distribution must be the product distribution. Thus, the knowledge that X and Y are independent makes the set of possible distributions on $\mathcal{X} \times \mathcal{Y}$ much smaller, and therefore, much easier to work with: if $\mathcal{X}$ has m_X elements and $\mathcal{Y}$ has m_Y elements, then each distribution on $\mathcal{X} \times \mathcal{Y}$ that is a product distribution can be described by its two marginal distributions. Thus, it can be identified with a point in $\Delta^{(m_X)} \times \Delta^{(m_Y)}$. Since any $(\alpha_1, \ldots, \alpha_m) \in \Delta^{(m)}$

is determined by its first $m - 1$ components, the product distribution can be described by a $(m_X + m_Y - 2)$-dimensional vector. In contrast, each element of the set of *all* distributions on $\mathcal{X} \times \mathcal{Y}$ may be viewed as a point in $\Delta^{(m_X \cdot m_Y)}$ and in order to describe it we need a vector of dimension $m_X \cdot m_Y - 1$, which can be much larger.

Sample Space of n Outcomes   We study scenarios in which we observe a sample of size n. Let $\mathcal{X}$ be a sample space and let $\mathcal{X}^n$ be its n-fold product space. Then $\mathcal{X}^n$ is itself a sample space; we typically call $\mathcal{X}$ the sample space *for one observation*. $\mathcal{X}^n$ is simply called "the sample space." A sample in $\mathcal{X}^n$ is of the form $(x_1, x_2, \ldots, x_n)$. We abbreviate this to x^n: $x^n := (x_1, \ldots, x_n)$. Note that each outcome x_i may itself be a vector $(x_{1i}, \ldots, x_{ki})^\top \in \mathbb{R}^k$ for some $k \geq 1$. We use *row* vectors to denote sequences of outcomes, and *column* vectors to denote components of a single outcome.

For a given distribution P on $\mathcal{X}^n$, we use X_i to denote the random variable (or vector) on $\mathcal{X}^n$ that for any sample $(x_1, \ldots, x_{i-1}, x_i, x_{i+1}, \ldots, x_n)$ takes the value x_i; formally, X_i is a function $\mathcal{X}^n \to \mathcal{X}$ with $X_i(x_1, \ldots, x_n) := x_i$. Above we implicitly gave an example for $\mathcal{X} = \{1, \ldots, 6\}$ and $n = 2$.

Let $x_i \in \mathcal{X}$. As is customary, we abbreviate $P(\{x \in \mathcal{X} : X_i(x) = x_i\})$ to $P(X_i = x_i)$. In the case of countable $\mathcal{X}$, we further abbreviate $P(X_i = x_i)$ to $P(x_i)$. We abbreviate $P(X_1 = x_1, \ldots, X_n = x_n)$ to $P(x_1, \ldots, x_n)$ and even to $P(x^n)$ – in other words, we consistently use the symbol P both to denote the probability distribution of the X_i and to denote the corresponding probability *mass* function.

As is customary, we abbreviate the statement "all $x_1, \ldots, x_n \in \mathcal{X}^n$ satisfy property Q" to "$X_1, \ldots, X_n$ satisfies property Q." By realizing that the X_i are formally *functions* we see that it is just an instance of the general custom in mathematics to write, for a function f, "f satisfies property Q" as abbreviation of "for all x, $f(x)$ satisfies Q." To give a concrete example, if $\mathcal{X}$ is finite or countable, then clearly, for all n, all $x_1, \ldots, x_n \in \mathcal{X}^n$, $P(x_1, \ldots, x_n) \geq 0$. We abbreviate this property of probability mass functions to "for all n, $P(X_1, \ldots, X_n) \geq 0$."

Indicator Functions   We often work with expectations of *indicator functions*. Formally, the indicator random variable (function) for event $\mathcal{E}$ is defined as

$$\mathbf{1}_{\mathcal{E}}(x) := \begin{cases} 1 & \text{if } x \in \mathcal{E} \\ 0 & \text{otherwise,} \end{cases} \tag{2.12}$$

so that $E[1_{\mathcal{E}}] = P(\mathcal{E})$ and the *relative frequency* of s in a sample $x_1, \ldots, x_n$ can be defined as:

$$\mathbb{P}(s) := \frac{1}{n} \sum_{i=1}^{n} 1_{\{x_i = s\}} = \frac{1}{n} |\{i \in \{1, \ldots, n\} \mid x_i = s\}|. \tag{2.13}$$

2.2.2 Probabilistic Sources

Many interesting models are *probabilistic* in the sense that each point hypothesis in the model represents a probability distribution over all possible data sequences. Examples are the model of all Bernoulli sources, the model class of all Markov chains, the model of all normal distributions, etc. Intuitively, by a *probabilistic source* we mean a probability distribution defined over arbitrarily long samples.[2] To make this precise, we first have to introduce some notation. For a given sample space $\mathcal{X}$, we use $\mathcal{X}^+ := \cup_{n \geq 1} \mathcal{X}^n$ as the set of *all possible samples of each length*. For convenience, we define $\mathcal{X}^0 = \{x^0\}$ where x^0 is a special sequence which we call the *empty sample*. Finally, $\mathcal{X}^* := \mathcal{X}^+ \cup \mathcal{X}^0$. We are now ready to define probabilistic sources:

Definition 2.1 Let $\mathcal{X}$ be a sample space. A *probabilistic source* with outcomes in $\mathcal{X}$ is a function $P : \mathcal{X}^* \to [0, \infty)$ such that for all $n \geq 0$, all $x^n \in \mathcal{X}^n$ we have:

1. $\sum_{z \in \mathcal{X}} P(x^n, z) = P(x^n)$
   (this is usually called the *compatibility condition*).

2. $P(x^0) = 1$.

The two conditions above simply say that the "event" that data (x^n, z) arrives is identical to the event that data x^n arrives first and data z arrives afterward. If $\mathcal{X}$ is continuous, then the sum in the definition above is replaced by an integral but otherwise nothing changes. In all cases we consider in this book, the "probabilistic sources" we will be working with could also have been defined as *probability distributions over infinite sequences*. However, this would require measure theory, which we want to avoid here. Nevertheless, we will from now on sometimes refer to them as *probability distributions on $\mathcal{X}^\infty$, the set of infinite sequences*, rather than as *sources*.

---

2. Our definition of a probabilistic source coincides with what information theorists (Rissanen 1989) call an *information source*. In the language of advanced probability theory, Definition 2.1 expresses that $(X_1, X_2, \ldots)$ is a *random process* where for all n, X_n has distribution $P(X_n = x_n) := \sum_{x^{n-1} \in \mathcal{X}^{n-1}} P(x^{n-1}, x_n)$.

Sequential Decomposition Property ("Chain Rule" for Log Probability)
Let P be a probabilistic source for $\mathcal{X}$. For all $m \leq n$ we can write, for all $x^m \in \mathcal{X}^m$,

$$P(x^m) = P(x^m | x^{m-1}) P(x^{m-1}). \tag{2.14}$$

By recursively applying (2.14), we obtain, for all $x^n \in \mathcal{X}^n$, properties (2.15) and (2.16), which are so important that they deserve a box around them:

Sequential Decomposition of Log-Likelihood

$$P(x^n) = \prod_{i=1}^{n} \frac{P(x^i)}{P(x^{i-1})} = \prod_{i=1}^{n} P(x_i | x_1, \ldots, x_{i-1}). \tag{2.15}$$

Similarly, for all $x^n \in \mathcal{X}^n$,

$$-\log P(x^n) = \sum_{i=1}^{n} [-\log P(x_i | x_1, \ldots, x_{i-1})]. \tag{2.16}$$

In words, the probability of a sequence of outcomes is the product of the individual probabilities at all times i, where each probability is conditioned on *the past until time i*.

This property will be used over and over again in this book.

A special but very important case of probabilistic sources is those in which the past plays no role in determining the probability of the present outcome: if for all n, all $x^n \in \mathcal{X}^n$ with $P(x^n) > 0$, and all $x \in \mathcal{X}$, $P(X_{n+1} = x | x^n) = P(X_1 = x)$, we say that the data are *i.i.d.* (independently and identically distributed) according to P.

Notation and Terminological Conventions   For a given source P on $\mathcal{X}$, we denote by $P^{(n)}$ the marginal distribution on the first n outcomes that is induced by P. Thus, $P^{(n)}$ is a distribution on $\mathcal{X}^n$, and we have for all $x^n \in \mathcal{X}^n$ that $P^{(n)}(x^n) = P(x^n)$. The notation $P^{(n)}$ will be useful when its argument x^n is not given explicitly.

At several places in this book we introduce a distribution P on $\mathcal{X}$ and then suddenly refer to P as a source. In that case, we invariably mean the i.i.d. source that can be constructed from P by independence, so that for all n,

$x^n \in \mathcal{X}^n$, $P(x^n) = P^{(n)}(x^n) := \prod P(x_i)$. Thus, in such a case, $P^{(n)}$ refers to a product distribution.

2.2.3   Limit Theorems and Statements

Probability 1-Statements   Let P^* be some probabilistic source for $\mathcal{X}$ and let $g : \mathcal{X}^+ \to \mathbb{R}$ be some function defined on sequences of arbitrary length > 0. Throughout this book, we frequently make statements of the form "with P^*- probability 1, $\lim_{n \to \infty} g(X^n) = g_0$." Strictly speaking, such statements are not well defined under our definition of probabilistic source. If P^* is defined as a distribution (which we did not do because we did not want to use measure theory), the meaning of the statement can be made clear after all. The worried reader may in all cases replace the statement by the (well defined) statement: for all $\epsilon > 0$, all $\delta > 0$, there exists an n_0, such that for *all* $n' > n_0$, it holds that

$$P^*(\text{ for } all \ n \in \{n_0, n_0 + 1, \ldots, n'\}, |g(X^n) - g_0| \leq \epsilon) \geq 1 - \delta.$$

The Strong Law of Large Numbers   Informally, the *law of large numbers* (LLN) says that, with high probability, "in the long run" averages of independent random variables tend to their expectations. By using indicator random variables, we see that this is a generalization of the well-known fact that observed frequencies tend to probabilities. To formalize this we have to be a bit more precise (Feller 1968a). Let P be a probabilistic source for sample space $\mathcal{X}$, such that $X_1, X_2, \ldots$ are i.i.d. with mean μ and finite variance σ^2.

Theorem 2.1 [The Strong Law of Large Numbers]
With P-probability 1,

$$\frac{1}{n} \sum_{i=1}^{n} X_i \to \mu.$$

Variations of the law of large numbers often still hold if the $X_1, X_2, \ldots$ are neither identically nor independently distributed. We give an example application of the LLN in Example 2.6.

Union Bound   The union bound (Feller 1968a) states that for any distribution P and any two events $\mathcal{E}_1$ and $\mathcal{E}_2$, we have

$$P(\mathcal{E}_1 \cup \mathcal{E}_2) \leq P(\mathcal{E}_1) + P(\mathcal{E}_2). \tag{2.17}$$

This follows immediately by setting $A_1 = \mathcal{E}_1 \setminus \mathcal{E}_2$, $A_2 = \mathcal{E}_2 \setminus \mathcal{E}_1$ and $A_3 = \mathcal{E}_1 \cap \mathcal{E}_2$. Then A_1, A_2, and A_3 are mutually exclusive events so

$$P(\mathcal{E}_1 \cup \mathcal{E}_2) = P(A_1 \cup A_2 \cup A_3) = P(A_1) + P(A_2) + P(A_3),$$

whereas
$$P(\mathcal{E}_1) + P(\mathcal{E}_2) = P(A_1) + P(A_2) + 2P(A_3).$$

The argument can be extended to more than two sets: for any (finite or countably infinite) list of sets $\mathcal{E}_1, \mathcal{E}_2, \ldots$, we have

$$P \left(\bigcup_{i \geq 1} \mathcal{E}_i \right) \leq \sum_{i \geq 1} P(\mathcal{E}_i). \tag{2.18}$$

Markov's Inequality   Markov's inequality (Feller 1968a) says that, for any random variable Y that cannot take on negative values and $c > 0$, we have $P(Y \geq c) \leq E[Y]/c$. It has a one-line proof:

$$c \cdot P(Y \geq c) = \sum_{y : y \geq c} P(y)c \leq \sum_{y : y \geq c} P(y)y \leq E[Y].$$

The Central Limit Theorem   Let $X_1, \ldots, X_n, P, \mu$ and σ^2 be as above. Broadly speaking, the central limit theorem (CLT) says that with increasing n, the distribution of the average $n^{-1} \sum_{i=1}^n X_i$ more and more resembles that of a normal distribution with *mean μ and variance σ^2/n*. Thus, the average is approximately distributed as a random variable with the same mean as the original random variables, but *with a variance that gets smaller and smaller as n increases*. To obtain a formally correct statement of this result, we have to be a bit more precise. Formally, let Y_n be the centralized and rescaled average

$$Y_n := \frac{\sum_{i=1}^n X_i - n\mu}{\sqrt{n}}.$$

Theorem 2.2 [The Central Limit Theorem] $Y_1, Y_2, \ldots$ converges to a normal distribution with mean 0 and variance σ^2, in the sense that for any interval $[a, b]$,

$$P(Y_n \in [a, b]) \rightarrow \int_a^b \frac{1}{\sqrt{2\pi\sigma^2}} e^{-\frac{x^2}{2\sigma^2}} \, dx.$$

The central limit theorem complements the law of large numbers: CLT implies a weak form of LLN, namely, it implies that for all $\epsilon > 0$, the probability of $n^{-1} \sum_{i=1}^{n} X_i$ diverging by more than ϵ from μ goes to 0 with increasing n. LLN is stronger than CLT in that it says that the convergence actually happens in a very strong sense (with probability 1); LLN is weaker than CLT in that in contrast to CLT, it tells us nothing about the distribution of $n^{-1} \sum_{i=1}^{n} X_i$ near the value to which it converges. We give an example application of the CLT in Example 2.6.

2.2.4   Probabilistic Models

Much of traditional statistics is concerned with families of probabilistic sources. Such families are often simply called "models." In many cases such models can be *parameterized* by a vector θ coming from some set of possible parameter vectors Θ.   The family of probabilistic sources can then be written as

$$\mathcal{M} = \{P_\theta \mid \theta \in \Theta\},$$

where the P_θ are all probabilistic sources defined over the same sample space $\mathcal{X}$. P_θ can be read as "the probability distribution of the data given that the source is (indexed by) θ"; examples are given below. Strictly speaking, θ does not denote a probabilistic source but a *name* for a source. It will be very helpful to make this distinction. Sometimes, we need to make explicit that Θ is actually a parameter set corresponding to model $\mathcal{M}$. In that case we write Θ as $\Theta_{\mathcal{M}}$. Similarly, we sometimes need to make explicit that $\mathcal{M}$ is a model indexed by parameter set Θ. In that case, we write $\mathcal{M}$ as $\mathcal{M}_\Theta$. Note that in order to know $\mathcal{M}$, it is not enough to know Θ. We also need to know the function $\Theta \to \mathcal{M}$, mapping each $\theta \in \Theta$ to $P_\theta \in \mathcal{M}$; in other words, we need to know the definition of P_θ for each θ. Motivated by this insight, we call (Θ, P_θ) the *parameterization of* $\mathcal{M}$. Nevertheless, for reasons of convenience, whenever P_θ is clear from the context, we refer to Θ as "the parameterization of $\mathcal{M}$" and we then say "$\mathcal{M}$ is parameterized by Θ."

We usually abbreviate $E_{P_\theta}[\cdot]$ (the expectation of a random variable under the distribution in $\mathcal{M}$ indexed by θ) to E_θ.

Maximum Likelihood (ML) Distribution   Given a model $\mathcal{M}$ and some data D, we will often be interested in the *maximum likelihood estimator*   (see any introductory textbook on statistics, for example (Bain and Engelhardt 1989)). In the case of finite or countable $\mathcal{X}$, this is just the probability distribution P_θ that maximizes the probability of D; in the continuous case, it is the distribution that maximizes the probability density of D. Here $D = (x_1, \dots, x_n)$ for some n. If such a P_θ exists, we call the corresponding parameter value θ the *maximum likelihood estimator* for data D and we denote it by $\hat\theta$. Sometimes we write $\hat\theta(D)$ rather than $\hat\theta$, in order to stress that $\hat\theta$ actually depends on D: it can be viewed as a function of D. If $\mathcal{M}$ is parameterized by Θ, we can write

$$\hat\theta(D) = \hat\theta = \underset{\theta \in \Theta}{\arg\max}\, P_\theta(D) = \underset{\theta \in \Theta}{\arg\max}\, \log P_\theta(D), \qquad (2.19)$$

where the rightmost ("log-likelihood") characterization is often useful in simplifying calculations.

Example 2.4 [Bernoulli sources] We consider the model of *Bernoulli sources* for the binary sequences given in Example 1.1 on page 4, defined in terms of *Bernoulli random variables*. First, let X be a random variable on some space $\mathcal{Z}$. Let $\theta \in [0,1]$. We say X is a *Bernoulli(θ)* random variable if for all $z \in \mathcal{Z}$, $X(z) \in \mathcal{X} = \{0,1\}$, and if $P(X=1) = \theta$. If X is Bernoulli(θ), we write

$$X \sim \mathrm{Ber}(\theta).$$

The Bernoulli model $\mathcal{B}^{(1)}$ is defined as the extension, by independence, of the Bernoulli distribution to probabilistic sources, so that, under the Bernoulli model P_θ, $X_1, X_2, \ldots$ are i.i.d., each of them being a Bernoulli(θ) random variable. Formally:

Definition 2.2 Let $\mathcal{X} = \{0,1\}$. The Bernoulli model $\mathcal{B}^{(1)}$ is defined as

$$\mathcal{B}^{(1)} := \{P_\theta \mid \theta \in [0,1]\},$$

where for each $\theta \in [0,1]$, P_θ is defined as follows: for all n, all $x^n \in \mathcal{X}^n$, $P(X_{n+1} = 1 | X^n = x^n) = P(X_1 = 1) = \theta$.

In words, we regard the data as being generated by independent tosses of a biased coin with probability θ of coming up heads (which we identify with 1). The probability of an initial sequence x^n with n_1 1s and $n_0 = n - n_1$ 0s is then given by $P_\theta(x^n) = \theta^{n_1}(1-\theta)^{n_0}$. Note that this is the probability of observing a particular, individual sequence x^n. The probability of observing *some* sequence of length n with n_1 1s is much larger, and given by $\sum_{x^n : \sum x_i = n_1} P_\theta(x^n) = \binom{n}{n_1}\theta^{n_1}(1-\theta)^{n_0}$.

As a first example, let us consider sequence (1.3) of Example 1.1, page 4, again. This sequence contains four times as many 0s as 1s. Intuitively, the ML estimator for this sequence is $\hat\theta = 1/5$. A simple calculation shows that this is indeed the case: for a sequence D of length n with a fraction of $\mathbb{P}(1)$ 1s, we have $\hat{\theta}(D) = \mathbb{P}(1)$: the ML Bernoulli model coincides with the frequency of 1s. (Verify by solving for θ in $(d/d\theta) \log P_\theta(x^n) = 0$ and checking that $\log P_\theta(x^n)$ reaches its maximum at the solution for θ.)

Example 2.5 [Multinomial Model] The Bernoulli example can be extended to the multinomial model $\mathcal{M}$, the set of all distributions on $\mathcal{X} = \{1, \dots, m\}$, extended to probabilistic sources by assuming independence. We parameterize the multinomial model by the vector $\theta = (\theta_1, \dots, \theta_{m-1})$ and define $\theta_m = 1 - \sum_{j=1}^{m-1} \theta_j$, such that, for $j = 1..m$, $P_\theta(X_i = j) = \theta_j$. Then for each sequence x^n, $P_\theta(x^n) = \prod_{j=1}^{m} \theta_j^{n_j}$, where n_j denotes the number of occurrences of outcome j in the sequence x^n.

It can be shown that the ML estimator is also consistent for the multinomial model. However, for each small $\epsilon > 0$, the smallest sample size at which we can expect the frequency of each outcome to be within ϵ of its probability, increases with the number of possible outcomes m.

Example 2.6 [Consistency of the ML Estimator for the Bernoulli model] Suppose now that data $X_1, X_2, \dots$ are actually i.i.d. according to some Bernoulli distribution with parameter θ^*. What can we say about the behavior of the ML estimator $\hat{\theta}$? By the law of large Numbers (Section 2.2.3, page 55), we know that with P_{θ^*}-probability 1, the frequency of 1s tends to its expectation $E_{\theta^*}[1_{X_1=1}] = E_{\theta^*}[X_1] = \theta^*$. Therefore, with P_θ-probability 1, the ML estimator $\hat{\theta}$ must converge to the 'true' parameter value θ^*. We say that the ML estimator is *consistent*: given enough data, with high probability the estimate gets more and more accurate (closer to the true value). We will say more about this desirable property in Section 2.5. In later chapters we shall see that for other, larger probabilistic models, the ML estimator does not always behave so nicely.

We can say something about the rate of convergence of the ML estimator by using the central limit theorem (Section 2.2.3, page 55). This theorem tells us that, for large samples, $\hat{\theta}$ is approximately distributed as a normal random variable with mean θ^* and variance $E[(X - E[X])^2]/n = \theta^*(1 - \theta^*)/n$. Thus, $\hat{\theta} - \theta^*$ is approximately distributed as a normal with mean 0 and variance $\theta^*(1 - \theta^*)/n$. Therefore, the probability that $|\hat{\theta} - \theta^*| > K\sqrt{\theta^*(1 - \theta^*)}/\sqrt{n}$ tends to $1 - \int_{-K}^{K} (2\pi)^{-0.5} e^{-0.5x^2} dx$. For $K = 3$, this probability is about 0.02; for $K = 4$, it is about 0.002. We can thus expect $|\hat{\theta} - \theta^*|$ to be no larger than a few times $1/\sqrt{n}$.

2.2.5   Probabilistic Model Classes

We frequently encounter model *classes* (sets of models, hence sets of families of probabilistic sources),

$$\mathcal{M} = \bigcup_{k \in \{k_1, k_2, \ldots\}} \mathcal{M}^{(k)}, \tag{2.20}$$

where $k_1 < k_2 < \ldots$ are all positive integers, and $\mathcal{M}^{(k)}$ is a "k-dimensional" parametric model $\mathcal{M}^{(k)} = \{P_\theta \mid \theta \in \Theta^{(k)}\}$, and $\Theta^{(k)} \subseteq \mathbb{R}^k$. In that case we denote the ML estimator for data D within submodel $\mathcal{M}^{(k)} \subset \mathcal{M}$ by $\hat{\theta}^{(k)}(D)$; but if k is fixed and understood from the context we simply use $\hat{\theta}$ rather than $\hat{\theta}^{(k)}$. We call a model class $\mathcal{M} = \cup_k \mathcal{M}^{(k)}$ *nested* if $\mathcal{M}^{(k_1)} \subset \mathcal{M}^{(k_2)} \subset \mathcal{M}^{(k_3)} \subset \ldots$. For some interesting model classes $\mathcal{M}$, it is inconvenient or ambiguous to denote the models contained in a class $\mathcal{M}$ by their number of parameters. An example is the selection-of-variables problem in regression, see page 25: there exist several submodels with the same number of parameters. In such cases, we denote these submodels as $\mathcal{M}_\gamma$ where γ is an element of the set of *indices* or *model parameters* Γ. Then k_γ is used to denote the number of parameters in $\mathcal{M}_\gamma$.

Below we provide a simple example of a model class: the *Markov chains*. We use this class in our first real implementation of MDL in Chapter 5.

Example 2.7 [Bernoulli Distributions and Markov Chains] By the sequential decomposition property (page 54) the following holds for an *arbitrary* probabilistic source P: for all n, all x^n,

$$P(x^n) = \prod_{i=1}^{n} P(x_i \mid x_1, \ldots, x_{i-1}). \tag{2.21}$$

The model $\mathcal{B}^{(1)}$ of Bernoulli sources restricts the probabilistic sources to those for which the following strengthening of (2.21) holds (for all n, x^n):

$$P(x^n) = \prod_{i=1}^{n} P(x_i),$$

so that the conditional probabilities do not actually depend on the past. In many realistic situations we would like to allow for the distribution of X_i to be dependent on the past, but only in such a way that knowledge of the *immediate* past (i.e. X_{i-1}) completely determines the distribution of X_i. In other words, we are interested in the model $\mathcal{B}^{(2)}$ consisting of all distributions P satisfying

$$P(x^n) = P(x_1) \prod_{i=2}^{n} P(x_i | x_{i-1}) \tag{2.22}$$

Usually, $n \gg 1$. In that case the probability of X_1 will not play an important role. Therefore, to simplify the analysis (and somewhat differently from other treatments, e.g. (Feller 1968b)), we will further impose that all distributions in $\mathcal{B}^{(2)}$ satisfy $P(X_1 = 1) = 1/2$. The resulting model $\mathcal{B}^{(2)}$ can be parameterized as follows:

$$\mathcal{B}^{(2)} = \{P_\theta \mid \theta = (\eta_{[1|0]}, \eta_{[1|1]}) \in [0,1]^2\},$$
$$P_{\eta_{[1|0]}, \eta_{[1|1]}}(x^n) = \tfrac{1}{2} \cdot \prod_{i=2}^{n} P_{\eta_{[1|0]}, \eta_{[1|1]}}(x_i | x_{i-1}), \tag{2.23}$$

where $P_{\eta_{[1|0]}, \eta_{[1|1]}}(X_i = 1 | X_{i-1} = 1) := \eta_{[1|1]}$ and $P_{\eta_{[1|0]}, \eta_{[1|1]}}(X_i = 1 | X_{i-1} = 0) := \eta_{[1|0]}$. Just like the ML distribution for the Bernoulli model exists for all sequences of data D and is given by the frequency of 1s, the ML distribution for the first-order Markov chain exists too, and is given by setting $\eta_{[1|1]}$ to the frequency in D of a 1 followed by a 1, and $\eta_{[1|0]}$ to the frequency in D of a 0 followed by a 1:

$$\hat{\eta}_{[1|1]} := \mathbb{P}(1|1) = \frac{\sum_{i=1}^{n-1} \mathbf{1}_{X_i=1} \mathbf{1}_{X_{i+1}=1}}{\sum_{i=1}^{n-1} \mathbf{1}_{X_i=1}} \;;\; \hat{\eta}_{[1|0]} := \mathbb{P}(1|0) = \frac{\sum_{i=1}^{n-1} \mathbf{1}_{X_i=0} \mathbf{1}_{X_{i+1}=1}}{\sum_{i=1}^{n-1} \mathbf{1}_{X_i=0}}. \tag{2.24}$$

Again, this can be easily verified by differentiation. We can generalize further by taking into account the γ previous outcomes (rather than just the immediately preceding outcome) in determining the probability of X_i. This leads to our general definition of γth-order Markov chains. Let $k = 2^\gamma$. We denote the γth-order Markov chain model by $\mathcal{B}^{(k)}$, in order to be consistent with the remainder of this book where we use the superscript index k to denote the number of parameters (dimension of $\Theta^{(k)}$). $\mathcal{B}^{(k)}$ is defined as

$$\mathcal{B}^{(k)} = \{P_\theta \mid \theta \in \Theta^{(k)}\} \;;\; \Theta^{(k)} = [0,1]^k, \tag{2.25}$$

where $\theta = (\eta_{[1|0...0]}, \eta_{[1|0...01]}, \ldots, \eta_{[1|1...10]}, \eta_{[1|1...11]})$, and for all n, x^n,

$$P_\theta(x^n) = \left(\frac{1}{2}\right)^\gamma \prod_{i=\gamma+1}^{n} P_\theta(x_i | x_{i-1}, \ldots, x_{i-\gamma}) \tag{2.26}$$

and

$$P_\theta(X_i = 1 | X_{i-1} = x_{i-1}, \dots, X_{i-\gamma} = x_{i-\gamma}) = \eta_{[1|x_{i-1}x_{i-2}\dots x_{i-\gamma}]}.$$

Finally, we define $\mathcal{B} = \cup_{\gamma \geq 0} \mathcal{B}^{(2^\gamma)}$.

2.3   Kinds of Probabilistic Models*

Throughout this book we encounter many different types of models. In this section we characterize these according to some of their distinguishing properties such as: do they consider the data i.i.d., is the likelihood function differentiable, and so on. This characterization will be highly useful later on. As an additional benefit, we see several examples of the types of models that MDL can be applied to. This section may be skipped at first reading.

1. i.i.d. models.   The first distinction we make is between i.i.d. and non-i.i.d. models. For example, the Bernoulli model is i.i.d., while the first-order Markov model is not.

---

i.i.d. Models
We call a family of probabilistic sources an *i.i.d. model* if it consists only of probabilistic sources under which the data are i.i.d. (independently and identically distributed).

If $\mathcal{M}$ is an i.i.d. model, then under any $P \in \mathcal{M}$ the distributions of $X_1, X_2, \dots$ are all identical: $P(X_1 = \cdot) = P(X_2 = \cdot) = \dots$. As is customary, in that case we use the generic letter "X" to indicate the distribution of X_1 (or $X_2, \dots$).

2. Conditional models.   Until now, all models we considered – i.i.d. or not – were defined as distributions over the full space of outcomes $\mathcal{X}$. In many applications, we are really interested in how a random variable Y taking values in $\mathcal{Y}$ depends on another variable U taking values in $\mathcal{U}$; we are not interested in the distribution of U itself. In some cases, no such distribution exists. For example, the values of U may be set by the experimenter. The prototypical examples are (probabilistic) regression, which we first encountered in Chapter 1, Example 1.4, and classification. We deal with this situation by introducing *conditional* probabilistic models as follows:

Definition 2.3 Let $\mathcal{Z} = \mathcal{U} \times \mathcal{Y}$. A function $P(\cdot \mid \cdot) : \mathcal{Z}^* \to [0, \infty)$ is called a *conditional probabilistic source* if, for all $n \geq 0, u^{n+1} \in \mathcal{U}^{n+1}, y^n \in \mathcal{Y}^n$,

1. $\sum_{z \in \mathcal{X}} P(y^n, z \mid u^{n+1}) = P(y^n \mid u^n)$.

   This is just the compatibility condition of probabilistic sources again, now required to hold for all sequences of input vectors $u_1, u_2, \ldots$.

2. $P(y^0 \mid u^0) = 1$.

A *conditional probabilistic model* is a family (set) of conditional probabilistic sources.

Example 2.8 [Regression] In regression problems we are interested in learning how the values $y_1, \ldots, y_n$ of a *regression* variable Y depend on the values $u_1, \ldots, u_n$ of the *regressor* variable or vector U, which takes values in a space $\mathcal{U}$. We assume or hope that there exists some function $h : \mathcal{U} \to \mathcal{Y}$ so that $h(U)$ predicts the value Y reasonably well, and we want to learn such an h from data. To this end, we assume a set of *candidate predictors* (functions) $\mathcal{H}$. In Example 1.4, we took $\mathcal{H}$ to be the set of all polynomials and we made no specific probabilistic assumptions. In this book we focus on a version of MDL that is only applicable to probabilistic models – for the nonprobabilistic case, we refer to Grünwald (1998). Thus, to make MDL applicable we somehow need to combine $\mathcal{H}$ with some probabilistic assumptions about the domain. If it is reasonable to assume Gaussian noise, we can do this in a straightforward manner: we take hypothesis h to express the *probabilistic* statement that

$$Y_i = h(U_i) + Z_i, \tag{2.27}$$

where the Z_i are i.i.d. Gaussian random variables with mean 0 and some variance σ^2, independent of U_i. (2.27) implies that the conditional density of $y_1, \ldots, y_n$, given $u_1, \ldots, u_n$, is equal to the product of n Gaussian densities:

$$f_{\sigma,h}(y^n \mid u^n) = \left(\frac{1}{\sqrt{2\pi}\sigma}\right)^n \exp\left(-\frac{\sum_{i=1}^n (y_i - h(u_i))^2}{2\sigma^2}\right). \tag{2.28}$$

Note that the smaller the sum of squared errors achieved by h on (u^n, y^n), the larger the density of y^n given u^n according to $f_{\sigma,h}(\cdot \mid \cdot)$. The analysis of such models is considerably simplified if the functions h are linear combinations of a (potentially infinitely large) set of "basis" functions. In that case we speak of *linear regression:*

Polynomial Regression Is Linear, although Polynomials Aren't

In *linear regression*, we restrict ourselves to $\mathcal{H}$ containing functions h that can be expressed as a linear combination of *basis functions* $h_j : \mathcal{U} \to \mathcal{Y}$. *Note that the basis functions themselves do not have to be linear!* For example, polynomial regression for polynomials of degree k, described in Example 2.9 below, is a special case of linear regression.

Example 2.9 [Polynomial Regression Model $\mathcal{P}$] Linear regression starts out with a set of basis functions $h_1, \ldots, h_k$ from $\mathcal{U}$ to $\mathcal{Y}$. The model $\mathcal{H}^{(k)}$ relative to this set of basis functions, is then defined as the set of functions h_μ such that $h_\mu(u) := \sum_{j=1}^{k} \mu_j h_j(u)$ for some $(\mu_1, \ldots, \mu_k) \in \mathbb{R}^k$. The corresponding *linear regression model* $\mathcal{M}^{(k)}$ is defined as the family of conditional probabilistic sources $\{ f_{\sigma^2, h} \mid h \in \mathcal{H}^{(k)} \}$ such that, given $u_1, u_2, \ldots$, the Y_i are i.i.d. with density given by (2.28), for some fixed value of the scale parameter σ^2. In general, the basis functions h_j can be anything. If $\mathcal{U} = \mathbb{R}$ they may, for example, be wavelets or trigonometric functions. In this book we shall take as our working example the case where $\mathcal{U} = \mathbb{R}$ and the h_j are polynomials, $h_j(u) = u^{j-1}$, so that each $h \in \mathcal{H}^{(k)}$ is a $(k-1)$-degree polynomial. We denote the corresponding linear regression model by the special notation $\mathcal{P}^{(k)}$. Note that, although it represents $(k-1)$-degree polynomials, $\mathcal{P}^{(k)}$ has k parameters, which explains the notation.

A formal definition of the linear regression models, often just called "linear models" is given in Chapter 12.

Readers familiar with regression analysis may wonder why we bother with conditional models, since one may regard the $u_1, u_2, \ldots$ as given in advance, and define an ordinary probabilistic source for $\mathcal{Y}$ in terms of the single, given sequence of u_i rather than all potential sequences in $\mathcal{U}^*$. It then seems that we do not need the above definition. While this can indeed be done for linear regression (Chapter 12), such a treatment would rule out comparison of nonlinear regression models such as Fechner's and Stevens's model (see Example 1.3, page 12).

3. (Non-) Parametric models. The third distinction we make is between parametric and nonparametric models:

Parametric and Smooth Models

Let $\mathcal{M}$ be a family of probabilistic sources parameterized by some connected set $\Theta \subseteq \mathbb{R}^k$ for some $k > 0$. We call the parameterization (Θ, P_θ) *continuous* if for all n, all $x^n \in \mathcal{X}^n$, $\log P_\theta(x^n)$ viewed as a function of θ is well defined and continuous. We call the parameterization *smooth* if, additionally, $\log P_\theta(x^n)$ is differentiable infinitely often on Θ.

We call a model $\mathcal{M}$ *parametric* if it can be continuously parameterized. We call a parametric model $\mathcal{M}$ *smooth* if it can be smoothly parameterized.

Broadly speaking, a parametric model is finite-dimensional: it is a model that can be continuously parameterized by some connected subset of $\mathbb{R}^k$ for some finite k. For example, the γth-order Markov chains are a parametric model (with $k = 2^\gamma$ parameters), for all fixed $\gamma \geq 0$. On the other hand, the model $\mathcal{B} = \cup_{\gamma \geq 0} \mathcal{B}^{(2^\gamma)}$ consisting of *all* Markov chains of *each* order is not parametric. In most beginner's courses on statistics, all models considered are parametric, and if one writes a "model", one really means a "parametric model." We will follow this common assumption in this text. Yet in modern statistics one frequently considers what statisticians call "nonparametric" models. These may sometimes be viewed as unions of parametric models, as in the Markov chain example above or in the case of Gaussian mixture models (Example 2.12) or histograms (Chapter 13, Section 13.3). In such cases, nonparametric models coincide with what in this text we call *CUP model classes* see model, class, CUP, Chapter 13, Section 13.2. But in general, nonparametric models may be of more abstract type such as "the set of all distributions on $\mathcal{X} = [0, 1]$ with twice differentiable densities." In principle, MDL can be applied to all of these, sometimes by approximating them by sequences of CUP model classes such as histograms (Chapter 13, Section 13.2), sometimes by approaching them more directly and abstractly, as with Gaussian processes (Chapter 13, Section 13.5).

Exponential Families   Of course, there is an enormous variety of smooth i.i.d. models around. But surprisingly many of these fall into one of relatively few categories. The most important of these categories is undoubtedly the class of *exponential families*.

Exponential families all share some pleasant properties which greatly facilitate their use in statistical and coding applications (Section 18.1, page 600). A prime example is the fact that they are smooth, and that, essentially, no mat-

---

The Exponential Families

Let Θ be some subset of $\mathbb{R}^k$ and let $\mathcal{M} = \{P_\beta \mid \beta \in \Theta\}$ be a family of probability distributions (not sources!) on sample space $\mathcal{X}$. $\mathcal{M}$ is an *exponential family* if there exist a function $\phi = (\phi_1, \dots, \phi_k) : \mathcal{X} \to \mathbb{R}^k$ and a function $r : \mathcal{X} \to [0, \infty)$ such that, for all $\beta \in \Theta$,

$$P_\beta(X) := \exp(\beta^\top \phi(X) - \psi(\beta)) r(X), \qquad (2.29)$$

where $\beta^\top \phi(X)$ is the (standard) inner product between β and $\phi(X)$, and $\psi(\beta) = \ln \sum_{x \in \mathcal{X}} \exp(\beta^\top \phi(x)) r(x)$. In this text we only consider exponential families that can be expressed in the form (2.29) such that the corresponding parameter set Θ is open and convex.

An exponential family defined in terms of a function $\phi = (\phi_1, \dots, \phi_k)$ is called *k-dimensional* if the representation (2.29) is *minimal*. This means that there exists no $\lambda_0, \lambda_1, \dots, \lambda_k \in \mathbb{R}^{k+1} \setminus \{0\}$ such that for all x with $r(x) > 0$, $\sum_{j=1}^k \lambda_j \phi_j(x) = \lambda_0$. Whenever we refer to an exponential family parameterized as (2.29), we assume that the parameterization is minimal.

These definitions and conventions are explained in detail in Chapter 18. The Bernoulli family with parameters in $(0, 1)$, the Poisson and geometric family, the families of gamma, beta, and Dirichlet distributions, and many other frequently used statistical models are exponential families. Standard linear and logistic regression can also be expressed in terms of exponential families, no matter what basis functions are chosen.

---

ter what data we observe, the likelihood $P_\beta(x^n)$ always achieves a unique maximum. as a function of β.

Exponential families are defined in the box on page 66. Note that the definition only applies to sample spaces of single outcomes. The simplest way to extend them to samples of arbitrary length is by taking product distributions. The resulting families then become i.i.d. models.

Example 2.10 [Bernoulli and Markov Models as Exponential Families] The Bernoulli model (Example 2.4) $\mathcal{B}^{(1)} = \{P_\theta \mid \theta \in [0, 1]\}$ is *not* a smooth model under our definition, because $\log P_\theta(x^n)$ is undefined for some combinations of θ and x^n. For example, take $\theta = 0$ and an x^n that contains a 1. If we restrict the Bernoulli model to parameters in the set $(0, 1)$ rather than $[0, 1]$, then it is a smooth model. It even becomes an exponential family. This can be seen by taking $\phi(X) = X = 1_{X=1}$ and defining

$$\beta_\theta \equiv \ln \frac{\theta}{1 - \theta}. \tag{2.30}$$

A straightforward calculation shows that $P_\theta(X) = \exp(\beta_\theta \phi(X) - \psi(\beta_\theta))$ where $\psi(\beta) = \ln(1 + e^\beta)$. Since (2.30) is a 1-to-1 transformation, we may parameterize the distributions by β rather than θ, with $\beta \in (-\infty, \infty)$.

In Chapter 18, Section 18.5, page 617, it is shown that also some non-i.i.d. models such as the γth order Markov sources can be constructed as sequences of exponential families; the many pleasant properties that hold for exponential families also transfer to such "non-i.i.d." exponential families.

Example 2.11 [Normal (Gaussian) Model as an Exponential Family] Let $\mathcal{M} = \{f_{\mu,\sigma^2} \mid (\mu, \sigma^2) \in \Theta\}$ with $\Theta = \mathbb{R} \times [0, \infty)$ and

$$f_{\mu,\sigma^2}(x) = \frac{1}{\sqrt{2\pi}\sigma} e^{-\frac{(x-\mu)^2}{2\sigma^2}}.$$

$\mathcal{M}$ is the family of normal distributions or Gaussians (identified with their densities). By the transformations

$$\beta_1 = \frac{\mu}{\sigma^2} \; ; \; \beta_2 = -\frac{1}{2\sigma^2}$$

we see that every normal distribution may be written as

$$f_{\mu,\sigma^2}(x) = \exp(\beta^\top \phi(X) - \psi(\beta)), \text{ where } \phi(X) = (X, X^2)^\top \text{ and } \beta^\top = (\beta_1, \beta_2).$$

Both in the Bernoulli and in the Gaussian example, we had to "reparameterize" the model to bring it in exponential form. The parameterization (2.29) is called the *canonical* parameterization of an exponential family. The canonical parameterization of the geometric, Poisson, and multinomial families is discussed in Example 18.1 on page 602.

Although a wide variety of parametric models can be expressed as exponential families, there certainly exist highly interesting parametric models that fall outside this class. These are often much harder to analyze. A prototypical example is the class of mixture families, defined below. MDL may be applied to select the, in some sense, "optimal" number of components of a mixture family for a given sequence of data (Li and Barron 2000), but we shall not consider such an application in detail since we will mainly be concerned with exponential families.

Mixture Models Let $\mathcal{M}_0$ be a family of distributions on sample space $\mathcal{X}$ with parameter set Θ_0. The family $\mathcal{M}$ of *m-component mixtures* of $\mathcal{M}_0$ consists of the distributions $P_{\alpha,\theta_1,\ldots,\theta_m}$ with for $j = 1..m$, $\theta_j \in \Theta_0$, and $\alpha = (\alpha_1,\ldots,\alpha_m) \in \Delta^{(m)}$ (the unit simplex, Equation 2.1, page 42). $P_{\alpha,\theta_1,\ldots,\theta_m}$ is defined as

$$P_{\alpha,\theta_1,\ldots,\theta_m}(X) := \sum_{j=1}^{m} \alpha_j P_{\theta_j}(X), \tag{2.31}$$

where $P_{\theta_j} \in \mathcal{M}_0$ is defined relative to parameterization Θ_0.

For example, the "Gaussian mixture model" defined below is a mixture family. m-component mixture models are appropriate if it is thought that there are really m different sources of data. The idea is that each outcome is generated as follows. First, independently of everything else, a source $j \in \{1,\ldots,m\}$ is chosen, where the probability of choosing source j is given by α_j. Then data are generated by the distribution P_{θ_j} associated with α_j. Mixture models are often used to model clusters of data. In principle, one can take mixtures of any family defined on single outcomes, including any exponential family.

Example 2.12 [The Gaussian Mixture Model] Let $\mathcal{X} = \mathbb{R}$. Let $\alpha \in \Delta^{(m)}$, $\mu \in \mathbb{R}^m$ and $\sigma \in [0,\infty)^m$ be m-dimensional vectors. The m-component Gaussian mixture model is given by the distributions with densities

$$f_{\alpha,\mu,\sigma^2}(X) = \sum_{j=1}^{m} \alpha_j \frac{1}{\sqrt{2\pi}\sigma_j} e^{-\frac{(x-\mu_j)^2}{2\sigma_j^2}}, \tag{2.32}$$

which can be depicted as a super-position of m bell-shaped Gaussian curves with different widths σ_j^2 and centers μ_j. This is clearly a mixture model as defined in (2.31). The distributions (2.32) are extended to probabilistic sources by taking product distributions, so that outcomes are independently distributed.

In practice, we often deal with situations where the number of components of the "best" Gaussian mixture is not known. If we simply pick the number of components that best fits the data $x_1,\ldots,x_n$ at hand, we will end up with an n-component Gaussian mixture, with means corresponding to the x_i and variances all equal to 0. Clearly, in most situations this distribution will be a terrible overfit - it assigns 0 density to any point different from the points already seen. This is a prototypical MDL application: we can use MDL to select the *number* of components of the given data. This will give us some tradeoff of goodness-of-fit and complexity (which is related to the number of components).

Unfortunately, mixtures of exponential families are mathematically not nearly as easy to analyze as exponential families.

This Book's Level of Generality

Most theorems about universal coding and MDL inference in this book belong to one of the following two types:

1. The result is stated for very general model classes, which can contain almost arbitrary sets of distributions, or arbitrary sets of i.i.d. distributions. In particular, the sets can be highly complex model classes (Chapter 13). Examples are the main MDL consistency theorems, Theorem 5.1 in Chapter 5 and Theorem 15.1 and Theorem 15.3 in Chapter 15.

2. The result is stated for exponential family models only. Examples are all theorems in Chapter 4 and in Part II, Chapter 7 through Chapter 12. Many of the results still hold for much more general parametric families, but they do not hold if the model class is not parametric. For each theorem, we shall indicate whether or not the (suitably modified) result still holds for more general families.

2.4 Terminological Preliminaries: Model Selection, Hypothesis Selection, Parameter Estimation, and Prediction

In order to make this text more accessible, let us contrast our terminology with that used in the various areas concerned with inductive inference: statistics, pattern recognition, and machine learning.

The task of inductive inference is to find laws or regularities underlying some given set of data D. These laws/regularities are then used to gain insight in the process underlying the data or to make predictions or decisions regarding other (future) data from the same or a similar source. In this book, we call the "laws underlying data" *hypotheses*. Hypotheses can be further subdivided into two categories: *point* hypotheses and composite hypotheses. Composite hypotheses are sets of point hypotheses.

A point hypothesis is also called a *singleton* or *individual* hypothesis. We deal with two kinds of point hypotheses: *probabilistic sources*, which are probability distributions over possible realizations of data; and *decision functions*, which arise when the data are of the form $D = ((x_1, y_1), \ldots, (x_n, y_n))$ and the task is to learn a functional relationship between x- and y-values. The underlying goal is often to learn how to predict y-values *given* x-values. Decision functions are functional relationships between x- and y-values or, more generally, rules which associate each x with an associated prediction or decision about y. An example of a class of decision functions is the polynomials that were used in various examples in Chapter 1.

We reserve the word *model* for sets of point hypotheses of the same functional form, e.g. the "model of second-degree polynomials." We reserve the word "model class" for a union of interrelated models, e.g. the "model class of all polynomials." The definitions of "model" and "model class" are chosen so that they agree with how these words are used in statistical practice. Therefore they are intentionally left somewhat imprecise.

A general theory of inductive inference should be able to deal with (at least) the following types of problems: *(1) hypothesis selection*, with its three special cases: (1a) *point hypothesis selection*, (1b) *model selection*, and (1c) *parameter estimation*; and (2) *prediction*. By a "hypothesis selection method" we mean a procedure that, when input data D of arbitrary length, outputs a hypothesis coming from some set C of candidate hypotheses. Point hypothesis selection is the case where all hypotheses in C are singletons. If $C = \mathcal{M}^{(k)}$ is some parametric model (see page 57), we use the term "parameter estimation." Much of traditional statistics is concerned with parameter estimation. A "model selection method" is a procedure that, when input data D of arbitrary length, outputs a model $\mathcal{M}$ from some set of candidate models $C = \{\mathcal{M}_1, \mathcal{M}_2, \ldots\}$. Hence, each hypothesis is a model rather than a point hypothesis. In Section 1.6, page 23 we explained why we are often interested in model rather than point hypothesis selection.

By a "prediction method" we mean a procedure that, when input data $X_1, \ldots, X_n$, directly outputs a prediction concerning the next (as yet unseen) observation X_{n+1}.

We note that in the statistics literature, what we here call "point hypothesis" is usually called "simple hypothesis." We cannot follow this terminology, since for us, a "simple hypothesis" means a "noncomplex" hypothesis, which is something quite different (see page 31).

Our use of "model selection" coincides with the use of the term in much of the statistics literature. However, in the information-theoretic literature (and specifically in Rissanen's work on MDL, (Barron, Rissanen, and Yu 1998)) what we here call "probabilistic source" is called "probabilistic model" and what we here call "model" is called "model class."

Example 2.13 [Hypotheses, Models and Parameters] To illustrate, let $\mathcal{B}^{(k)}$ be the model of k-parameter Markov chains over $\mathcal{X} = \{0, 1\}$ (page 60). If, based on data D, we try to infer an "optimal" $\mathcal{B}^{(k)}$ within the list $\mathcal{C} = \{\mathcal{B}^{(1)}, \mathcal{B}^{(2)}, \mathcal{B}^{(4)}, \ldots\}$, this is called *model* selection. If we try to infer the optimal $P_\theta \in \mathcal{B}^{(k)}$ for some fixed k, this is called both parameter estimation and point hypothesis selection. If we try to infer both k and $P_\theta \in \mathcal{B}^{(k)}$, this is called point hypothesis selection but not parameter estimation.

2.5 Modeling Preliminaries: Goals and Methods for Inductive Inference

We end this chapter by discussing what, according to different paradigms, the *goals* of statistical (inductive) inference should be, and how these goals relate to the primary goal implicit in MDL methods. In the boxes on the next two pages we give an overview of the terminology and goals of the currently most popular paradigms. Below we will say a bit more about *consistency*, a central concept in orthodox statistics, and about several basic concepts of *Bayesian statistics*. The reason is that we will use these concepts heavily in Part II and Part III of this book.

2.5.1 Consistency

We often want to find out whether a proposed method for inductive inference can be expected to actually do what it is supposed to do. One can check this in many different ways. One way which will repeatedly occur in this book is to check whether the method is *consistent*. Roughly speaking, a "consistent" inference method for a given model $\mathcal{M}$ has the following property: assuming that data are actually distributed (often the word *generated* is used) according to one of the $P^* \in \mathcal{M}$, then, as more and more data become available, the procedure should output distributions that are in some sense "closer and closer" to the *true* (as it is usually called) P^*. To formalize the notion of consistency, we need to specify what we mean by "closer." This can be done in many ways, and indeed, there exists a variety of notions of "consistency." For example, we can have "consistency in expected Hellinger distance," or "consistency in Euclidean distance between parameters, with probability 1." Every time we give a consistency statement for MDL inference in this book, we shall explicitly define the type of consistency that is involved. Such statements can be found in, for example, Chapter 5, Theorem 5.1; Chapter 15,

The Terminology Used in Fields Concerned with Inductive Inference
In the statistics literature, the data D are usually called the "sample" or
the "observations." The word "model" is usually used to denote a family of interrelated probability distributions or functions. The process of
finding, based on the given data, good hypotheses/models/predictors
is called "statistical inference." One usually assumes the existence of a
distribution P^* according to which D are distributed; we say that D *are
generated by* P^*. P^* is called the "true" distribution. When the data are of
the form $D = ((x_1, y_1), \ldots, (x_n, y_n))$ (where $x_i \in \mathcal{X}$ and $y_i \in \mathcal{Y}$) and the
goal is to learn a functional relationship between x- and y-values, this is
called *regression*. The special case where y takes values in a finite set $\mathcal{Y}$ is
called *classification*. In this case, a function $f : \mathcal{X} \to \mathcal{Y}$ is called a *classifier*.
In the part of the statistical literature that deals with *hypothesis testing*,
what we call a "point hypothesis" is called a *simple* hypothesis; "composite hypotheses" means the same as here.

In the information-theoretic literature, the word *model* is often used to
denote a (single) probabilistic source (rather than a set of them) and the
word *model class* is used to denote what we call a "model."

In the machine learning and neural network literature (Michalski, Carbonell, and Mitchell 1983; Michie, Spiegelhalter, and Taylor 1994; Hertz,
Krogh, and Palmer 1991), the sample is usually called the *training set*, and
future data are often called the *test set*. The process of finding, based on
the training data, good hypotheses/models/predictors is called "learning." When data are of the form $D = ((x_1, y_1), \ldots, (x_n, y_n))$ and the goal
is to learn a functional relationship between x and y, and/or to predict
y-values *given* x-values, this is called *supervised learning*. The special case
where y takes values in a finite set is called *classification*.

The field of *statistical learning theory* (Vapnik 1998) concentrates on learning functional relationships between x and y. The fields of *pattern recognition* (Ripley 1996; Devroye, Györfi, and Lugosi 1996; Duda, Hart, and
Stork 2000) and *computational learning theory* (Anthony and Biggs 1992)
further concentrate on *classification*, which computational learning theorists call "concept learning"; a "classifier" is then called a "concept".

A Note on the Goals of Inductive Inference

Orthodox In the (orthodox, non-Bayesian) statistics literature, the goal is often to provide inference procedures that are *consistent*. As some authors put it: "the goal of probability theory is to compute probabilities of events for some given probability measure; the goal of (orthodox) statistics is, given that some events have taken place, to infer what distribution P^* may have generated these events."

Bayesian In one form of Bayesian statistics, one considers a family of distributions (model) $\mathcal{M}$ and one represents one's uncertainty or "beliefs" by a prior probability distribution over all the distributions in $\mathcal{M}$. The first goal is then to update this distribution in the light of data; this transforms the prior into a *posterior* distribution, representing one's beliefs regarding the data-generating machinery *conditioned* on the data. The posterior is then used as a basis for predictions concerning the distributions in $\mathcal{M}$ and/or concerning new data coming from the same source.

Machine Learning In the decision-theoretic, machine learning, neural network, and pattern recognition literature, the goal is often to find a decision rule (e.g. a classifier) that *generalizes well* or equivalently, that has small *generalization error* under fairly general conditions. Roughly speaking, a decision rule that "generalizes well" is a hypothesis that has been inferred from "training data" D and that, when later tested on new "test data" D', fits these test data well, or leads to good predictions of D', where prediction error is measured using some *prediction error criterion* or *loss function*. (There may or may not be an assumption that D and D' are both generated by the same probability distribution P^*.)

MDL In the MDL literature, the primary goal is to find as many useful properties in the data as we can. This is realized by searching for the model that allows for as much compression of the data as possible, or in other words, that 'squeezes out' as much regularity, or useful information/properties, from the data as possible. The hope (but not the primary aim) is then that such a model also generalizes well and that, in the idealized case when some $P^* \in \mathcal{M}$ generates the data, the procedure of finding it is consistent - and we shall see that this often is the case.

Theorem 15.1 and Theorem 15.3; and the informal statements in Chapter 16.
These involve several variations of consistency.

We point out that the usual definition of consistency for *model selection*
needs extra care, because the true distribution P^* may be contained in more
than one of the models under consideration: Let $\mathcal{C} = \{\mathcal{M}_1, \mathcal{M}_2, \ldots\}$ be a
set of candidate models and let $\mathcal{M} = \bigcup \mathcal{M}_k$. We say that a *model* selection
method is consistent (relative to $\mathcal{C}$) if for all $P^* \in \mathcal{M}$, with P^*-probability 1,
there exists some n_0 (which may depend on P^*) such that for all n larger than
n_0, when input $X_1, \ldots, X_n$, the model selection method outputs k^* where k^*
is the *smallest* integer such that $P^* \in \mathcal{M}_{k^*}$. Again, there exist variations
where the statement is not required to hold with probability 1, but just with
probability converging to 1.

We should point out that one can certainly *not* say that "inconsistent methods are generally bad" and "consistent methods are generally good"; for one
thing, consistency only says something about "large sample" behavior, and
in some cases "large" may be extremely large indeed. Moreover, statisticians
of different schools attach different importance to the concept (see the box on
page 73). In this book the notion will often be used to give the reader some
preliminary idea of the behavior of a method under consideration.

2.5.2   Basic Concepts of Bayesian Statistics

Suppose we observe experimental data x^n that takes its value in some set
$\mathcal{X}^n$. We consider a (potentially infinite) set of probabilistic hypotheses Θ
as possible explanations of x^n. These hypotheses are probabilistic sources:
each θ defines a source P_θ for $\mathcal{X}$. Upon observing a particular x^n, we would
then like to calculate, for each θ, the probability that θ is the case *given* that
we observed x^n. That is, we are given $P_\theta(x^n)$, but we want to calculate the
probability of θ given x^n. In general, this probability is undefined, but if we
are willing to assign each $\theta \in \Theta$ an *a priori probability* $W(\theta)$, then we can
construct a new joint probability distribution $\bar{P}_{\text{Bayes}}$ on the space $\Theta \times \mathcal{X}^n$. We
define $\bar{P}_{\text{Bayes}}$ by setting its marginal distribution of θ equal to W,

$$\bar{P}_{\text{Bayes}}(\theta) = \sum_{x^n \in \mathcal{X}^n} \bar{P}_{\text{Bayes}}(\theta, x^n) := W(\theta),$$

and setting the conditional distribution to

$$\bar{P}_{\text{Bayes}}(x^n \mid \theta) := P_\theta(x^n).$$

By (2.6), page 50, this uniquely defines a joint distribution $\bar{P}_{\text{Bayes}}(\theta, x^n)$ on $\Theta \times \mathcal{X}^n$. In this space, the conditional distribution of θ given observation x^n, which is what we are after, is now well defined. By Bayes formula, (2.8), it is given by

$$\bar{P}_{\text{Bayes}}(\theta \mid x^n) = \frac{P_\theta(x^n)W(\theta)}{\sum_{\theta \in \Theta} P_\theta(x^n)W(\theta)}. \tag{2.33}$$

Example 2.14 Suppose you are dropped by parachute in a foreign country, which can be either Sweden, Germany, or France. You do not know which country you are in, and you do not speak the language, but you do know that the proportion of blond people in Sweden is 2/3, in Germany it is 1/2, and in France it is 1/3. You observe n people of which n_1 are blond, and would like to draw some conclusions about the probability of being in each country. Thus, $\mathcal{X} = \{B, NB\}$ and your set of hypotheses is $\{S, G, F\}$, and, assuming you observe an i.i.d. subset $(x_1, \ldots, x_n)$ of the population, the probability under this set under each hypothesis is given by

$$P_S(x^n) = \left(\frac{2}{3}\right)^{n_1} \left(\frac{1}{3}\right)^{n-n_1}, \ P_G(x^n) = \left(\frac{1}{2}\right)^n, \ P_F(x^n) = \left(\frac{1}{3}\right)^{n_1} \left(\frac{2}{3}\right)^{n-n_1}.$$

Suppose you want to use Bayes formula to calculate the probability that you are in Sweden, given that you meet five people all of whom are blond. This is only possible if you can assign an a priori probability W to Θ. Suppose you think that you are in each country with equal prior probability. Then the "a posteriori probability" that you are in Sweden is given by

$$\bar{P}_{\text{Bayes}}(S \mid x^n) = \frac{\frac{1}{2}\left(\frac{2}{3}\right)^5}{\frac{1}{2}\left(\frac{2}{3}\right)^5 + \frac{1}{2}\left(\frac{1}{2}\right)^5 + \frac{1}{2}\left(\frac{1}{3}\right)^5} = \frac{4^5}{4^5 + 2^5 + 3^5} = \frac{1024}{1299}.$$

Suppose that data are really i.i.d. according to P_{θ^*}, where θ^* indexes one of the three distributions P_S, P_G, or P_D. Then the "posterior" will, with high probability, concentrate on θ^* in the sense that $\bar{P}_{\text{Bayes}}(\theta \mid x^n)$ tends to 0 exponentially fast for $\theta \neq \theta^*$. If Θ is uncountably large, for example, if it represents all, rather than just three, Bernoulli sources, then typically, the posterior still converges to θ^*, but now only polynomially fast.

A strange aspect of our example is the "prior" probability $W(\theta)$. Where does this probability come from? When we look at more realistic examples, we can broadly distinguish between three types of applications of Bayes formula. In one type, the prior probabilities can be determined and have some frequentist interpretation. A prototypical example is medical testing.

Example 2.15 [Bayes Formula and Medical Testing] Suppose Mr. A performs
a medical test for some disease, and the test turns out positive. It is known
that the probability of a false test result is, say, 1%, both for false positives
and for false negatives. Naively, one would now assume that the probability
that Mr. A has the disease is 0.99. But now suppose it is also known that
the percentage of the population that has the disease is 0.1%. If Mr. A. is an
"average" person, then we can calculate the probability that he has the disease
using Bayes formula, where $\Theta = \{D, ND\}$, "D" representing that Mr. A has
the disease. Then the probability of a positive test result under P_D is 0.99, and
the probability of a positive test result under P_{ND} is 0.01. By Bayes formula,
the probability that Mr. A has the disease is really

$$\bar{P}_{\text{Bayes}}(D \mid \text{positive test result}) =$$
$$\frac{0.99 \cdot 0.001}{0.99 \cdot 0.001 + 0.01 \cdot 0.999} = \frac{0.00099}{0.00099 + 0.00999} \approx 0.09. \quad (2.34)$$

In the second type of application, one of the hypotheses θ^* is true and observable in principle; it may just not be observable to the experimenter. Yet,
the prior probabilities cannot be set equal to population statistics, because
the hypotheses cannot be viewed as the outcome of a sampling process. This
is the case in Example 2.14.

In the third type of application, the hypotheses cannot be viewed as the
outcomes of a sampling process, and, worse, they are unobservable *in principle*. Much of statistical inference deals with this type of hypotheses; a prototypical example is when θ represents the bias of some coin. Also the parameters in Stevens's and Fechner's models (Example 1.3, Chapter 1) can be
thought of in this manner.

Bayesian Statistics   *Bayesian statistics* is a paradigm of inductive inference
that starts with the premise that a statistician can *always* assign prior probabilities in some reasonable manner, even in the second and third type of applications discussed above (Berger 1985; Bernardo and Smith 1994; Gelman,
Carlin, Stern, and Rubin 2003). For example, such prior distributions may
represent prior belief or knowledge about the situation; in some subschools
of Bayesian statistics, one also allows "objective" priors representing "igno-
rance" about the parameter Θ. In Example 2.14, for symmetry reasons, the
"objective" prior would be the uniform prior $W(\theta) = 1/3$. The use of Bayes
formula in applications of the first type is not controversial. The essence of
Bayesian statistics is to assign prior probabilities and apply Bayes formula
even in applications of the second and third type. While such a stance is de-
batable, adopting it leads to a beautifully coherent statistical theory. Here we

just list the main quantities arising in this theory, since these quantities also play an important (though quite different) role in MDL inference:

1. **The posterior $W(\theta \mid x^n)$.** This is just the quantity (2.33) defined above. To emphasize the facts that (a) prior and posterior distributions can be viewed as "weights" of hypotheses; and (b), the "posterior" can itself be thought of as a "prior," to be used when new experimental data are observed, we usually write $W(\theta \mid x^n)$ rather than $\bar{P}_{\text{Bayes}}(\theta \mid x^n)$.

2. **The marginal distribution.** By (2.7), the marginal distribution of X^n based on the distribution $\bar{P}_{\text{Bayes}}$ is given by

$$\bar{P}_{\text{Bayes}}(x^n) := \sum_{\theta \in \Theta} P_\theta(x^n) W(\theta). \tag{2.35}$$

This distribution is sometimes called the *Bayesian marginal likelihood, Bayes mixture,* or *Bayesian evidence* given the model indexed by Θ, and the prior W.

3. **The predictive distribution.** Suppose we have already observed $n-1$ outcomes $x_1, \ldots, x_{n-1}$, and we would like to make some predictions about X_n. We can make such predictions based on the conditional distribution of X_n given x^{n-1}. By the definition of conditional probability, this distribution is given by

$$\bar{P}_{\text{Bayes}}(X_n = x \mid x^{n-1}) = \frac{\bar{P}_{\text{Bayes}}(x^n)}{\bar{P}_{\text{Bayes}}(x^{n-1})}.$$

For example, in Example 2.14, the probability that the third person is blond given that we have observed two blonds already, is given by

$$\frac{6^{-3}(4^3 + 2^3 + 3^3)}{6^{-2}(4^2 + 2^2 + 3^2)} = \frac{99}{6 \cdot 29} \approx 0.57.$$

Importantly, the predictive distribution can be rewritten as an average of the distributions $P_\theta(x_n)$, weighted by their posterior probability:

$$\bar{P}_{\text{Bayes}}(x_n \mid x^{n-1}) = \frac{\bar{P}_{\text{Bayes}}(x^n)}{\bar{P}_{\text{Bayes}}(x^{n-1})} = \frac{\sum P_\theta(x_n) P_\theta(x^{n-1}) W(\theta)}{\bar{P}_{\text{Bayes}}(x^{n-1})} =$$

$$\frac{\sum P_\theta(x_n) W(\theta \mid x^{n-1}) \bar{P}_{\text{Bayes}}(x^{n-1})}{\bar{P}_{\text{Bayes}}(x^{n-1})} = \sum P_\theta(x_n) W(\theta \mid x^{n-1}). \tag{2.36}$$

It explains why the predictive distribution is sometimes called "posterior predictive." Note that it also shows that, if all P_θ are i.i.d. sources, then *the predictive distribution of X_n is in fact equal to the marginal distribution of X_n, based on prior distribution $W'(\theta) = W(\theta \mid x^{n-1})$.* This fact, and (2.36) itself, can be generalized to the case where the P_θ are not i.i.d. sources.

As we will see, the marginal and predictive distributions play a crucial role in MDL inference, but the posterior – arguably the most important concept in Bayesian inference – is *not* an important concept in MDL!

2.6   Summary and Outlook

We have summarized all the probabilistic concepts that are needed in this book. In the next chapter, we will discuss all the information-theoretic (coding) theory needed to actually implement the MDL principle.

3 *Information-Theoretic Preliminaries*

Overview In order to make the MDL principle precise, we need to review some basic information theory, highlighting some essential ingredients of MDL. We define *coding systems, codes* and *description methods* and explain how they relate to *probability distributions*. We introduce the ideas of *uniform* and *quasi-uniform* codes/description methods. We also review the notions of *entropy* and *relative entropy*.

Contents Section 3.1 introduces all the coding (description) theory needed in this book. Section 3.2 discusses the fundamental relationship between probability distributions and codes *on which everything that is to follow will be built*. Section 3.3 gives a second connection between probabilities and code-lengths, and introduces the notions of entropy and relative entropy.

Fast Track Readers with no prior knowledge of information theory should probably read the whole chapter. Readers with some knowledge of information theory may just want to look at the boxes, specifically those on pages 88, 91, 96, 101, and 99. These highlight some facts about codes that are absolutely crucial in understanding MDL.

3.1 Coding Preliminaries

Definitions "Coding" means to describe sequences of *symbols* coming from some *alphabet* by other sequences of symbols coming from some potentially different alphabet. Formally, by an *alphabet* we mean any finite or countable set, whose elements we shall call *symbols*. The notation $\mathcal{X}^0$, $\mathcal{X}^n$, $\mathcal{X}^*$, $\mathcal{X}^+$ we introduced for sample spaces $\mathcal{X}$ (Chapter 2, Section 2.2.2) is extended to alphabets. In the MDL setting, we typically obtain a data sample $x^n \in \mathcal{X}^n$

where $\mathcal{X}$ is the space of observations. For now we assume that $\mathcal{X}$ is finite or countable, so that it can be viewed as an alphabet. Even if $\mathcal{X}$ is uncountable (e.g. $\mathcal{X} = \mathbb{R}$), in practice the x_i will always be recorded with finite precision so that essentially the same framework applies; we deal with the continuous case in the box on page 99.

We are interested in the length of some *encoding* or *description* of x^n. We shall always encode sequences x^n using the binary alphabet $\mathbb{B} = \{0, 1\}$. This is without any loss of generality, as will be explained in Section 3.2.2. In this way, each sequence x^n is mapped to some binary sequence or *string* in the set $\mathbb{B}^* = \cup_{k \geq 1} \mathbb{B}^k$. We now formally define the two main ways of associating sequences with descriptions, the "code" and the "description method."[1] Both notions are defined in terms of the fully general *coding system*:

Definition 3.1 [Coding Systems, Codes, Description Methods] (see also Figure 3.1). Let $\mathcal{A}$ be some alphabet.

Coding system: A *coding system* C is a relation between $\mathcal{A}$ and $\mathbb{B}^*$. If $(a, b) \in C$, we say b is a *code word* for *source symbol* or *source sequence* a.

We call a coding system *singular* or *lossy* if there exist $a, a' \in \mathcal{A}$, $a \neq a'$, that share a code word (i.e. there exist b such that $(a, b) \in C$ and $(a', b) \in C$).

We call a coding system *partial* if for some a, there is no b such that $(a, b) \in C$. In that case we say "a cannot be encoded under C."

Description method: A *description method* is a nonsingular coding system, that is, a coding system such that each $b \in \mathbb{B}^*$ is associated with at most one $a \in \mathcal{A}$.

A description method may be identified with a *decoding function* C^{-1} : $\mathbb{B}^* \rightarrow \mathcal{A} \cup \{\uparrow\}$ where $C^{-1}(b) = \uparrow$ means that b is not a code word for any source symbol. ("$\uparrow$" should be read as "undefined").

Code: A *code* is a description method such that each $a \in \mathcal{A}$ is associated with at most one $b \in \mathbb{B}^*$.

A code may be identified with a (possibly partial) *encoding function* C : $\mathcal{A} \rightarrow \mathbb{B}^* \cup \{\uparrow\}$ that maps each $a \in \mathcal{A}$ to its unique encoding $C(a) \in \mathbb{B}^*$. $C(a) = \uparrow$ indicates that $C(a)$ is undefined.

---

1. Perhaps surprisingly, the notion of "code" is defined differently in different texts on information theory. The definition of code in the standard textbook (Cover and Thomas 1991) coincides with what we here call a nonpartial code. The definition of code in the standard textbook (Li and Vitányi 1997) coincides with what we here call a nonpartial description method. Rissanen, in his 1989 monograph on MDL-type methods, defines a code as a mapping from $\mathcal{A}^*$ (the set of data sequences of arbitrary length, rather than length 1) to $\mathbb{B}^*$, and what he calls a "coding system" is what we call a (partial) description method! In this text we reserved the term "coding system" for the most general coding notion we could think of.

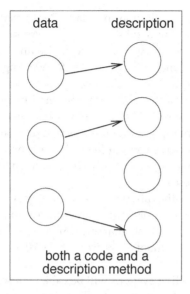

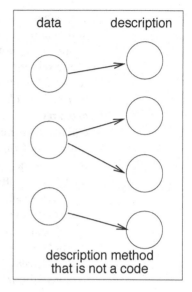

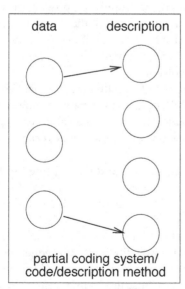

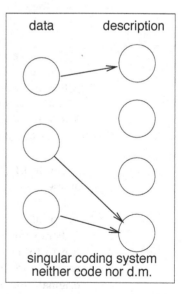

Figure 3.1 Coding systems, codes and description methods as defined in this book. MDL is only concerned with nonsingular codes/coding systems, allowing for lossless coding.

Let us explain this definition in detail. Recall that a *relation* R between $\mathcal{A}$ and $\mathcal{B}$ is by definition a subset of $\mathcal{A} \times \mathcal{B}$. We say that "the relation holds for (a, b)," or equivalently, "a is associated with b" or equivalently, "(a, b) is in the relation" if and only if $(a, b) \in R$. Viewing a coding system C as a relation, the interpretation is that the symbol a can be *encoded* or *described* as b iff $(a, b) \in C$. In our applications, the set $\mathcal{A}$ in Definition 3.1 will in some cases represent the set of "single" outcomes (then $\mathcal{A} = \mathcal{X}$: the alphabet is equal to the sample space). In other cases, it represents the set of *sequences* of outcomes of either given length (then $\mathcal{A} = \mathcal{X}^n$) or arbitrary length (then $\mathcal{A} = \mathcal{X}^+$). In some cases, $\mathcal{A}$ represents to-be-described hypotheses or parameters indexing hypotheses.

Figure 3.1 shows the different types of coding systems: *singular* coding systems map several symbols to the same description, so that there exist some descriptions that cannot be unambiguously decoded: given the description, it is not clear what symbol gave rise to it. *In MDL we never work with singular coding systems.*

Nonsingular coding systems will be called "description methods." By far the most important special case of a description method is the *code*. For a code, there should always be only *one* possible encoding of a data sequence. For a general description method, there may be data sequences that can be encoded in several ways. We shall generally use the symbol C to denote both codes and description methods, and, for a code, write $C(x)$ to denote the unique code word of x.

Partial codes are mainly needed for the case when $\mathcal{A}$ is uncountable; for example, we sometimes have to encode parameter values of (say), Bernoulli distributions (Chapter 2). These take values in $[0, 1]$, an uncountable set. In such a case, at most a countable subset of $\mathcal{A}$ can be encoded.

Example 3.1 [Example Code and Description Method] Here is a simple example (copied from (Rissanen 1989)) of a code C_0 for an alphabet $\mathcal{A}_0 = \mathcal{X}_0^+$ with $\mathcal{X}_0 = \{a, b, c\}$. C_0 is defined as follows: $C_0(a) = 0, C_0(b) = 10, C_0(c) = 11$; for all $x, y \in \mathcal{X}_0^+, C_0(xy) = C_0(x)C_0(y)$. We call $C_0(x)$ the *code word* of x. For example, data sequence $aabac$ is encoded as $C_0(aabac) = 0010011$. It is easy to see that no two different data sequences can have the same code word; hence from an encoded sequence $C_0(x)$ we can always retrieve the original sequence x. Thus, the coding system corresponding to C_0 is *nonsingular* – it allows for lossless rather than just lossy encoding. The code is also *nonpartial*, which means that all elements of $\mathcal{A}_0$ have an associated code word.

In general, description methods (nonsingular coding systems) cannot be defined in terms of a function from $\mathcal{A}$ to $\mathbb{B}^*$ since for some $x \in \mathcal{A}$ there may be different descriptions $b \in \mathbb{B}^*$. But since any encoding can map back to only one data sequence, description methods may be defined in terms of a *decoding function* from $\mathbb{B}^*$ to $\mathcal{A}$, which we denote by C^{-1}. As an example of a description method that is not a code, consider the method C for alphabet $\mathcal{A}_0$ defined by: $C^{-1}(00) = C^{-1}(01) = a$, $C^{-1}(10) = b, C^{-1}(11) = c$, $C^{-1}(xy) = C^{-1}(x)C^{-1}(y)$ if x and y are of even length.

Notational Conventions   Let C be some code for $\mathcal{A}$. For all $x \in \mathcal{A}$, we denote by $L_C(x)$ the length (number of bits) of the description of x when the description is done using code C.

If C is a partial code and $C(x)$ is not defined, we write $L_C(x) = \infty$.

If C is a description method that is not a code, we denote by $L_C(x)$ the length of the *shortest* description of x under C. In some cases we will use indexed codes/description methods C_i. We then use L_i as shorthand for L_{C_i}.

We frequently deal with codes of sequences $x_1, x_2, \ldots$ such that the codelengths $L(x_1, \ldots, x_n)$ increase in a certain manner with n. To concisely express how $L(x^n)$ grows with n, we use *order notation*, defined as in Chapter 2, Section 2.1. For example, $L(x^n) = O(n)$ means that the codelength of the sequence $x_1, x_2, \ldots$ grows linearly in n.

3.1.1   Restriction to Prefix Coding Systems; Descriptions as Messages

MDL is only concerned with nonsingular coding systems. It turns out that, to make the notion of coding system "reasonable," we should require one more property: the coding system should be *prefix*. This and many other aspects of coding can best be explained if we think of descriptions as *messages*, an interpretation which we now describe.

Descriptions as Messages   We can always view a description as a message that some sender or *encoder*, say Mr. A, sends to some receiver or *decoder*, say Mr. B. Before sending any messages, Mr. A and Mr. B meet in person. They agree on the set of messages that A may send to B; this is just the data alphabet $\mathcal{A}$. They also agree upon a coding system that will be used by A to send his messages to B. Once this has been done, A and B go back to their respective homes and A sends his messages to B in the form of binary strings. The fact that we restrict ourselves to nonsingular coding systems (page 80) implies that, when B receives a message, he should always be able to decode it in a unique manner.

Concatenating Messages/Codes   Suppose we want to describe two symbols, the first coming from alphabet $\mathcal{A}$ and the second from $\mathcal{A}''$. Suppose sender and receiver already agreed on a code for both alphabets, say C and C'. They may now construct a new code for the joint set of symbols $(x, x') \in \mathcal{A} \times \mathcal{A}'$. The most straightforward way of doing this is to define the *concatenation code C''* as follows: C'' encodes (x, x') simply as the concatenation of the individual code words $C(x), C'(x')$. Thus, for all $x, x', C''(xx'):=C(x)C'(x')$. This method was already used implicitly on page 82 in Example 3.1. In this book (as in most of lossless coding theory) we shall only consider (nonsingular) codes C such that for any other (nonsingular) codes C' on alphabet $\mathcal{A}'$, the concatenation coding system defined by $C''(xx'):=C(x)C'(x')$ is itself nonsingular. This means that there is no need to separate $C(x)$ and $C'(x')$ by a comma or any other "end-of-input" symbol. This is a very natural restriction: if it were necessary to use commas or end-of-input markers in our description, we would really be working with a ternary, not a binary alphabet as soon as we want to send more than a single message. So once we have decided to encode all our data in binary, it is only appropriate that we use only 0s and 1s and no other markers. We already implicitly demanded this in Definition 3.1 where a code was defined as a mapping into $\mathbb{B}^* = \{0, 1\}^*$, not $\{0, 1, ','\}^*$.

Prefix Codes   What are the nonsingular codes C that satisfy the requirement that for all (nonsingular) codes C', the coding system $C''(xx'):=C(x)C'(x')$ is itself nonsingular? It turns out that these are exactly the codes with the property that *no extension of a code word can itself be a code word*. Codes with this property are usually called *prefix* codes[2] (since no code word can be a *prefix* of any other code word) or *instantaneous* codes (since, if we de-code from left to right, we exactly know when we are done decoding – if the sequence of symbols we have seen so far is a code word, we must be done; otherwise, we should continue to read another symbol to the right and check again).

Clearly, prefix codes must be nonsingular. Moreover, if we concatenate another nonsingular code C' to a prefix code, the resulting coding system is itself nonsingular; and if C' is itself a prefix code, the resulting code C'' is again a prefix code. To see this, it is useful to think of codes in terms

---

2. Li and Vitányi (1997) call such codes, perhaps more justifiably, *prefix-free* codes.

of messages as explained above. Mr. A first encodes x using code C and then x' using code C'. Mr. B, upon receiving the message $C''(xx')$ starts decoding this message bit by bit from left to right. He knows that he has to start decoding using code C (A and B agreed on that before sending any message). After having read $L_C(x)$ bits, he can reconstruct x and, because C is prefix, he knows that he is done reading x and should now decode the remainder of the message based on code C'. He can then decode x' and, because C' is also prefix, he knows after how many bits he is done and the message has finished. Sending the message using the code C'' has taken $L_C(x) + L_{C'}(x')$ bits.

In contrast, if C were a nonsingular code that is not a prefix code, then we could have trivially constructed a nonsingular code C' such that for some (x_1, x_1') and (x_2, x_2') with $x_1 \neq x_2, x_1' \neq x_2', C(x_1 x_2) = C(x_1' x_2')$ (how?). This proves that the requirement that every concatenation (on the right) of C with another nonsingular code yields a new nonsingular code is satisfied for a code C if and only if C is a prefix code.

Prefix Description Methods   Just as the only codes that remain nonsingular under concatenation are the prefix codes, the only description methods that remain nonsingular under concatenation are the prefix description methods. These are simply those description methods C such that no code word can be a prefix of any other code word. That is, if b is a prefix of b' and $(a, b) \in C$ for some $a \in \mathcal{A}$, then there exists no $a' \in \mathcal{A}$ such that $(a', b') \in C$. Every prefix code is a prefix description method, but not vice versa.

Restriction to Prefix Codes/Description Methods

In MDL we only deal with nonsingular prefix coding systems, i.e. prefix description methods – these are the only nonsingular coding systems that are guaranteed to remain nonsingular under concatenation.

Henceforth, whenever we use the word "code" ("description method"), we really mean a "prefix code" ("description method").

Example 3.2 Consider the code C_0 of Example 3.1. Let $C^{(n)}$ be the restriction of this code to inputs (sequences to be encoded) of length n. For example, $C^{(1)} : \mathcal{X}_0 \rightarrow \{0, 10, 11\}$ is a code for the set $\mathcal{X}_0 = \{a, b, c\}$ with code words $C^{(1)}(a) = 0, C^{(1)}(b) = 10, C^{(1)}(c) = 11$. Note that the code $C^{(n)}$ encodes x^n by the code word $C^{(1)}(x_1) \ldots C^{(1)}(x_n)$. Because $C^{(1)}$ is a prefix code, there is no need in the code $C^{(n)}$ to separate the individual code words for the x_i by commas: a decoder, decoding from left to right, will always know at what point the subsequence used to encode one particular data symbol ends and the encoding of the next symbol starts, thus eliminating the need for commas.

Code Length Functions Are More Fundamental Than Codes   In MDL, we are concerned only with minimizing description *length*. Therefore, the *only* aspect of any description method C that will appear in our computations is the corresponding length function $L_C : \mathcal{A} \to \mathbb{N} \cup \{\infty\}$. If two codes C_1 and C_2 for the same alphabet use different code words, but in such a way that for all $x \in \mathcal{A}$, $L_{C_1}(x) = L_{C_2}(x)$, then from the point of view of MDL it makes no difference whether we work with C_1 or C_2. We will often be interested in the set $\mathcal{L}_\mathcal{A}$ of *all codelength functions* over alphabet $\mathcal{A}$. This is the set of all functions L for which there exists a (prefix!) code C such that for all $x \in \mathcal{A}, L(x) = L_C(x)$.

Terminology: Code Length Functions and Codes
We often speak of "codes" when we are really only interested in their length function. Similarly, a set $\mathcal{L}$ of codelength functions will often be called a "set of codes" rather than a set of "codelength functions."

3.1.2   Different Kinds of Codes

We now discuss some families of description methods that will play a fundamental role throughout this book.

Concatenating Description Methods   Suppose we want to describe two symbols, one coming from alphabet $\mathcal{A}_1$ and one from $\mathcal{A}_2$. Suppose we already have (prefix) description methods for both alphabets, say C_1 and C_2. We may construct a prefix description method for the joint set of descriptions $(x_1, x_2) \in \mathcal{A}_1 \times \mathcal{A}_2$ simply by declaring $b_1 b_2$ to be a code word for $x_1 x_2$ iff b_1 is a code word for x_1 and b_2 is a code word for x_2. We have already explained this method, and we have already seen that the resulting description method has the prefix property, and satisfies $L_C(x_1 x_2) = L_1(x_1) L_2(x_2)$. We now consider a more elaborate version of this construction.

Conditional Description Methods Consider now description methods for sequences $x^n = x_1, \ldots, x_n$ from alphabet $\mathcal{A}_1 \times \ldots \times \mathcal{A}_n$ which can be decomposed in the following way: x^n is encoded by first encoding x_1 using some (prefix) coding system C_1. Then x_2 is encoded using some description method C_{2,x_1} for $\mathcal{A}_2$ which is allowed to *depend* on the value of x_1. Then x_3 is encoded using some description method $C_{3,(x_1,x_2)}$ for $\mathcal{A}_3$, allowed to depend on both x_1 and x_2, and so on. Borrowing notation from probability theory (see Section 3.2), we will write $C(\cdot|x^{i-1})$ rather than $C_{i,x^{i-1}}(\cdot)$. $C(\cdot|x^{i-1})$ is to be read as "the description method used to encode x_i *given* that the previous symbols where $x_1, \ldots, x_{i-1}$." The resulting description method C is still prefix. To see this, think of our receiver Mr. B who has to decode the x_i one by one. After having decoded x_1 using C_1, he knows that Mr. A must have encoded x_2 using the coding system $C(\cdot|x_1)$, and he can use that fact to uniquely decode x_2. Mr. B then knows the values of x_1 and x_2 and can use this to decode x_3, and so on. In case C_1 and the $C(\cdot|x^i)$'s are all codes rather than just description methods, the resulting description length L_C is given by

$$L_C(x_1, \ldots, x_n) = L_C(x_1) + L_C(x_2|x_1) + \ldots + L_C(x_n|x^{n-1}). \qquad (3.1)$$

Uniform Codes – Minimizing Worst-case Description Length We now introduce a code that will be used over and over again in this book: the uniform code for encoding elements of a finite alphabet $\mathcal{A}$. Let us first consider the simplest case: the alphabet contains only one element, say $\mathcal{A} = \{a\}$. Then there is only one possible message to be sent. In this case, there is nothing to communicate: when A and B agreed upon the alphabet, B already knew what message was going to be sent to him — so no description method needs to be agreed upon and sending the "outcome" a to B takes 0 bits.

Next consider the case when the alphabet contains a finite number of elements. Suppose that A and B are both interested in minimizing the number of bits needed to send the message. If A and B have no idea whether any of the outcomes (symbols) is a priori more likely than any other, they may decide on a description method (which in this case is actually a code) which encodes all elements in $\mathcal{A}$ using the same length. Such a description method can be constructed as follows. First observe that we must have $2^{d-1} < |\mathcal{A}| \le 2^d$ for some $d \in \mathbb{N}$. We map the elements of $\mathcal{A}$ to binary strings of length d: we order all elements of $\mathcal{A}$ in some way and we order all binary strings of length d lexicographically. Then we assign the first element in $\mathcal{A}$ to the first binary string of length d, the second element to the second string, and so on.

Clearly, d bits are then needed to encode any single $x \in \mathcal{A}$. Also, the resulting code will have the prefix property: since all code words are different binary strings of the same length, none of them can be a prefix of one another. We call the resulting code the *uniform code* for $\mathcal{A}$. We denote the length of x when x is encoded using a uniform code by L_U. This length is given by

$$L_U(x) = \lceil \log |\mathcal{A}| \rceil, \tag{3.2}$$

where $\lceil \cdot \rceil$ denotes the ceiling operation, as defined on page 45. While (by ordering $\mathcal{A}$ in a different way), we can arrive at different uniform codes, the *codelength function* L_U is uniquely defined: (3.2) will hold whatever ordering of $\mathcal{A}$ we apply in devising our code.

It turns out that if A and B want to minimize the number of bits needed to communicate in the worst case, then they should use a uniform code. Indeed, $L_U(x)$ satisfies a *minimax property*: as before, let $\mathcal{L}_\mathcal{A}$ denote the set of all length functions for prefix description methods over $\mathcal{A}$. Then

$$\max_{x \in \mathcal{A}} L_U(x) = \min_{L \in \mathcal{L}_\mathcal{A}} \max_{x \in \mathcal{A}} L(x). \tag{3.3}$$

Uniform Codes Minimize Maximum Description Length
If we identify "optimal" with "short description length," then *the uniform code gives the worst-case optimal codelengths, where the worst case is over all* $x \in \mathcal{A}$.

Uniform codes are usually called "fixed-length" codes (Li and Vitányi 1997). We call them "uniform" here since we want to stress their correspondence to uniform probability distributions (Section 3.2.3).

Quasi-Uniform Description Methods   Let $\mathcal{M}$ be some finite or countable set and suppose we have a family of sets $\mathcal{M}_1 \subset \mathcal{M}_2 \subset \ldots$ with $\mathcal{M} = \bigcup_\gamma \mathcal{M}_\gamma$ where all the $\mathcal{M}_\gamma$ are finite and nonempty. We introduce a new type of description method that will be used throughout this book. Its rationale can best be explained for the case of infinite $\mathcal{M}$ even though it is often also useful for finite $\mathcal{M}$. Suppose then that $\mathcal{M}$ is infinite. Then there exists no uniform code over $\mathcal{M}$. We have seen that the uniform code has a minimum worst-case codelength interpretation. We are sometimes interested in a description method that is the "the next best thing," still retaining as much as possible of the minimum codelength properties of the uniform code.

Consider $\mathcal{M}_\gamma$ for some fixed γ. If we encoded the elements in $\mathcal{M}_\gamma$ with the uniform code, we would need $l_\gamma := \lceil \log |\mathcal{M}_\gamma| \rceil$ bits to encode one element. No matter what description method we use for the elements in $\mathcal{M}_\gamma$, "most" of them will be assigned a codelength at least as large as l_γ. This is because for every possible description method, only an exponentially small subset of $\mathcal{M}$ can be assigned small codelengths (Chapter 1, page 7). Hence, for "most" $x \in \mathcal{M}_\gamma$, we cannot do substantially better than the uniform code - in this sense the uniform code is the best we can achieve once we know that $x \in \mathcal{M}_\gamma$. We would like to come up with a special description method for $\mathcal{M}$ that achieves this "baseline" for every $x \in \mathcal{M}$. In other words, for every $x \in \mathcal{M}$, our description method should achieve a codelength only slightly larger than l_γ, where γ is the smallest γ such that $x \in \mathcal{M}_\gamma$. In this way, we obtain the following for every γ: for those x with $x \in \mathcal{M}_\gamma, x \notin \mathcal{M}_{\gamma-1}$, we do approximately as well as the uniform code for $\mathcal{M}_\gamma$. For those $x \in \mathcal{M}_\gamma$ which are also in $\mathcal{M}_{\gamma-1}$, we do approximately as well as the uniform code for $\mathcal{M}_{\gamma-1}$. For those $x \in \mathcal{M}_\gamma$ which are also in $\mathcal{M}_{\gamma-2}$, we do approximately as well as the uniform code for $\mathcal{M}_{\gamma-2}$, and so on. We now explain how to arrive at such a special code for the special case that, for all γ, $\mathcal{M}_\gamma$ is a *proper* subset of $\mathcal{M}_{\gamma+1}$, hence $\mathcal{M}_\gamma \neq \mathcal{M}_{\gamma+1}$. Let $m_\gamma = |\mathcal{M}_\gamma|$, so that $m_1 < m_2 < \ldots$.

Let $x \in \mathcal{M}$. Let $\gamma(x)$ be the smallest γ such that $x \in \mathcal{M}_\gamma$. We will encode x in two steps. We first encode $\gamma(x)$ using some prefix code C over the integers, which we describe below. We then encode x using the conditional code $C(\cdot | \gamma(x))$. $C(\cdot | \gamma(x))$ is defined to be identical to the uniform code over $\mathcal{M}_{\gamma(x)}$. Clearly, after having decoded $\gamma(x)$, the decoder knows that the uniform code for $\mathcal{M}_{\gamma(x)}$ has been used to encode x. He or she can now use this knowledge to decode x itself.

We still have to describe how to encode $\gamma(x)$ in a prefix-free manner. We first encode the number $\gamma'(x) = \lceil \log \gamma(x) \rceil$ in a prefix-free manner, using some code C' over the integers. We then use a conditional code $C(\cdot | \gamma'(x))$ to encode $\gamma(x)$. In this conditional code we can use the fact that $\gamma(x) \leq 2^{\gamma'(x)}$, so we can use the uniform code to encode $\gamma(x)$ and we need $\gamma'(x) = \lceil \log \gamma(x) \rceil$ bits to encode $\gamma(x)$. We thus encode x in three steps: we first encode $\gamma'(x)$, we then encode $\gamma(x)$ given $\gamma'(x)$, we then encode x given $\gamma(x)$.

We still have to describe how to encode $\gamma'(x)$ in a prefix-free manner. We could now repeat the same trick again, but then we would still not be done. Instead, we will simply encode $\gamma'(x)$ by a "trivial" prefix code. The code word of an integer y under such a code will simply be a concatenation of y 1s followed by a 0. Since we may safely assume $\gamma'(x) \geq 0$, we can encode all possible values of $\gamma'(x)$ in this way. Clearly the resulting code has the prefix property; we need $\gamma'(x) + 1 = \lceil \log \gamma(x) \rceil + 1$ bits for this. All in all, we end up with a code concatenating the trivial encoding of $\gamma'(x)$, the uniform encoding of $\gamma(x)$ given $\gamma'(x)$, and a uniform encoding of x given $\gamma(x)$, which takes

$$L(x) = \lceil \log m_{\gamma(x)} \rceil + 2\lceil \log \gamma(x) \rceil + 1 \text{ bits.} \qquad (3.4)$$

Since for all γ, $m_{\gamma+1} \geq m_\gamma + 1$, we have $\gamma \leq m_\gamma$. Therefore (3.4) gives

$$L(x) \leq \lceil \log m_{\gamma(x)} \rceil + 2\lceil \log \lceil \log m_{\gamma(x)} \rceil \rceil + 1 \leq$$
$$\log m_{\gamma(x)} + 2 \log \log m_{\gamma(x)} + 4. \quad (3.5)$$

We call the resulting code with lengths (3.5) a *quasi-uniform description method*; see also the box on page 91. We refine this description method and provide a precise definition in Section 3.2.3. One possible rationale for using general quasi-uniform description methods is given by the *luckiness principle*, described in the box on page 92. The name "luckiness principle" is not standard in the MDL area. I have adopted it from the computational learning theory community, where it expresses a superficially distinct but on a deeper level related idea, introduced by Shawe-Taylor, Bartlett, Williamson, and Anthony (1998); see also (Herbrich and Williamson 2002).

3.1.3   Assessing the Efficiency of Description Methods

We frequently need to compare description methods in terms of how well they compress particular sequences.

Definition 3.2 Let C_1 and C_2 be description methods for a set $\mathcal{A}$.

1. We call C_1 *more efficient* than C_2 if for all $x \in \mathcal{A}$, $L_1(x) \leq L_2(x)$ while for at least one $x \in \mathcal{A}$, $L_1(x) < L_2(x)$.

2. We call a code C for set $\mathcal{A}$ *complete* if there does not exist a code C' that is more efficient than C.

We note that a "complete" description method must always be a code; a code can be complete or not, as the case may be.

3.2   The Most Important Section of This Book: Probabilities and Code Lengths, Part I

All theory about MDL that we will develop builds on the following simple but crucial observation:

A Key Idea in Coding: Quasi-uniform Description Methods

Let $\mathcal{M}$ be a large finite or countably infinite set. Every description method for $\mathcal{M}$ can assign short (i.e., much shorter than $\log|\mathcal{M}|$) code-lengths only to an exponentially small subset of $\mathcal{M}$. Yet, for every family of sets $\mathcal{M}_1 \subseteq \mathcal{M}_2 \subseteq \ldots$ such that $\bigcup_\gamma \mathcal{M}_\gamma = \mathcal{M}$, one can construct a *quasi-uniform* description method C such that, for all γ, all $x \in \mathcal{M}_\gamma$, $L_C(x)$ is larger than $\log|\mathcal{M}_\gamma|$ only by a very small amount.

Most codes in this book are either refinements of the uniform code or of a quasi-uniform description method; see, for example, Chapter 5, Section 5.8.2; Chapter 11, Section 11.3 on "luckiness" codes; Chapter 13, Section 13.2; and, in particular, the box on page 236.

We can "carve up" (decompose) $\mathcal{M}$ into finite subsets $\mathcal{M}_1, \mathcal{M}_2, \ldots$ any way we like to. Every $x \in \mathcal{M}$ can be given an arbitrarily small codelength $L_C(x) \geq 1$ by carving up $\mathcal{M}$ in some way and using the quasi-uniform description method C corresponding to the decomposition; but, for every description method for $\mathcal{M}$, for every $l < \log|\mathcal{M}|$, only an exponentially small (in m) fraction of $x \in \mathcal{M}$ achieves codelength smaller than $l - m$.

As was discussed on page 7, a basic property of codes is the fact that each code for $\mathcal{X}$ can assign short codelengths only to "very few" elements in $\mathcal{X}$. Probability distributions P over $\mathcal{X}$ have the property that $\sum_{x\in\mathcal{X}} P(x) = 1$. Hence, each P can only assign high probability to very few elements in $\mathcal{X}$.

There is an analogy here. Indeed, it turns out that short codelengths can be formally related to high probabilities. The exact relation is given by the *Kraft inequality* (Kraft 1949). In Section 3.2.1 we give this inequality; the reader who just wants to learn about MDL proper may skip this section and read only about its consequences, described in Section 3.2.2.

3.2.1   The Kraft Inequality

Theorem 3.1 [Kraft Inequality] For any description method C for finite alphabet $\mathcal{A} = \{1, \ldots, m\}$, the code word lengths $L_C(1), \ldots, L_C(m)$ must satisfy

---

Luckiness Principle

Suppose we want to encode outcomes in a large but finite set $\mathcal{M}$. Carving up $\mathcal{M}$ into sets $\mathcal{M}_1 \subset \mathcal{M}_2 \subset \ldots \subset \mathcal{M}_{\gamma_{\max}} = \mathcal{M}$, and using a quasi-uniform code on $\bigcup_{\gamma=1}^{\gamma_{\max}} \mathcal{M}_\gamma$ means adhering to the *luckiness principle*:

- No matter what element of $\mathcal{M}$ we have to encode, we need less than $\log |\mathcal{M}| + 2 \log \log |\mathcal{M}| + 4$ bits, which is not much more than with the minimax optimal code for $\mathcal{M}$ (which takes $\log |\mathcal{M}|$ bits).

- If we are *lucky* and the element to be encoded is a member of some $\mathcal{M}_\gamma$ with $\gamma \ll \gamma_{\max}$, then we need *substantially less* bits than with the minimax optimal code for $\mathcal{M}$.

In other words, compared to minimax optimal, if we are *lucky*, we gain a lot. If we are not lucky, we hardly lose anything. This is the rationale of using quasi-uniform codes for a finite $\mathcal{M}$; the same reasoning extends to countably infinite $\mathcal{M}$ as well.

---

the inequality

$$\sum_{x \in \mathcal{A}} 2^{-L_C(x)} \leq 1. \tag{3.6}$$

Conversely, given a set of code word lengths that satisfy this inequality, there exists a prefix code with these code word lengths.

Proof: [adapted from (Cover and Thomas 1991)] We write $l_{\max}$ for the length of the longest code word in the set of code words: $l_{\max} = \max_{x \in \mathcal{A}} L_C(x)$. We write l_x as an abbreviation of $L_C(x)$. Consider the full binary tree of depth $l_{\max}$, where each branch is associated with either 0 or 1 (see Figure 3.2). In this tree, each code word corresponds to a unique path starting at the root node: the first (leftmost) bit of the code word determines which of the two children of the root node is visited; the second bit determines which of the two children of the first visited node is visited, etc. The length of the path is equal to the length of the code word. We label each node with the path leading to it. With each x we associate the node that is labeled $C(x)$. As an example, Figure 3.2 shows the paths for the code C_0 of Example 3.1. The

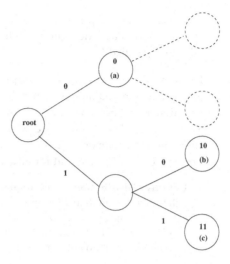

Figure 3.2 Binary code tree for the Kraft inequality using alphabet $\{a, b, c\}$ and code $C_0(a) = 0; C_0(b) = 10; C_0(c) = 11$.

node "10" is the node at the end of the path taking branch 1 at the root node and then taking branch 0. This node is associated with symbol "b," since $C_0(b) = 10$.

The prefix condition on the code words implies that no code word is an ancestor of any other code word on the tree. Hence, each code word eliminates its descendants as possible code words. For each $x \in \mathcal{A}$, the node associated with x, together with its descendants, defines a subtree of possible extensions of the code word $C(x)$ up to depth $l_{\max}$. If $l_x = l_{\max}$, this subtree coincides with the node x itself. If $l_x = l_{\max} - 1$, the subtree consists of the node associated with x together with its two children, and so on. Let D_x be the set of leafs of the subtree belonging to x. We have $2^{l_x}|\mathrm{D}_x| = 2^{l_{\max}}$, so that $2^{-l_x} = |\mathrm{D}_x| \cdot 2^{-l_{\max}}$. Since the prefix property implies that all D_x are disjoint, we have

$$\sum_{x \in \mathcal{A}} 2^{-L_C(x)} = \sum_{x \in \mathcal{A}} 2^{-l_x} = 2^{-l_{\max}} \sum_{x \in \mathcal{A}} |\mathrm{D}_x| \leq 2^{-l_{\max}} \cdot 2^{l_{\max}} = 1$$

which implies the Kraft inequality (3.6).

Conversely, given any set of code word lengths $l_1, \ldots, l_m$ satisfying the Kraft inequality, we can always construct a tree like the one in Figure 3.2. Label the first node (lexicographically) of depth l_1 as code word of 1. Label the first node (lexicographically) that has depth l_2 and that is not a descendant from the node 1 as code word of 2, etc. In this way, we construct a prefix code with the specified $l_1, \ldots, l_m$. $\square$

Let $\mathcal{X}$ be finite and C be a description method for $\mathcal{X}$. From the Kraft inequality we immediately see that there exists a "defective" probability distribution P defined over $\mathcal{X}$ such that for all $x \in \mathcal{X}$, $P(x) = 2^{-L_C(x)}$. By a "defective" distribution , we mean a "distribution" that may sum up to something less than one. That is, if $\mathcal{X}$ is countable, its mass function is a function $P : \mathcal{X} \to [0, 1]$ such that for all $x \in \mathcal{X}$, $P(x) \geq 0$, while $\sum_{x \in \mathcal{X}} P(x) \leq 1$.

Defective Distributions and Completeness of Codes We can always think of a defective distribution P as an ordinary probability distribution P over the extended sample space $\mathcal{X} \sqcup \{\square\}$, where $\square$ is an extra symbol used to ensure that $\sum_x P(x) = 1$. We may then have that $P(\square) > 0$, but we evaluate P only on sequences that do not contain $\square$.

Not surprisingly, defectiveness of distributions is related to (in)efficiency of codes as defined in Section 3.1.3. To be precise, a prefix code C is complete (page 90) if and only if the corresponding distribution P is not defective, i.e. if P is an ordinary distribution summing to 1. Let us indicate how to prove this.

Assume first that P is defective. We will show that C is not complete. If P is defective, then there exists another (possibly again defective) distribution P' on $\mathcal{X} \cup \{\square\}$ such that for all $x \in \mathcal{X}$, $P'(x) = P(x)$, and $P'(\square) = 2^{-k}$ for some $k < \infty$ such that $\sum_{x \in \mathcal{X} \cup \{\square\}} P'(x) \leq 1$. By the Kraft inequality, there must exist a prefix code C' such that, for all $x \in \mathcal{X}$,

$$L_{C'}(x) = L_C(x), \tag{3.7}$$

and $L_{C'}(\square) = k$. Consider the binary tree corresponding to C', constructed as in the proof of the Kraft inequality. One of the leaves of this tree corresponds to the source symbol $\square$. If this leaf has no sibling (the parent of $\square$ has only one child), then we can modify C' so that (3.7) still holds, and $L_{C'}(\square) = k - 1$. We do this by removing the leaf and making its parent the new leaf corresponding to $\square$. We can repeat this procedure until we end up with a tree corresponding to a prefix code C' satisfying (3.7), having $L_{C'}(\square) = k$ for some finite k, such that the leaf corresponding to $\square$ has a sibling. There are now two cases: either the sibling of $\square$ is a leaf or it is not. In case it is not, there exists some symbol x in $\mathcal{X}$ with codelength larger than k. Then we can modify the tree by changing the code word of x to the code word of $\square$. The resulting tree corresponds to a prefix code for $\mathcal{X}$ that is more efficient than C; therefore C is not complete, and we are done. In case the sibling is a leaf corresponding to some symbol x, we can modify the tree of C' by removing both siblings and making their parent a leaf, corresponding to the symbol x. The resulting tree corresponds to a prefix code for $\mathcal{X}$ that is more efficient than C, so C is not complete, and we are done.

It remains to be shown that if P is not defective, then C must be complete. We leave this as an exercise to the reader.

Similarly, let P be a probability distribution over the finite space $\mathcal{X}$. By the Kraft inequality (3.6) we see immediately that there exists a code C for $\mathcal{X}$ such that for all $x \in \mathcal{X}$: $L_C(x) = \lceil -\log P(x) \rceil$. This code is called the *Shannon-Fano code* (Cover and Thomas 1991).

We will ignore the effect of rounding up and drop the integer requirement for codelengths; this will be motivated at length in Section 3.2.2. Once we have done this, we obtain a *a correspondence between probability distributions and prefix description methods*: to every P, there is a corresponding C such that the codelengths $L_C(x)$ are equal to $-\log P(x)$ for *all* $x \in \mathcal{X}$. At the same time, for every C there is a corresponding P such that the codelengths $L_C(x)$ are equal to $-\log P(x)$ for *all* $x \in \mathcal{X}$.

Since an analogue to the Kraft Inequality can be proved for countably infinite alphabets, the correspondence still holds for countably infinite $\mathcal{X}$ (Cover and Thomas 1991). By discretizing in the appropriate way, we can achieve an analogue of the correspondence for continuous $\mathcal{X}$. Finally, by adapting the reasoning in the proof of the Kraft inequality (3.6) we obtain an analogue of the inequality for description methods rather than codes. The result is summarized in the box on page 96:

3.2.2   Code Lengths "Are" Probabilities

In the correspondence described in the box, probability distributions are treated as mathematical objects and *nothing else*. If we decide to use a code C to encode our data, this definitely does *not* necessarily mean that we assume our data to be drawn according to the probability distribution corresponding to C.

As will be seen in the coming chapters, the identification of probability distributions and codes allows for a probabilistic reinterpretation of the *minimum description length* principle as a *maximum probability* principle, since short codelengths correspond to high probabilities and vice versa.

Noninteger Code Lengths Are Harmless   In order to obtain an exact correspondence between probability distributions and codelength functions we decided to allow "idealized" codes with noninteger codelengths. In practi-

---

The Most Important Observation of this Book:
Correspondence between Probability Distributions and Prefix Description Methods

Let $\mathcal{X}$ be a finite or countable sample space. Let P be a probability distribution over $\mathcal{X}^n$, the set of sequences of length n. Then there exists a prefix code C for $\mathcal{X}^n$ such that for all $x^n \in \mathcal{X}^n$, $L_C(x^n) = -\log P(x^n)$. C is called the *code corresponding to* P.

Similarly, let C' be a prefix description method for $\mathcal{X}^n$. Then there exists a defective probability distribution P' such that for all $x^n \in \mathcal{X}^n$, $-\log P'(x^n) = L_{C'}(x^n)$. P' is called the *probability distribution corresponding to C'*.

Moreover, if (and only if) C' is a *complete prefix code* (page 90), then P' is a proper distribution ($\sum_{x^n} P'(x^n) = 1$).

This correspondence allows us to *identify* codelength functions and probability distributions, such that a short codelength corresponds to a high probability and vice versa.

Figure 3.3   The most important observation of this book.

cal problems, this will almost never make a difference: Suppose we have to encode some $a \in \mathcal{A}$ where $\mathcal{A}$ is some alphabet. For example, $\mathcal{A} = \mathcal{X}^n$, the set of all samples of length n. For any code or description method, the actual (integer) codelength will be within 1 bit of the idealized length. The codes we deal with in this book will, in all interesting cases, assign a description length of order n to sequences of length n. This means that for all but the smallest n, the differences in decription length when we drop the integer requirement will be negligible compared to the total description length of the data involved. Therefore, the hypothesis or model selected by MDL will not change if we do not round off the description lengths.

A Worry and Its Resolution Students new to information theory often seem very uncomfortable with the idea of noninteger codelengths. They fear that we can get very different codelengths after all if we ignore the effect of rounding up. Sometimes they come up with "counterexamples" such as the following:

consider a distribution over $\mathcal{X} = \{a, b, c\}$ with $P(a) = P(b) = P(c) = 1/3$. Each prefix code (defined in the original way, with the integer requirement; Section 3.1) over $\mathcal{X}$ has $L_C(x) \geq 2$ for at least two $x \in \mathcal{X}$. Let us fix one such C, for example the one given on page 82, with $L_C(c) = 2$. This C is one of the codes that correspond to the distribution P. Now consider P^n, the n-fold product distribution of P; and compare it to the n-fold concatenation $C^n(x_1, \ldots, x_n) = C(x_1) \ldots C(x_n)$. There exist sequences x^n (e.g. $x^n = ccc \ldots ccc$) with $L_{C^n}(x^n) = 2n$ whereas $-\log P^n(x^n) = -\log(1/3)^n = n \log 3$. Hence the difference between $-\log P^n(x^n)$ and $L_{C^n}(x^n)$ is much larger than 1. Since $L_{C^n}(x^n)$ *seems* to be the code corresponding to P^n, the integer requirement may seem important after all!

The flaw in this reasoning lies in the fact that C^n only *seems* to be the code corresponding to P^n; but in fact, P^n is defined over sample space $\mathcal{X}^n$ and the code corresponding to P^n is some quite different code, namely the uniform code C_U over sequences in $\mathcal{X}^n$. For this code, we do have $L_U(x^n) = \lceil -\log P(x^n) \rceil$ for all $x^n \in \mathcal{X}^n$.

Now let us extend the story to general distributions on $\mathcal{X}^n$. Suppose P is an arbitrary, not necessarily i.i.d. distribution on $\mathcal{X}^n$. For every sequence $x_1, \ldots, x_n$, the probabilities must satisfy (page 54):

$$-\log P(x^n) = \sum_{i=1}^{n} [-\log P(x_i \mid x^{i-1})]. \tag{3.8}$$

Every term involves a probability distribution $P(X_i = \cdot \mid x^{i-1})$ defined on the space $\mathcal{X}$. The actual codes corresponding to these conditional distributions, have lengths $L'(x_i \mid x^{i-1}) = \lceil -\log P(x_i \mid x^{i-1}) \rceil$; and the actual code corresponding to the joint distribution P on $\mathcal{X}^n$ has lengths $\lceil -\log P(x^n) \rceil$, Thus, in the worst case, the concatenation of the n codes with lengths $L'(x_i \mid x^{i-1})$ leads to a codelength of x^n that exceeds the codelength $L'(x^n)$ by $O(n)$ rather than 1. On the other hand, if we work with idealized codelengths $L(x_i \mid x^{i-1}) = -\log P(x_i \mid x^{i-1})$ without the integer requirement, then (3.8) immediately translates into

$$L(x^n) = \sum_{i=1}^{n} L(x_i \mid x^{i-1}). \tag{3.9}$$

The upshot is that we should not construct codes for sequences by transforming probability distributions on individual outcomes to codes, and then concatenating these codes. Instead, we should directly build a code based on the distribution on the full-length sequences. As long as we consequently use the notation $L(\cdot)$ for idealized instead of integer codelengths, all intuitive properties such as (3.9) continue to hold.

Noninteger Code Lengths are more more fundamental   We have seen that noninteger codelengths neatly correspond to probability distributions and that their use in MDL is generally harmless. But there are several other reasons for adopting them:

1. **Invariance.** Our notion of description length becomes invariant to the size of the encoding alphabet used.

> For example, if we use as our encoding alphabet $\{0, 1, 2\}$ rather than $\{0, 1\}$, then, if we drop the integer requirement, we can state: there exists a prefix code $C : \mathcal{A} \to \{0, 1\}^*$ with length function L if and only if there exists a prefix code $C' : \mathcal{A} \to \{0, 1, 2\}^*$ with length function $L' = (\log_3 2)L$. To see this, note that, assuming the exact correspondence between distributions and codelength functions, L is a codelength function iff there exists a defective distribution P with $-\log_2 P(X):=L(X)$. Repeating the entire chain of reasoning of Section 3.2.1 for alphabets $\{0, 1, 2\}$, we find that L' is a codelength function for a code over $\{0, 1, 2\}$ iff there exists a defective distribution P with $-\log_3 P(X):=L'(X)$. Taking the L and L' that correspond to the same distribution P, we then find
>
> $$\frac{L'(X)}{L(X)} = \frac{-\log_3 P(X)}{-\log_2 P(X)} = \frac{\ln P(X)/\ln 3}{\ln P(X)/\ln 2} = \frac{\ln 2}{\ln 3} = \log_3 2.$$
>
> With the integer requirement, it is impossible to achieve such an exact correspondence.

2. **Coding = Gambling.** We obtain an interpretation of description methods as gambling schemes which allows us to interpret the whole MDL principle in terms of sequential betting rather than codelength minimization. This interpretation is known as *Kelly gambling* (Kelly 1956; Cover and Thomas 1991). Even though this is a very fruitful way of looking at things, we shall not pursue it further in this book.

3. **Convenience.** The mathematics becomes a lot easier and more elegant.

Combined with the fact that the integer requirement will not make an essential difference in most applications, this strongly suggests that the idealized view of codelength functions is more fundamental than the concrete view with the integer requirement. We therefore take a bold step: we adopt the noninteger view as *basic*. From now on, we never require integer codelengths anymore, and (assuming some sample space $\mathcal{X}$) we redefine $\mathcal{L}_{\mathcal{X}}$ to be the set of all functions over the given sample space that satisfy the Kraft inequality:

Summary: Integers Don't Matter

There is **NO** practical application of MDL in which we worry about the integer requirement for codelengths; we *always* allow for codelength functions to take noninteger lengths. Instead, we call a function a "codelength function" if and only if it satisfies the Kraft inequality, that is, iff it corresponds to some defective probability distribution:

New Definition of Codelength Function/Completeness

In MDL we are **NEVER** concerned with actual encodings; we are only concerned with codelength functions. The set of all codelength functions for sample space $\mathcal{X}$ is redefined as:

$$\mathcal{L}_{\mathcal{X}} = \big\{ L : \mathcal{X} \to [0, \infty] \mid \sum_{x \in \mathcal{X}} 2^{-L(x)} \leq 1 \big\}. \tag{3.10}$$

This definition applies to finite, countable, and continuous sample spaces. It also holds for sample spaces $\mathcal{X} = \mathcal{Z}^n$ ($n \geq 1$) representing sequences of n outcomes in $\mathcal{Z}$.

We now call a codelength function defined as an element of $\mathcal{L}_{\mathcal{X}}$ *complete* if it satisfies $\sum_{x \in \mathcal{X}} 2^{-L(x)} = 1$.

3.2.3 Immediate Insights and Consequences

On page 87 we introduced the vertical-bar notation $L(X|Y)$ for conditional codes. We can now see the rationale behind this notation – it is simply inherited from the vertical-bar notation for conditional distributions. Also, we can now extend our result on the relation between uniform codes and minimax description length to probability distributions:

Uniform Distributions Achieve Minimax Description Length Let $\mathcal{A}$ be some finite set with m elements. P_U, the uniform distribution over $\mathcal{A}$, is defined as $P_U(x) = 1/m$ for all $x \in \mathcal{A}$. It corresponds to the uniform code with lengths $L_U(x) := = -\log m^{-1} = \log m$ (note there is no integer requirement anymore). The new definition of uniform code still achieves the minimax codelengths for our new definition of $\mathcal{L}_\mathcal{X}$:

$$\min_{L \in \mathcal{L}_\mathcal{X}} \max_{x \in \mathcal{A}} L(x) \tag{3.11}$$

is achieved for $L = L_U$. In fact, with our new definition of codelength functions (3.10), it is immediate that L_U *uniquely* achieves (3.11): for every code $L \neq L_U$, we have

$$\max_{x \in \mathcal{A}} L(x) > \max_{x \in \mathcal{A}} L_U(x) = \log |\mathcal{A}|.$$

Refining Quasi-Uniform Description Methods to Encode Positive Integers
We may use the correspondence between probability distributions and codes to refine our notion of a "quasi-uniform description method" as introduced on page 88. Suppose we are interested in describing an arbitrarily large number $n \in \mathbb{N}$. We need a code $C : \mathbb{N} \to \mathbb{B}^*$. Clearly, a uniform code does not exist in this case. We can use the idea of the quasi-uniform description method to devise a code such that $L(n)$ only increases extremely slowly with n. Let us first define $\mathcal{M}_N = \{1, \ldots, N\}$ and construct a quasi-uniform description method for $\cup_{N>0} \mathcal{M}_N$ in the manner outlined on page 88. This gives us a description method with lengths $L(n) \approx \log n + 2 \log \log n$, which for each n is within a logarithmic term of the worst-case optimal length $\log n$ which we would have obtained if we had known in advance that $n \in \mathcal{M}_N$. Codes of this type where first described by Levenstein (1968) and Elias (1975).

To achieve this length, we used a recursive procedure to encode n. Let $l(n) = \log n$ be the number of bits needed to encode n based on the uniform code for $\mathcal{M}_n$. We first encoded $x = l(l(n))$ in some trivial manner, namely by encoding $l(l(n))$ 1s and then a single 0. We then encoded $l(n)$ using the uniform code for $\{1, \ldots \lceil l(n) \rceil\}$. We finally encoded n using the uniform code for $\mathcal{M}_n$. If $l(l(n)) > 1$ we may repeat the recursion by starting with encoding $l(l(l(n)))$ in a trivial manner, and then encoding $l(l(n))$ using the uniform code. In this case we would need

$$\lceil \log n \rceil + \lceil \log \lceil \log n \rceil \rceil + 2 \lceil \log \lceil \log \lceil \log n \rceil \rceil \rceil + 1 \text{ bits.}$$

Rissanen (1983) refined this idea by allowing noninteger codelengths and repeating the recursion as often as possible. He showed that this leads to a code for the positive integers with lengths[3]

$$L_\mathbb{N}(n) = \log n + \log \log n + \log \log \log n + \ldots + \log c_0, \tag{3.12}$$

---

3. In some other texts such as (Li and Vitányi 1997), the symbol l^* rather than $L_\mathbb{N}$ is used for this code.

where the summation stops at the first negative term, and $c_0 \approx 2.865$ is chosen so that the Kraft inequality is satisfied with equality: $\sum_{j>1} 2^{-L_{\mathbb{N}}(j)} = 1$. We will call the code which achieves lengths $L_{\mathbb{N}}$ the *standard universal code for the integers* (why this code is called "universal" will become clear in Chapter 6). The corresponding distribution with lengths $\bar{P}_{\mathbb{N}}(j) = 2^{-L_{\mathbb{N}}(j)}$ is known as *the universal prior for the integers*. In this book we often use the fact that for all $n \geq 1$, $L_{\mathbb{N}}(n) \leq 2\log n + 2$.

3.3 Probabilities and Code Lengths, Part II

We have set up a correspondence between probability distributions P and description length functions L, such that for each P, the associated L satisfies $L(x) = -\log P(x)$ for all $x \in \mathcal{X}$. We know that a code with these lengths *exists* (we just *redefined* codelength functions in a way which guarantees this). But besides its existence, this code has an additional very important property:

The Second Most Important Observation of this Book:
The L That Corresponds to P Minimizes Expected Codelength
Let $\mathcal{X}$ be finite or countable, let P be a distribution over $\mathcal{X}$, and let L be defined by

$$L := \underset{L \in \mathcal{L}_{\mathcal{X}}}{\arg\min} \, E_P[L(X)]. \tag{3.13}$$

Then L exists, is unique, and is identical to the codelength function corresponding to P, with lengths $L(x) = -\log P(x)$.

This result may be recast as follows: for all distributions P and Q with $Q \neq P$,

$$E_P[-\log Q(X)] > E_P[-\log P(X)]. \tag{3.14}$$

In this form, the result is known as the *information inequality* (Cover and Thomas 1991). It will be proved in the following section.

The information inequality says the following: suppose X is distributed according to P ("generated by P"). Then, among all possible codes or description methods for $\mathcal{X}$, the code with lengths $-\log P(X)$ "on average" gives the shortest encodings of outcomes of P.

Why the average? — Part 1 Equation (3.14) suggests that we should use the code with lengths $-\log P(X)$ to model data if we think that data are distributed according to P. But it only says that this code is optimal on *average*. We would like some additional reassurance that the code will also be optimal on actually generated sequences. A first such reassurance can be obtained by the *law of large numbers* (Section 2.2.3, page 55). This theorem implies that, for large samples independently distributed according to P, with high P-probability, the code that gives the shortest expected lengths will also give the shortest *actual* codelengths, which is what we are really interested in.

> Let us briefly illustrate this. Let P^*, Q_A, and Q_B be three probability distributions on $\mathcal{X}$, extended to sequences of n outcomes by independence. Hence $P^*(x^n) = \prod P^*(x_i)$ and similarly for Q_A and Q_B. Suppose we obtain a sample generated by P^*. Mr. A and Mrs. B both want to encode the sample using as few bits as possible, but neither knows that P^* has actually been used to generate the sample. A decides to use the code corresponding to distribution Q_A and B decides to use the code corresponding to Q_B. Suppose that $E_{P^*}[-\log Q_A(X)] < E_{P^*}[-\log Q_B(X)]$. Then, by the law of large numbers , with P^*-probability 1,
>
> $$\frac{1}{n}[-\log Q_j(X_1,\ldots,X_n)] \to E_{P^*}[-\log Q_j(X)].$$
>
> (note $-\log Q_j(X^n) = -\sum_{i=1}^{n}\log Q_j(X_i)$) It follows that, with probability 1, Mr. A will need less (linearly in n) bits to encode $X_1,\ldots,X_n$ than Mrs. B.

The qualitative content of this result is not so surprising: in a large sample generated by P, the frequency of each $x \in \mathcal{X}$ will be approximately equal to the probability $P(x)$. In order to obtain a short codelength for x^n, we should use a code that assigns a small codelength to those symbols in $\mathcal{X}$ with high frequency (probability), and a large codelength to those symbols in $\mathcal{X}$ with low frequency (probability).

Why the average? — Part 2 We now know that the code with lengths $-\log P(X)$ will be optimal on average, and, in the long run, with very high probability. Both results still do not say much about the situation where we deal with an actual small sample distributed by P. Luckily, even in this situation the code with lengths $-\log P(X)$ is still optimal in a very strong sense:

No-Hypercompression-Inequality

Suppose $X_1, X_2, \ldots, X_n$ are distributed according to some distribution P^* on $\mathcal{X}^n$ ($X_1, X_2, \ldots$ are *not* necessarily i.i.d.!). Let Q be a (completely arbitrary) distribution on $\mathcal{X}^n$. Then for all $K > 0$,

$$P^*(-\log P^*(X^n) \geq -\log Q(X^n) + K) \leq 2^{-K}. \tag{3.15}$$

In words, the probability that a code *not* corresponding to P^* compresses the data substantially more (by more than K bits) than the code corresponding to P^* is negligible (exponentially small in K).

This generalizes the observation in the box on page 8 (Chapter 1), about the incompressibility of random sequences - a key to understanding the relationship between regularity and compression.

This simple inequality expresses that, in a sense, the idealized code that is optimal in expectation is also "competitively optimal" (Cover and Thomas 1991). The importance of this fact for the analysis of MDL was recognized early on by Barron (1985).

Proof: By Markov's inequality (page 56) applied to $Y := Q(X^n)/P^*(X^n)$, we have

$$P^*\left\{\frac{Q(X^n)}{P^*(X^n)} \geq c\right\} \leq \frac{E[\frac{Q(X^n)}{P^*(X^n)}]}{c} = \frac{\sum_{x^n} P^*(x^n)\frac{Q(x^n)}{P^*(x^n)}}{c} = \frac{1}{c}. \tag{3.16}$$

The result now follows by setting $c = 2^K$. $\square$

3.3.1 (Relative) Entropy and the Information Inequality

The information inequality allows us to give coding-theoretic interpretations to two fundamental quantities in information theory: the *entropy* and the *relative* entropy or *Kullback-Leibler (KL) divergence* (Cover and Thomas 1991). "Entropy" is a functional defined on probability distributions P measuring something like the "uncertainty inherent in P":

Definition 3.3 [Entropy] Let $\mathcal{X}$ be a finite or countable sample space, and let P be a distribution over $\mathcal{X}$. The *entropy* $H(P)$ of P is defined as

$$H(P) := E_P[-\log P(X)] = -\sum_{x \in \mathcal{X}} P(x)\log P(x), \tag{3.17}$$

where $0 \log 0$ is defined as $\lim_{x \downarrow 0} x \log x = 0$; if $- \sum_x P(x) \log P(x) = \infty$, then $H(P) = \infty$. If $\mathcal{X}$ is continuous, then there is no unique definition of entropy. As we explain below, the "right" definition depends on the application. Often, one can simply replace the sum in the definition above by an integral. The resulting expression is called the *differential* entropy.

By the results of the previous section, $H(P) = E_P[L(X)]$ where $L(X) = - \log P(X)$ are the codelengths of the code corresponding to P. This is the optimal (in an expected sense) code to use if X is distributed according to P. Therefore:

> **Coding Interpretation of Entropy**
> The entropy of P is the expected number of bits needed to encode an outcome generated by P when the optimal code is used to encode outcomes of P.

If $\mathcal{X} = \mathbb{R}$ is continuous, then we first have to discretize $\mathcal{X}$ before we can design a code for it. The differential entropy as defined above corresponds to a uniform discretization, where we first take grid points $\ldots, -2\epsilon, -\epsilon, 0, \epsilon, 2\epsilon, \ldots$ at equal distance ϵ, and then consider the limit of the, appropriately normalized, expected codelength for $\epsilon \to 0$. Different, nonuniform discretizations give rise to different versions of continuous entropy.

> There exist many variations of the concept of "entropy" in the literature. Even though $H(P)$ as defined in (3.17) is usually just called "entropy," a more precise name would be *Shannon entropy* if $\mathcal{X}$ is discrete and *differential Shannon entropy with respect to Lebesgue measure* if $\mathcal{X}$ is continuous.

We now move from entropy to relative entropy, also known as Kullback-Leibler divergence. The Kullback-Leibler divergence serves as a sort of "distance" between probability distributions. We call it divergence rather than distance since it is neither symmetric nor does it satisfy the triangle inequality. It is therefore not a distance in the formal, mathematical sense of the word.

Definition 3.4 [Relative entropy] Let $\mathcal{X}$ be a finite or countable sample space, and let P and Q be distributions over $\mathcal{X}$. The *relative entropy* or *Kullback-Leibler (KL) divergence* from P to Q, denoted $D(P\|Q)$, is defined as

$$D(P\|Q) := E_P[- \log Q(X)] - E_P[- \log P(X)] = \sum_{x \in \mathcal{X}} P(x) \log \frac{P(x)}{Q(x)} \quad (3.18)$$

where, for $a > 0$, $a \log 0$ is defined as ∞ and, once again, $0 \log 0$ is defined as 0. If both terms in (3.18) are infinite, $D(P\|Q)$ is undefined. If $\mathcal{X}$ is continuous, then the sum is replaced by an integral.

In general, $D(P\|Q)$ may be *very* different from $D(Q\|P)$ (Example 4.1). Using the results of the previous section again, $D(P\|Q)$ may be interpreted as a difference between two expected codelengths:

Coding Interpretation of Relative Entropy/KL Divergence
$D(P\|Q)$ is the expected *additional* number of bits needed to encode an outcome generated by P when the code that is optimal for Q is used to encode outcomes of P instead of the code that is optimal for P.

In contrast to the case for ordinary entropy, for continuous sample spaces, in the limit for small ϵ, the normalized codelength difference does *not* depend on the chosen discretization, so that the definition of KL divergence remains unique for continuous $\mathcal{X}$.

We may now rephrase the "information inequality" (sometimes also called *Gibbs' inequality* of the previous section as follows:

Information Inequality
$D(P\|Q) \geq 0$ with equality if and only if $P = Q$.

We prove this using *Jensen's inequality,* a standard result in mathematics. In our restricted context it says the following. Suppose f is a strictly convex function defined on $\mathcal{X}$, and let P be a probability distribution on $\mathcal{X}$ concentrated on at least two points (i.e., $P(x) > 0$ for at least two distinct x). Then $E_P[f(X)] > f(E_P[X])$.

If $P = Q$, then clearly $D(P\|Q) = 0$. If $P \neq Q$ and P is concentrated on a single point, then $D(P\|Q) = \infty$. If $P \neq Q$ and P is concentrated on at least two points, we can write by Jensen's inequality and the strict convexity of the $-\log$-function,

$$D(P\|Q) = E_P\left[-\log \frac{Q(X)}{P(X)}\right] > -\log E_P\left[\frac{Q(X)}{P(X)}\right] =$$

$$-\log \sum P(x)\frac{Q(x)}{P(x)} = 0, \quad (3.19)$$

which is what we had to prove.

(Relative) Entropy for Sources   For i.i.d. probabilistic sources P and Q, we define $H(P^{(1)})$ as the entropy of the corresponding distribution for X_1. $D(P\|Q)$ is defined as the relative entropy $D(P^{(1)}\|Q^{(1)})$ of the corresponding two distributions. For non-i.i.d. probabilistic sources P and Q, $D(P\|Q)$ is defined as $\lim_{n\to\infty} n^{-1} D(P^{(n)}\|Q^{(n)})$. If this quantity is undefined, then so is $D(P\|Q)$; similarly for $H(P)$. When we are interested in the entropy of a member θ of a parametric family $\mathcal{M}$, we write $H(\theta)$ as an abbreviation of $H(P_\theta)$. Similarly, we frequently use the abbreviation $D(\theta^*\|\theta)$:

$$D(\theta^*\|\theta) := D(P_\theta^*\|P_\theta).$$

3.3.2   Uniform Codes, Maximum Entropy, and Minimax Codelength

Suppose $\mathcal{X}$ is finite, say $\mathcal{X} = \{1, \ldots, m\}$. In practice, we often deal with a situation where it may be reasonable to assume that some Q generates X, but we do not know exactly what Q. In that case, we may use the uniform code, based on the uniform distribution. Since no matter what outcome obtains, $L_U(x) = -\log P_U(x) = \log m$, L_U is optimal in a worst-case sense where the worst case is over all data (page 87). But it is also optimal in a worst-case sense over all distributions Q that might generate data. This is highlighted in the box on page 107. To see that (3.20) in the box holds, take $Q = P_U$ and use the information inequality (3.14). Among all distributions over a finite sample space $\mathcal{X}$, the uniform distribution uniquely maximizes the entropy. This is not a coincidence, as we discuss further in Chapter 19, Section 19.5, page 637.

3.4   Summary, Outlook, Further Reading

We have introduced codes and description methods and we have discussed the fundamental relationship between probability distributions and codes. We have introduced uniform and quasi-uniform codes, as well as the notions of entropy and KL divergence. In the next chapter, these concepts are applied to the analysis of likelihood, entropy, and relative entropy for some frequently used statistical models.

   A much more detailed account of most topics treated in this chapter can be found in the exceedingly well-written standard textbook (Cover and Thomas 1991). We should also note that most of these topics were introduced, for the

---

The Third Most Important Observation of This Book: Using the Code Corresponding to Distribution P May Sometimes Be a Good Idea Even if the Data Are *Not* Distributed According to P. A Prime Example is the Uniform Code.

The uniform code L_U is sometimes good to use even if data are not uniformly distributed. If the sample space $\mathcal{X}$ has m outcomes, we are guaranteed a codelength of $\log m$ bits; *no matter what outcome actually obtains, and no matter what distribution generates the data*. Thus, for any distribution Q on $\mathcal{X}$,

$$E_Q[L_U(X)] = E_Q[-\log P_U(X)] = E_{P_U}[-\log P_U(X)] = H(P_U) = \log m.$$

For any other code (distribution used as code), we may need more bits on average in the worst case: for every $P \neq P_U$, there exists a Q such that

$$E_Q[-\log P(X)] > \log m = E_Q[-\log P_U(X)]. \tag{3.20}$$

Since the uniform code corresponds to the uniform distribution and is thus the optimal code to use if data are uniformly distributed, it is often thought that using the uniform code implicitly implies assuming that data are uniformly distributed. **This is wrong!**: Because of its optimal worst-case performance, using the uniform code is also a reasonable idea if it is *completely unknown* how the data are distributed, or if *no* distribution at all is assumed.

Figure 3.4   The third most important observation of this book.

first time, yet in essentially final form, in Claude Shannon's landmark paper (Shannon 1948), which is still well worth reading.

4 *Information-Theoretic Properties of Statistical Models*

Overview We consider some information-theoretic properties of standard statistical models. Specifically we introduce the *Fisher information*, a standard concept in statistics. We discuss its relation with *(maximum) log-likelihood, codelength, and relative entropy* for parametric models. We also consider the maximum likelihood estimator in some more detail, emphasizing the essential difference between varying data and parameters. This clarifies the relation between maximum likelihood, entropy, and probabilistic laws of large numbers.

Contents The chapter starts with an introduction. Section 4.2 relates the *observed* Fisher information to likelihood and codelength. Section 4.3 relates the *expected* Fisher information to expected codelength and relative entropy or Kullback-Leibler (KL) divergence. Section 4.4 discusses how the maximum likelihood estimator varies as a function of the data and the parameters.

Fast Track Most of the material in Chapter 5 and Part II and Part III of this book can be read without knowing the details of the derivations in this chapter. However, the *conclusions* of these derivations are of central importance. Therefore, at first reading, it may suffice to look at the boxes, in which these conclusions are summarized.

4.1 Introduction

In the first two sections of this chapter we discuss the relationship of log-likelihood and Fisher information, which are standard statistical concepts, to codelength and relative entropy, which are standard information-theoretic concepts. More specifically:

- First, in Section 4.2, we show that the likelihood $P_\theta(x_1, \ldots, x_n)$ as a function of θ may be locally approximated by a Gaussian-shaped curve centered at the maximum likelihood $\hat{\theta}$. This curve has width determined by n times a quantity known as *observed Fisher information*.

- Second, in Section 4.3 we show that the relative entropy (KL divergence), locally behaves like squared Euclidean distance with a rescaling determined by a quantity known as *expected* Fisher information.

These two results are close analogues: the first result can be restated as saying that, locally around its maximum, the *logarithm* of the *observed* likelihood at θ behaves like a quadratic. The second result can be restated as saying that, locally around its maximum, the *expected* log-likelihood behaves like a quadratic.

Both results are of central importance: they provide intuition regarding the relationship between expected and actual codelength and likelihood, and about the relationship between Kullback-Leibler divergence – the central "distance"-like notion in this book, and the familiar Euclidean distance.

Varying Parameters vs. Data   In Sections 4.2 and 4.3 the analysis focuses on the log- probability of a data sequence according to some distribution P_θ when the data are fixed and the parameter θ is varied. In Section 4.4 we consider the opposite situation where the data vary and θ remains fixed. Although this analysis is trivial, its outcome is somewhat surprising: the likelihood is typically maximized for extreme data, with frequency characteristics quite different from θ. We explain how this can be reconciled with, and, less trivially, even helps to explain, the laws of large numbers.

For reasons of convenience, throughout this chapter we analyze the behavior of $-\ln P_\theta$ rather than $-\log P_\theta$. Recall from Chapter 3 that $-\log P_\theta(x_1, \ldots, x_n)$ may be interpreted as the codelength of $x_1, \ldots, x_n$ when it is encoded using the Shannon-Fano code. Since for all x, $-\ln x = \ln 2(-\log x)$, we can view $-\ln P(x_1, \ldots, x_n)$ as the "codelength in nats (natural units),"[1] which is always a constant $(\ln 2)$ times the codelength in bits.

We use the symbol D to express the KL divergence in terms of the natural rather than the base-2 logarithm; and H to express the entropy in terms of the natural rather than the base-2 logarithm. We have for all distributions P, Q,

$$\mathrm{D}(P\|Q) = \ln 2 \cdot D(P\|Q) \quad ; \quad \mathrm{H}(P) = \ln 2 \cdot H(P).$$

---

1. Some authors prefer the abbreviation "nits" (Wallace 2005).

4.2 Likelihood and *Observed* Fisher Information

Suppose some source, not necessarily probabilistic, is generating a sequence of data $x_1, x_2, \ldots$. We observe an initial segment $x^n = (x_1, \ldots, x_n)$. Based on some parametric model $\mathcal{M}$ parameterized by Θ, we are going to analyze how $-\ln P_\theta(x_1, \ldots, x_n)$ varies with θ, particularly in small neighborhoods of the maximum likelihood point $\hat{\theta}$. Thus, in everything that follows in this section, $x_1, x_2, \ldots, x_n$ *is fixed and θ varies.*

Regularity Conditions Our analysis is based on performing Taylor expansions of $-\ln P_\theta(x_1, \ldots, x_n)$ around $\hat{\theta}$. For this, we must assume that the model $\mathcal{M}$ and the parameterization Θ are well behaved in several ways. For example, the first, second, and third derivative of the log-likelihood function $\ln P_\theta(x_1, \ldots, x_n)$ must exist. Also, there must be a unique $\theta \in \Theta$ achieving the maximum likelihood for $x_1, \ldots, x_n$. For pedagogical reasons, we shall simply discuss these conditions as they arise. In Part IV, Chapter 18 it will be seen that all conditions are automatically satisfied for the exponential families in their standard parameterizations. But in fact, the results hold much more generally – we return to this issue at the end of Section 4.3.

Single Parameter Case We first consider the 1-parameter case. Let $\mathcal{M} = \mathcal{M}^{(1)}$ be a model of probabilistic sources with a 1-parameter parameterization $\Theta^{(1)}$. For example, we could take the Bernoulli model, the Poisson model, or the set of all normal distributions with varying mean μ and constant variance $\sigma^2 = 1$. We use the Bernoulli model as our running example.

We assume that $x_1, \ldots, x_n$ are such that $\ln P_\theta(x_1, \ldots, x_n)$ achieves a unique maximum at $\hat{\theta}$, the maximum likelihood estimate. For example, for the Bernoulli model this assumption is automatically satisfied (Chapter 2). We can then Taylor-expand $-\ln P_\theta(x^n)$ around $\hat{\theta}$ as follows:

$$-\ln P_\theta(x^n) = -\ln P_{\hat{\theta}}(x^n) +$$
$$(\theta - \hat{\theta})\left\{\frac{d}{d\theta} - \ln P_\theta(x^n)\right\}_{\theta=\hat{\theta}} + \frac{1}{2}(\theta - \hat{\theta})^2\left\{\frac{d^2}{d\theta^2} - \ln P_\theta(x^n)\right\}_{\theta=\hat{\theta}} + R,$$

$$(4.1)$$

where R is a remainder term. Here

$$\left\{\frac{d}{d\theta} - \ln P_\theta(x^n)\right\}_{\theta=\hat\theta}$$

is to be read as "the first derivative of $-\ln P_\theta(x^n)$ evaluated at $\theta = \hat\theta$." Since $-\ln P_\theta(x^n)$ achieves its minimum at $\hat\theta$, this term must vanish, so (4.1) can be rewritten as

$$-\ln P_\theta(x^n) = -\ln P_{\hat\theta}(x^n) + \frac{1}{2}n(\theta-\hat\theta)^2 J(x^n) + R. \tag{4.2}$$

Here

$$J(x^n):=\left\{\frac{1}{n}\frac{d^2}{d\theta^2} - \ln P_\theta(x^n)\right\}_{\theta=\hat\theta} \tag{4.3}$$

is the so-called *observed information*, sometimes also called *observed Fisher information*.

> To be fully precise, what we call the "observed information (matrix)" is n^{-1} times the standard definition of observed information (matrix) (Kass and Voss 1997). The normalization achieved by the division by n is useful for our purposes, since we deal with models of probabilistic sources, defined for sequences of each n. In most treatments, one considers models that are distributions for a fixed sample size n.

Below we analyze $J(x^n)$ and the remainder term R in more detail. The latter can be written as

$$R = (\theta-\hat\theta)^3\frac{1}{6}\left\{\frac{d^3}{d\theta^3} - \ln P_\theta(x^n)\right\}_{\theta=\theta'} \tag{4.4}$$

where θ' lies between $\hat\theta$ and θ.

Our approximation of $-\ln P_\theta(x^n)$ will be valid only for values of θ sufficiently "close" to $\hat\theta$, more precisely, for values of θ in the region

$$\left\{\theta \mid |\theta - \hat\theta(x^n)| < \frac{K}{\sqrt{n}}\right\} \tag{4.5}$$

for some constant K. It turns out that, whenever our data are generated by a sufficiently regular probabilistic source (not necessarily in $\mathcal{M}$), this is precisely the region we are interested in.

Why a Region of Size $O(1/\sqrt{n})$**?** Suppose first that data are generated by a Bernoulli distribution. It is immediate from the central limit theorem (CLT) (Chapter 2, Theorem 2.2), that with high probability, for all large n, $\hat{\theta}$ will lie in the region (4.5): $\hat{\theta}$ is the relative frequency of 1s n_1/n, and θ is the probability of observing 1. By choosing K large enough, we can achieve that, for all large n, the probability that $|\theta - \hat{\theta}(x^n)| < K/\sqrt{n}$ is arbitrarily close to 1; see also Example 2.6. In Chapter 19, Section 19.4, we shall see that an analogous *multivariate* CLT for maximum likelihood (ML) estimators holds for many other models, including all exponential families.

Now suppose that (4.5) holds. As we shall see below, under further mild conditions on the model $\mathcal{M}$ and the sequence $x_1, x_2, \ldots$, there exist constants $K_2 > K_1 > 0$ and K_3, K_4 such that for all large n,

$$K_1 \leq J(x^n) \leq K_2 \quad \text{and} \quad K_3 \leq \left\{ -\frac{1}{n}\frac{d^3}{d\theta^3} \ln P_\theta(x^n) \right\}_{\theta = \theta'} \leq K_4. \tag{4.6}$$

Combining (4.4), (4.6) and (4.5), we see that $R = O(\frac{1}{\sqrt{n}})$, so that R tends to 0. (4.1) now becomes

$$-\ln P_\theta(x^n) = -\ln P_{\hat{\theta}(x^n)}(x^n) + \frac{1}{2}nJ(\theta - \hat{\theta})^2 + O\left(\frac{1}{\sqrt{n}}\right), \tag{4.7}$$

where J depends on the data x^n, but must lie in between K_1 and K_2. Exponentiating on both sides, we get the picture of Figure 4.1: to first order in the exponent, $P_\theta(x^n)$ behaves approximately like a Gaussian bell curve:

$$P_\theta(x^n) = P_{\hat{\theta}(x^n)}(x^n) \cdot e^{-(1/2)nJ(\theta - \hat{\theta})^2 + O(n^{-1/2})}, \tag{4.8}$$

where J lies in between K_1 and K_2.

Below we shall see that an analogous result holds for multivariate models $\mathcal{M}^{(k)}$, and that in many cases of interest, $J(x^n)$ stops fluctuating and converges to a single number K for large n. Summarizing and anticipating:

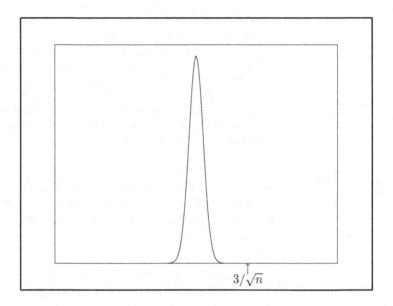

$3/\sqrt{n}$

Figure 4.1   The horizontal axis represents $\theta - \hat{\theta}(x^n)$ as a function of θ for a particular, fixed, x^n. The vertical axis represents $P_\theta(x^n)$. The function achieves its maximum at $\theta = \hat{\theta}$ and, near the maximum, has the shape of a Gaussian.

Likelihood near the Maximum and Observed Information
Let $\mathcal{M}$ be a 1-parameter model. Then,

- under weak regularity conditions on the model $\mathcal{M}$ and the sequence $x_1, x_2, \ldots$

- and if we consider θ in a small region around $\hat{\theta}$,

the averaged minus log-likelihood (Shannon-Fano codelength) $n^{-1} \ln P_\theta(x^n)$ behaves approximately like $0.5nJ(x^n)(\hat{\theta} - \theta)^2$ where for all n, $0 < K_1 < J(x^n) < K_2$. If, further, the sequence x_1, x_2 can be assumed to be generated by a "reasonable" probability distribution (not necessarily in $\mathcal{M}$), then $K_1 - K_2 \to 0$ as $n \to \infty$.
Thus, the likelihood itself behaves approximately like a Gaussian bell-shaped curve with width of order $O(1/\sqrt{n})$.

Similarly, for k-dimensional models $\mathcal{M}^{(k)}$, if $J(x^n)$ is positive definite, then the likelihood near $\hat{\theta}(x^n)$ behaves approximately like a k-dimensional Gaussian bell-shaped curve with widths of order $O(1/\sqrt{n})$.

Conditions   Before discussing the multivariate case, let us first investigate the conditions under which (4.6) and therefore also (4.8) holds. Obviously, these equations only hold for models that can be continuously parameterized in such a way that the first three derivatives of the log-likelihood exist. In particular, this will be the case if the models are smooth. Within the class of models with thrice differentiable parameterizations, let us first consider the simple case that $\mathcal{X}$ is finite and $\mathcal{M}$ is an i.i.d. model, so that for $m = 0, 1, 2, 3$,

$$-\frac{1}{n}\frac{d^{(m)}}{d\theta^{(m)}}\ln P_\theta(X^n) = -\frac{1}{n}\sum_{i=1}^{n}\frac{d^{(m)}}{d\theta^{(m)}}\ln P_\theta(X_i). \tag{4.9}$$

Then (4.6) must hold, as long as there is some compact (closed and bounded) subset R of the interior of the parameter space such that for all large n, $\hat{\theta}$ falls into R. To see this, consider for example the Bernoulli model for a sequence such that for some $\epsilon > 0$, for all large n, $\epsilon \leq \hat{\theta}(x^n) \leq 1 - \epsilon$. The mth derivative is easily seen to be

$$-\frac{d^m}{d\theta^m}\ln P_\theta(x^n) = -\frac{d^m}{d\theta^m}\sum_{i=1}^{n}\ln P_\theta(x_i) =$$
$$\frac{n_0((m-1)!)}{(1-\theta)^m} + \left(\frac{n_1((m-1)!)}{\theta^m}\right)\cdot(-1)^m, \tag{4.10}$$

where n_0 is the number of 0s in x^n. It follows that for every sequence x^n and every θ with

$$\epsilon \leq \theta \leq 1 - \epsilon, \tag{4.11}$$

we have

$$-\frac{2n}{\epsilon^3} \leq -\frac{d^3}{d\theta^3}\ln P_\theta(x^n) \leq \frac{2n}{\epsilon^3},$$

so that (4.6) and therefore, the expansion (4.8) holds. Note that if $\hat{\theta}$ can come arbitrarily close to the boundary of the space, then the θ' in (4.6) may violate (4.11) and the expansion does not hold anymore.

  The same type of reasoning can be easily extended to arbitrary i.i.d. $\mathcal{M}$ with finite $\mathcal{X}$, thrice differentiable parameterizations, and $\hat{\theta}$ falling into a compact subset of the interior of the parameter space.

Weaker Conditions   Equation (4.8) holds in much wider generality than just for finite sample spaces and i.i.d. models. For example it still holds if $\mathcal{M}$ is an i.i.d. exponential family with arbitrary sample space. It also holds for most standard recursive, non-i.i.d. exponential families such as the Markov chains.

For models that are not exponential families, (4.8) typically still holds, for arbitrary sample spaces, as long as the data are i.i.d. according to a "reasonable" distribution P^*. Here "reasonable" means that there exists some θ^* such that P_{θ^*} minimizes the KL divergence to P^*, among all $\theta^* \in \Theta$. In particular this will be the case if $P^* = P_{\theta^*}$, i.e. the data-generating distribution is in the model; but it holds much more generally.

If data are i.i.d. $\sim P^*$, then, applying the law of large numbers (Section 2.2.3, Theorem 2.1) to (4.9) we find the following: for all $\theta \in R$, where R is any compact subset of Θ, we have with probability 1, for $m = 0, 1, 2, 3$,

$$-\frac{1}{n}\frac{d^{(m)}}{d\theta^{(m)}} \ln P_\theta(X^n) \to E_{P^*}[-\frac{d^{(m)}}{d\theta^{(m)}} \ln P_\theta(X)], \qquad (4.12)$$

where, under mild conditions on $\mathcal{M}$ and its parameterization, the convergence is uniform in $\theta \in R$. Again, under mild conditions on $\mathcal{M}$ and P^*, the expectations in (4.12) exist and are continuous functions of θ. In that case, since the region (4.5) we are actually interested in becomes smaller and smaller as n increases, it follows that, for θ in this region, (4.6) and hence also (4.8) hold. Moreover, for large n, the interval $[K_1, K_2]$ in which $J(x^n)$ must lie, shrinks to 0. Thus, in the special case where the model is i.i.d., the parameter space compact, and the data are generated by a "reasonable" distribution (not necessarily inside the model), (4.8) and the corresponding statement in the box on page 114 hold. Even if the data are not i.i.d. under either the model $\mathcal{M}$ or the distribution P^*, then (4.8) may still hold; typically this will be the case as long as P^* is *stationary* and *ergodic* (Feller 1968b).

Multiple Parameter Case   By doing a multivariate Taylor expansion, we can extend the reasoning to k-parameter models $\mathcal{M}^{(k)}$. The first derivative in (4.1) is now replaced by the *gradient vector* of the negative log-likelihood. This is the row vector given by

$$\nabla\{-\ln P_\theta(x^n)\}_{\theta=\hat\theta} = \left\{\left(\frac{\partial}{\partial\theta_1} - \ln P_\theta(x^n), \ldots, \frac{\partial}{\partial\theta_k} - \ln P_\theta(x^n)\right)\right\}_{\theta=\hat\theta}, \quad (4.13)$$

and consisting of the partial derivatives of $-\ln P_\theta(x^n)$ with respect to the k components $\theta_1, \ldots, \theta_k$ of parameter vector θ. In the statistical literature, the negative of the gradient (4.13) is often called the *score* of the likelihood at $\hat\theta$.

The observed Fisher information (4.3) is replaced by the $(k \times k)$ *observed Fisher information matrix* $J(x^n)$ with entries

$$J_{ij}(x^n) := \left\{ \frac{\partial^2}{\partial \theta_i \partial \theta_j} - \frac{1}{n} \ln P_\theta(x^n) \right\}_{\theta = \hat{\theta}(x^n)}, \qquad (4.14)$$

where $\partial^2/\partial\theta_i\partial\theta_j$ is the partial derivative with respect to the ith and jth component of $\theta = (\theta_1, \ldots, \theta_k)$. This is the negative of the so-called *Hessian matrix* of the log-likelihood, evaluated at the maximum likelihood $\hat{\theta}$. We now get the expansion:

$$- \ln P_\theta(x^n) = - \ln P_{\hat\theta}(x^n) +$$
$$\nabla\{-\ln P_{\hat\theta(x^n)}\}_{\theta=\hat\theta}(\theta - \hat\theta) + \frac{1}{2}n(\theta - \hat\theta)^\top J(x^n)(\theta - \hat\theta) + O\left(\frac{1}{\sqrt{n}}\right) \quad (4.15)$$

where once again the second term on the right vanishes because we are evaluating at a minimum. If the matrix $J(x^n)$ is positive definite (Section 2.1), then the likelihood function $P_\theta(x^n)$ locally (around $\hat\theta(x^n)$) looks approximately like a k-dimensional multivariate Gaussian curve. This is guaranteed to be the case for, for example, the exponential families, as long as for all large n, $\hat\theta(x^n)$ lies in some compact subset of the parameter space.

> Suppose $\hat\theta$ lies in the interior of Θ. Then, if $J(x^n)$ is not positive definite, it must still be positive semidefinite. The reason is that $-\ln P_\theta(x^n)$ achieves a minimum at $\hat\theta$: assume, by contradiction, that $J(x^n)$ is not positive semidefinite. Then continuity arguments show that there is some θ' in a neighborhood of $\hat\theta$ with $-\ln P_{\theta'}(x^n) < -\ln P_{\hat\theta}(x^n)$; a contradiction.
>
> The fact that $J(x^n)$ is positive semidefinite implies that there is some hyperplane H going through $\hat\theta$ of dimension $k' < k$, such that within the plane H, the likelihood remains constant in a neighborhood around $\hat\theta$, or in any case it decreases so slowly that the second derivative at $\hat\theta$ along any line in the hyperplane is 0. In the $k - k'$–dimensional hyperplane that is orthogonal to H, the likelihood function $P_\theta(x^n)$ locally still looks like a k''-dimensional multivariate Gaussian curve, where $k'' = k - k'$.

4.3 KL Divergence and *Expected* Fisher Information

In the previous subsection we studied the behavior of the *actual* log-likelihood

$$\ln P_\theta(x^n)$$

near the value $\hat{\theta}$ that maximizes this likelihood for given *data* x^n. Wherever possible, we tried not to assume the existence of a distribution generating these data.

In the present section we assume that such a distribution, say $\theta^* \in \Theta^{(k)}$, does exist, and we study the behavior of the *expected* log-likelihood

$$E_{\theta^*}[\ln P_\theta(X)]$$

near the value of θ that maximizes the *expected* likelihood for the given *distribution* θ^*. By the information inequality (3.13), the unique P_θ that maximizes the expected likelihood is equal to the "true" P_{θ^*} generating the data. The treatment in this paragraph is entirely analogous to the previous one, with the maximum likelihood distribution $\hat{\theta}(x^n)$ (which depends on the actual data in an experiment) replaced by the maximum *expected* likelihood distribution θ^* (which does not depend on any data, but on an imagined data-generating distribution). Once we have an expansion for the expected log-likelihood, we automatically get a local approximation for the KL divergence. Note that the KL divergence can be viewed as an expected log-likelihood *ratio*. It will once again be convenient to study $-\ln P_\theta$ rather than $\ln P_\theta$.

Single Parameter, i.i.d. Case   Let $\mathcal{M} = \mathcal{M}^{(1)}$ be a 1-parameter i.i.d. model. As before, we may take the Bernoulli model as our running example. We can approximate the function $g(\theta) := E_{\theta^*}[-\ln P_\theta(X)]$ around $\theta = \theta^*$ by Taylor-expanding $-\ln P_\theta(X)$ *inside* the expectation. By linearity of expectation, this gives:

$$E_{\theta^*}[-\ln P_\theta(X)] = E_{\theta^*}[-\ln P_{\theta^*}(X)] +$$

$$(\theta - \theta^*) E_{\theta^*} \left\{ -\frac{d}{d\theta} \ln P_\theta(X) \right\}_{\theta=\theta^*} + \frac{1}{2}(\theta - \theta^*)^2 E_{\theta^*} \left\{ -\frac{d^2}{d\theta^2} \ln P_\theta(X) \right\}_{\theta=\theta^*}$$

$$+ R. \quad (4.16)$$

where R is a remainder term. Assuming that $E_{\theta^*}[-(d^3/d\theta^3) \ln P_\theta(X)]$ is continuous as a function of θ in a neighborhood of θ^*, it follows that $R = o((\theta - \theta^*)^2)$ and hence becomes negligible for θ close enough to θ^*. Assuming further that we are allowed to change the order of integration and differentiation in the first derivative term in (4.16), and using the information inequality (Equation (3.14), page 101) we see that the first derivative vanishes at the minimum θ^*, so that we can rewrite (4.16) as

$$E_{\theta^*}[-\ln P_\theta(X)] = E_{\theta^*}[-\ln P_{\theta^*}(X)] + \frac{1}{2}(\theta - \theta^*)^2 I(\theta^*) + (o(\theta - \theta^*)^2). \quad (4.17)$$

To arrive at (4.17), we assumed continuity of $E_{\theta^*}[-d^3/(d\theta^3)\ln P_\theta(X)]$ and interchangeability of the expectation and differentiation operations: $E_{\theta^*}[-(d/d\theta)$ $\ln P_\theta(X)] = (d/d\theta)E_{\theta^*}[-\ln P_\theta(X)]$. For smooth i.i.d. models with finite or compact sample spaces, such as the Bernoulli model, and θ^* in the interior of the parameter space, both assumptions can be verified immediately. For more general models, they typically still hold. For example, in the next chapter we shall see that they hold for the exponential families.

In (4.17), we wrote

$$I(\theta) := E_\theta\left[-\frac{d^2}{d\theta^2}\ln P_\theta(X)\right]. \quad (4.18)$$

This is the so-called *expected Fisher information* at θ (usually just called "Fisher information"), a definition and terminology explained further in Chapter 18, Section 18.6.

When we write "Fisher information," we always mean the expected version. In the statistical literature, the expected Fisher information is usually defined differently (Casella and Berger). For most standard parametric families, our definition (4.18) can be shown to *coincide* with the standard definition; see Chapter 18, Section 18.6.

Noting that

$$E_{\theta^*}[-\ln P_\theta(X)] - E_{\theta^*}[-\ln P_{\theta^*}(X)] = D(\theta^*\|\theta), \quad (4.19)$$

(4.17) shows that the KL divergence $D(\cdot\|\cdot)$ can be approximated as

$$D(\theta^*\|\theta) = \frac{1}{2}(\theta - \theta^*)^2 I(\theta^*) + o((\theta - \theta^*)^2). \quad (4.20)$$

Multiple Parameter, i.i.d. Case   A straightforward extension of this argument to the multidimensional case gives

$$E_{\theta^*}[-\ln P_\theta(X)] = E_{\theta^*}[-\ln P_{\theta^*}(X)] +$$

$$\nabla\{-\ln P_\theta(X)\}_{\theta=\theta^*}(\theta - \theta^*) + \frac{1}{2}(\theta - \theta^*)^\top I(\theta^*)(\theta - \theta^*) + o(\|\theta - \theta^*\|^2),$$

$$(4.21)$$

where $I(\theta^*)$ is now a matrix, the (expected) *Fisher information matrix*, with entries given by:

$$I_{ij}(\theta^*) := E_{\theta^*}\left[-\frac{\partial^2}{\partial\theta_i^* \partial\theta_j^*}\ln P_{\theta^*}(X) \right] = E_{\theta^*}\left\{ -\frac{\partial^2}{\partial\theta_i \partial\theta_j}\ln P_\theta(X) \right\}_{\theta=\theta^*}, \quad (4.22)$$

where we wrote the equation in two ways to prepare for a useful rewriting of the Fisher information below, (4.26). Once again, the first derivative vanishes at the minimum. Combining with (4.19) we now get:

Kullback-Leibler Divergence and Expected Fisher Information

For sufficiently regular 1-parameter models, in a small enough region around the "true" distribution θ^*, the KL divergence $D(\theta^*\|\theta)$ (viewed as a function of θ) behaves approximately like a quadratic with coefficient $(1/2)I(\theta^*)$. For models $\mathcal{M}^{(k)}$ with $k \geq 1$, we get

$$D(\theta^*\|\theta) = \frac{1}{2}(\theta - \theta^*)^\top I(\theta^*)(\theta - \theta^*) + o(\|\theta - \theta^*\|^2), \quad (4.23)$$

so that $D(\cdot\|\cdot)$ behaves like "rescaled" Euclidean distance (see below) with the particular rescaling depending on θ^*.

Positive Definiteness and Rescaled Euclidean (Mahalanobis) Distance   Let M be an arbitrary positive definite $k \times k$ matrix. We can think of the function $g : \mathbb{R}^k \to [0, \infty)$ defined by $g(v) := v^\top M v$ as a *rescaled Euclidean norm*, inducing a rescaled form of Euclidean distance. Such a distance measure is often called *Mahalanobis distance*.

To see this, fix some $\theta_0 \in \mathbb{R}^k$. Then $\{\theta : (\theta - \theta_0)^\top(\theta - \theta_0) < 1\}$ is the unit-distance ball around θ_0, where the distance metric is the plain Euclidean distance in k dimensions. It can be shown that for every symmetric positive definite $k \times k$ matrix M, $\{\theta : (\theta - \theta_0)^\top M(\theta - \theta_0) < 1\}$ is an ellipsoid around θ_0 whose axis points in the direction of the eigenvectors, and whose axis lengths are given by the square roots of the inverse eigenvalues of M. Indeed, it turns out that a matrix M is positive definite if and only if all its eigenvalues are larger than 0. Thus, defining the Mahalanobis distance relative to M as $d_M(\theta, \theta_0) := \sqrt{(\theta - \theta_0)^\top M(\theta - \theta_0)}$, d becomes a rescaled version of the Euclidean distance whose unit balls look like rotated ellipsoids in Euclidean space.

For many families of models, including all exponential families, $I(\theta^*)$ is guaranteed to be positive definite, so that $D(\cdot\|\cdot)$ locally behaves like rescaled squared (!) Euclidean distance. Even if $I(\theta^*)$ is not positive definite, existence of the third derivative of the likelihood implies that it must be positive semidefinite. In that case, $D(\cdot\|\cdot)$ effectively behaves locally like a rescaled Euclidean distance in $\mathbb{R}^{k'}$, where $k' < k$.

It will be useful for later chapters to determine the *volume* of Mahalanobis balls around θ_0, relative to $I(\theta_0)$. To this end, let

$$B_{I(\theta_0)}(\theta_0, \epsilon) := \{\theta \ : \ d_{I(\theta_0)}(\theta_0, \theta) \leq \epsilon\} =$$
$$\{\theta \ : \ (\theta - \theta_0)^\top I(\theta_0)(\theta - \theta_0) \leq \epsilon^2\} \quad (4.24)$$

be a ball of radius ϵ around θ_0. The volume of $B_{I(\theta_0)}(\theta_0, \epsilon)$ is the volume of a k-dimensional ellipsoid with axis lengths given by the square root of the inverse eigenvalues. Since $\det I(\theta_0)$ is equal to the product of the eigenvalues, this implies that $V(B_{I(\theta_0)}(\theta_0, \epsilon)) = 1/\sqrt{\det I(\theta_0)}V(B(\epsilon))$, where $B(\epsilon)$ is an ordinary k-dimensional Euclidean ball with radius ϵ. By circumscribing and inscribing the ball with a hypercube, it is clear that this latter volume is proportional to ϵ^k, so that

$$V(B_{I(\theta_0)}(\theta_0, \epsilon)) = \frac{c_k}{\sqrt{\det I(\theta_0)}}\epsilon^k \quad (4.25)$$

for some proportionality constant c_k. The value of c_k can be computed (Conway and Sloane 1993), and turns out to be equal to $\pi^{k/2}/\Gamma(1 + k/2)$, where Γ denotes the gamma function.

Assuming we can exchange the order of differentiation and integration (see Chapter 18, Section 18.6), (4.22) is clearly equivalent to

$$I_{ij}(\theta^*) = \left\{\frac{\partial^2}{\partial\theta_i\partial\theta_j}D(\theta^*\|\theta)\right\}_{\theta=\theta^*}. \quad (4.26)$$

For a concrete illustration, see Example 4.1 and Figure 4.3 below.

Non-i.i.d. Case For many non-i.i.d. models, such as the Markov chains of fixed order γ, essentially the same story can still be told. The main difference is that the definition of the Fisher information needs to be extended: $I_{ij}(\theta^*)$ is now defined as

$$I_{ij}(\theta^*) = \lim_{n\to\infty}\frac{1}{n}\left\{\frac{\partial^2}{\partial\theta_i\partial\theta_j}E_{\theta^*}[-\ln P_\theta(X_1,\ldots,X_n)]\right\}_{\theta=\theta^*}. \quad (4.27)$$

We omit further details.

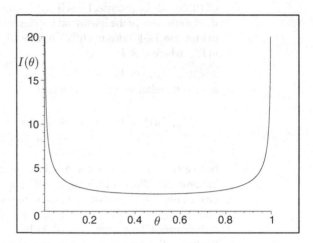

Figure 4.2 $I(\theta)$ as a function of θ for the Bernoulli model.

In most treatments, one considers models that are distributions for a fixed sample size n and then the Fisher information is defined as n times our definition (4.27). The normalization achieved by the division by n is useful for our purposes, since we deal with models of probabilistic sources, defined for sequences of each n. See also the remark on page 112.

Example 4.1 [Bernoulli and Fisher]   In Figure 4.2 we plotted the Fisher information $I(\theta)$ for the Bernoulli model $\mathcal{B}^{(1)}$. An easy calculation shows that in this case

$$I(\theta) = \frac{1}{\theta(1-\theta)}.$$

In words, the Fisher information is 1 over the variance $\theta(1-\theta)$. This means that the closer we get to the boundary of the parameter space, the more the KL divergence is affected by slight changes in θ.

Two examples of approximating $D(\theta^* \| \theta)$ by $0.5(\theta - \theta^*)^2 I(\theta^*)$ are shown in Figure 4.3. The figure shows that we have to be careful in applying our asymptotic expansions: the "size" of the region around θ^* for which the quadratic approximation is accurate depends strongly on θ^*.

Remark   Our analysis in this section and the previous one is only valid for models that satisfy certain regularity conditions. We repeatedly stressed that exponential families automatically satisfy these conditions. But they also

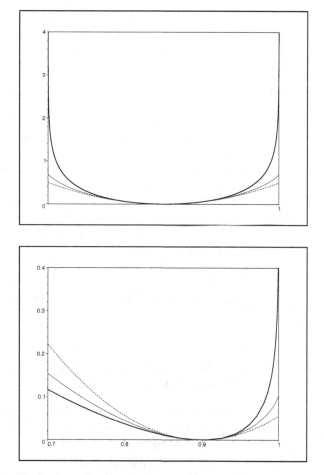

Figure 4.3   The horizontal axis represents θ. The vertical axis represents $D(\theta^*\|\theta)$ (solid thick line), $D(\theta\|\theta^*)$ (solid thin line), and $0.5(\theta - \theta^*)^2 I(\theta^*)$ (dotted line). In the upper picture, $\theta^* = 0.5$. In the lower picture, $\theta^* = 0.9$.

hold for many other i.i.d. and non-i.i.d. *parametric families* - typically, as soon as the likelihood is differentiable and, for all large n, the ML distribution is unique and converges to a point in the interior of the parameter space.

In some cases, such as mixture models, the results have to be slightly adjusted because the parameterization is not 1 to 1; also, the Fisher information may not be positive definite but only positive semidefinite at maxima in the likelihood. In that case, there may exist two or more parameter vectors indexing the same ML distribution, and we have to be clearer about what we mean by $\hat{\theta}(x^n)$ to get a precise result.

4.4   Maximum Likelihood: Data vs. Parameters

The previous two sections analyzed how the likelihood changes if the data are fixed and the parameters vary. We now look at the converse situation: how does the likelihood change when the data vary but the parameters remain fixed. The first situation (fixed data, varying θ) corresponds to statistical estimation, where we are given a set of data and have to infer parameter values. The situation we now consider (varying data) does not directly correspond to a practical setting, and its analysis is in some sense trivial. However, in my opinion, understanding it is essential for a proper appreciation of maximum likelihood and MDL inference.

To illustrate the issue, consider once more the Bernoulli model, Example 2.4, page 58, so that $P_\theta(X_i = 1) = \theta$ for some parameter θ. Then the probability (likelihood) of a sequence of n outcomes with n_1 1s is given by

$$\theta^{n_1}(1 - \theta)^{n - n_1}. \tag{4.28}$$

Note that

1. For fixed data $x_1, \ldots, x_n$ with n_1 1s, if we vary θ, then the likelihood is maximized for $\theta = n_1/n$ (Chapter 2).

2. If the data are distributed according to some fixed P_θ, then with high probability, the frequency of 1s converges to θ, so that $n_1/n \to \theta$ (law of large numbers, Chapter 2).

However, perhaps paradoxically:

The Data that Maximize the Likelihood

3. For *fixed* $\theta > 0.5$ and varying *data* (number of 1s), the likelihood increases with n_1/n and is maximized for $n_1 = n$ (analogously for $\theta < 0.5$, the likelihood is maximized for $n_1 = 0$).

Item 3 is the main point of this section: the data that maximize the likelihood is a degenerate, extreme sequence. To explain this, it is convenient to consider codelengths $-\ln P_\theta(x^n)$ rather than likelihoods, so that likelihood maximization becomes codelength minimization. Then (4.28) becomes

$$-\ln P_\theta(x^n) = n \cdot (-\nu \ln \theta - (1 - \nu)\ln(1 - \theta)), \tag{4.29}$$

where $\nu = n_1/n$. Item 1 above now states that, for given ν, (4.29) is minimized at $\theta = \nu$. Item 3 states that for given $\theta > 0.5$, (4.29) is minimized for $\nu = 1$ – which is of course trivial. Figure 4.4 illustrates the situation for various θ and values of ν (Note that n plays no role if we depict log-probabilities; large values of n correspond to a linear stretch of the y-axis. The fact that, for large n, the likelihood becomes a bell-shaped curve (Figure 4.1) only becomes visible if we depict the likelihood, rather than the log-likelihood.) We see, for example, that although $\theta = 0.7$ maximizes the likelihood for $\nu = 0.7$, it assigns a larger likelihood (smaller codelength) to data with $\nu = 0.8$.

Beyond Bernoulli   The discrepancy between likelihood maximization in terms of data and parameters is not limited to the Bernoulli model. As will become clear in Chapter 19 (Section 19.2, Propositions 19.1, and 19.3; Section 19.3, Example 19.4), essentially the same phenomenon takes place for all exponential families, including, for example the normal, Poisson, and geometric distributions: in the general case, the ML estimator is given by the average of a simple function $\phi(x_i)$ of the data; but for a given parameter value, the data that maximize the likelihood are data for which the average of the $\phi(x_i)$ is either maximal or minimal.

Laws of Large Numbers as a Balance between Two Opposite Forces   We now use the trivial observation we made above to gain some less trivial insights. At first sight, item 2 in our list above may seem to contradict item 3: if data are distributed according to $\theta = 0.7$, then the single sequence we are most likely to observe is the sequence consisting of only 1s. Yet by the law of large numbers, the sequence we will actually observe if data are distributed $\sim \theta$ must be a sequence with about 70% 1s. How is this possible? The reason is of course that there are exponentially many more sequences with about 70% 1s than sequences with only 1s. The *total* probability of a sequence with n_1 1s is given by

$$P_\theta\left(\hat{\theta}(X^n) = \frac{n_1}{n}\right) =$$

$$\sum_{x^n\,:\,\hat{\theta}(x^n)=n_1/n} \theta^{n_1}(1-\theta)^{n-n_1} = \binom{n}{n_1}\theta^{n_1}(1-\theta)^{n-n_1}, \tag{4.30}$$

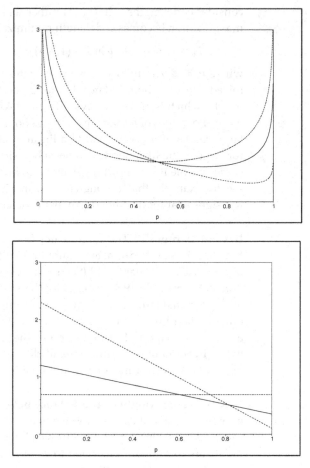

Figure 4.4 The top graph shows the negative log-likelihood $-\nu \ln \theta - (1-\nu) \ln(1-\theta)$ as a function of θ, where ν represents n_1/n. The graph shows the cases $\nu = 0.5$ (line that is lowest on the left, highest on the right), $\nu = 0.7$ (solid middle line), and $\nu = 0.9$. Note that for $\nu = 0.5$, θ achieves its minimum at 0.5: $\hat{\theta} = \nu$. Similarly for $\nu = 0.7$, $\hat{\theta} = 0.7$, and for $\nu = 0.9$, $\hat{\theta} = 0.9$. *Nevertheless*, $\theta = 0.7$ assigns a smaller description length to data with $\nu = 0.9$ than to data with $\nu = 0.7$. This is further illustrated in the bottom graph, which shows the negative log-likelihood $-\nu \ln \theta - (1-\nu) \ln(1-\theta)$ as a function of ν, for $\theta = 0.5$, $\theta = 0.7$, and $\theta = 0.9$. The corresponding functions are obviously linear. Note that we depict minus log rather than direct likelihoods here, which explains the difference in form between the top figure and the graph in Figure 4.1.

which, in contrast to the likelihood (4.28) involves the *sum* of the number of sequences achieving a particular frequency of 1s.

Thus, at least for $\theta \neq 0.5$, we may think of results like the law of large numbers as the large sample *balance* that is struck between two opposite driving forces: the *number* of sequences with a particular frequency of 1s $n \cdot \nu$, which is maximized at $\nu = 1/2$, and decreases exponentially in the size of $\delta := |\nu - 1/2|$; and the *probability* of such sequences according to the assumed distribution which *increases* exponentially in δ. Again, it turns out that an analogue of this result holds for general exponential families.[2] In this book we restrict our attention to the Bernoulli case, which we discuss in more detail below.

Second Interpretation of Entropy   The key to understanding the law of large numbers in terms of the "opposite forces" introduced above is the following fact: it turns out that, apart from its coding-theoretic interpretation, binary entropy is also a good approximation of the choose function:

Entropy as an Approximation of the Choose Function
Letting $\mathrm{H}(\nu) := -\nu \ln \nu - (1 - \nu) \ln(1 - \nu)$ represent the entropy of a Bernoulli distribution with parameter ν, measured in nats, we have

$$\mathrm{H}(\nu) = \lim_{n \to \infty} \frac{1}{n} \ln \binom{n}{\nu n}. \tag{4.31}$$

A more precise formula is given below: see (4.36).
While there is a close relationship between this combinatorial interpretation of entropy and the coding-theoretic interpretation (Chapter 4), the simplest proof of (4.31), given further below, uses Stirling's approximation rather than direct coding arguments.

It follows from (4.31) that the log of the probability (4.30) is approximately

---

2. The developments around Sanov's theorem and the conditional limit theorem in Chapter 12 of (Cover and Thomas 1991) can be interpreted in terms of the balance between number of sequences of a certain "type" (number of 1s) and the probability thereof, although Cover and Thomas do not emphasize this interpretation.

equal to

$$\ln \binom{n}{\nu n} + n\left(\nu \ln\theta + (1-\nu)\ln(1-\theta)\right) \approx$$

$$n \cdot \left[\, \mathrm{H}(\nu) - \left(-\nu\ln\theta - (1-\nu)\ln(1-\theta)\right) \,\right] = -n\mathrm{D}(\nu\|\theta), \quad (4.32)$$

where D stands for the relative entropy. The middle expression in (4.32) shows the two "opposite forces": the first term is the (log of the) number of sequences with given frequency, which turns out to be equal to the number of bits needed to encode a sequence with $n\nu$ 1s, if θ is set to the frequency ν which minimizes codelength; from this is subtracted the second term, which is the number of bits needed to encode a sequence with $n\nu$ 1s, if the original θ is used.

Exponentiating (4.32), we get

$$P_\theta\left(\hat{\theta}(X^n) = \nu\right) = e^{-n\mathrm{D}(\nu\|\theta)+o(n)},$$

which suggests that the probability that $|\hat{\theta} - \theta| > \epsilon$ is exponentially small in n. This in turn implies the law of large numbers: with probability 1, $\hat{\theta}$ converges to θ. Below we make the reasoning precise, and show that the entropy characterization of the choose function even gives rise to the central limit theorem for Bernoulli random variables.

Making Things Precise   Stirling's approximation of the factorial (Feller 1968a) says that $n! \sim \sqrt{2\pi n}\, n^n e^{-n}$ or more precisely:

$$\sqrt{2\pi}n^{n+1/2}e^{-n}e^{\frac{1}{12n+1}} \leq n! \leq \sqrt{2\pi}n^{n+1/2}e^{-n}e^{\frac{1}{12n}} \qquad (4.33)$$

Now suppose $\nu = n_1/n$ for some integer n_1 with $0 \leq n_1 \leq n$. We can rewrite the choose function as

$$\ln\binom{n}{\nu n} = \ln \frac{n!}{(n\nu)!(n(1-\nu))!} = \ln \sqrt{2\pi n}\, n^n e^{-n}$$

$$- \ln\sqrt{2\pi n\nu}(n\nu)^{n\nu}e^{-n\nu} - \ln\sqrt{2\pi n(1-\nu)}(n(1-\nu))^{n(1-\nu)}e^{-n(1-\nu)} + o(1)$$

$$= n(\ln n - \nu \ln n\nu - (1-\nu)\ln n(1-\nu))$$

$$- \frac{1}{2}\ln 2\pi - \frac{1}{2}\ln n - \frac{1}{2}\ln \nu(1-\nu) + R(n,\nu), \quad (4.34)$$

where the remainder term $R(n,\nu)$ satisfies

$$|R(n,\nu)| \leq 1/(6n\nu(1-\nu)).$$

The third line may be rewritten as

$$n(\nu \ln n + (1-\nu) \ln n - \nu \ln n\nu - (1-\nu)\ln n(1-\nu)) =$$
$$- n(\nu \ln \nu + (1-\nu)\ln(1-\nu)) = n\mathrm{H}(\nu). \quad (4.35)$$

Plugging this into (4.34) gives

$$\ln \binom{n}{\nu n} = n\mathrm{H}(\nu) - \ln \sqrt{2\pi n \mathrm{var}(\nu)} + R(n,\nu), \qquad (4.36)$$

where $\mathrm{var}(\nu) = \nu(1-\nu)$ is the variance of a Bernoulli random variable with parameter ν and the remainder term $R(n,\nu) = O(1/n)$ as long as, for increasing n, ν remains bounded away (stays farther than some small ϵ) from 0 and 1. If ν goes to 0 or 1 at rate slower than $1/n$, then we still have that $R(n,\nu) = o(1)$, i.e. it converges to 0 as $n \to \infty$.

> In Chapter 1, on page 5, we claimed that the fraction of binary sequences of length n with frequency of 1s equal to $n\nu$, for $\nu \neq 1/2$, is exponentially small in n. Since $\mathrm{H}(1/2) = \ln 2$, and for $0 < \nu < 1$, $\nu \neq 1/2$, $\mathrm{H}(\nu) < \ln 2$, this is now shown formally by (4.36). Equation (4.36) also shows that the fraction of sequences with $n/2$ 1s goes to 0 at a much smaller rate, at $O(1/\sqrt{n})$.

The Central Limit Theorem and (Relative) Entropy   Using the precise characterization (4.36) of the choose function to refine (4.32), we get

$$\ln P_\theta \left(\hat{\theta}(X^n) = \nu \right) = \ln \binom{n}{\nu n} + n \left(\nu \ln \theta + (1-\nu)\ln(1-\theta) \right) =$$
$$- n\mathrm{D}(\nu \| \theta) - \ln \sqrt{2\pi n \mathrm{var}(\nu)} + o(1). \quad (4.37)$$

Exponentiating (4.37) gives

$$P_\theta \left(\hat{\theta}(X^n) = \nu \right) = \frac{1}{\sqrt{2\pi n \mathrm{var}(\nu)}} e^{-n\mathrm{D}(\nu\|\theta)+o(1)}. \qquad (4.38)$$

Note that for all $\epsilon > 0$, if $|\nu - \theta| > \epsilon$ then we must have $\mathrm{D}(\nu\|\theta) > 0$. Thus, since for each n, ν can only take on $n+1$ values, by (4.38) and the union bound, we see that for every $\epsilon > 0$, the probability that $|\hat{\theta} - \theta| > \epsilon$ is exponentially small in n.

We now consider a scale that gets finer with increasing n: by looking at values of $\hat{\theta} = \nu$ that are within $O(1/\sqrt{n})$ of θ, it can be seen that (4.38) also implies the central limit theorem (Chapter 2) for Bernoulli random variables.

We now show this in an informal way. Since at the scale we consider, $\hat{\theta}$ converges to θ with increasing n, we can do a second-order Taylor expansion of $D(\nu\|\theta)$ as in Section 4.3, (4.20) and (4.23). Since for Bernoulli distributions $I(\theta) = 1/\mathrm{var}(\theta)$ (Example 4.1), the Taylor expansion gives

$$nD(\nu\|\theta) \approx n\frac{(\nu - \theta)^2}{2\mathrm{var}(\nu)}. \tag{4.39}$$

Now define $Y_n := \sqrt{n}(\nu - \theta)$. This is just the standard normalized average to which the CLT applies (Theorem 2.2, page 56). Using (4.38) and (4.39), we get, for all values of y that can be obtained from $\nu \in \{0, 1, \ldots, n\}$,

$$P_\theta\left(Y_n = y\right) = P_\theta\left(\nu - \theta - y\sqrt{\frac{1}{n}}\right) = \frac{1}{\sqrt{2\pi n\mathrm{var}(\nu)}}e^{-\frac{y^2}{2\mathrm{var}\nu} + o(y^2)}. \tag{4.40}$$

Now consider a fixed range $[a, b]$. As n increases, for $Y_n \in [a, b]$, the corresponding ν satisfies $\nu \to \theta$ and $\mathrm{var}(\nu) \to \mathrm{var}(\theta)$ and the number of values between a and b that can be taken by Y_n must be equal to $\lceil\sqrt{n}(b - a)\rceil$ plus or minus 1. Therefore (4.40) implies

$$P_\theta\left(Y_n \in [a, b]\right) \to \int_a^b \frac{1}{\sqrt{2\pi\mathrm{var}(\theta)}}e^{-\frac{y^2}{2\mathrm{var}(\theta)}}\,dy. \tag{4.41}$$

We see from Theorem 2.2 that (4.41) is just the CLT for Bernoulli random variables.

4.5   Summary and Outlook

In this chapter we have analyzed the likelihood of the data given a distribution taken from some parametric family of distributions. In Sections 4.2 and 4.3 we analyzed what happens if the data are given and the parameters are varied; Section 4.4 analyzed the opposite situation. The insights we gained will be used in the next chapter, where we study a simple form of MDL inference.

In Sections 4.2 and 4.3 we assumed that the models under consideration were sufficiently regular. In Section 4.4 we even restricted ourselves to the very simple Bernoulli model. It turns out that the analysis in all three sections is valid for – among others – the large class of *exponential family models*. These are treated in full detail in Part IV of this book.

5 *Crude Two-Part Code MDL*

Overview   MDL comes in several versions. The oldest but simplest and most well-known form is the *two-part code MDL principle for probabilistic models*. In this Chapter we introduce and make precise a crude form of the two-part code MDL, where "crude" means that the codelengths for hypotheses are not determined in an optimal manner (Chapter 1, Section 1.4, page 10). We defer the discussion of refined MDL and its central concept, the "universal model" to Part II and Part III of this book.

Contents   In Section 5.1 we formulate our crude two-part code MDL principle. In Section 5.2 we instantiate it to hypothesis/model selection for the class of Markov chains of arbitrary order. Generalizing from Markov chains to general model classes leads to a crude *simple two-part MDL criterion* for model selection which we present in Section 5.3. Sections 5.5 through 5.7 discuss various aspects of this criterion. Section 5.8 provides both justification and criticism of our simple form of MDL.

Fast Track   The main goal of this chapter is to discuss a very simple form of MDL that people often have used in practice. It is so simple that we can easily explain it in detail, so that it gives a good feel of what MDL "is really about." Yet, because it is so simple, it obviously has defects. Realizing what these defects are is a great introduction to the refined versions of MDL that we discuss in Part III of this book. However, readers with previous exposure to MDL may decide to confine their attention to the boxes and directly move on to Part II and Part III.

5.1   Introduction: Making Two-Part MDL Precise

In this chapter we give a precise description of a simple form of the two-part code MDL principle. It can be read as a continuation of Chapter 1, Section 1.5, where we introduced two-part MDL in an informal manner. We start right away with point hypothesis selection. In later sections we discuss model selection and parameter estimation.

Suppose then that we are given some candidate model or model class $\mathcal{M}$ (for example, $\mathcal{M} = \mathcal{B}$, the class of all Markov chains of each order) and some data D. All elements of $\mathcal{M}$ are probabilistic sources, so from now on we will refer to a point hypothesis as P (rather than H as we did in Section 1.5). We look for the $P \in \mathcal{M}$ that best explains the data. As we saw in Section 1.5, the two-part code MDL principle tells us to look for the (point) hypothesis $P \in \mathcal{M}$ that minimizes the sum of the description length of P plus the description length of the data when encoded with the help of P. In mathematical notation:

**MDL Principle for Point Hypothesis Selection
(Two-Part Version, Mathematical Notation)**
Suppose we are given data D. Then we should pick the $\ddot{P} \in \mathcal{M}$ minimizing

$$L_1(P) + L_2(D|P) = L_{1,2}(P, D). \tag{5.1}$$

If there is more than one $\ddot{P} \in \mathcal{M}$ for which $L_{1,2}(P, D)$ is minimized, we pick the one with minimum hypothesis complexity $L_1(P)$. If this still leaves us with several possible P, we do not have a further preference among them.

Let us explain the notation of (5.1) in detail. Let n be the sample size. We describe data $D = (x_1, \ldots, x_n)$ using a description method $C_{1,2}$. $C_{1,2}$ is a *partial description method*[1] for the joint alphabet of $\mathcal{M} \times \mathcal{X}^n$. It describes each pair (P, D) by concatenating the code words $C_1(P)$ and $C_2(D|P)$. Here C_1 is a code for $\mathcal{M}$ and $C_2(\cdot|P)$ is a family of codes for $\mathcal{X}^n$ (the notation $C_2(\cdot|P)$ was explained in Section 3.1). For each different P, C_2 will encode the data D in a different way: it encodes the data "with the help of P." The notation L_i is used to denote the length of the encoding under description method C_i.

---

1. Since $C_{1,2}$ is a *partial* description method, the fact that $\mathcal{M}$ is in general not countable poses no problem. See Definition 3.1.

This Chapter: Crude MDL The two-part code MDL principle looks more mathematical now but has not yet been formalized. For this, we have to instantiate the codes C_1 and C_2. In this chapter we content ourselves with intuitive choices for C_1 and C_2, leading to a specific "crude" version of two-part MDL. In Chapter 10 and Chapter 15, Section 15.3 we develop more precise guidelines for construction of C_1 – as will be seen, our choice for C_2 is essentially definitive and will remain unchanged. In the next section, we explain our current choices for C_1 and C_2 using the class of Markov Chains as a running example. In Section 5.3 we show that the same ideas can be applied to many other model classes. Sections 5.5-5.7 discuss various aspects of the resulting hypothesis selection criterion. Section 5.8 provides a justification as well as a criticism of our simple form of MDL, and provides a look ahead into the refined notions of MDL that we develop in Part III of this book.

5.2 Applying Two-Part Code MDL to Markov Chain Hypothesis Selection

Suppose we are given data $D \in \mathcal{X}^n$ where $\mathcal{X} = \{0, 1\}$. We seek a reasonable model for D that allows us to make good predictions of future data coming from the same source. We decide to model our data using the class $\mathcal{B}$ of all Markov chains.[2] Similarly to the case of learning polynomials (Example 1.4, page 14), we face the problem of overfitting: for a given sequence $D = (x_1, \ldots, x_n)$, there may be a Markov chain P of very high order that fits data D quite well but that will behave very badly when predicting future data from the same source. For example, suppose our data are generated by fair coin tosses. We would like an inference procedure that, given enough data, tells us that the data have been generated by the Bernoulli distribution $P_{0.5} \in \mathcal{B}^{(1)}$. However, with overwhelming probability, data distributed according to $P_{0.5}$ is such that there exists a Markov chain P' of order $\lceil n/2 \rceil$ which achieves $P'(x^n)2^{-\lfloor n/2 \rfloor}$, and therefore fits the data much better than $P_{0.5}$.

> Let us explain this in detail for even n. Suppose first that every subsequence of D of length $n/2$ is unique, i.e. D contains no repetitions of length $n/2$. Then there exists a Markov chain P' of order $n/2$ such that $P'(x_{n/2+1}, \ldots, x_n \mid$

---

2. This does *not* mean we think that our data are actually distributed as, or "generated by," some Markov chain; it only means that there exists some Markov chain which allows us to make reasonable predictions and decisions about future data coming from the same source; see Section 1.8, page 29.

$x^{n/2}) = 1$, so that $P'(x^n) = 2^{-n/2}$. It remains to be shown that the probability under $P_{0.5}$ of observing a D' which does contain a repetition of length $n/2$, is of order $2^{-(n/2)+O(\log n)}$. It is easy to construct a prefix code for sequences of length n that takes $2\log n + (n/2)$ bits to encode a sequence with a repetition of length $n/2$ (we leave the construction as an exercise for the reader). It now follows by the no-hypercompression inequality (box on page 103) that the probability under $P_{0.5}$ of observing such a D' is no more than $2^{-n/2+2\log n}$.

Since $P'(x^n)/P_{0.5}(x^n) \approx 2^{n/2}$, the probability of the data under P' is overwhelmingly larger than the probability under the distribution we are looking for; therefore, the naive procedure of simply picking the distribution in $\mathcal{B}$ that maximizes probability of the given D will, in general, lead to bad results ("overfitting"). This is shown formally in Section 5.6. Instead, we will use the two-part code MDL principle to find a Markov chain that is a tradeoff between complexity (related to the number of parameters k) and goodness-of-fit.

Two-Part Code MDL Principle for Markov Chains   Each $P \in \mathcal{B}$ is a probabilistic source $P = P_\theta \in \mathcal{B}^{(k)}$ for some $k > 0$. Below we explain the code C_1 (which tells us how to encode P) and the family of codes $C_2(\cdot|P)$ (which tell us how to encode D "with the help of P"). Some of the choices we make may seem disputable or arbitrary at this point; we discuss all these choices in later sections and for now content ourselves with footnotes referring to these sections.

We assume n, the length of the sample, is given. In the "descriptions-as-messages view" this means that, before any message is sent, n is known already to encoder and decoder.

> **Why n Can Be Safely Assumed to Be Known in Advance** The reader may worry that in practical applications, n is often unknown in advance: we have to decide on a description method before obtaining any data, and we may not know in advance how many data we will observe. While this is true, we now explain that it does not matter. Indeed, if we do not know n in advance, we may use a code that encodes data D by first encoding the sample size n using some prefix code C_0 - for example, the standard code for the integers. After encoding n, we encode D using the regular two-part code with codes C_1 and C_2. Then the total description length becomes
>
> $$L_0(n) + L_1(P) + L_2(D|P). \qquad (5.2)$$
>
> Adjusted to this new situation, the two-part code MDL principle tells us to pick the P minimizing (5.2). But since L_0 does not depend on P, this gives

exactly the same P as the original MDL principle (5.1). Therefore, nothing has changed, and we can safely assume that n is known in advance. This illustrates a line of reasoning we will use over and over again in this book: *parts of the description length that do not depend on the hypotheses P may be dropped without affecting the hypothesis output by MDL.* This is emphasized in the box on page 439.

However, some people may insist that all "reasonable" two-part codes should have the property that the coding of D can be done *on-line*; see Chapter 17, Section 17.5. By this we mean that it should be possible to already start encoding (and decoding) $x_1, x_2, \ldots$ before knowing how many x_i will be observed in the end. In that case, the fact that the two-part codes depend on the sample size n is more problematic; since it is unknown to the encoder when he starts to encode D, he cannot send n as a preamble to D. Nevertheless, the two-part codes that we introduce in this chapter can still be used, because they happen to be of a certain type that we call *semiprequential*, explained in Chapter 6, page 196. In later chapters we encounter two-part codes that cannot be used in the on-line setting and need to be modified.

5.2.1   The Code C_2

Let $P \in \mathcal{B}$. We can write $P = P_\theta \in \mathcal{B}^{(k)}$ for some $k > 0$ and some $\theta \in [0, 1]^k$. Note that $\mathcal{B}^{(k)}$, the $\log k$th order Markov chain model, is only defined for k such that $\log k$ is an integer. When k is not clear from the context, we write $P_{k,\theta}$. From Section 3.2.2, we know that for each $P_{k,\theta} \in \mathcal{B}$, there exists a code C such that

$$- \log P_{k,\theta}(D) = L_C(D) \text{ for all } D \text{ of length } n. \tag{5.3}$$

It is this code we will use for $C_2(\cdot \mid P_{k,\theta})$, the code we use to encode x^n based on the hypothesis $P_{k,\theta}$. We abbreviate $C_2(\cdot \mid P_{k,\theta})$ to $C_2(\cdot \mid k, \theta)$, and $L_2(\cdot \mid P_{k,\theta})$ to $L_2(\cdot \mid k, \theta)$.

   This choice for C_2 gives a short codelength to sequences which have high probability according to (k, θ) while it gives a high codelength to sequences with low probability. The codelength thus directly reflects the goodness-of-fit of the data with respect to (k, θ), measured in terms of the probability of D according to (k, θ). As explained in Chapter 1, our aim is a tradeoff between goodness-of-fit and complexity. This makes the present choice of C_2 a good *candidate* choice. Of course there are many other codes sharing C_2's property that better fit corresponds to shorter code lengths, and that are good "candidates" in this sense. But among all such codes, C_2 is the only one that would be optimal to use *under the assumption that P is true*. Here "P is true" means that data D are actually distributed according to P. "Optimal" means that C_2 minimizes expected codelength, and, for repeated outcomes, minimizes actual codelength with high probability; see Section 3.3, page 101.

Using (5.3) to define C_2, we see that the two-part code MDL principle thus tells us to pick the hypothesis $\ddot{P}$ given by

$$\ddot{P} := \underset{P \in \mathcal{B}}{\arg\min} \, \{ -\log P(D) + L_1(P) \}, \tag{5.4}$$

where C_1 (with lengths L_1) still has to be specified.

SUMMARY: Coding Data "with the Help of" a Hypothesis (Distribution)

When we say we "code data D with the help of probabilistic hypothesis P" we mean that we code D using the Shannon-Fano code corresponding to P:

$$L(D|P) := -\log \hat{P}(D). \tag{5.5}$$

Example 5.1 Coding Data with Markov Chains To get a better feel for the code C_2, we consider two examples. First, let $P_\theta \in \mathcal{B}^{(1)}$ be some Bernoulli distribution with $P_\theta(X = 1) = \theta$. Let $D = (x_1, \ldots, x_n)$. Since $P_\theta(D) = \prod P_\theta(x_i)$ and $\hat{\theta}$ is equal to the frequency of 1s in D, we get

$$-\log P_\theta(D) = -n_1 \log \theta - n_0 \log(1-\theta) = n[-\hat{\theta}\log\theta - (1-\hat{\theta})\log(1-\theta)], \tag{5.6}$$

where n_j denotes the number of occurrences of symbol j in D. Now consider some $P_\theta \in \mathcal{B}^{(k)}$, where

$$\theta = (\eta_{[1|0\ldots0]}, \eta_{[1|0\ldots01]}, \ldots, \eta_{[1|1\ldots10]}, \eta_{[1|1\ldots11]}).$$

Recall from Example 2.7, (2.24), that the maximum likelihood (ML) parameters $\hat{\eta}_{[1|y]}$ are equal to the conditional frequencies of 1 prefixed by y. By (2.26), $L_2(D \mid \theta)$ becomes

$$-\log P_\theta(D) = -n \sum_{y \in \{0,1\}^{\log k}} \hat{\eta}_{[1|y]} \log \eta_{[1|y]} + (1 - \hat{\eta}_{[1|y]}) \log(1 - \eta_{[1|y]}) + \gamma, \tag{5.7}$$

which generalizes (5.6). Here $\gamma = \log k$ is the number of bits needed to encode the first γ outcomes in D.

5.2.2   The Code C_1

The instantiation of the code C_2 we have just given has a unique status: the code with lengths (5.5) is the only one that would be optimal if P were true. It may therefore be regarded[3] as the *only* sensible choice for C_2. The situation for C_1 is more messy: several "reasonable" codes may be designed, and the question which of these is optimal and why will have to wait until Chapter 15, Section 15.3. Here we opt for a particularly simple choice of C_1 that is reasonable, yet certainly not "optimal" in any sense.

In order to describe a $P \in \mathcal{B}$, we really have to describe a pair (k, θ). We encode (k, θ) by first encoding k using some prefix code C_{1_a} and then code θ using some code $C_{1_b}(\cdot|k)$ depending on k. The resulting code C_1 is then defined by $C_1(k, \theta) = C_{1_a}(k)C_{1_b}(\theta|k)$. We instantiate C_{1_a} to the standard code for the integers. This gives[4]

$$L_{1_a}(k) = L_{\mathbb{N}}(k) = O(\log k). \tag{5.8}$$

The code $C_{1_b}(\cdot|k)$ must assign a code word to $\theta \in \Theta^{(k)}$. Since $\Theta^{(k)} = [0, 1]^k$ is an uncountably infinite set, we somehow have to "discretize" it first. More precisely, we will restrict $\Theta^{(k)}$ to some finite set $\ddot{\Theta}_d^{(k)}$ of parameters that can be described using a finite precision of d bits per parameter. To construct $\ddot{\Theta}_d^{(k)}$, we put a rectangular grid on $\Theta^{(k)}$ with equal side widths w, where (for reasons to become clear in a moment),

$$w = 2^{-d}. \tag{5.9}$$

$\ddot{\Theta}_d^{(k)}$ is now defined as the set of all the center points of the k-dimensional rectangles defined by this grid. In order to describe an element in $\ddot{\Theta}_d^{(k)}$, we first have to describe the precision d (otherwise a decoder cannot determine what the set $\ddot{\Theta}_d^{(k)}$ looks like). We can then describe which element in $\ddot{\Theta}_d^{(k)}$ has been used to encode the data. We encode d using the standard code for the integers, and $\theta \in \ddot{\Theta}_d^{(k)}$ using the uniform code. In case a particular θ can be encoded using several values of d, we will use the minimum d for which it can actually be encoded.

---

3. But see Chapter 10, Section 10.2, where we see that in some cases, another choice is sensible as well. This alternative choice will lead to very similar codelengths, though.

4. Of course, not all k are possible in our Markov chain example: we must have $k = 2^\gamma$ for some $\gamma \geq 0$, so somewhat shorter codelengths may be obtained by not reserving any code words for impossible values of k; see Problem III on page 161.

Note that the number of elements of $\ddot{\Theta}_d^{(k)}$ is $(1/w)^k$. Using a uniform code conditioned on k and d, we need $\log(1/w)^k = k \cdot d$ bits to describe any particular $\theta \in \ddot{\Theta}_d^{(k)}$; this explains why, by relating w and d as in (5.9), we may call d the "precision used to encode a parameter." Letting d_θ be the smallest d such that $\theta \in \ddot{\Theta}_d^{(k)}$, and $d_\theta = \infty$ if no such d exists, this gives

$$L_{1_b}(\theta|k) = \begin{cases} L_\mathbb{N}(d_\theta) + \log(\frac{1}{w})^k = L_\mathbb{N}(d_\theta) + kd_\theta & \text{if } d_\theta < \infty; \\ \infty & \text{otherwise.} \end{cases} \quad (5.10)$$

Combining this with (5.8), we get the following definition of the codelengths $L_1(P) = L_1(k, \theta)$:

$$L_1(k, \theta) = \begin{cases} L_\mathbb{N}(k) + L_\mathbb{N}(d_\theta) + kd_\theta & \text{if } d_\theta < \infty \\ \infty & \text{otherwise.} \end{cases} \quad (5.11)$$

Below we combine the codes C_1 and C_2 to make our definition of the two-part code MDL principle for Markov chain point hypothesis selection completely precise.

5.2.3   Exact Yet Simplistic Two-Part Code MDL for Markov Chains

In order to arrive at a precise definition of two-part code MDL for Markov chain hypothesis selection, it only remains to plug in (5.5), our expression for L_2, and (5.11), our expression for L_1, into (5.1). The resulting expression is:

$$\min_{k \in \mathbb{N}; d \in \mathbb{N}; \theta \in \ddot{\Theta}_d^{(k)}} \{ \overbrace{- \log P_{k,\theta}(D)}^{\text{error term}} + \overbrace{kd + L_\mathbb{N}(k) + L_\mathbb{N}(d)}^{\text{complexity term}} \}. \quad (5.12)$$

The two-part code MDL principle now tells us to pick the Markov chain $P_{k,\theta}$ minimizing (5.12). The definition is now mathematically precise (exactly defined).

As indicated before, (5.12) is by no means the best form of two-part code MDL that we could use. To give but one example: we discretized our parameter space using a uniform grid, with equal distances between discretized parameter values. This is not the the best thing to do (what "best" means will become clear in Part III of this book). However, as we will see, the present form of two-part code MDL, which we call *simplistic MDL*, behaves reasonably well. It therefore serves to illustrate many of the general ideas. Before discussing these, we formulate criterion (5.12) in a more general setting, not specifically tailored to Markov chains.

5.3   Simplistic Two-Part Code MDL Principle for Hypothesis Selection

Let $\mathcal{M} = \bigcup_{k \geq 1} \mathcal{M}^{(k)}$ be a family of probabilistic parametric models associated with parameter spaces $\Theta^{(1)}, \Theta^{(2)}, \ldots$. If, for all k, $\Theta^{(k)}$ is *compact* (closed and bounded), then we can use a uniform discretization of the space as for the Markov chains. For other models, the components of $\Theta^{(k)}$ may be unbounded. In that case, for each component we first encode an upper bound and a lower bound on its value, and we then encode an actual parameter value using a uniform grid. Both the lower bound and the upper bound will be represented as an integer, encoded by first encoding its sign $+$ or $-$ (which takes 1 bit), and then encoding its absolute value using the standard code for the positive integers. Thus, for each potentially unbounded parameter, encoding the range $[a, b]$ takes $2 + L_{\mathbb{N}}(a) + L_{\mathbb{N}}(b)$ bits.

Given then the models $\mathcal{M}^{(1)}, \mathcal{M}^{(2)}, \ldots$, the discretized parameter sets $\ddot{\Theta}_d^{(k)}$, and data D, the simplistic two-part MDL principle for hypothesis selection tells us the following:

Simplistic Two-Part Code MDL Point Hypothesis Selection for Families of Parametric Models

If, for all k, $\Theta^{(k)}$ is compact, then we should pick the $(\ddot{k}, \ddot{\theta}), \ddot{\theta} \in \ddot{\Theta}_d^{(\ddot{k})}$ minimizing

$$\min_{d \in \mathbb{N}} \{ \overbrace{-\log P_{k,\theta}(D)}^{\text{error term}} + \overbrace{kd + L_{\mathbb{N}}(k) + L_{\mathbb{N}}(d).}^{\text{complexity term}} \} \tag{5.13}$$

If there is more than one (k, θ) for which (5.13) is minimized, we pick the one with minimum hypothesis complexity $kd + L_{\mathbb{N}}(k) + L_{\mathbb{N}}(d)$. If this still leaves us with several possible (k, θ), we do not have a further preference among them.

In case for some k, $\Theta^{(k)}$ is not compact, then instead of (5.13) we minimize, over $d \in \mathbb{N}$ and $a_1, b_1, \ldots, a_k, b_k \in \mathbb{Z}$, the extended description length

$$-\log P_{k,\theta}(D) + kd + 2k + \sum_{j=1}^{k} (L_{\mathbb{N}}(|a_k|) + L_{\mathbb{N}}(|b_k|)) + L_{\mathbb{N}}(k) + L_{\mathbb{N}}(d). \tag{5.14}$$

Here the term $2k$ comes from encoding the $2k$ signs of $a_1, b_1, \ldots, a_k, b_k$.

We now have a precise definition of a simple form of MDL for hypothesis selection. How does it relate to other forms of MDL?

Crude and Simplistic MDL

In this book we use the following terminology:

Crude MDL MDL based on two-part codes in which the code C_1 for hypotheses is determined in an ad hoc manner.

> By "ad hoc" we mean that the codes are not specifically designed to make $C_{1,2}$ a universal code relative to the given model class; see Part II of this book.

Simplistic MDL This is one specific version of crude two-part MDL: the version we just defined in (5.13) and (5.14). For many model classes (for example, the Markov chains), the codes used in simplistic MDL are actually not that different from "refined" MDL codes; consequently for such model classes simplistic MDL behaves reasonably well. In the remainder of this chapter, when we use "MDL" we implicitly refer to simplistic MDL as defined here.

We warn the reader that none of this is standard terminology.

In order to understand simplistic MDL, it is useful to discuss the following issues:

1. **How to extend it.** We only formulated the two-part code MDL principle for hypothesis selection. How can we extend it to model selection and parameter estimation? (Section 5.4).

2. **What it does.** What will actually happen if we use formula (5.13) in a practical model selection problem? How does this depend on the sample size etc.? (discussed in Section 5.5).

3. **Comparison to ML.** How does it compare to methods that do not take into account model complexity, such as maximum likelihood? (Section 5.6).

4. **How to use it/compute it.** How can (5.13) be used in statistical applications? What additional, e.g. computational problems, are met in practice? (Section 5.7).

5. **Design principles:** What is the rationale for implementing the codes C_1 and C_2 the way we did? (Section 5.8).

6. **Asymptotic view.** To get a better feel for the tradeoff between goodness-of-fit and complexity implemented by two-part code MDL, it is useful to develop an asymptotic approximation to (5.13).

In the following sections we shall discuss all these issues except for the last one, which will have to wait until we have more powerful tools at our disposal (see Part II, Chapter 10). For the most part, the following sections may be read separately.

5.4   Two-Part MDL for Tasks Other Than Hypothesis Selection

Until now, we have focused on *hypothesis* selection for *nested* model classes. We discuss three more settings for which criterion (5.13) can be used: *model selection in nested/non-nested model classes and parameter estimation.*

Model Selection; Nested Models   Let $\mathcal{M} = \bigcup_{k \geq 1} \mathcal{M}^{(k)}$ be a nested model class as before. Two-Part Code MDL model selection is defined in the obvious manner: given data D, we should pick the model $\mathcal{M}^{(\ddot{k})}$ where $\ddot{k}$ is identical to the $\ddot{k}$ selected by (5.13). Hence, we simply ignore the selected $\ddot{\theta}$ and focus attention on $\ddot{k}$.

Model Selection; Non-Nested Models   Suppose we want to select between a finite (say, two) number of non-nested models $\mathcal{M}_A$ and $\mathcal{M}_B$ for the same data D. In contrast to the Markov chain example, we now allow $\mathcal{M}_A$ and $\mathcal{M}_B$ to be of entirely different nature; an example is given in Section 1.6, page 23. We can use a slight adjustment of the two-part criterion (5.13): we only have to replace the code for k. Since there are now only two possibilities for k (A and B), we can encode k using the uniform code over two outcomes. This will take 1 bit, no matter whether we encode A or B, and hence it does not influence which model is chosen. Let k_γ denote the number of parameters of model $\mathcal{M}_\gamma$ (note that it is possible that $k_A = k_B$). The MDL Two-Part criterion for model selection then tells us to pick the model $\mathcal{M}_\gamma$ for the $\gamma \in \{A, B\}$ achieving

$$\min_{d \in \mathbb{N}, \theta \in \ddot{\Theta}_d^{(\gamma)}} \{ -\log P_{\gamma, \theta}(D) + k_\gamma d + L_{\mathbb{N}}(d) \}.$$

Two-Part Code MDL for Parameter Estimation   Parameter estimation is the task of selecting a particular $\theta \in \Theta^{(k)}$ for a given, fixed k-dimensional parametric model $\mathcal{M}^{(k)}$. Once again we can adjust the two-part criterion for model selection (5.13) in an entirely straightforward manner to handle this situation. We now devise codes with lengths L_1 and L_2 similar as before, but for $\mathcal{M} = \mathcal{M}^{(k)}$ where $\mathcal{M} = \mathcal{M}^{(k)}$ is a *single* k-dimensional *model* (parametric family) $\mathcal{M}^{(k)}$, rather than a model *class* as was the case until now. We only have to adjust the code C_1 by "conditioning" on k. This gives a code C_1' with for all $\theta \in \Theta^{(k)}$, $L_1'(\theta) = L_{1_b}(\theta|k)$. The resulting two-part code MDL criterion for hypothesis selection tells us to pick, for given data D and model $\mathcal{M}^{(k)}$, the parameter $\ddot{\theta}$ achieving

$$\min_{\theta \in \ddot{\Theta}_d^{(k)};\; d \in \mathbb{N}} \{ -\log P_{k,\theta}(D) + kd + L_{\mathbb{N}}(d) \}. \tag{5.15}$$

We discuss in Section 5.6 whether or not it is reasonable to use such MDL-based (discretized) parameter estimators.

5.5   Behavior of Two-Part Code MDL

What happens if the two-part code MDL criterion is applied to some data set D? To get a first idea, we analyze how its behavior changes as the sample size n increases, i.e. where more and more data become available. Thus, with $D = (x_1, \ldots, x_n)$, we first look at the situation with $D_1 = (x_1)$, then we look at $D_2 = (x_1, x_2)$, and so on. We first study the codelength $L_2(D|k, \theta) + L_1(k, \theta)$ for some fixed k, d, and θ; later we see what happens if we minimize over θ, or k, or both.

Fixed k,θ   In this case, $L_1(k, \theta)$ does not depend on the data D. It can therefore be considered constant with increasing sample size. In contrast, the "error-term" $L_2(D|k, \theta) = -\log P_{k,\theta}(D)$ typically increases with n: as n increases, there are more data to be encoded and this takes more bits. Moreover, in the typical case that our data are nondegenerate, it increases *linearly* in n. By "nondegenerate" data we mean sequences such that none of the individual outcomes have probabilities arbitrarily close to 0 or 1, so that $P(x_1, \ldots, x_n) = \prod P(x_i \mid x_1, \ldots, x_{i-1})$ is exponentially small in n, whence $-\log P(x_1, \ldots, x_n)$ increases linearly.

Fixed k, Varying θ   Suppose now that we fix some k and minimize, for given D, (5.13) only over d and $\theta \in \ddot{\Theta}_d^{(k)}$. Let $\ddot{d}$ be the precision thus selected and let $\ddot{\theta} = \ddot{\theta}^{(k)} \in \ddot{\Theta}_d^{(k)}$ be the θ that is selected. We may now once more look at the error term $L_2(D|k, \ddot{\theta}) = -\log P_{k,\theta}(D)$ and the complexity term $L_1(k, \ddot{d}) = k\ddot{d} + L_{\mathbb{N}}(k) + L_{\mathbb{N}}(\ddot{d})$. In this case, at least for exponential families and most other sufficiently regular models $\mathcal{M}^{(k)}$ and nondegenerate data, $L_2(D|k, \ddot{\theta})$ *still* increases linearly in n. Just as $L_2(D|k, \ddot{\theta})$, $L_1(k, \ddot{d})$ will now also increase with n. This increase will be sublinear; for large n, and "regular" models, it will typically be logarithmic, i.e. $L_1(k, \ddot{d}) = O(\log n)$. As more data are observed, it becomes advantageous to encode θ at higher precision. The reasons for this behavior of L_2 are given in Chapter 7 and Chapter 10.

Goodness-of-Fit and Complexity
In practice, for each fixed k, the error term $-\log P_{k,\ddot{\theta}}(D)$ grows linearly with n; the complexity term $k\ddot{d} + L_{\mathbb{N}}(k) + L_{\mathbb{N}}(\ddot{d})$ grows sublinearly with n (for large n, it typically grows logarithmically).

We now investigate the behavior of MDL in more detail for the case that one of the distributions in $\mathcal{M}$ actually generated the data.

If There Is Something to Learn   Let us imagine the following situation: we receive more and more data coming from some probabilistic source. The source is some Markov chain P^* of order γ^* where (for concreteness, say, $\gamma^* = 5$, and $P^* = P_{\theta^*}$ for some $\theta^* \in \Theta^{(32)}$). Assume further that $P^* \notin \mathcal{B}^{(16)}$, so that P^* cannot be expressed as a "simpler" Markov chain of order 4. Imagine that we do not know that $\gamma^* = 5$. Instead, we repeatedly (for each n) use the two-part code MDL criterion to infer a Markov chain for the data. Then typically (with high "true" probability P^*) the following will happen: first, for small n, we select a Markov chain of order $\gamma < \gamma^*$; in the beginning, we typically even select one of order 1; that is, we initially *underfit*. Then, with increasing n, we start picking larger and larger γ, until we have reached $\gamma = \gamma^*$. At that point, we will fluctuate for a while around γ^*, selecting values like $\gamma^* - 1$ and $\gamma^* + 1$. But then, from some n_0 onward, we will pick γ^* and *we will keep picking γ^* for all $n > n_0$*. Indeed (under some conditions on the method used for discretizing parameters), *the two-part criterion is consistent for model selection of Markov chains*: suppose data are distributed according to some (any) Markov chain P^* and let k^* be the smallest number such that $P^* \in \mathcal{B}^{(k^*)}$. Then, with P^*-probability 1, for n larger than n_0, the two-part criterion will select the "correct model" $\mathcal{B}^{(k^*)}$, the smallest (simplest) model containing P^*.

Small Is Beautiful The reader may wonder why we should prefer γ^* over $\gamma^* + 1, \gamma^* + 2$, etc., since the models $\mathcal{B}^{(2^{\gamma^*+j})}, j \geq 0$ all contain P^*. There are several reasons: (a) knowledge that P^* resides in the smaller model gives a lot more information; and, relatedly, (b) if the selected model is further used to predict future data (for example, by predicting future data using $\hat{\theta}^{(j)}$ where $\mathcal{B}^{(j)}$ is the selected model), then, due to sampling variation, the ML estimator based on the "simpler" model will, with high probability, tend to give better predictions than the ML estimator based on the more complex model

The two-part criterion is also consistent for hypothesis selection of Markov chains in the sense defined in Section 2.5, page 71. These consistency results may be generalized to very general classes of models. In Section 5.8.1, we state and prove a simple version of such a theorem. Advanced, general consistency theorems are stated and proved in Part III, Chapter 15 (Theorem 15.1 and Theorem 15.3) and Chapter 16.

If There Is Something To Learn, but It is Not a Markov Chain In many realistic cases, the process underlying the data is such that some Markov chains give reasonable predictions, whereas it is very unrealistic to suppose that some "true" Markov chain has generated the data; an example is the use of Markov models in language modeling and speech recognition. In those cases, the hope is that the two-part criterion still converges to the Markov chain that is in some sense "closest" to the process generating the data. Such a closest Markov chain will in many cases still lead to reasonable predictions; see Chapter 15, Section 15.2.

5.6   Two-Part Code MDL and Maximum Likelihood

In this section we compare the two-part code MDL principle to the famous *Maximum Likelihood (ML) principle* of classical statistics. We first describe the behavior of the ML principle for parametric models; we then compare and contrast MDL with ML in various ways.

5.6.1   The Maximum Likelihood *Principle*

Given a set of candidate distributions $\mathcal{M}$ and data D, the maximum likelihood principle tells us to pick the distribution in $\mathcal{M}$ that maximizes the probability (for finite or countable $\mathcal{X}$) or probability density (for continuous $\mathcal{X}$) of D, and use that as an estimate of the unknown distribution that is supposed to generate the data. This method has been enormously influential in the development of statistics as a discipline. It was proposed as a principle in

(Fisher 1922) but it had been stated in some form at least a 100 years earlier (Gauss 1957).

ML for Parameter Estimation: Temporary Overfitting ; Consistency   For concreteness we focus on the class of all Markov models $\mathcal{B} = \mathcal{B}^{(1)} \cup \mathcal{B}^{(2)} \cup \dots$. We freely use notation and facts introduced in Example 2.7, page 60. Recall that the ML estimator $\hat{\theta}_k$ for $\mathcal{B}^{(k)}$ is the distribution in which all parameters (representing conditional probabilities) are set to the corresponding empirical frequencies in data D.

It can be shown that ML estimation for Markov chains $\mathcal{B}^{(k)}$ of fixed order k is *consistent*: Suppose $P^* \in \mathcal{B}^{(k)}$, and data are distributed according to P^*. Let $\hat{\theta} = \hat{\theta}(D) \in \mathcal{B}^{(k)}$ be the ML estimator in $\mathcal{B}^{(k)}$. Then, with P^*-probability 1, $P_{\hat{\theta}(D)}$ converges to P^* in the sense described in Section 2.5, page 71. Yet, due to the "complexity" of the model $\mathcal{B}^{(k)}$, the larger k, the longer the convergence will take. For example, let $k = 8$ ($\gamma = \log k = 3$) and suppose data are generated by $P^* \in \mathcal{B}^{(8)}$. Let θ^* be the parameter corresponding to P^*, such that $P^* = P_{\theta^*}$. Then for the first three observations, the ML estimator is undefined: for all $x_1, x_2, x_3 \in \{0,1\}^3$, for all $\theta \in \Theta^{(k)}$, we have $P_\theta(x_1, x_2, x_3) = 1/8$. Therefore, the ML is achieved for *all* $\theta \in \Theta^{(k)}$ and the ML estimator is undefined. For $n = 4$, the ML is achieved by any distribution $\hat{\theta} \in \Theta^{(k)}$ with

$$\hat{\eta}_{[x_4|x_1 x_2 x_3]} = 1. \tag{5.16}$$

If the corresponding "true" parameter value $\eta^*_{[1|x_1 x_2 x_3]}$ is bounded away from 0 and 1, then any $\hat{\theta}$ satisfying (5.16) is a lousy estimate of θ^*. Nevertheless, a distribution satisfying (5.16) always exists. It follows that we cannot trust the ML estimator for $n = 4$ to be a good approximation of the "true" distribution θ^*: $\hat{\theta}(x^4)$ terribly overfits the data. Similarly, for $n = 5, 6, 7, \dots$ the ML estimator still tends to overfit, but less and less so. Only as n grows really large, we have that $\hat{\theta}(x^n) \to \theta^*$.

If we take a larger value of k, say $k = 32$ ($\gamma = 5$), then the ML estimator $\hat{\theta} \in \Theta^{(32)}$ keeps overfitting the data for a longer time. This means the following: suppose $\theta^* \in \mathcal{B}^{(32)}$. Then substantially larger values of n are needed to be reasonably sure that $\hat{\theta}$ is reasonably close to θ^* than in the previous case with $\theta^* \in \mathcal{B}^{(8)}$ and $\hat{\theta} \in \Theta^{(8)}$.

ML for Selection between a Finite Number of Non-Nested Models: Temporary Overfitting; Consistency   Suppose we want to select between two parametric models $\mathcal{M}_A$ and $\mathcal{M}_B$. Suppose that the data are generated by a distribution $P^* \in \mathcal{M}_A$, $P^* \notin \mathcal{M}_B$. We may use ML for model selection in the following way: given data D of size n, we pick the model $\mathcal{M}_A$ if and only if

$$P_{\hat{\theta}_A}(D) > P_{\hat{\theta}_B}(D).$$

One can show that, under weak regularity conditions, with P^*-probability 1, for all n larger than some n_0, this procedure wil select $\mathcal{M}_A$ rather than $\mathcal{M}_B$. Thus, ML is consistent for model selection between a finite number of non-nested models. Nevertheless, its behavior can be quite problematic due to "temporary overfitting." For example, if model $\mathcal{M}_A$ has 1 parameter and model $\mathcal{M}_B$ has 100 free parameters, then even if $\mathcal{M}_A$ contains the true P^* but $\mathcal{M}_B$ does not, ML will typically select $\mathcal{M}_B$ for all samples of size < 100, and presumably even for much larger samples.

ML for Model and Hypothesis Selection within a Nested Model Class: Eternal Overfitting; Inconsistency   If the set of candidate models is infinite, or the models are nested, or both, then ML typically breaks down: it keeps overfitting the data, even as the sample size grows to infinity. We first illustrate this for the model class $\mathcal{B}$ of all Markov models, which is a countably infinite union of nested models. For given $D = (x_1, \ldots, x_n)$, let $\hat{k}(D)$ be the minimum k such that $\mathcal{B}^{(k)}$ contains a distribution maximizing the probability of the data:

$$P_{\hat{\theta}(\hat{k}(D))(D)}(D) = \max_{P \in \mathcal{B}} P(D).$$

We call $\hat{k}$ the maximum likelihood (ML) estimate of the number of parameters. Fix an arbitrary k^* and suppose data are generated according to some $P_\theta^* \in \mathcal{B}^{(k^*)}$, $P_\theta^* \notin \mathcal{B}^{(k^*-1)}$. Suppose P_θ^* is such that θ has no components equal to 0 or 1. Then, with P_θ^*-probability 1,

$$\lim_{n \to \infty} \hat{k}(X_1, \ldots, X_n) = \infty. \tag{5.17}$$

We explain further below why (5.17) holds. It expresses that, as n grows, $\hat{k}$ grows along - ML only takes into account how well a hypothesis fits the data, not its "complexity." No matter how large n, ML estimation will dramatically overfit. Thus, ML is inconsistent for model selection within the model class of all Markov chains. This example can be generalized to many other nested model classes.

The situation is a bit more subtle if we deal with a finite number of nested models. For example, suppose there are two candidate models: $\mathcal{B}^{(1)}$ (the

Bernoulli model) and $\mathcal{B}^{(2)}$ (the first-order Markov chains). Assume that data are generated by some $P^* \in \mathcal{B}^{(1)}$. Because $\mathcal{B}^{(1)} \subset \mathcal{B}^{(2)}$, we also have $P^* \in \mathcal{B}^{(2)}$. In this case, a "consistent" model selection method should prefer[5] $\mathcal{B}^{(1)}$ over $\mathcal{B}^{(2)}$ for all large n; see the definition of consistency, Section 2.5, page 71. But ML does not do this: if θ^* has no components that are equal to either 0 or 1, then, as n goes to infinity, the P^*-probability that $\mathcal{B}^{(2)}$ is preferred, i.e. that

$$P_{\hat{\theta}^{(2)}(D)}(D) > P_{\hat{\theta}^{(1)}(D)}(D) \tag{5.18}$$

goes to 1. Intuitively, this is because the distributions in $\mathcal{B}^{(1)}$ are a proper subset of the distributions in $\mathcal{B}^{(2)}$. More precisely, we only have $P_{\hat{\theta}^{(2)}(D)}(D) \le P_{\hat{\theta}^{(1)}(D)}(D)$ if the frequency of 1s preceded by a 0 in x^n is exactly equal to the frequency of 1s preceded by a 0. Even though, with high P^*-probability, these two frequencies will both converge to the same number $\theta^* = P^*(X = 1)$, one can show (using, for example, the *local* central limit theorem, as in (Grünwald 2001)) that the probability that they are *exactly* equal goes to 0 with increasing n. Extending the argument to $\mathcal{B}^{(k)}$ for $k > 2$ incidentally shows that (5.17) holds.

5.6.2   MDL vs. ML

We now contrast our findings about the behavior of MDL (Section 5.5) with our findings about the behavior of ML (Section 5.6.1).

MDL and ML, Part I   We have already indicated (page 143) that MDL is consistent for Markov chain model and hypothesis selection, based on the set $\mathcal{B}$ of all Markov chain models of each order: at least asymptotically, MDL neither over-, nor underfits. In general, it has been proved for a wide variety of finite and infinite, nested and non-nested model classes that MDL is consistent for such classes (Chapter 16). This stands in sharp contrast to ML estimation, which, when used for model selection, typically fails as soon as the model class contains an infinite set of nested models.

MDL and ML, Part II   In the case of parameter estimation within a k-dimensional parametric model $\mathcal{M}^{(k)}$ or for model selection between a finite number of non-nested models $\mathcal{M}_1, \ldots, \mathcal{M}_m$, both ML and MDL are consistent. Naively, one might now argue that in such cases there is no reason to prefer

---

5. One may ask why one should prefer a method to infer the simpler $\mathcal{B}^{(1)}$ rather than $\mathcal{B}^{(2)}$ if both models contain the "true" P^*. This is discussed on page 143, under *Small Is Beautiful.*

MDL over ML. But in fact, in many cases, two-part code MDL should still be preferred over ML. In the case of parameter estimation based on a parametric model with many parameters (such as $\mathcal{B}^{(32)}$), two-part code MDL will overfit much less than ML for small samples. We have already seen (Section 5.6.1) that ML will temporarily overfit in such cases. In contrast, MDL will typically pick a distribution $\ddot{\theta} \in \ddot{\Theta}_d^{(k)}$ with some small precision, much smaller than the precision needed to encode the ML parameter. Therefore, the *number of hypotheses* among which MDL selects is much smaller than the number of hypotheses among which ML selects. This leads to less overfitting, and, presumably, better behavior for the two-part code MDL estimator; see also Chapter 15, Section 15.3.

In the case of model selection between a finite number of non-nested models, a similar story can be told: even though ML is consistent, it may badly overfit on small samples. For example, if model $\mathcal{M}_A$ has 1 parameter and model $\mathcal{M}_B$ has 100 free parameters, then even if $\mathcal{M}_A$ contains the true P^* but $\mathcal{M}_B$ does not, ML will select $\mathcal{M}_B$ for all samples of size < 100. MDL tends to show the opposite behavior: if data are generated by some P^* in $\mathcal{M}_B$ but not in $\mathcal{M}_A$, then, for small samples, MDL will still prefer $\mathcal{M}_A$ rather than $\mathcal{M}_B$. In general, no matter whether the "true" distribution is in $\mathcal{M}_A$ or $\mathcal{M}_B$, MDL tends to start selecting the "right" model *based on a much smaller sample size* than ML. This follows from the consistency and rate of convergence results (see Chapter 15, Theorem 15.1 and Theorem 15.3).

For Parameter Estimation, MDL = ML *Asymptotically*   The differences between MDL and ML notwithstanding, it is an important fact that for parameter estimation within a parametric model $\mathcal{M}^{(k)}$, under the assumption that some $P^* = P_{\theta^*} \in \mathcal{M}^{(k)}$ generates the data, the ML estimator and the two-part code MDL estimator converge to the same value for large n. Namely, because both MDL and ML are consistent, both estimates must converge to the "true" parameter value θ^*.

5.6.3   MDL as a *Maximum Probability Principle*

We have just seen that MDL and ML may behave very differently when based on a model class (rather than a parametric model) $\mathcal{M}$. Nevertheless, the correspondence between probability distributions and codes indicates that they are still closely related:

To put it one way, MDL embodies something like a maximum *probability* rather than *likelihood* principle; put another way (Rissanen 1987), MDL can be viewed as a *global* version of the maximum likelihood principle. Let us briefly explain this.

In this chapter, we imposed a specific way of encoding the data (in terms of two-part codes with truncated parameter values). Within the class of codes that can be expressed this way, we looked for the one minimizing the code-length of the data. In terms of probability distributions, we used a model class such as the class of all Markov chains to arrive at a set of defective probability distributions for the data. Among all distributions defined in this way, we picked the one *maximizing the probability of the data.*

More precisely, we defined a distribution $\bar{P}$ as follows. First, we defined a *description method* (not a code) for $\mathcal{X}^n$ that allowed us to encode each data sequence $D \in \mathcal{X}^n$ in many different ways: one different encoding of D for each k and each $\theta \in \ddot{\Theta}^{(k)} := \bigcup_{d=1,2,\dots} \ddot{\Theta}_d^{(k)}$. For fixed k and θ, this gave rise to a code $L_{1,2}$ (for $\mathcal{M} \times \mathcal{X}^n$) satisfying, for all $D \in \mathcal{X}^n$,

$$L_{1,2}((k,\theta),D) := L_1(k,\theta) + L_2(D|k,\theta) = L_1(k,\theta) - \log P_{k,\theta}(D).$$

Then, the code $\bar{C}$ for $\mathcal{X}^n$ was defined by

$$\bar{L}(D) = \min_{k,\theta \in \Theta^{(k)}} L_{1,2}((k,\theta),D).$$

Finally, $\bar{P}$ was defined by

$$\bar{P}(D) := 2^{-\bar{L}(D)} = \max_{k,\theta \in \Theta^{(k)}} P_{k,\theta}(D) P(k,\theta)$$

where $P(k,\theta) := 2^{-L_1(k,\theta)}$.

> Note that $\bar{P}(\cdot)$ is in general "defective" (Section 3.2.2, page 95): in our Markov chain example, $\sum_{x^n \in \mathcal{X}^n} \bar{P}(x^n) < 1$. The reason is that the code to which $\bar{P}$ corresponds is not complete: each sequence D can be encoded in many different ways, one for each k and θ. For example, it can be encoded in a way that would be optimal if it were generated from a Bernoulli distribution, or in another way that would be optimal if it were generated by a first-order Markov chain, etc. $\bar{C}$ encodes D by picking the particular (k,θ) for which the total length is minimized; but code words are reserved for all other possible choices of k and θ too.

In Part II of this book, we shall formalize the idea of "maximizing probability with respect to a given model" and arrive at more sophisticated ways to associate models with codes/probability distributions. Whereas at this point, the maximum-probability interpretation may seem far-fetched, it will then become quite natural.

5.7   Computing and Approximating the Two-Part MDL Criterion in Practice

Equation 5.13 gives an exact formula for the two-part MDL principle for model and hypothesis selection. If we want to apply it in practice, we must somehow implement a procedure that when input a sample D, outputs the $(\ddot{k}, \ddot{\theta})$ minimizing (5.13), or at least some approximation thereof. In order to be practically useful, such a procedure should be reasonably fast. It turns out that for many, but certainly not all model classes, a computationally efficient procedure exists. Typically, the core of such a procedure consists of performing the following steps:

1. Compute ML estimators. Compute, for $k = 1, 2, \ldots$,

$$\min_{\theta \in \Theta^{(k)}} - \log P_\theta(D) = - \log P_{\hat{\theta}^{(k)}(D)}(D), \tag{5.19}$$

where $\hat{\theta}^{(k)}(D)$ is the ML estimator within $\mathcal{M}^{(k)}$ for $k = 1, 2, \ldots$.

2. Compute error terms, Now use (5.19) as a basis to compute the *error term* in (5.13). That is, for $k = 1, 2, \ldots, d = 1, 2, \ldots$, use (5.19) to compute

$$\min_{\theta \in \ddot{\Theta}^{(k)}_d} \{ - \log P_\theta(D) \}. \tag{5.20}$$

3. Compute complexity terms. Compute the *complexity term* of (5.13) for $k = 1, 2, \ldots, d = 1, 2, \ldots$.

4. Output. Output the k and d minimizing the sum of the error and complexity terms.

There are three obvious potential problems with this scheme:

1. Steps 1,2, and 3 need to be done for $k = 1, 2, \ldots$ and $d = 1, 2, \ldots$. Isn't this computationally prohibitive?

2. How can we compute the log-likelihood (5.19) evaluated at the maximum $\hat{\theta}^{(k)}(D)$ for fixed k and D?

3. How can we use (5.19) as a help in computing (5.20)?

In practice, problem 1 is usually not a problem. The reason is that for most model classes one encounters in practice, one can determine two numbers $k_{\max}$ and $d_{\max}$ such that no matter what data will be observed, MDL will output a $k \leq k_{\max}$ and a $d \leq d_{\max}$. For example, if we use the Markov chain model class $\mathcal{B}$, then for a sample of size n, we can a priori rule out that two-part MDL (5.13) will select a model index $\ddot{k} > n$. Problem 3 is usually solved by doing a Taylor expansion of (5.19) around $\hat{\theta}(x^n)$ as explained in Chapter 4, Section 4.2. We will not deal with it in more detail here since the problem is circumvented in most of the more sophisticated MDL methods that we discuss in Part III of this book.

This leaves us with problem 2. Since the maximum log-likelihood (5.19) needs to be computed also in some of the refined versions of MDL, we will consider this problem in more detail. Let $\hat{\theta}$ be the ML estimate for D within $\mathcal{B}^{(k)}$, and let $\theta_{z|y}$ be defined as in Example 2.7, page 60. One immediately verifies that

$$
-\log P_{\hat{\theta}^{(k)}(D)}(D) =
$$
$$
-n \sum_{y \in \{0,1\}^{\log k}} \hat{\eta}_{[1|y]} \log \hat{\eta}_{[1|y]} + (1 - \hat{\eta}_{[1|y]}) \log(1 - \hat{\eta}_{[1|y]}) + \gamma. \quad (5.21)
$$

Recall from Example 2.7, (2.24) that the ML parameters $\hat{\eta}_{[1|y]}$ are equal to the conditional frequencies of 1 prefixed by y. It follows that we need only record the k frequencies $\eta_{[1|y]}$ to compute (5.21). Thus, (5.21) can be computed very fast.

In general, we may say that the two-part code MDL criterion remains easy to evaluate *as long as for each k, finding $\hat{\theta}^{(k)}(D)$ is computationally easy*. For example, this is the case whenever $\mathcal{M}^{(k)}$ is an exponential family (Section 2.3, page 62). These all have a concave likelihood surface ($\log P_\theta(D)$ as a function of θ for fixed D). Therefore, all local maxima of the likelihood must be connected and also be global maxima. Therefore, the ML can, at least in principle, be found by local optimization methods such as hill-climbing. For some exponential families, such as the Markov models of fixed order, the ML estimator may even be found analytically by differentiation. For most models that are not exponential families, for example, multicomponent mixture models as defined in Section 2.3, page 62, there is no known algorithm that, given D, finds the ML estimator for D "efficiently," that is, in time polynomial in n. In such cases one can usually resort to approximation algorithms like the EM (expectation–maximization) algorithm (Ripley 1996; Duda, Hart, and Stork 2000) which can often find a *local* maximum of the likelihood surface after running for not too long. In Chapter 14, Example 14.8, we will have more to say about the consequences of using local instead of global maxima.

5.8   Justifying Crude MDL: Consistency and Code Design

In the previous section we introduced and analyzed simplistic two-part code MDL. Two very crucial issues were left open:

1. Justification. How can we justify the use of two-part code MDL?

2. Code design/arbitrariness. Why did we choose the codes the way we did? Couldn't we have chosen other codes with equal justification?

These two questions are interrelated. Concerning the first question, we would like to know why it should make any sense to use simplistic two-part MDL, or other forms of crude MDL in practice? The simple answer is this: we have argued that every regularity in the data can be used to compress the data; we take it as an axiom that "learning" is "finding regularity in data," and that "regularity" can be equated with "compressibility." Therefore, given our axiom, we should try to find the shortest description of the data. Since simplistic MDL does just this, it is justified in and of itself. There are at least three weaknesses to this answer:

1. We would have a much stronger case if we could justify crude versions of MDL in some *external* manner that does not involve any references to the axiom "compression is good." If we can justify MDL in such a different way, it would be much more convincing to an outsider who is not that convinced by the compression premise.

2. Even if one accepts the premise that learning should proceed by data compression, it is not clear

    (a) why the hypotheses in our two-part code should be encoded using the type of code that we actually used. Maybe there exist some codes which are in some way "better" or even "optimal," compared to the ad hoc codes we introduced for simplistic MDL?

    (b) why one should encode data in two stages at all. As we will see in the next chapters, the compression can proceed using other types of codes such as *one-part* and *predictive* codes as well.

In Section 5.8.1, we deal with issue 1, providing a partial external justification of MDL: crude MDL is *consistent* in the traditional statistical sense of the word. The justification will of necessity be partial, since, as we shall see, something crucial is still lacking in our crude MDL principle: in order to give a better external justification, we would need a principled, mathematically precise means of designing codes for actual problems. Thus, items 1 and 2 above are inextricably intertwined. In Section 5.8.2 we give a first idea of how code design should proceed, but we leave all details to the following chapters, where we introduce *refined MDL*, which gives explicit instructions for code design.

5.8.1   A General Consistency Result

Here we show that *no matter what description method is used*, all versions of crude two-part code MDL (not just our "simplistic" MDL) are, in a certain sense *consistent*: *if* the data happen to be distributed by one of the probabilistic sources in the model, *then*, given enough data, MDL will learn that this is the case, and output this "true" source. Thus, two-part code MDL does something reasonable, not just from a coding-theoretic, but also from a classical statistical point of view (Section 2.5, page 71). However, the result says nothing about whether MDL is in any sense better than other methods. Thus, it is really more of a "sanity check" than a complete justification.

Asymptotic Distinguishability   To state the result, we need the concept of "asymptotic distinguishability" between probabilistic sources. Suppose that data are distributed according to P^*. Intuitively, Q is asymptotically distinguishable from P^* if the probability that a sample generated by P^* looks as if it might have been generated by Q rather than P^* goes to 0 with increasing sample size. Formally, we say that Q *is asymptotically distinguishable from P^** if for all $\delta > 0$,

$$P^* \left(\frac{Q(X^n)}{P^*(X^n)} > \delta \right) \to 0 \text{ as } n \to \infty. \tag{5.22}$$

If P^* generates the data, but Q is not asymptotically distinguishable from P^*, then even if we observe an amount of data tending to infinity, the data never become overwhelmingly more plausible according to P^* than according to Q. In that case, no learning algorithm may ever be capable of finding out whether P^* or Q generated the data. For this reason, we are satisfied if, given enough data, a learning algorithm outputs as hypothesis any source that is asymptotically indistinguishable from P^*; it does not have to be P^* itself. In practice, we nearly always work with model classes $\mathcal{M}$ such that for all $P, Q \in \mathcal{M}, P \neq Q$, P and Q are asymptotically distinguishable. This is illustrated by the following example:

Example 5.2 Let $\mathcal{M}$ be some family of i.i.d. sources with finite variance, for example the Bernoulli model. Then all $P, Q \in \mathcal{M}, P \neq Q$ are asymptotically distinguishable. To see this, note that for all $P \in \mathcal{M}$, $\log P(X^n) = \sum_{i=1}^{n} \log P(X_i)$, so that

$$\frac{1}{n} \log P(X^n) - \frac{1}{n} \log Q(X^n) = \frac{1}{n} \sum_{i=1}^{n} \log \frac{P(X_i)}{Q(X_i)}.$$

Thus, by the law of large numbers (Section 2.2.3, page 55), with P-probability 1,

$$\frac{1}{n} \log P(X^n) - \frac{1}{n} \log Q(X^n) \rightarrow D(P\|Q),$$

where $D(\cdot\|\cdot)$ is the Kullback-Leibler divergence (Section 3.3.1, page 103). If $P \neq Q$, then $D(P\|Q) > 0$, so that (5.22) must hold. Similarly, one can show for many non-i.i.d. families $\mathcal{M}'$ (such as the Markov chains) that, for $P, Q \in \mathcal{M}', P \neq Q, P$ and Q must be asymptotically distinguishable.

> **Asymptotic Distinguishability and Mutual Singularity** Asymptotic distinguishability is not a standard concept. But it is implied by the standard notion of *mutual singularity* between distributions, as known from advanced, measure-theoretic probability (Feller 1968b). Two distributions P, Q are called mutually singular if there exists two sets E_1, E_2 such that P is concentrated on E_1 and Q is concentrated on E_2, and $E_1 \cap E_2 = \emptyset$. In the measure-theoretic framework, one can think of probabilistic sources as distributions defined over a sample space of infinite sequences. Given a suitable σ-algebra, one can then show that if P and Q are mutually singular, then P is asymptotically distinguishable from Q and vice versa (proof omitted). If we slightly strengthen the notion of asymptotic distinguishability, then it even becomes equivalent to mutual singularity: if P and Q are such that there exists a sequence $\delta_1, \delta_2, \ldots$ converging to 0 such that for all n, $P\left(\frac{Q(X^n)}{P(X^n)} > \delta_n\right) < \delta_n$ and $\sum_{j \geq 1} \delta_j < \infty$, then P and Q must be mutually singular (proof omitted). We do not know whether, under our weak definition, asymptotic distinguishability of P from Q implies asymptotic distinguishability of Q from P.

It turns out that asymptotic distinguishability between sources P and Q is intimately related to their Kullback-Leibler divergences. This fact, which we investigate in more detail in Part II, Chapter 7, Chapter 8, and Chapter 10, remains true for non-Bernoulli and non-i.i.d. models.

Consistency Consider the following scenario. Let $\mathcal{M}$ be any countable set of probabilistic sources for $\mathcal{X}$, and let $P^* \in \mathcal{M}$. Let L_1 be some codelength function, corresponding to a code over elements of $\mathcal{M}$. Let $X_1, X_2, \ldots$, be distributed according to P^*. Note that the X_i are *not* necessarily i.i.d. We define $\ddot{P}_{(n)}$ to be the probabilistic source selected by two-part code MDL for point hypothesis selection, as in (5.4), page 136.

Theorem 5.1 Let $\mathcal{M}^\circ \subset \mathcal{M}$ be the set of sources in $\mathcal{M}$ that are asymptotically distinguishable from P^*. If $L_1(P^*) < \infty$, then

$$P^*(\ddot{P}_{(n)} \in \mathcal{M}^\circ) \to 0 \tag{5.23}$$

as $n \to \infty$.

Example 5.3 makes clear why (5.23) expresses a form of consistency.

Proof Idea The proof is based on the *no-hypercompression-inequality*, see the box on page 103, Chapter 3. This fundamental inequality says that the probability that any given code C compresses the data by more than K bits compared to the code based on P^* is exponentially small: it is not greater than 2^{-K}. In particular, this must also hold for the two-part description method C with lengths $\min_{Q \in \mathcal{M}^\circ}\{L(Q) - \log Q(X^n)\}$. Thus, the minimum codelength achieved by first describing a Q that is asymptotically distinguishable from P and then encoding the data according to Q, is with overwhelming probability not substantially shorter than the codelength achieved by P itself. The proof slightly extends the reasoning to show that the codelength achieved by C must actually be *larger* than the codelength based on P, with probability tending to 1. The precise mathematical proof is given in the appendix to this chapter.

Comments Theorem 5.1 is a slight variation of Theorem 1 of (Barron and Cover 1991), which in turn uses ideas appearing in previous proofs of consistency of Bayes methods (Doob 1949; Blackwell and Dubins 1962; Barron 1985). The theorem has been formulated so as to admit an elementary proof. Using much more sophisticated arguments, much stronger theorems can be proved (for example, in (Barron and Cover 1991), (5.23) is replaced by the analogous "with probability 1, for all large n, $\ddot{P}_{(n)} \notin \mathcal{M}^\circ$" statement). The precise statement and proof of such "almost sure" versions are outside the scope of this book. We will consider other extensions though in Part III: Theorems 15.1 and 15.3 in Chapter 15, and the informal result in the box on page 506. These extended theorems still hold if P^* is not itself in $\mathcal{M}$, but $\mathcal{M}$

contains a sequence P_1, P_2, ... of sources converging to P^*. Here "converging" means that the Kullback-Leibler divergence (Section 3.3.1, page 103) $D(P^*\|P_m) \to 0$ as m tends to infinity. For example, such theorems allow us to prove consistency of two-part MDL with respect to *all* Bernoulli sources, or *all* Markov chains, and not just a countable (encodable) subset thereof. They also give explicit information on the *rate* (speed) with which $\ddot{P}_{(n)}$ converges to P^*.

Example 5.3 [Markov Chain Consistency] Let us apply Theorem 5.1 to the Markov model class. We encode parameters using the code C_1 of Section 5.2, (5.12), page 138. That is, we encode θ by first encoding the number of components k and the minimum precision d in which θ can be expressed. Then we encode the parameter itself, using a grid on parameter space $[0, 1]^k$ with widths 2^{-d}. Then $L_1(\theta) = L_{\mathbb{N}}(k) + L_{\mathbb{N}}(d) + kd$. Theorem 5.1 now says the following: suppose θ represents a γth order Markov chain with finite codelength under L_1, i.e. θ can be described in binary with finite precision. The order γ can be completely arbitrary. Then *if* the data happen to be distributed according to θ, two-part MDL will *learn* this: the probability that MDL selects some $\ddot{\theta} \neq \theta$ goes to 0 with increasing n. Note that the theorem says nothing about how fast the probability decreases with n – not surprisingly, it turns out that this depends on the order γ; Chapter 15, Theorem 15.1 and Theorem 15.3 deal with this issue explicitly. Also, the theorem says nothing about what happens if data are distributed according to some θ that cannot be finitely described using code C_1 (for example, the Bernoulli distribution with $\theta = 1/3$)– it turns out that MDL will still learn a good *approximation* of θ – again, Theorem 15.1 and Theorem 15.3 deal with this issue explicitly. Theorem 5.1 *does* say that, had we used a different code for encoding θ, then MDL would be able to learn all sources that have finite codelength under that different code. For example, consider the code C_1' that first encodes k, then encodes $2k$ integers $q_1, \ldots, q_k, r_1, \ldots, r_k$ using the standard code for the integers. These are then interpreted by the decoder as k parameters $\theta_1 = q_1/r_1, \ldots, \theta_k = q_k/r_k$. Using the code C_1', we can identify every rational-valued parameter, including, for example, $\theta = 1/3$.

Consistency of Crude, Two-Part Code MDL

No matter what code we use, as long as it assigns a code word to the true probabilistic source, then two-part code MDL will learn this source given enough data: two-part MDL is *consistent*. Note that

1. Not all commonly used learning methods have this desirable property. For example, maximum likelihood (ML) can be inconsistent; see Section 5.6, page 144.

2. Therefore, two-part code MDL is *not an arbitrary procedure.* Even though codes can be designed in many different ways, we cannot tweak MDL so as to give any answer we would like. For example, if we use the Markov chain model class, then we cannot design a code such that MDL does exactly the same thing as ML for all sample sizes. At least, this holds *as long as we are not allowed to change our two-part description method as the sample size increases.*

> There are versions of "refined" MDL, both based on two-part and other codes, in which the description method used to encode hypotheses is allowed to depend on the sample size. However, since we always require the resulting two-part code to be "universal" relative to some model class $\mathcal{M}$ (Part II, Chapter 6, Chapter 10), the dependency on the sample size is of a very restricted kind, and it remains the case that we cannot tweak MDL so as to give any answer we would like.

3. On the negative side, the result does not say anything about how many data are needed before MDL can find a (reasonable approximation to) the true source.

> In fact, if we use "stupid" codes, we may need arbitrarily large samples. Yet, as we shall see in Chapter 15, Theorem 15.1 and Theorem 15.3, even if we only have vague prior knowledge about the data-generating machinery, we may still construct "clever" codes that allow us to find a reasonable approximation fast.

5.8.2 Code Design for Two-Part Code MDL

We now know that no matter how we design our codes, MDL is consistent. But in order to be useful in practice, MDL should be able to learn reasonable approximations of the data-generating machinery relatively *fast*, i.e. based on *small* samples. We shall see in the next chapters that, not surprisingly, the sample size we need is closely related to the description length assigned to the source according to which the data happen to be distributed. Let us indicate why.

Clearly we are giving an advantage to distributions to which we assign a small codelength: if two distributions fit the data equally well, the one with shorter codelength will be selected. Thus, it seems that less data would be needed to identify such a distribution. Although this is not explicit in our simple consistency theorem, in Chapter 15 we show that this is indeed the case: the smaller the description length of the true distribution – our "target" in learning – the smaller the sample size needed before MDL gives, with high probability, a distribution sufficiently "close" to P^* (see Example 5.3). It therefore seems that we should design our codes so that the true distribution has a small code length. Of course, the very point of learning is that we do not know the true distribution, so we can never guarantee that it has small code length. Instead, *we may try to asssign code words to distributions in such a way that there is always a distribution with a short code length that is "close" (in some appropriate sense) to the true distribution.* Theorem 5.1 and Example 5.3 suggest, and the theorems of Chapter 15 in fact prove, that we will then be able to learn "reasonable approximations" of the true distributions relatively fast. But how should we implement such a "clever" code word assignment? In fact, we already did this in a primitive, suboptimal, way in our design of the code C_1 for "simplistic" two-part MDL:

Example 5.4 [Markov Chain Code Design, Fixed Order γ] Recall the code L_{1_b}, (5.10), that we used to encode parameters for the fixed-parameter model $\mathcal{B}^{(k)}$, $k = 2^\gamma$, of γth-order Markov chains. For a given precision d, we have 2^d code words available. Our new idea suggests that, to learn a good approximation to the true distribution as fast as possible *in the worst case* over all distributions in $\mathcal{B}^{(k)}$, we should discretize the 2^d parameter vectors in a way so as to minimize the maximum (worst-case) distance between a distribution in $\mathcal{M}^{(k)}$ and the closest discretized distribution. If $\mathcal{M}^{(k)}$ has just 1 parameter, and distance is measured by Euclidean distance between parameter values, then clearly we have to take a uniform grid on the parameter space Θ. Similarly, when the parameter space is $[0, 1]^k$, a good approximation to the optimal discretization is to take a rectangular grid with rectangle widths 2^{-d} and take the centers of those rectangles as our discretized parameter values. This is exactly what we did earlier in this chapter.

Now, the codelength we used to encode the particular discretized parameter values was taken uniformly as well. Because the uniform code is the minimax code (Section 3.1.2, page 88), this means that we minimize the worst-case codelength needed to encode a hypothesis at precision d; for any other choice of code, the description length of some of the hypotheses would have been higher, and we would have needed a larger sample to identify this distribution if it were true. This worst-case approach is justified by the fact that we have no idea whatsoever what distribution in $\mathcal{M}^{(k)}$ actually did generate the data.

While this simplistic approach for Markov chains is a step in the right direction, there is also a serious problem with it:

> **Problem I: Parameterization Dependence/Why the Euclidean Distance?** Models can be parameterized in arbitrary manners. For example, we might have parameterized the Markov model $\mathcal{B}^{(k)}$ in its "canonical" (exponential) parameterization rather than its mean-value parameterization (see Chapter 2, Example 2.10, page 66 and Chapter 18, Example 18.5, page 618). A uniform grid in one parameterization can be highly nonuniform in another parameterization. Clearly, "uniform" is a somewhat arbitrary notion.
>
> The underlying problem is the fact that the uniform grid leads us to minimize the worst-case *Euclidean* (standard) distance between a parameter and its discretized version, in the (arbitrary) parameterization we happen to have chosen. But why should the Euclidean distance be our metric of interest? As we shall see in Chapter 7, Section 7.3, we should really choose a grid that is minimax with respect to Kullback-Leibler divergence rather than Euclidean distance. Such a grid will lead to a discretization that is *parameterization invariant*: it does not depend on how we choose to parameterize our model.
>
> Unfortunately, we still lack the necessary insights to explain why we need a Kullback-Leibler grid and how it can be implemented. Indeed, *something crucial is still missing in our crude two-part code MDL principle*.

We thus have a (suboptimal) recipe for designing codes for discretized parameter values, given a precision d. We next have to encode the precision d itself. Since d is an arbitrary integer, we cannot use a uniform code. Therefore, we use a *quasi-uniform* code, achieving "almost" minimax codelengths (Section 3.1.2, page 91). Here we put in practice the *key idea in coding* as explained in the box on that page, and the *luckiness principle* explained on page 92.

Example 5.5 [Markov Chain Code Design, Varying Order γ] Now suppose our model class $\mathcal{B}$ is the set of *all* Markov chains. This set is too rich to determine a set of 2^d "minimax distance" discretized points for any d. Instead, we can carve up $\mathcal{B}$ into subsets $\mathcal{B}^{(1)} \subset \mathcal{B}^{(2)} \subset \mathcal{B}^{(4)} \subset \mathcal{B}^{(8)} \ldots$ where $\mathcal{B}^{(k)}$ is the $\log k$th-order Markov chain model. We then first code k using a quasi-uniform code for k, and then *given* k, we use the code for encoding discretized parameter values in $\mathcal{B}^{(k)}$, as described before. Once again, we put in practice the *key idea in coding* from the box on page 91; now combined with the *luckiness principle* (page 92): we use a coding strategy such that for any fixed large k, the number of bits needed to encode a parameter in $\mathcal{B}^{(k)}$ is only *slightly* (by an amount of approximately $\log k + 2 \log \log k$) larger than the number of bits we would have used if we had known k in advance. Therefore, in our two-part encoding of the data, no matter what the data are, we only need slightly more bits to encode the data than if we had fixed k in advance. Yet, and this is the "luckiness" idea, *if* the data happen to be such that for some $k' \ll k$, a Markov chain θ within the set $\mathcal{B}^{(k')}$ already provides a short codelength of the data, *then* we can encode the data using much less bits (about $(k - k')d$) than if we had fixed the order to the large value k in advance.

Problem II: How to Carve up Large Models The reader may wonder whether the whole scheme is not *arbitrary*: if we carve up the full, "union" model class $\mathcal{B}$ of all Markov chains of each order into submodels in a different manner (as done in Chapter 7, Section 7.3, Figure 7.1), we would obtain different codes and get different results. This important point is treated in detail in Chapter 17. For now, we only note that a minimax optimal (uniform) code over all fixed-precision hypotheses in $\mathcal{B}$ does not exist, since there is an infinite number of them.

By picking a uniform code over hypotheses conditioned on models, and *some* quasi-uniform code over models, we obtain a quasi-uniform code over hypotheses, which is the best we can obtain. However, the question remains why we should not pick a completely different quasi-uniform code over hypotheses... As we shall see, in many cases, some degree of subjectivity is unavoidable in choosing a good model class decomposition. Nevertheless, we can clearly distinguish between "reasonable" and "silly" decompositions (see Chapter 15).

The overall idea remains to design codes such that the description lengths are as small as possible, allowing us to find a reasonable approximation of the true distribution reasonably fast. Because we have no idea what the true distribution is, we should minimize codelengths of hypotheses in a worst-case sense. Thus, in designing codes for MDL we use a sort of *meta-MDL principle* for the code lengths of k, d, and the discretized parameter values.

We shall see in the introduction to Part III how obtaining short codelengths for parameters and obtaining short codelengths for data given parameters can be viewed as two consequences of a single, unified principle.

(Slight) Problem III: Inefficiency of Codes As already remarked on page 137, in the Markov chain example, we encoded the k of the Markov model $\mathcal{B}^{(k)}$ to be used using the universal code for the integers, with length $L_{\mathbb{N}}(k)$. This overlooks the fact that, for Markov chains, not all values of k are possible: we have to have $k = 2^\gamma$ for some integer $\gamma \geq 0$. So, if we were to take this into account, we could obtain uniformly *slightly* shorter codelengths by encoding γ instead of k using $L_{\mathbb{N}}(\gamma)$ bits. As expected from the discussion above, Theorem 15.3 in Chapter 15 indicates that this would lead to a identification of the correct model based on a slightly smaller sample. However, since, compared to the overall number of bits needed to encode data (which grows linearly in n for fixed k), the amount of saved bits is very small, the amount of data needed will only decrease slightly.

Code Design in MDL: A Provisional Strategy
The codes in two-part code MDL should *themselves be designed in order to minimize description length of the hypotheses*, in a worst-case sense. This leads to uniform and quasi-uniform codes for hypotheses. This design principle can be motivated in three interrelated ways, explained below:

1. **keeping with the general (MDL) principle;**
2. **trying to be "honest";**
3. **learning at a fast rate.**

On the other hand, it leaves open three key problems, discussed above:

1. **How should parameters be discretized?** This is Problem I above; uniform is arbitrary.

2. **How should models be carved up into submodels?** This is Problem II above: there seems to be a subjective (at best), or arbitrary (at worst) aspect.

3. **Why should we use a two-part coding scheme altogether?** Indeed we shall see in Part II that there are several entirely different coding schemes that we can use.

These problems will be resolved in Parts II and III of this book.

Let us briefly elaborate on the three rationales for our coding strategy:

1. **Keeping with the general (MDL) principle.** The MDL principle tells us to base hypothesis and model selection on minimizing the description length of a given set of data relative to some family of models $\mathcal{M}$. It then seems only reasonable to define "description length" in terms of codes that are themselves as efficient as possible. Since, when designing a code for the parameters, we cannot know in advance what parameters will be used in the actual encoding of data, we should minimize the description length of the parameters in a worst-case sense.

2. **Trying to be "honest".** Our goal is to devise a model selection criterion that treats all models $\mathcal{M}^{(1)}, \mathcal{M}^{(2)}, \ldots$ under consideration on the same footing. We try to avoid a built-in preference for any one of them. Similarly, *given* a model $\mathcal{M}^{(k)}$, we want to treat all $\theta \in \Theta^{(k)}$ on the same footing, avoiding a built-in preference for any one of them. By picking codes that are as uniform as possible, we try to be as honest as possible - we will be much more precise about this in the next chapters.

3. **Learning at a fast rate.** As suggested before and as will be shown in Chapter 15, Theorem 15.1 and Theorem 15.3, designing codes which minimize description length in a worst-case sense has the following advantage: *if* data are distributed according to some distribution that can be arbitrarily well approximated by the models under consideration, *then* such worst-case optimal codes are guaranteed to make MDL output a good approximation of the truth based on small samples.

   > The correspondence does not mean that, when applying MDL, we think that data are actually generated by one of the distributions in our class. It just reassures us that in the idealized case, where one of the distributions is (close to) true, we do something reasonable. This provides us with hope that MDL is still a reasonable principle to apply in situations where no "true" distribution can be assumed to exist.

This finishes our look ahead into clever code design for MDL. At this point we should emphasize that *in practice* simplistic two-part code MDL as defined here is suboptimal at best; general "crude" MDL (with arbitrary codes C_1) can be arbitrarily bad for samples unless they are unreasonably large. Yet we hope to have sparked enough interest in the reader to join us in our exploration of refined MDL methods, for which code design is the central issue!

5.9 Summary and Outlook

We gave a precise definition of "simplistic" two-part code MDL, first for the Markov chains and then for general model classes. We analyzed its behavior in detail, and explained that it was just one version of general "crude" two-part code MDL. We provided a consistency theorem for general crude two-part code MDL, indicating that it performs well "in the limit." This showed that crude two-part code MDL is not an arbitrary procedure, and it gave us some confidence that our idea of learning by minimizing description length is a reasonable one. However, in the last section we indicated several weaknesses of crude MDL in general and our simplistic form in particular. It seems our crude two-part MDL principle is still incomplete: we need to extend it such that it gives a principled way for *designing* codes that lead to learning of good models based on *small* samples. We are now ready for Part II of this book, where we shall investigate how this can be done.

5.A Appendix: Proof of Theorem 5.1

Let W be the (possibly defective) distribution corresponding to the code for hypotheses with lengths L_1, so that for all $Q \in \mathcal{M}$, $W(Q) = 2^{-L_1(Q)}$. Since $\mathcal{M}$ is countable, $\mathcal{M}°$ must be countable as well. Therefore we can order the elements in $\mathcal{M}°$ according to increasing description length $L_1(Q_j)$ (decreasing $W(Q_j)$) as $Q_1, Q_2, \ldots$. Now fix some π with $0 < \pi < 1$. Define $\underline{\mathcal{M}}°$ as the subset of $\mathcal{M}°$ consisting of the first N distributions in $\mathcal{M}°$, where N is chosen as the smallest number such that $\sum_{j=1}^{N} W(Q_j) \geq \pi$. Define

$$\overline{\mathcal{M}}° = \mathcal{M}° \setminus \underline{\mathcal{M}}° = \{Q_{N+1}, Q_{N+2}, \ldots\}.$$

In the derivation below we omit the subscripts 1 and 2 from the codelength functions L_1 and L_2. Note that

$$W(\overline{\mathcal{M}}°) = \sum_{j=N+1}^{\infty} W(Q_j) \leq 1 - \pi. \tag{5.24}$$

Note also that, for any $\mathcal{M}' \subseteq \mathcal{M}°$,

$$P^*\{\ddot{P}_{(n)} \in \mathcal{M}')\} =$$
$$P^*\{\text{for some } Q \in \mathcal{M}': L(P^*) + L(X^n \mid P^*) \geq L(Q) + L(X^n|Q)\} \leq$$
$$\sum_{Q \in \mathcal{M}'} P^*\{L(P^*) + L(X^n \mid P^*) \geq L(Q) + L(X^n|Q)\}. \tag{5.25}$$

Here the last line follows by the union bound (2.18), page 55. Now define, for $Q \in \mathcal{M}^\circ$,

$$f_n(Q) := P^* \left\{ -\log P^*(X^n) \geq -\log Q(X^n) + L(Q) - L(P^*) \right\},$$
$$\underline{g}_n := \sum_{Q \in \underline{\mathcal{M}}^\circ} f_n(Q) \; ; \; \overline{g}_n := \sum_{Q \in \overline{\mathcal{M}}^\circ} f_n(Q).$$

Applying (5.25) to both terms below, we can write

$$P^*\{\ddot{P}_{(n)} \in \mathcal{M}^\circ)\} = P^*\{\ddot{P}_{(n)} \in \underline{\mathcal{M}}^\circ)\} + P^*\{\ddot{P}_{(n)} \in \overline{\mathcal{M}}^\circ)\} \leq$$
$$\sum_{Q \in \underline{\mathcal{M}}^\circ} f_n(Q) + \sum_{Q \in \overline{\mathcal{M}}^\circ} f_n(Q) = \underline{g}_n + \overline{g}_n. \quad (5.26)$$

Each $Q \in \underline{\mathcal{M}}^\circ$ is asymptotically distinguishable from P^*, so that, by definition of asymptotic distinguishability, $\lim_{n\to\infty} f_n(Q) = 0$. Since $\underline{g}_n = \underline{\mathcal{M}}^\circ$ is the sum of a *finite* number of such Q's, we must have

$$\lim_{n\to\infty} \underline{g}(n) = 0. \quad (5.27)$$

(If every element of a finite sum tends to 0, the sum itself must tend to 0.) It only remains to bound $\overline{g}_n$. This is done by applying our fundamental coding inequality, (3.15), in the box on page 103, to each term $f_n(Q)$ in $\overline{g}_n$, with $K = L(Q) - L(P^*)$. This gives, for $Q \in \overline{\mathcal{M}}^\circ$,

$$f_n(Q) = P^* \left\{ -\log P^*(X^n) \geq -\log Q(X^n) + L(Q) - L(P^*) \right\} \leq 2^{-L(Q)+L(P^*)}. \quad (5.28)$$

so that $\overline{g}_n$ satisfies

$$\overline{g}_n \leq \sum_{Q \in \overline{\mathcal{M}}^\circ} f_n(Q) \leq \sum_{Q \in \overline{\mathcal{M}}^\circ} 2^{-L(Q)+L(P^*)} \leq (1-\pi)2^{L(P^*)}, \quad (5.29)$$

where the crucial last inequality follows from (5.24). Recall that this holds for every $0 < \pi < 1$. For every $\epsilon > 0$ we can choose $\pi = 1 - \epsilon 2^{-L(P^*)}$ giving that $\overline{g}_n \leq \epsilon$ for all large n. Combining with (5.27) and (5.26), we find that for all $\epsilon > 0$,

$$\lim_{n\to\infty} P^*\{\ddot{P}_{(n)} \in \mathcal{M}^\circ)\} < \epsilon,$$

which proves the theorem.

PART II

Universal Coding

Introduction to Part II

Part II of this book is about universal coding, the information-theoretic notion on which refined MDL is built. Broadly speaking, a *universal code* for a model $\mathcal{M}$ is a code that compresses the data almost as well as the element of $\mathcal{M}$ that compresses the data the most. We know from Chapter 3 that with each prefix code $\bar{L}$, we can uniquely associate a corresponding distribution $\bar{P}$ such that for all x, $\bar{L}(x) = -\log \bar{P}(x)$. The distributions that correspond to universal codes in this way are called *universal models*.

We have already seen one particular type of universal code:

Simplest Example of a Universal Code
The two-part MDL code, which was introduced informally in Chapter 1 and made precise in Chapter 5, is an example of a universal code.

Yet there exist several other types of universal codes, at least three of which are at least as important as the two-part codes:

2. The Bayesian universal codes

3. The Normalized Maximum Likelihood (NML) universal codes and variations thereof

4. The prequential plug-in universal code

These four types of universal codes and their corresponding universal models are introduced in Chapter 6. While most work reported in this book focuses on these four types of codes, the list is not exhaustive: we will also encounter *conditional two-part universal codes* and *Césaro universal codes*, introduced in Chapter 10 and Chapter 15 respectively.

The main message of Part II is that all these universal codes, while designed in completely different manners, usually achieve almost the same codelengths. This is of crucial importance when we discuss refined MDL inference in Part III of this book. *MDL inference always starts out by defining a universal code for the model class under consideration.* Thus, in order to define MDL inference, we first need to know about universal coding. Still, we stress that in Part II of the book, we are not at all concerned with inference; we only care about compressing data as much as possible. We reconnect our findings with inductive inference only in Part III, where we shall see that there exist several deep connections between universal coding and consistent statistical inference.

Structure of Part II

1. Chapter 6: The countable case. Part II starts with Chapter 6, which provides a general introduction to universal coding. For simplicity, in this chapter we restrict our attention to *countable* models. This allows us to focus on essential concepts rather than mathematical details. We give a brief introduction to, and comparison of, the four main types of universal codes mentioned above.

2. Chapters 7–10: The parametric case – finite COMP($\mathcal{M}$). The next four chapters, Chapter 7 through 10, are then each devoted to one particular type of universal code for *parametric* models $\mathcal{M}$. Such models contain uncountably many distributions, but are otherwise quite structured, especially if we restrict the parameter space to what we call *ineccsi sets*. This is a refinement of the notion of compact (closed and bounded) subsets of $\mathbb{R}^k$. With this restriction, the so-called *minimax regret* relative to a model $\mathcal{M}$ is guaranteed to exist. The minimax regret is, essentially, the worst-case additional number of bits one needs to encode a sequence of outcomes compared to the distribution in $\mathcal{M}$ that is optimal for that particular sequence. We then obtain the beautiful insight that the minimax regret for $\mathcal{M}$ can also be interpreted as a notion of *complexity* of $\mathcal{M}$, where "$\mathcal{M}$ is complex" means that "$\mathcal{M}$ contains many essentially different, or *distinguishable* distributions." This interpretation is so fundamental that we denote the minimax regret relative to $\mathcal{M}$ as COMP($\mathcal{M}$) and alternatively refer to it as *parametric complexity*. The related notion of distinguishability is a recurrent theme in Chapter 7 through 10. It will provide one of several justifications of the MDL procedures that we define in Part III of this book.

It turns out that the NML universal code is optimal in the sense that it achieves the minimax optimal codelength regret. This is the main theme of Chapter 7. The Bayesian universal code is in general not optimal, but can be made asymptotically optimal by choosing a particular prior distribution, the so-called *Jeffreys' prior*. This is the main theme of Chapter 8. The prequential plug-in code is not optimal, but provides an interesting reinterpretation of universal coding in terms of sequential prediction. That is the main theme of Chapter 9. Finally, by discretizing the parameter space in a clever way, the two-part code can be made close to optimal, and the "conditional" two-part code can even be made optimal. This is the theme of Chapter 10.

3. Chapters 11 and 12: The parametric case – infinite $\mathrm{COMP}(\mathcal{M})$. For some parametric models $\mathcal{M}$, the minimax regret is still finite if the parameter set is not ineccsi. But for most parametric models, if the parameter space is not restricted to an ineccsi set, the minimax regret $\mathrm{COMP}(\mathcal{M})$ is infinite. In that case, it is not always clear how one should define the quality of a universal code. Still, there exist weaker notions of optimality, and there exist some variations of the NML and the Bayesian universal codes which are optimal under this weaker notion. This is the theme of Chapter 11. A most important case of such models with infinite minimax regret is the *linear regression models*. They form the basis of MDL for linear regression model selection, for example based on the polynomial model that we encountered in Chapter 2. These linear regression models are the theme of Chapter 12.

4. Chapter 13: Beyond parametrics. In actual MDL applications we often aim to select a parametric model $\mathcal{M}_\gamma$ among an infinite union $\mathcal{M} = \bigcup_\gamma \mathcal{M}_\gamma$ of such models; or we aim to learn a distribution for our data from among a set of distributions $\mathcal{M}$ that is so large that it cannot be meaningfully parameterized by a finite-dimensional model. In both cases, MDL inference starts out with a universal code relative to $\mathcal{M}$. Such "nonparametric" universal codes are the theme of Chapter 13. Because the topic is quite abstract, we give two concrete examples: *histogram* and *Gaussian process* models.

6 *Universal Coding with Countable Models*

This chapter introduces universal coding. We only consider universal codes relative to countable (finite or countably infinite) sets of distributions. Also, the space of outcomes $\mathcal{X}$ is always assumed to be finite or countable. This considerably simplifies the mathematical treatment, and allows us to focus on ideas and concepts rather than mathematical detail. In practical applications of MDL, we are mostly concerned with universal codes relative to uncountably large sets of distributions. These will be the subject of all other chapters in Part II of this book.

In Section 6.1 we give a general introduction to the idea of universal coding and modeling. We give the formal definition of universal codes and models in terms of the *redundancy*. We then analyze the simple cases of finite $\mathcal{M}$ (Section 6.2) and countably infinite $\mathcal{M}$ (Section 6.3), introduce the second fundamental concept, the *regret*, and the third fundamental concept, the *minimax regret* or *model complexity* COMP($\mathcal{M}$). In Section 6.4, we explain the important difference between *prequential* (predictive) and nonprequential universal coding. Section 6.5 compares our notion of *individual sequence universality* with the *stochastic universality* that is more common in the information-theoretic literature.

It turns out that the following sections are natural places to introduce the four main types of universal codes:

1. **The two part codes** (Section 6.1.1)

2. **The Bayesian universal codes** (Section 6.1.2).

3. **The normalized maximum likelihood (NML) universal codes** (Section 6.2).

4. **The prequential plug-in universal code** (Section 6.4).

We will see that all these universal codes, while designed in completely different ways, usually achieve almost the same codelengths.

Fast Track   This chapter introduces universal codes, and discusses all general issues surrounding them. Some of these are quite advanced – they are only discussed in this chapter since they can be most easily explained within the simple context of countable models. Thus, for readers that are not familiar with universal coding, only Sections 6.1 and 6.2 are required reading. Concerning the remainder of the chapter, in order to quickly get to read about MDL proper in Part III, it should be sufficient to read the boxes.

6.1   Universal Coding: The Basic Idea

Like many other topics in coding, "universal coding" can best be explained if we think of descriptions as *messages*, an interpretation that was described in Chapter 3, page 83.

Suppose an encoder/sender is about to observe a sequence $x^n \in \mathcal{X}^n$ which he plans to compress as much as possible. Equivalently, he wants to send an encoded version of x^n to the receiver using as few bits as possible. Sender and receiver have a set of *candidate codes* $\mathcal{L}$ for $\mathcal{X}^n$ available.[1] They believe or hope that one of these codes will allow for substantial compression of x^n. However, they must decide on a code for $\mathcal{X}^n$ before sender observes the actual x^n, and they do not know *which* code in $\mathcal{L}$ will lead to good compression of the actual x^n. What is the best thing they can do? They may be tempted to try the following: upon seeing x^n, sender simply encodes/sends x^n using the $L \in \mathcal{L}$ that minimizes $L(x^n)$ among all $L \in \mathcal{L}$. But this naive scheme will not work: since decoder/receiver does not know what x^n has been sent before decoding the message, he or she does not know which of the codes in $\mathcal{L}$ has been used by sender/encoder. Therefore, decoder cannot decode the message: the resulting protocol does not constitute a uniquely decodable, let alone a prefix code. Indeed, as we show below, in general *no* code $\bar{L}$ exists such that for all $x^n \in \mathcal{X}^n$, $\bar{L}(x^n) \leq \min_{L \in \mathcal{L}} L(x^n)$: in words, there exists no code which, no matter what x^n is, always mimics the best code for x^n.

Example 6.1 Suppose we think that our sequence can be reasonably well compressed by a code corresponding to some biased coin model. For simplicity, we restrict ourselves to a finite number of such models. Thus, let

---

1. As explained in the box on page 99, we identify these codes with their length functions, which is the only aspect we are interested in.

$\mathcal{L} = \{L_1, \ldots, L_9\}$ where L_1 is the codelength function corresponding to the Bernoulli distribution P_θ with parameter $\theta = 0.1$, L_2 corresponds to $\theta = 0.2$, and so on. Since $P_\theta(x^n) = \theta^{n_1}(1 - \theta)^{n_0}$ (Example 2.4, page 58), we see that, for example,

$$L_8(x^n) = -\log P_{0.8}(x^n) = -n_0 \log 0.2 - n_1 \log 0.8$$
$$L_9(x^n) = -\log P_{0.9}(x^n) = -n_0 \log 0.1 - n_1 \log 0.9.$$

Both $L_8(x^n)$ and $L_9(x^n)$ are linearly increasing in the number of 1s in x^n. However, if the frequency n_1/n is approximately 0.8, then $\min_{L \in \mathcal{L}} L(x^n)$ will be achieved for L_8. If $n_1/n \approx 0.9$, then $\min_{L \in \mathcal{L}} L(x^n)$ is achieved for L_9. More generally, if $n_1/n \approx j/10$, then L_j achieves the minimum.[2] We would like to send x^n using a code such that for all x^n, we need $\hat{L}(x^n)$ bits. We already gave an informal explanation as to why such a code does not exist. We can now explain this more formally as follows: if such a code were to exist, it would correspond to some distribution P. Then we would have for all x^n, $L(x^n) = -\log P(x^n)$. But, by definition, $L(x^n) \le -\log P_{\hat{\theta}(x^n)}(x^n)$ where $\hat{\theta}(x^n) \in \{0.1, \ldots, 0.9\}$. Thus we get for all x^n, $-\log P(x^n) \le -\log P_{\hat{\theta}(x^n)}(x^n)$ or $P(x^n) \ge P_{\hat{\theta}(x^n)}(x^n)$, so that, since $|\mathcal{L}| > 1$,

$$\sum_{x^n} P(x^n) \ge \sum_{x^n} P_{\hat{\theta}(x^n)}(x^n) = \sum_{x^n} \max_\theta P_\theta(x^n) > 1, \tag{6.1}$$

where the last inequality follows because for any two θ_1, θ_2 with $\theta_1 \ne \theta_2$, there is at least one x^n with $P_{\theta_1}(x^n) > P_{\theta_2}(x^n)$. The argument can be extended beyond the Bernoulli model of the example above; as long as $|\mathcal{L}| > 1$, and all codes in $\mathcal{L}$ correspond to a nondefective distribution, (6.1) must still hold, so that there exists no code $\bar{L}$ with $\bar{L}(x^n) = \min_{L \in \mathcal{L}} L(x^n)$ for all x^n. The underlying reason that no such code exists is the fact that probabilities must sum up to something ≤ 1; or equivalently, that there exists no coding scheme assigning short code words to many different messages.

There exists no code which, no matter what x^n is, always mimics the best code for x^n. Therefore, it may make sense to look for the next best thing: does there exist a code which, for all $x^n \in \mathcal{X}^n$, is "nearly" (in some sense) as

---

2. The reason is that, in the full Bernoulli model with parameter $\theta \in [0, 1]$, the maximum likelihood estimator is given by n_1/n; see Example 2.4 on page 58. Since the likelihood $\log P_\theta(x^n)$ is a continuous function of θ, this implies that if the frequency n_1/n in x^n is approximately (but not precisely) $j/10$, then the ML estimator in the restricted model $\{0.1, \ldots, 0.9\}$ is still given by $\hat{\theta} = j/10$. Then $\log P_\theta(x^n)$ is maximized by $\hat{\theta} = j/10$, so that the $L \in \mathcal{L}$ that minimizes codelength corresponds to $\theta = j/10$.

good as $\hat{L}(x^n)$, where $\hat{L}(x^n)$ is defined as $\hat{L}(x^n) := \min_{L \in \mathcal{L}} L(x^n)$? It turns out that in many cases, the answer is *yes*: there typically exist codes $\bar{L}$ such that no matter what x^n arrives, $\bar{L}(x^n)$ is not much larger than $\hat{L}(x^n)$, which may be viewed as the code that is best "with hindsight" (i.e., after seeing x^n). Intuitively, codes $\bar{L}$ that satisfy this property are called universal codes - a more precise definition follows below. The simplest example of a universal code is the *two-part code* that we have encountered in Chapter 5.

6.1.1   Two-Part Codes as Simple Universal Codes

Example 6.2 [Finite $\mathcal{L}$] Let $\mathcal{L}$ be as in Example 6.1. We can devise a code $\bar{L}_{\text{2-p}}$ for all $x^n \in \mathcal{X}^n$ as follows: to encode x^n, we first encode the $j \in \{1, \ldots, 9\}$ such that $L_j(x^n) = \min_{L \in \mathcal{L}} L(x^n)$ using a uniform code. This takes $\log 9$ bits. We then encode x^n itself using the code indexed by j. This takes $L_j(x^n)$ bits. Thus, for *every possible* $x^n \in \mathcal{X}^n$, we obtain

$$\bar{L}_{\text{2-p}}(x^n) = \min_{L \in \mathcal{L}} L(x^n) + \log 9.$$

For all $L \in \mathcal{L}$, $\min_{x^n} L(x^n)$ grows linearly in n: $\min_{\theta, x^n} - \log P_\theta(x^n) = -n \log 0.9 \approx 0.15n$. Unless n is *very* small, no matter what x^n arises, the number of extra number of bits we need using $\bar{L}_{\text{2-p}}$ compared to $\hat{L}(x^n)$ is negligible.

More generally, let $\mathcal{L} = \{L_1, \ldots, L_M\}$ where M can be arbitrarily large, and the L_j can be any codelength functions we like; they do not necessarily represent Bernoulli distributions anymore. By the reasoning of Example 6.2, there exists a (two-part) code such that for *all* $x^n \in \mathcal{X}^n$,

$$\bar{L}_{\text{2-p}}(x^n) = \min_{L \in \mathcal{L}} L(x^n) + \log M. \qquad (6.2)$$

In most applications $\min L(x^n)$ grows linearly in n, and we see from (6.2) that, as soon as n becomes substantially larger than $\log M$, the relative difference in performance between our universal code and $\hat{L}(x^n)$ becomes negligible.

In the sections and chapters to come, we will also encounter two-part codes for arbitrary countably infinite sets, for parametric models such as the Bernoulli model, which have the cardinality of the continuum and are thus uncountable, and for unions of countably and uncountably infinite sets. For now we ask the reader to be patient, because the finite case is the easiest to explain the general ideas.

6.1.2   From Universal Codes to Universal Models

Instead of postulating a set of candidate codes $\mathcal{L}$, we may equivalently postulate a set $\mathcal{M}$ of candidate probabilistic sources, such that $\mathcal{L}$ is the set of codes corresponding to $\mathcal{M}$. We already implicitly did this in Example 6.1.

The reasoning is now as follows: we think that one of the $P \in \mathcal{M}$ will assign a high likelihood to the data to be observed. Therefore we would like to design a code that, for all x^n we might observe, performs essentially as well as the code corresponding to the best-fitting, maximum likelihood (minimum codelength) $P \in \mathcal{M}$ for x^n. Similarly, we can think of universal codes such as the two-part code in terms of the (possibly defective) *distributions* corresponding to them. Such distributions corresponding to universal codes are called *universal models*. The use of mapping universal codes back to distributions is illustrated by the *Bayesian universal model* which we now introduce.

> **Universal Model: Twice Misleading Terminology** The words "universal" and "model" are somewhat of a misnomer: first, these codes/models are only "universal" relative to a restricted "universe" $\mathcal{M}$. Second, the use of the word model will be very confusing to statisticians, who (as we also do in this book) call a family of distributions such as $\mathcal{M}$ a model. But the phrase originates from information theory, where a model often refers to a single distribution rather than a family. Thus, a universal model is a single distribution, representing a statistical "model" $\mathcal{M}$.

Example 6.3 [Bayesian Universal Model] Let $\mathcal{M}$ be a finite or countable set of probabilistic sources, parameterized by some parameter set Θ. Let W be a distribution on Θ. Adopting terminology from Bayesian statistics (Chapter 2, Section 2.5.2), W is usually called a *prior distribution*. We can construct a new probabilistic source $\bar{P}_{\text{Bayes}}$ by taking a weighted (according to W) average or mixture over the distributions in $\mathcal{M}$. That is, we define for all n, $x^n \in \mathcal{X}$,

$$\bar{P}_{\text{Bayes}}(x^n) := \sum_{\theta \in \Theta} P_\theta(x^n) W(\theta). \tag{6.3}$$

It is easy to check that $\bar{P}_{\text{Bayes}}$ is a probabilistic source according to our definition. In Bayesian statistics, $\bar{P}_{\text{Bayes}}$ is called the *Bayesian marginal likelihood* or *Bayesian mixture* (Bernardo and Smith 1994).

Second Example of a Universal Code/Model: The Bayesian Mixture
It is easy to see that $\bar{P}_{\text{Bayes}}$ is a universal model in the following sense: for all $\theta_0 \in \Theta$,

$$-\log \bar{P}_{\text{Bayes}}(x^n) := -\log \sum_{\theta \in \Theta} P_\theta(x^n) W(\theta) \leq -\log P_{\theta_0}(x^n) + c_{\theta_0} \quad (6.4)$$

where the inequality follows because a sum is at least as large as each of its terms, and $c_\theta = -\log W(\theta)$ depends on θ but not on n. Thus, the Bayesian mixture $\bar{P}_{\text{Bayes}}$ is a universal model or, equivalently, the code with lengths $-\log \bar{P}_{\text{Bayes}}$ is a universal code.
Variations of the derivation (6.4) will occur over and over again in this chapter and the next.

Example 6.4 [Bayes Is Better Than Two-Part] The Bayesian model is in a sense superior to the two-part code. Namely, in the two-part code we first encode an element of $\mathcal{M}$ or its parameter set Θ using some code L_0. Such a code must correspond to some "prior" distribution W on $\mathcal{M}$ so that the two-part code gives codelengths

$$\bar{L}_{\text{2-p}}(x^n) = \min_{\theta \in \Theta} -\log P_\theta(x^n) - \log W(\theta), \quad (6.5)$$

where W depends on the specific code L_0 that was used. Using the Bayes code with prior W, we get as in (6.4),

$$-\log \bar{P}_{\text{Bayes}}(x^n) = -\log \sum_{\theta \in \Theta} P_\theta(x^n) W(\theta) \leq \min_{\theta \in \Theta} -\log P_\theta(x^n) - \log W(\theta).$$

The inequality becomes strict whenever $P_\theta(x^n) > 0$ for more than one value of θ. Comparing to (6.5), we see that in general the Bayesian code is preferable over the two-part code: for all x^n it never assigns codelengths larger than $\bar{L}_{\text{2-p}}(x^n)$, and in many cases it assigns strictly shorter codelengths for some x^n.

This example raises two important issues: (1) What exactly do we mean by "better" anyway? (2) Can we say that "some prior distributions are better than others?" (3) Are there types of universal models that are even "better than Bayes?" In order to answer these questions, we first need a formal definition of universal models. This is given in the section below.

6.1.3   Formal Definition of Universality

Let $\bar{P}$ and P be two distributions on $\mathcal{X}^n$. Suppose we try to encode a sequence $x^n \in \mathcal{X}^n$ based on $\bar{P}$, and compare the number of bits we need with how well we would have done if we had used P. The difference may be called the excess codelength or *redundancy*[3] – note that it may be negative:

$$\mathrm{RED}(\bar{P}, P, x^n) := -\log \bar{P}(x^n) - [-\log P(x^n)]. \tag{6.6}$$

We may now consider the worst-case redundancy of $\bar{P}$ over P, over all possible sequences of length n:

$$\mathrm{RED}_{\max}(\bar{P}, P) := \max_{x^n \in \mathcal{X}^n} \mathrm{RED}(\bar{P}, P, x_n). \tag{6.7}$$

If P is nondefective (sums to 1 over x^n) and unequal to $\bar{P}$, then there must be a sequence with $\bar{P}(x^n) < P(x^n)$. Therefore, $\mathrm{RED}_{\max}(\bar{P}, P) > 0$; in some cases this quantity may even be infinite. Informally, we call a distribution $\bar{P}$ universal relative to $\mathcal{M}$ if for all $P \in \mathcal{M}$, $\mathrm{RED}_{\max}(\bar{P}, P)$ either grows slowly with n or becomes negative as n increases. Since we worked with $\bar{P}$ and P that were distributions on $\mathcal{X}^n$, it is not clear what we mean by "as n increases." To make the statement meaningful, we define a universal model as a *sequence* of distributions $\bar{P}^{(1)}, \bar{P}^{(2)}, \ldots$ on $\mathcal{X}^1, \mathcal{X}^2, \ldots$ respectively. Thus, the encoder may choose to use different codes for different n. This means that we assume that n is known in advance to encoder and decoder.[4] The consequences of this assumption and a stricter definition of universality which does not involve prior knowledge of n, is given in Section 6.4.

Here is the formal definition:

---

3. This is a slightly nonstandard use of the technical term "redundancy." See Section 6.5.
4. In an MDL model selection context, we can also think of such codes as being the second stage in a coding process where in the first stage, the number n is encoded separately; see Chapter 14, in particular the box on page 439.

Universal Models: Basic Definition

Let $\mathcal{M}$ be a family of probabilistic sources. A universal model relative to $\mathcal{M}$ is a sequence of distributions $\bar{P}^{(1)}, \bar{P}^{(2)}, \ldots$ on $\mathcal{X}^1, \mathcal{X}^2, \ldots$ respectively, such that for all $P \in \mathcal{M}$, the redundancy per outcome converges to 0. That is, for all $P \in \mathcal{M}$, for all $\epsilon > 0$, for all large enough n larger than some n_0 (which may depend on ϵ),

$$\tfrac{1}{n}\mathrm{RED}_{\max}(\bar{P}^{(n)}, P) \leq \epsilon \text{ or equivalently}$$
$$\max_{x^n \in \mathcal{X}^n} \left\{ -\log \bar{P}^{(n)}(x^n) - [-\log P(x^n)] \right\} \leq n\epsilon \qquad (6.8)$$

What we call a "universal model" is often called a "universal model in the individual-sequence sense" by other authors. When such authors write "universal model" without further qualification, they refer to what we call a "universal model in the expected sense"; see Section 6.5.

We see that $\bar{P}$ is universal if for every $P \in \mathcal{M}$, the codelength difference $-\log \bar{P}(x^n) + \log P(x^n)$ increases sublinearly in n. At this point, our definition may seem much too weak: if $\mathcal{M}$ is finite, then the two-part and Bayes distributions are universal in a much stronger sense: rather than just increasing sublinearly, the codelength difference is bounded by a constant. The weak definition becomes useful if we move to statistical models with uncountably many elements such as the Bernoulli model. Still, we do reserve a separate name for universal models with excess codelength bounded by some c for all n. These are the *c-uniformly universal models*, defined in the next section. There we will analyze the precise way in which one universal model can be "better" or "worse" than another, as long as the model $\mathcal{M}$ is finite. The case of countably infinite models is treated in Section 6.3. The case of parametric (uncountable) models and general, "nonparametric" models is treated in the following chapters.

6.2   The Finite Case

Unfortunately, at this point our analysis of universal codes requires several new definitions and much new terminology. These new concepts, however, are essential and will be used frequently in the remainder of this chapter as well as the following chapters.

6.2.1   Minimax Regret and Normalized ML

In the previous section we introduced the notion of redundancy RED. Redundancy stands at the root of all methods of measuring the performance of universal codes relative to a set of sources $\mathcal{M}$. In the case of finite and sufficiently simple parametric $\mathcal{M}$, it is useful to take a doubly worst-case approach, where we say a universal code is good if it achieves (uniformly) small redundancy on *all* sequences x^n compared to the *best* $P \in \mathcal{M}$ for that sequence. This is formalized as the regret. We start this section by defining regret and relating it to redundancy:

Definition 6.1 [Regret] Let $\mathcal{M}$ be a class of probabilistic sources. Let $\bar{P}$ be a probability distribution on $\mathcal{X}^n$ ($\bar{P}$ is not necessarily in $\mathcal{M}$). For given x^n, the *regret* of $\bar{P}$ relative to $\mathcal{M}$ is defined as

$$\text{REG}(\bar{P}, \mathcal{M}, x^n) := -\log \bar{P}(x^n) - \inf_{P \in \mathcal{M}} \{-\log P(x^n)\}. \tag{6.9}$$

The Regret
The regret of $\bar{P}$ relative to $\mathcal{M}$ for x^n is the additional number of bits needed to encode x^n using the code/distribution $\bar{P}$, as compared to the number of bits that had been needed if we had used the code/distribution in $\mathcal{M}$ that was *optimal ("best-fitting") with hindsight*.

For simplicity, in the remainder of this chapter, unless stated otherwise, we assume that for all models $\mathcal{M}$ under consideration, there is a single $\hat{\theta}(x^n)$ maximizing the likelihood for every $x^n \in \mathcal{X}^n$. In that case (6.9) simplifies to

$$\text{REG}(\bar{P}, \mathcal{M}, x^n) = \text{RED}(\bar{P}^{(n)}, P_{\hat{\theta}(x^n)}, x^n) =$$
$$-\log \bar{P}(x^n) - \{-\log P_{\hat{\theta}(x^n)}(x^n)\}. \tag{6.10}$$

Let $\bar{P}^{(1)}, \bar{P}^{(2)}, \ldots$ be a universal model. We fix some sample size n; whenever n is clear from the context, we will write $\bar{P}$ rather than $\bar{P}^{(n)}$ below. We would like to measure the quality of $\bar{P}$ as a universal model at sample size n in terms of its regret. However, $\bar{P}$ may have small (even negative) regret for some x^n, and very large regret for other x^n. We must somehow find a measure of quality that takes into account *all* $x^n \in \mathcal{X}^n$. We take a worst-case approach, and look for universal models $\bar{P}$ with small *worst-case* regret, where the worst case is over all sequences. Formally, the *maximum* or *worst-case regret* of $\bar{P}$ relative to $\mathcal{M}$ is defined as

$$\text{REG}_{\max}^{(n)}(\bar{P}, \mathcal{M}) := \max_{x^n \in \mathcal{X}^n} \left\{ -\log \bar{P}(x^n) - \{ -\log P_{\hat{\theta}(x^n)}(x^n) \} \right\} =$$

$$\max_{x^n \in \mathcal{X}^n} \text{RED}(\bar{P}, P_{\hat{\theta}}(x^n), x^n). \quad (6.11)$$

The Minimax Optimal Universal Model   If we use $\text{REG}_{\max}$ as our quality measure, then the optimal universal model relative to $\mathcal{M}$, for given sample size n, is the distribution achieving the *minimax regret*:

$$\min_{\bar{P}} \text{REG}_{\max}^{(n)}(\bar{P}, \mathcal{M}) =$$

$$\min_{\bar{P}} \max_{x^n \in \mathcal{X}^n} \left\{ -\log \bar{P}(x^n) - \{ -\log P_{\hat{\theta}(x^n)}(x^n) \} \right\}, \quad (6.12)$$

where the minimum is over *all* distributions on $\mathcal{X}^n$. The $\bar{P}$ minimizing (6.12) corresponds to the code minimizing the maximum regret, i.e. the additional number of bits compared to the code in $\mathcal{M}$ that is best in hindsight – in the worst case over all possible x^n. It turns out that we can find an elegant expression for the $\bar{P}$ achieving (6.12). To this end, we first define the *complexity* of a given model $\mathcal{M}$ as

$$\text{COMP}^{(n)}(\mathcal{M}) := \log \sum_{x^n \in \mathcal{X}^n} P_{\hat{\theta}(x^n)}(x^n). \quad (6.13)$$

The definition can be trivially generalized to cases where the ML estimator is not defined for some x^n, by setting

$$\text{COMP}^{(n)}(\mathcal{M}) := \log \sum_{x^n \in \mathcal{X}^n} \sup_{P \in \mathcal{M}} P(x^n). \quad (6.14)$$

$\text{COMP}^{(n)}(\mathcal{M})$ plays an important role in refined MDL model selection (Chapter 14). It is treated in much more detail in Chapter 7. To get a first idea of why $\text{COMP}^{(n)}$ is called model complexity, note that the more sequences x^n with large $P_{\hat{\theta}(x^n)}(x^n)$, the larger $\text{COMP}^{(n)}(\mathcal{M})$. In other words, the more sequences that can be fit well by an element of $\mathcal{M}$, that is, the "richer" $\mathcal{M}$, the larger $\mathcal{M}$'s complexity. If $\text{COMP}^{(n)}(\mathcal{M})$ is finite, then a $\bar{P}$ achieving (6.12) exists:

Third Example of a Universal Code: The Shtarkov or NML Code

Suppose that $\mathrm{COMP}^{(n)}(\mathcal{M})$ is finite. As demonstrated below, the minimax regret (6.12) is uniquely achieved for the distribution $\bar{P}_{\mathrm{nml}}^{(n)}$ on $\mathcal{X}^n$ given by

$$\bar{P}_{\mathrm{nml}}^{(n)}(x^n) := \frac{P_{\hat{\theta}(x^n)}(x^n)}{\sum_{x^n \in \mathcal{X}^n} P_{\hat{\theta}(x^n)}(x^n)}. \tag{6.15}$$

If $\hat{\theta}(x^n)$ is not defined for all x^n, we can generalize the definition analogously to (6.14).

$\bar{P}_{\mathrm{nml}}^{(n)}$ is an *equalizer strategy* (Ferguson 1967): it achieves the *same* regret on every sequence $x^n \in \mathcal{X}^n$. This regret is equal to $\mathrm{COMP}^{(n)}(\mathcal{M})$: *the minimax regret is equal to the model complexity.*

The distribution $\bar{P}_{\mathrm{nml}}^{(n)}$, introduced by Shtarkov (1987), is also known as the *Shtarkov distribution* or the *normalized maximum likelihood* (NML) distribution. The sequence of distributions $\bar{P}_{\mathrm{nml}}^{(1)}, \bar{P}_{\mathrm{nml}}^{(2)}, \ldots$ constitutes the *minimax optimal universal model* relative to $\mathcal{M}$.

To see that $\bar{P}_{\mathrm{nml}}$ achieves the minimax regret, we first show that it achieves the same regret, equal to $\mathrm{COMP}^{(n)}(\mathcal{M})$, *no matter what x^n actually obtains*. To see this, plug in $\bar{P}_{\mathrm{nml}}$ in (6.12) and notice that for all $x^n \in \mathcal{X}^n$,

$$- \log \bar{P}_{\mathrm{nml}}(x^n) - \{ - \log P_{\hat{\theta}(x^n)}(x^n) \} = \mathrm{REG}_{\max}^{(n)}(\bar{P}_{\mathrm{nml}}, \mathcal{M}) =$$
$$\mathrm{COMP}^{(n)}(\mathcal{M}). \quad (6.16)$$

Since clearly every distribution P on $\mathcal{X}^n$ with $P \neq \bar{P}_{\mathrm{nml}}$ must satisfy $P(z^n) < \bar{P}_{\mathrm{nml}}(z^n)$ for at least one $z^n \in \mathcal{X}^n$, it follows that for every $P \neq \bar{P}_{\mathrm{nml}}$,

$$\mathrm{REG}_{\max}^{(n)}(P, \mathcal{M}) \geq - \log P(z^n) + \log P_{\hat{\theta}(z^n)}(z^n) >$$
$$- \log \bar{P}_{\mathrm{nml}}(z^n) + \log P_{\hat{\theta}(z^n)}(z^n) = \mathrm{REG}_{\max}^{(n)}(\bar{P}_{\mathrm{nml}}, \mathcal{M}). \quad (6.17)$$

It follows that $\bar{P}_{\mathrm{nml}}^{(n)}$ achieves the minimax regret, and that this regret is equal to $\mathrm{COMP}^{(n)}(\mathcal{M})$. Since the core of this reasoning will reappear several times in later chapters, most notably Chapter 11 and Chapter 12, we repeat it here:

Equalizer Strategies and Minimax Regret

The fact that $\bar{P}_{\text{nml}}^{(n)}$ achieves the minimax regret follows directly from the fact that it achieves the same regret on all sequences.

$\bar{P}_{\text{nml}}$ is quite literally a "normalized maximum likelihood" distribution: it tries to assign to each x^n the probability of x^n according to the ML distribution for x^n. By (6.1), this is not possible: the resulting "probabilities" add to something larger than 1. But we can normalize these "probabilities" by dividing by their sum $\sum_{y^n \in \mathcal{X}^n} P_{\hat{\theta}(y^n)}(y^n)$, and then we obtain a probability distribution on $\mathcal{X}^n$ after all.

6.2.2   NML vs. Two-Part vs. Bayes

Let $\mathcal{M}$ be a finite model containing M distinct distributions with parameter set $\Theta = \{\theta_1, \ldots, \theta_M\}$. We can rewrite the sum in the model complexity $\text{COMP}^{(n)}(\mathcal{M}) = \log \sum P_{\hat{\theta}(x^n)}(x^n)$ as follows:

$$\sum_{x^n \in \mathcal{X}^n} P_{\hat{\theta}(x^n)}(x^n) = \sum_{j=1..M} \sum_{x^n : \hat{\theta}(x^n) = \theta_j} P_{\theta_j}(x^n) =$$

$$\sum_{j=1..M} \left(1 - \sum_{x^n : \hat{\theta}(x^n) \neq \theta_j} P_{\theta_j}(x^n) \right) = M - \sum_j P_{\theta_j}(\hat{\theta}(x^n) \neq \theta_j). \quad (6.18)$$

We may think of $P_{\theta_j}(\hat{\theta}(x^n) \neq \theta_j)$ as the probability, according to θ_j, that the data look as if they come from some $\theta \neq \theta_j$. Thus, it is the probability that θ_j is *mistaken* for another distribution in Θ. Therefore, for finite $\mathcal{M}$, the model complexity is the logarithm of the *number of models minus the summed probability that some θ_j is "mistaken" for some $\theta \neq \theta_j$*. Now suppose $\mathcal{M}$ is i.i.d. By the law of large numbers (Chapter 2), we immediately see that the "sum of mistake probabilities" $\sum_j P_{\theta_j}(\hat{\theta}(x^n) \neq \theta_j)$ tends to 0 as n grows. By using the Chernoff/Hoeffding bounds (Chapter 19) one can even show that the sum converges to 0 exponentially fast. It follows that as n tends to infinity, the model complexity converges to $\log M$. In other words, for large n, the distributions in $\mathcal{M}$ are "perfectly distinguishable" (the probability that a sample coming from one is more representative of another is negligible), and then the model complexity $\text{COMP}^{(n)}(\mathcal{M})$ of $\mathcal{M}$ is simply the log of the number of distributions in $\mathcal{M}$.

Example 6.5 [Distinguishability: NML vs. Two-Part] We have implicitly shown that for finite i.i.d. $\mathcal{M}$, the two-part code with uniform prior W on $\mathcal{M}$ is asymptotically minimax optimal: for all n, all x^n, the regret of the two-part code is $\log M$ (6.2), whereas we just showed that as $n \to \infty$, $\mathrm{REG}_{\max}^{(n)}(\bar{P}_{\mathrm{nml}}, \mathcal{M}) = \mathrm{COMP}^{(n)}(\mathcal{M}) \to \log M$. However, for small n, some distributions in $\mathcal{M}$ may be mistaken for one another; the number of "*distinguishable*" distributions in $\mathcal{M}$ is then smaller than the actual number of distributions, and this is reflected in $\mathrm{COMP}^{(n)}(\mathcal{M})$ being (sometimes much) smaller than $\log M$. This notion of distinguishability will be formalized for parametric models in Chapter 7, Section 7.3.4.

Example 6.6 [NML vs. Bayes] From Example 6.4 we know that, for all sequences $x^n \in \mathcal{X}^n$, Bayes with prior W has regret smaller than or equal to the regret of the two-part code with prior W. From Example 6.5 it thus follows that the worst-case regret of the Bayesian universal model with uniform prior must lie somewhere inbetween that of the two-part code and the NML code, and if $\mathcal{M}$ consists of M distinct i.i.d. distributions, then this worst-case regret must be asymptotically equal to $\log M$ as well.

If $\mathcal{M}$ is finite, then the NML, Bayes, and two-part universal models are all $O(1)$-uniformly universal, as long as the prior in the Bayes and two-part models is nowhere 0. This means the following:

Uniformly Universal Models

Let $f : \mathbb{N} \to [0, \infty)$ be a nondecreasing function. We call the universal model $\bar{P}^{(1)}, \bar{P}^{(2)}, \ldots$ $f(n)$-*uniformly universal* if for all n, $\mathrm{REG}_{\max}^{(n)}(\bar{P}, \mathcal{M}) \le f(n)$, i.e. if for all $P \in \mathcal{M}$, all n, all $x^n \in \mathcal{X}^n$,

$$-\log \bar{P}^{(n)}(x^n) - [-\log P(x^n)] \le f(n). \qquad (6.19)$$

Let c_{nml} be the smallest constant such that the NML universal model is c_{nml}-uniformly universal; let c_{Bayes} and $c_{\text{2-p}}$ be defined analogously, where the corresponding codes are defined with respect to the uniform prior. If $\mathcal{M}$ consists of M distinct i.i.d. sources, then Examples 6.5 and 6.6 show that

$$\lim_{n \to \infty} \mathrm{COMP}^{(n)}(\mathcal{M}) = c_{\mathrm{nml}} = c_{\mathrm{Bayes}} = c_{\text{2-p}} = \log M.$$

In contrast, if $\mathcal{M}$ is countably infinite, then the sum in $\mathrm{COMP}^{(n)}(\mathcal{M})$ will in many cases be infinite and then the NML distribution is undefined. In that case, there exists *no* universal model achieving constant regret as in (6.16). We now consider this countably infinite case in more detail.

6.3 The Countably Infinite Case

In this section we consider universal models defined relative to countably infinite sets of distributions $\mathcal{M}$. On the one hand, "countably infinite" may seem intuitively "small," which might suggest that the analysis is not very different from the finite case. For example, even the lowly Bernoulli model $\mathcal{B}^{(1)}$ is in one-to-one correspondence with the unit interval $[0,1]$ and therefore uncountably large. On the other hand, the countable sets include intuitively very "large" sets such as the *set $\mathcal{B}_{\mathbb{Q}}$ of all Markov distributions of each order with rational-valued parameters*, which we will use as our running example. Another even larger countable set is the *set of all computable distributions*. Here "computable" means "implementable by a computer program written in a standard language" (see Chapter 1). This latter set is so large that it presumably contains every distribution that humans or computers will ever use to make probabilistic predictions in practice! Thus, countably infinite models can, in a sense, be very large and therefore, their analysis is substantially different from the finite case after all. In general, the notion of regret, while still well defined, is no longer useful, whereas in many cases the minimax regret $\mathrm{COMP}^{(n)}$ is even undefined.

Below we first consider the two-part and Bayesian universal codes for countably infinite $\mathcal{M}$, and we discuss why for general countably infinite $\mathcal{M}$, the NML code is no longer universal nor even well-defined.

6.3.1 The Two-Part and Bayesian Codes

Extensions of the two-part and Bayesian codes to countably infinite $\mathcal{M}$ are entirely straightforward. Formally, let $\mathcal{M} = \{P_1, P_2, P_3 \ldots\}$ be a countably infinite set of probabilistic sources. Note that we can write $\mathcal{M} = \{P_\theta \mid \theta \in \Theta\}$, where $\Theta = \mathbb{N}$. Let W be a prior distribution on Θ. Using the code corresponding to W, we need $L(k) := -\log W(k)$ bits to encode integer k. We then encode x^n using the code $L(\cdot \mid k) := -\log P_k(\cdot)$ corresponding to P_k. $\bar{L}_{\text{2-p}}$ is now defined as the code we get if, for any x^n, we encode x^n using the L_k minimizing the total two-part description length $-\log W(k) + L(x^n \mid k)$.

In contrast to the case of finite $\mathcal{M}$, in general there does *not* exist a constant c any more such that for all $n, x^n \in \mathcal{X}^n$, $\bar{L}_{\text{2-p}}(x^n) \leq \inf_{k \in \mathbb{N}} L(x^n \mid k) + c$. Instead we have the following weaker, but still remarkable property: for all

k, all n, all x^n, $\bar{L}_{2\text{-p}}(x^n) \leq L(x^n \mid k) - \log W(k)$, so that also,

$$\bar{L}_{2\text{-p}}(x^n) \leq \inf_{k \in \mathbb{N}} \{L(x^n \mid k) + L(k)\}. \tag{6.20}$$

For any k, as n grows larger, the code $\bar{L}_{2\text{-p}}$ starts to mimic the code corresponding to the $P \in \{P_1, \ldots, P_k\}$ that compresses the data most. However, the larger k, the larger n has to be before this happens. We call this property "nonuniform" universality, since the additional number of bits needed compared to any P_k, although finite, depends on k, and is thus not uniform in k.

The notion of nonuniform universality is made precise in the box on the next page. Its importance can best be seen from an example:

Example 6.7 In Chapter 2, Example 2.7, we introduced the model class $\mathcal{B}$ of all Markov models of each order. Let us now consider the subclass $\mathcal{B}_{\mathbb{Q}}$ of all Markov models with rational-valued parameters. This is a countable set. Indeed, we can design a code L_1 for encoding an arbitrary $P \in \mathcal{B}_{\mathbb{Q}}$ as follows. First we encode the order K of P using the standard code for the integers. Next we encode the 2^K parameters $\theta_1, \ldots, \theta_{2^K}$ (here we deviate slightly from our notation in Example 2.7). Since we assume each parameter $\theta_j = p_j/q_j$ to be rational, we can encode each of them by encoding two natural numbers q_j and $p_j \leq q_j$. We encode q_j once again using the universal code for the integers, and then p_j using the uniform code with $\log q_j$ bits, where we use the fact that $p_j \leq q_j$ and ignore rounding. In this way, P is encoded using

$$L_1(P) = L_{\mathbb{N}}(K) + \sum_{j=1}^{2^K} (L_{\mathbb{N}}(q_j) + \log q_j).$$

We can now encode a sequence x^n by first encoding a Markov chain P, and then coding x^n using the code based on P. If we always pick the P that minimizes the total two-part codelength, we get

$$\bar{L}_{2\text{-p}}(x^n) = \inf_{P \in \mathcal{B}_{\mathbb{Q}}} \{-\log P(x^n) + L_1(P)\}. \tag{6.21}$$

Since the elements of $\mathcal{B}_{\mathbb{Q}}$ can be enumerated, this is an instance of (6.20). We see that for every *fixed* Markov chain $P \in \mathcal{B}_{\mathbb{Q}}$, the codelength we need is within $O(1)$ of the codelength needed using the code corresponding to P. However, x^n may be such that the order of the P chosen in (6.21) keeps increasing with n. In that case, for the *chosen* (rather than fixed) P, $L_1(P)$ may keep increasing with n. Thus, this notion of universality is considerably weaker than the uniform universality we encountered in the previous section. We develop a method for quantifying this 'nonuniform' universality in the box below.

In fact, the two-part MDL code for the Markov chains developed in Chapter 5 was closely related to the code we just introduced, the only essential difference being that in Chapter 5, we restricted the set of code words in the first part of the code to Markov chains whose parameters can be expressed with a finite precision in a binary expansion.

Nonuniform Universal Models

Let $\{\bar{P}^{(i)}\}_{i=1,2,\ldots}$ be a universal model relative to $\mathcal{M}$. Let $f : \mathbb{N} \to [0, \infty)$ be a nondecreasing function.

We call $\{\bar{P}^{(i)}\}_{i=1,2,\ldots}$ $f(n) + O(g(n))$-*universal* if for all $P \in \mathcal{M}$, for all n, $\mathrm{RED}_{\max}^{(n)}(\bar{P}^{(n)}, P) \leq f(n) + O(g(n))$, i.e.

$$\max_{x^n \in \mathcal{X}^n} \left\{ -\log \bar{P}^{(n)}(x^n) - [-\log P(x^n)] \right\} \leq f(n) + O(g(n)). \tag{6.22}$$

The constant hidden in the O-notation is allowed to depend on the distribution P.

We note that the terminology "$f(n) + O(g(n))$-(non-)uniform universal model" is not standard.

If we are not interested in the values of the constants, then we can re-express the difference between uniform and nonuniform universality in terms of the order of the quantifiers: it follows from the definitions above that a universal model $\bar{P}$ is $O(f(n))$-*uniformly universal* iff

there is a $C > 0$ such that for all $P \in \mathcal{M}$, $\mathrm{RED}_{\max}^{(n)}(\bar{P}^{(n)}, P) \leq Cf(n)$,

whereas $\bar{P}$ is already $O(f(n))$-*universal* if

for all $P \in \mathcal{M}$, there is a $C > 0$ such that $\mathrm{RED}_{\max}^{(n)}(\bar{P}^{(n)}, P) \leq Cf(n)$.

Example 6.8 ["Universal" Prior for the Integers] For the $L(k)$ in the code described above, we could have used $L(k) = L_{\mathbb{N}}(k)$, the standard code for the integers. We have $L_{\mathbb{N}}(k) = -\log W(k)$, where W is the "universal" prior on the integers (Chapter 3, Section 3.2.3). This prior is indeed a universal model relative to the sample space $\mathcal{X} = \mathbb{N}$ and the model $\mathcal{M}$ of *all* distributions on $\mathbb{N}$, but here a slightly different definition of "universality" is used - one tailored to single outcomes, rather than sequences of outcomes (Li and Vitányi 1997, Section 1.5.3). To see why universal prior would be an appropriate name, note that for any distribution P on $\mathbb{N}$, for all x, $L_{\mathbb{N}}(x) \leq -\log P(x) + O(\log x)$: the number of additional bits needed to encode outcome x increases only slowly with x. We will not go into this alternative notion of universality any further in this book.

In Chapter 3, we called the code with lengths $L_{\mathbb{N}}(k)$ a "quasi-uniform" code. Indeed, there is a strong relation between quasi-uniform codes and nonuniform universal models, as explained in the box below.

(Quasi-) Uniform Codes and (Non-) Uniform Two-Part Universal Codes

If the first part of a two-part code is a uniform code, the resulting two-part code must be a uniform universal code. If the first part of a two-part code is a quasi-uniform code and the model $\mathcal{M}$ is countable, then the resulting two-part code is a universal code that in many cases will be nonuniform.

Bayesian Code   The relation between the two-part and the Bayesian code for countably infinite $\mathcal{M}$ is the same as for finite $\mathcal{M}$, as discussed in Section 6.1.2. For a general prior W, we can construct the Bayesian mixture code as in (6.3). This code will then be universal by (6.4). Just as for the finite case, we can say that for any fixed prior W, the Bayesian code relative to that prior is uniformly better than the two-part code, since by (6.4), $\bar{L}_{\text{Bayes}}(x^n) \leq \bar{L}_{\text{2-p}}(x^n)$ for all $x^n \in \mathcal{X}^n$, with typically strict inequality for some x^n.

6.3.2 The NML Code

In general, the NML code with respect to countable $\mathcal{M}$ is not universal any more. This is shown in Example 6.9. In case $\mathcal{X}$ is itself infinite, the NML code may even be undefined, as shown in Example 6.11. Nevertheless, there do exist countably infinite $\mathcal{M}$ for which the NML code *is* defined and *is* universal (Example 6.10).

Example 6.9   Let $\mathcal{B}_{\mathbb{Q}}$ be the set of all Markov chain distributions of each order with rational-valued parameters. On page 134 we heuristically showed that, if $X_1, \ldots, X_n$ are i.i.d. according to the fair coin distribution $P_{0.5}$, and n is even, then with probability at least $1 - n^2 2^{-n/2}$, there exists a $P' \in \mathcal{B}_{\mathbb{Q}}$ of order $n/2$ such that $P'(X^n) = 2^{-n/2}$. Since all 2^n sequences of length n have the same probability under $P_{0.5}$, it follows that for at least $2^n - n^2 2^{n/2}$ sequences x^n, there exists a P' of order $n/2$ such that $P'(x^n) = 2^{-n/2}$. Then

$$
\mathrm{COMP}^{(n)}(\mathcal{M}) =
$$
$$
\log \sum_{x^n \in \{0,1\}^n} \max_{P \in \mathcal{M}} P(x^n) \geq \log \left(\left(2^n - n^2 2^{n/2} \right) 2^{-n/2} \right) = \frac{n}{2} + o(1).
$$

Therefore, if we choose to encode x^n based on the NML code relative to $\mathcal{M}$, the number of additional bits we need compared to an arbitrary $P \in \mathcal{M}$ grows on the order of n. Thus, the NML code is not universal according to the definition in the box on page 178. The rational-valued Markov model class is simply too large for the minimax optimal model to be of any use! Thus, if we are interested in universal coding with respect to $\mathcal{B}_{\mathbb{Q}}$, we cannot use the NML code, and should use a (universal) Bayesian or two-part code instead.

Example 6.10 [Rational Bernoulli] Let $\mathcal{B}_{\mathbb{Q}}^{(1)}$ be the set of Bernoulli distributions with rational-valued parameter. Since for any x^n, the ordinary Bernoulli ML estimate $\hat{\theta}(x^n)$ is rational-valued, in this case we have

$$
\max_{P \in \mathcal{B}_{\mathbb{Q}}^{(1)}} P(x^n) = \max_{P \in \mathcal{B}^{(1)}} P(x^n) = \hat{\theta}(x^n)^{n_1} (1 - \hat{\theta}(x^n))^{n-n_1},
$$

where n_1 is the number of 1s appearing in x^n. It follows that in this case,

$$
\mathrm{COMP}^{(n)}(\mathcal{B}_{\mathbb{Q}}^{(1)}) = \log \sum_{x^n \in \{0,1\}^n} \hat{\theta}(x^n)^{n_1} (1 - \hat{\theta}(x^n))^{n-n_1} =
$$
$$
\log \sum_{m \in \{0,1,\ldots,n\}} \binom{n}{m} \left(\frac{m}{n} \right)^m \left(\frac{n-m}{n} \right)^{n-m}. \qquad (6.23)
$$

In Chapter 7, Example 7.4, we show that this evaluates to

$$
\mathrm{COMP}^{(n)}(\mathcal{B}_{\mathbb{Q}}^{(n)}) = \frac{1}{2} \log n + O(1), \qquad (6.24)
$$

and we also calculate the $O(1)$-term. Note that by (6.24), according to the definition in the box on page 178, the NML code is uniformly universal for the rational Bernoulli model. More precisely, it is $(1/2) \log n + O(1)$- uniformly universal. It is also $O(1)$-universal, but it is not $O(1)$-uniformly universal. Apparently, the rational Bernoulli model is still simple enough to be uniformly universal, but, while finite for each n, the worst-case regret increases with the sample size n.

To get an initial idea of why the regret should increase as $O(\log n)$, note that in Example 6.7, we already gave a simple two-part recipe to encode x^n that achieves a uniform regret of $O(\log n)$. It follows that $\text{COMP}^{(n)}(\mathcal{B}_{\mathbb{Q}}^{(n)})$ must be $O(\log n)$. In the next chapter we shall see that by cleverly discretizing the parameters, we achieve a two-part code that achieves $1/2 \log n + O(1)$, and that this is the best that can be achieved by a two-part code. The NML code leads to a slightly smaller $O(1)$-term than the two-part code, but the log-term remains.

Example 6.11 [Rational Poisson; Infinite Complexity] Let $\mathcal{X} = \{0, 1, \ldots\}$, and let $\mathcal{M}_{\mathbb{Q}} = \{P_\theta \mid \theta \geq 0\}$ be the family of Poisson distributions on $\mathcal{X}$, given by $P_\theta(x) = \theta^x e^{-\theta}/x!$. An easy calculation shows that the ML estimator is the empirical average: $\hat{\theta}(x^n) = n^{-1} \sum_{i=1}^n x_i$.

Let us compute $\text{COMP}^{(1)}(\mathcal{M}_{\mathbb{Q}})$:

$$\text{COMP}^{(1)}(\mathcal{M}_{\mathbb{Q}}) = \log \sum_{x=0}^{\infty} P_{\hat{\theta}(x)}(x) = \log \sum \frac{e^{-x} x^x}{x!} = \infty.$$

To see that the last equation holds, apply Stirling's approximation (4.33) on page 128 to the denominator of each term. We see that for large x, the terms in the sum converge to $(2\pi x)^{-1/2}$, so that the series is divergent.

It is easy to show that for any i.i.d. model $\mathcal{M}$, $\text{COMP}^{(n)}(\mathcal{M})$ is nondecreasing in n:

$$\text{COMP}^{(n)}(\mathcal{M}) = \ln \sum_{x^n \in \mathcal{X}^n} P_{\hat{\theta}(x^n)}(x^n) \geq$$

$$\ln \sum_{x^{n-1}} \sum_{x_n \in \mathcal{X}} P_{\hat{\theta}(x^{n-1})}(x^{n-1}, x_n) = \ln \sum_{x^{n-1} \in \mathcal{X}^{n-1}} P_{\hat{\theta}(x^{n-1})}(x^{n-1}) =$$

$$\text{COMP}^{(n-1)}(\mathcal{M}). \quad (6.25)$$

It follows that for all n, the complexity of the Poisson model is infinite. Therefore, for all $n \geq 1$, the NML distribution $\bar{P}_{\text{nml}}^{(1)}$ relative to the Poisson family is ill-defined, the reason being that the denominator in (6.15) is undefined.

This completes our discussion of two-part, Bayesian, and NML codes for countably infinite models.

6.4   Prequential Universal Models

There are two major types of universal models/codes: those that can be interpreted as *sequential prediction strategies for sequences of arbitrary length horizon*,
and those that cannot. Universal codes with a predictive–sequential interpretation for arbitrary length sequences are often simply called "predictive" or
"on-line" codes. In this book, we call them *prequential* (predictive-sequential),
emphasizing the sequential aspect of the predictions. The term "prequential"
is due to A.P. Dawid (1984), who introduced it in the context of his general
theory of *prequential probability and statistics*; see Section 17.5, Chapter 17.

Among the three types of universal codes we have seen, two-part, NML,
and Bayes, only the Bayesian universal code is predictive. There is one other
major type of predictive universal model, the *prequential plug-in model*.

In this section we first introduce the predictive interpretation of probability distributions on sequences of given length (Section 6.4.1). We then discuss
the interpretation difference between prequential and nonprequential universal models (Section 6.4.2). Finally, we discuss a new type of universal
code whose design is explicitly based on the prequential idea: the prequential plug-in model (Section 6.4.3).

6.4.1   Distributions as Prediction Strategies

Let P be a distribution on $\mathcal{X}^n$. Applying the definition of conditional probability, we can write for every x^n:

$$P(x^n) = \prod_{i=1}^{n} \frac{P(x^i)}{P(x^{i-1})} = \prod_{i=1}^{n} P(x_i \mid x^{i-1}), \tag{6.26}$$

so that also

$$-\log P(x^n) = \sum_{i=1}^{n} -\log P(x_i \mid x^{i-1}) \tag{6.27}$$

Let us abbreviate $P(X_i = \cdot \mid X^{i-1} = x^{i-1})$ to $P(X_i \mid x^{i-1})$. $P(X_i \mid x^{i-1})$
is the *distribution* (not a single number) of X_i given x^{i-1}; $P(x_i \mid x^{i-1})$ is the
probability (a single number) of the actual outcome x_i given x^{i-1}.

Log Loss   We can think of $-\log P(x_i \mid x^{i-1})$ as the *loss* incurred when predicting x_i based on the conditional distribution $P(X_i \mid x^{i-1})$. Here "loss"
is measured using the so-called *logarithmic score*, also known simply as "log

loss." Note that the more likely x is judged to be, the smaller the loss incurred when x actually obtains. The log loss has a natural interpretation in terms of a type of sequential gambling known as *Kelly gambling* (Kelly 1956; Cover and Thomas 1991), but its main interpretation is still in terms of coding: by (6.27), the codelength needed to encode x^n based on distribution P is just the *accumulated log loss incurred when P is used to sequentially predict the ith outcome based on the past $i - 1$ outcomes.*

Prediction Strategies "Are" Distributions   Equation (6.26) gives a fundamental reinterpretation of probability distributions as prediction strategies, mapping each individual sequence of *past observations* $x_1, \ldots, x_{i-1}$ to a *probabilistic prediction of the next outcome* $P(X_i \mid x^{i-1})$. Conversely, (6.26) also shows that every probabilistic prediction strategy for sequential prediction of n outcomes may be thought of as a probability distribution on $\mathcal{X}^n$: a strategy is identified with a function mapping all potential initial segments x^{i-1} to the prediction that is made for the next outcome X_i, after having seen x^{i-1}. Thus, it is a function $S : \cup_{0 \leq i < n} \mathcal{X}^i \to \mathcal{P}_{\mathcal{X}}$, where $\mathcal{P}_{\mathcal{X}}$ is the set of distributions on $\mathcal{X}$. We can now define, for each $i < n$, all $x^i \in \mathcal{X}^i$, $P(X_i \mid x^{i-1}):=S(x^{i-1})$. We can turn these partial distributions into a distribution on $\mathcal{X}^n$ by sequentially plugging them into (6.26).

Log Loss for Universal Models   We see that for fixed n, the codelength $-\log P(x^n)$ can be interpreted as the sum of prediction errors when predicting with the conditional distributions $P(X_i \mid x^{i-1})$. It turns out to be very fruitful to analyze universal models from this predictive perspective. Thus, consider a universal model $\bar{P}^{(1)}, \bar{P}^{(2)}, \ldots$ and let $\bar{P} = \bar{P}^{(n)}$. In the prequential view, $\bar{P}$ is just a prediction strategy defined relative to a set of prediction strategies $\mathcal{M}$ so that, for all $P \in \mathcal{M}$, no matter what data x^n are observed, the accumulated log loss obtained by predicting with $\bar{P}$ is not much larger than the accumulated loss obtained by predicting with P. In this context, both $\bar{P}$ and P should really be thought of as a prediction strategy rather than as probability distributions.

What do the individual predictions $\bar{P}(X_i \mid x^{i-1})$ look like? Readers familiar with Bayesian statistics will realize that, when a Bayesian universal model is used, then $\bar{P}_{\text{Bayes}}(X_i \mid x^{i-1})$ is just the *Bayesian predictive distribution* (Chapter 2, Section 2.5.2). For finite and parametric i.i.d. models, $\bar{P}_{\text{Bayes}}(X_i \mid x^{i-1})$ converges (in an appropriate sense) to the ML distribution $P_{\hat{\theta}(x^{i-1})}$. Example 6.12 below provides a concrete case. Thus, the predictions $\bar{P}_{\text{Bayes}}(X_i \mid x^{i-1})$ adapt to or *learn* from the past, predicting similarly to – in fact, as we will see, even better than – the predictor within $\mathcal{M}$ that was optimal for the past data x^{i-1}. This latter predictor is just the maximum likelihood (ML) estimator of the past data x^{i-1}, which maximizes the probability of x^{i-1}, and therefore minimizes the log loss on x^{i-1} among all $P \in \mathcal{M}$. Something similar holds for other universal models such as the two-part and the NML model.

Log Loss for the Bayesian Universal Model   On behalf of readers not so familiar with Bayesian inference, we now explain the adaptive nature of the Bayesian universal models in more detail. Let us assume $\mathcal{M}$ is i.i.d., and let $\bar{P}_{\text{Bayes}} = \bar{P}_{\text{Bayes}}^{(n)}$, the Bayesian universal model relative to some prior W, restricted to n outcomes. By Chapter 2, Section 2.5.2, (2.36), the Bayesian predictive distribution $\bar{P}_{\text{Bayes}}(X_i \mid x^{i-1})$ can be rewritten as

$$\bar{P}_{\text{Bayes}}(x_i \mid x^{i-1}) = \sum_{\theta} P_\theta(x_i) W(\theta \mid x^{i-1}). \tag{6.28}$$

Here $W(\theta \mid x_1, \ldots, x_{i-1})$ is the posterior distribution (Bernardo and Smith 1994), which can be computed by Bayes formula, repeated here for convenience:

$$W(\theta \mid x^{i-1}) := \frac{P_\theta(x^{i-1}) W(\theta)}{\bar{P}_{\text{Bayes}}(x^{i-1})}. \tag{6.29}$$

We see that $\bar{P}_{\text{Bayes}}(x_i \mid x^{i-1})$ is a mixture of the distributions P_θ, where each θ is weighted by $W(\theta \mid x_1, \ldots, x_{i-1})$. If for some θ_0 and some $\epsilon > 0$, $-\log P_{\theta_0}(x^{i-1}) > -\log P_{\hat{\theta}}(x^{i-1}) + i \cdot \epsilon$, then the weight of θ_0 in the mixture $\bar{P}_{\text{Bayes}}(X_i \mid x^{i-1})$ will be exponentially smaller than the weight of $\hat{\theta}$. This suggests that, for large i, $\bar{P}_{\text{Bayes}}(X_i \mid x^{i-1})$ will be very close to the ML estimator $P_{\hat{\theta}(x^i)}(\cdot)$. Example 6.12 is a concrete illustration of this phenomenon.

We emphasize that if the model is not i.i.d., then the derivation (6.28) still holds, but with $P_\theta(x_i)$ replaced by $P_\theta(x_i \mid x^{i-1})$. Our focus on i.i.d. models is for simplicity only; the prequential story can be told for arbitrary models $\mathcal{M}$.

Example 6.12 Consider the model $\mathcal{M}$ of Example 6.1 with $\mathcal{M} = \{P_\theta\}$ and $\theta \in \Theta = \{0.1, 0.2, \ldots, 0.9\}$. Let W be any prior distribution with for all $\theta \in \Theta$, $W(\theta) > 0$. Suppose we observe a sequence $x_1, x_2, \ldots$ with $\sum x_i/n \to \theta^*$ for some $\theta^* \in \Theta$ – thus, the data clearly favor one particular θ^* over all others. As we know from Example 6.1, in that case $-\log P_\theta(x^i) - [-\log P_{\theta^*}(x^i)]$

increases linearly in i for all $\theta \in \Theta$, $\theta \neq \theta^*$, so that, using Bayes formula (6.29),

$$\frac{W(\theta \mid x^i)}{W(\theta^* \mid x^i)} = \frac{P_\theta(x^i)W(\theta)}{P_{\theta^*}(x^i)W(\theta^*)}$$

becomes exponentially small. Therefore for i large (but smaller than n), $W(\theta^* \mid x^{i-1}) \approx 1$. From (6.28) we then see that $\bar{P}_{\text{Bayes}}(x_i \mid x^{i-1}) \approx P_{\theta^*}(x_i)$: the Bayesian prediction of X_i becomes almost identical to the prediction according to θ^*, the ML distribution based on x^{i-1}.

The example shows that $\bar{P}_{\text{Bayes}}(X_i \mid x^{i-1})$ is adaptive, and learns to imitate whatever distribution in $\mathcal{M}$ has best predicted the past. Clearly, for other universal models such as two-part and NML, something similar must hold as well, otherwise there would be sequences where they would attain much larger regret than Bayes – and we have already seen (Example 6.5) that asymptotically they all achieve the same regret. Nevertheless, as we now explain, in contrast to two-part and NML, the Bayesian universal models do have a special status within the predictive framework.

6.4.2   Bayes Is Prequential; NML and Two-part Are Not

We have just seen that every probability distribution defined on a sample space $\mathcal{X}^n$ of n outcomes has a predictive interpretation. Since universal models are sequences of probability distributions, this holds in particular for the Bayes, NML, and two-part models restricted to outcomes of length n. However, in practical coding situations, the number of outcomes n is often unknown in advance. If we are to use distributions as prediction strategies in this situation, we do not know in advance how many predictions to make. It turns out that in this case the *predictive-sequential interpretation of two-part and NML codes breaks down, but the predictive-sequential interpretation of Bayes remains intact*. Intuitively, this is what we mean when we say: Bayes is prequential, two-part and NML are not. We will provide a precise definition below. We immediately note that the Bayesian universal model is by no means the only type of universal model that is "prequential": in the next subsection we encounter another one, the so-called "prequential plug-in model."

Why does the predictive interpretation break down for some universal models if n is unknown in advance? The reason is that with universal models, we code data using different codes/distributions $\bar{P}^{(n)}$ for different n. For each fixed n, the distribution $\bar{P}^{(n)}$ uniquely induces a set of conditional probabilities $\bar{P}^{(n)}(X_1), \bar{P}^{(n)}(X_2 \mid X_1), \ldots, \bar{P}^{(n)}(X_n \mid X^{n-1})$. But unfortunately, since $\bar{P}^{(n)}$ may be quite unrelated to $\bar{P}^{(n+1)}$, we may have that for some i, and some data x^i, that, for all $n > n' \geq i$,

$$\bar{P}^{(n)}(X_i \mid x^{i-1}) \neq \bar{P}^{(n')}(X_i \mid x^{i-1}).$$

In that case, the predictive distribution $\bar{P}^{(n)}(\cdot \mid x^{i-1})$ of X_i depends on the *horizon*, i.e. the number of outcomes that still have to predicted. If the horizon is unknown, then the predictive distribution is ill-defined.

Clearly, in order for a universal model to admit a predictive-sequential interpretation independently of the horizon, we must have, for all $i \geq 0$, all $x^i \in \mathcal{X}^i$ with $\bar{P}^{(i)}(x^i) > 0$, that for all $n > i$, $\bar{P}^{(n)}(x^i) > 0$ and

$$\bar{P}^{(n)}(x_i \mid x^{i-1}) = \bar{P}^{(i)}(x_i \mid x^{i-1}). \tag{6.30}$$

It is not hard to see that this is the case if and only if for all $n \geq 1$, $\bar{P}^{(n)}$ satisfies the "compatibility condition": for all $x^{n-1} \in \mathcal{X}^{n-1}$,

$$\sum_{x \in \mathcal{X}} \bar{P}^{(n)}(x^{n-1}, x) = \bar{P}^{(n-1)}(x^{n-1}), \tag{6.31}$$

i.e. if the sequence $\bar{P}^{(1)}, \bar{P}(2), \dots$ can be thought of as a single distribution over $\mathcal{X}^\infty$. We called such a distribution a *probabilistic source* in Chapter 2, page 53. This leads us to the following definition:

Definition 6.2 [Prequential Universal Models; Predictive Distributions] We call a universal model $\bar{P}^{(1)}, \bar{P}^{(2)}, \dots$ *prequential* if and only if it constitutes a probabilistic source (Chapter 2, page 53), i.e. if there exists a single probabilistic source $\bar{P}$ such that each $\bar{P}^{(i)}$ can be understood as $\bar{P}$'s marginal distribution for the first i outcomes.

In this case, the conditional distribution $\bar{P}^{(n)}(X_i \mid x^{i-1})$ does not depend on n and will be written as $\bar{P}(X_i \mid x^{i-1})$. It is called the *predictive distribution* of X_i given x^{i-1}.

While a prequential universal model is thus, by definition, a probabilistic "source," this terminology may be somewhat misleading: we think, for example, of a Bayesian "probabilistic source" as a predictor and not at all as a true "source" sequentially generating data.

Prequential universal models are in a way more natural than universal models, since if $\bar{P}$ is prequential, then there is a symmetry between $\mathcal{M}$ (a family of probabilistic sources) and $\bar{P}$ (a single probabilistic source acting as a representative of $\mathcal{M}$). In the example below we show that the Bayesian universal code is prequential. We also show that, although the distributions $\bar{P}_{\mathrm{nml}}(n)$ and $\bar{P}_{\mathrm{nml}}(n+1)$ are evidently closely related, it turns out that they do not always satisfy the compatibility condition (6.31), whence the NML models are not prequential in general. The same holds for the two-part code; we leave the details of showing this to the reader.

Example 6.13 [Bayes Is Prequential, NML Is Not] Let $\mathcal{M}$ be an arbitrary countable set of probabilistic sources, and let W be an arbitrary prior on this model. Then for all $n \geq 1$, all $x^{n-1} \in \mathcal{X}^{n-1}$,

$$\bar{P}_{\mathrm{Bayes}}^{(n)}(x^{n-1}) = \sum_{x \in \mathcal{X}} \bar{P}_{\mathrm{Bayes}}^{(n)}(x^{n-1}, x) =$$

$$\sum_{x \in \mathcal{X}} \sum_{\theta \in \Theta} W(\theta) P_\theta(x^{n-1}, x) = \sum_{\theta \in \Theta} W(\theta) \sum_{x \in \mathcal{X}} P_\theta(x^{n-1}, x) =$$

$$\sum_{\theta \in \Theta} W(\theta) P_\theta(x^{n-1}) = \bar{P}_{\mathrm{Bayes}}^{(n-1)}(x^{n-1}), \quad (6.32)$$

so that $\bar{P}_{\mathrm{Bayes}}$ is a probabilistic source, and hence (Definition 6.2) prequential. The important point is that this is *not* the case for the NML universal model. Indeed, consider once again the rational Bernoulli model $\mathcal{B}_{\mathbb{Q}}^{(1)}$ of Example 6.10. Then a straightforward calculation shows that $\bar{P}_{\mathrm{nml}}^{(2)}(X_1 = 1, X_2 = 1) = \frac{2}{5}$, whereas

$$\bar{P}_{\mathrm{nml}}^{(3)}(X_1 = 1, X_2 = 1) = \sum_{y \in \{0,1\}} \bar{P}_{\mathrm{nml}}^{(3)}(1, 1, y) = \frac{9}{24} \cdot \frac{31}{27} = \frac{31}{72} \neq \frac{2}{5}.$$

Interpretation Difference   To interpret the difference between prequential and nonprequential universal coding, recall the interpretation of coding in terms of communication between a sender and receiver (Chapter 3, Section 3.1.1). Nonpredictive universal coding corresponds to the case where n is known in advance. That is, sender and receiver agree on a code for sending n observations. They then split, sender observes the n observations, encodes them using the agreed-upon code, and transmits the encoding to receiver.

Predictive universal coding corresponds to the on-line setting where n is not known in advance, and remains unknown throughout: sender keeps receiving new outcomes, and has to communicate these to receiver. In particular, sender has to start encoding outcomes x_1, x_2 before knowing how many outcomes will have to be sent in total. Also, receiver wants to start decoding

x_i as soon as he or she receives x_i, and thus not want to wait until all x_i have been sent. Thus, sender and receiver have to agree on a code that works for all n. Clearly, this is a more general scenario: the set of situations in which one can use a prequential code is a superset of the set of situations in which one can use a nonprequential code. In our context universal codes will be used as the basis for MDL inference. It turns out that many applications of MDL can be interpreted as based on coding data in the on-line setting, where n is unknown in advance. This includes some applications involving two-part codes, because these are often still "semiprequential", see below. Applications of MDL based on NML or "sample size-dependent two-part codes" do not have an on-line interpretation; see the discussion in Chapter 17, Section 17.5 on the *infinite-horizon prequential principle*.

Two-part codes are sometimes *semi*-prequential; NML codes are not We can refine the prequential/nonprequential distinction as follows. We call a universal model $\bar{P}$ *semiprequential* if there exists another universal model $\bar{P}'$ such that for all n, all $x^n \in \mathcal{X}^n$, $\bar{P}'(x^n) \geq \bar{P}(x^n)$. Semiprequential codes for which one or more of these inequalities are strict are of course incomplete codes (see Chapter 3, box on page 99).

From Example 6.4 we see that two-part codes of the form we have considered in this and the previous chapter are semiprequential: for every two-part code $\bar{P}_{\text{2-p}}$, the Bayesian universal code $\bar{P}_{\text{Bayes}}$ based on the same prior assigns at least as much probability mass to every sequence. In Chapter 10 however, we will consider another type of two-part code for which the code L_1 used in the first stage changes with n. Like NML codes, such *sample size-dependent two-part codes* are not necessarily semiprequential.

Apart from their incompleteness, semiprequential codes have all the advantages of prequential codes. They can be used in all the cases where nonsemiprequential codes are used, but they can also be used in the on-line setting, where nonsemiprequential codes cannot be used.

Prequentialization Consider a nonsemiprequential universal code $\bar{L}$ such as an NML code or a sample size-dependent two-part code. Such a code can always be modified into a semi-prequential two-part code $\bar{L}'$ such that for all n, all $x^n \in \mathcal{X}^n$,

$$\bar{L}'(x^n) \leq \bar{L}(x^n) + L_{\mathbb{N}}(n) = \bar{L}(x^n) + O(\log n). \tag{6.33}$$

$\bar{L}'$ is constructed as a two-stage code, where in the first stage one encodes some m using the standard code for the integers; in the second stage, one encodes x^n using $\bar{L}^{(m)}(x^n)$ bits, where $\bar{L}^{(m)}$ is the original universal code-length function (which may itself be two-part) for sequences of length $m \geq n$.

Since the encoder can always decide to encode $m = n$ in the first stage, (6.33) holds.   Barron and Cover (1991, page 1046) present a variation of this argument which shows that (6.33) can sometimes be refined for i.i.d. model classes $\mathcal{M}$, when $\bar{L}$ is a two-part code, and when measuring the quality of universal codes using expected redundancy, a notion which we will define in Section 6.5. Barron and Cover construct a semiprequential universal code $\bar{L}''$ which is just like $\bar{L}'$, except that now in the first stage, an integer $m' = 2^m$ is encoded. This enforces an encoding x^n using $\bar{L}^{(m)}$ for an m that is some power of two. If for some $P^* \in \mathcal{M}$, the expected redundancy grows as an increasing function $f(n)$, i.e. $E_{X^n \sim P^*}[\bar{L}^{(n)}(X^n) + \log P^*(X^n)] = f(n)$, then it is easy to show that $E_{X^n \sim P^*}[\bar{L}''(X^n) + \log P^*(X^n)] \leq f(2n) + O(\log \log n)$. Thus, if $f(n)$ grows faster than $\log \log n$, then $\bar{L}''$ preserves the growth rate ORDER($f(n)$) of $\bar{L}$, though the constant in the ORDER-notation may be different in general. In later chapters, we often consider universal codes relative to k-dimensional parametric models $\mathcal{M}$ such that, for most or all $P \in \mathcal{M}$, $f(n) = (k/2) \log n + O(1)$. In that case, there is some advantage of using $\bar{L}''$ over $\bar{L}'$, since we now get $E_{X^n \sim P^*}[\bar{L}''(X^n) + \log P^*(X^n)] \leq (k/2) \log n + O(\log \log n)$, whereas from (6.33) we see that $E_{X^n \sim P^*}[\bar{L}'(X^n) + \log P^*(X^n)] = (k/2 + 1) \log n + O(\log \log n)$. Yet in other, nonparametric situations (Chapter 13) $f(n)$ grows faster than $\log n$, and in that case, $\bar{L}'$ may be preferrable over $\bar{L}''$.

6.4.3   The Prequential Plug-In Model

In many practical situations, $\bar{P}_{\text{Bayes}}(x^n)$ and $\bar{P}_{\text{nml}}(x^n)$ cannot be easily computed, but, for each $i > 0$, the ML estimator $\hat{\theta}(x^i)$ is uniquely determined and easy to compute. In Section 6.4.1 we argued that for large i, $\bar{P}_{\text{Bayes}}(X_i = \cdot \mid x^{i-1})$ will in some sense be very close to the ML estimator $P_{\hat{\theta}(x^{i-1})}(X_i)$. This suggests that we may try to approximate $\bar{P}_{\text{Bayes}}$ as follows. For an i.i.d. model $\mathcal{M}$ we recursively define the *maximum likelihood plug-in* distribution $\bar{P}_{\text{plug-in}}$ by setting, for $i = 2$ to n,

$$\bar{P}_{\text{plug-in}}(X_i = \cdot \mid x^{i-1}) := P_{\hat{\theta}(x^{i-1})}, \tag{6.34}$$

and setting $\bar{P}_{\text{plug-in}}(X_1)$ to some default value. If $\mathcal{X}$ is finite, this could, for example, be the uniform distribution. By the arguments of Section 6.4.1, (6.34) uniquely defines a joint distribution on $\mathcal{X}^n$ such that for all $x^n \in \mathcal{X}^n$, $\bar{P}_{\text{plug-in}}(x^n) := \prod_{i=1}^{n} P_{\hat{\theta}(x^{i-1})}(x_i)$. By doing this for every n, we obtain a sequence of distributions $\bar{P}_{\text{plug-in}}^{(1)}, \bar{P}_{\text{plug-in}}^{(2)}, \ldots$ It is easy to check that this sequence of distributions satisfies the compatibility condition (6.31), so that the sequence $\bar{P}_{\text{plug-in}}$ actually constitutes a probabilistic source.

The extension of (6.34) to non-i.i.d. models is immediate: we simply replace $P_{\hat{\theta}(x^{i-1})}$ by $P_{\hat{\theta}}(x^{i-1})(X_i = \cdot | x^{i-1})$ in the definition. It is straightforward to adjust the analysis below to this generalized definition.

Interestingly, the codelength of x^n according to the code corresponding to this source is the sum of the log loss prediction errors made by sequentially predicting X_i based on the predictor in $\mathcal{M}$ that would have been the best for sequentially predicting the previous outcomes $x_1, \ldots, x_{i-1}$:

$$-\log \bar{P}_{\text{plug-in}}(x^n) = \sum_{i=1}^{n} -\log P_{\hat{\theta}(x^{i-1})}(x_i). \qquad (6.35)$$

This suggests that the accumulated log loss (codelength) $-\log \bar{P}_{\text{plug-in}}(x^n)$ is "close" to the Bayesian codelength $-\log \bar{P}_{\text{Bayes}}(x^n)$. Indeed, it turns out that under some regularity conditions on $\mathcal{M}$, the resulting probabilistic source $\bar{P}_{\text{plug-in}}$ constitutes a prequential universal model. We discuss this in detail in Chapter 9. We call a universal model constructed as in (6.34) a *prequential plug-in model*. In general, there is no need to use the standard ML estimator $\hat{\theta}(x^{i-1})$ in the definition (6.34). Instead, we may try some other estimator with good asymptotic properties – it turns out that for many parametric models, with the standard ML estimator, the resulting source $\bar{P}_{\text{plug-in}}$ is well-defined but not a universal model, whereas with a slight modification of the ML estimator, $\bar{P}_{\text{plug-in}}$ becomes a very good uniformly universal model. In order to give interesting examples of plug-in universal models, we really need to work with parametric models with continuous parameter spaces. Therefore, we will defer all such examples to Chapter 9. There we will also discuss in detail the "start-up problem" (roughly, how should $\hat{\theta}$ be defined when the first prediction(s) have to be made?) and the type of modification needed to make $\bar{P}_{\text{plug-in}}$ competitive with other universal models.

The prequential plug-in universal model was discovered independently by Dawid (1984) and by Rissanen (1984). It is also known as the "predictive MDL code," a phrase coined by Rissanen (1984).

Fourth Example of a Universal Model: Prequential Plug-In

Let $\mathcal{M} = \{P_\theta \mid \theta \in \Theta\}$. A prequential plug-in universal model relative to $\mathcal{M}$ is implicitly defined by sequentially predicting the next outcome X_n using the $P \in \mathcal{M}$ that gave (almost) the best predictions on the previously seen data $x_1, \ldots, x_{n-1}$. Here "predicting using P" amounts to "coding using the code with length $-\log P(X_n)$."

6.5   Individual vs. Stochastic Universality*

6.5.1   Stochastic Redundancy

Until now, when defining and measuring the quality of universal models, we took an individual sequence approach: we required that, for each P in the model $\mathcal{M}$ under consideration, universal codes achieve small redundancy for *all* sequences $x_1, \ldots, x_n$. This is really an extremely worst-case view: although our universal code should compress data essentially as well as the code corresponding to P, we make no assumption at all that the data are actually distributed according to this P. As we explain in Chapter 17, one can argue that the underlying MDL philosophy that "data are never really generated by a distribution" naturally leads to the use of such individual-sequence universal codes in MDL inference. While Rissanen, the originator of MDL, strictly adheres to such a philosophy and therefore focuses his research on individual-sequence codes, the majority of information theorists are willing to make probabilistic assumptions after all. As a consequence, they typically investigate universal models under the assumption that the data are actually distributed according to some $P \in \mathcal{M}$. This leads to two alternative definitions of universal models, both of which are natural: the first says that, for all $P \in \mathcal{M}$, a universal model should achieve sublinear redundancy with respect to P, with P-probability 1, i.e. "almost surely"; the second one requires that sublinear redundancy is achieved in P-expectation. The definition of universal models in terms of P-expected redundancy is historically the first, and it is still the one adopted by most authors.

> We also note that some authors reserve the term "universal code" to mean "universal code for the integers", using a slightly modified definition of expected universality; see (Li and Vitányi 1997, Section 1.5.3) and Example 6.8. Such authors invariably use the terms "universal *source* codes" for what we call stochastic universal codes, and "universal codes for individual sequences" for what we call "individual-sequence universal codes". Unlike us, they never leave out the word "source" or "individual sequence".

Three Definitions of Universality

Let $\mathcal{M}$ be a family of probabilistic sources. Consider a sequence of distributions $\{\bar{P}^{(i)}\}_{i=1,2,\ldots}$ on $\mathcal{X}^1, \mathcal{X}^2, \ldots$ respectively.

1. If for all $P \in \mathcal{M}$, for all $\epsilon > 0$, for all large n, for all $X_1, \ldots, X_n \in \mathcal{X}^n$,

$$\frac{1}{n}\left[-\log \bar{P}^{(n)}(X_1, \ldots, X_n) - [-\log P(X_1, \ldots, X_n)]\right] \leq \epsilon, \qquad (6.36)$$

   then $\{\bar{P}^{(i)}\}_{i=1,2,\ldots}$ is a universal model in the (nonstochastic) *individual-sequence* sense. This is equivalent to the definition on page 178: in this book, when we refer to "universal model," we mean "universal model in the individual sequence sense."

2. If for all $P \in \mathcal{M}$, for all $\epsilon > 0$, with P-probability 1, (6.36) holds for all large n, then $\{\bar{P}^{(i)}\}_{i=1,2,\ldots}$ is a universal model in the (stochastic) *almost-sure* sense.

3. If for all $P \in \mathcal{M}$, for all $\epsilon > 0$, (6.36) holds in P-expectation, for all large n, then $\{\bar{P}^{(i)}\}_{i=1,2,\ldots}$ is a universal model in the (stochastic) *expected* sense. This requirement is equivalent to, for all $P \in \mathcal{M}$, all $\epsilon > 0$,

$$\frac{1}{n}D(P^{(n)}\|\bar{P}^{(n)}) \leq \epsilon, \text{ for all large } n,$$

   where $P^{(n)}$ is the marginal distribution of P on $\mathcal{X}^n$. Most authors, when they refer to "universal model," mean "universal model in the expected sense."

The definition of (uniform) $f(n)$-universality is extended from the nonstochastic (pages 183 and 186) case to the stochastic case in an analogous manner.

This settles the definition of expected and almost-sure universal codes. It turns out that stochastic redundancy is a weaker requirement than individual sequence redundancy:

Proposition 6.1 Let $\mathcal{M}$ be a set of probabilistic sources. Let $\{\bar{P}^{(i)}\}_{i=1,2,\ldots}$ be a universal model relative to $\mathcal{M}$ in the individual sequence sense. Then $\{\bar{P}^{(i)}\}_{i=1,2,\ldots}$ is a universal model relative to $\mathcal{M}$ in the almost-sure sense and in the expected sense. If $\{\bar{P}^{(i)}\}_{i=1,2,\ldots}$ is (uniformly) $f(n)$-universal in the individual sequence sense, then $\{\bar{P}^{(i)}\}_{i=1,2,\ldots}$ is (uniformly) $f(n)$-universal in the almost-sure sense and in the expected sense.

Proof: Fix some $P \in \mathcal{M}$ and let $f : \mathbb{N} \to [0, \infty)$ be any nondecreasing function such that $f(n) = o(n)$ and that for all n, all $x^n \in \mathcal{X}^n$,

$$- \log \bar{P}^{(n)}(x^n) + \log P(x^n) < f(n). \tag{6.37}$$

Such an f must exist by the fact that $\bar{P}$ is universal in the individual sequence sense. But because (6.37) holds for *all* x^n, it also holds with P-probability 1, and it also holds in expectation with respect to P, so that

$$E_{X^n \sim P}[- \log \bar{P}^{(n)}(X^n) + \log P(X^n)] < f(n).$$

The result now follows immediately from the definitions of basic, $f(n)$-, and uniformly $f(n)$-universality (pages 178, 183, 186. □

Note that it does not immediately follow that almost-sure universality implies expected universality. The reason is that we may have an almost-sure universal model $\bar{P}$, such that for some P, some sequences $X_1, X_2, \ldots$ with P-probability exponentially small in n achieves codelength $- \log \bar{P}^{(n)}(X^n)$ exponentially large in n, with a larger exponent. Such an almost-sure universal model would not be universal in the expected sense. Nevertheless, almost-sure universal models arising in practice are usually also universal in the expected sense.

Remark on Terminology   We already indicated that the meaning of the phrase "universal model" and "universal code," without any additions, depends on the context and the author. Similarly, there seems to be no standard definition of "redundancy." In this book, redundancy is defined as a codelength difference relative to a given sequence x^n. Some authors (Li and Yu 2000; Liang and Barron 2005) use redundancy the same way we do. But many other authors use redundancy to refer to redundancy in the expected sense (see e.g. (Haussler 1997)). Then the redundancy of $\bar{P}^{(n)}$ relative to P is just the Kullback-Leibler divergence $D(P^{(n)} \| \bar{P}^{(n)})$. Some authors define redundancy as the expected codelength difference divided by sample size n, i.e. $D(P^{(n)} \| \bar{P}^{(n)})/n$ (e.g. (Barron and Cover 1991)).

6.5.2   Uniformly Universal Models

How should we measure the quality of stochastic universal codes relative to a model $\mathcal{M}$? For simplicity we will answer this question only for the more commonly used stochastic universal codes in the expected sense. A similar treatment can be given for the almost-sure case.

Minimax Expected Regret   Analogously to the individual-sequence case, the straightforward way to measure the quality of a universal code "in expectation" is in terms of the defining property, the expected redundancy. Yet, again in analogy to the individual-sequence case, if the model is sufficiently simple to allow a uniformly universal code, then one can also look at the expected *minimax regret*. Let $P_{\hat{\theta}}$ be the ML estimator within the model $\mathcal{M}$. Recall that the individual-sequence minimax regret was given by

$$\min_{\bar{P}} \max_{x^n \in \mathcal{X}^n} \left\{ -\log \bar{P}(x^n) - \{-\log P_{\hat{\theta}(x^n)}(x^n)\} \right\}. \tag{6.38}$$

Similarly, the minimax expected regret is defined as

$$\min_{\bar{P}} \max_{P \in \mathcal{M}} E_{X^n \sim P} \left[-\log \bar{P}(X^n) - \{-\log P_{\hat{\theta}(X^n)}(X^n)\} \right]. \tag{6.39}$$

We may call the distribution achieving (6.39) the *minimax optimal universal model in the expectation sense*, at sample size n, relative to model $\mathcal{M}$.

Unrestricted Minimax Expected Regret Note that the maximum in (6.39) is over all $P \in \mathcal{M}$, and not over the much larger set of all distributions on $\mathcal{X}^n$. Instead, one may consider the *unrestricted minimax regret* defined by

$$\min_{\bar{P}} \max_{P:\ P\text{ is distribution on } \mathcal{X}^n} E_{X^n \sim P} \left[-\log \bar{P}(X^n) - \{-\log P_{\hat{\theta}(X^n)}(X^n)\} \right]. \tag{6.40}$$

However, it is easy to see that (6.40) is exactly equal to the individual-sequence minimax regret (6.38). Thus, the distribution $\bar{P}$ on $\mathcal{X}^n$ achieving (6.40) is equal to the NML distribution, and exists if and only if the NML distribution exists. Rissanen (2001) and Su, Myung, and Pitt (2005) define the NML distribution in terms of (6.40) rather than (6.38).

Minimax Expected Redundancy   Finally, we should mention a third method for measuring the quality of universal codes relative to models which allows uniformly universal codes. This is the *minimax expected redundancy*, defined as

$$\min_{\bar{P}} \max_{P \in \mathcal{M}} E_{X^n \sim P} \left[-\log \bar{P}(X^n) - \{-\log P(X^n)\} \right]. \tag{6.41}$$

Comparing to (6.39), we see that the ML estimator $P_{\hat{\theta}(X^n)}$ is replaced by the P according to which data are distributed. Comparing to the definition of expected redundancy, the reader can verify that the term "minimax expected redundancy" is appropriate. This quantity measures how much additional bits we need when coding with $\bar{P}$, on average, compared to the optimal (in expectation) code based on the true distribution P, in the worst case over all P. Both the minimax expected redundancy (6.41) and the minimax expected regret (6.39) are analogues to the minimax individual-sequence regret, but the minimax expected redundancy is arguably a more natural one: whereas in the minimax individual-sequence regret, one compares the *individual* codelength $-\log \bar{P}(X^n)$ on each sequence X^n with the code achieving the *smallest codelength for that sequence*, in the minimax expected redundancy, one compares the *expected* codelength $E_P[-\log \bar{P}(X^n)]$ on each $P \in \mathcal{M}$ with the code that has the smallest *expected codelength for that P*.

Asymptotic Equivalence of the Three Minimax Universal Codes   We thus end up with three different ways of measuring the goodness of a universal code with respect to a small probabilistic model: minimax individual-sequence regret, minimax expected regret, minimax expected redundancy (minimax individual redundancy is an ill-defined notion). Which of these three should we choose? Interestingly, in practice, it usually does not really matter a lot. Let us indicate why.

First, note that Proposition 6.1 may initially suggest that, for a given universal model $\bar{P}$, the minimax expected regret (6.39) may be much smaller than the minimax individual-sequence regret (6.39). Surprisingly, for finite models, as well as for simple parametric models, on which we focus in the next chapter, this turns out not to be the case: one can show that for large n, the difference between (6.38) and (6.39) tends to 0, and the NML distribution $\bar{P}_{\text{nml}}$ achieves not just the minimax individual sequence but also the minimax expected regret. This result is somewhat surprising: asymptotically, the best regret one can obtain if one makes no assumptions about the data at all is not smaller than the best regret under the much stronger assumption that some $P \in \mathcal{M}$ generated the data.

Second, note that for every sequence x^n and all $P \in \mathcal{M}$, it holds that

$$-\log P(x^n) \geq -\log P_{\hat{\theta}(x^n)}(x^n), \tag{6.42}$$

with strict (and substantial) inequality for most P. Therefore, for models containing more than one distribution, the minimax expected regret must be strictly smaller than the minimax expected redundancy. Initially, (6.42) may suggest that the difference can be quite large. But again, for finite models, as well as for simple parametric models, this turns out not to be the case: as we explain in Chapter 8, Section 8.4, one can show that for large n, the difference between (6.39) and (6.41) tends to a small constant (not 0, in this case), and the NML distribution $\bar{P}_{\text{nml}}$ achieves not just the minimax individual-sequence regret and expected regret, but also the minimax expected redundancy.

Thus, there exists a single code (the NML code) which is asymptotically minimax with respect to all three different approaches to universality. We take this fact to mean that there is some inherent meaning to the concept of "minimax optimal universal coding," which goes beyond the peculiarities of the three particular definitions that we proposed.

6.6   Summary, Outlook and Further Reading

In this chapter we introduced universal codes and models. We have encountered two methods for measuring the quality of universal models: the *redundancy*, which is their defining property, and the *regret*. Whereas the redundancy is a general performance measure, the regret only makes sense for so-called uniformly universal models. Uniformly universal models can only be defined relative to sufficiently "simple" models $\mathcal{M}$, including all finite models. In the next chapter, we shall see that uniformly universal models can also be defined relative to simple parametric models.

We have encountered an important distinction between types of universal models: the *prequential* vs. the *nonprequential* models. The prequential models have a natural interpretation as sequential prediction strategies for sequences whose length may be unknown in advance. The Bayesian and plug-in universal models have the prequential property, but the two-part and NML universal models do not. In this chapter we showed that for finite models $\mathcal{M}$, all these universal codes, while designed in completely different manners, typically achieve almost the same codelengths for large n. For small n, the NML model stands out as being minimax optimal in terms of regret. In the next chapter, we shall see that similar, but subtler, statements hold if $\mathcal{M}$ is a simple parametric family.

Finally, we noted that universality can be measured not just in terms of individual sequences, as we did throughout this chapter, but also, in two weaker "stochastic" senses: in terms of expected redundancy or regret, and in terms of almost-sure redundancy or regret.

Further Reading   There is a large amount of literature on universal coding and log loss prediction. In subsequent chapters we will only cite the literature that is most closely related to universal coding for the type of models we deal with in this book: statistical parametric and nonparametric models. A more general survey is presented by Merhav and Feder (1998). We should also note that general-purpose data compressors such as gzip are based on ideas closely related to universal coding. One of the most successful data compression algorithms, the *context tree weighting method* (Willems, Shtarkov, and Tjalkens 1995) is essentially based on a Bayesian universal code for context trees, a clever extension of the class of Markov chains of all orders. In the computational learning and game-theoretic communities, one also studies universal prediction with loss functions other than log loss. This is explored further in Chapter 17, Section 17.9.

7 *Parametric Models: Normalized Maximum Likelihood*

In this chapter, we analyze the minimax regret, or *parametric complexity*, for parametric exponential families with parameters restricted to *ineccsi* sets. This is the regret achieved by the *normalized maximum likelihood (NML) universal model*. First, in Section 7.1, we explain what ineccsi sets are. Then, in Section 7.2, we present Theorem 7.1, which gives an asymptotic expression for the minimax regret. In Section 7.3 we show that the theorem leads to an interpretation of the minimax regret as the logarithm of a (nonstandard) *volume* which is proportional to the *number of distinguishable distributions* in the model.

Fast Track The "ineccsi" terminology and the asymptotic expansion of the minimax regret are of crucial importance in the remainder of Part II and in Part III. The volume interpretation becomes important when the NML universal model is used for MDL model selection. It may be advisable to first read about MDL model selection (Chapter 14) before investigating the volume interpretation.

7.1 Introduction

For a given model $\mathcal{M}$ with parameterization Θ, the NML universal model $\bar{P}_{\mathrm{nml}}^{(1)}, \bar{P}_{\mathrm{nml}}^{(2)}, \dots$ is defined as in Chapter 6, Section 6.2.1, such that $\bar{P}_{\mathrm{nml}}^{(n)}$ achieves the minimax optimal regret (6.12) over all sequences $x^n \in \mathcal{X}^n$. Just as for countable Θ, $\bar{P}_{\mathrm{nml}}^{(n)}$ is well defined if and only if the minimax regret for sequences of length n with respect to Θ, given by

$$\mathrm{COMP}^{(n)}(\mathcal{M}) = \log \sum_{x^n \in \mathcal{X}^n} \sup_{\theta \in \Theta} P_\theta(x^n), \tag{7.1}$$

is finite. In that case, as long as $\hat{\theta}(x^n)$ exists for all $x^n \in \mathcal{X}^n$, we have

$$\bar{P}_{\text{nml}}^{(n)}(x^n) = \frac{P_{\hat{\theta}(x^n)}(x^n)}{\sum_{x^n \in \mathcal{X}^n} P_{\hat{\theta}(x^n)}(x^n)},$$

which achieves regret $\text{REG}(\bar{P}_{\text{nml}}^{(n)}, \mathcal{M}, x^n)$. For all $x^n \in \mathcal{X}^n$, this quantity is equal to the minimax regret $\text{COMP}^{(n)}(\mathcal{M})$. The main contribution of this chapter, to be found in Section 7.2, is to provide an asymptotic expansion of $\text{COMP}^{(n)}(\mathcal{M})$, which holds under some restrictions on the parameter space Θ. In Section 7.3 we show that this minimax regret is closely related to the "volume" of the model, with respect to a nonstandard geometry in which the volume of a set of distributions is proportional to *the number of distinguishable distributions that it contains*. We already established a relation between minimax regret and number of distinguishable distributions for finite models. Here, we establish the same type of relation for parametric models; as we will see in Part III, Chapter 14, this central result connects traditional statistical inference with minimax optimal universal coding.

7.1.1   Preliminaries

The Story of Chapters 7 through 10

This chapter is about the regret of the NML universal code. The next three chapters discuss, respectively, the Bayesian, plug-in, and two-part universal codes for parametric models. Each chapter starts with an analogue of Theorem 7.1, giving an asymptotic expression of the regret obtained with the universal code discussed in that chapter. In all three cases, these regrets come reasonably close to the minimax optimal regret that we study in the present chapter. In all cases, we give a precise theorem for i.i.d. exponential families, and later in each chapter, we outline extensions to nonexponential families. In all cases, we give a proof or proof sketch of the theorem. The proofs are invariably based on the Taylor expansions of the log-likelihood or the Kullback-Leibler (KL) divergence that we performed in Chapter 4, in combination with the robustness property of KL divergence for exponential families, expressed as Proposition 19.1 in Chapter 19, Section 19.2. In all cases (except Chapter 10), we give direct and much easier arguments showing that the theorem holds for the simple Bernoulli model.

When stating our theorems, we use a few concepts and insights about exponential families: we always assume they are given in a *diffeomorphic* parameterization Θ; in some cases, we assume that they are given in the *mean-value* parameterization, which is a special case of a diffeomorphic parameterization. A precise definition of exponential families, mean-value, and diffeomorphic parameterizations can be found in Chapter 18. Essentially, any "reasonable" 1-to-1 parameterization is diffeomorphic. We also tacitly use the fact that, for exponential families, if the ML estimator of x^n within Θ exists, then it must be unique.

Ineccsi Parameter Sets Let $\mathcal{M}$ be an exponential family, parameterized by some Θ. As we will see, quantities such as the regret may exhibit singular behavior in the limit for θ approaching either the boundaries of Θ or infinity. For this reason, we often want to study submodels $\Theta_0 \subset \Theta$ that exclude such θ. On the other hand, such Θ_0 should still be of the same dimensionality as the original Θ; otherwise – as we will see – the analysis changes completely. These considerations naturally lead to the notion of *ineccsi* subsets of Θ, and related *ineccsi models* and *ineccsi sequences* (the nonstandard terminology is mine). These are formally defined as follows:

1. Ineccsi subsets. Let $\mathcal{M}$ be a model with a smooth parameterization (Θ, P_θ). Let $\Theta_0 \subset \Theta$. We say that Θ_0 is an *ineccsi* subset of Θ if

1. the interior of Θ_0 is nonempty;

2. the closure of Θ_0 is a compact subset of the interior of Θ.

Thus, *ineccsi* stands for "interior (is) non-empty; closure (is) compact subset of interior." Intuitively, Θ_0 is an ineccsi subset of Θ if (i) it has the same dimensionality as Θ; but (ii) it does not come arbitrarily close to "boundary points" of Θ, where, if Θ is unbounded, boundary points may be vectors with infinite components. Because of (i), the interior of an ineccsi set Θ_0 must be nonempty; because of (ii), Θ_0 must be bounded (i.e. its closure must be compact), and its closure must not intersect with the boundary of Θ.

2. Ineccsi models. Relatedly, we say that a model $\mathcal{M}$ parameterized by some (Θ, P_θ) is ineccsi if there exists a model $\mathcal{M}'$ with $\mathcal{M} \subset \mathcal{M}'$ such that $\mathcal{M}'$ is parameterized by $(\Theta', P_{\theta'})$, where $\Theta \subset \Theta'$, the restriction of $P_{\theta'}$ to Θ is equal to P_θ, and Θ is an ineccsi subset of Θ'. In words, an ineccsi model parameterized by Θ is really a subset of another model parameterized by some Θ', such that Θ is an ineccsi subset of Θ'.

3. Ineccsi and Θ_0-sequences. Let Θ be the parameter space of some model $\mathcal{M}$, and let Θ_0 be an ineccsi subset of $\mathcal{M}$. We say that a sequence $x_1, x_2, \ldots$ is a Θ_0-*sequence* if for all large n, the ML estimator $\hat{\theta}(x^n)$ exists, is unique, and satisfies $\hat{\theta}(x^n) \in \Theta_0$. Stretching the definition of ineccsi, we say that a sequence $x_1, x_2, \ldots$ is ineccsi if there exists an ineccsi set $\Theta_0 \subset \Theta$ such that $x_1, x_2, \ldots$ is a Θ_0-sequence. If the ML estimator $\hat{\theta}(x^n)$ converges to some point θ^* in Θ, then this implies $x_1, x_2, \ldots$ is an ineccsi sequence, since for exponential families, Θ is required to be open, so there must be an ineccsi subset Θ_0 of Θ with $\theta^* \in \Theta_0$. But the ML estimators of ineccsi sequences do not necessarily converge to a single point; it is sufficient that, for all large n, they remain bounded away from the boundary of Θ.

Notation: Redefining ML, Regret and Complexity   To enable a smooth presentation of the material, we slightly change and extend some of our notation in this and all of the following chapters which deal with universal codes for parametric models (Chapters 7-12).

First of all, relative to a given model with parameter set Θ_0, we sometimes write $P_{\hat{\theta}(x^n)}(x^n)$ in cases where the ML estimator $\hat{\theta}(x^n)$ is undefined. In that case, $P_{\hat{\theta}(x^n)}(x^n)$ should be read as $\sup_{\theta \in \Theta_0} P_\theta(x^n)$. It is clear that, if $\hat{\theta}(x^n)$ is well defined, then both expressions coincide. The advantage of "acting as if the ML estimator existed" is that the resulting notation is easier to parse.

Second, we slightly change the notation of regret and represent the model $\mathcal{M}$ by its corresponding parameter set $\Theta_{\mathcal{M}}$. Whenever $\mathcal{M}$ is clear from the context, we simply write Θ rather than $\Theta_{\mathcal{M}}$. Thus, the regret of a universal model $\bar{P}$ on sequence x^n relative to Θ, is now written as $\mathrm{REG}(\bar{P}, \Theta, x^n)$, and defined as

$$\mathrm{REG}(\bar{P}, \Theta, x^n) := -\log \bar{P}(x^n) + \log P_{\hat{\theta}(x^n)}(x^n). \tag{7.2}$$

Let Θ_0 be any subset of Θ and let $\mathrm{COMP}^{(n)}$ represent the model complexity (7.1). In the context of parametric models, the complexity is usually called *parametric complexity.* Analogously to (7.2), we now write $\mathrm{COMP}^{(n)}(\Theta_0)$ rather than $\mathrm{COMP}^{(n)}(\mathcal{M}_{\Theta_0})$:

$$\mathrm{COMP}^{(n)}(\Theta_0) := \log \sum_{x^n \in \mathcal{X}^n} P_{\hat{\theta}(x^n)}(x^n), \tag{7.3}$$

where $\hat{\theta}(x^n)$ denotes the ML estimator within the set Θ_0. In case the sample space $\mathcal{X}$ is continuous-valued, the sum in (7.3) is to be replaced by an integral. This convenient change of notation is justified because *(7.3) does not depend on the chosen parameterization*: for any $\mathcal{M}_0$, and any parameterization Θ_0 such that $\{P_\theta \mid \theta \in \Theta_0\} = \mathcal{M}$, we have $\text{COMP}^{(n)}(\Theta_0) = \text{COMP}^{(n)}(\mathcal{M}_0)$.

7.2 Asymptotic Expansion of Parametric Complexity

The definition (7.3) does not give much intuition about the size of the minimax regret $\text{COMP}^{(n)}(\Theta_0)$. In Theorem 7.1 below we give an asymptotic formula for $\text{COMP}^{(n)}(\Theta_0)$ which does provide such an intuition. This theorem is of central importance in this and the next three chapters.

Theorem 7.1 Let $\mathcal{M}$ be a k-dimensional exponential family with parameter set $\Theta = \Theta_{\mathcal{M}}$ such that (Θ, P_Θ) is a diffeomorphic parameterization. Let Θ_0 be an ineccsi subset of Θ. Then $\text{COMP}^{(n)}(\Theta_0)$ is finite and satisfies

$$\text{COMP}^{(n)}(\Theta_0) = \frac{k}{2} \log \frac{n}{2\pi} + \log \int_{\theta \in \Theta_0} \sqrt{\det I(\theta)} d\theta + o(1), \qquad (7.4)$$

so that $\bar{P}_{\text{nml}}^{(n)}$ is well defined and satisfies

$$-\log \bar{P}_{\text{nml}}^{(n)}(x^n) = -\log P_{\hat{\theta}(x^n)}(x^n) + \frac{k}{2} \log \frac{n}{2\pi} + \log \int_{\theta \in \Theta_0} \sqrt{\det I(\theta)} d\theta + o(1). \qquad (7.5)$$

Here $\det I(\theta)$ stands for the determinant of the $k \times k$ Fisher information matrix I evaluated at θ. Although the theorem is stated in terms of the binary logarithm, and in fact holds for logarithms to arbitrary base, the Fisher information is defined in the usual way, relative to the natural logarithm. Since $o(1) \to 0$ as $n \to \infty$, this characterization of $\text{COMP}^{(n)}(\Theta_0)$ is asymptotically precise. We defer a heuristic derivation of (7.4) to Chapter 8, Section 8.3, because the proof makes a detour involving the Bayesian universal model, which we do not consider in this chapter. The precise proof is even postponed until Chapter 11, where we prove Theorem 11.4, of which Theorem 7.1 is a special case.

In the previous chapter we saw that for finite $\mathcal{M}$, $\text{COMP}^{(n)}(\mathcal{M})$ remains finite. Now we see that for parametric models, which contain uncountably many distributions, it generally grows logarithmically in n. On the other hand, if $\mathcal{M}$ is an i.i.d. exponential family, then it can be parameterized as in (2.29) (the "canonical parameterization," Chapter 18). This parameterization reveals that if $x_1, x_2, \ldots$ is ineccsi, then $P_{\hat{\theta}(x^n)}(x^n)$ is guaranteed to decrease exponentially in n. Therefore, although the regret $\text{COMP}^{(n)}(\Theta_0)$ grows log-arithmically in n, it is still very small compared to $-\log P_{\hat{\theta}(x^n)}(x^n)$, which grows linearly in n and makes up the bulk of the codelength (7.5).

As is to be expected, the minimax regret $\text{COMP}^{(n)}(\Theta_0)$ depends on the number of free parameters in the model: if one extends a model with an extra parameter, then it can fit every set of data at least as well and some data strictly better. Then the sum in (7.3) gets larger, and inevitably, so does the minimax regret. Indeed, the more parameters, the larger the factor in front of the logarithmic term. But complexity does not only depend on the number of parameters: the term $\int_{\Theta} \sqrt{\det I(\theta)}d\theta$ is important as well. It does not grow in n so that it can be ignored for large n; but in practice, for the sample sizes we are interested in, it may be quite large (Myung et al. 2000), see also Chapter 14, page 417. In Section 7.3 we explain the meaning of $\int_{\Theta} \sqrt{\det I(\theta)}d\theta$ in detail.

The regret of $\bar{P}_{\text{nml}}$ is equal to $\text{COMP}^{(n)}(\Theta_0)$ for *every* sequence $x^n \in \mathcal{X}^n$. Therefore, $\bar{P}_{\text{nml}}$ is a universal model in the strong, uniform sense, as defined in the box on page 183:

NML Model Is Uniformly Universal
The NML universal model with respect to a k-parameter exponential family model Θ restricted to an ineccsi parameter set Θ_0 is $\text{COMP}^{(n)}(\Theta_0)$-*uniformly universal*, where $\text{COMP}^{(n)}(\Theta_0)$ is given by

$$\frac{k}{2} \log \frac{n}{2\pi} + \log \int_{\theta \in \Theta_0} \sqrt{\det I(\theta)}d\theta + o(1).$$

Example 7.1 [Complexity of the Bernoulli Model] The Bernoulli model $\mathcal{B}^{(0)}$ can be parameterized in a one-to-one way by the unit interval $\Theta = [0, 1]$. Thus, its dimension k is equal to 1. From Example 4.1, Chapter 4, we know that the Fisher information is given by $I(\theta) = \theta^{-1}(1 - \theta)^{-1}$, so that

$$\int_{\Theta} \sqrt{\det I(\theta)}d\theta = \int_0^1 \frac{1}{\sqrt{\theta(1-\theta)}}d\theta = \pi. \tag{7.6}$$

Plugging this into (7.4) gives the following. Take an arbitrary $\epsilon > 0$. Then for Bernoulli models with parameters restricted to $\Theta_\epsilon := [\epsilon, 1 - \epsilon]$,

$$\text{COMP}^{(n)}(\Theta_\epsilon) = \frac{1}{2} \log \frac{n}{2\pi} + \log \int_\epsilon^{1-\epsilon} \sqrt{I(\theta)} d\theta + o(1) =$$
$$\frac{1}{2} \left(\log n - \log 2 + \log \pi \right) + f(\epsilon) + o(1), \quad (7.7)$$

for some function f with $\lim_{\epsilon \to 0} f(\epsilon) = 0$. The case $\epsilon = 0$ does not directly follow from our theorem. To see this, make the dependencies in the $o(1)$-term explicit by writing it as $g_{n,\epsilon}$, where for each $\epsilon > 0$, $\lim_{n \to \infty} g_{n,\epsilon} = 0$. It is important to realize that our theorem leaves open the possibility that the closer ϵ is to 0, the larger n must be before $g_{n,\epsilon}$ becomes really small. Xie and Barron (2000) show that for the Bernoulli model this possibility does not occur, and (7.7) continues to hold for the full Bernoulli model, with $\epsilon = 0$.

> More precisely, they show that (7.4) holds for the full parameter set Θ (rather than ineccsi subsets Θ_0) for i.i.d. multinomial models (Chapter 2, Example 2.5) and multinomial models with "side-information." They use a different proof technique than we use in proving Theorem 7.1. It is not clear whether their conclusion can be extended beyond the multinomial-type cases they consider.

In Example 7.4 on page 227, we compute the complexity of the Bernoulli model (7.7) directly, using Stirling's approximation of the factorial rather than Theorem 7.1.

The remainder of this chapter is fully devoted to further analysis of the statement made in Theorem 7.1. We consider the following issues in turn:

1. Extensions of the theorem.

2. Accuracy of the theorem

3. Usability of the theorem

4. Parameterization independence

5. The meaning of $\int_\Theta \sqrt{\det I(\theta)} d\theta$

6. Simplified/Alternative Computations of $\text{COMP}^{(n)}(\Theta_0)$

The last two issues are so important that we devote separate sections to them: Section 7.3 and Section 7.4.

1. Extensions of the theorem. Theorem 7.1 is a simplified version of the celebrated (Rissanen 1996, Theorem 1), with, however, a very different proof. Rissanen shows that (7.4) holds for all models satisfying a number of regularity conditions which are quite hard to verify. It turns out that these models include all i.i.d. exponential families and also non-i.i.d. exponential families such as Markov chains. As in our version of the theorem, the parameter space must always be restricted to ineccsi sets. The proof we give here is much simpler, but only works for i.i.d. exponential families. Rissanen's theorem was later extended by Takeuchi and Barron (1997, 1998a) and Takeuchi (2000). Essentially, Takeuchi and Barron show that if $\mathcal{M}$ behaves "asymptotically" like an i.i.d. exponential family, then (7.4) still holds. For example, (7.4) holds for *curved* i.i.d. exponential families (Kass and Voss 1997), for Markov models, and for AR and ARMA processes. Szpankowski (1998) develops methods for investigating the $o(1)$-term in more detail, for the special case of the Bernoulli and multinomial model. He finds that it converges to 0 at rate $O(1/\sqrt{n})$, and determines the precise rate up to order $O(n^{-3/2})$; see also (Drmota and Szpankowski 2004).

2. Accuracy. The expansion (7.4) is truly asymptotic. Under the conditions of Theorem 7.1, the expansion (7.4) never seems to hold exactly for finite sample sizes. However, this remark should be qualified:

- There are some models $\mathcal{M}$ relative to which (7.4) can be shown to be *almost* exact. This includes the normal location family, for which the results in Example 11.5, Chapter 11 imply that the error is smaller than $1/n$. Similarly, by Stirling's approximation of the factorial, using the reasoning of Example 7.4 below, one can show that the asymptotics (7.4) are still within $O(1/n)$ for the k-parameter multinomial model. In fact, the proof of Theorem 7.1 suggests that the approximation is also of order $O(1/n)$ for other exponential families, and perhaps even for more general models, but it is not clear how large the hidden constants are. Experiments show that in some cases (Poisson and geometric distributions), the approximation is very good already at very small samples (Lanterman 2005). But there are examples of parametric models for which the approximation is extremely bad for small samples. Navarro (2004) exhibits two models Θ_1 and Θ_2 so that Θ_1 is nested inside Θ_2, and hence automatically $\text{COMP}(\Theta_2) > \text{COMP}(\Theta_1)$. Yet for small n, (7.4) is smaller for Θ_2 than for Θ_1! We note that these models are not exponential families, yet they are such that the asymptotic expansion (7.4) should still hold.

- There is a generalization of (7.4) to certain models $\mathcal{M}$ and parameter sets $\Theta_{\mathcal{M}}$ for which $\mathrm{COMP}^{(n)}(\Theta_{\mathcal{M}})$ is infinite, to be discussed in Chapter 11, Theorem 11.3. As will then be shown in Chapter 12, Section 12.4, this extension of (7.4) *does* hold exactly for the normal location family, and for linear regression models with fixed variance. Using Stirling's approximation, as in Section 12.4.3, one can also show that it holds almost exactly (with error bounded by $1/(6n)$) for linear regression models with varying variance.

These issues are discussed further in Chapter 14, Section 14.4.1.

3a. Usability - I. Computing the Fisher determinant, let alone its integral, is not easy in general, but sometimes it can be done. For example, one can compute it for the Poisson and geometric families (Chapter 11, Example 11.4). Hanson and Fu (2005) compute the integral for several practically relevant models.

3b. Usability - II. Let Θ represent an exponential family and let Θ_0 be some ineccsi subset. In MDL applications based on NML universal codes, we are usually more interested in $\mathrm{COMP}^{(n)}(\Theta)$ than in $\mathrm{COMP}^{(n)}(\Theta_0)$, because it is often unclear how Θ_0 should be chosen (Chapter 14). Unfortunately, in many cases the more interesting quantity $\mathrm{COMP}^{(n)}(\Theta)$ is infinite for all n, due to the singular behavior of θ near the boundaries of Θ. This happens even for very simple models such as the Poisson, geometric, or normal families, as we show in Chapter 11, Section 11.1.1. Chapter 11 is devoted to solving this problem.

4. Parameterization independence. We have already indicated that the complexity associated with $\mathcal{M}_\Theta$ does not depend on the parameterization and can be written as $\mathrm{COMP}^{(n)}(\Theta)$ rather than $\mathrm{COMP}^{(n)}(\mathcal{M})$. As one would expect, the same holds for the asymptotic characterization given in Theorem 7.1. The following proposition implies that the asymptotic expression (7.4) does not depend on the chosen parameterization.

Proposition 7.1 Consider an exponential family $\mathcal{M}$ with two arbitrary diffeomorphic parameterizations Θ and Γ. Let $\theta(\gamma)$ denote the $\theta \in \Theta$ corresponding to γ. Let Θ_0 be an ineccsi subset of Θ and let $\Gamma_0 = \{\gamma : \theta(\gamma) \in \Theta_0\}$. Let $I(\theta)$ be the Fisher information of parameter $\theta \in \Theta$, and let $I_\Gamma(\gamma)$ be the Fisher information of parameter γ, defined with respect to parameterization

Γ. Then

$$\int_{\Gamma_0} \sqrt{\det(I_\Gamma(\gamma))}d\gamma = \int_{\Theta_0} \sqrt{\det(I(\theta))}d\theta.$$

Proof: (sketch) We only consider 1-parameter families. Thus, $\Theta \subseteq \mathbb{R}$ and $\Gamma \subseteq \mathbb{R}$. By Proposition 18.2 on page 612:

$$\int_{\Gamma_0} \sqrt{I_\Gamma(\gamma)}d\gamma = \int_{\Gamma_0} \sqrt{I(\theta(\gamma))^2 \left(\frac{d\theta(\gamma)}{d\gamma}\right)^2}d\gamma = \int_{\Theta_0} \sqrt{I(\theta)}d\theta. \tag{7.8}$$

Using the same proposition, it is straightforward to extend the argument to k-parameter families. We omit the details. $\square$

7.3   The Meaning of $\int_\Theta \sqrt{\det I(\theta)}d\theta$

In this key section we show that $\int_\Theta \sqrt{\det I(\theta)}d\theta$ may be interpreted as the contribution of the *functional form* of $\mathcal{M}$ to the model complexity (Balasubramanian 1997; 2005). As a result, the "exponentiated asymptotic complexity" $\mathrm{EACOMP}^{(n)}$,

$$\mathrm{EACOMP}^{(n)}(\Theta):= \left(\frac{n}{2\pi}\right)^{k/2} \int_\Theta \sqrt{\det I(\theta)}d\theta, \tag{7.9}$$

may be interpreted as an abstract version of "volume" of Θ, where the larger the volume, the more "distinguishable distributions" Θ_0 contains. As a by-product, the derivation will show that the KL divergence between distributions measures how "distinguishable" they are. $\mathrm{EACOMP}^{(n)}$ is just the exponentiated asymptotic minimax regret $(k/2)\log(n/2\pi)+\log\int_\Theta \sqrt{\det I(\theta)}d\theta$, so it satisfies

$$\mathrm{EACOMP}^{(n)}(\Theta) \sim \sum_{x^n} P_{\hat{\theta}(x^n)}(x^n), \tag{7.10}$$

where $\sim$ means that the ratio between the two sides tends to 1 with increasing n. In the remainder of this section we first give an intuitive explanation of the idea of "functional form" and how it relates to volume and distinguishability (Section 7.3.1). We then say more about distinguishability and its relation to KL divergence (Section 7.3.2). We then make the interpretations of $\int_\Theta \sqrt{\det I(\theta)}d\theta$ and $\mathrm{EACOMP}^{(n)}(\Theta)$ as volumes more precise (Section 7.3.3). Finally, we make a direct connection between $\mathrm{EACOMP}^{(n)}(\Theta)$ and the number of distinguishable distributions (Section 7.3.4).

A related interpretation of $\int_\Theta \sqrt{\det I(\theta)}d\theta$ is provided in Chapter 8, Section 8.2, when we discuss the special prior for which $\bar{P}_{\text{Bayes}}$ resembles $\bar{P}_{\text{nml}}$ the most. The interpretation of $\text{EACOMP}^{(n)}(\Theta)$ as volume is connected to two-part codes in Chapter 10, Section 10.1.2.

7.3.1 Complexity and Functional Form

Complexity, or equivalently, worst-case regret, does not only depend on the number of parameters. This can be seen as follows: suppose Θ_0 is some ineccsi subset of a model parameterized by $\Theta \subset \mathbb{R}^k$. Now take the submodel indexed by Θ_1, a small ineccsi subset of Θ_0. Because Θ_1 is of the same dimensionality as Θ_0, it has complexity of order $(k/2)\log n + O(1)$. But since the set of distributions it contains is a strict subset of Θ_0, we have for all sequences x^n that $P_{\hat{\theta}_1(x^n)}(x^n) \leq P_{\hat{\theta}_0(x^n)}(x^n)$ where the inequality will typically be strict for some sequences. Therefore the complexity of Θ_1 *must* be smaller. If we have two k-dimensional ineccsi subsets Θ_0, Θ_1 of Θ that are not nested, then the difference between their parametric complexity does not just depend on their volume in Euclidean space but also on the "functional form" of the model defining equations. Let us illustrate this with an example.

> **Example 7.2 [Bernoulli $\mathcal{B}^{(1)}$ vs. Crazy Bernoulli $\mathcal{C}^{(1)}$]** Let $\mathcal{B}^{(1)}$ be the Bernoulli model, and let $\mathcal{B}^{(2)}$ be the first-order Markov model, given in their usual parameterizations (Chapter 2, Example 2.7). The first-order Markov model is then parameterized by $(\eta_{[1|0]}, \eta_{[1|1]}) \in [0,1]^2$, and can thus be represented by the unit square $[0,1]^2$ where each point represents the corresponding distribution. This square is drawn in Figure 7.1. The Bernoulli model is a one-dimensional subset of the Markov model: it consists of those distributions in $\mathcal{B}^{(2)}$ for which $\eta_{[1|0]} = \eta_{[1|1]}$. Thus, it is represented by the diagonal line from the lower left to the upper right. But now consider a different one-dimensional subset of the Bernoulli model, which we may call the "crazy Bernoulli" model, say $\mathcal{C}^{(1)}$. It is defined as the set of all first-order Markov chain distributions represented by the folded curve in Figure 7.1. The picture shows that for each distribution in $\mathcal{B}^{(1)}$, there is a distribution in $\mathcal{C}^{(1)}$ that is very close by. This suggests that the sum $\sum_{x^n} P_{\hat{\theta}(x^n)}(x^n)$ with $\hat{\theta}$ the ML estimator restricted to lie in $\mathcal{C}^{(1)}$, is not much smaller than the sum $\sum_{x^n} P_{\hat{\theta}(x^n)}(x^n)$ with the ML estimator defined relative to $\mathcal{B}^{(2)}$, so that $\text{COMP}^{(n)}(\mathcal{B}^{(2)})$ is not much larger than $\text{COMP}^{(n)}(\mathcal{C}^{(1)})$. It turns out that if we define $\mathcal{C}^{(1)}$ such that the denseness of the foldings is high enough, then this is indeed the case. On the other hand, by Theorem 7.1, we already know that for large n, the complexity of $\mathcal{B}^{(2)}$ exceeds that of $\mathcal{B}^{(1)}$ by about $(1/2)\log n + O(1)$. This makes it clear that the crazy Bernoulli model $\mathcal{C}^{(1)}$ must have significantly larger complexity than the ordi-

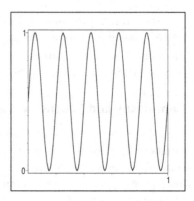

Figure 7.1 The crazy Bernoulli model.

nary Bernoulli model $\mathcal{B}^{(1)}$. More precisely, if the form of $\mathcal{C}^{(1)}$ remains fixed as n increases, then for large n, the leading term in its complexity will be $(1/2)\log n$, just as for the ordinary Bernoulli model: the difference in complexity between $\mathcal{B}^{(1)}$ and $\mathcal{C}^{(1)}$ is asymptotically just a constant. If we are allowed to change the form of of $\mathcal{C}^{(1)}$ with n, for example, by letting the number of folds increase with n, then we can make the complexity grow faster though. An explanation for this phenomenon is given further below.

The example and the figure suggest that the complexity $\text{COMP}^{(n)}(\Theta)$ of a one-dimensional model Θ should somehow depend on the *curvelength* of this model that one obtains if one embeds the model in some two-dimensional superset of it. More generally, if Θ is k-dimensional, then Θ becomes a curved surface in $\mathbb{R}^{k+1}$, and the complexity may be related to the *surface area*. This idea is partially, but not completely correct: we depicted the Bernoulli and first-order Markov distributions in their mean-value parameterizations, and we simply claimed that distributions which are close in terms of their parameter values are also similar in the sense that they provide about the same contribution to the sum $\sum_{x^n} P_{\hat{\theta}(x^n)}(x^n)$. To see that this is not completely correct, note that we could equally well have chosen another parameterization, for example, the canonical parameterization. Points which are close in the original parameterization may be quite far in the other parameterization. A more careful analysis, performed in Section 7.3.3, reveals that $\int_\Theta \sqrt{\det I(\theta)}d\theta$ and $\text{EACOMP}^{(n)}(\Theta) \propto n^{k/2}\int_\Theta \sqrt{\det I(\theta)}d\theta$ can indeed be interpreted as a curvelength, surface area, or volume, but in an abstract representation of the set of distributions $\mathcal{M}_\Theta$ where the distance between two distributions measures how *distinguishable* they are. This abstract representation is different from the mean-value parameterization depicted in Figure 7.1. Here "P is distinguishable from Q" essentially means that

$$P(Q(X^n) > P(X^n)) \text{ is small,}$$

so that, if a sample is distributed according to P, and we try to decide whether a sample comes from P or Q, we can actually *tell* from the sample that it comes from P, with high probability. The distance function measuring distinguishability turns out to be the familiar KL divergence between distributions, with a rescaling factor depending on sample size. This idea is made precise in Section 7.3.2. Since the KL divergence locally behaves like Euclidean distance, this also indicates that Figure 7.1 is not completely off the mark.

Both $\int_\Theta \sqrt{\det I(\theta)} d\theta$ and $\text{EACOMP}^{(n)}(\Theta)$ can be thought of as nonstandard "volumes," but under the rescaling in $\text{EACOMP}^{(n)}$, we get the additional interpretation that the "volume" of Θ is proportional to the *number of distinguishable distributions* contained in Θ. We heuristically develop this idea in Section 7.3.3. The insight unifies the interpretation of $\text{EACOMP}^{(n)}(\Theta)$ for parametric models with our previous interpretation for finite models, where a direct argument (Example 6.5 and the text above it) showed that $\text{EACOMP}^{(n)}(\mathcal{M})$ measures something like the number of distinguishable distributions in $\mathcal{M}$.

> **Example 7.3 [Example 7.2, Cont.]** Note that the total "volume" in terms of $\text{EACOMP}^{(n)}$ is multiplied by $(n/2\pi)^{k/2}$ as n increases. This implies that, to get a proper idea of the relation between the crazy Bernoulli and the first-order Markov model at sample size n, we should enlarge Figure 7.1 by a factor of $(n/2\pi)^{k/2}$. It is then clear that no matter how close the folds in the model $\mathcal{C}^{(1)}$, its denseness in the set $\mathcal{B}^{(2)}$ rapidly shrinks to 0 as n increases, which "explains" that the effect of functional form of the model can only be of size $O(1)$: Asymptotically, the dimensionality dominates the size of $\text{EACOMP}^{(n)}(\Theta)$.

7.3.2   KL Divergence and Distinguishability

In the remainder of this section, Θ_0 always represents an ineccsi subset of a k-dimensional exponential family given in any diffeomorphic parameterization (Θ, P_θ). In Section 7.3.3 we give a heuristic argument that $\int_{\Theta_0} \sqrt{\det I(\theta)} d\theta$ and $\text{EACOMP}^{(n)}(\Theta_0)$ can both be interpreted as "volumes." To prepare for this, in this subsection we relate KL divergence to distinguishability.

For two functions g and h, $g(\epsilon) \sim h(\epsilon)$ represents approximate equality for small ϵ, in the sense that $\lim_{\epsilon \to 0} g(\epsilon)/h(\epsilon) = 1$. Our arguments will not be precise, and at several places we will omit $o(1)$ terms without explicitly saying so.

Kullback-Leibler Balls   Define the ϵ-Kullback-Leibler ball around θ_0 as

$$B_{\mathrm{kl}}(\theta_0, \epsilon) = \{\theta \; : \; \mathrm{D}(\theta\|\theta_0) \le \epsilon\} \tag{7.11}$$

In contrast to ordinary Euclidean balls, the volume (defined in the standard manner) of the KL ball $B_{\mathrm{kl}}(\theta_0, \epsilon)$ depends on the location of θ_0. From the (local) convexity of KL divergence in any diffeomorphic parameterization, it is seen that KL balls are connected sets. From the Taylor expansion of KL divergence that we performed in Chapter 4 (box on page 120 and text underneath that box), we see that, for small ϵ, $B_{\mathrm{kl}}(\theta_0, \epsilon)$ essentially coincides with the Mahalanobis (rescaled Euclidean) ball around θ_0 with radius $\sqrt{\epsilon}$. The square root appears because KL divergence behaves like rescaled *squared* Euclidean distance.

Thus, it follows that, for small ϵ, the volume of $B_{\mathrm{kl}}(\theta_0, \epsilon)$ is approximately equal to that of the corresponding Mahalanobis ball $B_{I(\theta_0)}(\theta_0, \sqrt{\epsilon})$ We computed this latter volume on page 121:

$$V(B_{\mathrm{kl}}(\theta_0, \epsilon) \cap B_{I(\theta_0)}(\theta_0, \sqrt{\epsilon})) \sim V(B_{\mathrm{kl}}(\theta_0, \epsilon)) \sim V(B_{I(\theta_0)}(\theta_0, \sqrt{\epsilon})) =$$
$$V(\{\theta \; : \; (\theta - \theta_0)^\top M (\theta - \theta_0) \le \epsilon\}) = \frac{c_k}{\sqrt{\det I(\theta_0)}} \epsilon^{k/2}, \tag{7.12}$$

where c_k is as on page 121 and $\sim$ means that the ratio between the volumes converges to 1 as ϵ goes to 0. Using the fact that Θ_0 is ineccsi, it is easily shown that (7.12) holds uniformly for all $\theta_0 \in \Theta_0$.

Distinguishability Regions   Having thus gained some intuition about KL balls, we now relate them to *distinguishability regions*. For given θ_0, let Θ' be some set containing θ_0. We say that Θ' is a (δ, n)-*distinguishability region* for θ_0 if $P_{\theta_0}(\hat{\theta}(x^n) \in \Theta') = \delta$. Intuitively, if Θ' is a (δ, n)-distinguishability region for δ close to 1, then observing an x^n such that $\hat{\theta}(x^n)$ falls outside Θ' has probability close to 0, so the region of parameters *outside* Θ' is very "distinguishable" from θ_0. By the multivariate central limit theorem (Chapter 19, Theorem 19.1), and using (7.12) we see that, for $\epsilon > 0$, in the limit for large n, the KL ball

$$P_{\theta_0}\left(\hat{\theta}(x^n) \in B_{\mathrm{kl}}\left(\theta_0, \frac{\epsilon}{n}\right)\right) \sim P_{\theta_0}\left(\hat{\theta}(x^n) \in B_{I(\theta_0)}\left(\theta_0, \sqrt{\frac{\epsilon}{n}}\right)\right) \to g_k(\epsilon),$$

$$(7.13)$$

where

$$g_k(\epsilon) = \int_{z \in \mathbb{R}^k : \|z\| < \epsilon} \frac{1}{\sqrt{2\pi}^k} e^{-\frac{1}{2}\sum_{j=1}^k z_j^2} dz.$$

It is clear that the function g_k is continuous, monotonically increasing, and, being a probability, satisfies $g_k(0) = 0$, $\lim_{\epsilon \to \infty} g_k(\epsilon) = 1$. For small ϵ, a Taylor approximation gives

$$g_k(\epsilon) \sim c_k \epsilon^{k/2},$$

$$(7.14)$$

where c_k is a proportionality constant. Remarkably, the occurrence of Fisher information in the Euclidean volume of the KL ball $B_{\mathrm{kl}}(\theta_0, \epsilon/n)$ cancels with the occurrence of the Fisher information in the multivariate central limit theorem, so that (7.13) holds irrespective of the location of θ_0 in the parameter space. Therefore:

Kullback-Leibler Divergence and Distinguishability
For small ϵ and large n, the KL balls with radius ϵ/n effectively become $(g_k(\epsilon), n)$-distinguishability regions, *irrespective of the location of θ_0 in Θ, and irrespective of the details of the model Θ under consideration.* This suggests that the KL divergence can be interpreted as a basis for measuring distinguishability.

Henceforth we call the (δ, n)-distinguishability region for θ_0 that coincides with $g_k^{-1}(\delta)$-KL balls around θ_0 the "(δ, n)-distinguishability ball around θ_0." Strictly speaking, we only showed a relation between KL divergence and distinguishability relative to exponential families. Equipped with this relation, we can explain the volume interpretation of $\mathrm{EACOMP}^{(n)}(\Theta_0)$ in more detail.

> Balasubramanian (1997) pioneered the interpretation of $\int_{\Theta_0} \sqrt{\det I(\theta)} d\theta$ as a volume based on a metric that measures distance between distributions by their distinguishability. He makes a different connection between KL divergence and distinguishability via Stein's lemma (Cover and Thomas 1991). This has the advantage that it works for arbitrary pairs of distributions, not just

members of exponential families. It has the disadvantage that it only works if these distributions remain at a fixed KL divergence a as $n \rightarrow \infty$. In order to *directly* connect the number of KL balls to the number of distinguishable distributions, as we do in Section 7.3.4, we need to consider KL balls of size ϵ/n. Since this tends to 0, the KL divergence between distributions in those balls does not remain fixed, and it forces us to make the connection between KL divergence and distinguishability using the central limit theorem rather than Stein's lemma. This should not be taken as a criticism: I view (Balasubramanian 1997) as a major step forward. The developments in this section have been inspired by, and complement, Balasubramanian's analysis.

7.3.3   Complexity and Volume

Volume Defined Relative to a Metric   For any compact $\Theta_0 \subset \mathbb{R}^k$ and any $\epsilon > 0$, the *covering number* $N(\Theta_0, \epsilon)$ is defined as the minimum number of Euclidean balls with radius ϵ needed to cover Θ_0 (Conway and Sloane 1993). This is identical to the size of the smallest finite subset $\ddot{\Theta}_0$ of Θ_0 such that for all $\theta \in \Theta_0$, there exists $\ddot{\theta} \in \ddot{\Theta}_0$ with Euclidean distance $\|\ddot{\theta} - \theta\| \leq \epsilon$. We define the *packing number* $M(\Theta_0, \epsilon)$ as the maximum number of Euclidean balls with radius ϵ that one can put in Θ_0 such that no two balls overlap. Finally, let $H(\Theta_0, \epsilon)$ be the minimum number of hypercubes with side length 2ϵ needed to partition Θ_0.

The standard volume $V(\Theta_0)$ has the property that for each compact Θ_0, for small $\epsilon > 0$, both the covering number $N(\Theta_0, \epsilon)$ and the packing number $M(\Theta_0, \epsilon)$ are proportional to $V(\Theta_0)$, in the sense that

$$H(\Theta_0, \epsilon) \sim c_H \epsilon^{-k} V(\Theta_0), N(\Theta_0, \epsilon) \sim c_N \epsilon^{-k} V(\Theta_0), M(\Theta_0, \epsilon) \sim c_M \epsilon^{-k} V(\Theta_0),$$

$$(7.15)$$

where $c_H = 2^{-k}$, and $c_N \geq c_M > 0$ are two "proportionality constants." Since both the covering and the packing number are defined in terms of Euclidean balls, (7.15) shows that the ordinary volume is somehow related to the Euclidean distance.

Now, let $d : \Theta \times \Theta \rightarrow \mathbb{R}$ be some divergence measure, i.e. $d(\theta, \theta') \geq 0$, with equality iff $\theta = \theta'$. Under suitable conditions on d, one can define a generalized notion of "volume" relative to d such that, for any compact Θ_0, the volume relative to d is a number satisfying the properties expressed by (7.15), but now for the covering and packing numbers N_d and M_d defined in terms of the divergence d, rather than the Euclidean distance. In the special case of

$$d_I(\theta, \theta_0) := \sqrt{(\theta - \theta_0)^\top I(\theta_0)(\theta - \theta_0)},$$

giving Mahalanobis balls $B_{I(\theta_0)}(\theta_0, \epsilon)$ as defined above, the corresponding notion of volume satisfying (7.15) must be defined as

$$V_{d_I}(\Theta_0) = a \int_{\Theta_0} \sqrt{\det I(\theta)}d\theta, \tag{7.16}$$

where $a > 0$ can be freely chosen. Equation (7.16) was first shown by Balasubramanian (1997). For convenience, we will take $a = 1$. Since for small ϵ, the balls $B_{\text{kl}}(\theta_0, \epsilon)$ and $B_{I(\theta_0)}(\theta_0, \sqrt{\epsilon})$ essentially coincide (7.12), we can also think of $\int_{\Theta_0} \sqrt{\det I(\theta)}d\theta$ as a volume relative to the KL divergence $D(\cdot\|\cdot)$. In contrast to the situation for the ordinary volume, it is essential here that we only consider "small" ϵ. Luckily, we are mostly interested in the case where ϵ depends on the sample size n and shrinks to 0 automatically with increasing n.

> To see the need for small ϵ, suppose that Θ_0 has a simple form, say it is a rectangle centered at the origin, and consider $N(\Theta_0, \epsilon)$ and $M(\Theta_0, \epsilon)$. If we multiply ϵ by an arbitrary r, and we blow up the rectangle by a factor r, then the covering and packing numbers $N(r\Theta_0, r\epsilon)$ and $M(r\Theta_0, r\epsilon)$ will not be affected. But, because the KL divergence $D(\theta\|\theta')$ is asymmetric and its relation with the Euclidean distance depends on the location of θ in Θ_0, the covering and packing numbers N_{kl} and M_{kl} may change dramatically if we multiply both ϵ and Θ_0 by r. Therefore, the relation between N_{kl} and M_{kl} and volume only holds if ϵ is small.

All this implies that

A. $\int_{\Theta_0} \sqrt{\det I(\theta)}d\theta$ **as a volume** $\int_{\Theta_0} \sqrt{\det I(\theta)}d\theta$ is quite literally a volume relative to the KL divergence, and, for small ϵ, the number $N_{\text{kl}}(\Theta_0, \epsilon)$ of KL balls $B_{\text{kl}}(\theta, \epsilon)$ needed to cover Θ_0 is proportional to $\int_{\Theta_0} \sqrt{\det I(\theta)}d\theta$:

$$N_{\text{kl}}(\Theta_0, \epsilon) \sim N_{d_I}(\Theta_0, \sqrt{\epsilon}) \sim \epsilon^{-k/2} \int_{\Theta_0} \sqrt{\det I(\theta)}d\theta c_k, \tag{7.17}$$

where c_k is some proportionality constant.

B. EACOMP$^{(n)}(\Theta_0)$ **as a volume** Let $N_{\text{dist}}(\Theta_0, \delta, n)$ be the minimum number of (δ, n)-distinguishability balls needed to cover the space. From (7.13) and (7.14) we see that $N_{\text{dist}}(\Theta_0, \delta, n) \sim c_k N_{\text{kl}}(\Theta_0, \delta^{2/k}/n)$, where c_k is some proportionality constant. By (7.17), it follows that

$$N_{\text{dist}}(\Theta_0, \delta, n) \sim c_k' \left(\frac{n}{2\pi}\right)^{k/2} \int_{\Theta_0} \sqrt{\det I(\theta)}d\theta \delta^{-1} = c_k' \text{EACOMP}^{(n)}(\Theta_0)\delta^{-1}.$$

$$(7.18)$$

where c'_k is some proportionality constant. Stretching the meaning of volume somewhat, $\text{EACOMP}^{(n)}(\Theta_0)$ can be thought of as a "distinguishability" volume in the sense that it *measures the amount of δ-distinguishability balls needed to cover Θ_0 at sample size n.*

Caveat The proportionality constants relating our volumes to KL and distinguishability covering numbers depend on k, but not on Θ. Thus, suppose that $\mathcal{M}_A$ and $\mathcal{M}_B$ are two different non-nested ineccsi exponential families parameterized by Θ_A and Θ_B respectively. If both $\mathcal{M}_A$ and $\mathcal{M}_B$ have k parameters and $\text{EACOMP}^{(n)}(\Theta_A) > \text{EACOMP}^{(n)}(\Theta_B)$, then the proportionality constants are the same for both models and one can say that $\mathcal{M}_A$'s volume of distinguishability is larger than $\mathcal{M}_B$'s. However, if $\mathcal{M}_A$ does not have the same parameters as $\mathcal{M}_B$, then the proportionality constants are different and it does not seem very meaningful to say that $\mathcal{M}_1$'s volume of distinguishability is larger than $\mathcal{M}_0$'s.

Insights A and B above are sufficient motivation for the interpretation of $\int_{\Theta_0} \sqrt{\det I(\theta)} d\theta$ and $\text{EACOMP}^{(n)}(\Theta_0)$ as volumes. Insight B suggests that:

C. $\text{EACOMP}^{(n)}(\Theta_0)$ measures "something like" the number of distinguishable distributions in Θ_0.

However, it is not immediately clear whether the number of distinguishability balls can be related to the number of distinguishable distributions. Below we show that, under a reasonable definition of this concept, the two concepts can be related so that C is indeed the case.

7.3.4   Complexity and the Number of Distinguishable Distributions*

Let $\ddot{\Theta}_0$ be a finite subset of Θ. We define the *level of distinguishability* of $\ddot{\Theta}_0$ at sample size n as

$$\min_{\theta \in \ddot{\Theta}_0} P_\theta(\hat{\ddot{\theta}}(X^n) = \theta),$$

where $\hat{\ddot{\theta}}(x^n)$ is the ML estimator within the discrete set $\ddot{\Theta}_0$, achieving $\max_{\theta \in \ddot{\Theta}_0} P_\theta(x^n)$. This is the worst-case probability that the estimate $\hat{\ddot{\theta}}(x^n)$ is correct. If $\ddot{\Theta}_0$ achieves level of distinguishability close to 1, then the distributions it contains are all highly distinguishable from one another. Note that for each $\delta < 1$, a finite subset $\ddot{\Theta}_0$ of, say, two different $\theta \in \Theta_0$, will always achieve level of distinguishability δ for large n. Our goal is to find the *maximum* size subset such that its elements are still distinguishable at given level δ. Formally, we define the *number of distinguishable distributions* $M_{\text{dist}}(\Theta, \delta, n)$ at level δ and sample size n as the size of the largest $\ddot{\Theta}_0 \subset \Theta_0$ such that $\ddot{\Theta}_0$ has level of distinguishability δ. Thus,

$$M_{\text{dist}}(\Theta_0, \delta, n) := \max \left\{ |\ddot{\Theta}_0| \mid \min_{\theta \in \ddot{\Theta}_0} P_\theta(\hat{\ddot{\theta}}(X^n) = \theta) \geq \delta \right\}.$$

We would like to relate this quantity to our "volume" $\text{EACOMP}^{(n)}(\Theta_0)$. There may seem to be a difficulty here since $M_{\text{dist}}(\Theta_0, \delta, n)$ measures distinguishability between a finite set of isolated points, and therefore does not seem directly related to $(g_k(\epsilon), n)$-distinguishability balls, which concern the relation between a single point and all points in a connected set around it. Nevertheless, we can relate the two concepts. For simplicity, we only consider sequences x^n such that $\hat{\theta}(x^n) \in \Theta_0$. The robustness property of exponential families (see Chapter 19, in particular (19.12) on page 631), implies that for any such x^n we have

$$\ln P_{\hat{\theta}(x^n)}(x^n) - \ln P_{\hat{\ddot{\theta}}(x^n)}(x^n) = n\text{D}(\hat{\theta}\|\hat{\ddot{\theta}}).$$

Now let $\ddot{\Theta}_0$ be a finite subset of Θ_0 and define

$$\epsilon_0 = \sup_{\theta \in \Theta_0} \inf_{\ddot{\theta} \in \ddot{\Theta}_0} \text{D}(\theta\|\ddot{\theta}) \tag{7.19}$$

as the maximum KL divergence from any point in Θ_0 to the closest discretized point. If (7.19) holds for some given $\ddot{\Theta}_0$ and ϵ_0, then we say they *correspond* to each other. Then for every $\theta \in \ddot{\Theta}_0$,

$$P_\theta(\hat{\ddot{\theta}} \neq \theta) = P_\theta(\arg \min_{\ddot{\theta} \in \ddot{\Theta}_0} \{\text{D}(\hat{\theta}(X^n)\|\ddot{\theta})\} \neq \theta) \geq$$

$$P_\theta\left(\hat{\theta}(X^n) \notin B_{\text{kl}}\left(\theta, \frac{\epsilon_0}{n}\right)\right) \sim 1 - g_k(\epsilon_0). \tag{7.20}$$

This means that every set $\ddot{\Theta}_0$ with small corresponding ϵ_0 achieves level of distinguishability less than or equal to $g_k(\epsilon_0)$. In particular, this holds for the smallest $\ddot{\Theta}_0$ corresponding to some given ϵ_0. But the number of elements of the smallest such set is $N_{\text{kl}}(\Theta_0, \epsilon_0)$, the number of $g_k(\epsilon_0)$-distinguishability balls needed to cover Θ_0. It follows that the number of distinguishable distributions is bounded from above by this covering number: for all $\epsilon > 0$, for large enough n,

$$M_{\text{dist}}(\Theta_0, g_k(\epsilon), n) \leq N_{\text{kl}}(\Theta_0, \epsilon/n). \tag{7.21}$$

Completely analogously, one can show that, for large n, $M_{\text{dist}}(\Theta_0, g_k(\epsilon), n)$ is bounded from below by the packing number $M_{\text{kl}}(\Theta_0, \epsilon/n)$, which is the maximum number of KL balls of radius ϵ/n that one can put in Θ_0 in such a way that none of the balls overlap:

$$M_{\text{dist}}(\Theta_0, g_k(\epsilon), n) \geq M_{\text{kl}}(\Theta_0, \epsilon/n). \tag{7.22}$$

Just like $N_{\text{kl}}(\Theta_0, \epsilon/n)$, $M_{\text{kl}}(\Theta_0, \epsilon/n)$ can also be shown to be proportional to $\text{EACOMP}^{(n)}(\Theta_0)$: analogously to (7.17), we have

$$M_{\text{kl}}(\Theta_0, \epsilon/n) \sim \epsilon^{-k/2} \text{EACOMP}^{(n)}(\Theta_0) c_k.$$

Together with (7.22) and (7.21), and analogously to (7.18), this suggests that there exists a proportionality constant c'_k such that, for large n, for $\delta > 0$,

$$M_{\text{dist}}(\Theta_0, \delta, n) \sim c_k \text{EACOMP}^{(n)}(\Theta_0) \delta^{-1}.$$

Thus, we have made plausible that $\text{EACOMP}^{(n)}(\Theta_0)$ measures the number of distinguishable distributions in Θ_0 at each level δ, in a manner which avoids the concept of "distinguishability balls."

7.4   Explicit and Simplified Computations

When Θ_0 represents an exponential family, the expression for $\text{COMP}(\Theta_0)$ can be simplified. For many models, the simplified expression is still so complicated that no efficient algorithm for computing it exactly is known. However, the simplification does help to efficiently compute (appropriate modifications of) $\text{COMP}(\Theta_0)$ for linear regression models and their special case, the normal family, both for fixed and varying variance. At the time of writing this book, apart from the linear regression models, there are just two other models for which an efficient algorithm for precisely computing $\text{COMP}(\Theta_0)$ is known. These are the multinomial model (including its special case, the Bernoulli model), and the closely related finite-bin histogram model (Chapter 13).

We will first consider the simplified computations for exponential families, and then say a bit more about the multinomial model.

Simplified Computations for Exponential Families   Because exponential families admit sufficient statistics, the expression for $\text{COMP}^{(n)}(\Theta_0)$ can be simplified. For example, suppose $\mathcal{M}$ is an exponential family given in the mean-value parameterization Θ_{mean} (Chapter 18). Then $\Theta_0 \subset \Theta_{\text{mean}}$ represents a set of means, and the expression (7.3) simplifies to

$$\text{COMP}^{(n)}(\Theta_0) =$$
$$\log \sum_{\mu \in \Theta_0} \sum_{x^n \in \mathcal{X}^n : \hat{\theta}(x^n) = \mu} P_\mu(x^n) = \log \sum_{\mu \in \Theta_0} P_\mu(\hat{\theta}(X^n) = \mu). \quad (7.23)$$

In the continuous case, this becomes

$$\text{COMP}^{(n)}(\Theta_0) = \log \int_{\mu \in \Theta_0} f_\mu^{(n)}(\mu) d\mu, \qquad (7.24)$$

where $f_\mu(\cdot)$ is the density of the distribution $P_\mu(\hat{\theta}(X^n) = \cdot)$, i.e. $P_\mu(\hat{\theta}(X^n) \in [a,b]) = \int_{\mu' \in [a,b]} f_\mu(\mu') d\mu'$.

To see that the decompositions (7.23) and (7.24) can be quite useful, we now show how they lead to a direct proof of (a slight weakening of) Theorem 7.1 for the special case of the Bernoulli family. Another application will be given in Example 11.1, where we show that the complexity of the normal location family is infinite, and Section 11.2, where we calculate the complexity of a restricted normal location family. The latter is extended in Chapter 12, where we show how (7.24) can be used to calculate variations of $\text{COMP}^{(n)}(\Theta_0)$ for linear regression models, both with fixed and varying variance.

Example 7.4 [Explicit Calculation of $\text{COMP}^{(n)}$ for Bernoulli] Consider the Bernoulli model with $\Theta = (0,1)$. In this case, we have for $\mu = n_1/n$,

$$\sum_{x^n \in \mathcal{X}^n : \hat{\theta}(x^n) = \mu} P_\mu(x^n) = \binom{n}{n_1} \mu^{n_1}(1-\mu)^{n-n_1} = \binom{n}{n_1} e^{-n\text{H}(\mu)},$$

where the last equation follows because

$$n\text{H}(\hat{\theta}) = -n\hat{\theta} \ln \hat{\theta} - n(1-\hat{\theta}) \ln(1-\hat{\theta}) = -\ln \hat{\theta}^{n_1}(1-\hat{\theta})^{n-n_1} =$$
$$-\ln P_{\hat{\theta}(x^n)}(x^n). \quad (7.25)$$

Thus, $\text{COMP}^{(n)}(\theta)$ simplifies to

$$\text{COMP}^{(n)}(\Theta_{\mathcal{B}^{(0)}}) = \log \sum_{m=0}^{n} \binom{n}{m} e^{-n\text{H}(\frac{m}{n})},$$

which is interesting: of the two factors in the sum, one is exponentially large, the other exponentially small with the same rate, so that they "almost" cancel:

their ratio is of order $O(1/\sqrt{n})$; see Section 4.4, Chapter 4, page 125, Laws of Large Numbers as a Balance between Two Opposite Forces. The precise relation (4.35), derived by Stirling's approximation, shows that

$$\sum_{m=0}^{n} \binom{n}{m} e^{-n\mathrm{H}(\frac{m}{n})} = \sum_{\hat{\theta} \in \{0, 1/n, \dots, 1\}} \frac{1}{\sqrt{2\pi n \hat{\theta}(1-\hat{\theta})}} e^{R_{\hat{\theta}}},$$

where $R_{\hat{\theta}}$ is a remainder term. Working this term out in detail (in case $\hat{\theta} = 0$ or $\hat{\theta} = 1$ we cannot use Stirling's approximation and have to do this by hand), we find $|R_{\hat{\theta}}| \leq 1$, giving

$$\sum_{m=0}^{n} \binom{n}{m} e^{-n\mathrm{H}(\frac{m}{n})} = c \sum_{\hat{\theta} \in \{0, 1/n, \dots, 1\}} \frac{1}{\sqrt{2\pi n \hat{\theta}(1-\hat{\theta})}},$$

where $c \in [e^{-1}, e]$. As $n \to \infty$, the sum converges to n times the integral $\int_0^1 (2\pi n \nu (1-\nu))^{-0.5} d\nu$. Since, for Bernoulli models, the Fisher information is given by $I(\theta) = \theta^{-1}(1-\theta)^{-1}$ (Chapter 4, Example 4.1), we find

$$\mathrm{COMP}^{(n)}(\Theta_{B^{(0)}}) = \frac{1}{2} \log \frac{n}{2\pi} + \log \int_0^1 \det I(\theta) d\theta + R_n + o(1), \qquad (7.26)$$

where $|R_n| \leq 1$. This is in accordance with Theorem 7.1.

The simplification (7.23) of the complexity of the Bernoulli model still gave rise to an asymptotic formula (7.26). As we shall see in Chapter 11, when applied to the normal location family, the simplification (7.24) gives something better: it leads to a precise *nonasymptotic* expression of $\mathrm{COMP}^{(n)}(\Theta_0)$. Rissanen (2000) extends this computation to general linear regression models with fixed and varying variance, restricted to suitably parameterized ineccsi parameter sets Θ_0: in Chapter 14, Section 14.5.1, we shall encounter the corresponding explicit formulas.

Multinomial Complexity   In a series of papers, P. Kontkanen and collaborators showed that for the multinomial model (Chapter 2, Example 2.5) with $\mathcal{X} = \{1, \dots, m\}$, the precise, nonasymptotic minimax regret $\mathrm{COMP}^{(n)}(\Theta)$, where Θ now ranges over the full parameter set $\Delta^{(m)}$, can be efficiently computed as well (Kontkanen, Buntine, Myllymäki, Rissanen and Tirri 2003; Kontkanen and Myllymäki 2005a,b). Their algorithm can also be used to compute the nonasymptotic minimax regret for the closely related finite-bin histogram model of Chapter 13. The algorithm is not based on the simplification (7.23) for exponential families, but uses much more sophisticated techniques based on generating functions in a spirit that is reminiscent of the mysterious *umbral calculus*.

While Kontkanen and Myllymäki (2005b) provide an $O(n \log n \log m)$ algorithm, in recent, as yet unpublished work, a connection to the so-called *tree polynomials* is made, which leads to an improved algorithm of running time $O(n \log m)$ (Kontkanen and Myllymäki 2005a). An earlier, $O(n^2 \log m)$ algorithm was applied by (Kontkanen, Myllymäki, Buntine, Rissanen, and Tirri 2005) for NML-based clustering.

For other exponential families, despite the simplification (7.23), as far as we know, no efficient method to precisely compute $\text{COMP}^{(n)}(\Theta_0)$ is known, and (7.4) is typically the best approximation available.

8 *Parametric Models: Bayes*

In this chapter, we study the Bayesian universal model and its regret for parametric models. In Section 8.1, Theorem 8.1, we give an asymptotic expression for this regret. The remainder of the chapter is mostly devoted to an in-depth analysis of the regret. In Section 8.2 we discuss the crucial insight that with Jeffreys' prior, the regret of the Bayesian universal model becomes asymptotically equal to the minimax regret COMP(Θ). In Section 8.4 we compare the individual-sequence regret to the stochastic regret and redundancy.

Fast Track Section 8.1 and Section 8.2 until Subsection 8.2.1 are crucial for any understanding of MDL. The remainder of the chapter can be skipped at first reading.

8.1   The Bayesian Regret

With parametric models, the parameter set Θ is continuous-valued. The Bayesian universal model defined relative to prior distribution W is then given by

$$\bar{P}_{\text{Bayes}}(x^n) = \int_\Theta P(x^n \mid \theta) w(\theta) d\theta \tag{8.1}$$

where w is the *prior density* (often simply called "prior") corresponding to W, i.e. for $\Theta' \subseteq \Theta$, $W(\Theta') = \int_{\Theta'} w(\theta) d\theta$. Equation (8.1) is just the continuous analogue of (6.3) on page 175. As in the previous chapter, from now on we restrict attention to k-parameter exponential families, returning to more general setups at the end of Section 8.3. Thus, consider a k-parameter exponential family $\mathcal{M}$ and let (Θ, P_θ) be a diffeomorphic parameterization of $\mathcal{M}$. The following theorem characterizes the regret of the Bayesian universal model. It is just as important as, and should be compared to, Theorem 7.1 on the regret of the NML universal model.

Let Θ_0 be an *ineccsi* subset of Θ. We call a prior distribution on Θ with density w Θ_0-*compatible* if w is continuous on Θ and strictly positive on Θ_0, i.e. $\inf_{\theta \in \Theta_0} w(\theta) > 0$.

Theorem 8.1 Let Θ_0 be an *ineccsi* subset of Θ, let w be a Θ_0-compatible prior, and let $x_1, x_2, \ldots$ be any Θ_0-sequence. Then

$$\text{REG}(\bar{P}_{\text{Bayes}}, \Theta, x^n) = \frac{k}{2} \log \frac{n}{2\pi} - \log w(\hat{\theta}) + \log \sqrt{\det I(\hat{\theta})} + o(1). \qquad (8.2)$$

where the convergence is uniform in Θ_0.[1]

This theorem is well known. Different versions – weaker than this theorem in some sense, stronger in other senses – can be found in (Jeffreys 1961; Schwarz 1978; Kass and Raftery 1995; Balasubramanian 1997). In fact, the entire remainder of this chapter revolves around Theorem 8.1 and variations thereof. We consider the following issues:

Illustration We give a basic discussion of the theorem and illustrate it for the simple Bernoulli model with uniform prior (Section 8.1.1).

Bayes, NML, and Jeffreys' prior We compare the theorem to Theorem 7.1 on $\bar{P}_{\text{nml}}$, which leads to the minimax interpretation of *Jeffreys' prior* (Section 8.2) – the most important insight of this chapter.

Proof sketch In Section 8.3 we give a simple heuristic derivation of the result. A precise proof is in Appendix 8.A.

Extensions In Section 8.3 we also discuss extensions of the theorem beyond exponential families. In Section 8.4 we discuss variations of the theorem that hold for other types of universality such as stochastic redundancy and regret.

---

1. This means that the constants hidden in the o-notation do not depend on x^n, i.e. we actually show that

$$\lim_{n \to \infty} \sup_{x^n : \hat{\theta}(x^n) \in \Theta_0} \left| \text{REG}(\bar{P}_{\text{Bayes}}, \Theta, x^n) - \left[\frac{k}{2} \log \frac{n}{2\pi} - \log w(\hat{\theta}(x^n)) + \log \sqrt{\det I(\hat{\theta}(x^n))} \right] \right| = 0.$$

8.1.1 Basic Interpretation of Theorem 8.1

From (8.2) we see that, in contrast to the case with finite $\mathcal{M}$, for a parametric model the regret increases with n and tends to infinity, albeit only logarithmically. In contrast, as already noted in Chapter 7, $-\log P_{\hat{\theta}(x^n)}(x^n)$ increases linearly in n. This holds only as long as $\hat{\theta}$ remains in the set Θ_0, and thus away from the boundaries of the parameter set. Depending on the prior, (8.2) may be either grossly or mildly violated near the boundaries, as discussed in Example 8.2 and Section 8.2.1.

Note also that the influence of the prior is of $O(1)$ and becomes asymptotically negligible compared to the $(k/2)\log n$ term. Thus, the $(k/2)\log n$ term is common to all "reasonable" priors. Comparing to Theorem 7.1, we see that asymptotically, the regret of the Bayesian model is within $O(1)$ of the regret of the minimax optimal model, and thus, independently of the prior, close to minimax optimal. This raises the issue of whether there exist priors for which it really becomes minimax optimal, i.e. for which $\bar{P}_{\text{Bayes}}$ becomes a very good imitation of $\bar{P}_{\text{nml}}$. The answer is *yes*, as explained in Section 8.2.

> **Example 8.1 (Bayes for Bernoulli)** Let us illustrate Theorem 8.1 by directly calculating the regret of $\bar{P}_{\text{Bayes}}$ with respect to the Bernoulli model $\mathcal{B}^{(1)}$. We equip $\bar{P}_{\text{Bayes}}$ with the uniform prior $w(\theta):=1, \theta \in [0,1]$. Then
>
> $$\bar{P}_{\text{Bayes}}(x^n) = \int_0^1 P_\theta(x^n)d\theta = \int_0^1 \theta^{n_1}(1-\theta)^{n_0}d\theta,$$
>
> where n_1 denotes the number of 1s, and $n_0 = n - n_1$. Partial integration gives
>
> $$\int_0^1 \theta^{n_1}(1-\theta)^{n_0}d\theta = \left[\frac{1}{n_1+1}\theta^{n_1+1}(1-\theta)^{n_0}\right]_0^1 + \frac{n_0}{n_1+1}\int_0^1 \theta^{n_1+1}(1-\theta)^{n_0-1}d\theta,$$
>
> where the middle term is equal to 0. Repeating this step n_0 times leads to
>
> $$\bar{P}_{\text{Bayes}}(x^n) = \frac{1 \cdot 2 \cdot \ldots \cdot n_0}{(n_1+1) \cdot \ldots \cdot (n_1+n_0)}\int_0^1 \theta^n d\theta$$
>
> so that
>
> $$\bar{L}_{\text{Bayes}}(x^n) = -\log \bar{P}_{\text{Bayes}}(x^n) = \log\binom{n}{n_1} + \log(n+1). \tag{8.3}$$
>
> Recall that the ML estimator satisfies $\hat{\theta} = \hat{\theta}(x^n) = n_1/n$. Applying Stirling's approximation of the factorial as in (4.36) on page 129 shows that
>
> $$\ln\binom{n}{n_1} = n\mathrm{H}(\hat{\theta}) - \ln\sqrt{2\pi n\mathrm{var}(\hat{\theta})} + R(n,\hat{\theta}), \tag{8.4}$$

where $\text{var}(\hat{\theta}) = \hat{\theta}(1 - \hat{\theta})$ is the variance of a Bernoulli random variable with parameter $\hat{\theta}$. The remainder term satisfies $R(n, \nu) = o(1)$ as long as the sequence $x_1, x_2, \ldots$ is ineccsi. By (7.25), page 227, and because for the Bernoulli model, $\text{var}(\theta) = I^{-1}(\theta)$ (Example 4.1, page 122), (8.3) can be rewritten as

$$\bar{L}_{\text{Bayes}}(x^n) = -\log P_{\hat{\theta}(x^n)}(x^n) + \log \sqrt{I(\hat{\theta})} + \log \frac{n+1}{\sqrt{2\pi n}} + o(1). \qquad (8.5)$$

This coincides with (8.2) as long as $\hat{\theta}$ remains bounded away from 0 and 1, which is guaranteed to be the case if $x_1, x_2, \ldots$ is ineccsi.

The example shows that in the Bernoulli case, the Bayesian integral can be evaluated explicitly, and then (8.2) follows easily. In most cases, however, the integral cannot be solved analytically, and then Theorem 8.1 is of great help. The example also makes clear that the theorem does not necessarily hold for sequences that are not ineccsi:

> **Example 8.2 [Bayes at the Boundary]** Consider the previous example,. Suppose that n_1 remains equal to 0 for all n, so that x^n consists only of 0s. Then (8.3) becomes equal to $\ln(n + 1)$. Since then also $-\log P_{\hat{\theta}(x^n)}(x^n) = 0$, it holds that
>
> $$\bar{L}_{\text{Bayes}}(x^n) = -\log P_{\hat{\theta}(x^n)}(x^n) + \log(n + 1).$$
>
> Comparing to Theorem 8.1, we see that the regret is $(1/2) \log n + O(1)$ larger than the regret achieved for ineccsi sequences. This shows that in general, Theorem 8.1 only holds if the sequence $x_1, x_2, \ldots$ is ineccsi.

8.2   Bayes Meets Minimax – Jeffreys' Prior

In this key section we compare the regret of the Bayesian universal model $\bar{P}_{\text{Bayes}}$, as given by Theorem 8.1, to the minimax regret achieved by the NML model, given by Theorem 7.1. We already noted that, for ineccsi sequences and reasonable priors, the Bayesian regret (8.2) is within $O(1)$ of the minimax optimal NML regret, $\text{COMP}^{(n)}(\Theta)$. We may now ask whether there exist priors for which the worst-case regret achieved by $\bar{P}_{\text{Bayes}}$ is even closer to $\text{COMP}^{(n)}(\Theta)$. The answer is *yes*: if we equip the Bayesian universal model with a special prior known as the *Jeffreys' prior* (Jeffreys 1946; Bernardo and Smith 1994),

$$w_{\text{Jeffreys}}(\theta) = \frac{\sqrt{\det I(\theta)}}{\int_{\theta \in \Theta} \sqrt{\det I(\theta)} d\theta}, \qquad (8.6)$$

then Bayes and NML become very closely related: plugging (8.6) into (8.2), we find that the right-hand side of (8.2) now simply *coincides* with (7.4). More precisely:

The Most Important Insight of This Chapter:
NML $\approx$ Bayes with Jeffreys' Prior
Let (P_θ, Θ) be an exponential family such that (1) $\int \sqrt{\det I(\theta)}d\theta < \infty$, and (2), $\text{COMP}^{(n)}(\Theta) < \infty$. Then Jeffreys' prior is well defined, and so are $\bar{P}_{\text{Jeffreys}}$, the Bayesian universal model relative to Jeffreys' prior, and $\bar{P}_{\text{nml}}$, the minimax optimal universal model.
In that case, for any Θ_0 that is an ineccsi subset of Θ, and any Θ_0-sequence $x_1, x_2, \ldots$, we have

$$-\log \bar{P}_{\text{nml}}(x^n) = -\log \bar{P}_{\text{Jeffreys}}(x^n) + o(1),$$

where the convergence is uniform in Θ_0. This has important implications for MDL model selection (Chapter 14).
Conditions (1) and (2) above are both guaranteed to hold if Θ is itself an ineccsi model (see also the Open Problem in Chapter 11, Section 11.1.2).

As we discussed in Chapter 6, Section 6.4, in contrast to the NML universal code, the Bayesian universal codes have the elegant *prequential* property: they define a probabilistic source, rather than a sequence of incompatible distributions. In some applications of MDL (predictive estimation, Chapter 15, Section 15.2), one is actually forced to use prequential universal codes. In that case, the NML distribution cannot be used. Still, for large n, one can essentially achieve the minimax regret using the Bayesian code with Jeffreys' prior.

Three Interpretations of Jeffreys' Prior   Jeffreys introduced his prior as a "least informative prior", to be used when no useful prior knowledge about the parameters is available (Jeffreys 1946). As one may expect from such a prior, it is invariant under continuous 1-to-1 reparameterizations of the parameter space. The present analysis shows that when Θ represents an exponential family, then it also leads to asymptotically minimax codelength regret, giving it a universal coding interpretation. By the reinterpretation of $\text{EACOMP}^{(n)}$ and $\int_\Theta \sqrt{\det I(\theta)}d\theta$ as volumes (Chapter 7, Section 7.3), we obtain a third, at least equally important interpretation: for small ϵ, Jeffreys' prior is a distribution that puts equal mass on Kullback-Leibler balls of radius ϵ, irrespective of their location in the parameter space. While this provides another connection between Jeffreys' prior and data compression, it has the further consequence that, for large n, Jeffreys' prior also gives equal prior mass to ϵ-distinguishability balls. By the developments in Section 7.3.4, this means that, for large n, Jeffreys' prior puts equal mass on regions with the same number of "distinguishable" (essentially different) distributions.

We stress that if one decides to code the data with $\bar{P}_{\text{Jeffreys}}$, this does not imply a belief that, for $\Theta' \subset \Theta$, the probability that the "true state of the world" is in Θ' is given by $w_{\text{Jeffreys}}(\Theta')$. We use it because of its good compression properties in the worst case over all sequences. In reality, the true distribution may be any $\theta \in \Theta$, or a distribution outside Θ, or the data may be generated by some deterministic process. Therefore:

Jeffreys' Prior and the Third Most Important Observation of This Book (page 107)

On page 107 we claimed that "using the code corresponding to distribution P may sometimes be a good idea even if the data are *not* distributed according to P." There, we gave the uniform distribution on $\mathcal{X}^n$ as an example, which, when used as a code, achieves minimax *absolute* codelength. Another prime example is the code corresponding to $\bar{P}_{\text{Jeffreys}}$, which achieves minimax codelength (regret) *relative* to some Θ.

The analogy is strengthened by noting that Jeffreys' prior is also uniform, but not in the parameter space Θ: it is uniform in an abstract representation of $\mathcal{M}_\Theta$ in which the distance between two distributions measures how distinguishable they are.

We now give a concrete example of Jeffreys' prior. In Chapter 11, Section 11.1.2, we shall encounter some other examples.

Example 8.3 [Jeffreys' Prior for the Bernoulli Model] Consider Jeffreys' prior for the Bernoulli model with parameter set $\Theta = (0, 1)$. From example (7.1) we know that for the Bernoulli model, the Fisher information is given by $\theta^{-1/2}(1-\theta)^{-1/2}$ and $\int_\Theta \sqrt{\det I(\theta)}d\theta$ is equal to π, so that:

$$w_{\text{Jeffreys}}(\theta) = \frac{\sqrt{I(\theta)}}{\int_{\theta \in \Theta} \sqrt{I(\theta)}d\theta} = \frac{1}{\pi\sqrt{\theta(1-\theta)}}. \tag{8.7}$$

Suppose that x^n contains n_1 1s. Then the integral involved in computing

$\bar{P}_{\text{Jeffreys}}(x^n)$ can be evaluated and we get:

$$\bar{P}_{\text{Jeffreys}}(x^n) = \int \pi^{-1}\theta^{n_1-0.5}(1-\theta)^{n-n_1-0.5}d\theta =$$

$$\frac{\boldsymbol{\Gamma}(n_1+\tfrac{1}{2})\boldsymbol{\Gamma}(n-n_1+\tfrac{1}{2})}{\pi n!}. \quad (8.8)$$

Here $\boldsymbol{\Gamma}$ is the Gamma function (Chapter 2). In order to rewrite this in more explicit terms, it is useful to first calculate

$$\bar{P}_{\text{Jeffreys}}(X_{n+1}=1 \mid x^n) = \frac{\bar{P}_{\text{Jeffreys}}(x^n,1)}{\bar{P}_{\text{Jeffreys}}(x^n)} = \frac{n}{n+1}\frac{\boldsymbol{\Gamma}(n_1+1+\tfrac{1}{2})}{\boldsymbol{\Gamma}(n_1+\tfrac{1}{2})} =$$

$$\frac{1}{n+1}\left(n_1+\frac{1}{2}\right) = \frac{n_1+\tfrac{1}{2}}{n+1}. \quad (8.9)$$

Repeating the argument for $X_{n+1}=0$, one sees that for $j=0,1$:

$$\bar{P}_{\text{Jeffreys}}(X_{n+1}=j \mid x^n) = \frac{n_j+\tfrac{1}{2}}{n+1}. \quad (8.10)$$

Using (8.10) to Simplify (8.8) By the chain rule, $\bar{P}_{\text{Jeffreys}}(x^n) = \prod_{i=1}^{n} \bar{P}_{\text{Jeffreys}}(x_i \mid x^{i-1})$. Since $\bar{P}_{\text{Jeffreys}}(x^n)$ must be identical for all permutations of x^n, we can act as if x^n starts with n_1 consecutive 1s, followed by $n-n_1$ consecutive 0s. This gives:

$$\bar{P}_{\text{Jeffreys}}(x^n) = \prod_{i=1}^{n_1}\frac{i-1+\tfrac{1}{2}}{i} \prod_{i=n_1+1}^{n}\frac{i-n_1-1+\tfrac{1}{2}}{i} =$$

$$\frac{1}{n!}\prod_{i=1}^{n_1}\left(i-\frac{1}{2}\right) \prod_{i=n_1+1}^{n}\left(i-n_1-\frac{1}{2}\right). \quad (8.11)$$

In the box on page 258 we give a predictive interpretation of this formula.

8.2.1   Jeffreys' Prior and the Boundary

In this subsection we investigate what happens to the Bayesian codelength achieved with Jeffreys' prior if the sequence $x_1, x_2, \ldots$ is not ineccsi. $\hat{\theta}$ then comes arbitrarily close to the boundary of the parameter space Θ infinitely often. We already saw in Example 8.2 that in this case, with the uniform prior and the Bernoulli model, we achieve a different (larger) regret than the $(1/2)\log n + O(1)$ we achieve for ineccsi sequences. In Example 8.4 below, we show that something similar, but less dramatic, can happen with Jeffreys' prior for the multinomial model.

In both the Jeffreys and the uniform cases, the reason for the larger regret is that Theorem 8.1 does not hold if $x_1, x_2, \ldots$ is not an ineccsi sequence. To see how this comes about, suppose that, for large n, $\hat{\theta}(x^n)$ converges to some θ_0. Broadly speaking, the closer θ_0 is to the boundary, the larger n has to be before (8.2) becomes accurate. If Θ_0 is ineccsi, then (8.2) will at some point become accurate for *all* x^n with $\hat{\theta}(x^n) \in \Theta_0$, no matter how close to the boundary of Θ_0. But if Θ_0 is not ineccsi, then it may take "infinitely long" before (8.2) becomes accurate, and Theorem 8.1 does not hold anymore.

Example 8.4 [Jeffreys and Bernoulli at the Boundary] Consider the Bayesian universal code for the Bernoulli model with Jeffreys' prior. Suppose we observe a sequence x^n consisting only of 0s. By (8.11) we get

$$\text{REG}(\bar{P}_{\text{Jeffreys}}, \Theta, x^n) = -\log \bar{P}_{\text{Jeffreys}}(x^n) + \log P_{\hat{\theta}(x^n)}(x^n) =$$

$$-\log \bar{P}_{\text{Jeffreys}}(x^n) = -\log \frac{\Gamma(n+\frac{1}{2})\Gamma(\frac{1}{2})}{\pi\Gamma(n+1)}, \quad (8.12)$$

where the last equality follows from (8.8). Using two standard properties of the gamma function (Weisstein 2006), $\Gamma(1/2) = \sqrt{\pi}$ and $\Gamma(n+1/2)/\Gamma(n+1) = n^{-1/2}(1 - O(n^{-1}))$, this evaluates to

$$\frac{1}{2}\log \pi + \frac{1}{2}\log n + o(1).$$

Comparing to (7.7), the expression for $\text{COMP}^{(n)}(\Theta)$ for the Bernoulli model, we see that for this sequence, the regret achieved by Jeffreys' prior exceeds the minimax regret by 0.5 bit (see also (Freund 1996)). Admittedly this is not as much as with the uniform prior, but it is not $o(1)$. This implies that for nonineccsi sequences such as $0, 0, \ldots$, Theorem 8.1 does not hold. Xie and Barron (2000) extend this example to general k-dimensional multinomial models (Chapter 2, Example 2.5). Here k-dimensional means that there are $k+1$ outcomes, i.e. $\mathcal{X} = \{1, \ldots, k+1\}$. They show the following: (1) for multinomial models, $\text{COMP}^{(n)}(\Theta) = (k/2)\log(n/2\pi) + \int_\Theta \sqrt{\det I(\theta)}d\theta + o(1)$, even though $\Theta = [0,1]^k$ is not an ineccsi set, so that our Theorem 7.1 does not apply. On the other hand, (2), they show that $\bar{P}_{\text{Jeffreys}}$ achieves maximum regret for sequences with ML estimator at the boundary of the parameter space. The regret measured in bits is equal to $\text{COMP}^{(n)}(\Theta) + k/2 + o(1)$, so it asymptotically exceeds the minimax regret by $k/2$.

Xie and Barron (2000) also provide a means of slightly modifying Jeffreys' prior, so that the resulting prior $w_{\mathrm{XB},n}$ does achieve the minimax regret asymptotically, even for sequences with ML estimators at the boundaries of the parameter space. $w_{\mathrm{XB},n}$ is defined as follows: $w_{\mathrm{XB},n}(\theta) = (1 - \alpha_n)w_{\mathrm{Jeffreys}}(\theta) + \alpha_n w'_n(\theta)$, where $w'_n(\theta)$ is some prior that is concentrated near the boundary of the parameter space, and $\alpha_n = n^{-1/8}$. As n increases, the resulting prior resembles Jeffreys' prior more and more. We emphasize that, because the prior depends on n, the resulting universal model is not prequential, and therefore not a Bayesian universal model in the sense in which we defined it in Chapter 6. The main advantage in using $\bar{P}_{\mathrm{Bayes}}$ with the $w_{\mathrm{XB},n}$ prior over the NML code is that the corresponding codes and codelengths may be computed more efficiently, and can be mathematically analyzed more easily; see (Xie and Barron 1997).

Infinite $\int_\Theta \sqrt{\det I(\theta)}d\theta$ For the multinomial model and nonineccsi sequences, the Bayesian universal model with Jeffreys' prior may not achieve the minimax optimal regret. For most other exponential families, however, the situation is even worse than that: for such models, $\int_\Theta \det I(\theta)d\theta = \infty$, and then Jeffreys' prior, defined with respect to the full (non-ineccsi) parameter space Θ, is *undefined*. This situation will be considered in detail in Chapter 11.

8.3 How to Prove the Bayesian and NML Regret Theorems

8.3.1 Proof Sketch of Theorem 8.1

The proof of Theorem 8.1 is based on the *Laplace method* for integration (also known as "saddle point approximation"). The precise proof is found in Appendix 8.A. Below we provide a heuristic derivation. We start with the following proposition:

Proposition 8.1 Let $\mathcal{M}$ be a family of distributions parameterized by Θ. Let x^n be any sequence with $\hat{\theta}(x^n) \in \Theta$ and let w be an arbitrary prior distribution. Then

$$\mathrm{REG}_{\ln}(\bar{P}_{\mathrm{Bayes}}, \Theta, x^n) = -\ln \int_\Theta e^{-\mathrm{REG}(P_\theta, \Theta, x^n)} w(\theta)d\theta. \tag{8.13}$$

Moreover, if $\mathcal{M}$ is an exponential family, then

$$\mathrm{REG}_{\ln}(\bar{P}_{\mathrm{Bayes}}, \Theta, x^n) = -\ln \int_\Theta e^{-n\mathrm{D}(\hat{\theta}(x^n)\|\theta)} w(\theta)d\theta. \tag{8.14}$$

Here REG$_{\text{ln}}$ stands for the regret in nats (page 110), i.e. REG$_{\text{ln}}(\bar{P}_{\text{Bayes}}, \Theta, x^n)$- $= (\ln 2)\text{REG}(\bar{P}_{\text{Bayes}}, \Theta, x^n)$. Switching to natural units will be convenient in the further development below.

Proof: We have

$$
\begin{aligned}
\text{REG}_{\text{ln}}(\bar{P}_{\text{Bayes}}, \Theta, x^n) &:= -\ln \int_\Theta P(x^n \mid \theta)w(\theta)d\theta + \ln P(x^n \mid \hat{\theta}(x^n)) \\
&= -\ln \int \frac{P(x^n \mid \theta)}{P(x^n \mid \hat{\theta}(x^n))} w(\theta)d\theta \\
&= -\ln \int e^{\ln P(x^n \mid \theta) - \ln P(x^n \mid \hat{\theta}(x^n))} w(\theta)d\theta, \quad (8.15)
\end{aligned}
$$

and the first item follows. If $\mathcal{M}$ is an exponential family, we can use the robustness property for exponential families in the form of (19.12) on page 631, Chapter 19, to further rewrite this as

$$
-\ln \int e^{-n\text{D}(\hat{\theta}(x^n)\|\theta)} w(\theta)d\theta,
$$

which concludes the proof. $\square$

The characterization (8.14) is elegant, but does not directly give insight into the size of the regret. To obtain a more explicit expression, we can perform a straightforward Taylor approximation of $D(\hat{\theta}\|\theta)$ around θ as we did in Chapter 4, Section 4.3. To simplify matters, in our heuristic derivation we assume that Θ is compact, the prior $w(\theta)$ is uniform, $w(\theta) = w$ for some $w > 0$, for all $\theta \in \Theta$, and finally $\Theta \subset \mathbb{R}$ is one-dimensional. The Taylor approximation of the Kullback-Leibler divergence then gives

$$
\int e^{-n\text{D}(\hat{\theta}(x^n)\|\theta)} w(\theta)d\theta = w \int e^{-n\frac{1}{2}(\hat{\theta}-\theta)^2 I(\hat{\theta})+R}d\theta, \qquad (8.16)
$$

where R is some remainder term. Ignoring the remainder term and substituting $z := (\hat{\theta} - \theta)\sqrt{nI(\hat{\theta})}$, (8.16) becomes equal to

$$
\frac{w}{\sqrt{nI(\hat{\theta})}} \int e^{-\frac{1}{2}z^2}dz,
$$

where the factor in front of the integral is the Jacobian of the variable substitution. We recognize the integral as standard Gaussian. We assume further that the domain of integration for z (which we haven't determined) converges, for large n, to the full real line $\mathbb{R}$. Then in the large n limit, the integral becomes equal to $\sqrt{2\pi}$, so that

$$-\ln \int e^{-n\mathrm{D}(\hat{\theta}(x^n)\|\theta)} w(\theta)d\theta \to -\ln w \sqrt{\frac{2\pi}{nI(\hat{\theta})}} = \frac{1}{2}\ln \frac{n}{2\pi} - \ln w + \ln \sqrt{I(\hat{\theta})}.$$

In Appendix 8.A we make this argument precise, and extend it to nonuniform priors and multidimensional models. This leads to a precise proof of Theorem 8.1.

8.3.2   Beyond Exponential Families

If $\mathcal{M}$ is a parametric family that is not exponential, yet sufficiently regular in other respects, then we can still obtain an analogue of Theorem 8.1. We do this by performing a saddle point approximation of the integral of (8.13) rather than (8.14), that is, we directly consider the integral over the exponentiated regret. This regret is approximated by a Taylor expansion of the log-likelihood as in Chapter 4, Section 4.2. Because this Taylor expansion is analogous to that for the KL divergence of Section 4.3, it is not too surprising that we obtain a very similar result.

Under conditions on $\mathcal{M}$, Θ and the sequence x^n, we get the following generalization of (8.2) (Jeffreys 1961; Schwarz 1978; Kass and Raftery 1995; Balasubramanian 1997):

$$\begin{aligned} -\log \bar{P}_{\mathrm{Bayes}}(x^n \mid \mathcal{M}) = \\ -\log P(x^n \mid \hat{\theta}(x^n)) + \frac{k}{2}\log \frac{n}{2\pi} - \log w(\hat{\theta}) + \log \det \sqrt{J(x^n)} + o(1). \end{aligned}$$
$$(8.17)$$

Here $J(x^n)$ is the so-called *observed information*, sometimes also called *observed Fisher information*; see Chapter 4, Equation (4.14) on page 117. The most important condition that is needed for (8.17) to hold is that there is a closed subset $\Theta^{\circ} \subset \Theta$ and a $c > 0$, such that for all large n, $\hat{\theta}(x^n)$ is unique and lies in Θ°, and the observed Fisher information is positive definite, with determinant $c > 0$, for all sequences with ML estimators in Θ°. This is much weaker than the condition that $\mathcal{M}$ is an exponential family, but it is still a strong condition, as we explain at the end of this subsection.

If $\mathcal{M}$ is an exponential family, then the observed Fisher information at x^n coincides with the Fisher information at $\hat{\theta}(x^n)$, leading us back to (8.2). If $\mathcal{M}$

is not exponential, then, again under conditions on $\mathcal{M}$, if data are distributed according to one of the distributions in $\mathcal{M}$, the observed Fisher information still converges with probability 1 to the expected Fisher information. This is strongly suggested by the law of large numbers, but a rigorous proof is quite involved and we shall not give it here. This fact can be used to show that, if $\mathcal{M}$ satisfies (8.17), and data are i.i.d. according to $P^* \in \mathcal{M}$, then the *expected* regret still converges to the expression (8.2) of Theorem 8.1, even if $\mathcal{M}$ is not exponential; see also Section 8.4, page 245. However, (8.2) now does not hold in an individual-sequence sense anymore, since for individual sequences, I and J may be quite different. This has consequences for the validity of the central insight of this chapter: if Θ represents an exponential family, then $\bar{P}_{\text{Jeffreys}}$ and $\bar{P}_{\text{nml}}$ asymptotically achieve the same regret on ineccsi sequences. Since Jeffreys' prior is defined in terms of the expected rather than the observed Fisher information, this does not hold in an individual sequence sense any more, but only in expectation, if the family indexed by Θ is not exponential.

> Interestingly, Takeuchi and Barron (1998a,b) provide a modification $\bar{P}'_{\text{Jeffreys}}$ of $\bar{P}_{\text{Jeffreys}}$ so that $-\log \bar{P}'_{\text{Jeffreys}}$ and $-\log \bar{P}_{\text{nml}}$ do coincide to within $o(1)$ for all ineccsi sequences, even for sufficiently regular models $\mathcal{M}$ that are not exponential families. Essentially, $\bar{P}'^{(n)}_{\text{Jeffreys}}(x^n) = (1-\alpha_n)\bar{P}_{\text{Jeffreys}}(x^n) + \alpha_n P^{(n)}_{\text{TB}}(x^n)$, where $P^{(n)}_{\text{TB}}$ is a Bayesian universal code defined over a larger, $k + 2k^2$-dimensional model Θ' which has Θ as a proper subset. Here α_n decreases to 0 with increasing n, so that for large n, $\bar{P}'^{(n)}_{\text{Jeffreys}}$ resembles $\bar{P}_{\text{Jeffreys}}$ more and more. We note that, since α_n depends on n, the resulting universal model is not a Bayesian (prequential) universal code.

Beyond Nonsingular Models   The extended asymptotic expansion (8.17) does not necessarily hold if the parameterization has singularities (degenerate Fisher information with determinant 0; often caused by the parameterization not being one-to-one). Unfortunately, for a large class of practically important models, the standard parameterization (and perhaps even any useful parameterization) has such singularities. Such models include mixtures of exponential families (Chapter 2, Example 2.12, page 68), hidden Markov models and several types of neural network models. For such models, as far as I know, no general theorems about the individual sequence regret for all ineccsi sequences are available, and (8.17) will only hold for sequences with ML estimators in special sets $\Theta°$ as described above. However, using sophisticated tools from algebraic geometry related to the Riemann Zeta function, Watanabe (1999a,b) has studied the expected redundancy (page 245) for several models of this type, and is able to prove bounds on this redundancy even if the data are distributed according to P_θ with a "singular" θ. Briefly, Watanabe shows that, under (now very weak) conditions on $\mathcal{M}$ and its parameterization, the expected redundancy is given by

$$\frac{k'}{2} \log n + b \log \log n + O(1),$$

where *always* $k' \leq k$, the dimension of the model. For models without singularities, $b = 0$. In many cases, k' will be significantly smaller than k. . In a long series of papers, Watanabe and his coworkers have established bounds on the values of k' and b for a variety of singular models. Here, we only mention Yamazaki and Watanabe (2003), who establish the expected redundancy for various kinds of mixture models. To give but one very simple example, let $\mathcal{M}$ be the Gaussian mixture model as in Example 2.12, consisting of all distributions on $\mathbb{R}$ that are mixtures of m Gaussians, each with arrbitary mean μ and the same variance σ^2. Let us fix σ^2 to some value. The resulting model has dimensionality $k = (m-1)+m = 2m-1$. For this particular case, Theorem 1 of (Yamazaki and Watanabe 2003) says the following: suppose data are distributed according to some $P^* \in \mathcal{M}$ that can be expressed in m' components, i.e. P^* has density $f^*(x) = \sum_{j=1}^{m'} \alpha_j \sqrt{2\pi}^{-1} \sigma^{-1} e^{-(x-\mu_j)^2/(2\sigma^2)}$, for some $m' \leq m$, extended to n outcomes by independence. Then we have that

$$E_{X^n \sim P^*}[-\log \bar{f}_{\text{Bayes}}(X^n) + \log f^*(X^n)] \leq \frac{m+m'-1}{2} \log n + O(1).$$

We see that if $m' < m$, then the redundancy is $(k'/2) \log n + O(1)$ for some $k' < k$.

8.3.3   Proof Sketch of Theorem 7.1

Theorem 8.1 (the Bayesian regret) provides the basis of our proof of Theorem 7.1 (the NML regret). While the details of the proof of Theorem 7.1 are quite technical, it is easy to give a rough indication of how it follows from Theorem 8.1. Indeed, let Θ be an ineccsi model such that $\text{COMP}^{(n)}(\Theta)$ is finite, and let Θ_0 be an ineccsi subset of Θ. From the box on page 235, we see that for large n, under the Bayesian universal model based on Jeffreys' prior, the regret (8.2) becomes identical for all Θ_0-sequences. By picking Θ_0 "almost" as large as Θ, we see that the regret becomes constant for all sequences except for $x_1, x_2, \ldots$ that are not ineccsi. This suggests that we can

act as if the regret would become identical uniformly for *all* sequences of
length n. While this is in fact not at all true, let us act for the moment as if it
were the case. Then for all sequences x^n of length n, ignoring the $o(1)$-term,
we have

$$\text{REG}(\bar{P}_{\text{Bayes}}, \Theta, x^n) = \text{REG}(\bar{P}_{\text{nml}}, \Theta, x^n) + C_n = \text{COMP}^{(n)}(\Theta) + C_n$$

for some constant C_n. This must hold because the regret of the NML distribution $\bar{P}_{\text{nml}}$ is also the same for *all* sequences of length n, so the difference
between the two regrets must be a constant, not depending on x^n. If the
constant C_n is larger than 0, then for all x^n, $\bar{P}_{\text{Bayes}}(x^n) < \bar{P}_{\text{nml}}(x^n)$, which
is impossible since both distributions must sum to 1. Similarly, one shows
that C_n cannot be smaller than 0. It follows that $C_n = 0$ so the two regrets
are the same. To formalize this argument, we have to carefully analyze what
really happens close to the boundaries of the parameter space Θ. This is
done in Chapter 11, Appendix 11.A, where we provide a formal proof of
Theorem 11.4, an extension of Theorem 7.1. There we show that, although
(8.2) does not hold for sequences with $\hat{\theta}(x^n)$ close to the boundary, these
sequences are so sparse that the reasoning above essentially still holds.

8.4 Stochastic Universality*

The central Theorem 8.1 provides an expression of the Bayesian regret for
individual sequences, and all discussion thus far has focused on the quality of
$\bar{P}_{\text{Bayes}}$ as a universal model in the individual sequence sense. We now look at
the regret and the redundancy in a stochastic sense, as defined in Section 6.5.
As we will see, similar expressions hold for both regret and redundancy, and
in a sense, Jeffreys' prior is still minimax optimal.

1. Almost sure regret.   Let $\mathcal{M}$ be a k-parameter exponential familiy with
diffeomorphic parameterization (Θ, P_θ), and let w be a continuous prior with
$w(\theta) > 0$ for all $\theta \in \Theta$. Suppose that data are i.i.d. according to some $P^* = P_{\theta^*} \in \mathcal{M}$. Since Θ is convex and open, there must be some $\epsilon > 0$ such that
$\Theta_\epsilon = \{\theta \in \Theta : \|\theta - \theta^*\| < \epsilon\}$ is an ineccsi subset of Θ. It follows by the law of
large numbers (Chapter 2) that, with P^*-probability 1, for all large n, $\hat{\theta} \in \Theta_\epsilon$.
Together with our central Theorem 8.1, this shows that, for any (arbitrary)

$\theta^* \in \Theta$, with P_{θ^*}-probability 1,

$$\text{REG}(\bar{P}_{\text{Bayes}}, \Theta, X^n) =$$
$$\frac{k}{2} \log \frac{n}{2\pi} - \log w(\hat{\theta}(X^n)) + \log \sqrt{\det I(\hat{\theta}(X^n))} + o(1) =$$
$$\frac{k}{2} \log \frac{n}{2\pi} - \log w(\theta^*) + \log \sqrt{\det I(\theta^*(X^n))} + o(1), \quad (8.18)$$

where the final equality follows because we can take ϵ as small as we like, and w and I are continuous.

2. Expected regret.   The argument can be extended to the expected regret case, at least if we restrict ourselves to submodels $\mathcal{M}_0$ with parameters restricted to some ineccsi subset Θ_0 of Θ. Thus, let $\bar{P}_{\text{Bayes}}$ be a universal model defined with respect to a prior that is Θ_0-compatible, and let $\theta^* \in \Theta_0$. In the definition of regret, let $\hat{\theta}(x^n)$ denote the ML estimator within the restricted parameter set Θ_0.

Theorem 8.2 Under the conditions above, we have

$$E_{X^n \sim P_{\theta^*}}[\text{REG}(\bar{P}_{\text{Bayes}}, \Theta_0, X^n)] = \frac{k}{2} \log \frac{n}{2\pi} - \log w(\theta^*) + \log \sqrt{\det I(\theta^*)} + o(1),$$
$$(8.19)$$

where the convergence happens uniformly[2] for all $\theta^* \in \Theta_0$.

The proof (sketch) of this theorem is in Appendix 8.A.

3. Expected redundancy.   We now further extend the reasoning from stochastic regret to stochastic redundancy. The key to the extension is the following important result, which goes back to Wilks (1938): let $\mathcal{M}$ be an exponential family and (P_θ, Θ) be a diffeomorphic parameterization. Then for all $\theta \in \Theta$,

$$E_\theta[-\ln P_\theta(X^n) + \ln P_{\hat{\theta}(X^n)}(X^n)] = \frac{k}{2} + o(1). \quad (8.20)$$

To get some idea of why (8.20) holds, consider the special case $k = 1$ and reparameterize the model such that $\Theta \subset \mathbb{R}^1$ represents the mean-value parameterization. We can write

$$-\ln P_\theta(X^n) + \ln P_{\hat{\theta}(X^n)}(X^n) = n\text{D}(\hat{\theta}(X^n)\|\theta) \approx n\frac{1}{2}(\hat{\theta}-\theta)^2 I(\theta_0) + R_n, \quad (8.21)$$

---

2. See the footnote on page 232.

where θ_0 lies between $\hat{\theta}$ and θ. Here the first equation follows from the fundamental robustness property of exponential families in the form of (19.12) on page 631, Chapter 19. The second is the familiar second-order Taylor approximation of the log-likelihood (Chapter 4, Section 4.2). Now note that for exponential families in the mean-value parameterization, $E_\theta[(\hat{\theta}(X^n) - \theta)^2] = n^{-1}\text{var}[\phi(X)] = 1/(nI(\theta))$ (Chapter 18). Thus, if we further assume that (a) $I(\theta_0) \approx I(\theta)$ and (b), for large n, R_n is negligible, then the $I(\theta)$ factors cancel and the expectation under θ of (8.21) is equal to $1/2$, which is the special case of (8.20) for $k = 1$. The reasoning is easily extended to arbitrary k. Turning this reasoning into a formal proof requires proving (a) and (b), using, for example, techniques such as in (Grünwald and de Rooij 2005). In fact, since by the central limit theorem, $\hat{\theta} - \theta$ is asymptotically normal, the reasoning further suggests that the left-hand side of (8.21) is asymptotically χ^2-distributed with k degrees of freedom. It is shown in, for example, (Clarke and Barron 1990) that this is indeed the case, even for sufficiently regular models $\mathcal{M}$ that are not exponential families.

Combining the expression for the expected regret (8.19) with (8.20), and using continuity of $w(\theta)$ and $I(\theta)$, we immediately obtain the following:

Theorem 8.3 Let Θ_0 be an ineccsi subset of Θ, and let $\theta^* \in \Theta_0$. Let $\bar{P}_{\text{Bayes}}$ be defined with respect to a prior w that is Θ_0-compatible. Then

$$E_{\theta^*}[\text{RED}(\bar{P}_{\text{Bayes}}, P_{\theta^*}, X^n)] = \frac{k}{2} \log \frac{n}{2\pi e} - \log w(\theta^*) + \log \sqrt{\det I(\theta^*)} + o(1),$$
(8.22)

where the convergence is uniform in $\theta^* \in \Theta_0$.

Note that this differs from (8.19) by a $(k/2) \log e$ term. Equation (8.22) is a special case of a famous result of Clarke and Barron (1990), who show an analogue of (8.22) for general parametric families which are not necessarily exponential.

4. Almost sure redundancy. The fact that the Bayesian regret satisfies (8.18) both in expectation and almost surely suggests that the same holds for the redundancy, i.e. we may be tempted to think that, for exponential families, (8.22) also holds with P_{θ^*}-probability 1, for all $\theta^* \in \Theta$. This is almost, but not quite the case: as shown by Li and Yu (2000), for exponential families, with

P_{θ^*}-probability 1,

$$\mathrm{RED}(\bar{P}_{\mathrm{Bayes}}, P_{\theta^*}, X^n)] =$$
$$\frac{k}{2} \log \frac{n}{2\pi} - \log w(\theta^*) + \log \sqrt{\det I(\theta^*)} + C_n \log \log n + o(1), \quad (8.23)$$

where C_n is a random variable that with probability 1 is (a) nonnegative for all n, (b) is upper-bounded by k for all n, and (c) that takes on a value ≥ 1 for infinitely many n. In other words, fluctuations of order $\log \log n$ occur with probability 1.

These fluctuations are a consequence of the *law of the iterated logarithm*, (Feller 1968b), which complements the central limit theorem (CLT). To get an idea of why this is so, for simplicity let us restrict ourselves to the one-parameter case. For exponential families in their mean-value parameterization, the CLT implies that for each $c > 0$, as $n \to \infty$,

$$P_{\theta^*} \left((\hat{\theta}(X^n) - \theta^*)^2 \geq \frac{c}{n} \right) \to c', \qquad (8.24)$$

where $c' > 0$ depends on c. The Taylor approximation used in the approximate reasoning leading up to (8.20) now suggests that for each $c > 0$, the θ^*-probability that $nD(\hat{\theta}\|\theta^*) \geq c$ converges to c' as well. Thus, the probability that $nD(\hat{\theta}\|\theta^*)$ exceeds c does not go to 0, so that the probability that the redundancy differs from the expected redundancy by at least c is nonnegligible. Therefore, (8.22) cannot hold with probability 1. But, by the law of the iterated logarithm,

$$\text{With } P_{\theta^*}\text{-probability 1,} \lim_{n\to\infty} \sup_{n':n'>n} (\hat{\theta}(X^{n'}) - \theta^*)^2 = \frac{2\log\log n'}{n'}, \quad (8.25)$$

which indeed suggests that with probability 1, $nD(\hat{\theta}\|\theta^*)$ is of order $\log \log n$ infinitely often.

Jeffreys' Prior and Minimax Expected Redundancy   Theorem 8.3 suggests that Jeffreys' prior asymptotically is minimax optimal not only in the minimax expected regret sense but also in the minimax redundancy sense of (6.41), page 202, Section 6.5. Clarke and Barron (1994) show that, essentially, this is indeed the case for a general class of parametric families, including, but not limited to, the exponential families.

Again, the results of Clarke and Barron (1994) only hold for ineccsi Θ_0. Just as in the case for individual-sequence regret, Example 8.4, if Θ represents the multinomial model, then it is easy to show that Jeffreys' prior does not achieve the minimax redundancy relative to the full Θ. But, again as in the individual-sequence regret case, with a sample size-dependent modification of Jeffreys' prior like the one described underneath Example 8.4, the minimax redundancy can be achieved after all (Xie and Barron 1997). It is not clear to me whether such a construction can be extended to families other than the multinomial.

8.A   Appendix: Proofs of Theorem 8.1 and Theorem 8.2

In this appendix we freely use results about, and the notation for, exponential families introduced in Part IV, Chapter 18. We do not always refer to these results explicitly. For convenience, the proofs are based on codelengths measured in nats (page 110) rather than bits. The statements in the main text, which use bits, are immediate corollaries.

A useful concept throughout the proofs will be the idea of slightly extending the parameter set Θ_0. To this end, we define $\Theta_0^{[+\delta]}$ as the set obtained when "blowing up" Θ_0 such that its boundary moves a (Euclidean) distance of δ in all directions:

$$\Theta_0^{[+\delta]} := \{\theta \in \Theta \ : \ \text{There exists } \theta' \in \Theta_0 \text{ such that } \|\theta - \theta'\| \le \delta\}. \qquad (8.26)$$

Similarly, we define $\Theta_0^{[-\delta]}$ as the set obtained when excluding points within δ of the boundary:

$$\Theta_0^{[-\delta]} := \{\theta \in \Theta_0 \ : \ \text{There exists no } \theta' \in \Theta \setminus \Theta_0 \text{ such that } \|\theta - \theta'\| \le \delta\}. \qquad (8.27)$$

Proof of Theorem 8.1

We only give the proof for 1-parameter exponential families. Extension to the k-dimensional case is straightforward. After the proof, we present a slightly extended version of the theorem that will be useful for the proofs in the next subsection.

We first assume that (Θ, P_θ) is given in the canonical parameterization. Later we show how to extend the result to general smooth 1-to-1 parameterizations.

Let $\hat{\theta} = \hat{\theta}(x^n)$ be as in the theorem. Fix $0 < \alpha < 1/2$ and let $B_n = [\hat{\theta} - n^{-1/2+\alpha}, \hat{\theta} + n^{-1/2+\alpha}]$. To gain intuition, take α very small so that B_n is a neighborhood of $\hat{\theta}$ that shrinks to 0 at rate slightly slower than $1/\sqrt{n}$. Since the prior w must be continuous on Θ and strictly positive on the bounded set Θ_0, there must be some set Θ_1 such that w is strictly positive on Θ_1, and Θ_0 is an ineccsi subset of Θ_1. Since the boundary of Θ_1 and Θ_0 does not overlap, the minimum distance between any two points in Θ_0 and the boundary of Θ_1 is larger than some $\epsilon > 0$. Then for all n larger than some n_0, since we assume $\hat{\theta}(x^n) \in \Theta_0$, we must have $B_n \in \Theta_1$. We henceforth assume that n is larger than n_0. Then:

$$\text{REG}_{\ln}(\bar{P}^{(n)}_{\text{Bayes}}, \Theta, x^n) = -\ln(\mathcal{I}_1 + \mathcal{I}_2), \tag{8.28}$$

where

$$\mathcal{I}_1 = \int_{\theta \in \Theta \backslash B_n} e^{-n\text{D}(\hat{\theta}\|\theta)} w(\theta)d\theta, \text{ and } \mathcal{I}_2 = \int_{\theta \in B_n} e^{-n\text{D}(\hat{\theta}\|\theta)} w(\theta)d\theta.$$

To bound $\mathcal{I}_1$ and $\mathcal{I}_2$, we approximate $D(\hat{\theta}\|\theta)$ by performing a second-order Taylor expansion of $\theta \in B_n$ around $\hat{\theta}$, as in Chapter 4, Section 4.3, page 120: For all large n, all $\theta \in B_n$,

$$D(\hat{\theta}\|\theta) = \frac{1}{2}(\hat{\theta} - \theta)^2 I(\theta'), \tag{8.29}$$

where I is the Fisher information and $\theta' \in B_n$ lies inbetween θ and $\hat{\theta}$.

Stage 1: Bounding $\mathcal{I}_1$ As follows from Proposition 19.2, page 624), in the canonical parameterization, $D(\hat{\theta}\|\theta)$ as a function of θ is strictly convex and has a minimum at $\theta = \hat{\theta}$. $D(\hat{\theta}\|\theta)$ is increasing in $|\hat{\theta} - \theta|$, so that

$$0 < \mathcal{I}_1 < \int_{\theta \in \Theta \backslash B_n} e^{-n\delta_n} w(\theta)d\theta, \tag{8.30}$$

where

$$\delta_n = \min_{\theta \in \Theta \backslash B_n} D(\hat{\theta}\|\theta) = \min_{\theta \in \{\hat{\theta} - n^{-1/2+\alpha}, \hat{\theta} + n^{-1/2+\alpha}\}} D(\hat{\theta}\|\theta).$$

By (8.29),

$$\delta_n \geq \frac{1}{2} n^{-1+2\alpha} \min_{\theta \in \Theta_0} I(\theta),$$

so that, since $I(\theta)$ is continuous and > 0 for all $\theta \in \Theta$ (Section 18.3) and also $\int_{\Theta \backslash B_n} w(\theta)d\theta \leq 1$, by (8.30),

$$0 < \mathcal{I}_1 < e^{-cn^{2\alpha}} \tag{8.31}$$

for some $c > 0$.

Stage 2: Bounding $\mathcal{I}_2$ Let

$$\underline{I}_n:=\inf_{\theta'\in B_n} I(\theta')\,,\ \overline{I}_n:=\sup_{\theta'\in B_n} I(\theta')\,,\ \underline{w}_n:=\inf_{\theta'\in B_n} w(\theta')\,,\ \overline{w}_n:=\sup_{\theta'\in B_n} w(\theta').$$

By (8.29),

$$\mathcal{I}_2 = \int_{\theta\in B_n} e^{-\frac12 n(\hat\theta-\theta)^2 I(\theta')}w(\theta)d\theta,$$

where θ' depends on θ. Using the definitions above, we get

$$\underline{w}_n \int_{B_n} e^{-\frac12 n(\hat\theta-\theta)^2\overline{I}_n}d\theta \le \mathcal{I}_2 \le \overline{w}_n \int_{B_n} e^{-\frac12 n(\hat\theta-\theta)^2\underline{I}_n}d\theta.$$

We now perform the substitution $z:=(\hat\theta-\theta)\sqrt{n\overline{I}_n}$ on the left integral, and $z:=(\hat\theta\quad\theta)\sqrt{n\underline{I}_n}$ on the right integral, to get

$$\frac{\underline{w}_n}{\sqrt{n\overline{I}_n}} \int_{|z|<n^\alpha\sqrt{\underline{I}_n}} e^{-\frac12 z^2}dz \le \mathcal{I}_2 \le \frac{\overline{w}_n}{\sqrt{n\underline{I}_n}} \int_{|z|<n^\alpha\sqrt{\overline{I}_n}} e^{-\frac12 z^2}dz.$$

We recognize both integrals as standard Gaussian. Since, as $n\to\infty$, $\underline{I}_n\to I(\hat\theta)$ and $\overline{I}_n\to I(\hat\theta)$, the domain of integration tends to infinity for both integrals, so that they both converge to $\sqrt{2\pi}$. Since also $\underline{w}_n\to w(\hat\theta)$ and $\overline{w}_n\to w(\hat\theta)$, the constants in front of both integrals converge to $w(\hat\theta)/\sqrt{nI(\hat\theta)}$, and we get

$$\mathcal{I}_2 \sim \frac{\sqrt{2\pi}w(\hat\theta)}{\sqrt{nI(\hat\theta)}}, \tag{8.32}$$

where $\sim$ means that the ratio between the two sides goes to 1. Together with (8.31) we get further

$$\mathcal{I}_1 + \mathcal{I}_2 \sim \frac{\sqrt{2\pi}w(\hat\theta)}{\sqrt{nI(\hat\theta)}},$$

and (8.28) now gives

$$\mathrm{REG}_{\ln}(\bar{P}^{(n)}_{\mathrm{Bayes}},\Theta,x^n) = -\ln(\mathcal{I}_1+\mathcal{I}_2) \to \frac12 \ln\frac{n}{2\pi} + \ln\sqrt{I(\hat\theta)} - \ln w(\hat\theta)$$

and the result follows. To see that it holds uniformly for all $x^n\in\Theta_0$, note that our bound on $\mathcal{I}_1$ in (8.31) does not depend on x^n, whereas, because w and I are continuous functions over the compact set Θ_0, the convergence in (8.32) is also uniform.

This completes the proof for the case that $\Theta=\Theta_{\mathrm{can}}$ represents the canonical parameterization.

Stage 3: General Parameterizations We now extend the proof to arbitrary diffeomorphic parameterizations. Let (Γ, Q_γ) be any diffeomorphic parameterization of $\mathcal{M}$, and let the diffeomorphisms $\gamma(\beta)$ and $\beta(\gamma)$ be as in Section 18.4.2, so that $Q_\gamma = P_{\beta(\gamma)}$, where $(P_\beta, \Theta_{\text{can}})$ denotes the canonical parameterization. Let $\Gamma_0 = \{\gamma : \gamma = \gamma(\beta) \text{ for some } \beta \in \Theta_0\}$. We have

$$\int_{\Gamma_0} Q_\gamma(x^n) w(\gamma) d\gamma = \int_{\Gamma_0} P_{\beta(\gamma)}(x^n) w(\gamma) d\gamma =$$
$$\int_{\Theta_0} P_\beta(x^n) w(\gamma(\beta)) \frac{d}{d\beta} \gamma(\beta) d\beta = \int_{\Theta_0} P_\beta(x^n) v(\beta) d\beta, \quad (8.33)$$

where $v(\beta) = w(\gamma(\beta)) \cdot \frac{d}{d\beta} \gamma(\beta)$. We now apply the theorem that we proved above to the right-hand side of (8.33). This is possible because we are evaluating with respect to the canonical parameterization. We find

$$- \ln \int_{\Gamma_0} Q_\gamma(x^n) w(\gamma) d\gamma =$$
$$- \ln P_{\hat{\beta}(x^n)}(x^n) + \frac{k}{2} \ln \frac{n}{2\pi} + \ln \sqrt{I(\hat{\beta})} - \ln w(\gamma(\hat{\beta})) - \ln \frac{d}{d\beta} \gamma(\hat{\beta}) + o(1) =$$
$$= - \ln Q_{\hat{\gamma}(x^n)}(x^n) + \frac{k}{2} \ln \frac{n}{2\pi} + \ln \sqrt{I(\hat{\beta})} - \ln w(\hat{\gamma}) - \ln \frac{d}{d\beta} \gamma(\hat{\beta}) + o(1),$$
$$(8.34)$$

where $\hat{\gamma}(x^n) = \gamma(\hat{\beta}(x^n))$. Using Proposition 18.2 about the reparameterization of Fisher information, we see that $I(\hat{\beta}) = I(\gamma(\hat{\beta}))(\frac{d}{d\beta} \gamma(\hat{\beta}))^2$, so that (8.34) becomes

$$- \ln \int_{\Gamma_0} Q_\gamma(x^n) w(\gamma) d\gamma = - \ln Q_{\hat{\gamma}}(x^n) + \frac{k}{2} \ln \frac{n}{2\pi} + \ln \sqrt{I(\hat{\gamma})} - \ln w(\hat{\gamma}) + o(1),$$

which proves the theorem for general diffeomorphic parameterizations.

Extension We now present a slightly extended version of Theorem 8.1. This extended theorem will be needed in the proof of Lemma 11.1 on page 331, which in turn is needed to prove Theorem 11.4, of which Theorem 7.1, the central result of Chapter 7, is a special case.

Theorem 8.4 Let $\alpha \in (0, 1/2]$ and let Θ_0 be an ineccsi subset of Θ. Let $x_1, x_2, \ldots$ be any sequence such that for all large n, $\hat{\theta} = \hat{\theta}(x^n)$ exists and is contained in $\Theta_0^{[+0.5n^{-1/2+\alpha}]}$. Let $w_1, w_2, \ldots$ be a sequence of priors that are continuous and strictly positive on $\Theta_0^{[+n^{-1/2+\alpha}]}$, and let w be a prior such that $\lim_{n\to\infty} \sup_{\theta\in\Theta_0} |w_n(\theta) - w| = 0$. Let $\bar{P}_{\text{Bayes}}^{(n)}$ be the Bayesian mixture distribution on $\mathcal{X}^n$ based on prior w_n. Then

$$
\text{REG}_{\ln}(\bar{P}_{\text{Bayes}}^{(n)}, \Theta_0^{[+0.5n^{-1/2+\alpha}]}, x^n) = \frac{k}{2} \ln \frac{n}{2\pi} - \ln w_n(\hat{\theta}) + \ln \sqrt{\det I(\hat{\theta})} + o(1).
$$

(8.35)

where the convergence is uniform in $\Theta_0^{[+0.5n^{-1/2+\alpha}]}$.

The proof is identical to the proof of Theorem 8.1 with some obvious modifications and has been omitted.

Proof of Theorem 8.2

We only sketch the proof for the case that Θ is the mean-value parameterization. Because Θ_0 is an ineccsi subset of Θ, we must have that for all large n, $\Theta^{[+n^{-1/4}]}$ is also an ineccsi subset of Θ. Let $w^{(n)}$ be a prior that is continuous and strictly positive on $\Theta_0^{[+n^{-1/4}]}$, such that $w^{(n)}$ converges to w for large n, uniformly for $\theta \in \Theta_0$. We first consider the Bayesian marginal distribution $\bar{P}_{\text{Bayes}}^{\prime(n)}$ on $\mathcal{X}^n$, defined relative to prior $w^{(n)}$.

It follows from our version of the Chernoff-Sanov bounds (Chapter 19, Theorem 19.2) that the P_{θ^*}-probability that $\hat{\theta}$ lies on the boundary of Θ_0 must be exponentially small, i.e. smaller than e^{-cn} for some constant c. Because sequences with $\hat{\theta}(x^n)$ in the interior of Θ_0 uniformly satisfy (8.2), we get that

$$
E_{\theta^*}[\text{REG}_{\ln}(\bar{P}_{\text{Bayes}}^{\prime(n)}, \Theta_0, X^n)] \leq
$$
$$
(1 - e^{-cn}) \left(\frac{k}{2} \ln \frac{n}{2\pi} - \ln w^{(n)}(\theta^*) + \ln \sqrt{\det I(\theta^*)} + o(1) \right) + e^{-cn} R_n,
$$

(8.36)

where R_n is the regret of $\bar{P}_{\text{Bayes}}^{\prime(n)}$ on x^n with ML estimator on the boundary of Θ_0. These are sequences with sufficient statistic on the boundary or outside Θ_0. We distinguish two cases: (a) x^n is such that its sufficient statistic $n^{-1} \sum \phi(x_i)$ is inside $\Theta_0^{[+n^{-1/4}]}$; in case (b), $n^{-1} \sum \phi(x_i) \notin \Theta_0^{[+n^{-1/4}]}$. For sequences of type (a), the regret of $\bar{P}_{\text{Bayes}}^{\prime(n)}$ with respect to $\hat{\theta} \in \Theta_0$ cannot be greater than the regret of $\bar{P}_{\text{Bayes}}^{\prime(n)}$ with respect to $\hat{\theta} \in \Theta_0^{[+n^{-1/4}]}$. Because $\Theta_0^{[+n^{-1/4}]}$ are ineccsi sets that are shrinking with n, the regret R_n is uniformly bounded by $(k/2)\ln n + O(1)$ for all sequences of case (a). For sequences of case (b), in Lemma 8.1 below, it is shown that for all large n, the regret R_n must be 0. Combining cases (a) and (b), we see that the second term in (8.36) vanishes for large n. Since $w^{(n)}$ converges to w and $\bar{P}'^{(n)}_{\text{Bayes}}$ converges to $\bar{P}^{(n)}_{\text{Bayes}}$, (8.19) follows. $\square$

We proceed with the statement and proof of Lemma 8.1, which is used in the proof of Theorem 8.2 above, and in the proof of Theorem 11.4, given in Chapter 11, page 330.

Lemma 8.1 (Zero Regret if Substantially Outside Θ_0) Let (P_μ, Θ_μ) represent an exponential family in its mean-value parameterization, and let Θ_0 be an ineccsi subset of Θ. For each n, let $w^{(n)}$ be a prior that is continuous and strictly positive on $\Theta_0^{[+n^{-1/4}]}$. Let $S^{(n)} = \{x^n : n^{-1}\sum_{i=1}^n \phi(x_i) \notin \Theta_0^{[+0.5n^{-1/4}]}\}$. Let $\bar{P}^{(n)}$ be the Bayesian mixture on $\mathcal{X}^n$ defined with respect to prior $w^{(n)}$. Then for all large n,

$$\sup_{x^n \in S^{(n)}} \text{REG}_{\ln}(\bar{P}^{(n)}, \Theta_0, x^n) \leq 0.$$

Proof: Let $x^n \in S^{(n)}$ and let $t = t(x^n) = n^{-1}\sum_{i=1}^n \phi(x_i)$. Let $\hat{\mu}_0$ be the ML estimator of x^n within the closure of the set Θ_0. Let μ_1 be a point on the line segment joining $\hat{\mu}_0$ and t, such that $\mu_1 \in \Theta_0^{[+0.75n^{-1/4}]} \setminus \Theta_0^{[+0.5n^{-1/4}]}$. If n is large enough, then for each $x^n \in S^{(n)}$ and corresponding value of t, there must exist some μ_1 in the above set. Without loss of generality we assume n to be large enough for this to hold. With every possible t we associate an (arbitrary) such μ_1. Now let

$$B_{\mu_1, n} = \left\{ \mu' : |\mu_1 - \mu'| \leq \frac{1}{n} \right\},$$

where $|\cdot|$ denotes L_1-distance, i.e. all k components of μ' must be within $2/n$ of the corresponding component of μ_1. If n is large enough, then for each t the set $B_{\mu_1, n}$ is a subset of $\Theta_0^{[+n^{-1/4}]}$. Without loss of generality we assume n to be large enough for this to hold. We have

$$W^{(n)}(B_{\mu_1, n}) \geq \min_{\mu \in B_{\mu_1, n}} w^{(n)}(\mu) \left(\frac{1}{n} \right)^k \geq c\frac{1}{n^k},$$

where $W^{(n)}$ is the prior distribution with density $w^{(n)}$, and c depends on μ_1 but is constant for all large n.

Now for x^n with $t = t(x^n) \notin \Theta_0^{[+0.5n^{-1/4}]}$, we have

$$- \ln \bar{P}^{(n)}(x^n) \leq - \ln W^{(n)}(B_{\mu_1,n}) + \max_{\mu' \in B_{\mu_1,n}} - \ln P_{\mu'}(x^n) \leq$$

$$k \ln n + c_1 + \max_{\mu' \in B_{\mu_1,n}} - \ln P_{\mu'}(x^n), \quad (8.37)$$

where c_1 does not depend on n. Write $t = t(x^n)$ as $(t_1, \ldots, t_k)$. To bound (8.37) further, note that for all $\mu' \in B_{\mu_1,n}$, we have

$$- \ln P_{\mu'}(x^n) + \ln P_{\mu_1}(x^n) =$$

$$- n\beta(\mu')^\top t + n \ln Z(\beta(\mu')) + n\beta(\mu_1)^\top t - n \ln Z(\beta(\mu')), \quad (8.38)$$

where we switched to the canonical parameterization. Let, for $j \in \{1, \ldots, k\}$,

$$c_j = \sup_{\mu' \in \Theta_0^{[+n^{-1/4}]}} \left| \frac{\partial \beta_i(\mu')}{\partial \mu} \right|.$$

By a first-order Taylor approximation of $\beta(\mu') - \beta(\mu)$, we get

$$\sup_{\mu' \in B_{\mu_1,n}} |- \beta(\mu')^\top t + \beta(\mu_1)^\top t| < \frac{1}{n} \sum_{j=1}^{k} c_j |t_j|.$$

where the c_j are positive constants. Similarly, letting

$$c' = \sup_{\mu' \in \Theta_0^{[+n^{-1/4}]}} \left| \frac{\partial (\ln Z(\beta(\mu')) - \ln Z(\beta(\mu_1)))}{\partial \mu} \right|,$$

and doing a first order Taylor approximation of $\ln Z(\beta(\mu')) - \ln Z(\beta(\mu_1))$ in terms of μ', we find

$$\sup_{\mu' \in B_{\mu_1,n}} |\ln Z(\beta(\mu')) - \ln Z(\beta(\mu_1))| < \frac{c'}{n}$$

for some $c' > 0$. With these two bounds, (8.37) becomes

$$- \ln P_{\mu'}(x^n) \leq - \ln P_{\mu_1}(x^n) + \frac{c'}{n} + \frac{1}{n} \sum_{j=1}^{k} c_j \gamma_j |\mu_{1,j}| \quad (8.39)$$

where $\mu_{1,j}$ denotes the jth component of μ_1 and we defined $\gamma_j > 0$ by $|t_j| = \gamma_j |\mu_{1,j}|$.

We now express $-\ln P_{\mu_1}$ in terms of $-\ln P_{\hat\mu_0}$. By the reasoning of Chapter 19, (19.12) on page 631:

$$-\ln P_{\mu_1}(x^n) + \ln P_{\hat\mu_0}(x^n) = -n D_{P^*}(\mu_1 \| \hat\mu_0), \tag{8.40}$$

for P^* with $E_{P^*}[\phi(X)] = t$. Applying Proposition 19.3 with $t = \mu_\lambda$, we find

$$D_{P^*}(\mu_1 \| \hat\mu_0) = D(\mu_1 \| \hat\mu_0) + c''\alpha \tag{8.41}$$

for some $c'' > 0$ and $\alpha = \lambda - 1 > 0$, where λ is as in the proposition. Since $(t - \mu_1) = \alpha(\mu_1 - \hat\mu_0)$, we find that, for $j \in \{1, \ldots, k\}$,

$$\alpha = \left| \frac{t_j - \mu_{1,j}}{\mu_{1,j} - \hat\mu_{0,j}} \right| \geq \frac{|\gamma_j - 1| |\mu_{1,j}|}{c''_j},$$

where $c''_j = \max_{\mu_a, \mu_b \in \Theta_0^{[+n^{-1/4}]}} |\mu_{a,j} - \mu_{b,j}|$, so that by (8.40) and (8.41), for $j = 1..k$,

$$-\ln P_{\mu_1}(x^n) \leq -\ln P_{\hat\mu_0}(x^n) - n D(\mu_1 \| \hat\mu_0) - nc \sum_{j=1}^{k} \frac{|\gamma_j - 1| |\mu_{1,j}|}{c''_j} \tag{8.42}$$

where all constants are positive and not dependent on n. Because $|\mu_1 - \hat\mu_0| \geq 0.5n^{-1/4}$, by performing a second-order Taylor expansion of $\theta \in B_n$ around $\hat\theta$ as in Chapter 4, Section 4.3, page 120, we find $n D(\mu_1 \| \hat\mu_0) \geq cn^{1/2}$ for some $c > 0$, uniformly for all $\mu_1 \in \Theta_0^{[+0.75n^{-1/4}]} \setminus \Theta_0^{[+0.5n^{-/4}]}$ and $\hat\mu_0 \in \Theta_0$. n. Since μ_1 and $\hat\mu_0$ lie in a compact set, (8.42) implies that for all n larger than some n_0, for all values of $x^n \in \mathcal{X}^n$ with $t(x^n) \notin \Theta_0^{[]}$, we have (using (8.37),

$$\mathrm{REG}_{\ln}(\bar P^{(n)}, \Theta, x^n) = -\ln \bar P^{(n)}(x^n) - [-\ln P_{\hat\mu_0}(x^n)] \leq 0,$$

which proves the result. $\square$

9 *Parametric Models: Prequential Plug-in*

In general, the Bayesian universal codelengths $-\log \bar{P}_{\text{Bayes}}$ are not easy to compute. For small samples, the asymptotic expansion is not always reliable. In MDL applications, we sometimes need to calculate the codelength of the data based on a universal code at small samples. How should we proceed? In many cases, the prequential interpretation of Bayes comes to the rescue: it suggests that one can approximate the Bayesian universal codelengths by the codelengths achieved with the prequential plug-in model that we introduced in Chapter 6, Section 6.4.3. These codelengths are usually easier to compute than those based on Bayesian and NML codes. In this section, we first illustrate this using the Bernoulli model, a rare case for which, under a large class of priors, the Bayesian and prequential plug-in code actually *coincide*. We then show that, for other exponential families, the Bayesian and prequential plug-in, while not identical, still resemble each other in the sense that they both achieve the familiar $(k/2)\log n$ expected regret. In Section 9.2 we illustrate the relation using the multinomial and the Gaussian model. In Section 9.3 we discuss the relation in more detail.

Fast Track This chapter is of *major* importance, but all the main ideas can be found in Section 9.1.

9.1 Prequential Plug-in for Exponential Families

We first consider the prequential interpretation of the Bayesian universal codes for the Bernoulli model. This interpretation is of crucial importance in what follows. It is explained in the box:

Bayes, Laplace, and Jeffreys

Consider the Bayesian universal model $\bar{P}_{\text{Bayes}}$ relative to the Bernoulli model with uniform prior, as in Example 8.1. From (8.3) we see that

$$\bar{P}_{\text{Bayes}}(X_{n+1} = 1 \mid x^n)$$

$$= \frac{\bar{P}_{\text{Bayes}}(x_1, \ldots, x_n, 1)}{\bar{P}_{\text{Bayes}}(x_1, \ldots, x_n)} = \frac{n+1}{n+2} \frac{\binom{n}{n_1}}{\binom{n+1}{n_1+1}} = \frac{n_1 + 1}{n+2}. \qquad (9.1)$$

Thus, the Bayesian prediction for the next outcome is almost, but not quite the same as the prediction based on the ML estimator $\hat{\theta} = n_1/n$. The difference is that the Bayesian prediction is smoothed, corresponding to the ML estimator for data x^n augmented with two "virtual" initial data points 1 and 0. The prediction rule (9.1) is called the *Laplace rule of succession*. It was advocated by the great probabilist Pierre Simon de Laplace, co-originator of Bayesian statistics. It is a special case (with $\alpha = 2, \mu = 1/2$) of modified ML estimators of the form

$$\hat{\theta}_{\alpha,\mu}(x^n) := \frac{\alpha\mu + n_1}{\alpha + n}, \text{ where } 0 < \mu < 1, \alpha > 0. \qquad (9.2)$$

Sequential prediction with such estimators may be interpreted as ML estimation based on an *extended* sample, containing some initial virtual data sample of size α, consisting of $\alpha\mu$ 1s and $\alpha(1 - \mu)$ 0s. From (8.9), Example 8.3, we see that Jeffreys' prior is also of this form: as with the uniform prior, $\mu = 1/2$, but now $\alpha = 1$, corresponding to the ML estimator with one virtual data point that is "one-half 0, one-half 1." In the context of Bernoulli and multinomial models, this predictive Bayesian estimator based on Jeffreys' prior is also called the *Krichevsky-Trofimov estimator* (Krichevsky and Trofimov 1981).

It turns out that for each pair of (α, μ) with $\alpha > 0, 0 < \mu < 1$, there is a prior w on the Bernoulli model such that $\bar{P}_{\text{Bayes}}$ defined relative to w corresponds to $\hat{\theta}_{\alpha,\mu}$. These are the so-called *beta-*(λ_0, λ_1) priors (Berger 1985), where $\lambda_1 = \alpha\mu, \lambda_0 = \alpha(1 - \mu)$. The beta-$(\lambda_0, \lambda_1)$ distribution has a density on the set $\Theta' = \{(\theta_0, \theta_1) \mid \theta_0 \in [0, 1], \theta_1 = 1 - \theta_0\}$. We can think of this set as providing a redundant parameterization of the Bernoulli model; the point (θ_0, θ_1) represents the Bernoulli distribution with $P(X = 0) = \theta_0$, $P(X = 1) = \theta_1$, which we normally denote by P_{θ_1}. The density of the beta-

(λ_0, λ_1)-distribution on Θ' is given by

$$f(\theta_0, \theta_1) := \frac{\Gamma(\lambda_0 + \lambda_1)}{\Gamma(\lambda_0)\Gamma(\lambda_1)} \theta_0^{\lambda_0 - 1} \theta_1^{\lambda_1 - 1},$$

where Γ is the gamma function (Chapter 2). The uniform prior is a beta-$(1,1)$ distribution, and Jeffreys' prior is beta-$(1/2, 1/2)$. To see why the beta prior with parameter (λ_0, λ_1) leads to the predictive distribution $\hat{\theta}_{\alpha, \mu}$, consider Example 8.3 again. In the derivation leading up to (8.9), there was nothing special about $(\lambda_0, \lambda_1) = (1/2, 1/2)$. Any beta-$(\lambda_0, \lambda_1)$ prior can be plugged into (8.8), and then leads to (9.2).

$\bar{P}_{\text{Bayes}}$ **as a Prediction Strategy**   Consider the reinterpretation of distributions/codes as prediction strategies (Section 6.4). The example above shows that we can reinterpret the Bayesian universal codelength $-\log \bar{P}_{\text{Bayes}}(x^n)$ with the uniform prior as the sum of logarithmic prediction errors made on the sequence x^n, if we use the Laplace estimator for the subsequent predictions:

$$-\log \bar{P}_{\text{Bayes}}(x^n) = \sum_{i=1}^{n} -\log \bar{P}_{\text{Bayes}}(x_i \mid x^{i-1}) = \sum_{i=1}^{n} -\log P_{\hat{\theta}_{(2,1/2)}(x^{i-1})}(x_i).$$

This shows that for the Bernoulli model, the Bayesian codelengths *coincide* with the codelengths obtained with the prequential plug-in model with a slightly modified ML estimator: if we define $\bar{P}_{\text{plug-in}}(x_i \mid x^{i-1}) := P_{\hat{\theta}_{(2,1/2)}(x^{i-1})}(x_i)$, then

$$-\log \bar{P}_{\text{plug-in}}(x^n) = \sum_{i=1}^{n} -\log P_{\hat{\theta}_{(2,1/2)}(x^{i-1})}(x_i) = -\log \bar{P}_{\text{Bayes}}(x^n). \qquad (9.3)$$

General Exponential Families   In contrast to the Bernoulli case, for most other parametric families, the plug-in code is not precisely, but only approximately equivalent to a Bayesian universal code; yet it continues to be a reasonably good universal code. We only show this in more detail for the case where $\mathcal{M}$ is a k-parameter exponential family. Let (Θ, P_θ) represent the mean-value parameterization of $\mathcal{M}$. Then (Chapter 19, Section 19.3), the standard ML estimator satisfies

$$\hat{\theta}(x^n) = \frac{1}{n} \sum_{i=1}^{n} \phi(x_i),$$

where ϕ is the sufficient statistic of $\mathcal{M}$. Now let $\alpha > 0$, let $\mu_0 \in \Theta \subseteq \mathbb{R}^k$, and define

$$\hat{\theta}_{\alpha,\mu_0}(x^n) = \frac{\alpha\mu_0 + \sum_{i=1}^{n} \phi(x_i)}{\alpha + n}. \tag{9.4}$$

$\hat{\theta}_{\alpha,\mu_0}$ is once again an ML estimator that is modified by considering "virtual" data of mean μ_0 and size α. Here α may, but need not, be an integer. The estimator $\hat{\theta}_{\alpha,\mu}$ for the Bernoulli model is a special case of (9.4). We note that ML estimators modified according to (9.4) are special cases of the so-called *luckiness ML estimators* that we define in Chapter 11, Section 11.3, page 11.21.

We now define the prequential plug-in model for an arbitrary exponential family $\mathcal{M}$, relative to virtual data summarized by some (α, μ_0), as follows: for $i > 0$, we recursively set $\bar{P}_{\text{plug-in}}(x_i \mid x^{i-1}) := P_{\hat{\theta}_{\alpha,\mu_0}(x^{i-1})}(x_i)$, so that for all n, $x^n \in \mathcal{X}^n$,

$$-\log \bar{P}_{\text{plug-in}}(x^n) = -\sum_{i=1}^{n} \log P_{\hat{\theta}_{\alpha,\mu_0}(x^{i-1})}(x_i). \tag{9.5}$$

The resulting probabilistic source turns out to be a universal model relative to $\mathcal{M}$:

The Prequential Plug-In Model for Parametric Models
Let (Θ, P_θ) represent an ineccsi exponential family. Under weak conditions on (Θ, P_θ), we have that for all $\theta \in \Theta$, we have

$$E_{X^n \sim P_\theta} \left[-\log \bar{P}_{\text{plug-in}}(X^n) - [-\log P_{\hat{\theta}(X^n)}(X^n)] \right] = \frac{k}{2} \log n + O(1), \tag{9.6}$$

where $\hat{\theta}$ denotes the standard ML estimator. This shows that $\bar{P}_{\text{plug-in}}$ acts as a $(k/2) \log n + O(1)$-universal model relative to Θ in the *stochastic, expected regret* sense (Section 6.5, page 199). Note that

- the fundamental $(k/2) \log$–term appears again, indicating that the prequential plug-in model is within $O(1)$ of being minimax optimal. Yet:

- the result (9.6) only holds in expectation, and is weaker than the corresponding statement for Bayesian universal models, which holds for individual sequences – indeed, (9.6) does not hold for individual sequences (see Section 9.3 below).

At the end of Section 9.3, we give a rough proof sketch of the theorem for the special case that $k = 1$, and we indicate how to extend the proof for $k > 1$. The "weak conditions" we refer to above are quite technical, but they seem to hold for all common exponential families, including, for example, the normal, Poisson and geometric families; see (Grünwald and de Rooij 2005) for details.

Extensions The fact that (9.6) holds for some parametric families was discovered independently by Rissanen (1984) and Dawid (1984). Later, Rissanen (1986c, Theorem 3) established general conditions on parametric families under which (9.6) holds. This implies (9.6) for the exponential families we study here, as well as many other smooth parametric families that are not exponential; although in the latter case, the models do not admit sufficient statistics so that the modified ML estimator should explicitly be based on a virtual sample $z_1, \ldots, z_{n_0}$ rather than just a summary (α, μ_0).

The plug-in construction can easily be extended to non-i.i.d. models. In that case, we define the universal plug-in code by

$$\bar{P}_{\text{plug-in}}(X_i \mid x^{i-1}) = P_{\hat{\theta}(x^{i-1})}(X_i \mid x^{i-1}),$$

while otherwise nothing changes. Under a variety of conditions on the model $\mathcal{M}$, an analogue of (9.6) can still be proved (Rissanen 1989; Wei 1992), for example for ARMA models. Indeed, applications of the plug-in code in MDL are often more natural for non-i.i.d. models than for i.i.d. models, for reasons we explain in Chapter 14, Section 14.4.2.

Why Modify the ML Estimator? The plug-in model was defined relative to a slightly modified ML estimator. For many exponential families, including the Bernoulli model, this is essential, as the following example shows.

Example 9.1 [The Two Start-Up Problems] Consider the prequential plug-in model for the Bernoulli model. If we take $\hat{\theta}_{\alpha,\mu}$ in (9.3) equal to the ML estimator n_1/n ($\alpha = 0$), then $\bar{P}_{\text{plug-in}}$ is undefined for the first outcome. This first "start-up problem" can easily be solved by setting $\bar{P}_{\text{plug-in}}(x_1)$ to some default value, say $\bar{P}_{\text{plug-in}}(X_1 = 1) = \bar{P}_{\text{plug-in}}(X_1 = 0) = 1/2$. A second, more serious start-up problem (Rissanen 1989) is that we may get infinite codelengths for $n > 1$: Suppose that $n > 3$ and $(x_1, x_2, x_3) = (0, 0, 1)$ – a not-so-unlikely initial segment according to most θ. Then $\bar{P}_{\text{plug-in}}(X_3 = 1 \mid x_1, x_2) = P_{\hat{\theta}(x_1,x_2)}(X = 1) = 0$, so that by (9.5),

$$-\log \bar{P}_{\text{plug-in}}(x^n) \geq -\log \bar{P}_{\text{plug-in}}(x_3 \mid x_1, x_2) = \infty,$$

whence $\bar{P}_{\text{plug-in}}$ is not a universal model. Now let us consider $\bar{P}_{\text{plug-in}}$ defined relative to the modified ML estimator $\hat{\theta}_{\alpha,\mu}$ as defined above, for some $0 < \alpha, 0 < \mu < 1$. Then for all $i > 0$, all $x^i \in \mathcal{X}^i$, $\bar{P}_{\text{plug-in}}(x_i \mid x^{i-1}) > 0$ so that the codelength $- \log \bar{P}_{\text{plug-in}}(x^i)$ cannot become infinity.

The modification we proposed above is to add some "virtual data" to the original sample and include the virtual data when determining the ML estimator. Alternatively, one may decide to use the ML estimator after all, but only start using it at the first i such that, having observed x^{i-1}, for all $x_i \in \mathcal{X}$, $- \log P_{\hat{\theta}(x^i)}(x_i) < \infty$. In the Bernoulli example, this is the first i such that x^{i-1} contains both a 0 and a 1. In that case, the first $i - 1$ outcomes have to be encoded using some standard code that is nonadaptive. In the Bernoulli example, one could use a code based on $P(X_j = 1 \mid x^{j-1}) = 1/2$, independently of x^{i-1}, for all $j < i$. In model selection applications, under some circumstances it can be justified not to encode this initial "risky" data sequence x^{i-1} at all. This is what has been done in most practical implementations of MDL model selection based on prequential codes (Chapter 14, Section 14.4.3).

To avoid infinite codelengths, a modification of the ML estimator is essential for many, but not for all exponential families. For example, if $\mathcal{M}$ is the family of normal distributions, we can just start using the ML estimator after having observed the first outcome, without any danger of obtaining infinite codelengths.

9.2   The Plug-in vs. the Bayes Universal Model

We have shown that for the Bernoulli model, $\bar{P}_{\text{plug-in}}$ and $\bar{P}_{\text{Bayes}}$ can be made identical. In this section we show that this equivalence continues to hold for the multinomial model. We then informally argue that the equivalence cannot hold for any other exponential families. We end by showing that still, the equivalence "almost" holds for the Gaussian and linear regression models.

Example 9.2 [Multinomial Model] Consider the multinomial model with notation as in Chapter 2, Example 2.5. Let $\lambda = (\lambda_1, \ldots, \lambda_m)$ be a vector with positive components. Let $\alpha := \sum_{j=1}^{m} \lambda_j$, and let $\mu := (\mu_1, \ldots, \mu_m)$ with, for $j = 1..m$, $\mu_j = \lambda_j / \alpha$. It turns out that for each λ of this form, there exists a prior w_λ on the parameters $(\theta_1, \ldots, \theta_m)$ such that for all n, $x^n \in \mathcal{X}^n$,

$$\bar{P}_{\text{Bayes}}(X_{n+1} \mid x^n) = P_{\hat{\theta}_{\alpha,\mu}(x^n)}(X_{n+1}),$$

where

$$\hat{\theta}_{\alpha,\mu}(x^n) := \left(\frac{n_1 + \lambda_1}{n + \sum_{j=1}^m \lambda_j}, \ldots, \frac{n_m + \lambda_m}{n + \sum_{j=1}^m \lambda_j} \right) = \left(\frac{n_1 + \alpha\mu_1}{n + \alpha}, \ldots, \frac{n_m + \alpha\mu_m}{n + \alpha} \right).$$
$$(9.7)$$

The prior corresponding to the vector λ is the so-called *Dirichlet distribution* with parameter λ, defined by

$$w_\lambda(\theta_1, \ldots, \theta_m) := \frac{\Gamma(\alpha)}{\prod_{j=1}^m \Gamma(\lambda_j)} \prod_{j=1}^m \theta_j^{\lambda_j - 1},$$

where Γ is once again the gamma function. The beta distribution is the special case for $m = 2$. Once again $\lambda = (1, \ldots, 1)$ corresponds to the uniform, and $\lambda = (1/2, \ldots, 1/2)$ corresponds to Jeffreys' prior.

We conjecture below that the multinomial model (and its special case, the Bernoulli model) is the only finite dimensional exponential family for which a prior exists that makes $\bar{P}_{\text{plug-in}}$ identical to $\bar{P}_{\text{Bayes}}$. Nevertheless, as we show in Example 9.3, for some models, such as the fixed-variance Gaussian models, $\bar{P}_{\text{plug-in}}(x^n)$ is *nearly* identical to $\bar{P}_{\text{Bayes}}(x^n)$.

Why usually $\bar{P}_{\text{plug-in}} \neq \bar{P}_{\text{Bayes}}$. The reason why $\bar{P}_{\text{plug-in}}$ usually *cannot* be made equal to $\bar{P}_{\text{Bayes}}$ is that, as can be seen from (6.28), page 192, $\bar{P}_{\text{Bayes}}(x_i \mid x^{i-1})$ is a *mixture* of distributions in $\mathcal{M}$, whereas $\bar{P}_{\text{plug-in}}(x_i \mid x^{i-1})$ must be a single element of $\mathcal{M}$ – this is explored further when we discuss the difference between "in-model" and "out-model" estimators (page 462, Section 9.3, Chapter 15). Thus, in general, for all n, x^n,

$$\bar{P}_{\text{plug-in}}(X_{n+1} \mid x^n) \in \mathcal{M}, \text{ but } \bar{P}_{\text{Bayes}}(X_{n+1} \mid x^n) \text{ may not be in } \mathcal{M}. \quad (9.8)$$

Since the Bernoulli and multinomial models are convex (closed under taking mixtures), for those models we have $\bar{P}_{\text{Bayes}}(X_{n+1} \mid x^n) \in \mathcal{M}$ after all, and (9.8) is irrelevant. Now, if the sample space $\mathcal{X}$ is finite, then it is easy to see that a an exponential family $\mathcal{M} = \{P_\theta \mid \theta \in \Theta\}$ is convex if and only if there exists a partition $\mathcal{Z}$ of $\mathcal{X}$ such that $\mathcal{M}$ is the set of all distributions on $\mathcal{Z}$. This means that $\mathcal{M}$ is essentially a Bernoulli or multinomial model. All other exponential families on finite $\mathcal{X}$ are not convex, which suggests (but does not rigorously prove) that for all such families, and all Θ-compatible priors, we indeed must have $\bar{P}_{\text{Bayes}}(X_{n+1} \mid x^n) \notin \mathcal{M}$, and therefore, by (9.8), $\bar{P}_{\text{plug-in}}(X_{n+1} \mid x^n) \neq \bar{P}_{\text{Bayes}}(X_{n+1} \mid x^n)$, irrespective of the modification of the ML estimator used to define $\bar{P}_{\text{plug-in}}$.

Open Problem/Conjecture No. 1 We suspect that the same reasoning continuous to hold for arbitrary sample spaces $\mathcal{X}$, and we conjecture that all exponential families $\mathcal{M}$, except those that are multinomial on a partition of the sample space, are (a) nonconvex, and (b), when equipped with a Θ-compatible prior, satisfy, for all n, $\bar{P}_{\text{Bayes}}(X_{n+1} \mid x^n) \notin \mathcal{M}$.

Example 9.3 [Gaussian with Fixed Variance] Let $\mathcal{M} = \{f_{\mu,\sigma^2} \mid \mu \in \mathbb{R}\}$ be the set of all Gaussian distributions with some fixed variance σ^2, as defined in Chapter 2. An easy calculation shows that the ML estimator is equal to the observed average, i.e. $\hat{\mu}(x^n) = n^{-1} \sum_{i=1}^n x_i$. We consider a prior on parameter μ that is itself a Gaussian with mean μ_0 and variance τ_0^2, i.e. $w(\mu) \propto \exp(-(\mu - \mu_0)^2/2\tau_0^2)$. Let $\bar{P}_{\text{Bayes}}$ be defined with respect to that prior. Then one can show that the predictive distribution $\bar{P}_{\text{Bayes}}(X_{n+1} \mid x^n)$ is itself a Gaussian, given by

$$\bar{P}_{\text{Bayes}}(X_{n+1} \mid x^n) = f_{\mu_n, \tau_n^2 + \sigma^2}(X_{n+1}), \tag{9.9}$$

where

$$\mu_n = \frac{(\sum_{i=1}^n x_i) + \frac{\sigma^2}{\tau_0^2}\mu_0}{n + \frac{\sigma^2}{\tau_0^2}} \quad ; \quad \tau_n^2 = \frac{\sigma^2}{n + \frac{\sigma^2}{\tau_0^2}}. \tag{9.10}$$

This fact continues to hold for the rich class of linear regression models, and will be proved in full generality in Chapter 12, Section 12.3.1.

Since $\tau_n^2 = \text{ORDER}(1/n)$, we find that the Bayesian predictive distribution is itself a Gaussian, albeit with a sightly larger variance $\sigma^2 + \text{ORDER}(1/n)$. Thus, it is almost, but not quite, an element of the model $\mathcal{M}$. For example, if $\sigma^2 = 1$ and $\tau_0^2 = 1$, then $\mu_n = (n+1)^{-1}(\sum_{i=1}^n x_i + \mu_0)$ and $\tau_n^2 = 1/(n+1)$. The Bayesian predictive distribution is equal to the ML estimator obtained for the same data with additional data point μ_0, and a variance that is slightly (by a term of $\text{ORDER}(1/n)$) larger.

Because of its larger variance, the predictive distribution $\bar{P}_{\text{Bayes}}(X_{n+1} \mid x^n)$ is not an element of $\mathcal{M}$. Therefore, it cannot be equal to the prequential plug-in distribution $\bar{P}_{\text{plug-in}}(X_{n+1} \mid x^n)$, because the latter, by its definition, does belong to $\mathcal{M}$. Therefore, the Bayesian universal model with a Gaussian prior is almost, but not quite, equal to the prequential plug-in distribution with a correspondingly modified ML estimator.

9.3   More Precise Asymptotics

Work on the prequential plug-in model originated in the 1980s with Rissanen (1984) and Dawid (1984). In the late 1980s and early 1990s, versions of (9.6) were shown for a wide variety of models, including several non-i.i.d. models. All these theorems considered expected regret or redundancy (Chapter 6, Section 6.5). More recently, Li and Yu (2000) have shown that for i.i.d. exponential families, (9.6), with an additional $O(\log \log n)$ additive term, also holds in a much stronger sense, namely almost surely (with P_θ-probability 1). This mirrors the result for the almost-sure redundancy of the Bayesian universal code, where the $(k/2) \log n$ formula also had to be adjusted with an additional $O(\log \log n)$ term; see (8.22), Section 8.4.

This almost-sure result suggests that (9.6) also holds for individual sequences, under some conditions such as $\hat{\theta}(x^n)$ lying in an ineccsi subset of the parameter space. Interestingly, a recent result by Grünwald and de Rooij (2005) implies that this is *not* the case. More precisely, let $\mathcal{M}$ be a 1-parameter exponential family given in its mean-value parameterization Θ. Let $\phi(X)$ be the sufficient statistic, and let P^* be a distribution such that $E_{P^*}[\phi(X)] = \mu^*$ lies in the interior of Θ. We are especially interested in the case that $P^* \notin \mathcal{M}$ ("misspecification"). From Chapter 19, Section 19.2, we know that P_{μ^*} is the element of Θ that minimizes KL divergence to P^*. Grünwald and De Rooij show that under slight regularity conditions on P^*,

$$
E_{X^n \sim P^*}\left[-\log \bar{P}_{\text{plug-in}}(X^n) \right] =
$$
$$
E_{X^n \sim P^*}\left[-\log P_{\mu^*}(X^n) \right] + \frac{\text{var}_{P^*}[\phi(X)]}{\text{var}_{P_{\mu^*}}[\phi(X)]} \frac{1}{2} \log n + O(1). \quad (9.11)
$$

Thus, if $P^* \notin \mathcal{M}$, then the expected redundancy of $\bar{P}_{\text{plug-in}}$ is not of the form $(k/2) \log n + O(1)$ anymore. We note that the form of redundancy expressed by (9.11), evaluated under $P^* \notin \mathcal{M}$, has been called *relative redundancy*; the phrase has been coined independently by Takeuchi and Barron (1998b) and Grünwald and de Rooij (2005). After publication of (Grünwald and de Rooij 2005), it has come to my attention that a result analogous to (9.11) for misspecified linear regression models already appeared in (Wei 1992).

Grünwald and de Rooij (2005) further show that, under additional conditions on $\mathcal{M}$,

$$
E_{P^*}[-\log P_{\mu^*(X^n)}(X^n) + \log P_{\hat{\mu}(X^n)}(X^n)] = \frac{\text{var}_{P^*}[\phi(X)]}{\text{var}_{P_{\mu^*}}[\phi(X)]} \frac{1}{2} + o(1) = O(1),
$$
$$
(9.12)
$$

which should be compared to (8.20). Combining (9.11) and (9.12), and assuming $P^* \in \mathcal{M}$, we recover the special case of (9.6) for 1-parameter exponential families. But combining (9.11) and (9.12) also shows that, if data are distributed according to some $P^* \notin \mathcal{M}$, then $\bar{P}_{\text{plug-in}}$ still behaves like an $O(\log n)$-universal model, but with different constants in front of the logarithmic term. This implies that (9.6) cannot hold in an individual sequence sense either. Thus, the prequential plug-in model is somewhat of an outlier within the class of standard universal models considered in Part II of this book: in Theorem 7.1, Theorem 8.1, and Theorem 10.1, we show that for the NML, Bayes, and two-part code, (9.6) holds in an individual sequence sense.

Rough Proof Sketch of (9.11) Here we give a rough proof sketch of the result (9.11). At the heart of the proof lies the well-known fact from calculus that

$$\sum_{i=1}^{n} i^{-1} = \ln n + O(1). \tag{9.13}$$

The proof of the main result (9.6) in the box on page 260 for $k > 1$ as given by Rissanen (1986b) is quite different, but also makes use of (9.13) at some point.

To show (9.11), we first note that for exponential families as defined above, for all $\mu \in \Theta$, by the robustness property of exponential families, Proposition 19.1 in the box on page 625, the extended KL divergence $D_{P^*}(\mu^* \| \mu)$ is equal to the standard KL divergence $D(\mu^* \| \mu)$. Once again, just as in the proofs for the asymptotic expansions of $\bar{P}_{\text{nml}}$ and $\bar{P}_{\text{Bayes}}$ (and, as we shall see, $\bar{L}_{\text{2-p}}$), we now perform a second-order Taylor expansion of the KL divergence as in Chapter 4, Section 4.3. But, whereas in the other three cases we consider $D(\hat{\mu}(x^n) \| \mu)$, and expand it around $\hat{\mu}$, for the prequential result we consider $D(\mu^* \| \hat{\mu}(x^i))$ for some $i < n$, and expand around μ^*. Thus, in the current proof, ML estimators play a very different role. We have

$$D_{P^*}(\mu^* \| \hat{\mu}(x^i)) = D(\mu^* \| \hat{\mu}(x^i)) = \frac{1}{2} I(\mu^*)(\mu^* - \hat{\mu}(x^i))^2 + R, \tag{9.14}$$

where R is some remainder term. By linearity of expectation, it follows that

$$E_{P^*}[\text{RED}(\bar{P}_{\text{plug-in}}, P_{\mu^*}, X^n)] =$$
$$E_{X^n \sim P^*}\left[-\ln \bar{P}_{\text{plug-in}}(X^n) - [-\ln P_{\mu^*}(X^n)]\right] =$$
$$\sum_{i=1}^{n} E_{X_i \sim P^*} E_{X^{i-1} \sim P^*}[-\ln P_{\hat{\mu}(X^{i-1})}(X_i) + \ln P_{\mu^*}(X_i)], \tag{9.15}$$

which can be further rewritten as

$$\sum_{i=1}^{n} E_{X^{i-1} \sim P^*}[\mathrm{D}_{P^*}(\mu^* \| \hat{\mu}(X^{i-1}))] = \sum_{i=1}^{n} E_{X^{i-1} \sim P^*}[\mathrm{D}(\mu^* \| \hat{\mu}(X^{i-1}))] =$$

$$\sum_{i=1}^{n} E_{X^{i-1} \sim P^*}\left[\frac{1}{2} I(\mu^*)(\mu^* - \hat{\mu}(X^{i-1}))^2 + R_{i-1}\right] =$$

$$\frac{1}{2} I(\mu^*) \sum_{i=1}^{n} E_{X^{i-1} \sim P^*}[(\mu^* - \hat{\mu}(X^{i-1}))^2] + \sum_{i=1}^{\infty} E_{X^{i-1}}[R_{i-1}].$$

Here the R_{i-1} are the remainder terms in (9.14) corresponding to x^{i-1}. Since they correspond to the expectations of third-order terms in a Taylor-expansion, one would expect them to be of order $i^{-3/2}$ or smaller, and therefore, to have a finite sum. If $\hat{\mu}$ is a modified ML estimator of the form (9.4) for some $\alpha > 0$ ($\alpha > 0$ is crucial here), then under weak regularity conditions on the exponential family $\mathcal{M}$, this sum is indeed finite; see (Grünwald and de Rooij 2005) for the details. Assuming then that the remainder terms are summable, (9.15) becomes

$$E_{P^*}[\mathrm{RED}(\bar{P}_{\text{plug-in}}, P_{\mu^*}, X^n)] = \frac{1}{2} I(\mu^*) \sum_{i=1}^{n} E[(\mu^* - \hat{\mu}(X^{i-1}))^2] + O(1), \quad (9.16)$$

where we absorbed the first term ($i = 1$) of the sum into the $O(1)$-term, which is justified because $\alpha > 0$. The modified ML estimator satisfies $\hat{\mu} = n^{-1} \sum \phi(X_i) + O(1/n)$. It turns out that the $O(1/n)$ does not affect the remainder of the analysis (see (Grünwald and de Rooij 2005)) and below we will simply ignore it and act as if $\hat{\mu}$ were the ordinary ML estimator. Because $\mathcal{M}$ is an exponential family and μ is the mean-value parameter, we also have $\mu^* = E_{P^*}[\phi(X)]$ and $I(\mu^*) = 1/\mathrm{var}_{P_{\mu^*}}[\phi(X)]$. Then (9.16) becomes

$$E_{P^*}[\mathrm{RED}(\bar{P}_{\text{plug-in}}, P_{\mu^*}, X^n)] =$$

$$\frac{1}{2} \sum_{i=2}^{n} \frac{E_{X^{i-1} \sim P^*}[(E_{P^*}[\phi(X)] - (i-1)^{-1} \sum_{j=1}^{i-1} \phi(X_i))^2]}{\mathrm{var}_{P_{\mu^*}}[\phi(X)]} + O(1) =$$

$$\frac{1}{2} \sum_{i=2}^{n} \frac{1}{i-1} \frac{\mathrm{var}_{P^*}[\phi(X)]}{\mathrm{var}_{P_{\mu^*}}[\phi(X)]} = \frac{1}{2} \frac{\mathrm{var}_{P^*}[\phi(X)]}{\mathrm{var}_{P_{\mu^*}}[\phi(X)]} \ln n + O(1), \quad (9.17)$$

and the result follows.

Open Problem/Conjecture No. 2: in general, in-model estimators cannot achieve $(k/2) \log n$ The dependency of the redundancy (and regret) of the plug-in code on the variance of $\phi(X)$ under the true P^* is somewhat disturbing. Can we overcome this problem by defining a plug-in code relative to an estimator $\hat{\mu}'$ that is different from the modified ML estimator? We may consider Bayesian MAP or mean estimators relative to some priors, or unbiased estimators, or anything else. To address this question, we first note that *if $P^* \in \mathcal{M}$, then the plug-in code based on $\hat{\mu}'$ should achieve $(k/2) \log n + O(1)$ expected regret for all $P^* \in \mathcal{M}$*. The proof sketch of (9.11) suggests that, if $k = 1$, then for this to be the case, the variance of $\hat{\mu}'$ must be asymptotically approximately equal to $E_{X^n \sim P^*}[(\mu^* - \hat{\mu}'(X^n))^2] = n^{-1} \mathrm{var}_{P^*}[\phi(X)]$. This in turn suggests that asymptotically, the alternative $\hat{\mu}'$ must be essentially equivalent to a (modified) ML estimator of the form (9.4). Our proof of (9.11) implies however that if $P^* \notin \mathcal{M}$, then a plug-in code based on a modified ML estimator (9.4) inevitably incurs an expected redundancy that depends on $\mathrm{var}_{P^*}[\phi(X)]$. Therefore, we conjecture that *there exists no estimator (function from samples of arbitrary length to elements of $\mathcal{M}$) such that the corresponding plug-in code achieves $(k/2) \log n + O(1)$ P^*-expected redundancy for arbitrary i.i.d. sources P^* with positive, finite variance (where P^* is not required to lie in $\mathcal{M}$*. Formulating this conjecture in a precise manner and proving it is an open problem.

Open Problem/Conjecture No. 3: "almost" in-model estimators can achieve $(k/2) \log n$ **in general**[*] The notion of "estimator" we used above is called an *in-model estimator* in Chapter 15, Section 15.2.1. Alternatively we may consider "out-model" estimators, which estimate a $P \in \mathcal{M}$ by a distribution P' that is itself not necessarily in $\mathcal{M}$. As explained in Section 15.2.1, the Bayesian universal code may be thought of as a prequential plug-in code based on an out-model estimator. Now this Bayesian code does achieve expected redundancy $(k/2) \log n + O(1)$ for arbitrary i.i.d. sources P^* with positive, finite variance, including P^* that are not in $\mathcal{M}$. This shows that there do exist out-model estimators that achieve $(k/2) \log n + O(1)$ even if $P^* \notin \mathcal{M}$. From Example 9.3 we see that if $\mathcal{M}$ is the normal family with fixed variance σ^2, then the Bayesian out-model estimator is really "almost" an in-model estimator after all: it is a normal distribution with variance $\sigma^2 + \mathrm{ORDER}(1/n)$. This leads us to conjecture that something similar holds for general exponential families. More specifically, perhaps there exists a general method for extending a k-parameter exponential family $\mathcal{M} = \{P_\beta \mid \beta \in \Theta\}$ to $k + 1$-parameter model $\mathcal{M}_{\mathrm{disp}}$, parameterized as $P_{\beta,\lambda}$, by adding a special, dispersion-like parameter $\lambda > 0$, such that $\mathcal{M}_{\mathrm{disp}}$ has the following properties: (1) $P_{\beta,1}$ coincides with the original P_β; (2) for all λ, $E_{\beta,\lambda}[\phi(X)] = E_\beta[\phi(X)] = \mu(\beta)$ as for the standard exponential family; yet (3) the variance $\mathrm{var}_{\beta,\lambda}[\phi(X)]$ varies for different λ, and (4) there exists an out-model estimator $(\hat{\beta}', \lambda_n)$ for $\mathcal{M}$ which achieves expected redundancy $(k/2) \log n + O(1)$ even if $P^* \notin \mathcal{M}$, yet at the same time is "almost in-model" in the sense that $P_{\hat{\beta},\lambda_n}$ is always in the extended model $\mathcal{M}_{\mathrm{disp}}$, and $\mathrm{var}_{\beta,\lambda_n}[\phi(X)] = \mathrm{var}_\beta[\phi(X)] + O(1/n)$.

9.4   Summary

The main results of this chapter are so important they deserve a box around them:

The Prequential Plug-In Model: Summary
We summarize the main points about the plug-in model:

Start-up problems. In many cases we cannot define $\bar{P}_{\text{plug-in}}$ relative to the ML estimator; we use a slightly modified ML estimator instead (Example 9.1).

Stochastic universality. With such a modified ML estimator, $\bar{P}_{\text{plug-in}}$ becomes a universal code with good behavior in the stochastic sense. If data are drawn from $P \in \mathcal{M}$, then it behaves similarly (up to $O(1)$) to the Bayesian universal model $\bar{P}_{\text{Bayes}}$. For MDL applications, we are also interested in the individual sequence behavior; in those cases, it may behave quite differently from $\bar{P}_{\text{Bayes}}$. In MDL model selection applications, $\bar{P}_{\text{Bayes}}$ is then preferable (Chapter 14, Section 14.4.2).

Ease of computation. Still, for many parametric models, the prequential plug-in codelengths $- \log \bar{P}_{\text{plug-in}}(x^n)$ are significantly easier to compute than the Bayesian codelengths $- \log \bar{P}_{\text{Bayes}}(x^n)$, and may be the best universal code whose lengths are computable in practice, even in an MDL model selection context. This holds especially for time series models, where the data have a natural order (Chapter 14).

---

10 *Parametric Models: Two-Part*

In this chapter, we analyze the regret of cleverly designed two-part codes for exponential families. In Section 10.1, we consider standard, "ordinary" two-part codes. We present Theorem 10.1 which shows that they can be made to achieve regret not much larger than that of Bayesian universal codes. We give a proof sketch of Theorem 10.1 in the main text, since it contains an important idea: the two-level discretization process depicted in Figure 10.1. In Section 10.2, we describe a variation of the two-part coding idea that can be used to achieve the minimax optimal regret COMP($\mathcal{M}$). This is related to the interpretation of COMP($\mathcal{M}$) as "counting the number of distinguishable distributions" that we gave in Chapter 7.

Fast Track Except for the boxes, this chapter may be skipped at first reading.

10.1 The Ordinary Two-Part Universal Model

When introducing universal coding in Chapter 6, we first treated the two-part codes because they are conceptually the easiest to understand. In our treatment of optimal universal codes for parametric models they come last, since designing good universal codes relative to continuous parameter spaces is harder for two-part than for other universal codes.

Since two-part codes are incomplete (Chapter 6, Example 6.4), they cannot achieve the minimax regret. Nevertheless, as we show in this section, one can design two-part codes that come quite close to achieving it. In fact, we show something more general: we design a two-part code $\bar{L}_{2\text{-p}}$ relative to a given Bayesian universal code $\bar{L}_{\text{Bayes}}$, defined with respect to some prior W. The two-part code is designed such that, for all ineccsi x^n, the additional regret incurred by the two-part code compared to the Bayesian code is very small. By using Jeffreys' prior as the prior W, a two-part code that has minimax regret close to the optimal minimax regret arises as a special case.

Sample Size-Dependent Two-Part Codes   Let Θ represent an exponential family. As in Chapter 5 and Chapter 6, Section 6.1.1, $\bar{L}_{2\text{-p}}$ is based on a two-stage description method. In the first stage, some $\theta \in \Theta$ is encoded, using a code with length function $\dot{L}_n(\theta)$. In the second stage, the data x^n are encoded using the Shannon-Fano code relative to θ, which takes $-\log P_\theta(x^n)$ bits. We always use the θ minimizing the two-part codelength, so that the total codelength becomes

$$\bar{L}_{2\text{-p}}(x^n) = \min_\theta \{\dot{L}_n(\theta) - \log P_\theta(x^n)\}. \tag{10.1}$$

We henceforth use the notation $\dot{L}_n$ as the length function of the first part of the code. $\dot{L}_n$ *is allowed to depend on* n. In Chapter 5, we encoded θ using a code, denoted there as L_1, which was used for all n. Since universal codes are not required to be prequential, having $\dot{L}_n$ depend on n does not violate any of our definitions. We call two-part codes with $\dot{L}_n$ depending on n *sample size-dependent*; see also page 196, where we described how they can be modified to sample size independent two-part codes ath the cost of an additional $\log n + O(\log \log n)$ regret term.

Below we present Theorem 10.1, the analogue of Theorem 7.1 and Theorem 8.1 for the two-part codes. The theorem implies that there exist codes of form (10.1) which almost, but not quite, achieve the minimax regret. This is achieved by *discretizing* Θ to a countable set $\ddot{\Theta}_n$. indexkeywordsdiscretization of parameter set In contrast to the discretization in Chapter 5, the discretization depends on the sample size and, crucially, is not uniform: the density of discretized points in the vicinity of $\theta \in \Theta$ depends on θ. As we shall see in the proof, Sections 10.1.1 and 10.1.2, the optimal density near θ is given by the Jeffreys' prior density at θ. This is not surprising given the discussion on $\text{COMP}^{(n)}(\mathcal{M})$ in Section 7.3, Chapter 7: the more "distinguishable" distributions there are in the vicinity of θ, the more discretized points we should place in that area. This idea is discussed further in Section 10.2.2.

Theorem 10.1 Let Θ_0 be an *ineccsi* subset of Θ and let w be a Θ_0-compatible prior density on Θ. Then there exists a two-part code of form (10.1) such that for every Θ_0-sequence $x_1, x_2, \ldots,$

$$\mathrm{REG}(\bar{L}_{2\text{-}p}, \Theta, x^n) =$$

$$\frac{k}{2} \log \frac{n}{2\pi} - \log w(\hat{\theta}) + \log \sqrt{\det I(\hat{\theta})} + g(k) + o(1) =$$

$$\mathrm{REG}(\bar{L}_{\mathrm{Bayes}}, \Theta, x^n) + g(k) + o(1). \quad (10.2)$$

where the convergence is uniform[1] in Θ_0. Here $g(k)$ is a function that

1. for any fixed $a > 0$ satisfies $0 \leq g(k) \leq (k/2) \log 2\pi - k(\log e)\left(\ln a - \frac{a^2}{8}\right)$.
   In particular, by taking $a = 2$, we obtain

$$\mathrm{REG}(\bar{L}_{2\text{-}p}, \Theta, x^n) \leq$$

$$\frac{k}{2} \log n - \log w(\hat{\theta}) + \log \sqrt{\det I(\hat{\theta})} - k(\log e)\left(\ln 2 - \frac{1}{2}\right) + o(1).$$

$$(10.3)$$

   For $k = 1$, (10.3) holds with equality.

2. $\lim_{k \to \infty} g(k) = 0$.

The theorem has been stated in such a way that it remains valid if log were defined relative to a basis different from 2. It is very similar to our central result for the Bayesian asymptotic regret, Theorem 8.1. Comparing to that theorem, and taking log as logarithm to the base 2, we see that ((10.3)) gives

$$\mathrm{REG}(\bar{L}_{2\text{-}p}, \Theta, x^n) \leq \mathrm{REG}(\bar{L}_{\mathrm{Bayes}}, \Theta, x^n) + k\left(\frac{1}{2} \log 2\pi - 1 + \frac{1}{2} \log e\right) + o(1)$$

$$\approx \mathrm{REG}(\bar{L}_{\mathrm{Bayes}}, \Theta, x^n) + 1.05k, \quad (10.4)$$

showing the additional regret incurred by using the two-part code to be quite small, for small k. For large k, the difference with Bayes is even smaller, tending to 0 as k tends to infinity. It should be noted though that the $o(1)$ term in (10.2) depends on k, i.e. it may be that for large k, a larger sample size n is needed before the $o(1)$ term becomes negligible. Although this does not follow from our theorem, it seems that the actual value of $g(k)$ first increases with k, reaches a maximum for a certain dimension, and then decreases again.

---

1. See the footnote on page 232.

Theorem 10.1 has, to the best of our knowledge, not been published before. However, the proof is a simple adaption of a result by Barron and Cover (1991), who prove expected redundancy bounds of a form similar to (10.2). Their theorem is more general in that it also holds for some parametric models that are not exponential families. It seems quite likely that a variation of these results extends to our individual sequence regret setting as well, leading to a generalized form of Theorem 10.1 for general parametric families, in which, as in (8.17) on page 241, the (expected) Fisher information is replaced by the observed Fisher information.

Incompleteness   The fact that with a two-part code we can get so close to the Bayesian codelengths is somewhat surprising: Exponential families satisfy $P_\theta(x^n) > 0$ for all n, all $x^n \in \mathcal{X}^n$, all $\theta \in \Theta$. Therefore, by the reasoning of Example 6.4 ("Bayes is better than two-part"), the regret of any two-part code must be strictly larger on all sequences than the regret of the Bayesian code defined with respect to the same prior. Apparently, at least asymptotically, the difference is quite small, and for large k, even becomes negligible. Indeed:

The Two-Part Code for Simple Parametric Models
Theorem 10.1 shows that, for each k-dimensional exponential family Θ, there exists a two-part code that, for all ineccsi sequences, asymptotically achieves a regret within a small constant of the Bayesian code based on the same prior. In particular, if Θ is ineccsi and the two-part code is based on Jeffreys' prior, then the two-part code will asymptotically need only a few more bits than the NML code; for large k, the number of extra bits needed approaches 0. In practice, researchers have often used crude, ad hoc two-part codes that do not achieve the bounds of Theorem 10.1. In reality, cleverly designed two-part codes are surprisingly efficient – still, when working with continuous parameter sets, we tend to avoid them, mainly because nonasymptotic length calculation requires a complicated discretization procedure.

10.1.1   Derivation of the Two-Part Code Regret

The key to constructing a two-part code achieving Theorem 10.1 is to discretize Θ to a countable set of points $\ddot{\Theta}_n$ such that (a) the ML estimator restricted to $\ddot{\Theta}_n$ achieves almost the same codelength as the unrestricted ML estimator, i.e. $-\log P_{\ddot{\theta}}(x^n) - [-\log P_{\hat{\theta}}(x^n)]$ is small; whereas (b) the number of discretized points lying in areas with nonneglible prior mass is also small. The finer we take the discretization, the smaller the number of bits $-\log P(D \mid \ddot{\theta})$ needed in the second stage of the encoding, but the larger the number $\dot{L}_n(\ddot{\theta})$ needed in the first stage. Theorem 10.1 is based on choosing the discretization that gives the optimal tradeoff between these two description lengths.

We first give an informal derivation of a special case of Theorem 10.1, for 1-parameter models $\Theta \subset \mathbb{R}^1$ with Fisher information $I(\theta) = I_0$ constant on Θ. We then sketch the proof of the general result, for varying $I(\theta)$ and multi-parameter models. Both proofs are based on optimizing the aforementioned tradeoff.

Let $\Theta \subset \mathbb{R}$. Fix an arbitrary $a > 0$, and consider adjacent intervals of length $a/\sqrt{nI_0}$:

$$\ldots, \left[\frac{-a}{\sqrt{nI_0}}, 0\right), \left[0, \frac{a}{\sqrt{nI_0}}\right), \left[\frac{a}{\sqrt{nI_0}}, \frac{2a}{\sqrt{nI_0}}\right), \ldots.$$

Note that the set $\mathcal{R}$ of all these intervals is a partition of $\mathbb{R}$. For each $R \in \mathcal{R}$, let θ_R be the center (midpoint) of interval R. For each $\theta \in \Theta$, let $R(\theta)$ be the interval in which θ falls. Define

$$\ddot{\Theta}_n = \Theta \cap \{\theta : \theta = \theta_R \text{ for some } R \in \mathcal{R}\}.$$

This is our "discretization" of Θ at sample size n. Note that in Chapter 5, $\ddot{\Theta}_d^{(k)}$ referred to the discretized parameters for a k-parameter submodel of some model class $\mathcal{M}$, encoded at precision d. The discretization did not depend on the sample size n. Now, the situation is the opposite: the model $\mathcal{M}$ has a fixed number of parameters k, and the discretization depends on n. d is now taken as a fixed function of n (Section 10.1.3), and not as a parameter to be optimized.

With the discretized parameter set $\ddot{\Theta}_n$ we associate a discretization W_n of the prior W, letting, for $\ddot{\theta} \in \ddot{\Theta}_n$, $W_n(\ddot{\theta}) = \int_{\theta \in R(\ddot{\theta})} w(\theta)d\theta$. Our two-part code is based on first encoding some $\theta \in \ddot{\Theta}_n$, using the code based on W_n, and then encoding x^n using the Shannon-Fano code corresponding to θ. We always pick the $\ddot{\theta}$ minimizing this two-part codelength, so that we get

$$\bar{L}_{\text{2-p}}(x^n) = \min_{\theta \in \ddot{\Theta}_n} \{-\log W_n(\theta) - \log P_\theta(x^n)\} = -\log W_n(\ddot{\theta}) - \log P_{\ddot{\theta}}(x^n).$$

$$(10.5)$$

If several $\ddot{\theta}$ achieving the minimum two-part codelength exist, we can choose any one of them.

We further let $\hat{\hat{\theta}}$ denote the discretized point $\theta \in \ddot{\Theta}_n$ closest to the ML estimator $\hat{\theta}(x^n)$, so that $R(\hat{\theta}) = R(\hat{\hat{\theta}})$. The regret of $\bar{L}_{\text{2-p}}$ is bounded by

$$\text{REG}(\bar{L}_{\text{2-p}}, \Theta, x^n) =$$

$$- \log W_n(\ddot{\theta}) - \log \frac{P_{\ddot{\theta}}(x^n)}{P_{\hat{\theta}}(x^n)} \le - \log W_n(\hat{\hat{\theta}}) - \log \frac{P_{\hat{\hat{\theta}}}(x^n)}{P_{\hat{\theta}}(x^n)} =$$

$$- \log W_n(\hat{\hat{\theta}}) + n\text{D}(\hat{\theta}\|\hat{\hat{\theta}}), \quad (10.6)$$

where the last equation follows by the robustness property of exponential families in the form of (19.12), Chapter 19, Section 19.3.

Performing a second-order Taylor approximation of $\text{D}(\hat{\theta}\|\hat{\hat{\theta}})$ as in Chapter 4, just as we did to derive the Bayesian regret in Chapter 8, Section 8.3, we find

$$\text{REG}(\bar{L}_{\text{2-p}}, \Theta, x^n) \le - \log W_n(\hat{\hat{\theta}}) + \frac{1}{2}n(\hat{\theta} - \hat{\hat{\theta}})^2 I_0(\log e), \quad (10.7)$$

where the $\log e$ factor comes from the fact that the Fisher information I_0 is defined with respect to the natural logarithm $\ln$. Since I_0 is constant, there is no remainder term. We chose $\hat{\hat{\theta}}$ such that $|\hat{\theta} - \hat{\hat{\theta}}| \le a/(2\sqrt{nI_0})$, so that

$$\text{REG}(\bar{L}_{\text{2-p}}, \Theta, x^n) \le - \log W_n(\hat{\hat{\theta}}) + \frac{a^2}{8}\log e. \quad (10.8)$$

Since the size of the intervals $R(\hat{\hat{\theta}})$ shrinks to 0 with increasing n and w is continuous, for large n the density w becomes approximately constant within each interval. The prior mass $W_n(\hat{\hat{\theta}})$ can then be very well approximated by $w(\hat{\hat{\theta}})$ times the length $a/\sqrt{nI_0}$ of each interval. We now make this precise: as in the statement of Theorem 10.1, fix some ineccsi subset $\Theta_0 \subset \Theta$, and suppose that $x_1, x_2, \ldots$ is such that, for all large n, $\hat{\theta}(x^n) \in \Theta_0$, and w is bounded away from 0 on Θ_0, and $R(\hat{\theta}(x^n)) \subset \Theta_0$ (i.e. the discretization region of $\hat{\theta}$ is completely inside Θ_0 and does not lie at its boundary). Since the size of the intervals $R(\hat{\hat{\theta}})$ shrinks to 0 and w is continuous, we must have, uniformly for all such x^n,

$$\frac{\frac{a \cdot w(\hat{\theta}(x^n))}{\sqrt{nI_0}}}{W_n(\hat{\hat{\theta}}(x^n))} \to 1,$$

so that

$$\text{REG}(\bar{L}_{2\text{-p}}, \Theta, x^n) \le \frac{1}{2}\log n - \log \frac{w(\hat{\theta})}{\sqrt{I_0}} - \log a + \frac{a^2}{8}\log e + o(1). \qquad (10.9)$$

In the more precise proof below, we will see that, by slightly modifying the code for $\ddot{\theta}$, we can ensure that (10.9) even holds for x^n such that $R(\hat{\theta}(x^n))$ intersects with the boundaries of Θ_0. Thus, (10.9) holds uniformly for all x^n with $\hat{\theta}(x^n) \in \Theta_0$, in accordance with Theorem 10.1, (10.2).

For the second part of the theorem, note that we can choose the optimal grid with any a that we please. A natural choice is to pick $a = 2$, which minimizes the right-hand side of (10.9), giving

$$\text{REG}(\bar{L}_{2\text{-p}}, \Theta, x^n) \le \frac{1}{2}\log n - \log \frac{w(\hat{\theta})}{\sqrt{I_0}} + \frac{1}{2}\log e - 1 + o(1),$$

which is in accordance with Theorem 10.1, (10.3).

10.1.2 Proof Sketch of Theorem 10.1

The key to proving Theorem 10.1 in the multidimensional case, with $I(\theta)$ varying with θ, is to do the discretization in two stages: we first introduce a coarse partition $\mathcal{S}$ of $\mathbb{R}^k$, where each $S \in \mathcal{S}$ is a hypercube with side length $an^{-1/4}$. Here a is the number that appears in the statement of the theorem. Each S is further partitioned into a fine partition of rotated hyperrectangles R with side length $O(n^{-1/2})$, as in Figure 10.1. The idea is that, (a), S is chosen small enough so that, for large n, within each $S \in \mathcal{S}$, the Fisher information converges to a constant. Yet, (b), S is chosen large enough so that the number of rectangles within S tends to infinity with increasing n. As a consequence, the analysis within each S can essentially proceed as in the case we have seen before, where $I(\theta)$ was assumed constant.[2]

We now describe both partitions. The coarse partition $\mathcal{S}$ is constructed so that one of the hypercubes has the origin as its lower left corner, i.e. $S = [0, an^{-1/4})^k$. We now make a further, fine partition of each hypercube S, as follows. Let I_S be the Fisher information at the center point θ_S of S. Let

$$\Theta_S := \left\{ \theta : (\theta - \theta_S)^\top I(\theta_S)(\theta - \theta_S) \le \frac{a^2}{4n} \right\} \qquad (10.10)$$

---

2. This type of reasoning goes back at least to Ludwig Boltzmann (1844–1906), father of statistical mechanics.

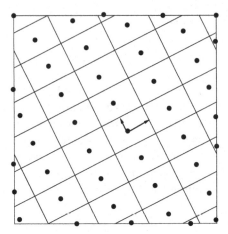

Figure 10.1   The structure of the discretization for the case $\Theta \subset \mathbb{R}^2$. The picture shows a single "large" hypercube S containing some "small" hyperrectangles R. The discretized points are the centers of the rectangles, if the rectangles lie completely inside S. Otherwise they are the closest points to the center that still lies within S. For the S that is shown here, the angle between the small and the large grid is 30 degrees; for other "large" S, the angle of the $R \subset S$ will be different. The arrows point in the direction of the eigenvectors of the Fisher information matrix. The length of the arrows is proportional to the square root of the inverse of the eigenvalues.

be a Mahalanobis ball relative to the metric induced by $I(\theta_S)$, as in Chapter 4, (4.24), page 121. From the box on page 120, we know that Θ_S is an ellipsoid (a generalization of "ellipse" to k dimensions), with axis given by the eigenvectors of $I(\theta_S)$, and axis lengths given by $a/2\sqrt{n}$ times the square root of the inverse eigenvalues. We now consider the smallest hyperrectangle $R(\theta_S)$ containing Θ_S. This rectangle lies parallel to the eigenvectors, and has side length $a/\sqrt{n}$ times the square root of the inverse eigenvalues (Figure 10.1). Since the determinant of I_{θ_S} is the product of the eigenvalues, the volume of $R(\theta_S)$ is given by $a^k n^{-k/2}/\sqrt{\det I_{\theta_S}}$. We now partition S by filling it up with adjacent copies of the rectangle $R(\theta_S)$, as in the figure. Here rectangles intersecting the boundaries are replaced by their intersection with S. Let $\mathcal{R}_S$ be the partition of S thus obtained. The elements R of $\mathcal{R}_S$ that do not intersect the boundary of S are parallel hyperrectangles with identical side lengths, as can be seen from the figure.

For each $R \in \mathcal{R}_S$ with $R \cap \Theta \neq \emptyset$, we define θ_R to be the point in $R \cap \Theta$

that is closest to the center of R (if such a point does not exist, then any other point in $R \cap S \cap \Theta$ will do as well). We now define

$$
\begin{aligned}
\ddot{\Theta}_{S,n} &= \{\theta \mid \theta = \theta_R \text{ for some } R \in \mathcal{R}_S \text{ with } R \cap \Theta \neq \emptyset\} \\
\ddot{\Theta}_n &= \cup_{S \in \mathcal{S}} \ddot{\Theta}_{S,n}.
\end{aligned}
\tag{10.11}
$$

In essence, the scale parameter a determines the *level of distinguishability* of the discretization $\ddot{\Theta}_n$. We defined this level in Chapter 7, Section 7.3.4. This intuition is explained in Section 10.2.2. The first part of Lemma 10.1 below is an analogue of (10.8). In the lemma, $\hat{\hat{\theta}}_n$ again stands for the discretized ML estimator, achieving $\max_{\theta \in \ddot{\Theta}_n} P_\theta(x^n)$.

Lemma 10.1 Fix an arbitrary $a > 0$. Let Θ_0 be an ineccsi subset of Θ. For all n, let W_n be an arbitrary distribution on the (countable) discretization $\ddot{\Theta}_n$. Then :

1. For all sequences $x_1, x_2, \ldots$ that are ineccsi relative to Θ_0, we have

$$
\text{REG}(\bar{L}_{\text{2-p}}, \Theta, x^n) \leq k\frac{a^2}{8}(\log e) - \log W_n(\hat{\hat{\theta}}_n) + o(1).
\tag{10.12}
$$

2. $\left|\ddot{\Theta}_{S,n}\right| \sim n^{k/4}\sqrt{\det I(\theta_S)}$, where $|\cdot|$ denotes the number of elements in a set. More precisely, there exists a continuous function $f : \Theta \to [0, \infty)$ such that, for all n, all $\theta \in \ddot{\Theta}_{S,n}$,

$$
1 - n^{-1/4}f(\theta) \leq \frac{\left|\ddot{\Theta}_{S,n}\right|}{n^{k/4}\sqrt{\det I(\theta_S)}} \leq 1 + n^{1/4}f(\theta).
\tag{10.13}
$$

Proof:(sketch) Item 1 is proved by performing, once again, a second-order Taylor approximation of the KL divergence (10.6), similar to Chapter 4; Chapter 8, Section 8.3; and (10.7), and using (10.10). Here we use the fact that for each $R \in \mathcal{R}_S$, for each $\theta \in R$, the Mahalanobis distance to θ_R is bounded by $\sqrt{k}a/(2n)$. This is derived by noting that (10.10) is an ellipsoid with radius $a/(2n)$, and then noting that each $\theta \in R$ must lie within the hyperrectangle that circumscribes this ellipsoid, which accounts for the factor $\sqrt{k}$.

To prove item 2, note that we already established that the volume of each small hyperrectangle $R \in \mathcal{R}_S$ is $V(R) = a^k n^{-k/2}(\det I_{\theta_S})^{-1/2}$. The volume of each large hyperrectangle S is $V(S) = (an^{-1/4})^k$. Thus approximately $V(S)/V(R) = n^{1/4}\sqrt{\det I_{\theta_S}}$ small rectangles fit in each large rectangle. Since each small rectangle contains one discretized point, this makes item 2 plausible. For a precise proof, we need to take into account that the grid of small rectangles is rotated and translated. Since this only affects points close to the boundary of the large rectangle S, the effect of this is asymptotically negligible; we omit further details. □

To turn Lemma 10.1 into Theorem 10.1, we need to cleverly choose the prior W_n as follows: for each S, each $\theta \in \ddot{\Theta}_{S,n}$, we set

$$W_n(\theta) = \frac{w(\theta_S)/\sqrt{\det I(\theta_S)}}{\sum_{S' \in \mathcal{S}} |\ddot{\Theta}_{S',n}| w(\theta_{S'})/\sqrt{\det I(\theta_{S'})}}. \tag{10.14}$$

Note that $|\ddot{\Theta}_{S,n}| = 0$ if $S \cap \ddot{\Theta}_n = \emptyset$. Now fix some ineccsi subset $\Theta_0 \subset \Theta$.

Let $\hat{\hat{\theta}}$ achieve $\min_{\theta \in \ddot{\Theta}_n} - \log W_n(\theta) - \log P_\theta(x^n)$, where we can resolve ties in an arbitrary fashion. Since $f(\theta)$ is continuous on the compact closure of Θ_0, item 2 of Lemma 10.1 implies that, for any sequence $x_1, x_2, \ldots$ with, for large n, $\hat{\theta}(x^n) \in \Theta_0$,

$$-\log W_n(\hat{\hat{\theta}}) = -\log w(\hat{\theta}(x^n)) + \log \sqrt{\det I(\hat{\theta})} + \log Z + o(1), \tag{10.15}$$

where

$$Z = \sum_{S \in \mathcal{S}} \frac{|\ddot{\Theta}_{S,n}| w(\theta_S)}{\sqrt{\det I(\theta_S)}}.$$

Here S is the hypercube containing $\hat{\hat{\theta}}$, and the equality follows by continuity of w and I. By item 2 of Lemma 10.1,

$$Z \approx \sum_{S \in \mathcal{S}} n^{k/4} w(\theta_S) = \sum_{S \in \mathcal{S}} n^{k/4}(a^{-k} n^{k/4})(a^k n^{-k/4} w(\theta_S))) =$$

$$n^{k/2} a^{-k} \sum_{S \in \mathcal{S}} a^k n^{-k/4} w(\theta_S) \approx n^{k/2} a^{-k} \int_{\theta \in \Theta} w(\theta) d\theta = n^{k/2} a^{-k}, \tag{10.16}$$

where $\approx$ means that the ratio between the two sides tends to 1 for large n. Here the final step follows because $a^k n^{-k/4}$ is the volume of S, and for large n, $w(\theta)$ is approximately constant within S, and equal to $w(\theta_S)$. It follows that

$$-\log W_n(\hat{\hat{\theta}}) = -\log w(\hat{\theta}(x^n)) + \log \sqrt{\det I(\hat{\theta})} + \frac{k}{2} \log n - k \log a + o(1), \tag{10.17}$$

where the convergence is uniform[3] in Θ_0. Combining this with Lemma 10.1,

---

3. See the footnote on page 232.

we get

$$\bar{L}_{2\text{-p}}(x^n) \leq -\log P_{\hat{\theta}}(x^n) + \frac{ka^2}{8}(\log e) - \log W_n(\hat{\hat{\theta}}(x^n)) = -\log P_{\hat{\theta}}(x^n) +$$

$$\frac{ka^2}{8}(\log e) - \log w(\hat{\theta}) + \log \sqrt{\det I(\hat{\theta})} - k\log a + \frac{k}{2}\log n + o(1). \quad (10.18)$$

This proves the first part of Theorem 10.1.

Proof Sketch of Second Part of Theorem 10.1[*] The key ingredient of the proof
of the first part was the discretization of the hyperrectangles S. Our goal
was really to obtain a discretization such that the maximum Mahalanobis distance between any point in S and a discretized point in $\ddot{\Theta}_{S,n}$ is bounded by
$\sqrt{k}a/(2n)$: Part 1 of Lemma 10.1 will hold for any discretization with this property. If we can obtain the same bound on the Mahalanobis distance from an alternative discretization of S that contains less points, then part 1 of Lemma 10.1
still holds, but clearly we need less bits to describe $\ddot{\theta} \in \ddot{\Theta}_{S,n}$ in the first part
of our two-part code, and thus the total two-part description length becomes
smaller. Indeed, it turns out that, if $k > 1$, than there exist slightly better methods of discretizing S than the one we used for Lemma 10.1. This is related to
the fact that, for $k > 1$, the smallest covering and packing of a hypercube in
k-dimensional Euclidean space is not by a set of balls whose centers form a
rectangular grid, but rather by a set of balls that are arranged slightly differently, making more efficient use of the space. Think, for example, about the
way oranges are packed into crates. More specifically, using results of (Conway and Sloane 1993) and others, Barron and Cover (1991, page 1053) show
the following: let J be a $k \times k$ positive definite symmetric matrix, and let S be
a hyperrectangle in $\mathbb{R}^k$. Then there exists a finite subset $\ddot{S}$ of S such that, for all
$\theta \in S$, for $\epsilon > 0$,
$$\min_{\ddot{\theta} \in \ddot{S}}(\theta - \ddot{\theta})^\top J(\theta - \ddot{\theta}) \leq \epsilon^2,$$
whereas at the same time $\left|\ddot{S}\right| \sim \lambda_k \epsilon^{-k} V(S)\sqrt{\det J}$, where λ_k is a constant that
satisfies $\lambda_k^{2/k}/k \sim 1/(2\pi e)$. We can apply this result to each hyperrectangle
$S \subset \Theta$, setting $J := I(\theta_S)$ and $\epsilon := (a/2)\sqrt{k/n}$, and setting $\ddot{\Theta}_{S,n}$ equal to $\ddot{S}$.
Then $V(S) = a^k n^{-k/4}$, and we find that

$$\left|\ddot{\Theta}_{S,n}\right| \sim \lambda_k \left(\frac{2\sqrt{n}}{a\sqrt{k}}\right)^k a^k n^{-k/4}\sqrt{\det I(\theta_S)} = \lambda_k 2^k k^{-k/2} n^{k/4}\sqrt{\det I(\theta_S)}.$$

For large k, we can use the asymptotics of λ_k to get

$$\left|\ddot{\Theta}_{S,n}\right| \sim \left(\frac{k}{2\pi e}\right)^{k/2} 2^k k^{-k/2} n^{k/4}\sqrt{\det I(\theta_S)} = (2\pi e)^{-k/2} 2^k n^{k/4}\sqrt{\det I(\theta_S)},$$

$$(10.19)$$

where we keep in mind that $\sim$ expresses the double limit $\lim_{k\to\infty} \lim_{n\to\infty}$, in that order. Thus, with the new, optimized discretization of the "large" rectangles S, item 1 of Lemma 10.1 still holds unchanged, whereas item 2 should now be replaced by (10.19). We now choose the discretized prior W_n just as before, as in (10.14). Reasoning just as in the proof of item 1, we find that (10.15) still holds, but now (10.16) is replaced by

$$Z \approx \sum_{S \in \mathcal{S}} 2^k (2\pi e)^{-k/2} n^{k/4} w(\theta_S) =$$

$$2^k (2\pi e)^{-k/2} \sum_{S \in \mathcal{S}} n^{k/4} (a^{-k} n^{k/4}) \left(a^k n^{-k/4} w(\theta_S)\right)) \approx$$

$$2^k (2\pi e)^{-k/2} n^{k/2} a^{-k}, \quad (10.20)$$

so that (10.17) becomes

$$- \log W_n(\hat{\hat{\theta}}) =$$

$$-\log w(\hat{\theta}(x^n)) + \log \sqrt{\det I(\hat{\theta})} + \frac{k}{2} \log \frac{n}{2\pi} + k \log 2 - \frac{k}{2} \log e - k \log a + o(1),$$

$$(10.21)$$

and (10.18) now becomes

$$\bar{L}_{\text{2-p}}(x^n) \leq -\log P_{\hat{\theta}}(x^n) - \log w(\hat{\theta}) + \log \sqrt{\det I(\hat{\theta})} + \frac{k}{2} \log \frac{n}{2\pi}$$

$$+ \frac{ka^2}{8} (\log e) - k \log a + k \log 2 - \frac{k}{2} \log e + o(1). \quad (10.22)$$

(10.22) holds for all $a > 0$. We find by differentiation that the minimum of the right hand side is achieved for $a = 2$. Plugging this into (10.22), the second line vanishes and the result follows.

10.1.3 Discussion

Comparison to the Code of Chapter 5 The code achieving the regret bound of Theorem 10.1 is similar to the "crude" code $L_{1_b}(\theta \mid k)$ that we used to encode $\log k$-parameter Markov chains in Chapter 5, Section 5.2.2. There are three important differences:

1. In Chapter 5, we carved up the parameter space in hypercubes of uniform size. Here, we use sophisticated, rotated hyperrectangles, the size and orientation of which depend on their location in the parameter space.

2. In Chapter 5, our coding was implicitly done relative to a prior that is uniform in the given parameterization, whereas in Theorem 10.1, the coding is done relative to arbitrary priors, although in practice we will mostly be interested in Jeffreys' prior, which is uniform on our sophisticated hyperrectangles, but not in the given parameterization.

> The combination of uniform hypercubes and the restriction to a uniform prior is what made the code in Chapter 5 somewhat "crude." The crudeness is not dramatic though: it is easy to adjust the proof of Theorem 10.1 to the code of Chapter 5, and this shows that that code still achieves a regret of $(k/2) \log n + O(1)$. However, the $O(1)$ term will increase as $\hat{\theta}$ moves closer to the boundary, even for large n (we omit the details of this calculation), so that, in contrast to the code of Theorem 10.1 equipped with Jeffreys' prior, the crude two-part code is not guaranteed to be within a few bits of minimax optimal.

3. Theorem 10.1 is based on a precision which is a fixed function of the sample size rather than a parameter to be optimized. As a consequence, the two-part code used in Theorem 10.1 is sample size-dependent.

Let us say a bit more about the third difference. It may seem that in this chapter, we have ignored the "precision" parameter d that appears in the codelength $L_{1_b}(\theta \mid k)$ in Section 5.2.2, representing the number of bits used to encode the side length. While it is true that we have not encoded d explicitly, this does not invalidate our coding scheme: d is a deterministic function of the sample size and a fixed number a. Since this number is available to both encoder and decoder before seeing the data, they can decide on such a sample size-dependent discretization scheme before seeing the data, so that our description method is a valid one.

Nevertheless, since our coding scheme is only optimal (in the sense that it achieves codelengths close to those achieved by the Bayesian code, for all sequences) asymptotically, for practical applications, it may be preferrable to explicitly encode a, which determines d, after all. For this we can use, for example, the universal code for the integers. Note that, if data are distributed according to some P_{θ^*}, $\theta^* \in \Theta$, then there will be some constant c such that, for large n, with high probability the number a that we will encode will not exceed c. For otherwise, the distances between discretized parameters would exceed ORDER$(n^{-1/2})$, and it is easy to show that then the expected regret compared to $\bar{P}_{\text{Bayes}}$ would be larger than (10.2). Encoding a will thus take a number of bits bounded by $\log c + 2 \log \log c$. This may sometimes, but not always, be compensated for by a shorter data codelength $-\log P_{\ddot{\theta}_n}(x^n)$. To

get the best of both worlds, we may reserve 1 extra bit to encode whether
we will use the asymptotically optimal partitions (fixed as a function of n)
or partitions with an explicitly encoded a. In that case, for large samples we
will need at most 1 extra bit compared to the two-part code described here,
but for some samples we may need considerably less.

10.2   The Conditional Two-Part Universal Code*

In this section we consider a new type of universal code which we call the
conditional two-part universal code. Having been mostly considered by Rissanen (2001) and Grünwald (2001), this code is not widely known, and the
name conditional two-part code is not standard. It should not be confused
with the "conditional NML" codes which we introduce in Chapter 11, and
which are quite different.

Like the ordinary two-part code, the conditional two-part code works by
coding the data in two stages. But in the conditional code, the number encoded in the first stage is primarily interpreted as the value of a *statistic* $T(x^n)$
(a property of the data), rather than as a *parameter* (a property of the model).
The phrase "conditional two-part code" refers to the second stage, in which
the data x^n are encoded using a code that is *conditioned* on the statistic $T(x^n)$
having the observed value. The distinction between "statistic" and "parameter" is subtle, and we return to it at the end of the section. We start with an
example.

Example 10.1 [Coding by Giving an Index] Although we did not call it that
way, in the very beginning of this book, on page 5, we already described a
conditional two-part code. We were considering sequences x^n that can be
substantiallly compressed using some Bernoulli distribution. For example,
we may take the Sequence 1.1 of Example 1.1 in the very beginning of this
book, containing four times as many 0s as 1s. From (10.2) we see that, using
the ordinary two-part code based on the Bernoulli model $\mathcal{B}^{(1)}$, we can code
this sequence using

$$\bar{L}_{\text{2-p}}(x^n) = -\log P(x^n|\hat{\theta}(x^n)) + \frac{1}{2}\log n + O(1) \text{ bits.} \tag{10.23}$$

This code works by first encoding a discretized parameter $\ddot{\theta}$ that is within
$O(1/\sqrt{n})$ of $\hat{\theta}$, and then coding the data based on $\ddot{\theta}$. The same codelength,
up to $O(1)$, can be obtained by the Bayesian code with a reasonable prior.
But on page 5 we described a more direct, and seemingly very different

method of encoding x^n. In this method we first encoded the relative frequency $\nu(x^n) = n_1/n$ of 1s in x^n. We then encoded the actual value of x^n by giving its *index* in the lexicographically ordered list of sequences of length n with frequency of 1s exactly equal to $\nu(x^n)$. We (implicitly) used a uniform, fixed-length code for both parts of the description. Let us abbreviate the resulting codelength function to $\bar{L}_{\text{cond-2-p}}$, standing for (length of) the *conditional two-part code*, a terminology to be explained further below. There are $n + 1$ distinct values that the frequency can take: $0, 1/n, \ldots, n/n$. Therefore, no matter what particular sequence we get, the description of ν takes $\log(n+1)$ bits. The number of sequences of length n with $n\nu = n_1$ 1s is equal to $\binom{n}{n_1}$. Therefore, the description of x^n given the frequency ν takes $\log \binom{n}{n_1}$ bits:

$$\bar{L}_{\text{cond-2-p}}(x^n) = \log(n + 1) + \log \binom{n}{n_1}. \tag{10.24}$$

$\bar{L}_{\text{cond-2-p}}$ seems a reasonable way to encode sequences x^n. But is it universal relative to the Bernoulli model? Lo and behold, the answer is yes: the codelengths obtained are in fact *identical* to the codelengths obtained with the Bayesian code $\bar{P}_{\text{Bayes}}$ with the uniform prior! This can be seen from (8.3), Example 8.1, which is identical to (10.24). Thus, the conditional two-part code is identical to the Bayes code with uniform prior. As explained in Section 10.1, the Bayes code with uniform prior achieves uniformly shorter codelengths than the two-part code with the same prior. Therefore, at least for the Bernoulli model, the conditional two-part code is even strictly preferable to the ordinary two-part code based on the uniform prior:

$$\text{For all } x^n \in \mathcal{X}^n \,, \bar{L}_{\text{cond-2-p}}(x^n) = \bar{L}_{\text{Bayes}}(x^n) < \bar{L}_{\text{2-p}}(x^n) \tag{10.25}$$

Incidentally, this shows that two seemingly quite different codes, based on quite different design principles, can sometimes be identical in terms of their length functions.

Let us compare the conditional two-part code to the standard two-part code of Chapter 5 and the previous section. Both codes consist of two parts. $\bar{L}_{\text{cond-2-p}}$ first encodes the ML estimator $\hat{\theta}$ (in this case: frequency of 1s) explicitly. It then encodes the sequence x^n by giving its index in the set of all sequences of length n with frequency $\hat{\theta}$, thereby making use of the fact that the ML estimator is $\hat{\theta}$. The ordinary two-part code first encodes a truncated ML estimator $\ddot{\theta}$, with $(1/2) \log n + O(1)$ precision. It then encodes x^n based on the Shannon-Fano code with lengths $- \log P(x^n|\ddot{\theta})$. Compared to $\bar{L}_{\text{cond-2-p}}$,

$\bar{L}_{\text{2-p}}$ saves about $1/2(\log n)$ bits in the first part of the description, since only the truncated rather than the precise ML estimator is encoded. But it loses bits in the second part of the description, since it reserves code words for *every* $x^n \in \mathcal{X}^n$, whereas (conditional on $\hat{\theta}(x^n)$), $\bar{L}_{\text{cond-2-p}}$ only reserves code words for a small subset of $\mathcal{X}^n$. Asymptotically, these two effects almost cancel and both codes yield approximately the same codelength; though, by (10.25), $\bar{L}_{\text{cond-2-p}}$ wins, achieving slightly smaller codelengths on all x^n.

10.2.1   Conditional Two-Part Codes for Discrete Exponential Families

We now extend the definition of $\bar{L}_{\text{cond-2-p}}$ beyond the Bernoulli model, to general exponential families $\mathcal{M}$ with discrete sample spaces $\mathcal{X}$, such as the Poisson and the geometric model. We assume that $\mathcal{M}$ is given in its mean-value parameterization Θ_μ, and that Θ_0 is an ineccsi subset of Θ_μ. The code consists of two stages. In the first stage we code the value τ of the *sufficient statistic $\hat{\mu}_n$ of the data* (see Chapter 18 for an explanation of "sufficient statistics").

$$\tau := \hat{\mu}(x^n) = n^{-1} \sum \phi(X_i).$$

Such a code must correspond to some probability mass function W_n which may depend on n.

> This is exactly what we did in Example 10.1: the Bernoulli model has sufficient statistic $\hat{\mu}(x^n) = n^{-1} \sum_{i=1}^n x_i$, i.e. ϕ is the identity function, and we encoded the statistic $\sum_{i=1}^n x_i$, which is in 1-to-1 correspondence with $\hat{\mu}$. The code we used for this was uniform, so the W_n in our example was the uniform prior on $n + 1$ outcomes.

Since for exponential families, the sufficient statistic $n^{-1} \sum \phi(x_i)$ happens to be identical to the ML estimator $\hat{\mu}(x^n)$, we effectively encode the ML estimator of the observed data. But the interpretation is that we are coding an aspect (summary) of the data, not (as in the ordinary two-part code), a potential model instance for the data. The difference is brought out by the second stage of the code: in the standard two-part code, we use the Shannon-Fano code with respect to the $\ddot{\mu}$ we encoded in the first stage, thereby typically allowing finite codelengths $-\log P_{\ddot{\mu}}(x^n)$ for *all* $x^n \in \mathcal{X}^n$. In the conditional two-part code, after encoding τ, we use a code that only allows us to encode those x^n with $\hat{\mu}(x^n) = \tau$. Such a code corresponds to a *conditional* distribution $Q(\cdot \mid \hat{\mu}(x^n) = \tau)$ on $\mathcal{X}^n$, which assigns probability 0 to $\{x^n : \hat{\mu}(x^n) \neq \tau\}$.

> Once again, this is exactly what we did in the Bernoulli example, where we set

the code $Q(\cdot \mid \hat{\mu}(x^n) = \tau)$ equal to the uniform code on all sequences x^n with $\hat{\mu}(x^n) = \tau$.

All in all, for data with $\hat{\mu}(x^n) = \tau$, we get the codelength

$$\bar{L}_{\text{cond-2-p}}(x^n) = -\log W_n(\tau) - \log Q(x^n \mid \hat{\mu}(x^n) = \tau).$$

We now investigate how we should choose W_n and Q for general discrete exponential families.

Choosing W_n and Q   Our goal is to make $\bar{L}_{\text{cond-2-p}}$ universal relative to $\mathcal{M}$, achieving comparable performance to a Bayesian code with prior W on the mean-value parameter space. In that case a natural choice is to use a discretized version of W to encode $\tau = \hat{\mu}(x^n)$. This leads to a discretized prior W_n on the set of values that $\hat{\mu}(x^n)$ can take — which depends on n.

> Again, this is exactly what we did in the Bernoulli example, where the uniform prior on $\Theta_\mu = [0, 1]$ translated into a uniform prior on
>
> $$\{\mu \in \Theta_\mu : \mu = \hat{\mu}(x^n) \text{ for some } x^n \in \mathcal{X}^n\}.$$
>
> But other choices than uniform are possible as well –an example is the "canonical prior" below.

It remains to choose the distribution Q. We will make the obvious choice, setting

$$Q(x^n \mid \hat{\mu}(x^n) = \tau) = P_\tau(x^n \mid \hat{\mu}(x^n) = \tau), \tag{10.26}$$

where P_τ is the member of $\mathcal{M}$ with parameter τ equal to the ML estimator $\hat{\mu}(x^n)$. But by momentarily expressing the exponential family in its canonical parameterization,

$$P_\tau(x^n) = Z(\beta_\tau)^{-n} \exp(\beta_\tau^\top \sum \phi(x_i)) r(x^n),$$

we see that (10.26) in fact simplifies and becomes

$$Q(x^n \mid \hat{\mu}(x^n) = \tau) = \frac{r(x^n)}{\sum_{x^n : \hat{\mu}(x^n) = \tau} r(x^n)},$$

where r is the carrier mass function of the exponential family $\mathcal{M}$. In the Bernoulli case, this distribution is uniform, so that, for x^n with $\hat{\mu}(x^n) = \mu$,

$$-\ln Q(x^n \mid \hat{\mu}(x^n) = \tau) = \ln |\{x^n : \hat{\mu}(x^n) = \tau\}| = \ln \binom{n}{n_1},$$

which coincides with the codelengths used in Example 10.1. If the carrier mass is not uniform, then Q will not be a uniform distribution. For example, if $\mathcal{M}$ is Poisson, we get

$$Q(x^n \mid \hat{\mu}(x^n) = \tau) = \frac{\prod \frac{1}{x_i!}}{\sum_{x^n : \hat{\mu}(x^n) = \tau} \prod \frac{1}{x_i!}},$$

In the Bernoulli example, the conditional two-part codes with uniform prior were *exactly* equal to the Bayesian codelengths based on the same prior. One can show that a similar result holds for the Poisson and geometric models (proof omitted). This is not true for general exponential families, but the central limit theorem (used as in (Grünwald 2001)) strongly suggests that, if the same prior is used for the Bayesian and for the conditional two-part codes, then the codelengths $\bar{L}_{\text{Bayes}}$ and $\bar{L}_{\text{cond-2-p}}$ will be within $o(1)$ for large n. In any case, the results of Grünwald (2001) imply that, if W_n is the discretized version of a prior distribution W which is ineccsi relative to Θ_0, then $\bar{L}_{\text{cond-2-p}}$ is a $(k/2) \log n + O(1)$ universal code.

The Canonical Prior   Following (Rissanen 2001), we define the *canonical prior* $\hat{W}_n$, relative to Θ_0, by

$$\hat{W}_n(\tau) = \frac{\sum_{x^n \in \mathcal{X}^n : \hat{\mu}(x^n) = \tau} P_{\hat{\mu}(x^n)}(x^n)}{\sum_{x^n \in \mathcal{X}^n} P_{\hat{\mu}(x^n)}(x^n)}. \tag{10.27}$$

We recognize the denominator as the denominator in the definition of the NML distribution $\bar{P}_{\text{nml}}$, which we already know to be well defined if Θ_0 is ineccsi. Therefore, $\hat{W}_n$ is a well defined "prior" distribution on Θ_0 (we put the word prior between quotation marks because it depends on n, and thus cannot really be interpreted as a prior in the Bayesian sense).

Using $\bar{L}_{\text{cond-2-p}}$ with the canonical prior, we get

$$\bar{L}_{\text{cond-2-p}}(x^n) =$$
$$- \log \frac{\sum_{x^n \in \mathcal{X}^n : \hat{\mu}(x^n) = \tau} P_{\hat{\mu}(x^n)}(x^n)}{\sum_{x^n \in \mathcal{X}^n} P_{\hat{\mu}(x^n)}(x^n)} - \log Q(x^n \mid \hat{\mu}(x^n) = \tau) = \bar{L}_{\text{nml}}(x^n),$$
$$\tag{10.28}$$

where the second equation follows from (10.26) and the definition of conditional probability. This means that:

The Canonical Prior
With the canonical prior $\hat{W}_n$, the codelength function $\bar{L}_{\text{cond-2-p}}$ of the two-part conditional code becomes identical to the codelength function $\bar{L}_{\text{nml}}$ of the minimax optimal NML code.

This raises the question whether the canonical prior can be approximated by another prior that can be more easily computed than by (10.27). The reader who has read through this chapter may not be surprised to hear that the answer is *yes*: for large n, $\hat{W}_n(\tau)$ becomes "essentially" identical to Jeffreys' prior defined on Θ_0 (Rissanen 2001).

To formalize this statement, we have to realize that $\hat{W}_n$ is discrete (at least if $\mathcal{X}$ is discrete), whereas Θ_0 is a continuous parameter space. In technical terms, we have a variation of "uniform weak convergence." To be precise, fix an arbitrary $c > 0$ and let $R_\mu \subset \Theta_0$ be a hyperrectangle centered at μ, with side length $c/\sqrt{n}$. Then it holds that

$$\max_{R_\mu : \mu \in \Theta_0} \left| \hat{W}_n(R_\mu) - \int_{\mu' \in R_\mu} w_{\text{Jeffreys}}(\mu') d\mu' \right| \to 0.$$

Proving this result involves a *uniform central limit theorem* (Rissanen 1996; 2001), and is beyond the scope of this book.

Extension to General Exponential Families   It is straightforward to extend the conditional two-part code to general exponential families, including the case of continuous-valued sufficient statistics; see (Rissanen 2001). Rissanen uses prior densities rather than probability mass functions in the continuous case. While these cannot be directly interpreted as corresponding to codes, an explicit two-part coding scheme can still be arrived at by discretizing $\hat{\mu}(x^n)$, but now we should select a precision of $\text{ORDER}(1/n)$ rather than the $\text{ORDER}(1/\sqrt{n})$ of the ordinary two-part code; we shall not go into this any further here.

Open Problem No. 4 If the model $\mathcal{M}$ is *not* an exponential family, then it is not clear exactly what statistic of the data we should encode in the first stage (the ML estimator may not even be unique, for example). Indeed, it is not clear to me whether the conditional code can be defined in a satisfactory way at all for general, nonexponential $\mathcal{M}$, or even for CUP or nonparametric model classes (Chapter 13). Here lies a potential topic for future research.

Advantage and Disadvantage of Conditional Two-Part Code   The main advantage over the ordinary two-part code is that the conditional code is *complete*: the ordinary two-part code reserves many code words to encode the same sequence x^n: basically, one code word for x^n is used for each parameter $\ddot{\mu} \in \ddot{\Theta}_\mu$ with $L_n(\ddot{\mu}) - \log P_{\ddot{\mu}}(x^n) < \infty$. Thus, it wastes code words and is therefore incomplete in the sense of Section 3.1.3, Chapter 3. In contrast, the conditional two-part code reserves only one code word for each sequence, and as we have just seen, by choosing the prior cleverly, it can even be made to coincide with the minimax optimal code.

The conditional code also has disadvantages. First and foremost, at least for the time being, it is only well defined if the model $\mathcal{M}$ is an exponential family. The second disadvantage is not relevant if we are only interested in data compression and not in learning: it only comes into play when we use a universal code in the context of MDL hypothesis selection and/or parameter estimation (Chapter 15). The conditional two-part code encodes a statistic $\hat{\mu}$ of the data, which should not be interpreted as an estimate of the parameter μ. Yet, $\hat{\mu}$ happens to coincide with the ML estimator for μ, and thus suggests that one select the ML parameters as the optimal parameters within the model. This is in general not the right thing to do: as we explain in Chapter 15, one should definitely prefer the ordinary two-part code estimates instead.

Fifth Example of a Universal Model: Conditional Two-Part Code
The conditional two-part code encodes data x^n by first encoding the value τ of the sufficient statistic $n^{-1} \sum_{i=1}^n \phi(x^n)$ of x^n, and then encoding the data using a code for all x^n satisfying $n^{-1} \sum_{i=1}^n \phi(x^n) = \tau$. In the case of the Bernoulli model with a uniform code for τ, $\bar{L}_{\text{cond-2-p}}$ coincides exactly with the Bayesian model with uniform prior.

10.2.2   Distinguishability and the Phase Transition*

Let Θ represent a k-dimensional ineccsi exponential family. In Section 10.1, we discussed the standard two-part code, in the first stage of which we always encode a $\ddot{\theta}$ coming from some set $\ddot{\Theta}_n$ of "distinguishable" distributions. This code is incomplete, and, for small k, cannot achieve the minimax regret $\text{COMP}^{(n)}(\Theta)$. Then, in Section 10.2.1, we discussed the conditional two-part code, which can achieve the minimax regret, but in the first stage of which we encode a θ from the set of ML estimates, which contains distributions that are "indistinguishably" close from one another.

In this section, we show that a variation of the conditional two-part code, in which only "distinguishable" distributions are encoded in the first stage, can achieve maximum regret arbitrarily close to the minimax $\text{COMP}^{(n)}(\Theta)$ after all, leading to interesting insights about the fundamental notion of "distinguishability."

Consider the standard two-part code MDL estimator $\ddot{\theta}_n(x^n) \in \ddot{\Theta}_n$ at sample size n, defined relative to the "distinguishability discretization" $\ddot{\Theta}_n$ with parameter a, as in Lemma 10.1. This standard two-part code is incomplete. Therefore, it cannot be minimax optimal, and must lead to codelengths different from those achieved by $\bar{L}_{\text{nml}}$.

The incompleteness arises because, in the second stage of the coding, we encode x^n using a Shannon-Fano code with lengths $L_\theta(x^n) := -\log P_\theta(x^n)$ for some $\theta \in \ddot{\Theta}_n$. While this code reserves code words for each $x^n \in \mathcal{X}^n$, we will only use it for those z^n for which $\ddot{\theta}(z^n) = \theta$, i.e. z^n with the same two-part MDL estimator as the one for the observed data $\theta = \ddot{\theta}(x^n)$. As noted by Rissanen (1996), we can remedy the incompleteness by changing the code L_θ: we now make it the Shannon-Fano code for the conditional distribution $P_\theta(\cdot \mid \ddot{\theta}(x^n) = \theta)$. Let us call the resulting code L'_θ. For x^n with $\ddot{\theta}(x^n) = \theta$, we have

$$L'_\theta(x^n) = -\log P_\theta(x^n \mid \ddot{\theta}(x^n) = \theta) = -\log P_\theta(x^n) + \log \sum_{x^n : \ddot{\theta}(x^n) = \theta} P_\theta(x^n).$$

Let, for each n, W_n be some prior on $\ddot{\Theta}_n$. We define the *modified two-part code* relative to W_n as follows. First, as before, we let

$$\ddot{\theta}(x^n) := \arg\min_{\theta \in \ddot{\Theta}_n} \{L_\theta(x^n) - \log W_n(\theta)\},$$

but now we code x^n by first encoding $\theta = \ddot{\theta}(x^n)$ and then coding x^n based on the conditional code $L'_\theta(x^n)$. The resulting codelength is

$$\bar{L}'_{2\text{-p}}(x^n) = -\log W_n(\theta) - \log P_\theta(x^n) + \log \sum_{x^n : \ddot{\theta}(x^n) = \theta} P_\theta(x^n). \tag{10.29}$$

We now define, for all $\theta \in \ddot{\Theta}_n$, the prior

$$W_n(\theta) = \frac{\sum_{x^n \in \mathcal{X}^n : \ddot{\theta}(x^n) = \theta} P_\theta(x^n)}{\sum_{x^n \in \mathcal{X}^n} P_{\ddot{\theta}(x^n)}(x^n)}.$$

This is a discretized version of the canonical prior $\hat{W}_n$ we introduced in the previous section. Now let Θ_0 be an ineccsi subset of Θ. Plugging this prior into (10.29) and using Lemma 10.1 and the fact that Θ_0 is ineccsi, we find that for all Θ_0-sequences $x_1, x_2, \ldots$, we have

$$\text{REG}(\bar{L}'_{2\text{-p}}, \Theta, x^n) \leq (\log e)\frac{a^2}{8} + \log \sum_{x^n \in \mathcal{X}^n} P_{\ddot{\theta}(x^n)}(x^n) + o(1) \leq$$

$$(\log e)\frac{a^2}{8} + \log \sum_{x^n \in \mathcal{X}^n} P_{\hat{\theta}(x^n)}(x^n) + o(1) = (\log e)\frac{a^2}{8} + \text{COMP}^{(n)}(\Theta) + o(1),$$

$$(10.30)$$

where the convergence is uniform[4] in Θ_0.

Thus, there exists a modified two-part code that performs almost as well as the minimax optimal NML universal code, restricted to sequences with $\hat{\theta}(x^n) \in \Theta_0$. Since this works for every ineccsi Θ_0, by choosing a small enough, our modified two-part code can be made to resemble the minimax optimal $\bar{P}_{\text{nml}}$ as much as we like, at least for sequences whose ML estimator does not come arbitrarily close to the boundary of Θ.

The Phase Transition   The importance of this result is that, to achieve the minimax regret with a conditional two-part code, one really only needs to encode *distinguishable* distributions (Chapter 7, Section 7.3.4), rather than all possible values for the ML distributions. We can cover the parameter space with points at KL distance ϵ/n, and achieve a regret that, for large n, is almost equal to the minimax regret $\text{COMP}^{(n)}(\Theta)$. If we let $\epsilon \to 0$, then the regret converges to $\text{COMP}^{(n)}(\Theta)$. But, in contrast to our first version of the conditional two-part code, for each $\epsilon > 0$, the points we choose lie at Mahalanobis, and therefore Euclidean, distance $\text{ORDER}(1/\sqrt{n})$ from each other (Chapter 7, Section 7.3.4). Recall that, at least for discrete exponential families such as the Bernoulli and Poisson models, in the first version of the conditional two-part code the distance was $\text{ORDER}(1/n)$. Apparently, nothing is gained by letting the distances between points be of order $O(n^{-\alpha})$ for any $\alpha > 1/2$. There is a phase transition at $\alpha = 1/2$, in the sense that $\alpha = 1/2$ is almost, but just not, enough to achieve the minimax regret, while for any $\alpha > 1/2$ the minimax regret will asymptotically be achieved.

Summarizing, we have obtained a two-part code interpretation of the parametric complexity $\text{COMP}^{(n)}(\Theta_0)$: asymptotically, it is the minimax regret one

4. See the footnote on page 232.

achieves by using a conditional two-part code that only encodes *distinguishable* distributions at level δ, for some δ that tends to 0 arbitrarily slowly with n.

Minimax Regret, Distinguishability, and Conditional Two-Part Codes
The minimax regret $\mathrm{COMP}^{(n)}(\Theta)$ can essentially be achieved by a conditional two-part code, in the first stage of which only a set of *distinguishable* distributions is encoded.

10.3 Summary and Outlook

We introduced two-part codes for exponential families, and showed that we can achieve asymptotically nearly optimal minimax regret with such codes. The codes implicitly make use of a "two-part MDL parameter estimator" $\hat{\hat{\theta}}$. The qualities of such an estimator will be considered in Chapter 15, Section 15.4.

This chapter ends our overview of universal codes for parametric models. We mostly analyzed the behavior of exponential families when the parameters were restricted to ineccsi subsets, and we showed that in that case, asymptotically, they all behaved very similarly. For the NML, Bayesian and two-part code, we gave an interpretation of the regret in terms of the *amount of distinguishable distributions* contained in the model indexed by Θ_0.

In the remainder of Part II of this book, the parameter space is not required to be ineccsi anymore. In that case, the NML distribution is often undefined, and we have to find a good replacement. That is the subject of the next chapter.

11 NML With Infinite Complexity

We already noted that for some of the most commonly used models, the parametric complexity $\mathrm{COMP}^{(n)}(\Theta)$ is infinite and the corresponding NML distribution $\bar{P}_{\mathrm{nml}}$ is undefined. Since MDL model selection, at least in its simplest form, is based on the NML codelength and uses $\mathrm{COMP}^{(n)}(\Theta)$ as a complexity measure, this is a serious problem. We refer to this issue as the *infinity problem*, and in this chapter, we shall try to solve it. We start with an overview of the problem, as well as examples of models with undefined NML distribution. Then, in Sections 11.2, 11.3, and 11.4, we discuss alternative solutions to this problem: metauniversal codes, luckiness codes, and conditional universal codes. All three types of codes can also be quite useful in cases where $\mathrm{COMP}^{(n)}(\Theta)$ is finite but large.

Fast Track For a first introduction to MDL inference, this chapter can be skipped. However, if one has all the basic knowledge and wants to apply MDL in practice, the infinity problem occurs all the time and the material of this chapter becomes quite important. In that case, I would suggest that one read at least the beginning of each section as well as the boxes.

11.1 Introduction

The Infinity Problem One may wonder whether the "infinity problem" simply means that the attempt to achieve minimax codelength regret is misguided. It is true that in some situations, the minimax approach is not very sensible. For example, if a model has many degrees of freedom and the sample size is small, then the minimax regret, if it is finite at all, will be quite large compared to the sample size. Then, at least if the goal is data compression, there is not much sense in trying to achieve the minimax regret, since it will be too large to be useful. In such cases, also if the goal is not data compression but model selection, it does not make a lot of sense to use MDL model selection based on the NML distributions; we return to this issue in Chapter 14.

Yet the models we deal with in this chapter can be intuitively quite "simple" 1-parameter models such as the Poisson family, and the sample sizes can be arbitrarily large. Still, the parametric complexity is infinite. This is strange: if we study the complexity $\text{COMP}(\Theta_K)$ where $\Theta_K = [0, K]$ is the restriction of the Poisson model to parameters within the range $[0, K]$, we find that it increases only logarithmically with K. A similar result holds for many other exponential families: if we blow up the parameter space, the complexity increases very slowly. This suggests that the complexity is infinite not because of inherent richness of the model, but because of singularities in the model geometry, taking place at extreme parameter values. This is confirmed by the analyses of Section 11.3 and Section 11.4, which imply that, by slightly changing the complexity measure, such models usually become simple after all. *Thus, the NML distribution is undefined even for some models which are intuitively very simple and for which we would really expect that there exist universal codes which achieve small regret uniformly for all data sequences.* Therefore, from a data compression point of view, and as we shall see later, also from a model selection point of view, it is really desirable to study the infinity problem in more detail, and to see whether we can somehow avoid it. It turns out that in many cases, we can.

Solutions   This chapter presents solutions to the infinity problem. By a solution we mean a method for designing universal codes for models Θ such that $\text{COMP}(\Theta) = \infty$ that, in some sense, are close to achieving minimax optimal regret. Part of the problem is, of course, how to define "in some sense" and "close." The solutions that have been proposed fall into three main groups: *metauniversal coding*, *luckiness universal coding*, and *conditional universal coding* – the terminology is ours. We present these three methods in order of their historical development. The only serious approach to the infinity problem that we know of and that does not clearly fall into any of the three groups is the competitive complexity ratio approach of Foster and Stine (2001). We will say a little bit more about it at the end of this chapter.

We start this chapter by giving some examples of models with infinite parametric complexity and, relatedly, undefined Jeffreys' prior. We then present the three solutions:

Metauniversal codes (Section 11.2). In this approach one first restricts the parameter space to an ineccsi set Θ_0. We have seen in Chapter 7 that this guarantees that $\mathrm{COMP}(\Theta_0)$ is finite, so that the NML code with lengths $-\ln \bar{P}_{\mathrm{nml}}(\cdot \mid \Theta_0)$ exists. One then treats Θ_0, or rather its boundaries, as a hyperparameter, and one designs a new universal code which tries to minimize regret relative to $-\ln \bar{P}_{\mathrm{nml}}(\cdot \mid \hat{\Theta}_0)$. Here $\hat{\Theta}_0$ is a "meta"-maximum likelihood estimate, which maximizes $\bar{P}_{\mathrm{nml}}(\cdot \mid \hat{\Theta}_0)$. This can be done in a variety of ways: meta-two-part coding, meta-Bayesian coding, or *re*normalized maximum likelihood coding.

Universal codes based on luckiness functions (Section 11.3). The ordinary NML distribution, whenever defined, achieves the same regret on all sequences. The regret achieved by metauniversal codes depends on the location of the ML estimator $\hat{\theta}(x^n)$ in the parameter space. In some cases, such a nonuniform regret is unavoidable, or, as we discussed at the beginning of this section, in the case of large models, even desirable. Yet, even if one accepts a nonuniform regret, there remains the problem that it is often hard to determine exactly how the regret varies as a function of $\hat{\theta}$. With luckiness coding we turn things on their head and start out with specifying a "luckiness function" that maps $\hat{\theta}$ to the corresponding regret. We first choose a function that we desire or can live with, and then – if possible – we design a universal code for which the regret achieves the function we specified.

Conditional universal codes (Section 11.4). These codes seek to avoid the dependency of the regret on the value of $\hat{\theta}$ altogether. This is often possible, at least to some extent: we describe the caveats in detail in Section 11.4. Interestingly, although at first their design principle appears to be quite different, conditional universal codes can be reinterpreted as luckiness codes with luckiness functions constructed in terms of the first few data points.

As discussed at the end of Section 11.2 and the beginning of Section 11.3, besides the complicated dependency of the regret on $\hat{\theta}$, there are a variety of other problems with metauniversal codes. These are solved to some extent by luckiness and conditional universal codes. Luckiness and conditional codes are recent concepts, and in this chapter I attempt to give the first unifying treatment. As a result, I develop several new concepts, and much of the material in Section 11.3 and Section 11.4 is as yet unpublished and of a tentative nature.

Throughout this chapter, codelengths are expressed in nats (Chapter 3, page 110) rather than bits. This is done mainly as a preparation for the next chapter, where it will be quite convenient to express luckiness and conditional NML codelengths in natural units.

11.1.1   Examples of Undefined NML Distribution

In this section we give a few simple, 1-parameter examples: the normal location family, which will serve as a running example throughout this chapter, and the Poisson and geometric families.

Example 11.1 [The Normal Location Family] Throughout this chapter $\mathcal{M}_{\text{loc}} = \{f_\mu \mid \mu \in \Theta\}$, $\Theta = \mathbb{R}$ denotes the family of normal distributions with fixed variance σ^2 and varying mean μ, identified by their densities $f_\mu(x) = (\sqrt{2\pi}\sigma)^{-1} e^{-\frac{(x-\mu)^2}{2\sigma^2}}$, and extended to sequences $x_1, \ldots, x_n$ by taking product densities. Recall that the ML estimator $\hat{\mu}(x^n)$ is equal to the sample mean: $\hat{\mu}(x^n) = n^{-1} \sum_{i=1}^{n} x_i$. Following Barron, Rissanen, and Yu (1998) and Foster and Stine (2001), we calculate $\text{COMP}^{(n)}(\Theta)$ by decomposing it into terms of the value of the sufficient statistics, (7.24) on page 227. This gives

$$\text{COMP}^{(n)}(\Theta) = \ln \int_{-\infty}^{\infty} f_\mu^\circ(\mu) d\mu,$$

where f_μ° is the density of the distribution of the ML estimator, $P_\mu(\hat{\mu}(X^n) = \cdot)$. Since $\hat{\mu}(X^n)$ is the average of n i.i.d. normal random variables with mean μ and variance σ^2, $\hat{\mu}(X^n)$ is itself normally distributed with mean μ and variance σ^2/n (Feller 1968a). Thus its density is given by

$$f_\mu^\circ(\hat{\mu}) = \frac{1}{\sqrt{2\pi(\sigma^2/n)}} e^{-\frac{(\hat{\mu}-\mu)^2}{2(\sigma^2/n)}} \; ; \; f_\mu^\circ(\mu) = \frac{1}{\sqrt{2\pi(\sigma^2/n)}}. \tag{11.1}$$

We then find

$$\int_a^b f_\mu^\circ(\mu) d\mu = \frac{b-a}{\sqrt{2\pi}\sigma} \cdot \sqrt{n}, \tag{11.2}$$

so that $\text{COMP}^{(n)}(\Theta) = \int_{-\infty}^{\infty} f_\mu(\mu) d\mu = \infty$.

Example 11.2 [Poisson and Geometric Families] . Let $\mathcal{M}$ be the Poisson model given in its mean-value parameterization Θ, as defined in Example 18.1. Since the ML estimator of the Poisson model is always rational-valued, we must have $\text{COMP}^{(n)}(\Theta) = \text{COMP}^{(n)}(\Theta \cap \mathbb{Q})$, where $\Theta \cap \mathbb{Q}$ represents $\mathcal{M}_{\mathbb{Q}}$, the restriction of the Poisson model to distributions with rational-valued parameters, as in Example 6.11, page 189. In that example, it was shown that $\text{COMP}^{(n)}(\Theta \cap \mathbb{Q}) = \infty$.

For the geometric model, given in its mean-value parameterization $\Theta = (0, \infty)$, (18.7) on page 605, we have

$$\text{COMP}^{(1)}(\Theta) = \ln \sum_{x=0}^{\infty} \frac{x^x}{(x+1)^{(x+1)}} = \sum \frac{1}{x}\left(1 - \frac{1}{x+1}\right)^{x+1} = \infty,$$

and by (6.25), it follows that $\text{COMP}^{(n)}(\Theta) = \infty$ for all n.

These examples all concerned 1-parameter families. An important example of a multidimensional model with infinite complexity is the linear regression model, Chapter 12.

11.1.2 Examples of Undefined Jeffreys' Prior

We have just seen that for many exponential families $\mathcal{M} = \{P_\theta \mid \theta \in \Theta\}$, $\text{COMP}^{(n)}(\Theta)$ is infinite. For such models, the NML distribution does not exist and there exists no distribution achieving the minimax regret. As an alternative that is "close" to achieving the minimax regret for ineccsi sequences, we may consider the code based on the Bayesian universal model $\bar{P}_{\text{Bayes}}$ equipped with Jeffreys' prior. However, if $\text{COMP}^{(n)}(\Theta) = \infty$, then usually $\int_\Theta \sqrt{\det I(\theta)}d\theta = \infty$ as well, so that Jeffreys' prior is ill-defined and this approach cannot be used either. Below we illustrate this for the three models that we considered in the previous section.

> **Open Problem No. 5** It may be the case that in general, at least for exponential families, $\text{COMP}^{(n)}(\Theta) = \infty$ for all n if and only if $\int_\Theta \sqrt{\det I(\theta)}d\theta = \infty$ as well. We do not know of any proof of this statement, however, and we are not 100% sure that it is true. The difficulty is as follows: if $\text{COMP}^{(n)}(\Theta)$ is finite and grows at rate $g(n) = (k/2)\ln n + O(1)$, then it is easy to show that $\int_\Theta \sqrt{\det I(\theta)}d\theta$ must be finite. But it is conceivable that for some $\mathcal{M}$ and Θ, $\text{COMP}^{(n)}(\Theta)$, while finite, grows at a rate *faster* than $g(n)$, and then $\int_\Theta \sqrt{\det I(\theta)}d\theta$ may be infinite. We have neither been able to disprove this statement nor to give an example of an $\mathcal{M}$ for which it holds.

Example 11.3 [Jeffreys' prior for All the Normal Families] Let $\mathcal{M}$, parameterized by $\Theta = \{(\mu, \sigma^2) \mid \mu \in \mathbb{R}, \sigma^2 \geq 0\}$, be the normal family of distributions. For $\sigma_0 > 0$, let $\Theta_{\sigma_0} = \{(\mu, \sigma_0^2) \mid \mu \in \mathbb{R}\}$ represent the 1-parameter normal location family $\mathcal{M}_{\text{loc}}$ with fixed variance σ_0^2. Let, for $\mu_0 \in \mathbb{R}$, $\Theta_{\mu_0} =$

$\{(\mu_0, \sigma^2) \mid \sigma^2 \geq 0\}$ represent the 1-parameter model of normal distributions with fixed mean μ_0. Let $I(\mu, \sigma^2)$ denote the Fisher information with respect to Θ, $I_{\sigma_0^2}(\mu)$ the Fisher information with respect to $\Theta_{\sigma_0^2}$, and $I_{\mu_0}(\sigma^2)$ the Fisher information with respect to Θ_{μ_0}. A simple calculation – a very special case of the general calculations of Section 12.3, Chapter 12 – gives the following useful facts:

Fisher Information/Jeffreys' Prior for the Normal Family
We have:

$$\det I(\mu, \sigma^2) = \frac{1}{2\sigma^4} \;\; ; \;\; \det I_{\sigma_0^2}(\mu) = \frac{1}{\sigma^2} \;\; ; \;\; \det I_{\mu_0}(\sigma^2) = \frac{1}{2\sigma^2}. \qquad (11.3)$$

Note in particular that $I_{\sigma_0^2}(\mu)$ is a constant function of μ. In all three models, Jeffreys' prior is undefined: $\sqrt{\det I(\cdot)}$ is proportional to, respectively, $1/\sigma^2$, $1/\sigma$ (or any other constant), and $1/\sigma$.

Example 11.4 [Jeffreys' Prior for the Poisson and Geometric Family] Consider the Poisson family, given in its standard parameterization $\Theta = (0, \infty)$, as in Example 11.2. Fix some $K > 0$ and let $\Theta_K = (0, K]$ represent the submodel of Poisson distributions with mean $\mu \leq K$. A straightforward calculation shows that, for $\mu \in \Theta$, $I(\mu) = \mu^{-1}$ so that (Lanterman 2005; De Rooij and Grünwald 2006)

$$\ln \int_0^K \sqrt{I(\mu)} d\mu = \ln 2\sqrt{K}. \qquad (11.4)$$

Thus, relative to the restricted model Θ_K, both the Bayesian universal model with Jeffreys' prior and the NML model are defined, and the two are asymptotically indistinguishable by Theorems 7.1 and 8.1. But if $K \to \infty$, the integral in (11.4) diverges. Then Jeffreys' prior becomes undefined, and, as we have seen in Example 11.2, also the NML model is undefined.

Similarly, for the geometric family, given, as in Example 11.2, in its mean-value parameterization $\Theta = (0, \infty)$, we get

$$\ln \int_0^K \sqrt{I(\mu)} d\mu = \ln 2 \ln(\sqrt{K} + \sqrt{K+1}),$$

which again tends to infinity with increasing K.

In both examples the reason for divergence may seem to be the fact that the domain of integration tends to infinity with increasing K. But this is not the right interpretation: for example, if we represent the geometric model in its standard parameterization (18.4), page 603, then the parameter set is given by $\Theta = (0, 1)$. Because of the parameterization independence of the quantity $\int_{\Theta} \sqrt{\det I(\theta)} d\theta$, the integral still diverges in that case, even though now the integral is taken over a bounded domain.

This ends our list of examples of "simple" models $\mathcal{M}$ for which the parametric complexity is infinite and Jeffreys' prior is undefined. The remainder of this chapter is devoted to finding "good" universal codes relative to such $\mathcal{M}$ anyway. We start with the most straightforward approach: metauniversal coding.

11.2   Metauniversal Codes

Consider an exponential family $\mathcal{M} = \{P_\theta \mid \theta \in \Theta\}$ and an $n > 0$ such that $\mathrm{COMP}^{(n)}(\Theta) = \infty$. In this section we describe a family of methods for defining good universal codes relative to such $\mathcal{M}$. Here "good" means that they should achieve regret that is somehow close to minimax optimal. Part of the problem here is to define what "close" means. Since the minimax optimal regret is infinite, there is no obvious meaning to the term. In the metauniversal coding approach that we describe below, the problem is solved by designing intuitively reasonable universal codes, without worrying too much about the definition of "close." In the next two sections, we consider approaches which are more precise on this issue.

Suppose first that it is known, for whatever reason, that the sequence x^n that will be observed is such that $\hat{\theta}(x^n) \in \Theta_0$, where Θ_0 is some closed ineccsi subset of Θ. For example, if Θ represents the mean-value parameterization, then this means that the average of the sufficient statistic of the data must fall in the set Θ_0. Below we shall see that, conditioned on this information, the minimax regret is finite after all, and a minimax optimal universal model exists. This is the cornerstone of the metauniversal coding approach. In its simplest form, *meta-two-part coding*, it amounts to encoding x^n in two stages: one first encodes some set Θ_0 that contains $\hat{\theta}(x^n)$. It turns out that this can often be done using only very few bits. One then encodes x^n using the minimax optimal model given that $\hat{\theta}(x^n) \in \Theta_0$.

Below we explain this approach in detail. We start with the *constrained parametric complexity*, which is the minimax optimal regret given that $\hat{\theta}(x^n) \in$

Θ_0. It was introduced by Foster and Stine (2001) under the name "conditional parametric complexity." To avoid confusion with the – different – conditional NML approach that we introduce in Section 11.4, we use a different name.

11.2.1   Constrained Parametric Complexity

As above, suppose that it is known that the sequence x^n that will be observed is such that $\hat{\theta}(x^n) \in \Theta_0$, where Θ_0 is some closed ineccsi subset of Θ. Given this information, the minimax regret is given by

$$\min_{\bar{P}} \quad \max_{x^n : \hat{\theta}(x^n) \in \Theta_0} \{-\ln \bar{P}(x^n) + \ln P_{\hat{\theta}(x^n)}(x^n)\}, \tag{11.5}$$

where the minimum ranges over all distributions on $\mathcal{X}^n$. The fact that Θ_0 is ineccsi implies that this quantity is finite; this is proved formally in Theorem 11.1 below. Because (11.5) is finite, we can reason exactly as in the box on page 182, Chapter 6, Section 6.2.1, to find that (11.5) is achieved by the following distribution, which we shall denote by $\bar{P}_{\text{nml}}^{(n)}(\cdot \mid \hat{\theta} \in \Theta_0)$:

$$\bar{P}_{\text{nml}}^{(n)}(x^n \mid \hat{\theta} \in \Theta_0) = \begin{cases} \dfrac{P_{\hat{\theta}(x^n)}(x^n)}{\sum_{y^n : \hat{\theta}(y^n) \in \Theta_0} P_{\hat{\theta}(y^n)}(y^n)} & \text{if } \hat{\theta}(x^n) \in \Theta_0 \\ 0 & \text{otherwise.} \end{cases} \tag{11.6}$$

If $\text{COMP}^{(n)}(\Theta)$ is finite, then $\bar{P}_{\text{nml}}(\cdot \mid \hat{\theta} \in \Theta_0)$ is just the ordinary NML distribution, conditioned on $\hat{\theta}(x^n) \in \Theta_0$. This explains our notation. Yet, if $\text{COMP}^{(n)}(\Theta) = \infty$, then $\bar{P}_{\text{nml}}(\cdot \mid \hat{\theta} \in \Theta_0)$ is still well defined even though $\bar{P}_{\text{nml}}$ itself is not.

We call the logarithm of the denominator the *constrained complexity* of Θ_0, and write it as

$$\text{CCOMP}^{(n)}(\Theta_0) := \ln \sum_{x^n : \hat{\theta}(x^n) \in \Theta_0} P_{\hat{\theta}(x^n)}(x^n). \tag{11.7}$$

Example 11.5 [Example 11.1, cont.] Let $[a, b]$ represent the normal location family with $a \le \mu \le b$. From (11.2), we see that

$$\exp(\text{CCOMP}^{(n)}([a, b])) = \int_a^b f_\mu^\circ(\mu) d\mu = \frac{b-a}{\sqrt{2\pi}\sigma} \cdot \sqrt{n} \tag{11.8}$$

$$\exp(\text{COMP}^{(n)}([a, b])) = \int_{-\infty}^a f_a^\circ(\mu) d\mu + \int_b^\infty f_b^\circ(\mu) d\mu + \int_a^b f_\mu^\circ(\mu) d\mu =$$

$$= \frac{b-a}{\sqrt{2\pi}\sigma} \cdot \sqrt{n} + 1. \tag{11.9}$$

Thus, for the normal family, the constrained complexity is smaller than the unconstrained complexity. This fact holds in general: for arbitrary families,

$$\text{CCOMP}^{(n)}(\Theta_0) \leq \text{COMP}^{(n)}(\Theta_0),$$

where in most cases the inequality is strict. The reason is that $\text{COMP}^{(n)}(\Theta_0)$ is the logarithm of a sum over all sequences $x^n \in \mathcal{X}^n$, where only the ML estimator for x^n is restricted to lie in Θ_0. On the other hand, in $\text{CCOMP}^{(n)}(\Theta_0)$ the sum is only over those sequences for which the unrestricted ML estimator $\hat{\theta}(x^n)$ lies in Θ_0. Still, although $\text{CCOMP}^{(n)}(\Theta_0) \leq \text{COMP}^{(n)}(\Theta_0)$, asymptotically the two quantities are indistinguishable:

Theorem 11.1 Let Θ_0 be a closed ineccsi subset of Θ. We have

$$\text{COMP}^{(n)}(\Theta_0) = \text{CCOMP}^{(n)}(\Theta_0) + o(1) = \frac{k}{2}\ln\frac{n}{2\pi} + \ln\int_{\Theta_0}\sqrt{\det I(\theta)}d\theta + o(1).$$

For example, in Example 11.5, as predicted by the theorem, the difference between the logarithms (!) of (11.8) and (11.9) tends to 0. Theorem 11.1, in the more general version of Theorem 11.4, as well as the proof, can be found in Appendix 11.A.

The Constrained Parametric Complexity $\text{CCOMP}^{(n)}(\Theta_0)$
Let Θ_0 be a closed ineccsi subset of Θ. The minimax regret over all sequences with $\hat{\theta}(x^n) \in \Theta_0$ is achieved by $\bar{P}_{\text{nml}}(\cdot \mid \hat{\theta} \in \Theta_0)$, as defined in (11.6). This minimax regret is equal to $\text{CCOMP}^{(n)}(\Theta_0)$, as defined in (11.7). By Theorem 11.1, $\text{COMP}^{(n)}(\Theta_0)$ is asymptotically equal to $\text{CCOMP}^{(n)}(\Theta_0)$, and satisfies the familiar asymptotic formula.

Having thus prepared the underlying notion of constrained complexity, we are now ready to define metauniversal codes. We start with the simplest one, called meta-two-part coding.

11.2.2 Meta-Two-Part Coding

Meta-two-part coding works by encoding x^n in two stages: we first encode a region Θ_0 such that $\hat{\theta}(x^n) \in \Theta_0$, and we then encode x^n based on $\bar{P}_{\text{nml}}(\cdot \mid \hat{\theta} \in \Theta_0)$. This can best be explained by an example:

Example 11.6 [Example 11.1, cont.] Let $\Theta_K = [-K, K]$. Then the NML density $\bar{f}_{\text{nml}}(\cdot \mid \hat{\mu} \in \Theta_K)$ for the constrained normal location family $\{f_\theta \mid \theta \in \Theta_k\}$

is given by

$$\bar{f}_{\text{nml}}(x^n \mid \hat{\mu} \in \Theta_K) := \frac{f_{\hat{\mu}(x^n)}(x^n)}{\int_{x^n \, : \, |\hat{\mu}(x^n)| \leq K} f_{\hat{\mu}(x^n)}(x^n) dx^n}.$$

By (11.8), we have

$$\text{CCOMP}^{(n)}(\Theta_K) = \ln \int_{|\hat{\mu}(x^n)| \leq K} f_{\hat{\mu}(x^n)}(x^n) dx^n =$$

$$\ln 2K + \frac{1}{2} \ln \frac{n}{2\pi} - \ln \sigma. \quad (11.10)$$

This suggests that we can obtain a reasonable universal code by first encoding K using some code with length function L, and then encoding x^n based on the constrained NML code $\bar{P}_{\text{nml}}(\cdot \mid \hat{\theta} \in \Theta_K)$. Taking the K which minimizes the resulting two-part codelength, we obtain a new universal model $\bar{f}_{\text{meta}}$ with corresponding length function

$$-\ln \bar{f}_{\text{meta}}(x^n) := \min_K \left\{ -\ln \bar{f}_{\text{nml}}(x^n \mid \hat{\theta} \in \Theta_K) + L(K) \right\}. \quad (11.11)$$

To make $\bar{f}_{\text{meta}}$ a "good" universal model, we need to choose L in a clever manner. A reasonable choice is to encode $K' = \ln K$ as an integer, using the standard code for the integers (Chapter 3, Section 3.2.3), so that $L_{\mathbb{N}}(K')$ (here expressed in nats) satisfies $L_{\mathbb{N}}(K) \leq 2 \ln K' + \ln 4 < 2 \ln K' + 2$. To see why this is a good choice, note that the regret of $\bar{f}_{\text{meta}}$ now becomes:

$$-\ln \bar{f}_{\text{meta}}(x^n) - [-\ln f_{\hat{\mu}(x^n)}(x^n)] \leq$$

$$\min_{K: \ln K \in \{1,2,\dots\}} \left\{ \ln K + \frac{1}{2} \ln \frac{n}{2\pi} - \ln \sigma + 2 \ln \ln K \right\} + 3 \leq$$

$$\ln |\hat{\mu}(x^n)| + 2 \ln \ln |\hat{\mu}(x^n)| + \frac{1}{2} \ln \frac{n}{2\pi} - \ln \sigma + 5 \leq$$

$$\text{CCOMP}^{(n)}(\Theta_{|\hat{\mu}|}) + 2 \ln \text{CCOMP}^{(n)}(\Theta_{|\hat{\mu}|}) + 5 + o(1). \quad (11.12)$$

If we had known a good bound K on $|\hat{\mu}|$ a priori, we could have used the conditional NML density $\bar{f}_{\text{nml}}(\cdot \mid \hat{\mu} \in \Theta_K)$. With "maximal" a priori knowledge, we would have even used the smallest model in which the observations have positive density, $\bar{f}_{\text{nml}}(\cdot \mid \theta \in \Theta_{|\hat{\mu}|})$, leading to regret $\text{CCOMP}^{(n)}(\Theta_{|\hat{\mu}|})$. The regret achieved by $\bar{f}_{\text{meta}}$ is *almost* as good as this "smallest possible regret-with-hindsight" $\text{CCOMP}^{(n)}(\Theta_{|\hat{\mu}|})$: the difference is much smaller than, in fact, logarithmic in $\text{CCOMP}^{(n)}(\Theta_{|\hat{\mu}|})$ itself, *no matter what x^n we observe.* This is the underlying reason why we choose to encode K with log-precision: the basic idea in refined MDL was to minimize worst-case regret, or *additional codelength* compared to the code that achieves the minimal codelength with hindsight. Here, we use this basic idea on a metalevel: we design a code such that the *additional regret* is minimized, compared to the code that achieves the minimal regret with hindsight. Note that we are effectively applying the *luckiness principle for coding* here. We first encountered this principle in Chapter 3, in the box on page 92. There, we considered luckiness codes with "quasi-uniform" *absolute* codelength; here, we consider luckiness codes with quasi-uniform regret, i.e. *relative* codelength. The connection will be explored further in Section 11.3.

The meta-two-part coding idea was introduced by Rissanen (1996). In principle, it can be applied to a wide range of models with infinite parametric complexity, including all exponential families $\mathcal{M} = \{P_\theta \mid \theta \in \Theta\}$ with $\text{COMP}^{(n)}(\Theta) = \infty$. For example, if the X_i represent outcomes of a Poisson or geometric distribution, one can encode a bound on μ just as in Example 11.1. If Θ represents the full Gaussian model with both μ and σ^2 allowed to vary, one has to encode both a bound on $\hat\mu$ and a bound on $\hat\sigma^2$.

Beyond Meta-Two-Part Codes   Meta-two-part coding is just one possible solution to the problem of undefined $\text{COMP}^{(n)}(\Theta)$. It can be criticized for a variety of reasons. One of these is the fact that it is based on two-part codes, which are not complete (Chapter 3, Section 3.1.3): they reserve several code words for the same data $x_1, \ldots, x_n$ (one for each integer value of $\ln K$); therefore, there must exist more efficient (one-part) codes $\bar{f}'_{\text{meta}}$ such that for all $x^n \in \mathcal{X}^n$, $\bar{f}'_{\text{meta}}(x^n) > \bar{f}_{\text{meta}}(x^n)$. To solve this suboptimality problem, one can use other, complete universal codes at the metastage such as a Bayesian universal model involving a prior W over K. In our example, W would be the distribution corresponding to the code $L(K)$, and we would get the universal model $\bar{f}'_{\text{meta}}(x^n) := \sum_{K:\ln K \in \{1,2,\ldots\}} W(K) \bar{f}_{\text{nml}}(x^n \mid \hat\theta(x^n) \in \Theta_K)$. The fact that we can construct such a Bayesian universal code at the metastage suggests that, perhaps, it is even possible to use a normalized ML universal code at the metastage. We now show that in some cases, this is indeed possible.

11.2.3   Renormalized Maximum Likelihood*

Rissanen's (2000) *renormalized maximum likelihood (RNML) distribution* is best
introduced using our normal location family example.

Example 11.7 [Gaussian Location, cont.] Consider the normal location fam-
ily with hyperparameter K, where $\Theta_K = \{\mu : |\mu| \leq K\}$. We will now
tentatively define the RNML universal model, or rather, its corresponding
density $\bar{f}_{\text{Rnml}}$. Let $\hat{K}(x^n)$ be the bound on $\hat{\mu}(x^n)$ that maximizes $\bar{f}_{\text{nml}}(x^n \mid$
$K) := \bar{f}_{\text{nml}}(x^n \mid \hat{\mu}(x^n) \leq K)$ for the actually given x^n. It is clear that $\hat{K}(x^n) =$
$|\hat{\mu}(x^n)|$. Then $\bar{f}_{\text{Rnml}}$ is tentatively defined by, for all $x^n \in \mathcal{X}^n$,

$$\bar{f}_{\text{Rnml}}(x^n) = \frac{\bar{f}_{\text{nml}}(x^n \mid \hat{K}(x^n))}{\int_{y^n \in \mathbb{R}^n} \bar{f}_{\text{nml}}(y^n \mid \hat{K}(y^n)) dy^n}. \tag{11.13}$$

This is an elegant idea: we simply perform the NML construction at a higher
level, now treating the boundary K of Θ_K as the (meta-)maximum likelihood
parameter.

A difficulty with this approach is that in many (or even most?) cases the
renormalized maximum likelihood distribution is still ill-defined, unless one
bounds the hyperparameter $\hat{K}$ to lie in some range. For example, we show
further below that the denominator in (11.13) is infinite, so that $\bar{f}_{\text{Rnml}}$ is still
ill-defined. One then has to keep re-renormalizing until the resulting distribution is well defined without restrictions on the hyperparameters. As
illustrated below, in some (or even most?) cases, this process gets stuck at
a certain level, because the renormalization becomes ill-defined. Nevertheless, as we explain after the example, even then the RNML approach can be
useful.

Example 11.8 [Gaussian Location, cont.] Let us restrict attention to a single
outcome $x_1 = x$. Note that, for x with $|x| \leq K$, we have by (11.2) that $f_\mu(\mu)$ is
uniform on the range $[-K, K]$, so that, for $x \in [-K, K]$:

$$\bar{f}_{\text{nml}}(x \mid K) = \frac{f_{\hat{\mu}(x)}(x)}{\int_{y:|y|<K} f_{\hat{\mu}(y)}(y) dy} = \frac{1}{2K}, \tag{11.14}$$

and $\bar{f}_{\text{nml}}(x \mid K) = 0$ if $|x| > K$. We would like to define $\bar{f}_{\text{Rnml}}$ as in (11.13),
which for $n = 1$ becomes:

$$\bar{f}_{\text{Rnml}}(x) = \frac{\bar{f}_{\text{nml}}(x \mid \hat{K}(x))}{\int_{y \in \mathbb{R}} \bar{f}_{\text{nml}}(y \mid \hat{K}(y)) dy} = \frac{\frac{1}{2|x|}}{\int_{y \in \mathbb{R}} \frac{1}{2|y|} dy}. \tag{11.15}$$

The denominator, which we might call the exponentiated "second-order complexity," is once again infinite, so the RNML distribution is still undefined. From Example 6.11, Chapter 6, we know that if $\mathrm{COMP}^{(1)}(\Theta) = \infty$, then, for all n, $\mathrm{COMP}^{(n)}(\Theta) = \infty$; the same holds for the second-order complexity, thus the infinity is not an artifact of the small sample. To get rid of this problem we may try to repeat the renormalization process: to make $\bar{f}_{\mathrm{Rnml}}$ well defined, we first introduce a hyper-hyperparameter to restrict the value of K. We plan to use this hyper-hyperparameter to define a re-renormalized $\bar{f}_{\mathrm{RRnml}}$. Since the denominator of (11.15) diverges both for $|y| \to 0$ and $|y| \to \infty$, we actually need to introduce two hyper-hyperparameters $R_1 > 0$ and $R_2 > 0$: for x with $|x| = \hat{K}(x) \in [R_1, R_2]$, we replace (11.15) by

$$\bar{f}_{\mathrm{Rnml}}(x \mid R_1, R_2) :=$$

$$\frac{\bar{f}_{\mathrm{nml}}(x \mid \hat{K}(x))}{\int_{y:\hat{K}(y)\in[R_1,R_2]} \bar{f}_{\mathrm{nml}}(y \mid \hat{K}(y))dy} = \frac{\frac{1}{2|x|}}{\int_{|y|\in[R_1,R_2]} \frac{1}{2|y|}dy} = \frac{\frac{1}{|x|}}{\ln \frac{R_2}{R_1}}. \quad (11.16)$$

This is a well defined quantity, but if we try to use it to define a re-renormalized complexity $\bar{f}_{\mathrm{RRnml}}$, then we are in trouble: for each fixed x, and fixed $R_2 > |x|$, the R_1 maximizing $\bar{f}_{\mathrm{Rnml}}(x \mid R_1, R_2)$ is equal to $\hat{R}_1(x) = |x|$. For each fixed $R_1 < |x|$, $\hat{R}_2(x) = |x|$. The denominator of $\bar{f}_{\mathrm{RRnml}}$ is an integral over $\bar{f}_{\mathrm{Rnml}}(y \mid \hat{R}_1(y), \hat{R}_2(y))$, for various values of y. But for every value of y over which we integrate, this quantity is infinite. Therefore, restricting the range of y with a hyper$^{(3)}$-parameter does not help: no matter how small we choose the range, the resulting integral is infinite. Thus, the renormalization gets stuck at the second level.

The example shows that the renormalization idea cannot be universally applied. Nevertheless, the exercise is useful: Rissanen (2000) performs a related, but much harder renormalization of the linear regression model. After the first renormalization, he ends up with a distribution of which (11.16) is a special case. While the resulting RNML distribution still has hyperparameters (corresponding to R_1 and R_2 in the example above), it turns out that these hyper-hyperparameters do not affect the solution of the model selection problem that Rissanen is interested in (Chapter 14, Section 14.5). In contrast, the first-order hyperparameter (corresponding to K in the example above) does affect the solution. Thus, by using the RNML universal code, Rissanen effectively trades in problematic hyperparameters for unproblematic hyper-hyperparameters.

Parameterization Dependence   Even in model selection problems where it can be used, the RNML approach is not without problems: just like the other metauniversal codes, it prefers some regions of the parameter space over others; had we chosen a different origin, i.e. had we defined $\Theta'_K = [-K + 1, K+1]$ rather than $\Theta_K = [-K, K]$, then we would have obtained a different regret for the same data. The choice between Θ_K and Θ'_K may sometimes be arbitrary though. The same phenomenon occurs in linear regression model selection (see Chapter 12). As we show in Section 11.4, sometimes such a dependency can be avoided with other variations of the NML idea, but we see no way to extend RNML to achieve this, even for models as simple as the normal location family.

Summary of Metauniversal Coding   There exist several versions of metauniversal codes. These invariably work by restricting the parameter space and treating its boundaries as a hyperparameter. Then each type of universal code, two-part, plug-in, Bayesian, and NML, can be applied on a metalevel, leading to good universal codes relative to the hyperparameters. A problem with the simplest ones, meta-two-part codes, is their incompleteness. A problem with the most sophisticated ones, the RNML codes, is that the renormalization process by which they are defined may get stuck. Some more fundamental problems with all the metauniversal approaches – including RNML – will be discussed in the next section.

11.3   NML with Luckiness

Metauniversal coding is essentially based on using the boundaries of the parameter space as hyperparameters and encoding these. This raises a number of problematic questions:

1. It seems too restrictive: why use "hard" boundaries on the parameter space as hyperparameters, rather than "soft" prior distributions on the main parameters?

2. It does not seem restrictive enough: the precision at which the boundaries of the parameter space should be encoded seems somewhat arbitrary.

3. The codes inherently prefer some region of the parameter space over others, in that the regret on a sequence depends on the value of the ML estimator of the sequence. This happens even for simple models such as the normal location family. Thus, these codes present us with exactly the same problem that the basic NML approach had been designed to avoid.

In this section we deal with a more general approach to the infinity problem: *luckiness NML* (LNML), based on the concept of a *luckiness function*. The luckiness approach solves problems 1 and 2. It gives a handle on, but does not solve, problem 3. In Section 11.4.2, we introduce the conditional NML (CNML) approach. This approach – which builds on the luckiness approach – is even capable of solving problem 3, at least to some extent.

Luckiness NML-1   Although the term "luckiness" seems new in this context, variations of the LNML idea were conceived of independently by various researchers: we mention (Kakade, Seeger, and Foster 2006; Roos, Myllymäki, and Tirri 2005; Zhang and Myung 2005; Clarke and Dawid 1999).

We introduce a *slack* or *luckiness function* $a : \Theta \to \mathbb{R}$. The terminology is explained below. We can now define the *luckiness NML-1 (LNML-1) model relative to luckiness function* a as the distribution $\bar{P}^{(n)}_{\text{Lnml-1}}$ on $\mathcal{X}^n$ achieving

$$\min_{\bar{P}} \max_{x^n \in \mathcal{X}^n} \left\{ -\ln \bar{P}(x^n) - \left[-\ln P_{\hat{\theta}(x^n)}(x^n) + a(\hat{\theta}(x^n)) \right] \right\}. \tag{11.17}$$

The notation LNML-1 will be explained further below. We postpone examples until Section 11.3.1. This approach was introduced by Roos (2004), who called it "generalized NML." Note that, if $a(\theta)$ is constant, then (11.17) is achieved by the standard NML distribution. For general continuous $a(\theta)$, the resulting distribution, if it exists, is an exponential tilting of the standard NML distribution:

$$\bar{P}^{(n)}_{\text{Lnml-1}}(x^n) := \frac{P_{\hat{\theta}(x^n)}(x^n)e^{-a(\hat{\theta}(x^n))}}{\sum_{y^n \in \mathcal{X}^n} P_{\hat{\theta}(y^n)}(y^n)e^{-a(\hat{\theta}(y^n))}}. \tag{11.18}$$

Example 11.9 below shows that choosing a appropriately makes this distribution well defined.

The approach is inspired by the, superficially distinct but on a deeper level related, notion of "luckiness function" in statistical and computational learning theory, introduced by Shawe-Taylor, Bartlett, Williamson, and Anthony (1998); see also (Herbrich and Williamson 2002) Since the minimax regret is infinite, any universal code we use will lead to large regret on some sequences. Depending on what sequence we observe, we may either be "lucky" (if the sequence leads to small regret) or "unlucky" (large regret). The idea is now to explicitly formalize how lucky we aim to be on what sequences: we design a function $a(\theta)$ such that on the sequences with large $a(\hat{\theta})$, we are prepared to incur large additional regret. Of course, not all functions $a(\theta)$ are possible, since the corresponding distribution (11.18) must be well defined. For example, if we only accept uniform $a(\theta):=c > 0$, then (11.18) will be the ordinary NML distribution, which is only well defined for special models. But if we allow $a(\theta)$ to vary, then there are suddenly a lot of new possibilities.

In Chapter 3, in the box on page 92, we mentioned the luckiness principle for the first time. There we said that, if we want to encode outcomes in a large or infinite set $\mathcal{S}$, it is a good idea to design a code L which, (a) for any finite subset $\mathcal{S}_0$ of $\mathcal{S}$, achieves codelengths "quite close" to the minimax optimal codelength $\ln |\mathcal{S}_0|$ for all elements in $\mathcal{S}_0$. Yet (b), L achieves much smaller codelengths on some special subsets of $\mathcal{S}$. If we are lucky, the actual outcome will lie in such a subset, and we gain a lot. If we are unlucky, we lose little. Now, we apply this idea to the regret, i.e. the relative rather than the absolute codelength, and with countable sets $\mathcal{S}$ replaced by parametric models $\mathcal{M}_\Theta$. The set $\mathcal{M}_\Theta$ is so large that a code with minimax optimal regret relative to $\mathcal{M}_\Theta$ does not exist – this corresponds to an infinite set $\mathcal{S}$. So, we define a code that, for every ineccsi subset Θ_0 of Θ, achieves regret "quite close" to the minimax optimal regret $\mathrm{COMP}^{(n)}(\Theta_0)$ relative to Θ_0. The set Θ_0 should be compared to a finite $\mathcal{S}$. For some special sets Θ_0 – sets such that $\max_{\theta \in \Theta_0} a(\theta)$ is small – our regret will be much smaller.

In our original formulation, we left open what we meant by "quite close." In the present context, the exact meaning depends on the chosen luckiness function (i.e., it is user-supplied), but we impose the following minimum requirement: for any ineccsi subset Θ_0 of Θ, the regret achieved with a universal code on a sequence with $\hat{\theta}(x^n) \in \Theta_0$ must be within some constant c_{Θ_0} of the minimax regret $\mathrm{CCOMP}^{(n)}(\Theta_0)$, where c_{Θ_0} is allowed to depend on Θ_0, *but not on the sample size* n. This requirement, which is also nicely in accord with the Kolmogorov complexity roots of MDL (see (Barron and Cover 1991)), will be motivated further in Section 14.6. Within subsets of parametric families, the requirement is automatically ensured when choosing any continuous luckiness NML code as universal code. This is because under our definition, the luckiness function $a(\theta)$ is not allowed to depend on n.

[Bayes and Luckiness] We note that imposing a luckiness function $a(\theta)$ is related to, but definitely not the same as assuming a prior distribution $w(\theta) \propto e^{-a(\theta)}$. This is explained in detail in Chapter 17, Section 17.2.1.

Just as with the meta-two-part code, the resulting distribution favors some parts of the parameter space over others, in that the regret depends on the region in which $\hat{\theta}$ falls. The advantage of luckiness NML is that the dependence is now very explicit, and we can design the codes such that a luckiness function $a(\theta)$ of our own choice gets implemented. Since we have a large freedom in choosing $a(\theta)$, we can often choose one that has particularly pleasant properties. For example, as we shall see in Section 11.4.2, in many cases it is possible to sacrifice some initial data points and base the choice of $a(\theta)$ on those points, thereby removing most of the dependence of $\bar{P}_{\text{Lnml-1}}$ on the region in which $\hat{\theta}$ falls.

Luckiness NML-2   Once we allow any slack for particular values of θ, we may wonder why we should compare the performance of the universal code to that of the ML distribution $\hat{\theta}$, rather than the distribution $\hat{\theta}_a(x^n)$ minimizing $-\ln P_\theta(x^n) + a(\theta)$. The latter option leads to the luckiness *NML-2 universal model* $\bar{P}_{\text{Lnml-2}}$, defined as

$$\min_{\bar{P}} \ \max_{x^n \in \mathcal{X}^n} \ \text{LREG}_a(\bar{P}, \Theta, x^n). \tag{11.19}$$

Here LREG_a is the *luckiness-adjusted regret*, defined as

$$\text{LREG}_a(\bar{P}, \Theta, x^n) := -\ln \bar{P}(x^n) - \inf_{\theta \in \Theta} \left\{ -\ln P_\theta(x^n) + a(\theta) \right\}. \tag{11.20}$$

If, for the given x^n, the infimum is achieved by a unique θ, we call this the *luckiness maximum likelihood (LML) estimator*, written as $\hat{\theta}_a$, and given by

$$\hat{\theta}_a := \arg \min_{\theta \in \Theta} \left\{ -\ln P_\theta(x^n) + a(\theta) \right\}. \tag{11.21}$$

Assuming the LML estimator exists for all x^n, we get the explicit expression

$$\bar{P}^{(n)}_{\text{Lnml-2}}(x^n) := \frac{P_{\hat{\theta}_a(x^n)}(x^n) e^{-a(\hat{\theta}_a(x^n))}}{\sum_{x^n \in \mathcal{X}^n} P_{\hat{\theta}_a(x^n)}(x^n) e^{-a(\hat{\theta}_a(x^n))}}. \tag{11.22}$$

The phrase "luckiness maximum likelihood estimator" is not standard. The "2" in $\bar{P}_{\text{Lnml-2}}$ refers to the fact that we measure regret relative to the minimum of *two* terms, $-\ln P_\theta(x^n)$ and $a(\theta)$. $\bar{P}_{\text{Lnml-1}}$ only considered the minimum relative to one term. $\bar{P}_{\text{Lnml-2}}$ was introduced by Kakade, Seeger, and Foster (2006), who called it the *NMAP (normalized maximum a posteriori)* distribution. Kakade et al. (2006) only considered functions $a(\theta)$ such that $\int_\Theta e^{-a(\theta)} d\theta < \infty$, so that

$$\pi_a(\theta) := \frac{e^{-a(\theta)}}{\int_\Theta e^{-a(\theta)} d\theta} \tag{11.23}$$

defines a probability density over Θ. This explains the term NMAP: if we think of $\pi_a(\theta)$ as a prior density, then, by first exponentiating and then applying Bayes formula, we see that

$$\hat{\theta}_a = \arg\max_\theta P_\theta(x^n)\pi_a(\theta) = \arg\max_\theta \frac{P_\theta(x^n)\pi_a(\theta)}{\int P_\theta(x^n)\pi_a(\theta)d\theta} =$$

$$\arg\max_\theta \pi_a(\theta \mid x^n),$$

where $\pi_a(\theta \mid x^n)$ is the posterior density of θ (see Chapter 2, Section 2.5.2), so that $\hat{\theta}_a$ looks like a (Bayesian) *MAP* estimator with respect to prior π_a. We did not adopt this terminology, because if we do a continuous 1-to-1 reparameterization of the model $\mathcal{M}$, then, as explained below, $\hat{\theta}_a$ becomes the MAP estimator relative to some *other* prior which may be quite different from π_a. Therefore, we cannot really think of $\hat{\theta}_a$ as a MAP estimator in the Bayesian sense. This is explained in detail in Chapter 15, beneath the box on page 494.

One may wonder whether, for a given slack function $a(\theta)$, to prefer LNML-1 or LNML-2 for MDL model selection (Chapter 14). Theorem 11.2 in the following subsection suggests (but does not prove) that it does not matter too much.

> Given the developments in Chapter 12, where we LNML-2 seems the mathematically more elegant, and therefore, perhaps the "right" choice; see the box on page 365. But one may also argue that the primary interest in constructing NML codes is the regret, which compares the universal codelength to the ML codelength. Therefore, it seems that the luckiness function should be evaluated at the ML estimate, which gives LNML-1. As an aside, one may also be interested in a luckiness function b that depends on the *data* x^n rather than the parameter θ (Clarke and Dawid 1999). We did not consider this – quite reasonable – possibility here; yet for exponential families, if the luckiness function $b(x^n)$ can be written as a function of the sufficient statistic $\hat{\theta}(x^n)$, we can simulate it with the LNML-1 approach: if $b(x^n) = a(\hat{\theta}(x^n))$ for some function a, then LNML with luckiness function b is equivalent to LNML-1 with luckiness function a.

11.3.1   Asymptotic Expansion of LNML

The Tilted Jeffreys' Prior   As can be seen from the box on page 235, the standard NML code, which is implicitly based on the uniform luckiness function, asymptotically achieves essentially the same regret on all ineccsi sequences as the Bayesian universal code based on Jeffreys' prior. Similarly,

we find that, under regularity conditions, the LNML-2 code based on luckiness function $a(\theta)$ asymptotically achieves essentially the same regret as the
Bayesian universal model based on a "luckiness-tilted" Jeffreys' prior, defined as

$$w_{\text{lucky-Jeffreys}}(\theta) := \frac{\sqrt{\det I(\theta)}\, e^{-a(\theta)}}{\int_\Theta \sqrt{\det I(\theta)}\, e^{-a(\theta)}\, d\theta}. \tag{11.24}$$

This prior was probably first used by Barron (1998) who considered codes optimizing expected redundancy rather than individual-sequence regret. For a
given luckiness function a, we define the *luckiness Bayesian universal model*
$\bar{P}_{\text{lucky-Jeffreys}}$ to denote the Bayesian universal model $\bar{P}_{\text{Bayes}}$ with prior given
by (11.24). Formally, we have the following:

Theorem 11.2 Let Θ represent an ineccsi exponential family, and assume
that $a(\theta)$ is continuous on Θ. Then $\bar{P}_{\text{Lnml-1}}$, $\bar{P}_{\text{Lnml-2}}$, and $\bar{P}_{\text{lucky-Jeffreys}}$ are all
well defined, and for any ineccsi $\Theta_0 \subset \Theta$, uniformly for all Θ_0-sequences
$x_1, x_2, \ldots$, we have

$$-\ln \bar{P}_{\text{Lnml-2}}(x^n) =$$
$$-\ln \bar{P}_{\text{Lnml-1}}(x^n) + o(1) = -\ln \bar{P}_{\text{lucky-Jeffreys}}(x^n) + o(1) =$$
$$-\ln P_{\hat{\theta}_a}(x^n) + a(\hat{\theta}_a) + \frac{k}{2}\ln\frac{n}{2\pi} + \ln\int\sqrt{\det I(\theta)}\,e^{-a(\theta)}\,d\theta + o(1) =$$
$$-\ln P_{\hat{\theta}}(x^n) + a(\hat{\theta}) + \frac{k}{2}\ln\frac{n}{2\pi} + \ln\int\sqrt{\det I(\theta)}\,e^{-a(\theta)}\,d\theta + o(1).$$

$$\tag{11.25}$$

Proof: The first and fourth equality are based on the following proposition,
which we state and prove first:

Proposition 11.1 Let (Θ, P_θ) be a diffeomorphic parameterization of a finite-
dimensional exponential family, and let Θ_0 be an ineccsi subset of Θ. Let $a(\theta)$
be continuous on Θ_0. Then, uniformly for all $x_1, x_2, \ldots$ with $\hat{\theta}(x^n) \in \Theta_0$, we
have

$$-\ln P_{\hat{\theta}(x^n)}(x^n) + a(\hat{\theta}(x^n)) = -\ln P_{\hat{\theta}_a(x^n)}(x^n) + a(\hat{\theta}_a(x^n)) + o(1). \tag{11.26}$$

Proof: Let $f(x^n) := a(\hat{\theta}_a(x^n)) - a(\hat{\theta}(x^n))$. By continuity of likelihood and $a(\theta)$,
uniformly for all x^n with $\hat{\theta}(x^n) \in \Theta_0$, we must have $f(x^n) \to 0$ as $n \to \infty$. But
we also have

$$-\ln P_{\hat{\theta}(x^n)}(x^n) + a(\hat{\theta}(x^n)) + f(x^n) = -\ln P_{\hat{\theta}(x^n)}(x^n) + a(\hat{\theta}_a(x^n)) \le$$
$$-\ln P_{\hat{\theta}_a}(x^n) + a(\hat{\theta}_a(x^n)) \le -\ln P_{\hat{\theta}(x^n)}(x^n) + a(\hat{\theta}(x^n)), \tag{11.27}$$

so that the result follows.□

The proposition immediately implies the fourth equality of (11.25), so it remains to prove only the first, second, and third equality. The first equality also follows from Proposition 11.1, by rewriting the terms within the denominator of $\bar{P}_{\text{Lnml-1}}$ as $\exp(-(-\ln P_{\hat{\theta}(x^n)} + a(\hat{\theta})))$ and similarly for $\bar{P}_{\text{Lnml-2}}$. The proposition implies that the numerators, as well as all the terms in the denominators, are equal to within a factor of $\exp(o(1))$, which, for large n, converges to 1. Since the sums are taken over an ineccsi set, the convergence is uniform and the first equality follows. The third equality follows by Theorem 8.1. Since $\bar{P}_{\text{lucky-Jeffreys}}$ is based on a prior with support Θ, we need to require here that $x_1, x_2, \ldots$ is a Θ_0-sequence for some Θ_0 that is an ineccsi subset of Θ, even though Θ is itself ineccsi. To finish the proof, it is sufficient to show that

$$-\ln \bar{P}_{\text{Lnml-1}}(x^n) + o(1) =$$
$$-\ln P_{\hat{\theta}_a}(x^n) + a(\hat{\theta}_a) + \frac{k}{2}\ln\frac{n}{2\pi} + \ln\int\sqrt{\det I(\theta)}e^{-a(\theta)}d\theta + o(1).$$

This follows by a straightforward extension of the proof of Theorem 7.1; we omit further details. □

Caveat and Open Problem No. 6 The theorem above is an analogue of Theorem 7.1 for luckiness NML. Just like that theorem, it is only defined for ineccsi parameter sets. However, one of the main points in introducing the luckiness framework was to define NML for nonineccsi parameter spaces. Thus, the implications of Theorem 11.2 are limited; the theorem suggests that LNML-1 and LNML-2 and the Bayesian approach with the tilted Jeffreys' prior are similar, but it does not really prove it for all relevant sequences. It would be desirable to have a version of the theorem that also holds for nonineccsi Θ. It is presently not clear to me how to prove this, or indeed, whether it even holds.

Perhaps the simplest case with nonuniform $a(\theta)$ arises in the context of the normal location family. In this case, the Fisher information $I(\mu) = 1/\sigma^2$ (page 300) is constant as a function of μ. Therefore, the "luckiness prior" π_a, defined as in (11.23) (in "NML space"), and the corresponding prior $w_{\text{lucky-Jeffreys}}$ (in "Bayes space") coincide:

$$\pi_a(\mu) \propto e^{-a(\mu)} \ ; \ w_{\text{lucky-Jeffreys}}(\mu) \propto \sqrt{\det I(\mu)}e^{-a(\mu)} \propto e^{-a(\mu)}. \tag{11.28}$$

(11.28) generalizes to linear regression models (Chapter 12, Section 12.4.2); for other models and parameterizations, π_a and $w_{\text{lucky-Jeffreys}}$ will typically be different.

Example 11.9 [Example 11.1, cont.] We illustrate (11.28) for the normal location family with a particularly convenient choice of $a(\mu)$: we fix some $m \in \mathbb{N}$, $\mu_0 \in \mathbb{R}$ and pick

$$a(\mu) = m \cdot \frac{(\mu_0 - \mu)^2}{2\sigma^2}, \text{ or equivalently, } \pi_a(\mu) = \sqrt{\frac{m}{2\pi\sigma^2}} e^{-m\frac{(\mu_0-\mu)^2}{2\sigma^2}}. \quad (11.29)$$

We see that π_a is the density of a normal distribution defined over m outcomes. Thus, the farther $\hat{\mu}(x^n)$ is from the "starting point" μ_0, the "less lucky" we are and the larger the regret on the sequence x^n will be. This choice of luckiness function may be reasonable if we have some prior idea that the mean of the data should be around μ_0. For example, we may have seen some data $x'_1, \ldots, x'_m$ in the past that came from the same source. If the mean of these data was μ_0, and the average distance $m^{-1} \sum_{i=1}^{m} (x'_i - \mu_0)^2$ was equal to σ^2, then this corresponds to $a(\mu)$ as in (11.29).

Evaluating $\bar{f}_{\text{lucky-Jeffreys}}$ **and** $\bar{f}_{\text{Lnml-2}}$ Irrespective of its practical relevance, the luckiness function (11.29) for the normal location family is convenient, because we can explicitly evaluate $- \ln \bar{f}_{\text{lucky-Jeffreys}}(x^n)$ based on $w_{\text{lucky-Jeffreys}}$. The remarkable result implies that, for the normal location family, $\bar{f}_{\text{Lnml-2}}(x^n)$ and $\bar{f}_{\text{lucky-Jeffreys}}$ must be identical for all sample sizes. To show this, we use the fact that for *all* $x^n \in \mathbb{R}^n$,

$$- \ln \bar{f}_{\text{lucky-Jeffreys}}(x^n) =$$

$$\frac{1}{2} \ln \frac{n+m}{m} + \frac{n}{2} \ln 2\pi\sigma^2 + \frac{1}{2\sigma^2} \left(\sum_{i=1}^{n} (\hat{\mu}_a(x^n) - x_i)^2 + m(\hat{\mu}_a(x^n) - \mu_0)^2 \right).$$

This formula is a very special case of (12.50), which is derived in detail in Chapter 12, Section 12.3.1. It implies that

$$\text{LREG}_a(\bar{f}_{\text{lucky-Jeffreys}}, \mathcal{M}_{\text{loc}}, x^n) =$$

$$- \ln \bar{f}_{\text{lucky-Jeffreys}}(x^n) + \ln f_{\hat{\mu}_a(x^n)}(x^n) - a(\hat{\mu}_a(x^n)) = \frac{1}{2} \ln \frac{n+m}{m}. \quad (11.30)$$

The first equation illustrates that the luckiness function can be interpreted in terms of m "virtual" outcomes with mean μ_0 and variance σ^2, that might have been observed in earlier experiments. The second equation shows that the luckiness regret of $\bar{f}_{\text{lucky-Jeffreys}}$ does not depend on the observed data x^n. It follows that it is the same for all sequences x^n. By the reasoning of the box on page 182, Chapter 6, Section 6.2, it then follows that $\bar{f}_{\text{lucky-Jeffreys}}$ must be identical to $\bar{f}_{\text{Lnml-2}}$, the density (11.22) that achieves the minimax luckiness regret (11.19). The same holds for general regression models with certain priors (Chapter 12, Section 12.4.2) and Gaussian process models with Gaussian noise (Kakade, Seeger, and Foster 2006) (Chapter 13, Section 13.5); but it certainly does not hold in general.

Asymptotics (11.30) can be rewritten as

$$- \ln \bar{f}_{\text{lucky-Jeffreys}}(x^n) + \ln f_{\hat{\mu}_a(x^n)}(x^n) = \frac{1}{2} \ln \frac{n+m}{m} + \frac{m}{2\sigma^2}(\hat{\mu}_a - \mu_0)^2, \quad (11.31)$$

which expresses the regret with respect to the LML estimator. Using (12.19), a special case of Lemma 12.2 in Chapter 12, we can also explicitly calculate the regret with respect to the ordinary ML estimator, which gives

$$- \ln \bar{f}_{\text{lucky-Jeffreys}}(x^n) + \ln f_{\hat{\mu}(x^n)}(x^n) = \frac{1}{2} \ln \frac{n+m}{m} + \frac{1}{2\sigma^2}\frac{nm}{n+m}(\hat{\mu}(x^n) - \mu_0)^2,$$

which, as expected, is slightly different, but within $O(1/n)$, from (11.31). (note that m stays fixed as n increases.) It is useful to compare this to the asymptotic expansion of $\bar{f}_{\text{lucky-Jeffreys}}$ that we developed in Theorem 8.1. A straightforward calculation shows that, when applied to the normal location model, it gives

$$- \ln \bar{f}_{\text{lucky-Jeffreys}}(x^n) + \ln f_{\hat{\mu}(x^n)}(x^n) = \frac{1}{2} \ln \frac{n}{m} + \frac{m}{2\sigma^2}(\hat{\mu}(x^n) - \mu_0)^2 + o(1).$$

We see that it is slightly different from, but very close (within $o(1)$) to, both nonasymptotic formulas.

So far we have avoided the main question: how should we choose the luckiness function $a(\theta)$? The previous example suggests that $a(\theta)$ may often be thought of as representing evidence from earlier experiments. This idea will be formalized in the next section.

11.4 Conditional Universal Models

All the approaches considered thus far slightly prefer some regions of the parameter space over others. We now discuss an approach that avoids this problem, at least to a large extent. It comes in two forms: first, there is a Bayesian approach, based on a so-called *improper* Jeffreys' prior. While the solution provided by this approach "looks reasonable," it has hitherto not been adopted in the MDL field – the only exception we know of being our own (De Rooij and Grünwald 2006). The reason for this lack of popularity may be that a straightforward interpretation of the improper Bayes-Jeffreys approach in terms of universal codes has been lacking. Here we present for the first time a related "conditional" NML approach, which both shows how to consider the problem from a minimax coding point of view, and which also re-establishes the connection between NML and the Bayes–Jeffreys approach for models with infinite parametric complexity. Our approach is inspired by, but different from, the important work of Liang and Barron (2004, 2005), who considered expected redundancy rather than individual-sequence regret. We compare our approach to Liang and Barron's in Section 11.4.3.

Below we treat both the Bayes–Jeffreys and the conditional NML approach in detail. For pedagogical reasons, it seems best to start with the Bayesian approach.

11.4.1 Bayesian Approach with Jeffreys' Prior

The basic idea behind the Bayesian approach is to use Jeffreys' prior anyway, even though it seems ill-defined. It turns out that this is possible if we are willing to *"sacrifice"* some initial data points $x_1, \ldots, x_{n_0}$. This leads to a Bayesian universal code for the remaining data $x_{n_0+1}, \ldots, x_n$, which allows us to achieve small regret compared to the ML estimator for $x_1, \ldots, x_n$. We now explain this approach step by step.

Improper Priors A measure on a parameter space Θ with density w is called *improper* if $\int_\Theta w(\theta) d\theta = \infty$. Improper prior measures are a well studied, but sometimes controversial, notion in Bayesian statistics (Berger 1985; Bernardo and Smith 1994). Although such measures have no interpretation as probability distributions, it is sometimes tempting to use them as "priors" after all. A good example is the normal location family: if we have no prior knowledge about the mean, then symmetry arguments suggest that we should adopt a uniform measure w_U on the set of means $\Theta = \mathbb{R}^1$. This seems to be the only assignment that does not depend on the location of the origin, and therefore the only assignment that does not either involve implicit prior knowledge or arbitrariness. Now, even though w_U is not a probability density, we may boldly try to use Bayes formula anyway to calculate a "posterior" of μ based on data $x_1, \ldots, x_n$. This way of proceeding is an instance of *generalized Bayes* (Ferguson 1967). Let us see what happens if the data consist of a single point x_1: we find that

$$w_U(\mu \mid x_1) = \frac{f_\mu(x_1) w_U(\mu)}{\int_{\mu \in \mathbb{R}} f_\mu(x_1) w_U(\mu) d\mu}.$$

Interestingly, the denominator is finite, so that the posterior $w_U(\mu \mid x_1)$ satisfies $\int_\mu w_U(\mu \mid x_1)d\mu = 1$. This means that the posterior $w_U(\mu \mid x_1)$ represents a proper probability distribution after all! In our particular case,

$$w_U(\mu \mid x_1) \propto e^{-\frac{(\mu - x_1)^2}{2\sigma^2}} \qquad (11.32)$$

represents a Gaussian distribution with variance σ^2 and mean given by the first data point. We may therefore proceed by conditioning on the first data point x_1 to obtain a proper posterior. Using this posterior as a prior, we then use standard Bayesian inference on $x_2, \ldots, x_n$. In general, for k-dimensional parametric families, we may need to condition on more than one outcome before the posterior becomes proper; for example, in the 2-parameter full Gaussian model, we need to condition on the first two observations. In all the examples I am aware of, the number of observations needed is never more than the dimension k.

Improper Jeffreys' Prior   As we illustrated in Section 11.1.2, for many exponential families $\mathcal{M} = \{P_\theta \mid \theta \in \Theta\}$ we have $\int_\Theta \sqrt{\det I(\theta)}d\theta = \infty$. If we accept the idea of improper priors, then in such cases we can simply define the improper Jeffreys' prior as $w_{\text{Jeffreys}}(\theta) = c\sqrt{I(\theta)}$ for some constant $c > 0$. The choice of c will not affect any of our results, so we fix it once and for all to be 1. For example, in the normal location family we just discussed, Jeffreys' prior becomes uniform: from the box on page 300, we see that $w_{\text{Jeffreys}}(\mu) = \sigma^{-1}$, which does not depend on μ. As another example, from Example 11.4 we see that for the Poisson family, $w_{\text{Jeffreys}}(\mu) = \mu^{-1/2}$.

Conditional Bayesian Universal Models   We proceed to define the universal code $\bar{P}_{\text{Bayes}}$ based on an improper prior w. We mostly study the case where w is Jeffreys' prior, but the formulas below hold more generally. We first note that, if w is improper, then $-\ln \bar{P}_{\text{Bayes}}(x^n)$ cannot be interpreted as a codelength: by interchanging summation over x^n and integration over θ, we see that

$$\sum_{x^n} \bar{P}_{\text{Bayes}}(x^n) = \int_\Theta \sum_{x^n} P_\theta(x^n)w(\theta)d\theta = \infty.$$

To obtain a proper code after all, we condition $\bar{P}_{\text{Bayes}}$ on the first n_0 outcomes, Here n_0 is the smallest number such that the posterior

$$w(\theta \mid x^{n_0}) = \frac{P_\theta(x^{n_0})w(\theta)}{\int P_\theta(x^{n_0})w(\theta)d\theta}, \qquad (11.33)$$

defines a probability density. This is just the smallest number n_0 such that the denominator in (11.33) is finite. In all examples I have seen, n_0 does not depend on the data x^n, but I have no proof that this is true in general. resulting conditional distribution $\bar{P}_{\text{Bayes}}(\cdot \mid x^{n_0})$ turns out to be a good universal code for the sequence $x_{n_0+1}, \dots, x_n$.

Notation for Conditional Universal Models It will be convenient to introduce some special purpose notation, to be used in the remainder of this chapter, and again in Chapter 12. We define $\mathbf{x} = (x_1, \dots, x_n)^{\top}$ as an abbreviation of the full data, $\mathbf{x}_0 = (x_1, \dots, x_{n_0})^{\top}$ as an abbreviation of the data on which to condition, and $\mathbf{x}_1 = (x_{n_0+1}, \dots, x_n)$ as an abbreviation of the remaining data to be encoded. We also let $n_1 = n - n_0$ be the size of the sample $\mathbf{x}_1$. For given prior w, we consider the conditional code with lengths

$$- \ln \bar{P}_{\text{Bayes}}(\mathbf{x}_1 \mid \mathbf{x}_0) := - \ln \frac{\bar{P}_{\text{Bayes}}(\mathbf{x}_0\mathbf{x}_1)}{\bar{P}_{\text{Bayes}}(\mathbf{x}_0)} = - \ln \int_{\Theta} P_{\theta}(\mathbf{x}_1) w(\theta \mid \mathbf{x}_0) d\theta. \quad (11.34)$$

This quantity is well defined since n_0 was chosen as the smallest number such that the denominator in (11.33) is finite, and $\bar{P}_{\text{Bayes}}(\mathbf{x}_0)$ is equal to this denominator. The first equality is a definition, the second then follows by (11.33). (11.34) can be interpreted as a codelength, since $\sum_{\mathbf{x}_1 \in \mathbb{R}^{n_1}} \bar{P}_{\text{Bayes}}(\mathbf{x}_1 \mid \mathbf{x}_0) = \int \sum_{\mathbf{x}_1 \in \mathbb{R}^{n_1}} P_{\theta}(\mathbf{x}_1) w(\theta \mid \mathbf{x}_0) d\theta = 1$.

Asymptotics By (11.33) and Theorem 8.1, we find that, for i.i.d. models satisfying the conditions of Theorem 8.1,

$$- \ln \bar{P}_{\text{Bayes}}(\mathbf{x}_1 \mid \mathbf{x}_0) =$$

$$- \ln P_{\hat{\theta}(\mathbf{x}_1)}(\mathbf{x}_1) + \frac{k}{2} \ln \frac{n_1}{2\pi} - \ln w(\hat{\theta}(\mathbf{x}_1) \mid \mathbf{x}_0) + \ln \sqrt{\det I(\hat{\theta}(\mathbf{x}_1))} + o(1).$$
$$(11.35)$$

In the special case that $w(\theta) = \sqrt{\det I(\theta)}$ is Jeffreys' prior, we have

$$w_{\text{Jeffreys}}(\theta \mid \mathbf{x}_0) = \frac{P_{\theta}(\mathbf{x}_0) w_{\text{Jeffreys}}(\theta)}{\int_{\Theta} P_{\theta}(\mathbf{x}_0) w_{\text{Jeffreys}}(\theta) d\theta} = \frac{P_{\theta}(\mathbf{x}_0) \sqrt{\det I(\theta)}}{\int_{\Theta} P_{\theta}(\mathbf{x}_0) \sqrt{\det I(\theta)} d\theta},$$
$$(11.36)$$

so that, since $\mathbf{x} = \mathbf{x}_0\mathbf{x}_1$ and we assume data are i.i.d., (11.35) becomes:

$$- \ln P_{\hat{\theta}(\mathbf{x}_1)}(\mathbf{x}_0\mathbf{x}_1) + \frac{k}{2} \ln \frac{n_1}{2\pi} + \ln \int_{\Theta} P_{\theta}(\mathbf{x}_0) \sqrt{\det I(\theta)} d\theta + o(1). \quad (11.37)$$

Example 11.10 [Normal Location, cont.] Consider the normal location family. Let $n_0 = 1$ and $\mathbf{x}_0 = (x_1)$. We then have

$$\int_{\mathbb{R}} f_\mu(\mathbf{x}_0)\sqrt{\det I(\mu)}d\mu = \sigma^{-1}\int_{\mathbb{R}}\frac{1}{\sqrt{2\pi\sigma^2}}e^{-\frac{1}{2\sigma^2}(\mu-x_1)^2}d\mu = \sigma^{-1}, \qquad (11.38)$$

so that (11.37) expresses that

$$-\ln \bar{f}_{\text{Jeffreys}}(x_2,\ldots,x_n \mid x_1) = -\ln f_{\hat\mu(\mathbf{x}_1)}(x^n) + \frac{1}{2}\ln\frac{n-1}{2\pi\sigma^2} + o(1).$$

Example 11.11 shows that this formula is almost exact.

Summary   We have seen that for models for which w_{Jeffreys} is improper, conditioning on some initial data $\mathbf{x}_0$ usually makes the posterior $w_{\text{Jeffreys}}(\theta \mid \mathbf{x}_0)$ a proper density on Θ. Then $-\ln \bar{P}_{\text{Jeffreys}}(\mathbf{x}_1 \mid \mathbf{x}_0)$ can be interpreted as a code-length function. This approach can only be used for coding a segment of the data $\mathbf{x}_1$ if n is larger than the minimum n_0 such that $w_{\text{Jeffreys}}(\theta \mid \mathbf{x}_0)$ is proper. In the next section, we show that this improper Jeffreys' prior approach can be connected to a modified version of NML, which we call *conditional NML*.

11.4.2   Conditional NML

From a universal coding perspective, the essence of the Bayesian approach with improper prior is not really the improperness. Rather, it is the idea of "sacrificing" some initial data, in order to be able to encode the remaining data in a special manner. Equivalently, if data from the same source are available that were obtained in an earlier experiment, then these data can be used to encode the entire new data sequence in a special manner. Here "special" means "using Jeffreys" parameterization-invariant prior measure." Now, we try to apply the same idea, but with "special" meaning "achieving minimax optimal regret." Thus, we accept that an initial part of the data, denoted by $\mathbf{x}_0$, will not be encoded in an optimal way. We can either assume that these data are given to the encoder for free, or that they are encoded using some standard code, which is not optimized to achieve minimax regret. We then encode the remaining data $\mathbf{x}_1 \in \mathcal{X}^{n_1}$ using a code $\bar{L}$ such that the length $\bar{L}(\mathbf{x}_1 \mid \mathbf{x}_0)$ depends on the previously seen $\mathbf{x}_0$, and at the same time, such that $\bar{L}(\cdot \mid \mathbf{x}_0)$ achieves small regret relative to $\mathcal{M}$, no matter what $\mathbf{x}_1$ we observe.

For many exponential families $\mathcal{M}$, there exists a code with length function $\bar{L}(\mathbf{x}_1 \mid \mathbf{x}_0)$ that, among all codes on $\mathbf{x}_1$, achieves minimax regret on $\mathbf{x}$, relative to $\mathcal{M}$. Although we have no proof, we suspect that such codes exist for *all k*-dimensional exponential families, with $\mathbf{x}_0$ of size $n_0 \geq k$, including all those families for which the ordinary NML code is undefined. We suspect that such codes exist even for much more general models, not just exponential families. We call such codes *conditional NML codes*. They come in (at least) two versions, depending on what exactly we mean by "minimax regret given that x begins with $\mathbf{x}_0$." Below we first explain conditional NML-2, because it is the most straightforward approach, leaving the definition of "regret" unchanged. We call it CNML-2 because, as we will see, it closely corresponds to a luckiness NML-2, rather than a luckiness NML-1 code.

Conditional NML-2   Here we take an arbitrary but fixed $\mathbf{x}_0$ of some length n_0, and we consider the minimax problem

$$\min_{\bar{P}} \max_{\mathbf{x}_1 \in \mathcal{X}^{n_1}} \left\{ -\ln \bar{P}(\mathbf{x}_1 \mid \mathbf{x}_0) - [-\ln P_{\hat{\theta}(\mathbf{x}_0\mathbf{x}_1)}(\mathbf{x}_0\mathbf{x}_1)] \right\}. \tag{11.39}$$

Thus, we try to find the code for $\mathbf{x}_1$ conditional on $\mathbf{x}_0$ that has minimax regret with respect to the full, combined data sequence $\mathbf{x} = \mathbf{x}_0\mathbf{x}_1$. Arguing as in the box on page 182, Section 6.2.1, Chapter 6, we see that the solution, if it exists, is given by

$$\bar{P}^{(n)}_{\text{Cnml-2}}(\mathbf{x}_1 \mid \mathbf{x}_0) := \frac{P_{\hat{\theta}(\mathbf{x}_0\mathbf{x}_1)}(\mathbf{x}_0\mathbf{x}_1)}{\sum_{\mathbf{z}_1 \in \mathcal{X}^{n_1}} P_{\hat{\theta}(\mathbf{x}_0\mathbf{z}_1)}(\mathbf{x}_0\mathbf{z}_1)}. \tag{11.40}$$

We suspect that, for k-dimensional exponential families, if we take $n_0 \geq k$, then the distribution (11.40) always exists. We illustrate CNML-2 in Example 11.11 below.

Equivalent Definition   We just defined $\bar{P}_{\text{Cnml-2}}$ as a conditional code on $\mathcal{X}^{n_1}$, dependent on $\mathbf{x}_0$. Equivalently, we may think of $\bar{P}_{\text{Cnml-2}}$ as a distribution/code on the full space $\mathcal{X}^n$, which is designed so that, for each fixed $\mathbf{x}_0$, it achieves minimax regret on $\mathbf{x}$; the way $\mathbf{x}_0$ is encoded does not matter to us. In this formulation, we look for the $\bar{P}$ achieving, for each fixed $\mathbf{x}_0$,

$$\min_{\bar{P}} \max_{\mathbf{x}_1 \in \mathcal{X}^{n_1}} \left\{ -\ln \bar{P}(\mathbf{x}_0, \mathbf{x}_1) - [-\ln P_{\hat{\theta}(\mathbf{x}_0, \mathbf{x}_1)}(\mathbf{x}_0, \mathbf{x}_1)] \right\},$$

which can be rewritten as

$$\min_{\bar{P}} \max_{\mathbf{x}_1 \in \mathcal{X}^{n_1}} -\ln \bar{P}(\mathbf{x}_1 \mid \mathbf{x}_0) - \ln \bar{P}(\mathbf{x}_0) - [-\ln P_{\hat{\theta}(\mathbf{x}_0, \mathbf{x}_1)}(\mathbf{x}_0, \mathbf{x}_1)]. \tag{11.41}$$

Since the second term does not depend on $\mathbf{x}_1$, the $\bar{P}$ achieving (11.41) is compatible with $\bar{P}_{\text{Cnml-2}}$, as promised.

Conditional NML-1 An alternative definition that, as we will see, leads to approximately the same solution, is to look for the $\bar{P}$ achieving

$$\min_{\bar{P}} \max_{\mathbf{x}_1 \in \mathcal{X}^{n_1}} \left\{ -\ln \bar{P}(\mathbf{x}_1 \mid \mathbf{x}_0) - [-\ln P_{\hat{\theta}(\mathbf{x}_1)}(\mathbf{x}_0\mathbf{x}_1)] \right\}. \tag{11.42}$$

We shall denote this $\bar{P}$ by $\bar{P}_{\text{Cnml-1}}$. Clearly, if it exists, it is given by

$$\bar{P}^{(n)}_{\text{Cnml-1}}(\mathbf{x}_1 \mid \mathbf{x}_0) := \frac{P_{\hat{\theta}(\mathbf{x}_1)}(\mathbf{x}_0\mathbf{x}_1)}{\sum_{\mathbf{z}_1 \in \mathcal{X}^{n_1}} P_{\hat{\theta}(\mathbf{z}_1)}(\mathbf{x}_0\mathbf{z}_1)}. \tag{11.43}$$

We concede that both alternatives $\bar{P}_{\text{Cnml-1}}$ and $\bar{P}_{\text{Cnml-2}}$ may look somewhat strange. Yet, as we show below, they are equivalent to each other, and to the Bayesian approach with Jeffreys' prior, all up to $o(1)$. For this reason, it may be that conditional NML-1 and -2 are steps in the right direction. On the other hand, the approach is not without its problems, as will be discussed at the end of this section.

CNML-i Is a Special Case of LNML-i The conditional NML-1 approach applied to data $\mathbf{x} = \mathbf{x}_0\mathbf{x}_1$ is really a special case of the luckiness NML-1 approach applied to data $\mathbf{x}_1$. We obtain it if we set the luckiness function $a(\theta)$ to $a(\theta) = -\ln P_\theta(\mathbf{x}_0)$. To see this, note that with this definition of $a(\theta)$, we can rewrite (11.43) as

$$\bar{P}^{(n)}_{\text{Cnml-1}}(\mathbf{x}_1) := \frac{P_{\hat{\theta}(\mathbf{x}_1)}(\mathbf{x}_1)e^{-a(\hat{\theta}(\mathbf{x}_1))}}{\sum_{\mathbf{x}_1' \in \mathcal{X}^{n_1}} P_{\hat{\theta}(\mathbf{x}_1')}(\mathbf{x}_1')e^{-a(\hat{\theta}(\mathbf{x}_1'))}}, \tag{11.44}$$

which is an instance of (11.18), the expression for $\bar{P}_{\text{Lnml-1}}$. Similarly, one can show that the conditional NML-2 approach is a special case of the luckiness NML-2 approach, again with $a(\theta)$ set to $-\ln P_\theta(\mathbf{x}_0)$. We omit the details of this calculation. By Theorem 11.2, it now follows that, for ineccsi data sequences, asymptotically, $-\ln \bar{P}^{(n)}_{\text{Cnml-1}}(\mathbf{x}_1 \mid \mathbf{x}_0) = -\ln \bar{P}^{(n)}_{\text{Cnml-2}}(\mathbf{x}_1 \mid \mathbf{x}_0) + o(1)$. This result is extended in Theorem 11.3 below.

[**Variations – Conditional NML-3**] Two other approaches suggest themselves: first of all, rather than solving for (11.42) (CNML-1) or (11.39) (CNML-2), we may look for the conditional distribution achieving

$$\min_{\bar{P}} \max_{\mathbf{x}_1 \in \mathcal{X}^{n_1}} \left\{ -\ln \bar{P}(\mathbf{x}_1 \mid \mathbf{x}_0) - [-\ln P_{\hat{\theta}(\mathbf{x}_1)}(\mathbf{x}_1 \mid \mathbf{x}_0)] \right\}. \tag{11.45}$$

Unfortunately, since for i.i.d. models, we have $P_\theta(\mathbf{x}_1 \mid \mathbf{x}_0) = P_\theta(\mathbf{x}_1)$, this approach does not lead to anything useful: (11.45) implies that for each fixed

$\mathbf{x}_0$, the conditional distribution $\bar{P}(\mathbf{x}_1 \mid \mathbf{x}_0)$ achieving (11.45) must be identical to the NML distribution $\bar{P}_{\mathrm{nml}}(\mathbf{x}_1)$, and we already know that this distribution is ill-defined – that was the very reason we tried to condition on the first few observations.

Conditional NML-3/Open Problem No. 7 Finally, rather than solving for (11.45), (11.39), or (11.42), we may try yet another, fourth possibility: we look for the conditional distribution on $\mathcal{X}^n$ achieving

$$\min_{\bar{P}} \max_{\mathbf{x}_1 \in \mathcal{X}^{n_1}} \left\{ -\ln \bar{P}(\mathbf{x}_1 \mid \mathbf{x}_0) - [-\ln P_{\hat{\theta}(\mathbf{x}_0 \mathbf{x}_1)}(\mathbf{x}_1 \mid \mathbf{x}_0)] \right\}. \tag{11.46}$$

Note the subtle difference with (11.39). Since we assume $\mathcal{M}^{(k)}$ is i.i.d., the expression can be simplified by noting that $P_{\hat{\theta}(\mathbf{x}_0 \mathbf{x}_1)}(\mathbf{x}_1 \mid \mathbf{x}_0) = P_{\hat{\theta}(\mathbf{x}_0 \mathbf{x}_1)}(\mathbf{x}_1)$. This approach, which we may call CNML-3, is perhaps more intuitive than either CNML-1 or CNML-2. It is also more in line with Liang and Barron's minimax expected redundancy approach, which we outline in Section 11.4.3 below. Unfortunately, (11.46), while it does seem to have a unique solution in most cases, does not seem easy to analyze, and we have not succeeded in determining its properties – such as whether, under some conditions, it coincides with Liang and Barron's approach.

Connecting Conditional NML and Jeffreys' Prior We are now ready to make the connection between CNML and the Bayes-improper Jeffreys' approach:

Theorem 11.3 Let Θ represent an ineccsi exponential family. Fix some $n_0 < n$ and some $\mathbf{x}_0 \in \mathcal{X}^{n_0}$. Then $\bar{P}_{\mathrm{Cnml\text{-}1}}(\cdot \mid \mathbf{x}_0)$, $\bar{P}_{\mathrm{Cnml\text{-}2}}(\cdot \mid \mathbf{x}_0)$ and $\bar{P}_{\mathrm{Jeffreys}}(\cdot \mid \mathbf{x}_0)$, the Bayesian universal model based on Jeffreys' prior, are well defined, and for every ineccsi subset Θ_0 of Θ, uniformly for all Θ_0-sequences $\mathbf{x}_1$, we have

$$-\ln \bar{P}_{\mathrm{Cnml\text{-}2}}(\mathbf{x}_1 \mid \mathbf{x}_0) =$$
$$-\ln \bar{P}_{\mathrm{Cnml\text{-}1}}(\mathbf{x}_1 \mid \mathbf{x}_0) + o(1) = -\ln \bar{P}_{\mathrm{Jeffreys}}(\mathbf{x}_1 \mid \mathbf{x}_0) + o(1) =$$
$$-\ln P_{\hat{\theta}(\mathbf{x}_1)}(\mathbf{x}_0 \mathbf{x}_1) + \frac{k}{2} \ln \frac{n_1}{2\pi} + \ln \int \sqrt{\det I(\theta)} P_\theta(\mathbf{x}_0) d\theta + o(1) =$$
$$-\ln P_{\hat{\theta}(\mathbf{x}_0 \mathbf{x}_1)}(\mathbf{x}_0 \mathbf{x}_1) + \frac{k}{2} \ln \frac{n}{2\pi} + \ln \int \sqrt{\det I(\theta)} P_\theta(\mathbf{x}_0) d\theta + o(1). \tag{11.47}$$

Proof: All equations of the theorem are immediate corollaries of the corresponding equations of Theorem 11.2, using the luckiness function $a(\theta) = -\ln P_\theta(\mathbf{x}_0)$. In the last equation we replaced n_1 by n. Since $n_1 = n - n_0$, and n_0 does not change with n, this changes the result only by $o(1)$. $\square$

Caveat The theorem above is an analogue of Theorem 7.1 and Theorem 11.2 for conditional NML. Just like those theorems, it is only defined for ineccsi models. For the reasons discussed under Theorem 11.2, the theorem is rather weak. It would be desirable to have a version of of the theorem that holds for nonineccsi Θ. It is presently not clear to me how to prove this, or indeed, whether it even holds.

Example 11.11 [The Normal Location Family] This example mirrors Example 11.9, in which we showed that with a normal prior, $\bar{f}_{\text{Bayes}}$ can be evaluated explicitly for the normal location model, and coincides exactly with $\bar{f}_{\text{Lnml-2}}$ with a corresponding luckiness function. Here, we show that with Jeffreys' prior, $\bar{f}_{\text{Jeffreys}}(\mathbf{x}_1 \mid \mathbf{x}_0)$ can also be evaluated explicitly for the normal location family, and is precisely equivalent to the conditional NML-2 density $\bar{f}_{\text{Cnml-2}}(\mathbf{x}_1 \mid \mathbf{x}_0)$. Here $\mathbf{x}_0 = (x_1)$ consists of the first observation only. First note that by (11.32), Jeffreys' posterior $w_{\text{Jeffreys}}(\mu \mid x_1)$ is normal with mean x_1 and variance σ^2. By (11.34) it follows that $\bar{f}_{\text{Jeffreys}}(\mathbf{x}_1 \mid \mathbf{x}_0) = \bar{f}_{\text{Bayes}}(\mathbf{x}_1)$, where $\bar{f}_{\text{Bayes}}$ is the marginal distribution of $\mathbf{x}_1 = (x_2, \ldots, x_n)^\top$ relative to Jeffreys' posterior $w_{\text{Jeffreys}}(\mu \mid x_1)$, which we now use as prior. We have

$$
\begin{aligned}
&\text{REG}_{\ln}(\bar{f}_{\text{Jeffreys}}(\cdot \mid \mathbf{x}_0), \mathcal{M}_{\text{loc}}, \mathbf{x}) = \\
&- \ln \bar{f}_{\text{Jeffreys}}(\mathbf{x}_1 \mid \mathbf{x}_0) + \ln f_{\hat{\mu}(\mathbf{x})}(\mathbf{x}) = \\
&\quad - \ln \bar{f}_{\text{Jeffreys}}(\mathbf{x}_1 \mid \mathbf{x}_0) - [-\ln f_{\hat{\mu}(\mathbf{x})}(\mathbf{x}_1) + a(\hat{\mu}(\mathbf{x})) + \ln \sqrt{2\pi\sigma^2}], \quad (11.48)
\end{aligned}
$$

where $a(\mu) = (\mu - x_1)^2/(2\sigma^2)$. From (11.30) we then see that

$$
\begin{aligned}
\text{REG}_{\ln}(\bar{f}_{\text{Jeffreys}}(\cdot \mid \mathbf{x}_0), \mathcal{M}_{\text{loc}}, \mathbf{x}) &= \text{LREG}_a(\bar{f}_{\text{Bayes}}(\cdot), \mathcal{M}_{\text{loc}}, \mathbf{x}_1) - \ln \sqrt{2\pi\sigma^2} = \\
&\frac{1}{2} \ln \frac{n}{2\pi\sigma^2}. \quad (11.49)
\end{aligned}
$$

The regret does not depend on $\mathbf{x}_1$, and is therefore constant for all $\mathbf{x}_1 \in \mathbb{R}^{n-1}$. Reasoning as in the box on page 182, Chapter 6, Section 6.2.1, it follows that $\bar{f}_{\text{Jeffreys}}(\cdot \mid \mathbf{x}_0)$ achieves the minimax luckiness regret over all $\mathbf{x}_1 \in \mathbb{R}^{n-1}$, relative to the normal location family. It follows that $\bar{f}_{\text{Jeffreys}}$ is equivalent to $\bar{f}_{\text{Cnml-2}}$.

Finally, let us compare (11.49) with the asymptotic formula (11.47) appearing in Theorem 11.3. By (11.38), $\ln \int f_\mu(\mathbf{x}_0) \sqrt{\det I(\mu)} d\mu = \sigma^{-1}$. Plugging this into (11.47), we see that it precisely coincides with (11.49). Thus, for the normal location family, the asymptotics of (the last line of) Theorem 11.3 hold for all sample sizes, and not just asymptotically. It turns out that the same holds for general linear regression models; see Chapter 12, Section 12.4.3.

11.4.3 Liang and Barron's Approach

Liang and Barron (2002, 2004, 2005) were probably the first to use conditional universal codes in an MDL context. In contrast to the CNML approach, their codes are optimized to achieve minimax conditional *expected* redundancy rather than individual sequence regret. At least in the cases we consider here, Liang and Barron's codes also achieve minimax expected regret (Liang and Barron 2005). Thus, the crucial difference to CNML methods lies in the use of stochastic rather than individual-sequence universal codes.

Formally, let $\mathcal{M} = \{P_\theta \mid \theta \in \Theta\}$ be some parametric family. Fix some n and $n_0 < n$. We define the *Liang-Barron universal model* $\bar{P}_{\text{LB}}$ as the universal model that achieves the minimax conditional expected redundancy relative to Θ. That is, $\bar{P}_{\text{LB}}^{(n)}$ is the distribution achieving

$$\min_{\bar{P}^{(n)}} \max_{\theta \in \Theta} E_{\mathbf{x}_0, \mathbf{x}_1 \sim P_\theta}[-\ln \bar{P}^{(n)}(\mathbf{x}_1 \mid \mathbf{x}_0) - [-\ln P_\theta(\mathbf{x}_1 \mid \mathbf{x}_0)]], \tag{11.50}$$

whenever such a distribution exists. Here $\mathbf{x}_0 = (X_1, \ldots, X_{n_0})$ and $\mathbf{x}_1 = (X_{n_0+1}, \ldots, X_n)$ are to be understood as random variables when inside the expectation operator. For the i.i.d. models we consider in this chapter, $P_\theta(\mathbf{x}_1 \mid \mathbf{x}_0)$ simplifies and is equal to $P_\theta(\mathbf{x}_1)$.

Liang and Barron (2004) show that for certain parametric families, the distribution achieving (11.50) can be expressed as a Bayesian marginal distribution $\bar{f}_{\text{Bayes}}$ with respect to an improper prior, and they identify this prior. The prior does not depend on n, so that the sequence $\bar{P}_{\text{LB}}^{(1)}, \bar{P}_{\text{LB}}^{(2)}, \ldots$ defines a probabilistic source, and $\bar{P}_{\text{LB}}$ is prequential. The families for which this holds include Gaussian, but also non-Gaussian, location and scale families, as well as linear regression models. For some other families, Liang and Barron (2004) show that (11.50) is achieved for a Bayesian marginal distribution as long as the set of distributions over which the minimum is taken is restricted to the set of "invariant" measures.[1] The families for which Liang and Barron prove their results include both some (but certainly not all) exponential families, and some nonexponential families such as the family of uniform distributions.

Liang-Barron vs. Bayes-Jeffreys It so happens that for the normal location family, and more generally, for the linear regression model with fixed variance, the Liang-Barron approach prescribes the use of Jeffreys' prior: the

---

1. The meaning of "invariant" depends on the family under consideration; for details see (Liang and Barron 2004).

universal code achieving (11.50) is the Bayesian code defined relative to Jeffreys' prior. As we already noted, the corresponding universal code coincides with the conditional NML-2 distribution. Therefore, in this case, the Bayes-Jeffreys, Liang-Barron, and conditional NML-2 approaches all coincide. For the normal family with fixed mean and varying variance, the prior such that $\bar{f}_{\text{Bayes}}$ achieves (11.50) also corresponds with Jeffreys' prior. However, if we consider the full normal family with both μ and σ varying, then the Liang-Barron prior is not equal to Jeffreys' prior, so that the approach becomes essentially different from the Bayes-Jeffreys/CNML approaches:

Example 11.12 [Bayes-Jeffreys and Liang-Barron for the Full Normal Family] From the box on page 300, we see that for the full normal family, Jeffreys' prior is improper and given by $w_{\text{Jeffreys}}(\mu, \sigma) \propto \sigma^{-2}$. On the other hand, Liang and Barron (2004) show that relative to this model, (11.50) is achieved for the distribution $\bar{P}_{\text{LB}}$ with density $\bar{f}_{\text{Bayes}}$ defined relative to the *scale-invariant* prior $w(\mu, \sigma) = \sigma^{-1}$. This makes the approaches inherently different: as a very special case of (12.68) and (12.71), Chapter 12, we find that

$$- \ln \bar{f}_{\text{Jeffreys}}(\mathbf{x}1 \mid \mathbf{x}_0) =$$
$$g(n, n_0) + \frac{n}{2} \ln \sum_{i=1}^{n} (x_i - \hat{\mu})^2 - \frac{n_0}{2} \ln \sum_{i=1}^{n_0} (x_i - \hat{\mu}_0)^2 + \ln \frac{\Gamma(\frac{n_0}{2})}{\Gamma(\frac{n}{2})}. \quad (11.51)$$

$$- \ln \bar{f}_{\text{LB}}(\mathbf{x}1 \mid \mathbf{x}_0) =$$
$$g(n, n_0) + \frac{n-2}{2} \ln \sum_{i=1}^{n} (x_i - \hat{\mu})^2 - \frac{n_0 - 2}{2} \ln \sum_{i=1}^{n_0} (x_i - \hat{\mu}_0)^2 + \ln \frac{\Gamma(\frac{n_0 - 2}{2})}{\Gamma(\frac{n-2}{2})}. \quad (11.52)$$

Here $g(n, n_0) = \frac{n - n_0}{2} \ln \pi + \frac{1}{2} \ln \frac{n}{n_0}$, $\hat{\mu}_0$ is the average of $\mathbf{x}_0$, and Γ is the gamma function (Chapter 2). It is clear that the distributions are different.

In Chapter 12 we also compute the regret of $\bar{f}_{\text{Jeffreys}}$. From (12.77) we see that it is given by

$$- \frac{n_0}{2} \ln \pi - \frac{n_0}{2} \ln \sum_{i=1}^{n_0} (x_i - \hat{\mu}_0)^2 + \frac{n}{2} \ln \frac{n}{2} - \frac{n}{2} + \frac{1}{2} \ln \frac{n}{n_0} + \ln \Gamma(\frac{n_0}{2}) - \ln \Gamma(\frac{n}{2}).$$

Thus, the regret of $\bar{f}_{\text{Jeffreys}}$ only depends on $\mathbf{x}_0$ and not on $\mathbf{x}_1$. Analogously to the reasoning in Example 11.11, it follows that $\bar{f}_{\text{Jeffreys}}$ is equal to $\bar{f}_{\text{Cnml-2}}$. In contrast, the regret of $\bar{f}_{\text{LB}}$ also depends on $\mathbf{x}_1$, so that it is not equal to $\bar{f}_{\text{Cnml-2}}$, and does not achieve the minimax regret (11.39).

The example raises the question of what to prefer in a model selection context: the Liang-Barron or the CNML-1/2 approaches? From an individual-sequence point of view — we want to be as close to the best distribution as possible, no matter what happens — we are naturally led to CNML-1 or CNML-2. From an expectation point of view — we want to be as close to the best distribution as possible, if data are distributed according to one of these distributions — we are naturally led to the Liang-Barron approach. If Θ is restricted to an ineccsi set Θ_0, then, as was shown in Chapter 8, Section 8.2, both the expectation and the individual sequence approaches asymptotically lead to the same regrets and similar minimax optimal universal codes. *Apparently, if we condition on initial data, the two approaches become mildly but essentially distinct.* To find the "best" approach, we may look at other motivations for using minimax optimal redundancy/regret codes in MDL learning. In Chapter 15, Section 15.2.3, we show that codes with minimax conditional expected redundancy have very good frequentist behavior: they can be used to learn a good approximation of the true distribution as fast as possible, in the worst case, if goodness is measured in terms of Kullback-Leibler divergence. This analysis immediately suggests the Liang-Barron approach as the best one can do. But if one takes the philosophical viewpoint of Rissanen (Chapter 1, Chapter 17), then there is no such thing as "a distribution generating the data" and we should be prepared for anything to happen; from that point of view, the CNML approaches seem preferable.

It could be that CNML-3 provides the best of both worlds; but it may also be the case that, in contrast to the case with ineccsi parameter sets, there is a mild but inherent conflict here between individual sequence and expected universality, so that no solution exists that is asymptotically optimal from both points of view.

> This parallels a discussion in Bayesian statistics. Jeffreys (1961) only advocated the prior that bears his name for 1-parameter models (so perhaps our phrase "Bayes-Jeffreys approach" is somewhat unfair). For the full normal family, he advocated the location-scale-invariant prior $w(\mu, \sigma) = \sigma^{-1}$, for he found the "Jeffreys' prior" $w_{\text{Jeffreys}}(\mu, \sigma) = \sigma^{-2}$ to have several undesirable properties. See Bernardo and Smith (1994), a Bayesian textbook advocating σ^{-2}, and (Gelman, Carlin, Stern, and Rubin 2003), a Bayesian textbook advocating σ^{-1}. The present development suggests that perhaps the situations in which Jeffreys' prior is problematic are not so much the multiparameter families, but rather the families where it becomes improper.

A pragmatic solution is to make a new universal code which, at a worst-case cost of 1 bit of additional regret, gives the best of both worlds: we first encode, using 1 bit, whether the data will be encoded using the Liang-Barron or the CNML-2 method. We then encode the data using whatever method gives the shortest codelength.

Summary and Discussion of Conditional Approaches   The approach based on conditional NML seems quite widely applicable. By conditioning on the first few examples it achieves conditional codes with optimal minimax regret. This goes halfway toward solving the infinity problem: on the good side, we have found a new notion of minimax regret that (in contrast to the standard notion) is finite for most parametric families, and is achieved by some (conditional) universal code. In contrast to the luckiness approach, the region of the parameter space in which we have small regret is determined by the data itself, so in this sense, there is no arbitrariness in the choice.

On the other hand, there remain two problems: first, as we have seen, there is a discrepancy between the Liang-Barron and the CNML approaches. Second, there is a problem which is inherent to both approaches: in general, the results one obtains depend on the order of the data. For i.i.d. models, the data really are unordered, so this is a strange (and probably undesirable) property: it is not clear on which points one should condition, and different points will give different results.[2] The problem is illustrated by the following example:

Example 11.13 [Permutation (In-) Variance] If data are i.i.d., and we use the conditional NML or the Liang-Barron approach, it is unclear whether we should condition our universal model on the first n_0 examples, or the last n_0 examples, or any other subset of n_0 examples. For the normal location family, where $n_0 = 1$, this does not matter: according to all versions of CNML, $\bar{f}_{\text{Jeffreys}}$, and $\bar{f}_{\text{LB}}$, the conditional codelength of $\mathbf{x}_1$ given $\mathbf{x}_0$ *is invariant under permutations of* x^n. Namely, by (12.64) of Section 12.3.2, Chapter 12, this length is given by

$$- \ln \bar{f}_{\text{Jeffreys}}(\mathbf{x}_1 \mid \mathbf{x}_0) = \frac{1}{2} \ln n + \frac{n-1}{2} \ln 2\pi\sigma^2 + \frac{1}{2\sigma^2} \sum_{i=1}^{n}(x_i - \hat{\mu})^2,$$

which clearly is not dependent on the order of the x_i. Unfortunately, this property does not generalize to arbitrary i.i.d. exponential families; for example, from (11.51) we immediately see that it does not hold for the full

---

2. In some cases we can avoid this problem by choosing the points on which to condition at random; see Section 14.4.3, Chapter 14.

normal family, with varying σ^2. Unlike the other properties of the normal location family discussed in this chapter, it does not even generalize to the linear regression model, for which the codelength does depend on how the sample is divided up into x_0 and x_1, as can be seen from (12.64).

11.5 Summary and Remarks

We gave a detailed discussion of metauniversal codes, luckiness NML codes, and conditional NML codes. To the best of our knowledge, this covers all serious attempts to deal with the infinity problem, with one exception: *Foster's and Stine's (2001) approach.* Briefly, Foster and Stine (2001) also consider the possibility of restricting the parameter values rather than the data, just as we did in Section 11.2.1. They then develop a general framework for comparing universal codes for models with undefined $\mathrm{COMP}^{(n)}(\Theta)$ relative to some given class of "experts." Once such a class of experts is given, a uniquely optimal universal code relative to the experts can be defined. This approach is similar, but not quite the same as luckiness NML. It may be interesting to compare the two approaches in more detail.

11.A Appendix: Proof of Theorem 11.4

Below we actually prove something more general than Theorem 11.1. For this, we first extend the notions of maximum regret, $\mathrm{REG}_{\mathrm{max}}$, and minimax regret, $\mathrm{REG}_{\mathrm{min\,max}}$, with an extra argument. Let $\mathcal{M}$ be a k-parameter exponential family and let (Θ, P_θ) be a diffeomorphic parameterization of $\mathcal{M}$. Let Θ_0, Θ_1 be subsets of Θ. We define

$$\mathrm{REG}_{\mathrm{max}}^{(n)}(\bar{P}, \Theta_0, \Theta_1) := \sup_{x^n\,:\,\hat{\theta}(x^n)\in\Theta_1} \left\{ -\ln \bar{P}(x^n) - \inf_{\theta\in\Theta_0} [-\ln P_\theta(x^n)] \right\}.$$

$$(11.53)$$

$$\mathrm{REG}_{\mathrm{min\,max}}^{(n)}(\Theta_0, \Theta_1) :=$$

$$\inf_{\bar{P}\in\mathcal{P}^{(n)}} \sup_{x^n\,:\,\hat{\theta}(x^n)\in\Theta_1} \left\{ -\ln \bar{P}(x^n) - \inf_{\theta\in\Theta_0} [-\ln P_\theta(x^n)] \right\}, \quad (11.54)$$

where $\mathcal{P}^{(n)}$ is the set of all distributions on $\mathcal{X}^n$. Note that, if Θ_0 is a closed ineccsi subset of Θ_1, with $\Theta_1 \subseteq \Theta$, then

$$\mathrm{COMP}^{(n)}(\Theta_0) =$$

$$\mathrm{REG}^{(n)}_{\min\max}(\Theta_0) \geq \mathrm{REG}^{(n)}_{\min\max}(\Theta_0, \Theta) \geq \mathrm{REG}^{(n)}_{\min\max}(\Theta_0, \Theta_0) =$$

$$\mathrm{CCOMP}^{(n)}(\Theta_0). \quad (11.55)$$

The superscript (n) will be omitted when clear from the context. We now make some further useful preliminary observations. If Θ_0 is any proper subset of Θ_0' and Θ_1 is any proper subset of Θ_1', then for all P,

$$\mathrm{REG}^{(n)}_{\max}(P, \Theta_0, \Theta_1) \;\leq\; \mathrm{REG}^{(n)}_{\max}(P, \Theta_0, \Theta_1') \qquad\qquad (11.56)$$

$$\mathrm{REG}^{(n)}_{\max}(P, \Theta_0, \Theta_1) \;\leq\; \mathrm{REG}^{(n)}_{\max}(P, \Theta_0', \Theta_1). \qquad\qquad (11.57)$$

Note also that

$$\mathrm{REG}^{(n)}_{\max}(P, \Theta_0, \Theta) \leq \mathrm{REG}^{(n)}_{\max}(P, \Theta_0). \qquad\qquad (11.58)$$

It is not a priori obvious whether we also have equality in (11.58), since there may be x^n such that $\hat{\theta}(x^n)$ is undefined. These can influence $\mathrm{REG}^{(n)}_{\max}(P, \Theta_0)$ but are not taken into consideration in $\mathrm{REG}^{(n)}_{\max}(P, \Theta_0, \Theta)$. The following theorem says that for exponential families, this cannot happen for the minimax optimal P: we asymptotically have equality in (11.58) and, more interestingly, also in (11.55).

Theorem 11.4 Let Θ be as above and let Θ_0 be any *ineccsi* subset of Θ. Then we have:

$$\mathrm{REG}^{(n)}_{\min\max}(\Theta_0) =$$

$$\mathrm{REG}^{(n)}_{\min\max}(\Theta_0, \Theta) + o(1) = \mathrm{REG}^{(n)}_{\min\max}(\Theta_0, \Theta_0) + o(1) =$$

$$\frac{k}{2}\ln\frac{n}{2\pi} + \ln\int_{\Theta_0}\sqrt{\det I(\theta)}d\theta + o(1). \quad (11.59)$$

The proof of Theorem 11.4 follows almost directly from the following lemma, which is interesting in its own right, and which we prove first. In the statement and proof of the lemma, we use the notation $\Theta_0^{[+\epsilon]}$ and $\Theta_0^{[-\epsilon]}$, introduced in the beginning of the proofs of Chapter 8, page 248.

Let $\mathcal{M}$ be a k-parameter exponential family with parameter set $\Theta = \Theta_{\mathcal{M}}$, such that the parameterization (Θ, P_θ) is smooth and 1-to-1. Let Θ_0 be an ineccsi subset of Θ. Define

$$w_{n,\text{Jef}+}(\theta) := \frac{\sqrt{\det I(\theta)}}{\int_{\Theta_0^{[+n^{-1/4}]}} \sqrt{\det I(\theta)}d\theta}$$

to be Jeffreys' prior restricted to domain $\Theta_0^{[+n^{-1/4}]}$, and let

$$\bar{P}_{n,\text{Jef}+}(x^n) := \int_{\Theta_0^{[+n^{-1/4}]}} P(x^n \mid \theta)w_{n,\text{Jef}+}(\theta)d\theta$$

be the Bayesian marginal distribution on $\mathcal{X}^n$ relative to this restricted Jeffreys' prior.

Lemma 11.1 We have (a), uniformly for all x^n with $\hat{\theta}(x^n) \in \Theta_0^{[+0.5n^{-1/4}]}$,

$$\text{REG}_{\text{ln}}^{(n)}(\bar{P}_{n,\text{Jef}+}, \Theta_0^{[+0.5n^{-1/4}]}, x^n) =$$
$$\text{REG}_{\max}(\bar{P}_{n,\text{Jef}+}, \Theta_0^{[+0.5n^{-1/4}]}, \Theta_0^{[+0.5n^{-1/4}]}) + o(1) =$$
$$\text{REG}_{\max}(\bar{P}_{n,\text{Jef}+}, \Theta_0, \Theta_0) + o(1) =$$
$$\frac{k}{2}\ln\frac{n}{2\pi} + \ln\int_{\Theta_0}\sqrt{\det I(\theta)}d\theta + o(1). \quad (11.60)$$

Further, (b),

$$\text{REG}_{\min\max}^{(n)}(\Theta_0, \Theta_0) = \frac{k}{2}\ln\frac{n}{2\pi} + \ln\int_{\Theta_0}\sqrt{\det I(\theta)}d\theta + o(1) \quad (11.61)$$

and (c),

$$\text{REG}_{\max}(\bar{P}_{n,\text{Jef}+}, \Theta_0) = \frac{k}{2}\ln\frac{n}{2\pi} + \ln\int_{\Theta_0}\sqrt{\det I(\theta)}d\theta + o(1). \quad (11.62)$$

We remark that part (a) does *not* hold if we replace the modified Jeffreys' prior by the ordinary Jeffreys' prior, or by its restriction to $\Theta_0^{[+0.5n^{-1/4}]}$. The reason is that then, in the second and third equation respectively, the boundary of the support of the prior coincides with the boundary of the set of ML estimators that we allow, which results in larger regret for x^n with $\hat{\theta}(x^n)$ very close $(O(n^{-1/2}))$ to this boundary.

Proof:
Part (a) The result follows immediately from Theorem 8.4, applied with $\alpha = 1/4$. To see that the leftmost expression is equal to the rightmost expression, apply the theorem with w_n equal to $w_{n,\text{Jef}+}$, the prior used to define $\bar{P}_{n,\text{Jef}+}$. To see that the rightmost equality holds, apply the theorem with w equal to Jeffreys' prior, restricted to Θ_0, and consider x^n with $\hat{\theta}(x^n) \in \Theta_0$.

Part (b)   If the result holds at all, it must hold for any diffeomorphic parameterization. Therefore, it is sufficient if we prove the result for the mean-value parameterization. For this, note first that

$$\bar{P}_{n,\text{Jef}^+}(\hat{\theta}(x^n) \notin \Theta_0) \le$$

$$\bar{P}_{n,\text{Jef}^+}(\theta \in \Theta_0^{[-n^{-1/4}]}) \max_{\theta \in \Theta_0^{[-n^{-1/4}]}} P_\theta(\hat{\theta}(x^n) \notin \Theta_0)+$$

$$\bar{P}_{n,\text{Jef}^+}(\theta \in \Theta_0^{[+n^{-1/4}]} \setminus \Theta_0^{[-n^{-1/4}]}) \max_{\theta \in \Theta_0^{[+n^{-1/4}]}\setminus\Theta_0^{[-n^{-1/4}]}} P_\theta(\hat{\theta}(x^n) \notin \Theta_0) \le$$

$$1 \cdot \max_{\theta \in \Theta_0^{[-n^{-1/4}]}} P_\theta(\|\hat{\theta}(x^n)-\theta\|^2 > n^{-1/2}) + \int_{\Theta_0^{[+n^{-1/4}]}\setminus\Theta_0^{[-n^{-1/4}]}} w_{n,\text{Jef}^+}(\theta)d\theta \cdot 1$$

$$\le \max_{\theta \in \Theta_0^{[-n^{-1/4}]}} \frac{\text{var}_\theta[\phi(X)]}{n^{1/2}} + \frac{\int_{\Theta_0^{[+n^{-1/4}]}\setminus\Theta_0^{[-n^{-1/4}]}} \sqrt{\det(I(\theta))}d\theta}{\int_{\Theta_0^{[-n^{-1/4}]}} \sqrt{\det(I(\theta))}d\theta} = o(1),$$

$$(11.63)$$

where in the final step we used Markov's inequality (Chapter 2). Now define, for x^n with $\hat{\theta}(x^n) \in \Theta_0$,

$$\bar{Q}^{(n)}(x^n) := \bar{P}_{n,\text{Jef}^+}(x^n \mid \hat{\theta}(x^n) \in \Theta_0) = \frac{\bar{P}_{n,\text{Jef}^+}(x^n)}{\bar{P}_{n,\text{Jef}^+}(\hat{\theta} \in \Theta_0)}.$$

$\bar{Q}^{(n)}$ is the Bayesian marginal distribution on $\mathcal{X}^n$ relative to Jeffreys' prior w_{n,Jef^+} restricted to domain $\Theta_0^{[+n^{-1/4}]}$, *conditioned* on the ML estimator lying in Θ_0. By the previous equation, the denominator in the definition converges to 1 so that, uniformly for x^n with $\hat{\theta}(x^n) \in \Theta_0$,

$$-\ln \bar{Q}^{(n)}(x^n) = -\ln \bar{P}_{n,\text{Jef}^+}(x^n) + \ln(1-o(1)) = -\ln \bar{P}_{n,\text{Jef}^+}(x^n) + o(1).$$

Combining this with part (a), we find that, *uniformly* for all x^n with $\hat{\theta}(x^n) \in \Theta_0$,

$$\text{REG}_{\ln}(\bar{Q}^{(n)}, \Theta_0, x^n) = \frac{k}{2} \ln \frac{n}{2\pi} + \ln \int_{\Theta_0} \sqrt{\det I(\theta)}d\theta + o(1). \quad (11.64)$$

Thus we must have

$$\text{REG}^{(n)}_{\text{min max}}(\Theta_0, \Theta_0) \le \text{REG}^{(n)}_{\text{max}}(\bar{Q}^{(n)}, \Theta_0, \Theta_0) =$$

$$\frac{k}{2} \ln \frac{n}{2\pi} + \ln \int_{\Theta_0} \sqrt{\det I(\theta)}d\theta + o(1). \quad (11.65)$$

For the reverse inequality, let P be an arbitrary distribution on the set $\{x^n : \hat{\theta}(x^n) \in \Theta_0\}$. Since $\bar{Q}^{(n)}$ is a distribution with $\bar{Q}^{(n)}(\hat{\theta}(x^n) \in \Theta_0) = 1$, we must have $P(x^n) \leq \bar{Q}^{(n)}(x^n)$ for at least one sequence x^n. Since (11.64) holds uniformly on this set, it follows

$$\text{REG}_{\max}^{(n)}(P, \Theta_0) \geq \text{REG}_{\max}^{(n)}(\bar{Q}^{(n)}, \Theta_0) - o(1),$$

so that the reverse inequality of (11.65) holds as well.

Part (c)   Without loss of generality, we can assume Θ and Θ_0 to represent the mean-value parameterization: for suppose they represent some other smooth 1-to-1 parameterization, then we map Θ and Θ_0 to their corresponding mean-value sets Θ_μ and $\Theta_{0,\mu}$. Then $\Theta_{0,\mu}$ will still be an ineccsi subset of Θ_μ, and by Proposition 7.1, we must have $\int_{\Theta_0} \sqrt{I(\theta)}d\theta = \int_{\Theta_{0,\mu}} \sqrt{I_\mu(\mu)}d\mu$, where I_μ represents Fisher information with respect to the mean-value parameterization. Thus, if the theorem holds for Θ_μ and $\Theta_{\mu,0}$, it must also hold for Θ and Θ_0.

Assume thus that Θ represents the mean-value parameterization. Since

$$\text{REG}_{\max}(\bar{P}_{n,\text{Jef}^+}, \Theta_0) \geq \text{REG}_{\max}(\bar{P}_{n,\text{Jef}^+}, \Theta_0, \Theta_0)$$

it follows from part (b) that

$$\text{REG}_{\max}(\bar{P}_{n,\text{Jef}^+}, \Theta_0) \geq \frac{k}{2} \ln \frac{n}{2\pi} + \ln \int_{\Theta_0} \sqrt{\det I(\theta)}d\theta + o(1).$$

To show the reverse inequality, we first look at x^n with $\hat{\mu}(x^n) \in \Theta_0^{[+0.5n^{-1/4}]}$. We have by (11.57),

$$\text{REG}_{\max}(\bar{P}_{n,\text{Jef}^+}, \Theta_0, \Theta_0^{[+0.5n^{-1/4}]}) \leq$$
$$\text{REG}_{\max}(\bar{P}_{n,\text{Jef}^+}, \Theta_0^{[+0.5n^{-1/4}]}, \Theta_0^{[+0.5n^{-1/4}]}) =$$
$$\frac{k}{2} \ln \frac{n}{2\pi} + \ln \int_{\Theta_0} \sqrt{\det I(\theta)}d\theta + o(1), \quad (11.66)$$

where the equality follows from part (a).

Let $t := t(x^n) := n^{-1} \sum_{i=1}^{n} \phi(x_i)$ be the average of the observed sufficient statistics. (If $t \in \Theta$, then $t = \hat{\mu}(x^n)$; but it may be that $t \notin \Theta$.) We now consider x^n with $t(x^n) \notin \Theta_0^{[+0.5n^{-1/4}]}$. By Lemma 8.1, page 253, on such x^n, $\bar{P}_{n,\text{Jef}^+}$ achieves regret ≤ 0 for large enough n. $\square$

We are now ready to prove Theorem 11.4:

Proof: We have

$$\text{REG}^{(n)}_{\min\max}(\Theta_0) \geq \text{REG}^{(n)}_{\min\max}(\Theta_0, \Theta) \geq \text{REG}^{(n)}_{\min\max}(\Theta_0, \Theta_0), \qquad (11.67)$$

and, by Lemma 11.1, part (a), we must have

$$\text{REG}^{(n)}_{\min\max}(\Theta_0, \Theta_0) \geq \frac{k}{2}\ln\frac{n}{2\pi} + \ln\int_{\Theta_0}\sqrt{\det I(\theta)}d\theta + o(1), \qquad (11.68)$$

so that it is sufficient to show

$$\text{REG}^{(n)}_{\min\max}(\Theta_0) \leq \frac{k}{2}\ln\frac{n}{2\pi} + \ln\int_{\Theta_0}\sqrt{\det I(\theta)}d\theta + o(1). \qquad (11.69)$$

To see that (11.69) holds, note that we must have, for all n, $\text{REG}^{(n)}_{\min\max}(\Theta_0) \leq$ $\text{REG}^{(n)}_{\max}(\bar{P}^{(n)}, \Theta_0)$ for any sequence of distributions $\bar{P}^{(1)}, \bar{P}^{(2)}, \ldots$. In particular this holds for the sequence of modified Jeffreys' marginal distributions defined in Lemma 11.1. The result now follows by that lemma, part (c). $\square$

12 *Linear Regression*

In this chapter we introduce universal codes for linear regression settings. The corresponding models are special cases of what is called the *linear model* in statistics. The goal is twofold: first, we want to prepare for the use of MDL in linear regression problems in Chapter 14, Section 14.5. This is one of the most well studied applications of MDL. The second goal is to illustrate some of the ideas introduced in Chapter 11, such as the luckiness NML (LNML) and the conditional NML (CNML) universal codes. Linear regression models lead to nontrivial, practically useful, yet mathematically remarkably clean examples of such codes.

Fast Track For a first introduction to MDL, this chapter may be skipped altogether, although readers may be interested in reading the "prelude," Section 12.1.1. Using the simple special case of the normal location family as an example, this section makes clear why the linear model really has a special status in universal coding. Also of interest may be the boxes in Section 12.4, which show that, for linear regression, Bayesian and normalized maximum likelihood methods *coincide*.

Overview In Section 12.2 we study least-squares estimation without any probabilistic interpretation. Section 12.3 discusses the basic linear model, a probabilistic model in which the maximum likelihood estimator always coincides with the least-squares estimator. In Section 12.3.1 we treat the linear model in a Bayesian way, by equipping it with a prior distribution. Section 12.4 then defines Bayesian and NML universal models for linear regression.

   Much of the material in this chapter has been known for a long time. Least-squares estimation was pioneered by Carl Friedrich Gauss in the early 1800s

(Gauss 1957), and Bayesian treatments of the linear model were already well established when the key reference (Lindley and Smith 1972) appeared. Our development of this material has been tailored to prepare for the last section, Section 12.4, where we discuss Bayesian and NML universal codes for regression. This is the only section containing recent results.

12.1   Introduction

Regression   In regression problems we are interested in learning how the values $y_1, \ldots, y_n$ of a *regression* variable Y depend on the values $u_1, \ldots, u_n$ of the *regressor* vector U. Sometimes the u_i are called *feature vectors* or *input vectors*, and the y_i are called *outputs*.

We assume or hope that there exists some function $h : \mathcal{U} \rightarrow \mathcal{Y}$ so that $h(U)$ predicts the value Y reasonably well, and we want to learn such an h from data. To this end, we assume a set of *candidate predictors* (functions) $\mathcal{H}$. For example, in Chapter 1, Example 1.4, we took $\mathcal{H}$ to be the set of all polynomials; but many other choices are possible as well. In this chapter, our aim is to design universal codes relative to such $\mathcal{H}$. To make this aim well defined, $\mathcal{H}$ needs to be transformed to a family of probabilistic sources rather than functions. If it is reasonable to assume Gaussian noise, we can do this in a straightforward manner: we take hypothesis h to express the *probabilistic* statement that

$$Y_i = h(U_i) + Z_i, \tag{12.1}$$

where the Z_i are i.i.d. Gaussian random variables with mean 0 and some variance σ^2, independent of U_i. Equation (12.1) implies that the conditional density of $y_1, \ldots, y_n$, given $u_1, \ldots, u_n$, is equal to the product of n Gaussian densities:

$$f_{\sigma,h}(y^n \mid u^n) = \left(\frac{1}{\sqrt{2\pi}\sigma} \right)^n \exp\left(-\frac{\sum_{i=1}^n (y_i - h(u_i))^2}{2\sigma^2} \right). \tag{12.2}$$

Note that the smaller the sum of squared errors achieved by h on (u^n, y^n), the larger the density of y^n given u^n according to $f_{\sigma,h}(\cdot \mid \cdot)$.

Linear Regression   In this chapter we restrict ourselves to settings where the functions h are linear combinations of a some set of "basis" functions. This is called *linear* regression. *Note that the basis functions themselves do not have to be linear!* For example, polynomial regression for polynomials of degree $k - 1$ (Chapter 2, box on page 64) is a special case of linear regression. Here $\mathcal{H} = \mathcal{H}^{(k)}$ consists of the set of functions $h_\mu(u) := \sum_{j=1}^{k} \mu_j u^{j-1}$ for $\mu = (\mu_1, \ldots, \mu_k) \in \mathbb{R}^k$. In other applications, the basis functions may for example be wavelets or trigonometric functions(Hanson and Fu 2005)..

The restriction to linear regression problems makes the treatment mathematically tractable. In our context, it even leads to remarkably clean examples of universal codes. One of the main reasons is that with linear models, the Kullback-Leibler (KL) divergence is a linear function of the squared Euclidean distance. The latter is both mathematically and intuitively easy to handle. Indeed, for some of the universal models we develop, the well known formula for regret, which normally only holds asymptotically, can be shown to hold for all finite sample sizes.

Least-Squares Estimation (Section 12.2) One can study linear regression in its own right, without making any probabilistic assumptions. Based on the set $\mathcal{H}$ and some data (u^n, y^n), one tries to learn a h_μ that describes the data well and/or leads to good predictions of new y-values, given new u-values. To measure the prediction quality or "fit" of a given h_μ, one needs to introduce an error measure or *loss function*. There are a variety of reasonable choices here. The most common choice is the *squared error*, under which the error hypothesis h_μ makes in predicting y_i given u_i, is given by $(y_i - h_\mu(u_i))^2$. The $\hat{\mu}$ that best fits the given data (u^n, y^n) is then the *least-squares estimator*, which minimizes the *sum of squared errors* $\sum_{i=1}^{n}(y_i - h_\mu(u_i))^2$. In Section 12.2 we study least-squares estimation in some detail. This serves as a preparation for the probabilistic treatment that we are really interested in.

Penalized Least-Squares It is often convenient to measure fit not directly in terms of the sum of squared errors, but rather as the sum of squared error plus an additional term, which depends on the distance between μ and some "base point" μ_0. μ_0 can be interpreted as summarizing previously observed data, and plays a fundamental role in avoiding overfitting. We discuss this "penalized" form of least-squares at the end of Section 12.2, in Section 12.2.3.

The Linear Model (Section 12.3) We can combine the Gaussian noise assumption, embedded in the probabilistic model (12.2), with the assumption that each $h \in \mathcal{H}$ is a linear combination of k basis functions. The result is a k-dimensional probabilistic model of a type known as the *linear model*. We discuss its main properties in Section 12.3.

Bayesian Linear Model Just as the section on least-squares estimation ended with a treatment of penalized least-squares, Section 12.3 ends with a treatment of the Bayesian linear model with Gaussian prior (Section 12.3.1). This Gaussian prior can be thought of as adding a form of penalization to the model, effectively decreasing the likelihood for distributions with means far from some "base" mean μ_0.

Universal Codes for Linear Regression (Section 12.4)   Here we consider Bayesian and NML universal codes for linear models. Neither the NML nor the Bayesian code with Jeffreys' prior are well defined for linear models, so we have to resort to LNML, CNML, or Bayesian codes with luckiness-tilted or improper Jeffreys' priors. Once we allow for this possibility, we find that we are really in a very pleasant situation: a particular luckiness NML approach precisely coincides with the corresponding Bayesian luckiness approach. The approaches are identical for all sample sizes, and not just asymptotically, as with other parametric families. Similarly, the conditional NML-2 approach precisely coincides with the Bayesian approach with the improper Jeffreys' prior. Again, the approaches are identical for all sample sizes.

Caveat   There exist many variations of linear regression: one can move beyond the squared error or the assumption of Gaussian noise; one can explicitly try to account for outliers, etc. The approach we present here is the simplest and mathematically the cleanest, but also the most unrealistic: Gaussian noise with variance independent of the u_i. We do not specifically advocate the use of the simple model we describe here; indeed, in data with outliers, it may perform quite poorly compared to other methods. The reason we present it in such detail is rather that (a) it provides a good starting point for exploring other, more sophisticated methods, and (b) its mathematical elegance leads to excellent examples of universal codes.

12.1.1   Prelude: The Normal Location Family

The normal location family (Example 11.1, page 298) is a very special case of a linear (regression) model. The remarkable properties of the linear regression models are often easiest to demonstrate using the normal location family, because it allows vector and matrix operations to be replaced by scalar operations.

The normal location family has several distinguishing features, nearly all of which generalize to the linear models. Three features which are particularly helpful in analyzing universal codes for this family are (1) the fact that the sum of n normally distributed random variables is itself normally distributed; (2), relatedly, the Fisher information is constant as a function of the parameter μ; and (3) the fact that the parameter μ and the data y play a symmetric role in the density $f_\mu(y) \propto \exp(-(y-\mu)^2/2\sigma^2)$: if they were interchanged, the formula would not change.

As a result of (2), the asymptotic expansions of the log-likelihood ratio and KL divergence that we performed in Chapter 4 are *exact*: they hold for all sample sizes, without any remainder terms. Indeed, the log-likelihood $-\ln f_\mu(y^n)$ is an affine (linear plus constant) function of $\sum_{i=1}^n (y_i - \mu)^2$ and the KL divergence between μ and μ' is equal to the rescaled Euclidean distance: $D(\mu\|\mu') = (\mu - \mu')^2/2\sigma^2$. Relatedly, Jeffreys' prior is uniform. This means that, everywhere in the space, distributions which are equally far in Euclidean distance are equally distinguishable (Chapter 7, Section 7.3; Chapter 8, Section 8.2). Distinguishability does not depend on the region of the space, so that the parameter space has no curvature, in terms of the "metric" induced by the KL divergence.

As a result of (3), the Bayesian marginal distribution, posterior and predictive distributions are all normally distributed, if the prior distribution is itself normal (Section 12.3.1). This has important consequences for Bayesian and NML universal codes: as we saw in Chapter 11, Example 11.9, the Bayesian luckiness code with squared luckiness function precisely, and not just asymptotically, coincides with the LNML-2 code with the same luckiness function. Similarly, the Bayesian code based on the improper prior precisely coincides with the CNML-2 code, and even with the asymptotic expansion for CNML codes given in Theorem 11.3 (see Example 11.11). As a consequence, the LNML-2 and CNML-2 codes constitute a probabilistic source, which is usually not the case for either NML, LNML, or CNML universal models.

All properties we mentioned here generalize to linear models, and will be encountered in the sections to follow. There is one more remarkable property of the normal location family which does *not* generalize: while for the normal location family, the conditional codelength achieved with the CNML-2 distribution $\bar{P}_{\text{Cnml-2}}(y_2, \ldots, y_n \mid y_1)$ remains invariant under permutations of $y_1, \ldots, y_n$ (Example 11.13), for general linear models it does not.

12.2   Least-Squares Estimation

We start with several definitions and notations. While perhaps burdensome now, this will be very helpful later on. Then, in Section 12.2.1 we describe the main concepts of least squares estimation, defined in terms of the basic definitions.

Let $y_1, \ldots, y_n$ be the realizations of the regression variables, and let $u_1, \ldots, u_n$ be the realizations of the regressor variables, which take values in some set $\mathcal{U}$. We fix some linear set of functions $\mathcal{H}^{(k)}$, defined in terms of k basis functions $h_1, \ldots, h_k$. We have $\mathcal{H}^{(k)} = \{h_\mu \mid \mu \in \mathbb{R}^k\}$, where $h_\mu : \mathcal{U} \to \mathbb{R}$ is defined as $h_\mu(u) := \sum_{j=1}^{k} \mu_j h_j(u)$, and $\mu = (\mu_1, \ldots, \mu_k)$.

Special Notation   We can represent the function h_μ by its associated parameter vector μ. Thus, we will henceforth refer to μ as a "hypothesis." It is extremely convenient to express the error of μ directly in terms of the values of $h_j(u_i)$, rather than in terms of u_i. For this, we define for each i,

$$
x_i := \begin{pmatrix} h_1(u_i) \\ \ldots \\ h_k(u_i) \end{pmatrix} \text{ and } \mathbf{X} := \begin{pmatrix} x_1^\top \\ \vdots \\ x_n^\top \end{pmatrix}. \tag{12.3}
$$

From now on, we will not refer to the u_i anymore in any of our equations: rather than $h_\mu(u_i)$ we write $x_i^\top \mu$, meaning the inner product of x_i and μ. Consequently, in this chapter (and in later chapters, when referring to regression) we use a notational convention that differs from the rest of this book: we use $\mathbf{X}$ to denote the matrix consisting of the x_i data. We also set $\mathbf{y} := (y_1, \ldots, y_n)^\top$.

The reason that we use boldface is that we normally use y and X to denote outcomes or random variables referring to a *single* observation. $\mathbf{y}$ and $\mathbf{X}$ refer to all n observations.

Design Matrix   Note that the so-called *design matrix* $\mathbf{X}$ has n rows and k columns. Whenever we refer to such a matrix in this book, we implicitly assume that $\mathbf{X}$ has *independent* columns (full rank), without mentioning this explicitly. The word "design" suggests that the u-values, and hence the x-values, are chosen at will by the experimenter. In practice, this is sometimes, but certainly not always the case. In many cases, the u_i, and hence the x_i, are best thought of as being independently generated by some distribution on $\mathcal{U}$, or $\mathcal{X}$, respectively. In yet other cases, the origin of the u- and x-values is completely unknown. The following analysis is applicable to all three situations.

Sum of Squared Errors   This fundamental quantity, denoted as $\mathrm{SSE}(\mu, \mathbf{y})$, is defined as

$$\mathrm{SSE}(\mu, \mathbf{y}) := \sum_{i=1}^{n}(y_i - \bar{y}_i)^2 = \|\mathbf{y} - \bar{\mathbf{y}}\|^2 = (\mathbf{y} - \bar{\mathbf{y}})^\top(\mathbf{y} - \bar{\mathbf{y}}),$$

where

$$\bar{\mathbf{y}} = \mathbf{X}\mu \text{ so that } \bar{y}_i = x_i^\top \mu.$$

Note that $\bar{\mathbf{y}}$ depends on μ, although this is not visible in the notation. $\bar{\mathbf{y}}$ can be thought of as the estimated value of the data $\mathbf{y}$ based on parameter μ. Also, $\mathrm{SSE}(\mu, \mathbf{y})$ depends on $\mathbf{X}$. Again, we do not make this explicit in the notation since $\mathbf{X}$ is considered fixed: we are interested in studying the behavior of SSE if we vary μ, or, later, in Section 12.3.1, if we vary $\mathbf{y}$; we are not directly concerned with the effects of varying $\mathbf{X}$.

We define the least-squares estimator $\hat{\mu}$ as

$$\hat{\mu} := \arg\min_{\mu \in \mathbb{R}^k} \mathrm{SSE}(\mu, \mathbf{y}). \tag{12.4}$$

The results below imply that if $\mathbf{X}$ has full rank, as we assume, then there is always a unique least-squares estimator. The estimate of $\mathbf{y}$ corresponding to $\hat{\mu}$ will be denoted as $\hat{\mathbf{y}}$:

$$\hat{\mathbf{y}} := \mathbf{X}\hat{\mu}.$$

Example 12.1 [Plain Averaging] The simplest case arises if $\mu \in \mathbb{R}$ with a $n \times 1$ design matrix $\mathbf{X} = (1, \ldots, 1)^\top$ consisting only of 1s. Then $\mathrm{SSE}(\mu, \mathbf{y}) = \sum_{i=1}^{n}(y_i - \mu)^2$, and differentiation shows that the least-squares estimate is just the average: $\hat{\mu} = n^{-1} \sum y_i$.

Example 12.2 [Polynomial Regression] Suppose we are interested in polynomial regression for polynomials of order $k - 1$. Then we have $\mathcal{H}^{(k)} = \{h_\mu \mid \mu \in \mathbb{R}^k\}$, and $h_\mu(u) = \sum_{j=1}^{k} \mu_j u^{j-1}$, where $\mu = (\mu_1, \ldots, \mu_k)^\top$, and we have data $(u_1, y_1), \ldots, (u_n, y_n)$. After the variable transformation, we get $x_i = (1, u_i, \ldots, u_i^{k-1})^\top$. If $k = 1$, then $x_1 = x_2 = \ldots = 1$, and we are back at Example 12.1: $\hat{\mu}$ is then just the average of the y_i.

12.2.1   The Normal Equations

We now provide an analytic solution for the $\hat{\mu}$ achieving (12.4), given as a list of equations known as the *normal equations*. We start by rewriting $\mathrm{SSE}(\mu, \mathbf{y})$ in two convenient ways ((12.5) is needed for the normal equations, (12.6) is needed later on):

$$
\begin{aligned}
\mathrm{SSE}(\mu, \mathbf{y}) &= \mathbf{y}^\top \mathbf{y} - 2\bar{\mathbf{y}}^\top \mathbf{y} + \bar{\mathbf{y}}^\top \bar{\mathbf{y}} & (12.5) \\
&= (\mathbf{y} - \bar{\mathbf{y}})^\top \mathbf{y} - \bar{\mathbf{y}}^\top (\mathbf{y} - \bar{\mathbf{y}}) & (12.6)
\end{aligned}
$$

Substituting $\bar{\mathbf{y}} = \mathbf{X}\mu$ in (12.5) and differentiating with respect to μ shows that the minimum of (12.5) is achieved at a unique $\hat{\mu}$, which satisfies $-2\mathbf{X}^\top \mathbf{y} + 2\mathbf{X}^\top \mathbf{X}\hat{\mu} = 0$, so that $\mathbf{X}^\top \mathbf{y} - \mathbf{X}^\top \hat{\mathbf{y}} = 0$. This gives:

The Normal Equations
The least-squares estimator $\hat{\mu}$, and $\hat{\mathbf{y}}$, the corresponding estimate of $\mathbf{y}$, satisfy

$$
\mathbf{X}^\top \mathbf{y} = \mathbf{X}^\top \hat{\mathbf{y}} = \mathbf{X}^\top \mathbf{X}\hat{\mu}, \tag{12.7}
$$

so that also

$$
\begin{aligned}
\hat{\mu} &= (\mathbf{X}^\top \mathbf{X})^{-1} \mathbf{X}^\top \mathbf{y} & (12.8) \\
\hat{\mathbf{y}} &= \mathbf{X}(\mathbf{X}^\top \mathbf{X})^{-1} \mathbf{X}^\top \mathbf{y} & (12.9)
\end{aligned}
$$

Least-squares Estimation as Projection The normal equations can also be derived by thinking of $\hat{\mathbf{y}}$ as a projection. This interpretation may be helpful for memorizing (12.9), especially for readers who are familiar with projection matrices but not with regression.

By its definition, for each μ, $\bar{\mathbf{y}}$ must be a linear combination of the columns of $\mathbf{X}$. Least-squares estimation amounts to finding the $\bar{\mathbf{y}} = \hat{\mathbf{y}}$ that is closest to $\mathbf{y}$ in the least-squares sense. Since $\bar{\mathbf{y}}$ is restricted to lie in the column space of $\mathbf{X}$, the $\bar{\mathbf{y}}$ that is closest to $\mathbf{y}$ must be the projection of $\mathbf{y}$ onto this column space. Indeed, (12.9) can be thought of as a generalization of the well known formula for projection on a line. To see this, let $\mathbf{a} \in \mathbb{R}^n$ represent a point in $\mathbb{R}^n$. Consider the line ℓ going through the origin $\mathbf{0}$ and the point $\mathbf{a}$. Suppose we want to project an n-dimensional point $\mathbf{y}$ onto the line ℓ. This can be done by multiplying $\mathbf{y}$ by the well known $n \times n$ *projection matrix* $P = \frac{\mathbf{a}\mathbf{a}^\top}{\mathbf{a}^\top \mathbf{a}}$ (Strang 1988): we have $\hat{\mathbf{y}} = P\mathbf{y}$, where $\hat{\mathbf{y}}$ is the projection of $\mathbf{y}$ onto ℓ, so that $\hat{\mathbf{y}}$ lies on

ℓ, the line through $\mathbf{y}$ and $\hat{\mathbf{y}}$ is perpendicular to ℓ, and $\hat{\mathbf{y}}$ is the point on ℓ that is closest in Euclidean distance to the point $\mathbf{y}$.

The complicated expression $\mathbf{X}(\mathbf{X}^\top\mathbf{X})^{-1}\mathbf{X}^\top$ appearing in (12.9) is just a generalization of the projection matrix P to a projection upon a k-dimensional subspace (hyperplane through the origin), rather than a one-dimensional line. Just as $\mathbf{a}$ represented the line to project upon, $\mathbf{X}$ represents the subspace to project upon: each column of $\mathbf{X}$ is a point in this subspace. Instead of dividing by the inner product $\mathbf{a}^\top\mathbf{a}$, we multiply by the inverse $(\mathbf{X}^\top\mathbf{X})^{-1}$. Note that the information matrix (see below) $\mathbf{X}^\top\mathbf{X}$ does *not* in itself play the role of a projection matrix P; rather it corresponds to the inner product $\mathbf{a}^\top\mathbf{a}$ occurring in the projection matrix P.

The Information Matrix $\mathbf{X}^\top\mathbf{X}$ A central quantity appearing in the normal equations is the $k \times k$ *information matrix* $\mathbf{X}^\top\mathbf{X}$, also known as the *cross-product matrix*. We call it information matrix since, as will be seen, in the context of the linear model, it becomes a constant times the Fisher information matrix. We now list some general properties of this matrix. More specific properties due to the Fisher information interpretation are given in Section 12.3. First, it is easy to show (Strang 1988, pages 157,158) that if $\mathbf{X}$ has full rank, as we assume, then $\mathbf{X}^\top\mathbf{X}$ is symmetric and positive definite, and hence also invertible. Second, direct calculation shows that

$$\mathbf{X}^\top\mathbf{X} = \sum_{i=1}^{n} x_i x_i^\top. \tag{12.10}$$

The fact that the transposes are reversed in the sum is an artifact of our notation, in which x_i always denotes a column vector. In Lemma 12.2, part 1, we generalize (12.10), and express $\mathbf{X}^\top\mathbf{X}$ as a sum of design matrices corresponding to subsets of the data $x_1, \ldots, x_n$.

Residual and Fitted Sum of Squares   The normal equations can be used to simplify the expression for $\mathrm{SSE}(\mu, \mathbf{y})$ when $\mu = \hat{\mu}$. The resulting expression represents the minimum squared error on the data $\mathbf{y} \mid \mathbf{X}$ that can be achieved within the model $\mathcal{M}^{(k)}$. It is called the *residual sum of squares* in the literature, and is denoted by RSS. It turns out that

$$\mathrm{RSS}(\mathbf{y}) := \mathrm{SSE}(\hat{\mu}, \mathbf{y}) = \mathbf{y}^\top\mathbf{y} - \hat{\mathbf{y}}^\top\mathbf{y} = \mathbf{y}^\top\mathbf{y} - \hat{\mathbf{y}}^\top\hat{\mathbf{y}}. \tag{12.11}$$

Let us prove (12.11). Substituting $\bar{\mathbf{y}}^\top = \hat{\mathbf{y}}^\top = \hat{\mu}^\top\mathbf{X}^\top$ in the second term of (12.6), we get $\mathrm{SSE}(\hat{\mu}, \mathbf{y}) = (\mathbf{y} - \hat{\mathbf{y}})^\top\mathbf{y} - \hat{\mu}^\top\mathbf{X}^\top(\mathbf{y} - \hat{\mathbf{y}})$. By the normal equations, the second term is zero, so that the middle equality of (12.11) follows.

For the final equality, first note that

$$\hat{y}^\top \hat{y} = (X(X^\top X)^{-1} X^\top y)^\top X(X^\top X)^{-1} X^\top y =$$
$$y^\top (X(X^\top X)^{-1} X^\top) y = y^\top \hat{y}. \quad (12.12)$$

Here the first equality follows by (12.9). The second uses the fact that $X^\top X$ is symmetric, so that, as is easy to see, $(X^\top X)^{-1}$ must also be symmetric, and hence equal to its own transpose. Note that, as a byproduct, we have proved the general identity

$$\hat{y}^\top \hat{y} = \hat{y}^\top y = y^\top \hat{y}. \quad (12.13)$$

Another related quantity sometimes encountered in the MDL literature is the *fitted sum of squares*, denoted as FSS. By definition, "the sum of squares is the fitted sum of squares plus the residual sum of squares":

$$y^\top y = \text{FSS}(y) + \text{RSS}(y),$$

so that by (12.11), we have $\text{FSS}(y) = y^\top \hat{y} = y^\top X \hat{\mu}$.

Squared Error as a Quadratic Form   We now present Lemma 12.1, which provides yet another expression for $\text{SSE}(\mu, y)$. It will play a central role in the coming two subsections. The lemma says that the squared error may be rewritten as a sum of two terms: first, a term that does not depend on μ, and second, a quadratic form, expressing a squared Mahalanobis distance between μ and $\hat{\mu}$. Since the first term plays no role when minimizing over μ, minimizing $\text{SSE}(\mu, y)$ amounts to minimizing a squared distance:

Lemma 12.1 If X has independent columns, then

$$\text{SSE}(\mu, y) = \text{RSS}(y) + (\hat{\mu} - \mu)^\top X^\top X(\hat{\mu} - \mu). \quad (12.14)$$

Proof: We have

$$
\begin{aligned}
\text{SSE}(\mu, y) &= y^\top y - 2\mu^\top X^\top y + \bar{y}^\top \bar{y} \\
&= y^\top y - 2\mu^\top X^\top \hat{y} + \bar{y}^\top \bar{y} \\
&= y^\top y - \hat{y}^\top \hat{y} + \hat{y}^\top \hat{y} - 2\bar{y}^\top \hat{y} + \bar{y}^\top \bar{y} \\
&= (y^\top y - \hat{y}^\top \hat{y}) + (\hat{y} - \bar{y})^\top (\hat{y} - \bar{y}) \\
&= (y^\top y - \hat{y}^\top \hat{y}) + (\hat{\mu} - \mu)^\top X^\top X(\hat{\mu} - \mu).
\end{aligned}
$$

Here the first equality follows from (12.5) and the definition of $\bar{y}$. The second equality follows by the normal equations. The remaining equalities are immediate. The result follows from combining the last equation with (12.11).
$\square$

12.2.2   Composition of Experiments

Suppose we have data $\mathbf{y}_0$ and $\mathbf{y}_1$ with design matrices $\mathbf{X}_0$ and $\mathbf{X}_1$. Let, for $j \in \{0, 1\}$, $\hat{\mu}_j$ denote the least-squares estimator corresponding to the subexperiment $\mathbf{y}_j \mid \mathbf{X}_j$, and let $\text{SSE}(\mu, \mathbf{y}_j) := \|\mathbf{y}_j - \mathbf{X}_j \mu\|^2$. We now consider what happens if we merge the two samples. That is, we consider a new joint data vector $\mathbf{y}$ and joint design matrix $\mathbf{X}$ defined by

$$\mathbf{y} = \begin{pmatrix} \mathbf{y}_1 \\ \mathbf{y}_0 \end{pmatrix} \text{ and } \mathbf{X} = \begin{pmatrix} \mathbf{X}_1 \\ \mathbf{X}_0 \end{pmatrix}. \tag{12.15}$$

What can we say about the sum of squared errors, the information matrix $\mathbf{X}^\top \mathbf{X}$, and the least-squares estimator $\hat{\mu}$ corresponding to the joint data $\mathbf{y}$ and joint design matrix $\mathbf{X}$? We have the following trivial, but important, lemma:

Lemma 12.2 [Composition Lemma] We have

1. $\mathbf{X}^\top \mathbf{X} = \mathbf{X}_0^\top \mathbf{X}_0 + \mathbf{X}_1^\top \mathbf{X}_1$.

2. $\text{SSE}(\mu, \mathbf{y}) = \text{SSE}(\mu, \mathbf{y}_0) + \text{SSE}(\mu, \mathbf{y}_1)$.

3. The least-squares estimator $\hat{\mu}$ satisfies

$$\begin{aligned}
\hat{\mu} &= (\mathbf{X}^\top \mathbf{X})^{-1} \mathbf{X}^\top \mathbf{y} \\
&= (\mathbf{X}_0^\top \mathbf{X}_0 + \mathbf{X}_1^\top \mathbf{X}_1)^{-1} (\mathbf{X}_1^\top \mathbf{y}_1 + \mathbf{X}_0^\top \mathbf{y}_0) \\
&= (\mathbf{X}_0^\top \mathbf{X}_0 + \mathbf{X}_1^\top \mathbf{X}_1)^{-1} (\mathbf{X}_1^\top \mathbf{X}_1 \hat{\mu}_1 + \mathbf{X}_0^\top \mathbf{X}_0 \hat{\mu}_0).
\end{aligned} \tag{12.16}$$

4. $\text{RSS}(\mathbf{y}) = \text{RSS}(\mathbf{y}_0) + \text{RSS}(\mathbf{y}_1) + (\hat{\mu}_1 - \hat{\mu}_0)^\top \mathbf{X}_0^\top \mathbf{X}_0 (\mathbf{X}^\top \mathbf{X})^{-1} \mathbf{X}_1^\top \mathbf{X}_1 (\hat{\mu}_1 - \hat{\mu}_0)$.

The characterization (12.16) of $\hat{\mu}$ as a weighted average between $\hat{\mu}_0$ and $\hat{\mu}_1$ plays an important role in the Bayesian treatment of Section 12.3.1.

Proof: The proof of parts 1, 2, and 3 is immediate. For Part 4, note that by Part 2 of the present lemma, and Lemma 12.1,

$$\text{RSS}(\mathbf{y}) = \text{SSE}(\hat{\mu}, \mathbf{y}) = \text{SSE}(\hat{\mu}, \mathbf{y}_0) + \text{SSE}(\hat{\mu}, \mathbf{y}_1) =$$
$$\text{RSS}(\mathbf{y}_0) + \text{RSS}(\mathbf{y}_1) + (\hat{\mu} - \hat{\mu}_0)^\top \mathbf{X}_0^\top \mathbf{X}_0 (\hat{\mu} - \hat{\mu}_0) + (\hat{\mu}_1 - \hat{\mu})^\top \mathbf{X}_0^\top \mathbf{X}_0 (\hat{\mu}_1 - \hat{\mu}). \tag{12.17}$$

Using (12.16) and some straightforward rewriting, we find

$$\begin{aligned}
\hat{\mu} - \hat{\mu}_0 &= (\mathbf{X}^\top \mathbf{X})^{-1} (\mathbf{X}_1^\top \mathbf{X}_1)(\hat{\mu}_1 - \hat{\mu}_0), \\
\hat{\mu}_1 - \hat{\mu} &= (\mathbf{X}^\top \mathbf{X})^{-1} (\mathbf{X}_0^\top \mathbf{X}_0)(\hat{\mu}_1 - \hat{\mu}_0).
\end{aligned} \tag{12.18}$$

We plug these equations into the last two terms of (12.17). The result then follows by straightforward but extensive rewriting, where at some point we re-express an occurrence of $\mathbf{X}_0^\top \mathbf{X}_0$ as $\mathbf{X}^\top \mathbf{X} - \mathbf{X}_1^\top \mathbf{X}_1$, and an occurrence of $\mathbf{X}_1^\top \mathbf{X}_1$ as $\mathbf{X}^\top \mathbf{X} - \mathbf{X}_0^\top \mathbf{X}_0$. We omit the details. □

Example 12.3 [Plain Averaging (Example 12.1, cont.)] Suppose that $\mathbf{X}_0$ consists of a single column of n_0 1s, and $\mathbf{X}_1$ is a single column of n_1 1s. Then $\mathbf{X}$ is a single column of $n = n_0 + n_1$ 1s, and $\hat{\mu}$ is just the average of $y_1, \ldots, y_n$, $\hat{\mu}_0$ is the average of $y_1, \ldots, y_{n_0}$, and $\hat{\mu}_1$ is the average of $y_{n_0+1}, \ldots, y_n$. Part 3 now expresses the intuitive fact that

$$\hat{\mu} = \frac{n_0\hat{\mu}_1 + n_1\hat{\mu}_0}{n_0 + n_1}.$$

Part 4 expresses that

$$\sum_{i=1}^{n}(y_i - \hat{\mu})^2 = \sum_{i=n_0+1}^{n}(y_i - \hat{\mu}_1)^2 + \sum_{i=1}^{n_0}(y_i - \hat{\mu}_0)^2 + \frac{n_0 n_1}{n_0 + n_1}(\hat{\mu}_0 - \hat{\mu}_1)^2. \quad (12.19)$$

In the sequel, we are mainly interested in cases where n_0 is small compared to n. Then $(n_0 n_1)/n \approx n_0$, and (12.19) says that the additional error made by $\hat{\mu}$ over the two partially optimal estimators $\hat{\mu}_0$ and $\hat{\mu}_1$ is on the order of the squared difference between $\hat{\mu}_0$ and $\hat{\mu}_1$. Equation (12.19) was used in this way in Example 11.9 of Chapter 11.

The lemma can be extended to the general case where $\mathbf{y} \mid \mathbf{X}$ represents a composition of m samples with $n_1, \ldots, n_m$ outcomes respectively. If each sample consists of only a single outcome, then part 1 of the lemma becomes equivalent to (12.10).

12.2.3   Penalized Least-Squares

Sometimes it is more appropriate to measure goodness-of-fit by a modification of the sum of squared errors, in which the fit of parameter μ depends not just on these errors, but also on the distance of μ to some base point μ_0. μ_0 can be interpreted as summarizing previously seen data. As will be seen in Chapter 14, Section 14.5, such a construction plays a fundamental role in avoiding overfitting.

To formalize this idea, we fix some positive definite, symmetric $k \times k$ matrix Σ_0, and some $\mu_0 \in \mathbb{R}^k$. We define the *penalization term relative to Σ_0 and μ_0*, denoted by $a(\mu)$, as

$$a(\mu) := (\mu - \mu_0)^\top \Sigma_0^{-1}(\mu - \mu_0). \quad (12.20)$$

Suppose we observe data $\mathbf{y}_1 \mid \mathbf{X}_1$. The reasons for including the subscript 1 will become clear below. We define the *penalized squared error* corresponding to these data and penalization $a(\mu)$ as

$$\text{SSE}_a(\mu, \mathbf{y}_1) := \text{SSE}(\mu, \mathbf{y}_1) + a(\mu). \tag{12.21}$$

Thus, the fit of μ is now "penalized" by its squared Mahalanobis distance (Chapter 4, page 120) to some "base point" μ_0, where the unit balls of the Mahalanobis distance are determined by Σ_0^{-1}. We define the *penalized least-squares estimator* $\hat{\mu}_a$ as

$$\hat{\mu}_a := \arg\min_{\mu \in \mathbb{R}^k} \text{SSE}_a(\mu, \mathbf{y}_1). \tag{12.22}$$

The positive definiteness of Σ_0 implies that $\hat{\mu}_a$ exists and is unique.

> **Terminology** In the literature, the phrase "penalized least-squares" does not necessarily refer to linear regression with quadratic penalizations of the kind we just described – it often refers to more general, nonparametric settings. What we call penalized least-squares estimator in this text is more widely known as the *ridge regression estimator* (Hoerl and Kennard 1970).

Virtual Data Interpretation We can interpret the penalized least-squares estimator $\hat{\mu}_a$ as the least-squares estimator $\hat{\mu}$ with respect to a joint sample, combining the original $\mathbf{y}_1 \mid \mathbf{X}_1$ together with some additional, "virtual" data $\mathbf{y}_0 \mid \mathbf{X}_0$. These data are chosen in such a way that $\hat{\mu}_0$, the least-squares estimator for $\mathbf{y}_0$, is equal to the μ_0 appearing in the definition of $a(\mu)$. We make this idea precise using the principal axis theorem of linear algebra (Strang 1988, Chapter 6, page 333), which implies that we can write $\Sigma_0^{-1} = \mathbf{X}_0^\top \mathbf{X}_0$ for some $k \times k$ matrix $\mathbf{X}_0$. We further define

$$\mathbf{y}_0 = \hat{\mathbf{y}}_0 = \mathbf{X}_0 \mu_0, \quad \bar{\mathbf{y}}_0 = \mathbf{X}_0 \mu. \tag{12.23}$$

Here $\bar{\mathbf{y}}_0$ is really a function (of μ) rather than a constant, although this is not visible in the notation.

With these definitions, we use Lemma 12.1 to establish equivalence between the quadratic form $a(\mu)$ and a sum of squared errors term $\text{SSE}(\mu, \mathbf{y}_0)$ for the $\mathbf{X}_0$ and $\mathbf{y}_0$ that we just defined. Applying the lemma with $\hat{\mu}$ substituted by $\hat{\mu}_0 = \mu_0$, $\mathbf{y}$ by $\mathbf{y}_0$, $\hat{\mathbf{y}}$ by $\hat{\mathbf{y}}_0$, and $\mathbf{X}$ by $\mathbf{X}_0$, we find that

$$\text{SSE}(\mu, \mathbf{y}_0) = \text{SSE}(\hat{\mu}_0, \mathbf{y}_0) + (\mu - \mu_0)^\top \Sigma_0^{-1}(\mu - \mu_0) =$$
$$0 + a(\mu) = a(\mu). \tag{12.24}$$

We now define $\mathbf{y}$ and $\mathbf{X}$ to be the combined data, as in (12.15), and combine (12.24) with the composition lemma (Lemma 12.2), giving

$$\text{SSE}_a(\mu, \mathbf{y}_1) = \text{SSE}(\mu, \mathbf{y}) = \text{SSE}(\mu, \mathbf{y}_1) + \text{SSE}(\mu, \mathbf{y}_0), \qquad (12.25)$$

and we find that, as promised, the penalized squared error is just the squared error for the combined data $\mathbf{y} \mid \mathbf{X}$. Also, the penalized least-squares estimator $\hat{\mu}_a$ is just the least-squares estimator $\hat{\mu}$ for the combined data $\mathbf{y} \mid \mathbf{X}$, so that $\hat{\mu}_a = (\mathbf{X}^\top \mathbf{X})^{-1} \mathbf{X}^\top \mathbf{y}$. By the composition lemma, $\hat{\mu}_a$ can conveniently be expressed in terms of μ_0, without explicitly mentioning the virtual data $\mathbf{X}_0$ and $\mathbf{y}_0$. Indeed, let $\hat{\mu}_1$ be the least-squares estimator for $\mathbf{y}_1 \mid \mathbf{X}_1$. Since $\mu_0 = \hat{\mu}_0$ is the least-squares estimator for $\mathbf{y}_0 \mid \mathbf{X}_0$, Lemma 12.2 gives

$$
\begin{aligned}
\hat{\mu}_a &= \left(\mathbf{X}_1^\top \mathbf{X}_1 + \Sigma_0^{-1} \right)^{-1} \left(\mathbf{X}_1^\top \mathbf{y}_1 + \Sigma_0^{-1} \mu_0 \right) && (12.26) \\
&= \left(\mathbf{X}_1^\top \mathbf{X}_1 + \Sigma_0^{-1} \right)^{-1} \left(\mathbf{X}_1^\top \mathbf{X}_1 \hat{\mu}_1 + \Sigma_0^{-1} \mu_0 \right). && (12.27)
\end{aligned}
$$

Example 12.4 [Polynomials (Example 12.2, cont.)] Let $\mathcal{H}^{(k)} = \{ h_\mu \mid \mu \in \mathbb{R}^k \}$ represent the set of $(k-1)$-degree polynomials, as in Example 12.2. If, as above, we interpret Σ_0 as representing previously seen data, then it must be possible to write $\Sigma_0^{-1} = c\mathbf{X}'^\top \mathbf{X}'$ where $\mathbf{X}'^\top = (x_1', \dots, x_m')$ for some $c > 0$ and $m \in \mathbb{N}$. For the current data $x_1, \dots, x_n$, we have, for $1 \leq i \leq n$, $x_i = (1, u_i^1, \dots, u_i^{k-1})^\top$, where u_i is the underlying input. Analogously, for $1 \leq j \leq m$, x_j' represents a vector of basis functions $x_j' = (1, u_j'^1, \dots, u_j'^{k-1})^\top$, and the "real" previous data is $u_1', \dots, u_m'$. We can think of c as measuring the amount of data or evidence summarized by Σ_0: if $c = 1$, then $\mathbf{X}' = \mathbf{X}_0$ as above, and n_0 (the number of rows of $\mathbf{X}_0$) is equal to m. If $c = 2$, then $n_0 = 2m$ and the $\mathbf{X}_0$ above is the $2m \times k$ matrix in which each row of $\mathbf{X}'$ is repeated. The simplest case of such a model, with $k = 1$, was already treated in Example 11.9 on page 315.

12.3   The Linear Model

As in the beginning of Section 12.2 on least-squares estimation, we fix k basis functions $h_1, \dots, h_k$, each mapping $\mathcal{U}$ to $\mathcal{Y} = \mathbb{R}$, and we let $\mathcal{H}^{(k)}$ be the set of functions $h : \mathcal{X} \to \mathbb{R}$ of the form $h(u) = \sum_{j=1}^k \mu_j h_j(u)$ for some $\mu = (\mu_1, \dots, \mu_k) \in \mathbb{R}^k$. Fix some $\sigma^2 > 0$ and let $\mathcal{M}^{(k)}$ be the set of conditional probabilistic sources $\{ f_{\sigma, h} \mid h \in \mathcal{H}^{(k)} \}$ as defined by (12.2), for some fixed value $\sigma^2 > 0$. For each $f_{\sigma, h}$, the marginal density for the first n outcomes is then given by

$$
f_{\sigma, h}(y^n \mid u^n) = \left(\frac{1}{\sqrt{2\pi}\sigma} \right)^n \exp\left(-\frac{\sum_{i=1}^n \left(y_i - \sum_{j=1}^k \mu_j h_j(u_i) \right)^2}{2\sigma^2} \right). \qquad (12.28)
$$

Just as for least-squares estimation, we can considerably simplify the treatment if, as in (12.3), we express $f_{\sigma,h}$ directly in terms of the transformed input variables $x_i = (h_1(u_i), \ldots, h_j(u_i))^\top$ and design matrix $\mathbf{X} = (x_1^\top, \ldots, x_n^\top)^\top$. We now define $\mathcal{M}^{\mathbf{X}} = \{P_\mu \mid \mu \in \mathbb{R}^k\}$ as the set of distributions on $\mathbb{R}^n$ with densities

$$f_\mu(\mathbf{y}) = \left(\frac{1}{\sqrt{2\pi}\sigma}\right)^n \exp\left(-\frac{\sum_{i=1}^n (y_i - \mu^\top x_i)^2}{2\sigma^2}\right) =$$
$$\left(\frac{1}{\sqrt{2\pi}\sigma}\right)^n \exp\left(-\frac{\mathrm{SSE}(\mu, \mathbf{y})}{2\sigma^2}\right), \quad (12.29)$$

which can be re-expressed as

$$-\ln f_\mu(\mathbf{y}) = \frac{1}{2\sigma^2}\mathrm{SSE}(\mu, \mathbf{y}) + \frac{n}{2}\ln 2\pi\sigma^2. \quad (12.30)$$

$\mathcal{M}^{\mathbf{X}}$ is just the instantiation of $\mathcal{M}^{(k)}$ for given data $x_1, \ldots, x_n$. This is now a family of ordinary distributions on $\mathbb{R}^n$, rather than conditional probabilistic sources for $\mathbb{R}$.

Similarly, we define $\mathcal{S}^{\mathbf{X}} = \{P_{\mu,\sigma^2} \mid \mu \in \mathbb{R}^k, \sigma^2 > 0\}$ as the set of distributions on $\mathbb{R}^n$ with densities (12.29), but now containing a distribution for all values $\sigma^2 > 0$. Thus, $\mathcal{S}^{\mathbf{X}}$ is described by $k + 1$ rather than k parameters.

Models of the form $\mathcal{M}^{\mathbf{X}}$ and $\mathcal{S}^{\mathbf{X}}$ are a special case of what is known as the *linear model* in the literature (Lindley and Smith 1972). Below we shall first give a very simple example of a linear model. We shall then list some important properties of the models $\mathcal{M}^{\mathbf{X}}$ and $\mathcal{S}^{\mathbf{X}}$. We treat the properties of models $\mathcal{M}^{\mathbf{X}}$ in great detail. We only list the – more involved – properties of models $\mathcal{S}^{\mathbf{X}}$ that are relevant to MDL model selection for regression (Chapter 14, Section 14.5).

> According to $\mathcal{M}^{\mathbf{X}}$ and $\mathcal{S}^{\mathbf{X}}$, the y_i are always i.i.d., but this is not required in the general definition of a linear model. There, it is only required that the vector $\mathbf{y} = (y_1, \ldots, y_n)^\top$ is normally distributed for each μ. The mathematics developed below can be readily extended to this more general case, which can be used to handle more sophisticated applications such as, for example, *denoising* (Rissanen 2000; Hansen and Yu 2000; Roos, Myllymäki, and Tirri 2005).

Example 12.5 [Normal (Location) Family] As announced in Section 12.1.1, the normal location family is a very special case of a linear model $\mathcal{M}^{\mathbf{X}}$, where, as in Example 12.1, $\mathbf{X} = (1, \ldots, 1)^\top$. The full normal family is the linear model $\mathcal{S}^{\mathbf{X}}$ with $\mathbf{X} = (1, \ldots, 1)^\top$ and σ^2 allowed to vary.

Example 12.6 If we equip the set $\mathcal{H}^{(k)}$ of $(k-1)$-degree polynomials with the Gaussian noise assumption, we obtain the $(k-1)$-degree polynomial regression model $\mathcal{P}^{(k)}$ of Example 2.9, Chapter 2. This is a set of conditional probabilistic sources. The corresponding linear model $\mathcal{P}^{\mathbf{X}}$ is the set of distributions on $\mathbb{R}^n$ obtained by defining $\mathbf{X}$ as in Example 12.2: we set $x_i = (1, u_i, \ldots, u_i^{k-1})^\top$, and $\mathbf{X} = (x_1^\top, \ldots, x_n^\top)^\top$.

1. ML estimator and regret. Consider the model $\mathcal{M}^{\mathbf{X}}$ for some fixed $\mathbf{X}$ and σ^2. From (12.30) is clear that, independently of the choice of σ^2, the least-squares estimator is equal to the ML estimator. Lemma 12.1 shows that for any $\mu, \mu' \in \mathbb{R}^k$, we have

$$-\ln \frac{f_\mu(\mathbf{y})}{f_{\mu'}(\mathbf{y})} = \frac{1}{2\sigma^2}\left((\hat{\mu}-\mu)^\top \mathbf{X}^\top \mathbf{X}(\hat{\mu}-\mu) - (\hat{\mu}-\mu')^\top \mathbf{X}^\top \mathbf{X}(\hat{\mu}-\mu')\right),$$
(12.31)

so that, in particular, the regret of using f_μ instead of $f_{\hat{\mu}}$ satisfies

$$-\ln f_\mu(\mathbf{y}) - [-\ln f_{\hat{\mu}(\mathbf{y})}(\mathbf{y})] = \frac{1}{2\sigma^2}(\hat{\mu}-\mu)^\top \mathbf{X}^\top \mathbf{X}(\hat{\mu}-\mu),$$
(12.32)

so that *the regret is given by the squared Mahalanobis distance between μ and $\hat{\mu}$.* Now consider the model $\mathcal{S}^{\mathbf{X}}$ with ML estimator $(\hat{\sigma}^2, \hat{\mu})$. It is clear that the $\hat{\mu}$-component of the ML estimator is still equal to the least-squares estimator. By differentiation we find that

$$\hat{\sigma}^2 = \frac{1}{n}\mathrm{RSS}(\mathbf{y}).$$
(12.33)

2. Expectations of y and $\hat{\mu}(\mathbf{y})$. We have

$$E_\mu[\mathbf{y}] = \bar{\mathbf{y}} = \mathbf{X}\mu \quad \text{and} \quad E_\mu[\hat{\mu}(\mathbf{y})] = \mu.$$
(12.34)

The equation on the left is immediately verified. It expresses that, in the context of linear models, $\bar{\mathbf{y}}$ may be explicitly thought of as the estimated value of the data $\mathbf{y}$ based on parameter μ. The equation on the right will be proved further below, in (12.38). It expresses that the ML estimator $\hat{\mu}$ is an unbiased estimate of μ.

3. Fisher information. Both the observed and the expected Fisher information matrices for data $\mathbf{y}$ depend on the design matrix $\mathbf{X}$. To emphasize this fact, they will be denoted as $J(\mathbf{y} \mid \mathbf{X})$ and $I(\mu \mid \mathbf{X})$, respectively. It turns out that, for all $\mathbf{y} \in \mathbb{R}^n$, all $\mu \in \mathbb{R}^k$,

$$J(\mathbf{y} \mid \mathbf{X}) = I(\mu \mid \mathbf{X}) = \frac{1}{\sigma^2} \mathbf{X}^\top \mathbf{X}. \tag{12.35}$$

so that $J(\mathbf{y} \mid \mathbf{X})$ *does not depend on the y-data* $\mathbf{y}$, and $I(\mu \mid \mathbf{X})$ *does not depend on* μ. We already encountered the special case of this phenomenon for the normal location model in the box on page 300, where we found that $I(\mu) = \sigma^{-1}$.

All this explains why we called $\mathbf{X}^\top \mathbf{X}$ the *information matrix*: if $\sigma^2 = 1$, it is equal to both the observed and the expected Fisher information matrix for the model $\mathcal{M}^\mathbf{X}$. We should be a bit careful here, since in Chapter 4, we defined the Fisher information $I(\theta)$ to correspond to one particular outcome. The present section is the only part of the book where a single outcome $\mathbf{y}$ for the model $\mathcal{M}^\mathbf{X}$ really corresponds to n outcomes in the experimental setting. Thus, in this chapter, the (i, j)-th entry of $I(\mu^* \mid \mathbf{X})$ is really defined as $E_{\mu^*}[-\{(\partial^2/\partial\mu_i\partial\mu_j) \ln f_\mu(\mathbf{y})\}_{\mu=\mu^*}]$ rather than n^{-1} times this amount, as in Chapter 4; see the remarks on pages 112 and 122.

4. KL divergence. It is easy to show that

$$D(\mu^* \| \mu) = \frac{1}{2\sigma^2} (\mu - \mu^*)^\top \mathbf{X}^\top \mathbf{X} (\mu - \mu^*). \tag{12.36}$$

Thus, for the linear model, the KL divergence is just a rescaling of the squared Mahalanobis distance. We give a direct proof of (12.36) further below. An indirect proof is as follows: since $I(\mu \mid \mathbf{X})$ is independent of μ, the asymptotic expansion of Chapter 4 – which, it turns out, is applicable to the model $\mathcal{M}^\mathbf{X}$ – must hold exactly for all sample sizes, and not just asymptotically. Indeed, (12.36) is equal to the quantity on the right of (4.23) on page 120, without the remainder term $o((\mu - \mu^*)^2)$. Let us elaborate on this for the case that $\mu \in \mathbb{R}^1$ and $\mathcal{M}^\mathbf{X}$ is the normal location family. The asymptotic expansion then says that for each μ, μ', $D(\mu^* \| \mu) = (1/2)(\mu - \mu^*)^2 I(\mu')$, where μ' is between μ and μ^*. Since, for the normal location family, $I(\mu) = \sigma^{-2}$ is constant as a function of μ, it follows that $D(\mu \| \mu^*)$ is exactly equal to $(1/2\sigma^2)(\mu - \mu^*)^2$.

We end this section by listing and proving some further, more advanced properties of linear models.

5. The linear model is an exponential family. $\mathcal{M}^\mathbf{X}$ is an exponential family, independently of the choice of $\mathbf{X}$. To see this, note that

$$f_\mu(\mathbf{y}) \propto e^{-\frac{1}{2\sigma^2}(\mathbf{y}^\top\mathbf{y} - 2\mathbf{y}^\top\mathbf{X}\mu + \mu^T\mathbf{X}^\top\mathbf{X}\mu)} \propto r(\mathbf{y}) e^{\frac{1}{\sigma^2}\mu^\top\mathbf{X}^\top\mathbf{y}} \tag{12.37}$$

with $r(\mathbf{y}) = \exp(-\frac{1}{2\sigma^2}\mathbf{y}^\top \mathbf{y})$. Since (12.37) is of the exponential form (2.29), this already shows that $f_\mu(\mathbf{y})$ is an exponential family with canonical parameter $\beta = \mu/\sigma^2 \in \mathbb{R}^k$ and sufficient statistic $\mathbf{X}^\top \mathbf{y}$. We now consider a linear transformation of this parameterization, which gives another, more convenient version of the canonical parameterization: since, by the normal equations (page 342), $\mathbf{X}^\top \mathbf{y} = \mathbf{X}^\top \hat{\mathbf{y}} = \mathbf{X}^\top \mathbf{X}\hat{\mu}(\mathbf{y})$, we have

$$f_\mu(\mathbf{y}) \propto r(\mathbf{y})e^{\frac{1}{\sigma^2}\mu^\top \mathbf{X}^\top \mathbf{X}\hat{\mu}(\mathbf{y})},$$

so that $\mathcal{M}^\mathbf{X}$ can also be viewed as an exponential family with canonical parameters $\beta^\top = \sigma^{-2}\mu^\top \mathbf{X}^\top \mathbf{X}$ and sufficient statistic $\phi(\mathbf{y}) = (\phi_1(\mathbf{y}), \dots, \phi_k(\mathbf{y})):= \hat{\mu}(\mathbf{y})$. Thus, the parameterization in terms of μ is a *mean-value parameterization* (Chapter 18, Section 18.4). This gives one other very special property of the normal family: up to linear transformations, the mean-value and the canonical parameterizations are identical.

The fact that μ is the mean-value parameter implies that, as in (12.34), for all $\mu \in \mathbb{R}^k$ we have $E_\mu[\hat{\mu}] = \mu$. This can also be shown directly:

$$E_\mu[\hat{\mu}] = \int \hat{\mu}(\mathbf{y}) \frac{1}{\sqrt{2\pi\sigma^2}^n} e^{-\frac{\|\mathbf{y}-\mathbf{X}\mu\|^2}{2\sigma^2}} \, d\mathbf{y} =$$

$$\int (\mathbf{X}^\top \mathbf{X}^\top)^{-1} \mathbf{X}^\top \mathbf{y} \frac{1}{\sqrt{2\pi\sigma^2}^n} e^{-\frac{\|\mathbf{y}-\mathbf{X}\mu\|^2}{2\sigma^2}} \, d\mathbf{y} =$$

$$(\mathbf{X}^\top \mathbf{X})^{-1}\mathbf{X}^\top \cdot E_\mu[\mathbf{y}] = (\mathbf{X}^\top \mathbf{X})^{-1}\mathbf{X}^\top \cdot (\mathbf{X}\mu) = \mu. \quad (12.38)$$

Finally, we note that the extended model $\mathcal{S}^\mathbf{X}$ is also an exponential family: to show this, we leave the definition of $\phi_1, \dots, \phi_k$ and $\beta_1, \dots, \beta_k$ unchanged, and we introduce the additional parameter $\beta_0:=1/\sigma^2$ and function $\phi_0(\mathbf{y}):=\mathbf{y}^\top \mathbf{y}$. By writing

$$f_\mu(\mathbf{y}) \propto e^{-\frac{1}{2\sigma^2}\mathbf{y}^\top \mathbf{y} + \frac{1}{\sigma^2}\mu^\top \mathbf{X}^\top \mathbf{X}\hat{\mu}(\mathbf{y})} = e^{-\sum_{j=0}^{k} \beta_j \phi_j(\mathbf{y})},$$

we see that $\mathcal{S}^\mathbf{X}$ is a $(k+1)$-parameter exponential family. We have more to say about the exponentiality of the linear model in Chapter 18, Section 18.5.

Let us now use the fact that $\mathcal{M}^\mathbf{X}$ is exponential to determine its Fisher information matrix $I(\mu \mid \mathbf{X})$. By definition, the (i, j)-entry of the *observed* matrix $J(\mathbf{y} \mid \mathbf{X})$ is given by

$$J(\mathbf{y} \mid \mathbf{X})_{ij} = \left\{ \frac{\partial^2}{\partial \mu_i \partial \mu_j} - \ln f_\mu(\mathbf{y}) \right\}_{\mu=\hat{\mu}(\mathbf{y})} =$$

$$\left\{ \frac{\partial^2}{\partial \mu_i \partial \mu_j} \frac{1}{2\sigma^2} \|\mathbf{y} - \mathbf{X}\mu\|^2 \right\}_{\mu=\hat{\mu}(\mathbf{y})} = \left\{ \frac{\partial^2}{\partial \mu_i \partial \mu_j} \frac{1}{2\sigma^2} \mu^\top \mathbf{X}^\top \mathbf{X}\mu \right\}_{\mu=\hat{\mu}(\mathbf{y})}$$

$$= \frac{1}{\sigma^2} \left(\mathbf{X}^\top \mathbf{X} \right)_{ij}, \quad (12.39)$$

so that $J(\mathbf{y} \mid \mathbf{X}) = \sigma^{-2}\mathbf{X}^{\top}\mathbf{X}$, independently of $\mathbf{y}$. The fact that $\mathcal{M}^{\mathbf{X}}$ is an exponential family with mean-value parameter μ implies that, for each $\mathbf{y}$, we have $I(\hat{\mu}(\mathbf{y}) \mid \mathbf{X}) = J(\mathbf{y} \mid \mathbf{X})$ (Chapter 19, page 632). This shows (12.35).

Let us now determine the $(k+1) \times (k+1)$ observed Fisher information matrix of $\mathcal{S}^{\mathbf{X}}$, which we shall denote by $J'(\mathbf{y} \mid \mathbf{X})$. The upper-left $k \times k$ submatrix of $J'(\mathbf{y} \mid \mathbf{X})$ is just equal to $J(\mathbf{y} \mid \mathbf{X})$. To calculate the other entries, first note that

$$-\frac{d}{d\sigma} \ln f_{\mu,\sigma}(\mathbf{y}) = \frac{n}{2}\left(\frac{2}{\sigma} - \frac{\frac{2}{n}\mathrm{SSE}(\mu,\mathbf{y})}{\sigma^3}\right). \tag{12.40}$$

For fixed σ, this quantity achieves its maximum at $\mu = \hat{\mu}$. Therefore, the partial derivative of this quantity with respect to μ, evaluated at $\hat{\mu}$, must be 0. It follows that, for $1 \le i \le k$, $J'_{i(k+1)}(\mathbf{y} \mid \mathbf{X}) = J'_{(k+1)i}(\mathbf{y} \mid \mathbf{X}) = 0$. It remains to evaluate the $(k+1, k+1)$-entry, which is given by the derivative of (12.40) with respect to σ, evaluated at $\hat{\sigma}^2$. Using (12.33), we find

$$-\left\{\frac{d^2}{d\sigma^2} \ln f_{\mu,\sigma}(\mathbf{y})\right\}_{\mu=\hat{\mu},\sigma^2=\hat{\sigma}^2} = \left\{\frac{d}{d\sigma}\frac{n}{2}\left(\frac{2}{\sigma} - \frac{2\hat{\sigma}^2}{\sigma^3}\right)\right\}_{\sigma^2=\hat{\sigma}^2} = \frac{2n}{\hat{\sigma}^2}. \tag{12.41}$$

Since $\mathcal{S}^{\mathbf{X}}$ is an exponential family, the expected Fisher information is once again equal to the observed information. The determinant of these Fisher informations is now given by

$$\det I'(\mu \mid \mathbf{X}) = \det J'(\mathbf{y} \mid \mathbf{X}) =$$
$$2n\sigma^{-2}\det I(\mu \mid \mathbf{X}) = 2n\sigma^{-2k-2}\det \mathbf{X}^T\mathbf{X}. \tag{12.42}$$

The fact that $\mathcal{M}^{\mathbf{X}}$ is an exponential family also leads to a direct proof of the expression for the KL divergence, (12.36), in terms of (12.32): since $\mathcal{M}^{\mathbf{X}}$ is exponential, the fundamental robustness property for exponential families (Chapter 19, Section 19.2) must hold, and we have

$$D(\mu\|\mu') = -\ln f_{\mu'}(\mathbf{y}) + \ln f_\mu(\mathbf{y}),$$

for any data $\mathbf{y}$ such that $\hat{\mu}(\mathbf{y}) = \mu$. The result then follows by plugging in (12.32).

6. Covariance of μ. The fact that $\mathcal{M}^{\mathbf{X}}$ is an exponential family also implies that the Fisher information must be the inverse of the covariance matrix of the parameters μ (Chapter 18, box on page 615). Note that this is *not* the same as the covariance matrix of the data $\mathbf{y} = (y_1, \ldots, y_n)^{\top}$. Indeed, let $\mu_0 = \hat{\mu}(\mathbf{y})$ be the ML estimator for the observed data $\mathbf{y}$. We have

$$\sigma^2(\mathbf{X}^{\top}\mathbf{X})^{-1} = I^{-1}(\mu_0 \mid \mathbf{X}) = E_{\mu_0}[(\hat{\mu} - \mu_0)(\hat{\mu} - \mu_0)^{\top}], \tag{12.43}$$

where $\hat{\mu}$ now denotes a random variable, namely the ML estimator when data are distributed according to μ_0. Since the left-hand side of (12.43) does not depend on μ_0, it follows that the covariance matrix of μ_0 does not depend on μ: given $\mathbf{X}$, the expected deviation of $\hat{\mu}$ from the true mean μ_0 is the same for all μ_0.

12.3.1   Bayesian Linear Model $\mathcal{M}^{\mathbf{X}}$ with Gaussian Prior

Suppose we observe data $\mathbf{y}_1 \mid \mathbf{X}_1$. We now study the behavior of a linear model $\mathcal{M}^{\mathbf{X}_1}$ equipped with a Bayesian prior. According to the linear model, $\mathbf{y}_1$ is Gaussian distributed with mean $\mathbf{X}_1\mu$ for some μ. It turns out to be mathematically most convenient to use a prior w_a that is itself Gaussian, with some mean, say, μ_0, and covariance matrix $\sigma^2\Sigma$. There are several reasons for this: first, with such a prior, the Bayesian maximum a posteriori (MAP) and mean estimators can be interpreted as ML estimators for data $\mathbf{y}_1$ together with some additional data $\mathbf{y}_0$. Thus, the approach is the probabilistic analogue of the penalized least-squares estimation of Section 12.2.3. Second, the posterior corresponding to such a prior is Gaussian as well, which is mathematically convenient. Third, with Jeffreys' prior, although uniform rather than Gaussian, the posterior will be Gaussian, so the mathematical analysis of using a Gaussian prior largely carries over to the Jeffreys' prior case, which we discuss in Section 12.3.2.

Formally, let $a(\mu)$ be a penalization term as in (12.20), and define a prior

$$w_a(\mu) := \frac{e^{-\frac{a(\mu)}{2\sigma^2}}}{\int_{\mu \in \mathbb{R}^k} e^{-\frac{a(\mu)}{2\sigma^2}}\, d\mu} \propto e^{-\frac{(\mu-\mu_0)^\top \Sigma_0^{-1} (\mu-\mu_0)}{2\sigma^2}}. \tag{12.44}$$

w_a is a normal distribution with mean μ_0 and covariance matrix $\sigma^2\Sigma_0$. w_a is also an instance of a Bayesian prior corresponding to luckiness function $a'(\mu) = a(\mu)/(2\sigma^2)$ as in (11.24), page 313. To obtain such priors, the exponentiated luckiness function has to be multiplied by the Fisher information. Since the Fisher information is constant for the linear model, this has no influence. The luckiness interpretation of w_a will be used in Section 12.4.2 to derive a luckiness NML code relative to $\mathcal{M}^{\mathbf{X}}$.

Suppose we observe data $\mathbf{y}_1 \mid \mathbf{X}_1$. Recall that, by Bayes formula (Chapter 2, Section 2.5.2), the posterior density of μ is then given by

$$w_a(\mu \mid \mathbf{y}_1) = \frac{f_\mu(\mathbf{y}_1) w_a(\mu)}{\bar{f}_{\text{Bayes}}(\mathbf{y}_1)} \propto e^{-\frac{\text{SSE}(\mu,\mathbf{y}_1) + a(\mu)}{2\sigma^2}}. \tag{12.45}$$

Here $\bar{f}_{\text{Bayes}}$ is the marginal distribution relative to prior w_a. From (12.22) it follows that the posterior density of μ is maximized for μ equal to the penalized least-squares estimator $\hat{\mu}_a$. Thus, for the chosen prior, *the penalized least-squares estimator coincides with the MAP estimator.*

The Posterior   To obtain an explicit formula for the posterior, we now rewrite (12.45) using the insights from Section 12.2.2 about the composition of experiments. Consider a virtual sample $\mathbf{y}_0 \mid \mathbf{X}_0$ corresponding to Σ_0 and μ_0 as in (12.23), and let the joint data $\mathbf{y} \mid \mathbf{X}$ be defined in terms of $\mathbf{y}_1, \mathbf{y}_0, \mathbf{X}_1$ and $\mathbf{X}_0$ as in (12.25). The equivalence between the MAP and the penalized least-squares estimator, together with (12.25), now implies that the MAP estimator is equal to the least-squares estimator for the joint data $\mathbf{y} \mid \mathbf{X}$, and that

$$w_a(\mu \mid \mathbf{y}_1) \propto e^{-\frac{\text{SSE}(\mu, \mathbf{y})}{2\sigma^2}}.$$

We can now apply Lemma 12.1 to this expression. Noting that $\text{RSS}(\mathbf{y}) = \text{SSE}(\hat{\mu}_a, \mathbf{y})$ does not depend on μ, we see that the first term in (12.14) can be ignored and we get

$$w_a(\mu \mid \mathbf{y}_1) \propto e^{-\frac{(\mu - \hat{\mu}_a)^\top \mathbf{X}^\top \mathbf{X}(\mu - \hat{\mu}_a)}{2\sigma^2}}. \tag{12.46}$$

This shows that the posterior $w_a(\mu \mid \mathbf{y}_1)$ is itself also a Gaussian distribution, with mean given by $\hat{\mu}_a$ and covariance matrix $\sigma^2(\mathbf{X}^\top \mathbf{X})^{-1} = \sigma^2(\mathbf{X}_1^\top \mathbf{X}_1 + \Sigma_0^{-1})^{-1}$:

$$\mu \mid \mathbf{y}_1 \sim \mathrm{N}(\hat{\mu}_a, \sigma^2(\mathbf{X}^\top \mathbf{X})^{-1}),$$

or, writing out (12.46) explicitly,

$$w_a(\mu \mid \mathbf{y}_1) = \frac{\det(\mathbf{X}^\top \mathbf{X})}{\sqrt{2\pi\sigma^2}^k} e^{-\frac{(\mu - \hat{\mu}_a)^\top \mathbf{X}^\top \mathbf{X}(\mu - \hat{\mu}_a)}{2\sigma^2}}. \tag{12.47}$$

We reiterate that $\hat{\mu}_a$ is not just the maximum, but also the mean of the posterior.

Example 12.7 [Normal Distributions, cont.]   In the special case where $\mathcal{M}^{\mathbf{X}}$ denotes the normal location family, $(\mathbf{X}^\top \mathbf{X})^{-1} = 1/n$, so (12.47) expresses that $w(\mu \mid \mathbf{y}_1)$ is a normal density around μ_0 with variance σ^2/n.

Marginal Density   Rewriting (12.45), we get

$$-\ln \bar{f}_{\text{Bayes}}(\mathbf{y}_1) = \ln w_a(\hat{\mu}_a \mid \mathbf{y}_1) - \ln f_{\hat{\mu}_a}(\mathbf{y}_1) - \ln w_a(\hat{\mu}_a). \tag{12.48}$$

Applying our formula for the posterior (12.47) to the right-hand side, this can be further rewritten as

$$\frac{1}{2}\ln\frac{\det(\mathbf{X}^\top\mathbf{X})}{(2\pi\sigma^2)^k} - \frac{1}{2}\ln\frac{\det\Sigma_0^{-1}}{(2\pi\sigma^2)^k} - \frac{n_1}{2}\ln\frac{1}{2\pi\sigma^2} +$$

$$\frac{1}{2\sigma^2}\left(\mathrm{SSE}(\hat{\mu}_a,\mathbf{y}_1) + a(\hat{\mu}_a)\right) =$$

$$\frac{1}{2}\ln\det(\mathbf{X}^\top\mathbf{X}) - \frac{1}{2}\ln\det(\mathbf{X}_0^\top\mathbf{X}_0) + \frac{n_1}{2}\ln 2\pi\sigma^2 + \frac{1}{2\sigma^2}\mathrm{RSS}(\mathbf{y}), \quad (12.49)$$

where n_1 is the number of components of $\mathbf{y}_1$. This gives

$$-\ln\bar{f}_{\mathrm{Bayes}}(\mathbf{y}_1) =$$

$$\frac{1}{2}\ln\det(\mathbf{X}^\top\mathbf{X}) - \frac{1}{2}\ln(\det\mathbf{X}_0^\top\mathbf{X}_0) + \frac{n_1}{2}\ln 2\pi\sigma^2 + \frac{1}{2\sigma^2}\mathrm{RSS}(\mathbf{y}) =$$

$$\frac{1}{2}\ln\det(\mathbf{X}_1^\top\mathbf{X}_1 + \Sigma_0^{-1}) + \frac{1}{2}\ln\det\Sigma_0 + \frac{n_1}{2}\ln 2\pi\sigma^2 + \frac{1}{2\sigma^2}\mathrm{RSS}(\mathbf{y}). \quad (12.50)$$

The first term is based on the joint design matrix $\mathbf{X}$; the second term is based on the virtual "prior" design matrix $\mathbf{X}_0$. Only the rightmost term depends on the data $\mathbf{y}_1$. Equations (12.57) and (12.58) give useful explicit expressions for the rightmost term $\mathrm{RSS}(\mathbf{y})$.

Marginal and Predictive Distribution*   Since only the rightmost term of (12.50) depends on $\mathbf{y}$, we have

$$\bar{f}_{\mathrm{Bayes}}(\mathbf{y}_1) \propto e^{-\frac{\mathrm{RSS}(\mathbf{y})}{2\sigma^2}}, \qquad (12.51)$$

where the residual sum of squares appearing in the exponent is taken with respect to the joint data $\mathbf{y} \mid \mathbf{X}$. To what distribution does this density correspond? It turns out that, once again, it is a normal distribution. Although we give a derivation in terms of (12.51) further below, we first give a direct argument (Lindley and Smith 1972) that bypasses (12.51): by the definition of the prior, the prior mean μ satisfies $\mu = \mu_0 + \nu$, where ν is normally distributed with mean 0 and covariance $\sigma^2\Sigma_0$. We also have $\mathbf{y}_1 = \mathbf{z}_1 + \bar{\mathbf{y}}_1$. Here the "noise vector" $\mathbf{z}_1$ is normally distributed with mean 0 and covariance $\sigma^2 I$, where (only in this subsection) I is the $n_1 \times n_1$ unit matrix. $\bar{\mathbf{y}}_1 := \mathbf{X}_1\mu$ is the vector of predictions for $\mathbf{y}_1$ given $\mu = \mu_0 + \nu$. Thus, $\mathbf{y}_1 = \mathbf{X}_1\mu_0 + \mathbf{z}_1 + \mathbf{X}_1\nu$, where the second and third terms are independently normally distributed with mean 0. It then follows by general properties of the normal distribution that $\mathbf{y}_1$ is itself normal with mean $\mathbf{X}_1 \mu_0$ and covariance matrix $\sigma^2(I + \mathbf{X}_1 \Sigma_0 \mathbf{X}_1^\top)$:

$$\bar{\mathbf{y}}_1 \;\sim\; \mathrm{N}(\mathbf{X}_1 \mu_0, \sigma^2 \mathbf{X}_1 \Sigma_0 \mathbf{X}_1^\top), \tag{12.52}$$

$$\mathbf{y}_1 \;\sim\; \mathrm{N}(\mathbf{X}_1 \mu_0, \sigma^2(I + \mathbf{X}_1 \Sigma_0 \mathbf{X}_1^\top)). \tag{12.53}$$

As a special case, we can now also calculate the posterior predictive distribution (Chapter 2, Section 2.5.2) $\bar{f}_{\text{Bayes}}(Y_{n+1} \mid \mathbf{y}_1)$ for a new data point Y_{n+1} given a new data point x_{n+1} and past data $\mathbf{y}_1 \mid \mathbf{X}_1$, as well as the distribution $\bar{f}_{\text{Bayes}}(\bar{Y}_{n+1} \mid \mathbf{y}_1)$ of the prediction $\bar{Y}_{n+1} := x_{n+1}^\top \mu$ given x_{n+1} and $\mathbf{y}_1 \mid \mathbf{X}_1$. Namely, we must have

$$\bar{f}_{\text{Bayes}}(Y_{n+1} \mid \mathbf{y}_1) = \bar{f}_{\text{Bayes}}^{\circ}(Y_{n+1}) \text{ and } \bar{f}_{\text{Bayes}}(\bar{Y}_{n+1} \mid \mathbf{y}_1) = \bar{f}_{\text{Bayes}}^{\circ}(\bar{Y}_{n+1}) \tag{12.54}$$

where $\bar{f}_{\text{Bayes}}^{\circ}$ is the Bayesian marginal distribution defined relative to the prior w_a° that is equal to the posterior given $\mathbf{y}_1, \mathbf{X}_1$: $w_a^{\circ}(\mu) := w_a(\mu \mid \mathbf{y}_1)$. By (12.53), we have that the random variables Y_{n+1} and $\bar{Y}_{n+1}$ are normally distributed:

$$\bar{Y}_{n+1} \mid \mathbf{y}_1 \;\sim\; \mathrm{N}(x_{n+1}^\top \hat{\mu}_a, \sigma^2(x_{n+1}^\top (\mathbf{X}^\top \mathbf{X})^{-1} x_{n+1})), \tag{12.55}$$

$$Y_{n+1} \mid \mathbf{y}_1 \;\sim\; \mathrm{N}(x_{n+1}^\top \hat{\mu}_a, \sigma^2(1 + x_{n+1}^\top (\mathbf{X}^\top \mathbf{X})^{-1} x_{n+1})). \tag{12.56}$$

Example 12.8 [Interpreting (12.56)] Equation (12.56) expresses that Y_{n+1} is normally distributed, with mean given by the expected value of Y_{n+1} given x according to the Bayesian MAP $\hat{\mu}_a$. If $x = 0$, then the variance of Y_{n+1} is equal to σ^2. One immediately sees this, since, according to each f_μ, Y_{n+1} is normally distributed with variance σ^2 and mean $x^\top \mu$. If $x = 0$, then the value of μ has no effect on the mean of Y_{n+1}, so according to each f_μ, Y_{n+1} has mean 0 and variance σ^2. Since the posterior predictive distribution of Y_{n+1} is a mixture over such f_μ, it must also have variance σ^2. However, if x takes on larger values, then the variance of Y_{n+1} increases. Under regularity conditions on $\mathbf{X}$, the scale at which it increases will be of order $O(1/n)$. To see this, consider the normal location family again. Then $\mathbf{X}_1 = (1, \ldots, 1)^\top$ and $\mathbf{X}^\top \mathbf{X} = \mathbf{X}_1^\top \mathbf{X}_1 + \Sigma_0^{-1} = n + \tau^{-2}$ for some $\tau > 0$, so that the variance of Y_{n+1} is equal to $\sigma^2(1 + 1/(n + \tau^{-2})) = \sigma^2 + O(1/n)$.

The Bayesian Linear Model: Normality Rules

Consider a linear model $\mathcal{M}^{\mathbf{X}_1}$, equipped with a Gaussian prior on $\mu \in \mathbb{R}^k$. The posterior $w_a(\mu \mid \mathbf{y}_1)$, the marginal distribution $\bar{f}_{\text{Bayes}}(\mathbf{y}_1)$, and the predictive distribution of a single new outcome Y_{n+1} are all Gaussian, with means and variances as given in (12.47), (12.53), and (12.56), respectively.

The derivation of the marginal distribution given above is not self-contained, in that it refers to "general properties" of the normal distribution. It is also possible to give a direct derivation based on (12.51): we first apply the formula for the residual sum of squares, (12.11), but with the translated data $\mathbf{y} - \mathbf{X}\mu_0$ rather than $\mathbf{y}$ itself. Letting $\hat{\mu}$ stand for the ML estimator relative to data $\mathbf{y}' = \mathbf{y} - \mathbf{X}\mu_0$, this gives:

$$\mathrm{SSE}(\hat{\mu}, \mathbf{y}') = \mathbf{y}'^{\top}\mathbf{y}' - \mathbf{y}'^{\top}(\hat{\mathbf{y}} - \mathbf{X}\mu_0) =$$
$$\mathbf{y}'^{\top}\mathbf{y}' - \mathbf{y}'^{\top}(\mathbf{X}(\mathbf{X}^{\top}\mathbf{X})^{-1}\mathbf{X}^{\top}\mathbf{y} - \mathbf{X}\mu_0) =$$
$$\mathbf{y}'^{\top}\mathbf{y}' - \mathbf{y}'^{\top}(\mathbf{X}(\mathbf{X}^{\top}\mathbf{X})^{-1}\mathbf{X}^{\top}(\mathbf{y}' + \mathbf{X}\mu_0) - \mathbf{X}\mu_0) =$$
$$\mathbf{y}'^{\top}\mathbf{y}' - \mathbf{y}'^{\top}\mathbf{X}(\mathbf{X}^{\top}\mathbf{X})^{-1}\mathbf{X}^{\top}\mathbf{y}' =$$
$$\mathbf{y}'^{\top}\mathbf{y}' - \begin{pmatrix} \mathbf{y}_1 - \mathbf{X}_1\mu_0 \\ \mathbf{y}_0 - \mathbf{X}_0\mu_0 \end{pmatrix}^{\top} \begin{pmatrix} \mathbf{X}_1 \\ \mathbf{X}_0 \end{pmatrix} (\mathbf{X}^{\top}\mathbf{X})^{-1} \begin{pmatrix} \mathbf{X}_1 \\ \mathbf{X}_0 \end{pmatrix}^{\top} \begin{pmatrix} \mathbf{y}_1 - \mathbf{X}_1\mu_0 \\ \mathbf{y}_0 - \mathbf{X}_0\mu_0 \end{pmatrix}.$$

Since $\mathbf{y}_0 - \mathbf{X}_0\mu_0 = \mathbf{0}$, both terms simplify and we obtain:

$$\mathrm{RSS}(\mathbf{y} - \mathbf{X}\mu_0) = \mathrm{SSE}(\hat{\mu}, \mathbf{y} - \mathbf{X}\mu_0) =$$
$$(\mathbf{y}_1 - \mathbf{X}_1\mu_0)^{\top}(\mathbf{y}_1 - \mathbf{X}_1\mu_0) - (\mathbf{y}_1 - \mathbf{X}_1\mu_0)^{\top}\mathbf{X}_1(\mathbf{X}_1^{\top}\mathbf{X}_1 + \Sigma_0^{-1})^{-1}\mathbf{X}_1^{\top}(\mathbf{y}_1 - \mathbf{X}_1\mu_0),$$

$$(12.57)$$

so that

$$\mathrm{SSE}(\hat{\mu}, \mathbf{y} - \mathbf{X}\mu_0) =$$
$$(\mathbf{y}_1 - \mathbf{X}_1\mu_0)^{\top}\left(I - \mathbf{X}_1(\mathbf{X}_1^{\top}\mathbf{X}_1 + \Sigma_0^{-1})^{-1}\mathbf{X}_1^{\top}\right)(\mathbf{y}_1 - \mathbf{X}_1\mu_0) =$$
$$(\mathbf{y}_1 - \mathbf{X}_1\mu_0)^{\top}(I + \mathbf{X}_1\Sigma_0\mathbf{X}_1^{\top})^{-1}(\mathbf{y}_1 - \mathbf{X}_1\mu_0). \quad (12.58)$$

Here the first equation follows from (12.57). The second follows from the fact that for any matrices $\mathbf{X}$ and Σ_0 of appropriate dimensions, and for which the inverses stated below exist, we have:

$$I - \mathbf{X}\left(\mathbf{X}^{\top}\mathbf{X} + \Sigma_0^{-1}\right)^{-1}\mathbf{X}^{\top} = \left(I + \mathbf{X}\Sigma_0\mathbf{X}^{\top}\right)^{-1}. \quad (12.59)$$

This is a special case of the *matrix lemma* of Lindley and Smith (1972). It is easily verified by multiplying both sides by $I + \mathbf{X}\Sigma_0\mathbf{X}^{\top}$. Then (12.59) becomes $I + \mathbf{X}\Sigma_0\mathbf{X}^{\top} - \mathbf{X}(I + \Sigma_0\mathbf{X}^{\top}\mathbf{X})(\mathbf{X}^{\top}\mathbf{X} + \Sigma_0^{-1})^{-1}\mathbf{X}^{\top} = I$, and this fact then proves (12.59). The last line of (12.58) proves (12.53).

12.3.2 Bayesian Linear Models $\mathcal{M}^{\mathbf{X}}$ and $\mathcal{S}^{\mathbf{X}}$ with Noninformative Priors

This subsection closely parallels the previous one. In the previous subsection, we observed data $\mathbf{y}_1 \mid \mathbf{X}_1$ and determined $\bar{f}_{\text{Bayes}}$ relative to a prior $w_a(\mu)$ corresponding to virtual data $\mathbf{y}_0 \mid \mathbf{X}_0$. In the present subsection, we denote the set of observed data as $\mathbf{y} \mid \mathbf{X}$ and we partition it into two subsets $\mathbf{y}_0 \mid \mathbf{X}_0$ and $\mathbf{y}_1 \mid \mathbf{X}_1$. We consider priors that are improper, but the posterior conditioned on $\mathbf{y}_0 \mid \mathbf{X}_0$ will be proper, and precisely equal to a prior $w_a(\mu)$ of the kind that we considered in the previous subsection. Thus, by the reasoning of Section 11.4.1, the marginal density

$$\bar{f}_{\text{Bayes}}(\mathbf{y}_1 \mid \mathbf{y}_0) = \frac{\bar{f}_{\text{Bayes}}(\mathbf{y})}{\bar{f}_{\text{Bayes}}(\mathbf{y}_0)}, \tag{12.60}$$

can be understood as a universal model for data $\mathbf{y}_1$. We are interested in computing (12.60) for the model $\mathcal{M}^{\mathbf{X}}$, and later also for the extended model $\mathcal{S}^{\mathbf{X}}$.

$\mathcal{M}^{\mathbf{X}}$ with Jeffreys' Prior We first restrict attention to the model $\mathcal{M}^{\mathbf{X}}$ with Jeffreys' prior, which is given by

$$w_{\text{Jeffreys}}(\mu) = \sqrt{\det I(\mu \mid \mathbf{X})} = \sigma^{-k}\sqrt{\det \mathbf{X}^\top \mathbf{X}}. \tag{12.61}$$

This quantity does not depend on μ, so Jeffreys' prior w_{Jeffreys} is uniform over $\mathbb{R}^k$, and therefore improper.

Suppose we observe an initial segment of data $\mathbf{y}_0$. It can be seen that the posterior $w_{\text{Jeffreys}}(\mu \mid \mathbf{y}_0)$ is improper if and only if the rank of $\mathbf{X}_0$ is smaller than k. In particular this will be the case if $\mathbf{y}_0$ contains less than k observations. Let us assume then that $\mathbf{y}_0, \mathbf{X}_0$ consists of $n_0 \geq k$ observations, and that the columns of $\mathbf{X}_0$ are linearly independent, so that $\mathbf{X}_0$ is of rank k. Then $w_{\text{Jeffreys}}(\mu \mid \mathbf{y}_0)$ is proper, and by first applying Bayes formula and then Lemma 12.1, we see

$$w_{\text{Jeffreys}}(\mu \mid \mathbf{y}_0) \propto f_\mu(\mathbf{y}_0) \propto e^{-\frac{1}{2\sigma^2}(\mu - \hat{\mu}_0)^\top \mathbf{X}_0^\top \mathbf{X}_0 (\mu - \hat{\mu}_0)}.$$

The posterior after observing initial data $\mathbf{y}_0$ is therefore proper and Gaussian, and we can apply (12.50), Section 12.3.1, to derive expressions for $-\ln \bar{f}_{\text{Bayes}}(\mathbf{y}_1 \mid \mathbf{y}_0)$. But we can also calculate $-\ln \bar{f}_{\text{Bayes}}(\mathbf{y}_1 \mid \mathbf{y}_0)$ directly, as follows: let w_{U} be the uniform prior over $\mathbb{R}^k$, $w_{\text{U}}(\mu){:=}1$. Let $n_0 \geq k$. Relative to w_{U}, we have

$$\bar{f}_U(\mathbf{y}_0) = \int_{\mu \in \mathbb{R}^k} \frac{1}{\sqrt{2\pi\sigma^2}^{n_0}} e^{-\frac{1}{2\sigma^2} \text{SSE}(\mu, \mathbf{y}_0)} w_U(\mu) d\mu =$$

$$\int_{\mu \in \mathbb{R}^k} \frac{1}{\sqrt{2\pi\sigma^2}^{n_0}} e^{-\frac{1}{2\sigma^2} \left(\text{RSS}(\mathbf{y}_0) + (\mu - \hat{\mu}_0)^\top \mathbf{X}_0^\top \mathbf{X}_0 (\mu - \hat{\mu}_0) \right)} d\mu =$$

$$\sqrt{\det(\mathbf{X}_0^\top \mathbf{X}_0)^{-1}} \left(\sqrt{2\pi\sigma^2} \right)^{k-n_0} e^{-\frac{1}{2\sigma^2} \text{RSS}(\mathbf{y}_0)}, \quad (12.62)$$

so that, with (12.61),

$$\bar{f}_{\text{Jeffreys}}(\mathbf{y}_0) = \sigma^{-n_0} \sqrt{\frac{\det \mathbf{X}^\top \mathbf{X}}{\det \mathbf{X}_0^\top \mathbf{X}_0}} \sqrt{2\pi}^{k-n_0} e^{-\frac{1}{2\sigma^2} \text{RSS}(\mathbf{y}_0)}. \quad (12.63)$$

It may seem strange that this expression refers to the full $\mathbf{X}^\top \mathbf{X}$, even though we evaluate $\bar{f}_{\text{Jeffreys}}$ only on $\mathbf{y}_0$ and not on the full $\mathbf{y}$. But note that $\bar{f}_{\text{Jeffreys}}(\mathbf{y}_0)$ is not a probability density. We now calculate $\bar{f}_{\text{Jeffreys}}(\mathbf{y}_1 \mid \mathbf{y}_0)$, which does represent a density and which does not refer to future design vectors. Using (12.60), applying (12.62) both to numerator (with $\mathbf{y}_0$ replaced by $\mathbf{y}$, and n_0 by n) and denominator, we get

$$- \ln \bar{f}_{\text{Jeffreys}}(\mathbf{y}_1 \mid \mathbf{y}_0) =$$

$$- \ln \bar{f}_U(\mathbf{y}_1 \mid \mathbf{y}_0) = - \ln \int f_\mu(\mathbf{y}_1 \mid \mathbf{y}_0) w(\mu \mid \mathbf{y}_0) d\mu =$$

$$\frac{1}{2} \ln \frac{\det(\mathbf{X}^\top \mathbf{X})}{\det(\mathbf{X}_0^\top \mathbf{X}_0)} + \frac{n - n_0}{2} \ln 2\pi\sigma^2 + \frac{1}{2\sigma^2} \left(\text{RSS}(\mathbf{y}) - \text{RSS}(\mathbf{y}_0) \right). \quad (12.64)$$

A concrete example is given in Example 11.11, page 324, and Example 11.13, page 328. Note that, if $n_0 = k$, then $\text{RSS}(\mathbf{y}_0) = 0$ and (12.64) must coincide with (12.50), as indeed it does.

$\mathcal{S}^\mathbf{X}$ **with Noninformative Priors**   We now consider what happens if we also treat the variance σ^2 as a freely varying parameter. Our derivation will hold for all improper priors of the form $w(\mu, \sigma) = \sigma^{-t}$, for some $t \geq 1$. As we shall see, this includes a prior proportional to Jeffreys' prior as a special case. Note that the number of parameters in $\mathcal{S}^\mathbf{X}$ is $k + 1$. Let $n_0 \geq k + 1$. Redefining $\bar{f}_{\text{Bayes}}$ relative to $\mathcal{S}^\mathbf{X}$ and prior $w(\mu, \sigma) = \sigma^{-t}$, we can now write

$$\bar{f}_{\text{Bayes}}(\mathbf{y}_0) = \int_{\mu \in \mathbb{R}^k, \sigma^2 \geq 0} f_{\mu, \sigma^2}(\mathbf{y}_0) \sigma^{-t} d\mu d\sigma = \int_0^\infty \bar{f}_{\text{Bayes}}(\mathbf{y}_0 \mid \sigma) \sigma^{-t} d\sigma,$$

where $\bar{f}_{\text{Bayes}}(\mathbf{y}_0 \mid \sigma)$ is given by (12.62), with the dependence on σ now made explicit. For any fixed t, $\bar{f}_{\text{Bayes}}$ satisfies

$$\bar{f}_{\text{Bayes}}(\mathbf{y}_0) = (\det \mathbf{X}_0^\top \mathbf{X}_0)^{-1/2} \sqrt{2\pi}^{-k-n_0} \int \sigma^{k-n_0-t} e^{-\frac{1}{2\sigma^2} \text{RSS}(\mathbf{y}_0)} d\sigma. \quad (12.65)$$

Evaluating this integral (see below) and taking logarithms, this becomes

$$-\ln \bar{f}_{\text{Bayes}}(\mathbf{y}_0) = \frac{n_0 - k - 1 + t}{2} \ln \text{RSS}(\mathbf{y}_0) + \frac{n_0 - k}{2} \ln 2\pi$$
$$- \frac{n_0 - k + t - 3}{2} \ln 2 + \frac{1}{2} \ln \det \mathbf{X}_0^\top \mathbf{X}_0 - \ln \Gamma \left(\frac{n_0 - k - 1 + t}{2} \right), \quad (12.66)$$

where Γ is the gamma function (Chapter 2, page 45).

Jeffreys' Prior By (12.42), Jeffreys' prior is given by $\sigma^{-k-1} \sqrt{2n \det \mathbf{X}^\top \mathbf{X}}$, so that, plugging in $t = k + 1$ into (12.66) and multiplying by $\sqrt{2n \det \mathbf{X}^\top \mathbf{X}}$, we get

$$-\ln \bar{f}_{\text{Jeffreys}}(\mathbf{y}_0) = \frac{n_0}{2} \ln \text{RSS}(\mathbf{y}_0) + \frac{n_0 - k}{2} \ln 2\pi$$
$$- \frac{n_0 - 2}{2} \ln 2 + \frac{1}{2} \ln \frac{\det \mathbf{X}_0^\top \mathbf{X}_0}{2n \det \mathbf{X}^\top \mathbf{X}} - \ln \Gamma \left(\frac{n_0}{2} \right) =$$
$$\frac{n_0}{2} \ln \text{RSS}(\mathbf{y}_0) + \frac{n_0 - k}{2} \ln \pi$$
$$- \frac{k - 1}{2} \ln 2 - \frac{1}{2} \ln n + \frac{1}{2} \ln \frac{\det \mathbf{X}_0^\top \mathbf{X}_0}{\det \mathbf{X}^\top \mathbf{X}} - \ln \Gamma \left(\frac{n_0}{2} \right). \quad (12.67)$$

We now evaluate the conditional codelength $-\ln \bar{f}_{\text{Bayes}}(\mathbf{y}_1 \mid \mathbf{y}_0)$ given by (12.60). We do this by applying (12.66) both to numerator and denominator. where $\mathbf{y}_0$ consists of the first n_0 observations. This gives:

$$-\ln \bar{f}_{\text{Bayes}}(\mathbf{y} \mid \mathbf{y}_0) = \frac{n - n_0}{2} \ln \pi + \frac{1}{2} \ln \frac{\det \mathbf{X}^\top \mathbf{X}}{\det \mathbf{X}_0^\top \mathbf{X}_0} +$$
$$\frac{n - k + t - 1}{2} \ln \text{RSS}(\mathbf{y}) - \frac{n_0 - k + t - 1}{2} \ln \text{RSS}(\mathbf{y}_0)$$
$$+ \ln \Gamma(\frac{n_0 - k + t - 1}{2}) - \ln \Gamma(\frac{n - k + t - 1}{2}). \quad (12.68)$$

Here k is the number of parameters of $\mathcal{M}^\mathbf{X}$, and one less than the number of parameters of $\mathcal{S}^\mathbf{X}$. Compared to (12.64), we see that the dependence on $\text{RSS}(\mathbf{y})$ is now *logarithmic* rather than linear. A concrete illustration of (12.68) based on the full normal family is given in Example 11.12, page 326.

[Evaluation of $\bar{f}_{\text{Bayes}}(\mathbf{y} \mid \mathbf{y}_0)$ for $\mathcal{S}^{\times}$] In order to derive (12.68), we used the following fact, which we state without proof: for all $m > 0, b > 0$, we have

$$\int_0^\infty \sigma^{-m-1} e^{-\frac{b}{2\sigma^2}} d\sigma = 2^{\frac{1}{2}m-1} b^{-\frac{1}{2}m} \Gamma(\frac{1}{2}m). \tag{12.69}$$

Evaluating (12.65), using (12.69) with $-m = k - n_0 - t + 1$, gives

$$\bar{f}_{\text{Bayes}}(\mathbf{y}_0) =$$
$$\frac{\sqrt{2\pi}^k}{\sqrt{2\pi}^{n_0}} \sqrt{\det(\mathbf{X}_0^\top \mathbf{X}_0)^{-1}} \frac{1}{\text{RSS}(\mathbf{y}_0)^{\frac{n_0-k+t-1}{2}}} \Gamma(\frac{n_0-k+t-1}{2}) 2^{\frac{n_0-k+t-3}{2}}, \tag{12.70}$$

from which (12.66) follows.

We highlight the instantiation of (12.68) for two specific priors. First we consider the prior $w(\sigma) = \sigma^{-1}$. This prior is a standard noninformative prior used in Bayesian statistics that is both location and scale invariant. With this prior, $\bar{f}_{\text{Bayes}}(\mathbf{y} \mid \mathbf{y}_0)$ achieves the minimax optimal conditional expected redundancy in the sense of Liang and Barron (2004); see Chapter 11, Section 11.4.3. The second prior we consider is Jeffreys' prior. Then $t = k + 1$ and (12.68) becomes

$$- \ln \bar{f}_{\text{Jeffreys}}(\mathbf{y} \mid \mathbf{y}_0) = \frac{n-n_0}{2} \ln \pi + \frac{1}{2} \ln \frac{\det \mathbf{X}^\top \mathbf{X}}{\det \mathbf{X}_0^\top \mathbf{X}_0} +$$
$$\frac{n}{2} \ln \text{RSS}(\mathbf{y}) - \frac{n_0}{2} \ln \text{RSS}(\mathbf{y}_0) + \ln \Gamma(\frac{n_0}{2}) - \ln \Gamma(\frac{n}{2}), \tag{12.71}$$

which can also be seen directly from (12.66).

The Posterior $w(\sigma \mid \mathbf{y}_0)$: Square-Root Inverted Gamma Although it is not needed in the development of universal codes for models $\mathcal{S}^{\times}$, it is of some interest to determine the posterior distribution of σ corresponding to improper priors of the form $w(\mu, \sigma) = \sigma^{-t}$. From (12.65) and Bayes formula, we see that

$$w(\sigma \mid \mathbf{y}_0) = \frac{\bar{f}_{\text{Bayes}}(\mathbf{y}_0 \mid \sigma) w(\sigma)}{\bar{f}_{\text{Bayes}}(\mathbf{y}_0)} \propto \sigma^{k-n_0-t} e^{-\frac{1}{2\sigma^2} \text{RSS}(\mathbf{y}_0)}.$$

This is the density of a *square-root inverted gamma distribution* (Bernardo and Smith 1994). Just as Jeffreys' prior for the model $\mathcal{M}^{\times}$ leads to a Gaussian posterior, Jeffreys' prior for $\mathcal{S}^{\times}$ leads to a square-root inverted gamma posterior. The Liang-Barron prior for $\mathcal{S}^{\times}$ also leads to such a posterior, but with different parameters. Not surprisingly, the linear models $\mathcal{S}^{\times}$ equipped with square-root inverted gamma priors on σ have been well studied in the Bayesian community. We note though that usually the model $\mathcal{S}^{\times}$ is either parameterized by

$\tau = \sigma^2$ (Hansen and Yu 2001), or by $\lambda = \sigma^{-2}$ (Bernardo and Smith 1994). In the first case, after performing the appropriate variable transformation, the square-root inverted gamma density for σ becomes the density of an ordinary inverted gamma distribution for τ. In the second case, it becomes the density of an ordinary (noninverted) gamma distribution for λ.

12.4   Universal Models for Linear Regression

After all preparations of the previous sections, it is now time to harvest. In this section we consider NML and Bayesian universal codes for linear models. Although we already developed explicit expressions for the Bayesian universal models $\bar{f}_{\text{Bayes}}$, we did not explicitly calculate their regret. Here, we calculate this regret, and show that, with a Gaussian or Jeffreys' prior, the Bayesian universal model coincides *exactly* (and not just asymptotically) with a luckiness and conditional NML universal model, respectively. Before we do this, however, we briefly consider the ordinary NML universal model.

12.4.1   NML

The NML distribution corresponding to $\mathcal{M}^{\mathbf{X}}$ is only well defined if we restrict μ to lie within some closed ineccsi parameter set $\Theta_0 \subset \mathbb{R}^k$. Calculation of the resulting $\bar{f}_{\text{nml}}(\mathbf{y} \mid \hat{\mu} \in \Theta_0)$ and minimax regret $\text{CCOMP}^{(n)}(\Theta_0)$ is done by a straightforward extension of the corresponding calculation for the normal location family, which we already did in Examples 11.1 and 11.5. As in those examples, we use the decomposition (7.24) of $\text{COMP}^{(n)}(\Theta_0)$ in terms of the value of the sufficient statistics, to find that $\text{CCOMP}^{(n)}(\Theta_0) = \ln \int_{\Theta_0} f_{\mu}^{\circ}(\mu) d\mu$. Here f_{μ}° is the density of the ML estimator $\hat{\mu}$ that arises if $\mathbf{y}$ is distributed according to $P_{\mu} \in \mathcal{M}^{\mathbf{X}}$. Because P_{μ} is a multivariate normal distribution, $\hat{\mu}$ is itself normal with mean μ and variance σ_n^2, so that, just as in (11.1), we find

$$f_{\mu}(\mu) = (2\pi(\sigma^2/n))^{-1/2}. \tag{12.72}$$

Therefore, analogously to (11.8), we get

$$\text{CCOMP}^{(n)}(\Theta_0) = \ln V(\Theta_0) + \frac{1}{2} \ln \frac{n}{2\pi\sigma^2},$$

where V denotes the standard, Euclidean volume of the set Θ_0. Using (12.72), the codelength achieved with the conditional NML density is given by

$$-\ln \bar{f}_{\text{nml}}(\mathbf{y} \mid \hat{\mu} \in \Theta_0) = \ln V(\Theta_0).$$

The NML code will not be of too much use in model selection contexts, since the codelength heavily depends on prior knowledge about the region in which $\hat{\mu}$ will fall. We can partially (not completely) avoid this dependency if we (a) treat σ^2 as an additional parameter, rather than a fixed constant, and (b) work with the renormalized NML (RNML) rather than the ordinary NML distribution. This will be explored further in Chapter 14, Section 14.5.

12.4.2   Bayes and LNML

Suppose we observe a sample $\mathbf{y}_1 \mid \mathbf{X}_1$. We consider the luckiness regret of $\bar{f}_{\text{Bayes}}$ with luckiness function $a'(\mu) := -\ln w_a(\mu)$, where $w_a(\mu)$ and $a(\mu)$ are as in (12.44). Note that $a'(\mu) = a(\mu) + c$, where c does not depend on μ, so that $\hat{\mu}_a = \hat{\mu}_{a'}$. By (12.48), the luckiness regret is given by

$$\text{LREG}_{a'}(\bar{f}_{\text{Bayes}}, \mathcal{M}^{\mathbf{X}}, \mathbf{y}_1) = -\ln \bar{f}_{\text{Bayes}}(\mathbf{y}_1) - [-\ln f_{\hat{\mu}_{a'}}(\mathbf{y}_1) + a'(\hat{\mu}_{a'})] =$$
$$\ln w(\hat{\mu}_{a'} \mid \mathbf{y}_1) = \frac{1}{2} \ln \frac{\det(\mathbf{X}^\top \mathbf{X})}{(2\pi\sigma^2)^k}, \quad (12.73)$$

where the second equality follows because we evaluate the posterior at its maximum, so that the exponent in the posterior density evaluates to 0.

Bayes = LNML-2   It can be seen that the luckiness regret does not depend on the Luckiness ML estimator $\hat{\mu}_a$: the luckiness regret takes on the same value, no matter what data we observe. By the reasoning of the box on page 182, Chapter 6, Section 6.2.1, this implies that $\bar{f}_{\text{Bayes}}$ is the solution to the minimax equation

$$\min_{\bar{f}} \sup_{\mathbf{y}_1 \in \mathbb{R}^n} -\ln \bar{f}(\mathbf{y}_1) - [-\ln f_{\hat{\mu}_{a'}}(\mathbf{y}_1) + a'(\hat{\mu}_{a'})].$$

Comparing with (11.19), we see that $\bar{f}$ is exactly (and not just asymptotically) equal to the luckiness NML-2 distribution on $\mathbb{R}^n$! A concrete illustration based on the normal location family can be found in Example 11.9, page 315. Kakade, Seeger, and Foster (2006) show the same result for the more general Gaussian process models with Gaussian noise (Chapter 13, Section 13.5). The present result can be seen as a special case of theirs. Because Bayesian universal models are prequential (Chapter 6, Section 6.4), the result implies that the luckiness NML-2 universal model for linear models is also prequential, i.e. it constitutes a probabilistic source. As we indicated in Chapter 6, Section 6.4, this certainly does not hold for every NML or luckiness NML-2 distribution.

For Linear Regression, Bayes with Normal Prior = Luckiness NML with Square Luckiness Function

For linear regression models $\mathcal{M}^{\mathbf{X}}$ with fixed variance, the Bayesian universal code based on a Gaussian prior coincides exactly with a particular LNML-2 code, for *all* sample sizes, and not just asymptotically.

This implies that the LNML-2 universal model for the linear regression models is *prequential*, i.e. it constitutes a probabilistic source.

12.4.3   Bayes-Jeffreys and CNML

In this section we consider both the model $\mathcal{M}^{\mathbf{X}}$ and the extended model $\mathcal{S}^{\mathbf{X}}$. We start with $\mathcal{M}^{\mathbf{X}}$:

The Model $\mathcal{M}^{\mathbf{X}}$ Consider the Bayesian universal code relative to Jeffreys' prior, with codelengths given by (12.64). If we take $n_0 = k$, then $\mathrm{RSS}(\mathbf{y}_0) = 0$ and the regret of $\bar{f}_{\mathrm{Jeffreys}}(\mathbf{y}_1 \mid \mathbf{y}_0)$ corresponding to (12.64) on the full sequence $\mathbf{y}$ can be calculated using the fact that it must be equal to the luckiness regret of $\bar{f}_{\mathrm{Jeffreys}}(\mathbf{y}_1 \mid \mathbf{y}_0)$ relative to $\mathbf{y}_1$, with luckiness function $a''(\mu) = -\ln f_\mu(\mathbf{y}_0)$. This was explained in Chapter 11, Section 11.4.2, before Theorem 11.3. Since $w_a(\mu) \propto f_\mu(\mathbf{y}_0)$, we have $w_a(\mu) = f_\mu(\mathbf{y}_0)/\int_{\mathbb{R}^k} f_\mu(\mathbf{y}_0)d\mu$. Since $a'(\mu) = -\ln w_a(\mu)$, we have $a''(\mu) = a'(\mu) + \ln \int_{\mathbb{R}^k} f_\mu(\mathbf{y}_0)d\mu$. By (12.62),

$$\int_{\mathbb{R}^k} f_\mu(\mathbf{y}_0)d\mu = \sqrt{\det(\mathbf{X}_0^\top \mathbf{X}_0)^{-1}}, \tag{12.74}$$

so that, by (12.74) and (12.73),

$$\mathrm{REG}_{\ln}(\bar{f}_{\mathrm{Jeffreys}}(\mathbf{y}_1 \mid \mathbf{y}_0), \mathcal{M}^{\mathbf{X}}, \mathbf{y}) = \mathrm{LREG}_{a''}(\bar{f}_{\mathrm{Jeffreys}}(\mathbf{y}_1 \mid \mathbf{y}_0), \mathcal{M}^{\mathbf{X}}, \mathbf{y}_1) =$$

$$\mathrm{LREG}_{a'}(\bar{f}_{\mathrm{Jeffreys}}(\mathbf{y}_1 \mid \mathbf{y}_0), \mathcal{M}^{\mathbf{X}}, \mathbf{y}_1) + \ln \int_{\mathbb{R}^k} f_\mu(\mathbf{y}_0)d\mu =$$

$$\frac{1}{2} \ln \frac{\det(\mathbf{X}^\top \mathbf{X})}{\det(\mathbf{X}_0^\top \mathbf{X}_0)} - \frac{k}{2} \ln 2\pi\sigma^2. \tag{12.75}$$

$\mathcal{M}^{\mathbf{X}}$: Bayes = CNML-2   Just as for the luckiness regret, the "conditional" regret does not depend on data $\mathbf{y}$. Therefore, it is the same for all data $\mathbf{y}$.

Reasoning as in the box on page 182, Chapter 6, Section 6.2.1, this shows that, among all conditional distributions of $\mathbf{y}_1$ given $\mathbf{y}_0$ and $\mathbf{X}$, $\bar{f}_{\text{Jeffreys}}(\mathbf{y}_1 \mid \mathbf{y}_0)$ achieves the minimax regret relative to $\mathbf{y}$. Thus, $\bar{f}_{\text{Jeffreys}}(\cdot \mid \mathbf{y}_0)$ must be identical to $\bar{f}_{\text{Cnml-2}}(\cdot \mid \mathbf{y}_0)$, the density of the CNML-2 distribution: for the linear models $\mathcal{M}^{\mathbf{X}}$, the Bayesian approach with Jeffreys' prior and the CNML-2 approach coincide exactly, for all sample sizes. This important fact is highlighted in the box at the end of this section. For a concrete illustration with the normal location family, see Example 11.11.

> $\mathcal{M}^{\mathbf{X}}$: **Bayes-Jeffreys = CNML-2 = Asymptotics** This situation clearly parallels the one for the luckiness regret. But in the conditional case, things are even better, since the regret relative to $\bar{f}_{\text{Cnml-2}}(\mathbf{y} \mid \mathbf{y}_0)$ and $\bar{f}_{\text{Jeffreys}}(\mathbf{y} \mid \mathbf{y}_0)$ is also equal to the corresponding asymptotic regret (11.47) appearing in Theorem 11.3. Strictly speaking, the theorem is not applicable to the present context since we only proved its correctness for (unconditional) i.i.d. models. But the result holds more generally than just under the circumstances under which we proved it; as we now show, for the linear model with Jeffreys' prior, the *asymptotic regret formula is exact for all sample sizes*.

First note that the Fisher information in (11.47) is defined with respect to a single outcome, whereas in the present context we have n outcomes. Therefore, we should plug in $I(\theta) = n^{-1}I(\mu \mid \mathbf{X})$ as $n^{-1}\sigma^{-2}\mathbf{X}^{\top}\mathbf{X}$ into (11.47). Then $\sqrt{\det I(\theta)}$ becomes $n^{-k/2}\sigma^{-k}\sqrt{\det \mathbf{X}^{\top}\mathbf{X}}$, and (11.47) can be rewritten as:

$$\text{REG}_{\ln}(\bar{f}_{\text{Cnml-2}}(\cdot \mid \mathbf{y}_0), \mathcal{M}^{\mathbf{X}}, \mathbf{y}) = -\ln \bar{f}_{\text{Cnml-2}}(\mathbf{y}_1 \mid \mathbf{y}_0) + \ln f_{\hat{\mu}}(\mathbf{y}) =$$

$$\frac{k}{2}\ln\frac{n}{2\pi} - \frac{k}{2}\ln(n\sigma^2) + \frac{1}{2}\ln\det(\mathbf{X}^{\top}\mathbf{X}) + \ln\int_{\mu\in\mathbb{R}^k} f_{\mu}(\mathbf{y}_0)d\mu + o(1) =$$

$$\frac{1}{2}\ln\frac{\det(\mathbf{X}^{\top}\mathbf{X})}{\det(\mathbf{X}_0^{\top}\mathbf{X}_0)} - \frac{k}{2}\ln(2\pi\sigma^2) + o(1), \quad (12.76)$$

where the third equality follows by (12.74). Comparing with (12.75), we see that the asymptotic formula for the regret is precisely correct for all $n > k$, and not just asymptotically.

$\mathcal{S}^{\mathbf{X}}$: **Bayes = CNML-2** We now repeat the analysis for the extended model $\mathcal{S}^{\mathbf{X}}$. Note that, by (12.33), relative to this model, the codelength of $\mathbf{y}$ obtained with the ML distribution $f_{\hat{\mu}(\mathbf{y}),\hat{\sigma}^2(\mathbf{y})}$, is given by

$$-\ln f_{\hat{\mu}(\mathbf{y}),\hat{\sigma}^2(\mathbf{y})}(\mathbf{y}) = -\ln\left(\frac{1}{\sqrt{2\pi\hat{\sigma}^2}}\right)^n e^{-\frac{n}{2}} = \frac{n}{2} - \frac{n}{2}\ln\frac{n}{2\pi} + \frac{n}{2}\ln\text{RSS}(\mathbf{y}).$$

Together with (12.71), this gives the following regret:

$$\text{REG}_{\ln}(\bar{f}_{\text{Jeffreys}}(\cdot \mid \mathbf{y}_0), \mathcal{S}^{\mathbf{X}}, \mathbf{y}) = -\frac{n_0}{2}\ln \pi - \frac{n_0}{2}\ln \text{RSS}(\mathbf{y}_0) +$$
$$\frac{n}{2}\ln\frac{n}{2} - \frac{n}{2} + \frac{1}{2}\ln\frac{\det \mathbf{X}^\top \mathbf{X}}{\det \mathbf{X}_0^\top \mathbf{X}_0} + \ln\mathbf{\Gamma}(\frac{n_0}{2}) - \ln\mathbf{\Gamma}(\frac{n}{2}). \quad (12.77)$$

Just as for $\mathcal{M}^{\mathbf{X}}$, by the reasoning of Chapter 6, Section 6.2.1, it follows that, conditional on each $\mathbf{y}_0$, $\bar{f}_{\text{Jeffreys}}(\cdot \mid \mathbf{y}_0)$ achieves the minimax regret among all sequences $\mathbf{y}_1 \in \mathbb{R}^{n-n_0}$. It must therefore be equal to the density of the CNML-2 distribution $\bar{P}_{\text{Cnml-2}}$. We note that this does *not* hold for the Liang-Barron universal code $\bar{f}_{\text{LB}}$: by (12.68) we can see that its regret depends slightly on $\mathbf{y}_1$. Therefore, although it is minimax in a stochastic sense (Chapter 11, Section 11.4.3), it cannot be conditionally minimax for individual sequences.

$\mathcal{S}^{\mathbf{X}}$: | **Bayes - Asymptotics** | $\leq 1/(6n)$: In contrast to the case of $\mathcal{M}^{\mathbf{X}}$, the regret (12.77) is now not exactly equal anymore to the corresponding asymptotic regret (11.47) given in Theorem 11.3. However, by rewriting the gamma function using Stirling's approximation (Chapter 4, page 128), we find that

$$\ln\mathbf{\Gamma}(\frac{n}{2}) = \ln\mathbf{\Gamma}(\frac{n}{2} + 1) - \ln\frac{n}{2} = \frac{n}{2}\ln\frac{n}{2} + \frac{1}{2}\ln 2\pi - \frac{1}{2}\ln\frac{n}{2} - \frac{n}{2} + r(n),$$

where $|r(n)| \leq 1/(6n)$. We can thus rewrite (12.77) as

$$-\frac{n_0 + 1}{2}\ln\pi - \frac{n_0}{2}\ln\text{RSS}(\mathbf{y}_0) + \frac{1}{2}\ln\frac{\det\mathbf{X}^\top\mathbf{X}}{\det\mathbf{X}_0^\top\mathbf{X}_0} + \ln\mathbf{\Gamma}(\frac{n_0}{2}) + \frac{1}{2}\ln n - \ln 2$$
$$+ O(1/n), \quad (12.78)$$

where $|O(1/n)| \leq 1/(6n)$. For a fair comparison to (11.47), we should realize that the number of parameters is $k + 1$, and that the matrix $I(\theta)$ occurring in (11.47) is equal to $n^{-1}I(\mu, \sigma^2 \mid \mathbf{X}^\top\mathbf{X})$ in our case. Thus the term $\ln\int P_\theta(\mathbf{x}_0)\sqrt{\det I(\theta)}d\theta$ is equal to $\ln\bar{f}_{\text{Jeffreys}}(\mathbf{y}_0) - ((k+1)/2)\ln n$. Using (12.67), (11.47) thus becomes:

$$\text{REG}_{\ln}(\bar{f}_{\text{Jeffreys}}(\cdot \mid \mathbf{y}_0), \mathcal{S}^{\mathbf{X}}, \mathbf{y}) =$$
$$\frac{k+1}{2}\ln\frac{n}{2\pi} - \frac{n_0 - k}{2}\ln\pi + \frac{k-1}{2}\ln 2 - \frac{k}{2}\ln n +$$
$$\frac{1}{2}\ln\frac{\det\mathbf{X}^\top\mathbf{X}}{\det\mathbf{X}_0^\top\mathbf{X}_0} - \frac{n_0}{2}\ln\text{RSS}(\mathbf{y}_0) + \ln\mathbf{\Gamma}(\frac{n_0}{2}) + o(1), \quad (12.79)$$

which can be seen to coincide with (12.78). Thus, the asymptotics do not hold precisely anymore, but they are very close.

Bayes with Jeffreys' Prior = Conditional NML-2, both for $\mathcal{M}^\mathbf{X}$ and $\mathcal{S}^\mathbf{X}$
For linear regression models, the Bayesian conditional universal code based on Jeffreys' prior coincides exactly with the CNML-2 code, for *all* sample sizes, and not just asymptotically. This holds both if the variance is kept fixed ($\mathcal{M}^\mathbf{X}$) and if it is allowed to vary ($\mathcal{S}^\mathbf{X}$).

This implies that the CNML-2 universal model for the linear regression models is *prequential*, i.e. it constitutes a probabilistic source.

[**Reconciliation with Standard** $(k/2) \ln n$ **Asymptotics**] There is an exact correspondence between Bayes with Jeffreys' prior and CNML-2. There is no such exact correspondence between Bayes with Gaussian prior and LNML-2: the expressions for the asymptotic Bayesian regret, (8.2) in Theorem 8.1 and (11.25) in Theorem 11.2, do not hold exactly, but only up to $o(1)$. There are two reasons for this. First, (8.2) involves the ML rather than the MAP estimator. With Jeffreys' prior, the MAP estimator for $\mathbf{y}_1$ coincides with the ML estimator for $\mathbf{y}$, and the discrepancy is resolved, but for the Gaussian prior, this is not the case. Second, both theorems involve the Fisher information defined only relative to the observed data $\mathbf{y}_1, \mathbf{X}_1$. To make the formulae hold precisely, we need to look at the Fisher information relative to the combined observed and virtual data $\mathbf{y} \mid \mathbf{X}$. In the improper Jeffreys' prior approach, the Fisher information is automatically defined in the "right" way and we get an exact match.

Nevertheless, under appropriate conditions on the sequence of regressors x_1, $x_2, \ldots$, (8.2) and (11.25) should still hold to within $o(1)$. Indeed, the regret will typically behave like $(k/2) \ln n + O(1)$, although this fact is somewhat hidden in the characterization (12.76). For example, this holds if all x_i are equal to 1 (the normal location family). As another example, suppose the regressors are sampled i.i.d. from some distribution concentrated on an ineccsi subset of $\mathbb{R}^k$. Then, by the law of large numbers, there exists $K_1, K_2 > 0$ such that with probability 1, for all large n, $K_1 \leq n^{-k} \det(\sum x_i x_i^\top) \leq K_2$, so that (12.76) now expresses the familiar $(k/2) \log n + O(1)$ asymptotics.

Nevertheless, as noted by Liang and Barron (2004), there are cases such as nonstationary time series where the x_i are not i.i.d., and $\det \mathbf{X}^\top \mathbf{X}$ may grow at a faster rater than n^k, e.g. it may grow as n^{2k}. In that case, $(1/2) \ln \det \mathbf{X}^\top \mathbf{X}$ does not grow as $(1/2) \ln n + O(1)$, but, for example, as $\ln n + O(1)$. Thus, in general, it is always better to use the exact formula rather than the possibly quite inaccurate approximation $(k/2) \ln n + O(1)$. See also the discussion in Section 13.5.3.

13 *Beyond Parametrics*

In this chapter, we consider model classes $\mathcal{M}$ that are so large that they cannot be continuously parameterized by a finite-dimensional space. We have to distinguish between so-called CUP model classes and (fully) "nonparametric" model classes. CUP model classes are really countable *unions* of *p*arametric models. An example is the union $\mathcal{P} = \bigcup_{k \geq 1} \mathcal{P}^{(k)}$, where $\mathcal{P}^{(k)}$ is the model of $(k-1)$-degree polynomials with Gaussian noise, Chapter 2, Example 2.9. "Fully nonparametric" model classes are even much larger than that. Nonparametric model classes $\mathcal{M}^*$ can often be understood as a kind of "closure" of a corresponding CUP model class $\mathcal{M}$. The CUP model class $\mathcal{M}$ is then viewed as an approximation of $\mathcal{M}^*$. For example, the closure of $\mathcal{P}$ contains all continuous functions that can be arbitrarily well approximated by polynomials. If the inputs are restricted to a finite closed interval, this includes *every* continuous function on this interval.

In this chapter, we first provide an overview of CUP and fully nonparametric model classes. We then, in Section 13.2, discuss CUP model classes, introducing terminology that will be heavily used in Part III of this book. Since fully nonparametric universal codes are rather abstract, we have chosen to introduce them by a simple, concrete. and important example: Section 13.3 deals with histogram density estimation, a prototypical example of a CUP approximation to a nonparametric model. After this example, in Section 13.4 we discuss the quality of nonparametric universal codes based on CUP approximations, and compare it to the minimax redundancy that is achievable for such codes. It turns out that the redundancy of the CUP histogram universal codes can be slightly suboptimal. As a second concrete example, in Section 13.5, we then discuss Gaussian processes, a powerful nonparametric method for regression which does appear to achieve minimax redundancy rates.

The Fast Track All of MDL model selection, and much of MDL prediction, are based on CUP model classes. Therefore, Section 13.2 is essential for Part III of this book. All other material in this chapter is rather advanced and can be skipped at first reading.

13.1 Introduction

CUP Model Classes In the first years after its inception, MDL inference was mostly used for model selection between a finite or countably infinite set of parametric models $\mathcal{M}_1, \mathcal{M}_2, \ldots.$. As we will see in Part III of this book, this requires defining a new universal code/model $\bar{P}(\cdot \mid \mathcal{M})$ for the model class $\mathcal{M} = \bigcup \mathcal{M}_\gamma$ consisting of the union of the models $\mathcal{M}_\gamma$ under consideration. We call $\mathcal{M}$ a *CUP* (countable union of parametric models) model class. In Section 13.2 we consider universal codes relative to CUP classes. There exists a standard way of designing universal codes relative to CUP classes, leading to what we will call "standard CUP universal codes." Standard CUP codes are very simple extensions of parametric universal codes. Essentially, they work by first encoding the model index γ, and then encoding the data using some standard universal code $\bar{P}(\cdot \mid \mathcal{M}_\gamma)$ relative to the parametric model $\mathcal{M}_\gamma$. Because of this simple construction, much of the analysis of parametric universal models still applies to CUP model classes.

Fully Nonparametric Model Classes The situation becomes more essentially different once we consider "fully" nonparametric model classes. For example, let $\mathcal{X} = [0, 1]$ be the unit interval and let $\mathcal{M}^*$ be the i.i.d. model class consisting of *all* distributions on $\mathcal{X}$ with densities f such that $f(x)$ is a differentiable function on $\mathcal{X}$. $\mathcal{M}^*$ is clearly "nonparametric": it cannot be meaningfully parameterized by a connected finite-dimensional parameter set $\Theta^{(k)} \subseteq \mathbb{R}^k$. As we shall see later, it cannot be parameterized by a countable union of such parametric models either, so $\mathcal{M}^*$ is more inherently nonparametric than a CUP model class. As is customary, we henceforth reserve the term "nonparametric model class" for classes such as $\mathcal{M}^*$ which can neither be viewed as parametric nor as a CUP model. To avoid confusion, we will never refer to CUP model classes as either parametric or nonparametric.

It is often quite possible to construct good universal codes relative to nonparametric $\mathcal{M}^*$. There are various strategies to achieve this:

1. **Approximate $\mathcal{M}^*$ by CUP $\mathcal{M}$, standard code.** The most straightforward, historically the oldest, but not necessarily always the best strategy is to

approximate $\mathcal{M}^*$ by a simpler CUP model class $\mathcal{M}$. In this strategy, one designs a standard universal code relative to $\mathcal{M}$, and uses it as a universal code relative to $\mathcal{M}^*$. It turns out that such a code often retains good universality properties relative to $\mathcal{M}^*$. This is done in, for example, polynomial regression where the target function is an arbitrary smooth function, not necessarily a polynomial, but the model is the union of all linear models based on polynomials of each degree. Another prototypical example, which we treat in detail in Section 13.3 below, is to approximate a set of densities $\mathcal{M}^*$ by the union $\mathcal{M}$ of all regular *histograms* with a finite number of bins.

2. **Approximate $\mathcal{M}^*$ by CUP $\mathcal{M}$, special code.** For regression and classification models, there exists an elegant method based on *Gaussian*[1] *processes* (Rasmussen and Williams 2006; Kakade, Seeger, and Foster 2006). We will discuss this method in great detail in Section 13.5. This method can be interpreted in many ways. In one interpretation, it is viewed as approximating a large, nonparametric set $\mathcal{M}^*$ by a CUP model class $\mathcal{M}$, but the universal code for this model is defined in a more holistic (and perhaps, more elegant) way, rather than explicitly encoding model indices γ. At least in some cases, the resulting universal code has better universality properties than those based on standard CUP codes.

3. **Other methods.** There exist various other methods for designing nonparametric universal codes. As we shall see in Section 13.4, sometimes these achieve better coding redundancy than the CUP approximations we just described. One method is to approximate $\mathcal{M}^*$ by a cleverly chosen countable subset $\ddot{\mathcal{M}}^*$, and design a two-part code over this set (Barron and Cover 1991). This two-part code is then used as a universal code for $\mathcal{M}^*$. Thus, once again, $\mathcal{M}^*$ is approximated by a simpler model class $\ddot{\mathcal{M}}^*$, but now the simpler model class does not have a straightforward interpretation as a CUP model class. Other methods are *kernel density estimators* or, in classification problems, *nearest neighbor methods*.

Why Bother about Nonparametric $\mathcal{M}^*$? Reverse Interpretation   Fully nonparametric models $\mathcal{M}^*$ often have abstract definitions, such as "the set of densities on $[0, 1]$ with bounded first derivative." Why should we be interested in designing univeral codes relative to such abstractly defined models

---

1. The use of the word "Gaussian" in Gaussian processes is confusing to some; see the remark on page 401.

$\mathcal{M}^*$ at all? The reasons for this can best be seen if we think of $\mathcal{M}^*$ in terms of a CUP model class $\mathcal{M}$ that may be used to approximate it. Indeed, researchers have often come to consider such $\mathcal{M}^*$ by first modeling data using a CUP model class $\mathcal{M}$. They then realized that in some cases, the assumption that data come from a source P^* in $\mathcal{M}$ is quite unrealistic, whereas the assumption that $P^* \in \mathcal{M}^*$, where $\mathcal{M}^*$ is a set of distributions whose members can be arbitrarily well approximated by members of $\mathcal{M}$, is much more realistic. In the linear model example, since every smooth function on a compact interval can be arbitrarily well approximated by a polynomial, it is only natural to consider what happens if the source of the data is a smooth function (such as a logarithm, or a square root), but it is approximated by polynomials. Thus, rather than starting out with $\mathcal{M}^*$ and approximating it by $\mathcal{M}$, researchers have often started out with $\mathcal{M}$ and then considered $\mathcal{M}^*$ as a natural extension of $\mathcal{M}$.

13.2   CUP: Unions of Parametric Models

Until about 1988, when Hall and Hannan (1988) published the first nonparametric MDL paper, most of the MDL literature was about selection between a finite or countably infinite set of parametric models $\mathcal{M}_1, \mathcal{M}_2, \ldots$, parameterized by $\Theta_1, \Theta_2, \ldots$ respectively. Here $\Theta_\gamma \subseteq \mathbb{R}^{k_\gamma}$, where k_γ denotes the number of free parameters in $\mathcal{M}_\gamma$. Denoting the set of model indices by Γ, we can define the model class $\mathcal{M} = \bigcup_{\gamma \in \Gamma} \mathcal{M}_\gamma$ as the union of such parametric models. As we shall see in Chapter 14, MDL model selection requires the construction of a universal code $\bar{L}(\cdot \mid \mathcal{M})$ relative to the model class $\mathcal{M}$. Since most basic applications of MDL involve such unions $\mathcal{M}$ of parametric models $\mathcal{M}_\gamma$, it is quite useful to reserve a special name for them: we call them *CUP* model classes. CUP stands for "countable union of parametric models." We shall mostly but not exclusively be interested in countably infinite unions of *nested* models, so that $\mathcal{M}_1 \subset \mathcal{M}_2 \subset \ldots \subset \mathcal{M}$. We will call such model classes $\mathcal{M}$ "NCUP" model classes, the "N" standing for nested. Each NCUP model class is also a CUP model class. In some cases though, the set Γ will be finite.

Terminology in the Context of CUP Model Classes   We shall often refer to the ML estimator for data x^n within model $\mathcal{M}_\gamma$. If it exists and is unique, this is denoted as $\hat{\theta}_\gamma$.

Sometimes, we assume the data are distributed according to a distribution

P^* in one of the models $\mathcal{M}_\gamma$. If there is only one γ^* such that $P^* \in \mathcal{M}_{\gamma^*}$, we call this $\mathcal{M}_{\gamma^*}$ the *true model* and generally denote its index as γ^*. If there are more γ such that $P^* \in \mathcal{M}_\gamma$, then we will invariably deal with a situation where there exists a unique γ^* such that for all γ with $P^* \in \mathcal{M}_\gamma$, we have $\mathcal{M}_{\gamma^*} \subset \mathcal{M}_\gamma$. In that case, if we refer to the "true model" without being more specific, then we refer to $\mathcal{M}_{\gamma^*}$ and not to any of its supersets. This terminology, as well as the one above, will be heavily used throughout Part III of this book.

Universal CUP Codes: Meta-Two-Part   One can associate universal codes with CUP model classes in various ways. In this book, with the exception of the Gaussian process universal codes (Section 13.5), we shall mostly consider just two types of such universal codes. The first type is called *meta-two-part universal CUP code*. Here we encode the data in two stages: we first encode the model index γ explicitly using some code $\dot{L}$ for the integers. We then encode the data x^n based on some universal model $\bar{P}(\cdot \mid \mathcal{M}_\gamma)$ relative to $\mathcal{M}_\gamma$, giving total codelength

$$\bar{L}_{\mathrm{CUP}}(x^n) = \min_\gamma \{ \, \dot{L}(\gamma) - \log \bar{P}(x^n \mid \mathcal{M}_\gamma) \, \}. \tag{13.1}$$

The reason for using the conditioning bar in the notation $\bar{P}(\cdot \mid \mathcal{M}_\gamma)$ is that, together with the code $\dot{L}(\gamma)$ for the model indices, we can think of

$$L(\gamma, x^n) := \dot{L}(\gamma) - \log \bar{P}(x^n \mid \mathcal{M}_\gamma)$$

as a joint code for data and model parameter γ. When no confusion can arise, we shall abbreviate $\bar{P}(\cdot \mid \mathcal{M}_\gamma)$ to $\bar{P}(\cdot \mid \gamma)$.

Here the universal models $\bar{P}(\cdot \mid \mathcal{M}_\gamma)$ can either be two-part, Bayesian, NML, or prequential plug-in. We always assume that the same type of universal code is used for each γ. Depending on our choice, we will refer to $\bar{L}_{\mathrm{CUP}}$ as a

$\mathrm{CUP}(\text{2-p}, \text{2-p})$, $\mathrm{CUP}(\text{2-p}, \mathrm{Bayes})$, $\mathrm{CUP}(\text{2-p}, \text{plug-in})$, or $\mathrm{CUP}(\text{2-p}, \mathrm{nml})$

universal code, respectively. The "2-p" on the left indicates that at a meta-level, the code is a two-part code, where γ is encoded explicitly. If we speak of a $\mathrm{CUP}(\text{2-p}, \cdot)$ universal code, we mean a universal code such that γ is encoded explicitly, and the code $\bar{P}(\cdot \mid \mathcal{M}_\gamma)$ in (13.1) can be any of the four standard choices.

Note that, whereas for ordinary two-part codes, we allow the code for distributions $\dot{L}_n(P)$ to depend on the sample size n, meta-two-part codes are defined such that the code for γ does not depend on sample size: $\dot{L}(\gamma)$ does not depend on n. We impose this additional restriction to enforce a correspondence to the meta-Bayes codes we introduce below.

Universal CUP Codes: Meta-Bayes The second type of universal codes will be called *meta-Bayes* standard CUP codes. These depend on some prior $W(\gamma)$ on the model indices γ. Analogously to (13.1), an implicit standard CUP code $\bar{L}_{\mathrm{CUP}}$ is defined as

$$\bar{L}_{\mathrm{CUP}}(x^n) = -\log \sum_{\gamma \in \Gamma} W(\gamma) \bar{P}(x^n \mid \mathcal{M}_\gamma), \qquad (13.2)$$

where the universal models $\bar{P}(\cdot \mid \mathcal{M}_\gamma)$ are of one of the standard types. We use the abbreviation $\mathrm{CUP}(\mathrm{Bayes}, \cdot)$ for any meta-Bayes code of the form (13.2); for example, $\mathrm{CUP}(\mathrm{Bayes}, \mathrm{Bayes})$ is a code where $\bar{P}(\cdot \mid \mathcal{M}_\gamma)$ are Bayesian universal codes relative to $\mathcal{M}_\gamma$.

Note that for each meta-two-part CUP code, there is a "corresponding" meta-Bayes CUP code with codelength function $\dot{L}(\gamma) = -\log W(\gamma)$. Our CUP terminology and notation is not standard, but will be very convenient in the sequel.

Standard CUP Codes: Meta-Bayes and Meta-Two-Part

There exist two standard types of universal codes for CUP model classes: meta-Bayesian standard CUP codes based on a prior distribution $W(\gamma)$ on the model indices γ, and meta-two-part standard CUP codes, based on explicitly encoding γ using a code with length function $\dot{L}(\gamma)$.

For each two-part code $\bar{P}_{\mathrm{CUP}(2\text{-}\mathrm{p}, \cdot)}$, there is a corresponding meta-Bayesian code $\bar{P}_{\mathrm{CUP}(\mathrm{Bayes}, \cdot)}$ and vice versa, such that for all γ, (a), $\dot{L}(\gamma) = -\log W(\gamma)$, and, (b), the universal models $\bar{P}_{\mathrm{CUP}(\mathrm{Bayes}, \cdot)}(\cdot \mid \mathcal{M}_\gamma)$ and $\bar{P}_{\mathrm{CUP}(2\text{-}\mathrm{p}, \cdot)}(\cdot \mid \mathcal{M}_\gamma)$ coincide. In this case, by Example 6.4, ("Bayes is better than two-part") we have for all n, x^n, that

$$-\log \bar{P}_{\mathrm{CUP}(\mathrm{Bayes}, \cdot)}(x^n) \leq -\log \bar{P}_{\mathrm{CUP}(2\text{-}\mathrm{p}, \cdot)}(x^n).$$

13.2.1 CUP vs. Parametric Models

Some, but of course not all, of the redundancy properties of universal codes for parametric models carry over to CUP model classes. To see this, let $\mathcal{M} = \bigcup_{\gamma \in \Gamma} \mathcal{M}_\gamma$ be a CUP model class consisting of i.i.d. exponential families $\mathcal{M}_\gamma$, given in some diffeomorphic parameterization $\Theta_\gamma \subseteq \mathbb{R}^{k_\gamma}$. Suppose that $P^* \in \mathcal{M}$. Then $P^* \in \mathcal{M}_{\gamma^*}$ for some finite γ^*, so that the codelength of a CUP(2-p, Bayes) universal model $\bar{P}_{\text{CUP}}$ satisfies, for all ineccsi sequences $x_1, x_2, \ldots,$

$$
-\log \bar{P}_{\text{CUP}}(x^n) + \log P^*(x^n) = \dot{L}(\gamma^*) - \log \bar{P}_{\text{Bayes}}(x^n \mid \mathcal{M}_{\gamma^*}) + \log P^*(x^n) \leq
$$
$$
\dot{L}(\gamma^*) - \log \bar{P}_{\text{Bayes}}(x^n \mid \mathcal{M}_{\gamma^*}) + \log P_{\hat{\theta}_{\gamma^*}(x^n)}(x^n) = \frac{k_{\gamma^*}}{2} \log n + O(1),
$$
(13.3)

where $\hat{\theta}_\gamma$ is the ML estimator within $\mathcal{M}_\gamma$, and the last line follows by the asymptotic expansion (8.2) of Chapter 8. Thus, the redundancy for the sequence $x_1, x_2, \ldots$ satisfies

$$
\text{RED}(\bar{P}_{\text{CUP}}, P^*, x^n)] = \frac{k_{\gamma^*}}{2} \log n + O(1).
$$
(13.4)

In Chapter 8, Theorem 8.2, we showed that the $(k/2) \log n$ regret formula does not just hold for individual ineccsi sequences, but also in expectation. Indeed, it turns out that (13.4) also holds in expectation. Theorem 8.2 implies that, for all $P^* \in \mathcal{M}_{\gamma^*}$ such that $P^* = P_{\theta^*}$ for some θ^* in the interior of the parameter set,

$$
E_{X^n \sim P^*}[\text{RED}(\bar{P}_{\text{CUP}}, P^*, X^n)] = \frac{k_{\gamma^*}}{2} \log n + O(1).
$$
(13.5)

The same can be shown to hold for the CUP(2-p, 2-p) and CUP(2-p, plug-in) universal models as long as $\bar{P}_{2\text{-p}}(\cdot \mid \mathcal{M}_\gamma)$ and $\bar{P}_{\text{plug-in}}(\cdot \mid \mathcal{M}_\gamma)$ are defined as explained in Chapter 10 and Chapter 9; whenever defined, it also holds if $\bar{P}(\cdot \mid \mathcal{M}_\gamma)$ is a (luckiness) NML code. Thus, the codelength achieved by the CUP-universal code $\bar{P}_{\text{CUP}}$, designed without knowledge of the optimal γ^*, is only slightly larger than the codelength achieved by the optimal universal code $\bar{P}(\cdot \mid \mathcal{M}_{\gamma^*})$. Here "slightly" means that the difference is bounded by the number $\dot{L}(\gamma^*)$, which increases logarithmically in γ^* if $\dot{L}(\gamma)$ is chosen to be the universal code for the integers.

(13.5) must also hold if $\bar{P}_{\text{CUP}}$ is a meta-Bayes code CUP(Bayes, $\cdot$). To see this, note that the codelength achieved by a meta-Bayes CUP code is (a) always bounded from above by the corresponding meta-two-part CUP code, whereas (b) the difference must be bounded by $L(\gamma^*)$.

Both the individual-sequence result (13.4) and the expectation result (13.5) continue to hold for every CUP model consisting of parametric families for which the Bayes universal code $\bar{P}_{\text{Bayes}}(\cdot \mid \mathcal{M}_\gamma)$ has asymptotic regret $(k_\gamma/2)$ $\log n$. As we explained in Chapter 8, this includes many nonexponential families.

Toward Nonparametric $\mathcal{M}^*$: The Information Closure We just showed that for CUP model classes $\mathcal{M}$, the redundancy relative to any $P^* \in \mathcal{M}$ is of order $O(\log n)$, which is the same order of magnitude as for parametric models. The situation becomes more essentially different if we consider P^* that are not in $\mathcal{M}$, but that can be *arbitrarily well approximated* by members of $\mathcal{M}$. To this end, following Barron and Cover (1991), we define the *information closure* $\langle \mathcal{M} \rangle$ of $\mathcal{M}$ as

$$\langle \mathcal{M} \rangle = \{P^* \| \inf_{P \in \mathcal{M}} D(P^* \| P) = 0\}. \tag{13.6}$$

The information closure of $\mathcal{M}$ can be much larger than $\mathcal{M}$ itself. For example, the information closure of the class of linear models based on polynomials is the set of all conditional densities such that $Y = g(X) + Z$ for any smooth function g, not necessarily a polynomial, and Z is normally distributed noise.

In many cases, standard CUP universal codes for $\mathcal{M}$ are still good universal codes for $\langle \mathcal{M} \rangle$, in a sense which we will make precise in Section 13.4. However, as we show there, they are sometimes not the optimal codes in terms of expected redundancy. The information closure may seem like a very abstract concept for now. It will become more concrete in the histogram example that we study in the next section.

13.3 Universal Codes Based on Histograms

Suppose we observe some data x^n such that the individual outcomes x_i take values in the interval $\mathcal{X} = [0, R)$ for some $R > 0$. Such data are often conveniently modeled by *histograms*. In this section, we study universal codes for nonparametric model classes $\mathcal{M}^*$ that can be well approximated by histogram models. Such universal codes can be put to use in *MDL-based histogram density estimation*, which we consider in Chapter 15, Section 15.2.3. The study of universal codes based on histograms was properly started by

Hall and Hannan (1988), and later significantly extended in (Rissanen, Speed, and Yu 1992; Yu and Speed 1992).

In the simplest form of histogram density estimation, we model the data by a *regular γ-bin histogram*, where typically the γ we choose depends on the sample size, the data itself, or both. The parametric model consisting of all regular γ-bin histograms is denoted by $\mathcal{M}_\gamma = \{P_{\theta,\gamma} \mid \theta \in \Delta^{(\gamma)}\}$ in this section.

In MDL histogram estimation, we use the model class $\mathcal{M} = \cup_{\gamma \geq 1} \mathcal{M}_\gamma$ of regular histograms with arbitrarily many bins. While this is a CUP model class, the universal code based on $\mathcal{M}$ will mostly be used as a universal code relative to a *larger* nonparametric class $\mathcal{M}^*$, a subset of the information closure $\langle \mathcal{M} \rangle$ of $\mathcal{M}$. This justifies calling universal coding based on histograms a nonparametric method. Below we first describe universal codes for $\mathcal{M}_\gamma$; then we describe universal codes for $\mathcal{M}$; and finally we make the connection to nonparametrics.

Regular γ-Bin Histogram $\mathcal{M}_\gamma$ is a family of probabilistic sources $P_{\theta,\gamma}$ with densities $f_{\theta,\gamma}$, identified by parameter vector $\theta = (\theta_1, \ldots, \theta_\gamma) \in \Delta^{(\gamma)}$. The data are i.i.d. according to $P_{\theta,\gamma}$, so that $f_{\theta,\gamma}(x^n) = \prod_{i=1}^n f_{\theta,\gamma}(x_i)$. For individual outcomes x, $f_{\theta,\gamma}$ is defined in terms of γ bins. These are consecutive intervals of $\mathcal{X} = [0, R)$ of length R/γ: the first bin is $[0, R/\gamma)$, the second bin is $[R/\gamma, 2R/\gamma)$, and so on. The histogram is called "regular" because all bins are of equal length. Each $P_{\theta,\gamma}$ is defined as a distribution on $[0, R)$ that is uniform within each of the bins, and with a total probability of θ_j for the region falling in bin j. Thus, introducing the function $B : \mathcal{X} \to \{1, \ldots, \gamma\}$ to denote the bin in which outcome X falls, $P_{\theta,\gamma}$ is defined by, for $j = 1, \ldots, \gamma$,

$$P_{\theta,\gamma}(B(X) = j) := \theta_j.$$

The conditional distribution $P_{\theta,\gamma}(X \mid B(X) = j)$ is uniform. Since the width of B_j is R/γ, this corresponds to a conditional uniform density $f_{\theta,\gamma}(X \mid B(X) = j) = \gamma/R$. Thus, $P_{\theta,\gamma}$ has density $f_{\theta,\gamma}$ defined by

$$f_{\theta,\gamma}(x) = \frac{\gamma}{R} Q_\theta(B(x)),$$

where Q_θ is the multinomial distribution on $\{1, \ldots, \gamma\}$ with parameter vector θ, i.e. $Q_\theta(j) = \theta_j$, see Example 2.5, Chapter 2. Since $\mathcal{M}_\gamma$ is i.i.d., we have

$$-\log f_{\theta,\gamma}(x^n) = n \log \frac{R}{\gamma} - \log Q_\theta(b_1 \ldots b_n), \tag{13.7}$$

where we abbreviated $B(x_i)$ to b_i. The first term does not depend on the data, so that the ML density $f_{\hat{\theta}(x^n),\gamma}$ can be calculated in the same way as that for a multinomial distribution. It corresponds to the distribution $Q_{\hat{\theta}(b^n)}$ assigning probability mass n_j/n to the jth bin.

Bayesian Universal Code for $\mathcal{M}_\gamma$ Let w be a prior on $(\theta_1,\ldots,\theta_\gamma) \in \Delta^{(\gamma)}$. From (13.7) we see that the Bayesian universal code relative to prior w is given by

$$-\log \bar{f}_{\text{Bayes}}(x^n \mid \mathcal{M}_\gamma) = n\log \frac{R}{\gamma} - \log \int_{\theta \in \Delta^{(\gamma)}} Q_\theta(b_1 \ldots b_n)w(\theta)d\theta. \quad (13.8)$$

Since the first term does not depend on the prior it follows that Jeffreys' prior relative to the γ-bin regular histogram is identical to Jeffreys' prior for the γ-outcome multinomial model. From Example 9.2, Chapter 9, we know that this prior is given by $w(\theta) \propto \theta_1^{-1/2} \cdot \ldots \cdot \theta_\gamma^{-1/2}$.

NML Universal Code for $\mathcal{M}_\gamma$ The parametric complexity of the model $\mathcal{M}_\gamma$ is given by

$$\text{COMP}^{(n)}(\mathcal{M}_\gamma) = \log \int_{x^n \in [0,R]^n} f_{\hat{\theta}(x^n),\gamma}(x^n)dx^n. \quad (13.9)$$

Since the sequence of bins $b_1,\ldots,b_n$ is a sufficient statistic of x^n, we can use the device explained in Chapter 7, Section 7.4, Equation (7.23), to simplify (13.9): it must be equal to the sum over all $b^n \in \{1,\ldots,\gamma\}^n$, of the maximized probability of the sequence b^n:

$$\text{COMP}^{(n)}(\mathcal{M}_\gamma) = \log \sum_{b^n \in \gamma^n} Q_{\hat{\theta}(b^n)}(b^n) = \text{COMP}^{(n)}(\mathcal{M}'_\gamma),$$

where $\mathcal{M}'_\gamma$ denotes the multinomial model for outcome space $\mathcal{X}' = \{1,\ldots,\gamma\}$. Therefore, the NML distribution is given by

$$\bar{f}_{\text{nml}}(x^n \mid \mathcal{M}_\gamma) = \frac{f_{\hat{\theta}(x^n),\gamma}(x^n)}{\int_{x^n \in [0,R]^n} f_{\hat{\theta}(x^n),\gamma}(x^n)dx^n} =$$

$$\left(\frac{\gamma}{R}\right)^n \frac{Q_{\hat{\theta}(B^n),\gamma}(x^n)}{\exp(\text{COMP}^{(n)}(\mathcal{M}'_\gamma))} = \left(\frac{\gamma}{R}\right)^n \bar{P}_{\text{nml}}(b^n \mid \mathcal{M}'_\gamma). \quad (13.10)$$

Thus, if we manage to compute $\bar{P}_{\text{nml}}(b^n \mid \mathcal{M}'_\gamma)$ for the multinomial model, we can also compute $\bar{P}_{\text{nml}}(b^n \mid \mathcal{M}_\gamma)$ for the γ-bin regular histogram model.

Therefore, the efficient algorithm introduced by Kontkanen and Myllymäki (2005b) for computing $\bar{P}_{\text{nml}}(x^n \mid \mathcal{M}'_\gamma)$ exactly (not just asymptotically), can also be used for computing the histogram NML codelength $\bar{f}_{\text{nml}}(x^n \mid \mathcal{M}_\gamma)$ exactly. Unfortunately, this was not yet known at the time of (Hall and Hannan 1988) and (Rissanen, Speed, and Yu 1992), on which the following material is based. Their theoretical analysis is in terms of the Bayesian codelength (13.8) with a uniform prior; the fact that Jeffreys' prior is more appropriate in an MDL context was not fully realized in 1992 either.

CUP Universal Code for All Histograms: Meta-Bayes Approach   We now want to design a universal code relative to the model class $\mathcal{M} = \cup_{\gamma \geq 1} \mathcal{M}_\gamma$ of all regular histograms with an arbitrary number of bins. This is a CUP model class. Recall from Section 13.2 that there are two standard types of universal codes for such a class: the meta-Bayesian code and the meta-two-part code. From a compression perspective, the meta-Bayes code is to be preferred (box on page 374), so we consider it first. We put a prior distribution W on the model index γ, and then define

$$\bar{f}_{\text{CUP(Bayes,Bayes)}}(x^n) = \sum_{\gamma=1}^{\infty} W(\gamma)\bar{f}_{\text{Bayes}}(x^n \mid \mathcal{M}_\gamma). \tag{13.11}$$

To make sure that, for each γ, the regret of $-\log \bar{f}_{\text{CUP(Bayes,Bayes)}}$ is small relative to $-\log \bar{f}_{\text{Bayes}}(\cdot \mid \mathcal{M}_\gamma)$, we should take a prior W on γ that is close to uniform, such as, for example, the universal prior on the integers (Chapter 3).

   The reason we focus on $\bar{f}_{\text{CUP(Bayes,Bayes)}}$ rather than, say, $\bar{f}_{\text{CUP(Bayes,nml)}}$, is that $\bar{f}_{\text{CUP(Bayes,Bayes)}}$ is a prequential universal model (Chapter 6, Section 6.4). This will be advantageous in our application of histogram universal codes for predictive MDL estimation in Chapter 15, Section 15.2.3.

Semiprequential Approach   Rissanen, Speed, and Yu (1992) focus on a meta-two-part code rather than a meta-Bayesian code. The corresponding lengths $\bar{L}_{\text{CUP(2-p,Bayes)}}(x^n)$ correspond to a defective density $\bar{f}_{\text{CUP(2-p,Bayes)}}$, defined as

$$\bar{L}_{\text{CUP(2-p,Bayes)}}(x^n) = -\log \bar{f}_{\text{CUP(2-p,Bayes)}}(x^n) :=$$
$$\min_{\gamma}\{L_{\mathbb{N}}(\gamma) - \log \bar{f}_{\text{Bayes}}(x^n \mid \mathcal{M}_\gamma)\}. \tag{13.12}$$

Here $\bar{f}_{\text{Bayes}}(x^n \mid \mathcal{M}_\gamma)$ is once again defined relative to the uniform rather than Jeffreys' prior, for the historical reason we already gave above.

13.3.1   Redundancy of Universal CUP Histogram Codes

Following Rissanen, Speed, and Yu (1992), we now study the quality of the CUP universal codes $\bar{f}_{\text{CUP(Bayes,Bayes)}}$ and $\bar{f}_{\text{CUP(2-p,Bayes)}}$ in terms of their redundancy.

Equation (13.12) implies that, for all γ, all $P \in \mathcal{M}_\gamma$, the regret of $\bar{f}_{\text{CUP(2-p,Bayes)}}$ relative to the density f of P is bounded by

$$\text{RED}(\bar{f}_{\text{CUP(2-p,Bayes)}}, f, x^n) =$$
$$-\log \bar{f}_{\text{CUP(2-p,Bayes)}}(x^n) + \log f(x^n) \leq L_{\mathbb{N}}(\gamma) + \text{RED}(\bar{f}_{\text{Bayes}}(\cdot \mid \mathcal{M}_\gamma), f, x^n)$$
$$\leq 2\log\gamma + \frac{k_\gamma}{2}\log n + O(1), \quad (13.13)$$

the latter equation following by the asymptotic expansion (8.2) of $\bar{f}_{\text{Bayes}}(\cdot \mid \mathcal{M}_\gamma)$ for k_γ-dimensional parametric models. Here $k_\gamma = \gamma - 1$ is the number of free parameters in $\mathcal{M}_\gamma$. The box on page 374 states that for all n, x^n, $\bar{f}_{\text{CUP(Bayes,Bayes)}}(x^n) \geq \bar{f}_{\text{CUP(2-p,Bayes)}}(x^n)$. Therefore (13.13) also holds for the fully prequential $\bar{f}_{\text{CUP(Bayes,Bayes)}}$. Thus, for any $P \in \mathcal{M} = \cup_{\gamma \geq 1} \mathcal{M}_\gamma$, the regret is of order $O(\log n)$. However, we often use histograms to model data that are best viewed as coming from a distribution P^* having a continuous density. On such data P^*, or rather its density f^*, may achieve asymptotically much smaller codelengths than (the density f of) any fixed $P \in \mathcal{M}$, since every $P \in \mathcal{M}$ (except for the uniform distribution) has a discontinuous density. However, we would still expect that the codes $\bar{f}_{\text{CUP(Bayes,Bayes)}}$ and $\bar{f}_{\text{CUP(2-p,Bayes)}}$ are good universal codes relative to such $P^* \notin \mathcal{M}$, as long they can somehow be "arbitrarily well approximated" by $P \in \mathcal{M}$. To this end, we consider the information closure $\langle \mathcal{M} \rangle$ given by (13.6). If $\mathcal{M}$ is the model class of histograms, then $\langle \mathcal{M} \rangle$ is the set of distributions that have densities that can be arbitrarily well approximated, in the KL sense, by sequences of more and more complex histograms. But now we face the opposite problem: whereas the set $\mathcal{M}$ was too poor to be used in a realistic analysis, the set $\langle \mathcal{M} \rangle$ is too rich: it contains essentially every distribution with a continuous density, and many more besides. Therefore, we cannot expect that $\bar{f}_{\text{CUP(Bayes,Bayes)}}$ and $\bar{f}_{\text{CUP(2-p,Bayes)}}$ achieve small redundany with respect to *all* $P^* \in \langle \mathcal{M} \rangle$. To overcome this problem, we restrict $\langle \mathcal{M} \rangle$ to some subset $\mathcal{M}^* \subseteq \langle \mathcal{M} \rangle$, containing only sufficiently "smooth" $P^* \in \langle \mathcal{M} \rangle$. It turns out that for such $\mathcal{M}^*$, we can prove that our CUP codes are still good universal codes in the *expectation* sense – not much is known about their behavior in the individual-sequence sense. Importantly, $\mathcal{M}^*$ still consists of continuous densities, so $\mathcal{M}^*$ is not a subset of $\mathcal{M}$. We just disallow these densities to have arbitrarily wild fluctuations.

The underlying idea extends beyond histogram models: for many types of CUP model classes $\mathcal{M}$, one can identify interesting nonparametric subsets $\mathcal{M}^*$ of $\langle \mathcal{M} \rangle$ on which standard CUP codes achieve good redundancy. In general, different CUP model classes $\mathcal{M}$ will lead to different classes $\mathcal{M}^*$. In the present case, we take $\mathcal{M}$ to be the regular histogram model class relative to $\mathcal{X} = [0,1]$. Then it is useful to define $\mathcal{M}^*$ as the set of i.i.d. sources for $\mathcal{X}$ having densities f^* that are uniformly bounded from above and below, and whose first derivative also has a uniform bound, i.e. $\mathcal{M}^*$ consists of all P^* with f^* satisfying

$$0 < c_0 \leq f^*(x) \leq c_1 < \infty, \left| \frac{d}{dx} f^*(x) \right| \leq c_2, \tag{13.14}$$

where c_0, c_1, c_2 are some fixed positive constants. For this definition of $\mathcal{M}^*$, Yu and Speed (1992) prove some very precise results on the stochastic redundancy achieved by the universal code $\bar{f}_{\text{CUP(2-p,Bayes)}}$. Theorem 2.4 of Yu and Speed (1992) shows that for all $P^* \in \mathcal{M}^*$ except if P^* is the uniform distribution,

1. With P^*-probability 1, the $\ddot{\gamma}(X^n)$ achieving the minimum in (13.12) satisfies

$$\ddot{\gamma}(X^n) = (3c_{f^*} n / \log n)^{1/3}(1 + o(1)) = \text{ORDER}((n/\log n)^{1/3}). \tag{13.15}$$

2. We have

$$\frac{1}{n} E_{X^n \sim P^*}[-\log \bar{f}_{\text{CUP(2-p,Bayes)}}(X^n) + \log f^*(X^n)] =$$

$$\frac{1}{2}(3c_{f^*})^{1/3} n^{-2/3}(\log n)^{2/3}(1 + o(1)) = \text{ORDER}\left(\left(\frac{\log n}{n} \right)^{2/3} \right). \tag{13.16}$$

Here $c_f = \frac{1}{12} \int_0^1 \frac{f'(x)^2}{f(x)} dx$, where f' is the derivative of f. Clearly, c_f is a measure of the smoothness of the density f, but it is 0 if f is uniform. For this case, Yu and Speed (1992) provide a separate result.

(13.16) shows that the histogram-based $\bar{f}_{\text{CUP(2-p,Bayes)}}$ is a universal code relative to $\mathcal{M}^*$ in the expectation sense, even though $\mathcal{M}^*$ contains (gigantically) many distributions that are not in $\mathcal{M}$. For such distributions, the number of bins $\ddot{\gamma}(X^n)$ chosen in the definition of $\bar{f}_{\text{CUP(2-p,Bayes)}}$ will increase with n at a rate slightly below $n^{1/3}$. With respect to any fixed $P^* \in \mathcal{M}^*$, the expected redundancy grows at a rate slightly exceeding $n \cdot n^{-2/3} = n^{1/3}$.

Although not mentioned by Rissanen, Speed, and Yu (1992), it is easy to extend this result to the meta-Bayesian universal model $\bar{f}_{\text{CUP(Bayes,Bayes)}}$. For this universal model, we also have expected redundancy growing as $n\text{ORDER}(n^{-2/3}(\log n)^{2/3}) = \text{ORDER}(n^{1/3}(\log n)^{2/3})$:

$$\frac{1}{n} E_{X^n \sim P^*}[-\log \bar{f}_{\text{CUP(Bayes,Bayes)}}(X^n) + \log f^*(X^n)] =$$

$$\text{ORDER}\left(\left(\frac{\log n}{n}\right)^{2/3}\right). \quad (13.17)$$

CUP Codes Are Almost Optimal   We may now ask ourselves whether this redundancy rate is, in some sense, optimal. It turns out that the answer is "no, but almost": there exist universal codes which achieve a slightly better expected redundancy of order $n^{1/3}$, uniformly for all $P^* \in \mathcal{M}^*$, and without any log factors. This is the *minimax optimal* order, as shown in (Yu and Speed 1992, Theorem 3.2). What this means is explained in Section 13.4.2. Intuitively, it means that no universal code can have expected redundancy $o(n^{1/3})$ for all $P^* \in \mathcal{M}^*$. Rissanen, Speed, and Yu (1992) prove the related result that for any universal code, the subset of $\mathcal{M}^*$ at which it achieves expected redundancy $o(n^{1/3})$ must be, in a sense, negligibly small. This result is especially interesting because a priori, one might expect that $\mathcal{M}^*$ contains many distributions that are best not modeled by sequences of histograms at all, but rather by some other finite-dimensional approximations. The minimax result shows that no other approximations can lead to universal codes that converge at a much (superlogarithmic) faster rate.

A Modified Minimax Optimal Prequential Approach   Rissanen, Speed, and Yu (1992) exhibit a prequential universal code $\bar{f}_{\text{RSY}}$ which does provably achieve the minimax optimal redundancy up to leading order. This code is a modification of $\bar{f}_{\text{CUP(2-p,Bayes)}}$ that works as follows. $\bar{f}_{\text{RSY}}$ is defined by recursively defining $\bar{f}_{\text{RSY}}(X_{n+1} \mid x^n)$ for all n, all $x^n \in [0,1]^n$. These predictive distributions are defined as

$$\bar{f}_{\text{RSY}}(X_{n+1} \mid x^n) := \bar{f}_{\text{Bayes}}(X_{n+1} \mid x^n, \mathcal{M}_{\gamma(n)}), \quad (13.18)$$

where $\gamma(n)$ is defined as $\gamma(n) := \lceil (n+1)^{1/3} \rceil$. As $\bar{f}_{\text{Bayes}}(\cdot \mid \mathcal{M}_\gamma)$ is based on the uniform prior, (13.18) is, crucially, *not* the ML estimator for $\gamma(n)$-bin histograms, which could assign probably 0 to some bins and then achieve infinite redundancy for some sequences with positive probability, and hence also infinite expected redundancy. Instead, the probability that $\bar{f}_{\text{RSY}}$ assigns to the jth bin, $j \in \{1, \ldots, \gamma(n)\}$ is equal to $(n_j + 1)/(n + \gamma(n))$; with Jeffreys' prior, it would have been $(n_j + 0.5)/(n + 0.5\gamma(n))$ (Example 9.2 in Chapter 9). Rissanen, Speed, and Yu (1992) show that, for the code $\bar{f}_{\text{RSY}}$ defined by (13.18), for all $P^* \in \mathcal{M}^*$,

$$\frac{1}{n} E_{X^n \sim P^*}[-\log \bar{f}_{\text{RSY}}(X^n) + \log f^*(X^n)] \leq Cn^{-2/3}(1 + o(1)), \qquad (13.19)$$

where f^* is the density of P^*, $C > 0$ is a constant depending on the constants c_0, c_1, c_2 in (13.14), and $o(1)$ converges to 0 uniformly for all P^* in $\mathcal{M}^*$.

> **Open Problem No. 8: Does There Exist a More Natural Universal Code Which Achieves Minimax Expected Redundancy Relative to $\mathcal{M}^*$?** We see that, perhaps surprisingly, the optimal number of estimators, needed to achieve the minimax redundancy, is not the number of estimators minimizing the two-part codelength, but slightly larger. This implies that *MDL model selection* does not always converge at the minimax optimal rate; see Chapter 16, Section 16.5. To achieve the optimal rate, we have to impose a fixed rule that determines the number of bins on which $\bar{f}_{\text{RSY}}(X_{n+1} \mid x^n)$ is based as a function of n. This is not satisfactory: first of all, we would expect that selecting the number of bins which minimizes codelength is automatically optimal. The fact that it is not suggests that there may a deeper underlying problem for MDL in nonparametric contexts. We consider this further at the end of Section 13.4.2. The (admittedly somewhat vaguely stated) question is, whether there exists an alternative and "natural" universal code which does determine the number of bins automatically in terms of the data, and at the same time leads to a code which achieves the minimax expected redundancy. A first step in this direction is given by Barron, Yang, and Yu (1994).

13.4 Nonparametric Redundancy

In this section, we analyze the quality of universal codes in nonparametric settings. Recall from Chapter 6 that we can measure this quality in two ways: by the *regret* and by the *redundancy*. Since the ordinary regret is not well suited to nonparametric models, we concentrate on analyzing the redundancy. Probably because its analysis is more straightforward, most writings on nonparametric universal codes have been on expected rather than individual-sequence redundancy. For these reasons, we exclusively consider the expected redundancy below.

To see the problems with the notion of regret, consider a nonparametric model class $\mathcal{M}^*$ that is approximated by a standard CUP universal code for some CUP model class $\mathcal{M}$. $\mathcal{M}$ usually contains, for each sequence x^n of each length n, some element $\hat{P}_n$ that fits the data exceedingly well. In the histogram case of Section 13.3, this is the n-bin histogram that puts each observed x_i into its own bin. One cannot expect that a universal code $\bar{P}(\cdot \mid \mathcal{M})$ achieves small excess codelength relative to $\hat{P}_n$, for all n. Thus, the regret of $\bar{P}(\cdot \mid \mathcal{M})$ will invariably be too large to be a useful quantity. It does make sense to consider *luckiness regret* for nonparametric models, as we will do in Section 13.5; but this is such a recent idea that there is not much literature about it yet.

13.4.1 Standard CUP Universal Codes

Consider some nonparametric class $\mathcal{M}^*$, to be approximated by a standard CUP universal code relative to a CUP model class $\mathcal{M} = \mathcal{M}_1 \cup \mathcal{M}_2 \cup \ldots$ such that $\mathcal{M}^* \subset \langle \mathcal{M} \rangle$. For example, $\mathcal{M}^*$ could be the class (13.14) of densities with bounded derivatives, and $\mathcal{M}$ could be the set of regular histogram densities. Below we perform a very crude analysis of the redundancy of CUP codes; the intention is to explain the general idea of how such an analysis can be done rather than getting the details right. We will make several implicit assumptions, such as the existence of unique minima and so on.

It is convenient for our analysis to rename $\mathcal{M}_\gamma$ such that $k_\gamma = \gamma$; thus, the number of parameters of model $\mathcal{M}_k$ is k. For simplicity we assume that for each $k \in \mathbb{N}$, $\mathcal{M}$ contains exactly one parametric submodel $\mathcal{M}_k$ with k parameters. The fundamental quantity is the *approximation function* $g : \mathbb{N} \to \mathbb{R}^+$ defined as

$$g(k) = \min_{P \in \mathcal{M}_k} D(P^* \| P).$$

If $P^* \in \langle \mathcal{M} \rangle$, then $\lim_{k \to \infty} g(k) = 0$. Yet the crucial factor when determining the redundancy of a universal code relative to $\mathcal{M}^*$ is the *rate* at which $g(k)$ tends to 0. Roughly, the faster the rate, the smaller the redundancy that will be achieved. We now consider the expected redundancy of a meta-two-part CUP(2-p, $\cdot$) code $\bar{P}_{\mathrm{CUP}}$. Here $\bar{P}(\cdot \mid \mathcal{M}_\gamma)$ can be a Bayes, two-part or NML universal code; it is not clear whether the analysis carries over when $\bar{P}(\cdot \mid \mathcal{M}_\gamma)$ is a plug-in code. We use a meta-two-part rather than a meta-Bayes code because its redundancy is easier to analyze. It is clear that the redundancy of a CUP(Bayes, $\cdot$) code is bounded from above by the redundancy of the corresponding CUP(2-p, $\cdot$) code (see the box on page 374).

We consider two cases: (1) $g(k) = 0$ for all large k; (2) $g(k) = \mathrm{ORDER}(k^{-t})$ for some $t > 0$.

Case 1: $g(k) = 0$ for large k   This is just the case that $P^* \in \mathcal{M}$ and hence $P^* \in \mathcal{M}_{k^*}$ for some finite k^*. Then under conditions on $\mathcal{M}_{k^*}$ which hold if, e.g., $\mathcal{M}_{k^*}$ is an exponential family, we have from (13.5), Section 13.2,

$$E_{X^n \sim P^*}[\text{RED}(P^*, \bar{P}_{\text{CUP}}, X^n)] = \frac{k^*}{2} \log n + O(1),$$

and the expected redundancy is of order $\log n$.

Case 2: $g(k) = \text{ORDER}(k^{-t})$ This is the inherently nonparametric case. To analyze it, we first recall from Chapters 7 through 10 that, under conditions on $\mathcal{M}_k$ which hold if, e.g., all $\mathcal{M}_k$ are exponential families, we have, for all k, for all $P^* \in \mathcal{M}_k$, and all ineccsi sequences $x_1, x_2, \ldots$, that

$$\text{REG}(\bar{P}_{\text{CUP}}(\cdot \mid \mathcal{M}_k), \mathcal{M}_k, x^n) = \frac{k}{2} \log n + O(1). \tag{13.20}$$

This suggests that, if data are i.i.d. $\sim P^*$, where P^* is a distribution in $\langle \mathcal{M} \rangle$, that

$$E_{X^n \sim P^*}[\text{REG}(\bar{P}_{\text{CUP}}(\cdot \mid \mathcal{M}_k), \mathcal{M}_k, X^n)] = \frac{k}{2} \log n + O(1). \tag{13.21}$$

Theorem 8.2 essentially showed that (13.21) holds if $P^* \in \mathcal{M}_k$. Equation (13.21) is the stronger statement that it holds for the $P^* \in \langle \mathcal{M} \rangle$ that we try to approximate. Since (13.20) only holds for ineccsi sequences, and not for "degenerate" sequences, (13.20) only suggests, and does not prove, that (13.21) holds.

Let $\tilde{P}_k$ achieve $\min_{\tilde{P} \in \mathcal{M}_k} D(P^* \| \tilde{P})$. Letting $P_{\hat{\theta}_k(x^n)}$ denote the ML estimator within $\mathcal{M}_k$ for data x^n, we have for all $x^n \in \mathcal{X}^n$, that $P_{\hat{\theta}_k(x^n)}(x^n) \geq \tilde{P}_k(x^n)$. Then (13.21) implies

$$E_{X^n \sim P^*}[-\log \bar{P}_{\text{CUP}}(X^n \mid \mathcal{M}_k) + \log \tilde{P}_k(X^n)] = \frac{k}{2} \log n + O(1),$$

so that

$$E_{X^n \sim P^*}[-\log \bar{P}_{\text{CUP}}(X^n) + \log \tilde{P}_k(X^n)] = \frac{k}{2} \log n + \dot{L}(k) + O(1). \tag{13.22}$$

To get some idea of the achievable redundancy, we will now make the further simplifying assumption that (13.22) holds uniformly for k, i.e. we assume that the constant hidden in the $O(1)$ term does not depend on k. This is, in fact, not true, but will serve us well for a first approximation. We later discuss the repercussions of the assumption.

Thus, under our new assumption that (13.21) holds uniformly in k, we have

$$E_{P^*}[-\log \bar{P}_{\text{CUP}}(X^n) + \log P^*(X^n)] \leq$$

$$E_{P^*}\left[\min_k\left\{-\log \tilde{P}_k(X^n) + \log P^*(X^n) + \frac{k}{2}\log n + \dot{L}(k)\right\}\right] + C \leq$$

$$\min_k E_{P^*}\left[-\log \tilde{P}_k(X^n) + \log P^*(X^n) + \frac{k}{2}\log n + \dot{L}(k)\right] + C \quad (13.23)$$

for some $C > 0$. Usually, if $\dot{L}(k)$ is based on a slowly decaying prior such as the universal code for the integers, $\dot{L}(k)$ is so small that it can be ignored. Thus, to crudely analyze (13.23) further, we ignore the $\dot{L}(k)$ and $O(1)$ terms. Equation (13.23) now becomes

$$\frac{1}{n}E_{X^n \sim P^*}[\text{RED}(P^*, \bar{P}_{\text{CUP}}, X^n)] \leq \min_k\left\{g(k) + \frac{k}{2}\frac{\log n}{n}\right\}.$$

We also treat k as a continuous variable, so that we can find the minimum of (13.23) by differentiation. Simplifying further, let us assume that $g(k) = ck^{-t}$ for some $c > 0$ and $t > 0$. Differentiation shows that the minimum is then achieved by

$$k = c'\left(\frac{\log n}{n}\right)^{-\frac{1}{t+1}} \quad \text{so that} \quad k^{-t} = c''\left(\frac{\log n}{n}\right)^{\frac{t}{t+1}}$$

for some $c', c'' > 0$. Then (13.23) becomes

$$\frac{1}{n}E_{X^n \sim P^*}[\text{RED}(P^*, \bar{P}_{\text{CUP}}, X^n)] = O\left(\left(\frac{\log n}{n}\right)^{\frac{t}{t+1}}\right). \quad (13.24)$$

If t tends to infinity, then (13.24) converges to the CUP/parametric redundancy of $nO((\log n/n)) = O(\log n)$.

In many cases, upper bounds on the expected redundancy such as (13.24) can be formally shown to hold. For example, for the class $\mathcal{M}^*$ of densities (13.14) that we considered in the histogram example, the approximation function $g(k)$ had the form n^{-t} for $t = 2$. This explains why we obtained a redundancy of $nO((\log n/n)^{2/3}) = O(n^{1/3}(\log n)^{2/3})$. Note, however, that (13.24) provides only an upper bound; (Rissanen, Speed, and Yu 1992) show that in the case of (13.14) and the histogram model class, the bound is tight. But it is not clear whether this is true in general. In the next subsection we investigate how good the bound (13.24) is compared to the best that can be achieved.

13.4.2 Minimax Nonparametric Redundancy

Recall that, for samples of length n, the minimax expected redundancy (6.41), defined on page 202, is defined as

$$\text{RED}^{(n)}_{\min\max}(\mathcal{M}^*) = \inf_{\bar{P}} \sup_{P \in \mathcal{M}^*} E_{X^n \sim P}\left[-\log \bar{P}(X^n) + \log P(X^n)\right], \quad (13.25)$$

where the infimum ranges over all distributions $\bar{P}$ on $\mathcal{X}^n$. We may ask whether the universal codes we discussed in this chapter and the previous one achieve, or at least come close to, the minimax expected redundancy. For parametric models $\mathcal{M}$, under mild regularity conditions on $\mathcal{M}$, the answer is yes, as already indicated in Chapter 8, Section 8.4, at least if $\mathcal{M}$ is an exponential family restricted to an ineccsi parameter set. In that case, the Bayesian universal code with Jeffreys' prior and the NML universal code achieve the redundancy (13.25) to within $o(1)$ and are thus "asymptotically minimax optimal." By the familiar asymptotic expansion of the NML code, the minimax redundancy must then be equal to $(k/2)\log n + O(1)$.

For nonparametric $\mathcal{M}^*$, the situation is more complicated. If we take a countably infinite nested CUP model class $\mathcal{M}$, then the minimax redundancy relative to its closure $\langle \mathcal{M} \rangle$ is usually infinite; the model class $\langle \mathcal{M} \rangle$ is simply too large to allow a uniform universal code. But if we take a subset of $\langle \mathcal{M} \rangle$ that satisfies some smoothness constraints, then the minimax redundancy is often finite, but now grows polynomially, rather than logarithmically. For example, if $\mathcal{M}$ is the class of finite-bin regular histograms, then if we take $\langle \mathcal{M} \rangle$ to be the set of bounded densities with bounded first derivatives as in (13.14), then, as indicated on page 382, the minimax regret is of order $n^{1/3}$. We shall content ourselves with establishing the behavior of the minimax expected redundancy *per outcome*, which is the minimax redundancy divided by n. Formally, we say that the *minimax redundancy per outcome converges at rate $g(n)$* if

$$\frac{1}{n}\text{RED}^{(n)}_{\min\max}(\mathcal{M}^*) = \text{ORDER}(g(n)).$$

Let us now return to case 2 of the previous subsection: assume data are i.i.d. $\sim P^*$ such that $\inf_{P \in \mathcal{M}_k} D(P^*\|P) = \text{ORDER}(k^{-t})$ for some $t > 0$. It turns out that in such cases, under further regularity conditions on $\mathcal{M}$, the minimax redundancy per outcome rate is given by

$$n^{-t/(t+1)} = \left(\frac{1}{n}\right)^{\frac{t}{t+1}}. \quad (13.26)$$

Example 13.1 Let $\mathcal{X}$ be the unit interval, let $s \in \mathbb{N}$ and let $c_0, c_1, \ldots, c_{s+1}$ be positive constants. We define $\mathcal{M}^*_{s,(c_0,\ldots,c_{s+1})}$ to be the set of distributions on $\mathcal{X}$ with densities f^* satisfying

$$0 < c_0 \le f^*(x) \le c_1 < \infty, \left| \frac{d}{dx} f^*(x) \right| \le c_2, \ldots, \left| \frac{d^s}{dx^s} f^*(x) \right| \le c_{s+1}. \quad (13.27)$$

For each $s > 0$, this is a set of densities that are uniformly bounded from above and below, and whose first s derivatives also have a uniform bound. For $s = 2$, the condition is equal to (13.14). It turns out that for the class $\mathcal{M}^*_{s,c_0,\ldots,c_{s+1}}$, the minimax expected redundancy per outcome converges at rate $n^{-2s/(2s+1)}$ (Yu and Speed 1992), which is an instance of (13.26), with $t = 2s$.

> **Prequential vs. Nonprequential Minimax Rate** Note that our definition of minimax expected redundancy is for a given sample size n. Therefore, the distributions $\bar{P}^{(n)}, \bar{P}^{(n+1)}$ achieving minimax expected redundancy at sample sizes n and $n + 1$ may theoretically be wildly different, and incompatible in the sense that $\bar{P}^{(1)}, \bar{P}^{(2)}, \ldots$ does not define a probabilistic source. Since prequential universal codes $\bar{P}_{\text{preq}}$ must have compatible marginal distributions $\bar{P}^{(1)}_{\text{preq}}, \bar{P}^{(2)}_{\text{preq}}, \ldots$, it is therefore conceivable that the minimax redundancy per outcome for prequential universal codes is of larger order than the minimax redundancy per outcome for general universal codes. However, it turns out that if $\mathcal{M}^*$ is such that the minimax redundancy per outcome is of order $g(n)$ where $g(n) \ge n^{-\alpha}$ for some $\alpha < 1$, then the minimax redundancy per outcome among all prequential universal codes must also be of order $g(n)$. Namely, let $\bar{P}^{(1)}, \bar{P}^{(2)}, \ldots$ achieve the minimax redundancy for $n = 1, 2, \ldots$. We can turn each $\bar{P}^{(n)}$ into a probabilistic source $\bar{P}'_n$ by fixing any arbitrary distribution Q on $\mathcal{X}$ and defining $\bar{P}'_n(X^n) = \bar{P}^{(n)}(X^n)$ and for all $m > n$, $\bar{P}'_n(X_{n+1}, \ldots, X_m \mid X^n) = Q^{(m-n)}(X_{n+1}, \ldots, X_m)$. We now define a Bayesian (hence prequential) universal code by, for all n, $\bar{P}_{\text{Bayes}}(X^n) = \sum_{j=1}^{\infty} W(j) \bar{P}'_j(X^n)$. If we take W to be the universal prior for the integers, then $-\log \bar{P}_{\text{Bayes}}(X^n) \le -\log \bar{P}'_n(X^n) + O(\log n)$ so that $-n^{-1} \log \bar{P}_{\text{Bayes}}(X^n) \le g(n) + O((\log n)/n)$. Since we assume $g(n) \ge n^{-\alpha}$ for some $\alpha > 1$, it follows that the minimax redundancy per outcome of the prequential $\bar{P}_{\text{Bayes}}$ is of order $g(n)$.

Comparing (13.26) with (13.24), we see that the bound on the redundancy of the meta-two-part code, which is also a bound on the redundancy of the meta-Bayes code, is a $\log n$-factor larger than the minimax rate. This can mean any of the following three things:

1. The bound (13.24) is loose.

2. There are cleverer meta-two-part codes, which do achieve the minimax rate.

3. There is an inherent problem with some meta-two-part and meta-Bayes codes for standard CUP models.

Which of the three is the case depends on the details of the standard CUP code that is used. For CUP(2-p, Bayes) and CUP(Bayes, Bayes) codes, the bound is, at least in some cases, not loose. This was shown (see (13.16)) for CUP(2-p, Bayes)-codes with the histogram CUP model $\mathcal{M}$ and $t = 2$ by Rissanen, Speed, and Yu (1992), extending work of (Hall and Hannan 1988). The theorem of Rissanen et al. also implies (13.17), which shows the same for CUP(Bayes, Bayes)-codes.

For CUP(2-p, 2-p) codes, it seems that the bound is not loose if the precision with which parameters are encoded is imposed as a fixed function of the sample size, as in the construction in Chapter 10, Section 10.1. The bound may be loose though if the precision is allowed to be determined by the data, such that for each x^n, the precision is chosen such to minimize the description length of d plus the description length of the parameters when encoded with precision d. This is similar to the "crude" MDL method of Chapter 5, but now with a clever, specially designed parameterization and a clever, nonuniformly spaced grid on the parameter space. The precision d then determines the denseness of this grid. Indeed, it is known that there do exist some CUP model classes $\mathcal{M}$ for which a clever CUP(2-p, 2-p) code with flexible precision avoids the logarithmic dilation and does achieve the minimax rates (Barron, Yang, and Yu 1994), but it is unclear whether the techniques used in this paper can be generalized to arbitrary CUP model classes.

In any case, the fact that for some CUP(2-p, Bayes) and CUP(Bayes, Bayes)-codes, the bound is tight, suggests that there is indeed an inherent problem with some of the most standard CUP codes. Whether there is also an inherent problem with all the other versions of the CUP codes is unclear, and needs further investigation.

In the next section, we will see that in regression problems, the issue of potentially suboptimal minimax redundancy rates can often be sidestepped: we exhibit a completely different type of universal model that can be applied to many CUP models, and that holds promise to achieve the minimax rates in case 2 ($g(k) = \text{ORDER}(k^{-t})$), although at the time of writing this book, this has not been formally proved.

13.5   Gaussian Process Regression*

Gaussian processes provide a powerful method for nonparametric regression
and classification (Rasmussen and Williams 2006; Seeger 2004). Here we focus on their simplest form, in which they implicitly define model classes for
nonparametric regression with i.i.d. Gaussian noise. Our treatment will be
very informal, emphasizing the underlying ideas rather than the mathematical details. A Gaussian process is really a conditional probabilistic source
for $\mathcal{Y}$ given $\mathcal{U}$ defined in terms of a *kernel function* $\kappa : \mathcal{U}^2 \rightarrow \mathbb{R}^+$. Different
kernels κ lead to different conditional sources. The Gaussian process defined
in terms of a kernel κ can be interpreted in many ways. Here we show that
one valid interpretation is as a universal model relative to a model class $\mathcal{M}_\kappa$
of conditional probabilistic sources, defined implicitly by the κ. For each γ,
there are kernels which make the Gaussian process equivalent to a Bayesian
universal model relative to the linear model with Gaussian noise based on
the γ-degree polynomials, and a Gaussian prior. However, there also exist kernels for which the model class $\mathcal{M}_\kappa$ is gigantic, containing, essentially,
arbitrarily good approximations to any continuous regression function. In
such cases, $\mathcal{M}_\kappa$ can still be written as a CUP model class (Section 13.2), but
the Gaussian process is a universal code that has entirely different properties from the standard meta-two-part and meta-Bayes CUP codes. These
properties ensure that, at least for some kernels, the Gaussian process has
excellent redundancy properties if data are distributed according to some
P^* in the information closure of $\mathcal{M}_\kappa$ – unlike for some standard CUP codes,
there is no extra $\log n$-factor in the redundancy. Thus, just like the regular
histogram model class, Gaussian processes have an interpretation in terms
of CUP model classes, but will mostly be applied in nonparametric settings;
this justifies calling them a nonparametric method.

Below we first, in Section 13.5.1, show how Bayesian universal codes for
ordinary Bayesian linear regression, as treated in Chapter 12, Section 12.3,
can be reinterpreted in terms of a kernel function. We then, in Section 13.5.2,
introduce general Gaussian processes. In Section 13.5.3 we show how to interpret them as universal codes.

13.5.1   Kernelization of Bayesian Linear Regression

We start by considering a k-dimensional linear model $\mathcal{M}^{\mathbf{X}_1}$. As in Chapter 12, Section 12.3.1, we denote the design matrix by $\mathbf{X}_1$ and the observed
y-values $y_1, \ldots, y_n$ by $\mathbf{y}_1$, the subscript 1 emphasizing that the prior may

represent an earlier sample/design matrix $\mathbf{y}_0/\mathbf{X}_0$. Recall that each vector x_i occurring in the design matrix $\mathbf{X}_1$ is really a transformation of the underlying input vectors or values u_i: for $1 \leq i \leq n$, $x_i = \phi(u_i)$, where $\phi : \mathcal{U} \to \mathbb{R}^k$.

Rather than considering $\mathcal{M}^{\mathbf{X}_1}$ for fixed design matrix $\mathbf{X}_1$, we switch back to our original interpretation of $\mathcal{M}^{(k)}$ as a set of conditional probabilistic sources for data $(u_1, y_1), (u_2, y_2), \ldots$; see the beginning of Section 12.3. As in Section 12.3.1, we consider Bayesian universal models with densities $\bar{f}_{\text{Bayes}}$ for $\mathcal{M}^{(k)}$, defined with respect to a Gaussian prior with some covariance matrix Σ_0. Viewed as a universal code for $\mathcal{M}^{(k)}$ rather than $\mathcal{M}^{\mathbf{X}_1}$, the density $\bar{f}_{\text{Bayes}}(y^n)$ should now be written as $\bar{f}_{\text{Bayes}}(y^n \mid u^n)$, where u^n is such that $\mathbf{X}_1^\top = (\phi(u_1), \ldots, \phi(u_n))$. In (12.56), page 357, we showed that the conditional density for a new data point Y_{n+1},

$$\bar{f}_{\text{Bayes}}(Y_{n+1} \mid \mathbf{y}_1) = \bar{f}_{\text{Bayes}}(Y_{n+1} \mid u_{n+1}, u^n, y^n), \qquad (13.28)$$

is Gaussian, and we gave a formula for computing its mean and variance. The first expression in (13.28) uses the notation of Chapter 12; the second uses our notation for conditional sources. It will be convenient to mix both notations below. To calculate (13.28), we use the input values u^n by assessing the design matrix $\mathbf{X}_1^\top$. We proceed to develop an alternative formula for computing (13.28) which uses the u^n in an entirely different way.

The Kernel For the given covariance matrix Σ_0, we define the *kernel* $\kappa :$ $\mathcal{U} \times \mathcal{U} \to \mathbb{R}$ relative to ϕ and Σ_0 by

$$\kappa(u, u') = \phi(u)^\top \Sigma_0 \phi(u'). \qquad (13.29)$$

Example 13.2 [Polynomial Kernel] Suppose that $\mathcal{P}^{(3)}$ is the 3-parameter regression model based on the 2nd-degree polynomials (Example 2.9), and Σ_0 is the unit matrix. Then $\phi(u) = (1, u, u^2)^\top$, so $\kappa(u, u') = 1 + uu' + u^2 u'^2$.

It turns out that the predictive density (13.28) can be calculated from y^n, u^n and u_{n+1} as long as one has access to the function κ, even if the function ϕ and the design matrix $\mathbf{X}_1$ are themselves unknown. This makes the kernel a highly useful concept. For example, it allows us to deal with ϕ that are complex nonlinear transformations of the u_i, such that the range of ϕ becomes infinite-dimensional (and $x_i = \phi(u_i)$ impossible to compute), whereas the function κ is still easy to compute. To prepare for a more precise statement of this fact, we first show that the mean of Y_{n+1} under the Bayesian predictive distribution $\bar{f}_{\text{Bayes}}(Y_{n+1} \mid \mathbf{y}_1)$ can be written as a linear combination of an alternative set of n basis functions $\{\kappa(\cdot, u_1), \ldots, \kappa(\cdot, u_n)\}$. Note that these basis functions are defined in terms of the input *data* $u_1, \ldots, u_n$. The new expression only uses the transformation function ϕ in terms of the kernel κ.

We will assume that the prior has mean $\mu_0 = \mathbf{0}$ (if not, translate all data so that it has), and covariance matrix Σ_0. It will be convenient to write $\Sigma_0 = \sigma^2 \Sigma_0'$, where σ^2 is the variance that is shared by all members (conditional densities) $f_{\sigma^2, \phi}(y_i \mid u_i)$ of $\mathcal{M}^{(k)}$. Then $\Sigma_0' = \sigma^{-2} \Sigma_0$. We have by the composition lemma (Lemma 12.2), that the MAP estimator is given by $\hat{\mu}_a = (\mathbf{X}_1^\top \mathbf{X}_1 + \Sigma_0'^{-1})^{-1} \mathbf{X}_1^\top \mathbf{y}_1$. We can rewrite this as

$$\hat{\mu}_a = \Sigma_0 \mathbf{X}_1^\top \alpha = \Sigma_0 \left(\sum_{i=1}^n \alpha_i x_i \right), \tag{13.30}$$

where $\alpha = (\alpha_1, \ldots, \alpha_n) \in \mathbb{R}^n$ is given by

$$\alpha = \sigma^{-2} (\mathbf{X}_1 \Sigma_0' \mathbf{X}_1^\top + I)^{-1} \mathbf{y}_1 = \sigma^{-2} (K \sigma^{-2} + I)^{-1} \mathbf{y}_1 = (K + \sigma^2 I)^{-1} \mathbf{y}_1. \tag{13.31}$$

Here K is the $n \times n$ matrix with $K_{ij} = \kappa(u_i, u_j)$.

To derive (13.30), notice that

$$\mathbf{X}_1^\top (\mathbf{X}_1 \Sigma_0' \mathbf{X}_1^\top + I) = (\mathbf{X}_1^\top \mathbf{X} + \Sigma_0'^{-1}) \Sigma_0' \mathbf{X}_1^\top,$$

where I denotes the identity matrix. Multiplying both sides by $(\mathbf{X}_1^\top \mathbf{X}_1 + \Sigma_0'^{-1})^{-1}$ on the left and $(\mathbf{X}_1 \Sigma_0' \mathbf{X}_1^\top + I)^{-1}$ on the right, we get

$$(\mathbf{X}_1^\top \mathbf{X}_1 + \Sigma_0'^{-1})^{-1} \mathbf{X}_1^\top = \Sigma_0' \mathbf{X}_1^\top (\mathbf{X}_1 \Sigma_0' \mathbf{X}_1^\top + I)^{-1},$$

and (13.30) follows.

Rewriting $\hat{\mu}_a$ as in (13.30) will prove very useful. We can now write for the expectation of Y_{n+1} given a new data point $x_{n+1} = \phi(u_{n+1})$, according to the predictive distribution (12.56) based on data $\mathbf{y}_1$:

$$E_{\bar{P}_{\text{Bayes}}}[Y_{n+1} \mid \mathbf{y}_1] = x_{n+1}^\top \hat{\mu}_a = x_{n+1}^\top \Sigma_0 (\sum_{i=1}^n \alpha_i x_i) = \sum_{i=1}^n x_{n+1}^\top \Sigma_0 (\alpha_i x_i) =$$

$$\sum_{i=1}^n \alpha_i \kappa(u_{n+1}, u_i). \tag{13.32}$$

Thus, the posterior predictive mean of Y_{n+1} given x_{n+1} can be expressed as a linear combination of n basis functions $\kappa(\cdot, u_i)$, which are defined in terms of the observed inputs $u_1, \ldots, u_n$. Moreover, in order to compute (13.32), we only need to access the function ϕ in terms of the function κ. This follows by (13.32) and (13.31), the latter equation showing that also the α_i can

be computed from $u_1, \ldots, u_n$ and $\mathbf{y}$ using the function κ rather than ϕ. It
follows (with some work, see (Rasmussen and Williams 2006), (2.12)) from
(12.56) that also the variance of Y_{n+1} given y^n, u^{n+1} can be calculated assessing the u_i only in terms of κ, and not directly in terms of ϕ: defining
$\mathbf{k}_{n+1} = (\kappa(u_1, u_{n+1}), \ldots, \kappa(u_n, u_{n+1}))^\top$, and K as before, we have

$$
\begin{aligned}
\operatorname{var}[\bar{Y}_{n+1} \mid \mathbf{y}_1] &= \kappa(u_{n+1}, u_{n+1}) - \mathbf{k}_{n+1}^\top \left(K + \sigma^2 I\right)^{-1} \mathbf{k}_{n+1}, \\
\operatorname{var}[Y_{n+1} \mid \mathbf{y}_1] &= \operatorname{var}[\bar{Y}_{n+1}] + \sigma^2.
\end{aligned}
\tag{13.33}
$$

Here $\bar{Y}_{n+1}$ is the posterior predicted value for Y_{n+1}, and $\operatorname{var}[\bar{Y}_{n+1} \mid \mathbf{y}_1]$ is
the variance of $\bar{Y}_{n+1}$ under the distribution $\bar{P}_{\text{Bayes}}(Y_{n+1} \mid u_{n+1}, u^n, y^n)$; see
page 357.

Kernel Trick   Since the predictive distribution $\bar{f}_{\text{Bayes}}(Y_{n+1} \mid \mathbf{y}_1)$ is normal,
it is completely determined by its mean and variance. Thus, we have just
shown that the predictive distribution $\bar{f}_{\text{Bayes}}(Y_{n+1} \mid \mathbf{y}_1)$ can be calculated
by an algorithm that only has access to κ, and not to ϕ. This is one instance of what is called the *kernel trick* in the literature (Schölkopf and Smola
2002). It becomes useful if we turn it on its head, and think of the equations (13.32) and (13.33) simply as describing an *algorithm* for predicting Y_{n+1}
given u^{n+1}, y^n and an input transformation given by the function κ. Namely,
as long as all quantities appearing in (13.32) and (13.33) are well defined, it
does not matter how the kernel function $\kappa : \mathcal{U} \times \mathcal{U} \to \mathbb{R}^+$ arises. κ may be
based on ϕ which we do not know, or which may be infinite-dimensional
and therefore hard to compute or imagine. If we use such general kernels,
not necessarily based on finite-dimensional ϕ, then the corresponding $\bar{f}_{\text{Bayes}}$
describes a so-called *Gaussian process*, a notion which we describe in the next
section.

Symmetric Positive Definite Kernels   As long as for any $n \in \mathbb{N}$, any vectors
$(u_1, \ldots, u_n) \in \mathcal{U}^n$, the $n \times n$ matrix K with $K_{ij} = \kappa(u_i, u_j)$ is a symmetric,
positive definite matrix, the quantities in (13.32) and (13.33) are well defined.
We call a kernel function $\kappa : \mathcal{U} \times \mathcal{U} \to \mathbb{R}^+$ satisfying this property a *symmetric positive definite κ*. Whenever we speak of "kernel" below, we implicitly
assume it is symmetric positive definite.

Example 13.3 [RBF Kernel] The symmetric positive definite kernels indeed
include many functions κ which are easy to describe, but for which it is not
immediately clear what the corresponding function ϕ is. A prototypical example is the *radial basis function (RBF)* kernel with parameter b, defined, for

$\mathcal{U} = \mathbb{R}^d$, as $\kappa(u, u') = e^{-b\|u-u'\|^2}$. Since $\kappa(\cdot, u)$ is a (nonnormalized) Gaussian around u, this kernel has also been called Gaussian, but we will avoid this name since it is quite unrelated to the use of Gaussian in the phrase Gaussian process; see below.

One can show that this kernel is symmetric positive definite. It is also easy to see that there exists no function $\phi : \mathcal{U} \rightarrow \mathbb{R}^k$ with finite k, such that the RBF kernel satisfies (13.29) for some matrix Σ. However, it turns out that there exist some ϕ with *infinite-dimensional range*, effectively mapping each $u \in \mathcal{U}$ into a corresponding point in an infinite-dimensional Hilbert space, such that (13.29) holds after all. Such a reinterpretation of symmetric positive definite κ as a dot product in an infinite-dimensional space is always possible, although it is often hard to imagine or determine what the functions ϕ look like (Schölkopf and Smola 2002).

13.5.2   Gaussian Processes

Let κ be an arbitrary symmetric positive definite kernel. We have just seen that we can compute the conditional distribution $\bar{f}_{\text{Bayes}}(Y_{n+1} \mid u_{n+1}, y^n, u^n)$ based on such a kernel, using the fact that it must be a normal density with mean (13.32) and variance (13.33). Therefore, we can also compute the product distribution

$$\bar{f}_{\text{Bayes}}(y^n \mid u^n) := \prod_{i=1}^{n} \bar{f}_{\text{Bayes}}(y_i \mid u_i, u^{i-1}, y^{i-1}). \tag{13.34}$$

It turns out that, essentially, the probabilistic source that is given, for each n, by (13.34) is a universal code relative to some i.i.d. model class $\mathcal{M}_\kappa$ that is implicitly defined by the kernel κ. For some kernels, the model class $\mathcal{M}_\kappa$ is infinite-dimensional. For example, in the case of the RBF kernel, it can be thought of as a CUP model class that is infinitely richer than finite-dimensional linear regression models: for essentially every continuous function $h : \mathcal{U} \rightarrow \mathbb{R}$ that converges to 0 if one of the components of u tends to plus or minus infinity, $\mathcal{M}_\kappa$ contains conditional sources $Y = h'(U) + Z$, where Z is normally distributed noise, for functions h' that are arbitrarily good approximations of h. Yet, crucially, at the same time, automatically $\bar{f}_{\text{Bayes}}$ achieves a surprisingly small redundancy if there exist "simple" elements of $\mathcal{M}_\kappa$ that compress the observed data well, as we explain in Section 13.5.3.

The conditional probabilistic source with density (13.34) describes what is called a *Gaussian process* on the input space $\mathcal{U}$. Gaussian processes are an important notion in advanced probability theory that has been around for a long time, at least since the 1940s (Kolmogorov 1941; Wiener 1949). While their importance in statistics was recognized a long time ago, more recently people have come to realize that such Gaussian processes have an important role in machine learning as well, and have applied them in several regression and classification contexts; see (Seeger 2004; Rasmussen and Williams 2006) for recent overviews of Gaussian processes in statistics and machine learning. Section 2.8 of (Rasmussen and Williams 2006) discusses the history of the subject. Here we neither give a precise formal definition nor the classical probabilistic interpretation of Gaussian processes; the interested reader is referred to (Rasmussen and Williams 2006). Instead, we content ourselves with a description of the more recent (Kakade, Seeger, and Foster 2006) interpretation of Gaussian processes as prequential estimators, or, equivalently, prequential universal codes relative to some model class $\mathcal{M}_\kappa$ determined by the kernel function.

Gaussian Process with RBF Kernel   To make all this more concrete, let us now focus on a particular case, the Gaussian process based on the RBF kernel. We first consider the case where we set σ^2 infinitesimally close to 0 in the definition of $\bar{f}_{\text{Bayes}}$. Then, for fixed data u^n, y^n, $\bar{f}_{\text{Bayes}}(Y_{n+1} \mid u_{n+1}, u^n, y^n)$, viewed as a function of u_{n+1}, becomes a conditional density which puts essentially all its mass on (an infinitesimally small band around) some continuous function $h(u)$ going through all the points $(u_1, y_1), \ldots, (u_n, y_n)$. While constrained to go through all these points, $h(u)$ typically looks surprisingly smooth (see Figure 2.2, page 15 of (Rasmussen and Williams 2006)). In fact, $h(u)$ is a linear combination of the kernel function, evaluated at a subset of the points $(u_1, \ldots, u_n)$: there exist $\alpha_1, \ldots, \alpha_n$ such that for each $u \in \mathcal{U}$,

$$h(u) = \sum_{i=1}^{n} \alpha_i \kappa(u_i, u) = \sum_{i=1}^{n} \alpha_i e^{-b\|u_i - u\|^2}, \tag{13.35}$$

where the α_i are themselves determined by u^n, y^n, as in (13.31). Note that the α_i may be negative, so $h(u)$ does not necessarily look like a mixture of Gaussian probability densities.

If we now apply the algorithm for some $\sigma^2 > 0$, then the α_i change: for $\sigma^2 \to \infty$, $\alpha \to 0$. As σ^2 increases, $h(u)$ becomes smoother – it will not go exactly through all the y_i anymore. $h(u)$ is now the *mean* of $\bar{f}_{\text{Bayes}}(Y_{n+1} \mid u_{n+1}, u^n, y^n)$, viewed as a function of u_{n+1}. It is of interest to consider the case where u_{n+1} is very far from any of the earlier observed u_i, i.e., one of the d components of the vector u_{n+1} tends to plus or minus infinity. In that case, $h(u_{n+1})$, the mean of $\bar{f}_{\text{Bayes}}(Y_{n+1} \mid u_{n+1}, u^n, y^n)$, will be close to 0; but more interestingly, the *variance* of $\bar{f}_{\text{Bayes}}(Y_{n+1} \mid u_{n+1}, u^n, y^n)$ will also tend to infinity. This is an intuitively pleasing locality property: essentially, the data indicate that for u_{n+1} near another u_i, the observed value of Y_{n+1} should with nonnegligible probability be close to the observed y_i; but if u_{n+1} is far from any observed u_i, then not much can be said about Y_{n+1}, so it makes sense that its variance becomes very large.

13.5.3   Gaussian Processes as Universal Models

We can think of Gaussian processes as individual-sequence universal codes relative to some model class $\mathcal{M}_\kappa$ that is implicitly defined by the choice of kernel κ. The connection to stochastic universal coding was recognized early on by Haussler and Opper (1997); the connection to individual-sequence coding was made more recently by Kakade, Seeger, and Foster (2006). Making the connection completely precise requires the notion of a reproducing kernel Hilbert space (RKHS). Instead, we only give an informal treatment, and refer to Kakade, Seeger, and Foster (2006) for details.

The model class $\mathcal{M}_\kappa$ induced by the kernel κ is the set of i.i.d. conditional probabilistic sources where the density of a single outcome Y given input u, $f(Y \mid u)$, is Gaussian with some mean function $h(u)$ and fixed variance σ^2. Here $h(u)$ is any function that can be written as a linear combination of the kernel evaluated at a finite (but arbitrarily large) number of points $(u_1, \ldots, u_\gamma)$. Thus, $\mathcal{M}_\kappa = \{f_{\sigma^2, h} \mid h \in \mathcal{H}_\kappa\}$, where $\mathcal{H}_\kappa = \mathcal{H}_{\kappa,1} \cup \mathcal{H}_{\kappa,2} \cup \ldots$. Here $\mathcal{H}_{\kappa,\gamma}$ is the 2γ-dimensional set of all functions $h : \mathcal{U} \to \mathbb{R}$ that can be written as

$$h(u) = \sum_{j=1}^{\gamma} \alpha_j \kappa(u, v_j), \tag{13.36}$$

parameterized by $(\alpha_1, \ldots, \alpha_\gamma, v_1, \ldots, v_\gamma) \in \mathbb{R}^{2\gamma}$. For convenience, we define $\mathcal{M}_{\kappa,\gamma} = \{f_{\sigma^2, h} \mid h \in \mathcal{H}_{\kappa,\gamma}\}$. Note that $\mathcal{M}_{\kappa,\gamma}$ has 2γ parameters, and is itself a union of γ-dimensional linear models. In the RBF kernel example, $\mathcal{H}_{\kappa,\gamma}$ contains all functions that can be written as $h(u) = \sum_{j=1}^{\gamma} \alpha_j e^{-b\|u - v_j\|^2}$ for some $\gamma > 0$, so that $\mathcal{H}_\kappa$ and $\mathcal{M}_\kappa$ are gigantic. Nevertheless, as was shown by Kakade, Seeger, and Foster (2006, Theorem 2), the luckiness regret of the Gaussian process $\bar{f}_{\text{Bayes}}$ relative to $f_{\sigma^2, h}$ such that h is "simple," is remarkably small. Here by a "simple" h we mean an $h \in \mathcal{H}_{\kappa,\gamma}$ for small γ. Thus, $\mathcal{M}_\kappa$ may be viewed as a CUP model class, since it is a union of parmetric models. Yet the Gaussian process/universal model $\bar{f}_{\text{Bayes}}$ has completely different properties from the standard meta-Bayes and meta-two-part CUP codes that we discussed in Section 13.2.

We now describe the theorem of Kakade et al., which applies to general positive definite symmetric kernels, not just RBF kernels. We then show how it can be applied to RBF kernels.

The Result of Kakade et al.   Suppose that $\bar{f}_{\text{Bayes}}$ is defined by (13.32), (13.33), (13.28) and (13.34), with respect to a symmetric positive definite kernel κ. Theorem 2 of (Kakade, Seeger, and Foster 2006) expresses that, for all individual sequences u^n, y^n,

$$-\log \bar{f}_{\text{Bayes}}(y^n \mid u^n) = \min_{h \in \mathcal{H}_\kappa} \left\{ -\log f_{\sigma^2, h}(y^n \mid u^n) + \frac{1}{2}\|h\|_\kappa^2 \right\} + R(u^n), \quad (13.37)$$

where

$$R(u^n) = \frac{1}{2}\log\det(I + \sigma^{-2}K). \quad (13.38)$$

Here I is the $n \times n$ unit matrix and K is the $n \times n$ matrix with $K_{ij} = \kappa(u_i, u_j)$. Equation (13.37) really expresses the individual-sequence luckiness regret achieved by $\bar{f}_{\text{Bayes}}$, where the luckiness function $a(\sigma, h)$ is given by $0.5\|h\|_\kappa^2$, and the luckiness regret ((11.20), page 311) is $R(u^n)$. Below we first describe $R(u^n)$, and then $\|h\|_\kappa^2$. Following the reasoning of Chapter 6, Section 6.2.1, we note that, since the luckiness regret does not depend on y^n, the Gaussian process achieves *the minimax luckiness regret*; therefore, it coincides with the LNML-2 code for the model class $\mathcal{M}_\kappa$.

Luckiness Regret $R(u^n)$ $R(u^n)$ depends crucially on both the kernel and on $u_1, \ldots, u_n$. To evaluate whether $\bar{f}_{\text{Bayes}}$ is a good universal model relative to $\mathcal{M}_\kappa$, we should get some idea of how large this term is. Whereas there exist sequences $u_1, \ldots, u_n$, for which the term grows linearly in n, it turns out that if we are willing to assume that the $u_1, u_2, \ldots$ are really random variables $U_1, U_2, \ldots$, distributed i.i.d. according to some distribution P_U^*, then, under conditions on P_U^*, we can bound the expected size of $R(U^n)$. Kakade, Seeger, and Foster (2006) show the following for the RBF kernel: if the U_i are independently distributed according to a multivariate normal distribution on $\mathcal{U} = \mathbb{R}^d$ with mean 0 and diagonal covariance matrix Σ_U, then

$$E[R(U^n)] = \text{ORDER}((\log n)^{d+1}). \quad (13.39)$$

Here the leading constant hidden in the order notation depends on Σ_U and the kernel parameter b. Interestingly, it does not depend on either the dimensionality or the norm $\|h\|_\kappa^2$ of the h achieving the minimum in (13.37); see Example 13.5. I conjecture that, as long as the RBF kernel is used, similar logarithmic regret bounds hold for a wide variety of input distributions P_U^*, including all distributions with bounded support. The constant in the order notation, as well the precise dependence on the input dimensionality d will depend on the details of P_U^* though. Assuming this conjecture to be true, it follows that $\bar{f}_{\text{Bayes}}$ is an $O((\log n)^c)$ universal model for some $c > 0$ under assumptions on the U_i that in many situations are quite reasonable.

Luckiness Function $0.5\|h\|_\kappa^2$ This term is defined as follows. Since $h \in \mathcal{H}_\kappa$, we can write it in the form (13.36) for some vectors $\alpha \in \mathbb{R}^\gamma, v \in \mathbb{R}^\gamma$, for some $\gamma \in \mathbb{N}$ such that $h \in \mathcal{H}_{\kappa,\gamma}$. Then $\|h\|_\kappa^2$ is defined as $\alpha^\top K \alpha$, K being the $\gamma \times \gamma$ matrix with $K_{ij} = \kappa(v_i, v_j)$. It turns out that this definition is unambiguous: if we consider some $\gamma' > \gamma$, then $h \in \mathcal{H}_{\gamma'}$, and we can also write $\|h\|_\kappa^2$ in terms of $\alpha'^\top K' \alpha'$, where K' is now a $\gamma' \times \gamma'$ matrix. The resulting $\|h\|_\kappa^2$ is still the same, as will be illustrated in Example 13.4 below. To get some idea of what it means, consider an h that is simple in the sense that it can be written as in (13.36) for some small γ. In such a case, $\|h\|_\kappa^2$ will be very small as well; roughly, for all h defined by α_j's and v_j's in some bounded set around 0, $\|h\|_\kappa^2$ is on the order of the minimum number of basis functions γ by which h can be expressed. Thus, $\|h\|_\kappa^2$ measures something like the complexity of h relative to the kernel κ: its size depends on how many basis functions are needed to express h, as well as on how large the coefficients of these basis functions must be to express h.

Example 13.4 [Finite-Dimensional Kernels] Consider the special case where the kernel κ is based on a k-dimensional ϕ as in (13.29), and Σ_0 is the $k \times k$ identity matrix. In this case, $\mathcal{M}_\kappa$ and $\mathcal{H}_\kappa$ are not gigantic as with the RBF kernel, but rather, finite-dimensional parametric.

For each $h \in \mathcal{H}_\kappa$, we can then write $h(u) = \mu^\top \phi(u)$ for some $\mu \in \mathbb{R}^k$. If we have k linearly independent points $x_1 = \phi(u_1), \ldots, x_k = \phi(u_k)$, then $\mathbf{X}_1^\top = (\phi(u_1), \ldots, \phi(u_k))$ is a $k \times k$ matrix of full rank and some straightforward rewriting shows that we can express h as $h(u) = \sum_{j=1}^k \alpha_j \kappa(u, u_j)$, where we set $\alpha = \left(\mathbf{X}_1^\top\right)^{-1} \mu$. Then

$$\|h\|_\kappa^2 = \alpha^\top \mathbf{X}_1 \mathbf{X}_1^\top \alpha = \mu^\top \mu,$$

which is the Mahalanobis distance between μ and the origin. Note that, as promised, $\|h\|_\kappa^2$ does not depend on the choice of $\mathbf{X}_1$, as long as $\mathbf{X}_1$ has an inverse.

Example 13.5 [Gaussian Processes for Finite-Dimensional Kernels] Consider a k-dimensional linear regression model $\mathcal{M}^{(k)}$, based on a ϕ with k-dimensional range, as in the previous example. Then the Gaussian process $\bar{f}_{\text{Bayes}}$ is really the Bayesian universal code relative to $\mathcal{M}^{(k)}$ equipped with a Gaussian prior. The reader may check that, indeed, in this case, by rewriting $\mathbf{X}_1$ in terms of κ, the result (13.37), giving the codelength of the Gaussian process, agrees with (12.73), giving the codelength of the ordinary Bayesian universal code. We have already discussed (Chapter 12, Section 11.4.3) that, if the U_i are i.i.d., then under mild conditions on the function ϕ, both the standard and the luckiness regret of the Bayesian universal code relative to a linear model $\mathcal{M}^{(k)}$ will be of the familiar size $(k/2)\log n + O(1)$. Since the regret of the Gaussian process density must be identical, it should also be of order $(k/2)\log n$.

Example 13.6 In contrast to the previous example, with the RBF kernel the function ϕ is infinite rather than k-dimensional; yet the kernel turns out to be such a "strong regularizer" that the luckiness regret of $\bar{f}_{\text{Bayes}}$ is still logarithmic. Let κ be the RBF kernel. Let us compare the redundancy relative to $\mathcal{M}_\kappa$, achieved by the Gaussian process $\bar{f}_{\text{Bayes}}$, to the redundancy of a standard meta-Bayes or meta-two-part CUP universal model $\bar{f}_{\text{CUP}}$, as defined in Section 13.2. To avoid confusion we rename $\bar{f}_{\text{Bayes}}$ to $\bar{f}_{\text{GP}}$. Now, assume that (U_i, Y_i) are i.i.d. according to some distribution P^* on $\mathcal{U} \times \mathcal{Y}$. First suppose that the conditional distribution $P^*(Y \mid Y)$ is an element of $\mathcal{M}_\kappa$. Let γ^* be the smallest γ such that $P^* \in \mathcal{M}_{\kappa,\gamma}$. Then, asymptotically, the P^*-expected redundancy of the code $\bar{f}_{\text{CUP}}$ will be equal to $(k_{\gamma^*}/2)\log n + O(1) = \gamma^* \log n + O(1)$. On the other hand, the redundancy of $\bar{f}_{\text{GP}}$ will be of $\text{ORDER}((\log n)^{d+1}) \geq \text{ORDER}((\log n)^2)$. It seems that the standard CUP code is preferable, since the expected redundancy of $\bar{f}_{\text{GP}}$ will become infinitely larger for large n. However, if k_{γ^*} is large, then, since the constant in front of the $(\log n)^{d+1}$ term does not depend on k_{γ^*}, there may be a substantial range of sample sizes for which the expected redundancy of $\bar{f}_{\text{GP}}$ is much lower than that of $\bar{f}_{\text{CUP}}$. Thus, for *practical* sample sizes, $\bar{f}_{\text{GP}}$ may well be preferrable.

If, as in Section 13.4, we now make a milder, nonparametric assumption that $P^*(Y|U) \in \mathcal{M}_t^*$ for some $\mathcal{M}_t^* \subset \langle \mathcal{M} \rangle$, where $\mathcal{M}_t^*$ ($t > 0$) consists of the set of distributions P^* such that $\inf_{P \in \mathcal{M}_\gamma} D(P^* \| P) = k_\gamma^{-t}$, then the analysis under case 2 of that section suggests that the redundancy of $\bar{f}_{\text{CUP}}$ is given by

$$E_{X^n \sim P^*}[\text{RED}(P^*, \bar{f}_{\text{CUP}})] =$$

$$E_{P^*}[-\log \bar{f}_{\text{CUP}}(Y^n \mid U^n) + \log f^*(Y^n \mid U^n)] = \text{ORDER}\left(\left(\frac{\log n}{n}\right)^{t/(t+1)}\right),$$

$$(13.40)$$

where f^* is the density of $P^*(Y \mid U)$. On the other hand, in the expression for the expected redundancy of $\bar{f}_{\text{GP}}$, the $\log^{d+1}$-term in the regret is swamped by the luckiness term $\|h\|_\kappa^2$. A similar analysis as under case 2 of Section 13.4, based on differentiation, now suggests that the redundancy of $\bar{f}_{\text{GP}}$ is given by

$$E_{X^n \sim P^*}[\text{RED}(P^*, \bar{f}_{\text{GP}})] = E_{P^*}[-\log \bar{f}_{\text{GP}}(Y^n \mid U^n) + \log f^*(Y^n \mid U^n)] =$$

$$\text{ORDER}\left(\left(\frac{1}{n}\right)^{t/(t+1)}\right), \quad (13.41)$$

so in this "inherently nonparametric" situation, it seems that $\bar{f}_{\text{GP}}$ will outperform $\bar{f}_{\text{CUP}}$ for all large n. We should point out that we have no formal proof of either (13.40) or (13.41).

> We strongly suspect that (13.40) holds if $\bar{f}_{\text{CUP}}$ is a fully two-part code CUP(2-p, 2-p). If, however, $\bar{f}_{\text{CUP}}$ is a CUP(Bayes, lnml)-code, then this is not so certain: for k-parameter models $\mathcal{M}$, the regret of $\bar{f}_{\text{Lnml-2}}(x^n \mid \mathcal{M})$ is of size $(k/2) \log n$ only if k is fixed and $n \to \infty$. It is known (Foster and Stine 2005) that for some models $\mathcal{M}$, if k is close to n, then the regret essentially becomes an increasing function of k only, that does not depend on n. Thus, it may be that if γ grows as n^α for some $0 < \alpha < 1$, the regret of $\bar{f}_{\text{CUP}}(\cdot \mid \mathcal{M}_{\kappa,\gamma})$ is already significantly smaller than $(k_\gamma/2) \log n$, and then the rough derivation leading up to (13.40) does not hold anymore.

Extensions I   For other kernels, partially the same story can be told, as long as they belong to the general class of *Mercer kernels* (Schölkopf and Smola 2002): Suppose $\bar{f}_{\text{Bayes}}$ is defined with respect to an arbitrary Mercer kernel κ. Then (13.35) and the middle equation of (13.36) still hold, so that the mean of Y_{n+1} given y^n, u^{n+1} is still given by a linear combination of the kernel evaluated at some or all of the data points u^n. Theorem 2 of (Kakade, Seeger, and Foster 2006) still holds. However, the quantity $R(u^n)$ depends strongly on the kernel, and may be quite different. For example, if κ is one of the so-called *Matérn kernels* with smoothness parameter $\nu > 0$ (Rasmussen and

Williams 2006), and the U_i are i.i.d. according to some distribution P^* with bounded support, then we get

$$E_{P^*}[R(U^n)] = \text{ORDER}\left(n^{\frac{d}{2\nu+d}}(\log n)^{\frac{2\nu}{2\nu+d}}\right),$$

which gives a much larger luckiness regret: it is now polynomial rather than logarithmic in n.

Extensions II   Just as finite-dimensional linear regression models can be generalized to deal with different output spaces and noise distributions (they are then called "generalized linear models," see (Hansen and Yu 2002)) the Gaussian process distributions can be generalized in this way as well. For example, if $\mathcal{Y}' = \{0,1\}$, and the goal is to encode Y'_{n+1} based on u^n, y^n and u_{n+1}, we may take a Gaussian process density $\bar{f}_{\text{Bayes}}$ relative to some kernel and transform its output by the *logistic link function* $P(Y'_{n+1} = 1) := 1/(1 + e^{-\bar{y}})$, where $\bar{y}$ is the mean of $\bar{f}_{\text{Bayes}}(Y_{n+1} \mid u_{n+1}, y^n, u^n)$. In this way we create a conditional probabilistic source for $\mathcal{Y}'$ rather than $\mathcal{Y}$, but clearly the underlying model is still a Gaussian process. Theorem 1 of Kakade, Seeger, and Foster (2006) essentially shows that for such generalizations of Gaussian processes, the regret is still bounded by (but now not exactly equal to) the quantity on the right side of (13.37).

> **Three Uses of the Word "Gaussian"**   In many applications of Gaussian processes, the noise is assumed to be Gaussian, and the kernel function is assumed to be Gaussian (RBF). But with other kernels, the resulting conditional sources are still "Gaussian processes"; and with other output spaces (e.g. $\mathcal{Y} = \{0,1\}$, classification) or noise functions, the underlying sources are still "Gaussian processes" (Rasmussen and Williams 2006).

Other Kernel Methods   The idea to apply linear statistical algorithms in a nonlinear way by transforming input variables into an infinitely high-dimensional space by means of a kernel, and to apply the linear algorithm there, is by no means restricted to Gaussian processes. Perhaps the most well known alternative application is the *support vector machine* for regression and classification (Vapnik 1998). In recent years there has been enormous interest in Gaussian processes, support vector machines, and many other kernel-based learning methods, witnessed by the fact that there are now at least three introductory textbooks around (Herbrich 2002; Schölkopf and Smola 2002; Shawe-Taylor and Cristianini 2004).

13.6   Conclusion and Further Reading

The study of nonparametric MDL seems to have started properly with the publication of (Hall and Hannan 1988). There exists quite a lot of – often quite complicated – work on nonparametric universal codes, and this chapter only covers a small part of it. For further reading, see, for example, (Barron and Cover 1991; Barron, Yang, and Yu 1994; Yu 1996; Rissanen, Speed, and Yu 1992; Yu and Speed 1992; Speed and Yu 1993; Haussler and Opper 1997; Barron 1998).

PART III

Refined MDL

Introduction to Part III

In this part of the book, we describe the minimum description length principle as it has been understood since the first grand overview article by Barron, Rissanen, and Yu (1998). We call this form of MDL *refined MDL*. For brevity, we will simply refer to it as MDL throughout most of Part III of this book. Refined MDL is not standard terminology; we choose it to stress the difference with the ad hoc, two-part code versions of MDL that have often been used in practice, and that were discussed in Chapter 5; see also Chapter 1. Below, we give an overview of the refined MDL idea. Again, our description of refined MDL is somewhat subjective, based on what researchers have actually recently done under the banner of MDL rather than on anyone's formal definition of MDL – indeed, such a formal definition does not exist; see Chapter 17, Section 1.9.1, for some alternative views and definitions of MDL.

A central concept in both crude two-part and in refined MDL is the idea of "coding the data D with the help of a hypothesis." In the crude MDL of Chapter 5, the hypothesis was always a probability distribution P, and the idea was formalized as "coding D with the Shannon-Fano code relative to P." In refined MDL, the hypothesis can also be a *set* of distributions: a model or model class $\mathcal{M}$. "Coding the data with the help of $\mathcal{M}$" is now formalized as "using a universal code relative to $\mathcal{M}$." This is the core of the refined MDL idea:

The Refined MDL Principle for Learning and Prediction

We want to find structure in the observed data $D = (x_1, \ldots, x_n)$, based on some model class $\mathcal{M}$, a family of (possibly conditional) probabilistic sources. These sources are to be interpreted primarily as *codes* or *description languages* for the data. In the cases we consider in this book, $\mathcal{M}$ is either a parametric model, a CUP model class (union of parametric models), or a nonparametric model class.

Refined MDL invariably starts by designing a "top-level" universal model $\bar{P}_{\text{top}}$ relative to the model class $\mathcal{M}$. This universal code is then used to achieve one of the following tasks:

1. **Model selection (Chapter 14).** In case the goal is to identify a *model* (interesting subfamily of model class $\mathcal{M}$), the universal code $\bar{P}_{\text{top}}$ should be a meta-two-part code (a concept explained in Chapter 13, Section 13.2).

2. **Prediction (Chapter 15, Section 15.2).** In case the goal is to predict future data coming from the same source, the universal code should be a one-part prequential code, for example, a meta-Bayesian code.

3. **Point hypothesis selection (Chapter 15, Section 15.3).** If the goal is to identify a single element of $\mathcal{M}$ (point hypothesis or parameter selection), the universal code should be a full (and not just "meta"-) two-part code, in which an element of $\mathcal{M}$ is explicitly described.

The general principle is as follows. First, $\bar{P}_{\text{top}}$ should be a good universal code. The definition of "good" is partially subjective, and depends on a "luckiness function," except in special cases, where minimax optimal codes exist. However, if we can choose between two universal models $\bar{P}_{\text{top}}$ and $\bar{P}'_{\text{top}}$ such that for all $n, x^n \in \mathcal{X}^n$, $\bar{P}_{\text{top}}(x^n) \geq \bar{P}'_{\text{top}}(x^n)$, and for some x^n, $\bar{P}_{\text{top}}(x^n) > \bar{P}'_{\text{top}}(x^n)$, then we always prefer $\bar{P}_{\text{top}}$.

$\bar{P}_{\text{top}}$ must be chosen such that those patterns in the data that we want to identify *explicitly*, have to be encoded explicitly, as part of a two-part code. These are the "models" in model selection and the "point hypothesis" in point hypothesis selection. Those patterns in the data that we do not need to identify explicitly, but that can still be used to compress the data, can be encoded *implicitly*, in a one-part code. For such patterns we use a one-part code rather than a two-part code, because two-part codes are incomplete: for every two-part code, there exists a one-part code that assigns uniformly shorter codelengths.

We should immediately add that one can broadly distinguish between two *types* of refined MDL, each of which can be used to any of the three tasks described above:

Individual-Sequence- vs. Expectation-Based MDL

In the individual-sequence-based version of refined MDL, one requires the universal model $\bar{P}_{\text{top}}$ to be *universal in an individual-sequence sense.*

In the expectation-based version of refined MDL, one merely requires $\bar{P}_{\text{top}}$ to be *universal in the expected sense.*

J. Rissanen, the originator of MDL, explicitly intended it to be a statistical method that has a clear interpretation that remains valid *even if no probabilistic assumptions about the data are made at all.* Therefore, whenever we refer to MDL in Part III of this book, we implicitly refer to the individual-sequence-based version. When we want to refer to expectation-based MDL, we shall say so explicitly.

A few remarks on this informal description of refined MDL are in order:

1. **Density estimation.** Apart from the three tasks in the box above, refined MDL is also often used for *parametric and nonparametric density estimation.* While at this point it may seem that this is an instance of point hypothesis selection (item 3 above), it turns out that there exists an alternative "predictive" MDL method for density estimation based on sequential prediction (item 3 above). Both methods are described in Chapter 15.

2. **Overlapping categories.** The division of refined MDL applications into the three categories given above is somewhat rough. For example, nonparametric density estimation based on histograms, Section 15.2.3 of Chapter 15, is best viewed as a combination of predictive MDL estimation and MDL model selection.

3. **Other applications.** In this book we focus on refined MDL applications to model selection, prediction, and point hypothesis selection. The reason is that these three applications have been most extensively developed. But in principle, the refined MDL idea, or more specifically, what we called the "general principle" above, should be applicable to *every* type of inductive inference, including tasks such as *denoising* (Roos et al. 2005) or *clustering* (Kontkanen, Myllymäki, Buntine, Rissanen, and Tirri 2005). We will not discuss such applications in this book.

4. Occam's razor. All forms of refined MDL start by designing a universal
code for the data, relative to a model class $\mathcal{M}$. The selected model, hypothesis, or prediction can always be related to the shortest obtainable
codelength for the data, based on the universal code, and hence based
on the set of description languages $\mathcal{M}$. As a result, all these versions of
MDL can be related to Occam's razor, although intriguingly, in some cases
(MDL for prediction, for example, with Gaussian processes; see Chapter 17, Section 17.2.2), a "simple" prediction can sometimes be obtained
by averaging over many "complex" ones.

Structure of Part III   This third part of the book is structured as follows: in
Chapter 14, we introduce and extensively discuss what is arguably the most
important application of refined MDL: model selection between parametric
models. Chapter 15 introduces MDL for prediction and point hypothesis selection, the second and third forms of refined MDL discussed above. This
chapter contains justifications of these two forms of MDL in terms of classical, *frequentist* statistics in the form of *statistical consistency* and associated
rate-of-convergence theorems. These are extensively discussed in Chapter 16,
which is fully devoted to consistency and rate-of-convergence issues. There
we also give consistency theorems for MDL model selection; these are left out
of the model selection Chapter 14 because they are more complicated than
the consistency theorems for prediction and point hypothesis selections, and
are best discussed after these. Finally, in Chapter 17, we extensively compare
MDL to other methods of inductive inference, and speculate about its future.

14 MDL Model Selection

14.1 Introduction

In this introductory section, we start right away with a high-level description of the refined MDL method for model selection. Based on this description, we then give an overview of the contents of this chapter.

Suppose we observe some data D consisting of n outcomes. Our goal is to select a model from a list $\mathcal{M}_1, \mathcal{M}_2, \ldots$ that is a good explanation for data D. According to refined MDL model selection, we should first design a universal model $\bar{P}(\cdot \mid \gamma)$ for each $\mathcal{M}_\gamma$, as well as a code on the model indices γ, with some length function $\dot{L}(\gamma)$. We then define the MDL model selection code as the code with lengths

$$\bar{L}_{\text{CUP}}(D) := \min_\gamma \left\{ \dot{L}(\gamma) - \log \bar{P}(D \mid \gamma) \right\}. \tag{14.1}$$

We then adopt, as best explanation of data D, the model $\mathcal{M}_\gamma$ that minimizes (14.1). This leaves open the choices for $\bar{P}(\cdot \mid \gamma)$ and $\dot{L}(\gamma)$. This chapter is mostly about what choices should be made in what situation.

Together, $\bar{P}(\cdot \mid \gamma)$ and $\dot{L}(\gamma)$ define $\bar{L}_{\text{CUP}}$, which represents the lengths of a universal code for $\mathcal{M}$, where $\mathcal{M} = \cup_\gamma \mathcal{M}_\gamma$. We usually consider a finite or countably infinite list of parametric models $\mathcal{M}_1, \mathcal{M}_2, \ldots$. Thus, $\mathcal{M}$ is a *CUP* model class, and $\bar{L}_{\text{CUP}}$ is really a meta-two-part code, which could more explicitly be denoted as $\bar{L}_{\text{CUP}(2\text{-p},\cdot)}$; see Chapter 13, Section 13.2. $\bar{L}_{\text{CUP}}$ is the "top-level" universal code, corresponding to the distribution that, in the introduction to Part III, page 406, we called $\bar{P}_{\text{top}}$. We use the more specific subscript CUP rather than TOP in this chapter, since in the context of model selection, $\bar{P}_{\text{top}}$ will always be a CUP model class. The notation for the parameterization Θ_γ of $\mathcal{M}_\gamma$, the number of parameters k_γ, the "true" model $\mathcal{M}_{\gamma^*}$ (if it exists), and so on, were all introduced in Chapter 13, Section 13.2, page 372. The only novelty is that observed data are denoted as D. D always consists of n outcomes. Usually, these are denoted as x_i, so that $D = (x_1, \ldots, x_n)$, but in a regression context, we denote them as (x_i, y_i), so that $D = ((x_1, y_1), \ldots, (x_n, y_n))$. The parametric complexity of a model $\mathcal{M}_\gamma$ is denoted as $\mathrm{COMP}(\mathcal{M}_\gamma)$. In this chapter, we leave out the superscript n, since it will always be clear from the context.

Simple Model Selection: Four Interpretations (Section 14.2)   As said, to make MDL model selection well defined, we should make choices for $\bar{P}(\cdot \mid \gamma)$ and $\dot{L}(\gamma)$. The preferred choice for $\bar{P}(\cdot \mid \gamma)$ is always to take the NML distribution $\bar{P}_{\mathrm{nml}}(\cdot \mid \gamma)$, whenever this is defined for $\mathcal{M}_\gamma$. If the number of models under consideration is finite and small, in particular if it is just two, the preferred code for $\dot{L}$ is the uniform code. We begin our treatment with the case where the number of models under consideration is just two, and the NML distribution for both models is defined. We call this case *simple* refined MDL model selection. It is treated in Section 14.2 below. We argue that simple refined MDL model selection is a good idea by interpreting it in four, quite different, ways.

General Model Selection (Section 14.3)   We discuss how to deal with large numbers of models in Section 14.3. By a "large" number of models we either mean that the number of potentially interesting models is finite but grows with the sample size n, or that the number of such models is infinite. Section 14.3 also explains how to deal with the – common – case of models $\mathcal{M}$ with infinite parametric complexity $\mathrm{COMP}(\mathcal{M})$.

Practical Issues in MDL Model Selection (Section 14.4)   When applying MDL model selection in practice, a number of additional difficulties come into play. In this section we explain how the most common difficulties should be resolved.

MDL Model Selection in Linear Regression (Section 14.5)   Here we illustrate the MDL method on perhaps the most well studied practical example: model selection for linear regression. Three variations of MDL have been proposed for this problem, and we study each of them in detail. We also report how these methods perform in practice.

Worst Case or Average Case? (Section 14.6*) MDL model selection as defined in this chapter is based on using universal codes that are optimal in a worst-case sense. One may wonder why the methodology should not be based on average case behavior instead. This issue is discussed in detail in this section.

14.2 Simple Refined MDL Model Selection

In this section we consider the simple case where, for the given data D, we want to choose between just two parametric models $\mathcal{M}_A$ and $\mathcal{M}_B$, both of which are assumed to have finite parametric complexities $\text{COMP}(\mathcal{M}_A)$ and $\text{COMP}(\mathcal{M}_B)$. These complexities are defined as in Chapter 7, (7.1) on page 207. Since the complexities are finite, the NML universal models $\bar{P}_{\text{nml}}(D \mid \gamma)$ are well defined for $\gamma \in \{A, B\}$.

As our running example, we take binary data $D = x^n \in \{0, 1\}$, and let $\mathcal{M}_A$ and $\mathcal{M}_B$ be the first- and second-order Markov models (Chapter 2, Example 2.7).

According to the refined MDL principle for model selection, we should pick the model $\mathcal{M}_\gamma$ achieving the minimum codelength of the data in (14.1). We will take $\dot{L}(\gamma)$ to be uniform, so this amounts to picking the $\mathcal{M}_\gamma$ maximizing the *normalized* maximum likelihood $\bar{P}_{\text{nml}}(D \mid \gamma)$, or equivalently, minimizing

$$- \log \bar{P}_{\text{nml}}(D \mid \gamma) = - \log P(D \mid \hat{\theta}_\gamma(D)) + \text{COMP}(\mathcal{M}_\gamma). \tag{14.2}$$

We call this procedure *simple refined MDL model selection*. The *confidence* in the decision is given by the codelength difference

$$\left| - \log \bar{P}_{\text{nml}}(D \mid \mathcal{M}_A) - [- \log \bar{P}_{\text{nml}}(D \mid \mathcal{M}_B)] \right|.$$

We have already indicated in Chapter 6, Section 6.2.1, and Chapter 7, Section 7.3, that $\text{COMP}(\mathcal{M}_\gamma)$ measures something like "complexity" of model $\mathcal{M}_\gamma$. As we already know from Chapter 7, $\text{COMP}(\mathcal{M}_\gamma)$ is called the *parametric complexity* of $\mathcal{M}_\gamma$. In the context of model selection, it is sometimes also called the *model cost*. On the other hand, $- \log P(D \mid \hat{\theta}_\gamma(D))$ is minus the maximized likelihood of the data, so it measures something like (minus) fit or *error* – in the linear regression case (Chapter 12), it can be directly related to the mean-squared error. Thus, (14.2) embodies a tradeoff between lack of fit (measured by minus log-likelihood) and complexity (measured by $\text{COMP}(\mathcal{M}_\gamma)$.

In analogy to Kolmogorov complexity, the codelength $-\log \bar{P}_{\mathrm{nml}}(D \mid \gamma)$ has been called the *stochastic complexity of the data D relative to model $\mathcal{M}_\gamma$* (Rissanen 1987,1996). With this definition, we can say that simple refined MDL tells us to select the model that minimizes the stochastic complexity of the data. Note that "parametric complexity" is a property of a model, and "stochastic complexity" is a property of data relative to a model.

In the remainder of this section, we first provide some basic intuition about simple refined MDL model selection by comparing it to classical hypothesis testing. We then, in Section 14.2.1 through 14.2.4, argue that simple refined MDL model selection is a good idea, by interpreting it in four quite different ways. In Section 14.4.1 we consider how to calculate or approximate $-\log \bar{P}_{\mathrm{nml}}(D \mid \mathcal{M})$.

Example 14.1 [Refined MDL and Naive GLRT] Generalized likelihood ratio testing (GLRT) is a hypothesis testing method from traditional statistics. It first requires that we give one of the two models the special status of "null hypothesis," so let us rename our two models as $\mathcal{M}_0$ (the null hypothesis) and $\mathcal{M}_1$. GLRT tells us to "reject" $\mathcal{M}_0$ if the value of the *test statistic*

$$-\ln P(D \mid \hat{\theta}_0(D)) + \ln P(D \mid \hat{\theta}_1(D))$$

exceeds some "critical value" t. In a naive form of GLRT (not really advocated by anyone), we would set $t = 0$ and simply pick the $\mathcal{M}_\gamma$ maximizing $\log P(D \mid \hat{\theta}_\gamma(D))$. This amounts to ignoring the complexity terms $\mathrm{COMP}(\mathcal{M}_\gamma)$ in (14.2). If the two models are nested, $\mathcal{M}_0 \subset \mathcal{M}_1$, then it is impossible that $-\log P_{\hat{\theta}_1}(D) > -\log P_{\hat{\theta}_0(D)}(D)$, so that model $\mathcal{M}_0$ can never be selected with confidence larger than 0. Clearly, this cannot be right. In contrast to naive GLRT, MDL tries to avoid overfitting by picking the model maximizing the *normalized* rather than the ordinary likelihood. The more distributions in $\mathcal{M}$ that fit the data well, the larger the normalization term will be, and the larger the corresponding critical value t.

Example 14.2 [MDL and Point Null Hypothesis Testing] The version of GLRT that is advocated within the hypothesis testing literature (Casella and Berger) requires that we specify some desired significance level $0 < \alpha < 1$. One then calculates a "critical value" t, dependent on both α and n, such that

$$\sup_{P^* \in \mathcal{M}_0} P^*(-\log P_{\hat{\theta}_0(X^n)}(X^n) \geq -\log P_{\hat{\theta}_1(X^n)}(X^n) + t) = \alpha, \qquad (14.3)$$

and one "rejects" the null hypothesis if the log-likelihood ratio achieved by the two ML estimators on the actually observed data $D = (x_1, \ldots, x_n)$ exceeds the value t. If no t exists for which (14.3) holds precisely, one rejects if the log-likelihood ratio exceeds the smallest t for which (14.3) holds with $=$ replaced by $\leq$.

If $\mathcal{M}_0$ consists of a single distribution or source, $\mathcal{M}_0 = \{P_0\}$, then GLRT becomes an instance of point null hypothesis testing. Interestingly and very importantly, in this case, MDL model selection can be directly related to classical, significance-level based, GLRT point null hypothesis testing. To see this, note that if $\mathcal{M}_0 = \{P_0\}$, then for all x^n, $-\log \bar{P}_{\mathrm{nml}}(x^n \mid \mathcal{M}_0) = -\log P_0(x^n)$. Fix some significance level $0 < \alpha < 1$ and suppose that we observe data D such that

$$-\log P_0(D) \geq -\log \bar{P}_{\mathrm{nml}}(D \mid \mathcal{M}_1) - \log \alpha. \tag{14.4}$$

Then MDL model selection would select the model $\mathcal{M}_1$ with confidence at least $-\log \alpha$. By the no-hypercompression inequality of Chapter 3, the probability that we observe (14.4) if $\mathcal{M}_0$ is true must be smaller than or equal to $2^{-(-\log \alpha)} = \alpha$. Therefore, we have

$$P_0(-\log P_0(D) \geq -\log P_{\hat{\theta}_1(X^n)}(X^n) + t') \leq \alpha,$$

where $t' = \mathrm{COMP}^{(n)}(\mathcal{M}_1) - \log \alpha$. It follows that the critical value t for which (14.3) holds must be no larger than t. Therefore, if we perform a traditional GLRT test, and we observe (14.4), then we would reject $\mathcal{M}_0$ with confidence level α. Summarizing: if MDL model selection selects $\mathcal{M}_1$ with confidence at least $-\log \alpha$, the corresponding traditional test rejects $\mathcal{M}_0$ for the given confidence level α. For example, if $\alpha = 0.05$, then $-\log \alpha = \log 20 < 5$. So if the NML universal code for $\mathcal{M}_1$ compresses the data by more than 5 bits compared to $\mathcal{M}_0$, then the traditional hypothesis test we just defined would have rejected $\mathcal{M}_0$, if the significance level had been set at 0.05.

> **Open Problem No. 9** Such a direct relation between MDL model selection and null hypothesis testing does not seem to exist if both hypotheses are composite. It would be interesting to investigate whether natural universal codes (different from NML codes) exist, such that the relation to null hypothesis testing can be re-established in the composite case, and whether there is any practical advantage in using such codes.

Example 14.3 [The Basic Sanity Check: Do I Compress at All?] Suppose the sample space $\mathcal{X}$ is finite, say $|\mathcal{X}| = m$. Then we can always use the uniform code to encode the sample $D = (x_1, \ldots, x_n)$ literally. This takes $n \log m$ bits. This codelength $n \log m$ is achieved no matter what data D are encoded. Therefore, if MDL selects a model $\mathcal{M}_{\ddot{\gamma}}$, it is of interest to see whether this model really achieves much more compression than the code that encodes the data literally. If it does not, then the model $\mathcal{M}_{\ddot{\gamma}}$ does not compress the data very well. This means that it has failed to identify any patterns in the data (Chapter 1), and this means that it should definitely not be adopted as "best available explanation of the data."

In other words, when comparing two models $\mathcal{M}_A$ and $\mathcal{M}_B$, it is always a good idea to consider a third, "trivial" model $\mathcal{M}_0 = \{P_0\}$, where P_0 is the uniform distribution on $\mathcal{X}^n$. $\mathcal{M}_0$ is not intended as a serious explanation of the data, but as a sanity checker: if we cannot compress the data substantially more with $\mathcal{M}_{\ddot{\gamma}}$, than with $\mathcal{M}_0$, this does not mean that $\mathcal{M}_0$ is a good explanation of the data; but it does mean that, at the given sample size, none of the models under consideration provide good explanations of the data. $\mathcal{M}_0$ plays an analogous role to a null hypothesis in hypothesis testing: if one cannot "reject" the null hypothesis, this does not necessarily mean that one believes it is true. In the MDL context, one never believes that any model is true, but one can say: if one cannot compress the data substantially more than with $\mathcal{M}_0$, this does not necessarily mean that one believes $\mathcal{M}_0$ is a good explanation of the data, but it does mean that neither $\mathcal{M}_A$ nor $\mathcal{M}_B$ is a good explanation of the data.

> If $\mathcal{X}$ is continuous, then it is not clear what it means to encode the data "literally." Still, since data invariably are stored as a file in a computer, they are always discretized, and there is always some code used to store the discretized data D' on the computer. This code corresponds to some distribution P_0, and we may take $\mathcal{M}_0 = \{P_0\}$ to be our sanity-check model in this case. It is still a good idea to compare $-\log P_0(D')$ to the codelength $-\log \bar{P}_{\mathrm{nml}}(D' \mid \mathcal{M}_{\ddot{\gamma}})$ obtained by MDL model selection. Note that, in contrast to the usual situation, in this comparison, $\bar{P}_{\mathrm{nml}}(\cdot \mid \mathcal{M}_{\ddot{\gamma}})$ is not equal to the density $\bar{f}_{\mathrm{nml}}(\cdot \mid \mathcal{M}_{\ddot{\gamma}})$. Instead, it must be set equal to the probability mass function on the discretized data D', which can be deduced from $\bar{f}_{\mathrm{nml}}(\cdot \mid \mathcal{M}_{\ddot{\gamma}})$.

> More generally, both with continuous and discrete $\mathcal{X}$, if one has prior knowledge about the code by which the data is stored on the computer, then one can use this to refine the trivial null model $\mathcal{M}_0$. For example, if the data are a sequence of letters encoded in the standard ASCII form, then each byte (unit of 8 bits) will have its leftmost bit 0. Then a compression by a factor of 7/8 can be trivially achieved, and we can only have any confidence at all in our selected model $\mathcal{M}_A$ or $\mathcal{M}_B$ if they compress substantially more than that.

This ends our comparison of simple refined MDL to hypothesis testing.

Four Interpretations of Simple Refined MDL   The hope is that the normalization term $\text{COMP}(\mathcal{M}_\gamma)$ strikes the right balance between complexity and fit. Whether it really does depends on whether COMP is a "good" measure of complexity. In the remainder of this section we argue that it is, by giving four different interpretations of COMP and of the resulting tradeoff (14.2):

1. Compression interpretation (Section 14.2.1)

2. Counting interpretation (Section 14.2.2)

3. Bayesian interpretation (Section 14.2.3)

4. Prequential interpretation (Section 14.2.4)

These interpretations correspond to alternative universal codes that achieve codelengths close to that of $\bar{P}_{\text{nml}}$: the two-part codes yield the counting interpretation, Bayesian codes yield the Bayesian interpretation, and prequential plug-in codes lead to the prequential interpretation.

There is one more justification of the tradeoff (14.2) in traditional, frequentist terms: in many cases, estimating the model $\mathcal{M}_\gamma$ by (14.2) can be proved to be statistically consistent: for all large n, the true model $\mathcal{M}_{\gamma^*}$ is selected with probability 1. We will postpone derivation of this result to Chapter 16, Section 16.3. The reason is that, for a proper understanding of MDL model selection consistency, one should already know about the – much simpler – consistency proofs for the fully one-part code MDL for prediction, and the fully two-part code MDL for hypothesis selection, to be introduced in Chapter 15.

14.2.1   Compression Interpretation

Rissanen's original goal was to select the model that detects the most regularity in the data; he identified this with the "model that allows for the most compression of data x^n." To make this precise, he needed to associate a code with each model. The NML code with lengths $-\log \bar{P}_{\text{nml}}(\cdot \mid \mathcal{M}_\gamma)$ seems to be a very reasonable choice because of the following two properties:

1. The better the best-fitting distribution in $\mathcal{M}_\gamma$ fits the data, the shorter the codelength $-\log \bar{P}_{\text{nml}}(D \mid \mathcal{M}_\gamma)$.

2. No distribution in $\mathcal{M}_\gamma$ is given a prior preference over any other distribution, since the regret of $\bar{P}_{\text{nml}}(\cdot \mid \mathcal{M}_\gamma)$ is the same for all $D \in \mathcal{X}^n$ (see

(6.16) on page 181). $\bar{P}_{\mathrm{nml}}$ is the *only* complete prefix code with this property, which may be restated as: $\bar{P}_{\mathrm{nml}}$ treats *all distributions within each* $\mathcal{M}_{\gamma}$ *on the same footing!*

Therefore, if one is willing to accept the basic ideas underlying MDL as *first principles*, then the use of NML in model selection is now justified, at least to some extent. Below we give additional justifications that are not directly based on data compression; but we first provide some further interpretation of $-\log \bar{P}_{\mathrm{nml}}$.

Compression and Separating Structure from Noise   We present the following ideas in an imprecise fashion – Rissanen and Tabus (2005) recently showed how to make them precise. The stochastic complexity of data D relative to $\mathcal{M}$, given by (14.2) can be interpreted as the amount of information in the data relative to $\mathcal{M}$, measured in bits. Although a one-part codelength, it still consists of two parts: a part $\mathrm{COMP}^{(n)}(\mathcal{M})$ measuring the amount of *structure* or *meaningful information* in the data (as "seen through $\mathcal{M}$"), and a part $-\log P(D \mid \hat{\theta}(D))$ measuring the amount of *noise* or *accidental information* in the data. To see that this second part measures noise, consider the regression example, Example 1.3, again. As we showed in Chapter 12, in that case $-\log P(D \mid \hat{\theta}(D))$ becomes equal to a linear function of the mean-squared error of the best-fitting polynomial in the set of kth degree polynomials – quite literally "noise." To see that the first part measures structure, we reinterpret it below as the number of bits needed to specify a "distinguishable" distribution in $\mathcal{M}$, using a uniform code on all distinguishable distributions.

14.2.2   Counting Interpretation

Intuitively, the more distributions a model contains, the more patterns it can fit well and thus the larger the risk of overfitting. However, if two distributions are very close in the sense that they assign high likelihood to the same patterns, they do not contribute so much to the complexity of the overall model. It seems that we should measure complexity of a model in terms of the number of distributions it contains that are "essentially different" (distinguishable). We already indicated in Chapter 6, Section 6.2.2, and Chapter 7, Section 7.3, that $\mathrm{COMP}^{(n)}(\mathcal{M})$ measures something like this. In Section 7.3.4 we even showed that it is directly proportional to the number of distinguishable distributions in the model $\mathcal{M}$. The derivation was based on the asymptotic expansion (7.4) of $\bar{P}_{\mathrm{nml}}$ which we repeat here for convenience:

$$\mathrm{COMP}(\mathcal{M}_\gamma) = \frac{k_\gamma}{2} \log \frac{n}{2\pi} + \log \int_{\theta \in \Theta_\gamma} \sqrt{\det I(\theta)} d\theta + o(1). \qquad (14.5)$$

To illustrate, consider Example 1.3, Fechner's and Stevens's model. Both models have two parameters, yet the $\int_\Theta \sqrt{\det I(\theta)} d\theta$-term is much larger for Fechner's than for Stevens's model. In the experiments of Myung, Balasubramanian, and Pitt (2000), the parameter set was restricted to $0 < a < \infty, 0 < b < 3$ for Stevens's model and $0 < a < \infty, 0 < b < \infty$ for Fechner's model. The variance of the error Z was set to 1 in both models. With these values, the difference in $\int_\Theta \sqrt{\det I(\theta)} d\theta$ is 3.804, which is nonnegligible for small samples. Thus, Stevens's model contains more distinguishable distributions than Fechner's, and is better able to capture random noise in the data, as Townsend (1975) already speculated more than 30 years ago.

Example 14.4 [MDL, AIC, and BIC Model Selection] Two benchmark methods for model selection are the *Akaike information criterion* or *AIC* (Akaike 1973), and the *Bayesian* or *Schwarz information criterion* or *BIC* (Schwarz 1978). According to BIC, we should pick the model minimizing

$$- \log P_{\hat{\theta}}(D \mid \gamma) + \frac{k_\gamma}{2} \log n. \qquad (14.6)$$

According to the simplest form of AIC, we should pick the model minimizing

$$- \log P_{\hat{\theta}}(D \mid \gamma) + k_\gamma. \qquad (14.7)$$

We see that in AIC and BIC, the penalty of each model only depends on the number of parameters and the sample size. In MDL model selection, it also depends on the functional form of the model $\mathcal{M}_\gamma$, expressed by the term $\mathrm{COMP}(\mathcal{M}_\gamma)$. This makes MDL a more flexible, adaptive criterion, as discussed in Section 14.5.4 in a regression context. If both models have the same number of parameters, then in contrast to MDL, both AIC and BIC reduce to crude generalized likelihood ratio testing.

From the asymptotic expansion (14.5) we see that for a large enough sample, MDL and BIC will select the same model. But, as illustrated in Section 14.5.4, this is not at all the case when the sample size is small. Crucially, as first pointed out by Foster and Stine (1999), when the number of models under consideration is infinite or grows with n, then MDL and BIC need not select the same model even if the sample size tends to infinity.

We will compare MDL more thoroughly with AIC and BIC in Chapter 17, Section 17.3.

14.2.3   Bayesian Interpretation

The Bayesian method of statistical inference provides an alternative approach to model selection based on *Bayes factors* (Kass and Raftery 1995). The Bayes factor method is very closely related to the refined MDL approach.

Suppose we want to select between models $\mathcal{M}_1$ and $\mathcal{M}_2$. According to the Bayesian approach, we should specify a prior distribution on $\mathcal{M}_1$ and $\mathcal{M}_2$. Then, conditioned on each model, we should specify prior densities w_1 and w_2. As in (6.4), the Bayesian marginal likelihood is defined as

$$\bar{P}_{\text{Bayes}}(x^n \mid \mathcal{M}_\gamma) = \int P(x^n \mid \theta) w_\gamma(\theta) d\theta. \tag{14.8}$$

Bayes then tells us to select the model with the maximum a posteriori probability $P(\mathcal{M}_\gamma \mid D)$. This can be computed from Bayes formula as

$$P(\mathcal{M}_\gamma \mid D) = \frac{\bar{P}_{\text{Bayes}}(D \mid \mathcal{M}_\gamma) W(\gamma)}{\sum_{k=1,2} P(D \mid \mathcal{M}_k) W(k)}.$$

Since the denominator does not depend on γ, Bayes tells us to pick the $\mathcal{M}_\gamma$ maximizing $\bar{P}_{\text{Bayes}}(D \mid \mathcal{M}_\gamma) W(\gamma)$. By asymptotic expansion of $-\log \bar{P}_{\text{Bayes}}$, Theorem 8.1 of Chapter 8 (see also the box on page 235), we have that

$$-\log \bar{P}_{\text{nml}}(D \mid \mathcal{M}_\gamma) + \log \bar{P}_{\text{Bayes}}(D \mid \mathcal{M}_\gamma) =$$

$$\ln w(\hat{\theta}_\gamma) - \ln \frac{\sqrt{\det I(\hat{\theta}_\gamma)}}{\int_{\Theta_\gamma} \sqrt{\det I(\hat{\theta}_\gamma)} d\theta_\gamma} + o(1). \tag{14.9}$$

It follows that Bayes factor model selection with Jeffreys' prior, MDL model selection based on $\bar{P}_{\text{CUP}(2\text{-}p, \text{Bayes})}$ with Jeffreys' prior, and NML model selection between $\mathcal{M}_A$ and $\mathcal{M}_B$ are asymptotically based on an *identical* minimization: a close relation indeed. If a prior different from Jeffreys' is used, and the number of parameters of $\mathcal{M}_A$ and $\mathcal{M}_B$ is different, then, asymptotically, still the same model will be chosen. But for small sample sizes, or if the number of parameters of both models is the same, Bayes and NML model selection may select a different model if the prior is not Jeffreys'. If a large or infinite number of models are compared, then it is not clear anymore whether Bayes and NML are equivalent, since the $o(1)$-term in (14.9) depends on γ.

14.2.4   Prequential Interpretation

The prequential view gives a fourth interpretation of refined MDL model selection: given models $\mathcal{M}_1$ and $\mathcal{M}_2$, MDL tells us to pick the model that minimizes the accumulated prediction error resulting from sequentially predicting future outcomes given all the past outcomes. This interpretation is immediate if we use a prequential plug-in code as an approximation of $-\log \bar{P}(\cdot \mid \mathcal{M}_\gamma)$, as the following example shows.

Example 14.5 [GLRT and Prequential Model Selection] In generalized likelihood ratio testing (GLRT, Example 14.1), we associate with each model the log-likelihood (minus log loss) that is obtained by the ML estimator. This is the predictor within the model that minimizes log loss *with hindsight, after* having seen the data; if the model $\mathcal{M}$ is large enough, the fact that such an ML estimator achieves small log loss tells us nothing about its quality on future data, whence GLRT is prone to overfitting. In contrast, prequential model selection associates with each model the log-likelihood (minus log loss) that can be obtained by using a sequence of estimators (usually, luckiness ML estimators) $\hat{\theta}(x^{i-1})$ to predict data x_i. Crucially, the data on which ML estimators are evaluated has not been used in constructing the ML estimators themselves. Thus, we select the model that, when used for sequentially predicting *unseen* data given parameters fitted on previously seen data, achieves the best prediction performance. Intuitively, this seems like a very reasonable way to measure a model's fit without risking overfitting. It is clear that this prequential procedure, and therefore, MDL model selection, is closely related to cross-validation, a popular model selection method that is commonly used in practice. We discuss the connections in more detail in Chapter 17, Section 17.6.

It may seem that the prequential interpretation is not valid for the NML or two-part codes, since these are not prequential. Nevertheless, even in that case, if we consider a single batch of data of some fixed sample size n, then the prequential interpretation remains valid. Let us illustrate this for NML. The conditional probabilities $\bar{P}_{\mathrm{nml}}(X_i \mid x^{i-1})$ can be interpreted as predictions, and $\sum -\log \bar{P}_{\mathrm{nml}}(x_i \mid x^{i-1})$ can be interpreted as the accumulated prediction error made when sequentially predicting x_i on the basis of x^{i-1}, using the prediction strategy $\bar{P}_{\mathrm{nml}}$ that achieves the minimax optimal regret on sequences of length n. It follows that the predictive interpretation is still valid, although the prediction strategy now has built-in knowledge of the "horizon" (sample size, total number of predictions to be made) n.

14.3   General Parametric Model Selection

In the previous section we introduced a simple version of the refined MDL principle for model selection, applicable when the set of models under consideration is "small" and their parametric complexities $\mathrm{COMP}(\mathcal{M}_\gamma)$ are finite. In this section, we extend the (refined) MDL model selection to general model selection problems, where the complexities of the models may be infinite (Section 14.3.1) or the number of models themselves may be large or infinite (Section 14.3.2). This leads to a general MDL principle for model selection, which we describe and motivate in Section 14.3.3.

14.3.1   Models with Infinite Complexities

In practice, even when we just compare a small, finite number of models $\mathcal{M}_1, \ldots, \mathcal{M}_m$, the complexity $\mathrm{COMP}(\mathcal{M}_\gamma)$ will often be infinite for at least one of the models $\mathcal{M}_\gamma$, $\gamma \in \{1, \ldots, m\}$. In that case, the simple approach based on $\bar{P}_{\mathrm{nml}}$ cannot be used. Instead, we have to associate $\mathcal{M}_\gamma$ with some other universal code. This could, for example, be a conditional NML (CNML) or luckiness NML (LNML) code, see Chapter 11. Otherwise, one could use a Bayesian code with an improper Jeffreys' prior or an informative prior, or a prequential plug-in code, or a two-part code, or any other type of code, as long as it is a universal code for $\mathcal{M}_\gamma$ in the individual-sequence sense. Often, the best available approximations of the NML code are the CNML-1 and CNML-2 codes.

1. Using the Luckiness Principle.   Most such alternatives to NML codes make use of the luckiness principle at some level, in that the regret they achieve depends on the observed sequence. Despite their minimax regret interpretation, this even holds for some CNML codes. For example, in nested model selection problems such as polynomial regression, they have to be combined with luckiness codes to become effective; see Section 14.4.3.

How does the use of the luckiness principle influence the result of the model selection procedure? At first sight it may seem to make the result less trustworthy at best and arbitrary at worst. But fortunately, at least in the case where one of the models is a point hypothesis, the results are just as trustworthy as before: depending on how "lucky" one is, more or less data may be needed to obtain a given level of confidence in the result. But, as the following example shows, *if* one is lucky and obtains a high confidence in the result, this is just as meaningful as in the simple case where only NML distributions are used.

Example 14.6 [MDL Model Selection, Point Null Hypothesis Testing, and Luckiness] Suppose we compare two models, $\mathcal{M}_0$ and $\mathcal{M}_1$. As in Example 14.2, $\mathcal{M}_0 = \{P_0\}$ consists of a single distribution, but now $\mathcal{M}_1$ is a parametric family such that $\mathrm{COMP}(\mathcal{M}_1)$ is infinite, so that we cannot base MDL model selection on the NML distributions. Instead, we associate some other universal model $\bar{P}$ with $\mathcal{M}_1$, for example, a luckiness NML or a prequential plug-in model. Crucially, the resulting procedure can *still* be interpreted as a point null hypothesis test, just as in Example 14.2: suppose we observe that

$$- \log P_0(D) = - \log \bar{P}(D \mid \mathcal{M}_1) + a$$

for some $a > 0$. According to the no-hypercompression inequality, the P_0-probability that $a \geq -\log \alpha$ cannot be larger than α. This means that we can transform the MDL model selection into a null hypothesis test in the same way as in Example 14.2. Thus, we can still think of the observed confidence a as a measure of how confident we should be in the decision that $\mathcal{M}_1$ is the best explanation of the data, even though the code we used for $\mathcal{M}_1$ is not minimax optimal: the regret it achieves depends on the ML estimator $\hat{\theta}_1$, so that it prefers some distributions within $\mathcal{M}_1$ over others. The consequence of this is only that if we are *unlucky* and observe "bad" data D, so that $-\log \bar{P}(D \mid \mathcal{M}_1)$ has large regret, we will have less confidence in our decision than if we are lucky and observe data D' with small regret. Equivalently, the use of luckiness codes implies that in the unlucky case, we need more data before we obtain a confident decision. But the hypothesis testing interpretation shows that *even in the unlucky case*, the probability that we will make the wrong decision and be confident about it by degree a is still smaller than 2^{-a}. Thus, while luckiness codes are in a sense suboptimal, their use in model selection is not "dangerous."

> **Open Problem No. 10** If all models under consideration are composite (contain more than one distribution), then the interpretation of MDL model selection in terms of traditional hypothesis testing is lost. We still have consistency results for the resulting procedures (Section 16.3, Chapter 16), but it is conceivable that, from a traditional, significance level interpretation, the confidence (amount of compression) in the decision may perhaps be misleadingly high for small samples.

2. You Don't Have to Use NML. After the introduction of the NML codes in the MDL context, a few authors (including myself) have stressed the advantages of using NML over other universal codes. As an unfortunate by-product, this has led some authors to conclude that prequential plug-in, two-part, or even Bayesian codes are necessarily crude, and that their use should be avoided.[1] This is far from true: Bayesian codes achieve asymptotically the same minimax luckiness regret as LNML codes, and have the advantage of being prequential. Two-part codes can be designed to have luckiness regret within a few bits of LNML codes; and prequential plug-in codes, while having less desirable regret properties, are sometimes the only computationally tractable alternative.

14.3.2 Comparing Many or Infinitely Many Models

Suppose we want to compare more than two models for the same data. If the number to be compared is "small," we can proceed as before and pick the model $\mathcal{M}_k$ with smallest $-\log \bar{P}_{\mathrm{nml}}(x^n \mid \mathcal{M}_k)$. Here "small" means that the set of contemplated models $\{\mathcal{M}_\gamma \mid \Gamma\}$ is finite, and does not depend on the sample size n. In such a case, it is reasonable to assign a uniform code to γ, for reasons we discuss in Section 14.3.3.

However, if the number of models is "large," i.e. Γ is countably infinite or is finite but grows with the sample size n, we have to be more careful. Consider first the case that $\Gamma = \{1, 2, \ldots\}$ is infinitely large. We compare models $\mathcal{M}_1, \mathcal{M}_2, \ldots$ for data x^n. We may be tempted to pick the model minimizing $-\log \bar{P}_{\mathrm{nml}}(x^n \mid \mathcal{M}_k)$ over all $k \in \{1, 2, \ldots\}$, but in some cases this gives unintended results. To illustrate, consider the extreme case that every $\mathcal{M}_k$ contains just one distribution. For example, let $\mathcal{M}_1 = \{P_1\}, \mathcal{M}_2 = \{P_2\}, \ldots$ where $\{P_1, P_2, \ldots\}$ is the set of *all* Markov chains with rational-valued parameters. In that case, $\mathrm{COMP}(\mathcal{M}_k) = 0$ for all k, and we would always select the maximum likelihood Markov chain. As we explained in Chapter 5, typically this will be a chain of very high order, severely overfitting the data. This cannot be right! Instead, we should realize that all along, we were really picking the model $\mathcal{M}_\gamma$ minimizing

$$\dot{L}(\gamma) - \log \bar{P}_{\mathrm{nml}}(x^n \mid \mathcal{M}_\gamma), \tag{14.10}$$

where $\dot{L}$ is the codelength function of some code for encoding model indices γ. Since now γ ranges over an infinite set, we cannot pick a uniform code anymore. Instead, we should pick a *quasi-uniform* code of the

---

1. I have heard this opinion expressed by several people at several conferences.

type considered in Chapter 3; see the box on page 91. We could, for example, choose the "universal" prior for the integers (Chapter 3, page 100) with $L_{\mathbb{N}}(\gamma) \approx \log \gamma + 2 \log \log \gamma$. Equation (14.10) avoids the overfitting problem mentioned above: in case $\mathcal{M}_1, \mathcal{M}_2, \dots$ represent all the rational-parameter Markov chains, (14.10) would reduce to two-part code MDL (Chapter 5) which is asymptotically consistent.

Thus, if Γ is "large," then in *general*, $\dot{L}(\gamma)$ cannot be ignored. Yet for many model classes $\mathcal{M}$, the term $\dot{L}(\gamma)$ will have a negligible influence on (14.10) after all, and so can be ignored after all. This is the case if, for example, $\mathcal{M}_\gamma$ represents the set of γth-order Markov chains or the linear model with Gaussian noise based on polynomials of degree γ. In such cases, $\dot{L}(\gamma)$ is typically negligible compared to $\mathrm{COMP}(\mathcal{M}_\gamma)$, the complexity term associated with $\mathcal{M}_\gamma$ that is hidden in $- \log \bar{P}_{\mathrm{nml}}(\mathcal{M}_\gamma)$: thus, the complexity of $\mathcal{M}_\gamma$ comes from the fact that for large γ, $\mathcal{M}_\gamma$ contains many distinguishable distributions; not from the much smaller term $\dot{L}(\gamma) < \log \gamma + O(\log \log \gamma)$.

However, there do exist situations in which $\dot{L}(\gamma)$ really has to be taken into account. The following example illustrates that these include not just artificial examples such as the countable Markov chains above, but also real-world situations.

Example 14.7 [MDL Denoising: $\dot{L}(\gamma)$ Is Important] In one variation (Rissanen 2000) of MDL denoising (Rissanen 2000; Hansen and Yu 2000; Roos et al. 2005), one actually performs a type of model selection between numerous linear regression-type models. The number of potentially interesting parameters grows linearly with the sample size n. For simplicity, let us assume it is equal to n. For each parameter, we can decide whether or not to include it in the model. Thus $\gamma = (\gamma_1, \dots, \gamma_n)$ may be taken as a vector in $\{0, 1\}^n$, where $\gamma_j = 1$ means that the jth parameter should be included. This corresponds to model selection between 2^n models. While this number is finite, the number of bits needed to encode γ grows linearly in n. If one ignored the codelength $\dot{L}(\gamma)$, this is equivalent to using a fixed-length code for $\dot{L}(\gamma)$, where γ is encoded in $\log 2^n = n$ bits. That is really too large: the redundancy of $\bar{L}_{\mathrm{top}}(x^n)$ relative to every distribution P in the model class $\mathcal{M}$ is then linear in the sample size n, so the code with lengths $\bar{L}_{\mathrm{top}}$ is then not a universal code for the model class $\mathcal{M}$ anymore. Therefore, as is quite clear from the box on page 406 which describes refined MDL, the resulting procedure cannot be called an MDL procedure anymore.

Indeed, as discovered by Roos et al. (2005), in the first publication on model selection-based MDL denoising, Rissanen (2000) ignored $\dot{L}(\gamma)$ and thus implicitly took it to be uniform, and the resulting procedure did not work very well in practice. Roos et al. (2005) show that if one modifies the encoding of γ as follows, then the resulting procedure works quite well on real-world data sets: one takes $\dot{L}(\gamma):=L_{\mathbb{N}}(k_\gamma) + L'(\gamma \mid k_\gamma)$, where k_γ is the number of nonzero parameters in $\mathcal{M}_\gamma$. $L_{\mathbb{N}}$ is the universal code for the integers, and $L'(\gamma \mid k) = \log \binom{n}{k}$ is the uniform code on all $\binom{n}{k}$ γ's with k parameters. This code gives much shorter codelengths to model indices for models with very few or very many parameters, and is thus an instantiation of a "luckiness code."

In practice, the number of models $\mathcal{M}_\gamma$ under consideration may sometimes be finite and grow with n, but it is not clear whether it is so large that this will make the regret of the code $\bar{L}_{\text{top}}$ be too large to be useful. In that case, one may proceed by designing two codes: one with a fixed-length code $L_1 = L_U$ for γ, and one with a luckiness code L_2 for γ, which encodes some specially stated subsets of γ with a (much) smaller codelength. One then defines $\dot{L}(\gamma)$ as the codelength resulting from first encoding whether code L_1 or L_2 will be used, and then encoding γ with that code. This takes

$$\min_\gamma \{ \dot{L}(\gamma) - \log \bar{P}_{\text{nml}}(x^n \mid \gamma) \} = \min_\gamma \min_{j=1,2} \{ L_j(\gamma) + 1 - \log \bar{P}_{\text{nml}}(x^n \mid \gamma) \} \quad (14.11)$$

bits, so that one gets the best (within 1 bit) of both codes. Note that the code L_2 must be chosen in advance of seeing the data, or based on previous data from the same source, not on x^n. Equation (14.11) is a prime example of the luckiness principle: we will never do worse than 1 bit of worst-case optimal, but in some cases, we will do substantially better.

Let us summarize the main insights of this subsection:

Coding the Model Index

MDL model selection *always* proceeds by selecting the model $\mathcal{M}_{\ddot{\gamma}}$ with index $\ddot{\gamma}$ minimizing

$$\dot{L}(\gamma) + \bar{L}(D \mid \gamma). \quad (14.12)$$

In many applications, the codelength $\dot{L}(\gamma)$ for encoding the model index is either, as in (14.2), chosen to be the same for all models under consideration, or has a a negligible influence on the total codelength. For this reason, in the majority of papers on MDL model selection, $\dot{L}(\gamma)$ is is omitted from the equations.

Still, there are situations where it is inappropriate or even impossible to choose $\dot{L}$ uniform, and an appropriate choice for $\dot{L}$ varies so much among γ that it does influence the γ minimizing (14.12).

14.3.3 The General Picture

Section 14.3.2 illustrates that, in *all* applications of MDL, we first define a *single* universal code with lengths $\bar{L}_{\text{top}}$. If the set of models is small and finite, we use the uniform prior/code for $\dot{L}(\gamma)$. We do this in order to be as "honest" as possible, treating all models under consideration on the same footing. But if the set of models is infinite, there exists no uniform prior on γ anymore. Therefore, we must choose a quasi-uniform code to encode the model index, thereby resorting to the luckiness principle. Even if the set of models is finite but "large" in the sense of Section 14.3.2, we should not use a uniform code for γ, for then $\bar{L}_{\text{top}}$ may lose the universality property (Example 14.7). Then the $\mathcal{M}_{\ddot{\gamma}}$ minimizing $\dot{L}(\gamma) - \log \bar{P}(D \mid \gamma)$ does not compress the data, and cannot be considered a good explanation of the data. In that case, we have to use a code $\dot{L}$ that prefers some γ over others, thereby once again resorting to the luckiness principle.

> We can also directly motivate the prescription of (quasi-) uniform codes in terms of data compression rather than as an attempt to treat models on an equal footing. (Quasi-) uniform codes for γ achieve *absolute* codelengths $\dot{L}(\gamma)$ that are (close to) minimax optimal (Chapter 3). When encoding x^n based on $\mathcal{M}_\gamma$, we achieve regret $- \log \bar{P}(D \mid \gamma) + \dot{L}(\gamma) - \ln P_{\hat{\theta}_\gamma}(D)$ on data D. Thus, the smaller the absolute codelength $L(\dot{\gamma})$, the smaller the relative codelength (regret) when encoding D based on γ: small *absolute* codelengths of model indices lead to small *relative codelengths* of the data. This gives a universal-coding motivation for using (quasi-) uniform codes.

We can choose the code $\dot{L}$ because we have prior knowledge (similar to the choice of a Bayesian prior), or because it is easy to compute, or for some other reason; see Chapter 17, Section 17.2. But we cannot use just any arbitrary code to implement $\dot{L}(\gamma)$: the fact that $\dot{L}(\gamma)$ must be quasi-uniform severely restricts the choices. While we have not formalized what types of codes still count as quasi-uniform and what not, it should be clear that some choices cannot be right. For example, if $\gamma \in \Gamma = \{1, 2, \ldots\}$, we are not allowed to take $\dot{L}(\gamma)$ that increases linearly in γ; the increase should be logarithmic. This is further motivated by the results on MDL consistency (Chapter 16, Section 16.3), which show that the rate of convergence of estimators based on MDL model selection is directly related to the redundancy of the universal code $\bar{L}_{\text{top}}$.

After having encoded a γ, we encode data x^n based on model $\mathcal{M}_\gamma$. Section 14.3.1 shows that we design the code $\bar{P}(\cdot \mid \mathcal{M}_\gamma)$ using essentially the same ideas as in the design of $\dot{L}$, but implemented at a metalevel: we try to

The "Refined" MDL Principle for Model Selection

Suppose we plan to select between models $\{\mathcal{M}_1, \mathcal{M}_2, \ldots\} = \{\mathcal{M}_\gamma \mid \gamma \in \Gamma\}$ for data $D = (x_1, \ldots, x_n)$. We do this by designing a universal code with lengths $\bar{L}_{\text{top}}$ for $\mathcal{X}^n$. If the goal is model selection, then this should be a mixed one-part/two-part code for the model class $\mathcal{M} = \cup_\gamma \mathcal{M}_\gamma$, in which the index γ of $\mathcal{M}_\gamma$ is encoded explicitly. The resulting code has two parts, the two subcodes being defined such that

1. All models $\mathcal{M}_\gamma$ are treated on the same footing, as long as the number of models $|\Gamma|$ is "small." In that case, we assign a uniform prior to γ. This prior achieves the minimax codelength $\log|\Gamma|$ for encoding any $\gamma \in \Gamma$. If the number of models is large, we put a quasi-uniform code ("luckiness prior") on γ. This code should be such that there exists a sequence of finite sets $\Gamma_1 \subset \Gamma_2 \subset \ldots$ with $\cup_{j \geq 1} \Gamma_j = \Gamma$ such that for each Γ_j, the codelength for any $\gamma \in \Gamma_j$ is close to the minimax optimal $\log|\Gamma_j|$.

2. All distributions within each $\mathcal{M}_\gamma$ are treated on the same footing, as much as possible: we use the minimax regret universal model $\bar{P}_{\text{nml}}(D \mid \mathcal{M}_\gamma)$. If this model is too hard to compute or leads to a very large or infinite regret, we instead use a different universal model $\bar{P}(\cdot \mid \mathcal{M}_\gamma)$ based on the luckiness principle. We should do this in such a way that for each submodel $\mathcal{M}' \subset \mathcal{M}_\gamma$ with finite $\text{COMP}^{(n)}(\mathcal{M}')$, $\max_{x^n : \hat{\theta}(x^n) \in \Theta_{\mathcal{M}'}} - \log \bar{P}(x^n \mid \mathcal{M}_\gamma) + \log \bar{P}_{\text{nml}}(x^n \mid \mathcal{M}') = O(1)$. This is guaranteed if we pick the LNML-1 or LNML-2 universal models relative to any luckiness function for which they are well defined. If we want to avoid the use of a luckiness function, we can sometimes sacrifice a few data points and use a CNML-1 or CNML-2 universal model relative to $\mathcal{M}_\gamma$.

In the end, we encode data D using a hybrid two-part/one-part universal model, explicitly encoding the models we want to select between and implicitly encoding any distributions contained in those models.

Figure 14.1   The Refined MDL Principle for Model Selection

associate with $\mathcal{M}_\gamma$ a code for encoding outcomes in $\mathcal{X}^n$ that achieves uniform (= minimax) regret for every sequence x^n. If this is not possible, either because $\text{COMP}^{(n)}(\mathcal{M}_\gamma)$ is infinite or so large, that, at the given sample size, $-\log \bar{P}_{\text{nml}}(x^n \mid \gamma)$ is not smaller than the number of bits needed to code the data literally, then once again we have to resort to the luckiness principle: we use a code with a preference for some regions of the parameter space over others, but we try to to keep this preference as small as possible. In some cases we can apply conditional codes which do achieve a "conditional" minimax regret, but even in those cases, the luckiness principle is often implicitly applied (Section 14.4.3).

The general idea is summarized in the box on page 426, which provides something like a definition of MDL model selection, but only in a quite restricted context. If we go beyond that context, these prescriptions cannot be used literally, but extensions in the same spirit suggest themselves. Here is a first example of such an extension:

Example 14.8 [MDL and Local Maxima in the Likelihood] In practice we often work with models for which the ML estimator cannot be calculated efficiently; or at least, no algorithm for efficient calculation of the ML estimator is known. Examples are finite and Gaussian mixtures (Example 2.12 on page 68) and hidden Markov models. In such cases one typically resorts to methods such as expectation-maximization (EM) or gradient descent, which find a *local* maximum of the likelihood surface (function) $P(x^n \mid \theta)$, leading to a *local* maximum likelihood estimator $\theta^\circ(x^n)$. Suppose we need to select between a finite number of such models. We may be tempted to pick the model $\mathcal{M}$ maximizing the normalized likelihood $\bar{P}_{\text{nml}}(x^n \mid \mathcal{M})$. However, if we then plan to use the local estimator $\theta^\circ(x^n)$ for predicting future data, then, from an MDL perspective, this is *not* the right thing to do. To see this, note that, if suboptimal estimators θ° are to be used, the ability of model $\mathcal{M}$ to fit arbitrary data patterns may be severely diminished! Rather than using $\bar{P}_{\text{nml}}$, we should redefine it to take into account the fact that θ° is not the global ML estimator:

$$\bar{P}'_{\text{nml}}(x^n) := \frac{P(x^n \mid \theta^\circ(x^n))}{\sum_{x^n \in \mathcal{X}^n} P(x^n \mid \theta^\circ(x^n))}, \tag{14.13}$$

leading to an adjusted parametric complexity

$$\text{COMP}'(\mathcal{M}) := \log \sum_{x^n \in \mathcal{X}^n} P(x^n \mid \theta^\circ(x^n)), \tag{14.14}$$

which, for every estimator $\dot{\theta}$ different from $\hat{\theta}$ *must* be strictly smaller than $\mathrm{COMP}(\mathcal{M})$.

14.4   Practical Issues in MDL Model Selection

14.4.1   Calculating Universal Codelengths

In general, $-\log \bar{P}_{\mathrm{nml}}(x^n \mid \mathcal{M})$ can only be evaluated numerically, but there are some exceptions. When $\mathcal{M}$ is a linear regression model, either with fixed or varying σ^2, then, although the basic NML distributions are not defined, we can obtain precise, nonasymptotic analytic expressions for its natural replacements, luckiness universal codes with quadratic luckiness functions and conditional NML-2 approaches, as defined in Chapter 12. The same holds of course for the special case where $\mathcal{M}$ is the Gaussian location or the full Gaussian family. As we noted in Chapter 7, Section 7.2, Kontkanen and Myllymäki (2005b) provided efficient algorithms for computing the precise codelengths and regret for k-parameter multinomial models, for arbitrary k.

For all other parametric families that we know of, there is no analytically closed-form expression for $\mathrm{COMP}^{(n)}(\mathcal{M})$, at least no such expression is known to us. Hence, there is no precise expression for $\bar{P}_{\mathrm{nml}}(x^n \mid \mathcal{M})$ available either. We may then resort to numerical evaluation. However, even using the simplification for exponential families described in Chapter 7, Equations (7.23) and (7.24), such numerical evaluation is often still computationally problematic, since the sum involved in computing $\mathrm{COMP}(\mathcal{M})$ may have infinitely many terms. In such cases, in order to compute codelengths, one may resort to the asymptotic expansion (14.5), but, as was discussed in Chapter 7, Section 7.2 on page 214, the quality of this approximation strongly depends on the model $\mathcal{M}$. While it seems to work well for, for example, multinomial models and linear regression with fixed and varying variance (with $\mathrm{COMP}^{(n)}(\mathcal{M})$ defined relative to the luckiness or conditional regret), Poisson and geometric models (with a restricted parameter space), there are also models for which it is quite bad.

The problem gets worse if the number of models under consideration is infinite or "large" in the sense of Section 14.3.2, for the asymptotics generally only hold if the number of parameters k is very small compared to n: for a sequence of models $\mathcal{M}_1, \mathcal{M}_2, \ldots$ with number of parameters $k_\gamma = \gamma$, the $o(1)$-term in (14.5) for model $\mathcal{M}_\gamma$ strongly depends on the model order k_γ, and, for fixed n, the complexity penalty incurred by adding an additional parameter usually decreases with k (Foster and Stine 2005). But the four reinterpretations of $\bar{P}_{\text{nml}}$ that we provided in Section 14.2 indicate that in many cases, Bayesian, two-part, and prequential plug-in universal codes achieve codelengths that are quite close to those of $- \log \bar{P}_{\text{nml}}(D \mid \mathcal{M})$; in the first two cases, with Jeffreys' prior they even come close to achieving the minimax regret. For some models, one or more of these codelengths can be calculated precisely or at least be well approximated. Rather than approximating $- \log \bar{P}_{\text{nml}}(D \mid \mathcal{M})$ by a potentially bad asymptotic formula, in such cases it is preferable to replace it by the codelength achieved by some other (suboptimal) universal code, which does not achieve minimax regret, but the lengths of which can be calculated precisely or almost precisely.

The Asymptotic Expansion of COMP **should be used with care!**
Equation (7.4) does *not* hold for all parametric models; and for some models for which it does hold, the $o(1)$ term may converge to 0 only for quite large sample sizes (Navarro 2004). Foster and Stine (1999, 2005) show that the approximation (7.4) is, in general, only valid if k is much smaller than n. If this is not the case, the approximation may fail dramatically.

14.4.2 Computational Efficiency and Practical Quality of Non-NML Universal Codes

Since we are advocating that NML codes should sometimes be replaced by other universal codes, we will study the computational efficiency and practical quality of such alternative codes in more detail.

Bayesian Universal Codes The Bayesian universal codelengths can be efficiently calculated for several combinations of models and priors. In some cases, this can even be done for Jeffreys' (possibly improper) prior. Examples are the multinomial model (Chapter 9, Example 9.2), the linear models with Gaussian priors (Chapter 12, Section 12.3.2), but also the Poisson and geometric families (De Rooij and Grünwald 2006).

   In general though, and certainly if the model $\mathcal{M}$ is not an exponential family, the computation of $- \log \bar{P}_{\text{Bayes}}(D \mid \mathcal{M})$ may be difficult. A popular and very powerful tool that can be used to approximate it is the *Markov chain Monte Carlo* (MCMC) method (see Gelman, Carlin, Stern, and Rubin (2003)). MCMC was used in an MDL context by Hansen and Yu (2001).

Two-Part Codes and COMP($\mathcal{M}$)   In Section 10.1, we showed that *optimally designed* two-part codes achieve regret almost as good as the minimax regret COMP($\mathcal{M}$). The problem with two-part MDL is that finding the optimal discretization for the parameter space of $\mathcal{M}$ at a given sample space is,however, conceptually (and probably computationally) daunting. For this reasons, two-part code MDL is that *in practice*, people often use much cruder ad-hoc codes with much worse worst-case regret properties. This is bad practice if better alternatives are available; but it can also be good practice if we are dealing with exotic models such as context-free grammars (Solomonoff 1964), decision forests (Breiman 2001), taut string representations of probability distributions (Davies and Kovac 2001), and so on. An advantage of the two-part code is precisely its "engineering" flavor: one can design clever (though not in any sense optimal) two-part codes for arbitrarily exotic parametric and nonparametric models.

Prequential Plug-in Codes   For many parametric models, the prequential plug-in codelength of the data can be calculated precisely. This is an important advantage over the Bayesian universal models, which for many models involve integrals that have no analytic solution, and the two-part models, which invariably involve a complicated discretization, Nevertheless, model selection based on the prequential plug-in codes can be computationally quite expensive: for each model $\mathcal{M}_\gamma$ under consideration, we have to calculate n predictions $\bar{P}_{\text{plug-in}}(X_1 \mid \gamma), \bar{P}_{\text{plug-in}}(X_2 \mid x_1, \gamma), \ldots, \bar{P}_{\text{plug-in}}(X_n \mid x^{n-1}, \gamma)$. Often, calculating the prediction $\bar{P}_{\text{plug-in}}(X_i \mid x^{i-1}, \gamma)$ takes time of ORDER(i), so that the total computation time for each model becomes quadratic in n. In many cases though, if $\bar{P}_{\text{plug-in}}(X_{i-1}, \mid X^{i-2}, \gamma)$ has already been computed, then the result of this computation can be used to compute $\bar{P}_{\text{plug-in}}(X_i \mid X^{i-1}, \gamma)$ in time $O(1)$. In those cases, prequential plug-in model selection is quite efficient.

In practical applications of prequential plug-in model selection, it is important to condition on the first few examples or use modified (luckiness) ML estimators such as those described in Chapter 9, rather than the standard, unmodified ML estimator. This certainly holds for models such as the multinomial model where both "start-up problems" (Example 9.1, Chapter 9) occur. As we report in Section 14.5.4, empirical evidence suggests that it even holds for models such as the linear regression model, where the start-up problems do not occur.

Both empirical evidence and theoretical analysis (De Rooij and Grünwald

2006) show that, at least in model selection with *non-nested* models, prequential plug-in model selection may converge somewhat slower than Bayesian and NML methods. This means that one needs a (slightly) larger sample before the true model is selected with high probability. The underlying reason is that the prequential plug-in models, while close to minimax optimal in the expected regret sense, are not close to minimax optimal in the individual-sequence sense. This is explained in detail in (De Rooij and Grünwald 2006). Still, prequential plug-in model selection can be proved to be consistent in a wide variety of situations (Chapter 16, Section 16.3).

For many models $\mathcal{M}$, including, for example, some popular time series models, there seems to be no known algorithm for which exact computation of $-\ln \bar{P}_{\text{Bayes}}(D \mid \mathcal{M})$, $-\ln \bar{P}_{\text{2-p}}(D \mid \mathcal{M})$ or $-\ln \bar{P}_{\text{nml}}(D \mid \mathcal{M})$ is feasible. Then the prequential plug-in code is the only standard universal code with lengths that can be computed both exactly and reasonably efficiently – even if the computation cost is quadratic. In such cases, it should definitely be used, even though its behavior in model selection problems may be slightly worse than that of the full Bayesian or NML universal models. Hannan and Rissanen (1982) and Lai and Lee (1997) propose some methods for reduction of computational cost in time series contexts.

Indeed, the prequential plug-in codes are especially suited for time series, where the data have a natural order. If the data are i.i.d., however, then there is no such order and some additional problems for plug-in codes arise. These are treated in the next section.

14.4.3 Model Selection with Conditional NML and Plug-in Codes

Suppose we intend to do model selection based on conditional NML or conditional prequential plug-in universal codes. The corresponding codelengths only become well defined if we condition on part of the data. There are two issues here which need to be discussed: (1) what data should we condition on, and (2) how many data points should we condition on. Finally, with plug-in codes (both conditional and luckiness ones), there is the further issue (3) of how to choose the order of the data when the data come in unordered. Let us discuss these issues in turn.

1. What data to condition upon? This problem can best be explained by example.

Example 14.9 Let $\mathcal{M}_1$ be the family of Poisson distributions and let $\mathcal{M}_2$ be the family of geometric distributions on $\mathcal{X} = \{1, 2, \ldots\}$. The NML code is undefined for both $\mathcal{M}_1$ and $\mathcal{M}_2$, but the CNML-2 code, conditioned on the first example, does exist. A straightforward extension of MDL model selection to this situation would be to choose the $\gamma \in \{1, 2\}$ minimizing

$$- \log \bar{P}_{\text{Cnml-2}}(x_2, \ldots, x_n \mid x_1, \mathcal{M}_\gamma). \tag{14.15}$$

The codelength (14.15) depends on the order of the data: if we permute the data and exchange, say x_1 and x_2, (14.15) may become different. But this seems wrong: since data are i.i.d. under both $\mathcal{M}_1$ and $\mathcal{M}_2$, they have no natural order and this suggests that our model selection procedure should not depend on the order in which these data are given. Technically speaking, the data are *exchangeable* under both models.

We see two reasonable ways to deal with this issue: either we leave the order as is, and use (14.15), admitting that conditional NML codes have some imperfections compared to ordinary NML codes; or we choose the second, perhaps better, option, which is to pick an order uniformly at random. In our example, this means the following: for given x^n, let $Z \sim Q$, where Q is the uniform distribution on $\{1, \ldots, n\}$. We should pick the model $\mathcal{M}_\gamma$ minimizing

$$E_{Z \sim Q}[- \log \bar{P}_{\text{Cnml-2}}(x_2, \ldots, x_{Z-1}, x_{Z+1}, \ldots, x_n \mid x_Z, \mathcal{M}_\gamma)] + \dot{L}(\gamma). \tag{14.16}$$

Does this conflict with the individual-sequence MDL philosophy (Chapter 1) which says that we should minimize codelength on individual, actually observed sequences, and never take expectations thereof? No: crucially, the expectation in (14.16) is of the statistician's own making, reflecting a randomness device under his or her control. It does not arise from an assumption of randomness in nature – it is the latter kind of assumption that the MDL philosophy is suspicious about.

One may wonder: why not condition on the x_i that minimizes the conditional codelength $- \log \bar{P}_{\text{Cnml-2}}(x_1, \ldots, x_{i-1}, x_{i+1}, \ldots, x_n \mid x_i, \mathcal{M}_\gamma)$. The problem here is that the x_i that minimizes this expression will in general be different for different γ. Thus, one would end up with a procedure where one encodes first a model index γ, and then the sequence of $n - 1$ data points that are actually encoded would depend on γ. Such a procedure is not formally a code or description method as we defined it in Chapter 3. This leads to problems: for example, the no-hypercompression inequality (Chapter 3) does not hold anymore, and as a result, the proofs of the various MDL consistency theorems of the next chapter break down, and it is not clear whether these theorems still hold.

In contrast, if the x_i on which to condition is the same for all models under consideration, then the resulting procedure does define a prefix code on $\mathcal{X}^{n-1}$, since what is actually encoded does not depend on γ. Thus, the order of the data should either be left as is or be randomized, but not optimized to minimize codelength, since the latter option destroys the codelength interpretation of the inference procedure.

We stress that this issue only arises if *all* the models $\mathcal{M}_\gamma$ are i.i.d. If at least for one value of γ, $\mathcal{M}_\gamma$ is not i.i.d., then any reasonable universal code relative to the model class $\mathcal{M} = \bigcup_\Gamma \mathcal{M}_\gamma$ should assign codelengths that are order dependent.

2. How many points to condition on? Combining luckiness and conditional codes. In Example 14.9 above, both conditional codes became well defined when we conditioned on a single observation. In practice, it will often be the case that the minimum number of observations n_0 needed to make $-\log \bar{P}(x_{n_0+1}, \ldots, x_n \mid x^{n_0}, \mathcal{M}_\gamma)$ a codelength, depends on γ. In such cases, it is crucial that we *encode the same number of data points* in all models under consideration. The reason is the same as the reason why we are not allowed to optimize the order of the data when using conditional codes: if n_1 depends on γ, then the resulting sum, $\min_\gamma \{\dot{L}(\gamma) - \log \bar{P}(x_{n+1}, \ldots, x_n \mid x^{n_1}, \mathcal{M}_\gamma)\}$, has no codelength interpretation anymore.

Example 14.10 Suppose $\mathcal{M}_0 = \{P_4\}$ consists of a single Poisson distribution with mean 4. $\mathcal{M}_1$ is the set of all Poisson distributions. For $\mathcal{M}_0$, the NML code is well defined, and $\bar{P}_{\mathrm{nml}}(\cdot \mid \mathcal{M}_0)$ is equal to P_4. For $\mathcal{M}_1$, the NML code is not well defined, and we need to sacrifice a single data point x_Z (for example, randomly selected) to make the CNML-2 code well defined. This means that, when doing model selection between $\mathcal{M}_0$ and $\mathcal{M}_1$, we should also sacrifice the same point when coding with $\mathcal{M}_0$. That is, we still use (14.16), with $\bar{P}_{\mathrm{Cnml-2}}(\cdot \mid \mathcal{M}_0)$ set equal to P_4:

$$- \log \bar{P}_{\mathrm{Cnml-2}}(x_1, \ldots, x_{Z-1}, x_{Z+1}, \ldots, x_n \mid x_Z, \mathcal{M}_0) :=$$
$$- \log P_4(x_1, \ldots, x_{Z-1}, x_{Z+1}, \ldots, x_n). \quad (14.17)$$

Such a method is feasible as long as the minimum number of points on which one has to condition is small for all models under consideration. In nested model selection, such as linear regression, this is not the case: for a k-parameter linear model $\mathcal{M}^{(k)}$ (Chapter 12, see also this chapter, Section 14.5), we need to sacrifice k points. Hence, when doing model selection relative to, say, the polynomials ($\mathcal{M}^{(k)} = \mathcal{P}^{(k)}$, Example 2.9), we need to choose between models $\mathcal{M}^{(1)}, \mathcal{M}^{(2)}, \ldots$ including the model $\mathcal{M}^{(n)}$, for which we need to sacrifice all our data points. Then the approach of (14.10) cannot be applied anymore, and we are forced to resort to the luckiness principle. One reasonable way of proceeding, which combines luckiness and conditional NML, is to define, for $k \geq 1$, the universal code $\bar{P}$ corresponding to $\mathcal{M}^{(k)}$ recursively as follows:

$$
\begin{aligned}
\bar{P}(x_{k+1}, \ldots, x_n \mid x^k, \mathcal{M}^{(k)}) &:= \bar{P}_{\text{Cnml-2}}(x_{k+1}, \ldots, x_n \mid x^k, \mathcal{M}^{(k)}) \\
\bar{P}(x_1, \ldots, x_k \mid \mathcal{M}^{(k)}) &:= \bar{P}(x_1, \ldots, x_k \mid \mathcal{M}^{(k-1)}).
\end{aligned}
\tag{14.18}
$$

3. Order dependence for prequential plug-in codes. With the prequential plug-in code, there is a further issue: the codelength of the actually encoded data $x_{n_1}, \ldots, x_n$ can still depend on the order of these data, even if all models under consideration are i.i.d[2]. For this case, Rissanen (1989, page 132) suggests that, since the order is irrelevant anyway, we can reorder the data and, for each γ, pick the order that minimizes codelength $-\log \bar{P}(x_{n_1}, \ldots, x_n \mid \mathcal{M}_\gamma)$. We disagree: as we argue below, just as in the situation where we have to choose data to condition on, the order should either be left as is or chosen randomly, because otherwise the codelength interpretation can be lost.

> Let us explain this in more detail. It is true that, if data are exchangeable, their order should be irrelevant to the decoder. Below we formalize this intuition. We will see then though, that coding under the assumption that the order is irrelevant changes the whole situation, and the conclusion that data can be reordered to minimize codelength is not justified.

> For simplicity, let $\mathcal{X} = \{0, 1, 2, \ldots\}$ and consider models $\mathcal{M}_1, \mathcal{M}_2$ on $\mathcal{X}$, both of which are i.i.d. Assume we observe some $x^n \in \mathcal{X}^n$. Let $\mathcal{Z} \subset \mathcal{X}^n$ be the set of all sequences of length n that are ordered from small to large, so that if $\mathbf{z} = (z_1, \ldots, z_n) \in \mathcal{Z}$, then $z_1 \leq z_2 \leq \cdots \leq z_n$. We let $\mathbf{z}(x^n)$ denote the permutation of x^n that makes x^n ordered. If we want to encode data x^n without taking its order into account, it is sufficient to encode $\mathbf{z}(x^n)$ rather than x^n; note that $\mathbf{z}(x^n)$ may be viewed as a sufficient statistic relative to the model class $\mathcal{M} = \mathcal{M}_1 \cup \mathcal{M}_2$. Coding $\mathbf{z}(x^n)$ rather than x^n saves a considerable amount of bits. Each source P_θ in each model $\mathcal{M}_\gamma$ defines a distribution P'_θ on $\mathcal{Z}$ with mass function

$$
P'_\theta(\mathbf{z}(x^n)) = |\Pi(x^n)| P_\theta(x^n),
\tag{14.19}
$$

---

2. Note that this problem does not occur for the CNML universal codes.

where $\Pi(x^n)$ is the set of permutations of x^n. It is clear from their definitions that Bayesian and luckiness universal models relative to $\mathcal{M}_\gamma$ preserve exchangeability. For example, $\bar{P}_{\text{Bayes}}(x^n \mid \mathcal{M}_\gamma) = \bar{P}_{\text{Bayes}}(y^n \mid \mathcal{M}_\gamma)$ if y^n is a permutation of x^n. By analogy with (14.19) it follows that the mass function on reordered outcomes $\mathbf{z}$ is given by

$$\bar{P}_{\text{Bayes}}(\mathbf{z}(x^n) \mid \mathcal{M}_\gamma) = |\Pi(x^n)|\bar{P}_{\text{Bayes}}(x^n \mid \mathcal{M}_\gamma). \tag{14.20}$$

Taking logarithms, it follows that, if $\mathbf{z}(x^n)$ rather than x^n is encoded, then the codelength differences $- \log \bar{P}_{\text{Bayes}}(\mathbf{z}(x^n) \mid \mathcal{M}_1) + \log \bar{P}_{\text{Bayes}}(\mathbf{z}(x^n) \mid \mathcal{M}_2)$ will remain the same for all γ, γ'. Therefore, Bayesian (and LNML) model selection on the level $\mathbf{z}(x^n)$ will always lead to the same choice of models, as well as the same confidence, as Bayesian/LNML model selection on the level x^n. This holds even though the absolute codelengths based on $\bar{P}_{\text{Bayes}}$ become much smaller. Clearly the example can be extended to model selection between any countable set of models. So far so good.

But now consider an order-dependent universal model $\bar{P}$ relative to some $\mathcal{M}_\gamma$. If we were to encode x^n by reordering it, as Rissanen (1989) suggests, then we obtain a new universal code with $\bar{P}_0(x^n) = \max_{y^n \in \Pi(x^n)} \bar{P}(y^n)$. Now clearly the receiver/decoder cannot receive the data in their original order. This is reflected by the fact that in general, $\sum_{x^n \in \mathcal{X}^n} \bar{P}_0(x^n) \gg 1$. Thus, $\bar{P}_0$ should be understood as a (defective) probability mass function on $\mathcal{Z}$ rather than $\mathcal{X}$, and we should really write $\bar{P}_0(\mathbf{z}(x^n))$. But now, in general we will get $\sum_{\mathbf{z} \in \mathcal{Z}} \bar{P}_0(\mathbf{z}) \ll 1$: the code based on $\bar{P}_0$ on level $\mathbf{z}(x^n)$ will be incomplete, and in general, it seems that it can be very inefficient. To see this, consider a universal model $\bar{P}$ that is order dependent for most y^n, but for which there also exists a sequence x^n such that $\bar{P}(x^n)$ is invariant under permutations. Then $\bar{P}_0(\mathbf{z}(x^n)) = \bar{P}(x^n)$, but we know from (14.19) that $\sum_{\mathbf{z} \in \mathcal{Z}: \mathbf{z} \neq \mathbf{z}(x^n)} \bar{P}_0(\mathbf{z} \mid \mathcal{M}_\gamma) + |\Pi(x^n)| \bar{P}_0(\mathbf{z}(x^n) \mid \mathcal{M}_\gamma) \leq 1$.

Thus, if we encode data on level $\mathcal{X}^n$, then $\bar{P}_0$ is not a probability mass function, and therefore, does not correspond to codelength function, and cannot be used in MDL model selection. If we encode data on level $\mathcal{Z}$, then $\bar{P}_0$ does correspond to a codelength function, but now it may represent a very inefficient code. It is therefore doubtful whether it can serve as a universal model relative to $\mathcal{M}_\gamma$, and therefore, whether it should be used in MDL model selection. Since we see no other possibilities for representing the data than either at the level $\mathcal{X}^n$ or at the level $\mathcal{Z}$, the conclusion is that the code $\bar{P}_0$ should probably not be used in MDL model selection.

14.4.4   General Warnings about Model Selection

From the development of MDL model selection, it may appear that the process is very simple: one defines the code with lengths $\bar{L}_{\text{top}}$ using the guidelines given in the previous sections, and then one simply picks the model with index $\ddot{\gamma}$ minimizing the two-part codelength $\bar{L}_{\mathrm{top}}(x^n)$ of the data x^n, and outputs that as the inferred hypothesis. In reality, just following these rules is not nearly sufficient to get a meaningful result.

First, as we already explained in Example 14.3, if $\bar{L}_{\mathrm{top}}(x^n) = L(x^n \mid \ddot{\gamma}) + \dot{L}(\ddot{\gamma})$ is not significantly smaller than the number of bits needed to code the data literally, then the result is not to be trusted altogether: although $\ddot{\gamma}$ may be optimal among all models under consideration, it still does not compress the data. Therefore, it has not detected any regularity in the data, and cannot be taken seriously as an explanation of the data.

Second, there is always the possibility that with another model $\mathcal{M}^*$ that was not on the list $\mathcal{M}_1, \mathcal{M}_2, \ldots$, one could have obtained a much larger compression of the data. Indeed, according to the MDL philosophy (Chapter 1, Section 1.7), one can never be sure whether all regularity in the data has truly been detected: it may always be the case that some $\mathcal{M}^*$ exists which allows for much more compression of the data.

> Of course, *after* having seen the data x^n, one can always construct a model $\mathcal{M}^*$ that assigns probability 1 to the observed data and hence yields a very short codelength for it; but this is not what we mean. Instead, we refer to the following possibility: another researcher, who has *not* seen the data but who may have better knowledge or intuition about the physical machinery comes along, and says: "why haven't you considered model $\mathcal{M}^*$?" If you can be reasonably sure that $\mathcal{M}^*$ has not been postulated with hindsight, after having seen the same set of data as you did, and it turns out that $-\log \bar{P}_{\mathrm{nml}}(x^n \mid \mathcal{M}^*)$ is much smaller than $\bar{L}_{\mathrm{top}}(x^n)$, then you should better abandon the model $\mathcal{M}_{\ddot{\gamma}}$ and switch to $\mathcal{M}^*$ instead; this idea is made more precise in Example 17.4 on page 545. As argued by Rissanen (1989), the theory of Kolmogorov complexity implies that in principle, a scenario like this can never be ruled out, unless the codelength of the data given $\mathcal{M}_{\ddot{\gamma}}$ is about 0. Thus, the inferred model, unless it assigns codelength close to 0, is never to be fully trusted.

Third, relatedly, even if one can obtain substantial compression of the data with $\mathcal{M}_{\ddot{\gamma}}$, one should not state that the model is "the best possible explanation of the data," but rather that it is "the best explanation relative to (a) the given sample size n' and (b) the given model class $\mathcal{M}$. The dependency (a) on the sample size becomes clear if we consider nonparametric model selection situations (Chapter 16, Section 16.3.2): in such settings, MDL will select more and more complex models, leading to better and better predictors, with increasing sample size. We already explained in Chapter 1 that this can be quite reasonable; it just implies that in some cases, every explanation of the data is suboptimal, to be replaced by a better one when more data become available.

The dependency (b) on the given model class is especially important if one does not fully understand why the model compresses the data so well. A good example is speech recognition: human speech can be compressed quite substantially by large-order hidden Markov models, but it would be quite silly to assume that human speech is generated by a hidden Markov process.

> Indeed, hidden Markov models can predict some features of human speech quite well (i.e. they are state-of-the-art methods in automated speech recognition), but they are quite bad in predicting other features of speech. For example, they may predict that the probability that a speaker uses the word "USA" in a sentence is independent of whether he used the words "Bill Clinton" ten sentences earlier. In reality, the probability is highly dependent on this earlier event.

> In general, models that allow for substantial compression of the data are often completely wrong, but, with very high probability, they *must* be good at predicting *some* aspects of future data from the same source. This point is much elaborated upon by Grünwald (1998).

Fourth, it is in general not sufficient to just report the model $\mathcal{M}_{\ddot{\gamma}}$ that achieves the minimum codelength $\bar{L}_{\text{top}}(x^n)$. Often, there are models $\mathcal{M}_{\gamma'}$ "close by" that compress the data nearly as well, and these should be reported as well, together with the codelengths $\dot{L}(\gamma') - \log \bar{P}(x^n \mid \gamma')$. For example, in model selection for linear regression, as described in the next section, it is very well possible that, for some $\ddot{\gamma}, \gamma'$,

$$\min_{\gamma}\{\dot{L}(\gamma) - \log \bar{f}(y^n \mid x^n, \mathcal{M}_{\gamma})\} = \dot{L}(\ddot{\gamma}) - \log \bar{f}(y^n \mid x^n, \mathcal{M}_{\ddot{\gamma}}) =$$
$$\dot{L}(\gamma') - \log \bar{f}(y^n \mid x^n, \mathcal{M}_{\gamma'}) - a, \quad (14.21)$$

for some very small a, i.e. $a = 0.5$. For example, the minimizing $\mathcal{M}_{\ddot{\gamma}}$ may correspond to the kth-degree polynomials with Gaussian noise, for some k, and $\mathcal{M}_{\gamma'}$ may correspond to the $(k+1)$st-degree polynomials (Hansen and Yu 2001). If a is less than a few bits, then it would of course be silly to just report $\ddot{\gamma}$, and not γ'. If the models $\mathcal{M}_{\gamma}$ can be linearly ordered in some logical way, e.g. $\mathcal{M}_{\gamma}$ represents the polynomials of degree γ, then it is often useful to report the full graph depicting $\dot{L}(\gamma) - \log \bar{f}(y^n \mid x^n, \mathcal{M}_{\gamma})$ as a function of γ, in a region near $\ddot{\gamma}$. This curve will often look convex, but in some model selection situations may exhibit local minima (Nannen 2003), which would be another reason for treating the winner $\mathcal{M}_{\ddot{\gamma}}$ with some suspicion: if more

data were observed from the same source, the winner could soon become a
very different γ'.

14.5   MDL Model Selection for Linear Regression

Consider the linear regression problem of Chapter 2, Example 2.8, and Chapter 12. In a fixed-variance regression model selection problem, we are given
data $D = (u_1, y_1), \ldots, (u_n, y_n)$ and a set of candidate linear models $\{\mathcal{M}_\gamma :
\gamma \in \Gamma\}$, where Γ is the set of model indices. Each model $\mathcal{M}_\gamma$ is a fam-
ily of conditional probabilistic sources. For given $\mathbf{u} = (u_1, \ldots, u_n)^\top$, it is
equivalent to the linear model $\mathcal{M}^{\mathbf{X}_\gamma}$, with design matrix $\mathbf{X}_\gamma$ depending on
$\mathbf{u} = (u_1, \ldots, u_n)^\top$ and the index γ.

> **Example 14.11** [Polynomial Regression] In polynomial regression, Chapter 2,
> Example 2.9, $\Gamma = \{0, 1, 2, \ldots\}$, and, using the notation of that example, $\mathcal{M}_\gamma =
> \mathcal{P}^{(\gamma+1)}$ is the linear model based on polynomials of degree γ. This $\gamma + 1$-
> dimensional model may be viewed as the linear model $\mathcal{M}^{\mathbf{X}_\gamma}$ with the $n \times
> (\gamma + 1)$ design matrix $\mathbf{X}_\gamma$, the rows of which are given by $(1, u_i, u_i^2, \ldots, u_i^\gamma)^\top$.

We want to select the model $\mathcal{M}_\gamma$ that best explains the observed data D. The
MDL principle for model selection tells us to pick the model $\mathcal{M}_\gamma$ minimizing

$$- \ln \bar{f}(y^n \mid \mathcal{M}_\gamma, u^n) + \dot{L}(\gamma) = - \ln \bar{f}(y^n \mid \mathcal{M}^{\mathbf{X}_\gamma}) + \dot{L}(\gamma). \qquad (14.22)$$

Below we also consider the varying-variance linear model selection problem, which is identical to (14.22), but with universal codes for the models
$\mathcal{S}_\gamma = \mathcal{S}^{\mathbf{X}_\gamma}$ rather than $\mathcal{M}^{\mathbf{X}_\gamma}$ (Chapter 12, Section 12.3). In both cases, $\bar{f}$ is
some universal code for $y_1, y_2, \ldots$ given $u_1, u_2, \ldots$, relative to $\mathcal{M}_\gamma$. $\dot{L}(\gamma)$ is
based on some code for encoding model indices. To make this precise, $\dot{L}(\gamma)$
and $\bar{f}$ have to be specified further. We cannot simply instantiate $\bar{f}$ to the
NML distribution and/or the Bayesian universal model with Jeffreys' prior,
since, as was shown in Chapter 12, Section 12.4, these are undefined. Thus,
the most straightforward approach cannot be applied, and there are now several reasonable options for instantiating $\bar{f}$. Indeed, (14.22) has been the basis
of several versions of linear MDL regression, all of which differ in their in-
stantiations of $\bar{f}(y^n \mid \mathcal{M}^{\mathbf{X}})$ or $\bar{f}(y^n \mid \mathcal{S}^{\mathbf{X}})$ for given design matrix $\mathbf{X}$. Here
we review the three most recent, state-of-the-art approaches, each of which
has been (co-)developed by one of the three main contributors to MDL: Rissanen's (2001) RNML approach, Hansen and Yu's (2001, 2002) gMDL approach,
and Liang and Barron's (2004, 2005) conditional approach. As in Chapter 12,

---

When Parts of the Codelength Can Be Ignored

Suppose that for each D, $\bar{L}(D \mid \gamma)$ can be written as $\bar{L}'(D) + \bar{L}''(D \mid \gamma)$, where $\bar{L}'$ is a function that does not depend on γ. Then $\bar{L}'(D)$ does not influence the model selected by MDL and can be dropped from the minimization. As a special case of this phenomenon, if all models under consideration represent *conditional* sources $P(Y \mid U)$, then the codelength for $u_1, \ldots, u_n$ can be ignored in model and parameter selection. Examples are applications of MDL in *classification* and *regression*.

The phenomenon also explains why, when designing two-part code MDL estimators, we may safely assume that the sample size n is given in advance; see Chapter 5, page 134.

Figure 14.2 Ignoring codelengths.

we abbreviate y^n to **y** and we assume that the design matrices $\mathbf{X}_\gamma$ have independent columns.

> Note that we ignore the codelength of $u_1, \ldots, u_n$. Indeed, we are only interested in coding the sequence of y_i's given the sequence of u_i's. Intuitively, this is because we are only interested in learning how the y_i *depend* on the u_i; therefore, we do not care how many bits are needed to send the u_i.
>
> Formally, this may be understood as follows: we really *are* encoding the u_i-values as well, but we do so using a fixed code that does not depend on the model $\mathcal{M}_\gamma$ under consideration. Thus, we look for the γ minimizing
>
> $$-\ln \bar{f}(y^n \mid \mathcal{M}_\gamma, u^n) + L'(u^n) + \dot{L}(\gamma), \qquad (14.23)$$
>
> where L' represents some code for $\mathcal{U}^n$. But, since this codelength does not depend on $\mathcal{M}_\gamma$, it can be dropped from the minimization without affecting the choice of γ; see the box on this page.

14.5.1   Rissanen's RNML Approach

The starting point of Rissanen's RNML approach is the NML density defined relative to data **y**, restricted to lie within a certain subset $Y(\tau_0, R)$ of $\mathbb{R}^n$. This subset is parameterized by two hyperparameters τ_0 and R. We first treat a precursor to the RNML approach, called *nMDL* by Hansen and Yu (2001), in which τ_0 and R are simply set to the values $\hat{\tau}_0, \hat{R}$ that minimize the codelength of the data. Since these values themselves are then not encoded, the resulting criterion cannot be interpreted as a codelength anymore, so that the approach is strictly speaking not an MDL approach.

Rissanen's approach builds on nMDL by renormalizing the normalized likelihood. The idea behind such *renormalized* NML (RNML) approaches was explained in Section 11.2.3, Chapter 11. As we will see, the resulting criterion does have a codelength interpretation, and is therefore truly a form of MDL.

1. nMDL. Fix some linear model $\mathcal{S}^{\mathbf{X}}$ with varying σ^2 and $n \times k$ design matrix $\mathbf{X}$. Note that $\mathcal{S}^{\mathbf{X}}$ is a $k+1$-dimensional model. For fixed $\tau_0 > 0, R > 0$, we define

$$Y(\tau_0, R) = \{\mathbf{y} \mid \hat{\sigma}^2(\mathbf{y}) \geq \tau_0, n^{-1}\hat{\mu}(\mathbf{y})^\top \mathbf{X}^\top \mathbf{X}\hat{\mu}(\mathbf{y}) \leq R\}.$$

The division by n is not essential for the results, but we included it so that our definition of $Y(\tau_0, R)$ precisely coincides with Rissanen's. For $\mathbf{y} \in Y(\tau_0, R)$, we define the constrained NML density relative to $\mathcal{S}^{\mathbf{X}}$ as

$$\bar{f}_{\mathrm{nml}}(\mathbf{y} \mid \mathbf{y} \in Y(\tau_0, R)) = \frac{f_{\hat{\mu}(\mathbf{y})}(\mathbf{y})}{\int_{\mathbf{y}:\hat{\mu}(\mathbf{y})\in Y(\tau_0,R)} f_{\hat{\mu}(\mathbf{y})}(\mathbf{y})d\mathbf{y}}. \tag{14.24}$$

Equation (14.24) is in accordance with our definition of constrained NML distributions in Section 11.2.1; the set Θ_0 in (11.6) corresponds to the set

$$\Theta(\tau_0, R) := \{(\mu, \sigma^2) \mid \sigma^2 \geq \tau_0, n^{-1}\mu^\top \mathbf{X}^\top \mathbf{X}\mu \leq R\}. \tag{14.25}$$

The integral in the denominator of (14.24) corresponds to the constrained complexity of $\Theta(\tau_0, R)$ as defined in Section 11.2.1:

$$\mathrm{CCOMP}^{(n)}(\Theta(\tau_0, R)) = \ln \int_{\mathbf{y}:\hat{\mu}(\mathbf{y})\in Y(\tau_0,R)} f_{\hat{\mu}(\mathbf{y})}(\mathbf{y})d\mathbf{y}.$$

Note that in this subsection, rather than $\mathrm{COMP}^{(n)}(\mathcal{M})$, we use the notation $\mathrm{COMP}^{(n)}(\Theta)$ as in Chapters 7 through 12. By an ingenious calculation, Barron, Rissanen, and Yu (1998) managed to find an analytic, nonasymptotic expression for $\mathrm{CCOMP}^{(n)}(\Theta(\tau_0, R))$:

$$\mathrm{CCOMP}^{(n)}(\Theta(\tau_0, R)) = \ln \frac{4}{k^2} + \frac{n}{2}\ln\frac{n}{2e} + \frac{k}{2}\ln\frac{R}{\tau_0} - \ln\boldsymbol{\Gamma}(\frac{n-k}{2}) - \ln\boldsymbol{\Gamma}(\frac{k}{2}),$$
$$\tag{14.26}$$

where Γ denotes the gamma function, Chapter 2, page 45. Essentially, the calculation is based on *twice* using the decomposition of $\mathrm{COMP}(\Theta(\tau_0, R))$ in terms of the value of the sufficient statistics ((7.24), page 227): once for the parameter vector $\hat{\mu}$, and once for the parameter $\hat{\sigma}^2$. Rissanen (2000) and Roos (2004) explain the argument in detail.

Using (14.26), the codelength corresponding to (14.24) can also be evaluated explicitly. It is given by

$$-\ln \bar{f}_{\mathrm{nml}}(\mathbf{y} \mid \mathbf{y} \in Y(\tau_0, R)) =$$
$$\frac{n}{2} \ln \mathrm{RSS}(\mathbf{y}) - \ln \Gamma(\frac{n-k}{2}) - \ln \Gamma(\frac{k}{2}) + \ln \frac{4}{k^2} + \frac{k}{2} \ln \frac{R}{\tau_0} + \frac{n}{2} \ln n\pi,$$
$$(14.27)$$

where $\mathrm{RSS}(\mathbf{y}) = n\hat{\sigma}^2(\mathbf{y})$ (Chapter 12, (12.33) on page 350). Suppose we want to select between models $\mathcal{S}_1, \mathcal{S}_2, \ldots$ for given data $(\mathbf{u}, \mathbf{y})$. We may try to determine a priori some τ_0 and R such that, for each $\mathcal{S}_\gamma$ under consideration, the corresponding ML estimator $(\hat{\mu}_\gamma, \hat{\sigma}_\gamma^2)$ will fall in the region $\Theta_\gamma(\tau_0, R)$ given by (14.25). We may then try to pick the $\mathcal{S}_{\hat{\gamma}}$ for which the resulting codelength

$$-\ln \bar{f}_{\mathrm{nml}}(\mathbf{y} \mid \mathbf{y} \in Y(\tau_0, R), \gamma) + \dot{L}(\gamma) \qquad (14.28)$$

is smallest. Here $\bar{f}_{\mathrm{nml}}$ is given by (14.27), and depends on $\mathcal{S}_\gamma = \mathcal{S}^{\mathbf{X}_\gamma}$ through $\mathrm{RSS}(\mathbf{y})$ and $k = k_\gamma$. Equation (14.28) is not satisfactory, since it heavily depends on the chosen values for R and τ_0, which determine the volume of the parameter space. In practice, such a choice will often be arbitrary, and the resulting criterion cannot be trusted.

An immediate fix to this problem (Rissanen 1999; Hansen and Yu 2001) is to replace, for each model $\mathcal{S}_\gamma$ under consideration, its corresponding R and τ_0 by the "maximum normalized likelihood values" $\hat{R}$ and $\hat{\tau}_0$ that minimize the value of (14.27) for the given data $\mathbf{y}$. This was called the "nMDL approach to regression" by Hansen and Yu (2001). The problem with this approach is that the resulting model selection criterion does not have a codelength interpretation anymore, since the values of $\hat{\tau}_0$ and $\hat{R}$ depend on the data.

2. RNML. To obtain a criterion that does have a proper codelength interpretation, Rissanen (2000) performs a second (re-)normalization of the normalized ML (14.27), using the RNML technique that we described in Section 11.2.3. As in Example 11.7, for each fixed model $\mathcal{S}_\gamma = \mathcal{S}^{\mathbf{X}_\gamma}$, Rissanen introduces hyper-hyperparameters $0 < \tau_1 < \tau_2$ and $0 < R_1 < R_2$. Analogously to (11.13), he then defines, for data $\mathbf{y}$ with $\hat{\sigma}^2(\mathbf{y}) = \hat{\tau}_0(\mathbf{y}) \in [\tau_1, \tau_2]$, and $\hat{R} \in [R_1, R_2]$, the *renormalized ML distribution* with density given by

$$\bar{f}_{\text{Rnml}}(\mathbf{y} \mid \hat{\tau}_0(\mathbf{y}) \in [\tau_1, \tau_2], \hat{R} \in [R_1, R_2]) :=$$

$$\frac{\bar{f}_{\text{nml}}(\mathbf{y} \mid \mathbf{y} \in Y(\hat{\tau}_0(\mathbf{y}), \hat{R}(\mathbf{y})))}{\int_{\mathbf{y}:\hat{\tau}_0(\mathbf{y}) \in [\tau_1, \tau_2], \hat{R}(\mathbf{y}) \in [R_1, R_2]} \bar{f}_{\text{nml}}(\mathbf{y} \mid \mathbf{y} \in Y(\hat{\tau}_0(\mathbf{y}), \hat{R}(\mathbf{y})))d\mathbf{y}}. \quad (14.29)$$

Rissanen (2001) manages to evaluate this integral as well.[3] The denominator turns out to be equal to $\frac{k^2}{4} \ln \frac{\tau_2}{\tau_1} \ln \frac{R_2}{R_1}$. The codelength corresponding to (14.29) is given by

$$- \ln \bar{f}_{\text{Rnml}}(\mathbf{y} \mid \hat{\tau}_0(\mathbf{y}) \in [\tau_1, \tau_2], \hat{R}(\mathbf{y}) \in [R_1, R_2]) =$$

$$\frac{n-k}{2} \ln \text{RSS}(\mathbf{y}) + \frac{k}{2} \ln \hat{R} +$$

$$- \ln \Gamma(\frac{n-k}{2}) - \ln \Gamma(\frac{k}{2}) + \frac{n}{2} \ln n\pi + \ln \left(\ln \frac{\tau_2}{\tau_1} \ln \frac{R_2}{R_1} \right). \quad (14.30)$$

Once again, an extensive explanation of the calculation can be found in (Roos 2004). The result is reminiscent of the simple calculation we did for the Gaussian location family, (11.16).

RNML Model Selection   We may now perform model selection by fixing some code $\dot{L}$ over model indices γ, and then selecting the model $S_{\hat{\gamma}}$ minimizing

$$\dot{L}(\gamma) - \ln \bar{f}_{\text{Rnml}}(\mathbf{y} \mid \hat{\tau}_0(\mathbf{y}) \in [\tau_1, \tau_2], \hat{R}(\mathbf{y}) \in [R_1, R_2]). \quad (14.31)$$

Here $\bar{f}_{\text{Rnml}}(\cdot \mid \gamma)$ is given by (14.30), instantiated to the model S_γ. To make the approach feasible, we set the values of $\tau_1, \tau_2, R_1,$ and R_2 such that for all S_γ under consideration,

$$\hat{\tau}_0(\mathbf{y}) \in [\tau_1, \tau_2] \text{ and } \hat{R}(\mathbf{y}) \in [R_1, R_2]. \quad (14.32)$$

It may seem that, just as for nMDL, the resulting procedure does not define a universal code, since it depends on values $\tau_1, \tau_2, R_1,$ and R_2 which are determined in terms of the data, yet not encoded. However, remarkably, from (14.30) we see that, in contrast to the nMDL case, the values that we choose for $\tau_1, \tau_2, R_1,$ and R_2 do not influence which S_γ is chosen, as long as we

---

3. There is a little mistake in the original calculation, which is corrected in (Roos 2004) and in (Rissanen 2007).

choose them such that (14.32) holds for all $\mathcal{S}_\gamma$ under consideration. Therefore, if we make the mild assumption that, before seeing the data, they can be fixed to some values such that (14.32) holds for all $\mathcal{S}_\gamma$, then the resulting criterion (14.31) does have a direct codelength interpretation.

Note, however, that the criterion is *not* invariant under reparameterization: the size of the term $(k/2) \ln \hat{R}$ depends on the chosen origin and favors distributions with $\hat{\mu}$ near the origin. In the present context, it is not clear whether this is really a weakness, as we elaborate in the discussion of the g-prior in the next section.

> **Reinterpretation of RNML as LNML-1** The RNML approach is elegant, but it is also hard to interpret. In practice, it seems that the more recent luckiness (LNML) approaches (Section 11.3) are easier to interpret: when using the LNML-1 approach, it is explicitly stated through the luckiness function $a(\hat{\theta})$ how much additional regret one is prepared to incur if the ML estimator for data $\mathbf{y}$ turns out to be equal to $\hat{\theta}$. Interestingly, Roos (2004) has shown that the RNML density (14.29) has an equivalent interpretation in terms of an LNML-1 approach with a particular luckiness function $a(\mu, \sigma^2)$. The result is also mentioned in (Roos et al. 2005). Namely, take
>
> $$a(\mu, \sigma^2) = \begin{cases} \frac{k}{2} \ln \frac{\mu^\top \mathbf{X}^\top \mathbf{X} \mu}{2\sigma^2} & \text{if } \tau_1 \leq \sigma^2 \leq \tau_2, R_1 \leq \mu^\top \mathbf{X}^\top \mathbf{X} \mu \leq R_2, \\ \infty & \text{otherwise.} \end{cases}$$
>
> Let $\bar{f}_{\text{Lnml-1}}$ be the LNML-1 density, defined as in (11.18), relative to a model $\mathcal{S}^{\mathbf{X}}$ and the luckiness function $a(\mu, \sigma^2)$. With the above choice of $a(\mu, \sigma^2)$, we get, for all $\mathbf{y} \in \mathbb{R}^n$, $\bar{f}_{\text{Rnml}}(\mathbf{y} \mid \hat{\tau}_0(\mathbf{y}) \in [\tau_1, \tau_2], \hat{R} \in [R_1, R_2]) = \bar{f}_{\text{Lnml-1}}(\mathbf{y})$.

14.5.2   Hansen and Yu's gMDL Approach

The approach of Hansen and Yu (2001) is based on combining sophisticated Bayesian universal codes with a simple meta-two-part code. In the first approach, they use fixed-variance models $\mathcal{M}_\gamma$. In their second approach, they use varying-variance models $\mathcal{S}_\gamma$. We outline both approaches below. Hansen and Yu (2002) extend the approach to *generalized* linear models, where the y_i are not necessarily continuous-valued anymore and the noise is not necessarily Gaussian. We will not go into that extension here.

Fixed σ^2   We start with a fixed, k-dimensional linear model. As in Section 12.3.1, Chapter 12, it will be convenient to denote the observed data as $\mathbf{y}_1 = (y_{n_0+1}, \ldots, y_n)^\top$ and the corresponding design matrix as $\mathbf{X}_1$. The model $\mathcal{M}$ may then be denoted as $\mathcal{M}^{\mathbf{X}_1}$. As in Section 12.3.1, let $\bar{f}_{\text{Bayes}}$ represent the Bayesian universal model relative to model $\mathcal{M}^{\mathbf{X}_1}$, with a Gaussian prior with some mean μ_0 and covariance matrix Σ_0. The prior can be interpreted as representing previously seen data $\mathbf{y}_0 = (y_1, \dots, y_{n_0})^\top$ with design $\mathbf{X}_0$. We already gave an analytic expression for $\bar{f}_{\text{Bayes}}(\mathbf{y}_1)$ in (12.50). This involved the quantity $\text{RSS}(\mathbf{y})$ for the extended data $\mathbf{y} \mid \mathbf{X}$, which, in general, is not so easy to deal with. We can simplify this expression considerably if we choose a so-called *g-prior*. This is a prior with $\mu_0 = \mathbf{0}$ and $\Sigma_0^{-1} = c(\mathbf{X}_1^\top \mathbf{X}_1)$, for some constant c. From (12.57), we see that the expression (12.50) for $\bar{f}_{\text{Bayes}}$ now simplifies to

$$- \ln \bar{f}_{\text{Bayes}}(\mathbf{y}_1 \mid c) = \frac{k}{2} \ln(1 + c) + \frac{1}{2\sigma^2} \left(\mathbf{y}_1^\top \mathbf{y}_1 - \frac{c}{1+c} \text{FSS}(\mathbf{y}_1) \right), \quad (14.33)$$

where $\text{FSS}(\mathbf{y}_1) = \mathbf{y}_1^\top \hat{\mathbf{y}}_1^\top$ is the fitted sum of squares, defined in Section 12.2. Here we put c in the conditional, since different values of c lead to different codes. To obtain a universal model for $\mathbf{y}_1$, Hansen and Yu (2001) now use a meta-two-part coding approach: they define the code $\bar{L}_{\text{HY}}$ by first encoding a value for c using some code with length function L_0, and then encoding $\mathbf{y}$ using the code corresponding to $\bar{f}_{\text{Bayes}}(\cdot \mid c)$: $\bar{L}_{\text{HY}}(\mathbf{y}_1) := \min_c \{ - \ln \bar{f}_{\text{Bayes}}(\mathbf{y}_1 \mid c) + L_0(c) \}$.

How should the code L_0 be designed? By differentiating we find that the c minimizing (14.33) is given by $\hat{c} = \max\{\text{FSS}(\mathbf{y}_1)/k\sigma^2 - 1, 0\}$. Thus, the value 0 plays a special role, and it is useful to account for it explicitly: L_0 works by first encoding, in 1 bit, whether $c = 0$ or not. If $c \neq 0$, then a discretized value $\ddot{c}$ of $\hat{c}$ is encoded. By the arguments of Chapter 10, Section 10.1, it can be shown that the optimal precision to encode $\ddot{c}$ is $(1/2) \log n + O(1)$, and with this precision, $- \ln \bar{f}_{\text{Bayes}}(\mathbf{y}_1 \mid \ddot{c}) = \bar{f}_{\text{Bayes}}(\mathbf{y}_1 \mid \hat{c}) + O(1)$. Since both $O(1)$-terms can be made very small, Hansen and Yu (2001) simply ignore them. They end up with the codelength

$$\bar{L}_{\text{HY}}(\mathbf{y}_1) =$$
$$\begin{cases} \left(\frac{\mathbf{y}_1^\top \mathbf{y}_1 - \text{FSS}(\mathbf{y}_1)}{2\sigma^2} \right) + \frac{k}{2} \left(1 + \ln \frac{\text{FSS}(\mathbf{y}_1)}{\sigma^2 k} \right) + \frac{1}{2} \ln n & \text{if } \text{FSS}(\mathbf{y}_1) > k\sigma^2 \\ \frac{1}{2\sigma^2} \mathbf{y}_1^\top \mathbf{y}_1 & \text{otherwise.} \end{cases}$$
$$(14.34)$$

Note that, if it is encoded that $c = 0$, then this essentially means that the "null model," in which all effects are 0, is to be preferred over the model Θ_k.

Equation (14.34) is the basis of Hansen and Yu's model selection method for known σ^2: for each model $\mathcal{M}_\gamma$ under consideration, they define $\bar{L}_{\text{HY}}(\mathbf{y}_1 \mid$

γ) by (14.34), which depends on $\mathcal{M}_\gamma$ through $\text{FSS}(\mathbf{y}_1)$ and $k = k_\gamma$. They then pick the γ minimizing the codelength $\bar{L}(\mathbf{y} \mid \gamma)$, ignoring the codelength $\dot{L}(\gamma)$. They note that George and Foster (2000) present an "empirical Bayes approach" that leads to essentially the same criterion, but without the $(1/2) \ln n$ term. According to Hansen and Yu (2002), this extra term is essential to guarantee consistency of the selection method when the null model is true.

> **The g-Prior** The idea to take $\Sigma_0 = c(\mathbf{X}_1^\top \mathbf{X}_1)^{-1}$ apparently goes back to Zellner (1986), who christened the prior with mean $\mathbf{0}$ and covariance matrix Σ_0 the "g-prior." It is easy to show that with this prior, the Bayesian MAP estimator $\hat{\mu}$ can be expressed in terms of the ML estimator $\hat{\mu}_1$ for the observed data $\mathbf{y}_1$: $\hat{\mu} = \frac{c}{1+c}\hat{\mu}_1$.
>
> The g-prior is centered at $\mathbf{0}$, which may seem arbitrary. In the case of nested model selection, such a choice is often quite reasonable, as we discuss in Section 14.5.4.

Varying σ^2   For models $\mathcal{S}^{\mathbf{X}_1}$ with varying σ^2, Hansen and Yu (2001) set $\sigma^2 = \tau$, and define a prior on (μ, τ) as follows. First, fix two hyperparameters c and a. Conditional on each fixed τ, the prior $w(\mu \mid \tau)$ on μ is the g-prior with hyperparameter c as defined above, with mean $\mu_0 = \mathbf{0}$ and covariance matrix $c(\mathbf{X}_1^\top \mathbf{X}_1)^{-1}$. The prior on τ is an inverted gamma distribution with hyperparameter a, i.e. $w(\tau) := a^{1/2}(2\pi)^{-1/2}\tau^{-3/2}e^{-\frac{a}{2\tau}}$. The joint prior density is then defined as $w(\tau, \mu) = w(\tau)w(\mu \mid \tau)$.

> This approach is equivalent to assigning a *square-root* inverted gamma distribution to the parameter $\sigma = \tau^{1/2}$ (see Chapter 12 at the end of Section 12.3.2), and is thus more closely related to the improper Jeffreys' prior and Liang-Barron approaches (Chapter 12, Section 12.4) than it might at first seem.

This leads to a Bayesian universal model $\bar{f}'_{\text{Bayes}}$ depending on hyperparameters a and c. The corresponding codelength can be evaluated explicitly. Here, we only give the equation resulting for the $\hat{a}$ that minimizes the codelength; see (Hansen and Yu 2001,20002) for the general treatment. It turns out that

$$-\ln \bar{f}'_{\text{Bayes}}(\mathbf{y}_1 \mid \hat{a}, c) = \min_{a>0} -\ln \bar{f}'_{\text{Bayes}}(\mathbf{y}_1 \mid a, c) =$$
$$\frac{k}{2}\ln(1+c) + \frac{n}{2}\ln\left(\mathbf{y}_1^\top\mathbf{y}_1 - \frac{c}{1+c}\text{FSS}(\mathbf{y}_1)\right). \quad (14.35)$$

Just as was done for $\hat{c}$ in the fixed σ^2 case, Hansen and Yu (2001) proceed by encoding discretizations of the optimizing values $\hat{a}$ and $\hat{c}$ explicitly. Thus, they end up with a universal code with lengths

$$\bar{L}'_{\text{HY}}(\mathbf{y}_1) = \min_{a,c}\{ -\ln \bar{f}'_{\text{Bayes}}(\mathbf{y}_1 \mid a, c) + L_0(c) + L_1(a) \}$$

for some codes L_0 and L_1. The code L_1 encodes a at optimal precision, which turns out to be $(1/2)\log n + O(1)$, as in Chapter 10, Section 10.1. This leads to an increase of (14.35) of $O(1)$. The code L_0 for c is again found by determining the $\hat{c}$ minimizing (14.35). It turns out that $\hat{c} = \max\{F - 1, 0\}$, where $F = (\text{FSS}(\mathbf{y}_1)/\text{RSS}(\mathbf{y}_1))(n - k)/k$. This F is also known as the F-ratio and is used in traditional statistical tests for testing the hypothesis that all components of μ are 0. The optimum $\hat{c}$ is encoded as in the fixed-variance case, reserving 1 bit to determine whether $\hat{c} = 0$ or not. Taking everything together and ignoring the (small) $O(1)$ terms, we get

$$\bar{L}'_{\text{HY}}(\mathbf{y}_1) = \begin{cases} \frac{n-k}{2} \ln \frac{\text{RSS}(\mathbf{y}_1)}{n-k} + \frac{k}{2} \ln \frac{\text{FSS}(\mathbf{y}_1)}{k} + \ln n & \text{if } F > 1 \\ \frac{n}{2} \ln \frac{\mathbf{y}_1^\top \mathbf{y}_1}{n} + \frac{1}{2} \ln n & \text{otherwise.} \end{cases} \quad (14.36)$$

Ignoring the code length for $\dot{L}(\gamma)$, (Hansen and Yu 2001) now define *gMDL* as the model selection procedure selecting the model $\mathcal{S}_\gamma$ with the smallest associated codelength $\bar{L}'_{\text{HY}}(\mathbf{y}_1 \mid \gamma)$, given by (14.36), instantiated to $\mathcal{S}_\gamma$.

14.5.3   Liang and Barron's Approach

In this subsection, we denote the observed data as $\mathbf{y} = (y_1, \ldots, y_n)^\top$ and the design matrix as $\mathbf{X}$. Just as in Section 12.3.2, $\mathbf{y}$ consists of an initial part $\mathbf{y}_0 = (y_1, \ldots, y_{n_0})$ with design matrix $\mathbf{X}_0$, and a remaining part $\mathbf{y}_1$ with design matrix $\mathbf{X}_1$. Note the difference in notation to Hansen and Yu's version of MDL for regression, where we denoted the observed data as $\mathbf{y}_1 \mid \mathbf{X}_1$, and $\mathbf{y}_0$ and $\mathbf{X}_0$ were implicitly defined in terms of the prior on the model. Liang and Barron (2004) provide an instantiation of $\bar{f}(\mathbf{y}_1 \mid \mathbf{y}_0, \gamma)$ for linear models $\mathcal{M}_\gamma$ with fixed variance, and for models $\mathcal{S}_\gamma$ with varying variance. We first treat the fixed-variance case.

Fixed Variance; Conditional NML   Recall from Chapter 11, Section 11.4.3, that a Liang-Barron universal model $\bar{f}_{\text{LB}}$, conditioned on n_0 outcomes and relative to a k-dimensional linear model $\mathcal{M}^{\mathbf{X}}$, is defined to achieve the *minimax conditional expected redundancy*, given by

$$\min_{\bar{f}} \max_{\mu \in \mathbb{R}^k} E_{\mathbf{y}_0, \mathbf{y}_1 \sim f_\mu}[-\ln \bar{f}(\mathbf{y}_1 \mid \mathbf{y}_0) - [-\ln f_\mu(\mathbf{y}_1)]], \quad (14.37)$$

where both $\mathbf{y}_1 \in \mathbb{R}^{n-n_0}$ and $\mathbf{y}_0 \in \mathbb{R}^{n_0}$ are to be understood as random variables. The conditional density $f(\mathbf{y}_1 \mid \mathbf{y}_0)$ is well defined if and only if $n_0 \geq k$ (Chapter 12, Section 12.3.2).

Liang and Barron (2004) show that (14.37) is exactly achieved by the Bayesian universal model with the improper Jeffreys' prior (12.61), which in this case is uniform. Thus, in this case we get, as in (12.64),

$$-\ln \bar{f}_{\text{LB}}(\mathbf{y}_1 \mid \mathbf{y}_0) = -\ln \bar{f}_{\text{Jeffreys}}(\mathbf{y}_1 \mid \mathbf{y}_0) = -\ln \bar{f}_{\text{Cnml-2}}(\mathbf{y}_1 \mid \mathbf{y}_0) =$$

$$\frac{1}{2} \ln \frac{\det \mathbf{X}^\top \mathbf{X}}{\det \mathbf{X}_0^\top \mathbf{X}_0} + \frac{n}{2} \ln 2\pi\sigma^2 + \frac{1}{2\sigma^2} \left(\text{RSS}(\mathbf{y} \mid \mathbf{X}) - \text{RSS}(\mathbf{y}_0 \mid \mathbf{X}_0) \right).$$

$$(14.38)$$

The Liang-Barron universal code for the linear model $\mathcal{M}^{\mathbf{X}}$ with fixed σ^2 is thus *identical* to the Bayesian codelength achieved with the improper Jeffreys' prior. As we have seen in Section 12.4.3, this is also equal to the codelength achieved with the CNML-2 universal code, and the asymptotic codelengths/regrets of Theorem 11.3 hold exactly for all sample sizes $n > k$.

Varying Variance Let $\mathbf{y}_0 \in \mathbb{R}^{n_0}$, where $n_0 \geq k+1$, and consider a $k+1$-parameter linear model $\mathcal{S}^{\mathbf{X}}$ with $n \times k$ design matrix $\mathbf{X}$. The formula (14.37) for minimax expected conditional redundancy relative to $\mathcal{M}_\gamma$ is easily adjusted to this case, by letting the maximum range over all $\mu \in \mathbb{R}^k, \sigma^2 \geq 0$, and replacing μ by (μ, σ^2) at all appropriate places. Liang and Barron (2004) show that in this case, the minimax conditional expected redundancy is exactly achieved by the code $\bar{f}_{\text{LB}}^\circ$ with lengths

$$-\ln \bar{f}_{\text{LB}}^\circ(\mathbf{y}_1 \mid \mathbf{y}_0) = \frac{n-n_0}{2} \ln \pi + \frac{1}{2} \ln \frac{\det \mathbf{X}^\top \mathbf{X}}{\det \mathbf{X}_0^\top \mathbf{X}_0} - \ln \frac{\Gamma\left(\frac{n-k}{2}\right)}{\Gamma\left(\frac{n_0-k}{2}\right)}$$

$$+ \frac{n-k}{2} \ln \text{RSS}(\mathbf{y}) - \frac{n_0-k}{2} \ln \text{RSS}(\mathbf{y}_0). \quad (14.39)$$

This is just (12.68) evaluated for the improper prior $w(\sigma) = \sigma^{-1}$. In contrast to the situation for fixed variance, this approach is *not* equal to a CNML approach or a Bayes-Jeffreys prior approach, which gives codelengths (12.71). We already noted this in Chapter 11, Example 11.12, for the special case where $\mathcal{S}^{\mathbf{X}}$ represents the full normal family.

Model Selection Suppose we have two k-dimensional fixed-variance linear models $\mathcal{M}_1$ and $\mathcal{M}_2$, with associated design matrices $\mathbf{X}_1$ and $\mathbf{X}_2$. In this simple case, where both models have the same number of parameters, model selection may proceed by selecting the model $\mathcal{M}_\gamma$ minimizing $-\ln \bar{f}_{\mathrm{LB}}(\mathbf{y}_1 \mid \mathbf{y}_0, \gamma)$, where $\mathbf{y}_0$ consists of the first $n_0 = k$ observations. Here $\bar{f}_{\mathrm{LB}}(\cdot \mid \gamma)$ is the instantiation of (14.38) to model $\mathcal{M}_1$ and $\mathcal{M}_2$ respectively. We implicitly assume uniform codelengths for the models $\mathcal{M}_1$ and $\mathcal{M}_2$. The same procedure can be applied for selecting between the corresponding $\mathcal{S}_1$ and $\mathcal{S}_2$, using (14.39) instead of (14.38). Things become more complicated if we want to select between models with a different number of parameters or a large number of parameters. In that case, one can use the procedure based on (14.18), described in Section 14.4.3.

14.5.4   Discussion

Alternative MDL Approaches   We have described three MDL-based approaches for model selection in linear regression. The approaches differed in how the universal code $\bar{f}(\mathbf{y} \mid \gamma)$ associated with model $\mathcal{M}_\gamma$ or $\mathcal{S}_\gamma$ was defined. There exist at least three other, somewhat older, approaches. First, Lee (2000) presents a two-part code MDL approach in a nonparametric context; see also (Lee 2002c), where the approach is extended to recover *discontinuous* regression functions. Second, Rissanen (1989) presents an approach that is quite similar to gMDL. It is called *iMDL* by Hansen and Yu (2001). The difference to gMDL is that instead of the g-prior $\Sigma_0 = c(\mathbf{X}_1^\top \mathbf{X}_1)$, one takes a prior with $\Sigma_0 = cI$, I being the unit matrix. The development proceeds as in (Hansen and Yu 2001), where the optimal $\ddot{c}$ can be found numerically (Rissanen 1989). The final approach we discuss is the *predictive least-squares (PLS) method*, which is based on plug-in prequential universal codes for the models $\mathcal{M}_\gamma$ or $\mathcal{S}_\gamma$. It was first described by Rissanen (1986a,b); an extensive description can be found in (Rissanen 1989); see also (Wei 1992; Qian, Gabor, and Gupta 1996; Modha and Masry 1998). We should add that related methods such as *forward validation* (Hjorth 1982) have appeared in the literature on Gaussian regression even before the development of either MDL or Dawid's prequential approach. However, until Rissanen's (1984, 1986c) work on predictive coding, it was unknown that such methods could be given a codelength interpretation. We do not describe the PLS method in detail, but we should note one appealing aspect: the PLS method defined relative to fixed-variance models $\mathcal{M}_\gamma$ does not depend on the choice of σ^2. If we had chosen a different value for σ^2, we would have ended up with exactly the same predictions. Because the choice for σ^2 is often somewhat arbitrary, this is a desirable property. It is not shared by the other fixed-variance methods that we considered: as can be seen from (14.34) and (14.38), the models selected by the fixed-variance criteria of both Hansen and Yu (2001) and of Liang and Barron (2004) depend on the chosen value of σ^2.

In all five approaches, noise is modeled as being normally distributed. Hansen and Yu (2002) consider generalized linear models, which may have a different noise distribution. Alternatively, in the spirit of statistical learning theory (Chapter 17, Section 17.10) it has been tried to *directly* try to learn functions $h \in \mathcal{H}$ from the data, without making any probabilistic assumptions about the noise (Rissanen 1989; Barron 1990; Yamanishi 1998; Grünwald 1998; Grünwald 1999). We now compare the five main approaches in more detail.

Theoretical Comparison It seems that the Liang–Barron approach is the "cleanest": it employs conditional universal codes, which do not depend on potentially arbitrary aspects of the problem such as the chosen parameterization. On the other hand, in a model selection context with nested models, this conditioning can be problematic, since to define the codelength for a model with k parameters, one must either ignore a potentially substantial amount (k outcomes) of data, or first encode the first $k - 1$ outcomes using a suboptimal code, such as the codes used in (14.18), page 434. Since it is not exactly clear what code should be used here, this amounts to using some form of the luckiness principle again. Also, these codes depend on the order of the data, which seems arbitrary (see Section 14.4.3).

RNML and gMDL have a different arbitrary aspect: they have a built-in preference for parameter values near the origin. However, such a preference may actually be quite reasonable when doing nested model selection. To see this, suppose that $\mathcal{M} = \bigcup_\gamma \mathcal{M}_\gamma$, where $\mathcal{M}_\gamma$ is the restriction of $\mathcal{M}_{\gamma+1}$ with the parameter $\mu_{\gamma+1}$ restricted to 0. This is the case, if, for example, $\mathcal{M}_\gamma = \mathcal{P}^{(\gamma+1)}$ represents the polynomials of degree γ. In such a case, the Bayesian universal model $\bar{P}_{\text{top}}$ for the union $\mathcal{M}$ of all models already assigns infinitely more prior density to distributions with $\mu_\gamma = 0$ than to distributions with any other choice of μ_γ. Therefore, it may be reasonable to take a prior density of μ in $\mathcal{M}_{\gamma+1}$ that decreases as a function of $\|\mu - \mathbf{0}\| = \|\mu\|$.

All in all, it seems that all three state-of-the-art approaches, RNML, gMDL, and Liang-Barron MDL, depend on the "luckiness principle" at some level. This is even more so for the iMDL and the PLS method that we did not discuss in detail. On the other hand, using the developments of Chapter 16, Section 16.3, all five methods can be shown to be asymptotically consistent

(Hansen and Yu 2001). Thus it is not clear which method should be preferred on a theoretical basis.

Practical Comparison Hansen and Yu (2001) performed some illuminating experiments with gMDL, nMDL (Section 14.5.1), and iMDL. They compared these procedures on a variety of model selection problems. They used various simulated data sets and also two real-world data sets, concerning the genetics of fruit flies and the color of fruits sold in supermarkets, respectively. At the sample sizes considered by Hansen and Yu, the behavior of gMDL, nMDL and iMDL is dramatically different from the two most well known benchmark model selection procedures AIC and BIC; see Chapter 17, Section 17.3. In the context of linear regression between models $\{S_\gamma : \gamma \in \Gamma\}$ for data D, AIC and BIC take on the form

$$\mathrm{AIC}(D) \;=\; \arg\min_\gamma \left\{ k_\gamma + \frac{n}{2} \ln \mathrm{RSS}(\gamma) \right\}$$

$$\mathrm{BIC}(D) \;=\; \arg\min_\gamma \left\{ \frac{k_\gamma}{2} \ln n + \frac{n}{2} \ln \mathrm{RSS}(\gamma) \right\}, \tag{14.40}$$

where k_γ is the number of parameters in S_γ, and $\mathrm{RSS}(\gamma)$ is the residual sum of squares obtained on data D with model S_γ. The various MDL criteria are more adaptive than AIC and BIC: as can be seen from (14.30), (14.36), and (14.39), for each given data set D, each MDL criterion chooses a model which essentially minimizes the sum of $\frac{n}{2} \ln \mathrm{RSS}(\gamma)$ plus some penalty, which depends not just on the number of parameters and the least-squares fit, but also on various other aspects of the relation between models and data. For example, as discussed by Hansen and Yu, if data are distributed such that there is a large number of small effects (k_γ large but most parameters near 0), the penalty implicit in iMDL typically shrinks below that of AIC, which in turn is always below that of BIC. But if there is a single strong effect (k_γ small, but one very large parameter), then the penalty implicit in iMDL becomes even stronger than that of BIC.

In nearly all experiments, it was found that the behavior of the three MDL methods was much more reasonable than that of AIC and BIC. Yet, there were nonnegligible differences between the three forms of MDL, and there was no clear winner among them.

Predictive Least Squares As shown in a simulation study by Rissanen (1986a), and later confirmed by other authors such as Wei (1992), when the sample is small and the unmodified ML estimator is used, then PLS tends to select simpler models than model selection based on other model selection criteria such as two-part code MDL and BIC. Wei (1992)'s simulations show that, for small samples, some other model selection methods tend to select the model containing the "true" distribution more often than PLS. It is not clear whether this is still the case if one bases the criterion on a luckiness rather than an ordinary ML estimator.

RNML/CNML/Liang-Barron At the time of writing this book, not very much was known about the practical behavior of the RNML and the Liang-Barron/ CNML methods. Roos et al. (2005) found that the RNML-denoising method, which is closely related to RNML regression, worked very well in denoising problems as long as $\dot{L}(\gamma)$ was not taken to be uniform (Example 14.7); this nonuniformity of $\dot{L}(\gamma)$ does not seem to be relevant in regression contexts though. Liang and Barron (2005) use their method for predictive coding of a sequence of real-world data based on the full normal family, and find that they obtain quite short codelengths even though the data contain a few outliers, which indicates that their approach is quite robust. On the other hand, Nannen (2003) experimented with the Liang-Barron method for model selection using various synthetic data sets. His experiments were based on the polynomial linear regression models $\mathcal{P}^{(k)}$, $k = 0, 1, 2, \ldots$, and he obtained rather mixed results.

Open Problem No. 11/Project   Since all of the approaches mentioned here are based on the Gaussian noise assumption, none of them deals very well with data containing outliers. For that, one would need to develop a "robustified" method in which the error distribution has much heavier tails, or in which outliers are identified and coded separately. It would be both interesting and practically useful to develop MDL concepts such as NML and prequential coding for such robustified models. A first step in this direction has been taken by Qian and Künsch (1998).

14.6   Worst Case vs. Average Case*

Readers that first read about MDL model selection are often worried that the approach may be too much worst case-oriented. Real data are usually not designed to make the life of the statistician or data compressor as hard as possible, so why should one devise methods based on a minimax (=worst-case) analysis?

Short Answer   There are a short, a medium, and a long answer. The short answer is as follows: broadly speaking, worst case analyses can be applied in two very different types of situations. One is the type of situation where the worst case is inherently different from the typical case; and the other is the type of situation where the worst case and the typical case do not differ very much. It turns out that universal coding deals with a situation of the second type: considering "typical" rather than worst-case data shows that worst-case optimal, NML-type codes are still quite close to being optimal in the typical case. Here "optimal" means "achieving small regret"; when such codes are used to define estimators (Chapter 15, Section 15.2.1), it also means "converging to the data-generating distribution at a fast rate." Thus, while worst-case optimal codes perform reasonably well in "typical" cases, on the other hand, one can design codes which are arbitrarily close to optimal in the "typical" case, yet extremely bad in the worst-case over all sequences. Therefore, there is not much harm, but potentially significant gain in using codes that are worst-case (minimax) optimal for individual sequences.

Medium Answer   We now substantiate the claim above that NML-type codes are close to optimal in the typical case. First, we provide an informal argument. Let $\bar{L}$ be a universal code relative to model $\mathcal{M}$ with parameterization Θ. We formalize the "typical situation" as the average codelength $\bar{L}(X^n)$ that is obtained if data $X_1, X_2, \ldots X^n$ are i.i.d. $\sim P_\theta$, and we then take a second, weighted average over $\theta \in \Theta$, where the weights are given by some density $w(\theta)$ which we assume to be continuous and strictly positive on Θ. Then

$$\int_\Theta w(\theta) E_{P_\theta}[\bar{L}(X^n)]d\theta = E_{\bar{P}_{\text{Bayes}}}[\bar{L}(X^n)],$$

where $\bar{P}_{\text{Bayes}}$ is the Bayesian marginal distribution relative to prior w. This means that formally, the average codelength is the same as the expected codelength relative to a Bayesian marginal distribution. But then, by the information inequality (Chapter 3, Section 3.3), for all distributions P on $\mathcal{X}^n$,

$$E_{\bar{P}_{\text{Bayes}}}[-\log P(X^n)] \geq E_{\bar{P}_{\text{Bayes}}}[-\log \bar{P}_{\text{Bayes}}(X^n)], \tag{14.41}$$

so that the Bayesian universal distribution $\bar{P}_{\text{Bayes}}$ with respect to prior w would give optimal expected codelengths in the "average" sense. On the other hand, by Theorem 8.1, the *actual* codelengths achieved by a Bayesian universal code with prior w' will be within $-\log w'(\hat{\theta}) + \log w(\hat{\theta}) = O(1)$, as long as the prior w' is itself continuous and the sequence $x_1, x_2, \ldots$ is also "typical" in that it remains bounded away from the boundaries of the parameter space. This means that any two "reasonable" Bayesian codes will achieve codelengths within $o(1)$ of each other. Because of the asymptotic equivalence of NML, luckiness NML, and conditional NML approaches with Bayesian universal codes with certain specific priors, these NML approaches will also achieve codelengths within $O(1)$ of the optimal code with lengths $-\log \bar{P}_{\text{Bayes}}(x^n)$.

In other words: if we take an average over data-generating distributions, then, if one uses a Bayesian universal code, there is *some* gain in adopting the "right" prior. If one uses an NML universal code, there is some gain in adopting a luckiness-function that is well adopted to the prior. Indeed, if prior knowledge (for example, in the form of earlier data coming from the same source) is available, we would advocate the use of luckiness NML distributions for exactly this reason. But the size of this gain is bounded by a constant - the constant can be large enough to make the gain highly useful, but it is important to note that the gain cannot keep increasing with n. Compare this to the situation where one restricts a k-dimensional model $\mathcal{M}^{(k)}$ to a $k-1$-dimensional subset $\mathcal{M}^{(k-1)}$, using prior knowledge that $P_\theta^* \in \mathcal{M}^{(k-1)}$: here the gain will be $(1/2)\log n + O(1)$, which increases with sample size.

Averages and Approximations Thus, adopting a worst-case approach one may need a finite number of bits more than by adopting an approach that is optimal in the expected sense. On the other hand, it is easy to construct an alternative to $\bar{P}_{\text{Bayes}}$ which is negligibly worse than $\bar{P}_{\text{Bayes}}$ in the expected sense, but infinitely worse in a worst-case sense. For an (admittedly contrived) example, fix some θ_0 in the interior of Θ and consider the distribution $\bar{P}'_{\text{Bayes}}(x^n) = c\bar{P}_{\text{Bayes}}(x^n)e^{-\sqrt{n}}$ if $\hat{\theta}(x^n) = \theta_0$, and $\bar{P}'_{\text{Bayes}}(x^n) = c\bar{P}_{\text{Bayes}}(x^n)$ otherwise, where c is chosen so that the distribution sums to 1. It is easy to show that, if $\mathcal{M}$ has more than one free parameter, then $E_{\bar{P}_{\text{Bayes}}}[-\log \bar{P}'_{\text{Bayes}}(X^n) - [-\log \bar{P}_{\text{Bayes}}(X^n)]]$ $= o(1)$, whereas in the worst case over all x^n, $-\log \bar{P}'_{\text{Bayes}}(x^n) = -\log \bar{P}_{\text{Bayes}}(x^n)$ $+\sqrt{n} + o(1)$. The MDL approach (at least the individual-sequence version), is based on the premise that any sequence at all may be observed. Thus, it would never allow "good approximations" such as $\bar{P}'_{\text{Bayes}}$.

Long Answer We now present Theorem 14.1, a precise, nonasymptotic version of the argument above, based on the no-hypercompression inequality (Chapter 3, Section 3.3) rather than the information inequality (14.41). Related results can be found in (Barron, Rissanen, and Yu 1998), using earlier ideas of Barron (1985). In the theorem, $V(\Theta)$ denotes the volume of the set

$\Theta \subset \mathbb{R}^k$, for some $k \geq 1$. The theorem uses the notation $\text{COMP}^{(n)}(\Theta)$ as in Chapters 7 through 12.

Theorem 14.1 Let Θ_0 be an *ineccsi* subset of a k-dimensional exponential family $\mathcal{M}$, given in a diffeomorphic parameterization $(\Theta_{\mathcal{M}}, P_\theta)$. Let, for every n, $\bar{P}^{(n)}$ be an arbitrary distribution on $\mathcal{X}^n$. Define for $\epsilon, c > 0$:

$$\check{\Theta}_{c,\epsilon}^{(n)} := \{\theta \in \Theta_0 \mid P_\theta(\text{REG}(\bar{P}^{(n)}, \Theta_0, x^n) \leq \text{COMP}^{(n)}(\Theta_0) - c) \geq \epsilon\}.$$

Then $V(\check{\Theta}_{c,\epsilon}^{(n)}) \leq \frac{2^{-c}}{\epsilon} K_{\Theta_0} + o(1)$, where $o(1)$ tends to 0 with increasing n, and

$$K_{\Theta_0} := \frac{\int_{\Theta_0} \sqrt{I(\theta)} d\theta}{\inf_{\theta \in \Theta_0} \sqrt{I(\theta)}}$$

is a constant that does not depend on either n or k.

The proof can be found at the end of this section. The theorem tells us that, for *any* code, the volume of $\theta \in \Theta$ for which it outperforms the minimax optimal code/regret by more than c bits is exponentially small in c. The setting of this proposition is contrary to the individual-sequence MDL philosophy of analyzing data in terms of individual sequences, rather than probabilistic assumptions. But now we adopt this setting on purpose, just to see what happens *if* we are in the probabilistic rather than worst-case sequence situation.

Relation to Rissanen's Celebrated Lower Bound Theorem 14.1 is related to a celebrated theorem by Rissanen (1984, 1986c) about expected codelength rather than "probability of compressing more than c bits." Rissanen's theorem holds more generally than just for exponential families. Restricted to our setting, it says the following:

Theorem 14.2 [Rissanen 1986], Special Case Let $\mathcal{M}$ and Θ_0 be as above. Let Q be an arbitrary probabilistic source, and let $Q^{(n)}$ be its restriction to the first n outcomes. Define

$$g_n(\theta) = \inf_{n' \geq n} \left\{ \frac{D(P_\theta^{(n')} \| Q^{(n')})}{\frac{k}{2} \log n'} \right\}.$$

Then the limit $\lim_{n \to \infty} g_n(\theta)$ exists for all $\theta \in \Theta_0$ and we have

$$V(\theta \in \Theta_0 \mid \lim_{n \to \infty} g_n(\theta) \geq 1) = 1.$$

(Rissanen 1986c) calls this a "grand Cramér-Rao bound," and indeed, close connections with the classical Cramér-Rao bound of statistics and related notions can be established. For example, Barron and Hengartner (1998) relate Rissanen's result to the classical statistical notion of "superefficiency."

Based on Theorem 14.1, it is easy to show the following simplified version of Rissanen's theorem: for all $\epsilon > 0$, as $n \rightarrow \infty$,

$$V\left(\theta \in \Theta_0 \mid \frac{\mathrm{D}(P_\theta^{(n)} \| Q^{(n)})}{\frac{k}{2} \log n} > 1 - \epsilon\right) \rightarrow 1. \tag{14.42}$$

Essentially, this follows from Theorem 14.1 by writing out the expectation in $\mathrm{D}(P_\theta^{(n)} \| Q^{(n)})$ in terms of probabilities, and bounding each probability using Theorem 14.1. We omit the details.

Note that Rissanen's theorem expresses something much stronger than (14.42). Equation (14.42) allows the "exceptional" set of θ for which Q has expected redundancy bounded by $(1 - \epsilon)(k/2) \log n$ to vary with n. Rissanen's theorem rules out this possibility, and says that for almost all $\theta \in \Theta_0$, there exists an n_θ such that Q will not achieve expected redundancy of $(1 - \epsilon)(k/2) \log n$ or smaller, for all $n > n_\theta$. Rissanen's result has a very complicated proof, much more complicated than the proof of Theorem 14.1.

We end this section with the proof of Theorem 14.1.

Proof of Theorem 14.1   We actually state and prove a more general theorem, which makes use of the concept of the volume of a set $\Theta' \subseteq \mathbb{R}^k$, *relative to a measure q*, where $q : \mathbb{R}^k \rightarrow [0, \infty)$ is a function that must be continuous on Θ'. This is denoted by $V_q(\Theta')$ and defined as

$$V_q(\Theta') = \int_{\theta \in \mathbb{R}^k} q(\theta) \mathbf{1}_{\theta \in \Theta'} d\theta.$$

In case we take q the uniform (Lebesgue) measure, $q(x) := 1$, then the resulting notion of volume is just the ordinary volume, and the theorem below becomes Theorem 14.1.

Theorem 14.3   Let Θ_0 be an *ineccsi* subset of a k-dimensional exponential family $\mathcal{M}$, given in a diffeomorphic parameterization $(\Theta_{\mathcal{M}}, P_\theta)$. Fix some measure q. Let, for every n, $\bar{P}^{(n)}$ be an arbitrary distribution on $\mathcal{X}^n$. Define for $\epsilon, c > 0$:

$$\check{\Theta}_{c,\epsilon}^{(n)} := \{\theta \in \Theta_0 \mid P_\theta(\mathrm{REG}(\bar{P}^{(n)}, \Theta_0, x^n) \leq \mathrm{COMP}^{(n)}(\Theta_0) - c) \geq \epsilon\}.$$

Then $V_q(\check{\Theta}_{c,\epsilon}^{(n)}) \leq \frac{2^{-c}}{\epsilon} K_{\Theta_0,q} + o(1)$, where $o(1)$ tends to 0 with increasing n, and $K_{\Theta_0,q} := \int_{\Theta_0} \sqrt{I(\theta)} d\theta \sup_{\theta \in \Theta_0} \frac{q(\theta)}{\sqrt{I(\theta)}}$ is a constant that does not depend on either n or k.

Proof: Let

$$\check{\mathcal{X}}^n := \{x^n : \text{REG}(\bar{P}^{(n)}, \Theta_0, x^n) \leq \text{COMP}(\Theta_0) - c\}. \tag{14.43}$$

By Lemma 11.1, part(a), we can choose a sequence $a_1, a_2, \ldots$ tending to 0 such that, for all n,

$$\text{REG}(\bar{P}_{n,\text{Jef}+}, \Theta_0, x^n) = \text{COMP} - a_n.$$

where $\bar{P}_{n,\text{Jef}+}$ is the modified Jeffreys' prior with prior $w_{n,\text{Jef}+}$. Also,

$$\text{REG}(\bar{P}^{(n)}, \Theta_0, x^n) - \text{REG}(\bar{P}_{n,\text{Jef}+}, \Theta_0, x^n) = \text{RED}(\bar{P}^{(n)}, \bar{P}_{n,\text{Jef}+}, x^n).$$

Taking these two equations together, we find that

$$\check{\mathcal{X}}^n = \{x^n : \text{RED}(\bar{P}^{(n)}, \bar{P}_{n,\text{Jef}+}, x^n) \leq -c - a_n\}.$$

By the no-hypercompression inequality (Chapter 3, Section 3.3), we have

$$\bar{P}_{n,\text{Jef}+}(\check{\mathcal{X}}^n) \leq 2^{-c-a_n}. \tag{14.44}$$

On the other hand, we have

$$\bar{P}_{n,\text{Jef}+}(\check{\mathcal{X}}^n) = \bar{P}_{n,\text{Jef}+}(\theta \in \check{\Theta}_{c,\epsilon}) \bar{P}_{n,\text{Jef}+}(\check{\mathcal{X}}^n \mid \theta \in \check{\Theta}_{c,\epsilon}) +$$
$$\bar{P}_{n,\text{Jef}+}(\theta \notin \check{\Theta}_{c,\epsilon}) \bar{P}_{n,\text{Jef}+}(\check{\mathcal{X}}^n \mid \theta \notin \check{\Theta}_{c,\epsilon}) \geq$$
$$\bar{P}_{n,\text{Jef}+}(\theta \in \check{\Theta}_{c,\epsilon})\epsilon, \tag{14.45}$$

where the last inequality follows by ignoring the second term and noting that the second factor in the first term is a mixture of θ, all of which satisfy $P_\theta(\check{\mathcal{X}}^n) > \epsilon$. Taking (14.44) and (14.45) together, we get

$$\bar{P}_{n,\text{Jef}+}(\theta \in \check{\Theta}_{c,\epsilon})\epsilon \leq 2^{-c-a_n} = 2^{-c} + o(1). \tag{14.46}$$

Now for $\theta \in \Theta_0$,

$$w_{n,\text{Jef}+}(\theta) = \frac{\sqrt{I(\theta)}}{\int_{\Theta_0^{[+n^{-1/4}]}} \sqrt{I(\theta)} d\theta} = \frac{\sqrt{I(\theta)}}{\int_{\Theta_0} \sqrt{I(\theta)} d\theta} + o(1),$$

so that with (14.46),

$$V_q(\check{\Theta}_{c,\epsilon}) \leq \sup_{\theta \in \check{\Theta}_{c,\epsilon}} \frac{q(\theta)}{w_{n,\mathrm{Jef}^+}(\theta)} \bar{P}_{n,\mathrm{Jef}^+}(\theta \in \check{\Theta}_{c,\epsilon}) \leq$$

$$\sup_{\theta \in \check{\Theta}_{c,\epsilon}} \frac{q(\theta) \int_{\Theta_0} \sqrt{I(\theta)} d\theta}{\sqrt{I(\theta)}} \cdot \frac{2^{-c}}{\epsilon} + o(1), \quad (14.47)$$

and the result follows. $\square$

15 *MDL Prediction and Estimation*

15.1 Introduction

As we stated in the introduction to Part III of this book, refined MDL is always based on designing a universal code $\bar{L}_{\text{top}}$ relative to some model class $\mathcal{M}$, which may be arbitrarily complex. In the previous chapter, we worked out the details of $\bar{L}_{\text{top}}$ when the goal is model selection. In that case, $\bar{L}_{\text{top}}$ should be a meta-two-part code, in which the "models" between which we want to choose are encoded explicitly. In this chapter, in Section 15.2, we first consider MDL for *prediction*. In prediction applications, $\bar{L}_{\text{top}}$ should invariably be a one-part code. In Section 15.3, we consider MDL for *point hypothesis selection*. Since we now want to choose a single distribution, we have to encode this distribution explicitly, and $\bar{L}_{\text{top}}$ will be a two-part code.

Two MDL Convergence Theorems In Section 15.2, we state and prove Theorem 15.1, which shows that the prediction quality of MDL prediction based on a universal code $\bar{L}_{\text{top}}$ is directly related to the data compression capabilities of $\bar{L}_{\text{top}}$: if $\bar{L}_{\text{top}}$ compresses data well relative to some P^*, then, if P^* happens to generate the data, we can learn it fast. Here "learning" means learning to predict future data just as well as somebody who knows that data are sampled from P^*. Theorem 15.1 is our first main connection between MDL and frequentist statistics.[1]

In Section 15.3, we state and prove Theorem 15.3, which shows that the convergence rate of two-part MDL for hypothesis selection is also directly related to the data compression capabilities of $\bar{L}_{\text{top}}$: if $\bar{L}_{\text{top}}$ compresses data well

---

1. Although one may also view the point null hypothesis testing interpretation of MDL model selection as an MDL-frequentist connection. We already established this connection in the previous chapter, Examples 14.2 and 14.6.

relative to some P^*, then, if P^* happens to generate the data, we can learn it quickly, i.e. based on a small sample only. Here "learning" means outputting a distribution which in some sense resembles the "true" P^*. Theorem 15.3 is our second main connection between MDL and frequentist statistics.

Both theorems are mainly due to A. Barron (Barron and Cover 1991; Barron 1998), and in fact, this whole chapter relies heavily on Barron's work. The theorems provide a strong justification of refined MDL: the more we can compress data coming from P^*, the faster we can learn P^*. This justification is convincing even if one does not adhere to the MDL philosophy that learning should always proceed by data compression, but instead one believes in the concept of a "true" distribution. The theorems show that if one thinks that the true distribution lies in a model class $\mathcal{M}$, then it makes a lot of sense to base learning and prediction on universal codes relative to $\mathcal{M}$.

MDL Parametric Density Estimation   Both two-part MDL hypothesis selection and MDL for prediction can be used for density estimation. For two-part MDL point hypothesis selection, this is obvious. We show in Section 15.2.1 that the predictions output by MDL for prediction can be interpreted as estimates as well. Thus, there are two different ways to do MDL density estimation. In Section 15.4 we consider the special case of *parametric density estimation* in detail: we formally define two types of MDL estimators, and we compare them to maximum likelihood (ML) estimators.

15.2   MDL for Prediction and Predictive Estimation

Let $\mathcal{M}$ be an arbitrary set of distributions, and let $\bar{P}$ be a prequential universal model relative to $\mathcal{M}$. Recall from Chapter 6, Section 6.4, Definition 6.2, that $\bar{P}(X_i \mid x^{i-1})$ is called the *predictive distribution* of X_i, given initial data x^{i-1}. In this section, we first consider a setting where the sole goal is to make predictions of future data, given previous data coming from the same source. In such a case, as the terminology already suggests, it makes eminent sense to predict future data X_i using the predictive distribution $\bar{P}(X_i \mid x^{i-1})$. If we measure prediction quality by the logarithmic loss, then this is evident (see Chapter 6, Section 6.4): since $\bar{P}$ is a universal model relative to $\mathcal{M}$, it must be the case that if *some* $P \in \mathcal{M}$ lead to good predictions of the data, then predicting based on $\bar{P}(X_i \mid x^{i-1})$ will eventually lead to predictions that are at least almost as good, or even better than those made by P. But even if we measure prediction quality by some different, user-specified loss function, basing predictions on the predictive distribution often makes sense (see Beyond log loss, page 464). This is related to the fact that, if we assume that some $P^* \in \mathcal{M}$ actually generated the data, then it turns out that the predictive distribution $\bar{P}(X_i \mid x^{i-1})$ may be viewed as an estimator of this P^*. Thus, the form of MDL discussed in this section, while primarily aimed at prediction, also leads to a notion of "prequential MDL estimation" . In the remainder of this section we first (Section 15.2.1) discuss the interpretation of prequential universal models as estimators. Then, in Section 15.2.2, we show – and this is perhaps the most important insight of Part III of this book – that such prequential MDL estimators are *necessarily* statistically consistent, thereby establishing a strong connection between MDL and traditional statistics. In Section 15.2.3 we illustrate the theory using two practical examples: nonparametric density estimation via histograms, and nonparametric regression via Gaussian processes.

Preliminaries The version of MDL we discuss in this section only works for prequential universal models, as defined in Chapter 6, Section 6.4. The reason is that its central tool is the predictive distribution $\bar{P}(X_i \mid x^{i-1})$, which is undefined for nonprequential universal models. Thus, in this section $\bar{P}$ invariably denotes a prequential universal model relative to some given set of distributions $\mathcal{M}$.

15.2.1 Prequential MDL Estimators

Prequential MDL estimators are best introduced by example:

Example 15.1 [Parametric Cases: Bayes, Bernoulli, and Gauss] Let $\bar{P}_{\text{Bayes}}$ be the Bayesian universal model relative to the Bernoulli model as in the box on page 258. As explained in the box, if $\bar{P}_{\text{Bayes}}$ is defined relative to Jeffreys' prior (Example 8.3), then the corresponding predictive distribution

$$\bar{P}_{\text{Bayes}}(X_i = 1 \mid X^{i-1}) = P_{\hat{\theta}_{1/2,1/2}}(X_i = 1) = \frac{n_1 + \frac{1}{2}}{n+1},$$

is a slight smoothing of the ML estimators $\hat{\theta}(x^n) = n_1/n$. If we imagine that X^n is sampled from some $P^* \in \mathcal{M}$, then obviously $\bar{P}_{\text{Bayes}}(X_i \mid X^{i-1})$ can be interpreted as an estimate of P^*.

Similarly, let $\mathcal{M}$ be the Gaussian model with fixed variance σ^2, as in Example 9.3, equipped with a prior on μ that is Gaussian with mean μ_0 and variance τ_0^2. As explained in the example, the Bayesian predictive distribution $\bar{P}_{\text{Bayes}}(X_i \mid X^{i-1})$ is Gaussian with mean very close to the ML estimator $\hat{\mu} = n^{-1} \sum x_i$, and variance that differs from σ^2 by a term of $O(1/n)$. Once again, if we can assume that $P^* \in \mathcal{M}$, the predictive distribution may be interpreted as an estimate of the "true" data-generating distribution P^*.

In Section 15.2.3, we consider more ambitious examples where the model $\mathcal{M}$ is infinite-dimensional and, in some sense, extremely large.

We shall call estimators derived from a prequential universal model in this way *prequential MDL estimators*. They are more commonly known as "predictive MDL estimators" in the literature, e.g. in (Barron, Rissanen, and Yu 1998).

Plug-in Prequential Codes as Estimators   The connection between the predictive distribution and parameter estimation is even more direct if the universal model $\bar{P}$ is of the plug-in rather than the Bayesian type: in Chapter 6, Section 6.4.2, and Chapter 9, page 9.4 we *defined* prequential plug-in codes $\bar{P}_{\text{plug-in}}$ as probabilistic sources for which the predictive distribution $\bar{P}_{\text{plug-in}}(X_n \mid x^{n-1})$ is equal to $P_{\hat{\theta}_a(x^{n-1})}$, where $\hat{\theta}_a$ is a (usually slightly modified) maximum likelihood estimator. Of course, there is no need to restrict ourselves to ML-type estimators: we can use any estimator we like to define prequential plug-in codes. In this chapter, we are often interested in estimators for nonparametric model classes $\mathcal{M}$ that cannot be meaningfully parameterized by a finite-dimensional Θ. For such $\mathcal{M}$, the ML estimator will often severely overfit the data and cannot be used. It is useful to introduce some new terminology for such estimators:

Definition 15.1 Let $\mathcal{P}_\mathcal{X}$ be the set of *all* distributions on $\mathcal{X}$, and let $\mathcal{M} \subset \mathcal{P}_\mathcal{X}$. We call any function $S : \bigcup_{n \geq 0} \mathcal{X}^n \rightarrow \mathcal{P}_\mathcal{X}$ an *estimator*. We call any function $S : \bigcup_{n \geq 0} \mathcal{X}^n \rightarrow \mathcal{M}$ an "in-model estimator" relative to $\mathcal{M}$.

Thus, an in-model estimator S maps each sequence x^n of each length n to a corresponding estimate $S(x^n)$, a distribution in the model class $\mathcal{M}$. This definition essentially corresponds to what in statistics is simply called an "estimator." We call it "in-model" because we also consider estimators with estimates outside $\mathcal{M}$ (see below).

Comparing to Chapter 6, Section 6.4.1, we see that under our definition, an "estimator" is just what in that section we called a *sequential probabilistic prediction strategy*. Every prediction strategy S corresponds to an estimator, although, of course, many such strategies will correspond to bad estimators.

From the developments of Chapter 6, Section 6.4.3, it is clear that every pre-diction strategy/estimator S uniquely defines a probabilistic source $\bar{P}$ on $\mathcal{X}^\infty$, with conditional probabilities given by $\bar{P}(X_i = \cdot \mid x^{i-1}):=S(x^{i-1})$. In the remainder of this chapter, we will make heavy use of this correspondence and *identify* estimators S with probabilistic sources $\bar{P}$ such that for all n, all $x^n \in \mathcal{X}^n$, $\bar{P}(X_{n+1} \mid x^n):=S(x^n)$. Just as for universal models, we use the notation $\bar{P}$ with the bar on top of P. The reason is that we may expect that "good" estimators S, when used as prediction strategies/universal codes, lead to small logarithmic loss relative to $\mathcal{M}$. Hence, if the estimator is good, then the corresponding $\bar{P}$ should be not just a probabilistic source, but a uni-versal model for $\mathcal{M}$. In the next section we formalize this intuition. It will be useful to introduce new notation for general estimators, since in general neither the $\hat{\ }$ nor the θ in "$\hat{\theta}$" are meaningful anymore. From now on, we re-fer to an estimator as $\bar{P}$, thinking of it as a probabilistic source. Whenever x^n is clear from the context, we use the following abbreviation of the estimate $\bar{P}(X_{n+1} \mid x^n)$ for the distribution of $\mathcal{X}$ based on x^n:

$$\bar{P}_{|n}:=\bar{P}(X_{n+1} \mid x^n) \tag{15.1}$$

Example 15.2 We saw in Chapter 9 that for exponential families $\mathcal{M}$, mod-ified ML estimators $\hat{\theta}_{\alpha,\mu_0}(x^n)$ define a prequential plug-in universal code $\bar{P}$ relative to $\mathcal{M}$. In our new notation, whenever x^n and the definition of the estimator $\hat{\theta}_{\alpha,\mu_0}(x^n)$ are clear from the context, we write $\bar{P}_{|n}$ rather than $P_{\hat{\theta}_{\alpha,\mu_0}(x^n)}$.

In-Model vs. Out-Model Estimators   The definition of in-model estima-tor requires that the estimated distribution $\bar{P}_{|n}$ is always an element of the model $\mathcal{M}$ under consideration. This condition is not necessarily satisfied by prequential MDL estimators that are derived from universal models that are not of the plug-in type. Specifically, if we use a Bayesian universal model, then the resulting prequential MDL estimates $\bar{P}_{|n}:= \bar{P}_{\text{Bayes}}(X_{n+1} \mid x^n)$ are *mixtures* of elements of $\mathcal{M}$. If $\mathcal{M}$ is not convex, then these mixtures will typi-cally not lie in $\mathcal{M}$ (see Chapter 6, Section 6.4.3, page 263). Nevertheless, they can be very good estimators relative to $\mathcal{M}$. We call such estimators *out-model estimators*. Summarizing, $\bar{P}$ is an *in-model estimator*, if for every n, X^n, $\bar{P}_{|n}$ lies in $\mathcal{M}$; $\bar{P}_{|n}$ is an *out-model estimator* if this is not the case.

The terms in-model and out-model estimators were introduced by Grünwald and de Rooij (2005). A similar distinction in a parametric context is made by Barron and Hengartner (1998), where in-model estimation is called "parameter estimation" and out-model estimation is called "parametric density estimation."

Beyond Log Loss Let $\bar{P}$ be a prequential universal model relative to $\mathcal{M}$. We have seen that $\bar{P}(X_i \mid x^{i-1})$ is particularly suitable for making predictions if the prediction quality is measured in terms of log loss. The fact that $\bar{P}(X_i \mid x^{i-1})$ may be thought of as an estimator of P^* based on x^{i-1} implies that it is useful to base predictions on $\bar{P}(X_i \mid x^{i-1})$ even relative to other, user-specified loss functions. More precisely, let $\mathbf{L} : \mathcal{X} \times \mathcal{A} \to \mathbb{R} \cup \{\infty\}$ be any loss function defined relative to some space of "actions" or "predictions" $\mathcal{A}$. Then, given data X^{i-1}, we can predict X_i using the decision

$$\delta(x^{i-1}) := \arg\min_{a \in \mathcal{A}} \{ E_{X_i \sim P(\cdot \mid x^{i-1})}[\mathbf{L}(X, a)] \}, \tag{15.2}$$

that is optimal in expectation relative to $P(X_i \mid x^{i-1})$. This means that we act just as we would if data were distributed according to $P(X_i \mid x^{i-1})$. The reason that this makes sense is the following: suppose we are willing to assume that the data $X_1, X_2, \ldots$ are actually sampled i.i.d. from some $P^* \in \mathcal{M}$. Since $\bar{P}_{|i-1}$ is an estimator of P^*, we expect it to converge, in some sense, to P^*. In the next section we show that this convergence will indeed take place. Therefore, as n increases, if the loss function $\mathbf{L}$ is not too ill-behaved, then we may expect the quality of the predictions based on (15.2) to converge to the quality of the optimal predictions based on P^*.

We end this subsection by a summary that further fixes our terminology:

> **Estimators and Prequential Universal Models**
> Let $\mathcal{M}$ be a set of distributions. A prequential universal model $\bar{P}$ relative to $\mathcal{M}$ uniquely defines a corresponding "estimator" relative to $\mathcal{M}$, which we also denote by $\bar{P}$. We call such an estimator a *prequential MDL estimator*. If $\bar{P}$ is universal in expectation, then the corresponding estimator is called a prequential expectation MDL estimator. If $\bar{P}$ is universal in the individual-sequence sense, the estimator is called a prequential individual-sequence MDL estimator. If, for all n, $x^n \in \mathcal{X}^n$, $\bar{P}_{|x^n} \in \mathcal{M}$, then $\bar{P}$ is an "in-model" estimator, i.e. an estimator of the type usually considered in statistics.
> Conversely, every estimator S for $\mathcal{M}$ uniquely defines a probabilistic source. Under some conditions on the estimator, this source will be a prequential universal model relative to $\mathcal{M}$.

15.2.2   Prequential MDL Estimators Are Always Consistent

In this key section we investigate the quality of prequential MDL estimators. It turns out that, because of an intrinsic relation between prequential universal codes and statistical consistency, the prequential MDL estimators are automatically consistent. Here "consistency" is defined in a nonstandard way, in terms of the so-called Césaro KL risk. Below we first introduce the chain rule of relative entropy, and explain how it gives rise to the notion of Césaro KL risk. Then, in Theorem 15.1, we prove the Césaro KL consistency of prequential MDL estimators.

The Chain Rule Revisited   Let P^* and $\bar{P}$ be two probabilistic sources. Recall from Chapter 6 that the redundancy of $\bar{P}$ over P^* on data $x^n = x_1, \ldots, x_n$ is given by the codelength difference

$$\text{RED}(\bar{P}, P^*, x^n) = -\log \bar{P}(x^n) + \log P^*(x^n).$$

For ease of exposition we shall now assume that, under P^*, the data are i.i.d. The extension of the derivation to the non-i.i.d. case is entirely straightforward. Using the familiar sequential decomposition rule for probability distributions (Chapter 2, box on page 54, (2.16)), the redundancy can be rewritten as

$$-\log \frac{\bar{P}(x^n)}{P^*(x^n)} = \sum_{i=1}^{n} \left[-\log \frac{\bar{P}(x_i | x_1, \ldots, x_{i-1})}{P^*(x_i)} \right]. \tag{15.3}$$

Here and in the remainder of the derivation we assume that for all x^n, $P^*(x^n) > 0$. The same argument can be generalized to cases with $P^*(x^n) = 0$ for some x^n, but we shall not do so here. Taking expectations over P^* on both sides, (15.3) becomes

$$D(P^{*(n)} \| \bar{P}^{(n)}) = E_{X^n \sim P^*}[\text{RED}(\bar{P}, P^*, X^n)] =$$

$$E_{X^n \sim P^*} \left[\sum_{i=1}^{n} \left[-\log \frac{\bar{P}(X_i | X_1, \ldots, X_{i-1})}{P^*(X_i)} \right] \right], \tag{15.4}$$

where $P^{*(n)}$ and $\bar{P}^{(n)}$ are the marginal distributions of P^* and $\bar{P}$, respectively, over the first n outcomes. Rewriting the right-hand side further using the linearity of expectation, this becomes something quite interesting:

$$E_{X^n \sim P^*} \left[\sum_{i=1}^{n} \left[-\log \frac{\bar{P}(X_i \mid X^{i-1})}{P^*(X_i)} \right] \right] =$$

$$\sum_{i=1}^{n} E_{X^n \sim P^*} \left[-\log \frac{\bar{P}(X_i \mid X^{i-1})}{P^*(X_i)} \right] = \sum_{i=1}^{n} E_{X^i \sim P^*} \left[-\log \frac{\bar{P}(X_i \mid X^{i-1})}{P^*(X_i)} \right] =$$

$$\sum_{i=1}^{n} E_{X^{i-1} \sim P^*} \left[E_{X_i \sim P^*} \left[-\log \frac{\bar{P}(X_i \mid X^{i-1})}{P^*(X_i)} \right] \right] =$$

$$\sum_{i=1}^{n} E_{X^{i-1} \sim P^*} \left[D(P^*_{|i-1} \| \bar{P}_{|i-1}) \right] = E_{X^n \sim P^*} \sum_{i=1}^{n} \left[D(P^{*(1)} \| \bar{P}_{|i-1}) \right], \quad (15.5)$$

where $P^*_{|i-1} = P^*(X_i = \cdot \mid X^{i-1}) = P^*(X_i = \cdot)$ is the marginal distribution under P^* of a single X_i, and $\bar{P}_{|i-1} := \bar{P}(X_i \mid X^{i-1})$ is the predictive distribution of X_i under $\bar{P}$. It can be seen that the same derivation except for the last equation still holds if data are not i.i.d. according to P^*, since in that case, of course, $P^*_{|i-1} \neq P^*(X_i = \cdot)$. Combining the general, non-i.i.d. case with (15.4), we get what is commonly referred to as the *chain rule for relative entropy*:

The Chain Rule of Relative Entropy
Let P^* and $\bar{P}$ be probabilistic sources. Then

$$D(P^{*(n)} \| \bar{P}^{(n)}) = \sum_{i=1}^{n} E_{X^{i-1} \sim P^*} \left[D(P^*_{|i-1} \| \bar{P}_{|i-1}) \right]. \qquad (15.6)$$

Césaro, Cumulative, and Standard KL Risk   Now let $\bar{P}$ be a prequential universal model for some arbitrary model class $\mathcal{M}$ and recall that $\bar{P}_{|i-1} = \bar{P}(X_i \mid X^{i-1})$ is then a prequential MDL estimator. Thus, the right-hand side of (15.6) is the sum of the expected KL divergences between the estimator $\bar{P}_{|i-1}$ and the "true" distribution P^*. This is usually called the *(standard) Kullback-Leibler (KL) risk* of the prequential MDL estimator at time i (Barron 1998). The rationale for this terminology is that in statistics, an expected discrepancy (such as KL divergence) between distributions is usually called a "risk." We call the sum over the n expected KL divergences the *cumulative*

KL risk associated with the prequential universal model $\bar{P}$, and we call the cumulative KL risk up till the nth outcome divided by n the *time-average* or *Césaro-average* KL risk, abbreviated to Césaro KL risk. We denote the standard KL risk by RISK and the Césaro KL risk by $\overline{\text{RISK}}$. The definitions are

$$\text{RISK}_n(P^*, \bar{P}) \ := \ E_{X^{n-1} \sim P^*}[D(P^*_{|n-1} \| \bar{P}_{|n-1})] \tag{15.7}$$

$$D(P^{*(n)} \| \bar{P}^{(n)}) \ = \ \sum_{i=1}^{n} \text{RISK}_i(P^*, \bar{P}) \tag{15.8}$$

$$\overline{\text{RISK}}_n(P^*, \bar{P}) \ := \ \frac{1}{n} D(P^{*(n)} \| \bar{P}^{(n)}). \tag{15.9}$$

If the ordinary risk tends to 0, this means that, in expectation, the estimator $\bar{P}_{|n}$ converges to P^*. If this happens, we call the estimator *KL consistent*. The rate at which $\bar{P}_{|n}$ tends to P^* is called the *rate of convergence* relative to P^*:

Definition 15.2 [KL Consistency, Rate of Convergence] We say that an estimator $\bar{P}$ is *KL consistent* relative to model $\mathcal{M}$ if the KL risk goes to 0 for all $P^* \in \mathcal{M}$, i.e. if $\text{RISK}_n(P^*, \bar{P}) \to 0$. For $f : \mathbb{N} \to \mathbb{R}$ a nonnegative function, we say that $\bar{P}$ converges to P^* at rate $f(n)$ in terms of KL risk if $\text{RISK}_n(P^*, \bar{P}) = \text{ORDER}(f(n))$.

It is clear that small cumulative risk relative to P^* implies some kind of convergence of the estimator $\bar{P}_{|n}$ to the estimand P^*. Unfortunately, we cannot show that small cumulative risk implies ordinary KL consistency. However, it does imply another type of consistency, which we now define:

Definition 15.3 [Césaro consistency] We say that $\bar{P}$ is *Césaro consistent* relative to model $\mathcal{M}$ if the Césaro KL risk goes to 0 for all $P^* \in \mathcal{M}$, i.e. if $\overline{\text{RISK}}_n(P^*, \bar{P}) \to 0$. In this case, let $f : \mathbb{N} \to \mathbb{R}$ be some nonnegative function. We say that $\bar{P}$ converges to P^* at rate $f(n)$ in terms of Césaro KL risk if $\overline{\text{RISK}}_n(P^*, \bar{P}) = \text{ORDER}(f(n))$.

Césaro consistency is really shorthand for "consistency in terms of the Césaro KL risk." It was introduced by Barron (1998) who called it "consistency in information." We can now formulate the *convergence theorem for prequential MDL estimators*:

Theorem 15.1 (Barron 1998) Let $\mathcal{M}$ be an arbitrary set of probabilistic sources and let $\bar{P}$ be a prequential universal model relative to $\mathcal{M}$, either in the individual-sequence or in the expected sense. Then (a) the prequential MDL estimator is Césaro consistent relative to $\mathcal{M}$. Moreover, (b), for every $P^* \in \mathcal{M}$, the rate of convergence in terms of Césaro risk of the prequential MDL estimator is given by the time-averaged expected redundancy, i.e.

$$\overline{\mathrm{RISK}}_n(P^*, \bar{P}) = n^{-1}D(P^{*(n)}\|\bar{P}^{(n)}) \to 0. \tag{15.10}$$

The proof is immediate: the equation in part (b) is just the definition (15.9)! The fact that the right-hand side converges to 0, as well as part (a), follows from the definition of expected universality, and the fact (Chapter 6, Proposition 6.1) that individual-sequence universality implies expected universality.

Theorem 15.1 expresses consistency in a rather unusual way: rather than taking the standard KL risk, a variation of a common procedure in statistics, we consider its time average. Proposition 15.1 below shows that KL consistency implies Césaro consistency. Whether the converse holds is not known, but reassuringly, as will be shown in Section 15.2.4, consistency at rate $f(n)$ in terms of Césaro KL risk implies a form of "essential" consistency in terms of standard KL risk.

Proposition 15.1 (a) If $\mathrm{RISK}_n(P^*, \bar{P}) \to 0$, then $\overline{\mathrm{RISK}}_n(P^*, \bar{P}) \to 0$.

(b) In more detail, let $f : \mathbb{R}^+ \to \mathbb{R}^+$ be a differentiable function such that $\lim_{x\to\infty} f(x) = 0$ and the derivative $f'(x) = O(x^{-\alpha})$ for some $\alpha > 1$. Let $F(x) := \int_0^x f(t)dt$. Then, if $\mathrm{RISK}_n(P^*, \bar{P}) = O(f(n))$, then $\overline{\mathrm{RISK}}_n(P^*, \bar{P}) = O((F(n) + 1)/n)$. In particular,

1. If $\mathrm{RISK}_n(P^*, \bar{P}) = O(1/n)$ then $\overline{\mathrm{RISK}}_n(P^*, \bar{P}) = O((\log n)/n)$.

2. If $\mathrm{RISK}_n(P^*, \bar{P}) = O(n^{-\gamma})$ for some $0 < \gamma < 1$, then $\overline{\mathrm{RISK}}_n(P^*, \bar{P}) = O(n^{-\gamma})$.

Part (b) of the Proposition will become useful in the next chapter, where it will be seen that relative to most models $\mathcal{M}$ that we study , the best KL risk that any universal model can achieve for all $P^* \in \mathcal{M}$ satisfies $\mathrm{RISK}_n(P^*, \bar{P}) = \mathrm{ORDER}(n^{-\gamma})$ for some $0 < \gamma \le 1$. **Proof:** (a) If $\mathrm{RISK}_n(P^*, \bar{P}) \to 0$, then for all $\epsilon > 0$, there exists n_0 such that for all $n \ge n_0$, $\mathrm{RISK}_n(P^*, \bar{P}) < \epsilon$. Then for all sufficiently large n, $\overline{\mathrm{RISK}}_n(P^*, \bar{P}) < 2\epsilon$. Since this holds for all $\epsilon > 0$, $\overline{\mathrm{RISK}}_n(P^*, \bar{P}) \to 0$.

(b) By our condition on f', we have $F(n) = \sum_{i=1}^n f(i) + O(1)$, so that $\overline{\mathrm{RISK}}_n(P^*, \bar{P}) = O(n^{-1} \sum_{i=1}^n f(i)) = O(n^{-1}(F(n)+O(1)))+O((F(n)+1)/n)$. $\square$

As the examples below show, Theorem 15.1 has interesting implications both for parametric and nonparametric $\mathcal{M}$. In a sense its implications are strongest when it is applied to huge, nonparametric models of infinite dimensionality, where overfitting is a very serious concern: the theorem then establishes a very direct connection between data compression and statistical estimation: Since for *every* statistical estimator (both in- and out-model), there is a corresponding probabilistic source (box on page 464), Theorem 15.1 really leads to the following two insights:

MDL and Traditional Statistics I

Let $\mathcal{M}$ be a set of distributions. *Every* estimator that is Césaro KL consistent relative to $\mathcal{M}$ defines a corresponding prequential universal model in the expected sense and is therefore an expectation-based MDL estimator. By Proposition 15.1 it follows that *every KL consistent estimator is a prequential expectation-based MDL estimator.*

MDL and Traditional Statistics II:
Good Compression Implies Fast Learning

Conversely, let $\bar{P}$ be a prequential universal code relative to $\mathcal{M}$. If $\bar{P}$ has expected redundancy $f(n)$ relative to P^*, then $\bar{P}$ converges to P^* at rate at least as good as $f(n)/n$, where the convergence is in terms of Césaro KL risk. Thus: *The better $\bar{P}$ compresses data from P^*, the faster the corresponding MDL estimator $\bar{P}_{|n}$ converges to P^*.*

We proceed to give three examples of prequential MDL estimators with good rates of Césaro convergence.

15.2.3   Parametric and Nonparametric Examples

Parametric Models: Césaro KL risk of $O((\log n)/n)$ Let $\mathcal{M}$ be a finite-dimensional parametric model, and let $P^* \in \mathcal{M}$. In Chapter 8, Section 8.4, we saw that, under regularity conditions which hold, for example, if $\mathcal{M}$ is an exponential family, the expected redundancy of Bayesian universal codes to continuous and strictly positive priors is given by $(k/2) \log n + O(1)$. By Theorem 15.1, this implies that the Bayesian predictive distribution converges at rate ORDER$((\log n)/n)$ in terms of Césaro risk. By (9.6) on page 260 of Chapter 9, it also implies that the prequential plug-in model equipped with a modified (luckiness) ML estimator also achieves ORDER$((\log n)/n)$.

In Chapter 11, Section 11.4.3, we discussed two conditional methods for defining "optimal" universal codes for parametric models $\mathcal{M}$ for which the ordinary NML is undefined: the conditional NML and the Liang-Barron universal codes. Recall that the Liang-Barron universal model $\bar{P}_{\text{LB}}$ is a prequential universal code that achieves the minimax conditional redundancy ((11.50), page 325). Translating (11.50) into Césaro risk by Theorem 15.1, this says that there is some (usually small) n_0 such that for all $n > n_0$, $\bar{P}_{\text{LB}}^{(n)}$ achieves

$$\min_{\bar{P}} \max_{P^* \in \mathcal{M}} E_{X_{n_0+1}, \ldots, X_n \sim P^*} \left[\frac{1}{n - n_0} \sum_{j=n_0+1}^{n} \text{RISK}_j(P^*, \bar{P}) \right],$$

where the minimum is over all distributions on $\mathcal{X}^n$. It follows that if we treat $x_1, \ldots, x_{n_0}$ as start-up data and start counting at $n_0 + 1$, then the minimax accumulated risk, and hence the minimax Césaro risk, for sequentially predicting $X_{n_0+1}, \ldots, X_n$, is achieved by predicting with $\bar{P}_{\text{LB}}$. Thus, in a sense. $\bar{P}_{\text{LB}}(X_i \mid X^{i-1})$ is the prequential estimator which, among all estimators, converges the fastest in the worst case over all $P^* \in \mathcal{M}$. From an expectation-based MDL point of view, this provides some motivation for basing universal codes on $\bar{P}_{\text{LB}}$ rather than $\bar{P}_{\text{Cnml-2}}$ – see the discussion below Example 11.12, page 326.

Nonparametric Density Estimation   Sometimes the model class $\mathcal{M}^*$ is so large that it cannot be finitely parameterized (Chapter 13). We may still try to learn a distribution from such a nonparametric $\mathcal{M}^*$ in various ways, for example by *histogram density estimation* (Rissanen, Speed, and Yu 1992) or *kernel density estimation* (Rissanen 1989). In a regression setting, nonparametric $\mathcal{M}^*$ are often modeled by *Gaussian processes* (Rasmussen and Williams 2006; Seeger 2004; Kakade, Seeger, and Foster 2006). Following the general MDL principle (page 406), the MDL strategy to approach such problems is invariably to design a universal code/model $\bar{P}_{\text{top}}$ relative to the given model class $\mathcal{M}^*$, and base all inferences on $\bar{P}_{\text{top}}$. The analysis is easiest if $\bar{P}_{\text{top}}$ is prequential, because then the fact that $\bar{P}_{\text{top}}$ is universal means by definition that for all $P \in \mathcal{M}^*$, the prequential MDL estimator $\bar{P}_{\text{top}}(X_i \mid X^{i-1})$ will eventually predict future data almost as good or even better than P.

Histogram Density Estimation   In Chapter 13, Section 13.3 we discussed three ways of designing universal codes relative to the CUP model class $\mathcal{M}$

of all regular histograms with arbitrarily many bins: the meta-Bayesian code $\bar{f}_{\text{CUP(Bayes,Bayes)}}$ (13.11), the meta-two-part code $\bar{f}_{\text{CUP(2-p,Bayes)}}$ (13.12), and the modified prequential estimator $\bar{f}_{\text{RSY}}$ (13.18). Let us first consider the consistency properties of $\bar{f}_{\text{CUP(Bayes,Bayes)}}$. If data are i.i.d. $\sim P^*$, where $P^* \in \mathcal{M}$ has a density that is a histogram with an arbitrary but finite number of bins, then, by (13.14), $\bar{f}_{\text{CUP(2-p,Bayes)}}$ and hence $\bar{f}_{\text{CUP(Bayes,Bayes)}}$ achieve expected redundancy no larger than $(k/2) \log n + O(1)$, so $\bar{f}_{\text{CUP(Bayes,Bayes)}}$ is Césaro KL consistent relative to n and converges at rate $O((\log n)/n)$, just as in the parametric case above.

As we noted in Section 13.3.1, it is more interesting to study the behavior of $\bar{f}_{\text{Bayes}}$ if $P^* \in \mathcal{M}^*$, where $\mathcal{M}^*$ is a nonparametric, "sufficiently smooth" subset of the information closure $\{P^* : \inf_{P \in \mathcal{M}} D(P^* \| P) = 0\}$ of $\mathcal{M}$. As in that section, (13.14), we take $\mathcal{M}^*$ to be the set of i.i.d. sources with densities bounded away from 0 and infinity, and with bounded first derivative. *In this case, the number of histograms $\ddot{\gamma}(x^n)$ that minimizes the meta-two-part codelength $- \ln \bar{f}_{\text{CUP(2-p,Bayes)}}(x^n)$ increases with n,* and the Bayesian prediction $\bar{P}(x_{n+1} \mid x^n, \mathcal{M}_{\ddot{\gamma}(x^n)})$ becomes an ever better approximation of P^*. We have by (13.16) that $\bar{f}_{\text{CUP(2-p,Bayes)}}$, and hence $\bar{f}_{\text{CUP(Bayes,Bayes)}}$, have expected redundancy bounded by $O(n^{1/3} (\log n)^{2/3})$. Since $\bar{f}_{\text{CUP(Bayes,Bayes)}}$ is fully Bayesian and hence prequential, by Theorem 15.1 we see that the corresponding prequential MDL estimator converges at Césaro rate $O((\log n/n)^{2/3})$.

Since $\bar{f}_{\text{CUP(2-p,Bayes)}}$ is not prequential, it does not define a prequential MDL estimator and Theorem 15.1 cannot be applied. By (13.19), the prequential estimator corresponding to $\bar{f}_{\text{RSY}}$ converges at the minimax optimal rate $O(n^{-2/3})$.

Alternative MDL Histogram Estimators Rissanen, Speed, and Yu (1992) consider two other variations of MDL histogram density estimators: one is defined as the uniform average of $\bar{f}_{\text{Bayes}}(X_{n+1} \mid x^n, \mathcal{M}_\gamma)$ for $\gamma \in \{1, \ldots, M\}$, where M is an additional parameter, to be encoded and optimized explicitly. Note that this is not the same as the fully predictive approach we described above, where the average is taken with respect to the posterior rather than uniformly. While this estimator still corresponds to a universal model relative to the model class $\mathcal{M}$, and appears to deliver very smooth-looking estimates, we do not see any advantage over taking the posterior average. The third estimator considered by Rissanen, Speed, and Yu (1992) is based on *irregular* histograms with nonequal bin widths. This estimator is quite interesting, since, even though it offers more flexibility than the ordinary histogram estimator, it is still efficiently computable. For the nontrivial details, we refer to Rissanen, Speed, and Yu (1992).

Nonparametric Regression via Gaussian Processes   As in Chapter 13, Section 13.5, let $\bar{f}_{\text{Bayes}}$ represent the Gaussian process defined with respect to the RBF kernel $\kappa(u, u') = \exp(-b\|u - u'\|)^2$. Let $\mathcal{H} = \mathcal{H}_{\kappa,1} \cup \mathcal{H}_{\kappa,2} \ldots$ be the corresponding set of functions. By the consistency Theorem 15.1, we see that the results of Kakade et al., (13.37) and (13.39), imply the following: when used as a prequential MDL estimator, using the RBF kernel and assuming the U_i are distributed such that (13.39) holds, then $\bar{f}_{\text{Bayes}}(Y_{n+1} \mid u_{n+1}, u^n, y^n)$ converges at the Césaro KL rate $O(n^{-1}(\log n)^{d+1})$. From the derivation of (13.39) in (Kakade, Seeger, and Foster 2006), it follows that the leading constant in the O-notation does not depend on the number of parameters of the f achieving the minimum in (13.37). Thus, suppose data (X_i, Y_i) are i.i.d. $\sim P^*$, where X_i is normal with mean 0 and $Y_i = h(X_i)$ for some $h \in \mathcal{H}_{\kappa,\gamma}$ for some finite γ. Even if γ is very large, the multiplicative factor in the Césaro risk does not depend on on the number of parameters (2γ) of $\mathcal{H}_\gamma$. This makes it intrinsically different from parametric estimation, where the Césaro risk has a multiplicative factor of $(\gamma/2)(\log n)/n + O(1/n)$.

15.2.4   Césaro KL consistency vs. KL consistency*

Open Problem No. 12: Does Césaro KL Consistency Imply KL Consistency?   Let $\bar{P}$ be a prequential MDL estimator relative to some $\mathcal{M}$. Since our theorem shows convergence of the Césaro KL risk $\overline{\text{RISK}}_n(P^*, \bar{P})$ rather than the standard KL risk $\text{RISK}_n(P^*, \bar{P})$, it may be that for some n and $n' > n$, the KL risk at time point n' is actually *larger* than at time n. While this is probably a rather unusual thing to happen, it is not impossible: Barron (1998) (in Section 7, "Some surprises") gives an example where for some Bayesian universal model, the KL risk at $n = 1$ is smaller than at $n = 2$.

Theorem 15.1 does not even rule out a more dramatic variation of this anomaly: it may be that, for some prequential MDL estimators, while the Césaro risk converges to 0, the standard KL risk does not converge to 0. Thus, for some $\epsilon > 0$, at infinitely many n the risk $E[D(P^{*(n)}\|\bar{P}_n)]$ is larger than ϵ. It seems unlikely this can happen at all for practically useful model classes, but it has not been proved that it is impossible. Barron (1998), in his excellent reply to the discussion following the main article, raises the question of identifying general conditions under which consistency in information provably implies that the ordinary KL risk converges to 0 as well. At the time of writing this book, this is still an interesting open question. However, Theorem 15.2, or rather its Corollary 15.1, shows that Césaro consistency implies a form of "essential" standard consistency.

Essential Consistency   We start with two definitions: an increasing sequence $n_1, n_2, \ldots$ is called *gappy* if $\sup_{m \in \mathbb{N}} \{n_{m+1} - n_m\} = \infty$. We say that an estimator $\bar{P}$ *essentially converges* to P^* at rate at least $f(n)$ if there exists a $c > 0$ and a gappy or finite sequence $n_1, n_2, \ldots$ such that for all $n \in \mathbb{N} \setminus \{n_1, n_2, \ldots\}$, $\text{RISK}_n(P^*, \bar{P}) \leq cf(n)$. This means that convergence takes place except for some "exceptional" set of points, where, as n increases, there are longer and longer periods of nonexceptional behavior.

Theorem 15.2 Let $F : \mathbb{R}^+ \to \mathbb{R}^+$ be a smooth increasing function satisfying $\lim_{x \to \infty} F(x) = \infty$, and with a derivative $f(x) = F'(x)$ that is convex and decreasing in x. If $\bar{P}$ converges to P^* at rate at least $n^{-1}F(n)$ in terms of Césaro KL risk, i.e. if $\sum_{i=1}^n \text{RISK}_i(P^*, \bar{P}) = O(F(n))$, then $\bar{P}$ essentially converges to P^* at rate at least $f(n)$ in terms of standard risk.

For $0 < \alpha < 1$, if $F(n) = n \cdot n^{-\alpha} = n^{1-\alpha}$ then $f(n) = (1 - \alpha)^{-1} n^{-\alpha}$, and if $F(n) = \ln n$, then $f(n) = 1/n$. Plugging this into Theorem 15.2, we find that

Corollary 15.1 Let $0 < \alpha < 1$. If $\bar{P}$ converges at rate $n^{-\alpha}$ to P^* in terms of Césaro KL risk, then it essentially converges at rate $n^{-\alpha}$ in terms of standard KL risk. If $\bar{P}$ converges at rate $n^{-1} \log n$ to P^* in terms of Césaro KL risk, then it essentially converges at rate n^{-1} in terms of standard KL risk.

> **Proof (of Theorem 15.2):** Fix some $c' > 0$, and let $n_1, n_2, \ldots$ be the increasing sequence of all n such that
>
> $$\text{RISK}_n(P^*, \bar{P}) > c'f(n). \tag{15.11}$$
>
> We prove the theorem by showing that there exists a finite value of c' such that the corresponding sequence $n_1, n_2, \ldots$ becomes either finite or gappy.
>
> By assumption, there exists a $c > 0$ such that for all n, $\sum_{i=1}^n \text{RISK}_i(P^*, \bar{P}) \leq cF(n)$, so that, for all $m > 0$,
>
> $$\sum_{j=1}^m c'f(n_j) < \sum_{j=1}^m \text{RISK}_{n_j}(P^*, \bar{P}) \leq cF(n_m) \leq cF(n_1) + \sum_{i=n_1+1}^{n_m} cf(i),$$
>
> where the rightmost inequality follows by convexity of f and approximating the integral F by a sum. On the other hand
>
> $$\sum_{j=1}^m c'f(n_j) \geq \sum_{j=1}^{m-1} c'f(n_j) \geq \sum_{j=1}^{m-1} \sum_{n=1+n_j}^{n_{j+1}} \frac{c'}{n_{j+1} - n_j} f(n),$$
>
> where the latter inequality follows because f is decreasing. Combining these two equations gives
>
> $$\sum_{j=1}^{m-1} \sum_{n=n_j+1}^{n_{j+1}} \frac{c'}{n_{j+1} - n_j} f(n) \leq cF(n_1) + \sum_{i=n_1+1}^{n_m} cf(i). \tag{15.12}$$

Now suppose that $n_1, n_2, \ldots$ is neither gappy nor finite. We prove the theorem by showing that this leads to a contradiction. If $n_1, n_2, \ldots$ is neither gappy nor finite, then there exists an $a > 0$ such that for all m, $n_{m+1} - n_m < a$. It follows that the left-hand side of (15.12) is at least $(c'/a) \sum_{m=n_j+1}^{n_m} f(n)$. The fact that $\lim_{n\to\infty} F(n) = \infty$ implies that $\lim_{n\to\infty} \sum_{i=1}^{n} f(i) \to \infty$. Since (15.12) holds for all m, it follows that there exists a finite $c' > 0$ such that (15.12) does not hold. Thus, for that c', the sequence $n_1, n_2, \ldots$ must be gappy.

Example 15.3 If P^* is an arbitrary element of a parametric model $\mathcal{M}$, prequential MDL estimators based on the Bayesian universal code achieve a redundancy of $(k/2)\log n + O(1)$, and therefore, by Theorem 15.1, a Césaro risk of $O(\log n/n)$. By the corollary, they essentially converge at rate $O(1/n)$. Indeed, under regularity conditions on $\mathcal{M}$, one can show (Barron 1998) that in this case the risk is bounded by a constant times $1/n$ for every n, so they actually, and not just essentially, converge at rate $O(1/n)$.

The Césaro Universal Model Theorem 15.2 indicates that convergence in terms of Césaro risk implies essential convergence in terms of ordinary risk: in a sense, a violation of the risk bound will occur ever more rarely as n increases; therefore, one may just decide to live with the fact that for ordinary prequential MDL estimators, convergence rates in terms of ordinary risk usually cannot be proved. If one is not so complacent, one may consider the possibility of *modifying* any given prequential MDL estimator $\bar{P}$ so that it is guaranteed to have standard, and not just Césaro KL risk converging to 0. It turns out that if the data are i.i.d.[2] according to the model class $\mathcal{M}$ with respect to which $\bar{P}$ is universal, then such a modification is possible. We simply replace the prequential estimators $\bar{P}_{|n-1} = \bar{P}(X_n \mid X^{n-1})$ by their *Césaro averages*: for each n, for all $x \in \mathcal{X}$, we define

$$\bar{P}_{\text{Cesaro}}(X_n = x \mid X^{n-1}) := \frac{1}{n} \sum_{i=1}^{n} \bar{P}(X_i = x \mid X^{i-1}).$$

It turns out that, if $\bar{P}$ has small Césaro risk relative to any given P^*, then $\bar{P}_{\text{Cesaro}}$ has small standard risk:

Proposition 15.2 Let P^* be an arbitrary distribution on $\mathcal{X}$, let $\bar{P}$ be a probabilistic source, and let $\bar{P}$ be the corresponding Césaro source. For all n, $\text{RISK}_n(P^*, \bar{P}_{\text{Cesaro}}) \leq \overline{\text{RISK}}_n(P^*, \bar{P})$.

---

2. This is the only place in this chapter where it is not clear whether the ideas can be extended beyond the i.i.d. setting.

Proof: Abbreviating $\bar{P}(X_i = x \mid X^{i-1})$ to $\bar{P}(x \mid X^{i-1})$, we have

$$D(P^* \| \bar{P}_{\text{Cesaro}|n-1}(X_n \mid X^{n-1})) =$$
$$E_{X_n \sim P^*}[-\log \bar{P}_{\text{Cesaro}}(X_n \mid X^{n-1}) + \log P^*(X_n)] =$$
$$\sum_x P^*(x) \left[-\log \frac{1}{n} \sum_{i=1}^{n} \bar{P}(x \mid X^{i-1}) + \log P^*(x) \right] \leq$$
$$\sum_x P^*(x) \left[-\frac{1}{n} \sum_{i=1}^{n} \log \bar{P}(x \mid X^{i-1}) + \log P^*(x) \right],$$

where the inequality is Jensen's. Note that $D(P^* \| \bar{P}_{\text{Cesaro}|n-1})$ is a *function* from $\mathcal{X}^{n-1}$ to $\mathbb{R}$. It follows that

$$\text{RISK}_n(P^*, \bar{P}_{\text{Cesaro}})$$
$$= E_{X^{n-1} \sim P^{*(n-1)}}[D(P^* \| \bar{P}_{\text{Cesaro}|n-1}(X_n \mid X^{n-1}))]$$
$$\leq E_{X^{n-1} \sim P^{*(n-1)}} \sum_x P^*(x) \left[-\frac{1}{n} \sum_{i=1}^{n} \log \bar{P}(x \mid X^{i-1}) + \log P^*(x) \right]$$
$$= E_{X^n \sim P^{*(n)}} \left[\sum_{i=1}^{n} D(P^* \| \bar{P}_{|i-1}) \right] = \frac{1}{n} \sum_{i=1}^{n} E_{X^{i-1} \sim P^{*(i-1)}}[D(P^* \| \bar{P}_{|i-1})]$$
$$\overset{(a)}{=} \frac{1}{n} D(P^{*(n)} \| \bar{P}^{(n)}) \overset{(b)}{=} \overline{\text{RISK}}_n(P^* \| \bar{P}), \tag{15.13}$$

where equality (a) is just (15.6), and equality (b) is (15.9). □

Several authors have independently introduced variations of César universal codes as well as variations of Proposition 15.2; see (Helmbold and Warmuth 1995, Section 9) and (Barron 1998; Yang and Barron 1999; Yang 2000).

César Risk, Standard KL Risk, and the César Universal Model
Let $\bar{P}$ represent a prequential MDL estimator. Convergence of $\bar{P}$ in terms of César KL risk at rate at least $n^{-\alpha}$ for $0 < \alpha < 1$ implies "essential" convergence of $\bar{P}$ at rate at least $n^{-\alpha}$ in terms of standard risk. It is not known whether, and if so, under what conditions and at what rate, it also implies true convergence of $\bar{P}$ in terms of standard risk.
If $\mathcal{M}$ is i.i.d., then the estimator/universal model $\bar{P}$ can be modified into a corresponding "César universal model" which is guaranteed to converge in terms of KL risk at at least the same rate as $\bar{P}$ converges in terms of César risk.

It is unclear whether a large temporary upward jump in risk ever occurs in practical situations. Therefore, it is unclear whether it is really useful in practice to modify an estimator into its corresponding Césaro estimator.

15.3   Two-Part Code MDL for Point Hypothesis Selection

We have already encountered two-part code MDL in Chapter 5 and in Chapter 10. In Chapter 5 we used two-part code MDL for general point hypothesis selection using ad hoc codes to encode hypotheses (singleton distributions) P. In Chapter 10 we used a two-part code for point hypothesis selection restricted to finite-dimensional exponential families. In this parametric case, "point hypothesis selection" amounted to "parameter selection." The two-part code we used in Chapter 10 was not ad hoc but rather designed such that its worst-case regret or luckiness regret is close to minimax optimal.

In this section, we let the model class $\mathcal{M}$ be an arbitrary set of i.i.d. probabilistic sources on $\mathcal{X}$. We analyze the behavior of a version of two-part code MDL relative to $\mathcal{M}$ assuming data are i.i.d. according to some distribution $P^* \in \mathcal{M}$. Since we assume throughout the analysis that such a P^* actually exists, the hypothesis selected by two-part MDL point hypothesis selection may be interpreted as an *estimator* of the unknown P^*. Therefore, we shall refer to the selected hypothesis as the *two-part MDL estimator*. Our analysis leads to Theorem 15.3, which states that, the smaller the expected redundancy of the two-part code relative to P^*, the faster the two-part MDL estimator converges to P^*. This shows that, just as for the prequential MDL estimators, the more we compress, the faster we learn, and it guides the design of "refined" two-part codes which guarantee small redundancy and therefore fast convergence.

While in most (not all) situations where two-part code MDL is of interest, $\mathcal{X} = \mathbb{R}^d$ for some d and the distributions in $\mathcal{M}$ are described by densities on $\mathcal{X}$, we still follow our usual convention, and use the same notation $P(x)$ both for density and probability mass.

For each n, we fix a countable subset $\ddot{\mathcal{M}}_{(n)}$ of $\mathcal{M}$, which we call the discretization of $\mathcal{M}$ at time n. We also fix a code for the elements of $\ddot{\mathcal{M}}_{(n)}$ with length function $\dot{L}_n$. We define the *two-part description method* relative to $\dot{L}_n$ as the description method that encodes data x^n by first encoding some $P \in \ddot{\mathcal{M}}_{(n)}$, using $\dot{L}_n(P)$ bits, and then encoding x^n using the code with lengths $-\log P(x^n)$. The shortest encoding of x^n is then given by

$$\bar{L}_{\text{2-p}}^{(n)}(x^n) = \min_{P \in \dot{\mathcal{M}}_{(n)}} \{\dot{L}_n(P) - \log P(x^n)\}. \tag{15.14}$$

Theorem 15.3 below is stated in terms of a variation of this quantity: for $\alpha \geq 1$, we define the α-*two-part codelength* to be

$$\bar{L}_{\alpha\text{2-p}}^{(n)}(x^n) = \min_{P \in \dot{\mathcal{M}}_{(n)}} \{\alpha\dot{L}_n(P) - \log P(x^n)\}. \tag{15.15}$$

Suppose that $\bar{L}_{\alpha\text{2-p}}$ is a universal code for $\mathcal{M}$. In that case we denote the P achieving the minimum in (15.15) by $\ddot{P}_n$ and call it the α-*two-part code MDL estimator* relative to code $\bar{L}_{\alpha\text{2-p}}$. If the minimum is achieved by more than one P, we take the one with smallest $\dot{L}_n(P)$. If there is still more than one such P, we have no further preference.

Example 15.4 [Examples of MDL for General Hypothesis Selection] If $\alpha = 1$, then the two-part code MDL estimator coincides with a crude two-part MDL hypothesis selector of Chapter 5, with the additional requirement that $\bar{L}_{\text{2-p}}$ be universal. The two-part code for exponential families $\mathcal{M}$ defined in Chapter 10, Section 10.1, is also a special case of the two-part code $\bar{L}_{\text{2-p}}$, with α equal to 1. It is obtained by setting $\dot{L}_n(P_\theta)$ equal to $-\log W_{(n)}(\theta)$, where $W_{(n)}(\theta)$ is the discretized prior of Section 10.1.1.

Consistency and Rate of Convergence It turns out that, essentially, the universality of $\bar{L}_{\text{2-p}}$ is sufficient to make $\ddot{P}_n$ consistent in a weak sense (Barron and Cover 1991). Such universality will typically already hold for "crudely designed" two-part codes such as those discussed in Chapter 5. We can make such codes more refined by making sure that the two-part code is a good universal model achieving small redundancy. The reason is that, just as for prequential MDL estimators, the rate-of-convergence of two-part MDL estimators relative to any distribution P^* is directly related to the expected coding redundancy that $\bar{L}_{\alpha\text{2-p}}$ achieves for data coming from P^*. Once again, *the better* $\bar{L}_{\alpha\text{2-p}}$ *compresses data coming from* P^**, the faster* $\ddot{P}_{(n)}$ *converges.* However, the argument that shows this is more involved than in the prequential MDL case, and furthermore there are two complications:

1. In order to get good rates of convergence, we need to take $\alpha > 1$. Any $\alpha > 1$ will do , but it has to be larger than 1. We discuss this issue in detail in Section 15.3.1.

2. The expected divergence between $\ddot{P}_n$ and P^*, while *bounded* by the KL divergence, is *measured* by the *(squared) Hellinger distance* and the *Rényi divergences*, both of which are defined below and discussed in detail in Section 15.3.1.

Definition 15.4 Let P_1, P_0 be two distributions on $\mathcal{X}$. The *squared Hellinger distance* is defined as

$$\text{He}^2(P_1\|P_0) = \sum_{x\in\mathcal{X}}(\sqrt{P_1(x)} - \sqrt{P_0(x)})^2. \tag{15.16}$$

Now let $\lambda > 0$. The *Rényi divergence of order* λ is defined as

$$\bar{\text{d}}_\lambda(P_1\|P_0) := -\frac{1}{1-\lambda}\ln\sum_x P_1(x)^\lambda P_0(x)^{1-\lambda}, \tag{15.17}$$

with $\bar{\text{d}}_1(P_1\|P_0) := \lim_{\lambda\uparrow 1}\bar{\text{d}}_\lambda(P_1\|P_0)$.

We are now ready to present the two-part MDL consistency/rate-of-convergence theorem:

Theorem 15.3 Let $\alpha > 1$. Consider an arbitrary set of i.i.d. sources $\mathcal{M}$, and an arbitrary prefix code with length function $\dot{L}_n$ on a subset of $\mathcal{M}$. Let $\ddot{P}_n$ be the α-two-part MDL estimator achieving (15.15). Let $\bar{P}^{(n)}_{\alpha 2\text{-p}}$ be the distribution corresponding to the code $\bar{L}^{(n)}_{\alpha 2\text{-p}}$, i.e. $-\log \bar{P}^{(n)}_{\alpha 2\text{-p}}(X^n) = \bar{L}^{(n)}_{\alpha 2\text{-p}}(X^n)$. Then for all λ with $0 < \lambda \le 1 - 1/\alpha$, we have

$$E_{X^n\sim P^*}[\bar{\text{d}}_\lambda(P^*\|\ddot{P}_n)] \le \frac{1}{n}\text{D}(P^{*(n)}\|\bar{P}^{(n)}_{\alpha 2\text{-p}}). \tag{15.18}$$

If we choose $\alpha = 2$, then also

$$E_{X^n\sim P^*}[\text{He}^2(P^*, \ddot{P}_n)] \le \frac{1}{n}\text{D}(P^{*(n)}\|\bar{P}^{(n)}_{\alpha 2\text{-p}}). \tag{15.19}$$

Note that D refers to KL divergence expressed in nats rather than bits (Chapter 4). The proof of this theorem is in Appendix 15.A. It is a minor extension of theorems due to A. Barron, J. Li, and T. Zhang; at the end of the section we discuss its history in more detail.

15.3.1 Discussion of Two-Part Consistency Theorem

Theorem 15.1 bounds the expected divergence between the α-two-part MDL estimator and the "true" P^*. While the bound is itself in terms of the KL divergence between P^* and the α-two-part MDL universal model $\bar{P}_{\alpha2\text{-p}}$, the quantity being bounded is either any expected $\bar{d}_\lambda$ divergence for λ with $0 < \lambda \leq 1 - 1/\alpha$, (15.18), or the expected squared Hellinger distance, (15.19).

Let us compare this to Theorem 15.1, (15.10), which expresses the analogous result for prequential MDL estimators $\bar{P}$. On the left of (15.10) we see the Césaro KL risk, which is just the expected time-averaged KL divergence between P^* and $\bar{P}$. In Theorem 15.3 this is replaced by the expected $\bar{d}_\lambda$ divergence. The right-hand side of both equations is identical. Thus, the quantity bounded in Theorem 15.3 is, in one sense, more natural than in Theorem 15.1, since it does not involve a time average; but in another sense it is less natural, since it involves a notion of divergence which is not as directly related to compression as the KL divergence.

We now discuss the theorem in more detail by first discussing the quantities on the left of equations (15.19) and (15.18): Hellinger and $\bar{d}_\lambda$ divergences. We then discuss the meaning of the KL divergence on the right-hand side. But we start with the mysterious α-factor in the definition of two-part MDL.

1. Comparison to Theorem 5.1 of Chapter 5. In Chapter 5 we already gave a two-part MDL consistency theorem. How does that theorem relate to Theorem 15.3? There are two crucial differences: first of all, Theorem 5.1 gave no rates of convergence. Second, Theorem 5.1 only proved consistency if data were distributed by some $P^* \in \mathcal{M}$ such that, for all large n, $\dot{L}_n(P^*) < \infty$. These are P^* that can be encoded precisely, and there can only be countably many of those. In contrast, the present theorem shows that for *all* P^* in the much larger, uncountable set $\mathcal{M}$, consistency and good rates of convergence can be achieved. This is possible because, for all $\epsilon > 0$, we have for all large n, $\dot{L}_n(P) < \infty$ for some P with $\mathrm{d}(P^*\|P) < \epsilon$: we can approximate each P^* arbitrarily well by P that do have a finite codelength.

2. The α-factor. We note that for $\alpha = 1$, a weak form of consistency still holds (Zhang 2004b), but in general, good convergence rates such as in Theorem 15.3 cannot be achieved anymore.

The α-factor arises naturally when trying to prove convergence of two-part MDL. From the proof of Theorem 15.3 this may not be so clear. But it can be clearly seen from the proof of an earlier, weaker version of Theorem 15.3, which was given by Barron and Cover (1991), the paper in which the α-factor was introduced. Thus, from a frequentist point of view (proving convergence), $\alpha > 1$ is natural. From a purely coding-theoretic point of view, picking $\alpha > 1$ still has a clear interpretation, but why it should be necessary to get good results is not directly clear. This coding interpretation of α follows if we suppose that we use a code $\dot{L}_n$ for $\ddot{\mathcal{M}}_{(n)}$ such that, for some $\alpha > 1$,

$$\sum_{P \in \ddot{\mathcal{M}}_{(n)}} 2^{-\frac{\dot{L}_n(P)}{\alpha}} < \infty. \tag{15.20}$$

Then there exists a $c \in \mathbb{R}$ and an idealized code $\dot{L}'_n$ such that for all $P \in \ddot{\mathcal{M}}_{(n)}$, $\dot{L}'_n(P) = \alpha^{-1}\dot{L}_n(P) + c$. This means that applying the α-two-part code MDL with code $\dot{L}'_n$ for the hypotheses is equivalent to applying ordinary two-part code MDL with code $\dot{L}_n$. Thus, if we use a code $\dot{L}_n$ satisfying (15.20), then the α-correction is not necessary. This means that the $\alpha > 1$ requirement may also be seen as a requirement on $\dot{L}_n$ to have "light tails." For example, if $\ddot{\mathcal{M}}_n = \{P_1, P_2, \ldots\}$ and $\dot{L}_n(P_i) = L_{\mathbb{N}}(i)$, where $L_{\mathbb{N}}$ is the universal code for the integers, then the corresponding prior distribution $W_{(n)}(i) = 2^{-\dot{L}_n(i)}$ decays so slowly with i that the restriction is violated. But if $W(i) = i^{-1}(i + i)^{-1}$, then $\sum_i \pi(i)^{\alpha^{-1}} < \infty$ as long as $\alpha < 2$, and Theorem 15.3 applies to ordinary two-part code MDL with the code $\dot{L}_n = -\ln W_{(n)}$, as long as $\lambda < 1/2$.

3. Hellinger distance on the left. Good things about the Hellinger distance are (a) it is well known among statisticians, (b) it is often considered in statistical convergence proofs, and (c) in its nonsquared form $\mathrm{He}(P, Q)$ $:= (\mathrm{He}^2(P, Q))^{1/2}$, it defines a real distance: it is nonnegative, it is 0 only if $P = Q$, and it satisfies the triangle inequality. The disadvantage of the Hellinger distance is that it has no direct information-theoretic interpretation. In fact, the proof of Theorem 15.3 only makes use of Rényi divergences, which do have an information-theoretic interpretation – the proof can be extended to the Hellinger distance simply because, by a straightforward calculation (see Chapter 19, Section 19.6, (19.41)), we have for all P, Q that

$$\mathrm{He}^2(P, Q) \le \bar{\mathrm{d}}_{1/2}(P\|Q).$$

Together with (15.21) and (15.22), this implies that for any P, Q,

$$\mathrm{He}^2(P, Q) \le \mathrm{D}(P\|Q).$$

The inequality is usually strict, so that (15.19) cannot be used to bound the expected KL divergence. For more on the Hellinger distance and how it relates to other distances between probability distributions, we refer to (Gibbs and Su 2002; Haussler and Opper 1997); see also the box on page 518.

4. Rényi divergence on the left. The Rényi divergences are also known as I-divergences. They were introduced by Rényi (1960); see also (Haussler and Opper 1997). Since Rényi divergences are more fundamentally involved in the analysis of two-part MDL, we discuss them in more detail here. In Section 19.6 of Chapter 19 we extensively discuss their various connections to exponential family theory.

It is straightforward to show that for all $\lambda \in (0,1)$, $\bar{d}_\lambda(P_1, P_0) \geq 0$, where the latter inequality becomes an equality iff $P_1 = P_0$; thus, just like the Kullback-Leibler divergences, the Rényi divergences behave as "something like a distance," which justifies the term "divergence." Indeed, it turns out that for $\lambda = 1$, the Rényi divergence is just the KL divergence: for all P_1, P_2, we have

$$D(P_1\|P_2) = \lim_{\lambda \uparrow 1} \bar{d}_\lambda(P_1\|P_2). \tag{15.21}$$

In fact, for all $0 < \lambda < \lambda' \leq 1$, all P, P', we have

$$\bar{d}_\lambda(P\|P') \leq \bar{d}_{\lambda'}(P\|P'), \tag{15.22}$$

so that KL divergence upper-bounds Rényi divergences. This is proved in Section 19.6 of Chapter 19. Since in Theorem 15.3, $\lambda = 1$ implies $\alpha = \infty$, (15.18) cannot be used to bound the expected KL divergence. Indeed, the expected KL divergence of $\ddot{P}_n$ need not converge to 0. This is illustrated in the example below. Therefore, a general analogue of Theorem 15.3 for KL divergence cannot exist.

Example 15.5 [Nonconvergence of Expected KL Divergence] Consider the Bernoulli model and a two-part code based on a discretization of $\Theta = [0,1]$ that includes boundary values: for example, $\ddot{\mathcal{M}}_{(n)} = \{P_0, P_{0.1}, \ldots, P_{0.9}, P_1\}$. Let $\dot{L}_n$ be a uniform code on $\ddot{\mathcal{M}}_{(n)}$. Suppose the data are i.i.d. according to some P_{θ^*}, $\theta^* \in (0,1)$. Then with small but nonzero probability, the first n outcomes are only 0s. In that case, $\ddot{P}_n$ will be equal to P_θ with $\theta = 0$, so that $D(P_{\theta^*}\|\ddot{P}_n) = \infty$. Therefore, the P_{θ^*}- expected KL divergence between P_{θ^*} and $\ddot{P}_n$ must also be infinity.

This example notwithstanding, in some special cases, convergence of expected KL divergence does take place. Namely, if there exist $c, c' > 0$ such that for all $P \in \mathcal{M}$, $c < P(x) < c'$ for all $x \in \mathcal{X}$, then the above problem does not occur. This will often be the case if $\mathcal{X}$ is a compact continuous-valued set such as $\mathcal{X} = [0,1]$, and then, by our notational conventions $c < P(x) < c'$ really means that $c < f(x) < c'$, where f is the density of P. In that case, the

KL divergence is bounded from above by a constant $C_{c,c'}$ times the squared Hellinger distance, and convergence in Hellinger distance implies convergence in KL divergence, as explained in the box on page 518. For example, in the histogram density estimation setting, Chapter 13, Section 13.3, one may consider the set of distributions $\mathcal{M}^*$ on $\mathcal{X} = [0, 1]$ with densities bounded away from 0, as given by (13.14). In that setting, for $\alpha > 1$, any α-two-part MDL estimator must also converge in expected KL divergence, and the convergence will be bounded by the same rate as the convergence in terms of squared Hellinger distance.

5. KL divergence on the right.   Analogously to Theorem 15.1, the quantity on the right-hand sides of Theorem 15.3 is the Kullback-Leibler divergence between the true distribution, extended to n outcomes, and the universal code on which the inference is based, in this case the defective distribution $\bar{P}_{\alpha 2\text{-p}}$ corresponding to $\bar{L}_{\alpha 2\text{-p}}$. This is equal to the *expected redundancy* between P^* and $\bar{P}_{\alpha 2\text{-p}}$, which is bounded in terms of the individual sequence redundancy. Thus, we get the following analogue of the box on page 469:

MDL and Traditional Statistics III:
Good Compression Implies Fast Learning, Also for Two-Part Code MDL
The better $\bar{P}_{\alpha 2\text{-p}}$ compresses data from P^*, the faster the corresponding two-part MDL estimator $\ddot{P}_n$ converges to P^*.

Example 15.6 In Theorem 10.1, Chapter 10, Section 10.1, we showed that for k-dimensional exponential families $\mathcal{M}$, the individual-sequence regret is equal to $(k/2) \log n + O(1)$, as long as the sequence $x_1, x_2, \ldots$ is ineccsi and the prior w is $\mathcal{M}$-compatible. This suggests that for all $P^* \in \mathcal{M}$, the P^*-expected redundancy of the corresponding universal α-two-part code is also equal to $(k/2) \log n + O(1)$. This can indeed be shown to be true; see (Barron and Cover 1991). As a result, Theorem 15.3 says that the Hellinger distance between $\ddot{P}_n$, which in the notation of Section 10.1 would be written as $P_{\ddot{\theta}(x^n)}$, converges at a rate at least $\log n / n$. The result can be generalized beyond exponential families: Barron and Cover (1991) show that a rate $\log n / n$ can be achieved for a wide variety of finite-dimensional parametric families. The log-factor is not included in the optimal rate-of-convergence of, for example, the ML estimator; see Example 16.3. Indeed, Zhang (2004b) presents a (difficult) refinement of Theorem 15.3 which shows that α-two-part code MDL in fact achieves a rate of $O(1/n)$ rather than $O(\log n/n)$.

Note that Theorem 15.1 also gives a rate $\log n/n$, but in terms of the time-average risk, and Theorem 15.2 shows that this implies an essential rate of $1/n$ in terms of standard KL risk.

> **Historical Note** The results in this section are based on (Barron and Cover 1991; Li 1999) and (Zhang 2004b). The ground-breaking (Barron and Cover 1991) introduced the *index of resolvability* (a variation of the expected redundancy which we do not consider further in this book), and provided a convergence proof of two-part MDL in terms of it. It seems that this was also the first paper that considered α-two-part MDL for $\alpha > 1$. The original theorem (Theorem 4 of (Barron and Cover 1991)) states convergence in probability rather than expectation, and has a much more complicated proof than the proof of Theorem 15.3 provided in the appendix. Theorem 15.3 is a minor strengthening of an unpublished theorem shown to me by A. Barron when I first met him at Stanford University in 1999. Barron's version bounds the expected Rényi divergences in terms of the *index of resolvability* rather than the expected redundancy. The index of resolvability, introduced by Barron and Cover (1991), is an upper bound on expected redundancy that is sometimes easier to analyze than the redundancy itself. Barron never published his theorem, but a simplified version (for $\lambda = 1/2$) can be found as Theorem 5.5, page 78, in the Ph.D. thesis of his former student J. Li (1999). Essentially the same theorem, with a similar proof, was later published by Zhang (2004b). Zhang (2004b) also discovered various improvements of the theorem, including the fact that the $\log n$-factor in the rate of convergence for parametric models is not needed.

15.4   MDL Parameter Estimation

In this section, we study prequential and two-part MDL estimation for the special case of parametric models $\mathcal{M} = \{P_\theta \mid \theta \in \Theta\}$. In the more general, nonparametric case, there is a large variety in the codes we can use for the distributions $P \in \mathcal{M}$. Many different codes will lead to good rates in the convergence Theorems 15.1 and 15.3, and we can give no general prescription for designing such codes. But in the simple, parametric case, we can assume that the person who wants to do estimation can provide us with a luckiness function $a(\theta)$ (see Chapter 11, Section 11.3). Once such a luckiness function is specified, there is essentially only one correct code on which to base either prequential or two-part individual-sequence MDL estimators. This allows us to give formal definitions of these estimators below. We note that the luckiness function is a relatively new concept in MDL theory, and therefore our definitions differ somewhat from earlier, more restricted definitions of "parametric MDL estimation" as given by Rissanen and others. The following definitions should be viewed as tentative rather than definitive. We first treat the prequential, and then the two-part case. Whenever we write MDL in the remainder of this section, we refer to individual-sequence MDL. Whenever we write prediction, we refer to prediction with respect to the log loss. For convenience, we work with natural logarithms in this section.

Prequential Parametric MDL Estimation   The central goal in all applications of individual-sequence MDL is to compress data as much as possible relative to a model $\mathcal{M}$, either in a minimax regret sense or in a minimax "luckiness-adjusted" regret sense, see Chapter 11, Section 11.3, page 311. If $\mathcal{M} = \{P_\theta \mid \theta \in \Theta\}$ is parametric, then we can formalize the idea of luckiness regret by a luckiness function $a(\theta)$. Recall from Section 11.3, page 311 that the luckiness-adjusted regret for a universal model $\bar{P}$ is then defined as

$$\mathrm{LREG}_a(\bar{P}, \Theta, x^n) := -\ln \bar{P}(x^n) - \inf_{\theta \in \Theta} \left\{ -\ln P_{\theta(x^n)}(x^n) + a(\theta) \right\} =$$
$$-\ln \bar{P}(x^n) + \ln P_{\hat{\theta}_a(x^n)}(x^n) - a(\hat{\theta}(a)), \quad (15.23)$$

where $\hat{\theta}_a$ is the luckiness ML (LML) estimator (page 311), defined as

$$\hat{\theta}_a := \arg \min_{\theta \in \Theta} \left\{ -\ln P_\theta(x^n) + a(\theta) \right\}. \quad (15.24)$$

If a uniform luckiness function is used, this is just the ordinary ML estimator.

Henceforth we assume that $a(\theta)$ is such that the minimax luckiness-adjusted regret is finite. We simply require the statistician to supply us with a luckiness function for which it is. Then the LNML-2 universal model $\bar{P}_{\text{Lnml-2}}$ is well defined and achieves the minimax luckiness-adjusted regret. In order to design a prequential MDL estimator, we need a prequential universal model, but unfortunately, $\bar{P}_{\text{Lnml-2}}$ is not prequential in general. By the arguments of Section 11.3.1, in particular Theorem 11.2, the best (in the sense that it asymptotically achieves the same regret on all ineccsi sequences) prequential approximation of $\bar{P}_{\text{Lnml-2}}$ is given by the Bayesian universal model $\bar{P}_{\text{lucky-Jeffreys}}$ based on the "luckiness-tilted" Jeffreys' prior, defined as

$$w_{\text{lucky-Jeffreys}}(\theta) := \frac{\sqrt{\det I(\theta)}e^{-a(\theta)}}{\int_\Theta \sqrt{\det I(\theta)}e^{-a(\theta)}d\theta}. \quad (15.25)$$

Thus, it makes eminent sense to define the prequential MDL estimator relative to parametric model $\mathcal{M}$ and luckiness function $a(\theta)$ as the prequential estimator corresponding to the universal code $\bar{P}_{\text{lucky-Jeffreys}}$, i.e. it is given by

$$\bar{P}_{\text{lucky-Jeffreys}}(X_{i+1} \mid X^i). \tag{15.26}$$

In general, this will be an out-model estimator. It can also be shown to be reparameterization invariant, i.e. it is not affected by 1-to-1 continuous transformations of the parameter space.

> **Uniform Luckiness** If we have no inherent preference for any region in the parameter space, we may be tempted to use the uniform luckiness function. The corresponding $\bar{P}_{\text{Lnml-2}}$ is just the standard NML distribution $\bar{P}_{\text{nml}}$, and will often be undefined. However, if n is large enough, we can often still use such a uniform luckiness function, since the *conditional* NML model $\bar{P}_{\text{Cnml-2}}(X_{m+1} \mid x^m)$ will be well defined even for the uniform luckiness function, if m is large enough. In that case, the prequential MDL estimator $\bar{P}_{\text{lucky-Jeffreys}}(X_{n+1} \mid x^n)$ is well defined for all $n \geq m$, see Section 11.4. Thus, in practice, we can often work with the uniform luckiness function after all.

Two-Part Parametric MDL Estimation The two-part story closely mirrors the prequential one. We now want to base our estimator on a two-part code that achieves small luckiness-adjusted regret in the worst-case over all sequences. Thus, rather than the best prequential approximation of $\bar{P}_{\text{Lnml-2}}$, we now look for the best two-part code approximation of $\bar{P}_{\text{Lnml-2}}$, using a two-part code of the form (15.14). Since two-part codes are not required to be prequential, the code we use can depend on the sample size n. Therefore, the best two-part code approximation of $\bar{P}_{\text{Lnml-2}}$ is just the two-part code that, among all two-part codes, achieves minimax luckiness-adjusted regret. Thus, for each n, we are looking for the code $\bar{L}_{\text{2-p, opt}}^{(n)}$ on $\mathcal{X}^n$ which achieves

$$\min_{\bar{L}_{\text{2-p}}} \sup_{x^n \in \mathcal{X}^n} \left\{ \bar{L}_{\text{2-p}}^{(n)}(x^n) + \ln P_{\hat{\theta}_a(x^n)}(x^n) \right\} =$$

$$\min_{\bar{L}_{\text{2-p}}} \sup_{x^n \in \mathcal{X}^n} \left\{ \bar{L}_{\text{2-p}}^{(n)}(x^n) + \ln \bar{P}_{\text{Lnml-2}}^{(n)}(x^n) \right\}. \tag{15.27}$$

where the minimum is over all two-part codes on $\mathcal{X}^n$ of form (15.14). The leftmost expression is just the defining formula (11.19) for the LNML-2 code, but now the set of codes over which the minimum is taken is restricted to two-part codes. If more than one two-part code achieves (15.27), we need some way to resolve ties; any such way will do. Note that the $\bar{L}_{\text{2-p, opt}}^{(n)}$ achieving (15.27) implicitly defines an optimal discretization grid $\ddot{\Theta}_{\text{opt},n}$, an optimal first-stage code $\dot{L}_{\text{opt},n}$ for encoding $\theta \in \ddot{\Theta}_{\text{opt},n}$, and a corresponding two-part estimator $\ddot{\theta} : \mathcal{X}^n \to \Theta$, which maps x^n to the $\theta \in \ddot{\Theta}_{\text{opt},n}$ used to encode x^n:

$$\ddot{\theta}_{\text{opt}}(x^n) := \arg \min_{\theta \in \ddot{\Theta}_{\text{opt},n}} \{ \dot{L}_n(\theta) - \ln P_\theta(x^n) \}. \tag{15.28}$$

We define $\ddot{\theta}(\cdot)_{\text{opt}}$, viewed as a function on $\mathcal{X}^*$, as the *parametric two-part MDL estimator*. Just like the prequential MDL estimator, the two-part parametric estimator does not depend on the chosen parameterization. It may, however, be exceedingly hard to compute. Therefore, in practical applications, we should settle for a feasible approximation of it.

Approximating the Two-Part MDL Estimator Let us first consider an approximation that works well for large samples. For simplicity, we now assume that Θ represents a k-dimensional exponential family. For any two-part code $\bar{L}_{\text{2-p}}$ (not just the minimax optimal one), we can rewrite (15.14) as

$$\bar{L}_{\text{2-p}}(x^n) = \min_{\ddot{\theta} \in \ddot{\Theta}_n} \{ -\ln W_n(\ddot{\theta}) - \ln P_{\ddot{\theta}}(x^n) \}, \tag{15.29}$$

where $\ddot{\Theta}_n$ is a discretization of Θ that depends on n, and W_n is the distribution on $\ddot{\Theta}_n$ that corresponds to $\dot{L}_n$. Now let W be an arbitrary Θ-compatible prior, and let $\bar{P}_{\text{Bayes}}$ be the corresponding Bayesian universal code. By Theorem 10.1 on page 272, there exists a two-part code $\bar{L}_{\text{2-p}}$ that, uniformly on all ineccsi sequences x^n, achieves codelengths within just a few bits of $-\ln \bar{P}_{\text{Bayes}}(x^n)$. From the proof of Theorem 10.1 ((10.17), page 280), we see that for this two-part code, W_n is a discretization of the prior W with density w that satisfies, for large n, for $\ddot{\theta} \in \ddot{\Theta}$,

$$W_n(\ddot{\theta}) \propto \frac{w(\ddot{\theta})}{\sqrt{\det I(\ddot{\theta})}} \left(n^{-k/2} \right), \tag{15.30}$$

where we ignore $(1 + o(1))$-factors. The Bayesian universal code $\bar{P}_{\text{lucky-Jeffreys}}$ based on the luckiness-tilted Jeffreys' prior (15.25) asymptotically achieves the minimax luckiness-adjusted regret (15.23). Therefore, a good strategy to approximate the two-part code $\bar{L}_{\text{2-p, opt}}$ is to use the construction of Theorem 10.1 to design a two-part code such that its minimax regret is within a few bits of $\bar{P}_{\text{lucky-Jeffreys}}$. This means that the prior density w of (15.30) now becomes equal to the luckiness-tilted Jeffreys prior (15.25): $w = w_{\text{lucky-Jeffreys}}$. The precise definition of the corresponding $\ddot{\Theta}_n$ and W_n is now given by (10.11) and (10.14), in the proof of Theorem 10.1. For each x^n, the resulting two-part code is based on using a particular $\ddot{\theta}_a(x^n)$, achieving the minimum in (15.29). This $\ddot{\theta}_a$ will be good approximation of $\ddot{\theta}_{\text{opt}}$, in the sense that the two-part code $\bar{L}_{\text{2-p}}$ on which $\ddot{\theta}_a$ is based and the two-part code $\bar{L}_{\text{2-p, opt}}$ on which $\ddot{\theta}_{\text{opt}}$ both satisfy, uniformly for all ineccsi sequences $x_1, x_2, \ldots,$

$$0 \le \bar{L}_{\text{2-p}}^{(n)}(x^n) - [-\ln \bar{P}_{\text{Lnml-2}}^{(n)}(x^n)] \le g(k) + o(1),$$

$$0 \le \bar{L}_{\text{2-p, opt}}^{(n)}(x^n) - [-\ln \bar{P}_{\text{Lnml-2}}^{(n)}(x^n)] \le g(k) + o(1), \tag{15.31}$$

where $g(k)$ is the bounded function mentioned in Theorem 10.1. If we construct $\bar{L}_{\text{2-p}}$ using the discretization mentioned in the proof of the second part of Theorem 10.1, page 281, then it even seems likely that $|\bar{L}_{\text{2-p}}^{(n)}(x^n) - \bar{L}_{\text{2-p, opt}}^{(n)}(x^n)| = o(1)$, although we have no formal proof that this is the case. (15.31) shows that for large samples, $\ddot{\theta}_a$ is a very good approximation of $\ddot{\theta}_{\text{opt}}$. Since $\ddot{\theta}_a$ is based on a parameter precision (density of grid points in $\ddot{\Theta}$) that is only optimal for large n, it is not clear whether it is also a good approximation for small samples. As written at the end of Section 10.1.3, page 284, for small n, one may perhaps obtain smaller codelengths (and therefore, according to the MDL philosophy, better estimators than $\ddot{\theta}_a$), by explicitly encoding a precision d as an additional parameter, and then choosing the d minimizing the total description length of x^n.

We give more intuition about the two-part parametric MDL estimator in the next subsection, where we compare it to the LML estimator.

15.4.1 Parametric MDL Estimators vs. (Luckiness) ML Estimators

Let $\hat{\theta}_a$ be the LML estimator as in (15.24). $P_{\hat{\theta}_a(x^n)}$ is the distribution in $\mathcal{M}$ which achieves the minimum luckiness-adjusted codelength *with hindsight*, after seeing the data. Since, for $i = 0, 1, \ldots, n - 1$, the parametric prequential MDL estimator $\bar{P}_{\text{lucky-Jeffreys}}(\cdot \mid x^i)$ is used to predict X_{i+1} without knowledge of x^n, it is clear that it should not be equal to $P_{\hat{\theta}_a(x^i)}$: in general, that would lead to suboptimal predictions. Similarly, since the parametric two-part MDL estimator has to be decoded as the first stage of a code by a decoder who has no knowledge of x^n, encoding $\hat{\theta}_a(x^n)$ rather than $\ddot{\theta}_{\text{opt}}(x^n)$ in the first stage will in general be suboptimal. Thus, both types of parametric MDL estimators are inherently different from the luckiness ML estimator and its special case, the standard ML estimator. Whereas the luckiness ML estimator for a sequence x^n is optimal *with hindsight*, the parametric MDL estimators define (almost) minimax optimal prediction and coding algorithms that do not have the benefit of hindsight.

Nevertheless, there is a close relation between the two-part code MDL and the LML estimator. This can best be explained if instead of $\ddot{\theta}_{\text{opt}}$, we consider its asymptotic approximation $\ddot{\theta}_a$. From (15.30) and (15.25), we see that $\ddot{\theta}_a$ is based on a discretized prior W_n satisfying, for large n,

$$W_n(\ddot{\theta}) \propto \frac{e^{-a(\ddot{\theta})}\sqrt{\det I(\ddot{\theta})}}{\sqrt{\det I(\ddot{\theta})}}\left(n^{-k/2}\right) = e^{-a(\ddot{\theta})}\left(n^{-k/2}\right). \tag{15.32}$$

Thus, the Fisher factors cancel, and since the grid $\ddot{\Theta}_n$ becomes dense for large n, we see from (15.29) that, for large n, $\ddot{\theta}_a$ is really just a discretized version of $\hat{\theta}_a$, without any further modification or adjustment.

Parametric MDL Estimators vs. ML Estimators

Both types of parametric MDL estimators are inherently *different* from the luckiness ML estimator and its special case, the standard ML estimator. It is true though that, if Θ represents an exponential family in a diffeomorphic parameterization, then, for each continuous strictly positive luckiness function $a(\theta)$, for all ineccsi sequences,

1. The parametric two-part, parametric prequential and luckiness ML estimators all asymptotically converge to the ordinary ML estimator, the KL divergence between any two of these being of order $O(n^{-2})$.

2. The parametric two-part MDL estimator (at least its approximate version $\ddot{\theta}_a$) and the luckiness ML estimator are even "closer" in that the first may be viewed as a discretized luckiness ML estimator on an asymptotically dense grid; thus, the luckiness ML estimator is the "continuum limit" of the two-part estimator.

It has sometimes been implicitly suggested (Rissanen 1987; Hansen and Yu 2001) that, for parametric models, MDL estimators are identical to ML estimators. Taken literally, this is wrong. What is true is that, with a uniform luckiness function, the ML estimator is the "continuum limit" of the two-part estimator.

Why the LML Estimator Should Not Be Used   Since neither the LML estimator nor its special case, the ML estimator, have a clear coding interpretation, according to MDL they should *not* be used as estimators.

This point is often disputed. It is sometimes argued that two-part code MDL estimators are inherently inferior to ML estimators, because they are based on a discretization of the data.[3] The argument is as follows:

1. Because the two-part estimator involves a discretization, it is not "continuous," which seems inherently wrong.

2. Because of this discretization, the two-part estimator is not based on all the information in the data. Some information is lost in the discretization procedure. Again, this seems wrong.

3. The optimal two-part estimator $\ddot{\Theta}_{opt}$ is infeasible to compute. In practice we try to approximate it, but then we invariably end up with an estimator such as $\ddot{\theta}_a$ based on a particular discretization grid $\ddot{\Theta}_n$ the choice of which is somewhat *arbitrary*: if we were to shift it relative to the origin of Θ, nothing would change in our analysis. Indeed, for small sample sizes, $\ddot{\theta}_a$ is slightly dependent on the chosen parameterization.

In contrast, at least for exponential families, both the ordinary ML and the LML estimators (1) are a continuous function of a sufficient statistic of the data; (2) do not discard any information; and (3) involve no arbitrary discretization. Therefore, even though the (L)ML estimator has no coding-theoretic interpretation, it must be a better estimator than (approximations of) the two-part MDL estimator.

These are valid concerns. However, they are all overridden by the following fact: *even for parametric models, for small samples, the (L)ML estimator overfits, whereas the two-part MDL estimator does not.* We argued this extensively in Chapter 5 (see, e.g., page 147) in the context of Markov chain learning based on two-part MDL vs. ordinary ML. It is also substantiated by empirical evidence, for example, concerning the EM algorithm (see below). We note that the argument given in Chapter 5 on page 147 crucially depends on the assumption that, for small samples, two-part MDL will tend to select a $\ddot{\theta}$ with very coarse precision, i.e. effectively taken from a very small set. It is not clear whether this happens if we use the approximate estimator $\ddot{\theta}_a$, whose parameter precision depends on n in a fixed manner and is only optimal asymptotically. It may be that, to have practical two-part MDL really behaving better than ML on small samples, we need to approximate $\ddot{\theta}_{opt}$ by an estimator based on a two-part code in which the parameter precision is

---

3. I have heard this point made by several people at several talks I gave.

encoded explicitly. It would be useful to empirically investigate this issue using simulated data.

Early Stopping and Two-Part Codes The EM (expectation-maximization) algorithm (Duda, Hart, and Stork 2000), is an iterative method to numerically find a (possibly local) maximum of the likelihood. It is often used in the context of parametric models such as mixture models, whose ML distribution cannot be determined analytically. At each iteration, EM outputs a current estimate θ_{EM}. One can run EM for many iterations, until θ_{EM} converges to some (local) maximum $\hat{\theta}_0$, but in practice, one often runs it only for a few iterations and stops well before it has converged. It is well known that the resulting θ_{EM} often has better predictive properties (measured, by, for example, the squared error) than the $\hat{\theta}_0$ one obtains if one keeps running until convergence. One may think of the results of running EM only a few iterations as being somewhat analogous to two-part MDL estimation with a coarse $\ddot{\Theta}$ with a uniform codelength function $\dot{L}_n$ on it. In both cases, one severely restricts the set of points that the estimator can possibly output when input a sequence of length n, thereby preventing overfitting.

Open Problem No. 13: Show Convincingly That Two-Part MDL Outperforms ML Estimator Even for Low-Dimensional Families We would really like to go beyond mere arguing and prove formally that even with small parametric models, for small samples, ML estimators overfit to some extent, whereas two-part MDL estimators do not. But this is hard, because it is not so clear what "overfitting" exactly means in this context. The usual definition of overfitting as "having a good fit on the data x^i but making bad predictions of x_{i+1}, for successive i," does not work here. The reason is that, as we explain further below, *both* the ML estimator $\hat{\theta}(x^i)$ and the two-part MDL estimator $\ddot{\theta}(x^i)$ may incur infinite log loss when used for sequential prediction of X_{i+1}. Instead, one may look at the small sample expected Hellinger risk of the two-part MDL vs. the two-part ML estimator, as in Theorem 15.3. A first attempt to formalize the argument of Chapter 5 would run as follows, where for simplicity, we assume $\mathcal{X}$ is discrete. For such discrete $\mathcal{X}$, the ML estimator $\hat{\theta}$ can be thought of as a suboptimal MDL estimator, based on a uniform first-stage code $\hat{L}_n$ defined on an overly dense grid $\ddot{\Theta}_n$. This grid contains every possible value that the ML estimator $\hat{\theta}(x^n)$ can take on for a sample of size n. For the Bernoulli model, $\ddot{\Theta}_n$ would be equal to $\{0, 1/n, \ldots, n\}$, using a precision of $1/n$ instead of the optimal $\text{ORDER}(1/\sqrt{n})$. If $\dot{L}_n$ is set equal to $\hat{L}_n$, and $\ddot{\Theta}_n$ is set equal to $\hat{\Theta}_n$, then the resulting two-part MDL estimator would coincide with the ML estimator. This two-part estimator would lead to a code with expected redundancy $k \ln n + o(\ln n)$ rather than the optimal $(k/2) \ln n + o(\ln n)$. Thus, if one believes that the more one compresses, the faster one learns, it is clear that with the ML estimator, one does not learn as fast as with the optimal two-part MDL estimator. The problem is that Theorem 15.3 on the convergence rate of two-part MDL estimator shows that good compression implies fast learning, but it does *not* show that bad compression implies slow or no learning; for this, the inequality in the theorem would have had to be an equality. This makes it hard to show that for small samples, the optimal two-part MDL estimator outperforms the ML estimator in terms of Hellinger risk. It would be interesting to do some experiments with simulated data to investigate this in more detail.

15.4.2 What Estimator To Use?

We have introduced two types of parametric MDL estimators. We now explain which of the two to prefer in what the situation.

1. Goal is prediction. If the sole goal of the inference process is to make predictions of future data, then one obviously should predict using the predictive distribution of a prequential universal model. In the case of a parametric model, relative to a given luckiness function $a(\theta)$, one should use the corresponding prequential estimator $\bar{P}_{\text{lucky-Jeffreys}}$ based on the tilted Jeffreys prior (15.25), which is asymptotically minimax optimal. Note that in some cases, $\bar{P}_{\text{lucky-Jeffreys}}(\cdot \mid X^n)$ strongly outperforms both the two-part estimator $P_{\ddot{\theta}_{\text{opt}}}$ and the LML estimator $P_{\hat{\theta},a}$. Indeed, when the luckiness function is uniform, LML is ML, and using ML for sequential prediction can incur infinite loss, as we argued in Example 9.1 on page 261. This happens, for example, if Θ represents the Bernoulli model and our first few outcomes are all zeroes. The basic design principle of the optimal two-part estimator does not rule out the possibility that some of the discretized points in $\ddot{\Theta}_n$ are very close to, or lie at, the boundary of the parameter space. In that case, just as for the ML estimator, sequential prediction based on the two-part estimator may also incur very large, or even infinite, log loss. This is reflected by the fact that, if data are i.i.d. by some $P^* \in \mathcal{M}_{\Theta}$, then neither the ML estimator nor the two-part estimator necessarily converge to P^* in terms of expected KL divergence; they only converge in terms of Rényi divergences and Hellinger distance (Example 15.5).

2. Goal is to gain insight. What if the main goal is to gain insight in the phenomenon one is trying to model? In such cases, one often wants to use an in-model estimator. Since the prequential estimator $\bar{P}_{\text{lucky-Jeffreys}}$ is in general out-model, it usually cannot be used. This is easiest to see for large, nonparametric model classes. For example, in biological applications, the models under consideration are often evolutionary trees, where the nodes in the trees stand for different species, each represented by a DNA sequence of a particular animal belong to that species. Given data that consists of DNA sequences of several different species, one tries to infer a model of how these species may have evolved from a single ancestor species. In such cases, if we were to use a Bayesian prequential estimator, our model estimate would be a mixture of many different trees. Such a mixture is more confusing than helpful if the goal is to gain insight in the evolution of the considered species. One prefers a single tree, even if this tree has worse predictive properties than the mixture of trees. Therefore, one needs an in-model rather than an out-model estimator. One can argue similarly (but perhaps less forcefully) if the goal is to learn parameters rather than structural information such as trees.

Thus, if our goal is to gain insight, we should use the two-part estimator, because it is in-model. In this case, when the model $\mathcal{M}$ is parametric, we should use the two-part parametric MDL estimator as defined above. Whereas the prequential MDL estimator is minimax optimal for individual-sequence sequential *prediction* of the given data, the optimal two-part estimator is minimax optimal among all "nonpredictive" *succinct descriptions* of the given data.

3. Goal is both prediction and insight (Open Problem No. 14). In this case, we (a) prefer to use an in-model estimator, but at the same time, (b), we want a guarantee that, when used for sequential prediction, our in-model estimator performs well in terms of log loss. Because of (a), except when our model is Bernoulli, multinomial, or Markov, we cannot use the prequential MDL estimator. Because of (b), as was discussed above, we cannot use either the two-part code MDL estimator or its continuum limit, the LML estimator. What should we do in this case? Unfortunately, we have no completely satisfactory solution. To see why, note that we are really looking for an in-model estimator $\hat{\theta}'_a$ with good minimax prequential properties. Given the ubiquitous $(k/2)\ln n$ formula for parametric universal codes, a minimum requirement for such an estimator would be the following: on all ineccsi sequences relative to the given exponential family (Θ, P_θ), the corresponding prequential plug-in model $\bar{P}_{\text{plug-in}}$ achieves luckiness regret, and hence standard regret, $(k/2)\ln n + O(1)$:

$$-\ln \bar{P}_{\text{plug-in}}(x^n) := \sum_{i=1}^{n} -\ln P_{\hat{\theta}'_a(x^{i-1})}(x_i) = \frac{k}{2}\ln n + O(1). \tag{15.33}$$

Yet, as we conjectured in Chapter 9, page 267, for most exponential families, estimators achieving (15.33) on all ineccsi sequences probably do not exist: for any given estimator, the actual regret may be of order $O(\ln n)$, but the constant in front of $\ln n$ will depend on the empirical variance of the sufficient statistic of the given exponential family model. As a result, if we restrict to prequential plug-in in-model universal models, there seems to be no meaningful analogue of the notion of "universal model achieving the minimax optimal luckiness-adjusted regret," and we cannot define a "minimax optimal prequential in-model MDL estimator." However, as we also conjecture in Chapter 9 on page 268, there may be some kind of "almost in-model estimator," which does achieve (15.33) on all ineccsi sequences. This almost in-model estimator could then be used as a third kind of MDL estimator, that is "essentially" in-model and still has good log loss prediction properties. Whether such a third kind of MDL estimator exists, is unknown at the time of writing this book.

15.4.3   Comparison to Bayesian Estimators*

Let us compare the estimators we have just discussed to some standard estimators that have been derived in the Bayesian and the MML (see Chapter 17) literature.

The Bayesian MAP Estimator   Even though most Bayesians consider it a poor substitute of an analysis involving the full posterior distribution, the Bayesian MAP (maximum a posteriori) estimator $\hat{\theta}_{\mathrm{map}}$ is often applied in statistical practice. For a given prior density π on a model parameterized by some Θ, $\hat{\theta}_{\mathrm{map}}$ is defined as the θ achieving $\max \pi(\theta \mid x^n)$. By Bayes formula, we have

$$\hat{\theta}_{\mathrm{map}} = \arg\max_{\theta \in \Theta} \ \pi(\theta \mid x^n) = \arg\max_{\theta \in \Theta} \ P_\theta(x^n)\pi(\theta). \tag{15.34}$$

Now consider a luckiness function $a(\theta)$ such that $\int_\Theta e^{-a(\theta)} d\theta < \infty$, so that

$$\pi_a(\theta) := \frac{e^{-a(\theta)}}{\int_\Theta e^{-a(\theta)} d\theta} \tag{15.35}$$

defines a probability density over Θ. Superficially, it may seem that the LML estimator based on luckiness function $a(\theta)$ is really equivalent to the MAP estimator based on the prior π_a. Namely, if we think of $\pi_a(\theta)$ as a prior density, then we see that

$$\hat{\theta}_a = \arg\max_{\theta} P_{\theta}(x^n)\pi_a(\theta),$$

which coincides with (15.34). Therefore, $\hat{\theta}_a$ *looks like* a MAP estimator with respect to prior π_a.

However, closer inspection reveals that the identification of MAP and LML estimators is incorrect. Namely, if we do a continuous 1-1 reparameterization of the model $\mathcal{M}$, then, as explained below, $\hat{\theta}_a$ becomes the MAP estimator relative to some *other* prior which may be quite different from π_a. Relatedly:

MAP vs LML Estimators

Although superficially, MAP and LML estimators seem identical concepts, in reality they are not. Indeed, the LML estimator is invariant under continuous 1-to-1 reparameterizations of the parameter space, but the MAP estimator is not.

MAP vs. LML in Detail Suppose that, instead of Θ, we choose another diffeomorphic representation Γ for the model $\mathcal{M}$. For given $\theta \in \Theta$, let $\gamma(\theta)$ denote the parameter $\gamma \in \Gamma$ that indexes the same distribution as θ. Similarly, for given $\gamma \in \Gamma$, let $\theta(\gamma)$ denote the parameter in Θ that indexes the same distribution as γ. Let $a(\theta)$ be the luckiness function in the original parameterization. The corresponding luckiness function a° in the Γ-parameterization is simply given by $a^{\circ}(\gamma) = a(\theta(\gamma))$. Then the LML estimator relative to Γ satisfies

$$\hat{\gamma}_{a^{\circ}}(x^n) = \arg\max_{\gamma \in \Gamma} P_{\theta(\gamma)}(x^n)e^{-a^{\circ}(\gamma)} =$$

$$\arg\max_{\gamma \in \Gamma} P_{\theta(\gamma)}(x^n)\pi_a(\theta(\gamma)) = \gamma(\hat{\theta}_a(x^n)), \quad (15.36)$$

where π_a is as in (15.35). This makes the LML estimator reparameterization invariant. It also guarantees that $\bar{P}_{\text{Lnml-2}}$ defined with respect to Γ will be identical to $\bar{P}_{\text{Lnml-2}}$ defined with respect to Θ.

But now let us compute the Bayesian MAP estimator defined relative to the new parameterization Γ and the distribution Π_a on Θ corresponding to prior density π_a on Θ. To compute this MAP estimator, we need to transform the prior distribution Π_a on Θ to another distribution Π_a° on Γ such that for every subset $\Theta_0 \subset \Theta$,

$$\Pi_a(\Theta_0) = \Pi_a^{\circ}(\{\gamma \in \Gamma : \theta(\gamma) \in \Theta_0\}).$$

In the one-dimensional case, the density π_a° corresponding to Π_a° will then satisfy $\pi_a(\theta) = \pi_a^{\circ}(\gamma(\theta))\frac{d}{d\theta}\gamma(\theta)$, so that the MAP estimator relative to Γ, achieving

$\max_{\gamma} P_{\theta(\gamma)}(x^n)\pi_a^{\circ}(\gamma)$ will in general be different from the LNML estimator relative to Γ, given by (15.36).

The Bayesian Posterior Mean Estimator   Another popular Bayesian estimator is the posterior mean $\hat{\theta}_{\text{mean}}$ (Berger 1985). For a model parameterized by $\Theta \in \mathbb{R}^k$, $\hat{\theta}_{\text{mean}}(x^n)$ is defined as the posterior expectation of θ. Formally, suppose w is a prior density on Θ. Let $w(\theta \mid x^n)$ denote the posterior density given data x^n. Then

$$\hat{\theta}_{\text{mean}}(x^n):=E_{\theta \sim w(\cdot \mid x^n)}[\theta].$$

This estimator is not reparameterization invariant. Whether or not $\hat{\theta}_{\text{mean}}$ is meaningful depends on the application and the chosen parameterization. For exponential families, it usually makes sense to take the mean-value parameterization Θ_{μ}. It is of some interest to study this case in some detail. This will lead up to a characterization of the posterior mean estimator that immediately makes clear how it is related to the other estimators that we discuss here. Let then (P_{μ}, Θ_{μ}) be an exponential family with sufficient statistic $\phi(X)$, given in its mean-value parameterization. Let w be a differentiable prior density on Θ_{μ} that is strictly positive for all $\mu \in \Theta_{\mu}$, and let $\bar{P}$ be the Bayesian universal code that corresponds to w. Interestingly, in this case, we obtain

$$\hat{\mu}_{\text{mean}}(x^n):=E_{\mu \sim w(\cdot \mid x^n)}[\mu] = \arg \min_{\mu \in \Theta_{\mu}} E_{X_{n+1} \sim \bar{P}_{\text{Bayes}}(\cdot \mid x^n)}[-\ln P_{\mu}(X_{n+1})] =$$

$$\arg \min_{\mu \in \Theta_{\mu}} D(\bar{P}_{\text{Bayes}}(\cdot \mid x^n)\|P_{\mu}). \quad (15.37)$$

These equalities follow by the robustness property of exponential families, Proposition 19.1 on page 625, which says that exponential families with sufficient statistic X satisfy, for all μ^* in Θ_{μ}, all P^* with $E_{P^*}[\phi(X)] = \mu^*$,

$$\arg \min_{\mu \in \Theta_{\mu}} E_{P^*}[-\ln P_{\mu}(X)] = \mu^*.$$

(15.37) implies that, if X_{n+1} were distributed according to the predictive distribution $\bar{P}_{\text{Bayes}}(\cdot \mid x^n)$, then the Bayesian posterior mean $\hat{\mu}_{\text{mean}}(x^n)$ would coincide with the in-model estimator that would minimize expected codelength, which in turn is the in-model estimator that minimizes KL risk.

Example 15.7 [Bernoulli Model] Suppose Θ_{μ} represents the Bernoulli model, and w is a beta prior corresponding to a virtual sample of λ_1 initial ones and λ_0 initial zeroes; see underneath the box on page 258. This is one of the rare cases where $\bar{P}_{\text{Bayes}}$ is an in-model estimator. From the analysis in Chapter 9 we see that $\bar{P}_{\text{Bayes}}(X_{n+1} \mid x^n) = P_{\hat{\mu}_a}$, where $\hat{\mu}_a := (\sum_{i=1}^{n} x_i + \lambda_1)/(n + \lambda_0 + \lambda_1)$. In the case of Jeffreys' prior, $\lambda_0 = \lambda_1 = 1/2$. Since $\bar{P}_{\text{Bayes}}(X_{n+1} \mid x^n) = P_{\hat{\mu}_a}$, we must have that $D(\bar{P}_{\text{Bayes}}(X_{n+1} \mid x^n) \| P_{\hat{\mu}_a}) = 0$, so that by (15.37) we have that $\hat{\mu}_a$ coincides with the posterior mean estimator $\hat{\mu}_{\text{mean}}$. Note that $\hat{\mu}_a$ also happens to coincide with the μ' achieving

$$\mu' := \arg \max_{\mu \in \Theta_\mu} \frac{P_\mu(x^n) w(\mu)}{I(\mu)}, \tag{15.38}$$

where $I(\mu) = \mu^{-1}(1-\mu)^{-1}$ is the Fisher information. This is not a coincidence, as we shall now see.

It turns out that for large n, $\hat{\mu}_{\text{mean}}(x^n)$ can easily be approximated, at least for a large class of one-dimensional exponential families. This is done by adjusting and extending an ingenious argument found on page 74 of Hartigan (1983). To apply the argument, we need to move to the canonical parameterization (Θ_β, β) of the given one-dimensional exponential family. We can write $\Theta_\beta = [a, b]$ for some a, b with $a \in \mathbb{R} \cup \{-\infty\}$ and $b \in \mathbb{R} \cup \{\infty\}$. Typically, for all sequences x^n with $\hat{\beta}(x^n) \in (a, b)$, one-dimensional families satisfy

$$\lim_{\beta \uparrow b} P_\beta(x^n) = \lim_{\beta \downarrow a} P_\beta(x^n) = 0. \tag{15.39}$$

This holds, for example, for the Bernoulli, normal, Poisson and geometric families. Now consider the MAP estimator $\hat{\beta}_{\text{map}}$, given by

$$\hat{\beta}_{\text{map}}(x^n) := \arg \max_{\beta \in \Theta_\beta} P_\beta(x^n) w_0(\beta). \tag{15.40}$$

Here w_0 is the prior density on β corresponding to the prior density w on μ, i.e. $w_0(\beta(\mu)) = w(\mu)/((d/d\mu)\beta(\mu)) = w(\mu)/I(\mu)$, where $I(\mu)$ denotes the Fisher information. This expression for w_0 follows from (18.36) on page 614. Let $\hat{\mu}'$ be the corresponding estimator in the mean-value parameterization, i.e. $\hat{\mu}'(x^n) = \mu(\hat{\beta}_{\text{map}}(x^n))$. It is seen that

$$\hat{\mu}'(x^n) := \arg \max_{\mu \in \Theta_\mu} \frac{P_\mu(x^n) w(\mu)}{I(\mu)}. \tag{15.41}$$

Now, let $\hat{\mu}_{\text{mean}}(x^n)$ be the posterior mean estimator based on prior w. Extending Hartigan's arguments, one can show that under condition (15.39),

$$|\hat{\mu}_{\text{mean}}(x^n) - \hat{\mu}'(x^n)| = O(n^{-3/2}). \tag{15.42}$$

(we omit the details of this calculation). Since normally, the absolute difference between two efficient estimators (e.g., luckiness estimators) is of ORDER

(n^{-1}), we see that $\hat{\mu}_{\text{mean}}$ and $\hat{\mu}'$ are much closer, and we may say that they asymptotically coincide.

> **Example 15.8 [Bernoulli, cont.]** (15.42) says that for general one-parameter exponential families, $\hat{\mu}'$ and $\hat{\mu}_{\text{mean}}$ will be very close. From (15.38) we see that in the special case of the Bernoulli model, things are even better, and $\hat{\mu}'$ and $\hat{\mu}_{\text{mean}}$ actually coincide.

Concluding, for 1-parameter exponential families, the posterior mean estimator, defined relative to the mean-value parameterization, is asymptotically given by (15.41). By (15.40), this is equal to the MAP estimator in the canonical parameterization. In general, it is substantially different from MAP estimators in other parameterizations, as well as from LML, two-part MDL and predictive MDL estimators. However, in the special case of the Bernoulli and multinomial model, for some luckiness functions – including the uniform one – the predictive MDL estimator coincides with the Bayesian posterior mean estimator based on the tilted Jeffreys' prior.

The Wallace-Freeman Estimator   In Chapter 17, Section 17.4, we briefly consider the *strict minimum message length (SMML) estimator*, introduced by Wallace and Boulton (1975). This estimator is at the same time Bayesian and based on trying to describe the data using as few bits as possible. It avoids most of the problems with more standard Bayesian estimators such as the MAP and the mean estimators defined above (Wallace 2005); see Section 17.4 for further details.

Recall that, for parametric models, the LML estimator can be viewed as the continuum limit of the two-part parametric MDL estimator based on luckiness function $a(\theta)$. Similarly, one can derive a sort of "continuum limit" of the SMML estimator for parametric models. We call the resulting estimator the Wallace-Freeman estimator and denote it by $\hat{\theta}_{\text{wf}}$. It was originally simply called "MML estimator" by Wallace and Freeman (1987), who introduced it. For standard parametric families, it is given by

$$\hat{\theta}_{\text{wf}}(x^n) := \arg\max_{\theta \in \Theta} \frac{P_\theta(x^n) w(\theta)}{\sqrt{\det I(\theta)}}. \tag{15.43}$$

Note that this is reminiscent of the asymptotic formula for the Bayesian posterior mean, given by (15.41), but the division is now by $\sqrt{\det I(\theta)}$ rather than $\det I(\theta)$. This subtle difference makes the Wallace-Freeman estimator reparameterization invariant: for any diffeomorphic parameterization, it indexes the same distribution.

There is a more interesting relationship with the LML estimator. To see this, suppose a friend wants to do Bayesian inference relative to Θ, but is unsure about what prior to use. He asks us, MDL people, for advice. We are unsure about how Bayesian priors should be interpreted, but if we want our friend to make good predictions, we would advice to use the Bayesian marginal distribution based on the tilted Jeffreys' prior $w_{\text{lucky-Jeffreys}}(\theta) \propto e^{-a(\theta)}\sqrt{\det I(\theta)}$. Equipped with this prior, our friend may suddenly be asked to make a parameter estimate. He decides to use the Wallace-Freeman estimator relative to his prior. This means that he adopts the estimator

$$\arg\max_{\theta\in\Theta} \frac{P_\theta(x^n)w_{\text{lucky-Jeffreys}}(\theta)}{\sqrt{\det I(\theta)}} = \arg\min_{\theta\in\Theta}\{-\ln P(\theta) + a(\theta)\},$$

which is just the LML estimator! Thus: while we cannot say that the LML estimator coincides with the WF estimator in general, we *can* say the following:

Wallace-Freeman and Luckiness ML Estimators
The WF estimator relative to a prior that is designed to achieve minimax optimal luckiness regret with respect to luckiness function $a(\theta)$, is equal to the LML estimator for $a(\theta)$. If a is uniform, then the corresponding WF estimator becomes the ordinary ML estimator.

Just as we do not think that the LML estimator is a good replacement for MDL estimators, we also have doubts on whether the Wallace-Freeman estimator is a good replacement of Wallace's original MML estimator. Wallace and Freeman (1987) do advocate the use of this estimator as a replacement of SMML, although Wallace (2005) warns that the approximation may not work very well for some models; see the remark on page 562.

15.5   Summary and Outlook

We have thoroughly studied MDL prediction and estimation, introducing prequential and two-part estimators. We considered the simple but important case of parameter estimation in considerable detail. We also presented the fundamental convergence Theorems 15.1 and 15.3. In the next chapter, we look in more detail at consistency and convergence of MDL model selection, prediction and estimation.

15.A   Appendix: Proof of Theorem 15.3

Proof: We first prove the theorem for the case $\lambda = 1 - \alpha^{-1}$, so that $\alpha = 1/(1 - \lambda)$. Our proof uses the λ-Hellinger affinity, defined in Chapter 19, Section 19.6, Definition 19.1, as $A_\lambda(P_1 \| P_0) = \sum_{x \in \mathcal{X}} P_1^\lambda(x) P_0^{1-\lambda}(x)$. In the derivation below, $\bar{P}_{\alpha 2\text{-p}}$ stands for the (defective) distribution corresponding to the codelength function $\bar{L}_{\alpha 2\text{-p}}$ defined in (15.15). We leave out the superscript (n) of $\bar{P}_{\alpha 2\text{-p}}$ as well as subscript n of $\ddot{P}_n$ and $\dot{L}_n$, and the subscript λ of A_λ. All codelengths are expressed in nats, which explains the occurrence of e rather than 2 in the equations below. For every $x^n \in \mathcal{X}^n$ we have

$$\bar{d}_\lambda(P^* \| \ddot{P}) := -\frac{1}{1-\lambda} \ln A(P^* \| \ddot{P}) =$$

$$\frac{1}{n} \ln \frac{\ddot{P}(x^n) e^{-\alpha L(\ddot{P})}}{\bar{P}_{\alpha 2\text{-p}}(x^n)} + \frac{\alpha}{n} \ln \frac{1}{A^n(P^* \| \ddot{P})} = \tag{15.44}$$

$$\frac{1}{n} \ln \frac{P^*(x^n)}{\bar{P}_{\alpha 2\text{-p}}(x^n)} + \frac{\alpha}{n} \ln \frac{\left(\frac{\ddot{P}(x^n)}{P^*(x^n)}\right)^{1/\alpha} e^{-L(\ddot{P})}}{A^n(P^* \| \ddot{P})} = \tag{15.45}$$

$$\frac{1}{n} \ln \frac{P^*(x^n)}{\bar{P}_{\alpha 2\text{-p}}(x^n)} + \frac{\alpha}{n} \ln \frac{\left(\frac{\ddot{P}(x^n)}{P^*(x^n)}\right)^{1-\lambda} e^{-L(\ddot{P})}}{A^n(P^* \| \ddot{P})} \leq \tag{15.46}$$

$$\frac{1}{n} \ln \frac{P^*(x^n)}{\bar{P}_{\alpha 2\text{-p}}(x^n)} + \frac{\alpha}{n} \ln \sum_{Q \in \mathcal{M}} \frac{\left(\frac{Q(x^n)}{P^*(x^n)}\right)^{1-\lambda} e^{-L(Q)}}{A^n(P^* \| Q)}, \tag{15.47}$$

where $A^n(P^* \| Q)$ is short for $(A(P^* \| Q))^n$. Here the first equality follows by noting that, for every $Q \in \mathcal{M}$, the fraction in the first term in (15.44) must be equal to 1. Equations (15.45) and (15.46) follow by straightforward rewriting. Equation (15.47) follows because a sum is larger than each of its terms.

Taking the expectation under P^* over sequences $X_1, \ldots, X_n$ in all terms of (15.47), this becomes

$$E_{X^n \sim P^*}[\bar{d}_\lambda(P^* \| \ddot{P})] \leq$$

$$\frac{1}{n} D(P^{*(n)} \| \bar{P}_{\alpha 2\text{-p}}^{(n)}) + \frac{\alpha}{n} E_{X^n \sim P^*} \left[\ln \sum_{Q \in \mathcal{M}} \frac{\left(\frac{Q(X^n)}{P^*(X^n)}\right)^{1-\lambda} e^{-L(Q)}}{A^n(P^* \| Q)} \right]. \tag{15.48}$$

We prove the theorem by showing that the rightmost term is no greater than

0. To see this, note that by Jensen's inequality, the term is bounded by

$$
\frac{\alpha}{n} \ln \sum_{Q \in \mathcal{M}} \frac{E_{P^*}\left[\left(\frac{Q(X^n)}{P^*(X^n)}\right)^{1-\lambda} e^{-L(Q)}\right]}{A^n(P^* \| Q)} =
$$

$$
\frac{\alpha}{n} \ln \sum_{Q \in \mathcal{M}} e^{-L(Q)} \frac{E_{P^*}\left[\left(\frac{Q(X)}{P^*(X)}\right)^{1-\lambda}\right]^n}{A^n(P^* \| Q)} = \frac{\alpha}{n} \ln \sum_{Q \in \mathcal{M}} e^{-L(Q)} \le 0,
$$

where the inequality is Kraft's, and we used the fact that $\mathcal{M}$ is i.i.d. to rewrite the expectation of an n-fold product as the n-fold product of an expectation. This proves the theorem for the case that $\lambda = \lambda_{\max} = 1 - \alpha^{-1}$. The general result for $0 < \lambda \le \lambda_{\max}$ now follows from (15.22). $\square$

16 MDL Consistency and Convergence

16.1 Introduction

In the previous chapter we provided MDL consistency results for prequential and two-part code MDL estimators. This was done in Theorem 15.1 and Theorem 15.3, respectively. In this chapter, first, in Section 16.2, we discuss these MDL consistency results in more detail, and then, in Section 16.3, we also provide consistency results for the third form of MDL, MDL model selection. While there are thus strong consistency results for all three forms of MDL, there are also – interrelated – peculiarities regarding each of the three results. These are discussed in Section 16.4.

Having established that the three forms of MDL are consistent in a variety of situations, the next question to ask is the speed or *rate* at which they converge. To make this question precise, in Section 16.5 we provide formal definitions of statistical *risk* relative to some given divergence function; rate of convergence in terms of a risk function; and minimax rate of convergence. We end, in Section 16.6, with an analysis of the rates of convergence attained by the three forms of MDL.

16.1.1 The Scenarios Considered

Not surprisingly, the behavior of the various forms of MDL strongly depends on the situation for which we analyze it. We can broadly distinguish six relevant, but inherently different situations:

1(a) Countable truth, countable model. We design a universal model $\bar{P}$ for model class $\mathcal{M} = \{P_1, P_2, \ldots\}$. We analyze its behavior under the assumption that $X_1, X_2, \ldots \sim P^*$, with $P^* \in \mathcal{M}$.

1(b) Parametric truth, parametric model. We design a universal model $\bar{P}$ for model class $\mathcal{M}_\gamma$, where $\mathcal{M}_\gamma$ is a finite-dimensional parametric model, such as an exponential family. We analyze the behavior of $\bar{P}$ under the assumption that $X_1, X_2, \ldots \sim P^*$, with $P^* \in \mathcal{M}$.

1(c) Parametric truth, CUP model class. We design a universal model $\bar{P}$ for model class $\mathcal{M} = \bigcup_{\gamma \in \mathbb{N}} \mathcal{M}_\gamma$, where each $\mathcal{M}_\gamma$ is a finite-dimensional parametric model. We analyze its behavior under the assumption that $X_1, X_2, \ldots \sim P^*$, with $P^* \in \mathcal{M}$.

Recall (Chapter 13, page 376) that the *information closure* of a model class $\mathcal{M}$ is defined as $\langle \mathcal{M} \rangle = \{P^* \mid \inf_{P \in \mathcal{M}} D(P^* \| P) = 0\}$.

2(a) Nonparametric truth, CUP model class. We design a universal model $\bar{P}$ for model class $\mathcal{M} = \bigcup_\gamma \mathcal{M}_\gamma$, where each $\mathcal{M}_\gamma$ is a smooth finite-dimensional parametric model. We analyze its behavior under the assumption that $X_1, X_2, \ldots \sim P^*$, with either, when studying consistency, $P^* \in \langle \mathcal{M} \rangle$, or, when studying rates of convergence, $P^* \in \mathcal{M}^*$. Here $\mathcal{M}^*$ is some subset of $\langle \mathcal{M} \rangle$ of distributions that are sufficiently smooth so that a uniform minimax rate of convergence exists relative to $\mathcal{M}^*$.

2(b) Nonparametric truth, direct approximation. We directly consider some $\mathcal{M}^*$ that cannot be meaningfully parameterized in a finite number of dimensions. We explicitly design a universal model $\bar{P}$ relative to $\mathcal{M}^*$. We analyze the behavior of $\bar{P}$ under the assumption that $P^* \in \mathcal{M}^*$.

3. Misspecification. $\bar{P}$ is designed as a universal model for either $\mathcal{M}$ or $\langle \mathcal{M} \rangle$, and we investigate what happens if $X_1, X_2, \ldots \sim P^*$, where $P^* \notin \langle \mathcal{M} \rangle$.

16.2   Consistency: Prequential and Two-Part MDL Estimators

In this section, we study whether prequential and two-part MDL estimators are consistent in the three situations described above.

Cases 1(a), (b), and (c). Prequential MDL estimators $\bar{P}(X_n \mid X^{n-1})$ relative to a model class $\mathcal{M}$ are defined as the predictive distributions corresponding to a prequential universal model $\bar{P}$ for $\mathcal{M}$. This is the case irrespective of whether $\mathcal{M}$ is countable, parametric, or a union of parametric models. Since $\bar{P}$ is universal for $\mathcal{M}$ by definition, it immediately follows from Theorem 15.1 that we have Césaro KL consistency for each prequential MDL estimator.

Similarly, from Theorem 15.3 we immediately see that we have consistency in terms of expected Hellinger distance for each α-two-part MDL estimator, $\alpha > 1$. We already proved a weaker form of consistency for ordinary two-part MDL in Theorem 5.1 of Chapter 5, which is applicable to case 1(a).

Whether such consistency results are practically meaningful depends on whether it is always (irrespective of the details of $\mathcal{M}$) possible to design universal models relative to $\mathcal{M}$. In cases 1(a),(b), and (c), this is easy: we start by designing a prior W on the set of distributions in $\mathcal{M}$. In the countable case 1(a), we make sure $W(j) > 0$ for each $P_j \in \mathcal{M}$. In the parametric case 1(b), we make sure that the density w of W is smooth and $w(\theta) > 0$ for all $\theta \in \Theta_\gamma$. In case 1(c), we use a prior $W(\gamma)$ as in case 1(a) on the model index, and a prior $w(\theta \mid \gamma)$ as in case 1(b) on the parameters given the index. We can now base prequential MDL estimators on the Bayesian universal model relative to any such prior W. We can base two-part estimators on the two-part code based on any such W, where $w(\theta \mid \gamma)$ is discretized as in Chapter 10, Section 10.1. The resulting universal models have expected redundancy of $O(1)$ in the countable case 1(a), and $O(\log n)$ in cases 1(b) and 1(c), so that Césaro KL consistency of prequential MDL estimators, and Hellinger consistency of α-two-part MDL, both follow.

Case 2(a).   In this case, we cannot directly apply Theorem 15.1 (consistency for prequential MDL estimator) or Theorem 15.3 (two-part consistency), because it is not a priori clear whether the universal model constructed for $\mathcal{M}$ is also a universal model for $\langle \mathcal{M} \rangle$ or $\mathcal{M}^*$. Yet in all situations I have ever encountered, standard meta-two-part and meta-Bayes CUP universal models for $\mathcal{M}$ turn out to also be universal models for the classes $\mathcal{M}^*$. In such cases, consistency (Césaro KL vs. Hellinger, respectively) of both forms of MDL follows. We encountered an example of this in Chapter 13, where $\mathcal{M}$ was the union of all finite-bin regular histograms, and $\mathcal{M}^*$ was the class of densities with bounded first derivative satisfying (13.14). Other examples are regression setups, where each $\mathcal{M}_\gamma$ is a parametric linear model, e.g. defined by the γ-degree polynomials, the prior on γ is discrete, and the prior $w(\theta \mid \gamma)$ is defined by any of the means described in Chapter 12, Section 12.4.

Case 2(b).   Here the model class $\mathcal{M}^*$ is nonparametric. For example, take the set of densities with bounded first derivative satisfying (13.14) of Chapter 13, Section 13.3. Since $\bar{P}$ is constructed as a universal model relative to

$\mathcal{M}^*$, Theorems 15.1 and 15.3 imply consistency of prequential and two-part MDL estimators.

Hence, *if* we manage to construct a universal code relative to $\mathcal{M}^*$, we have consistency as in cases 1(a), (b), and (c). But, unlike in case 1, there is no obvious recipe for constructing such universal codes. Thus, while true, the statement "prequential and two-part MDL are automatically consistent relative to nonparametric $\mathcal{M}^*$" is not very informative. Instead, the real question of interest is: "is there a general recipe for constructing universal codes relative to nonparametric $\mathcal{M}$?" To answer this question, we need to distinguish various subcases:

i. If we are only interested in *expectation-based MDL* and do not care about individual-sequence universality, then *every* estimator that is consistent in the expected KL sense can be turned into a prequential universal code, using the construction we already described in the box MDL and Traditional Statistics I on page 469. Every such estimator is thus a "prequential (expectation-based) MDL estimator," and MDL consistency is achieved trivially.

ii. If we are interested in *expectation-based MDL based on two-part codes*, then universal codes relative to $\mathcal{M}^*$ can often be constructed by decomposing $\mathcal{M}^*$ into a set of parametric or finite submodels $\mathcal{M}_1, \mathcal{M}_2, \ldots$, such that $\mathcal{M}^* \subset \langle \mathcal{M} \rangle$, where $\langle \mathcal{M} \rangle = \cup_\gamma \mathcal{M}_\gamma$. If the $\mathcal{M}_\gamma$ are finite-dimensional parametric, we are back to case 2(a), and MDL based on two-part codes relative to $\mathcal{M}$ is usually consistent. In some cases, it is also convenient to construct $\mathcal{M}$ such that each $\mathcal{M}_\gamma$ is finite or countably large, and design a two-part code directly for $\mathcal{M}_\gamma$. If the $\mathcal{M}_\gamma$ are constructed cleverly, then the two-part code will be a universal model relative to $\mathcal{M}^*$ whence two-part MDL will be consistent in the Hellinger sense (Barron and Cover 1991).

iii. Apparently, at the time of writing this book not very much was known about the construction of two-part codes or prequential universal codes that are universal in an individual-sequence sense, relative to nonparametric $\mathcal{M}^*$, the only exception being the Gaussian process models we defined in Chapter 13, Section 13.5.

Case 3: Misspecification. In this case, the model class $\mathcal{M}$ is incorrect ("misspecified"). Even so, we may hope that two-part or prequential MDL estimators "converge," in some useful sense, to the distribution $\tilde{P} \in \mathcal{M}$ that is, in some useful sense, "closest" to the true P^* generating the data. It turns out that if the model $\mathcal{M}$ is convex or finite-dimensional parametric, then, under mild additional conditions on $\mathcal{M}$, one can prove that this indeed happens. For example, the expected KL divergence between the prequential MDL estimator and P^* converges to the minimum obtainable $\inf_{P \in \mathcal{M}} D(P^* \| P)$ (Grünwald and Langford 2004; Li 1999). However, Grünwald and Langford (2004) show that this does not necessarily happen if $\mathcal{M}$ is neither convex nor parametric: they exhibit a model $\mathcal{M}$ and a true conditional probabilistic i.i.d. source P^* such that $\min_{P \in \mathcal{M}} D(P^* \| P) = \epsilon$ for some small $\epsilon > 0$. Yet, for the prequential estimator based on a prequential universal code relative to $\mathcal{M}$, with P^*-probability 1, $\lim_{n \to \infty} D(P^*, \bar{P}(X_n \mid X^{n-1})) = \infty$. Essentially the same holds for two-part code estimators based on α-two-part codes that are universal relative to $\mathcal{M}$.

16.3   Consistency: MDL Model Selection

In this section, we provide and discuss two general consistency results for MDL model selection. These results apply to cases 1(c) and 2(a) in the list of relevant scenarios of Section 16.1.1. We do not consider cases 1(a), 1(b), and 2(b). The reason is that for these cases, model selection is not a well defined concept. In case 3, just like two-part and prequential MDL estimation, MDL model selection can be inconsistent (Grünwald and Langford 2004), and we will not consider it any further here. This leaves us with cases 1(c) and 2(a), which we discuss in turn. We will only consider the "standard" type of model selection that we discussed in Chapter 14, which is invariably based on a meta-two-part CUP universal code CUP(2-p, ·).

16.3.1   Case 1(c): Selection between a Union of Parametric Models

We further distinguish between two subcases of case 1(c):

1. Γ finite.   In this case, $\mathcal{M}$ is a union of a finite number of, possibly nonnested, parametric models, usually, but not necessarily i.i.d. For example, we could have $\mathcal{M} = \mathcal{M}_a \cup \mathcal{M}_b$ where $\mathcal{M}_a$ is Fechner's and $\mathcal{M}_b$ is Stevens's model (see Chapter 1, Example 1.3). Let $\ddot{\gamma}(x^n)$ denote the $\gamma \in \mathbb{N}$ that is selected by the MDL model selection procedure based on data x^n. Then, MDL is consistent in the following sense: under mild conditions on the models $\mathcal{M}_\gamma$, it holds that for all $P^* \in \mathcal{M}$, the probability that MDL model selection picks a $\ddot{\gamma}(X^n)$ such that $P^* \notin \mathcal{M}_{\ddot{\gamma}(X^n)}$ goes to 0 exponentially fast in n. In addition, the probability that there exists another $\gamma' \neq \ddot{\gamma}(X^n)$ such that $P^* \in \mathcal{M}_{\gamma'}$ while $\mathcal{M}_{\gamma'}$ has fewer free parameters than $\mathcal{M}_{\ddot{\gamma}_n}$, goes to 0 polynomially fast in n. For details about the rates with which the probabilities converge to 0, see (Barron, Rissanen, and Yu 1998).

2. Γ countably infinite. We will only consider the common situation where $\mathcal{M}$ is a union of a countably infinite number of smooth parametric models $\mathcal{M}_\gamma$ such that for all γ, $\mathcal{M}_\gamma$ is 1-to-1 parameterized by $\Theta_\gamma \subset \mathbb{R}^{k_\gamma}$, and the list $\mathcal{M}_1, \mathcal{M}_2, \ldots$ satisfies $k_1 < k_2 < k_3 < \ldots$. Consider the MDL model selection procedure based on a meta-two-part CUP universal code CUP(2-p, Bayes). Under mild regularity conditions on the $\mathcal{M}_\gamma$, which hold, for example, if all $\mathcal{M}_\gamma$ are i.i.d. models, the following can be shown:

MDL Model Selection Consistency for Countably Infinite Union of Parametric Models – Central Result
For all $\gamma^* \in \mathbb{N}$, for all $\theta^* \in \Theta_{\gamma^*}$, except for a subset of Θ_{γ^*} of Lebesgue measure 0, it holds that: if data $X_1, X_2, \ldots \sim P_{\theta^*}$, then with P_{θ^*}-probability 1, for all large n, $\ddot{\gamma}(X^n) = \gamma^*$.

This result goes back to (Barron 1985; Dawid 1992; Barron, Rissanen, and Yu 1998) and others. A few remarks are in order:

1. "Lebesgue measure 0" can be read as "0 volume," where volume in $\mathbb{R}^{k_{\gamma^*}}$ is defined in the usual, standard way. The qualification "except for a subset of Lebesgue measure 0" thus means that there may exist some "exceptional" $\gamma \in \mathbb{N}$, $\theta \in \Theta_\gamma$ such that, if data $X_1, X_2, \sim P_\theta$, then MDL model selection is inconsistent: even as n tends to infinity, it will tend to choose some $\ddot{\gamma}$ such that $P_\theta \notin \mathcal{M}_{\ddot{\gamma}}$. However, if this is the case for some $P_\theta \in \mathcal{M}_\gamma$, then there must still be infinitely many $\theta' \in \Theta_\gamma$ in arbitrarily small neighborhoods of θ, such that, under $P_{\theta'}$, MDL model selection is consistent after all. Even so, the Csiszár-Shields inconsistency result that we present in Section 16.4 shows that, at least for some model classes, there do exist θ that make MDL model selection inconsistent.

2. Suppose that data $X_1, X_2, \ldots \sim P^* \in \mathcal{M}$. In the common case where $\mathcal{M}$ is nested, there exists some γ^* such that $P^* \notin \mathcal{M}_{\gamma^*-1}, P^* \in \mathcal{M}_{\gamma^*}$, and $P^* \in \mathcal{M}_{\gamma^*+1}$. The result may seem to imply that $\ddot{\gamma}(X^n)$ converges both to γ^* and $\gamma^* + 1$. But this does not happen: by the construction of $\mathcal{M}$, the set of θ in Θ_{γ^*+1} such that P_θ is also in $\mathcal{M}_{\gamma^*}$, has 0 volume; indeed, this is

part of the "exceptional" measure 0 set for Θ_{γ^*+1}. Thus, for all $P^* \in \mathcal{M}_{\gamma^*}$, $\ddot{\gamma}$ will converge to γ^* rather than $\gamma^* + 1$ (except, once more, for a subset of 0 volume, now measured with respect to Θ_{γ^*}).

3. The result holds irrespective of the details of the priors $W(\gamma)$ and $w(\theta \mid \gamma)$.

4. Although we have no formal proof of this fact, the similarity between the (luckiness) NML, the two-part and the Bayesian universal codes for parametric models strongly suggests that the result continues to hold if we use a CUP(2-p, lnml) or CUP(2-p, 2-p) universal code. For CUP(2-p, plug-in) codes, there do exist variations of the model consistency result above, which in some cases prove consistency for *all* P^* rather than "almost all" P^*; see below.

Proof Sketch (Very Simplified): For simplicity, let us assume that all $\mathcal{M}_\gamma$ are i.i.d. models. We usually interpret the Bayesian universal models $\bar{P}_{\text{Bayes}}(\cdot \mid \mathcal{M}_1), \bar{P}_{\text{Bayes}}(\cdot \mid \mathcal{M}_2), \ldots$ as prediction strategies or universal codes. In contrast, the proof of the result above works by thinking of them as distributions that might have generated the data. In Theorem 5.1 of Chapter 5, we already showed that, if data are distributed by any P^* in a countable set $\mathcal{M} = \{P_1, P_2, \ldots\}$ of distributions that are asymptotically distinguishable, then the probability that the $\ddot{P}_n$ minimizing $-\log W(\gamma) - \log P_\gamma(X^n)$ is equal to any $P \in \mathcal{M}$ that is distinguishable from P^* goes to 0 with increasing n. The distributions

$$\{\bar{P}_{\text{Bayes}}(\cdot \mid \mathcal{M}_1), \bar{P}_{\text{Bayes}}(\cdot \mid \mathcal{M}_2), \ldots\} \tag{16.1}$$

turn out to be all mutually asymptotically distinguishable. Roughly, this is because for any $\gamma \neq \gamma'$, for each $\theta \in \Theta_\gamma$, the set of $\theta' \in \Theta_{\gamma'}$ such that P_θ is indistinguishable from P_θ has measure 0 under $w(\theta \mid \gamma)$ (if $\gamma' < \gamma$) or measure 0 under $w(\theta' \mid \gamma')$ (if $\gamma' > \gamma$). It turns out that this implies that $\bar{P}_{\text{Bayes}}(\cdot \mid \mathcal{M}_\gamma)$ is asymptotically distinguishable from $\bar{P}_{\text{Bayes}}(\cdot \mid \mathcal{M}_{\gamma'})$.

The distributions (16.1) thus being mutually asymptotically distinguishable, Theorem 5.1 implies that, if data are distributed according to $\bar{P}_{\text{Bayes}}(\cdot \mid \mathcal{M}_{\gamma^*})$ for any $\gamma^* \in \mathbb{N}$, then the $\ddot{\gamma}(X^n)$ selected by MDL, which is just the two-part code estimator for $\bar{P}_{\text{Bayes}}(\cdot \mid \mathcal{M}_\gamma)$, will be equal to γ^* with probability tending to 1. By replacing our notion of "mutually asymptotically distinguishable" with the related but stronger notion of "mutually absolutely singular," one can strengthen this result further: for all $\gamma^* \in \mathbb{N}$, with probability 1 according to $\bar{P}_{\text{Bayes}}(\cdot \mid \mathcal{M}_{\gamma^*})$, for all large n, $\ddot{\gamma}(X^n) = \gamma^*$. Now for each γ^*, the prior $w(\theta \mid \gamma^*)$ is strictly positive on Θ_{γ^*}, and the mass $W(\gamma^*)$ is larger than 0. Thus, if for some γ_0, there would exist a region R in Θ_{γ_0} of nonzero Lebesgue volume such that, for all $\theta \in R$, with some P_θ- probability $\epsilon > 0$, there exist infinitely many n such that $\ddot{\gamma}(X^n) \neq \gamma^*$, then we would have

$$\bar{P}_{\text{CUP}(2\text{-p,Bayes})}(P^* \in \mathcal{M}_{\gamma_0}, \text{for infinitely many } n, \ddot{\gamma}(X^n) \neq \gamma_0) \geq \epsilon,$$

which would contradict the previous probability 1 statement. The result follows.

Further Consistency Results for Case 1(c).   Apart from the central result we discussed above, there exist various consistency results for MDL model selection based on CUP(2-p, plug-in) codes. These papers are usually concerned with the same scenario as the central result above, namely, it is assumed that data are distributed according to some $P^* \in \mathcal{M}_{\gamma^*}$ for some finite γ^*. A substantial part of this literature is about time-series modeling, where each $\mathcal{M}_\gamma$ is a parametric, non-i.i.d. time-series model such as an ARMA process. For such models, it is quite natural to use prequential plug-in universal codes. Consistency of model selection based on such codes is investigated by (Hannan and Rissanen 1982; Gerenscér 1987; Wax 1988; Hannan, McDougall, and Poskitt 1989; Hemerly and Davis 1989b; Hemerly and Davis 1989a; Gerencsér 1994). (Wei 1992) considers model selection in linear regression with prequential plug-in codes. Wei studies consistency in various situations, including cases where the design matrix behaves in strange, nonstationary ways. Related consistency results for linear regression are in (Speed and Yu 1993). Generalized linear models are considered by Qian, Gabor, and Gupta (1996).

16.3.2   Case 2(a): Nonparametric Model Selection Based on CUP Model Class

This is the case where $P^* \in \mathcal{M}^*$, where $\mathcal{M}^* \subset \langle \mathcal{M} \rangle$, and $\langle \mathcal{M} \rangle$ is the information closure of the CUP class $\mathcal{M} = \mathcal{M}_\gamma$. In general $P^* \notin \mathcal{M}$, and then there is no smallest γ^* such that $P^* \in \mathcal{M}_\gamma$. This raises the question of how we should define consistency in this case.

The usual way to proceed is to define a new estimator, which for each sample x^n of each size n is based on first choosing $\gamma = \ddot{\gamma}(x^n)$ (using MDL model selection), and then adopting some standard MDL estimator for x^n relative to the model $\mathcal{M}_{\ddot{\gamma}}$. Then we can say that MDL model selection is consistent if the risk of this new estimator converges to 0. To achieve this, the $\ddot{\gamma}(X^n)$ selected by the meta-two-part code should increase with n. If it increases too fast, we will overfit – the models $\mathcal{M}_{\ddot{\gamma}}$ we select are then so large that the estimators within these models do not converge to the optimal distribution $\breve{P}_\gamma = \arg\min_{P \in \mathcal{M}_\gamma} D(P^* \| P)$ within these models, so that the risk does not converge to 0. If $\ddot{\gamma}(X^n)$ does not increase at all, then our estimator cannot converge to P^*, and the risk will not converge to 0 either. If $\ddot{\gamma}(X^n)$ increases, but too slowly, then we will get consistency, but the risk of some other, non-MDL-based estimator may go to 0 much faster. In this subsection, we are only concerned with consistency and do not care about this latter possibility, which will be discussed in Section 16.6.

We formalize this idea as follows: let $\{\mathcal{M}_\gamma \mid \gamma \in \Gamma\}$ be the set of models under consideration. A *model selection criterion* is a function $S : \mathcal{X}^* \rightarrow \Gamma$, which, for each n, each sequence of outcomes x^n, selects (outputs) a model $\mathcal{M}_{S(x^n)}$.

Let S be a model selection criterion, and let $\{\bar{P}(\cdot \mid \gamma) \mid \gamma \in \Gamma\}$ be a family of estimators, using the notation of Section 15.2.1. In the development below, $\bar{P}(\cdot \mid \gamma)$ is usually a prequential universal code relative to $\mathcal{M}_\gamma$, which represents an estimator for the model $\mathcal{M}_\gamma$. But we shall make no formal requirements about $\bar{P}(\cdot \mid \gamma)$ except that it is a probabilistic source.

For all $n > 0$, $x^{n-1} \in \mathcal{X}^{n-1}$, we define

$$\bar{P}_{\text{modsel}}(X_n \mid x^{n-1}) := \bar{P}(X_n \mid x^{n-1}, S(x^{n-1})), \qquad (16.2)$$

and call it the *model selection-based estimator* relative to model selection criterion S and estimators $\bar{P}(\cdot \mid \gamma), \gamma \in \Gamma$. We call a model selection-based estimator an *MDL model selection-based estimator* if (a) the model selection criterion $S(x^n) = \ddot{\gamma}(x^n)$ is based on MDL model selection; and (b) the estimator $\bar{P}(X_n \mid x^{n-1}, \ddot{\gamma}(x^{n-1}))$ is either an (α-) two-part or a prequential MDL estimator.

> The model selection criterion must thus be based on a CUP(2-p, $\cdot$)-universal code, with $\cdot$ either Bayes, (L)NML, two-part or plug-in. Any allowed type of meta-two-part code can in principle be combined with any two-part or prequential MDL estimator, but it is clear that there are two natural options. One is to use a CUP(2-p, Bayes) code in combination with a prequential MDL estimator $\bar{P}(X_n \mid x^{n-1}, \ddot{\gamma}(x^{n-1})) := \bar{P}_{\text{Bayes}}(X_n \mid x^{n-1}\ddot{\gamma}(x^{n-1}))$, where $\bar{P}_{\text{Bayes}}(\cdot \mid \gamma)$ is the same universal model that was used in the meta-two-part universal code. This is illustrated in Example 16.2. The other natural option is to use a CUP(2-p, 2-p) code in combination with a two-part code estimator based, for each $\mathcal{M}_\gamma$, on the universal model $\bar{P}_{\text{2-p}}(\cdot \mid \gamma)$, where $\bar{P}(\cdot \mid \gamma)$ is the same universal model that was used in the meta-two-part universal code. This is explained in more detail in Example 16.1.

Example 16.1 [CUP(2-p, 2-p) **codes**] Using a CUP(2-p, 2-p) code, the code-length of the data becomes

$$\min_{\gamma \in \Gamma} \{\dot{L}(\gamma) - \log \bar{P}_{\text{2-p}}(x^n \mid \mathcal{M}_\gamma)\} =$$

$$\min_{\gamma} \min_{\theta \in \Theta_\gamma} \{\dot{L}(\gamma) + \dot{L}_n(\theta \mid \gamma) - \log P_\theta(x^n)\} \quad (16.3)$$

for some length functions $\dot{L}$ and $\dot{L}_n$. The corresponding MDL model selection criterion picks the γ achieving the minimum in (16.3). The two-part MDL estimator based on $\bar{P}_{\text{2-p}}(\cdot \mid \mathcal{M}_\gamma)$ picks, for each γ, the $\ddot{\theta}_\gamma$ achieving the minimum in the second line of (16.3). Together, this MDL model selection criterion and two-part estimator are an instance of an MDL model selection-based estimator.

Note that the codelength $\dot{L}(\gamma) + \dot{L}_n(\theta \mid \gamma)$ can also be interpreted as a code-length $\dot{L}_n(\gamma, \theta)$ relative to a joint code for (γ, θ). If this joint code has "light tails" (Chapter 15, Section 15.3.1), then this MDL model selection-based estimator will actually be identical to some α-two-part estimator $\ddot{P}_{n-1}$ for some $\alpha > 1$, so that $\bar{P}_{\text{modsel}}(\cdot \mid x^{n-1}):=\ddot{P}_{n-1}$.

Example 16.2 [CUP(2-p, Bayes) **Codes**] Consider the meta-two-part code of the Speed-Rissanen-Yu method of histogram density estimation of Chapter 13, Section 13.3, based on the CUP(2-p, Bayes) universal model defined in (13.12), page 379. Let $\bar{f}_{\text{Bayes}}(\cdot \mid \mathcal{M}_\gamma)$ denote the universal code used in (13.12), relative to the parametric submodels $\mathcal{M}_\gamma$. Let $\ddot{\gamma} : \mathcal{X}^* \to \Gamma$ be the function mapping each n, x^n to the γ that is encoded for x^n, i.e. the γ min-imizing (13.12) for the given x^n. This is an MDL model selection criterion. The prequential estimator

$$\bar{P}_{\text{modsel}}(X_{n+1} \mid x^n):=\bar{f}_{\text{Bayes}}(X_{n+1} \mid x^n, \ddot{\gamma}(x^n)) \quad (16.4)$$

defines an MDL model selection-based estimator.

We say that an MDL model selection criterion $\ddot{\gamma} : \mathcal{X}^* \to \Gamma$ is *consistent for prediction tasks* in terms of KL risk, relative to some given $\mathcal{M}^*$, if there exist a family of prequential or two-part MDL estimators $\{\bar{P}(\cdot \mid \gamma) \mid \gamma \in \Gamma\}$ such that, for all $P^* \in \mathcal{M}^*$, the model selection-based estimator based on criterion $\ddot{\gamma}$ and the estimators $\bar{P}(\cdot \mid \gamma), \gamma \in \Gamma$, is consistent in terms of KL risk. The definition is extended to consistency in terms of Césaro KL risk and expected Hellinger distance in the obvious way.

In Example 16.1 we showed that MDL model selection-based estimators based on CUP(2-p, 2-p) codes can often be reinterpreted as α-two-part code

MDL estimators. The reverse is true as well: α-two-part codes can often be viewed as MDL model selection-based estimators. Therefore, Theorem 15.3, which gives conditions for consistency for α-two-part MDL, transfers to MDL model selection based on CUP(2-p, 2-p) codes. The theorem implies that if model selection is based on a CUP(2-p, 2-p) code which is universal relative to $\mathcal{M}^*$, then consistency is guaranteed. Barron and Cover (1991) and Barron, Yang, and Yu (1994) show that, for a wide variety of CUP model classes $\mathcal{M}$ and nonparametric $\mathcal{M}^* \subset \langle \mathcal{M} \rangle$, standard two-part codes for $\mathcal{M}$ are also universal relative to $\mathcal{M}^*$, thus establishing consistency for prediction of MDL model selection based on CUP(2-p, 2-p) codes in a variety of situations. (Hall and Hannan 1988) consider an MDL estimator for histograms similar to (16.4), and show that it is consistent for prediction. Apart from these papers, we do not know of any other works in which consistency of MDL model selection for prediction tasks is shown. We conjecture though that it holds very generally – there are no known cases where it does not hold.

16.4   MDL Consistency Peculiarities

We have seen that the three main forms of MDL are usually consistent. We shall now see that the results are not perfect: there are some peculiarities with each of the three approaches. We show that these peculiarities are interrelated: it seems that the complexity penalty implicit in standard, unmodified forms of the three MDL procedures is slightly insufficient in some cases. An interesting question is therefore whether there exists some natural, simple way to avoid this problem. This question is posed in a more detailed way at the end of the section, as Open Problem No. 15. We shall now consider the three peculiarities in turn.

1. Prequential MDL: Posterior concentration $\neq$ convergence of predictive distribution. Let $\bar{P}_{\text{Bayes}}$ be a Bayesian universal code for model class $\mathcal{M} = \bigcup_{\gamma \in \Gamma} \mathcal{M}_\gamma$. Theorem 15.1 shows that for each $P^* \in \mathcal{M}$, $\bar{P}_{\text{Bayes}}(X_n \mid X^{n-1})$ converges, in the Césaro KL risk sense, to P^*. Since the predictive distribution can be written as a mixture according to the posterior (Chapter 2, Section 2.5.2),

$$\bar{P}_{\text{Bayes}}(X_{n+1} \mid x^n) := \sum_{\gamma \in \Gamma} W(\gamma) \int P_\theta(X_{n+1}) w(\theta \mid x^n, \gamma) d\theta,$$

we see that our estimator is really a weighted combination of $P \in \mathcal{M}$. We may now ask whether, for large n, there is a small ball (in KL or some other divergence) around P^* such that the posterior mass of this ball will be close to 1. In that case, the Bayesian predictive estimator is really asymptotically close to an "in-model" estimator, and we say that the posterior *concentrates* on neighborhoods of P^*.

Alternatively, it is conceivable that for some P^*, no matter how large n, there are sets $\mathcal{S}_n$ of P with nonnegligible posterior weight such that all $P \in \mathcal{S}_n$ are quite different from P^*. This does not necessarily contradict Theorem 15.1, since the $P \in \mathcal{S}_n$ may also be very different from each other, and their mixture, with components weighted according to the posterior distribution, may be a distribution that is close to P^* in KL divergence after all. Barron (1998, Section 7) shows that this can indeed happen: there exist $\mathcal{M}$ and priors W such that (a) $\bar{P}_{\text{Bayes}}$ is a universal mode relative to $\mathcal{M}$, so that $\bar{P}_{\text{Bayes}}(X_n \mid X^{n+1})$ converges to P^* for all $P^* \in \mathcal{M}$, yet for some $P^* \in \mathcal{M}$, the posterior never concentrates on neighborhoods of P^*.

Later, Zhang (2004a) showed that by slightly modifying the predictive distribution, we get a version of predictive MDL/Bayes that does guarantee concentration of the posterior in neighborhoods of the true distribution. For countable i.i.d. models $\mathcal{M} = \{P_1, P_2, \ldots\}$ with parameterization $\Theta = \{1, 2, \ldots\}$, and any $0 < \rho \leq 1$, Zhang (2004a) defines the ρ-posterior to be

$$W^{(\rho)}(\theta \mid x^n) := \frac{\prod_{i=1}^n (P(x_i \mid \theta))^\rho W(\theta)}{\sum_{\theta \in \Theta} \prod_{i=1}^n (P(x_i \mid \theta))^\rho W(\theta)}. \tag{16.5}$$

For arbitrary, uncountable models the definition is extended accordingly. Comparing this to the standard definition of a posterior (2.33) (Chapter 2, Section 2.5.2), we see that the effect of the prior is slightly larger than in standard Bayesian inference.

Among many other things, Zhang shows that, under weak conditions on the prior W, for all $0 < \rho < 1$, for all $P^* \in \langle \mathcal{M} \rangle$, i.e. $\inf_{P \in \mathcal{M}} D(P^* \| P) = 0$, if data are i.i.d. $\sim P^*$, then the posterior (16.5) concentrates, with high P^*-probability, on ever smaller neighborhoods of P^*. Here "neighborhood" is defined in terms of what Zhang calls the "ρ-divergence," which is a constant times the generalized squared $(1 - \rho)$-Hellinger divergence (Chapter 19, Section 19.6). For $\rho = 1/2$, it coincides with the ordinary squared Hellinger distance.

2. Two-part MDL: the mysterious α.   We have already seen the "problem" with two-part MDL: consistency with good rates of Hellinger or Rényi divergence can only be proved if we take some $\alpha > 1$. As we discussed on page 479, while the requirement $\alpha > 1$ can be interpreted as a condition on the prior W_n corresponding to the code $\dot{L}_n$ having "light tails," it is not clear why this requirement is really needed.

The α-two-part MDL estimator (15.15) can be rewritten as the minimizer over $P \in \mathcal{M}$ of

$$\dot{L}_n(P) - \rho \ln P(x^n) = -\ln W_n(P)(P(x^n))^\rho,$$

where $\rho = 1/\alpha$, leading to the consistency in terms of Rényi divergence of order $1 - \rho$, and, by (19.41), also to consistency in terms of $(1 - \rho)$-generalized Hellinger divergence. It seems clear that the $\alpha > 1$ needed to guarantee two-part MDL convergence corresponds exactly to the $\rho = 1/\alpha < 1$ needed to guarantee concentration of the posterior in neighbourhoods of the true P^*!

3. MDL model selection: Csiszár-Shields inconsistency result. Csiszár and Shields (2000) prove a very surprising result for MDL model selection of Markov chains: they show that it can be inconsistent in the simplest of all cases, namely if data $X_1, X_2, \ldots$ are generated independently by fair coin tosses.

More precisely, let $\mathcal{X} = \{0, 1\}$ and consider the Markov model class $\mathcal{B} = \cup_\gamma \mathcal{B}_\gamma$, where $\mathcal{B}_\gamma$ denotes the γ-order Markov model, as in Chapter 2.

We apply refined MDL model selection to this problem in a standard manner: we associate each submodel $\mathcal{M}_\gamma$ with the universal distribution $\bar{P}_{\text{Jeffreys}}$ $(\cdot \mid \gamma)$, which is just the Bayesian universal distribution based on Jeffreys' prior. We encode γ by the universal code for the integers. We then select the model $\mathcal{M}_{\ddot{\gamma}}$, where $\ddot{\gamma}$ is the γ minimizing the total codelength $L_\mathbb{N}(\gamma) - \log \bar{P}(x^n \mid \gamma)$. Now let $X_1, X_2, \ldots \sim P^*$, where $P^* \in \mathcal{B}_0$ is the Bernoulli source with parameter $1/2$. We would expect that, for large n, the MDL model selection procedure selects $\mathcal{B}_0$. But Csiszár and Shields (2000) show that this does not happen: with P^*-probability 1, we have that $\lim_{n \to \infty} \ddot{\gamma}(X^n) = \infty$. Exactly the same phenomenon occurs if we leave the code for γ unchanged, but replace the Bayesian universal distributions $\bar{P}_{\text{Jeffreys}}(\cdot \mid \gamma)$ by the minimax optimal NML distributions $\bar{P}_{\text{nml}}(\cdot \mid \gamma)$.

This result may seem to contradict our earlier MDL model selection consistency result on page 506. But we recall that model selection consistency only holds for a set of distributions $\mathcal{M}' \subset \mathcal{M}$ such that $\mathcal{M}'$ has prior probability 1. Since the singleton set $\{P^*\}$ has prior probability 0, the consistency result does not rule out that MDL model selection is inconsistent if P^* generates the data. In fact, Csiszár and Shields (2000) conjecture that the Bernoulli($1/2$) distribution may be the *only* distribution in the model class $\mathcal{M}$ for which

MDL model selection may be inconsistent. They further remark that, if this conjecture holds true, then the problem could be remedied by defining a new model $\mathcal{B}_0 = \{P^*\}$ containing only the Bernoulli$(1/2)$ source, and put some positive prior mass on $\mathcal{B}_0$ as well.

Do I Compress at All? As remarked by T. van Erven, there is an intriguing connection with the basic sanity check that we proposed in Chapter 14, Example 14.3, under the name "Do I compress at all?" There we stated that, in MDL model selection problems, it is always a good idea to add a special "null model" $\mathcal{M}_0 = \{P_0\}$ to the data, and assign it a positive codelength/prior. Here P_0 is the distribution corresponding to the code that is used to store the data on the computer. For binary data, we may assume the data are stored literally, and then P_0 would be the Bernoulli source with parameter $1/2$. If we would apply this sanity check to the Ciszár-Shields example, then $P^* = P_0$ would achieve positive prior probability, and would be selected by MDL model selection for all large n. Hence, the problem would be solved. It is not clear whether this "solution" can still be used if $\mathcal{X}$ is infinite. It is not known whether in such situations, MDL model selection can be inconsistent at all, but if it can be, then it would not always be obvious how the "sanity check distribution P_0" should be defined.

We can conclude from this example that the qualification "except for a subset of Lebesgue measure 0" is quite relevant: first of all, at least for some model classes, there do exist distributions $P^* \in \mathcal{M}$ for which MDL model selection is inconsistent. Second, these distributions are not necessarily results of strange constructions with, say, uncomputable parameters – they can be most straightforward indeed.

MDL and Consistency

The three main forms of refined MDL are usually consistent in a wide variety of situations. However, in none of the three cases is the consistency perfect; in MDL model selection, we can even get real inconsistency in a rare but simple case. The problem with all three forms of MDL seems to be that in some cases, the complexity penalty implicit in MDL/universal codes is slightly too small.

Open Problem No. 15 In prequential MDL estimation with Bayesian universal codes and in two-part estimation, we can avoid these problems by using the α-factor to slightly increase (implicit) model complexity. But it seems that this is not always necessary, and perhaps in cases where it is not needed, picking $\alpha > 1$ unnecessarily slows down the convergence of the learning procedures. Also, it is not clear what α should be picked, and why. With MDL model selection, we could perhaps remedy the Csiszár-Shields inconsistency by adding an additional singleton model $\mathcal{B}_0$ to $\mathcal{B}$, as explained above; but again, it is not clear for exactly what model classes this should be done, and why. The (non-mathematical) question is: does there exist a simple, natural restriction on the universal codes used in MDL procedures, which avoids MDL's slight under-penalization? In the spirit of individual-sequence-based MDL, this restriction should have a natural coding-theoretic interpretation, rather than a fine-tuning of the procedure to achieve consistency.

16.5   Risks and Rates

We start by introducing the notions of *statistical risk* and *(minimax) rate of convergence*. Let $\mathcal{P}$ be the set of distributions on $\mathcal{X}$. A *divergence* for $\mathcal{P}$ is a function $d : \mathcal{P} \times \mathcal{P} \to [0, \infty]$ such that for all P, P', $d(P, P') \geq 0$, with equality if and only if $P = P'$. While in the context of this section, d will usually (but not always) refer to the KL divergence, the following definitions make sense for general divergences d. In statistics one typically considers either squared Euclidean or Hellinger distance, which we encountered in Section 15.3. Throughout this section, $f : \mathbb{N} \to \mathbb{R}$ invariably denotes a non-negative function, and $\bar{P}$ is a probabilistic source that represents an estimator, as in Chapter 15, Section 15.2.1.

As a generalization of (15.7), for a given divergence d, we define the *statistical risk* at sample size n as

$$\text{RISK}_n(P^*, \bar{P}) := E_{X^{n-1} \sim P^*}[d(P^*_{|n-1} \| \bar{P}_{|n-1})]. \tag{16.6}$$

We usually refer to this function as "risk." If it is not clear from the context what the divergence d is, we refer to it as "d-risk." It expresses the expected divergence between P^* and the estimator $\bar{P}$. For simplicity, in the remainder of this section we assume that data are i.i.d. under P^*. Therefore we can simplify the notation, using that $d(P^*_{|n-1} \| \bar{P}_{|n-1}) = d(P^* \| \bar{P}_{|n-1})$.

We now move to the central definitions of this section: rate of convergence of estimator $\bar{P}$ to a true distribution P^*; rate of convergence of $\bar{P}$ relative to a set of distributions $\mathcal{M}^*$; and (uniform) minimax rate of convergence.

Convergence Rate to P^*   We say that $\bar{P}$ converges to P^* at rate $f(n)$ in terms of risk function RISK if there exist positive constants c_1, c_2 such that for all n, $c_1 f(n) \leq \mathrm{RISK}_n(P^*, \bar{P}) \leq c_2 f(n)$.

Convergence Rate Relative to $\mathcal{M}^*$ Let $\mathcal{M}^*$ be a set of distributions on $\mathcal{X}$. We extend these to probabilistic sources by independence. We say that estimator $\bar{P}$ achieves convergence rate $f(n)$ in terms of RISK, relative to $\mathcal{M}^*$, if for all $P^* \in \mathcal{M}^*$, there is a $c > 0$ such that for all n,

$$\mathrm{RISK}_n(P^*, \bar{P}) \leq cf(n). \qquad (16.7)$$

We say that $\bar{P}$ uniformly achieves rate $f(n)$ relative to $\mathcal{M}^*$, if there is a $c > 0$ such that for all $P^* \in \mathcal{M}^*$, all n, (16.7) holds; or equivalently:

$$\sup_{P^* \in \mathcal{M}^*} \mathrm{RISK}_n(P^*, \bar{P}) \leq cf(n). \qquad (16.8)$$

Minimax Convergence Rate   We say that $f(n)$ is the minimax convergence rate in terms of given risk function RISK relative to $\mathcal{M}^*$ if there exists an estimator $\bar{P}$ which uniformly achieves rate $f(n)$, but for any function g with $g(n) = o(f(n))$, there is no estimator which uniformly achieves rate $g(n)$. Note that $f(n)$ is the uniform minimax convergence rate relative to $\mathcal{M}^*$ if and only if there exist $c_1 > 0, c_2 > 0$ such that for all n,

$$c_1 f(n) < \inf_{\bar{P}^{(n)}} \sup_{P^* \in \mathcal{M}^*} \mathrm{RISK}_n(P^*, \bar{P}) < c_2 f(n),$$

which explains the term "minimax."

> **Nonuniform Minimax Rate**   As is customary, the word "convergence" in our definition of minimax convergence rate really means *uniform* convergence. A better phrase would thus perhaps be "uniform minimax convergence rate." One could then also define a "not-necessarily-uniform minimax convergence rate" as follows: $f(n)$ is the not-necessarily-uniform minimax convergence rate in terms of RISK relative to $\mathcal{M}^*$ if there exists an estimator $\bar{P}$ which achieves rate $f(n)$, but for any function g with $g(n) = o(f(n))$, there is no estimator which achieves rate $g(n)$. Equivalently, $f(n)$ is the not-necessarily-uniform minimax convergence rate relative to $\mathcal{M}^*$, if there exists some function $g : \mathcal{M}^* \to \mathbb{R}^+$ such that
>
> $$\inf_{\bar{P}} \sup_{P^* \in \mathcal{M}^*} \sup_{n \in \mathbb{N}} \frac{\mathrm{RISK}_n(P^*, \bar{P})}{f(n)} < g(P^*) \ ; \ \inf_{\bar{P}} \sup_{P^* \in \mathcal{M}^*} \inf_{n \in \mathbb{N}} \frac{\mathrm{RISK}_n(P^*, \bar{P})}{f(n)} > 0.$$

Finally, we note that all the above definitions are extended to the Césaro risk $\overline{\mathrm{RISK}}_n(P^*, \bar{P}) := \frac{1}{n} \sum_{i=1}^n \mathrm{RISK}_i(P^*, \bar{P})$ by replacing each occurrence of RISK by $\overline{\mathrm{RISK}}$.

16.5.1   Relations between Divergences and Risk Measures

In the next two subsections we consider rates of convergence of various MDL and non-MDL estimators. Depending on the type of estimator we investigate, the risks are measured in terms of KL divergence, Hellinger divergence, Rényi divergence of some order λ, integrated squared error between densities, or squared Euclidean or Mahalanobis distance between parameters. There is a simple reason for this confusing state of affairs: for each type of estimator, the mathematical proofs of convergence theorems naturally give rise to a particular divergence measure, and usually consistency and convergence rates are easiest to prove using that measure, and sometimes may not even hold using other measures. To be able to relate the different results, we summarize the relations between the divergences under consideration in the box on page 518. Part of these relations were already stated in Section 15.3.1. The box mentions two new divergence measures that we have not encountered before: the *integrated squared error* between P and Q, given by $\sum_{x \in \mathcal{X}}(P(x) - Q(x))^2$, and the χ^2-divergence D_{χ^2} between P and Q, given by $D_{\chi^2}(P\|Q) = \sum_{x \in \mathcal{X}}(P(x) - Q(x))^2/Q(x)$. These two divergences will mainly be used when P and Q are densities, and then the sum is replaced by an integral. As an example of the implications of the relations described in the box, if the risk of an estimator $\bar{P}$ relative to P^* converges at a rate at least $f(n)$ in terms of KL divergence $D(P^*\|\bar{P}_{|n})$, this automatically implies that the risk in terms of squared Hellinger distance also converges at a rate at least $f(n)$. If $\mathcal{M}$ is a model class such that all $P \in \mathcal{M}$ are uniformly bounded away from 0 and infinity, then (16.10) must hold for some $c > 0$ and convergence at rate $f(n)$ in terms of any of the divergence measures mentioned (squared Hellinger, KL, χ^2, integrated squared error, Rényi-divergence for $\lambda \geq 1/2$), implies convergence at the same rate $f(n)$ in terms of any of the other measures. The constants c^2 and c^4 appearing in (16.11) are very rough. For example, a more precise upper bound on KL divergence in terms of Hellinger divergence under condition (16.10) is given in (Yang and Barron 1998, Lemma 4). Equation (16.12) shows that, on ineccsi parameter sets, the squared Euclidean and Mahalanobis distances and the KL divergence are within constants of each other. By the smoothness properties of exponential families, on ineccsi parameter sets, all probability mass/density functions are bounded away from 0 and infinity, so that by (16.11), the squared Euclidean distance can also be related to the χ^2, Rényi, and (not surprisingly) the integrated squared error divergences.

Relations between Divergences

For *all* distributions P and Q on $\mathcal{X}$, as long as they have mass functions or densities, and for all $0.5 \leq \lambda \leq 1$, we have, (Barron and Cover 1991),

$$\text{He}^2(P,Q) \leq \bar{\text{d}}_\lambda(P\|Q) \leq D(P\|Q) \leq D_{\chi^2}(P\|Q). \tag{16.9}$$

Now, let $\mathcal{M}$ be a set of distributions on $\mathcal{X}$ and suppose that there exists a $c > 1$ such that for all $P \in \mathcal{M}$, all x,

$$\frac{1}{c} \leq P(X) \leq c. \tag{16.10}$$

Then for all $P, Q \in \mathcal{M}$, in addition to (16.9), we also have

$$D_{\chi^2}(P\|Q) \leq c^2 \sum_{x \in \mathcal{X}} (P(x) - Q(x))^2 \leq 4c^4 \text{He}^2(P,Q). \tag{16.11}$$

Further, in the very special case that $\mathcal{M}$ is a k-dimensional exponential family given in a diffeomorphic parameterization Θ, and Θ_0 is an ineccsi subset of Θ, and M is a $k \times k$ symmetric positive definite matrix, then there exists a constant $C > 1$ such that for all $\theta, \theta' \in \Theta_0$,

$$\frac{1}{C}(\theta' - \theta)^\top M(\theta' - \theta) \leq D(P_\theta\|P_\theta') \leq C(\theta' - \theta)^\top M(\theta' - \theta). \tag{16.12}$$

Finally, if $\mathcal{M}$ is a parametric linear (regression) model, for some fixed variance σ^2, then the KL divergence is a fixed multiple of the Mahalanobis distance between parameter vectors (see Chapter 12, page 351).

Proof Sketch: The first two inequalities of (16.9) are proved in Chapter 19, Section 19.6. The third follows by a Taylor approximation of the KL divergence $D(P\|Q)$ (Barron and Sheu 1991, Section 3). The first inequality of (16.11) follows because under (16.10), for all x, $1/q(x) \leq c \leq c^2$. The second inequality follows by some calculus as in (Barron and Cover 1991, page 1045). Equation (16.12) follows by the general properties of exponential families as outlined in Chapter 18; we omit the details.

16.5.2   Minimax Rates

The following examples summarize some standard facts about convergence rates.

Example 16.3 [Parametric Families: Minimax Rate of $1/n$] For finite-dimensional parametric families, the minimax rate of convergence is usually equal to n^{-1}. This holds for the risk function defined with respect to the squared Hellinger distance, the Rényi divergences of order λ, and the KL divergence. Under conditions on the parameterization, it also holds for the squared Euclidean and Mahalanobis distance between the parameters. For finite dimensional exponential families in diffeomorphic parameterizations, combined with squared Euclidean, Mahalanobis, Hellinger, or Rényi divergence risks with $\lambda < 1$, the maximum likelihood estimator achieves the minimax rate n^{-1}. This fact is particularly easy to see with squared Euclidean distance, for one-dimensional exponential families $\mathcal{M} = \{P_\mu \mid \mu \in \Theta\}$, where (P_μ, Θ) represents the mean-value parameterization. In that case, there exists a sufficient statistic $\phi(X)$ of X (Chapter 18, Section 18.2), and the ML estimator satisfies $\hat{\mu}(x^n) = n^{-1} \sum \phi(x_i)$, whereas for all $\mu^* \in \Theta$, $E_{\mu^*}[\phi(X)] = \mu^*$. Then the risk in terms of squared Euclidean distance becomes

$$\mathrm{RISK}_{n+1}(P^*, \bar{P}) = E[(\hat{\mu}(X^n) - \mu^*)^2] =$$

$$\frac{1}{n^2} E\left[\left(\sum_{i=1}^{n} \phi(X_i) - n E_{\mu^*}[\phi(X)] \right)^2 \right] = \frac{1}{n} \mathrm{var}_{\mu^*}[\phi(X)] = \frac{1}{n} I(\mu^*)^{-1} =$$

$$\mathrm{ORDER}\left(\frac{1}{n+1} \right), \quad (16.13)$$

where the expectation is of $X^n \sim P_{\mu^*}$ and $I(\mu^*)$ is the Fisher information evaluated at μ^*, which is equal to $1/\mathrm{var}_{\mu^*}[\phi(X)]$; see Chapter 18, box on page 615. This shows that the ML estimator achieves rate $1/n$. The result can be extended to Hellinger and Rényi divergences by performing Taylor expansions; we omit the details. With the KL divergence, for some exponential families such as the Bernoulli model, the ordinary ML estimator can have infinite risk at all n. This was shown in Example 15.5. For such models, the ML estimator does not achieve the minimax KL rate. Yet, if, as in Chapter 9, we slightly modify the ML estimator by adding some virtual data, then the resulting luckiness ML estimator will once again achieve the rate of $1/n$.

Not surprisingly, it turns out that also the Bayesian prequential MDL estimator based on the Bayesian universal code with a Θ-compatible prior, achieves the minimax rate of $1/n$: using the familiar $(k/2) \log n$ expansion of the redundancy, we showed in Example 15.3 that the Césaro KL risk converges as $n^{-1} \log n$, so that the standard KL risk essentially achieves rate $1/n$. It can be shown (Barron 1998) that the convergence is not just in the essential, but also in the standard sense.

Similarly to the ML estimator, the two-part code MDL estimator does not converge in the KL risk sense (Chapter 15, Example 15.5), but it does converge at the optimal $1/n$ rate in terms of squared Hellinger distance (Example 15.6).

Example 16.4 [Nonparametric Density Estimation: Often Minimax Rate of $n^{-\alpha}$, $1/2 \leq \alpha \leq 1$] The situation for nonparametric model classes $\mathcal{M}^*$ is more complicated. One often considers models $\mathcal{M}^*$ consisting of distributions with densities satisfying some smoothness constraints, which imply that at least the first derivative of the density exists. For example, if $\mathcal{M}^*$ is the smoothness class $\mathcal{M}^*_{s,(c_0,\ldots,c_{s+1})}$ as defined in Chapter 13, Example 13.1, then, as claimed there, the minimax expected redundancy per outcome rate is $n^{-2s/(2s+1)}$. By the remark on page 388, the minimax expected redundancy per outcome among all prequential universal codes is also of order $n^{-2s/(2s+1)}$. This shows that the minimax KL Césaro convergence rate of any estimator is $n^{-2s/(2s+1)}$. This, in turn, suggests (but does not prove) that also the minimax "ordinary" KL convergence rate is $n^{-2s/(2s+1)}$. Because the model $\mathcal{M}^*_{s,(c_0,\ldots,c_{s+1})}$ satisfies (16.10), the minimax Hellinger, Rényi, and integrated squared-error risk is also of order $n^{-2s/(2s+1)}$. It turns out that this is indeed the case. One often considers somewhat different smoothness constraints on $\mathcal{M}^*$ in the literature, but still, in many cases, the minimax risk in any of the divergence measures mentioned above is of order $n^{-t/(t+1)}$ for some $t > 0$ (Barron and Cover 1991).

16.6 MDL Rates of Convergence

16.6.1 Prequential and Two-Part MDL Estimators

We consider all scenarios discussed in Section 16.1.1, except case 3. Since in case 3, both forms of MDL can be inconsistent, it does not make much sense to consider their rates of convergence.

Case 1(a) In this case, $\mathcal{M}$ is countable. From the arguments in Chapter 6 we see that there exists a Bayesian universal code relative to $\mathcal{M}$ that has finite expected redundancy bounded by $-\log W(P^*)$ with respect to each $P^* \in \mathcal{M}$. Thus, we can apply Theorem 15.1 to find that for the prequential MDL estimators based on a Bayesian universal code $\bar{P}_{\text{Bayes}}$, the Césaro KL risk is of order $1/n$. This implies that the sum $\sum_{n=1}^{\infty} \text{RISK}_n(P^*, \bar{P}_{\text{Bayes}}) \leq -\log W(P^*)$ is finite, so that the KL risk converges faster than $1/n$. It turns out that, for the two-part code MDL, under some regularity conditions on $\mathcal{M}$, we also get such a fast rate of convergence, though in general the sum of risks can only be bounded by $1/W(P^*)$, which can of course be much larger than $-\log W(P^*)$ (Poland and Hutter 2005).

Cases 1(b), 1(c) As has already been pointed out at the end of Example 16.3, in all cases that have been investigated, α-two-part MDL estimators, prequential Bayes, and prequential plug-in MDL estimators all achieve the minimax optimal parametric rate $1/n$ in case 1(b). It is easy to show that they also achieve this rate in case 1(c).

Case 2(a) The histogram example showed that neither CUP(Bayes, Bayes) nor CUP(2-p, Bayes) achieves the minimax optimal redundancy rate. Given these two results, it seems very likely that CUP(2-p, 2-p) does not achieve the minimax optimal rate either. Since CUP(Bayes, Bayes) defines a prequential MDL estimator, this estimator does not converge at the optimal Césaro rate, which implies that it also does not converge at the optimal KL rate, and, by (16.10), not at the optimal Hellinger, Rényi and integrated squared-error rates. There exist some model classes $\mathcal{M}^*$ for which a type of two-part MDL estimator, defined on an approximating CUP model class $\mathcal{M}$, does achieve the minimax expected redundancy rate (Barron, Yang, and Yu 1994), which implies that it also achieves minimax optimal Hellinger rate $n^{-2s/(2s+1)}$. But this two-part estimator is defined in a different, more complicated way than a CUP(2-p, 2-p)-universal code. It is not clear whether this minimax optimal version of the two-part code can be applied to general CUP model classes.

Case 2(b) If we take the expectation-based MDL point of view, and we accept that universal codes have to be universal only in the expectation sense, then we trivially achieve the minimax or uniform minimax rate of convergence here: given any estimator which achieves the minimax rate of convergence, we turn it into a probabilistic source $\bar{P}$ as in Chapter 15, Section 15.2.1. Then $\bar{P}$ will be a prequential universal code, so it will be a prequential MDL estimator in the expectation sense. By construction, it automatically achieves the minimax rate. The same can be done for an estimator achieving the minimax uniform rate.

If we insist on MDL (prequential or two-part) estimators that are based on individual-sequence universal codes, then it is not clear whether something like this can be done.

> **Open Problem No. 16** Can we always design universal codes *in an individual-sequence sense* that achieve the minimax rate of convergence?

16.6.2   MDL Model Selection

Among the scenarios considered in Section 16.1.1, MDL model selection is only meaningful in cases 1(c) and 2(a) and case 3. In case 3 it can be inconsistent, so it does not make much sense to consider its rate of convergence. In case 1(c), if $P^* \in \mathcal{M}_{\gamma^*}$ for some finite γ^*, then, if MDL is consistent at all, this means that for all large n, some γ^* will be chosen such that $\mathcal{M}_{\gamma^*}$ contains the true distribution. In that case, it is not really meaningful to talk of a "rate of convergence." This leaves us with case 2(a). In this case, MDL model selection is based on a meta-two-part code $\text{CUP}(2\text{-p}, \cdot)$ relative to some CUP model class $\mathcal{M}$, and we investigate its behavior if $P^* \in \mathcal{M}^*$, for some $\mathcal{M}^* \subset \langle \mathcal{M} \rangle$.

In case we base model selection on a $\text{CUP}(2\text{-p}, \text{Bayes})$-universal code, then, as we already know from the histogram example (Example 16.2), the MDL model selection-based estimator does not always converge at the minimax optimal rate, and, just as for the prequential MDL estimator above, may lose a factor of $\log n$ compared to the minimax optimal estimator. If the model selection is based on a $\text{CUP}(2\text{-p}, 2\text{-p})$ code, then, under conditions on the length functions $\dot{L}$ and $\dot{L}_n$ (Example 16.1 and the discussion at the end of Section 16.3.2), MDL model selection-based estimation reduces to α-two-part MDL estimation, and the rate of convergence of MDL model selection is equal to that of α-two-part MDL; we stated above that in some special cases, this achieves the minimax optimal rate, but it is not clear whether it does in general. In fact, we very strongly suspect that it does not. Both the histogram analysis of (Yu and Speed 1992) and the analysis of two-part codes in Barron and Cover (1991) strongly suggests that in general, just like the $\text{CUP}(2\text{-p}, \text{Bayes})$-universal code, the α-two-part MDL converges at a rate that exceeds the minimax optimal rate by a logarithmic factor.

17 *MDL in Context*

In this chapter, we compare refined MDL to various other statistical inference methods. We start in Section 17.1, with a comparison between MDL and various frequentist approaches. Section 17.2 considers the relation between MDL and Bayesian inference in great detail. Section 17.3 compares MDL model selection to the two popular default model selection approaches AIC and BIC. Section 17.4 compares MDL to the similar Minimum *Message* Length Principle. Section 17.5 compares MDL to Dawid's prequential approach. Sections 17.6 through 17.10 consider cross-validation, maximum entropy, idealized MDL, individual sequence prediction and statistical learning theory, respectively. The latter two comparisons make clear that there do exist some problems with the MDL approach at its current stage of development. These are discussed in Section 17.11, in which I also suggest how the MDL approach might or should develop in the future.

Unless mentioned otherwise, whenever we write "MDL," we refer to the individual-sequence version of MDL; see the introduction to Part III of this book.

A Word of Warning Some of the differences between MDL and other approaches simply concern details of algorithms that are used for practical inference tasks. Others concern the difference in underlying principles. Discussion of such philosophical differences is inherently subjective, and therefore, some comparisons (especially MDL-Bayes, Section 17.2) will be quite opinionated. When referring to the underlying principles, I use phrases such as "From an MDL perspective, . . .," "the MDL view," and so on. In those cases where I strongly agree with the MDL perspective, I have permitted myself to use first-person phrases such as "in my opinion." I have tried to restrict the use of phrases involving the word "we" (such as "we now see that") to "objective" facts, such as mathematical derivations. These safeguards notwith-standing, it is inevitable that in this chapter, my personal viewpoints become entangled with those of Rissanen and other MDL researchers.

17.1   MDL and Frequentist Paradigms

Against Principles?   Frequentist or "orthodox" statisticians (Chapter 2, page 73) are often suspicious of anything calling itself a "principle."

> I have heard several well-known statisticians say this. One well-known sta-tistical learning theorist even told me that "MDL and Bayes are just *recipes* for doing inferences; these may work in some, but not in other situations. In contrast, in learning theory we design algorithms that are provably optimal."

They argue that, when designing methods for learning, rather than dogmat-ically adhering to principles, we should focus on what counts: making sure that our algorithms learn a good approximation to the true distribution fast, based on as few data as possible. Researchers who dismiss principles such as MDL on such grounds tend to forget that they themselves strongly rely on another principle, which one might call *the frequentist principle*: the idea that it is realistic to view real-world data as sampled from some P^* in some model class $\mathcal{M}$. This is just as much a "principle" as the basic MDL idea that "the more you can compress data, the more you have learned from the data." From an MDL perspective, there are at least three problems with the frequentist principle:

1. **Too unrealistic.** The frequentist principle is often quite unrealistic in prac-tice. In Section 17.1.1 we illustrate this using a detailed example, and we emphasize that frequentist ideas can be used either as a sanity check for algorithms based on other principles, or as a principle for *designing* learn-ing algorithms. From the MDL stance, only the latter type of frequentist principle is truly problematic.

2. **Too restrictive.** The frequentist design principle is unnecessarily restric-tive. The reason is that frequentist procedures usually violate the *prequen-tial principle*, which we discuss in Section 17.1.2.

3. **Too much work.** Designing optimal frequentist procedures involves a lot of work, which may sometimes be unnecessary. This is explained in Sec-tion 17.1.3.

In the sections below we discuss each issue in turn. Before we start, we note that the first issue (unrealistic probabilistic assumptions) is mostly resolved in *statistical learning theory*, which we further discuss in Section 17.10. This is a frequentist approach to learning from data that only makes very mild assumptions about the data generating distribution. The price to pay is that it can be applied only in restricted settings.

17.1.1 Frequentist Analysis: Sanity Check or Design Principle?

Frequentist Assumptions Are Unrealistic   We already argued in Chapter 1, Section 1.7, that frequentist assumptions are often unrealistic. It is sometimes argued that the frequentist principle becomes more realistic if one takes a nonparametric approach. Thus, one assumes that data are sampled from some P^* in some large nonparametric class $\mathcal{M}^*$. For example, as in Chapter 13, Section 13.3, one could choose to "merely" assume that P^* has a differentiable density f^* on its support $\mathcal{X} = [0,1]$, where $f^*(x)$ is bounded away from 0 and infinity. While this is evidently a weaker assumption than the parametric requirement that P^* is a member of some finite-dimensional model, it is still problematic from an MDL perspective. Namely, such nonparametric modeling is often applied in settings where it is unclear whether the assumption of a "true" P^* makes sense at all. And even if one does assume that such a P^* exists, the assumption that its density be differentiable is still very strong, and one would need an infinite amount of data to test whether it truly holds. Often, it will simply not hold, as Example 17.1 illustrates: data may be sampled from a distribution P^* which has no density, yet $\mathcal{M}^*$ may contain distributions with differentiable densities that predict data sampled from P^* very well. However, if we design our estimators so as to be optimal from a frequentist perspective, we may end up with a brittle algorithm that only works well (learns P^* fast) if P^* truly has a density, and fails dramatically if P^* has no density.

> For example, consider any learning algorithm for histogram density estimation that achieves the minimax optimal convergence Hellinger rate (Chapter 13, Chapter 16). We can always modify such an algorithm such that, if for some $n, n' > n$, $x_n = x_{n'}$, then for *all* $n'' > n'$, the algorithm outputs the uniform distribution on $\mathcal{X}$. Hence the algorithm breaks down as soon as two times the same outcome is observed. Since such an event has probability 0 under any $P^* \in \mathcal{M}^*$, it will still achieve the minimax optimal convergence rate.
>
> While most nonparametric estimators used in practice will not do anything strange like this, and will be reasonably robust against P^* that do not admit

a density, the point is that there is nothing in the frequentist paradigm which requires one to avoid brittle algorithms like the one above.

To me, it seems a much better strategy to design a learning method which leads to good predictions whenever some $P \in \mathcal{M}^*$ leads to good predictions, no matter what particular sequence is observed. By Theorem 15.1, the resulting algorithms then also lead to consistent estimates, such that *if* data are i.i.d. $\sim P^*$ according to some $P^* \in \mathcal{M}^*$, *then* the estimator converges to P^* at reasonably fast rate. This is a fantastic sanity check of such an individual-sequence method; but one should never turn the world on its head, and design estimators solely to converge fast if $P^* \in \mathcal{M}^*$; for then one cannot really say anything about their performance on the sequence that actually arrives.

> **Example 17.1** [**Models with, and Distributions without Densities**] One often adopts the normal family as one's statistical model because one has reason to believe that each outcome X_i is really the normalized sums of a number of bounded i.i.d. random variables $Y_{i,1}, \ldots, Y_{i,m}$. It then follows by the central limit theorem that the X_i are approximately normally distributed. However, if the $Y_{i,j}$ are discrete (for example, Bernoulli) random variables, then the X_i will have a discrete rather than a continuous distribution. In particular, the X_i will not have a differentiable density. Modeling such data by a normal distribution is harmless as long as one considers individual sequences: with high probability, $\hat{\theta}(x^n)$ will achieve small log loss $- \log f_{\hat{\theta}(x^n)}(x^n)$, and universal models relative to the normal family will lead to good predictions of future data in the log loss sense. Thus, even in a parametric context, a model $\mathcal{M}$ of distributions with densities can be a very good model for the data even though the "true" distribution does not have a density, but only if the estimators based on such models do not crucially rely on the existence of such a density. One would expect that the same is the case for nonparametric models.

Summarizing, from an MDL perspective, the frequentist principle may very well serve as a sanity check, but never as a design principle (an explicit example of the frequentist design principle at work is given in Section 17.10). To be fair, I should immediately add that many frequentist statisticians have been working in a way consistent with the "weakly frequentist" sanity-check view. They accept that some of the most clever statistical procedures in history have been suggested by external ideas or principles, and they make it their business to analyze the frequentist behavior of such procedures. This type of research, which may analyze methods such as moment-based estimators, Bayes procedures, cross-validation, MDL, and many others, is generally illuminating and often quite sophisticated. However, one surprising aspect from an MDL point of view is that a substantial fraction of this research still concentrates on the maximum likelihood method and its direct extensions.[1]

The Strange Focus on Maximum Likelihood   Fisher's ideas on maximum likelihood estimation provided an enormous breakthrough in the 1920s and 1930s. While at that time, there was ample justification to study its frequentist properties, I think that now, in 2006, it is time to move on. The ML method suffers from a number of problems: (1) it does not protect against overfitting; (2) in some quite simple problems (such as the Neyman-Scott problem (Wallace 2005)), its performance is simply dismal; (3) even if one analyzes its behavior for quite simple parametric families, it is sometimes not "admissible" (Ferguson 1967). Finally, (4), it provides no clue as to why there exist phenomena such as "superefficiency." A superefficient estimator relative to a parametric Θ is one which, like the ML estimator, achieves the minimax (squared Hellinger) convergence rate $O(n^{-1})$, but achieves much faster rates on a subset of Θ of Lebesgue measure 0. None of these four issues are a problem for MDL. Given this insight, it seems strange to focus so much effort on proving consistency and convergence rate results for ML estimators.

> For example, overfitting is taken care of automatically by MDL, witness the convergence results Theorem 15.1 and Theorem 15.3; its behavior on Neyman-Scott is just fine (Rissanen 1989); admissibility is guaranteed for two-part MDL estimators (Barron and Cover 1991), and finally, the superefficiency phenomenon is easily explained from an MDL point of view (Barron and Hengartner 1998): as we already pointed out in Chapter 6, one can easily design a Bayesian universal code relative to a parametric model Θ with a discrete prior, that puts nonzero prior mass on all rational-valued parameter values. One can define a meta-universal code relative to this code, combined with the ordinary Bayesian universal code based on a continuous prior. Such a meta-universal code will achieve standard expected redundancy $O(\log n)$ if $X_1, X_2, \ldots \sim P_\theta$ for all $\theta \in \Theta$, but it will achieve expected redundancy $O(1)$ for θ with rational-valued parameters. It follows that for rational parameters, the KL, and therefore, the Hellinger risk, of the corresponding prequential Bayesian estimator must essentially converge (Chapter 15, Corollary 15.1, page 473) at rate faster than $O(f(n))$, where $\sum_{i=1,2,\ldots} f(i) < \infty$, so that $f(n) = o(1/n)$.

---

1. To witness, I have once taken part in a discussion with several well-known non-Bayesian statisticians, who simply could not believe (a) that in the MDL approach to histogram estimation, histograms are determined by a Jeffreys' or Laplace estimator, rather than an ML estimator (Chapter 13, Section 13.3); and (b) that this matters.

ML Is Fundamental - in a Different Sense The ML estimator plays a fundamental role in statistics: it pops up in a wide variety contexts, it has a natural
feel to it, and it has many pleasant properties. To give but one example of such
a property, in exponential families, it is equal to the average sufficient statistic
of the observed data. Because of its fundamental role, it is sometimes argued
that there is ample justification to continue studying the convergence properties of ML estimators. From an MDL point of view, the ML estimator is indeed
a most fundamental notion, so there is no contradiction here. But it is invariably seen as a quantity that is optimal *with hindsight*. Thus, the MDL goal is
to design estimators or predictors that predict almost as well as the ML estimator constructed with hindsight from the data that needs to be predicted. As
explained in Chapter 15, Section 15.4.1, this goal is *not* achieved by predicting
with, or estimating by, the ML estimator itself.

Of course, one can extend the ML method to deal with complex models by
adding complexity penalties, as is done, in, for example, the AIC model
selection criterion (Section 17.3.2). Such complexity penalties are typically
designed such as to achieve good rates of convergence in terms of (e.g.,
Hellinger) risk. Thus, they are designed so as to achieve good performance
in expectation, where the expectation is under one of the distributions in the
assumed model class. The problem with such extensions is that now the
frequentist paradigm is once more used as a design principle, rather than
merely as a sanity check.

17.1.2   The Weak Prequential Principle

Inference methods based on the frequentist design principle often violate
the *weak prequential principle (WPP)*. The WPP was introduced in essence by
Dawid (1984), and investigated in detail by Dawid and Vovk (1999).

Let us consider a hypothesis P for data $x_1, \ldots, x_n$ that can be used for
sequentially predicting x_i given x^{i-1}. For example, P may be a probabilistic source, or a universal code representing a set of probabilistic sources.
According to the WPP, the quality of P as an explanation for given data
$x^n = x_1, \ldots, x_n$ should only depend on the actual outcomes $x_1, \ldots, x_n$, as
well as the predictions that the distribution P makes on x^n, i.e. on the set of
n conditional probabilities $P(x_i \mid x^{i-1})$, $i = 1, \ldots n$. It should not depend on
any other aspect of P. In particular, the conditional probability of any $x \in \mathcal{X}$
conditioned on data y^{i-1} that did *not* occur in the sequence $x_1, \ldots, x_n$ should
not play any role at all.

There are at least two reasons why this might be a good idea: first, intuitively, it would be strange or even irrational, if predictions *that were never made* would somehow influence any decision about whether P is a suitable model for the observed data. Second, we may sometimes want to consider a "hypothesis" P whose predictions conditional on unseen data are simply *unknowable*. A prototypical example is weather forecasting.

> **Example 17.2 [Weather Forecasters and the WPP]** Here we let P represent a weather forecaster, in the following sense: let data $(x_1, y_1), \ldots, (x_n, y_n)$ represent consecutive days. On each day $i-1$, based on previous data x^{i-1}, y^{i-1}, the weather forecaster announces the probability that it will rain on day i. Thus, $y_i \in \mathcal{Y}$ indicates whether it rains (1) or not (0) on day i, and the weather forecaster's predictions can be thought of as conditional distributions $P(Y_i \mid x^{i-1}, y^{i-1})$. Here each x_i can be thought of as a gigantic vector summarizing all the observable data on day i that the forecaster makes use of in her prediction algorithm. This may include air pressure, humidity, temperature and other related quantities measured at various places around the world.
>
> In the Netherlands we have two weather forecasters (one working for public television, the other for commercial television). Both make daily predictions about the precipitation probability for the next day. If we want to know who of the two we should listen to, we would like to compare their predictions on some sequence of days, say, the entire previous year. If we use a comparison procedure which needs to look at their prediction for day y_i in contexts that have not taken place (i.e. for values of x^{i-1} and y^{i-1} different from those observed), then we are in trouble, for it would be exceedingly hard to obtain this information.

The WPP is violated by many classical statistical procedures, including standard null hypothesis testing. As a result, standard hypothesis testing cannot be used to determine the quality of a weather forecaster, merely by watching her make predictions on television. Instead, one would need to know what she *would* have predicted in all possible situations that might have, but did not occur. The relation between the WPP and MDL is explored in Section 17.5.

17.1.3 MDL vs. Frequentist Principles: Remaining Issues

As claimed by the frequentist in the beginning of this section, page 524, principles like MDL and Bayes do provide recipes to "automatically" approach all kinds of statistical problems. But unlike the frequentist, I think this is good rather than bad. The alternative offered by the frequentist design principle is to design separate, possibly entirely different algorithms for each of the many different types of inductive inference tasks, such as classification, regression, sequential prediction, model selection, clustering, similarity analysis... For each of these tasks, one should design an algorithm with good properties for exactly that task. To me, such an approach seems neither very elegant nor very robust. I'd much rather use a "principle" (such as MDL or Bayes) that is widely applicable, always yields reasonable answers, even if in any particular application, the method induced by the principle is not 100% optimal. For example, it is not clear to me whether one should be particularly concerned about the fact that the risk of MDL inference with CUP model classes in nonparametric contexts does not always converge at the optimal rate (Chapter 16, Section 16.6). MDL sometimes needs an extra $\log n$ factor in expectation compared to the minimax optimal algorithm, under some assumptions on the true distribution P^*. This may not be a very large price to pay, given that we have designed our MDL algorithm without making any assumptions about this P^* whatsoever!

However, the fact that I (and most other individual-sequence MDL adherents) embrace the use of frequentist analysis as a sanity check, does imply the following: suppose that an MDL procedure has *really bad* frequentist behavior, e.g. suppose that it would be inconsistent under a wide variety of conditions. Then I am in trouble: my basic principle suggested a method which fails my sanity check. Luckily, the convergence results Theorem 15.1 and 15.3 guarantee that this never happens when the model class contains the true data-generating distribution. However, such inconsistency can sometimes occur if the model class is misspecified; see Section 17.10.2.

Expectation-Based vs. Individual-Sequence MDL   As discussed in Chapter 6, Section 6.5, a majority of information theorists works with stochastic rather than individual-sequence universal codes, where usually, "universality" is defined in expectation with respect to some P in one of the models under consideration. According to the individual-sequence MDL philosophy, one really should not use expectation-based MDL procedures, which are based on such expected-redundancy universal models. Nevertheless, I have to admit that from a certain point of view, the use of such codes is quite natural. To see this, first note that if we code data using the code corresponding to a distribution P, then the code would be optimal in expectation sense if indeed the data were distributed $\sim P$. That is, we associate each distribution P with the code Q achieving

$$\min_Q D(P\|Q),$$

where Q ranges over all codelength functions. The Q achieving this minimum happens to be equal to P. Starting from that consideration, if we want to associate a code with a *set* of distributions $\mathcal{M}$, the natural extension seems to be to require that the code would be optimal in expectation sense if indeed the data were distributed $\sim P$, in the worst-case over all $P \in \mathcal{M}$. Thus, we should pick the code minimizing

$$\min_{Q} \max_{P \in \mathcal{M}} D(P\|Q).$$

This is exactly what we do if we base model selection on the minimax optimal expected redundancy code ((6.41) on page 202) rather than the minimax optimal individual-sequence regret code $\bar{P}_{\text{nml}}$.

Thus, one may reason that the proper type of universal code to use in MDL inference is of the expected rather than the individual sequence kind. In my own personal view, expectation-based MDL is an interesting variation of MDL where the frequentist principle is elevated from its sanity check status, and put on the same footing as the compression principle. I prefer the individual-sequence principle, but think it is reassuring that in practice, individual-sequence MDL procedures are usually also minimax optimal in an expectation sense, and *intuitive*[2] expectation-based MDL procedures often also turn out to work well in an individual sequence sense; see, however, the discussion in Chapter 11, the discussion below Example 11.12, page 326. In the remainder of this chapter, the term "MDL" keeps referring to the individual-sequence version.

17.2 MDL and Bayesian Inference

Bayesian statistics is one of the most well-known, frequently and successfully applied paradigms of statistical inference (Berger 1985; Bernardo and Smith 1994; Lee 1997; Gelman et al. 2003). It is often claimed that "MDL is really just a special case of Bayes."[3] Although there are close similarities, this is simply not true. To see this quickly, consider the basic quantity in refined MDL: the NML distribution $\bar{P}_{\text{nml}}$, (6.15) on page 181. There is no mention of anything like this code/distribution in any Bayesian textbook!

---

2. The word "intuitive" is meant to rule out brittle procedures such as those described on page 525 which, for example, crash if the same observation occurs twice.

3. The author has heard many people say this at many conferences. The reasons are probably historical: while the underlying philosophy has always been different, until Rissanen introduced the use of $\bar{P}_{\text{nml}}$, most actual implementations of MDL "looked" quite Bayesian.

Thus, it must be the case that Bayes and MDL are somehow different. While a Bayesian statistician may still think of NML as an approximation to the log marginal likelihood (see below), this cannot be said for the "localized" NML distribution (14.14) on page 427. While natural from an MDL point of view, this version of NML cannot even be interpreted as an approximation to any Bayesian quantity. The differences become more dramatic if one considers expectation-based MDL as well. In Section 17.3.2 below we describe an expectation-based MDL method that combines the best of the AIC and BIC model selection criteria, and that does not seem to resemble any Bayesian procedure.

In the remainder of this section, we analyze the differences between MDL and Bayes in considerable detail. We first give a high-level overview, emphasizing the difference in underlying principles. Then, in Section 17.2.1 through 17.2.3, we investigate the practical consequences of these underlying differences of principle.

The MDL vs. the Bayesian Principles   Two central tenets of modern Bayesian statistics are: (1) probability distributions are used to represent uncertainty, and to serve as a basis for making predictions, rather than merely standing for some imagined "true state of nature"; and, (2), all inference and decision-making is done in terms of prior and posterior distributions and utility functions. MDL sticks with (1) (although here the "distributions" are primarily interpreted as "codelength functions"), but not (2): MDL allows the use of arbitrary universal models such as NML and prequential plug-in universal models; the Bayesian universal model does not have a special status among these. Such codes are designed according to the minimum compression (or "maximum probability") principle and the luckiness principle, both of which have no direct counterpart in Bayesian statistics.

MDL's Two Principles: Maximum Probability and Luckiness   The first central idea of MDL is to base inferences on universal codes that achieve small codelength in a minimax sense, relative to some class of candidate codes ("model") $\mathcal{M}$. This minimum codelength paradigm may be reinterpreted as a *maximum probability principle*, where the maximum is relative to some given models, in the worst case over all sequences (Rissanen (1987) uses the phrase "*global* maximum likelihood principle"). Thus, whenever the Bayesian universal model is used in an MDL application, a prior (usually Jeffreys') should be used that minimizes worst-case codelength regret, or equivalently, maximizes worst-case relative probability.

In practice, the minimax optimal prior is often not well defined. Then MDL approaches have to resort to a second idea: the luckiness principle. The procedure now becomes "subjective,"[4] just like a Bayesian approach. Still, there remain some essential differences between MDL and Bayes. The most important of these are:

1. **Types of universal codes.** MDL is not restricted to Bayesian universal codes; for example, LNML and plug-in codes may be used as well.

2. **Hope vs. expectation.** The luckiness-type subjectivity of MDL is of an inherently different, weaker type than the subjectivity in Bayesian approaches. This is explained in Section 17.2.1 below. As a consequence, many types of inferences and decisions that are sometimes made in Bayesian inference are meaningless from an MDL perspective. This is perhaps the most crucial, yet least understood difference between MDL and Bayes.

3. **Priors must compress.** Even when luckiness functions are allowed, if a Bayesian marginal likelihood is used in an MDL context, then it has to be interpretable as a universal code, i.e. it has to compress data. This rules out the use of certain priors. For example, the Diaconis-Freedman type priors, which make Bayesian inference inconsistent, cannot be used in MDL approaches, as explained in Section 17.2.2.

The first difference illustrates that in some respects, MDL is less restrictive than Bayes.[5] The second and third difference illustrate that in some respects, MDL is more restrictive than Bayes; yet, as I argue below, the MDL-imposed restrictions make eminent sense. In the remainder of this section, we first, in Section 17.2.1, explain the differences between MDL's luckiness approach and the Bayesian prior approach. Section 17.2.2 explains how MDL's insistence on data compression helps avoid some problems and interpretation difficulties with Bayesian inference. In Section 17.2.3 we discuss the relation between MDL and various sub-brands of Bayesian inference.

---

4. It is sometimes claimed that MDL inference has no subjective aspects. This is wrong: subjectivity enters MDL through the luckiness principle. This fact was somewhat hidden in earlier treatments of MDL, because "luckiness functions" were not made explicit there.

5. From a Bayesian point of view, one may dismiss this difference by claiming that LNML, two-part and plug-in codes should merely be viewed as approximations of the Bayesian universal code, which is what really should be used. The other two differences cannot be dismissed on such grounds.

17.2.1   Luckiness Functions vs. Prior Distributions

Let Θ represent some parametric model $\{P_\theta \mid \theta \in \Theta\}$. Suppose we are interested in parameter estimation relative to Θ, or in model selection between Θ and some other parametric model Θ°. To apply MDL inference, we impose a luckiness function $a(\theta)$. While this is related to adopting a prior $\pi(\theta)$, we now explain why it is really not the same. First of all, recall that the prior $\pi(\theta)$ corresponding to $a(\theta)$ is in general *not* proportional to $e^{-a(\theta)}$. Rather, it is given by the luckiness-tilted Jeffreys' prior $\pi(\theta) \propto \sqrt{\det I(\theta)}e^{-a(\theta)}$.

Three Reasons for Choosing a Particular Luckiness Function   A second and more important difference with Bayesian priors is that we may choose a particular luckiness function for all kinds of reasons: first, it may indeed be the case that we choose a particular $a(\theta)$ because we have prior beliefs that data for which $a(\hat\theta(x^n))$ is large are improbable. A second reason for imposing a certain luckiness function is that it may make our universal codes mathematically simpler or more efficiently computable, so that our inference problem becomes tractable. A third reason to impose a particular luckiness function arises when we deal with an inference problem for which some region $\Theta' \subset \Theta$ is simply of no interest to us. We can then make the corresponding model selection problem a lot easier by imposing a luckiness function with large $a(\theta)$ for $\theta \in \Theta'$.

Example 17.3 Let Θ represent the Poisson model, given in the mean-value parameterization. Suppose, for the sake of argument, that data are distributed according to some $\mu^* \in \Theta$. Let $\Theta' = \{\mu \mid \mu > 1000\}$. It may be that μ^* represents the average time between two phone calls in a particular neighborhood. A phone company may be interested in estimating μ^* because it can optimize its resources if it has a better idea of the length of phone calls. If μ^* is very large, than P_{μ^*} also has large variance (the Poisson model satisfies $\mathrm{var}_{\mu^*}[X] = \mu^*$), and then knowing μ^* or a good approximation thereof may not be very useful, and will not save a lot of money. So, the company may be interested in good estimates of μ^*, but only if μ^* is small.

Only the first of these three reasons for using luckiness functions truly corresponds to the use of a prior in Bayesian statistics. The second reason – choosing a luckiness function for computational reasons – corresponds to the use of pragmatic priors, which, as explained further below, is standard Bayesian practice, yet, in my view, cannot be justified by Bayesian theory. From a Bayesian point of view, the third reason may seem strange, since it mixes up probability and utility considerations.[6] From an MDL point of view, this is as it should be, as we now explain.

The Rationale of Luckiness   Suppose we have chosen a luckiness function $a(\theta)$. We then observe data x^n, and end up with a luckiness ML estimator $\hat{\theta}_a(x^n)$ which achieves a certain luckiness value $a(\hat{\theta}_a(x^n))$. What are the consequences of this for decision-making? If $a(\hat{\theta}_a(x^n))$ is small, then our universal code $\bar{P}$ based on $a(\theta)$ achieved small regret. This means we are *lucky*: because we were able to compress the observed data a lot, we have a lot of confidence in any inferences we may draw from our universal code. For example, if we use the predictive distribution $\bar{P}(\cdot \mid x^n)$ as an estimator, then small $a(\hat{\theta}_a(x^n))$ means high confidence that $\bar{P}(\cdot \mid x^n)$ will lead to good predictions of future data. This conclusion can also be motivated from a frequentist perspective by Theorem 15.1, which relates good compression to fast learning. On the other hand, if the data were such that $a(\hat{\theta}_a(x^n))$ is large, then we were unlucky: we do not compress a lot, and we cannot trust predictions of future data based on our current predictive distribution $\bar{P}(\cdot \mid x^n)$ to be accurate. Another connection to frequentist analysis can be made in a model selection context, when comparing the model (Θ, P_θ) to a point hypothesis P_0. In that case, observing data with small $a(\hat{\theta}_a(x^n))$ implies that in a frequentist hypothesis test, we would have rejected P_0. This is implied by the no-hypercompression inequality, as we explained in Chapter 14, Example 14.6, page 421. It is crucial to note that *observing "lucky" data with small $a(\hat{\theta}_a(x^n))$ implies large confidence in estimates and predictions irrespective of whether our luckiness function corresponds to prior beliefs or not!* This shows that it is *safe* to choose a luckiness function completely at will – if it is chosen for mathematical convenience, and the corresponding prior puts large mass at parameter values that do not turn out to fit the data well, then we will simply conclude that we were "unlucky," and not have any confidence in our future predictions. We will see below that the same cannot be said for pragmatically chosen Bayesian priors.

Pragmatic Priors vs. Luckiness Functions: Expectation vs. Hope   Most practical Bayesian inference is based on pragmatic priors, which, rather than truly representing the statistician's prior degree of belief, are chosen mostly

---

6. But see Rubin (1987), who mathematically shows that Bayesian prior and utility considerations are, in a sense, logically inseparable. This is, however, not the way Bayesian theory is usually presented.

for their mathematical convenience. An example is the frequent adoption in Bayesian practice of conjugate priors relative to exponential families (Berger 1985). One may argue that the use of such pragmatic priors corresponds exactly to the use of luckiness function in MDL priors. There is, however, a crucial difference. To see this, suppose we adopt some convenient, pragmatic prior π on the model Θ. For example, let Θ be the Bernoulli model in its standard parameterization, and suppose a pragmatic Bayesian adapts the uniform prior for convenience. Now the prior probability that θ will fall into the interval $[0, 0.9]$, is nine times as large as the prior probability that θ will fall in the region $[0.9, 1.0]$. Then strictly speaking, a Bayesian should be prepared to pay up to ten dollars for a lottery ticket which pays 100 dollars if, in a long sequence of outcomes, more than 90% ones are observed, and which pays 0 dollars otherwise. But why would this make sense if the uniform prior has been chosen for pragmatic, e.g. computational reasons, and does not *truly and precisely* reflect the Bayesian's subjective prior belief? To me, it does not make much sense. The same argument holds for most other decisions that can be made on the basis of pragmatic priors and posteriors.

Note that MDL inference with luckiness functions is immune to this problem. For example, suppose we use MDL with a Bayesian universal code relative to the Bernoulli model. We decide to use Jeffreys' prior (and use a uniform luckiness function), because it achieves codelengths that are close to minimax optimal. Now, once Jeffreys' prior has been adopted, one can formally calculate the prior probability that θ will fall into the interval $[0.5, 0.51]$, and the prior probability that θ will fall in the region $[0.99, 1.0]$. The latter probability is more than 5 times the former, but this certainly does not mean that an MDL statistician deems data with 99% or more 1s as a priori five times as likely than data with about 50% ones; he or she would certainly not be willing to take part in a betting game which would be fair if this proposition were true. From the MDL viewpoint, Jeffreys' prior has been adopted only because it leads to minimax optimal relative codelengths, *no matter what the data is*, and no statement about which parameters are "more likely" than others can ever be based on it.

According to MDL, all decision-making should be directly based on the universal code, which is a distribution on sequences of data. Thus, we can use the marginal likelihood $\bar{P}_{\text{Bayes}}(x^n)$ as a basis for decisions in model selection problems, and the predictive distribution $\bar{P}_{\text{Bayes}}(X_{n+1} \mid x^n)$ as a predictor of future data or as an estimator of θ. We are only willing to place bets on events whose expected payoffs can be expressed directly in terms of

$\bar{P}_{\text{Bayes}}$. The luckiness-Jeffreys' posterior of θ has no meaning in and of itself.[7] Whereas in Bayesian inference, confidence in decisions is measured based on the posterior, in MDL it is solely measured by the amount of bits by which $\bar{P}_{\text{Bayes}}(x^n)$ compresses data x^n. Thus, with a very small sample, say, $n = 1$, $\bar{P}_{\text{Bayes}}(X_{n+1} \mid x^n)$, is of course still strongly dependent on the luckiness function, and hence very "subjective," we are allowed to use it for prediction of X_2. But our confidence in the prediction is measured by the amount of bits by which $\bar{P}_{\text{Bayes}}(x^n)$ compresses data x^n relative to some null model $\mathcal{M}_0$ (Chapter 14, Example 14.3); for small n, this will usually give us very small confidence. For $n = 0$ (no data observed, distribution fully determined by luckiness function), it will give us no confidence at all — which is exactly how it should be, according to the luckiness principle.

Summarizing and rephrasing the previous paragraphs:

Bayesian Priors vs. MDL Luckiness Functions

From a Bayesian point of view, adopting a prior π implies that we a priori *expect* certain things to happen; and strictly speaking, we should be willing to accept bets which have positive expected pay-off given these expectations. For example, we always believe that, for large n, with high probability, the ML estimator $\hat{\theta}(x^n)$ will lie in a region Θ_0 with high prior probability mass. If this does not happen, a low-probability event will have occurred and we will be surprised.

From an MDL point of view, adopting a luckiness function a implies that we a priori *hope* certain things will happen. For example, we hope that the ML estimator $\hat{\theta}(x^n)$ will lie in a region with small luckiness function (i.e., high luckiness) $a(\theta)$, but we are not willing to place bets on this event. If it does not happen, then we do not compress the data well, and therefore, we do not have much confidence in the quality of our current predictive distribution when used for predicting future data; but we will not necessarily be surprised.

Bayes and Gzip In prequential MDL approaches, we predict X_{n+1} using $\bar{P}_{\text{Bayes}}$ $(X_{n+1} \mid x^n)$. Our predictions would be optimal in posterior expectation, *if*

---

7. Note that $\bar{P}_{\text{Bayes}}(x^n)$ and $\bar{P}_{\text{Bayes}}(x_{n+1} \mid x^n)$ can be written as expectations taken over the prior and the posterior, respectively. Thus, we cannot say that MDL considers *all* expectations over prior/posterior to be meaningless; the problematic ones are those which cannot be rewritten in terms of $\bar{P}_{\text{Bayes}}$ only.

data were really sampled by first sampling θ from the prior π_a, and then sampling data from θ. Does this imply that MDL secretly assumes that π_a is a prior in the Bayesian sense after all? Certainly not. To see why, consider the widely used data compression program *gzip*. Gzip is really just a prefix code, and by the Kraft inequality, there must be a (possibly defective) probability distribution $\bar{P}_{\text{gzip}}$ such that for all files, represented as a string x^n, the number of bits needed to encode x^n by gzip is given by $-\log \bar{P}_{\text{gzip}}(x^n)$. Thus, gzip would be the optimal code in expectation to use if data were actually sampled according to P_{gzip} or if, as a Bayesian would think of it, P_{gzip} would truly express our subjective uncertainty about the data. But it would be absurd to assume that either of these two is the case. This would imply that the entropy $H(P_{\text{gzip}}^{(n)})$ is a reliable estimate of the number of bits we would need for encoding an actual file x^n. Now some people use gzip only for the compression of pdf files, and others use gzip only for the compression of postscript files. These two groups achieve different compression rates, so for at least one of them, $H(P_{\text{gzip}}^{(n)})$ must be a very bad indicator of how well they can compress their files. Just like gzip can compress well even if one does not believe that $\bar{P}_{\text{gzip}}$ truly represents one's uncertainty, it is also the case that $\bar{P}_{\text{Bayes}}$ based on prior π_a can compress well, even if one does not believe that $\bar{P}_{\text{Bayes}}$, or equivalently, π_a truly represents one's uncertainty. $\bar{P}_{\text{Bayes}}$ may even be the best compressor one can think of, in the limited computation time that one has available. Note that we are really reiterating the "third-most important observation" of this book here, see Chapter 3, page 107.

This difference between MDL and Bayesian inference is also brought out if $\bar{P}_{\text{Bayes}}(x^n)$ cannot be computed, and we have to use an approximation instead. What constitutes a valid approximation? As we already described in Section 14.6 on page 453, an approximation which performs well apart for data with ML estimators that fall in a region with very small prior probability is acceptable from a Bayesian point of view, but not from an MDL (and not even from an expectation-based MDL) point of view.

Some Bayesians agree that, if a pragmatic convenience prior is used, then expectations defined with respect to the prior are not very meaningful, and even expectations over the posterior should be treated with some care. Yet the point is that, in contrast to MDL, there is nothing in Bayesian statistics which explicitly rules out taking such expectations. Moreover, many Bayesian procedures are explicitly based on taking such expectations. We give a particular example (DIC) below. Finally, even if a Bayesian admits that her prior may be "wrong," and only intends to use Bayes if the sample is so large that the prior hardly matters, there remains a huge conceptual problem if not just the prior, but the model itself is wrong. We very often want to use such models which we *a priori* know to be wrong; see Example 1.6. If we use Bayes for such models, then we are forced to put a prior distribution on a set of distributions which we know to be wrong - that is, we have degree-of-belief 1 in something we know not to be the case. From an MDL viewpoint, these priors are interpreted as tools to achieve short codelengths rather than degrees-of-belief and there is nothing strange about the situation; but from a Bayesian viewpoint, it seems awkward (but see Section 17.2.3 on purely subjective Bayes).

DIC An example of a Bayesian procedure that explicitly relies on expectations over the posterior, even when the sample is small, is the Bayesian *deviance information criterion (DIC)* for model selection (Spiegelhalter, Best, Carlin, and van der Linde 2002). DIC is based on the posterior expected *deviance*

$$E_{\theta \sim w(\cdot | X^n)}[-\log P_{\theta}(X^n) + \log P_{\hat{\theta}_{\text{mean}}(X^n)}(X^n)], \tag{17.1}$$

where $w(\cdot \mid X^n)$ represents the posterior distribution of θ and $\hat{\theta}_{\text{mean}}$ is the posterior mean estimator. The latter is arrived at by taking expectations over the posterior (Chapter 15, Section 15.4.3). The examples in (Spiegelhalter et al. 2002) are based on standard, pragmatic priors (such as the normal prior for the linear model), which may be called "weakly informative" or "essentially flat" (see Bernardo's comment on (Spiegelhalter et al. 2002, page 625)). Such priors usually do not truly reflect the statistician's beliefs. Therefore, expectations taken over the posterior, and hence, the entire derivation leading up to the DIC criterion, are essentially meaningless from an MDL perspective.

Note that we chose this particular example because it is recent and directly related to model selection and regret; numerous other examples could be given as well.

17.2.2 MDL, Bayes, and Occam

Bayesian model selection can be done in various ways. One of the most straightforward and popular of these is the *Bayes factor* method (Kass and Raftery 1995). The Bayes factor method automatically implements a form of Occam's razor. This "Occam factor" phenomenon has been independently observed by several researchers; see (MacKay 2003, Chapter 28) for a detailed account, and (Jeffereys and Berger 1992) for a list of references. Below we shall see that in some other contexts such as nonparametric estimation and prediction, Bayesian inference can sometimes become disconnected from Occam's razor, and that this can cause trouble. Bayesian statisticians often view Bayesian inference as the more fundamental concept, and use the Occam factor phenomenon to argue that a form of Occam's razor is implied, and therefore justified, by the deeper principle that rational learning and inference should be done in a Bayesian manner. In this subsection I argue that one may just as well turn the argument on its head and view Occam's razor, formalized as MDL inference based on universal coding, as the deeper principle. It justifies aspects of Bayesian inference by showing that they are implied by MDL's universal coding approach; but it also rules out some other, problematic aspects of Bayesian inference which contradict MDL ideas.

Bayes Factors: Direct Occam   As we showed in Chapter 14, Section 14.2.3, page 418, Bayes factor model selection ends up being very similar to MDL model selection. This is all the more remarkable since the motivation for both methods is entirely different. Let us describe the motivation for the Bayes factor method. For simplicity, we restrict to the simple case where there are just two parametric models $\mathcal{M}_1$ and $\mathcal{M}_2$ under consideration. From a Bayesian perspective, we can assign each of these a prior probability W. Fortunately, the precise probabilities we assign will hardly affect the result, unless they are very close to zero or one, or the sample is exceedingly small. So, just for simplicity, we set $W(\mathcal{M}_1) = W(\mathcal{M}_2) = 0.5$. We now observe some data x^n and our task is to select a model $\mathcal{M}_1$ or $\mathcal{M}_2$. In the Bayes factor method, the goal of model selection is to find the true state of nature. This can be formalized by using a 0/1-loss (minus utility) function $\mathbf{L} : \{1,2\}^2 \rightarrow \{0,1\}$: suppose $\mathcal{M}_\gamma$ is the "true" model, and we select model with index $\hat{\gamma}$. Then $\mathbf{L}(\gamma, \hat{\gamma}):=0$ if $\gamma = \hat{\gamma}$ (our guess is correct), and $L(\gamma, \hat{\gamma}):=1$ if $\gamma \neq \hat{\gamma}$ (our guess is wrong). According to Bayesian statistics, upon observing data $x^n \in \mathcal{X}^n$, we should take the decision $\hat{\gamma} \in \{1,2\}$ that minimizes the posterior expected loss, i.e. we set

$$\hat{\gamma} = \arg \min_{\gamma \in \{1,2\}} E_{Z \sim W(\cdot | x^n)}[\mathbf{L}(Z, \gamma)], \tag{17.2}$$

where

$$E_{Z \sim W(\cdot | x^n)}[\mathbf{L}(Z, \gamma)] = \sum_{\gamma' \in \{1,2\}} W(\mathcal{M}_{\gamma'} \mid x^n)\mathbf{L}(\gamma', \gamma).$$

Evidently, $\hat{\gamma}$ is achieved for the γ with the maximum posterior probability $W(\mathcal{M}_\gamma \mid x^n)$. This is exactly the γ picked by the Bayes factor method. In Section 14.2.3 we explained how to calculate $W(\gamma \mid x^n)$, and why it usually leads to the same results as MDL model selection.

The derivation makes clear why Bayes factors are sometimes criticized on the grounds that they strongly depend on one of the models being true in the sense of being identical to the data generating process (Gelman et al. 2003), and that they have no "predictive interpretation"(Spiegelhalter, Best, Carlin, and van der Linde 2002).

Bayesian Model Selection and Prediction Our MDL analysis shows that both criticisms are unjustified: Bayes factor model selection can be viewed as a form of MDL model selection, which has a predictive (prequential) interpretation that is valid no matter what sequence is observed, and which does not depend on any underlying "true distribution."

Intriguingly however, Bernardo and Smith (1994, Chapter 6) consider alternative utility functions that correspond to viewing model selection in predictive rather than truth-hunting terms. They find that Bayesian model selection with such alternative utility functions behaves quite differently from Bayes factor model selection. More precisely, they replace the 0/1 loss function in (17.2) by the log loss $-\log \bar{P}_{\text{Bayes}}(X_{n+1} \mid x^n, \mathcal{M}_{\hat{\gamma}})$. Here $\bar{P}_{\text{Bayes}}(X_{n+1} \mid x^n, \mathcal{M}_{\hat{\gamma}})$ is the Bayesian predictive distribution for the next outcome based on model $\mathcal{M}_{\gamma}$. Thus, they select the model $\hat{\gamma}$ such that the Bayesian prequential estimator based on $\mathcal{M}_{\hat{\gamma}}$ has the smallest posterior expected log loss. Their analysis suggests that asymptotically, the resulting "predictive Bayesian" model selection method will behave like leave-one-out cross-validation (Section 17.6) and the AIC criterion (Section 17.3.2). Also, unlike the Bayes factor method, their heuristic analysis still makes sense if the "true" data generating machinery is unknown, and none of the models under consideration is true. In this case, the models $\mathcal{M}_{\gamma}$ are simply viewed as sets of predictors. More precisely, they assume a "true" model class $\mathcal{M}^*$ and a prior W^* on $\mathcal{M}^*$, where $\mathcal{M}^*$ does not necessarily contain any of the $\mathcal{M}_{\gamma}$. Their analysis suggests that, under some conditions, asymptotically, someone who performs Bayesian model selection based on the loss function $-\log \bar{P}_{\text{Bayes}}(X_{n+1} \mid x^n, \mathcal{M}_{\hat{\gamma}})$ relative to model class $\mathcal{M}^*$ and prior W^*, would select the same model $\mathcal{M}_{\hat{\gamma}}$ as would be selected by leave-one-out cross-validation, which can be implemented without knowledge of $\mathcal{M}^*$. Thus, while Bayes factor model selection has a *sequential* predictive interpretation, the Bayesian method suggested by Bernardo and Smith (1994) may have a leave-one-out style predictive interpretation.

Because of its correspondence to MDL model selection, it is clear that the Bayes factor method "automatically" implements some form of Occam's razor. If Bayes is used for estimation or prediction rather than model selection, then this connection may sometimes be lost. For example, in nonparametric estimation, the question whether or not Bayes has a built-in Occam's razor strongly depends on the chosen model and prior. Diaconis and Freedman (1986) provide combinations of models and priors for which Bayesian inference becomes inconsistent. As we argue below, this is really implied by the fact that with such priors, the Bayesian universal code does not compress, and hence, does not implement a form of Occam's razor. On the other hand, the Gaussian processes that we introduced in Chapter 13 define models and priors for which the Bayesian universal code compresses very well, and, as a consequence, the Bayesian predictive distribution predicts exceedingly well. Taken together, these two facts illustrate why one might prefer the principles underlying MDL over those underlying Bayesian inference.

Gaussian Processes: Hidden Occam   In nonparametric contexts, Bayesian prediction is sometimes based on a mixture of infinitely many arbitrarily complex distributions. Yet, in many such cases, Bayesian methods predict exceedingly well in practice. Therefore, it is sometimes argued that nonparametric Bayes violates the spirit of Occam's razor, but that also, this is as it should be. Take, for example, the Gaussian processes with RBF kernel. Regression based on such highly nonparametric models is very successful in practice (Rasmussen and Williams 2006). As we described in Section 13.5, such Gaussian process regression is based on a Bayesian predictive distribution which itself is essentially a mixture of infinitely many Gaussians. Therefore, it seems to violate Occam's razor.

I strongly disagree with this interpretation. When Gaussian processes are combined with the RBF kernel, then the Bayesian marginal likelihood has excellent, almost magical universal coding properties – the developments in Chapter 13, Section 13.5.3 show that it can be viewed as an excellent data compressor, with small coding regret even relative to high-dimensional regression functions. Using the prequential MDL convergence theorem, Theorem 15.1, this implies that, even if the data are distributed by some quite complex process, the Gaussian process predictions converge to the optimal predictions at a very fast (logarithmic) rate. Therefore, an MDL analysis of the Gaussian process model shows that, when used to sequentially code the data, it leads to very short descriptions thereof, and therefore does implement some form of Occam's razor after all; because good compression implies fast learning, it is exactly its good compression behavior which explains why it works so well in practice (a related point is made by (Rasmussen and Ghahramani 2000)).

In a nonparametric Bayesian modeling context, Neal (1996) states that:

"For problems where we do not expect a simple solution, the proper Bayesian approach is therefore to use a model of a suitable type that is as complex as we can afford computationally, regardless of the size of the training set."

Our analysis suggests that this is true *only* if the chosen model has good universal coding properties. We proceed to confirm this suggestion by reviewing an example with a model/prior combination that has bad universal coding properties, and for which Bayesian inference leads to bad results.

Bayesian Inconsistency: No Occam For some nonparametric i.i.d. model classes $\mathcal{M}$, there exist priors such that the corresponding Bayesian marginal likelihood $\bar{P}_{\text{Bayes}}$ is not a universal model relative to $\mathcal{M}$. More precisely, there exists $P^* \in \mathcal{M}$ and $c > 0$ such that, if data are i.i.d. $\sim P^*$, then no matter how large the sample n, the expected redundancy $E_{X \sim P^{*(n)}}[-\log \bar{P}_{\text{Bayes}}(X^n) + \log P^*(X^n)] > cn$. Thus, $\bar{P}_{\text{Bayes}}$ is not universal relative to P^*. Since MDL is *defined* as inference based on universal models, it is clear that from an MDL point of view, such priors can *never* be used.

Now interestingly, there exist some (in)famous theorems by Diaconis and Freedman (1986), which show that for some nonparametric contexts and with some priors, Bayesian inference can be inconsistent, in the sense that for some P^*, if data are i.i.d. $\sim P^*$, then the posterior concentrates on (smaller and smaller Hellinger neighborhoods of) a distribution P' with nonzero Hellinger distance to P^*. Bayesians often dismiss these results as irrelevant, since they are based on "silly" combinations of models and priors, that one would never use in practice. There is, however, nothing in standard Bayesian statistics which gives any clue about the conditions under which a model/prior combination is "silly." MDL provides exactly such a clue: it turns out that the combination of priors and true distributions used by Diaconis and Freedman are invariably such that the resulting $\bar{P}_{\text{Bayes}}$ is not a universal code relative to P^*. Thus, from an MDL point of view, one would never use such priors! To see this, note that Theorem 15.1 immediately implies the following: if $\bar{P}_{\text{Bayes}}$ is a universal code relative to P^*, then Bayes must be Césaro-consistent in KL, and therefore, also in Hellinger distance. The Diaconis-Freedman results imply that with the Diaconis-Freedman prior, the Bayesian predictive distribution $\bar{P}_{\text{Bayes}}$ is *not* Césaro consistent in Hellinger distance. It follows that under the Diaconis and Freedman prior, $\bar{P}_{\text{Bayes}}$ cannot be universal. In his comment on Diaconis and Freedman (1986), Barron (1986) already brings up a related point.

Bayesian vs. MDL Inconsistency
Suppose that data are sampled from a distribution P^* in the model class $\mathcal{M}$ under consideration. As a direct consequence of its focus on data compression, in prediction and estimation contexts, MDL is 100% immune to inconsistency by Theorem 15.1 and Theorem 15.3. In contrast, Bayesian inference can be inconsistent for some combinations of nonparametric $\mathcal{M}$ with some priors. In *model selection contexts*, both MDL and Bayes can be inconsistent in at least one case (Chapter 16, Section 16.4). If the model class is wrong, then MDL and Bayes can both be inconsistent in the sense of (Grünwald and Langford 2004).

17.2.3 MDL and Brands of Bayesian Statistics

In the previous subsections, we criticized the "pragmatic" version of Bayesian statistics that is most often used in practice. But perhaps Bayes was never intended to be used in such a pragmatic way; if we use Bayesian inference as it was intended by its founding fathers, then maybe our criticisms become invalid. Matters are complicated by the fact that there exist various brands of pure, "nonpragmatic" Bayesian statistics. Here we examine the main brands, (purely) subjective Bayes, mostly associated with the work of De Finetti (1937) and Savage (1954), and objective Bayes, mostly associated with Jeffreys (1961) and Jaynes (2003). We also look into Solomonoff's (1964) approach, a specific version of objective Bayes that forms a middle ground between Bayes and MDL. Below, we characterize each brand by the type of prior that it uses.

Nonpragmatic Subjective Priors If a decision-maker thinks about a problem long enough, then she may avoid pragmatic priors and instead use priors that truly reflect her degrees of belief that various events occur. Assuming that the decision-maker can come up with such priors, some of the problems with Bayes that we mentioned above will disappear. In particular, expectations taken over the prior will be meaningful, at least in a subjective sense. Based on the "Dutch Book Argument" of De Finetti (1937), or on the axiomatic approach of Savage (1954), one may claim that subjective Bayes is the only rational ("coherent") approach to decision-making and should be preferred over MDL; in this view, the problems we mentioned are all due to the use of pragmatic priors. I have two problems with this position. First, while I find De Finetti's and Savage's results very interesting, I am not at all convinced that they imply that a rational decision-maker should act like a Bayesian.[8] Second, I do not think that humans have sufficient imaginative power to come up with a prior distribution that truly represents their beliefs, as the following example illustrates.

> **Example 17.4 [Mercury's Perihelion Advance]** Suppose that, after having observed data x^n, you selected some model $\mathcal{M}_0$ as a best explanation of the data. Later you learn that another research group found an entirely different explanation $\mathcal{M}_1$ of the data, such that
>
> $$-\log \bar{P}_{\text{Bayes}}(x^n \mid \mathcal{M}_1) \ll -\log \bar{P}_{\text{Bayes}}(x^n \mid \mathcal{M}_0).$$
>
> If you can be reasonably sure that $\mathcal{M}_1$ has not been constructed with hindsight, after seeing data x^n (so that there was no "cheating" going on), then you may well want to abandon the model $\mathcal{M}_0$ in favor of $\mathcal{M}_1$, *even if you had put no prior probability on $\mathcal{M}_1$ in the first place*. According to the subjective Bayesian viewpoint, this is not possible: if your prior probability of $\mathcal{M}_1$ was 0, the posterior is 0, and you can never embrace $\mathcal{M}_1$. But how can you put a prior on all possible models $\mathcal{M}_1$? Surely the imagination of individuals and research groups is limited, and they cannot think of all possible explanations – which may be provided by other research groups – in advance. For example, it was discovered in the 19th century that Mercury's perihelion does not exactly follow the predictions of Newton's theory of gravitation. As astronomers gathered more and more data about this phenomenon, various explanations ("models") were suggested, such as the existence of an unknown planet "Vulcan." The matter was finally settled when it turned out that Einstein's theory of general relativity, discovered only in 1916, explained Mercury's perihelion perfectly well. If astronomers had been using subjective priors on models, then it seems quite unlikely that, before 1916, anyone except Einstein would have had a nonzero prior probability on the theory of general relativity. This implies that they would not have believed this theory after 1916, no matter how well it had accounted for the data. This problem is closely related to the "old evidence" problem in Bayesian confirmation theory (Hutter 2006).

In the MDL approach, we can effectively avoid this "zero prior problem." We mentioned this possibility already in Chapter 14, Section 14.4.4, page 436; see also Example 17.5. For example, suppose we want to select a model $\mathcal{M}_\gamma$ from a CUP model class $\mathcal{M} = \cup_\gamma \mathcal{M}_\gamma, \gamma \in \Gamma$. We can use a meta-two-part code in which $\dot{L}(\gamma)$, the codelength function for γ, corresponds to a defective distribution W that sums to $1/2$ rather than 1. If later somebody proposes a new model

---

8. To mention just one, of many, problems: in my opinion, the *Ellsberg* paradox convincingly shows that sometimes uncertainty about an event cannot be represented by a single number; see (Ellsberg 1961) and (Halpern 2003, Example 2.3.2).

$\mathcal{M}_a, a \notin \Gamma$ for the data x^n that we were trying to model, and we are confident that that person has not peeked at x^n, then we can assign a code word with length $\dot{L}(a) = 1/4$ to $\mathcal{M}_a$; now $\dot{L}$ corresponds to a distribution W summing to $3/4$ rather than $1/2$. Now if another trustworthy person comes along and proposes some model $\mathcal{M}_b, b \notin \Gamma$, we can set $\dot{L}(b) = 1/8$; now W sums to $7/8$. The process can be repeated infinitely often. From an MDL perspective, there is nothing strange about this procedure. From a Bayesian point of view, however, it seems awkward: if we use a defective prior such as W before we are told about any of the alternative models $\mathcal{M}_a, \mathcal{M}_b, \ldots$, then we are effectively basing our decisions on the posterior $W(\mathcal{M}_\gamma \mid x^n, \gamma \notin \{a, b, \ldots\})$. Thus, it seems as if we have already decided that the true state of the world is a model $\mathcal{M}_\gamma$ on the original list, with $\gamma \in \Gamma$. If we are then told to consider the newly proposed model $\mathcal{M}_a$, we would have to "decondition" and assume that $\mathcal{M}_a$ may contain the true state of the world after all.

Solomonoff's Nonpragmatic, "Universal" Priors   In the earliest version of what we called "idealized MDL" in Chapter 1, Section 1.4, Solomonoff (1964) proposed a prior $\mathbf{M}$ on a countable set $\mathcal{M}$ that includes all computable probabilistic sources. Broadly speaking, this prior assigns large mass to sources P that can be implemented by a short computer program. More precisely, there is some constant C such that for all computable sources P, $-\log \mathbf{M}(P) \leq K(P) + C$, where $K(P)$ is the length of the shortest computer program that, when input n, x^n and precision d, outputs the first d bits of $P(x^n)$ and then halts. It is natural to extend the definition of Kolmogorov complexity and call $K(P)$ the Kolmogorov complexity of the distribution P (Li and Vitányi 1997). Here we consider Solomonoff's approach from a Bayesian perspective. We will have more to say about its relation to (practical, nonidealized) MDL in Section 17.8.

One can show that the Bayesian universal model $\bar{P}_{\text{Solomonoff}}$ relative to such a prior is $O(1)$-universal relative to any other computable probabilistic source, including any other universal model (Li and Vitányi 1997). Since we may assume that in practice, any universal model we will ever use in MDL or Bayesian inference is computable, $\bar{P}_{\text{Solomonoff}}$ may serve as a replacement for any other universal model that we might be interested in. Similarly, it may be reasonable for a decision-maker to use the prior $\mathbf{M}$ as a proxy of the subjective prior that he would really like to use, but cannot formulate for lack of time and imagination. If $\mathbf{M}$ is used in this way, then the problem of zero prior (Example 17.4) disappears: $\mathbf{M}$ assigns positive prior mass on any computable theory that can be formulated at all. Hutter (2006) forcefully argues that M solves various other problems of subjective Bayesianism as well.

Still, this approach is not without its problems. As mentioned in Chapter 1, Solomonoff's and other idealized MDL approaches are inherently uncomputable, and it is not clear whether sufficiently general computable approximations exist. Second, if we apply it to small samples (as, in statistical practice, we often must),[9] then the choice of programming language on which it is based has a significant impact on the Bayesian predictive distribution. We may choose the language that best suits the phenomenon that we are trying to model, but then subjectivity enters again, and the problems of the strictly subjective approach reappear.

Finally, it seems that using Solomonoff's approach, we violate the weak prequential principle. For example, it is not clear how we can use it for universal prediction in the weather forecasting example (Example 17.2), where the Kolmogorov complexity of the various forecasters is unknowable.

The relation between MDL inference, subjective priors, and Solomonoff's objective priors, is discussed further in Example 17.5.

Other "Objective" Priors   In the *objective Bayesian* approach, one replaces subjective or pragmatic priors by more "objective" ones, which may be used if no or very little prior knowledge is available. Examples are the Jeffreys' prior (Jeffreys 1961), and Bernardo's *reference priors*, which sometimes, but not always, coincide with Jeffreys' prior (Bernardo and Smith 1994). Various other possibilities are explored by Berger and Pericchi (2001). In contrast to Solomonoff's approach, the focus here is usually on parametric estimation or model selection between parametric models, and the priors are computable in practice. It is generally recognized (even by Jeffreys and Bernardo) that the choice of "objective" prior should depend on, for example, the loss function of interest: a prior which works as a good proxy for an unknown prior in one context (e.g., model selection), may not be such a good proxy in another context (e.g., parameter estimation). Some objective Bayes approaches to Bayes factor model selection are almost identical to MDL approaches with Bayesian universal codes.

In my view, there is still some advantage in interpreting these procedures from an MDL universal coding point of view, rather than as Bayesian. When

---

9. Consider, for example, experiments where each subject has to be paid in order to take part. In such experiments, one often has to make do with about 30 sample points. These are common in, e.g., the field of psychology.

Jim Berger recently (2005) gave an excellent tutorial on objective Bayes methods in Amsterdam, a member of the audience asked: "In both frequentist methods and subjective Bayesian methods, the interpretation of probability is clear, albeit very different. But how should we interpret the probabilities appearing in objective Bayesian methods?" Berger answered: "In many cases, both interpretations are valid." My answer would have been: "In *all* cases, these probabilities can be interpreted as *codelengths!*"

17.2.4   Conclusion: a Common Future after All?

In the previous section, I have criticized several aspects of the Bayesian approach. I do, however, see problems with the MDL approach as well — such as the lack of a proper accompanying decision theory; see Section 17.11 — and I do recognize that the two approaches are often similar in practice. As said, MDL methods often resemble objective Bayes methods. I should also mention that there is a nontrivial overlap between Rissanen's individual-sequence philosophy and De Finetti's original motivation for subjective Bayesian analysis, which is still shared by some Bayesians. Such subjectivists prefer not to speak about nonobservable things such as "θ, the true probability, or long-term frequency of heads." (Diaconis 2003). In fact, the preface of the magnum opus (De Finetti 1974) opens with the following memorable lines:

> "My thesis, paradoxically, and a little provocatively, but nonetheless genuinely, is simply this: PROBABILITY DOES NOT EXIST.
>
> The abandonment of superstitious beliefs about the existence of Phlogiston, the Cosmic Ether, Absolute Space and Time, ..., or Fairies and Witches, was an essential step along the road to scientific thinking. Probability, too, if regarded as something endowed with some kind of objective existence, is no less a misleading misconception [...]."

Subjectivists such as De Finetti only want to speak about probabilities of events that will eventually be observed (such as the probability that it will rain tomorrow), and they interpret these as degrees of belief, operationalized as the amount of money one is willing to place on certain bets. This is quite similar to Rissanen's ideas, who also restricts probabilist statements to observable events, and regards them as indicating the code one would use to code the data if the goal were to compress data as much as possible.

> In practice, subjective Bayesians then often speak about quantities like "θ, the true bias of the coin" after all, motivated either by De Finetti's exchangeabil-

ity theorem, or by Savage's treatment of subjective probability, which show that under certain circumstances, a rational decision maker should act *as if* data were distributed accorded to some $P_\theta \in \mathcal{M}$. From this point of view, individual-sequence MDL is like De Finetti-type subjectivist Bayesian statistics, but even more radical: any talk of a true θ is now truly avoided, and no inference is based on the presumption that such a θ exists.

Given these considerations, it may certainly be possible that one day, Bayesian and MDL approaches to statistics will merge into one. In such a joint approach, the contribution of MDL theory could be a proper interpretation of probabilities and expectations when pragmatic priors (now viewed as luckiness functions) are used, as well as some restrictions on the priors in non-parametric problems.

17.3   MDL, AIC and BIC

In this section, we specialize to MDL model selection. We compare it to two popular benchmark model selection methods: the *Bayesian Information Criterion* (BIC) and the *Akaike Information Criterion*, both of which we already encountered in Chapter 14, Example 14.4, page 417, and, in a regression context, in Section 14.5.4 on page 450.

17.3.1   BIC

In the first paper on MDL, Rissanen (1978) used a two-part code and showed that, asymptotically, and under regularity conditions, the two-part code-length of x^n based on a parametric model $\mathcal{M}_\gamma = \{P_\theta \mid \theta \in \Theta_\gamma\}$ with k_γ parameters, using an optimally discretized parameter space is given by

$$- \log P_{\hat\theta_\gamma(x^n)}(x^n) + \frac{k_\gamma}{2} \log n, \tag{17.3}$$

where $\hat\theta_\gamma$ is the ML estimator within Θ_γ, and $O(1)$-terms (depending on k_γ, but not on n) are ignored. As we have discussed in Chapter 14, these terms can be quite important in practice. In the same year Schwarz (1978), ignoring $O(1)$-terms as well, showed that, for large enough n, Bayes factor model selection between two exponential families amounts to selecting the model minimizing (17.3). As a result of Schwarz's paper, model selection based on (17.3) became known as the *BIC (Bayesian Information Criterion)*. Not taking into account the functional form of the model $\mathcal{M}$, it often does not work very well in practical settings with small or moderate samples.

Consistency   BIC does tend to perform well if the sample size gets really large: Suppose BIC is used to select a model $\mathcal{M}_\gamma$ coming from some CUP model class $\mathcal{M} = \cup_{\gamma \in \Gamma}\mathcal{M}_\gamma$ (Case 1(c) of Chapter 16, Section 16.1.1). Then BIC is asymptotically consistent under a wide variety of conditions on the model class $\mathcal{M}$. Here we refer to consistency in the sense of Chapter 16, Section 16.3.1. Often, consistency will hold for *all* P^* in *all* $\mathcal{M}_\gamma$: there is no need to exclude subsets of measure 0, as there was with MDL model selection based on CUP(2-p, Bayes)-codes (Barron, Rissanen, and Yu 1998; Csiszár and Shields 2000).

On the other hand, consider the nonparametric context where data are distributed according to some $P^* \in \mathcal{M}^*$, $P^* \notin \mathcal{M}$, where $\mathcal{M}^*$ is some smooth subset of $\langle\mathcal{M}\rangle$ (Case 2(a) of Chapter 16, Section 16.1.1). Then BIC model selection combined with maximum likelihood inference in the chosen model often does not achieve the minimax rate of convergence (Speed and Yu 1993; Yang 2005a; Yang 2005b). More precisely, the model selection-based estimator based on BIC and ML (defined analogously to (16.2) on page 509) typically does converge in terms of Hellinger risk for all $P^* \in \mathcal{M}^*$, but the rate of convergence exceeds the minimax rate by a factor of ORDER$(\log n)$; see (Yang 2005b, Section 4) and (Shao 1997). Here the "minimax rate" is the minimax optimal rate where the minimum is over all estimators, i.e. all functions from $\mathcal{X}^*$ to $\mathcal{M}$, and the maximum is over all $P^* \in \mathcal{M}$. This minimax rate is often of the form $n^{-2s/(2s+1)}$, where s is the degree of smoothness of the distributions in P^*; see Chapter 16, Example 16.4.

17.3.2   AIC

The *Akaike Information Criterion* was introduced and developed by Akaike in a series of papers starting with (Akaike 1973). It can be used for model selection with finite or countably infinite CUP model classes $\mathcal{M} = \cup_{\gamma \in \Gamma}\mathcal{M}_\gamma$. For given data x^n, it tells us to select the model with index γ_{aic} that minimizes, over all $\gamma \in \Gamma$,

$$-\log P_{\hat{\theta}_\gamma(x^n)}(x^n) + k_\gamma. \tag{17.4}$$

If $\mathcal{M}$ is countably infinite, then for large n, this criterion tends to select more complex models than BIC, the reason being that the complexity penalty does not depend on n.

Consistency   The consistency properties of AIC are quite different from those of BIC. In the case where data are distributed according to some $P^* \in$

$\mathcal{M}_{\gamma^*}$ for some $\gamma^* \in \Gamma$ (Case 1(c) of Chapter 16, Section 16.1.1), AIC is often inconsistent (Shibata 1976; Hannan 1980; Woodroofe 1982). Recall from the previous subsection that BIC is typically consistent in such cases. On the other hand, consider the nonparametric context where data are distributed according to some $P^* \in \mathcal{M}^*$, $P^* \notin \mathcal{M}$, where $\mathcal{M}^*$ is some smooth subset of $\langle\mathcal{M}\rangle$ (Case 2(a) of Chapter 16, Section 16.1.1). Then, under a variety of conditions on $\mathcal{M}^*$, AIC combined with maximum likelihood estimation is not only consistent; it also converges at the minimax rate of convergence (Speed and Yu 1993; Yang 2005a; Yang 2005b). Relatedly, when used for predictions, the AIC-MDL squared prediction error converges to 0 at the minimax optimal rate (Shao 1997; Li 1987). Recall that in such cases, BIC is often slower than minimax by a factor of ORDER$(\log n)$. The upshot is that there exist cases for which BIC is asymptotically optimal whereas AIC is not, and vice versa.

The reason why AIC achieves these optimal convergence rates can be seen from a reinterpretation of Akaike's original derivation of AIC. In this reinterpretation, AIC is really an easily computable approximation of another criterion which we will call AIC*. AIC* is defined as the model selection criterion γ (see page 509) that, for each n, achieves

$$\max_{P^* \in \mathcal{M}^*} \min_{\gamma: \mathcal{X}^n \to \Gamma} E_{X^n \sim P^*}[D(P^* \| P_{\hat{\theta}_{\gamma(X^n)}})]$$

where the minimum is over all model selection criteria, i.e. all functions from $\mathcal{X}^*$ to Γ, and $\mathcal{M}^* \subset \langle\mathcal{M}\rangle$ is a subset of $\mathcal{M}$'s information closure that satisfies some smoothness conditions. By definition, AIC* attains the minimax optimal KL risk among all model selection-based estimators that use the ML estimator within the selected model. This makes it plausible (but by no means proves) that, under some conditions on $\mathcal{M}$ and $\mathcal{M}^*$, AIC, which can be seen to be an approximation of AIC*, achieves the minimax convergence rate among *all* (and not just model-selection based) estimators.

AIC achieves the minimax optimal convergence rate under certain regularity conditions on $\mathcal{M} = \cup_{\gamma \in \Gamma}\mathcal{M}_\gamma$ and $\mathcal{M}^*$. For example, these hold if, for each γ, $\mathcal{M}_\gamma$ is a linear model (Chapter 12) with γ covariates, (X_i, Y_i) are i.i.d., and $\mathcal{M}^*$ satisfies certain smoothness assumptions. They also hold for a wide variety of other models, including some time series models. However, we do have to restrict $\mathcal{M}^*$, i.e. we have to make assumptions about the $P^* \in \langle\mathcal{M}\rangle$ that is supposed to have generated the data; see (Yang and Barron 1999). Various modifications of AIC have been proposed for the case where such conditions on $\mathcal{M}$ and $\mathcal{M}^*$ are violated, or for the case of small samples. For the latter, see (Burnham and Anderson 2002).

We further note that if all the appropriate conditions hold, then the AIC-based estimator achieves the minimax optimal convergence rates both if (a) data are distributed according to some $P^* \in \mathcal{M}_{\gamma^*}$ for finite $\gamma^* \in \Gamma$ (this holds even if Γ is itself finite); and also if (b) $P^* \in \mathcal{M}^*, P^* \notin \mathcal{M}$. In case (a), the rate is $O(1/n)$. Also, under the same conditions, even though it achieves the minimax optimal convergence rate, AIC is inconsistent if $P^* \in \mathcal{M}_{\gamma^*}$ for some finite γ^*, both if Γ is finite and if Γ is countably infinite. In both cases, the inconsistency is of a curious type: as n increases, the P^*-probability that $\gamma_{\text{aic}}(X^n) > \gamma^*$ goes to some number p with $0 < p < 1$. Thus, AIC is only inconsistent with a certain probability; this probability neither tends to 1 nor to 0.

17.3.3   A Version of MDL that Combines the Best of AIC and BIC

AIC As Expectation-Based MDL   From the *expectation-based* MDL point of view, the AIC idea makes a lot of sense. Indeed, it defines a prequential coding system, given by

$$\bar{P}_{\text{mdl-aic}}(X_{n+1} \mid x^n) := P(X_{n+1} \mid \hat{\theta}_{\gamma_{\text{aic}}(x^n)}(x^n)). \tag{17.5}$$

Under the conditions for which AIC is a good approximation of AIC*, $\bar{P}_{\text{mdl-aic}}$ will actually be a very good universal code relative to $\mathcal{M}^*$. Namely, by its definition, AIC* chooses the model index γ such that the worst-case expected codelength of encoding a new value X_{n+1} using the code with lengths $- \log P_{\hat{\theta}_\gamma(x^n)}(X)$ is minimized. If we were to look for the prequential plugin code relative to $\mathcal{M}$, that, assuming $P^* \in \mathcal{M}^*$, asymptotically achieves the minimax optimal redundancy, and under the constraint that the estimator to be used in the plugin code is model-selection based, then we would arrive at almost the same estimator/universal code as (17.5), but with two differences: (1) γ_{aic} is replaced by γ_{aic^*}; and, (2), rather than predicting by the ML estimator $\hat{\theta}_\gamma$ for the selected γ, it would be better to predict using a prequential MDL estimator $\bar{P}(\cdot \mid \mathcal{M}_\gamma)$ defined relative to $\mathcal{M}_\gamma$, for example, the Bayesian universal code with the luckiness-tilted Jeffreys' prior. Presumably however, such a modification would not affect the minimax convergence rate of $\bar{P}_{\text{mdl-aic}}$.

MDL Is Not BIC...   It has sometimes been claimed that MDL = BIC; for example, Burnham and Anderson (2002, page 286) write "Rissanen's result is equivalent to BIC." This is wrong, even for the 1989 version of MDL that Burnham and Anderson refer to – as pointed out by Foster and Stine (2005), the BIC approximation only holds if the number of parameters k is kept fixed and n goes to infinity. If we select between nested families of models where the maximum number of parameters k considered is either infinite or grows with n, then model selection based on both CUP(2-p, Bayes) and CUP(2-p, nml) tends to select quite different models than BIC; if k gets closer to n, the contribution to $\text{COMP}^{(n)}(\mathcal{M})$ of each additional parameter becomes much smaller than $(1/2) \log n$ (Foster and Stine 2005). Similarly, in CUP(2-p, 2-p)-MDL, if the discretized value of a parameter chosen by two-part MDL is close to 0, then, at least for some models, again the MDL procedure may actually behave more like AIC than BIC; see Foster and Stine (1999). Similarly, Hansen and Yu (2001) show that some versions of MDL model selection in linear regression punish even less for complexity than AIC (Chapter 14, page 450) for some data and models, and Hansen and Yu (2002) conjecture that their gMDL procedure actually combines the strengths of AIC and BIC. They prove gMDL consistent for the situation that $P^* \in \mathcal{M}_{\gamma^*}$ (Case 1(c) of Chapter 16), thus showing it has the strength of BIC; but the statement about AIC is only based on experimental results.

> We note that researchers who claim MDL = BIC do have an excuse: in early work, Rissanen himself has used the phrase "MDL criterion" to refer to (17.3), and, unfortunately, the phrase has stuck.

Sometimes, MDL Is Asymptotically BIC After All   We just indicated that in many situations, at least some variations of CUP(2-p, $\cdot$)-code MDL model selection seem to behave more like AIC than BIC. But unfortunately, the fact remains that in other situations, asymptotically CUP(2-p, Bayes)-code MDL model selection does not achieve the minimax optimal rate of convergence, whereas AIC does. As we remarked in Chapter 16, in some nonparametric contexts such as histogram density estimation (Case 2(a) of Chapter 16), prequential MDL estimation based on the CUP(Bayes, Bayes)-codes, as well as MDL model selection based on CUP(2-p, Bayes)-codes, does not achieve the minimax rate of convergence. Like BIC, it is too slow by a factor of ORDER($\log n$).

> **Open Problem No. 17** Although this log-factor is probably not that relevant for practical applications, we do consider this a serious issue: the fact that universal codes designed in standard ways such as CUP(2-p, Bayes) are sometimes not asymptotically optimal, is not so surprising. What is more worrying is that nobody knows how to design an alternative *individual-sequence* universal code based on $\mathcal{M}^*$, that, when used for model selection and analyzed in expectation under some $P^* \in \mathcal{M}$, does achieve the minimax optimal rate. It seems

that the common strategies for designing universal codes – NML, two-part, Bayes, plugin – all fail here, and something entirely new is needed.

Although there is no known individual-sequence based universal code that achieves the minimax optimal rate in all cases where AIC is known to achieve this rate, there does exist an expectation-based universal code that achieves it. This is just the code $\bar{P}_{\text{mdl-aic}}$ that we described above. Using this code for prequential estimation will lead to an estimator that, like AIC, is sometimes inconsistent if $P^* \in \mathcal{M}$. On the other hand, $\text{CUP}(2\text{-p}, \text{Bayes})$-estimators, which may not achieve the minimax optimal rate, are consistent if $P^* \in \mathcal{M}$ (Section 16.3). We now sketch a variation of MDL that is likely to combine the best of both worlds – although we have not formally proven that it does. Let, for the given model class $\mathcal{M}$, $\bar{P}_{\text{mdl-aic}}$ be the universal code that embodies AIC, as described above. Let $\bar{P}_{\text{CUP}(2\text{-p},\text{Bayes})}$ be a $\text{CUP}(2\text{-p}, \text{Bayes})$-universal code, where $\bar{P}_{\text{Bayes}}(\cdot \mid \gamma)$ is a Bayesian universal code relative to some given luckiness function or prior. We define a new, nonprequential code as follows. For any data sequence x^n, we first encode whether $-\log \bar{P}_{\text{mdl-aic}}(x^n)$ or $-\log \bar{P}_{\text{CUP}(2\text{-p},\text{Bayes})}$ is smaller. This takes one bit. We then encode x^n using whichever of the two codes compresses x^n more. The first bit can be thought of as part of our hypothesis: if $-\log \bar{P}_{\text{mdl-aic}}(x^n) < -\log \bar{P}_{\text{CUP}(2\text{-p},\text{Bayes})}$, this can interpreted as stating the hypothesis that "we are in a nonparametric situation; AIC is better." If the reverse inequality holds, this can be interpreted as stating the hypothesis "parametric situation; $\text{CUP}(2\text{-p}, \cdot)$-MDL is better." In the first case, model selection should proceed by AIC; in the second case, it should proceed by our $\text{CUP}(2\text{-p}, \cdot)$-MDL code. In essence, we are doing MDL model selection between two-universal codes, just as in Chapter 14. But the two universal codes now represent the hypotheses $P^* \in \mathcal{M}^* \setminus \mathcal{M}$ vs. $P^* \in \mathcal{M}$.

We do not regard this new universal code as a perfect solution to the AIC-BIC dilemma, since it only has an expectation-based, and not an individual-sequence MDL interpretation. It does illustrate, however, the power of basing learning on universal data compression – we simply use the fact that any two universal codes (in this case, the MDL-AIC code, which is optimal in nonparametric settings, and the $\text{CUP}(2\text{-p}, \text{Bayes})$-code, which is optimal in parametric settings) can be trivially combined into a new universal code that, on any given sequence performs essentially as well as the code that is best on that sequence.

It is sometimes claimed that the question whether to prefer AIC or BIC is irrelevant, since the two procedures have been developed with different goals in mind – optimal prediction of future data vs. hunting for the true model, containing P^*; see, for example, (Forster 2001, page 90) and (Sober 2004, page 649). From this perspective, it may seem to be impossible or irrelevant to craft new methods that combine the strengths of AIC and BIC. Yet, BIC is an approximation of Bayes factor model selection, and as we showed in Section 17.2.2, Bayes factor model selection has a very clear predictive interpretation as well – it can be thought of as a prequential MDL method. Thus, both AIC and BIC are approximations to procedures with predictive interpretations and this suggests that it may be both possible and desirable to combine the strengths of both procedures after all. We are not the first to notice this: De Luna and Skouras (2003) propose a somewhat similar *model meta-selection method* which holds promise to asymptotically combine the best of both methods. Such a method was used earlier by Clarke (1997), and was extended by Clarke (2003), who also provides a theoretical analysis. Yang (2005b) uses a form of cross-validation to select between AIC and BIC and proves that, in a certain sense, it achieves the best of both worlds. This is a subtle issue though – Yang (2005a) shows that it is only possible to "combine the strengths of AIC and BIC" under a restricted definition of what exactly one means by "combining the strengths."

17.4 MDL and MML

MDL shares some ideas with the *Minimum Message Length (MML) Principle* which predates MDL by 10 years. Some key references are (Wallace and Boulton 1968; Wallace and Boulton 1975; Wallace and Freeman 1987) and (Wallace 2005); a long list of references is in (Comley and Dowe 2005). Just as in MDL, MML chooses the hypothesis minimizing the code-length of the data. But the *codes* that are used are quite different from those in MDL. First of all, in MML one always uses two-part codes, so that, like two-part code MDL, MML automatically selects both a model family and parameter values. Second, while MDL codes such as $\bar{P}_{\mathrm{nml}}$ minimize *worst-case (minimax)*, expected or individual sequence, *relative* code-length (i.e. redundancy or regret), the two-part codes used by MML are designed to minimize *a priori* expected *absolute* code-length. Here the expectation is taken over a subjective prior distribution on the collection of models and parameters under consideration; see the summary in Figure 17.1 on page 562. Note that such an approach flagrantly contradicts Rissanen's individual-sequence MDL philosophy: first, it is based on expectation rather than individual sequences; second, it is based on expectations taken over a prior distribution, which, as we explained in Section 17.2.1, cannot be justified from an MDL perspective — nevertheless, in practice it often leads to similar results.

Indeed, Wallace and his co-workers stress that their approach is fully (subjective) *Bayesian*. Strictly speaking, a Bayesian should report his findings by citing the full posterior distribution. But, as we explained in Chapter 15, Section 15.4.2, sometimes one is interested in a single model, or hypothesis for the data. In that case, Bayesians often use the MAP (Maximum A Posteriori) hypothesis; or the posterior mean parameter vector; or the posterior median. The first two approaches were described in Chapter 15, Section 15.4.3. As explained by Wallace (2005), all three approaches have some unpleasant properties. For example, the MAP and the mean approach are parameterization dependent. The posterior mean and median approaches cannot be used if different model families are to be compared with each other. The MML method provides a method for Bayesian estimation that avoids most of the problems of these standard methods.

Below we describe the main ideas behind MML in more detail, and we compare them to corresponding notions in MDL.

17.4.1   Strict Minimum Message Length

Let $\mathcal{M}$ be some given model class of probabilistic sources. MML takes a subjective Bayesian approach, and assumes that the statistician is able to formulate a subjective prior distribution W on the given model class $\mathcal{M}$, representing his subjective beliefs about the domain under consideration. $\mathcal{M}$ is usually either a parametric model or a CUP model class $\cup_{\gamma \in \Gamma} \mathcal{M}_{\gamma}$. In the latter case, W will be a hierarchical prior, consisting of a discrete distribution on Γ, and, for each $\gamma \in \Gamma$, a prior on the parametric model $\mathcal{M}_{\gamma} = \{ P_{\theta} \mid \theta \in \Theta_{\gamma} \}$, given by some density $w(\theta \mid \gamma)$.

The basic idea behind MML modeling is then to find (a) a two-part description method and (b) an associated estimator, minimizing the *expected* two-part description length of the data. Here the expectation is taken according to the statistician's subjective distribution of X^n, which is just the Bayesian marginal likelihood $\bar{P}_{\text{Bayes}}$, defined with respect to the prior W. Formally, let $\dot{\mathcal{L}}$ be the set of partial codes for $\mathcal{M}$. If for some $\dot{L} \in \dot{\mathcal{L}}$, some $P \in \mathcal{M}$ cannot be encoded under $\dot{L}$, then we write $\dot{L}(P) = \infty$. For each n, for each code(length function) $\dot{L}$ in the set $\dot{\mathcal{L}}$, we can examine the expected length of the corresponding two-part code, where the two-part code is defined just as in Chapter 10, (10.1), page 272 (if $\mathcal{M}$ is parametric), and more generally, in

Chapter 15, (15.14), page 477:

$$E_{P \sim W} E_{X^n \sim P}[\min_{\ddot{P} \in \mathcal{M}} \{ \dot{L}(\ddot{P}) - \log \ddot{P}(X^n) \}] =$$

$$E_{X^n \sim \bar{P}_{\text{Bayes}}}[\min_{\ddot{P} \in \mathcal{M}} \{ \dot{L}(\ddot{P}) - \log \ddot{P}(X^n) \}] =$$

$$\sum_{x^n \in \mathcal{X}^n} \bar{P}_{\text{Bayes}}(x^n)(\min_{\ddot{P} \in \mathcal{M}} \{ \dot{L}(\ddot{P}) - \log \ddot{P}(x^n) \}). \quad (17.6)$$

We define $\dot{L}_{\text{smml},n}$ to be the code in $\dot{\mathcal{L}}$ that minimizes (17.6). In the sequel we shall simply assume that there is a unique $\dot{L}_{\text{smml},n}$ achieving the minimum in (17.6). Let $\ddot{\mathcal{M}}_{\text{smml},n}$ denote the domain of $\dot{L}_{\text{smml},n}$. $\ddot{\mathcal{M}}_{\text{smml},n}$ is a countable subset of the set $\mathcal{M}$. $\ddot{\mathcal{M}}_{\text{smml},n}$ is the analogue of the discretized parameter set $\ddot{\Theta}_n$ defined in Chapter 10, but it contains distributions rather than parameters. For each individual x^n, the two-part codelength obtained when using the expectation-optimal code $\dot{L}_{\text{smml},n}$,

$$\min_{P \in \ddot{\mathcal{M}}_{\text{smml},n}} \{\dot{L}_{\text{smml},n}(P) - \log P(x^n)\},$$

is achieved for a particular $P \in \ddot{\mathcal{M}}_{\text{smml},n}$. For simplicity, we shall assume that for each x^n there is a unique such P, and denote it by $\ddot{P}_{\text{smml},n}$. Thus, $\ddot{P}_{\text{smml},n} : \mathcal{X}^n \to \ddot{\mathcal{M}}_{\text{smml},n}$ is a function mapping data sequences x^n to corresponding elements of $\mathcal{M}$. The function $\ddot{P}_{\text{smml},n}$ is called the *strict MML (SMML) estimator*. Note that it once again depends on the sample size n. It was introduced in this form by Wallace and Boulton (1975).

It is of some interest to determine a more explicit relation between $\dot{L}_{\text{smml},n}$ and $\ddot{P}_{\text{smml},n}$. For this, note first that the SMML estimator achieves the minimum a priori expected two-part codelength

$$\min_{\ddot{P}_n:\mathcal{X}^n \to \mathcal{M}} \min_{\dot{L} \in \dot{\mathcal{L}}} E_{P \sim W} E_{X^n \sim P}[\dot{L}(\ddot{P}_n) - \log \ddot{P}_n(X^n)] =$$

$$\min_{\mathcal{M}} \min_{\ddot{P}_n:\mathcal{X}^n \to \ddot{\mathcal{M}}} \min_{\dot{L} \in \dot{\mathcal{L}}} E_{X^n \sim \bar{P}_{\text{Bayes}}}[\dot{L}(\ddot{P}_n) - \log \ddot{P}_n(X^n)(X^n)] =$$

$$\min_{\mathcal{M}} \min_{\ddot{P}_n:\mathcal{X}^n \to \ddot{\mathcal{M}}} \{E_{X^n \sim \bar{P}_{\text{Bayes}}}[- \log \ddot{P}_n(X^n)] + \min_{\dot{L} \in \dot{\mathcal{L}}} E_{X^n \sim \bar{P}_{\text{Bayes}}}[\dot{L}(\ddot{P}_n)]\}.$$

$$(17.7)$$

Here the leftmost minimum in the first line is over all estimators, i.e. functions from samples to elements of $\mathcal{M}$. $\ddot{P}_n(X^n)$ should be read as "the probability of X^n under the distribution to which X^n is mapped by the estimator $\ddot{P}_n$."[10]

---

10. If $\mathcal{M}$ had been parametric, we could have used the clearer notation $P_{\ddot{\theta}(X^n)}(X^n)$.

The leftmost minimum in the second line is over all countable subsets of $\mathcal{M}$, and the second minimum in the second line is over all "discretized" estimators mapping samples to elements of $\ddot{\mathcal{M}}$. The right-hand side of the final expression in (17.7) shows that the first-stage SMML codelength function $\dot{L}_{\text{smml},n}$ must be equal to the $\dot{L} \in \dot{\mathcal{L}}$ achieving

$$\min_{\dot{L} \in \dot{\mathcal{L}}} E_{X^n \sim \bar{P}_{\text{Bayes}}} [\dot{L}(\ddot{P}_{\text{smml},n})] = \min_{\dot{L} \in \dot{\mathcal{L}}} \sum_P \bar{P}_{\text{Bayes}}(\ddot{P}_{\text{smml},n} = P) \cdot \dot{L}(P). \quad (17.8)$$

It now follows by the information inequality that $\dot{L}_{\text{smml},n}$ is given by

$$\dot{L}_{\text{smml},n}(P) \coloneqq -\log \bar{P}_{\text{Bayes}}(\ddot{P}_{\text{smml},n} = P) = -\log \sum_{x^n : \ddot{P}_{\text{smml},n} = P} \bar{P}_{\text{Bayes}}(x^n). \quad (17.9)$$

Given a model class $\mathcal{M}$, the MML method ideally proceeds by (i) formulating a subjective prior W on $\mathcal{M}$, (ii) determining the corresponding strict MML code $\dot{L}_{\text{smml},n}$ and corresponding strict MML estimator, $\ddot{P}_{\text{smml},n}$, and, (iii) for the given data sequence x^n, compute the value of the corresponding $\ddot{P}_{\text{smml},n}$. It can be seen that this coincides with the P that, among all $P \in \ddot{\mathcal{M}}_{\text{smml},n}$, minimizes the two-part codelength $\dot{L}_{\text{smml},n}(P) - \log P(x^n)$ of the actually given data.

17.4.2   Comparison to MDL

There are three immediate differences with MDL codelength design: first, whereas MDL universal codes need not be two-part, the SMML code is always a two-part code, explicitly encoding a single distribution in $\mathcal{M}$. Second, whereas MDL codes are designed to minimize a worst-case quantity, the SMML code minimizes an *expected* quantity.[11] Third, whereas MDL universal codes seek to minimize luckiness redundancy or regret (relative codelength), the SMML code directly minimizes absolute codelengths. Of these three differences, only the first two are essential. Namely, given the fact that in SMML we take expectations over a prior (the second difference), the third difference disappears.

The Second Difference Makes the Third Disappear To see this, note that the strict MML code achieves

$$\min_{\dot{L} \in \dot{\mathcal{L}}} E_{P \sim W} E_{X^n \sim P} [\min_{\ddot{P} \in \mathcal{M}} (\dot{L}(\ddot{P}) - \log \ddot{P}(X^n))], \quad (17.10)$$

---

11. Even in expectation-based MDL, one takes the *worst-case* expected regret or redundancy, where the worst-case is over all distributions in the given model. SMML is based on a double expectation instead: the prior-expectation of the expected codelength.

whereas a two-part code minimizing expected (relative) redundancy rather than (absolute) log loss would achieve

$$\min_{\dot{L}\in\dot{\mathcal{L}}} E_{P\sim W} E_{X^n\sim P}[\min_{\ddot{P}\in\mathcal{M}} (\ \dot{L}(\ddot{P}) - \log \ddot{P}(X^n)\ ) \ - [-\log P(X^n)]] =$$

$$\min_{\dot{L}\in\dot{\mathcal{L}}} E_{P\sim W} E_{X^n\sim P}[\min_{\ddot{P}\in\mathcal{M}} (\ \dot{L}(\ddot{P}) - \log \ddot{P}(X^n)\ ) \ ] - E_{P\sim W}[H(P^{(n)})],$$

$$(17.11)$$

where $H(P^{(n)})$ is the entropy of the restriction of the source P to the first n outcomes. The last equality, which follows by the linearity of expectation, shows that the $\dot{L}$ achieving the minimum in (17.11) is identical to the $\dot{L}$ achieving the minimum in (17.10), which is just the SMML codelength function $\dot{L}_{\text{smml},n}$. Thus, the two-part code achieving minimum expected codelength is also the code that achieves minimum expected redundancy. It then immediately follows that the two-part estimator minimizing expected two-part codelength (the SMML estimator) is identical to the two-part estimator minimizing expected redundancy. Whereas in the minimax framework, minimizing codelength vs. the redundancy leads to wildly different codes, in the prior expectation framework, the resulting codes coincide.

Philosophical Differences In my view, both the MDL and the MML philosophies are internally consistent, but much more different than is usually thought. This has caused a lot of confusion in debates about the merits of either approach. To give but one example, Rissanen (1989, page 56) writes

> "[Wallace and Freeman] advocate the principle of minimizing the mean codelength [with respect to the prior] ... which strictly speaking does not allow it to be used to select the model class. Indeed, take a model class which assigns the probability $1 - \epsilon$ to the string consisting of $0s$ only and the rest equally to all remaining strings. For a small enough ϵ the mean relative to a model can be made as small as we like."

This remark has caused some bewilderment in the MML camp, but from Rissanen's strict MDL point of view it makes sense: Rissanen views a prior on hypotheses as a purely pragmatic tool to be used when designing codes. In this book, we have made this view on priors more precise by introducing the more fundamental concept of a "luckiness function" in Chapter 11. The luckiness function indicates how much codelength regret you are willing to accept if your data falls in a certain region. If your data are aligned with the prior/luckiness function you chose, then you will make good inferences already for small samples and you are "lucky." From this point of view, it makes no sense to design a code that minimizes prior-expected codelength: since you are free to choose the prior, you will always pick a point prior on a low entropy distribution, allowing for an expected codelength approaching 0. Of course, from the subjective Bayesian MML point of view, the prior is seen as something that cannot be chosen at will; it has to seriously reflect one's personal beliefs.

17.4.3   Approximating SMML by the Wallace-Freeman (MML) Estimator

Although (17.7) represents a well-defined optimization problem, in practice, the SMML estimator is very hard to find, and various approximations have been suggested. The most well-known of these is the *Wallace-Freeman estimator* (15.43), also simply known as "(nonstrict) MML estimator." We already defined this estimator in Chapter 15, Section 15.4.3. Because I find the derivation of this estimator in Wallace and Freeman (1987) almost impossible to comprehend, I will give a simplified heuristic derivation based on the two-part MDL codes of Chapter 10, Section 10.1. I do this for the special case where $\mathcal{M}$ is a k-dimensional exponential family given in a diffeomorphic parameterization (P_θ, Θ). Note that this is a severe restriction to the general setup, in which $\mathcal{M}$ is often a CUP rather than a parametric model class.

Let W be a prior and let Θ_0 be an arbitrary ineccsi subset of Θ. Theorem 10.1 (see, in particular, (10.4) below the theorem), showed that there exists a 2-part code $\bar{L}_{\text{2-p}}$ such that uniformly for *every* sequence x^n with $\hat{\theta}(x^n) \in \Theta_0$ for n larger than some n_0,

$$\bar{L}_{\text{2-p}}(x^n) \leq -\log \bar{P}_{\text{Bayes}}(x^n) + g(k) + o(1),$$

where $g(k)$ is bounded by $1.05k$ and converges to 0 for large k. Since this holds for every sequence in an arbitrary compact set, we may reasonably conjecture that it also holds in expectation over $\bar{P}_{\text{Bayes}}$. Assuming this is indeed the case, and using the information inequality, it follows that

$$E_{\bar{P}_{\text{Bayes}}}[\bar{L}_{\text{2-p}}^{(n)}(X^n)] \leq E_{\bar{P}_{\text{Bayes}}}[-\log \bar{P}_{\text{Bayes}}(X^n)] + 1.05k + o(1) \leq$$
$$E_{\bar{P}_{\text{Bayes}}}[\bar{L}_{\text{smml}}^{(n)}(X^n)] + 1.05k + o(1). \quad (17.12)$$

Here $\bar{L}_{\text{smml}}$ represents the codelength function corresponding to the two-part SMML code, i.e. $\bar{L}_{\text{smml}}^{(n)}(x^n) = \dot{L}_n(\ddot{\theta}_{\text{smml},n}) - \log P_{\ddot{\theta}_{\text{smml},n}(x^n)}(x^n)$. Here, for convenience, we switched to the parametric notation of Chapter 10, where we denote distributions P_θ by their parameter θ.

(17.12) shows that *asymptotically* the two-part code of Chapter 10, Section 10.1 is indeed a reasonably good approximation to $\bar{L}_{\text{smml}}$, and in particular that $\bar{L}_{\text{smml}}$ must exhibit the familiar $(k/2 \log n)$ asymptotics shared by both $-\log \bar{P}_{\text{Bayes}}$ and $\bar{L}_{\text{2-p}}$. As a consequence, asymptotically, the two-part estimator $\ddot{\theta}_n$ achieving the minimum codelength in $\bar{L}_{\text{2-p}}$ should behave about as well as the two-part estimator $\ddot{\theta}_{\text{smml},n}$ based on $\bar{L}_{\text{smml}}$.

> The essential difference between $\bar{L}_{\text{2-p}}$ and $\bar{L}_{\text{smml}}$ is as follows. $\bar{L}_{\text{2-p}}$ encodes the discretized values $\ddot{\theta} \in \ddot{\Theta}_n$ using the code based on the prior density w, so that $\dot{L}_n(\ddot{\theta}) \approx -\log \int_{\theta \in R(\ddot{\theta})} w(\theta)d\theta$, where $R(\ddot{\theta})$ is the rectangle with center point $\ddot{\theta}$, see Section 10.1. In contrast, from (17.9) we see that $\bar{L}_{\text{smml}}$ encodes $\ddot{\theta}$ based on the probability that some data sequence x^n occurs with $\ddot{\theta}_{\text{smml},n}(x^n) = \ddot{\theta}$.

Wallace and Freeman (1987) were looking, essentially, for an approximation to the SMML estimator that is a continuous function of some statistic of the data, and that would be easy to compute. While the two-part estimator $\ddot{\theta}_n$ is a good approximation of the SMML estimator, it still lacks these two properties. One way to obtain an easily computable continuous estimator is to do a second approximation, and replace $\ddot{\theta}_n$ by its continuum limit. From the proof of Theorem 10.1 ((10.17), page 280), we see that $\ddot{\theta}_n$ is essentially a "discretized MAP estimator," with a prior W_n given by

$$W_n(\ddot{\theta}) \propto \frac{w(\ddot{\theta})}{\sqrt{\det I(\ddot{\theta})}} \left(n^{-k/2} \right), \tag{17.13}$$

where we ignore $(1 + o(1))$-factors. Because for large n, the grid from which the values $\ddot{\theta}$ are taken becomes dense, we see from (17.13) that the continuum limit of the two-part estimator must be given by

$$\hat{\theta}_{\text{wf}}(x^n) := \arg\max_{\theta \in \Theta} \frac{P_\theta(x^n)w(\theta)}{\sqrt{\det I(\theta)}}, \tag{17.14}$$

Here we reason in exactly the same way as we did when showing that the luckiness ML estimator is the continuum limit of the parametric two-part estimator (Chapter 15, Section 15.4.1). (17.14) is just the Wallace-Freeman estimator $\hat{\theta}_{\text{wf}}$ that we defined in Section 15.4.3.

An Apologetic Remark The conference paper (Kontkanen, Myllymäki, Silander, Tirri, and Grünwald 1998) as well as my Ph.D. thesis (Grünwald 1998) contained a theoretical and experimental comparison between MDL and MML approaches. There were two serious mistakes in both works, and in both cases

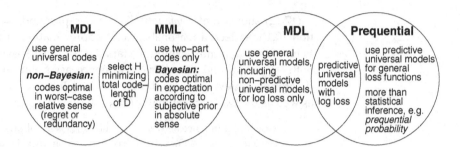

Figure 17.1   Rissanen's MDL, Wallace's MML and Dawid's Prequential Approach

these were caused by myself. First, it was wrongfully claimed that the continuum limit of the two-part code MDL estimator (with uniform luckiness function) would be given by the Bayesian MAP estimator with Jeffreys' prior. This is false: if there is a uniform luckiness function, then the limiting two-part MDL estimator is just the ML estimator, and the ML estimator is not equal to the MAP estimator with Jeffreys prior, except in a parameterization where Jeffreys' prior is uniform; see Section 15.4.1.

Second, while it was correctly claimed that the basic Wallace-Freeman estimator provided silly results when used in combination with the naive Bayes model and small data sets, we did not realize at the time that, in exactly this case, the basic Wallace-Freeman estimator is actually a very bad approximation of the SMML estimator. The latter certainly does provide reasonable estimates. Wallace (2005) explicitly addresses the problems with the Wallace-Freeman approximation for the naive Bayes model. Briefly, even though the naive Bayes model is an exponential family, the sample sizes at which the asymptotics start to play any meaningful role whatsoever are thoroughly unrealistic. Wallace (2005, page 227) shows how the problem can be circumvented by approximating the SMML estimator in a slightly different manner. The problem of unrealistic asymptotics also arises if one replaces the two-part MDL estimator for the naive Bayes model by its continuum limit, the LML estimator.

17.5   MDL and Prequential Analysis

In a series of papers, A.P. Dawid (1984, 1992, 1997) put forward a methodology for probability and statistics based on sequential prediction which he called the *prequential approach*. When applied to model selection problems, it is closely related to MDL: Dawid proposes to construct, for each model $\mathcal{M}^{(j)}$

under consideration, a "probability forecasting system" (a sequential prediction strategy) where the $i + 1$-st outcome is predicted based on either the Bayesian posterior $\bar{P}_{\text{Bayes}}(\theta|x^i)$ or on some estimator $\hat{\theta}(x^i)$. Then the model is selected for which the associated sequential prediction strategy minimizes the accumulated prediction error. Related ideas were put forward by Hjorth (1982) under the name *forward validation*.. From Chapter 15, Section 15.2.1 we see that this is just a form of MDL: *every* universal code can be thought of as as prediction strategy, and therefore, in this strict sense, every instance of MDL model selection is also an instance of prequential model selection. It would, however, be strange to call two-part MDL or NML model selection an instance of the prequential approach, since for these methods, in general the horizon n needs to be known in advance; see page 196. Dawid mostly talks about Bayesian and the plug-in universal models for which the horizon does not need to be known, so that the prequential interpretation is much more natural (Chapter 6, Section 6.4). For this reason, I call such codes "prequential" in this book. The terminology is mine: Dawid reserves the term "prequential" for the general framework.

The Infinite-Horizon Prequential Principle From a prequential viewpoint, one may view codes that are neither prequential nor semiprequential as unnatural (Chapter 6, page 196). This may lead one to insist that the only "reasonable" applications of refined MDL are those based on (semi-) prequential codes. One may call this the *infinite-horizon prequential principle*. The terminology is ours; it is different from the weak prequential principle introduced in Section 17.1.2. Note that MDL model selection as defined in Chapter 14 satisfies the infinite-horizon prequential principle, as long as it is based on CUP(2-p, Bayes) or CUP(2-p, plug-in) codes (the use of a meta-two part code does no harm, since we insisted such codes to be independent of the sample size, which makes them semiprequential). CUP(2-p, 2-p) codes only satisfy the infinite horizon principle if the two-part code $\bar{L}(\cdot \mid \mathcal{M}_\gamma)$ relative to model $\mathcal{M}_\gamma$ is sample size independent. CUP(2-p, nml) codes cannot be used in general – except for the linear regression case where the CNML and NML codes are prequential.

Thus, prequential analysis is usually understood to be "infinite horizon" prequential analysis, and in this sense, it is less general than MDL. On the other hand, Dawid's framework allows for adjusting the sequential prediction loss to be measured in terms of arbitrary loss functions, not just the log loss. In this sense, it is more general than MDL, and is related to the individual sequence prediction literature; see Section 17.9.

There is also a "prequential approach" to probability theory developed by Dawid (Dawid and Vovk 1999) and Shafer and Vovk (2001). Prequential probability and prequential statistics are based on a set of underlying ideas, which one might call the prequential "paradigm" or "philosophy." The prequential philosophy has a lot in common with Rissanen's MDL philosophy, especially the focus on individual sequences rather than ensemble averages. One of its central tenets is the weak prequential principle, which we already introduced in Section 17.1.2. The similarities and difference between MDL and the prequential approach are summarized in Figure 17.1.

MDL and The Weak Prequential Principle   The WPP makes eminent sense from the individual-sequence MDL point of view, being reminiscent of Rissanen's tenet that there is no such thing as a true distribution, and "we only have the data," page 28. In a sense it is even more radical, saying that, indeed, when judging the quality of our model, performance of the model on other data than the data at hand may play no role whatsoever. Indeed, MDL inference based on two-part, Bayesian and prequential plug-in universal codes or combinations thereof satisfies the WPP. MDL model selection based on NML codes, however, violates the WPP: since

$$- \log \bar{P}_{\mathrm{nml}}(x^n \mid \mathcal{M}) = - \log P_{\hat{\theta}(x^n)}(x^n) + \log \sum_{y^n \in \mathcal{X}^n} P_{\hat{\theta}(y^n)}(y^n),$$

in order to assess the quality of the model $\mathcal{M}$ (viewed as a prediction strategy with finite horizon $\bar{P}_{\mathrm{nml}}$), one needs to know the distributions $P_{\hat{\theta}(y^n)}(y^n)$ for $y^n \neq x^n$.

> **Two-Part codes and the WPP** Even though sample-size dependent two-part codes, in our terminology, are neither prequential nor semiprequential, they satisfy the WPP. To see this, let $\mathcal{M}$ be some model class, let x^n be the data and suppose we do MDL model or hypothesis selection using a sample-size dependent two-part code. If we consider n to be fixed, we can think of them as defining a sequential prediction strategy with finite horizon (Chapter 6, Section 6.4.1). The log loss of this strategy is the two-part codelength, and to calculate it we only need to know $P(x^n)$ for all $P \in \mathcal{M}$. In particular, we do not need to know $P(y^n)$ for any $y^n \neq x^n$.

Thus, if we want to apply MDL and adhere to the weak prequential principle, we are forced to use two-part codes or (indeed) prequential universal codes such as Bayes and plug-in.

> I myself am not sure whether there are any truly undesirable consequences of violating the WPP (except in the situation where $P(y^n)$ for unobserved y^n is

simply unknowable, such as the weather forecasting example), so I have no problems in using (luckiness) NML codes. However, I can sympathize with people who think they should be avoided, and in all cases be replaced by semiprequential universal codes.

17.6 MDL and Cross-Validation

It is well known that one cannot confirm a hypothesis by testing on the data that led one to adopt the hypothesis in the first place. Thus, if Θ represents some complex model with many degrees of freedom, and $-\log P_{\hat{\theta}(x^n)}(x^n)$ is small (achieving a good fit on data x^n), this does not mean anything by itself. To investigate whether Θ is really a good hypothesis for the data, we must either somehow correct for its inherent complexity (as we do in NML model selection), or we must test its behavior on a *distinct* set of data coming from the same source, say $y_1, \ldots, y_m$. This is the rationale for model selection by *cross-validation (CV)* (Stone 1974). In this section we briefly consider CV for selecting between a set of candidate i.i.d. models for the data $D = x^n$. For simplicity, assume n is even. In its simplest form, CV amounts to splitting the data into a *training set* D_1 and a *test set* D_2, both of size $n/2$. D_1 is constructed by randomly selecting $n/2$ elements of D. We then determine the ML estimator $\hat{\theta}(D_1)$ based on the training set and use it to sequentially predict the outcomes in D_2. We record the total prediction error $\hat{\theta}(D_1)$ made on D_2. To make the procedure more robust, we repeat it a few, say M, times, each time making a new random split into training and test set. The M test set prediction errors obtained in this way are then averaged. This procedure is repeated for all models $\mathcal{M}_\gamma$ under consideration. Finally, one selects the model with the smallest average test set prediction errors.

Leave K-out CV In variations of the CV scheme, one may use estimators other than the ML estimator, or loss functions other than log loss. Here we will restrict to (luckiness) ML estimators and log loss. Even with this restriction, the procedure can be substantially varied by changing the relative sizes of training and test set. In *leave-K-out CV*, the size of each test set is set to K outcomes. The simple case we just described corresponds to leave $n/2$-out CV. The consistency and rate of convergence properties of CV strongly depend on whether or not K is allowed to grow with n, and if so, how fast (Shao 1993). For example, in the case we just described, K grows linearly with n. Here we study the case where K remains constant in n, since, as we now show, this case is most closely related to MDL. The most extreme and most popular version of this case is *leave-one-out cross validation (LOO CV)*. Here, the test set consists of only one outcome. The procedure is usually repeated for all n splits of x^n into a training set with $n-1$ and a test set with 1 outcome. Thus, each model $\mathcal{M}_\gamma$ is associated with its *leave-one-out error*

$$\sum_{i=1}^{n} \left[-\log P_{\hat{\theta}(x^n \setminus x_i)}(x_i) \right], \tag{17.15}$$

where $\hat{\theta}$ is the ML estimator within $\mathcal{M}_\gamma$, and $x^n \setminus x_i$ is the sequence x^n with outcome x_i removed. Model selection proceeds by picking the γ for which (17.15) is minimized. This is obviously related to prequential model selection, as well as to MDL model selection based on the prequential plug-in model, in which we select a model $\mathcal{M}_\gamma$ based on the *accumulated* prediction error

$$\sum_{i=1}^{n} \left[-\log P_{\hat{\theta}(x^{i-1})}(x_i) \right]. \tag{17.16}$$

The main difference is that in MDL, all predictions are done *sequentially*: the future is never used to predict the past.

Shao (1993) shows that LOO CV can be inconsistent for selection between linear models. On the other hand, Li (1987) shows that, under weak conditions, LOO achieves the asymptotically optimal convergence rate for CUP linear models. Thus, in both cases, LOO CV asymptotically behaves like AIC. This was already suggested by Stone (1977), who shows that, under some conditions on the models under consideration, AIC and leave-one-out CV asymptotically select the same model when the number of models under consideration is finite. As we already discussed in Section 17.3.2, the convergence properties of MDL model selection are quite different: it is usually consistent, but not always minimax optimal in terms of the rate.

One underlying reason for this different behavior seems to be the following. It is clear that, if we let training set and test set fully overlap and the model is complex, then a good fit on the test set (small $-\log P_{\hat{\theta}(y^n)}(y^n)$) is meaningless. This is just the overfitting phenomenon. If the test set partially overlaps with the training set, then the larger the overlap, the less meaningful a good fit on the test set is.

If we do not have additional data available, then we can sequentially test the x_i based on $\hat{\theta}(x^{i-1})$ and add the n resulting prediction errors; this is the prequential idea. Just like with a separate test set, we still have the property that we can test x_i before we see it. But with leave-one out cross-validation, for $j < i$, x_i is used in the prediction of x_j *and* vice versa. This means that no matter how we order the data, one of the two predictions is made on data that has already been seen and used for other predictions. Thus we cannot maintain that we always test on *unseen data*: in the words of Rissanen (1987), the cross-validation prediction errors are not "honest." Indeed, with a prequential scheme, at the time we predict x_i we have no information at all on how good our prediction for x_i will be; but with a leave-one-out scheme, the prediction errors are correlated: the size of the prediction error for each x_j involves all $x_i, i \neq j$, and therefore does give us some information (albeit admittedly not much) about the prediction errors we will make for x_i with $i \neq j$. Thus, there is some very indirect type of "overlap" between training set and test set after all, which apparently can cause a mild form of overfitting.

17.7 MDL and Maximum Entropy

There are some intriguing connections between MDL and the *Maximum Entropy Principle* ("MaxEnt") for inductive inference, which was first proposed by E.T. Jaynes (1957, 2003). Such connections have been observed by a number of researchers; we mention (Feder 1986; Li and Vitányi 1997; Grünwald 1998) and (Grünwald 2000). Here we follow and extend the observations of (Grünwald 2000). We explain MaxEnt and its relation to minimax codelengths in detail in Chapter 19, Section 19.5. In this section we assume that the reader is familiar with that material. MaxEnt is very frequently applied in practice. To explore the connection to MDL, we need to distinguish between two types of applications. First, MaxEnt can be applied directly on the data; second, it can be applied to select a prior distribution.

1. MaxEnt on the data. This type of application is popular in, for example, computational linguistics (Rosenfeld 1996). Here one has a large sequence of data $x_1, \ldots, x_n$ (for example, a long text written in English), and one records certain statistics of the data (for example, for each pair of words w_1, w_2 appearing in the text, one records the number of times that w_1 is followed by w_2). These statistics are then reformulated as a list of constraints, expressed in terms of a large number of functions $\phi_1, \ldots, \phi_k$, each mapping $\mathcal{X}^*$ to $\mathbb{R}$. For each $j = 1, \ldots, k$, the corresponding constraint is of the form $\sum_{i=1}^n \phi_j(x^i) = t_j$. This can be written as one equation in vector form by defining $\phi = (\phi_1, \ldots, \phi_k)^\top$ and $t = (t_1, \ldots, t_k)^\top$ and writing

$$\sum_{i=1}^{n} \phi(x^i) = t. \tag{17.17}$$

In our natural language example, there would be one ϕ_j for each pair of words w_1, w_2, such that $\phi_j(x^i) = 1$ if $x_{i-1}x_i = w_1 w_2$, and $\phi_j(x^i) = 0$ otherwise. Then t_j would be set to the number of times $w_1 w_2$ occurred as a subsequence in x^n. This leads to a long list of constraints (on the data) of form (17.17). In the next step, these are reinterpreted as constraints on the underlying *distribution* P^*, by rewriting them as

$$E_{X^n \sim P^*}\left[\sum_{i=1}^{n} \phi(X^i)\right] = t. \tag{17.18}$$

Such a step may be justifiable if n is large and the functions ϕ only depend on a few of the X_i.

> An important special case arises if for each j, there exists a function $\phi'_j : \mathcal{X} \to \mathbb{R}$ so that $n^{-1}\sum_{i=1}^{n}\phi_j(x^i) = t/n$ can be rewritten as $n^{-1}\sum \phi'_j(x_i) = t/n$. Then (17.18) can be rewritten as $E_{P^*}[\phi'(X)] = t/n$, and the rewriting step amounts to replacing a time average over the data by an ensemble average, which is intuitively reasonable. This makes it plausible that the rewrite (17.18) remains reasonable if ϕ_j does not depend on just one, but only a few of the x_i.

As a "best guess" for the underlying distribution P^*, one now adopts the distribution P_{me} that maximizes the entropy among all distributions that satisfy all given constraints (17.18). As explained in Section 19.5, the maximum entropy will typically be achieved for a distribution $P_{\mathrm{me}} = P_\beta$ that is a member of the exponential family with sufficient statistic $\phi = (\phi_1, \ldots, \phi_k)^\top$. Within this family, the maximum entropy is achieved for the $\hat{\beta}$ that maximizes the likelihood of x^n. Thus, one may reinterpret this form of MaxEnt as consisting of two steps: first, a kind of model "selection," where the set of models to be selected from contains *all* models (sets of probabilistic sources) that can be defined on $\mathcal{X}$. This is followed by maximum likelihood estimation within the chosen model.

We explain in Section 19.5 that P_{me} is the distribution minimizing worst-case expected *absolute* codelength. As explained in Chapter 15, Section 15.4, MDL estimation for a given model $\mathcal{M}$ can be viewed as sequential coding with the goal of minimizing worst-case individual sequence *relative* codelength (regret). There is clearly a relation. To clarify this relation, we first note that at least if $\mathcal{X}$ is finite, then P_{me} also has an individual sequence interpretation. Namely, in that case, the *conditional limit theorem* (Csiszár 1984; Cover and Thomas 1991; Grünwald 2001) implies that, under regularity conditions, the maximum entropy distribution is, in a sense, almost identical to the distribution P'_{me} on $\mathcal{X}^n$ that minimizes absolute codelength of individual sequences, in the worst-case over all sequences x^n that satisfy (17.17). Note that P'_{me} is just the uniform distribution on the set of all x^n that satisfy (17.17). With this new insight, we can connect MDL and MaxEnt more closely.

Both MDL estimators[12] relative to a model $\mathcal{M}$ and ME distributions relative to constraints (17.17) may be thought of as (approximations to) codes on $\mathcal{X}^n$. The MDL estimator is the code that tries to achieve codelength $\bar{L}(x^n)$ as close as possible to the shortest expected codelength $L_{\hat{\theta}}(x^n)$ that is obtainable by a code within $\mathcal{M}$, in the worst-case over all sequences on $\mathcal{X}^n$. The maximum entropy distribution is the code that tries to achieve codelength $L_{\mathrm{me}}(x^n)$ as close as possible to the shortest expected codelength $\hat{L}(x^n) = 0$ that is obtainable by a code within the set of all codes on $\mathcal{X}^n$, in the worst-case over all sequences on $\mathcal{X}^n$ that satisfy (17.17).

Thus, in MDL inference, we restrict the class of comparison codes to those that lie within a given model or model class, and we do not restrict the data. In MaxEnt inference, we do not restrict the class of comparison codes at all, so that absolute and relative log loss coincide, but we do restrict the data. Essentially the same story can be told if $\mathcal{X}$ is infinite and the constraints are such that no MaxEnt distribution P_{me} exists. In that case, MaxEnt adherents often assume some "default" or "background" distribution Q on $\mathcal{X}^n$, and adopt the distribution P_{mre} that, among all distributions satisfying (17.17) minimizes the relative entropy relative to Q. Whether such maximum entropy and minimum relative entropy inferences on the data can be justified on external grounds or not seems to depend on the situation one uses them in; see (Grünwald 2000) and (Grünwald and Halpern 2003).

2. MaxEnt on the prior: open problem No. 18. Suppose maximum entropy we are given a model (P_θ, Θ) equipped with some prior density w. Suppose that before we apply this model, we are given some additional information about θ, namely that $\theta \in \Theta_0$ for some convex set $\Theta_0 \subset \Theta$. As an example, Θ may represent the normal family of distributions, and Θ_0 is the subfamily with mean $\mu \geq 4$. How should we update our prior given this information? According to the MaxEnt principle, we should now adopt the prior w' that,

---

12. For simplicity, we consider MDL estimators restricted to samples of length less than n here.

among all w' satisfying the constraint $\theta \in \mathcal{C}$, is closest to w in relative entropy (KL) distance. This type of MaxEnt application is often interpreted as a tool for objective Bayesian inference (Berger 1985): it tells the Bayesian how to adjust his or her prior given additional information about this prior. Its formal relation to MDL inference has not been investigated. However, if the original prior is a (luckiness-adjusted) Jeffreys' prior, then it seems that the resulting prior will be the luckiness-adjusted prior relative to the set of Θ that satisfy the given constraint. If this is true, then minimum relative entropy inference on the prior would be perfectly consistent with MDL inference. Determining whether something like this is really the case seems an interesting open problem.

17.8   Kolmogorov Complexity and Structure Function; Ideal MDL

Kolmogorov complexity (Li and Vitányi 1997) has played a large but mostly inspirational role in Rissanen's development of MDL. Over the last fifteen years, several "idealized" versions of MDL have been proposed, which are more directly based on Kolmogorov complexity theory. These include extensions of Solomonoff's (1964) original work (Hutter 2003; Hutter 2004), as well as extensions of Kolmogorov's (1965,1974a,1974b) approach (Barron and Cover 1991; Li and Vitányi 1997; Gács, Tromp, and Vitányi 2001; Vereshchagin and Vitányi 2002; Vereshchagin and Vitányi 2004; Vitányi 2005). In both Solomonoff's and Kolmogorov's approaches, hypotheses are described using a universal programming language such as C or PASCAL. Solomonoff's work and its extensions are based on prequential one-part codes, and was discussed in Section 17.2.3 on page 546. Here we very briefly describe Kolmogorov's work and its extensions, which are invariably based on two-part codes. At the end of the section, in Example 17.5, we further investigate the essential difference between coding hypotheses by using a programming language (idealized MDL) and coding hypotheses by implicitly giving their index in some predefined list (two-part MDL as described in this book).

Kolmogorov's Minimum Sufficient Statistic   Barron and Cover (1991) describe what is perhaps the most straightforward variation of Kolmogorov's proposal. Given data D, they pick the distribution minimizing

$$K(P) - \log P(D), \tag{17.19}$$

where the minimum is taken over *all* computable probability distributions, and $K(P)$ is the length of the shortest computer program that, when input (x, d), outputs $P(x)$ to d bits precision and halts. While such a procedure is mathematically well-defined, it cannot be used in practice. The reason is that in general, the P minimizing (17.19) cannot be effectively computed. Kolmogorov himself used a variation of (17.19) in which one adopts, among all P with $K(P) - \log P(D) \approx K(D)$, the P with smallest $K(P)$. Here $K(D)$ is the Kolmogorov complexity of D, that is, the length of the shortest computer program that prints D and then halts. This P is known as the *Kolmogorov minimum sufficient statistic*. The resulting method is called the *Kolmogorov structure function* approach (Kolmogorov 1974a,b). As explained by Vitányi (2005), it has several advantages over merely minimizing (17.19). In the structure function approach, the idea of separating data and noise (Section 14.2.1) is taken as basic, and the hypothesis selection procedure is defined in terms of it. The selected hypothesis may now be viewed as capturing all structure inherent in the data; given the hypothesis, the data cannot be distinguished from random noise. Therefore, it may be taken as a basis for *lossy* data compression: rather than sending the whole sequence, we only send the hypothesis representing the "structure" in the data. The receiver can then use this hypothesis to generate "typical" data for it - this data should then look just the same as the original data D. Rissanen views this separation idea as perhaps the most fundamental aspect of "learning by compression." Therefore, in recent work with I. Tabus he has tried to define an analogue of the Kolmogorov structure function for hypotheses that, as in refined MDL, are encoded in a way that is designed to achieve minimax optimal (luckiness) regret. In this way, he connects refined MDL — originally concerned with lossless compression only — to lossy compression, thereby, as he puts it, "opening up a new chapter in the MDL theory" (Vereshchagin and Vitányi 2002; Vitányi 2005; Rissanen and Tabus 2005). Another connection between refined and Kolmogorov-style MDL is due to Poland and Hutter (2005,2006), who consider two-part MDL under the assumption that the data are distributed according to some P in a countable set. They study the predictive properties of two-part MDL estimators, and define variations of two-part estimators with improved prediction quality.

Practical MDL is sometimes seen merely as an approximation to idealized MDL, hampered by the use of less powerful codes to encode hypotheses. The following example shows that the difference is really more subtle than that.

Example 17.5 [Does MDL Allow Cheating?] Suppose we want to do model selection or universal prediction relative to two singleton models $\mathcal{M}_0 = \{P_0\}$ and $\mathcal{M}_1 = \{P_1\}$. Suppose that P_0 has low, but P_1 has very high Kolmogorov complexity. For concreteness, imagine that P_0 represents a weather forecaster (Example 17.2) who always predicts that the probability that it will rain tomorrow is $1/3$, whereas P_1 is the weather forecaster appearing on Dutch TV, whose predictions are based on a meteorological theory that cannot be implemented by a program of length less than 100 megabytes. From a "practical" MDL perspective, we can design a two-part code relative to $\{P_0, P_1\}$ where both P_0 and P_1 are encoded using just 1 bit. Based on data x^n, we then select the P_j minimizing the two-part codelength, which is just the P_j maximizing the likelihood of the sequence. To some adherents of idealized MDL, this is unacceptable: they argue that instead, we should choose the P_j minimizing $K(P_j) - \log P_j(x^n)$. As a consequence, for small samples, we would never select the complex weather forecaster. This reasoning is incorrect: when we do model selection between two hypotheses such as the weather forecasters, the predictions of the hypotheses can be regarded as *given*, and we can sequentially code data using a "conditional" code (Chapter 3), conditioned on the predictions of the individual hypotheses.

Idealized MDL adherents sometimes dismiss this counterargument on the grounds that practical MDL would then allow for *cheating*: given data x^n, one first looks at the data, then one designs a distribution P_1 that assigns probability 1 to the data x^n, then one performs model selection between $\{P_1\}$ and some other model $\mathcal{M}_0$, using a uniform code on the model index $\{0, 1\}$. In this way one would always choose $\{P_1\}$, now matter how large its Kolmogorov complexity $K(P_1) \approx K(x^n)$ is. Worse, one would even have a large confidence in the result!

Again, the reasoning is not correct: if we design P_1 after seeing data x^n, then P_1 depends on x^n, and therefore $-\log P_1(x^n)$ cannot be interpreted as a codelength function. In the two-stage coding setup, in the sender-receiver interpretation of coding (Chapter 3), this can be seen as follows: when a receiver receives index 1 in the first stage of the code, he cannot decode the remainder of the message, since to decode x^n, he needs to know what P_1 is, and to know what P_1 is, he already needs to know what x^n is.

Concluding, in some cases one can encode hypotheses P_1 with high Kolmogorov complexity using only a few bits, but only if the predictions (probability assignments) of such hypotheses are given in advance (available to both encoder and decoder).

This line of thought does show, however, that there is a crucial difference between practical MDL on the one hand, and both idealized MDL and purely subjective Bayes on the other hand: suppose that we observe data x^n about an entirely unknown phenomenon, for which we initially have no idea how to model it (see also Example 17.4). In this case, from a practical MDL perspective, it seems a good idea to split the data in two parts, say $x_1, \ldots, x_m$ and $x_{m+1}, \ldots, x_n$, with $m \approx n/2$. Then, based on the first part, one starts thinking and exploring what might be a good model class for the data at hand. Having determined a model class (set of candidate models) $\mathcal{M}$, one proceeds to design a universal code $\bar{L}(\cdot \mid \mathcal{M})$ relative to $\mathcal{M}$, to be used to encode the second part of the data $x_{m+1}, \ldots, x_n$. MDL inference then proceeds as usual, and the confidence in any decision one might make is determined by the amount by which $L(x_{m+1}, \ldots, x_n \mid \mathcal{M})$ compresses data $x_{m+1}, \ldots, x_n$ relative to some null model $\mathcal{M}_0$ (Chapter 14, Example 14.3). Since the model $\mathcal{M}$ is used to encode only a part of the data, the number of bits by which it compresses data relative to $\mathcal{M}_0$ will be smaller than it would have been if the full data $x_1, \ldots, x_n$ had been taken into account. Thus, there will be less confidence in the result of the model selection than there would have been if the full data had been used, but this is how it should be: we used $x_1, \ldots, x_m$ to construct the model $\mathcal{M}$, so then $x_1, \ldots, x_m$ should of course not be used to test the quality of $\mathcal{M}$ as a model for the phenomenon at hand. The first half of the data must be ignored, otherwise cheating would be possible after all. In contrast, in idealized MDL and purely subjective Bayesian approaches, one's prior for the models under consideration is fixed once and for all, before seeing *any* data. Therefore, with these approaches, one can always use the full data sequence $x_1, \ldots, x_n$, and there is a never a need to remove an initial part of it for exploratory purposes. Another way to say this is that the premise "we observe data about which we initially have no idea how to model it" cannot be true from a subjective Bayes or idealized MDL perspective.

17.9 MDL and Individual Sequence Prediction

In its prequential guise, MDL may be viewed as being based on sequential prediction with respect to the logarithmic loss function. In the computational learning and game-theoretic communities, one also studies universal prediction with loss functions other than log loss. Here we compare MDL to this generalized notion of universal prediction; for an overview of the extensive research in this field, see the excellent recent textbook (Cesa-Bianchi and Lugosi 2006).

Suppose one sequentially observes $x_1, x_2, \ldots$, where each $x_i \in \mathcal{X}$. At each point in time, one wants to predict x_i based on the previous data x^{i-1}. The prediction quality is measured by some loss function $\mathbf{L} : \mathcal{X} \times \mathcal{A} \rightarrow [0, \infty]$.

Here $\mathcal{A}$ is a space of *actions* or *predictions*. A prediction algorithm is a (computable) function $h : \mathcal{X}^* \to \mathcal{A}$ which maps each initial sequence x^i to an action $h(x^i)$ used to predict x_{i+1}. The loss a prediction algorithm incurs on a sequence x^n is defined to be the sum of the individual losses, i.e. it is given by $\mathbf{L}(x^n, h) := \sum_{i=1}^{n} \mathbf{L}(x_i, h(x^{i-1}))$.

If the goal is to compress $x_1, x_2, \ldots,$, then the logarithmic loss function $\mathbf{L}(x, P) = -\log P(x)$ is appropriate. In many other situations, one may be more interested in, say, the squared loss function, where $\mathcal{A} = \mathcal{X} = \mathbb{R}$ and $\mathbf{L}(y, a) = (y - a)^2$, or, if $\mathcal{X}$ is discrete, the 0/1-loss or *classification loss* function. The latter is defined by setting $\mathcal{A} = \mathcal{X}$, and

$$\mathbf{L}(x, a) = \begin{cases} 1 & \text{if } x \neq a \\ 0 & \text{if } x = a. \end{cases} \tag{17.20}$$

Whereas the log loss is based on probabilistic predictions ($\mathcal{A} = \mathcal{P}$, the set of distributions on $\mathcal{X}$), the squared and the 0/1-loss correspond to point prediction. As an example of a 0/1-loss problem, one may think of a weather forecaster who, at each day, only says "it will rain tomorrow" or "it will not rain tomorrow," and one measures her performance by observing how often she predicts correctly.

Let $\mathcal{H}$ be a set of sequential predictors with respect to some known loss function $\mathbf{L}$. The predictors may be hypotheses, but they may also be "experts," such as in the weather forecasting example. Our goal is to design a prediction algorithm $\bar{h}$ that is universal with respect to these predictors for the given loss function $\mathbf{L}$. That is, for all $h \in \mathcal{H}$, the algorithm should satisfy

$$\max_{x^n \in \mathcal{X}^n} \sum_{i=1}^{n} \mathbf{L}(x_i, \bar{h}(x^{i-1})) \leq \sum_{i=1}^{n} \mathbf{L}(x_i, h(x^{i-1})) + o(n). \tag{17.21}$$

Entropification It may seem that the type of universal prediction expressed by (17.21) is beyond the scope of MDL approaches, as soon as $\mathbf{L}$ is not the log loss. It turns out, however, that there is a method to "transform" arbitrary sequential prediction problems to log loss sequential prediction problems. Namely, one fixes some $\beta > 0$, say, $\beta = 1$, and, for each action $a \in \mathcal{A}$, one defines the distribution P_a on $\mathcal{X}$ by

$$P_a(x) := \frac{1}{Z(\beta)} e^{-\beta \mathbf{L}(x, a)}, \tag{17.22}$$

where $Z(\beta) = \sum_{x \in \mathcal{X}} e^{-\beta \mathbf{L}(x, a)}$. Note that we implicitly assume here that $Z(\beta)$ does not depend on a. Loss functions for which this holds were called *simple* by Grünwald (1998) and Rissanen (2001). Examples of simple loss functions are the $0/1$-loss and other symmetric loss functions such as the squared error loss. Assuming then that $\mathcal{H}$ is a set of predictors to be used against a simple loss function $\mathbf{L}$. We use (17.22) to define, for each $h \in \mathcal{H}$, a corresponding probabilistic source P_h, by

$$P_h(x_i \mid x^{i-1}):=P_{h(x^{i-1})}(x_i) = \frac{1}{Z(\beta)} e^{-\beta \mathbf{L}(x_i, h(x^{i-1}))}. \tag{17.23}$$

Using $P_h(x^n) = \prod P_h(x_i \mid x^{i-1})$ (Chapter 2, page 54), the code L_h corresponding to P_h satisfies

$$L_h(x^n) = -\ln P_h(x^n) = \beta \sum_{i=1}^{n} \mathbf{L}(x_i, h(x^{i-1})) + n \ln Z(\beta). \tag{17.24}$$

We see that the codelength (log loss) of x^n under L_h is an *affine (linear plus constant) function of the loss that h makes on x^n, as measured in the loss function* $\mathbf{L}$ *of interest*. Such a transformation of predictors h into probabilistic prediction strategies P_h was suggested by Rissanen (1989), and studied in detail by Grünwald (1998,1999), who called it "entropification." We note that it usually does not make sense to think of P_h as candidates for sources that might have generated the data. They should first and foremost be thought of as log loss prediction strategies or, equivalently, codes. In Section 17.10 we connect entropification to the correspondence between least-squares estimation and ML estimation under the assumptions of Gaussian noise, and we consider what happens if β is allowed to vary, or to be learned from the data.

> It turns out that one can also construct codes L_h with a linear relation to the original loss $\mathbf{L}$ for nonsimple loss functions for which $Z(\beta)$ does depend on $h(x^{i-1})$, but the construction is more complicated (Grünwald 2007).

If we "entropify" each $h \in \mathcal{H}$, we end up with a model of "sources" $\mathcal{M}_{\mathcal{H}}:=\{P_h \mid h \in \mathcal{H}\}$, where P_h is given by (17.24). Now suppose we have designed a prequential plug-in universal model $\bar{P}_{\text{plug-in}}$ relative to $\mathcal{M}_{\mathcal{H}}$, that satisfies, for each $P_h \in \mathcal{M}_{\mathcal{H}}$, for all n, x^n,

$$-\ln \bar{P}_{\text{plug-in}}(x^n) \leq -\ln P_h(x^n) + f(n), \tag{17.25}$$

for some slowly growing function $f(n)$, say, $f(n) = O(\ln n)$. Then $\bar{P}_{\text{plug-in}}$ is $f(n)$-universal relative to $\mathcal{M}_{\mathcal{H}}$. Now note that, while until now we used (17.23) to construct sources corresponding to given predictors h, we can also apply it the other way around: starting from $\bar{P}_{\text{plug-in}}$, we can construct a prediction algorithm $\bar{h}$ such that we have $\bar{P}_{\text{plug-in}} = P_{\bar{h}}$, i.e. for each n, x^n, $P_{\bar{h}}(x^n) = \bar{P}_{\text{plug-in}}(\cdot \mid x^n)$. It then follows immediately from (17.24) and (17.25) that for all $h \in \mathcal{H}$,

$$\sum_{i=1}^{n} \mathbf{L}(x_i, \bar{h}(x^{i-1})) \leq \sum_{i=1}^{n} \mathbf{L}(x_i, h(x^{i-1})) + \beta^{-1} f(n),$$

so that $\bar{h}$ is $O(f(n))$-universal relative to $\mathcal{H}$. It seems that we have succeeded to translate arbitrary-loss universal prediction problems to log loss universal prediction, and that MDL is a more general idea than we thought!

The Catch   Unfortunately though, there is a catch: it is crucial in the reasoning above that we looked at a *plug-in* universal model $\bar{P}_{\text{plug-in}}$, or equivalently, an "in-model estimator" (Chapter 15, Section 15.2). For many probabilistic model classes $\mathcal{M}$, the best universal models relative to $\mathcal{M}$ are not of the plug-in type. For example, the prediction $\bar{P}_{\text{Bayes}}(X_{n+1} \mid x^n)$ corresponding to the Bayesian universal code is a *mixture* of elements of $\mathcal{M}$, which often does not lie itself in $\mathcal{M}$. As already indicated in Chapter 9, for universal prediction in the individual sequence sense, there seems to be an inherent advantage if one is allowed to predict with mixtures. Thus, to get good universal prediction schemes, one would often want to use Bayesian universal models rather than plug-in universal models relative to $\mathcal{M}_{\mathcal{H}}$. But now there is a problem: if the Bayesian prediction $\bar{P}_{\text{Bayes}}(X_{n+1} \mid x^n)$ is *not* an element of $\mathcal{M}_{\mathcal{H}}$, there may be no action (prediction) $a \in \mathcal{A}$ such that (17.22) holds, i.e. such that for all $x_{n+1} \in \mathcal{X}$,

$$- \ln \bar{P}(x_{n+1} \mid x^n) = \beta \mathbf{L}(x_{n+1}, a) + \ln Z(\beta). \qquad (17.26)$$

In that case, we cannot translate the universal code $\bar{P}$ "back" to a universal prediction algorithm $\bar{h}$ with respect to the original model and loss. At first sight, it seems that the correspondence (17.22) has become useless. In some cases though, entropification can still be useful. Whether or not this is the case, depends on whether the loss function of interest is *mixable*. The concept of mixable loss functions was introduced and developed by V. Vovk and his coworkers in a remarkable series of papers; some highlights are (Vovk 1990; Vovk 2001; Kalnishkan and Vyugin 2002); see also (Littlestone and Warmuth 1994). Roughly speaking, if the loss function is mixable, then a variation of the entropification method can still be used, and the existence of an $f(n)$-universal model for $\mathcal{M}_{\mathcal{H}}$ relative to log loss implies the existence of an $O(f(n))$ universal model for $\mathcal{H}$ relative to loss function **L**. For example, the squared loss function is mixable as long as it is defined relative to a compact set of outcomes $\mathcal{X} = [-R, R]$ rather than the full real line. Unfortunately, the important $0/1$-loss is *not* mixable. Indeed, if $\mathcal{H}$ consists of a fixed number of N experts, and if we allow the prediction algorithm to randomize (i.e. use a biased coin to determine whether to predict 0 or 1), then the optimal universal $0/1$-loss predictor has worst-case regret (in the worst-case over all types of experts and all sequences x^n) of $\text{ORDER}(\sqrt{n})$, whereas the log loss predictor has a much smaller worst-case regret $\ln N$, independently of n and x^n (Cesa-Bianchi, Freund, Helmbold, Haussler, Schapire, and Warmuth 1997). The latter fact can be seen by noting that the worst-case regret of $\bar{P}_{\text{Bayes}}(\cdot \mid \mathcal{M}_{\mathcal{H}})$ with the uniform prior is bounded by $\ln N$. The upshot is that there exist important nonmixable loss functions **L** such as the $0/1$-loss, which have the property that universal prediction with respect to **L** *cannot* be seen as universal prediction with respect to log loss.[13]

Mixability On an informal level, we may say that a loss function is mixable[14] if the following holds. Let $\mathcal{P}_{\mathcal{A}}$ be the set of distributions P_a on $\mathcal{X}$ given by (17.22), so that $\mathcal{P}_{\mathcal{A}}$ contains one distribution for each $a \in \mathcal{A}$. Now let $\overline{\mathcal{P}}_{\mathcal{A}}$ be the convex closure of $\mathcal{P}_{\mathcal{A}}$, i.e. the set of all distributions on $\mathcal{X}$ that can be written as mixtures of elements of $\mathcal{P}_{\mathcal{A}}$. We say that **L** is mixable if we can choose a $\beta > 0$ such that for *any* mixture $P_{\text{mix}} \in \overline{\mathcal{P}}_{\mathcal{A}}$, there exists an $a \in \mathcal{A}$ such that for all $x \in \mathcal{X}$,

$$- \ln P_{\text{mix}}(x) \geq \beta \mathbf{L}(x, a) + \ln Z(\beta). \tag{17.27}$$

If this condition holds, we can modify an $f(n)$-universal code $\bar{P}$ for $\mathcal{M}_{\mathcal{H}}$ into an $O(f(n))$-universal prediction strategy $\bar{h}$ for the loss function **L**, as long as the predictions $\bar{P}(\cdot \mid x^n)$ can be written as mixtures over the elements of $\mathcal{M}_{\mathcal{H}}$. Thus, unlike in the original entropification approach, we can now also use Bayesian universal codes $\bar{P}_{\text{Bayes}}$. To see this, suppose that $\bar{P}$ is an $f(n)$-universal code for $\mathcal{M}_{\mathcal{H}}$ such that for all $n, x^n, \bar{P}(\cdot \mid x^n) \in \overline{\mathcal{P}}_{\mathcal{A}}$. For each n, x^n, we first set P_{mix} in (17.27) to $\bar{P}(\cdot \mid x^n)$, and then we set $\bar{h}(x^n)$ equal to the a for which (17.27) holds. From (17.27) it is immediate that, for each n, x^n, each

---

13. Nevertheless, some universal predictors that achieve the minimax optimal $0/1$-regret to within a constant, are still based on entropification-related ideas. The important difference is that in such algorithms, the β used in (17.23) varies as a function of n. To get good worst-case performance, one needs to take $\beta = O(1/\sqrt{n})$.

14. Vovk's technical definition is more complicated.

$h \in \mathcal{H}$,

$$\beta \sum_{i=1}^{n} \mathbf{L}(x_i, \bar{h}(x^{i-1})) + n \ln Z(\beta) \leq -\sum_{i=1}^{n} \ln \bar{P}(x_i \mid x^{i-1}) =$$

$$- \ln \bar{P}(x^n) \leq$$

$$- \ln P_h(x^n) + f(n) \leq \beta \sum_{i=1}^{n} \mathbf{L}(x_i, h(x^{i-1})) + n \ln Z(\beta) + f(n), \quad (17.28)$$

from which it follows that

$$\sum_{i=1}^{n} \mathbf{L}(x_i, \bar{h}(x^{i-1})) \leq \sum_{i=1}^{n} \mathbf{L}(x_i, h(x^{i-1})) + \beta^{-1} f(n).$$

As an example, if $\mathcal{X} = [-1, 1]$ and the squared loss is used, then the best achievable β is given by $\beta = 1/2$, and an $f(n)$-universal model relative to $\mathcal{P}_{\mathcal{H}}$ with respect to log loss becomes a $2f(n)$-universal model relative to $\mathcal{H}$ with respect to squared loss. This type of correspondence was initiated by Vovk (1990). Further examples of such correspondences, as well as many other relations between log loss and general universal prediction, are discussed by Yamanishi (1998) in the context of his notion of *extended stochastic complexity*.

MDL Is Not Just Prediction   The analysis above suggests that MDL should simply be thought of as the special case of the sequential universal prediction framework, instantiated to log loss, and that all references to data compression may be dropped. This reasoning overlooks three facts. First, Theorem 15.1 tells us that in statistical contexts, there is something special about log loss: in contrast to many other loss functions, with probabilistic predictions, it leads to consistent (prequential) estimators $\bar{P}(\cdot \mid X^n)$. Thus, if a "true" distribution P^* exists, the KL divergence between $\bar{P}(\cdot \mid X^n)$ and P^* will quickly tend to 0 as n increases. This suggests that, even if we are interested in loss functions $\mathbf{L}$ that are not equal to the log loss, predicting X_{n+1} by $\arg\min_{a \in \mathcal{A}} E_{X_{n+1} \sim \bar{P}(\cdot \mid X^n)}[\mathbf{L}(X_{n+1}, a)]$ will still be a good idea, at least if n is large enough, at least *if* the data are actually distributed according to a distribution in our model class.

Viewing MDL simply as a special case of universal prediction also ignores the existence of two-part MDL estimation. This form of MDL also has excellent frequentist properties (Theorem 15.3), and is just as fundamental as the other ones. Nevertheless, it is purely based on "nonpredictive" data compression, and interpreting it prequentially is a bit far-fetched. The third problem with the exclusive universal prediction view is model selection. If we compare a finite number of models, and our end goal is to predict future data using a loss function **L** that is not equal to the log loss, then it makes perfect sense to judge each model based on accumulated prediction error of an estimator for the model in terms of **L** rather than log loss. This is explicitly advocated by the prequential approach, see Section 17.5. It is indeed problematic that MDL does not account for this. However, what if we want to compare an infinite number of models? Then MDL proceeds by adding the codelength needed to encode the models themselves, and we have seen in Chapter 14 that this is sometimes essential. It is not clear how the prequential non-log-loss approach can be extended to deal with this situation.

17.10   MDL and Statistical Learning Theory

Statistical learning theory (Vapnik 1998) is an "agnostic" approach to classification, regression and other conditional prediction problems. One observes a sample $D = (x_1, y_1), \ldots, (x_n, y_n)$ where each $x_i \in \mathcal{X}$ and each $y_i \in \mathcal{Y}$. In regression problems, $\mathcal{Y} = \mathbb{R}$; in classification, $\mathcal{Y}$ is finite; the goal is to match each *feature* X (for example, a bit map of a handwritten digit) with its corresponding *label* or *class* (e.g., a digit); in other words, we want to predict y assuming that x is given. Just as in the individual-sequence prediction framework of the previous section, the prediction quality is measured in terms of a loss function $\mathbf{L} : \mathcal{Y} \times \mathcal{A} \to [0, \infty]$. One usually starts out with a hypothesis class $\mathcal{H}$ consisting of functions $h : \mathcal{X} \to \mathcal{A}$ mapping input values x to corresponding actions a. A standard loss function for regression is the squared loss, $\mathcal{A} = \mathcal{Y}$ and $\mathbf{L}(y, a) = (y - a)^2$. A standard loss for classification is the 0/1-loss, defined as in (17.20), with $\mathcal{X}$ replaced by $\mathcal{Y}$. Based on a sample D, one wants to learn a $h \in \mathcal{H}$ that makes good predictions on future data. In learning theory, this is formalized by assuming that data (X_i, Y_i) are jointly i.i.d. according to some unknown source P^*. In the basic framework, one makes *no assumptions at all about P^**, except that data are *i.i.d.* according to P^*. Thus, just like in MDL, one takes an "agnostic" stance, but this is realized in a totally different way.

We may view P^* as a joint distribution on $\mathcal{X} \times \mathcal{Y}$ and define the *risk* of a hypothesis h as $E_{X,Y \sim P^*}[\mathbf{L}(Y, h(X))]$. In the machine learning community, the risk is often called "error function," and the risk of h is called the *generalization error* of h. By the law of large numbers, a hypothesis with small generalization error will, with very high probability, make good predictions on future data from P^*. For a given hypothesis class $\mathcal{H}$, we further define

$$\mathbf{L}^* := \inf_{h \in \mathcal{H}} E_{X,Y \sim P^*}[\mathbf{L}(Y, h(X))]. \tag{17.29}$$

$\mathbf{L}^*$ is the best expected loss that can be obtained by a hypothesis in $\mathcal{H}$. Thus, the goal of learning theory can now be rephrased as: find a good learning algorithm mapping, for each n, data $(x_1, y_1), \ldots, (x_n, y_n)$ to hypotheses $\dot{h}_n \in \mathcal{H}$ such that $E_{P^*}[\mathbf{L}(Y, \dot{h}_n(X))] \rightarrow \mathbf{L}^*$, *no matter what the distribution P^* is.* Here the convergence may be in P^*-expectation, or with high P^*-probability. If $\mathcal{H}$ is sufficiently simple, then this goal can be achieved by *empirical risk minimization* (ERM): for sample $(x_1, y_1), \ldots, (x_n, y_n)$, we simply pick any $\hat{h} \in \mathcal{H}_\gamma$ minimizing the *empirical risk* $n^{-1} \sum_{i=1}^n \mathbf{L}(Y_i, h(X_i))$. This is just the $\hat{h}$ that achieves the smallest error on the sample.

Example 17.6 [Polynomial Regression] Let $\mathcal{X} = \mathcal{Y} = \mathbb{R}$ and let $\mathcal{H}_\gamma$ be the set of polynomials of degree γ. For simplicity, assume that $\gamma = 2$. Suppose we are interested in predicting y given x against the square loss. Given points $(x_1, y_1), \ldots, (x_n, y_n)$, ERM tells us to pick the polynomial $\hat{h}_n$ that achieves the optimal least-squares fit $\min_{h \in \mathcal{H}_\gamma} \sum (y_i - h(x_i))^2$. The optimal polynomial $\tilde{h} \in \mathcal{H}$ is the polynomial achieving $\min_{h \in \mathcal{H}_\gamma} E_{P^*}[(Y - h(X))^2] = L^*$. By the *uniform law of large numbers* (Vapnik 1998), it holds that $\hat{h}_n \rightarrow \tilde{h}$, in the sense that

$$E_{P^*}[(Y - \hat{h}_n(X))^2] \rightarrow L^*.$$

in P^*-probability and in P^*-expectation. This holds no matter what P^* is, so that ERM can be used to learn a good approximation of $\tilde{h}$, no matter what P^* is. P^* may of course be such that even the optimal $\tilde{h} \in \mathcal{H}$ predicts Y quite badly. This happens, for example, if $P^*(Y \mid X)$ is essentially flat (has fat tails) and does not depend on X. So we cannot always guarantee that, based on a small sample, we will learn, with high probability, a $\hat{h}_n$ which predicts well. We can guarantee however that, based on a small sample, we will learn a $\hat{h}_n$ which predicts almost as well as the best predictor $\tilde{h} \in \mathcal{H}$.

Now consider the model $\mathcal{P}^{(\gamma+1)}$ (Example 2.9, page 64). This is the linear model corresponding to $\mathcal{H}^\gamma$, i.e. it assumes that Y_i are independent given X_i, and normally distributed with mean $h(X_i)$ for some $h \in \mathcal{H}^\gamma$, and some fixed variance σ^2. As we pointed out in Chapter 12, Section 12.3, least-squares estimation for $\mathcal{H}_\gamma$, which is what ERM amounts to in this case, corresponds to ML estimation for $\mathcal{P}^{(\gamma+1)}$. Yet there is an important interpretation difference: rather than modeling the noise as being normally distributed, ERM seeks to learn functions $h \in \mathcal{H}_\gamma$ in a way that leads to good predictions of future data with respect to the squared loss, *even if P* is such that the noise is very different from the normal distribution, i.e. even if P*(Y|X) is not normal at all.* Implementing this goal leads to algorithms that differ significantly with MDL and Bayes once we consider larger classes of hypotheses such as the set of all polynomials considered. This is the topic of the next subsection.

17.10.1   Structural Risk Minimization

If $\mathcal{H}$ contains predictors of arbitrary complexity, then ERM will fail. For example, this happens if $\mathcal{H}$ is the set of all polynomials of each degree. Then for a sample of size n, ERM will tend to select a polynomial of degree $n - 1$ that perfectly fits the data. As we already saw in Chapter 1, Example 1.3, such a polynomial will severely overfit the data and will not lead to good generalization performance. This is of course analogous to the maximum likelihood estimator for the linear model defined relative to the set of all polynomials, which also corresponds to a polynomial of degree $n - 1$. For this situation, Vapnik (1982,1998) proposed the *structural risk minimization (SRM)* method; see also (Bartlett, Boucheron, and Lugosi 2001). The idea is to carve up a hypothesis class $\mathcal{H}$ into subsets $\mathcal{H}_1, \mathcal{H}_2, \ldots$ such that $\bigcup_\gamma \mathcal{H}_\gamma = \mathcal{H}$. The subclasses $\mathcal{H}_\gamma$ are typically nested, $\mathcal{H}_\gamma \subset \mathcal{H}_{\gamma+1}$, and correspond to what we call "models" in this book. In our polynomial example, $\mathcal{H}_\gamma$ would be the set of polynomials of degree γ. The idea is to first select a model $\mathcal{H}_{\hat{\gamma}}$ for the given data $(x_1, y_1), \ldots, (x_n, y_n)$ by minimizing some tradeoff between the complexity of $\mathcal{H}_\gamma$ and if the fit of $\hat{h}_\gamma$, the best-fitting predictor within $\mathcal{H}_\gamma$. In the simplest forms of SRM, this tradeoff is realized by picking the $\dot{\gamma}_n$ achieving

$$\min_{\gamma \in \Gamma} \quad f_n(\hat{\mathbf{L}}_\gamma, \text{COMP}_{\text{srm}}(\mathcal{H}_\gamma)). \tag{17.30}$$

Here

$$\hat{\mathbf{L}}_\gamma := \inf_{h \in \mathcal{H}_\gamma} \frac{1}{n} \sum_{i=1}^n \mathbf{L}(y_i, h(x_i))$$

measures the empirical error that is achieved by the $h \in \mathcal{H}_\gamma$ that minimizes this empirical error; note that this is analogous to the quantity $-\log P_{\hat{\theta}(x^n)}(x^n)$ appearing in MDL complexity tradeoffs. $f_n : \mathbb{R} \times \mathbb{R} \to \mathbb{R}$ is some function that is increasing in both arguments. $\text{COMP}_{\text{srm}}(\mathcal{H}_\gamma)$ is some function that measures the complexity of the set of predictors $\mathcal{H}_\gamma$. Intuitively, the more patterns for which there is an $h \in \mathcal{H}_\gamma$ that fits them well, the larger the complexity. As we show below, the complexity measures used in SRM are often directly or indirectly related to the number of bits needed to describe an element of $\mathcal{H}_\gamma$ using a worst-case optimal code. Thus, (17.30) is reminiscent of two-part code MDL: we pick the $\mathcal{H}_\gamma$ optimizing a tradeoff between loss on the data and hypothesis class complexity. Different forms of SRM use different definitions of $\mathrm{COMP}_{\mathrm{srm}}$; some of these definitions are *data-dependent*, in the sense that $\mathrm{COMP}_{\mathrm{srm}}(\mathcal{H}_\gamma)$ is really a function not just of $\mathcal{H}_\gamma$ but also of x^n. Again this is reminiscent of MDL, where the parametric complexity of regression models also depends on the design matrix $\mathbf{X}$.

In two-part MDL, both the loss and the complexity are measured in bits, and they are simply added to one another. In SRM, the loss and the complexity are measured in different units, and rather than just adding them, the tradeoff is in terms of a more complicated function f_n which depends on the sample size n, and which increases both if the empirical loss $\check{L}$ and if the complexity $\mathrm{COMP}_{\mathrm{srm}}(\mathcal{H}_\gamma)$ increase. We postpone giving explicit examples of f_n until the next subsection, where we discuss a variation of SRM that is more closely related to MDL. The tradeoff (17.30), the complexity measures $\mathrm{COMP}_{\mathrm{srm}}$ and the function f_n are all designed so as to make sure that $\hat{h}_{\hat{\gamma}}$ converges to the best hypothesis in $\mathcal{H}$ as fast as possible, in the sense that

$$E_{P^*}[\mathbf{L}(Y, \hat{h}_{\hat{\gamma}_n})] \to \mathbf{L}^*,$$

with high P^*-probability, or in P^*-expectation. Here $\mathbf{L}^*$ is defined as in (17.29). Again, this will be explained in detail in Section 17.10.2, where we give an explicit example. The "best possible" choices for $\mathrm{COMP}_{\mathrm{srm}}$ may depend on the hypothesis class $\mathcal{H}$ under consideration.

Complexity Measures for Classification   We now give some examples of complexity measures $\mathrm{COMP}_{\mathrm{srm}}$ that have been used in the SRM literature. We concentrate on classification settings with $\mathcal{Y} = \{0, 1\}$ and the 0/1-loss function as defined by (17.20). This is the type of SRM application that has most often been studied in practice.

For a given sample x^n, we may partition any given $\mathcal{H}$ into N equivalence classes $\{\mathcal{H}_1, \ldots \mathcal{H}_N\}$, where hypotheses fall into the same class $\mathcal{H}_j$ if and only if they agree on all given x_i. That is, for all $j \in \{1, \ldots, N\}$, for all $h, h' \in \mathcal{H}_j$, for all x_i with $1 \le i \le n$, $h(x_i) = h'(x_i)$; and for each $h \in \mathcal{H}_j, h' \in \mathcal{H} \setminus \mathcal{H}_j$, there is an x_i with $h(x_i) \neq h'(x_i)$. $N = N(x^n)$ depends on the input data x^n, and must satisfy $N(x^n) \le 2^n$, since y^n can only take on 2^n distinct values. The *Vapnik-Chervonenkis (VC) dimension* of $\mathcal{H}$ is defined as the largest n for which there exists a sample x^n with $N(x^n) = 2^n$ (Vapnik and Chervonenkis 1971). This is the largest n for which there exists a sample that can be classified in all 2^n possible ways by elements of $\mathcal{H}$. Clearly, this measures something like the "richness" of $\mathcal{H}$. The VC dimension was historically the first complexity notion used in SRM approaches. These were based on applications of (17.30) with $\text{COMP}_{\text{srm}}(\mathcal{H})$ instantiated to the VC dimension of $\mathcal{H}$.

According to *Sauer's lemma* (Vapnik and Chervonenkis 1971), if $\mathcal{H}$ has VC-dimension d, then for all n, x^n, $N(x^n)$ is bounded by $\sum_{j=0}^{d} \binom{n}{j}$, so that, for $n > 1$, $N(x^n) \le n^d$. Thus, suppose there is a $h \in \mathcal{H}$ that fits the data perfectly, i.e. $h(x_i) = y_i$ for $i = 1, \dots, n$. Then $h \in \mathcal{H}_j$ for some j, and in order to encode y^n given x^n and hypothesis class $\mathcal{H}$, it suffices to describe the number j. This takes at most $d \log n$ bits, since we must have $j \in \{1, \dots, N(x^n)\}$ and by Sauer's lemma, $N(x^n) \le n^d$.

More Relations between Complexities in Learning Theory and in MDL Interestingly, the VC-dimension was originally introduced to provide a distribution-independent upper bound for what Vapnik calls the *annealed entropy*, defined, for given $\mathcal{H}$, as $\log E_{X^n \sim P^*}[N(X^n)]$. This quantity cannot be computed directly because it depends on the unknown distribution P^*, but by Sauer's lemma, it is bounded, for all $n > 1$, by $d \log n$, where d is the VC-dimension of $\mathcal{H}$. Most other authors call the annealed entropy simply "entropy," which I think is less fortunate because, unlike the Shannon entropy, it does not have a direct expected codelength interpretation. However, it would have such an interpretation if we exchanged log and expectation, just like Rényi entropy (no direct coding interpretation) becomes equal to Shannon entropy (direct coding interpretation) if we exchange log and expectation.

Open Problem No. 19: Rademacher vs. Parametric Complexity The *empirical Rademacher complexity* (Bartlett, Boucheron, and Lugosi 2001; Boucheron, Bousquet, and Lugosi 2005) is a more recent complexity notion used in SRM approaches. It bears a resemblance to the parametric complexity $\text{COMP}^{(n)}(\mathcal{M})$ although it is unclear whether it can be given a coding interpretation. The empirical Rademacher complexity is used in classification problems where $\mathcal{Y} \in \{-1, 1\}$, and $\mathcal{H}$ consists of real-valued predictors $h : \mathcal{X} \to \mathbb{R}$. Many classification models used in practice employ such h to predict y against the 0/1-loss, and then $h(x) > 0$ is interpreted as a prediction of 1, and $h(x) < 0$ is interpreted as a prediction of -1. This is the case in, for example, feedforward neural networks and in support vector machines (SVMs; see (Schölkopf and Smola 2002)). To simplify definitions, we will assume that for each $h \in \mathcal{H}$, there is a $h' \in \mathcal{H}$ such that for all x, $h(x) = -h'(x)$. This condition is satisfied for SVMs and feedforward neural networks. In such cases, the empirical

Rademacher complexity of $\mathcal{H}$, relative to inputs $x_1, \ldots, x_n$, is defined as

$$\hat{R}^{(n)}(\mathcal{H}) := n^{-1} 2^{-n+1} \sum_{y^n \in \{-1,1\}} \sup_{h \in \mathcal{H}} \sum_{i=1}^{n} y_i h(x_i)$$

Just like $\mathrm{COMP}^{(n)}(\mathcal{M})$ in regression problems (Chapter 14, Section 14.5), this quantity is data-dependent: it depends on the input values $x_1, \ldots, x_n$. Let us compare it more closely to the parametric complexity of an i.i.d. conditional probabilistic model $\mathcal{M} = \{P_\theta(Y \mid X) \mid \Theta\}$ for $\mathcal{Y}$, which, for given x^n, may be written (Chapter 7) as

$$\mathrm{COMP}^{(n)}(\mathcal{M}) = \log \sum_{y^n \in \{-1,1\}} \sup_{P \in \mathcal{M}} e^{-\sum_{i=1}^{n} [-\log P(y_i|x_i)]}.$$

In both cases, one takes the sum over all possible realizations of the data y^n, of the best fit that can be achieved for that particular y^n. In the MDL case, the fit is measured in terms of the exponent of minus log loss . In the structural risk minimization case, the fit is measured in terms of a "smoothed" version of the 0/1-loss.

A final connection between complexity notions in learning theory for classification and MDL is provided by the so-called *compression schemes* (Floyd and Warmuth 1995). Here, one focuses on hypothesis classes $\mathcal{H}$ such that each $h \in \mathcal{H}$ can be uniquely identified by a finite number of input values x_i. For example, we may have $\mathcal{X} = \mathbb{R}^2$ and $\mathcal{Y}$ is the class of 'rectangles' on $\mathcal{X}$. That is, each $h \in \mathcal{H}$ has $h(x) = 1$ if and only if x falls in some rectangle with sides running parallel to the axis of $\mathcal{X}$. Then each h may be identified by two points in the plane (its lower left and upper right corner). Given a sample of input points $x_1, \ldots, x_n$, one can now "encode" a hypothesis h by giving the indices (j_1, j_2) of two of the x_i-points, which are interpreted as the lower left and upper right corner of h. Thus, one needs $\log \binom{n}{2}$ bits to encode a rectangle. Such a method of representing h is called a compression scheme; the complexity of a class $\mathcal{H}$ may be measured by the number of x-values that must be provided in order to identify an element of h uniquely.

Such relations between learning and coding complexity notions notwithstanding, there is usually no direct interpretation of (17.30) in terms of minimizing a codelength. This is due to the fact that the function f_n depends on n, $\hat{L}_\gamma$ and $\mathrm{COMP}_{\mathrm{srm}}$ in a complicated manner. Below we clarify this issue in the context of the PAC-Bayesian approach to learning theory, a variation of SRM which has complexity penalties that resemble those of MDL even more closely.

17.10.2   PAC-Bayesian Approaches

In the PAC-Bayesian method of McAllester (1998,1999,2002), complexity penalties are measured by a user-supplied prior distribution W, or equivalently,
a codelength function L, on *hypotheses* $\mathcal{H}$. Although this prior distribution
may be chosen subjectively, its interpretation is quite different from that of
a subjective prior in Bayesian statistics. It is (much) more closely related to
MDL's luckiness interpretation of codelength functions.[15] For our purposes,
it is sufficient to discuss a simplified version of the method, with a level of
sophistication inbetween that of the so-called "Occam's Razor bound" (a precursor to PAC-Bayes due to Blumer, Ehrenfeucht, Haussler, and Warmuth
(1987)) and the PAC-Bayes method itself. Below we describe this simplification and its rationale, highlighting similarities and differences with MDL.
For simplicity we restrict to hypothesis selection in a classification setting,
$\mathcal{Y} = \{0,1\}$ with the 0/1-loss function, and a countable set of hypotheses $\mathcal{H}$.
The set of hypotheses may be arbitrarily complex though, in the sense of hav-
ing infinite VC-dimension; for example, $\mathcal{H}$ may be the set of all decision trees
with an arbitrary depth and arbitrary number of leaves, and with decision
functions based on rational numbers. See (McAllester 2003) for extensions
to uncountable hypothesis classes, stochastic hypothesis "averaging," and
other loss functions.

Simplified PAC-Bayes Hypothesis Selection   Let $\mathbf{L}$ be the 0/1-loss function. In the remainder of this section, we abbreviate $n^{-1} \sum_{i=1}^{n} \mathbf{L}(Y_i, h(X_i))$ to
$\mathbf{e}_{\mathrm{emp}}(h)$, and $E_{X,Y \sim P^*}[\mathbf{L}(Y, h(X))]$ to $\mathbf{e}(h)$.

In order to apply the PAC-Bayesian method, we must first fix some *confidence level* δ, the meaning of which will become clear later. For concreteness,
we could take $\delta = 0.05$. We could also choose δ as a function of the sample
size n, say, $\delta = 1/n$. With this choice, the influence of δ becomes almost negligible for large n. We must also fix a "prior" W on the countable set $\mathcal{H}$, and
define the codelength function (measured in nats) $L(h) = -\ln W(h)$. Now
suppose we are given data $(x_1, y_1), \ldots, (x_n, y_n)$. Then according to simplified
PAC-Bayes, we should pick the hypothesis $\hat{h}$ minimizing, over all $h \in \mathcal{H}$,

$$n\mathbf{e}_{\mathrm{emp}}(h) + 2L(h) + \sqrt{n} \cdot \sqrt{\mathbf{e}_{\mathrm{emp}}(h)(8L(h) - \ln \delta)}. \tag{17.31}$$

Why would this be a good idea? The hypothesis selection rule (17.31) is

---

15. Indeed, some of the bounds on which PAC-Bayesian model selection and averaging are
based have been called *PAC-MDL* bounds in the literature (Blum and Langford 2003).

based on a *generalization bound* expressed in Proposition 17.1 below. As we will see below, the best performance guarantee on the generalization error $\mathbf{e}(h)$ given by that bound is achieved for the $\ddot{h}$ minimizing (17.31). This is a typical instance of what we called the *frequentist design principle* and criticized in Section 17.1.1: one proves a certain frequentist property of sets of classifiers, and then one designs a hypothesis selection algorithm that is optimal relative to the proven property. In the case of PAC-Bayes and other statistical learning methods, I have not much objections against this principle, since the sole assumption on which it is based is that the data are i.i.d. Indeed, this is one of the few examples of a modeling assumption which may actually be quite realistic in some situations.

Proposition 17.1 Let $\mathcal{H}$ be an arbitrary countable set of classifiers. Assume $(X_1, Y_1), \ldots, (X_n, Y_n)$ are i.i.d. P^*. Then no matter what P^* is, for all $h \in \mathcal{H}$, in particular, for the $\ddot{h}$ minimizing (17.31), we have, with P^*-probability at least $1 - \delta$, that

$$n\mathbf{e}(h) \leq n\mathbf{e}_{\mathrm{emp}}(h) + 2L(h) - \ln \delta + \sqrt{n} \cdot \sqrt{8\mathbf{e}_{\mathrm{emp}}(h)(L(h) - \ln \delta)}.$$

Results of this type, but with cruder notions of complexity, were originally called *probably approximately correct (PAC)* generalization bounds. This explains the term "PAC-Bayes." The bound says that, simultaneously for *all* hypotheses $h \in \mathcal{H}$, their generalization error is not much larger than their error on the training set plus a slack, which depends on the prior on h: the bound holds for all h at the same time, but is stronger for h with a large "prior" $W(h) := e^{-L(h)}$. This means that, for each hypothesis h, with high P^*-probability, if $L(h)$ is small, then its performance on a future test set is not much worse than its performance on the training set. Since our goal is to find a hypothesis with small generalization error $\mathbf{e}(h)$, it may be a good idea to pick the h for which Proposition 17.1 provides the smallest *upper bound* on the generalization error. This is exactly the h we pick in the PAC-Bayesian method. Note that there is an analogy to our luckiness approach: if there exists a h with small empirical error $\mathbf{e}_{\mathrm{emp}}(h)$ and large "prior" $W(h)$, then we were *lucky* and get a good (small) upper bound on future performance. If there exists no such h, than we are not lucky, but, by Proposition 17.1, we *know* in that case that the h chosen in (17.31) may predict badly in the future. The main difference to our notion of "luckiness" is that here it refers to generalization error for future data (an expected quantity), whereas in individual-sequence MDL, it refers to individual sequence codelength of the given data;

17.10 MDL and Statistical Learning Theory 587

although we do use it as an indication of how much confidence we have in the prediction quality (codelength) that we achieve on future data.

Proof: For each $h \in \mathcal{H}$, let $Z_{h,i} := |Y_i - h(X_i)|$. Then $Z_{h,1}, Z_{h,2}, \ldots$ are i.i.d. Bernoulli distributed, with mean $\mu_h^* = P^*(Z_{h,1} = 1)$. Let $\hat{\mu}_h$ be the corresponding ML estimator based on data Z^n. It follows from Theorem 19.2 in Chapter 19 that, for all $K > 0$,

$$P^*(n\mathrm{D}(\hat{\mu}_h\|\mu_h^*) \geq K) \leq e^{-K}.$$

Therefore,

$$P^*(\exists h \in \mathcal{H} \ : \ n\mathrm{D}(\hat{\mu}_h\|\mu_h^*) \geq L(h) - \ln \delta) \leq$$
$$\sum_{h \in \mathcal{H}} P^*(n\mathrm{D}(\hat{\mu}_h\|\mu_h^*) \geq L(h) - \ln \delta) \leq \sum_{h \in \mathcal{H}} e^{-L(h)} e^{\ln \delta} \leq \delta. \quad (17.32)$$

where the first inequality is the union bound, the final inequality is Kraft's, and we set $K = L(h) - \ln \delta$. Now if $Z_1, \ldots, Z_n$ are i.i.d. Bernoulli with mean μ^* and $\hat{\mu}$ represents the ML estimator, then we must have

$$\mathrm{D}(\hat{\mu}\|\mu^*) \geq \frac{(\hat{\mu} - \mu^*)^2}{2\mu^*}.$$

This follows by a Taylor approximation of the type we performed in Chapter 4, Section 4.3, using the fact that the Fisher information is given by $I(\mu^*) = 1/(\mu^*(1 - \mu^*))$. Using the fact that $\mu_h^* = \mathbf{e}(h)$ and $\hat{\mu}_h = \mathbf{e}_{\mathrm{emp}}(h)$, together with (17.32), taking square roots, and rearranging terms, we get

$$P^* \left(\exists h \in \mathcal{H} \ : \ \frac{|\mathbf{e}(h) - \mathbf{e}_{\mathrm{emp}}(h)|}{\sqrt{\mathbf{e}(h)}} \geq \sqrt{\frac{2(L(h) - \ln \delta)}{n}} \right) \leq \delta. \quad (17.33)$$

If $\mathbf{e}_{\mathrm{emp}}(h) < \mathbf{e}(h)$, then $\mathbf{e}_{\mathrm{emp}}(h)/\sqrt{\mathbf{e}(h)} < \sqrt{\mathbf{e}_{\mathrm{emp}}(h)}$. With this observation, (17.33) implies that

$$P^* \left(\exists h \in \mathcal{H} \ : \ \sqrt{\mathbf{e}(h)} - \sqrt{\mathbf{e}_{\mathrm{emp}}(h)} \geq \sqrt{\frac{2(L(h) - \ln \delta)}{n}} \right) \leq \delta.$$

The result now follows by moving $\sqrt{\mathbf{e}_{\mathrm{emp}}(h)}$ to the right of the inequality inside the probability, and squaring both sides inside the probability. $\square$

Relation to SRM The overall strategy to arrive at the hypothesis selection criterion (17.31) was to first derive a uniform generalization bound, relating empirical error to generalization error, that holds for *all* $h \in \mathcal{H}$ simultaneously. This bound then motivates an algorithm that selects the h which, for the given data, gives, with high probability, the smallest upper bound on generalization error. The SRM method which we described further above is invariably based on exactly the same idea: one first proves a generalization bound which holds for all $h \in \mathcal{H}$ simultaneously; this bound may depend on complexity notions such as VC-dimension applied to subclasses $\mathcal{H}_\gamma \subset \mathcal{H}$. One then designs an algorithm that selects the $\mathcal{H}_\gamma$ containing the h for which the bound is optimal.

17.10.3   PAC-Bayes and MDL

MDL and learning theory approaches may seem to be very different: in the former, hypotheses are probability models; in the latter, they are (sets of) predictors relative to arbitrary loss functions (most often, the $0/1$-loss). In the former, no probabilistic assumptions are made; in the latter, it is assumed that data are sampled from an i.i.d., but otherwise arbitrary, unknown source.

The first difference is less essential than it seems: the probabilistic sources appearing in MDL are first and foremost interpreted not as probability distributions but rather as *codes* or equivalently, predictors relative to the log loss function. Just as we did for the individual sequence prediction (Section 17.9), we may "entropify" any arbitrary hypothesis class $\mathcal{H}$ together with a loss function $\mathbf{L}$, so that it becomes a model class $\mathcal{P}_\mathcal{H}$ consisting of conditional i.i.d. sources such that for some $\beta > 0$, for each $h \in \mathcal{H}$, there is exactly one $p_h \in \mathcal{P}_\mathcal{H}$ satisfying, for all n, x^n, y^n,

$$- \ln P_h(y^n \mid x^n) = \beta \sum_{i=1}^{n} \mathbf{L}(y_i, h(x_i)) + n \ln Z(\beta). \qquad (17.34)$$

Thus, the log loss that P_h achieves on any sequence of data is a fixed affine (linear plus constant) function of the loss achieved by h as measured in the original loss function $\mathbf{L}$. To construct P_h, we use an analogue of (17.23):

$$P_h(x_i \mid y_i) := \frac{1}{Z(\beta)} e^{-\beta \mathbf{L}(x_i, h(y_i))}, \qquad (17.35)$$

where $Z(\beta) = \sum_{x \in \mathcal{X}} e^{-\beta \mathbf{L}(x, h(y_i))}$. P_h is extended to a conditional source by taking product distributions. Note that P_h is an i.i.d. conditional source here, whereas in the individual sequence prediction, $P_h(x_i \mid x^{i-1})$ strongly depended on x^{i-1}. The difference arises because in the present setup, the predictors h only use side information x_i rather than information about the past. In the case where $\mathcal{H}$ is a set of functions from $\mathcal{X}$ to $\mathbb{R}$ and $\mathbf{L}$ is the squared error loss function, $\mathcal{P}_{\mathcal{H}}$ is just the linear regression model with Gaussian noise with fixed variance $\sigma^2 = 1/2\beta^{-1}$.

Now suppose we have a countable set of classifiers $\mathcal{H}$. Equation (17.34) suggests the following MDL approach to hypothesis selection for classification: first, we fix some $\beta > 0$ and we transform each $h \in \mathcal{H}$ into the corresponding source (or, more appropriately, log loss prediction strategy) P_h. Second, we perform two-part code MDL on the resulting model $\mathcal{P}_{\mathcal{H}}$, using some code $L(h)$ for encoding hypotheses in $\mathcal{H}$ (Of course, we may use minimax and luckiness principles to guide our choice of $L(h)$, but the details of this choice do not matter below). Using the abbreviations for 0/1-loss introduced above, this amounts to selecting the $\ddot{h}$ minimizing the two-part codelength

$$n\beta \mathbf{e}_{\mathrm{emp}}(h) + n\ln Z(\beta) + L(h).$$

This is closely related to, but much simpler than, the PAC-Bayes hypothesis selection as embodied by (17.31). If we set $\beta = 1$ and, as suggested in Chapter 15, Section 15.3, Theorem 15.3, we use α-two part MDL for $\alpha = 2$, then we are effectively picking the h minimizing

$$n\mathbf{e}_{\mathrm{emp}}(h) + 2L(h). \tag{17.36}$$

Comparing this to (17.31), we see that the only difference is the additional term in (17.31) involving the square root of n. To illustrate the difference, suppose $\mathcal{X} = [0,1]$, and P^* is such that $P^*(Y = 1 \mid X = x) = 1$ if $x \in [0, 0.1]$, whereas for each $h \in \mathcal{H}$, $h(x) = 0$ if $x \in [0.0.1]$. If $P^*(X \in [0, 0.1]) = 1/10$, then on approximately 10% of the sample, *all* $h \in \mathcal{H}$ will make a wrong prediction of Y_i. Then in a typical run, no $h \in \mathcal{H}$ will achieve empirical error $\mathbf{e}_{\mathrm{emp}}(h)$ much smaller than 0.1, and then the second term in (17.31) becomes dominant: it is nonzero, and multiplied by $\sqrt{n}$. In such cases, hypothesis selection based on (17.31) will be *much* more conservative than model selection based on MDL, since in the former the weight of the "complexity" $L(h)$ of hypothesis h is multiplied by $\sqrt{n}$, and in the latter, it remains constant.

From an MDL point of view, one may now think that this additional complexity penalty implicit in PAC-Bayes is not really necessary. Indeed, the two-part MDL consistency result Theorem 15.3 suggests that two-part MDL will be consistent. If this were the case, then it might be advantageous to drop the additional term in PAC-Bayes and use MDL instead: if all hypotheses h with smallest generalization error have large complexity $L(h)$, then PAC-Bayes will only start selecting good approximations of h for much larger sample size than two-part MDL.

Unfortunately though, Theorem 15.3 does not apply in the present situation. The reason is that the entropified model class $\mathcal{M}_{\mathcal{H}}$ will in general be severely *misspecified*: it has been artificially constructed, and there is no reason at all why it should contain the assumed true distribution P^*. Indeed, Grünwald and Langford (2007) show that the two-part MDL approach to classification (17.36) can be *inconsistent*: they give an example of a true distribution P^*, a hypothesis class $\mathcal{H}$ and a codelength function L such that there exists a $\tilde{h} \in \mathcal{H}$ with small codelength $L(\tilde{h})$ and with generalization error $\mathbf{e}(\tilde{h}) = \epsilon$ close to 0 relative to P^*; yet with P^*-probability 1, as n increases, the two-part MDL criterion (17.36) will keep selecting h with larger and larger $L(h)$, and all of these h will have generalization error $\mathbf{e}(h) \gg \epsilon$. The difference between $\mathbf{e}(\tilde{h})$ and the generalization error for all of the h selected by MDL can be as large as 0.15. One consequence of this phenomenon is that MDL as well as Bayesian inference can be inconsistent under misspecification, even with countable model classes; see (Grünwald and Langford 2007). The underlying reason for the inconsistency is, once again, the *nonmixability* of the 0/1-loss. In the individual sequence prediction framework with finite $\mathcal{H}$, this nonmixability implied worst-case regrets of ORDER($\sqrt{n}$). This implies that MDL based on the entropification procedure (which, if it worked, would promise worst-case regrets of constant order) cannot be applied on all sequences. In the statistical learning framework (data i.i.d. P^*, P^* unknown), the nonmixability implies that consistent hypothesis selection algorithms need $\sqrt{n}$-factors in front of the hypothesis complexities. Thus, MDL based on the entropification procedure (which would promise complexity penalties without sample-size dependent multiplicative factors) does not converge for all P^*.

Not surprisingly then, earlier approaches that try to combine learning theory and MDL-type inference for classification (Barron 1990; Yamanishi 1998) also end up with a factor in front of the hypothesis complexity $L(h)$ that can be as large as $\sqrt{n}$, and the resulting criteria have no natural coding interpretation any more; see also Meir and Merhav (1995), who do classification with one-part universal codes based on the entropification–construction (17.35).

By now, the reader may have come to wonder why we chose $\beta = 1$. From an MDL point of view, a much more natural approach is to try to *learn* β from the data. This idea was investigated by Grunwald (1998,1999), who showed that the β learned from the data has an interesting interpretation as a 1-to-1 transformation of an unbiased estimate of the generalization error of the h selected by MDL. Adjusting (17.36) to learn β as well, (17.36) becomes:

minimize, over $h \in \mathcal{H}$,

$$
n\mathrm{H}(\mathsf{e}_{\mathrm{emp}}(h)) + 2L(h) + \frac{1}{2}\log n, \tag{17.37}
$$

where the $(1/2)\log n$ term is used to encode β. It plays no role in the minimization and can be dropped. The value of β that is adopted is given by $\ddot{\beta} = \ln(1 - \mathsf{e}_{\mathrm{emp}}(\ddot{h})) + \ln(\mathsf{e}_{\mathrm{emp}}(\ddot{h}))$; its occurrence in (17.37) is not visible because we have rewritten $\mathsf{e}_{\mathrm{emp}}(h)$ in terms of β. Grünwald (1998) shows that several versions of MDL for classification that have been proposed in the literature (Quinlan and Rivest 1989; Rissanen 1989; Kearns, Mansour, Ng, and Ron 1997) can all be reduced to variations of (17.37). Unfortunately though, learning β from the data does not solve the serious inconsistency problem mentioned above. In fact, in their main result Grünwald and Langford (2007) show that (17.37) can be inconsistent; the inconsistency for fixed β follows as a corollary.

Summary: MDL and Learning Theory   We have seen that the algorithms used in learning theory are based on the frequentist design principle, which we criticized in Section 17.1. Nevertheless, the approach is quite "agnostic," in the sense that very few assumptions are made about the underlying P^*. Therefore, it is worrying that MDL approaches to learning classifiers relative to the 0/1-loss can fail asymptotically when investigated within the learning theory framework. The underlying reason seems to be the nonmixability of the 0/1-loss function that we discussed in Section 17.9.

MDL and Learning Theory
In learning theory, complexity of a class of functions $\mathcal{H}$ is usually still measured in terms of quantities related to bits; in the PAC-Bayesian approach, it is directly measured in bits. But to get algorithms with guaranteed consistency, one needs to combine the complexity with the empirical loss in a more subtle way than by merely adding them.

Apart from the advantage of guaranteed consistency, the learning theory approach also has significant drawbacks compared to MDL. One problem is that its domain of application is quite limited. For example, if the x_i are set by humans (as they often are in regression problems, viz. the term "design matrix"), then the learning theory analysis is not valid anymore, since it requires the X_i to be i.i.d. In practice, MDL and Bayesian approaches to classification often work just fine, even under misspecification. In contrast, approaches based on learning bounds such as (17.31) often need a lot more data before they produce a reasonable hypothesis than either MDL or Bayes.

> In 2002, I attended a workshop called "Generalization Bounds < 1." The title says it all: researchers at this workshop presented some of the rare cases where bounds such as those in Proposition 17.1 actually produced a nontrivial bound ($\mathbf{e}(h) < 1$) on some real-world data set. At the workshop, it turned out that in some cases, the bound was still larger than 0.5 — larger than the trivially obtained bound by randomly guessing Y using a fair coin flip!

It seems that learning theory approaches are often too pessimistic, whereas the MDL approach can sometimes be too optimistic.

17.11   The Road Ahead

Problems with MDL   In this chapter we argued that from a theoretical perspective, MDL approaches compare favorably to existing approaches in several respects. In many cases, MDL methods also perform very well in practice. Some representative examples are Hansen and Yu (2000,2001), who report excellent behavior of MDL in regression contexts; the studies in (Allen, Madani, and Greiner 2003; Kontkanen, Myllymäki, Silander, and Tirri 1999; Modha and Masry 1998) demonstrate excellent behavior of prequential coding in Bayesian network model selection and regression; many more such examples could be given. Also, "objective Bayesian" model selection methods are frequently and successfully used in practice (Kass and Wasserman 1996). Since these are based on noninformative priors such as Jeffreys', they often coincide with a versions of "refined" MDL and thus indicate successful performance of MDL.

   Yet there is also practical work in which MDL is not competitive with other methods (Kearns, Mansour, Ng, and Ron 1997; Clarke 2004; Pednault 2003).[16] Not surprisingly then, there are also some problems with MDL from a theoretical perspective. These are mostly related to MDL's behavior under frequentist assumptions. A related problem is that in its current state of development, MDL lacks a proper *decision theory*. Let us discuss each of these in turn.

---

16. But see (Viswanathan., Wallace, Dowe, and Korb 1999) who point out that the problem of (Kearns, Mansour, Ng, and Ron 1997) disappears if a more reasonable coding scheme is used. Clarke (2004) actually considers Bayesian methods, but MDL methods would work similarly in his examples.

MDL Consistency Peculiarities In Chapter 16 we showed that the three main applications of MDL, prediction, hypothesis selection and model selection, generally have very good consistency properties: the prequential, two-part or model-selection based MDL estimator typically converges to the true distribution at near optimal rate. In Section 17.2.2 of this chapter we even saw that in nonparametric settings, consistency of predictive MDL estimators is guaranteed, even in cases where Bayesian inference can be inconsistent. Yet, as we also argued in Chapter 16, each of the three versions of MDL has its own peculiarity: for prequential MDL, we get consistency in terms of Césaro rather than ordinary KL risk; for two-part MDL, we have the $\alpha > 1$-phenomenon; and for MDL model selection, there is the curious Csiszár-Shields inconsistency result. It seems that in nonparametric cases, straightforward implementations of all three versions of MDL sometimes incur an additional $\log n$-factor compared to the risk of the minimax optimal estimation procedure. All this may not be of too much practical interest, but from a theoretical perspective, it does show that some aspects of MDL are currently not fully understood.

The problem is more serious, and presumably, much more relevant in practice, if the true distribution P^* is not in the (information closure of) the model class $\mathcal{M}$; indeed, this seems to be the main cause of the suboptimal behavior reported by (Clarke 2004; Pednault 2003). As explained in the previous section, in that case, MDL (and Bayes) may be inconsistent, no matter how many data are observed (Grünwald and Langford 2007). This is a bit ironic, since MDL was explicitly designed *not* to depend on the untenable assumption that some $P^* \in \mathcal{M}$ generates the data. Indeed, if we consider the *accumulated log loss* of the prequential MDL estimator in the inconsistency example of Grünwald and Langford (2007), we find that MDL behaves remarkably well. In fact, the problem is caused because for large n, the prequential MDL estimator $\bar{P}_{\text{Bayes}}(X_{n+1} \mid X^n)$ is a distribution on $\mathcal{X}$ that is *closer* to P^* in KL divergence than the $\tilde{P} \in \mathcal{M}$ that achieves $\min_{P \in \mathcal{M}} D(P^* \| P)$. While $\bar{P}_{\text{Bayes}}(X_{n+1} \mid X^n)$ is a better predictor than $\tilde{P}$ in terms of expected log loss (KL divergence), it is a mixture of $P \in \mathcal{M}$ each of which is extremely far from P^* in terms of KL divergence. Therefore, the posterior puts nearly all its mass on very bad approximations of P^*, and we cannot say that $\bar{P}_{\text{Bayes}}$ is consistent. Also, if $\bar{P}_{\text{Bayes}}(X_{n+1} \mid x^n)$ is used for 0/1-loss prediction, then it will become much *worse* than $\tilde{P}$; see (Grünwald and Langford 2007) for a thorough explanation of why this is problematic. The strange phenomenon that inconsistency is caused by $\bar{P}_{\text{Bayes}}(X_{n+1} \mid X^n)$ predicting *too well* is related to what I see as the second main problem of MDL: the lack of a proper decision theory.

Lack of MDL Decision Theory   It is sometimes claimed that MDL is mostly like Bayesian inference, but with a decision theory restricted to using the logarithmic utility function.[17] This is not true: via the entropification device, it is possible to convert a large class of loss functions to the log loss, so that predicting data well with respect to log loss becomes equivalent to predicting data well with respect to the loss function of interest. Nevertheless, as we discussed in the previous section, this is not without its problems. It can only be used if the loss function is given in advance; and it can fail for some important loss functions that may be defined on the data, such as the 0/1-loss.

More generally speaking, in Section 17.2.1 we made clear that parts of Bayesian statistical decision theory (maximize expected utility according to the posterior) are unacceptable from an MDL perspective. But this was a negative statement only: we did not give a general MDL rule of exactly how one should move from inferences based on the data (two-part MDL or prequential MDL estimators) to decisions relative to some given loss or utility function. The entropification idea gives a partial answer, but we do not know how this should be done in general. To me, it seems that what is really lacking here is a general MDL decision theory.

Conclusion   Personally, I feel that the two problems mentioned above are strongly interrelated. The main challenge for the future is to modify and extend the MDL ideas in a non-ad hoc manner, in a way that avoids these problems. I am confident that this can be done — although the resulting theory may perhaps become a merger of MDL, the most agnostic brands of Bayesian statistics, prequential analysis, and some types of universal individual sequence prediction, and those statistical learning theory approaches in which complexity is measured in bits. All these alternative methods have some overlap with MDL, and they may all have something to offer that current MDL theory cannot account for. One aspect of MDL that I do not sufficiently recognize in any of the alternative approaches, is the view that models can be thought of as languages, and the consequence that *noise* relative to a model should be seen as the number of bits needed to describe the data once the model is given.

---

17. Again, I have heard people say this at several conferences.

As a final note, I strongly emphasize that none of the problems mentioned above invalidates the fundamental idea behind the MDL Principle: *any regularity in a given set of data can be used to compress the data, i.e. to describe it using fewer symbols than needed to describe the data literally*. The problems mentioned above suggest that this statement cannot be strengthened to "every good learning algorithm should be based on data compression." But, motivated by Theorem 15.3 and the entropification idea, I firmly believe the following, weaker statement: "every statistical estimation algorithm, every sequential prediction algorithm with respect to any given loss function, and every learning algorithm of the type considered in statistical learning theory, can be transformed into a sequential data compression algorithm. If this algorithm does not compress the given data at all, it hasn't really learned any useful properties about the data yet, and one cannot expect it to make good predictions about future data from the same source. Only when the algorithm is given more data, and when it starts to compress this data, can one expect better predictive behavior. Summarizing:

Concluding Remark on The MDL Philosophy
One cannot say: "all good learning algorithms should be based on data compression." Yet one *can* say: *if one has learned something of interest, one has implicitly also compressed the data.*

PART IV

Additional Background

18 *The Exponential or "Maximum Entropy" Families*

Exponential families form a group of statistical models that share several properties which greatly facilitate their mathematical analysis; they also admit a clear interpretation as minimax codelength functions, which further simplifies their treatment in information-theoretic contexts. For these two reasons, many (not all) theoretical properties about MDL inference that we presented in Part II of this book, have been restricted to exponential families. In this chapter we provide a list of statistical properties of exponential families. This serves mainly as a reference for Part II. In the next chapter, we focus on information-theoretic properties of exponential families. These play a crucial role in the proofs in Part II, and are not treated explicitly in most existing introductions to exponential family theory such as (Barndorff-Nielsen 1978) and (Brown 1986).

Contents   Section 18.1 and Section 18.2 provide an introduction, a definition of exponential families, and an informal overview of their most important properties. We then provide some easy rules to calculate mean, variance, and Fisher information (Section 18.3). Section 18.4 shows that exponential families can always be parameterized in terms of *sufficient statistics*. Section 18.5 shows how exponential families can represent general probabilistic sources rather than distributions, and Section 18.6 gives some details about the calculation of the Fisher information for exponential families.

Fast Track   Most results in this chapter and the next have only been used in the *proofs* (not the statements) of results in Part II of this text. One idea that does appear repeatedly in the main text of Part II are the alternative parameterizations used for exponential families. These are first described on page 604, and then in more detail in Section 18.4.

18.1   Introduction

In Chapter 2 we introduced the remarkable *exponential* or *maximum entropy* families. These families comprise statistical models as diverse as the Zipf, binomial, normal, Dirichlet, gamma, and Poisson distributions and the linear regression models. These models all share an enormous number of properties which greatly facilitates both their mathematical analysis and their practical application. The reason behind these "nice" properties is that exponential families admit *sufficient statistics*, a central concept in statistical theory and practice. In this book we are interested in exponential families for the following reasons:

1. They are often easy to use in practice (to give but one example, the log-likelihood function for an exponential family is guaranteed to have no local maxima).

2. They arise in many relevant contexts, ranging from maximum entropy inference to proving large deviation bounds.

3. They can be interpreted as worst-case optimal codes.

4. Most (not all) theoretical results about MDL that we presented in Part II of this book were proved for model classes consisting of exponential families, the reason being that theoretical analysis of nonexponential models is usually much harder.

Items (1) and (2) are well-known facts among statisticians. A much more extensive treatment of such properties, which, however, requires measure theory, may be found in, e.g., (Barndorff-Nielsen 1978).

In the next chapter, we emphasize the much less well-known fact (3): the interpretation of maximum entropy in terms of minimax codelength, going back to (Topsøe 1979).

Ordering the Chaos   Although exponential families comprise a wide variety of distributions, it is easy to get lost in and confused by the large amount of properties they share. For this reason, we separate these properties into different types. Each type is treated in one of the sections of this and the next chapter. Each of these sections is organized in the same way: first the main results are presented, then an example is given, and the proofs of the results are postponed until the end of the section. The next section gives an overview of all properties. At the end of that section we provide a road map that should help the reader to select what further sections he or she wants to read.

18.2   Definition and Overview

Recall from Section 2.3, (2.29), that an *exponential family with sufficient statistic* ϕ is a collection of distributions that can be written in the form

$$P_\beta(X) := \exp(\beta^\top \phi(X) - \psi(\beta)) r(X) \tag{18.1}$$

for some vector-valued function $\phi(x) = (\phi_1(x), \ldots, \phi_k(x))^\top$, $\phi_i : \mathcal{X} \to \mathbb{R}$ and a nonnegative function $r : \mathcal{X} \to \mathbb{R}$ known as the "carrier" mass or density function. An exponential family $\{P_\beta \mid \beta \in \Theta_{\mathrm{can}}\}$ is fully determined by the function ϕ, the carrier r, and a *parameter set* $\Theta_{\mathrm{can}} \subseteq \mathbb{R}^k$. The subscript "can" will be explained in Section 18.4. For each $\beta \in \Theta_{\mathrm{can}}$, the family contains a distribution P_β. Since P_β must be well defined, the *partition function* $Z(\beta)$ must be finite for all $\beta \in \Theta_{\mathrm{can}}$. $Z(\beta)$ is defined as

$$Z(\beta) := \sum_{x \in \mathcal{X}} e^{\beta^\top \phi(x)} r(x) = \exp(\psi(\beta)).$$

(If $\mathcal{X}$ is continuous, then the sum is replaced by an integral.) We can write any P_β as

$$P_\beta(X) = \frac{1}{Z(\beta)} e^{\beta^\top \phi(X)} r(X)$$

so that we have $\psi(\beta) = \ln Z(\beta)$.

k-Dimensional Exponential Family   We say that an exponential family is k-dimensional if the representation (18.1) is *minimal*. This means that there exist no $\lambda_0, \lambda_1, \ldots, \lambda_k \in \mathbb{R}^{k+1} \setminus \{\mathbf{0}\}$ such that for all x with $r(x) > 0$, it holds that $\sum_{j=1}^{k} \lambda_j \phi_j(x) = \lambda_0$. Minimality means that none of the functions ϕ are redundant: if a family does not satisfy this requirement, there exists a $k' \in \{1, \ldots, k\}$ with $\lambda_{k'} \neq 0$ such that $\phi_{k'}$ is a linear combination of the ϕ_j's, for $j \neq k'$. Thus, such a family can be reexpressed using only $k - 1$ of the ϕ_j functions, requiring 1 parameter less.

CONVENTIONS: Θ_{can} Open and Convex, $(P_\beta, \Theta_{\text{can}})$ Minimal

Condition on family: Whenever we refer to an exponential family in this text, we really mean a family that can be expressed in the form (18.1) in such a way that Θ_{can} is open and convex. This requirement rules out local maxima in the likelihood, as will be shown in Section 19.4.

Condition on parameterization: Whenever we refer to a parameterization of an exponential family in the form (18.1), we assume that this parameterization is minimal.

In the advanced literature (Barndorff-Nielsen 1978), one considers more general Θ_{can} and what we call "exponential family" would be called an *open convex* exponential family. Following standard terminology (Barndorff-Nielsen 1978), we call an exponential family *full* if Θ_{can} contains all β with $Z(\beta) < \infty$. In that case, Θ_{can} is called the *natural parameter space*.

Example 18.1 [Bernoulli, Multinomial, Normal, Poisson and Geometric Families] In Example 2.10 we saw that the Bernoulli family with open parameter set $(0, 1)$ is an exponential family with carrier $r(X) \equiv 1$. The sufficient statistic is $\phi(X) = X$ (ϕ is the identity) and the distribution with $P(X = 1) = \theta$ is given by $P_\beta(X = 1)$ with

$$\beta = \ln\theta - \ln(1 - \theta) \tag{18.2}$$

and $\psi(\beta) = \ln(1 + e^\beta)$. More generally, let $\mathcal{X} = \{1, \ldots, m\}$. The *multinomial family for one outcome* is the set of all distributions on $\mathcal{X}$. The one-outcome multinomial family restricted to distributions with $P(x) > 0$ for all $x \in \mathcal{X}$ is equal to the full exponential family with carrier $r(x) := 1$ and sufficient statistic $(\phi_1(X), \ldots, \phi_{m-1}(X))^\top$ with $\phi_j(X) = 1_{X=j}$, 1 denoting the indicator function that is 1 iff $X = j$, and 0 otherwise. The Bernoulli family is the special case with $m = 2$.

In Example 2.11 the family of *normal distributions* was seen to be an exponential family with sufficient statistic $\phi(X) = (X, X^2)^\top$ and carrier $r(X) \equiv 1$.

As an example of an exponential family with nonconstant carrier, consider the *Poisson* family $\{P_\theta \mid \theta \in (0, \infty)\}$ for sample space $\mathcal{X} = \{0, 1, 2 \ldots\}$ with

$$P_\theta(X) = \frac{1}{x!}e^{-\theta}\theta^x. \tag{18.3}$$

By setting $\beta = \ln\theta$ we see that this is an exponential family with sufficient statistic $\phi(X) = X$ (the identity function), $\psi(\beta) = e^\beta$, and $r(x) = 1/x!$.

As a final example, again by setting $\beta := \ln\theta$, we see that the geometric family of distributions for sample space $\mathcal{X} = \{0, 1, 2 \ldots\}$ with

$$P_\theta(X) = \theta^x(1 - \theta) \tag{18.4}$$

is an exponential family with carrier $r(x) \equiv 1$, $\phi(X) = X$ and $\psi(\beta) = -\ln(1 - \theta) = -\ln(1 - \exp(\beta))$. Thus, the Poisson and geometric family share the same sample space and sufficient statistic, but differ in their carrier, making them quite different families in the end: whereas the geometric distribution characterizes the number of outcomes in a sequence of Bernoulli trials before the first 0 is observed, the Poisson distribution can be used to model such things as the number of phone calls received by an operator in a 10-minute period of time.

I.I.D. Exponential Families   In the definition above, exponential families were defined as distributions on a single outcome $\mathcal{X}$. For a given exponential family $P_\beta(X) = \exp(\beta^\top \phi(X) - \psi(\beta))r(X)$, we can set $\mathcal{Z} = \mathcal{X}^n$ and define $P_\beta^{(n)}(X^n) := \prod_{i=1}^n P_\beta(X_i)$. We immediately see that $P_\beta^{(n)}$ is an exponential family on $\mathcal{Z}$ with sufficient statistic $\phi^{(n)}(X^n) := \sum_{i=1}^n \phi(X_i)$ and carrier $r(X^n) := \prod r(X_i)$. We see that exponential families remain exponential under taking product distributions. In general, we define the *i.i.d. model corresponding to an exponential family (18.1)* as a probabilistic model $\mathcal{M} = \{P_\beta \mid \beta \in \Theta_{\mathrm{can}}\}$ such that, for each $n, x^n \in \mathcal{X}^n$, $P_\beta(x^n) = \prod P_\beta(x_i)$, and $P_\beta(x_i)$ is defined as in (18.1).

Exponential families can be extended to probabilistic models (distributions on $\mathcal{X}^\infty$), not just by taking product distributions: in Section 18.5, we discuss *conditional*, including *non-i.i.d.*, models based on exponential families. These include, for example, the Markov chain models.

Sufficient Statistics   Underlying most of the remarkable properties that we are about to present is the fact that exponential families have finite-dimensional *sufficient statistics*. Roughly speaking, this means that all relevant information in the sample $x_1, \ldots, x_n$ about the parameter β is contained in the value of the function $\phi^{(n)}(x^n) := \sum_{i=1}^n \phi(x_i)$. Indeed, consider two distributions $P_\beta(X)$ and $P_{\beta'}(X)$ from the same exponential family. The log-likelihood ratio between these distributions is given by

$$(\beta - \beta')^\top \sum_{i=1}^n \phi(x_i) + \psi(\beta) - \psi(\beta'), \tag{18.5}$$

a quantity *which only depends on the sample $x_1, \ldots, x_n$ through the values that the function $\phi^{(n)} = \sum \phi(x_i)$ takes on $x_1, \ldots, x_n$. It does not depend on any other* *aspect of the data.* Hence, to determine the relative likelihood of two members of the same exponential family, we need not care about any details of the sample except those that are summarized in the "sufficient statistic" $\phi^{(n)}$; all other aspects of the sample are irrelevant. For example, for the normal family (Example 2.11, page 67), the sufficient statistics are given by the vector $\phi(X) = (X, X^2)^\top$: only the first two moments (that is, the mean and the variance) are relevant for inference. Example 18.2 below gives further examples.

The celebrated Pitman-Koopman-Darmois theorem says that, with some caveats, the *only* families with sufficient statistics that remain finite-dimensional as n increases are the exponential families (Jeffreys 1961). This means, again with some caveats, that if a family $\mathcal{M}$ of distributions on $\mathcal{X}$ is extended to a family of sources for $\mathcal{X}$ by independence, then, in order for (18.5) to hold for some function ϕ, $\mathcal{M}$ must be an exponential family. This implies that, again with some caveats, many of the properties we are about to list *only* hold for exponential families and not for any other models.

Mean-Value Parameterization   The same exponential family can be parameterized in many different ways. We call a parameterization in terms of β, used in the defining Equation (18.1), the *canonical* parameterization; see Section 18.4 for details. It turns out that all exponential families can be parameterized in a second standard and useful way, taking the mean of the sufficient statistic $E[\phi(X)]$ as the identifying parameter. In the Bernoulli case, this is the usual parameterization with $\theta = P(X = 1)$ (Example 2.4).

In Section 18.3 we provide basic properties of exponential families in terms of a canonical parameterization; in Section 18.4 we do the same in terms of a mean-value parameterization. By using tools from *convex analysis* (Rockafellar 1970), we can exploit symmetries between the two parameterizations to derive the corresponding properties.

Example 18.2 For the Bernoulli distribution, we have $E_\theta[X] = P_\theta(X = 1) = \theta$, so the standard parameterization *is* a mean-value parameterization. The same holds for the binomial distribution on n outcomes. Noting that,

$$P_\theta(X^n) = \theta^{\sum_{i=1}^n X_i} (1 - \theta)^{n - \sum_{i=1}^n X_i},$$

we immediately see that $\phi^{(n)}(X^n) = \sum_{i=1}^n X_i$ is a sufficient statistic: the likelihood as a function of θ only depends on the observed number of 1s.

For the Poisson distribution (18.3), $E[X] = \theta$, so again the standard parameterization is a mean-value parameterization.

For the geometric distribution, a simple calculation shows that

$$E_\theta[X] = \theta/(1 - \theta), \tag{18.6}$$

so that the standard parameterization is neither a mean-value nor a canonical one. Since (18.6) implies that $\theta = E_\theta[X]/(E_\theta[X] + 1)$, by (18.4), a mean-value parameterization is

$$P_\mu(X) = \left(\frac{\mu}{\mu + 1}\right)^x (1 - \frac{\mu}{\mu + 1}) = \frac{\mu^x}{(\mu + 1)^{x+1}}. \tag{18.7}$$

Similarly, for the normal family the standard parameterization is $(\mu, \sigma^2) = (E[X], E[(X - E[X])^2])$ which is neither equal to a mean-value nor to a canonical parameterization.

Robustness Property   In the next chapter, we consider what happens if we encode data based on the codes corresponding to an exponential family. It turns out that such codes are surprisingly *robust*, meaning that the expected codelength that is achieved does not depend on whether or not the data are generated according to a member of the family.

This remarkable property has consequences for maximum likelihood estimation and large deviation probabilities, and it connects exponential families to maximum entropy and minimum relative entropy inference. We discuss these properties in more detail in the introduction to the next chapter. This finishes our overview of exponential family properties. In the coming sections, we will discuss these properties in detail. We start with a listing of the most basic properties.

18.3 Basic Properties

Below we compute the mean, variance, and Fisher information corresponding to exponential families. We then (Example 18.3) illustrate our findings using the Bernoulli and geometric family. All computations rely on the fact that the function $\psi(\beta)$ is differentiable infinitely often, and coincides with the so-called *cumulant generating function*: the nth derivative of ψ gives the nth *cumulant* of P_β, the first cumulant being the mean and the second being the variance (Barndorff-Nielsen 1978). In this as well as in all further sections, we postpone all proofs and derivations to the end of the section.

1. Computing mean and variance/   The mean (expected value) of the jth component of $\phi(x) = (\phi_1(x), \ldots, \phi_k(x))^\top$ is given by the first partial derivative of ψ:

$$E_\beta[\phi_j(X)] = \frac{\partial}{\partial \beta_j} \psi(\beta). \tag{18.8}$$

Defining the function $\mu : \mathbb{R}^k \to \mathbb{R}^k$ mapping each β to the corresponding means $(\mu_1(\beta), \dots, \mu_k(\beta))^\top$, with $\mu_j(\beta) := E_\beta[\phi_j(X)]$, we can summarize the k equations (18.8) as

$$\mu(\beta)^\top = \nabla \psi(\beta). \tag{18.9}$$

Whereas the mean is given by the first derivative of ψ, the covariance between ϕ_i and ϕ_j (entry i, j in the covariance matrix of P_β) is given by the second derivative:

$$\mathrm{cov}[\phi_i, \phi_j] := E_\beta[\phi_i \phi_j] - E_\beta[\phi_i] E_\beta[\phi_j] =$$

$$E_\beta\big[(\phi_i(X) - E_\beta[\phi_i(X)])(\phi_j(X) - E_\beta[\phi_j(X)])\big] = \frac{\partial^2}{\partial \beta_i \beta_j} \psi(\beta). \tag{18.10}$$

2. Computing Fisher information.   The covariance matrix with entries given by (18.10) is in fact *equal* to the Fisher information $I(\beta)$ at β:

$$I_{ij}(\beta) = \frac{\partial^2}{\partial \beta_i \beta_j} \psi(\beta) = E_\beta[\phi_i \phi_j] - E_\beta[\phi_i] E_\beta[\phi_j]. \tag{18.11}$$

Moreover, it turns out that the Fisher information matrix is *positive definite* (Section 2.1, page 41):

3. Fisher information is positive definite.   For a one-dimensional family, this simply means that $I(\beta)$ is strictly positive for all $\beta \in \Theta_{\mathrm{can}}$. Since $I(\beta) = \mathrm{var}[\phi(X)] = E[(\phi(X) - E[\phi(X)])^2]$, we obviously have $I(\beta) \geq 0$; we show further below that we have strict inequality.

Positive definiteness of Fisher information has three direct consequences:

3(a) ψ is strictly convex. This follows directly from the fact that the Fisher information is the matrix of second derivatives of ψ, and positive definiteness of this matrix implies convexity of ψ (Section 2.1).

3(b) $\mu(\beta) := E_\beta[\phi(X)]$ is **strictly increasing**.

Consider the mapping $\mu : \beta \to E_\beta[\phi(X)]$. If Θ_{can} is one-dimensional, then $\mu(\beta)$ strictly increases with β. For general k-dimensional Θ_{can}, we mean the following by "strictly increasing": we have for all $\beta, \beta' \in \Theta_{\mathrm{can}}$:

$$(\beta' - \beta)^\top (\mu' - \mu) \geq 0, \tag{18.12}$$

where $\mu = \mu(\beta)$ and $\mu' = \mu(\beta')$. Equality holds iff $\beta' = \beta$. Another way of stating this is as follows: for all β, β', there exists a continuously differentiable and strictly increasing function $f : [0, 1] \rightarrow [0, 1]$ with $f(0) = 0$ and $f(1) = 1$ such that for all $\lambda \in [0, 1]$ and $\gamma = f(\lambda)$, we have

$$\mu((1 - \lambda)\beta + \lambda\beta') = (1 - \gamma)\mu + \gamma\mu'. \tag{18.13}$$

A consequence of property 3(b) is that:

3(c) The mapping $\mu : \beta \rightarrow E_\beta[\phi(X)]$ is **1-to-1**; therefore, the parameterization $(\Theta_{\mathrm{can}}, P_\beta)$ is also **1-to-1**.

Example 18.3   [Bernoulli and Geometric] For the Bernoulli model, we have

$$P_\beta(X) = \frac{1}{Z(\beta)} \exp(\beta X)$$

where $Z(\beta) = 1 + \exp(\beta)$. Taking the first derivative of $\psi(\beta) = \ln Z(\beta)$ with respect to β, we find

$$\frac{d}{d\beta}\psi(\beta) = \frac{\exp\beta}{1 + \exp\beta},$$

so by (18.9) we must have

$$E_\beta[X] = P_\beta(X = 1) = \mu = \frac{\exp\beta}{1 + \exp\beta}, \tag{18.14}$$

as can indeed be verified from (18.2). Equation (18.14) also confirms that μ is increasing as a function of β.

By (18.11), the Fisher information must be equal to the variance of X:

$$I(\beta) = E_\beta[X^2] - (E_\beta[X])^2 = \mu - \mu^2 = \mu(1 - \mu),$$

where $\mu = \mu(\beta) = E_\beta[X]$. However, in Example 4.1 we showed that the Fisher information in terms of the mean parameter μ is $\mu^{-1}(1-\mu)^{-1}$. Apparently the Fisher information can depend on the parameterization; in the next section we shall see that generally, $I(\mu) = 1/I(\beta)$ for $\mu = \mu(\beta)$.

For the geometric model (18.4), we have $\psi(\beta) = -\ln(1-\exp\beta)$ (Example 18.1), so that

$$\frac{d}{d\beta}\psi(\beta) = \frac{d}{d\beta} - \ln(1 - \exp\beta) = \frac{\exp\beta}{1 - \exp\beta}.$$

By (18.9) this must be equal to $\mu(\beta)$. This can be verified by recalling that $\beta = \ln\theta$ (Example 18.1). Then, by (18.6), $E_\theta[X] = \theta/(1 - \theta)$.

For the Fisher information, we have

$$I(\beta) = \frac{d^2}{d\beta^2}\psi(\beta) = \frac{d}{d\beta}\frac{\exp\beta}{1 - \exp\beta} = \frac{\exp\beta}{(1 - \exp\beta)^2}, \tag{18.15}$$

which, as promised, is always positive.

We leave the corresponding calculations for the multinomial, normal, and Poisson distributions as an exercise.

Proof Sketches: In all our derivations we make use of the following fact:

Proposition 18.1 The function $Z(\beta)$ is differentiable infinitely often on the open set Θ_{can}. In case X is a continuous random variable or vector, we have for the first partial derivatives $\partial/\partial\beta_j, j = 1, \ldots, k$:

$$\frac{\partial}{\partial\beta_j} Z(\beta) = \int \frac{\partial}{\partial\beta_j} e^{\beta^\top \phi(x)} r(x) dx,$$

and the same holds for all nth partial derivatives, $n > 2$. That is, the order of differentiation and integration can always be exchanged.

For a proof, see (Barndorff-Nielsen 1978, Theorem 8.1, Corollary 7.2).

Now to prove (18.8), note that

$$\frac{\partial}{\partial\beta_j} \psi(\beta) = \frac{\partial}{\partial\beta_j} \ln Z(\beta) = \frac{\frac{\partial}{\partial\beta_j} Z(\beta)}{Z(\beta)} = \frac{1}{Z(\beta)} \frac{\partial}{\partial\beta_j} \sum_x e^{\beta^\top \phi(x)} r(x) \overset{(*)}{=}$$

$$\frac{1}{Z(\beta)} \sum_x \frac{\partial}{\partial\beta_j} e^{\beta^\top \phi(x)} r(x) = \frac{1}{Z(\beta)} \sum_x \phi_j(x) e^{\beta^\top \phi(x)} r(x) = \sum_x P_\beta(x) \phi_j(x) =$$

$$E_\beta[\phi_j(X)], \quad (18.16)$$

where, for continuous x, the sum is replaced by an integral. By Proposition 18.1, the order of integration and differentiation (Equality $(*)$) can then be exchanged and the result still holds.

To show that (18.10) holds, first compute the partial derivative $(\partial/\partial\beta_j)$, as in (18.8), and then perform a straightforward second partial differentiation to $(\partial/\partial\beta_i)$; we omit details.

Equation (18.11) follows because, by the definition of Fisher information, Section 4.3, (4.22),

$$I_{ij}(\beta) = E_\beta\left[-\frac{\partial^2}{\partial\beta_i\beta_j} \ln P_\beta(X)\right] = E_\beta\left[\frac{\partial^2}{\partial\beta_i\beta_j} \beta^\top\left(-\phi(X) + \psi(\beta)\right)\right] =$$

$$E_\beta\left[-\frac{\partial^2}{\partial\beta_i\beta_j} \beta^\top \phi(X)\right] + \frac{\partial^2}{\partial\beta_i\beta_j} \psi(\beta) = 0 + \text{cov}[\phi_i, \phi_j],$$

where the last equality follows from (18.10).

To see that the Fisher information matrix is positive definite, assume, by means of contradiction, that it is not. Then there exists some vector $\lambda \neq \mathbf{0}$ with

$$\lambda^\top I(\beta)\lambda \leq 0. \quad (18.17)$$

Let $Y := \sum \lambda_j \phi_j(X)$. By writing out $\mathrm{var}[Y] = E[Y^2] - E[Y]^2$ in terms of λ and ϕ, one finds that, by (18.17), $\mathrm{var}[Y] \le 0$. Since $\mathrm{var}[Y] \ge 0$ by definition, it must be the case that $\mathrm{var}[Y] = 0$. But this implies that for some constant K, with probability 1 according to P_β, $\sum \lambda_j \phi_j(X) = K$. This contradicts the requirement (page 602) for exponential families, that $\phi_1, \dots, \phi_k$ are minimal.

It remains to show property 3(b), $\mu(\beta)$ is strictly increasing. Pick any $\beta, \beta' \in \Theta_{\mathrm{can}}$ with $\beta \ne \beta'$. Fix a small $\epsilon > 0$ and define, for $\lambda \in (0 - \epsilon, 1 + \epsilon)$,

$$P'_\lambda(X) := P_{\lambda\beta' + (1-\lambda)\beta}(X).$$

It is seen that $P'_\lambda(X)$ is a 1-parameter exponential family with canonical parameter set $(0 - \epsilon, 1 + \epsilon)$ and sufficient statistic

$$\phi^* \equiv (\beta' - \beta)^\top \phi. \tag{18.18}$$

Abbreviating $E_{P'_\lambda}$ to E_λ, by positive definiteness (which we proved above),

$$\frac{d}{d\lambda} E_\lambda[\phi^*(X)] = \frac{d^2}{d\lambda^2} \psi(\lambda) = I(\lambda) > 0 \tag{18.19}$$

on $\lambda \in [0, 1]$. Hence, there exists a continuously differentiable and strictly increasing function $f : [0, 1] \to [0, 1]$ with $f(0) = 0$ and $f(1) = 1$ such that for all $\lambda \in [0, 1]$ and $\gamma = f(\lambda)$,

$$E_\lambda[\phi^*] = (1 - \gamma) E_0[\phi^*] + \gamma E_1[\phi^*]. \tag{18.20}$$

Since by (18.18) we have

$$E_\lambda[\phi^*] = (\beta' - \beta)^\top E_\lambda[\phi], \tag{18.21}$$

it follows that for all $\lambda \in [0, 1]$ and $\gamma = f(\lambda)$

$$E_\lambda[\phi] = (1 - \gamma) E_0[\phi] + \gamma E_1[\phi] = (1 - \gamma)\mu + \gamma\mu',$$

which proves (18.13). Equation (18.12) follows because, by (18.19), $E_\lambda[\phi^*(X)]$ is strictly increasing on $[0, 1]$. Then (18.18) gives that $(\beta' - \beta)^\top \mu' > (\beta - \beta)^\top \mu$.

To show that $\mu(\beta)$ is 1-to-1, take any $\beta, \beta' \in \Theta_{\mathrm{can}}$ with $\beta \ne \beta'$. By (18.12), we have $(\beta' - \beta)(\mu(\beta') - \mu(\beta)) > 0$ so that $\mu(\beta) \ne \mu(\beta')$. Thus, all $P_\beta(\cdot)$ have different means, so that the parameterization must be 1-to-1. □

18.4 Mean-Value, Canonical, and Other Parameterizations

18.4.1 The Mean Value Parameterization

Property 3(c) of Section 18.3 has a profound consequence:

Mean-Value Parameterization
Each member P_β of an exponential family is identified by the expectation (mean value) of the sufficient statistic $\phi(X)$. Therefore we can *parameterize exponential families by these mean values!*

More precisely, let

$$\Theta_{\text{mean}} := \{\mu : \exists \beta \in \Theta_{\text{can}} \text{ such that } \mu(\beta) = \mu\}, \tag{18.22}$$

where $\mu(\cdot)$ is once again the mapping $\mu : \beta \to E_\beta[\phi(X)]$. We can view $\mu(\cdot)$ as a 1-to-1 mapping from Θ_{can} to Θ_{mean}. We use the notation $\beta(\cdot)$ to denote its inverse: for $\mu^* \in \Theta_{\text{mean}}$, $\beta(\mu^*)$ is the (unique!) value β^* such that $\mu(\beta^*) = E_{\beta^*}[\phi(X)] = \mu^*$. For all $\mu \in \Theta_{\text{mean}}$, we write P_μ as shorthand for $P_{\beta(\mu)}$, that is,[1]

$$P_\mu := P_{\beta(\mu)}, \tag{18.23}$$

and we write $E_\mu[\phi]$ as shorthand for $E_{\beta(\mu)}[\phi] = E_{X \sim P_{\beta(\mu)}}[\phi(X)]$. Then the exponential family under consideration is equal to

$$\{P_\mu \in \Theta_{\text{mean}}\} = \{P_\beta \in \Theta_{\text{can}}\}, \tag{18.24}$$

so that $(\Theta_{\text{mean}}, P_\mu)$ is a parameterization of the family. This is called the *mean-value* parameterization of the exponential family. Following (Barndorff-Nielsen 1978), we call parameterizations of the form $(\Theta_{\text{can}}, P_\beta)$ that we hitherto considered *canonical parameterizations*.[2]

Are The Mean-Value and Canonical Representations Unique? Strictly speaking, there is neither a single mean-value, nor a single canonical representation. The reason is that any invertible linear transformation ϕ' of the function ϕ gives rise to an alternative minimal parameterization of the same exponential family, now in terms of ϕ' rather than ϕ. More precisely, given any invertible $k \times k$ matrix A, we may define the function $\phi' = (\phi'_1, \ldots, \phi'_k)$ as $\phi'(x) := A\phi(x)$. Let $\Theta'_{\text{can}} = \{\beta' : \exists \beta \in \Theta_{\text{can}} : \beta' = A^{-1}\beta\}$. Then the family $\{P_\beta \mid \beta \in \Theta_{\text{can}}\}$ is equal to the family $\{P'_{\beta'} \mid \beta' \in \Theta'_{\text{can}}\}$, where $P'_{\beta'}$ is defined as P_β, but relative

---

1. While this notation would become ambiguous if we were to plug in actual numbers for μ and β, in practice parameters will always be denoted by the symbol μ or β so that there can be no confusion.
2. Often the term "natural parameterization" is used, but then it is usually assumed that Θ_{can} ranges over all β for which $Z(\beta) < \infty$. Since we often deal with restricted Θ_{can}, we use the word "canonical."

to the function ϕ' rather than ϕ. Not surprisingly, the mean-value parameterization corresponding to $P'_{\beta'}$ is a linear transformation of the mean-value parameterization corresponding to P_β: we have $P'_{\mu'} = P_\mu$ iff $\mu' = A\mu$.

In practice though, we often consider exponential families relative to a given, fixed function ϕ and when we speak of the mean-value or canonical parameterization, we really mean the mean-value or canonical parameterization relative to the given ϕ.

In practice, exponential families are more often given in their mean-value rather than their canonical parameterizations. Examples are the Bernoulli, multinomial, and Poisson models (Example 18.2, page 604). While μ as a function of β is given by (18.9), an easy way to calculate β as a function of μ, given only the mean-value parameterization, is by the following identity:

$$\beta(\mu')^\top = \nabla_\mu \{E_\mu[\ln P_{\mu'}(X)]\}_{\mu=\mu'}, \tag{18.25}$$

which holds because

$$\nabla_\mu \{E_\mu[\ln P_{\mu'}(X)]\}_{\mu=\mu'} = \nabla_\mu \{E_\mu[\ln P_{\beta(\mu')}(X)]\}_{\mu=\mu'} =$$
$$\nabla_\mu \{\beta(\mu')^\top \mu - \psi(\beta(\mu'))\}_{\mu=\mu'} = \beta(\mu')^\top.$$

18.4.2 Other Parameterizations

Some exponential families are usually given neither in their mean-value nor in their canonical parameterization. An example is the family of geometric distributions, as already pointed out in Example 18.2. Such parameterizations are usually *diffeomorphisms* of the canonical parameterization (Kass and Voss 1997), which we now define.

Definition 18.1 [diffeomorphism] Let $f(\theta):=(f_1(\theta), \ldots, f_k(\theta))^\top$ be a function $f : \Theta \to \mathbb{R}^k$. f is a *diffeomorphism* if it is smooth (infinitely often differentiable), 1-to-1 on its image $\{\eta : \eta = f(\theta) \text{ for some } \theta \in \Theta\}$, and for all $\theta \in \Theta$, the *Jacobi matrix* of first derivatives

$$D_{\text{Jacobi}}(\theta) := \begin{pmatrix} \nabla f_1(\theta) \\ \ldots \\ \nabla f_k(\theta) \end{pmatrix} = \begin{pmatrix} \frac{\partial}{\partial \theta_1} f_1(\theta) & \cdots & \frac{\partial}{\partial \theta_k} f_1(\theta) \\ & \ldots & \\ \frac{\partial}{\partial \theta_1} f_k(\theta) & \cdots & \frac{\partial}{\partial \theta_k} f_k(\theta) \end{pmatrix} \tag{18.26}$$

has rank k, that is, $\det D_{\text{Jacobi}}(\theta) \neq 0$.

In Part II of this book, we encountered several theorems involving exponential families $\mathcal{M}$. In these theorems, we always assumed that $\mathcal{M}$ is given in a parameterization $(\Theta_\gamma, Q_\gamma)$ such that there is a diffeomorphism $\gamma(\mu)$ from Θ_{mean} to Θ_γ. We call such parameterizations *diffeomorphic*.

That is, for all $\mu \in \Theta_{\text{mean}}$, $Q_{\gamma(\mu)} = P_\mu$, in particular, $E_{Q_{\gamma(\mu)}}[\phi(X)] = \mu$. It follows from the inverse function theorem that the inverse of a diffeomorphism is also a diffeomorphism (see (Kass and Voss 1997), Appendix A). This implies that there is also a diffeomorphism $\mu(\gamma)$ such that for all $\gamma \in \Theta_\gamma$, $P_{\mu(\gamma)} = Q_\gamma$. Since $\mu(\beta)$ is smooth and its Jacobi matrix is equal to $I(\beta)$, which is positive definite, it follows that $\mu(\beta)$ is a diffeomorphism, so that $\beta(\mu)$ is also a diffeomorphism (Kass and Voss 1997).

Why do we restrict attention to diffeomorphic parameterizations? It is intuitively clear that it is useful to consider parameterizations such that the mapping $\gamma(\mu)$ is smooth and 1-to-1. The additional requirement that the Jacobian matrix is of full rank, ensures that the inverse mapping $\gamma(\mu)$ is smooth as well. To get some intuition, consider the example $\Theta_\gamma = \Theta_{\text{mean}} = [-1, 1]$, and $\gamma(\mu) = \mu^3$. Then $\gamma(\mu)$ is smooth but not a diffeomorphism, since the rank at $\mu = 0$ is 0. Indeed, we see that $\mu(\gamma)$ is not differentiable at $\mu = 0$ and hence not smooth.

The following proposition relates the Fisher information between two arbitrary diffeomorphic representations Θ_γ and Θ_η. It is useful in proving some of the theorems in Part II of this book.

Proposition 18.2 Let (Θ_η, P_η) and $(\Theta_\gamma, Q_\gamma)$ be two diffeomorphic parameterizations of exponential family $\mathcal{M}$. Let $I(\gamma)$ denote the Fisher information in parameterization Θ_γ, and let $I(\eta)$ denote the Fisher information in parameterization Θ_η. Then the function $\eta : \Theta_\gamma \rightarrow \Theta_\eta$ defined by $\eta\gamma_0 = \eta_0$ for the η_0 such that $P_{\eta_0} = Q_{\gamma_0}$ is a diffeomorphism. For all $\gamma \in \Theta_\gamma$, we have

$$I(\gamma) = (D_{\text{Jacobi}}\eta(\gamma))^\top I(\eta(\gamma))(D_{\text{Jacobi}}\eta(\gamma)). \tag{18.27}$$

Proof(sketch): $\eta(\gamma)$ can be rewritten as the composition of $\mu(\gamma)$, the mapping from Θ_γ to the mean-value parameterization Θ_{mean}, and $\eta(\mu)$, the mapping from Θ_{mean} to Θ_η. Since both $\mu(\gamma)$ and $\eta(\mu)$ are diffeomorphisms, and the composition of two diffeomorphisms is itself a diffeomorphism (Kass and Voss 1997), it follows that $\eta(\gamma)$ is a diffeomorphism. The proof of (18.27) follows by the chain rule of differentiation. Here we only sketch the proof for 1-parameter families. Extension to the k-parameter version is straightforward and has been omitted.

$$I(\gamma) = E_{\theta(\gamma)} \left(\frac{d}{d\gamma} - \ln P_{\theta\gamma}(X) \right)^2 =$$

$$E_{\theta(\gamma)} \left(\frac{d}{d\theta} - \ln P_{\theta}(X) \right)^2 \left(\frac{d\theta}{d\gamma} \right)^2 = I(\theta) \left(\frac{d\theta}{d\gamma} \right)^2, \quad (18.28)$$

where we rewrote the Fisher information as in (18.49). □

18.4.3 Relating Mean-Value and Canonical Parameters**

In Section 18.3 we expressed the mean μ and the Fisher information in terms of β. We would now like to express β and the Fisher information in terms of μ. We already gave a characterization of β in terms of μ in (18.25), but as we shall see, more characterizations are possible. To develop the corresponding equations, we use another remarkable property of exponential families, which has its roots in the theory of *convex duality* (Rockafellar 1970). First we note (see below) that every exponential family has a canonical parameterization such that $0 \in \Theta_{\mathrm{can}}$ and $\sum_x r(x) = 1$ (that is, r is a probability mass or density function).

If $0 \notin \Theta_{\mathrm{can}}$ or $\sum_x r(x) \neq 1$, we can pick any $\beta_0 \in \Theta_{\mathrm{can}}$ and set

$$r'(x) = \frac{r(x) \exp(\beta_0^\top \phi(x))}{\sum_{x \in \mathcal{X}} r(x) \exp(\beta_0^\top \phi(x))}. \quad (18.29)$$

Then the exponential family corresponding to r' instead of r with parameters $\Theta'_\beta = \Theta_{\mathrm{can}} - \beta_0$ is identical to the original family, but now contains the "origin" $\beta = 0$ and satisfies $\sum_x r'(x) = 1$.

For such families we define

$$\xi(\mu) := \mathrm{D}(\beta(\mu)\|0) = \mathrm{D}(P_{\beta(\mu)}\|P_0).$$

Since $\ln P_\beta(X) = \beta^\top X - \psi(\beta)$, we have

$$\xi(\mu) = E_\mu[\beta^\top X - \psi(\beta)] = \beta^\top \mu - \psi(\beta), \quad (18.30)$$

where $\mu = \mu(\beta)$ is the μ corresponding to β.

To help interpret ξ, note that in many interesting cases, $\mathcal{X}$ is finite, say of size M, and $r(x) \equiv 1$, so that after the transformation (18.29), for all x, $r(x) = 1/M$. Then we see from (18.30) that

$$\xi(\mu) = E_\mu[\ln P_\mu(X)] + \ln M,$$

so that we can think of $\xi(\mu)$ as minus the entropy of $P(\cdot\mu)$ plus some constant.

Duality   Since $\beta = \beta(\mu)$ is a 1-to-1 function from Θ_{mean} to Θ_{can}, (18.30) implies that *for all $\beta \in \Theta_{\text{can}}$ and all $\mu \in \Theta_{\text{mean}}$ such that β corresponds to μ,*

$$\xi(\mu) + \psi(\beta) = \beta^{\top}\mu. \tag{18.31}$$

Equation (18.31) expresses that ξ with domain Θ_{mean} and ψ with domain Θ_{can} are each other's *Legendre transform*[3] (Rockafellar 1970; Barndorff-Nielsen 1978). From (18.31) we immediately see that there is a strong symmetry between ξ and ψ. This implies that, broadly speaking, essential properties which hold for one function also hold for the other, with the role of variables exchanged. For example, (18.9) established that for all β,

$$\mu(\beta)^{\top} = \nabla\psi(\beta), \tag{18.32}$$

which suggests that for all μ,

$$\beta(\mu)^{\top} = \nabla\xi(\mu), \tag{18.33}$$

and this is indeed the case, providing an alternative characterization of $\beta(\mu)$ next to the one we established in (18.25). Similarly, (18.11) established that

$$I_{ij}(\beta) = \frac{\partial^2}{\partial\beta_i\beta_j}\psi(\beta), \tag{18.34}$$

which suggests that

$$I_{ij}(\mu) = \frac{\partial^2}{\partial\mu_i\partial\mu_j}\xi(\mu), \tag{18.35}$$

which can once again be verified. What is the relation between these Fisher information matrices $I(\beta)$ and $I(\mu)$? In the 1-parameter case, by (18.33) and (18.35), we can rewrite $I(\mu)$, and by (18.32) and (18.34) we can rewrite $I(\beta)$:

$$I(\mu) = \frac{d}{d\mu}\beta(\mu) \quad \text{and} \quad I(\beta) = \frac{d}{d\beta}\mu(\beta), \tag{18.36}$$

where $\mu(\beta)$ is the inverse of $\beta(\mu)$. Further below we show how this implies that

$$I(\mu) = I^{-1}(\beta(\mu)). \tag{18.37}$$

---

3. In a more general treatment, we can extend the functions ξ and ψ to all of $\mathbb{R}^k$ by setting their values to ∞ outside their domain; they then become each other's *convex conjugate*.

To finalize this section, we list three more properties of the mean-value parameterization which arise from the duality relation (18.31). Note how these properties correspond to the properties listed in Section 18.3 for the canonical parameterization.

Properties of Mean-Value Parameterization

1. Θ_{mean} **is convex.**

2. $I(\mu) = I^{-1}(\beta(\mu))$ **is positive definite.**

3. ξ is strictly convex, from which it follows that for all $\mu' \in \Theta_{\text{mean}}$, $D(\mu\|\mu')$ **is strictly convex as a function of** μ. ($D(\mu\|\mu')$ is not necessarily convex as a function of μ'; see Example 19.2.)

Example 18.4 [Bernoulli] Let us check (18.33) and (18.35) for the Bernoulli model. For this model, $\xi(\mu) = D(P_\mu \| P_{\frac{1}{2}})$ where P_μ is the Bernoulli distribution with $P_\mu(X = 1) = \mu$. Using the definition of the KL divergence $D(\cdot\|\cdot)$ this becomes

$$\xi(\mu) = \mu \ln \mu + (1 - \mu) \ln(1 - \mu) + \mu \ln 2 - (1 - \mu) \ln 2 = \ln 2 - H(P_\mu),$$

where H is the Shannon entropy measured in nats. Differentiating gives

$$\frac{d}{d\mu}\xi(\mu) = -\frac{d}{d\mu}H(P_\mu) = \log \frac{\mu}{1 - \mu}, \tag{18.38}$$

which coincides with (18.2) and confirms (18.33) for the Bernoulli model. Similarly, differentiating (18.38) once more, we find

$$\frac{d^2}{d\mu^2}\xi(\mu) = \frac{d}{d\mu} \log \frac{\mu}{1 - \mu} = \frac{1}{\mu} + \frac{1}{1 - \mu} = \frac{1}{\mu(1 - \mu)},$$

which coincides with the Fisher information $I(\mu)$ for the Bernoulli model and confirms (18.35).

Proof Sketches: Paralleling Proposition 18.1, we first establish

Proposition 18.3 $\xi(\cdot)$ is "smooth," i.e. continuous and infinitely often differentiable on Θ_{mean}.

Proof: Since $\psi(\beta)$ is smooth, $\mu(\beta) = \nabla\psi(\beta)$ must also be smooth. We already established in Section 18.4 that $\mu(\beta)$ is also a 1-to-1 mapping from an open set to another open set. The Jacobian matrix of $\mu(\beta)$ is the matrix of partial second derivative of $\psi(\beta)$, and we also established that this matrix is positive definite. It follows that $\mu(\beta)$ is a diffeomorphism, so its inverse $\beta(\mu)$ must also be smooth. Since we have $\xi(\mu) = \beta(\mu)^\top \mu - \psi(\beta(\mu))$, $\xi(\mu)$ is the sum of two smooth functions and hence must itself be smooth. $\square$

We now have to show (18.33). For simplicity, we verify the 1-parameter case only:

$$\frac{d}{d\mu}\xi(\mu) = \frac{d}{d\mu}E_\mu[-\ln P_{\beta(\mu)}(X)] =$$

$$\frac{d}{d\mu}E_\mu[\beta(\mu)X - \psi(\beta(\mu))] = \frac{d}{d\mu}\mu\beta(\mu) - \frac{d}{d\mu}\psi(\beta(\mu)) =$$

$$\beta(\mu) + \mu\frac{d}{d\mu}\beta(\mu) - \left\{\frac{d}{d\beta}\psi(\beta)\right\}_{\beta=\beta(\mu)} \cdot \frac{d}{d\mu}\beta(\mu) =$$

$$\beta(\mu) + (\mu - \mu)\frac{d}{d\mu}\beta(\mu) = \beta(\mu), \quad (18.39)$$

where the third equality follows by the product rule and the chain rule for differentiation. Now for (18.35). Again we only show the 1-parameter case:

$$I(\mu') =$$

$$E_{\mu'}\left\{\frac{d^2}{d\mu^2} - \ln P_{\beta(\mu)}(X)\right\}_{\mu=\mu'} = \left\{\frac{d}{d\mu}\left[\frac{d}{d\mu}(-\mu'\beta(\mu) + \psi(\beta(\mu)))\right]\right\}_{\mu=\mu'} \overset{(*)}{=}$$

$$\left\{\frac{d}{d\mu}\left[\left[\frac{d}{d\beta}(-\beta\mu' + \psi(\beta))\right]_{\beta=\beta(\mu)} \cdot \frac{d}{d\mu}\beta(\mu)\right]\right\}_{\mu=\mu'} =$$

$$\left\{\frac{d}{d\mu}\left[(-\mu' + \mu) \cdot \frac{d}{d\mu}\beta(\mu)\right]\right\}_{\mu=\mu'} = \left\{\frac{d}{d\mu}\beta(\mu)\right\}_{\mu=\mu'} = \left\{\frac{d^2}{d\mu^2}\xi(\mu)\right\}_{\mu=\mu'},$$

$$(18.40)$$

where $(*)$ follows by the chain rule for differentiation and the last equality follows from (18.33).

Now for (18.37). Again we only show the 1-parameter case. Fix any point $(\mu_0, \beta_0) = (\mu_0, \beta(\mu_0))$ and fix some small $\epsilon > 0$. The first derivatives at μ_0 and β_0 can be written as

$$\frac{d}{d\beta}\mu(\beta_0) = \lim_{\epsilon\downarrow 0} \frac{\mu(\beta_0 + \epsilon) - \mu(\beta_0)}{\epsilon}$$

and

$$\frac{d}{d\mu}\beta(\mu_0) = \lim_{\epsilon\downarrow 0} \frac{\epsilon}{\mu(\beta_0 + \epsilon) - \mu(\beta_0)},$$

showing that $I(\beta_0) = 1/I(\mu_0)$. The argument can be easily formalized and generalized to multivariate families. It then becomes an instance of the *inverse function theorem* of calculus and leads to (18.37).

Finally, we show the three properties listed in the box. Convexity of Θ_{mean} is a direct consequence of property 3(b) of Section 18.3, (18.13), and the fact that Θ_{can} is convex (see box on page 602).

Since $I(\beta)$ is positive definite on all $\beta \in \Theta_{\text{can}}$ (Section 18.3), by (18.37) $I(\mu)$ must be positive definite on Θ_{mean}. By (18.35) it now follows that $\xi(\mu) = D(\mu\|\mu(\mathbf{0}))$ is strictly convex. By appropriately modifying the carrier $r(x)$, one can use the same argument to show that for all $\mu' \in \Theta_{\text{mean}}$, $D(\mu\|\mu')$ is strictly convex in its first argument. $\square$

18.5   Exponential Families of General Probabilistic Sources*

Most of the special mathematical properties of a k-parameter exponential family $\mathcal{M}$ defined on sample space $\mathcal{X}$ really become useful only if we consider a sample $x^n = x_1, \ldots, x_n \in \mathcal{X}^n$ and model it by the set $\mathcal{M}^{(n)}$ of n-fold product distributions of elements of $\mathcal{M}$. The distributions in $\mathcal{M}^{(n)}$ can still be described using only k parameters, and the sufficient statistic of x^n remains of dimension k, no matter how large n; this is what makes exponential families so convenient in practice.

However, in practice we often deal with models of probabilistic sources such that data are either not independent (such as the Markov models) or not identically distributed (such as the linear regression model). Such models of sources, when restricted to the first n outcomes, can often still be represented as exponential families, defined on the space $\mathcal{X}^n$ rather than $\mathcal{X}^1$; we showed this for linear regression models in Chapter 12, Section 12.3, page 351. For the Markov models, it is shown below. This shows that both Markov and linear regression models, when viewed as families of (conditional) probabilistic sources, are in a sense "exponential families of probabilistic sources." It seems desirable to me to formalize this notion. Since I found no formalization in the literature, I tried to do it myself, leading to the definition below.

Let $\mathcal{Z} = \mathcal{X} \times \mathcal{Y}$. Let $\phi : \mathcal{Z}^* \to \mathbb{R}^k$ and $r : \mathcal{Z}^* \to (0, \infty)$ be some functions on sequences $z^n = ((x_1, y_1), \ldots, (x_n, y_n))$ of arbitrary length n. Let $\Theta_{\text{can}} \subset \mathbb{R}^k$. We define the conditional probabilistic source P_β relative to ϕ and carrier r as the source satisfying for all n, $z^n = ((x_1, y_1), \ldots, (x_n, y_n)) \in \mathcal{Z}^n$:

$$P_\beta(y_n \mid z^{n-1}, x_n) := \frac{e^{\beta^\top \phi(z^{n-1}, x_n, y_n)} r(z^{n-1}, x_n, y_n)}{Z(\beta \mid z^{n-1}, x_n)}, \tag{18.41}$$

where

$$Z(\beta \mid z^{n-1}, x_n) = \sum_{y \in \mathcal{Y}} e^{\beta^\top \phi(z^{n-1}, x_n, y)} r(z^{n-1}, x_n, y).$$

A conditional exponential family of probabilistic sources $\mathcal{M} = \{P_\beta \mid \beta \in \Theta_{\mathrm{can}}\}$ relative to ϕ and r as above is a set of sources $\{P_\beta \mid \beta \in \Theta_{\mathrm{can}}\}$ as defined in (18.41), such that for each $\beta \in \Theta_{\mathrm{can}}$, all $n \geq 1$, all $z^{n-1} \in \mathcal{Z}^{n-1}, x_n \in \mathcal{X}$, $Z(\beta \mid z^{n-1}, x^n)$ is finite. As for ordinary exponential families, we require that Θ_{can} is open and convex. We call $\mathcal{M}$ *k-dimensional* if the representation (18.41) is minimal. This means that there exists no $\lambda_0, \lambda_1, \ldots, \lambda_k \in \mathbb{R}^k \setminus \{\mathbf{0}\}$ such that for all $y \in \mathcal{Y}$, $\sum_{j=1}^k \lambda_j \phi_j(y) + \lambda_0 = 0$.

Example 18.5 [γth-order Markov Model $\mathcal{B}^{(k_\gamma)}$] The γth order Markov model $\mathcal{B}^{(\gamma)}$ with $k = 2^\gamma$ parameters is a simple example of a non-i.i.d. exponential family. In this case, the x_i's play no role, and they will be omitted from the following equations. We can formally achieve this by defining $\mathcal{B}^{(k)}$ as a set of probabilistic sources on $\mathcal{Y}$, taking an $\mathcal{X}$ containing only one element that occurs at every outcome. It is easy to see that, for any $n > \gamma$, the restriction of $\mathcal{B}^{(k)}$ to distributions on n outcomes is an exponential family model for the sample space $\mathcal{Y}^n$. But we can also view $\mathcal{B}^{(k)}$ as an exponential family of sources: we set $r(y^n):=1$ for all n, all $y^n \in \{0,1\}^n$. We can now represent the elements of $\mathcal{B}^{(k)}$ as

$$P_\beta(y_n \mid y^{n-1}) = \frac{e^{\beta^\top \phi(y^{n-1}, y_n)}}{Z(\beta \mid y^{n-1})},$$

where ϕ is a 2^γ-dimensional vector $(\phi_1, \ldots, \phi_k)$. Rather than giving the general definition of the ϕ_j we will restrict to the case $\gamma = 3$; the reader can easily figure out the general case. For $y_1, y_2, y_3 \in \{0,1\}^3$, we set $\phi(y_1) = \mathbf{0}, \phi(y_1, y_2) = \mathbf{0}, \phi(y_1, y_2, y_3) = \mathbf{0}$. For $n \geq 4$, $\phi(y^n)$ only depends on the current outcome y_n and the previous three outcomes $y_{n-1}, \ldots, y_{n-k}$ as follows. First, we rename the functions $\phi_1, \ldots, \phi_8$ to $\phi_{[1|000]}, \phi_{[1|001]}, \ldots, \phi_{[1|111]}$. Then $\phi_{[1|x_1 x_2 x_3]}$ is defined as

$$\phi_{[1|x_1 x_2 x_3]}(y^n):= \begin{cases} 1 & \text{if } y_{n-3} = x_1, y_{n-2} = x_2, y_{n-1} = x_3, y_n = 1. \\ 0 & \text{otherwise.} \end{cases} \tag{18.42}$$

In this way, setting

$$\beta_{[1|x_1 x_2 x_3]}:= \ln \theta_{[1|x_1 x_2 x_3]} - \ln(1 - \theta_{[1|x_1 x_2 x_3]}),$$

we get $P_\beta(Y_n = 1 \mid y^{n-1}) = \theta_{[1|x_1 x_2 x_3]}$, in accordance with Chapter 2, Example 2.7.

A conditional exponential family model is called *i.i.d.* if there exist functions $f_0, f_1, \ldots f_k$ with for $j = 1, \ldots, k$, $f_j : \mathcal{X} \times \mathcal{Y} \to \mathbb{R}$ such that for all n, $z^n = ((x_1, y_1), \ldots, (x_n, y_n)) \in \mathcal{Z}^n$, all $j = 1, \ldots, k$, we have

$$\phi_j(z^{n-1}, (x_n, y_n)) = f_j(x_n, y_n) \quad \text{and} \quad r(z^n) = \prod_{i=1}^{n} f_0(x_i, y_i).$$

Example 18.6 [Linear Regression] Consider linear regression models $\mathcal{M}^{\mathbf{X}}$ and $\mathcal{S}^{\mathbf{X}}$, defined as in Chapter 12, Section 12.3. These are families of distributions $\mathcal{Y}^n$, and we already showed on page 351 that they are exponential families. The argument can be extended to show the exponentiality of the model of conditional sources $\mathcal{M}^{(k)}$ and $\mathcal{S}^{(k+1)}$ from which they derive. Let us verify this for $\mathcal{S}^{(k+1)}$. We can write $\mathcal{S}^{(k+1)} = \{P_{(\sigma^2, \mu)}) \mid \sigma^2 \in (0, \infty), \mu \in \Theta\}$, with, for each n, $P_{\sigma^2, \mu} \in \mathcal{S}^{(k+1)}$ having density $f_{\sigma^2, \mu}$ given by (12.2). We now reparameterize the $P_{(\sigma^2, \mu)})$ so that they are given in exponential family form. Define the mapping $\beta : (0, \infty) \times \mathbb{R}^k \to \mathbb{R}^{k+1}$ by

$$\beta(\sigma^2, \mu_1, \ldots, \mu_k) := (-\frac{1}{2\sigma^2}, \frac{1}{\sigma^2}\mu_1, \ldots, \frac{1}{\sigma^2}\mu_k)^\top \tag{18.43}$$

and let Θ_{can} be the range of $\beta(\cdot)$. It is easy to see that Θ_{can} is open and convex. Now define

$$\begin{aligned} \phi_0(x, y) &= y^2 \\ \phi_j(x, y) &= -yx_{(j)} \text{ for } j \in \{1, \ldots, k\}, \end{aligned} \tag{18.44}$$

where $x_{(j)}$ represents the jth component of the input vector x. Rewriting (12.2) for $n = 1$, using (18.44) and (18.43) gives

$$f_{(\sigma^2, \mu)}(Y \mid X) = \frac{1}{Z(\beta \mid X)} e^{\beta^\top \phi(X, Y)}, \tag{18.45}$$

where $Z(\beta \mid X)$ depends only on β and X, not on Y. It follows that $\mathcal{S}^{(k+1)}$ is an i.i.d. conditional exponential family.

18.6   Fisher Information Definitions and Characterizations*

1. Our definition. Let $\mathcal{M}$ be a model with k-dimensional smooth parameterization Θ. For $\theta \in \Theta$, and $i, j \in 1..k$, let $I_{ij}(\theta)$ be the corresponding entry in the Fisher information matrix $I(\theta)$. In (4.22) we defined this matrix in a slightly nonstandard fashion, as

$$I_{ij}(\theta^*) := E_{\theta^*}\left\{-\frac{\partial^2}{\partial\theta_i\partial\theta_j} \ln P_\theta(X)\right\}_{\theta=\theta^*}. \tag{18.46}$$

2. First KL divergence characterization.   If we are allowed to exchange the order of differentiation and integration over X in E_{θ^*}, then (18.46) becomes equivalent to the following definition of Fisher information as the second derivative of the KL divergence with the second argument varying: for $i, j \in 1..k$,

$$I_{ij}(\theta^*) = \left\{ \frac{\partial^2}{\partial \theta_i \partial \theta_j} \mathrm{D}(\theta^* \| \theta) \right\}_{\theta = \theta^*}. \tag{18.47}$$

Using the fact that for exponential families in their canonical parameterizations, we can write $-\ln P_\beta(X) = -\beta^\top \phi(X) + \psi(\beta)$, we immediately see that (18.47) is implied by our definition (18.46). The argument is easily extended to show that (18.47) also holds for exponential families in their mean parameterization. Yet (18.47) holds more generally; in our experience, it seems to hold for most parametric models encountered in practice.

3. Standard definition.   If additionally, for all n,

$$\int_{x_1, \ldots, x_n \in \mathcal{X}^n} \Big[\frac{\partial^2}{\partial \theta_i \partial \theta_j} P_\theta(x_1, \ldots, x_n) \Big] dx_1 \ldots dx_n =$$

$$\frac{\partial^2}{\partial \theta_i \partial \theta_j} \int_{x_1, \ldots, x_n \in \mathcal{X}^n} P_\theta(x_1, \ldots, x_n) dx_1 \ldots dx_n, \quad (18.48)$$

then our definition of Fisher information coincides with the standard definition in the statistical literature of *the Fisher information in one observation* (Casella and Berger), which is given by

$$I'_{ij}(\theta) := E_\theta \left(\frac{\partial}{\partial \theta_i} \ln P_\theta(X) \right) \left(\frac{\partial}{\partial \theta_j} \ln P_\theta(X) \right). \tag{18.49}$$

For non-i.i.d. models, the defining equation (4.27) is modified analogously.

   Once again, (18.48) expresses that we are allowed to change the order of differentiation and integration, but now the integral is over a different function as compared to (18.46). By Proposition 18.1, this exchange is possible for exponential families in their mean and canonical parameterizations. Equation (18.48) holds more generally though; in our experience, it seems to hold for most parametric models encountered in practice.

4. Second KL divergence characterization.   Finally, recall (Section 18.4.3) that for exponential families in their mean-value parameterization, we have for all $\theta^*, \theta_0 \in \Theta_{\text{mean}}$,

$$I_{ij}(\theta^*) = \left\{ \frac{\partial^2}{\partial\theta_i \partial\theta_j} D(\theta \| \theta_0) \right\}_{\theta=\theta^*}. \tag{18.50}$$

Note that (18.47) characterizes Fisher information as a second derivative with respect to the second argument of the KL divergence; (18.50) characterizes it as the second derivative with respect to the first argument. Equation (18.50) is highly specific to mean-value parameterizations of exponential families and does not hold generally.

19 *Information-Theoretic Properties of Exponential Families*

Overview The previous chapter listed standard statistical properties of exponential families. In this chapter, we concentrate on properties with an information-theoretic flavor. We present several results that are needed in the proofs of the main theorems of Part II of this text. The results also serve as an illustration that some of the concepts introduced in Chapter 2 (such as the central limit theorem for maximum likelihood estimators) and Chapter 3 (the minimax interpretation of uniform codes) hold in fact much more generally than for Bernoulli models.

Contents The parameterization in terms of sufficient statistics lies at the root of various *robustness properties* of exponential families. These are discussed in Section 19.2. These in turn can be used to precisely analyze the behavior of maximum likelihood estimation (Sections 19.3 and 19.4) and to interpret exponential families in terms of minimax codelength functions (Section 19.5). The latter section also discusses the relation between exponential families, maximum entropy, and minimum codelength. In Section 19.6 we consider a special exponential family that we call the *likelihood ratio family*, and we explain its connection to Rényi divergences.

Fast Track This chapter may be skipped at first reading. Nevertheless, it may be useful to glance at Section 19.5 on the connection between maximum entropy, minimax codelength, and exponential families. This serves as a very strong illustration of a central theme in this book: it is sometimes useful to encode data using the code based on distribution P, even if this P is not the data-generating distribution.

19.1   Introduction

In this chapter, we consider what happens if we encode data based on the codes corresponding to an exponential family. It turns out that such codes are surprisingly *robust*, meaning that the expected codelength that is achieved does not depend on whether or not the data are generated according to a member of the family.

We introduce the basic robustness property in Section 19.2. This remarkable property has several important consequences, which are the subjects of subsequent sections:

1. **Maximum likelihood estimation** is considered in Section 19.3. It turns out that the likelihood has a unique maximum depending only on the sufficient statistic of the data.

2. **Large deviation probabilities.** Suppose we observe a value of the sufficient statistic that is much larger or smaller than its expected value. What is the probability of such an event? The answer is related to the robustness property above and can be given in terms of the KL divergence, as we show in Section 19.4. There we also consider the *central limit theorem* for exponential families.

3. **Maximum entropy inference.** Jaynes's celebrated maximum entropy and minimum relative entropy principles lead to inference of exponential families. This is a direct consequence of the robustness property mentioned above (Section 19.5).

4. **Minimax codelength.** It also follows directly from the robustness property that exponential families, when used as codes, achieve minimax codelength among all codes for a given constraint. This fact can be used to reinterpret maximum entropy in coding theoretic terms (Section 19.5).

Finally, in Section 19.6, we discuss a particular kind of 1-parameter exponential family that we call the *likelihood ratio family*. This family is really a theoretical construct that helps to understand abstract notions such as Rényi divergences (Chapter 15, Section 15.3) in concrete coding-theoretic terms.

19.2   Robustness of Exponential Family Codes

Consider an exponential family given in the mean-value parameterization $(P_\mu, \Theta_{\text{mean}})$ and with $r(x) > 0$ for all $x \in \mathcal{X}$. Let P^* be any distribution on

$\mathcal{X}$. We specifically do *not* require that P^* be a member of the family represented by Θ_{mean}. In this section we investigate the behavior of the expected log-likelihood/codelength $-\log P_\mu(x)$ under the assumption that data are distributed according to such an arbitrary P^*. To this end, it is useful to extend the notion of KL divergence:

Extended KL Divergence   We define *extended Kullback-Leibler divergence* as:

$$D_{P^*}(\mu_1 \| \mu_2) = E_{P^*}\left[-\ln P_{\mu_2}(X) - (-\ln P_{\mu_1}(X))\right] \tag{19.1}$$

Since we require that, for all x, $r(x) > 0$, we also have $P_{\mu_1}(x) > 0$ and $P_{\mu_2}(x) > 0$, so the extended KL divergence is well defined.

This quantity can be interpreted as follows: suppose we want to encode outcomes coming from some distribution P^*. We have no idea what P^* is, and we only have at our disposal codes corresponding to exponential family Θ_{mean}. Then $D_{P^*}(\mu_1 \| \mu_2)$ is the expected additional bits we need to encode X using the code based on μ_2, compared to the number of bits we would need using the code based on μ_1. D_{P^*} can be negative, since clearly,

$$D_{P^*}(\mu_1 \| \mu_2) = -D_{P^*}(\mu_2 \| \mu_1) = D(P^* \| P_{\mu_2}) - D(P^* \| P_{\mu_1}),$$

where the first equality holds in general and the second equality holds whenever P^* is such that the quantity on the right is well defined. The following important proposition is a direct consequence of the fact that exponential families admit sufficient statistics:

Robustness Property
Proposition 19.1 Let $\mu^* \in \Theta_{\text{mean}}$, let $\beta^* = \beta(\mu^*)$ and let P^* be an *arbitrary* distribution with $E_{P^*}[\phi(X)] = \mu^*$. Then

1. For all $\mu \in \Theta_{\text{mean}}$,

   $$D_{P^*}(\mu^* \| \mu) = D(\mu^* \| \mu), \tag{19.2}$$

   or equivalently, for all $\beta \in \Theta_{\text{can}}$, $D_{P^*}(\beta^* \| \beta) = D(\beta^* \| \beta)$.

2. Moreover, if $r(x) \equiv c$ for some constant c, then

   $$E_{P^*}[-\ln P_\mu(X)] = E_{\mu^*}[-\ln P_\mu(X)], \tag{19.3}$$

   or equivalently, $E_{P^*}[-\ln P_\beta(X)] = E_{\beta^*}[-\ln P_\beta(X)]$.

Part 2 of the proposition is easiest to explain. It says that, for exponential families with $r(x) \equiv c$, using the code P_μ, the number of bits needed to encode an outcome from P^* is equal to the number of bits needed to encode an outcome from P_{μ^*}! In particular, if we use P_{μ^*} to encode the data, *the expected codelength behaves just as if P_{μ^*} would generate the data*. This holds no matter what P^* actually generates the data, as long as $E_{P^*}[\phi(X)] = \mu^*$.

Part 1 is a variation of part 2 for the case where $r(x)$ varies with x. It says that in that case, the *additional* number of bits needed to code the data using P_μ rather than the P_{μ^*} that is optimal within the set Θ_{mean} only depends on the data-generating distribution P^* through the mean μ^* and not on any other aspects of P^*.

> **Example 19.1** **[Normal Family]** Consider for example the family of normal distributions $P_{\nu,\sigma^2}(X)$ with mean ν and variance σ^2. Since this is an exponential family, Proposition 19.1 must hold. Indeed, let P^* be an arbitrary distribution on $\mathcal{X} = \mathbb{R}$ with mean ν and variance σ^2. Direct calculation shows that
>
> $$E_{P^*}[-\ln P_{\nu,\sigma}(X)] = \frac{1}{2} + \frac{1}{2}\ln 2\pi\sigma^2,$$
>
> which does not depend on the details of P^*. This is an instance of Proposition 19.1 with $\mu^* = (\nu, \sigma^2)$.

In the remainder of this section we provide two additional results that refine Proposition 19.1. The first tells us how $D_{P^*}(\cdot\|\cdot)$ varies as a function of its second argument:

Proposition 19.2 Assume the setting of Proposition 19.1. We have:

1. $E_{P^*}[-\ln P_\beta(X)]$ is a strictly convex function of β, achieving its unique minimum at β^*.

   $E_{P^*}[-\ln P_\mu(X)]$ as a function of μ achieves its unique minimum at $\mu = \mu^*$. It has no local minima: for all $\mu' \in \Theta_{\mathrm{mean}}, \mu' \neq \mu^*$, all $\lambda \in [0,1]$, $E_{P^*}[-\ln P_{\lambda\mu^*+(1-\lambda)\mu'}(X)]$ is strictly decreasing in λ.

2. $D_{P^*}(\beta^*\|\beta)$ is a strictly convex function of β, achieving its minimum at β^*.

   $D_{P^*}(\mu^*\|\mu)$ as a function of μ achieves its unique minimum at $\mu = \mu^*$. It has no local minima: for all $\mu' \in \Theta_{\mathrm{mean}}, \mu' \neq \mu^*$, all $\lambda \in [0,1]$, $D_{P^*}(\mu^*\|\lambda\mu^* + (1-\lambda)\mu')]$ is strictly decreasing in λ.

Proof (of Proposition 19.1): Note first

$$E_{P^*}[-\ln P_\beta(X)] = E_{P^*}[-\beta^\top\phi(X) + \psi(\beta) - \ln r(X)] =$$
$$- \beta^\top\mu^* + \psi(\beta) + E_{P^*}[-\ln r(X)]. \quad (19.4)$$

For part 1, using (19.4), note that for arbitrary μ^* and arbitrary $\mu \in \Theta_{\text{mean}}$, and $\beta^* = \beta(\mu^*), \beta = \beta(\mu)$,

$$D_{P^*}(\mu^* \| \mu) = D_{P^*}(\beta^* \| \beta) = (\beta^* - \beta)^\top \mu^* - \psi(\beta^*) + \psi(\beta),$$

whereas

$$D(\mu^* \| \mu) = D(\beta^* \| \beta) = (\beta^* - \beta)^\top \mu^* - \psi(\beta^*) + \psi(\beta),$$

so that the two divergences are identical. Note that the terms $E_{P^*}[-\ln r(X)]$ and $E_{P_{\mu^*}}[-\ln r(X)]$ cancel in both equations. Part 2 is shown analogously, using the fact that if $r(x)$ is constant, then $E_{P^*}[-\ln r(X)] = E_{P_{\mu^*}}[-\ln r(X)]$. $\square$

Proof (of Proposition 19.2): We first show the first half of part 1. Differentiating (19.4) gives

$$\frac{\partial}{\partial \beta_j} E_{P^*}[-\ln P_\beta(X)] = \mu^* - \mu,$$

which is 0 iff $\mu = \mu^*$, i.e. if $\beta = \beta^*$. Similarly,

$$\frac{\partial^2}{\partial \beta_i \partial \beta_j} E_{P^*}[-\ln P_\beta(X)] = \frac{\partial^2}{\partial \beta_i \partial \beta_j} \psi(\beta) = I(\beta),$$

which was shown to be positive definite in Section 18.3. It therefore follows that $E_{P^*}[-\ln P_\beta(X)]$ is strictly convex, and that $E_{P^*}[-\ln P_\beta(X)]$ reaches its unique minimum at $\beta = \beta(\mu^*)$.

Now for the second half of part 1, the mean-value parameterization. Let $\beta' = \beta(\mu')$. Property 3(b) of exponential families, Equation (18.13), implies that there exists a differentiable function g with $g(0) = 0, g(1) = 1$ that is strictly increasing on $[0,1]$ and satisfies, for all $\lambda \in [0,1]$, $\beta((1 - \lambda)\mu' + \lambda\mu^*) = (1 - \gamma)\beta' + \gamma\beta^*$, where $\gamma = g(\lambda)$. So we have

$$\frac{d}{d\lambda} E_{P^*}[-\ln P_{\lambda\mu^* + (1-\lambda\mu')}(X)] =$$

$$\frac{d}{d\gamma} E_{P^*}[-\ln P_{\gamma\beta^* + (1-\gamma)\beta'}(X)]_{\gamma=g(\lambda)} \cdot \frac{d}{d\lambda} g(\lambda) < 0. \quad (19.5)$$

By noting that the functions of part 2 of the proposition are equal to the corresponding functions in part 1 plus a constant term, we see that part 2 follows in the same way. $\square$

19.2.1 If Θ_{mean} Does Not Contain the Mean**

In Section 19.4 we will deal with combinations of P^* generating the data and exponential families whose mean-value parameter sets are restricted to sets that may not contain a μ with $E_{P^*}[\phi(X)] = \mu$. To analyze the situation, we will need the following variation of Proposition 19.1. In this proposition, P^* can be any distribution such that $E_{P^*}[\phi(X)]$ is well defined; in particular, $E_{P^*}[\phi(X)]$ is not necessarily in Θ_{mean}.

Proposition 19.3 Let $\mu_0, \mu_1 \in \Theta_{\text{mean}}$ and let, for some $\lambda \geq 1$, $\mu_\lambda = \lambda\mu_1 + (1 - \lambda)\mu_0$. Let P^* be any distribution with $E_{P^*}[\phi(X)] = \mu_\lambda$. Then

1. $D_{P^*}(\mu_1 \| \mu_0) = D_{\mu_\lambda}(\mu_1 \| \mu_0)$.

2. $D_{\mu_\lambda}(\mu_1 \| \mu_0)$ increases linearly in λ:

$$D_{P^*}(\mu_1 \| \mu_0) - D(\mu_1 \| \mu_0) = (\beta_1 - \beta_0)^\top (\mu_1 - \mu_0)(\lambda - 1), \qquad (19.6)$$

where the right-hand side is always positive. Equality holds iff $E_{P^*}[\phi(X)] = \mu_1$.

To understand what this means, consider for example a two-dimensional exponential family. We draw a straight line between any two parameter vectors μ_1 and μ_0, and we extend the line from μ_1 in the opposite direction of μ_0 to some point μ_λ (which may lie outside Θ_{mean}). Proposition 19.3 says the following: The expected codelength difference between the code based on P_{μ_1} and the code based on P_{μ_0} when encoding a distribution P^* with mean μ_λ *increases* in λ. Thus, the farther the mean of P^* is from μ_1 and μ_0, the larger the gain is in using μ_1 over μ_0. This is somewhat surprising since, at $\lambda = 1$, the code based on P_{μ_1} is optimal among all codes P_μ. As λ increases, P_{μ_1} loses its optimality, but *relative* to μ_0, its coding performance becomes better and better.

Example 19.2 [Geometric] For the geometric family (18.4) in the canonical pa-rameterization, we have by (18.15)

$$\frac{d^2}{d\beta^2} E_{P^*}[-\ln P_\beta(X)] = I(\beta) = \frac{\exp\beta}{(1 - \exp\beta)^2},$$

which is positive for all β, in accordance with Proposition 19.2. However, for the mean-value parameterization (18.7), we have

$$E_{P^*}[-\ln P_\mu(X)] = E_{P^*}[X](\ln(\mu + 1) - \ln\mu) + \ln(\mu + 1).$$

Taking the second derivative and setting $E_{P^*}[X] = \mu^*$, we find

$$\frac{d^2}{d\mu^2} E_{P^*}[-\ln P_\mu(X)] = \mu^* \left(\frac{1}{\mu^2} - \frac{1}{(\mu+1)^2} \right) - \frac{1}{(\mu+1)^2}.$$

which becomes negative for small enough μ^*.

Thus, while $E_{P^*}[-\ln P_\beta(X)]$ and $D(\beta^*\|\beta)$ are strictly convex for the geometric and all other exponential families, $E_{P^*}[-\ln P_\mu(X)]$ and $D(\mu^*\|\mu)$ are convex for some (e.g., the Bernoulli) but not all (e.g., not for the geometric family) exponential families.

Proof(of Proposition 19.3): The first part of the proposition follows in exactly the same way as the first part of Proposition 19.1. For the second part, let $\beta_\lambda = \beta(\mu_\lambda)$ and let $\alpha = \lambda - 1$. Note that for all P^* with mean $E_{P^*}[\phi(X)] = \mu_\lambda$, including $P^* = P_{\mu_\lambda}$,

$$D_{P^*}(\mu_1\|\mu_0) - D(\mu_1\|\mu_0) = D_{P^*}(\beta_1\|\beta_0) - D(\beta_1\|\beta_0) =$$
$$\beta_1^\top(\mu_\lambda - \mu_1) - \beta_0^\top(\mu_\lambda - \mu_1) = (\beta_1 - \beta_0)^\top((1+\alpha)\mu_1 - \alpha\mu_0 - \mu_1) =$$
$$(\beta_1 - \beta_0)^\top(\mu_1 - \mu_0)\alpha. \quad (19.7)$$

Here the second equality follows by writing out the log-likelihood in the canonical parameter form $-\ln P_\beta(X)$; the other equalities are straightforward. The Proposition now follows since, by (18.12), the last line in (19.7) is linearly and strictly increasing in $\alpha \geq 0$. $\square$

19.3   Behavior *at* the ML Estimate $\hat{\beta}$

In this section we consider the following scenario: we observe a sequence $x^n = x_1, \ldots, x_n$ and we look for the ML estimator within some exponential family on $\mathcal{X}^n$ with sufficient statistic $\sum \phi(X_i)$. Note from Section 18.3 that according to this family, $X_1, \ldots, X_n$ are i.i.d. $\sim P_\beta^{(1)}$, where $P^{(1)}$ is the exponential family on $\mathcal{X}$ with sufficient statistic $\phi(X)$. As a consequence of Propositions 19.1, 19.2, and 19.3, the ML estimator is very well behaved for exponential families. Its behavior is easily analyzed by setting $P^* = \mathbb{P}$ and then applying Proposition 19.1. Here $\mathbb{P}$ is the *empirical distribution* of data x^n. This distribution was introduced on page 53, (2.13), as follows: for all $x \in \mathcal{X}$, we set

$$\mathbb{P}(x) = \frac{|\{i \in \{1, \ldots, n\} : x_i = x\}|}{n}.$$

Then for all $\beta \in \Theta_{\text{can}}$, the log-likelihood $\ln P_\beta(x^n)$ satisfies

$$\ln P_\beta(x^n) = nE_{\mathbb{P}}[\ln P_\beta(X)], \quad (19.8)$$

since

$$\ln P_\beta(x^n) = \beta^\top n E_\mathbb{P}[\phi(X)] - n \ln Z(\beta) + n E_\mathbb{P}[\ln r(X)] =$$
$$n E_\mathbb{P}[\ln P_\beta(X)]. \quad (19.9)$$

Using (19.8) and applying Proposition 19.2, part 1, with $P^* = \mathbb{P}$, we immediately get the following result:

1. Log-likelihood surface $\log P_\beta(x^n)$ Is strictly concave. Thus, because we also assume the parameter set Θ_{can} is convex, if a $\hat\beta$ maximizing the likelihood within Θ_{can} exists at all, it is unique. Because the mapping $\beta(\mu)$ is 1-to-1, the ML estimator $\hat\mu$ exists iff the ML estimator $\hat\beta$ exists. Again by Proposition 19.2, part 1, applied with $P^* = \mathbb{P}$, we find that:

2. ML estimator is average sufficient statistic. The ML estimator satisfies

$$\hat\mu(x^n) = E_{\hat\mu(x^n)}[\phi(X)] = E_{\hat\beta(x^n)}[\phi(X)] = \frac{1}{n}\sum_{i=1}^{n} \phi(x_i), \quad (19.10)$$

and it exists whenever $n^{-1}\sum \phi(x_i) \in \Theta_{\text{mean}}$. The rightmost equality follows because the mean of $\phi(X)$ under the empirical distribution $\mathbb{P}$ is equal to $n^{-1}\sum_{i=1}^{n} \phi(x_i)$, which must therefore be equal to $\hat\mu(x^n)$. Thus, the likelihood is maximized by setting the mean (*expected* value) of $\phi(X)$ according to P_μ to the empirical (*observed*) average of $\phi(x_i)$. This may seem "obviously right" but it should be noted that for probability models which are not exponential families (for example, mixture models), there exist no sufficient statistics and no analogue of (19.10) holds.

Equation (19.10) suggests that for any given set of data, the ML estimator (19.10) can be found by counting statistics of the data, without using any search techniques. While this is true in many cases, there do exist exponential families with many variables for which the sufficient statistics are hard to compute, and one has to resort to local optimization methods to find $\hat\mu$. An example is *logistic regression models*, which can be written in the exponential family form (Roos et al., 2005b) . Since there are no local maxima in the likelihood, such methods are guaranteed to converge, although they can be slow in practice.

3. Expected codelength is Observed average codelength. Suppose $r(x) \equiv 1$. Using (19.8) and Proposition 19.1, part 2, applied with $\mu = \mu^*$ and $P^* = \mathbb{P}$, we see that for all $x^n \in \mathcal{X}^n$ with $n^{-1} \sum \phi(x_i) \in \Theta_{\text{mean}}$, we have

$$-\frac{1}{n} \ln P_{\hat{\beta}(x^n)}(x^n) = E_{\hat{\beta}(x^n)}[-\ln P_{\hat{\beta}(x^n)}(X)] = \text{H}(\hat{\beta}(x^n)). \qquad (19.11)$$

In words, *no matter what sequence we observe*, the *average* number of bits per sample outcome that we need to encode a sequence x^n, using the code based on the ML distribution for x^n, is *precisely* equal to the *expected* number of bits needed to encode a sequence X^n generated by $\hat{\beta}(x^n)$. This is a remarkable property that, with some caveats, holds only for the exponential families: the mean (an "ensemble," or average over *all* possible sequences) is exactly equal to an average over a *single* sequence. Some of the consequences of this fact are explored in (Grünwald 1998, Chapter 4) and (Grünwald 1999).

Example 19.3 [Normal Family, Example 19.1, cont.] Since the normal family is an exponential family with $r(x) \equiv 1$, (19.11) must hold. Indeed, fix any $\mu_0 \in \mathbb{R}, \sigma_0^2 > 0$ and let $x_1, \dots, x_n$ be any sequence of data with maximum likelihood estimate $(\hat{\mu}, \hat{\sigma}^2) = (\nu_0, \sigma_0^2)$. Then the empirical average $n^{-1} \sum x_i$ must be equal to μ_0 and the empirical variance $n^{-1} \sum (x_i - n^{-1} \sum x_i)^2$ must be equal to σ_0^2. Direct calculation shows that the normal density f_{μ,σ^2} satisfies, as promised,

$$-\ln f_{\mu_0,\sigma_0^2}(x^n) = E_{\mu_0,\sigma_0^2}[-\ln f_{\mu_0,\sigma_0^2}(X)] = \text{H}(\mu_0,\sigma_0^2) = \frac{1}{2} + \frac{1}{2} \log 2\pi\sigma_0^2.$$

For general $r(x)$ that are not necessarily constant, Proposition 19.1, part 1, gives a *relative* analogue of (19.11): for all $\beta \in \Theta_{\text{can}}$, all data x^n with $\hat{\beta}(x^n) \in \Theta_{\text{can}}$,

$$\ln \frac{P_{\hat{\beta}(x^n)}(x^n)}{P_\beta(x^n)} = nE_{\hat{\beta}(x^n)}\left[\ln \frac{P_{\hat{\beta}(x^n)}(X)}{P_\beta(X)}\right] = n\text{D}(\hat{\beta}\|\beta). \qquad (19.12)$$

Example 19.4 [Extreme Data Maximizes Likelihood Ratio] In the next section, and in the proofs of theorems of Part II we sometimes need an analogue of (19.12) for restricted 1-parameter families with a compact parameter set $[\mu^-, \mu^+]$ that lies in the interior of the original parameter set Θ_{mean}. In that case, we can still get an analogue of (19.12) using Proposition 19.3: suppose x^n is such that $\hat{\mu}(x^n) = n^{-1} \sum \phi(x_i) \geq \mu^+$. Then μ^+ must be the ML estimator within the restricted set $[\mu^-, \mu^+]$. Fix some $\mu < \mu^+$. Then for all x^n with $\hat{\mu}(x^n) = n^{-1} \sum \phi(x_i) \geq \mu^+$, we have

$$\frac{1}{n} \ln \frac{P_{\mu^+}(x^n)}{P_\mu(x^n)} = \text{D}_{\hat{\mu}(x^n)}(\mu^+\|\mu) \geq \text{D}(\mu^+\|\mu), \qquad (19.13)$$

with equality iff $\mu^+ = \hat{\mu}(x^n)$. Equation (19.13) is a direct consequence of Proposition 19.3, applied with $P^* = \mathbb{P}$. In fact, it follows from the proposition that

$$\frac{1}{n} \ln \frac{P_{\mu^+}(x^n)}{P_\mu(x^n)} \text{ increases linearly in } \hat{\mu}(x^n). \tag{19.14}$$

This incidentally generalizes the observation we made in Section 4.4, in the box on page 124: there, we noted that for the Bernoulli model, if $\mu > 0.5$ remains fixed, then $-\log P_\mu(x^n)$ is maximized for extreme data consisting of only 1s, so that $\hat{\mu}(x^n) = 1$. This is just the special case of (19.14) for the Bernoulli model with μ set to $1/2$. With a little more work, we can extend the idea to exponential families with more than 1 parameter; we omit the details.

4. Expected information is observed information. The observed information $J(x^n)$ plays a central role in the evaluation of the likelihood near its maximum (Section 4.2). The expected Fisher information $I(\beta)$ plays a central role in the evaluation of the KL divergence near its minimum (Section 4.3). For exponential families they are related as follows. For all x^n for which $\hat{\mu}(x^n)$ exists (i.e. for which $n^{-1} \sum \phi(x_i) \in \Theta_{\text{mean}}$), we have

$$J(x^n) = I(\hat{\beta}(x^n)). \tag{19.15}$$

where J is the observed information expressed in the canonical parameterization. To see this, note that

$$J_{ij}(x^n) = \left\{ \frac{\partial^2}{\partial \beta_i \partial \beta_j} \left[-\frac{1}{n} \ln P_\beta(x^n) \right] \right\}_{\beta = \hat{\beta}(x^n)} =$$
$$\left\{ \frac{\partial^2}{\partial \beta_i \partial \beta_j} E_{\hat{\beta}(x^n)} [- \ln P_\beta(X)] \right\}_{\beta = \hat{\beta}(x^n)} = I_{ij}(\hat{\beta}(x^n)), \tag{19.16}$$

where the second equality follows by (19.8) and the third follows by exchanging the order of differentiation and integration, which is allowed by Proposition 18.1. By appropriately modifying (19.16), using the fact that $I(\hat{\beta}) = I^{-1}(\hat{\mu})$ (box on page 615), we see that (19.15) continues to hold if we replace $\hat{\beta}$ by $\hat{\mu}$ and consider the two matrices in the mean-value parameterization.

19.4   Behavior *of* the ML Estimate $\hat{\beta}$

In this section we study how the ML estimator $\hat{\mu}$ behaves if the data are actually distributed according to some distribution P_μ in the exponential family under consideration, given in its mean-value parameterization. It turns out that $\hat{\mu}$ satisfies the central limit theorem. As we discuss below, this implies that, with large probability, it will fluctuate around the "true" mean μ with deviations of order $O(1/\sqrt{n})$. We then study the probability that $\hat{\mu}$ is at a large distance from μ. While by the central limit theorem, this probability must be small, we would like to know exactly *how* small. It turns out that the KL divergence plays a crucial role in analyzing this situation. The results have implications that go far beyond modeling with exponential families.

19.4.1 Central Limit Theorem

One-Parameter Case Suppose that $(P_\mu, \Theta_{\text{mean}})$ is a 1-dimensional exponential family with sufficient statistic ϕ, given in its mean-value parameterization. Let $X_1, X_2, \ldots$ be i.i.d. $\sim P_\mu$ for some $\mu \in \Theta_{\text{mean}}$. If $n^{-1} \sum \phi(X_i) \in \Theta_{\text{mean}}$, then $\hat{\mu}(x^n) = n^{-1} \sum \phi(X_i)$ (Section 19.3). By the central limit theorem (CLT), Theorem 2.2 on page 56, we find that $\hat{\mu} - \mu$ is asymptotically normally distributed with mean 0 and variance σ^2/n. Here σ^2 is the variance of P_μ. We have already seen a special case of this result in Example 2.6, page 59, where it was argued that the Bernoulli ML estimator is asymptotically normal with mean μ and variance σ^2/n, where $\sigma^2 = \mu(1-\mu)$ is the variance of the data-generating Bernoulli distribution.

Multivariate Case By Section 18.3, $\sigma^2 = I(\beta(\mu)) > 0$. By Section 18.4, $I(\beta(\mu)) = I^{-1}(\mu)$. Thus, another way to express the behavior of the ML estimator is to say that $\sqrt{n}(\hat{\mu} - \mu)$ is asymptotically normal with mean 0 and variance $I^{-1}(\mu)$. It turns out that this form is the most convenient to generalize the result to multivariate exponential families and canonical parameterizations:

Let (P_θ, Θ) be a k-dimensional exponential family given in either its mean-value or its canonical parameterization. Let $\Theta_\square \subset \Theta$ be a compact (closed and bounded) subset of Θ, and suppose $X_1, X_2, \ldots$ are i.i.d. $\sim P_\theta$ for some θ in the interior of $\Theta_\square$. Let $\hat{\theta}(x^n)$ be the ML estimator for x^n within $\Theta_\square$.

Theorem 19.1 [Central Limit Theorem for ML Estimators]
For all n, $x^n \in \mathcal{X}^n$, $\hat{\theta}(x^n)$ exists, and the distribution of $\sqrt{n}(\hat{\theta} - \theta)$ converges to a k-dimensional normal with mean 0 and covariance matrix $I^{-1}(\theta)$, in the sense that for any rectangle $R = [a_1, b_1] \times \ldots \times [a_k, b_k]$, $R \subset \Theta_\square$,

$$P(\sqrt{n}(\hat{\theta} - \theta) \in R) \to \int_{\sqrt{n}(\hat{\theta}-\theta) \in R} \sqrt{\frac{\det I(\theta)}{(2\pi)^k}} e^{-\frac{1}{2}(\hat{\theta}-\theta)^\top I(\theta)(\hat{\theta}-\theta)} d\hat{\theta}. \quad (19.17)$$

The expression under the integral is just the multivariate normal density $f_{\mu,\Sigma}(z)$ as in (2.9), page 50, applied to the transformed variable $z = \sqrt{n}(\hat{\theta}-\theta)$, with mean $\mu = 0$ and covariance matrix $\Sigma(\theta) = I^{-1}(\theta)$.

Theorem 19.1 holds if P_θ is given in its mean-value parameterization; it is then a direct corollary of the standard multivariate CLT, since the ML estimators are just the averages of ϕ over the data, and the Fisher information is just the covariance matrix of P_θ. However, it also holds if θ represents the canonical parameter β. Intuitively, this is the case because β is a smooth function of μ, so that small deviations in $\hat{\mu}$ correspond to small deviations in $\hat{\beta}$.

We will not prove Theorem 19.1 here. The theorem can, in fact, be extended to many statistical families beyond the exponential ones; for a general theorem and its proof, see for example (van der Vaart 1998).

19.4.2   Large Deviations

Suppose data are i.i.d. according to some distribution Q. Let $\phi : \mathbb{R} \to \mathbb{R}$ be some function on $\mathcal{X}$ and let $\mu = E_Q[\phi(X)]$. We want to evaluate the probability that the observed average of ϕ, is farther than δ from its expected value μ:

$$Q\left(\frac{1}{n}\sum \phi(X_i) > \mu + \delta\right) \tag{19.18}$$

for some $\delta > 0$. The central limit theorem suggests – but does not prove – that this probability will be exponentially small in n. Here we prove that, under regularity conditions on Q, the probability (19.18) is indeed exponentially small, and in Theorem 19.2 we provide an explicit nonasymptotic upper bound on it. This bound will be quite strong: it follows from *Cramér's theorem* (Cramér 1938) that it is asymptotically optimal to within first order in the exponent. We will not state Cramér's theorem here; see, for example (Kallenberg 2002). As we will see, standard bounds on large deviations such as the Chernoff and Hoeffding bounds (Hoeffding 1963; Vapnik 1998) arise as approximations and special cases of our bound.

Remarkably, our bound involves the KL divergence between Q and members of the exponential family with carrier $r \equiv Q$ and sufficient statistic ϕ. Indeed, the proof is based on the robustness properties of KL divergence that we discussed in Section 19.2. Thus, we introduce the 1-parameter exponential family

$$P_\beta(X) = \exp(\beta\phi(X) - \psi(\beta))Q(x) \tag{19.19}$$

with canonical parameter set Θ_{can} containing some $\tilde{\beta}$ with $E_{\tilde{\beta}}[\phi(X)] = \mu + \delta$. Define $\tilde{\mu} = \mu + \delta = \mu(\tilde{\beta})$. Such a family is called the exponential family *generated by ϕ and Q* (Barndorff-Nielsen 1978). Note that this family automatically contains Q. The result we are about to present only holds if a distribution of form (19.19) with parameter $\tilde{\beta}$ exists. In particular, such a distribution will always exist if $\phi(X)$ is bounded above.

Theorem 19.2 Suppose that $P_{\tilde{\beta}}$ with $E_{\tilde{\beta}}[\phi(X)] = \mu + \delta$ exists. Then we have:

$$Q\left(\frac{1}{n}\sum \phi(X_i) \geq \mu + \delta\right) = Q(\hat{\mu}(X^n) \geq \tilde{\mu}) \leq e^{-n D(\tilde{\mu}\|\mu)}, \tag{19.20}$$

where $D(\tilde{\mu}\|\mu)$ is the Kullback-Leibler divergence between $P_{\tilde{\mu}} = P_{\tilde{\beta}}$ and $P_{\mu} = Q$.

This result is by no means new – Chernoff (1952) already contains a very similar result. However, our proof is quite different from the standard proofs:

Proof: We have

$$Q\left(\frac{1}{n}\sum \phi(X_i) \geq \mu + \delta\right) = Q(\hat{\mu}(X^n) \geq \tilde{\mu}) =$$

$$P_{\mu}(\hat{\mu}(X^n) \geq \tilde{\mu}) = \sum_{x^n : \hat{\mu}(x^n) \geq \tilde{\mu}} P_{\tilde{\mu}}(x^n)\frac{P_{\mu}(x^n)}{P_{\tilde{\mu}}(x^n)} =$$

$$\sum_{x^n : \hat{\mu}(x^n) \geq \tilde{\mu}} P_{\tilde{\mu}}(x^n) e^{-n\left[\frac{1}{n}\ln \frac{P_{\tilde{\mu}}(x^n)}{P_{\mu}(x^n)}\right]} \leq$$

$$\sum_{x^n : \hat{\mu}(x^n) \geq \tilde{\mu}} P_{\tilde{\mu}}(x^n) e^{-n D(\tilde{\mu}\|\mu)} \leq e^{-n D(\tilde{\mu}\|\mu)}. \tag{19.21}$$

Here the first inequality follows from Equation (19.13) in Section 19.3. Note that it is a consequence of the robustness of the KL divergence discussed in Section 19.2. The second inequality follows because $\sum_{x^n \in \mathcal{E}} P_{\tilde{\mu}}(x^n) \leq 1$ for any event $\mathcal{E}$. This finishes the proof.

> Usually (19.20) is proved differently, based on applying Markov's inequality to the random variable $Y := \exp(\beta\phi(X))$. Instead, (19.21) uses an extension of one of the ideas behind Sanov's theorem (Cover and Thomas 1991).

$\square$

Theorem 19.2 can be interpreted in two ways: first of all, note that, for every β such that (19.19) is well defined, by setting $Q'(X) := Q(X) \exp \beta\phi(X)$ and applying (19.20) to Q' rather than Q, we can show that for every member P_β of every 1-parameter exponential family, the probability of observing an average $\hat\mu$ such that the ML estimator is farther than ϵ in KL divergence from the data-generating distribution μ_0, is exponentially small in $n\epsilon$.

In the second interpretation, the result transcends exponential family theory: it tells us that for *every* Q for which we can artificially construct an exponential family "around" Q, we can obtain exponentially small tail bounds.

Relation to Central Limit Theorem By a second-order Taylor approximation of $\mathrm{D}(\tilde\mu\|\mu)$ as in Section 4.3, (4.17), we find that for all $\mu, \tilde\mu \in \Theta_{\mathrm{mean}}$,

$$\mathrm{D}(\tilde\mu\|\mu) - \frac{1}{2}(\tilde\mu - \mu)^2 I(\mu')$$

with μ' between μ and $\tilde\mu$. As shown in Section 18.4.3, for exponential families, we have $I(\mu) = 1/\sigma^2$ where σ^2 is the variance of P_μ. Therefore, our bound (19.20) implies

$$Q\left(\frac{1}{n}\sum \phi(X_i) \geq \mu + \delta\right) = Q(\hat\mu(X^n) > \tilde\mu) \leq e^{-n\frac{(\tilde\mu-\mu)^2}{2\max_{\mu' \in [\mu,\tilde\mu]} \sigma^2_{\mu'}}}. \quad (19.22)$$

It is instructive to compare this with the corresponding probability according to the normal distribution. If the $\phi(X_i)$ were i.i.d. according to a normal distribution with mean μ and variance σ^2 (Example 2.2), we would get

$$P(\hat\mu(X^n) \geq \tilde\mu) = \int_{\hat\mu > \tilde\mu} f(n) e^{-n\frac{(\hat\mu-\mu)^2}{2\sigma^2_{\hat\mu}}} d\hat\mu, \quad (19.23)$$

where $f(n) = O(1/\sqrt{n})$. The quantities on the right-hand sides of (19.22) and (19.23) are very similar. Comparing the two equations, we see that (19.22) is weaker in the sense that the $O(1/\sqrt{n})$-factor is missing, and the variance is replaced by a supremum over variances. On the other hand, while the central limit theorem *suggests* that (19.23) may hold for $X^n \sim Q$, it certainly does not prove it. Indeed, if Q is such that no exponential family with Q as carrier and ϕ as sufficient statistic exists, then the central limit theorem may still hold but in general neither (19.20) nor (19.22) holds.

Hoeffding and Chernoff The well-known Hoeffding-Chernoff bounds (Vapnik 1998), as well as the Bernstein inequality (van der Vaart 1998) and one direction in Sanov's theorem (Cover and Thomas 1991), can all be seen as consequences of (19.20). We give the basic intuition behind such results by showing this for a particular, simplified version of the Chernoff bound that is often used in the learning theory literature (Vapnik 1998):

Theorem 19.3 [Simplified Chernoff/Hoeffding] Let $X, X_1, X_2, \ldots$ be i.i.d. Bernoulli random variables, with $P(X = 1) = \mu$ for some $0 < \mu < 1$. Then

$$P\left(\left| \frac{1}{n} \sum_{i=1}^{n} X_i - \mu \right| \geq \epsilon \right) \leq 2e^{-2n\epsilon^2}. \tag{19.24}$$

To see that (19.24) is a consequence of (19.20), note that for the Bernoulli model in its mean-value parameterization, we have

$$\sup_{\mu' \in [\mu, \tilde{\mu}]} \sigma_{\mu'}^2 \leq \sup_{\mu' \in (0,1)} \sigma_{\mu'}^2 = \sup_{\mu' \in (0,1)} \mu'(1 - \mu') = \frac{1}{4}.$$

Plugging this into (19.22) gives $P(n^{-1} \sum_{i=1}^{n} X_i - \mu \geq \epsilon) \leq \exp(-2n\epsilon^2)$. Repeating the same reasoning for the random variables $Y_i := - X_i$, we get the same bound for the average of the Y_i. The result now follows by combining these two statements using the union bound (2.17), page 55.

19.5   Maximum Entropy and Minimax Codelength

In this section we are concerned with various aspects of the following scenario: suppose $X_1, X_2, \ldots$ are i.i.d. according to some unknown distribution P. In many practical applications, especially in physics, the following type of problem arises: we observe some statistics $\mu = n^{-1} \sum_{i=1}^{n} \phi(x_i)$ of a very large sample $x_1, \ldots, x_n$. For example, these statistics may be obtained using some measurement device. However, the individual outcomes x_i remain unknown. We would like to make an informed guess about the distribution P underlying the data, based on this very limited type of information. In Section 19.5.1 we introduce a celebrated but controversial way to deal with this problem: the *maximum entropy (MaxEnt) principle*, which was proposed by Jaynes (1957, 2003) and his followers. We show that, under weak conditions, it leads us to infer a P that is a member of the exponential family with sufficient statistic ϕ. This gives an interesting interpretation of exponential families. In Section 19.5.2 we show that the maximum entropy distribution can be reinterpreted as the minimax codelength distribution. Section 19.5.3 reinterprets our findings in terms of a two-player zero-sum game.

19.5.1   Exponential Families and Maximum Entropy

As indicated above, we are given the information that $n^{-1} \sum \phi(x_i) = \mu$. The goal of the MaxEnt principle is to provide us with a guess about the distribution P underlying the data. Let $\mathcal{P}$ be the set of distributions that satisfy the *constraint* $E[\phi(X)] = \mu$:

$$\mathcal{P} = \{P \ : \ E_P[\phi(X)] = \mu\}. \tag{19.25}$$

According to Jaynes's MaxEnt principle, we should adopt some $P \in \mathcal{P}$. This is, of course, reasonable, assuming that n is large. But, much more controversially, the MaxEnt principle tells us to adopt as a "best guess" for P the distribution $P_{\mathrm{me}} \in \mathcal{P}$ that, among all distributions in $\mathcal{P}$, maximizes the entropy $\mathrm{H}(P)$.

Example 19.5 [Uniformity] Let $\mathcal{X}$ be finite, with, say, N elements. Suppose that no further constraints are given. We can embed this in our framework, for example, as a trivial constraint $E[\phi(X)] = 0$ for the function ϕ which is 0 for all x. Then $\mathcal{P}$ consists of the set of all distributions on $\mathcal{X}$. We shall see that the maximum entropy distribution within $\mathcal{P}$ is the uniform distribution with probabilities $1/N$.

Example 19.6 [Independence] Let p_1 be the bias of some coin, and let p_2 be the bias of a second coin. We may, for example, have established these numbers by flipping both coins a million of times and recording the observed frequencies. Let $X_1 \in \{0, 1\}$ denote the outcome of the first coin, and let $X_2 \in \{0, 1\}$ denote the outcome of the second coin. Let $\mathcal{P}$ be the set of all distributions on the joint space $\{0, 1\}^2$ that satisfy the constraints, i.e. $P(X_1 = 1) = p_1$ and $P(X_2 = 1) = p_2$. It turns out that the maximum entropy distribution within $\mathcal{P}$ is the distribution according to which X_1 and X_2 are independent, i.e. $P_{me}(X_1 = 1, X_2 = 1) = p_1 p_2$ and similarly for the other three values of (X_1, X_2). This result is a straightforward consequence of Proposition 19.4 below.

Example 19.7 [Brandeis dice] Consider a six-sided die, so that the space of outcomes is $\mathcal{X} = \{1, 2, \ldots, 6\}$. We are given the information that the expected number of spots coming up in a throw is 4.5 rather than 3.5. That is, $E[X] = \sum_{x=1}^{6} P(x)x = 4.5$. Jaynes (1957) calculated that the maximum entropy distribution under this constraint is given by

$$(P_{me}(1), \ldots, P_{me}(6)) =$$
$$(0.05435, 0.07877, 0.11416, 0.16545, 0.23977, 0.34749). \tag{19.26}$$

How do we calculate MaxEnt distributions as in (19.26)? Consider the set $\mathcal{P}$ as in(19.25).

Proposition 19.4 *If* a distribution $P(X) = \exp(\beta\phi(X) - \psi(\beta))$ of the exponential family form with uniform carrier $r(X) \equiv 1$ exists such that $E_P[\phi(X)] = \mu$, *then* P *maximizes the entropy within the set* $\mathcal{P}$.

The proposition partially explains why exponential families are sometimes also called *maximum entropy families* (Jaynes 2003; Grünwald 1998).

Proof: Let $\beta = \beta(\mu)$. Then, since $P_\beta \in \mathcal{P}$,

$$\mathrm{H}(\beta) \leq \max_{P \in \mathcal{P}} \mathrm{H}(P). \tag{19.27}$$

where $\mathrm{H}(\beta)$ denotes the entropy of P_β. On the other hand,

$$\mathrm{H}(\beta) \overset{(1)}{=} E_\beta[-\ln P_\beta(X)] \overset{(2)}{=} \max_{P \in \mathcal{P}} E_P[-\ln P_\beta(X)]$$

$$\overset{(3)}{\geq} \max_{P \in \mathcal{P}} \min_Q E_P[-\ln Q(X)] \overset{(4)}{=} \max_{P \in \mathcal{P}} \mathrm{H}(P). \tag{19.28}$$

Here (1) is just the definition of entropy; (2) uses the robustness property of exponential families, Proposition 19.1 of Section 19.2: for all $P \in \mathcal{P}$, we must have that $E_P[-\ln P_\beta(X)]$ is constant; (3) is straightforward; (4) holds by the information inequality, (3.14), Section 3.3. Together, (19.27) and (19.28) show that

$$\mathrm{H}(\beta) = \max_{P \in \mathcal{P}} \mathrm{H}(P). \tag{19.29}$$

$\square$

Example 19.8 [Brandeis dice, cont.] In the Brandeis dice example, the constraint is of the form $E[\phi(X)] = \mu$ with $\phi(X) = X$. Thus, the MaxEnt distribution must be of the form

$$P_{me}(X = x) = \frac{1}{Z(\beta)} e^{\beta x} \tag{19.30}$$

with $Z(\beta) = \sum_{x=1}^{6} e^{\beta x}$, where β is chosen so that $E_\beta[\phi(X)] = \mu$. For a given value of μ, β must be a strictly increasing function of μ (18.12). This fact can be used to determine β numerically. If $\mu = 4.5$, then calculating β and substituting into (19.30) gives (19.26).

Example 19.9 [Normal Distribution as a Maximum Entropy Distribution]
Suppose we are given that the mean of P is μ and the variance is σ^2. Otherwise nothing is known about P. The maximum entropy distribution under this constraint is a member of the exponential family with sufficient statistic $\phi(X) = (X, X^2)$:

$$P_\beta(X) = e^{\beta_1 X + \beta_2 X^2 - \psi(\beta)},$$

where β is chosen so that $E[X] = \mu$ and $E[X^2] - \mu = \sigma^2$. As we have seen in Example 2.11, this is just the normal distribution with mean μ and variance σ^2.

Minimum Relative Entropy Distributions   The maximum entropy principle is a special case of the more flexible *minimum relative entropy principle*. Here one starts out with a prior measure P_0 on $\mathcal{X}$. We first consider the most straightforward case, where P_0 is to be interpreted as a probability distribution on $\mathcal{X}$. Thus, the scenario is now as follows: the statistician's initial guess of the distribution on $\mathcal{X}$ is P_0. He then observes that $n^{-1} \sum_{i=1}^{n} \phi(x_i) = \mu$, typically for some μ that is not equal to $E_{P_0}[\phi(X)]$. Thus, somehow the situation has changed and P_0 needs to be updated in the light of the new information. The minimum relative entropy principle tells the statistician to pick the distribution with $E_P[\phi(X)] = \mu$ that is closest in KL divergence to P_0:

$$P_{\mathrm{mre}} = \arg\min_{P \in \mathcal{P}} \mathrm{D}(P \| P_0),$$

where $\mathcal{P}$ is defined as in (19.25). Using exactly the same argument as above, it can once again be shown that *if a distribution of exponential form $P_\beta = \exp(\beta\phi(X) - \psi(\beta))P_0(X)$ exists such that $\mu(\beta) = \mu$, then P_{mre} is achieved for P_β*. Thus, as long as the full exponential family with carrier $r = P_0$ and sufficient statistic ϕ has an element with mean μ, this element will be the minimum relative entropy distribution. We immediately see that the maximum entropy procedure is the special case of the minimum relative entropy procedure, based on the uniform prior P_0.

In the second form of the minimum relative entropy principle, P_0 is not necessarily a probability distribution. Rather it is a measure without any probabilistic interpretation. For example, we may have $\mathcal{X} = \mathbb{R}$ and P_0 is uniform, the measure with density $P_0(x) \equiv 1$ for all x. This is not a probability distribution since it does not integrate to 1. In this case, the interpretation is that P_0 represents the symmetries of the problem, which amounts to determining how outcomes should be *counted*. In the dice example, our physical knowledge of dice tells us that there is a symmetry between all six faces, which suggests using the uniform measure. But in other problems with $\mathcal{X} = \mathbb{R}$ we may, for example, have information that the measure should be uniform on a log-scale, leading to a highly nonuniform P_0.

19.5.2   Exponential Families and Minimax Codelength

This section extends the ideas of Section 3.3.2, where we argued that if we have no idea at all about the data-generating machinery, then the code corresponding to the uniform distribution may be a reasonable code to use because it is minimax optimal - even if data are highly nonuniform, we are guaranteed a reasonable codelength. Here, we look at the slightly more informed case of the beginning of this section: we know that data are distributed according to some P with $E_P[\phi(X)] = \mu$ for some given value of μ. Otherwise, we know nothing at all about P. It turns out that in this case, the minimax optimal code typically corresponds to the maximum entropy distribution for the given constraint. The latter, as we just showed, is a member of the exponential family with sufficient statistic ϕ.

More precisely, suppose we are interested in coding an outcome of P using as few bits as possible. Since we have no idea what P actually generates the data, we may consider a worst-case approach. That is, we look for the codelength function L minimizing, over all codelength functions for $\mathcal{X}$, the worst-case expected codelength $\max_{P \in \mathcal{P}} E_P[L(X)]$, where $\mathcal{P}$ is given by (19.25). From Chapter 3, Section 3.2, we know that for every L, there is a corresponding distribution Q with $-\log Q(X) = L(X)$, and vice versa. Therefore, we are equivalently looking for the Q achieving

$$\min_{Q} \max_{P \in \mathcal{P}} E_P[-\ln Q(X)] \tag{19.31}$$

where the minimum is over all probability mass functions on $\mathcal{X}$, both defective and normal. In analogy to Proposition 19.4, we have

Proposition 19.5 *If a distribution of the exponential family form* $P_\beta(x) = \exp(\beta\phi(x) - \psi(\beta))$ *exists with* $\mu(\beta) = \mu$, *then the* Q *achieving* (19.31) *is once again equal to* P_β.

Proof: By the robustness property of exponential families, Proposition 19.1, (19.3),

$$\max_{P \in \mathcal{P}} E_P[-\ln P_\beta(X)] = E_\beta[-\ln P_\beta(X)] = \mathrm{H}(\beta). \tag{19.32}$$

On the other hand, for any distribution $Q \neq P_\beta$, (here Q is not necessarily in $\mathcal{P}$),

$$\max_{P \in \mathcal{P}} E_P[-\ln Q(X)] \overset{(1)}{\geq} E_\beta[-\ln Q(X)] \overset{(2)}{>} E_\beta[-\ln P_\beta(X)] \overset{(3)}{=} H(\beta). \quad (19.33)$$

Here (1) follows because $P_\beta \in \mathcal{P}$ and the maximum over $\mathcal{P}$ must be greater or equal than each of its elements; (2) follows by the information inequality. (3) is just the definition of entropy.

Together, (19.32) and (19.33) show that (19.31) is uniquely achieved for P_β, such that $\beta = \beta(\mu)$. □

In the previous subsection the distribution P_μ was shown to be the maximum entropy distribution for the given constraint:

$$\arg\min_Q \max_{P \in \mathcal{P}} E_P[-\ln Q(X)] = P_{me}.$$

It turns out that a similar result, the maximum entropy distribution minimizes worst-case expected codelength, continues to hold for general convex $\mathcal{P}$, even if they cannot be expressed in the "linear" form (19.25). Summarizing:

Exponential Families, Maximum Entropy and Minimax Codelength
Let $\mathcal{P}$ be a convex set of distributions.

- Under weak conditions on $\mathcal{P}$, the maximum entropy distribution within $\mathcal{P}$ coincides with the distribution Q that, when used as a code, minimizes the worst-case expected codelength

$$\max_{P \in \mathcal{P}} E_P[-\log Q(X)].$$

- As we just proved, the result is guaranteed to hold if $\mathcal{P}$ is of the form $\{P : E_P[\phi(X)] = \mu\}$ and the full exponential family with sufficient statistic ϕ and uniform carrier has an element P_β with $E_\beta[\phi(X)] = \mu(\beta) = \mu$. In that case, P_β is both the maximum entropy and the minimax codelength distribution.

- Thus, the distribution P_β is useful for coding the data if it is only known that $E_P[\phi(X)] = \mu$; even if the true data-generating distribution is *not* equal to P_β.

Example 19.10 [Brandeis dice, cont.] What does our result say for the Brandeis dice problem? It says that for *every* distribution P for a die with $E_P[X] = 4.5$, we have $E_P[-\log P_{me}(X)] = H(P_{me}) \approx 2.33$: the expected codelength of coding an outcome with P_{me} is the same whether the data-generating distribution has $P(X = 4) = P(X = 5) = 0.5$, or $P(X = 6) = 1/4, P(X = 4) = 3/4$, or any other P with $E_P[X] = 4.5$. However, for every such P, as long as it is not equal to P_{me}, there exist data-generating distributions Q with $E_Q[X] = 4.5$ so that the expected codelength based on Q is *larger* than $H(P_{me})$, and an example of such a Q happens to be P_{me} itself: if $P \neq P_{me}$, then

$$E_{P_{me}}[-\log P(X)] > H(P_{me}).$$

Minimum Worst-Case *Relative* Codelength The minimum worst-case codelength scenario may be generalized to minimum worst-case *relative* codelength: suppose we have a "reference code" (corresponding to distribution) P_0 available. Rather than the minimax code under constraint $E[\phi(X)] = \mu$, we look for the minimax *relative* codelength under the constraint, i.e.

$$\min_Q \max_{P \in \mathcal{P}} E_P[-\log Q(X) - (-\log P_0(X))]. \tag{19.34}$$

Why should we be interested in such a Q? For example, consider $\mathcal{X} = \mathbb{R}$, constraint $E[X] = \mu$, so ϕ is the identity. In this case (as well as many others), (19.31) has no solution, so a code with minimax optimal absolute lengths does not exist. Therefore, being minimax optimal relative to some "standard reference" is the best we can hope for.

Using exactly the same reasoning as in (19.32) and (19.33), it turns out that the relative minimax code achieving (19.34) is identical to the $P \in \mathcal{P}$ that minimizes $D(P\|P_0)$.

19.5.3 The Compression Game

The previous results indicate that worst-case codelength minimization and entropy maximization are closely related. We now show that they are in fact two sides of the same coin: By (19.29) we have

$$H(\beta) = \max_{P \in \mathcal{P}} H(P) = \max_{P \in \mathcal{P}} \min_Q E_P[-\ln Q(X)]$$

and, together, (19.32) and (19.33) give that

$$\min_{Q} \max_{P \in \mathcal{P}} E_P[-\ln Q(X)] = \mathrm{H}(\beta),$$

so that, as originally observed by Topsøe (1979), we have

$$\min_{Q} \max_{P \in \mathcal{P}} E_P[-\ln Q(X)] = \max_{P \in \mathcal{P}} \min_{Q} E_P[-\ln Q(X)]. \tag{19.35}$$

Equation (19.35) is a variation of von Neumann's (1928) celebrated minimax theoremminimax for zero-sum games. The corresponding game-theoretic interpretation is as follows: we imagine a two-player game between Nature and Statistician. Nature first picks a distribution and then generates an outcome X according to it; Statistician picks a code and uses it to describe X. Nature is allowed to select any distribution she likes, as long as it satisfies $E[\phi(X)] = \mu$, and Statistician is allowed to use any code whatsoever. Nature's goal is to maximize Statistician's expected codelength, and Statistician's goal is to minimize it. Equation (19.35) expresses that the best (maximum codelength) Nature can achieve if she has to move first, is equal to the best (minimum codelength) that Statistician can achieve if he has to move first. Surprisingly, by the results above, under weak conditions both Nature's maximin and Statistician's minimax strategy turn out to be equal to the MaxEnt distribution $P_\beta \in \mathcal{P}$ – even though Statistician's distribution (code) was not required to lie in $\mathcal{P}$. That the minimax code is a member of $\mathcal{P}$ is a consequence, not a restriction, of the analysis.

Discussion   Although it has often been applied in practice (Kapur and Kesavan 1992), the rationale for the maximum entropy principle has always been controversial. The results in this section give a clear rationale for using maximum entropy distributions in coding problems: even if in reality the data are *not* distributed according to the MaxEnt P, using the code based on the MaxEnt P will still lead to reasonable (worst-case optimal) codelengths (Topsøe 1979; Harremoës and Topsøe 2001; Topsøe 2007; Grünwald 2000). However, the justification for the use of MaxEnt distributions in other types of decision problems remains problematic in many researcher's views, including mine; see (Seidenfeld 1986; Uffink 1995; Grünwald and Halpern 2003).

19.6 Likelihood Ratio Exponential Families and Rényi Divergences*

In Chapter 15, Section 15.3, Theorem 15.3, we gave the fundamental two-part code MDL consistency result. This result showed that both the expected Rényi divergence and the expected squared Hellinger distance of the α-two-part MDL estimator converge as long as the two-part code $\bar{L}_{2\text{-p}}$ is universal. In this section, we show in detail how the Hellinger distance is related to the Rényi divergence, and we give several information-theoretic interpretations of the Rényi divergences. We do this by showing that the Rényi divergence $d_\lambda(P_1\|P_0)$ is the cumulant generating function of a certain exponential family, which has as its sufficient statistic the likelihood ratio between P_1 and P_0, and which may also be interpreted as a family of "log-convex mixtures" between P_1 and P_0, with $P_\lambda(X) \propto P_1^\lambda(X)P_0^{1-\lambda}(X)$.

We start with a formal definition of the four quantities of interest (Rényi 1960; Haussler and Opper 1997):

Definition 19.1 Let P_1, P_0 be two distributions on $\mathcal{X}$ and let $\lambda \in [0,1]$. The λ-*affinity* is defined as

$$A_\lambda(P_1\|P_0) = \sum_{x\in\mathcal{X}} P_1(X)^\lambda P_0(x)^{1-\lambda}. \tag{19.36}$$

The λ-generalized squared Hellinger divergence is defined as

$$\mathrm{He}_\lambda^2(P_1\|P_0) := \frac{1}{1-\lambda}\left(1 - \sum_{x\in\mathcal{X}} P_1(X)^\lambda P_0(x)^{1-\lambda}\right). \tag{19.37}$$

The *unnormalized Rényi divergence of order* λ is defined as

$$d_\lambda(P_1\|P_0) := -\ln \sum_x P_1(x)^\lambda P_0(x)^{1-\lambda}. \tag{19.38}$$

The *Rényi divergence of order* λ is defined as

$$\bar{d}_\lambda(P_1\|P_0) := -\frac{1}{1-\lambda}\ln \sum_x P_1(x)^\lambda P_0(x)^{1-\lambda}, \tag{19.39}$$

with $d_1(P_1\|P_0) := \lim_{\lambda\uparrow 1} \bar{d}_\lambda(P_1\|P_0)$.

Note that the generalized squared Hellinger divergence and the Rényi divergences can be directly expressed as functions of λ and the affinity A_λ.

Terminology   "Generalized squared Hellinger divergences" appear under various names, and sometimes without a name, in the literature; our terminology is not standard. They are essentially the same as the ρ-divergences considered in (Zhang 2004b), but Zhang's ρ corresponds to $1 - \lambda$ rather than λ; see further below. For $\lambda = 1/2$, we get the ordinary Hellinger distance, since

$$\text{He}^2(P_1\|P_0) := \sum_x \left(\sqrt{P_1(x)} - \sqrt{P_0(x)} \right)^2 =$$

$$\sum_x (P_1(x) + P_0(x)) - \sum_x 2\sqrt{P_1(x)P_0(x)} = 2 \left(1 - \sum_x \sqrt{P_1(x)P_0(x)} \right) =$$

$$\text{He}^2_{0.5}(P_1\|P_0). \quad (19.40)$$

Similarly, $A_{1/2}$ is sometimes called the *Hellinger affinity* or *Hellinger sum* in the literature (Gibbs and Su 2002). d_λ is not often encountered in the literature, and the term "unnormalized Rényi divergence" is not standard. It seems that sometimes the term *"Chernoff divergence* of order λ" has been used. Still, this will turn out to be a useful concept below. The Rényi divergences are also known as *I*-divergences or *Rényi's I-divergences* (Haussler and Opper 1997). They are defined for all $\lambda > 0$, including $\lambda > 1$, but here we shall only be interested in the case $0 < \lambda \leq 1$.

Hellinger vs. Rényi   Generalized Hellinger divergences are never larger than the corresponding Rényi divergences: for all $\lambda \in (0,1)$, all distributions P_1, P_0 on $\mathcal{X}$, we have

$$\text{He}^2_\lambda(P_1\|P_0) \leq \bar{d}_\lambda(P_1\|P_0). \quad (19.41)$$

To see that (19.41) holds, note first that for all $z > 0$, $\log z \leq z - 1$. Using this fact, we get

$$\text{He}^2_\lambda(P_1\|P_0) = \frac{1}{1-\lambda} \left(1 - \sum_x P_1(X)^\lambda P_0(X)^{1-\lambda} \right) \leq$$

$$\frac{1}{1-\lambda} \left(-\ln \sum_x P_1(X)^\lambda P_0(X)^{1-\lambda} \right) = \bar{d}_\lambda(P_1\|P_0). \quad (19.42)$$

It is clear that for any pair of distributions P_0, P_1, $\text{He}^2_\lambda(P_1\|P_0) \leq 1/(1-\lambda)$, so that the Hellinger divergence is bounded. It follows from the results below, that for all P_1, P_0, we have $\text{He}^2_\lambda(P_1\|P_0) \leq D(P_1\|P_0)$. Since for some

$P_0, P_1, D(P_1 \| P_0) = \infty$, in general, the KL divergence is not bounded by a constant times the squared or nonsquared Hellinger distance. However, as we indicated in the box on page 518, if there exist $c, c' > 0$ such that for all P in some set $\mathcal{M}$, $\min_x P(x) > c, \max_x P(x) < c'$, then we do have that for all $P_0, P_1 \in \mathcal{M}$, $D(P_1 \| P_0) \le C_{c,c'} \mathrm{He}^2(P_1 \| P_0)$, where $C_{c,c'} > 0$ is a constant depending on c and c'.

For more on generalized Hellinger divergences, see, for example, Haussler and Opper (1997). In the remainder of this section, we shall concentrate on Rényi divergences.

Rényi vs. Kullback-Leibler   If P_0 has full support, i.e. for all $x \in \mathcal{X}$, $P(x) > 0$, then straightforward rewriting gives

$$\bar{\mathrm{d}}_\lambda(P_1 \| P_0) = -\frac{1}{1-\lambda} \ln E_{X \sim P_1} \left[\left(\frac{P_0(X)}{P_1(X)} \right)^{1-\lambda} \right].$$

Note that if we were to exchange expectation and $-\ln$, then we would end up with the familiar KL divergence. Because of Jensen's inequality (Chapter 3), this shows that for all $\lambda \in (0, 1)$,

$$\bar{\mathrm{d}}_\lambda(P_0 \| P_1) \le D(P_0 \| P_1). \tag{19.43}$$

Indeed, as we prove further below, for $\lambda \uparrow 1$, $\bar{\mathrm{d}}_\lambda$ and D become equal. We can extend the reasoning leading to (19.43) to find that for every P_0, P_1, the Rényi divergence $\bar{\mathrm{d}}_\lambda(P_1 \| P_0)$ is a strictly increasing function of λ.

To see this, define

$$g(\eta) = \left(E_{P_1} \left[\left(\frac{P_0(X)}{P_1(X)} \right)^\eta \right] \right)^{1/\eta},$$

so that $\bar{\mathrm{d}}_\lambda(P_1 \| P_0) = -\ln g(1 - \lambda)$. Using Jensen's inequality, one can show that for $\alpha' > \alpha$, $g(\alpha') > g(\alpha)$, from which the claim follows.

19.6.1   The Likelihood Ratio Family

We just gave a first interpretation of $\bar{\mathrm{d}}_\lambda$ as a variation of KL divergence (with log and expectation interchanged) that serves as a lower bound on the KL divergence. This interpretation, as well as the other interpretations discussed below, can best be understood by defining, for any two P_0, P_1 whose Rényi divergence we want to determine, a 1-parameter exponential family $\{P_\lambda \mid$

$\lambda \in (0,1)\}$ interpolating between P_0 and P_1. For this, we define

$$P_\lambda(x):=\frac{P_1^\lambda(x)P_0^{1-\lambda}(x)}{\sum_x P_1^\lambda(x)P_0^{1-\lambda}(x)}.$$

This is an exponential family with sufficient statistic

$$\phi(X):=\ln\frac{P_1(X)}{P_0(X)}.$$

To make this well defined, we shall assume that $P_0(x) > 0$ for all x, although the ideas can be generalized to P_0 with $P_0(x) = 0$ for some x.

We can rewrite P_λ as

$$P_\lambda(X) = e^{\lambda\phi(X)-\psi(\lambda)}r(X),$$

where

$$\psi(\lambda) = \ln\sum_x P_1^\lambda(x)P_0^{1-\lambda}(x) = -\mathrm{d}_\lambda(P_1\|P_0)$$

is a function not depending on X and $r(X) = P_0(X)$ is a function not depending on λ. It follows that $\mathrm{d}_\lambda(P_1\|P_0)$ is minus the cumulant generating function (Section 18.3, page 605) of the family $\{P_\lambda\}$, as well as the Legendre transform of the KL divergence $D(P_\lambda\|P_0)$ (Section 18.4.3, page 613). This immediately implies a number of useful properties of d_λ. We mention its strict concavity, as well as the following three identities, which are also easily verified directly:

$$\frac{d}{d\lambda}\mathrm{d}_\lambda(P_1\|P_0) = -E_{P_\lambda}[\phi(X)] = E_{P_\lambda}\left[\ln\frac{P_0(X)}{P_1(X)}\right] =$$
$$\mathrm{D}_{P_\lambda}(P_0\|P_1) = \mathrm{D}(P_\lambda\|P_1) - \mathrm{D}(P_\lambda\|P_0). \quad (19.44)$$

$$\left\{\frac{d}{d\lambda}\mathrm{d}_\lambda(P_1\|P_0)\right\}_{\lambda=0} = \mathrm{D}(P_0\|P_1) \;\; ; \;\; \left\{\frac{d}{d\lambda}\mathrm{d}_\lambda(P_1\|P_0)\right\}_{\lambda=1} = -\mathrm{D}(P_1\|P_0).$$
$$(19.45)$$

We note that, while $\bar{\mathrm{d}}_\lambda(P_1\|P_0)$ is 0 at $\lambda = 0$ and then increases in λ, d_λ is 0 at $\lambda = 0$, then increases in λ until it reaches its maximum $\mathrm{d}_{\lambda^*}(P_1\|P_0)$ at the λ such that $\mathrm{D}(P_\lambda\|P_1) = \mathrm{D}(P_\lambda\|P_0)$, and then it decreases again, with $\mathrm{d}_1(P_1\|P_0) = 0$.

Since $d_1(P_0\|P_1) = 0$, it follows that

$$\lim_{\lambda\uparrow 1}\bar{d}_\lambda(P_1\|P_0) = \lim_{\lambda\uparrow 1}\frac{1}{1-\lambda}(d_\lambda(P_0\|P_1) - d_1(P_0\|P_1)) =$$

$$-\lim_{\lambda\uparrow 1}\frac{d_1(P_0\|P_1)) - d_\lambda(P_0\|P_1)}{1-\lambda} = D(P_1\|P_0), \quad (19.46)$$

as we claimed before.

Various Interpretations of Rényi Divergences We just saw that Rényi divergence can be interpreted as a version of KL divergence with ln and expectation interchanged. Unnormalized Rényi divergence has an interpretation as the cumulant generating function in an exponential family. I now provide a second interpretation of the unnormalized divergence as a difference between two codelengths; I have come up with this interpretation myself, but recently I discovered that I am not the only one; see (Harremoës 2004; Harremoës 2006) for an extension of this interpretation that directly involves Rényi divergence rather than the unnormalized version, as well as for a discussion of its consequences.

Suppose we have doubts whether X is distributed according to P_0 or P_1. For this reason, we may decide (not too cleverly) to use a *randomized* code: we toss a coin with bias λ, and if the coin lands heads, we code using the code based on P_1; otherwise we use the code based on P_0. Let $X \sim Q$, where Q is arbitrary. Then the expected number of nats needed to encode X is

$$E_Q[-\lambda \ln P_1(X) - (1-\lambda)\ln P_0(X)] = E_Q[-\ln R(X)],$$

where $R(X):=P_1^\lambda(X)P_0^{1-\lambda}(X)$. But now we note that, if $0 < \lambda < 1$, then $\sum_x R(x) < 1$. Hence, the code corresponding to R is incomplete, and we can obtain strictly shorter codelengths by normalizing, i.e. using the code corresponding to $R'(x):=R(x)/\sum_x R(x)$. The number of nats we win by this normalization is given by

$$E_Q[-\ln R(X) + \ln R'(X)] = -\ln\sum_x R(x) = d_\lambda(P_0\|P_1), \quad (19.47)$$

which gives an interpretation of d_λ as an expected coding gain. This holds no matter what Q is; it need not be equal to P_λ. However, in the special case where $Q = P_\lambda$, a straightforward rewriting of (19.47) gives the useful identity

$$d_\lambda(P_1\|P_0) = \lambda D(P_\lambda\|P_1) + (1-\lambda)D(P_\lambda\|P_0). \quad (19.48)$$

Relations to Other Divergence Measures   We have already seen the relation between Rényi divergences, KL divergence, and generalized Hellinger divergences. There is also a close relation to the so-called *Rényi entropies*, a particular generalization of the Shannon entropy (Cover and Thomas 1991): the relation between Rényi divergence and Kullback-Leibler divergence is the same as the relation between Renyi entropies and Shannon entropy. More precisely, for finite sample spaces $\mathcal{X}$, the Shannon entropy $H(P)$ can be written as $H(P) = -D(P\|P_U) + \ln |\mathcal{X}|$, where P_U is the uniform distribution. Similarly, the *Rényi entropy of order* λ is be equal to $H_\lambda(P) = -\bar{d}_\lambda(P\|P_U) + \ln |\mathcal{X}|$. We note that the term "relative Rényi entropy" is already in use for a different notion; see (Lutwak, Yang, and Zhang 2005).

Zhang (2004a) employs the ρ-divergence D_ρ between P_0 and P_1, defined as $D_\rho(P_1\|P_0) = \rho^{-1}(1-\rho)^{-1}(1 - \sum (P_0(x))^{1-\rho}(P_1(x))^\rho)$. Clearly this is equal to $\rho^{-1}\mathrm{He}_{1-\rho}^2(P_1\|P_0)$.

For given P_0, P_1, $d_{\lambda *}(P_0, P1) = \max_{\lambda \in (0,1)} d_\lambda(P_0, P_1)$ is also known as the "Chernoff information" (Cover and Thomas 1991). It plays a fundamental role in frequentist analysis of the asymptotic error probability in Bayesian hypothesis testing.

19.7   Summary

In this chapter we have extensively discussed various information-theoretic properties of exponential families, emphasizing the robustness property of KL divergence. All these properties are mainly used in the *proofs* of the theorems appearing in Part II of this book. These theorems usually make claims that hold for all exponential families at the same time.

References

Adriaans, P., and C. Jacobs (2006). Using MDL for grammar induction. In *Proceedings of the Eighth International Colloquium on Grammatical Inference (ICGI-2006)*. To appear.

Akaike, H. (1973). Information theory and an extension of the maximum likelihood principle. In B. N. Petrov and F. Csaki (Eds.), *Second International Symposium on Information Theory*, pp. 267–281.

Allen, T. V., and R. Greiner (2000). Model selection criteria for learning belief nets: An empirical comparison. In *Proceedings of the Seventeenth International Conference on Machine Learning (ICML-97)*.

Allen, T. V., O. Madani, and R. Greiner (2003). Comparing model selection criteria for belief networks. Submitted.

Anthony, M., and N. Biggs (1992). *Computational Learning Theory*. Cambridge, UK: Cambridge University Press.

Bain, L., and M. Engelhardt (1989). *Introduction to Probability and Mathematical Statistics*. Boston: PWS-Kent.

Balasubramanian, V. (1997). Statistical inference, Occam's razor, and statistical mechanics on the space of probability distributions. *Neural Computation 9*, 349–368.

Balasubramanian, V. (2005). MDL, Bayesian inference and the geometry of the space of probability distributions. In P. D. Grünwald, I. J. Myung, and M. A. Pitt (Eds.), *Advances in Minimum Description Length: Theory and Applications*. Cambridge, MA: MIT Press.

Barndorff-Nielsen, O. (1978). *Information and Exponential Families in Statistical Theory*. Chichester, UK: Wiley.

Barron, A. (1985). *Logically Smooth Density Estimation*. Ph. D. thesis, Department of Electrical Engineering, Stanford University, Stanford, CA.

Barron, A. (1986). Discussion on Diaconis and Freedman: the consistency of Bayes estimates. *Annals of Statistics 14*, 26–30.

Barron, A. (1990). Complexity regularization with application to artificial neural networks. In G. Roussas (Ed.), *Nonparametric Functional Estimation and Related Topics*, pp. 561–576. Dordrecht, the Netherlands: Kluwer Academic Publishers.

Barron, A. (1998). Information-theoretic characterization of Bayes performance and the choice of priors in parametric and nonparametric problems. In A. D. J.M. Bernardo, J.O. Berger and A. Smith (Eds.), *Bayesian Statistics*, volume 6, pp. 27–52. Oxford: Oxford University Press.

Barron, A., and T. Cover (1991). Minimum complexity density estimation. *IEEE Transactions on Information Theory 37*(4), 1034–1054.

Barron, A., and N. Hengartner (1998). Information theory and supereffiency. *Annals of Statistics 26*(5), 1800–1825.

Barron, A., J. Rissanen, and B. Yu (1998). The minimum description length principle in coding and modeling. *IEEE Transactions on Information Theory 44*(6), 2743–2760. Special Commemorative Issue: Information Theory: 1948-1998.

Barron, A., and C. Sheu (1991). Approximation of density functions by sequences of exponential families. *Annals of Statistics 19*(3), 1347–1369.

Barron, A., Y. Yang, and B. Yu (1994). Asymptotically optimal function estimation by minimum complexity criteria. In *Proceedings of the 1994 International Symposium on Information Theory*, pp. 38. Trondheim, Norway.

Bartlett, P., S. Boucheron, and G. Lugosi (2001). Model selection and error estimation. *Machine Learning 48*, 85–113.

Berger, J. (1985). *Statistical Decision Theory and Bayesian Analysis*, revised and expanded 2nd edition. Springer Series in Statistics. New York: Springer-Verlag.

Berger, J., and L. Pericchi (2001). Objective Bayesian methods for model selection: introduction and comparison. In P. Lahiri (Ed.), *Model Selection*, volume 38 of *IMS Lecture Notes – Monograph Series*, pp. 135–207. Beachwood, Ohio: Institute of Mathematical Statistics.

Bernardo, J., and A. Smith (1994). *Bayesian Theory*. Chichester: Wiley.

Blackwell, D., and L. Dubins (1962). Merging of opinions with increasing information. *Annals of Mathematical Statistics 33*, 882–886.

Blum, A., and J. Langford (2003). PAC-MDL bounds. In *Proceedings of the Sixteenth Conference on Learning Theory (COLT' 03)*, pp. 344–357.

Blumer, A., A. Ehrenfeucht, D. Haussler, and M. Warmuth (1987). Occam's razor. *Information Processing Letters 24*, 377–380.

Boucheron, S., O. Bousquet, and G. Lugosi (2005). Theory of classification: a survey of recent advances. *ESAIM: Probability and Statistics 9*, 323–375.

Breiman, L. (2001). Statistical modeling: the two cultures (with discussion). *Statistical Science 16*(3), 199 –215.

Brown, L. (1986). *Fundamentals of Statistical Exponential Families, with Applications in Statistical Decision Theory*. Hayward, CA: Institute of Mathematical Statistics.

Burnham, K., and D. Anderson (2002). *Model Selection and Multimodel Inference*. New York: Springer-Verlag.

Casella, G., and R. Berger. *Statistical Inference*. Belmont, CA: Wadsworth.

Cesa-Bianchi, N., Y. Freund, D. Helmbold, D. Haussler, R. Schapire, and M. Warmuth (1997). How to use expert advice. *Journal of the ACM 44*(3), 427–485.

Cesa-Bianchi, N., and G. Lugosi (2006). *Prediction, Learning and Games*. Cambridge, UK: Cambridge University Press.

Chaitin, G. (1966). On the length of programs for computing finite binary sequences. *Journal of the ACM 13*, 547–569.

Chaitin, G. (1969). On the length of programs for computing finite binary sequences: Statistical considerations. *Journal of the ACM 16*, 145–159.

Chernoff, H. (1952). A measure of asymptotic efficiency of test of a hypothesis based on the sum of observations. *Annals of Mathematical Statistics 23*, 493–507.

Cilibrasi, R., and P. Vitányi (2005). Clustering by compression. *IEEE Transactions on Information Theory 51*(4), 1523–1545.

Clarke, B. (1997). Online forecasting proposal. Technical report, University of Dortmund. Sonderforschungsbereich 475.

Clarke, B. (2003). Combining model selection procedures for online prediction. *Sankhyā: The Indian Journal of Statistics, Series A 63*, 229–249.

Clarke, B. (2004). Comparing Bayes and non-Bayes model averaging when model approximation error cannot be ignored. *Journal of Machine Learning Research 4*(4), 683–712.

Clarke, B., and A. Barron (1990). Information-theoretic asymptotics of Bayes methods. *IEEE Transactions on Information Theory IT-36*(3), 453–471.

Clarke, B., and A. Barron (1994). Jeffreys' prior is asymptotically least favorable under entropy risk. *Journal of Statistical Planning and Inference 41*, 37–60.

Clarke, B., and A. Dawid (1999). Online prediction with experts under a log-scoring rule. Unpublished manuscript.

Comley, J. W., and D. L. Dowe (2005). Minimum message length and generalized Bayesian nets with asymmetric languages. In P. D. Grünwald, I. J. Myung, and M. A. Pitt (Eds.), *Advances in Minimum Description Length: Theory and Applications*. Cambridge, MA: MIT Press.

Conway, J., and N. Sloane (1993). *Sphere Packings, Lattices and Groups*. New York: Springer-Verlag.

Cover, T., and J. Thomas (1991). *Elements of Information Theory*. New York: Wiley-Interscience.

Cramér, H. (1938). Sur un nouveau théorème-limite de la théorie des probabilités. *Actualités Scientifiques et Industrielles 736*, 5–23.

Csiszár, I. (1984). Sanov property, generalized *I*-projection and a conditional limit theorem. *Annals of Probability 12*(3), 768–793.

Csiszár, I., and P. Shields (2000). The consistency of the BIC Markov order estimator. *Annals of Statistics 28*, 1601–1619.

Davies, P., and A. Kovac (2001). Modality, runs, strings and multiresolution (with discussion). *Annals of Statistics 29*, 1–65.

Dawid, A. (1984). Present position and potential developments: Some personal views, statistical theory, the prequential approach. *Journal of the Royal Statistical Society, Series A 147*(2), 278–292.

Dawid, A. (1992). Prequential analysis, stochastic complexity and Bayesian inference. In J. Bernardo, J. Berger, A. Dawid, and A. Smith

(Eds.), *Bayesian Statistics*, volume 4, pp. 109–125. Oxford: Oxford University Press.

Dawid, A. (1997). Prequential analysis. In S. Kotz, C. Read, and D. Banks (Eds.), *Encyclopedia of Statistical Sciences*, volume 1 (Update), pp. 464–470. New York: Wiley-Interscience.

Dawid, A. P., and V. G. Vovk (1999). Prequential probability: Principles and properties. *Bernoulli 5*, 125–162.

De Finetti, B. (1937). La prevision: ses lois logiques, ses sources subjectives. *Annales Institut H. Poincaré 7*, 1–68.

De Finetti, B. (1974). *Theory of Probability. A Critical Introductory Treatment.* London: Wiley.

De Luna, X., and K. Skouras (2003). Choosing a model selection strategy. *Scandinavian Journal of Statistics 30*, 113–128.

De Rooij, S., and P. D. Grünwald (2006). An empirical study of MDL model selection with infinite parametric complexity. *Journal of Mathematical Psychology 50*(2), 180–192.

Devroye, L., L. Györfi, and G. Lugosi (1996). *A Probabilistic Theory of Pattern Recognition.* New York: Springer-Verlag.

Diaconis, P. (2003). The problem of thinking too much. *Bulletin of the American Academy of Arts and Sciences 16*(3), 26–38.

Diaconis, P., and D. Freedman (1986). On the consistency of Bayes estimates. *The Annals of Statistics 14*(1), 1–26.

Domingos, P. (1999). The role of Occam's razor in knowledge discovery. *Data Mining and Knowledge Discovery 3*(4), 409–425.

Doob, J. (1949). Application of the theory of martingales. In *Le Calcul de Probabilités et ses Applications. Colloques Internationaux du Centre National de la Recherche Scientifique*, pp. 23–27.

Drmota, M., and W. Szpankowski (2004). Precise minimax redundancy and regret. *IEEE Transactions on Information Theory 50*, 2686–2707.

Duda, R., P. Hart, and D. Stork (2000). *Pattern Classification.* New York: Wiley.

Elias, P. (1975). Universal codeword sets and representation of the integers. *IEEE Transactions on Information Theory 21*(2), 194–203.

Ellsberg, D. (1961). Risk, ambiguity, and the Savage axioms. *Quarterly Journal of Economics 75*, 643–649.

Feder, M. (1986). Maximum entropy as a special case of the minimum description length criterion. *IEEE Transactions on Information Theory 32(6)*, 847–849.

Feller, W. (1968a). *An Introduction to Probability Theory and Its Applications*, 3rd edition, volume 1. New York: Wiley.

Feller, W. (1968b). *An Introduction to Probability Theory and Its Applications*, 3rd edition, volume 2. New York: Wiley.

Ferguson, T. (1967). *Mathematical Statistics – a decision-theoretic approach*. San Diego: Academic Press.

Figueiredo, M., J. Leitão, and A.K.Jain (2000). Unsupervised contour representation and estimation using b-splines and a minimum description length criterion. *IEEE Transactions on Image Processing 9(6)*, 1075–1087.

Fisher, R. (1922). On the mathematical foundations of theoretical statistics. *Philosophical Transactions of the Royal Society of London, Series A 222*, 309–368.

Floyd, S., and M. Warmuth (1995). Sample compression, learnability and the Vapnik-Chervonenkis dimension. *Machine Learning 21*, 269–304.

Forster, M. (2001). The new science of simplicity. In A. Zellner, H. Keuzenkamp, and M. McAleer (Eds.), *Simplicity, Inference and Modelling*, pp. 83–117. Cambridge: Cambridge University Press.

Foster, D., and R. Stine (1999). Local asymptotic coding and the minimum description length. *IEEE Transactions on Information Theory 45*, 1289–1293.

Foster, D., and R. Stine (2001). The competitive complexity ratio. In *Proceedings of the 2001 Conference on Information Sciences and Systems*. WP8 1-6.

Foster, D. P., and R. A. Stine (2005). The contribution of parameters to stochastic complexity. In P. D. Grünwald, I. J. Myung, and M. A. Pitt (Eds.), *Advances in Minimum Description Length: Theory and Applications*. Cambridge, MA: MIT Press.

Freund, Y. (1996). Predicting a binary sequence almost as well as the optimal biased coin. In *Proceedings of the Ninth Annual ACM Conference on Computational Learning Theory (COLT' 96)*, pp. 89–98.

Friedman, N., D. Geiger, and M. Goldszmidt (1997). Bayesian network classifiers. *Machine Learning 29*, 131–163.

Gács, P., J. Tromp, and P. Vitányi (2001). Algorithmic statistics. *IEEE Transactions on Information Theory 47*(6), 2464–2479.

Gao, Q., and M. Li (1989). An application of minimum description length principle to online recognition of handprinted alphanumerals. In *Proceedings of the Eleventh International Joint Conference on Artificial Intelligence (IJCAI-89)*, pp. 843–848.

Gauss, C. (1957). *Gauss's Work on the Theory of Least Squares (1803-1826)*. Princeton, NJ: Princeton University Press. Translated by H.F. Trotter.

Gelman, A., B. Carlin, H. Stern, and D. Rubin (2003). *Bayesian Data Analysis*. Boca Raton, FL: CRC Press.

George, E., and D. Foster (2000). Calibration and empirical Bayes variable selection. *Biometrika 84*(4), 731–747.

Gerenscér, L. (1987). Order estimation of stationary Gaussian ARMA processes using Rissanen's complexity. Technical report, Computer and Automation Institute of the Hungarian Academy of Sciences.

Gerencsér, L. (1994). On Rissanen's predictive stochastic complexity for stationary ARMA processes. *Journal of Statistical Planning and Inference 41*, 303–325.

Gibbs, A., and F. Su (2002). On choosing and bounding probability metrics. *International Statistical Review 70*(3), 419–435.

Goodman, N. (1955). *Fact, Fiction, and Forecast*. Cambridge, MA: Harvard University Press.

Grünwald, P. D. (1996). A minimum description length approach to grammar inference. In S. Wermter, E. Riloff, and G. Scheler (Eds.), *Connectionist, Statistical and Symbolic Approaches to Learning for Natural Language Processing*, Number 1040 in Lecture Notes in Artificial Intelligence, pp. 203–216. New York: Springer-Verlag.

Grünwald, P. D. (1998). *The Minimum Description Length Principle and Reasoning under Uncertainty*. Ph. D. thesis, University of Amsterdam, the Netherlands. Available as ILLC Dissertation Series 1998-03.

Grünwald, P. D. (1999). Viewing all models as "probabilistic". In *Proceedings of the Twelfth ACM Conference on Computational Learning Theory (COLT' 99)*, pp. 171–182.

Grünwald, P. D. (2000). Maximum entropy and the glasses you are looking through. In *Proceedings of the Sixteenth Conference on Uncertainty in Artificial Intelligence (UAI 2000)*, pp. 238–246.

Grünwald, P. D. (2001). Strong entropy concentration, game theory and algorithmic randomness. In *Proceedings of the Fourteenth Annual Conference on Computational Learning Theory (COLT' 01)*, pp. 320–336.

Grünwald, P. D. (2005). A tutorial introduction to the minimum description principle. In P. D. Grünwald, I. Myung, and M. Pitt (Eds.), *Advances in Minimum Description Length: Theory and Applications*, pp. 3–79. Cambridge, MA: MIT Press.

Grünwald, P. D. (2007). Prediction is coding. Manuscript in preparation.

Grünwald, P. D., and S. de Rooij (2005). Asymptotic log-loss of prequential maximum likelihood codes. In *Proceedings of the Eighteenth Annual Conference on Computational Learning Theory (COLT 2005)*, pp. 652–667.

Grünwald, P. D., and J. Y. Halpern (2003). Updating probabilities. *Journal of Artificial Intelligence Research 19*, 243–278.

Grünwald, P. D., and J. Langford (2004). Suboptimality of MDL and Bayes in classification under misspecification. In *Proceedings of the Seventeenth Conference on Learning Theory (COLT' 04)*.

Grünwald, P. D., and J. Langford (2007). Suboptimal behavior of Bayes and MDL in classification under misspecification. *Machine Learning*. To appear.

Grünwald, P. D., I. J. Myung, and M. A. Pitt (Eds.) (2005). *Advances in Minimum Description Length: Theory and Applications*. MIT Press.

Hall, P., and E. Hannan (1988). On stochastic complexity and nonparametric density estimation. *Biometrika 75*, 705–714.

Halpern, J. (2003). *Reasoning about Uncertainty*. Cambridge, MA: MIT Press.

Hannan, E. (1980). The estimation of the order of an ARMA process. *Annals of Statistics 8*, 1071–1081.

Hannan, E., A. McDougall, and D. Poskitt (1989). Recursive estimation of autoregressions. *Journal of the Royal Statistical Society, Series B 51*, 217–233.

Hannan, E., and J. Rissanen (1982). Recursive estimation of mixed autoregressive-moving average order. *Biometrika 69*, 81–94.

Hansen, M., and B. Yu (2000). Wavelet thresholding via MDL for natural images. *IEEE Transactions on Information Theory 46*, 1778–1788.

Hansen, M., and B. Yu (2001). Model selection and the principle of minimum description length. *Journal of the American Statistical Association 96*(454), 746–774.

Hansen, M., and B. Yu (2002). Minimum description length model selection criteria for generalized linear models. In *Science and Statistics: Festschrift for Terry Speed*, volume 40 of *IMS Lecture Notes – Monograph Series*. Hayward, CA: Institute for Mathematical Statistics.

Hanson, A. J., and P. C.-W. Fu (2005). Applications of MDL to selected families of models. In P. D. Grünwald, I. J. Myung, and M. A. Pitt (Eds.), *Advances in Minimum Description Length: Theory and Applications*. Cambridge, MA: MIT Press.

Harremoës, P. (2004). The weak information projection. In *Proceedings of the 2004 International Symposium on Information Theory (ISIT 2004)*, pp. 28.

Harremoës, P. (2006). Interpretations of Rényi entropies and divergences. *Physica A 365*(1), 57–62.

Harremoës, P., and F. Topsøe (2001). Maximum entropy fundamentals. *Entropy 3*, 191–226. Available at http://www.mdpi.org/entropy/.

Hartigan, J. (1983). *Bayes Theory*. New York: Springer-Verlag.

Haussler, D. (1997). A general minimax result for relative entropy. *IEEE Transactions on Information Theory 43*(4), 1276–1280.

Haussler, D., and M. Opper (1997). Mutual information, metric entropy, and cumulative relative entropy risk. *Annals of Statistics 25*(6), 2451–2492.

Helmbold, D., and M. Warmuth (1995). On weak learning. *Journal of Computer and System Sciences 50*, 551–573.

Hemerly, E., and M. Davis (1989a). Recursive order estimation of stochastic control systems. *Mathematical Systems Theory 22*, 323–346.

Hemerly, E., and M. Davis (1989b). Strong consistency of the PLS criterion for order determination of autoregressive processes. *Annals of Statistics 17*(2), 941–946.

Herbrich, R. (2002). *Learning Kernel Classifiers*. Cambridge, MA: MIT Press.

Herbrich, R., and R. C. Williamson (2002). Algorithmic luckiness. *Journal of Machine Learning Research 3*, 175–212.

Hertz, J., A. Krogh, and R. Palmer (1991). *Introduction to the theory of neural computation*. Lecture Notes of the Santa Fe Institute. Boston: Addison-Wesley.

Hjorth, U. (1982). Model selection and forward validation. *Scandinavian Journal of Statistics 9*, 95–105.

Hoeffding, W. (1963). Probability inequalities for sums of bounded random variables. *Journal of the American Statistical Association 58*, 13–30.

Hoerl, A., and R. Kennard (1970). Ridge regression: Biased estimation of non-orthogonal components. *Technometrics 12*, 55–67.

Hutter, M. (2003). Optimality of universal Bayesian sequence prediction for general loss and alphabet. *Journal of Machine Learning Research 4*, 971–1000.

Hutter, M. (2004). *Universal Artificial Intelligence: Sequential Decisions based on Algorithmic Probability*. Berlin: Springer-Verlag.

Hutter, M. (2006). On the foundations of universal sequence prediction. In *Proceedings of the Third Annual Conference on Theory and Applications of Models of Computation (TAMC 2006)*, pp. 408–420.

Jaynes, E. (1957). Information theory and statistical mechanics. *Physical Review 106*(4), 620–630.

Jaynes, E. (2003). *Probability Theory: The Logic of Science*. Cambridge, UK: Cambridge University Press. Edited by G. Larry Bretthorst.

Jeffereys, W., and J. Berger (1992). Ockham's razor and Bayesian analysis. *American Scientist 80*, 64–72.

Jeffreys, H. (1946). An invariant form for the prior probability in estimation problems. *Proceedings of the Royal Statistical Society (London) Series A 186*, 453–461.

Jeffreys, H. (1961). *Theory of Probability*, 3rd edition. London: Oxford University Press.

Jornsten, R., and B. Yu (2003). Simultaneous gene clustering and subset selection for classification via mdl. *Bioinformatics 19*(9), 1100–1109.

Kakade, S., M. Seeger, and D. Foster (2006). Worst-case bounds for Gaussian process models. In *Proceedings of the 2005 Neural Information Processing Systems Conference (NIPS 2005)*.

Kallenberg, O. (2002). *Foundations of Modern Probability*, 2nd edition. New York: Springer-Verlag.

Kalnishkan, Y., and M. Vyugin (2002). Mixability and the existence of weak complexities. In *Proceedings of the Fifteenth Conference on Computational Learning Theory (COLT' 02)*, pp. 105–120.

Kapur, J. N., and H. K. Kesavan (1992). *Entropy Optimization Principles with Applications*. San Diego: Academic Press.

Kass, R., and A. E. Raftery (1995). Bayes factors. *Journal of the American Statistical Association 90*(430), 773–795.

Kass, R., and P. Voss (1997). *Geometrical Foundations of Asymptotic Inference*. New York: Wiley-Interscience.

Kass, R., and L. Wasserman (1996). The selection of prior distributions by formal rules. *Journal of the American Statistical Association 91*, 1343–1370.

Kearns, M., Y. Mansour, A. Ng, and D. Ron (1997). An experimental and theoretical comparison of model selection methods. *Machine Learning 27*, 7–50.

Kelly, J. (1956). A new interpretation of information rate. *Bell System Technical Journal*, 917–926.

Kolmogorov, A. (1941). Interpolation und Extrapolation von stationären zufälligen Folgen. *Isvestiia Akademii Nauk SSSR 5*, 3–14.

Kolmogorov, A. (1965). Three approaches to the quantitative definition of information. *Problems of Information Transmission 1*(1), 1–7.

Kolmogorov, A. (1974a). Talk at the Information Theory Symposium in Tallinn, Estonia, 1974, according to P. Gács and T. Cover who attended it.

Kolmogorov, A. (1974b). Complexity of algorithms and objective definition of randomness. A talk at Moscow Mathematical Society meeting, April 16th, 1974. A 4-line abstract is available in *Uspekhi Matematicheskih Nauk* 29:4(1974), 155 (in Russian).

Kontkanen, P., W. Buntine, P. Myllymäki, J. Rissanen, and H. Tirri (2003). Efficient computation of stochastic complexity. In C. Bishop and B. Frey (Eds.), *Proceedings of the Ninth International Workshop on Artificial Intelligence and Statistics (AISTATS 2003)*, pp. 181–188.

Kontkanen, P., and P. Myllymäki (2005a). Analyzing the stochastic complexity via tree polynomials. Unpublished manuscript.

Kontkanen, P., and P. Myllymäki (2005b). A fast normalized maximum likelihood algorithm for multinomial data. In *Proceedings of the Nine-*

teenth International Joint Conference on Artificial Intelligence (IJCAI-05), pp. 1613–1616.

Kontkanen, P., P. Myllymäki, W. Buntine, J. Rissanen, and H. Tirri (2005). An MDL framework for data clustering. In P. D. Grünwald, I. J. Myung, and M. A. Pitt (Eds.), *Advances in Minimum Description Length: Theory and Applications*. Cambridge, MA: MIT Press.

Kontkanen, P., P. Myllymäki, T. Silander, and H. Tirri (1999). On supervised selection of Bayesian networks. In K. Laskey and H. Prade (Eds.), *Proceedings of the Fifteenth International Conference on Uncertainty in Artificial Intelligence (UAI'99)*.

Kontkanen, P., P. Myllymäki, T. Silander, H. Tirri, and P. D. Grünwald (1998). Bayesian and information-theoretic priors for Bayesian network parameters. In C. Nedellec and C. Rouveirol (Eds.), *Machine Learning: ECML-98, Proceedings of the Tenth European Conference*, volume 1398 of *Lecture Notes in Artificial Intelligence*, pp. 89–94.

Kraft, L. (1949). A device for quantizing, grouping and coding amplitude modulated pulses. Master's thesis, Department of Electrical Engineering, MIT, Cambridge, MA.

Krichevsky, R., and V. Trofimov (1981). The performance of universal encoding. *IEEE Transactions on Information Theory 27*, 199–207.

Lai, T., and C. Lee (1997). Information and prediction criteria for model selection in stochastic regression and ARMA models. *Statistica Sinica 7*, 285–309.

Lanterman, A. (2001). Schwarz, Wallace, and Rissanen: Intertwining themes in theories of model order estimation. *International Statistical Review 69*(2), 185–212.

Lanterman, A. D. (2005). Hypothesis testing for Poisson versus geometric distributions using stochastic complexity. In P. D. Grünwald, I. J. Myung, and M. A. Pitt (Eds.), *Advances in Minimum Description Length: Theory and Applications*. Cambridge, MA: MIT Press.

Lee, M. (2002a). Generating additive clustering models with minimal stochastic complexity. *Journal of Classification 19*(1), 69–85.

Lee, M. (2002b). A simple method for generating additive clustering models with limited complexity. *Machine Learning 49*, 39–58.

Lee, P. (1997). *Bayesian Statistics — An Introduction*. London and Oxford: Arnold & Oxford University Press.

Lee, T. (2000). Regression spline smoothing using the minimum description length principle. *Statistics and Probability Letters 48*(71–82).

Lee, T. (2002c). Automatic smoothing for discontinuous regression functions. *Statistica Sinica 12*, 823–842.

Levenstein, V. (1968). On the redundancy and delay of separable codes for the natural numbers. *Problems of Cybernetics 20*, 173–179.

Li, J. (1999). *Estimation of Mixture Models*. Ph. D. thesis, Yale University, New Haven, CT.

Li, J., and A. Barron (2000). Mixture density estimation. In S. Solla, T. Leen, and K.-R. Müller (Eds.), *Advances in Neural Information Processing Systems*, volume 12, pp. 279–285.

Li, K. (1987). Asymptotic optimality of c_p , c_l, cross-validation and generalized cross-validation: Discrete index set. *Annals of Statistics 15*, 958–975.

Li, L., and B. Yu (2000). Iterated logarithmic expansions of the pathwise code lengths for exponential families. *IEEE Transactions on Information Theory 46*(7), 2683–2689.

Li, M., and P. Vitányi (1997). *An Introduction to Kolmogorov Complexity and Its Applications*, revised and expanded 2nd edition. New York: Springer-Verlag.

Liang, F., and A. Barron (2005). Exact minimax predictive density estimation and MDL. In P. D. Grünwald, I. J. Myung, and M. A. Pitt (Eds.), *Advances in Minimum Description Length: Theory and Applications*. Cambridge, MA: MIT Press.

Liang, F., and A. R. Barron (2002). Exact minimax strategies for predictive density estimation, data compression, and model selection. In *Proceedings of the 2002 IEEE International Symposium on Information Theory (ISIT 2002)*.

Liang, F., and A. R. Barron (2004). Exact minimax strategies for predictive density estimation, data compression, and model selection. *IEEE Transactions on Information Theory 50*, 2708–2726.

Lindley, D., and A. Smith (1972). Bayes estimates for the linear model. *Journal of the Royal Statistical Society, Series B 34*, 1–41. With discussion.

Littlestone, N., and M. Warmuth (1994). The weighted majority algorithm. *Information and Computation 108*(2), 212–261.

Liu, J., and P. Moulin (1998). A new complexity prior for multiresolution image denoising. In *Proceedings of IEEE Workshop on Time-Frequency Time-Scale Analysis*, pp. 637–640.

Lutwak, E., D. Yang, and G. Zhang (2005). Cramér-Rao and moment-entropy inequalities for Rényi entropy and generalized Fisher information. *IEEE Transactions on Information Theory 51*, 473–478.

MacKay, D. (2003). *Information Theory, Inference, and Learning Algorithms.* Cambridge, UK: Cambridge University Press.

McAllester, D. (1998). Some PAC-Bayesian theorems. In *Proceedings of the Eleventh ACM Conference on Computational Learning Theory (COLT' 98)*, pp. 230–234.

McAllester, D. (1999). PAC-Bayesian model averaging. In *Proceedings of the Twelfth ACM Conference on Computational Learning Theory (COLT' 99)*, pp. 164–171.

McAllester, D. (2003). PAC-Bayesian stochastic model selection. *Machine Learning 51*(1), 5–21.

Mehta, M., J. Rissanen, and R. Agrawal (1995). MDL-based decision tree pruning. In *Proceedings of the First International Conference on Knowledge Discovery and Data Mining (KDD '95)*, pp. 216–221.

Meir, R., and N. Merhav (1995). On the stochastic complexity of learning realizable and unrealizable rules. *Machine Learning 19*, 241–261.

Merhav, N., and M. Feder (1998). Universal prediction. *IEEE Transactions on Information Theory IT-44*(6), 2124–2147. Special Commemorative Issue: Information Theory: 1948-1998.

Michalski, R., J. Carbonell, and T. Mitchell (1983). *Machine Learning, An Artificial Intelligence Approach.* San Francisco: Morgan Kaufmann.

Michie, D., D. Spiegelhalter, and C. Taylor (Eds.) (1994). *Machine Learning, Neural and Statistical Classification.* London: Ellis Horwood.

Modha, D. S., and E. Masry (1998). Prequential and cross-validated regression estimation. *Machine Learning 33*(1), 5–39.

Myung, I., V. Balasubramanian, and M. Pitt (2000). Counting probability distributions: Differential geometry and model selection. *Proceedings of the National Academy of Sciences USA 97*, 11170–11175.

Myung, I. J., M. A. Pitt, S. Zhang, and V. Balasubramanian (2000). The use of MDL to select among computational models of cognition. In

Advances in Neural Information Processing Systems, volume 13, pp. 38–44. Cambridge, MA: MIT Press.

Nannen, V. (2003). The paradox of overfitting. Master's thesis, University of Groningen, Groningen, the Netherlands.

Navarro, D. (2004). A note on the applied use of MDL appproximations. *Neural Computation 16*, 1763–1768.

Ndili, U., R. Nowak, and M. Figueiredo (2001). Coding-theoretic approach to image segmentation. In *Proceedings of the 2001 IEEE International Conference on Image Processing - ICIP'2001*.

Neal, R. (1996). *Bayesian learning for neural networks*. New York: Springer-Verlag.

Nowak, R., and M. Figueiredo (2000). Unsupervised segmentation of Poisson data. In *Proceedings of the International Conference on Pattern Recognition - ICPR'2000*, volume 3, pp. 159–162.

Osborne, M. (1999). MDL-based DCG induction for NP identification. In *Proceedings of the Third Conference on Computational Natural Language Learning (CoNLL '99)*, pp. 61–68.

Pednault, E. (2003). Personal communication, June 2003.

Poland, J., and M. Hutter (2005). Asymptotics of discrete MDL for online prediction. *IEEE Transactions on Information Theory 51*(11), 3780–3795.

Poland, J., and M. Hutter (2006). MDL convergence speed for Bernoulli sequences. *Statistics and Computing 16*, 161–175.

Qian, G., G. Gabor, and R. Gupta (1996). Generalised linear model selection by the predictive least quasi-deviance criterion. *Biometrika 83*, 41–54.

Qian, G., and H. Künsch (1998). Some notes on Rissanen's stochastic complexity. *IEEE Transactions on Information Theory 44*(2), 782–786.

Quinlan, J., and R. Rivest (1989). Inferring decision trees using the minimum description length principle. *Information and Computation 80*, 227–248.

Rasmussen, C., and Z. Ghahramani (2000). Occam's razor. In *Advances in Neural Information Processing Systems*, volume 13, pp. 294–300.

Rasmussen, C., and C. Williams (2006). *Gaussian Processes for Machine Learning*. Cambridge, MA: MIT Press.

Rényi, A. (1960). On measures of entropy and information. In *Proceedings of the Fourth Berkeley Symposium on Mathematical Statistics and Probability*, volume 1, pp. 547–561.

Rice, J. (1995). *Mathematical Statistics and Data Analysis*. Duxbury Press.

Ripley, B. (1996). *Pattern Recognition and Neural Networks*. Cambridge, UK: Cambridge University Press.

Rissanen, J. (1978). Modeling by the shortest data description. *Automatica 14*, 465–471.

Rissanen, J. (1983). A universal prior for integers and estimation by minimum description length. *Annals of Statistics 11*, 416–431.

Rissanen, J. (1984). Universal coding, information, prediction and estimation. *IEEE Transactions on Information Theory 30*, 629–636.

Rissanen, J. (1986a). Order estimation by accumulated prediction errors. In J. Gani and M. B. Priestley (Eds.), *Essays in Time Series and Allied Processes*, pp. 55–61. Sheffield, UK: Applied Probability Trust.

Rissanen, J. (1986b). A predictive least squares principle. *IMA Journal of Mathematical Control and Information 3*, 211–222.

Rissanen, J. (1986c). Stochastic complexity and modeling. *Annals of Statistics 14*, 1080–1100.

Rissanen, J. (1987). Stochastic complexity. *Journal of the Royal Statistical Society, Series B 49*, 223–239. Discussion: 252–265.

Rissanen, J. (1989). *Stochastic Complexity in Statistical Inquiry*. Hackensack, NJ: World Scientific.

Rissanen, J. (1996). Fisher information and stochastic complexity. *IEEE Transactions on Information Theory 42(1)*, 40–47.

Rissanen, J. (1999). Hypothesis selection and testing by the MDL principle. *Computer Journal 42(4)*, 260–269.

Rissanen, J. (2000). MDL denoising. *IEEE Transactions on Information Theory 46(7)*, 2537–2543.

Rissanen, J. (2001). Strong optimality of the normalized ML models as universal codes and information in data. *IEEE Transactions on Information Theory 47(5)*, 1712–1717.

Rissanen, J. (2007). *Information and Complexity in Statistical Modeling*. New York: Springer-Verlag.

Rissanen, J., and E. Ristad (1994). Language acquisition in the MDL framework. In E. Ristad (Ed.), *Language Computations*. Philadelphia: American Mathematical Society.

Rissanen, J., T. Speed, and B. Yu (1992). Density estimation by stochastic complexity. *IEEE Transactions on Information Theory 38*(2), 315–323.

Rissanen, J., and I. Tabus (2005). Kolmogorov's structure function in MDL theory and lossy data compression. In P. D. Grünwald, I. J. Myung, and M. A. Pitt (Eds.), *Advances in Minimum Description Length: Theory and Applications*. Cambridge, MA: MIT Press.

Rissanen, J., and B. Yu (1995). MDL learning. In D. Kueker and C. Smith (Eds.), *Learning and Geometry: Computational Approaches, Progress in Computer Science and Applied Logic*, volume 14, pp. 3–19. Boston: Birkhäuser.

Rockafellar, R. (1970). *Convex Analysis*. Princeton, NJ: Princeton University Press.

Roos, T. (2004). MDL regression and denoising. Unpublished manuscript.

Roos, T., P. Myllymäki, and H. Tirri (2005). On the behavior of MDL denoising. In *Proceedings of the Tenth International Workshop on Artificial Intelligence and Statistics (AISTATS '05)*, pp. 309–316.

Roos, T., H. Wettig, P. Grünwald, P. Myllymäki, and H.Tirri (2005). On discriminative Bayesian network classifiers and logistic regression. *Machine Learning 59*(3), 267 – 296.

Rosenfeld, R. (1996). A maximum entropy approach to adaptive statistical language modeling. *Computer, Speech and Language 10*, 187–228.

Ross, S. (1998). *A First Course in Probability*. Upper Saddle River, NJ: Prentice-Hall.

Rubin, H. (1987). A weak system of axioms for "rational" behavior and the nonseparability of utility from prior. *Statistical Decisions 5*, 47–58.

Savage, L. (1954). *The Foundations of Statistics*. Dover Publications.

Schölkopf, B., and A. J. Smola (2002). *Learning with Kernels*. Cambridge, MA: MIT Press.

Schwarz, G. (1978). Estimating the dimension of a model. *Annals of Statistics 6*(2), 461–464.

Seeger, M. (2004). Gaussian processes for machine learning. *International Journal of Neural Systems 14*(2), 69–106.

Seidenfeld, T. (1986). Entropy and uncertainty. *Philosophy of Science 53*, 467–491.

Shafer, G., and V. Vovk (2001). *Probability and Finance – It's Only a Game!* New York: Wiley.

Shaffer, C. (1993). Overfitting avoidance as bias. *Machine Learning 10*, 153–178.

Shannon, C. (1948). The mathematical theory of communication. *Bell System Technical Journal 27*, 379–423, 623–656.

Shao, J. (1993). Linear model selection by cross-validation. *Journal of the American Statistical Association 88*, 486–494.

Shao, J. (1997). An asymptotic theory for linear model selection (with discussion). *Statistica Sinica 7*, 221–242.

Shawe-Taylor, J., P. Bartlett, R. Williamson, and M. Anthony (1998). Structural risk minimisation over data-dependent hierarchies. *IEEE Transactions on Information Theory 44*(5), 1926–1940.

Shawe-Taylor, J., and N. Cristianini (2004). *Kernel Methods for Pattern Analysis*. Cambridge, UK: Cambridge University Press.

Shibata, R. (1976). Selection of the order of an autoregressive model by Akaike's information criterion. *Biometrika 63*(1), 117–126.

Shtarkov, Y. M. (1987). Universal sequential coding of single messages. *Problems of Information Transmission 23*(3), 3–17.

Sober, E. (2004). The contest between parsimony and likelihood. *Systematic Biology 4*, 644–653.

Solomonoff, R. (1964). A formal theory of inductive inference, part 1 and part 2. *Information and Control 7*, 1–22, 224–254.

Solomonoff, R. (1978). Complexity-based induction systems: comparisons and convergence theorems. *IEEE Transactions on Information Theory 24*, 422–432.

Speed, T., and B. Yu (1993). Model selection and prediction: Normal regression. *Annals of the Institute of Statistical Mathematics 45*(1), 35–54.

Spiegelhalter, D., N. Best, B. Carlin, and A. van der Linde (2002). Bayesian measures of model complexity and fit (with discussion). *Journal of the Royal Statistical Society, Series B 64*(4), 583–639.

Starkie, B. (2001). Programming spoken dialogs using grammatical inference. In *Advances in Artificial Intelligence (AI 2001)*. Berlin: Springer.

Stone, M. (1974). Cross-validatory choice and assessment of statistical predictions. *Journal of the Royal Statistical Society, Series B 36*(2), 111–147.

Stone, M. (1977). An asymptotic equivalence of choice of model by cross-validation and Akaike's criterion. *Journal of the Royal Statistical Society, Series B 39*, 44–47.

Strang, G. (1988). *Linear Algebra and its Applications*, 3rd edition. Philadelphia: W.B. Saunders.

Su, Y., I. J. Myung, and M. A. Pitt (2005). Minimum description length and cognitive modeling. In P. D. Grünwald, I. J. Myung, and M. A. Pitt (Eds.), *Advances in Minimum Description Length: Theory and Applications*. Cambridge, MA: MIT Press.

Szpankowski, W. (1998). On asymptotics of certain recurrences arising in universal coding. *Problems of Information Transmission 34*(2), 142–146.

Tabus, I., J. Rissanen, and J. Astola (2002). Normalized maximum likelihood models for Boolean regression with application to prediction and classification in genomics. In W. Zhang and I. Shmulevich (Eds.), *Computational and Statistical Approaches to Genomics*.

Tabus, I., J. Rissanen, and J. Astola (2003). Classification and feature gene selection using the normalized maximum likelihood model for discrete regression. *Signal Processing 83*(4), 713–727. Special issue on Genomic Signal Processing.

Takeuchi, J. (2000). On minimax regret with respect to families of stationary stochastic processes [in Japanese]. In *Proceedings IBIS 2000*, pp. 63–68.

Takeuchi, J., and A. Barron (1997). Asymptotically minimax regret for exponential families. In *Proceedings SITA '97*, pp. 665–668.

Takeuchi, J., and A. Barron (1998a). Asymptotically minimax regret by Bayes mixtures. In *Proceedings of the 1998 International Symposium on Information Theory (ISIT 98)*.

Takeuchi, J., and A. R. Barron (1998b). Robustly minimax codes for universal data compression. In *Proceedings of the Twenty-First Symposium on Information Theory and Its Applications (SITA '98)*.

Topsøe, F. (1979). Information-theoretical optimization techniques. *Kybernetika 15*(1), 8–27.

Topsøe, F. (2007). Information theory at the service of science. In I. Csiszár, G. Katona, and G. Tardos (Eds.), *Entropy, Search, Complexity*, volume 16 of *Bolyai Society Mathematical Studies*. New York: Springer-Verlag.

Townsend, P. (1975). The mind-body equation revisited. In C.-Y. Cheng (Ed.), *Psychological Problems in Philosophy*, pp. 200–218. Honolulu: University of Hawaii Press.

Uffink, J. (1995). Can the maximum entropy principle be explained as a consistency requirement? *Studies in History and Philosophy of Modern Physics 26B*, 223–261.

van der Vaart, A. (1998). *Asymptotic Statistics*. Cambridge Series in Statistical and Probabilistic Mathematics. Cambridge, UK: Cambridge University Press.

Vapnik, V. (1982). *Estimation of Dependencies Based on Empirical Data*. Berlin: Springer-Verlag.

Vapnik, V. (1998). *Statistical Learning Theory*. New York: Wiley.

Vapnik, V., and A. Chervonenkis (1971). On the uniform convergence of relative frequencies of events to their probabilities. *Theory of Probability and Its Applications 16*(2), 264–280.

Vereshchagin, N., and P. Vitányi (2002). Kolmogorov's structure functions with an application to the foundations of model selection. In *Proceedings Fourty-Seventh IEEE Symposium on the Foundations of Computer Science (FOCS'02)*.

Vereshchagin, N., and P. Vitányi (2004). Kolmogorov's structure functions and model selection. *IEEE Transactions on Information Theory 50*(12), 3265–3290.

Viswanathan., M., C. Wallace, D. Dowe, and K. Korb (1999). Finding cutpoints in noisy binary sequences - A revised empirical evaluation. In *Proceedings of the Twelfth Australian Joint Conference on Artificial Intelligence*, volume 1747 of *Lecture Notes in Artificial Intelligence (LNAI)*, pp. 405–416.

Vitányi, P. M. (2005). Algorithmic statistics and Kolmogorov's structure function. In P. D. Grünwald, I. J. Myung, and M. A. Pitt (Eds.), *Advances in Minimum Description Length: Theory and Applications*. Cambridge, MA: MIT Press.

von Neumann, J. (1928). Zur Theorie der Gesellschaftsspiele. *Mathematische Annalen 100*, 295–320.

Vovk, V. (1990). Aggregating strategies. In *Proceedings of the Third Annual ACM Conference on Computational Learning Theory (COLT' 90)*, pp. 371–383.

Vovk, V. (2001). Competitive on-line statistics. *International Statistical Review 69*, 213–248.

Wagenmakers, E., P. D. Grünwald, and M. Steyvers (2006). Accumulative prediction error and the selection of time series models. *Journal of Mathematical Psychology 50*(2), 149–166.

Wallace, C. (2005). *Statistical and Inductive Inference by Minimum Message Length*. New York: Springer-Verlag.

Wallace, C., and D. Boulton (1968). An information measure for classification. *Computer Journal 11*, 185–195.

Wallace, C., and D. Boulton (1975). An invariant Bayes method for point estimation. *Classification Society Bulletin 3*(3), 11–34.

Wallace, C., and P. Freeman (1987). Estimation and inference by compact coding. *Journal of the Royal Statistical Society, Series B 49*, 240–251. Discussion: pages 252–265.

Wallace, C., and J. Patrick (1993). Coding decision trees. *Machine Learning 11*, 7–22.

Watanabe, S. (1999a). Algebraic analysis for non-regular learning machines. In *Advances in Neural Information Processing Systems*, pp. 356–363.

Watanabe, S. (1999b). Algebraic analysis for singular statistical estimation. In *Tenth International Conference on Algorithmic Learning Theory (ALT'99)*, volume 1720 of *Lecture Notes in Computer Science*, pp. 39–50.

Wax, M. (1988). Order selection for AR models by predictive least squares. *IEEE Transactions on Acoustics, Speech and Signal Processing 36*(4), 581–588.

Webb, G. (1996). Further experimental evidence against the utility of Occam's razor. *Journal of Artificial Intelligence Research 4*, 397–417.

Wei, C. (1992). On predictive least squares principles. *Annals of Statistics 20*(1), 1–42.

Weisstein, E. (2006). Gamma function. From MathWorld–A Wolfram Web Resource.

Wiener, N. (1949). *Extrapolation, Interpolation and Smoothing of Stationary Time Series*. Cambridge, MA: MIT Press.

Wilks, S. (1938). The large sample distribution of the likelihood ratio for testing composite hypothesis. *Annals of Mathematical Statistics 9*, 60–62.

Willems, F., Y. Shtarkov, and T. Tjalkens (1995). The context-tree weighting method: basic properties. *IEEE Transactions on Information Theory 41*, 653–664.

Woodroofe, M. (1982). On model selection and the arcsine laws. *Annals of Statistics 10*, 1182–1194.

Xie, Q., and A. Barron (1997). Minimax redundancy for the class of memoryless sources. *IEEE Transactions on Information Theory 43*, 646–657.

Xie, Q., and A. Barron (2000). Asymptotic minimax regret for data compression, gambling and prediction. *IEEE Transactions on Information Theory 46*(2), 431–445.

Yamanishi, K. (1998). A decision-theoretic extension of stochastic complexity and its applications to learning. *IEEE Transactions on Information Theory 44*(4), 1424–1439.

Yamazaki, K., and S. Watanabe (2003). Singularities in mixture models and upper bounds of stochastic complexity. *International Journal of Neural Networks 16*, 1029–1038.

Yang, Y. (2000). Mixing strategies for density estimation. *Annals of Statistics 28*(1), 75–87.

Yang, Y. (2005a). Can the strengths of AIC and BIC be shared? A conflict between model indentification and regression estimation. *Biometrica 92*(4), 937–950.

Yang, Y. (2005b). Consistency of cross-validation for comparing regression procedures. Submitted for publication.

Yang, Y., and A. Barron (1998). An asymptotic property of model selection criteria. *IEEE Transactions on Information Theory 44*, 117–133.

Yang, Y., and A. Barron (1999). Information-theoretic determination of minimax rates of convergence. *Annals of Statistics 27*, 1564–1599.

Yu, B. (1994). Lower bound on the expected redundancy for classes of continuous Markov sources. In S. Gupta and J. Berger (Eds.), *Statistical Decision Theory and Related Topics*, volume V, pp. 453–466.

Yu, B. (1996). Lower bounds on expected redundancy for nonparametric classes. *IEEE Transactions on Information Theory 42*, 272–275.

Yu, B., and T. Speed (1992). Data compression and histograms. *Probability Theory and Related Fields 92*, 195–229.

Zellner, A. (1986). On assessing prior distributions and Bayesian regression analysis with g-prior distributions. In P. Goel and A. Zellner (Eds.), *Bayesian Inference and Decision Techniques: Essays in Honor of Bruno de Finetti*, pp. 223–243. Amsterdam: North–Holland.

Zhang, J., and J. Myung (2005). A note on informative normalized maximum likelihood with data prior. Manuscript in preparation.

Zhang, T. (2004a). Learning bounds for a generalized family of Bayesian posterior distributions. In S. Thrun, L. K. Saul, and B. Schölkopf (Eds.), *Advances in Neural Information Processing Systems*, volume 16. Cambridge, MA: MIT Press.

Zhang, T. (2004b). On the convergence of MDL density estimation. In Y. Singer and J. Shawe-Taylor (Eds.), *Proceedings of the Seventeenth Conference on Learning Theory (COLT' 04)*, Lecture Notes in Computer Science. New York: Springer-Verlag.

List of Symbols

$\mathbf{0}$: null vector in $\mathbb{R}^l$, 43
$\mathbf{1}$: indicator function, 52

$\mathcal{A}$: data alphabet, 6
A_λ: λ-affinity, 645
$a(\theta)$: luckiness function, 309
$\ddot{\alpha}$ where $\alpha \in \{P, k, \gamma, \theta, (\theta, k)\}$:
    two-part code estimator,
    132
$\hat{\alpha}$, with $\alpha \in \{\theta, \mu, \beta\}$: ML
    parameter, 58
α^* where $\alpha \in \{P, k, \theta, \mu, \beta, \gamma\}$:
    "truth", 143
arg: argument of min/max, 44

$\mathcal{B}$: Bernoulli/Markov model, 58
$\mathcal{B}_\mathbb{Q}$: rational Markov models, 185
$B(\epsilon)$: ϵ-ball, 44
$B_{I(\theta)}$: Mahalanobis ball, 121
B_{kl}: KL ball, 220
$\mathbb{B}$: Booleans, i.e. $\{0, 1\}$, 6
β: canonical parameter, 601
$\hat{\beta}$, *see* $\hat{\alpha}$

C: code, coding system, 80
CCOMP$^{(n)}$: constrained
    complexity, 302
COMP$^{(n)}$: model complexity, 180
CUP$(\cdot, \cdot)$: CUP universal model,
    373
cov: covariance, 48

D: KL divergence, 104
D: data sequence, 6
D: KL div. rel. to ln, 111
$\Delta^{(m)}$: m-dimensional unit
    simplex, 42

D_{P^*}: extended KL divergence,
    625
$\bar{d}_\lambda$: Rényi divergence, 478
d_λ: unnormalized Rényi
    divergence, 645
$d, d(x^n)$: parameter precision, 137
det: determinant of matrix, 43

E: expectation, 48
E_θ: expectation under P_θ, 57
EACOMP$^{(n)}$: exponentiated
    asymptotic complexity,
    216

f: probability density function, 46
$\bar{f}_{\text{IND}}$ with IND $\in$ { meta, plug-in,
    nml, Bayes, Jeffreys,
    two-part }, *see* $\bar{P}_{\text{IND}}$
ϕ: sufficient statistic, 601
FSS: fitted sum of squares, 344

Γ: Gamma function, 45
γ: model index, 61
γ^*, *see* α^*

$\mathcal{H}$: hypoth. class of functions, 63
H: (Shannon) entropy, 103
$H(\Theta_0, \epsilon)$: hypercube fill up
    number, 222
H: entropy rel. to ln, 111
h^*, *see* α^*
He^2: squared Hellinger distance,
    478
He$_\lambda^2$: generalized squared
    Hellinger divergence,
    645

I: Fisher information, 112

Subject Index